THE 1996 FRANCHISE ANNUAL

"THE ORIGINAL" FRANCHISE HANDBOOK AND DIRECTORY

PUBLISHED BY

INFO FRANCHISE NEWS, INC.

EDITOR/PUBLISHER: TED DIXON

EDITOR: DENISE MUIR

ASSISTANT EDITOR: HEATHER MAGUIRE

SUBSCRIPTION MANAGER: LORI MARSH

9 DUKE ST., P.O. BOX 670
ST. CATHARINES, ONTARIO
CANADA
L2R 6W8
TELEPHONE: (905) 688-2665   FAX: (905) 688-7728

728 CENTER ST., P.O. BOX 550
LEWISTON, NEW YORK
U.S.A.
14092-0550
TELEPHONE: (716) 754-4669

E-MAIL: infopress@infonews.com
WWW Site: http://infonews.com/franchise

® FRANCHISE NEWS INC.
a Division of INFO PRESS, INC.

INTERNATIONAL FRANCHISE OPPORTUNITIES
LIBRARY OF CONGRESS CATALOG CARD NUMBER 76-17321

ISBN: 0-96 92267-4-8
ISSN: 0318-8752

COPYRIGHT © 1996 by INFO PRESS, INC.

Reprinting, reproduction, or adaptation of the material contained herein for any purpose other than critical reviews is expressly forbidden without permission of the publisher.

PRINTED IN CANADA

TABLE OF CONTENTS

HANDBOOK

Categorical Index	H3
Editor's Introduction	H4
Franchising	H5
Investigating the Franchisor	H7
The Franchisor	H9
The Product or Service	H9
The Franchisee	H10
The Territory	H10
The Contract	H10
Business Opportunity Fraud	H11
State Regulations	H14
News From The Info Franchise Newsletter	H16
The Info Franchise Newsletter	H17

DIRECTORY

American Listings	1
Canadian Listings	176
Overseas Listings	245
Alphabetical Index	275
Advertiser List	315
Blank Questionnaire	316
Mailing List Rentals	317
Order Coupons	318

(Special Note: All new listings are marked with *)

We believe that all the information which is contained in the directory is from reliable sources, but we accept no responsibility for transactions that result from the use of it. Information contained in the directory section has been supplied to Info Press, Inc. by the companies listed.

CATEGORICAL INDEX

AMERICAN LISTINGS

Accounting and Tax Services	1
Advertising/Publishing Services	2
Automobile Rental & Leasing	6
Automotive Lubrication & Tune Up	7
Automotive Muffler Shops	9
Automotive Products and Services	10
Automotive Transmission Repair	16
Beverages	17
Building Products and Services	17
Burglar & Fire Prevention	23
Business Products & Services	23
Carpet, Drapery and Upholstery Cleaning	32
Children's Products and Services	33
Cleaning Products & Services	37
Consumer Buying Services	43
Distributors	43
Employment & Personnel	50
Entertainment	55
Food: Convenience Stores, Specialty Shops & Supermarkets	56
Food: Donut, Bakery & Coffee Shops	60
Food: Ice Cream & Yogurt	65
Food: Restaurants & Quick Service	69
Franchise Consultants & Services	102
Franchise Consultants - Legal	112
Furniture Refinishing & Repair	117
Greeting Services	117
Hairstyling & Cosmetics	118
Health Aids & Services	121
Home Furnishings	127
House/Pet Sitting Services	129
Laundry & Dry Cleaning	129
Lawn, Garden Care & Florists	131
Motels, Hotels & Campgrounds	133
Pet Products & Services	136
Photo, Framing & Art	137
Printing & Copying Services	139
Real Estate Services	141
Rental Services	144
Retail	145
Retail: Clothing & Shoes	154
Retail: Computer, Electronics & Video	155
Schools & Teaching	158
Sign Products & Services	160
Sports & Recreation	162
Travel	165
Water Treatment	167
Wedding Related Services	168
Miscellaneous	168

CANADIAN LISTINGS

Accounting and Tax Services	176
Advertising/Publishing Services	177
Automobile Rental & Leasing	178
Automotive Lubrication & Tune Up	179
Automotive Muffler Shops	179
Automotive Products and Services	180
Automotive Transmission Repair	183
Beverages	183
Building Products and Services	183
Burglar & Fire Prevention	186
Business Products & Services	186
Carpet, Drapery and Upholstery Cleaning	189
Children's Products and Services	190
Cleaning Products and Services	191
Distributors	193
Employment & Personnel	196
Entertainment	197
Food: Convenience Stores, Specialty Shops & Supermarkets	197
Food: Donut, Bakery & Coffee Shops	199
Food: Ice Cream & Yogurt	203
Food: Restaurants & Quick Service	203
Franchise Consultants & Services	214
Franchise Consultants - Legal	219
Greeting Services	222
Hairstyling & Cosmetics	222
Health Aids and Services	223
Home Furnishings	226
House/Pet Sitting Services	227
Laundry & Dry Cleaning	227
Lawn, Garden Care & Florists	228
Motels, Hotels & Campgrounds	228
Pet Products & Services	229
Photo, Framing & Art	230
Printing & Copying Services	231
Real Estate Services	231
Rental Services	232
Retail	232
Retail: Clothing & Shoes	236
Retail: Computer, Electronics & Video	237
Schools & Teaching	238
Sign Products & Services	240
Sports & Recreation	241
Travel	242
Water Treatment	243
Miscellaneous	243

OVERSEAS LISTINGS

Automotive Products and Services	245
Building Products and Services	247
Business Products and Services	249
Cleaning Products and Services	252
Foods and Beverages	253
Franchise Consultants	259
General	261
Health and Beauty Aids and Services	267
Photo, Printing and Art	269
Retail	270

EDITOR'S INTRODUCTION

This is INFO'S 27th Edition of the ***FRANCHISE ANNUAL DIRECTORY***. We stand alone as the major source of independent and reliable information about business format franchising. This edition includes **4,210** listings. There are **534** new listings. *All new listings are marked with *.*

There are:
- **2,338** *American* franchisors, plus **129** *distributors*, plus **240** *franchise consultants;*
- **820** *Canadian* franchisors, plus **54** *distributors*, plus **165** *franchise consultants;* and
- **470** *Overseas* franchisors plus **52** *franchise consultants.*

(The most complete directory of franchisors in the world.)

Details about our rental list of directory purchasers as well as information about the continuously **updated franchisor mailing list** can be found on page 317.

Franchising remains a strong and ever growing major financial force throughout the world. **MAKE SURE THAT YOU WRITE TO MANY DIFFERENT COMPANIES AND COMPARE THE SYSTEMS THAT EACH OFFERS.** This is the purpose of this directory when used by the prospective franchisee. We want to provide basic information in order to help make general comparisons. However it is finally a personal choice. In order to make informed judgements, prospective franchisees must write to the franchisors and compare the offerings which they provide and then investigate, investigate, investigate.

Because every potential franchisee has different needs (some need financial assistance, some may not be able to relocate) the final choice of franchisor must be a personal decision. Anyone who claims to be able to make this decision for you will do more harm than good.

Beware of franchisor rating systems. These are usually compiled using arbitrary values fed into a computer. They seldom even reflect whether or not the franchisees are actually successful. Each prospective franchisee must make his/her own evaluation of possible franchisors. **READ THE HANDBOOK SECTION CAREFULLY** and with your own common sense your chance of success as a franchisee will be greatly increased. Good luck.

Ted Dixon

Ted Dixon
Editor/Publisher

Ted Dixon has been editor/publisher of the award-winning *Info Franchise Newsletter* and the *Franchise Annual Directory* for nineteen years. He first became involved with franchising in 1969 when he helped edit the first Franchise Annual while still a university student.

FRANCHISING

Franchising is a method of distribution of goods and services. Some people refer to the franchise "industry". There really is no such thing. There is just this method of distribution, although franchisors have formed associations such as the **Canadian Franchise Association** and the **International Franchise Association**.

Essentially, franchising works due to such things as shared advertising costs and economies of scale attained through increased purchasing power. The franchisee purchases the right to run a business (the franchise fee) which the franchisor has shown to be successful. A franchisor must have a concept which is inherently franchiseable. This means that it must be possible to duplicate the business format in many different locations.

This is not possible if the pilot's success depends on its totally unique location, or a specific personality. Ultimately, a franchisee is hoping to purchase "risk reduction". The franchisor is providing the franchisee with the "know-how" to succeed. The franchisor benefits because he is using other people's money to expand his system.

In the last year, *The Info Franchise Newsletter* has reported on new studies which suggest that franchising isn't very successful (see page H16). These studies contradict older studies which were based on a few successful franchisors.

Really, there are no all-encompassing statistics available concerning the success rate of franchising. This does not preclude you from creating your own success by carefully studying the franchisor, the business, as well as your own financial position and personality. Diligent research in your own specific area raises the prospect of success even if broad-based statistics are not really available.

It is very important to establish clearly in your mind that <u>it does not matter what the statistics say either positively or negatively</u>. Each prospective franchisee must do their own homework! You cannot rely on studies. You cannot rely on a franchisor being listed in a top 500 list. You cannot even rely on a franchisor's success in locations other than your own. You must know your own proposed location. You must understand the type of business you are entering. You must investigate the franchisor, closely question the franchisees, see if the economic niche in which the franchisor is operating is a secure one and finally ascertain if you could succeed at your location.

In the last year, for instance, INFO has been saying that franchises which offer time-saving services for two-income families, such as fast-food restaurants, children's products & services, computer training, software & games, lawn & garden care, pet products/care, temporary employment services, reselling used goods and automotive care/repair are steady sectors to enter. This might change. <u>You</u> must find out.

It's hard work investigating a franchise opportunity. Running a franchise is hard work. The good news is that you can do hard work. If you have made it this far you probably have what it takes to succeed if you <u>don't rush</u>.

Franchising works, no matter what the studies say either pro or con.

It is important to remember that we are in an age that is entirely brand driven. It is another important plus for franchising. People trust brands and recognize logos as indicating a company whose philosophy espouses such things as quality, cleanliness and service. Many people today do not remember what it was like just thirty years ago travelling with children. Unfamiliar restaurants made parents feel that making a decision to have lunch was like playing Botulism Roulette. When you took your car into the local gas station to have your muffler repaired, you were often told to come back in two or three days.

Right now in North America, there are approximately 3,200 franchisors responsible for approximately 600,000 franchised locations accounting for at least one-third of the North American economy. In the words of **John Naisbitt**, author of *Megatrends* and *Megatrends 2000*, "Franchising is the single most successful marketing concept ever." It really is. But that doesn't mean if you attempt to create a franchise in a faulty part of the economy that you will succeed anyway!

There are many good reasons to think seriously about buying a franchise. <u>It is the only type of job you can buy where your hard work will generate equity which you can sell after twenty years.</u> But you must also <u>work hard before you buy</u> in order to see if there are going to be problems down the road.

Problems can arise when, for example, after the contract has expired, the franchisor wishes to take over the store. Company stores are often more profitable to the franchisor simply because head office receives all the profits and not simply a percentage of the monthly gross. Will the franchisor make it difficult for you to profit from your years of hard work?

Also, from the franchisee's point of view, it seems to be just human nature, four or five years into the contract, to start wondering why he or she needs the franchisor. You might start to feel that you know it all and begin to forget the initial fears of going into business alone.

It is up to the franchisor to continually reinforce his importance to the franchisee with new research and development, innovative advertising campaigns, supportive and educational newsletters, etc.

It is very important to beware of franchisor rating systems found in magazines, the top 500 etc. These have little basis in reality. Some of the top 500 franchisors are out of business the next year. The ratings are compiled using arbitrary values fed into a computer, so many points for number of franchisees, years in business etc. These simple-minded ratings may help sell magazines, but can be very misleading to a prospective franchisee. Just because a franchisor is in some supposed top 500, doesn't even mean its franchisees are making any money. No one has ever asked them. They are not part of the rating system.

While franchising has provided a successful means of marketing for many corporations, relationships between franchisors and franchisees are sometimes strained. One reason for this is that the franchisee typically owns only a limited-term license to operate a business according to the requirements of the franchisor's operating manual. An established franchisee may think that it has a right to continue to operate under the same terms, but a franchisee is only a party to a limited term contract. To the extent that franchisees are successful, the market values of their franchises are likely to increase. Thus, conflicts may arise between the franchisor and the franchisee at the time of contract renewal.

The last few years have been particularly interesting as many of the twenty year contracts signed in the late sixties and early seventies have come up for renewal.

A source of friction in some franchise relationships is that franchisors are developing alternative approaches to distributing their goods or services that bypass, and compete with, franchisees selling the same goods or services. For example, some food service companies now sell in grocery stores, from push carts, or at kiosks, the same products their franchisees sell only in the franchised outlet. Thus, while franchisors may increase market penetration and market share through the use of alternative distribution systems, franchisees may actually lose business. Mail order and telemarketing are also viewed as forms of encroachment.

Franchisees are often angered by franchisors entering what they consider to be their territory. As noted Atlanta franchise lawyer, **Rupert Barkoff (Kilpatrick & Cody)**, says:

"...The encroachment phenomenon is given various 'handles'.
1. Franchisors use the words 'system expansion'. For example, the recent International Franchise Association Code of Principles and Standards of Conduct uses this term. In a prior draft, the term 'encroachment' had appeared.
2. Franchisees use the colorful term 'cannibalization'...
3. While the fast food industry seems to have grown accustomed to the word encroachment, the hotel industry uses the word 'impact'.
4. It has been reported that the McDonald's system has coined its own term, impaction, to describe encroachment...

Encroachment, traditionally thought of in geographic terms...is today thought of in broader terms...

Franchisors want their profits to increase. Use of alternative markets (e.g., supermarkets) and marketing approaches (catalog sales) may, on the whole, increase market penetration without having a serious impact on franchisees. This is particularly true where there are distinct markets that can be easily differentiated. For example, a perfume shop franchisor may be limited to franchising in malls in urban and suburban areas; however, by selective postal code mailings to rural areas, the franchisor could capture a market that was otherwise not being captured by franchisees or company retail outlets...
Franchisors justify expansion in several ways.

a) If that franchisor does not take the site, his competitor will. (The franchisee will customarily respond to this argument by saying that he can compete with a different product or service, but it is difficult, if not impossible, to compete with the same products or services.)

b) Expansion will result in greater sales in the marketplace, which usually means more marketing dollars from which existing units will benefit. As a result, expansion may lead to increased sales for the existing units...

As value pricing in the fast-food and other industries has demonstrated, 'it's a jungle out there'. Most franchisees believe that profit margins have dropped over the last several years. As a result, any additional lost sales can have devastating results on the franchisee's bottom line, and quickly turn a profitable unit into a losing proposition...

Many franchisors have grown to such a size that within certain geographical markets, expansion is not possible without some infringement...on existing units..."

As a result of concerns such as these two franchisee associations have emerged in the U.S.

The **American Association of Franchisees and Dealers** is a non-profit trade association which was founded to support and protect franchisees. The Association's goal is to bring what it terms "fairness" to franchising. The **American Franchisee Association** is another broad-based organization of business format franchisees. It had an initial membership of more than 10,000 franchisees.

In Canada, with the exception of Alberta, the franchisor is not required to provide a disclosure document to the prospective franchisee, detailing the history of the company.

For years, INFO has been advocating that there be disclosure guidelines for all provinces, in order that Canada may eventually have uniform disclosure requirements. Victims of franchise fraud are going to get so outraged that they will demand disclosure requirements and it would be wisest to avoid duplication of legislation such as the federal/state situation in the U.S.

In 1995, Ontario's **Franchise Sector Working Team (FSWT)** submitted its report to **Norman W. Sterling**, Minister of Consumer & Commercial Relations. The members of the FSWT were unanimous in recommending franchise legislation along the lines of the new Alberta Act (which now does not require franchise registration). There was common ground among the members of the FSWT regarding the desirability of a self-governing mechanism for franchising. However, there were substantial differing views about the form and extent of such self-governance. It was relatively easy to agree on a code of ethics and the fact that such a code must be mandatory to be effective. The other provinces have all reviewed the new Alberta legislation and received copies of the report of the Ontario FSWT. They are apparently waiting to see how Ontario reacts. If Ontario follows Alberta's lead, it is very likely that many of the other provinces would do likewise, particularly because there is a trend among the provinces to harmonize their legislation which can affect interprovincial commerce.

Because the world of franchising is not only growing but also changing rapidly, pre-sale disclosure of all material terms and conditions of the franchise agreement is more important than ever. Franchisees who understand their rights and obligations before they purchase their franchise are far less likely to experience strained relationships with their franchisors. The franchisor can also actually use a disclosure document as a marketing tool.

Ultimately, it is important to remember that by purchasing a franchise you are going to end up, not so much a franchisee, but as a muffler shop owner, printer or tax consultant etc., who has entered the business by purchasing a franchise in the hopes of risk-reduction.

People always ask what's the best franchise? The only way to really ask this is "What's the best franchise for me?" The answer is a combination of four things.
1) What is the kind of business you would like to be in?
2) What types of businesses are succeeding these days, with every indication that they will continue to succeed?
3) Is someone offering a franchise in your area of interest, that you believe will help you to succeed, and that you can afford?
4) Can you work within the limits of a franchise system? Franchisors are not looking for real entrepreneurs, but more entrepreneurial sergeants who can fit into the system.

There is no magic in franchising. It works for good economic and social reasons. If you fully investigate the franchisor, there is every hope that you can make a choice that will significantly increase your chance of success in business.

INVESTIGATING THE FRANCHISOR

The new **Uniform Franchise Offering Circular (U.F.O.C.)** is now in effect. It was overhauled by the **North American Securities Administrators Association (N.A.S.A.A.)**.

The **Federal Trade Commission** requires franchisors in the U.S. to provide a disclosure statement based on either the F.T.C. Franchise Rule or the U.F.O.C. to the prospective franchisee at the appropriate time. (In Canada, only Alberta requires this, but Ontario is considering it.)

Briefly the Franchise Rule requires that a franchisor provide a prospective franchisee with a history of the company (the disclosure document) as well as a copy of the franchise agreement in time for them to be studied before the agreement is signed.

The new U.F.O.C. requires franchisors to disclose more information than ever before in "plain English" with easy to read tables etc. The new requirements mean that prospective franchisees will have a better idea of how many legal battles the franchisor has been involved in.

An earnings claim by the franchisor is any statement which tells you how much money you are going to earn. Under the F.T.C. Franchise Rule and the U.F.O.C., earnings claims can be made if they meet certain guidelines. Often franchisors prefer not to make any formal claims that they may later regret. This can result in "table napkin" outlines of profits that may be misleading.

Also, a franchisor may call a franchise a success when the franchisee would claim he is barely staying in business. Or a franchisor may call a unit a success, even if it was closed and then re-sold. Obviously, the failed franchisee would not call it a success. The new U.F.O.C. rules require the franchisor to include a clear outline of exactly what has happened to its franchisees each year.

Sometimes people think that because a franchisor has prepared a U.F.O.C. in compliance with Federal Trade Commission requirements, or in accordance with state registration regulations, that these documents amount to a stamp of approval by the government. This is false. Receiving a U.F.O.C. document should be just the starting point for the prospective franchisee. The first thing a prospective franchisee should do is contact present and past franchisees listed in the document.

When investigating the franchisor your aim should be to independently obtain information. You can obtain assistance in your investigation from many sources.

But, be aware that different sources have unique points of view. A franchisor association will look at things differently than a franchisee association. You must weigh the facts.

Important Worldwide Sources

1) **Alberta Securities Commission**, 21st Floor, 10025 Jasper Ave., Edmonton, AB, T5J 3Z5. Tel: (403) 427-5201 (Alberta is the only Canadian province with disclosure legislation.)
2) **The Ministry of Consumer and Commercial Relations** in your province.
3) **The Small Business Branch**, Ontario Ministry of Industry, Trade & Technology provides seminars entitled "Purchasing A Franchise" at different communities. Contact: 1-800-567-2345.
4) **American Franchisee Association** (AFA), 53 W. Jackson, Ste. 205, Chicago, IL, 60604. Tel: (312) 431-0545.
5) **American Association of Franchisees & Dealers** (AAFD), P.O. Box 81887, San Diego, CA, 92138-1887. Tel: (800) 733-9858.
6) **Federal Trade Commission**, Division of Marketing Practices, Bureau of Consumer Protection, 6th and Pennsylvania Ave., N.W., Washington, DC, 20580. Tel: (202) 326-3128.
7) **North American Securities Administrators Association** (NASAA), 1 Massachusetts Ave. N.W., Ste. 310, Washington, DC, 20001, Contact: Mr. Jeff Himstreet, Tel: (202) 737-0900.

Franchisor Associations

Argentine Franchising Association
Santa Fe 995, Piso 4, Buenos Aires 1059, Argentina
Tel: 54-1-393-9260, Fax: 54-1-393-5263

Austrian Franchise Association
Nonntaler Hauptstraße 48 Salzburg 5020-A, Austria
Tel: 0662-835303, Fax: 0662-832164

Franchise Association of Australia & New Zealand
Unit 9, 2-6 Hunter St., Parramatta, NSW, 2150, Australia
Tel: 61 2 891 4933, Fax: 61 2 891 4474

Belgian Franchise Federation
Groot Molenveldlaan, 52-1850, Grimbergen, Belgium
Tel: 02/253.27.12, Fax: 02/253.40.37

Brazilian Franchise Association
Av. Prof. Ascendino Reis 1548, Cep 04027-000, Sao Paulo, Brazil
Tel: 55-11-571-1303, Fax: 55-11-575-5590

The British Franchise Association
Thames View, Newtown Road, Henley-on-Thames, Oxon, RG9 1HG, England
Tel: 44 491 578 049, Fax: 44 491 573 517

Bulgarian Franchise Association
25A Ochrid St., 9000 - Varna, Bulgaria
Tel: 359 256 891, Fax: 359 256 891

Canadian Franchise Association,
5045 Orbitor Dr., Bldg. 12, Unit 201, Mississauga, ON, L4W 4Y4, Canada
Tel: (905) 625-2896 or (800) 665-4CFA, Fax: (905) 625-9076

Columbian Franchise Association
Apartado Aeoeo 25200, Cali, Columbia
Tel: 57 23 317 138, Fax: 57 23 311 086

Franchisors Association of the Czech Republic
Rytirska 31, POB 7067-110 00, Praha 1, Czech Republic

Danish Franchise Association
Amaliegade 31-A, 1256 Copenhagen, Denmark
Tel: 45-33156011, Fax: 45-33910346

European Franchise Federation
c/o Federation Francaise de la Franchise,
60, rue la Boétie, 75008, Paris, France
Tel: 53 75 2225, Fax: 53 75 2220
Finnish Franchising Association
PL 39, Helsinki SF-08501, Finland
French Franchise Federation
60, rue la Boétie, 75008, Paris, France
Tel: 53 75 2225, Fax: 53 75 2220
German Franchise Association
Paol Heyse Str. 33-35, Munchen 8033G, Germany
Tel: 49-89535027, Fax: 49-89531323
Hong Kong Franchise Association
22/F United Centre, 95 Queensway, Hong Kong
Tel: 2529 9229, Fax: 2527 9843
Hungarian Franchise Association
Secretariat, P.O. Box 446, Budapest H-1537, Hungary
Tel: 361-212-4124, Fax: 361-212-5712
Indonesia Franchise Association
JI Pembangunan 1/7, Jakarta, 10130, Indonesia
Tel: 62 21 3800233, Fax: 62 21 3802448
International Franchise Association
1350 New York Ave., N.W., Ste. 900, Washington, DC, 20005
Tel: (202) 628-8000
Irish Franchise Association
13 Frankfield Terrace, Summerhill South, Cork, Ireland
Italian Franchising Association
Corso Di Porta Nuova 3, 20121 Milano, Italy
Tel: 39-2-2900-3779, Fax: 39-2-655-5919
Japan Franchise Association
Elsa Bldg. 602, Roppongi 3-13-12, Minato-Ku, Tokyo 106, Japan
Tel: 81-3-401-0421, Fax: 81-33-423-2019
Malaysian Franchise Association
Implementation Coord. Unit, Jalan Dato' Onn
Fran. Dev. Dir., PM's Dept., Kuala Lumpur 50502, Malaysia
Tel: 60 3 2321957, Fax: 60 3 2301951
Mexican Franchise Association
Insurgentes Sur 1783 #303, Col. Guadalupe Inn,
Mexico City 01020, Mexico
Tel: 525-661-0655, Fax: 525-661-0655
Netherlands Franchise Association
Boomberglaan 12, 1217 RR, Hilversum, Netherlands
Tel: 31-35-6243444, Fax: 31 35 6249194
Franchise Association of Nigeria
P.O. Box 71729, Victoria Island, Lagos, Nigeria
Tel/Fax: 011-234-1-883585
Norwegian Franchise Federation
Postboks 2483 Solli, 0202 Oslo 2, Norway
Tel: 47-2-558220, Fax: 47-2-558225
Philippine Franchise Association
2/F Collins Int'l. Bldg., 167 ESDA Mandaluyong City,
Metro Manila, Philippines
Tel: 63-2-532-5644, Fax: 63-2-531-3894
Polish Franchise Association
UI. Krolewska 27, Pok. 340, 00-060, Warsaw, Poland
Franchise Association of Portugal
Rua Castilho, 14 Lisboa 1250, Portugal
Tel/Fax: (+351-1) 315 18 45
Romanian Franchise Association
Calea Victorieri Nr. 95, Et. 4, Ap. 16, Sect.1,
Bucharest, Romania
Tel: 401 312 6889/6180186, Fax: 401 312 6890
Singapore International Franchise Association
71 Sophia Rd., 0922, Singapore
Tel: 65 334 8200, Fax: 65 334 8211
Franchise Association of Southern Africa
P.O. Box 31708, 2017 Braamfontein, Republic of South Africa.
Tel: 27-11-403-3468, Fax: 27-11-403-1279
Asociacion Espanola de Franquiciadores
Avda. de las Ferias S/N, P.O. Box 476, 46080 Valencia, Spain
Tel: 96 386-11 23, Fax: 96 363 61 11
Swedish Franchise Association
Box 5512 - S. 114 85, Stockholm, Sweden
Tel: (46) 86608610, Fax: (46) 86627457
Swiss Franchise Association
Pilatussetrasse 55, Luzern 6003, Switzerland
Tel: 414 1222001, Fax: 414 1222004
UFRAD - Turkish Franchise Assoc.
Istiklal Cad No. 65, Emgentlar, 80600, Beyoglu, Istanbul, Turkey
Tel: 90212 252 5561, Fax: 90212 252 5561

The wise prospective franchisee should be looking for a franchisor who has been successfully doing business for several years and/or who can show that he will be doing a healthy business in the years to come. Franchising is essentially a "two-way street," with both parties entering into the franchise contract knowing that each has certain obligations to the other.

Real confidence can only be gained by your own thorough investigation of any franchisor. The franchise method is continually being adopted by small, growing, honest franchisors, one of whom might meet your needs, according to your business background, personality and financial resources.

Here are some of the questions which you should have obtained answers to before signing the franchise contract. Some of these questions help to give you a general idea of the franchisor's ability, which is of use when comparing him with other franchisors who are offering the same type of franchise. It is important to COMPARE FRANCHISORS IF MORE THAN ONE HAS THE PRODUCT/SERVICE IN WHICH YOU ARE INTERESTED.

The following questions cover more than is needed in order to investigate most franchisors but the questions do not fully cover all that is needed to investigate every franchisor.

THE FRANCHISOR

- Does the franchisor have the proper financial backing?
- Is the franchisor a subsidiary of another company? What are their assets?
- Who is the parent company? Have they ever franchised other products or services?
- Is it a similar product?
- Would they be in competition with you?
- Was, or is, the other franchise operation successful?
- Can you see any of the franchisor's recently audited financial statements?
- When do you get to see the contract, and disclosure document if there is one? Is there a profit projection?
- Is it based on company run or franchisee run outlets?
- How long have each of the outlets used as a basis for the projection been in operation? Are they rural or urban?
- How long has the franchisor been in business? How long has he been offering franchises?
- What is the business experience of the franchise company's directors and officers?
- Have any of the franchisor's partners or company members ever gone bankrupt?
- Have any of them been involved in litigation recently?
- Is it a public company? (If it is a public company you can obtain copies of their annual reports and also get copies of the detailed 10K reports.)
- When can you read the prospectus?
- Does the franchisor help you finance the purchase of the franchise?
- Does the franchisor have the kind of reputation and credit rating which would help you to obtain the financial backing needed to purchase the franchise?
- How many franchisees does the franchisor have? How many does he plan on having?
- Where will these be located?
- Does he have a good marketing plan?
- Does he provide a useful initial training program? Who pays for this?
- Does the franchisor provide post-opening training, if necessary, and other continuing assistance?
- Does the franchisor have a system for the inspection of the franchisees?
- Is he always available for on-the-spot counseling? Will he help recruit your personnel?
- Who pays for the initial opening supplies?
- Does the franchisor design store layouts and displays?
- Does the franchisor exercise good quality control?
- Does the franchisor provide inventory control?
- Does the franchisor provide volume purchasing discounts?
- Are the administrative and bookkeeping procedures simple and well run?
- What is the advertising program? What do you pay towards local advertising? What do you pay towards national advertising?
- Do you have any say in the advertising format?
- Is the franchisor up-to-date in all his operations?
- Are his sales techniques modern?
- What innovations has the franchisor introduced since first starting?
- Does the franchisor provide a helpful and fully explanatory manual for the training of the staff and the operation of the franchise?
- Is the price of the franchise variable? If so, how?
- Can you purchase used equipment for a discount?

THE PRODUCT OR SERVICE

- What is the demand for the product/service?
- Would **you** buy the product or require the service?
- How long has it been on the market? Is the product/service seasonable?
- Is it a staple or a luxury?
- Will the franchisee depend on the tourist trade? To what extent?
- Is the product/service a fad?
- Is it marketable in your territory?
- Is the quality of the product/service acceptable?
- Are there federal or state/provincial requirements for the product/service?
- Are there product warranties or guarantees? Who backs them?
- Who makes the repairs? Who pays for the repairs?
- Is the price competitive with similar products or services on the market?
- Who controls the price?
- Can you purchase any of your stock from a source other than the franchisor or his designated suppliers?
- What percent of the population will be attracted to the product/service?
- Is its appeal limited to certain age groups?
- Is it properly packaged?
- Is it protected by trademark or copyright?
- Has the product been patented? Can it be easily copied?
- Is a well known person involved in selling the product? Is this celebrity involved financially?
- What would be the effect on the marketing of the product if the celebrity withdrew support?

THE FRANCHISEE

The following questions (and most of the previous ones) could be directed to franchisees who are already operating. Get the franchisor to give you a list of present franchisees and visit or phone them. You can also question franchisees in rival franchise systems!

- ❏ What was the total (not simply the downpayment) investment required by the franchisor?
- ❏ Were there hidden or unexpected costs?
- ❏ Has the merchandise, machinery and other equipment which the franchisor supplied been of good quality?
- ❏ Is the franchisor prompt with his deliveries?
- ❏ How long was it before you hit the break-even point?
- ❏ How long before the franchise was able to support you?
- ❏ Were you trained? Was the training adequate?
- ❏ Were the projected sales of the franchise, which the franchisor supplied, accurate?
- ❏ Was the general profit projection accurate?
- ❏ Do you have a guaranteed (not right to) buy-back agreement in your contract on inventory and equipment?
- ❏ Have you ever had a serious disagreement with the franchisor?
- ❏ What about? Was it settled amicably?
- ❏ Do you know whether the franchisor has ever had to settle any problem through arbitration?
- ❏ Do you have to send a periodic report to the company? What does it include?
- ❏ Does the franchisor actively respond to the reports?
- ❏ Are you satisfied with the marketing, promotional and advertising assistance that you receive from the company?
- ❏ If you could change your contract, what would you change?
- ❏ Would you advise anyone to start a franchise with this franchisor?

THE TERRITORY

- ❏ Is it exclusive?
- ❏ What assurance do you have that it is exclusive?
- ❏ Can you choose the location or territory?
- ❏ Will the franchisor help you select a location?
- ❏ Has the franchisor conducted feasibility studies of the market potential in your proposed territory?
- ❏ Do you lease or buy the location?
- ❏ Are the equipment and fixtures specified?
- ❏ Can you buy or lease equipment and fixtures from someone other than the franchisor?
- ❏ Is the layout of the location specified?
- ❏ Can you change the layout?
- ❏ How near to you is the franchisor's next franchisee or company owned unit going to be? Can the franchisor tell you when this other new unit will be set up? (Will this hinder your development, i.e. competition, or will it help your development, i.e. more money in your area for advertising?)
- ❏ Is the territory well defined? Is it large enough? What are your expansion possibilities?
- ❏ What is the present population? What is the proposed population for five years from now?
- ❏ Are there any new highways planned?
- ❏ What is the industrial growth?
- ❏ What are the zoning laws? (Strict zoning laws in some areas may forbid opening a franchise at all.) Will these laws be changed?
- ❏ Are zoning licenses required?
- ❏ What is the average income level in the area?
- ❏ What is the competition in the area?
- ❏ How are other businesses doing in the area?
- ❏ What is the traffic count near your location? (both auto and pedestrian)
- ❏ What kind of insurance is available for the area? Is it expensive?

THE CONTRACT

There is usually a standard contract. However, do not hesitate to have your lawyer/attorney add any extra clauses which you feel are necessary. Do not be afraid to "haggle" a little. There has been a lot of talk about a David and Goliath situation existing between the franchisee and the franchisor. Whether this is the case or not in some instances, it is not the case with you as a prospective franchisee. When you sit down with your legal representative and the franchisor to draw up the contract there is no reason why you can't get up and walk away if you don't like the deal you are getting. However, it is important to understand that most franchisors will be adamant about keeping the standard contract for the sake of uniformity.

- ❏ Does the contract protect both parties?
- ❏ Are the nature, duration and extent of your training outlined in the contract?
- ❏ Is a franchise cost hidden in a minimum purchase of merchandise per year?
- ❏ Are there any additional fixed payments?
- ❏ Is the monthly royalty reasonable?
- ❏ Is there a monthly percentage of gross required for advertising?
- ❏ Does the franchisee have to pay a royalty when business is poor?
- ❏ What constitutes the "poor" business level?
- ❏ Is the sales quota at a minimum?
- ❏ What are the conditions for renewal of the contract?
- ❏ Does the franchisor agree to maintain a good reputation? (He could lose his trademark if he does not properly supervise the quality of the product/service).

- ❏ If a signed lease with the franchisor is involved, is it at a competitive price?
- ❏ Does your lease correspond in duration to the contract?
- ❏ Are there parallel renewal options for the contract and the lease?
- ❏ Does the contract cover in detail all the franchisor's verbal promises?
- ❏ Have you a right to the franchisor's latest innovations?
- ❏ Will the franchisor maintain any necessary Federal and State/Provincial registrations?
- ❏ Do you have the right to assign the franchise?
- ❏ Must the franchisor approve the new franchisee? Under what conditions?
- ❏ How can you terminate the franchise?
- ❏ When and how can the franchisor terminate your franchise?
- ❏ How will you be compensated for the "goodwill" which you have built up?
- ❏ What happens in the event of illness or death?
- ❏ What time have you to correct defaults?
- ❏ Is there an arbitration clause? Is there a mediation clause?
- ❏ If there is a legal dispute, must your attorneys journey to the franchisor's legal district?
- ❏ Must you promise not to enter into a business similar to the franchisor's for a period of time after you have separated from the franchisor (covenant not to compete)?
- ❏ Must you promise not to enter into any other business while you are a franchisee (full time and attention clause)?
- ❏ In what other business activities may you engage?

Get a Lawyer/Attorney. Get an Accountant. (And maybe even an Urban Economist.) Do you have a bank affiliation? No matter how much investigation you have done, you will need to consult a Lawyer and Accountant before investing. You probably will need to consult them during your investigation. And don't forget to consult your Insurance Agent. He may be aware of a few hidden costs about which you do not know. Investing in the cost of a lawyer and accountant is the best way to protect your final franchise investment. You need to invest in professional advice. **Do it.** There is no reliable alternative. But make sure your investigation has been a thorough one in order that you will be able to bring to your lawyer and accountant as much information as possible. It is only in this way that you can take full advantage of their services. You should know what you are investing in and you should have your own facts.

BUSINESS OPPORTUNITY FRAUD

The **North American Securities Administrators Association (NASAA)** reports: "...con artists are cashing in on the rapidly changing North American workplace. A record number of people are now self-employed business owners. Millions more find themselves out of work as the result of corporate downsizing. Still others must seek second jobs in order to make ends meet. All are prime targets for the growing ranks of fast-buck operators pushing worthless "business opportunity" schemes involving vending machines, amusement games, pay telephones, and display racks for greeting cards, CD-ROM computer software, and other items.

Lured by deceptive promises of independence and easy income, many would-be entrepreneurs are jumping into the arms of con artists who claim: **"we are not just selling you a business, we put you IN business."** The recent rise of dozens of telemarketing "boiler rooms" pushing pre-packaged small business "deals" has yielded an astounding surge in business opportunity scams across America. Though precise numbers are not available, state and federal regulators estimate that **well over $100 million a year** is now disappearing into worthless business opportunity rip-offs. The actual figure most likely is substantially higher; in just three recent cases handled by the **Federal Trade Commission (FTC)**, almost $64 million in losses were sustained by the unwary victims.

Enter "Project Telesweep"

On July 18, 1995, the FTC, the **U.S. Department of Justice**, 20 state securities regulators, attorneys general, franchise and business opportunity regulators, and consumer protection offices, announced an unprecedented federal-state assault on business opportunity scams. This coordinated crackdown effort is known as "Project Telesweep." The following cases illustrate the nature and extent of the business opportunity fraud epidemic in North America:

• *Staggering Losses.* A Mercer Island, Washington, woman who is the single mother of three daughters fell into a business opportunity trap in late 1993 when she resolved to supplement her income to pay for her children's education, according to the Securities Division of the State of Washington, Department of Financial Institutions. After responding to a classified ad in the *Seattle Times* and traveling to Colorado to meet the promoter, she invested more than $13,000 in "video pool" and "video bowling" games that broke down within 90 days. Rather than fixing the equipment, the promoter sent her two new units that she had not ordered. The machines are now gathering dust in the woman's garage.

In a case brought by the FTC, a woman from Pennsylvania responded to an advertisement for a pizza vending machine business opportunity. The promoter promised huge earnings and the best locations in the area. The woman ended up losing her entire investment of $72,000. In order to make up the loss, she and her husband had to mortgage their home and sell off a dairy cow herd. They are now working multiple jobs in a struggle to avoid losing their family farm.

• *Promises of instant riches.* One trademark of a business

opportunity scam is an overblown promise of easy money. In one ad for a pay telephone scheme, a promoter promises: **"Get 96 sites for $7,795. Then Retire! Call 1-800/XXX-XXXX."** A brochure for a Utah snack vending machine company reads: **"Many People Earn $36,000/year in Income, But...Very Few Earn $30,000/year working only five-six hours per week."** In another case, a promoter for a gumball machine business opportunity claimed that one operator had earned $14,000 from four machines...in just seven days!

• *Unproven concepts.* In a case handled by the Securities Division of the Maryland Attorney General, an in-state company ran ads in *Income Plus* magazine and other publications for a business opportunity involving an overhyped solar-powered car battery recharger. According to the *Income Plus* ad, distributors for the company were **"making in excess of $200,000 in their first year with the business."** The state handled more than 70 complaints from investors around the United States, many of whom reported that the solar-powered rechargers did not work at all. When one investor took the recharger to an electrician, he was told that it would take weeks to recharge a battery with the device. Nonetheless, the recharger had been touted in ads with the line: **"In seconds, you're off and running..."**

In one case brought by the Federal Trade Commission, a promoter touting a vending machine known as the **"Alcohol Neutralizer"** offered investors packages of five machines for $4,500. Installed in taverns and other places where liquor is served, the "Alcohol Neutralizer" was to dispense an herbal pill containing an active ingredient that was **supposed to be able to reduce blood alcohol count (BAC) levels**. Supposedly, the pills had been endorsed as safe and efficacious by the Food and Drug Administration and were backed up by the work of Harvard Medical School researchers. In fact, the FDA had taken action to stop the manufacturing of the pills and the Ivy League scientists in questions denied ever having produced the supportive findings linked to them by the promoter. An independent study by an Indiana University scientist found that the herbal ingredient in the pills might actually keep BAC levels **higher** for a longer period of time than if a drinker had never taken the pill!

• *Shoddy merchandise.* In one investigation of a business opportunity scheme, investors complained about a soda vending machine that looked like a small refrigerator. Not only did the vending machine have to be opened from the front, but customers had to turn a crank in order to get out their sodas. Complicating matters was the fact that the inferior vending machines required exact change...and only in a certain combination of coins!

Another business opportunity scheme promising six-figure earnings in the display rack sale of discount CD-ROM computer software lured customers with promotional materials implying that the low-priced software in question would feature such major brand names as IBM, Corel, and Microsoft. In fact, the business opportunity, for which some customers paid up to $40,000, featured "junk software", including cheap shareware, service and installation disks, and promotional samples marked "not for resale."

What Are Business Opportunities?

A business opportunity involves the sale of goods or services that enable the novice entrepreneur to begin a business. Typical business opportunities involve vending machines, amusement games, pay telephones, and display racks for such items as greeting cards and CD-ROM computer software. Ideally, the vending machines or display racks are located in high-traffic areas, such as malls, airports, or bowling alleys.

The promoter of a business opportunity is responsible for providing vending machines or display racks and finding locations for investors. The promoter may offer to locate the machines for investors, may assist the investor in locating the machines, or may refer the investor to a professional locating service. The promoter may also represent that it will repair or replace broken machines. The promoter may also supply marketing plans, training, or other general guidance. Generally, the operator of the business opportunity is responsible for cleaning and restocking the machines or display racks, making sure needed repairs get done, and collecting the money.

Under federal law, the promoter of a business opportunity is required to provide potential investors with complete pre-sale information in the form of a disclosure document. Some states impose additional licensing and disclosure requirements.

In a world where McDonald's is one of the best known of all household names, the "franchise" is probably the most familiar type of business venture package. A business opportunity is considered a franchise when its name is identified by a common trademark or trade name and the promoter offers investors significant assistance in operating a business or exercises significant control over the investor's method of operation. Federal law deals with franchises and business opportunities in much the same way. A total of 15 states have some type of franchise disclosure regulation; 24 states have laws that specifically address business opportunity promotions.

The Surge in Bogus Business Opportunities

Business opportunities have received considerable attention in recent years, owning in large part to the decline of traditional job security and the increasing number of individuals who have lost jobs due to corporate downsizing. Always quick to seize on a new way to make an illicit buck, con artists have picked up on the changes in the traditional American job. The result: fraudulent telemarketing operations are now pushing overhyped or worthless small business deals on unsuspecting entrepreneurs, individuals looking for a second income to make ends meet, and people who have lost jobs and cannot find replacements for them.

Investigations show that victims are lured into the telemarketing "boiler room" by small ads that appear in the classified sections of newspapers and magazines. If an unwary investor makes the mistake of calling, the high-pressure "boiler room" sales tactics begin immediately. In the typical illicit telemarketing operation, the phone operators play a number of different roles. The first person to take the call is known as the **"fronter"** and has the task of making the initial pitch and determining if the potential "mooch" has the money to invest. Once qualified, the caller encounters a second person, usually referred to as the **"owner/manager"**, who turns up the heat and urges the caller to check out the firm's references. The call may also be handed off to a **"closer"** who pulls out all the stops in attempting to extract payment.

Peddlers of bogus business opportunities do not seem to have a care in the world about a potential investor contacting existing operators. That is because many rely upon what we know as **"singers"**, people who get paid to pose as reference givers or who are existing operators enticed with the prospect of additional goods and services in exchange for their high praise. In the case of one Miami company offering a business opportunity deal involving candy vending machines, existing operators were promised one free vending machine for each positive testimonial.

Signs of Business Opportunity Scams

How can you tell a legitimate business opportunity from a promotion that is a scam? Investigators in "Project Telesweep" report that the following are hallmarks of fraudulent business opportunity schemes today:

- **Use of classified ads that urge the prospect to call an "800" number.**
- **Wild and unsubstantiated claims about potential earnings.**
- **Claims about "proven" concepts.**
- **Suggestions that no experience is necessary.**
- **Promises about exclusive territories.**
- **Assurances about good locations for vending machines or display racks, or the assistance of a professional locator.**
- **Reliance on references handpicked by the company (instead of being provided a list of current business opportunity owners).**
- **Failure to provide prospective investors with a complete disclosure document containing pre-sale disclosures about their experience, lawsuit history, audited financial statements, and substantiation for any representations made about earnings.**

Steps You Can Take To Protect Yourself

If you detect signs of a problem in a business opportunity that you are reviewing, you should proceed with **extreme** caution. If you have concerns about how you are faring with an existing business opportunity and believe that some of these hallmarks are at work in your deal, it may be time for you to complain to a regulator. Unfortunately, the nature of business opportunity fraud is that it may take six or more months for an operator to recognize that he or she has been duped. The problems may drag on because of stalling tactics on the part of promoters who promise to make repairs or partial refunds.

The best way to avoid being taken by a business opportunity scam to begin with is to research any potential investment thoroughly with an eye to signs of possible trouble. Anyone who is considering an investment in a business opportunity should review the following key pieces of advice:

- ***Be skeptical about earnings claims that sound too good to be true.*** The "bait" on the "hook" of a business opportunity scam is that a person with no experience may be able to work only a few hours a week and earn $50,000, $100,000 ... or more ... a year. The truth is that making money almost always requires hard work ... and lots of it.

- ***Exercise caution when it comes to newspaper and magazine ads that contain little more than glowing promises and an "800" number.*** This is very likely a "come-on" pitch to lure you into calling a high-pressure telemarketing boiler room operation! Keep in mind that just because an ad appears in a reputable newspaper or magazine does not mean that the information it contains is accurate or legitimate. As in recent sweepstakes and travel scams, the phone con artists pushing bogus business opportunities will make any statement necessary to separate an unwary individual from his or her savings.

- ***Obtain and review the required disclosure document before money changes hands.*** Keep in mind that business opportunity and franchise promoters are required to present you with a disclosure document **before** you sign a contract or pay a fee. If this document is not made readily available, beware! When you get the document, carefully review the portions dealing with: risks; the business experience of the company and directors; history of lawsuits; including those alleging fraud; fees to be paid and conditions under which fees and deposits will be returned; audited financial statements containing balance sheets for the three previous years; and substantiation for any earnings claims made to you.

- ***Make sure that the business opportunity has complied with applicable state registration laws.*** Even if a business opportunity promoter complies with the laws in your state governing such deals, there is no guarantee that you will make money. However, it is one easy way to screen out bogus operators who are trying to "fly below radar" in order to evade detection by regulators.

- ***Talk to current investors..and watch out for "singers."*** You should always take the time to speak with several people who are current investors in the business opportunity that you are considering. The disclosure document must contain a list of the business opportunities' current operators. But be on your guard! A scheming promoter of a bogus business opportunity may line up "singers" who provide phony testimonials.

Be suspicious if you cannot reach references by phone. In one case investigated by the FTC, a promoter used three aliases and out-of-state voice mail boxes to return calls in which he posed

as an investor to woo prospects. The best way to avoid "singers," is to get the names and addresses of the retail locations where the vending machines or rack display are purportedly located and visit the locations in person. You can then judge for yourself the quality of the machines, their state of repair, and the traffic volume in the store. Take the time to interview at least five references. You may wish to ask them the following questions:
Are you happy with your investment?
Has the promoter come through for you?
Are you making the money you thought you'd be making?
Would you make this investment again, knowing what you now know?
What do you like and dislike about this business opportunity?
What are the names and addresses of the retail locations where your machines are currently located?

- **Research the business and the market.** Make sure that you have a clear grasp of how the business opportunity will work and what demand (if any) there is likely to be in your territory. Don't rely only on glowing promises from telemarketers who claim that consumers are clamoring to get your product. In one case where a business opportunity claimed to have a "worst case" net return of $1,220 a month, investigators found that the investor who was doing the best only made about $200-$300 monthly.

- **Get professional advice if you need it.** Don't lose your life savings just because you failed to spend a few hundred dollars to talk to a lawyer, an accountant or other expert. These people will sometimes be able to spot key details that you are missing. Since they are not caught up in your dream and hope for success, outsiders are also in a better position to review a business opportunity from a neutral vantage point.

- **Don't automatically assume that promises of prime sites, speedy repairs, and ongoing assistance will be there when you need them.** Remember that a bogus business opportunity promoter will promise you the sun and the moon in order to get your money. Be cautious when you sign up with a firm that is supposed to identify prime sites for your vending machines, pay telephones, display racks, or other items. Keep in mind that many who get burned in business opportunities lose their money when promoters fail to come through with promised repairs and other ongoing assistance.

If you want to check out a business opportunity scam, contact your state securities division or attorneys general office. You may also file a complaint with the FTC."

STATE REGULATIONS

The Following is a summary of the states which have legislation which directly concerns general business format franchising as well as pertinent government bodies to contact. (Auto, truck, beer, liquor and gasoline marketing legislation has been omitted.) For further details of state laws and other franchise legislation see "Franchising" by Glickman. Matthew Bender & Company. (235 E. 45th St., New York, NY, 10017.)

ARKANSAS: Franchise Practices Act prevents termination of franchisee without good cause and governs renewal of franchise contract. Forbids fraud and deceit in sale of franchises.

CALIFORNIA: Franchise Investment Law requires registration and disclosure by franchisor. The modification of Existing Franchise amendment makes a material modification of an existing franchise the equivalent of a sale subject to the disclosure and registration provisions of the Franchise Investment Law. Another amendment, the Franchisee's Right to Join Trade Association, makes it a violation of the Act for a franchisor to restrict the right of franchisees to join a trade association or to prohibit free association among franchisees for any lawful purposes. The Seller Assisted Marketing Plan statute requires certain sellers of business opportunities to register with the Secretary of State (Legal Review) a disclosure statement and its salesmen before advertising or selling an opportunity and to give each purchaser, at least forty-eight hours prior to the execution of any agreement or the receipt of consideration, a copy of the disclosure statement (franchises covered by the Franchise Investment Law are excluded). Franchise Relations Act covers termination and renewal of franchisee. It prevents termination without good cause and requires franchisor to give 180 days notification to franchisee if the franchisor does not intend to renew contracts and prohibits converting a non-renewed franchise to a company owned unit without compensating the franchisee. (Good Cause is defined as including but not limited to the failure of the franchisee to comply with any lawful requirements of the franchise agreement after being given notice and a reasonable opportunity, which in no event need be more than 30 days, to cure the failure). Contact: Department of Corporations, 3700 Wilshire Blvd., Ste. 600, Los Angeles, CA, 90010. Tel: (213) 736-2741.

CONNECTICUT: Registration and disclosure by franchisor under Business Opportunity Investment Act. Franchising Fairness Law governs termination and non-renewal. Contact: Department of Banking, Securities Division, 260 Constitution Plaza, Hartford, CT, 06106, Tel: (203) 240-8299.

DELAWARE: Under Prohibited Trade Practices the Franchise Security Act prohibits unjust or bad faith termination of franchisee or refusal to renew a franchise.

DISTRICT OF COLUMBIA: Franchising Act establishes uniform standards for franchising agreements.

FLORIDA: Franchises and Distributorship Law forbids intentional misrepresentation in the sale of franchises and distributorships. Contact: Consumer Services Div., 209 Mayo Bldg., Tallahassee, FL, 32399-0800. Tel: (904) 488-2221. Business Opportunity Act requires registration and disclosure by franchisor.

Contact: Office of Attorney General. Dept. of Legal Affairs, Consumer Division, The Capitol, TL-01, Tallahassee, FL, 32399-1050, Tel: (904) 488-9105.

GEORGIA: Business Opportunity statute aimed at preventing fraudulent and deceptive practices in the sale of business opportunities. Governs disclosure and registration. Office of Consumer Affairs, 2 Martin Luther King Dr. S.E., Ste. 356, Atlanta, GA, 30334, Tel: (404) 656-3790, Fax: (404) 651-9018. The Georgia Sale of Business Opportunities Act may include certain franchisors and sub-franchisors depending on whether the exemption under the law applies.

HAWAII: Franchise Investment Law outlines registration, disclosure, termination and renewal. Contact: Department of Commerce and Consumer Affairs, P.O. Box 40, Honolulu, HI, 96810. Tel: (808) 586-2722.

ILLINOIS: The Franchise Disclosure Act regulates disclosure, registration, termination and non-renewal. Contact: Franchise Division, Attorney General's Office, 500 S. Second St., Springfield, IL, 62706. Tel: (217) 782-4465.

INDIANA: Franchise Disclosure Law. Deceptive Franchise Practices Act regulates the terms of franchise agreements and practices arising out of the relationship under the contracts. Contact: Securities Commissioner, 302 W. Washington St., Ste. E111, Indianapolis, IN, 46204. Tel: (317) 232-6681.

IOWA: Franchise Relationship Law and Business Opportunity Laws. Contact: Iowa Division of Insurance. Securities Division, Lucas State Office Bldg., Des Moines, IA, 50319, Tel: (515) 281-5705.

KENTUCKY: Business Opportunity Disclosure and Registration Act.

LOUISIANA: Business Opportunity Sellers and Agents Act.

MAINE: Business Opportunity Act outlines registration and disclosure requirements for sale of any business opportunity. Contact: Securities Division. Dept. of Professional & Financial Regulation. State House Station 121, Augusta, ME, 04333. Tel: (207) 624-8551.

MARYLAND: Franchise Registration and Disclosure Act. Contact: Office of Attorney General, Division of Securities, 200 St. Paul Pl., 20th Flr., Baltimore, MD, 21202-2020. Tel: (410) 576-6360. Business Opportunities Sales Act.

MICHIGAN: Franchise Investment Law. Contact: Attorney General Department, Consumer Protection Division, 525 W. Ottawa, 670 Law Bldg., Lansing, MI, 48913. Tel: (517) 373-7117. Michigan Franchise Investment Law Reform Act.

MINNESOTA: Franchise Law. Contact: Department of Commerce, 133 E. 7th St., St. Paul, MN, 55101. Tel: (612) 296-6328.

MISSOURI: Merchandising Practices Act.

NEBRASKA: Franchise Practices Act governs termination and renewal. Business Practices Act governs seller-assisted marketing plans. Contact: Division of Securities, P.O. Box 95006, Lincoln, NE, 68509-5006. Tel: (402) 471-2171.

NEW HAMPSHIRE: Distributorship Disclosure Act governs registration and disclosure. Contact: Consumer Protection and Antitrust Bureau, 33 Capital St., Concord, NH, 03301. Tel: (603) 271-3641.

NEW JERSEY: Franchise Practices Act concerns termination and renewals.

NEW YORK: Franchise Sales Act. Contact: New York State, Department of Law, 120 Broadway, Room 23-122, New York, NY, 10271. Tel: (212) 416-8800. Also Rule 5-60 of the Rules of the City of New York, Vol. 3, Titles 6-8, enforced by Department of Consumer Affairs. Contact: Assistant Commissioner, Legal Affairs, Susan Kassapian, 42 Broadway, New York, NY, 10004. Tel: (212) 487-3961.

NORTH CAROLINA: Business Opportunity Sales Law requires disclosure. Contact: Secretary of State, Securities Division, 300 N. Salsbury St., Room 100, Raleigh, NC, 27603. Tel: (919) 733-3924.

NORTH DAKOTA: Franchise Investment Law governs registration, disclosure, termination and renewal. Contact: Securities Commission, 5th Floor, 600 East Boulevard Ave., Bismarck, ND, 58505-0510. Tel: (701) 328-2910.

OHIO: Business Opportunity Law. Contact: Assistant Attorney General, Consumer Protection Division, State Office Tower, 25th Floor, 30 E. Broad St., Columbus, OH, 43215. Tel: (614) 466-8831.

OKLAHOMA: Business Opportunity Sales Act.

OREGON: Franchise Law requires disclosures from franchisor. Contact: Department of Insurance and Finance, Div. of Finance and Corporate Securities, Securities Section, 21 Labour & Industries Building, 350 Winter St. N.E., Room 21, Salem, OR, 97310. Tel: (503) 378-4387.

RHODE ISLAND: Franchise and Distributorship Investment Regulation Act requires full disclosure. Contact: State of Rhode Island, Department of Business Regulation, Securities Division, 233 Richmond St., Ste. 232, Providence Rhode Island, 02903-4232. Tel: (401) 277-3048.

SOUTH CAROLINA: Business Opportunity Sales Act covers disclosure. Contact: Attn: Caroline Hatcher, Secretary of State's Office, P.O. Box 11350, Columbia, SC, 29211. Tel: (803) 734-2166.

SOUTH DAKOTA: The South Dakota Franchise Law requires registration and disclosure. Contact: Franchise Administrator, Division of Securities, 118 W. Capitol, Pierre, SD, 57501-2017, Tel: (605) 773-4823.

TEXAS: Business Opportunity Disclosure Act requires disclosure and registration. (Franchisors who comply with F.T.C. requirements are exempt.)

UTAH: Business Opportunity Act requires a disclosure statement.

VIRGINIA: Retail Franchising Act covers termination, renewal, registration and disclosure. Contact: State Corporation Commission, Division of Securities and Retail Franchising, 1300 E. Main St., 9th Flr., Richmond, VA, 23219, Tel: (804) 371-9051.

WASHINGTON: Franchise Investment Protection Act requires disclosure and registration. It also governs termination and renewal. Contact: Department of Financial Institutions Securities Division, P.O. Box 9033, Olympia, WA, 98507-9033. Tel: (360) 902-8760. Also: Business Opportunity Fraud Act covering disclosure and registration.

WISCONSIN: Franchise Investment Law requires registration and disclosure. Contact: Securities Commission, P.O. Box 1768, Madison, WI, 53701. Tel: (608) 266-3431. Also Dealership Practices Act covers termination and renewal.

PUERTO RICO: Dealer's Contracts Law covering termination and non-renewal of contract.

NEWS FROM THE INFO FRANCHISE NEWSLETTER

Here are two excerpts from the *INFO Franchise Newsletter* concerning franchise statistics:

Franchisee Survival Rates
(Vol. 19, No. 6, Pg. 1)

Dr. Timothy Bates, professor of labor and urban affairs at **Wayne State University** *(Tel: (313) 577-5071, Fax: (313) 577-8800)* has produced a paper entitled *Analysis of Survival Rates Among Franchise and Independent Small Business Startups* (See also INFO, Vol. 18, No. 3, Pg. 6). The research reported in the study was conducted on-site at the **Center for Economic Studies, U.S. Bureau of the Census.** Findings addressed are those of Mr. Bates, and do not necessarily reflect the views of the U.S. Bureau of the Census. The paper notes:

"Findings of this study indicate that young franchise startups exhibit both higher rates of firm discontinuance and lower mean profitability than cohort independent business startups. When owner and firm traits are controlled for statistically in logistic regression exercises, the franchise characteristic is found to be negatively related to firm survival prospects...

The findings of this study are consistent with the hypothesis that popular franchising niches have become saturated, leaving diminished prospects for newcomers...

Relative to all small business startups, franchises are heavily concentrated in retailing and it is the retail franchises that most often fit the high risk, low return profile...

Franchise discontinuance rates reported in this study differ dramatically from those cited by various franchisors and franchisors associations. According to research sponsored by the **International Franchise Association,** 96.9 percent of franchised units opened nationwide within the past five years are still in operation (**Arthur Andersen & Co., 1992**). This survival rate information was compiled by surveying franchisors, the corporations that sell franchises, rather than the actual franchisee owners of the operations whose survival is at issue. The approach of this study, in contrast, is to rely upon franchisee owners to self-report information about the continuity of operations in the small businesses that they own and operate...

Franchisees are generally better endowed with traits linked to survival than nonfranchise young firms...sales five times larger than...independent businesses...Capitalization...three times greater... Only in the area of owner educational background do the franchise firms appear to be weaker than the independents: 9.1 percent of the former and 16.2 percent of the latter had pursued graduate studies beyond the bachelor's degree... Yet, despite the obvious strengths of the young franchise firms, they are dramatically less profitable than independent firms of the same age...and they exhibit a lower survival rate, 65.3 percent (versus 72.0 percent for nonfranchise firms), over the 1987-late 1991 time period...

Could this lower incidence of graduate-educated owners account for the fact that the franchise group exhibited a lower rate of survival than independent business startups?...

The surviving firms active in late 1991 are disproportionately those headed by highly educated owners who worked full-time in the business. The surviving firms, further, were the larger firms in the sense that they began operations with greater owner financial capital investments; labor input, measured by number of employees, was higher among the survivors...

Young retail firms are much less profitable and much more likely to go out of business than franchises operating in nonretailing fields. This pattern is consistent with the hypothesis that saturation exists in the franchise retailing industry.

One possible cause of poor franchise performance is the costs specific to this organizational form, upfront fees to the franchisor, royalty fees, marketing fees, and the like. Do these costs exceed the benefits accruing to young firms choosing the franchise route? Are low margin lines of retailing particularly burdened by such fees? The potential research agenda is just beginning to emerge."

Castrogiovanni on Franchise Failure
(Vol. 19, No. 8, Pg. 3)

Professor Gary Castrogiovanni *(Department of Management, College of Business Administration, **University of Houston**, Houston, TX, 77204-6283, Tel: (713) 743-4657, Fax: (713) 743-4652)* in conjunction with **Robert T. Justis**, and **Scott D. Julian** authored a paper entitled *Franchise Failure Rates: An Assessment of Magnitude and Influencing Factors*, which appeared in the April, 1993 issue of the *Journal of Small Business Management*... The paper noted:

"The relevant issue is whether a particular individual would be better off buying a particular franchise. The following are some factors that prospective business owners should consider.

Buying a franchise may not be a better option if:

✖ the particular franchisor is new and small, without a well-known brand name;

✖ the nature of the business is such that a large proportion of customers are local rather than transient (and thus likely to make repeat purchases);

✖ the franchisor has had a high percentage of unit closures in recent years;

✖ it is impossible to imitate the successful practices of established competitors;

✖ it is possible to buy an established, successful independent business;

✖ the prospective business owner has substantial management experience in the type of business under consideration;

✖ the prospective business owner has an extensive network of business associates with knowledge of the type of business under consideration;

✖ price competition is intense in the local market being considered; or

✖ local market conditions are very different from those faced by most other units in the franchised chain.

Prospective buyers need to scrutinize the particular opportunity being considered. They should not rely on general rules of thumb.

...Though important, knowledge of franchise failure rates on average is, however, of limited usefulness to aspiring business owners. The more germane question is 'How likely is it that my franchise will fail if I do acquire one?'..."

| BUYING A FRANCHISE? | EXPANDING YOUR BUSINESS? | SELLING FRANCHISES? |

Call *Women in* FRANCHISING

Women in Franchising, Inc. (WIF) offers
- Franchise applicant self-assessment
- Assistance locating, selecting and evaluating a franchise
- Legal referral service
- Help with your business plan
- Help finding financing
- One-on-one consulting
- Seminars / workshops

Women in Franchising, Inc. (WIF) offers
- Feasibility studies
- Development of offering circular
- Operations manuals
- Sales & marketing plan
- Brochure/collateral materials
- "Is Your Business Franchisable?" workshops
- Strategic planning

Become a WIF Corporate Member! Benefits include:
- Recruit and retain women & minorities
- "Marketing to Women & Minorities" seminars
- Free public relations
- 2,000 leads per year
- Franchisor-Franchisee Relations
- Native American Franchise Initiatives
- International trade missions

Call 1-800-222-4WIF (4943)

...for free "get started" kit. | ...for free initial consultation. | ...to join or for information.

DON'T BE LEFT IN THE DARK!

FRANCHISEES...
Join YOUR trade association today! 14,000 franchise owners have discovered that AFA represents their interests. Benefits include:
- *Network with other Franchisees*
- *Regional Meetings*
- *Annual Convention*
- *Legal Referral Service*
- *AFA Quarterly Newsletter*
- *AFA Purchasing Group*
- *Influence Your Lawmakers*

For a complimentary copy of the AFA Quarterly and information about services and membership, call
1-800-334-4AFA

BEFORE YOU INVEST...
Ask the nation's oldest franchisee trade association for help evaluating any franchise. Services available:
- *Business Review of the Uniform Franchise Offering Circular (UFOC)*
- *Comparative Analysis of two or more Franchise Companies*

THE AMERICAN FRANCHISEE ASSOCIATION

AMERICAN LISTINGS

ACCOUNTING AND TAX SERVICES

ACCOUNTABILITIES ACCOUNTING AND TAX SERVICE
151 Wymore Rd., Ste. 550-B7, Altamonte Springs, FL, 32714. Contact: Jim Bell, CEO - Tel: (407) 774-0014. Full service accounting and tax services specializing in providing business growth alternatives for clients. Established: 1987 - Franchising Since: 1993 - No. of Units: Company Owned: 1 - Franchised: 14 - Franchise Fee: $6,500 - Royalty: None (update/ support $150/month) - Total Inv: $6,500 - $15,000 - Financing: No.

ACCOUNTANT'S CHOICE
401 St. Francis St., Talahassee, FL, 32301. Contact: President - Tel: (904) 681-1941. A full service accounting practice. Established: 1989 - Franchising Since: 1991 - No. of Units: Company Owned: 12 - Franchised: 195 - Franchise Fee: $12,000 - Royalty: 6%, 2% adv. - Total Inv: $12,000 - $25,000 - Financing: Yes.

ADVANTAGE PAYROLL SERVICE
P.O. Box 3188, Auburn, ME, 04212. Contact: Michael Nadeau, Fran. Dir. - Tel: (207) 782-2844. Producing paychecks, filing payroll tax forms, and making payroll tax deposits to federal, state, and local agencies. Established: 1967 - Franchising Since: 1983 - No. of Units: Company Owned: 1 - Franchised: 25 - Franchise Fee: $14,500 - Total Inv: $20,000 - $40,000 - Financing: Yes.

AMERICOUNT BUSINESS CONSULTANTS, INC.
3800 Douglas, Des Moines, IA, 50310. Contact: Leon Ebling, Pres. - Tel: (515) 274-4195, Fax: (515) 274-6411. Accounting and business consulting for small to medium size business. Established: 1963 - Franchising Since: 1993 - No. of Units: Company Owned: 1 - Franchised: 1 - Franchise Fee: $40,000 - Royalty: 5% of monthly billings on first $5,000, then graduates down to 1% - Total Inv: $40,000 fran. fee, $10,000 equip. - work. cap. - Financing: Assist franchisees in obtaining financing.

BECK, VILLATA & CO., P.A. CERTIFIED PUBLIC ACCOUNTANTS
1390 Northeast 162nd St., North Miami Beach, FL, 33162. Contact: Frank Beck, Partner - Tel: (305) 944-5900. Senior partners are both extremely well versed and knowledgeable in franchise accounting and are available for consultations on issues relating to taxes, estate planning, new business setup, and financial statement preparation & projections as well as new business valuations & litigation support. We are a full service accounting office able to meet all your accounting needs. Established: 1990.

BECK, VILLATA & CO., P.C. CERTIFIED PUBLIC ACCOUNTANTS
28 West Grand Ave., P.O. Box 470, Montvale, NJ, 07645. Contact: Frank Beck, Partner - Tel: (800) 395-BECK. Our 23 years of franchise accounting experience, both in the U.S. and Overseas has enabled us to acquire and handle the needs of hundreds of franchises. Our service is personalized to your needs. We also have developed a special expertise in tax and estate planning. Some of our other services include: personal, partnership & corporate income taxes, financial statements & projections, new business setup & consultation, and payroll & sales taxes. Established: 1972.

CHUNOWITZ, TEITELBAUM & BAERSON, LTD., CERTIFIED PUBLIC ACCOUNTANTS
401 Huehl Rd., Northbrook, IL, 60062. Contact: Martin Magida - Tel: (708) 498-9620. Personal and timely service throughout the country and the Virgin Islands. Over twenty years of franchise accounting, tax planning, cash flow analysis, appraisals and valuations, personal financial planning and litigation support. Established: 1973.

COMPREHENSIVE BUSINESS SERVICES
1925 Palomar Oaks Way, Ste. 105, Carlsbad, CA, 92008. Contact: Jack Frampton, VP - Tel: (800) 323-9000. The Comprehensive system enables an accountant to build a practice offering monthly accounting, bookkeeping and tax services to small and medium sized businesses. Support and training in marketing, practice management and processing is included. Established: 1949 - Franchising Since: 1965 - No. of Units: Franchised: 280 - Franchise Fee: $12,500 - Royalty: 6%, 2% adv. - Total Inv: $30,500 + work. cap. & equip. - Financing: Yes.

DELOITTE & TOUCHE
1200 Two Ruan Center, 601 Locust St., Des Moines, IA, 50309. Contact: John L. Allbery, Dir. of Fran. Ind. Svcs. - Tel: (515) 288-1200. Independent CPA's and business advisors with significant experience in the franchise industry through involvement in franchise trade organizations and consulting with many international franchise clients. Work with start-up franchise organizations and other established companies evaluating franchising as an alternative operational and growth strategy. Develop innovative and cost-effective planning strategies for franchise industry companies.

ECONOTAX
Taxpro Inc.
P.O. Box 13829, Jackson, MS, 39236-3829. Contact: Jeffrey T. Williams, Pres./V.P. - Tel: (800) 748-9106, (601) 373-2651, Fax: (601) 956-0583. Provides the public professional tax services including tax preparation, electronic filing, refund loans, audit representation, and tax planning. Established: 1965 - Franchising Since: 1968 - No. of Units: Company Owned: 11 - Franchised: 80 - Franchise Fee: $5,000 - Royalty: 15% - Total Inv: $6,000 - $10,000.

ELECTRONIC TAX FILERS, INC.
P.O. Box 2077, Cary, NC, 27512-2077. Contact: Rachel Wishon, Fran. Dev. - Tel: (919) 469-0651. Data entry of federal and state income tax information furnished by the taxpayer, for the purpose of transmitting electronically to the IRS the taxpayer's income tax return. This service enables the taxpayer to obtain their refund more rapidly. No tax preparation. Franchisor provides training. Established: 1990 - Franchising Since: 1990 - No. of Units: Company Owned: 2 - Franchised: 22 - Franchise Fee: $22,500 - Royalty: 9%, 4% adv. fee - Total Inv: $20,000 working cap.

H & R BLOCK, INC.
4410 Main St., Kansas City, MO, 64111. Contact: Fran. Dept. - Tel: (816) 753-6900, Ext. 461. Income tax return preparation and electronic filing. Established: 1955 - Franchising Since: 1956 - No. of Units: Company Owned: 4,087 worldwide - Franchised: 4,868 worldwide. No longer offering franchises.

JACKSON HEWITT TAX SERVICE
4575 Bonney Rd., Virginia Beach, VA, 23462. Contact: Cynthia Peroe, Dir. of Fran. Dev. - Tel: (804) 473-3300. Computerized income tax preparation service. Established: 1960 - Franchising Since: 1986 - No. of Units: Company Owned: 88 - Franchised: 1,100 - Franchise Fee: $17,500 - Royalty: 12%, 6% adv. - Total Inv: $28,300 - $38,600 - Financing: Yes.

LEDGERPLUS
401 St. Francis St., Tallahassee, FL, 32301. Contact: Arden Harrison, Mktg. Dir. - Tel: (904) 681-1941. Provides accounting, tax and financial consulting services to small businesses. Established: 1989 - Franchising Since: 1991 - No. of Units: Company Owned: 18 - Franchised: 195 - Franchise Fee: $12,000 - Royalty: 6% + 2% adv. - Total Inv: $12,400 - $25,000 incl. fran. fee - Financing: Yes.

NATIONWIDE INCOME TAX SERVICE COMPANY
14507 W. Warren, Dearborn, MI, 48126. Contact: Carl Gilbert, Pres. - Tel: (313) 584-7640. Preparation of income tax returns. Established: 1965 - Franchising Since: 1967 - No. of Units: Company Owned: 8 - Franchised: 32 - Franchise Fee: $5,000 - $15,000 - Royalty: 8% - Total Inv: $15,000 - $25,000 - Financing: No.

PADGETT BUSINESS SERVICES
Padgett Business Services USA, Inc.
160 Hawthorne Park, Athens, GA, 30606. Contact: Greg Williams, V.P. Sales - Tel: (800) 323-7292, Fax: (706) 543-8537. Licenses individuals to operate their own accounting, income tax and business consulting practice. Four weeks of initial training, including in-area field support by home office are provided. Continuing support with yearly seminars. Established: 1966 - Franchising Since: 1975 - No. of Units: Franchised: 332 - Franchise Fee: $22,000 plus $12,500 training fee - Royalty: 9% - Total Inv: fee $34,500, work. cap. $20,000 - $40,000 - Financing: Yes, $20,000.

PEYRON TAX SERVICES
Peyron Associates, Inc.
3212 Preston St., Louisville, KY, 40213. Contact: Dan Peyron, Pres. - Tel: (502) 637-7483 . Tax return preparation in home, malls, stores, storefronts. Also electronic filing & refund loans, tax newsletters & service booths in malls. "Our most successful operators are not accountants or tax preparers." Established: 1960 - Franchising Since: 1965 - No. of Units: Franchised: 500 - Franchise Fee: $3,000 - Royalty: 5% to Peyron - Financing: With 10% down.

TAX MAN INC.
678 Massachusetts Ave., Room 202, Cambridge, MA, 02139. Contact: Mr. Garon, Exec. V.P. - Tel: (617) 868-1374. Tax preparation. Available in New England Only. Established: 1967 - No. of Units: 23 - Franchise Fee: $2,000 - Total Inv: $5,000.

TRIPLE CHECK INCOME TAX SERVICE
727 S. Main St., Burbank, CA, 91506. Contact: David Lieberman, Pres. - Tel: (800) 283-1040. Franchisor offers full range of support services to build a quality tax and small business consulting/accounting practice. Through Triple Check Financial Services, franchisees are able to add a separate profit center providing their clients with need-oriented, conservative financial planning. Established: 1941 - Franchising Since: 1978 - No. of Units: Company Owned: 2 - Franchised: 284 - Franchise Fee: None - Royalty: Varies - Total Inv: $5,000 - $15,000 - Financing: Yes.

ADVERTISING/PUBLISHING SERVICES

ADVERTISING SOLUTION
9699 N. Hayden Rd., Ste. 108, Scottsdale, AZ, 85258. Contact: Cameron Latrell, Dir. of Mktg. - Tel: (602) 860-1488. #1 advertising business opportunity. Coupon, receipt and placemat advertising programs. Established: 1987 - Franchising Since: 1989 - No. of Units: Company Owned: 11 - Franchised: 900+ - Franchise Fee: $500 - $1,500 - Royalty: 3% - Total Inv: $500 - $1,500 - Financing: No.

AMERICAN VENTURES GROUP
130 North Vutte St., Ste. A, Willows, CA, 95988. Contact: Roger Memmott, V.P. - Tel: (916) 934-8827. Placing advertising on the exterior and inside of video cassette cases. Established: 1987 - Franchising Since: 1989 - No. of Units: Company Owned: 2 - Franchised: 27 - Franchise Fee: under $1,000 - Royalty: 5% - Total Inv: under $1,000 - Financing: No.

AUTO SHOW MAGAZINE
Fantasy Publications, Inc.
6030 S. Lindbergh Blvd., St. Louis, MO, 63123. Contact: Jim Smoot, President/Founder - Tel: (314) 487-0054. A spectacular photo showcase of vehicles for sale by private owners & licensed dealers. Publishes bi-weekly & sold at major newsstands for 95¢. Established: 1991 - Franchising Since: 1993 - No. of Units: Company Owned: 1 - Franchise Fee: $5,975 - Royalty: $75 per week, $25 per week adv. - Total Inv: $20,000 - $35,000 - Financing: No.

$AVE-A-BUCK
P.O. Box 290837, Port Orange, FL, 32129-0837. Contact: M.V. Biro, Dir. - Tel: (904) 767-7523. Discount coupons advertising mailer (book & coupons) sales, production and mailing. Established: 1992 - Franchising Since: 1993 - No. of Units: Franchised: 1 - Franchise Fee: $1,000 - Royalty: 5% gross - Total Inv: $3,000 - Financing: No.

BENCH AD
4839 E. Greenway Rd., Ste. 339, Scottsdale, AZ, 85254. Contact: John Sachs, V.P. - Tel: (602) 443-9740. Bus bench advertising. Established: 1976 - Franchising Since: 1985 - No. of Units: Company Owned: 5 - Franchised: 25 - Franchise Fee: $5,000 - Royalty: 2% - Financing: Yes.

BINGO BUGLE NEWSPAPER
K & O Publishing, Inc.
P.O. Box 51189, Seattle, WA, 98115-1189. Contact: Warren Kraft, Pres. - Tel: (206) 527-4958. Monthly publication for bingo players. Franchisee is responsible for sales, publishing, and distribution. A 2-day training is provided to franchisees, along with manuals and start-up materials. Established: 1981 - Franchising Since: 1983 - No. of Units: Franchised: 72 - Franchise Fee: $1,500 - $10,000 - Royalty: 10% of monthly gross revenues, except first month of publication - Total Inv: $2,500 - $10,000, plus cost of telephone, camera, automobile, typewriter and/or computer if franchisee doesn't own.

BOULDER BLIMP COMPANY
2840 Wilderness Place, Ste. E, Boulder, CO, 80301. Contact: Terry Goodhart, Sales Mgr. - Tel: (303) 449-2190. Manufactures the highest quality cold-air inflatables. We have been in business for over 14 years. We will produce inflatables to meet all of your requirements, no matter what size or shape. We specialize in custom shapes, product replicas to characters in sizes from 10 to 50 feet! Established: 1980 - Total Inv: $3,250 plus misc. expenses, one High-Rider 24'.

BREAD BOX, THE
Superior Marketing Services, Inc.
P.O. Box 46405, Little Rock, AR, 72214-6405. Contact: John Reynolds, Pres. - Tel: (501) 666-6742. Co-op direct mail advertising - selling advertising to local businesses to be mailed in an envelope with other non-competing businesses to area residents at a much more economical cost than utilizing individual direct mail. Established: 1976 - Franchising Since: 1985 - No. of Units: Company Owned: 1 - Franchised: 5 - Franchise Fee: $7,000 - Total Inv: additional $8,000 - $12,000 work cap. - Financing: Partial.

BRIGHT BEGINNINGS
Artistic Horizons, Inc.
1150 Main St., #D, Irvine, CA, 92714. Contact: Melanie Hodgson - Tel: (714) 752-2772. Advertising and community service. Neighborhood welcoming service. Business involves welcoming newcomers to an area w/civic information as well as gifts & gift certificates & word of mouth sales message from local businesses. Established: 1986 - Franchising Since: 1989 - No. of Units: Company Owned: 7 - Franchise Fee: $11,000 - Royalty: 10%, 2% adv. - Total Inv: fran. fee, computer, laser printer $4,000, misc. $3,000.

BUSINESS ADVERTISING SPECIALTIES CORP. (BASCO)
9351 De Soto Ave., Dept. B783-0592, Chatsworth, CA, 91311-4948. Contact: Mike Seingstein - Tel: (818) 718-1506. Direct sales, mail order, manufacturer. Put you in your own advertising specialty business as a supplier, distributor & imprinter. Full-time or part-time, earn up to 10 times your cost. Everything supplied including color catalogs, complete step-by-step instructions & hundreds of ad specialty items, all warehoused for immediate delivery. Established: 1987 - Capital Requirements: $24.95 to start. Training and support provided.

BUYING & DINING GUIDE
Community Publications of America, Inc.
80 8th Ave., New York, NY, 10011. Contact: Allan Horwitz, Pres. - Tel: (212) 243-6800. Buying & Dining Guide is a unique money-maker for the publisher and the advertiser offering total market coverage of the active buyers and diners throughout the area. Publishing and distribution costs are minimal, and the advertiser receives 14 days of effective advertising, for the price of a single ad. Established: 1980 - Franchising

Since: 1989 - No. of Units: 12 - Franchise Fee: $29,900 with money-back guarantee - Royalty: $200+ per issue - Total Inv: $29,900 incl. fran. fee plus $3,000 work. cap. - Financing: Yes, with down payment of 20%.

CARTOON CARTOGRAPHICS & CALENDARS
Alternative Media Group
P.O. Box 1952, Grand Jct., CO, 81502. Contact: Kevin Van Gundy, Pres. - Tel: (970) 242-6030. America's highest quality cartoon promotional maps & calendars. Established: 1982 - Franchising Since: 1989 - No. of Units: Company Owned: 3 - Franchised: 3 - Franchise Fee: $4,995 - Royalty: 10% - Financing: Yes.

CASUALTY ADJUSTER'S GUIDES
3801 Mountainview Pl., Gig Harbor, WA, 98332. Contact: R.A. Hourigan, Pres. - Tel: (206) 858-6153. Licensing copyrights and trademark for publication of local editions of the insurance claims publication. Established: 1958 - Franchising Since: 1966 - No. of Units: Franchised: 28 - Franchise Fee: $4,000 - Royalty: 10% of gross adv. sales - Total Inv: $4,000 acquisition fee covers all manuals, forms & training - Financing: No.

CATHEDRAL DIRECTORIES FRANCHISES, INC.
1401 W. Girard Ave., Madison Heights, MI, 48071. Contact: Jack Frye, Fran. Sales Dir. - Tel: (800) 544-6903. U.S. publisher of church, homeowners & organization directories. Franchisee will offer the service on a no-charge basis to the church and will sell advertisements to support it. No royalties. No competition. Enjoy 95% renewal. Build a long term, profitable, home-based business. Established: 1948 - Franchising Since: 1993 - No. of Units: Company Owned: 4 - Franchised: 6 - Franchise Fee: $14,500 - Total Inv: Fran. fee, living expenses and computer - Financing: 3rd party assistance, SBA.

CHILD CARE & SCHOOL PUBLISHING CO. *
Southeastern Directory Association, Inc.
P.O. Box 16055, Huntsville, AL, 35802. Contact: Sylvia Elrod, Pres., CEO - Tel: (205) 883-1382. Publishing franchise for a child care/school listing magazine/directory. Established: 1988 - Franchising Since: 1993 - No. of Units: Company Owned: 1 - Franchised: 4 - Franchise Fee: $25,000 - $60,000 - Royalty: 10% - Total Inv: $10,650 - $20,050 - Financing: No.

CONSUMER NETWORK OF AMERICA *
15965 Jeanette, Southfield, MI, 48075. Contact: Colleen McGaffey - Tel: (810) 557-2784, Fax: (810) 557-7931. An innovative alternative advertising program for short term advertising for retailers. Extremely strong track record of performance. Unique franchise with no direct competition. A very profitable home-based business. Established: 1990 - Franchising Since: 1995 - No. of Units: Company Owned: 13 markets - Franchise Fee: $15,000 - Royalty: $10,000 per market.

COUPON-CASH SAVER
Coupon-Cash Saver Franchise Corp.
925 N. Milwaukee Ave., Wheeling, IL, 60090. Contact: Myrna O'Reilly, Pres. - Tel: (708) 537-6420, Fax: (708) 537-6499. Direct mail coupon advertising booklet. Established: 1984 - Franchising Since: 1990 - No. of Units: Company Owned: 5 - Franchised: 4 - Franchise Fee: $9,500 - Royalty: 8% - Total Inv: $22,600 - Financing: Yes.

CREATE-A-BOOK - PRESTO BOOKS - GRACE CHRISTION
Hefty Publishing
1232 Paula Cir., Gulf Breeze, FL, 32561. Contact: Dave Redden, Mktg. - Tel: (800) 732-3009. Personalizing children's books using your computer & laser printer. Provide marketing programs, manuals & ongoing support. Over $400 mark-up. Part-time or full-time from home. Established: 1980 - No. of Dealerships: 995 - Franchise Fee: $995 - Royalty: None - Financing: No.

DESIGN SHOP, THE *
507 S. Thornton Ave., Dalton, GA, 30720. Contact: Sharon Jernigan, Pres. - Tel: (706) 226-4541. A direct mail advertising coupon mailer for small or local businesses. Established: 1994 - Franchising Since: 1995 - No. of Units: Company Owned: 1 - Franchised: 1 - Franchise Fee: $5,000 minimum - Royalty: flat fee $125 per mailer - Total Inv: $10,000 to $15,000.

DOLPHIN PUBLICATIONS OF AMERICA, INC.
800 3rd St., Windsor, CO, 80550. Contact: Kristie Straube, Mktg. Dir. - Tel: (800) 426-1056. Four color/high gloss/quality coupon - display ad, direct mail magazine. Franchisees sell ads to local businesses. Franchisor handles all production & distribution. Established: 1984 - Franchising Since: 1992 - No. of Units: Company Owned: 75 - Franchised: 14 - Franchise Fee: $2,950 min. investment - Royalty: None - Total Inv: $3,450 - Financing: Yes.

EFFECTIVE MAILERS *
Effective Direct Marketing Systems, Inc.
1151 Allen Dr., Troy, MI, 48083. Contact: Jai Gupta, Pres. - Tel: (810) 588-9880, Fax: (810) 588-4299. Direct mail advertising business. We design, print, insert and mail coupons in envelopes. In technology, we are either at par or ahead of competitors. Clients advertising with us get one of the best responses. We train franchisees in coupon design, selling and all other aspects of the business. Established: 1982 - Franchising Since: 1993 - No. of Units: Company Owned: 1 - Franchised: 3 - Franchise Fee: $500 plus territory fee - Royalty: None - Total Inv: $25,000+ (fran. fee $500, territory $18,000, training & travel $3,000, initial supplies $1,100, plus misc.) - Financing: None.

EXECUTIVE, THE
1655 McFarland Blvd. N., #123, Tuscaloosa, AL, 35406-2212. Contact: Kevin Foote, Pres. - Tel: (800) 264-3932. A business magazine full of coupons for executives. Magazines are distributed by large and small companies for their employees. Revenues are received through the sale of advertising. Established: 1987 - Franchising Since : 1989 - No. of Units: Company Owned: 1 - Franchised: 4 - Franchise Fee: $5,995 - Royalty: $200 monthly.

FELIX RUSLIN DIRECT RESPONSE, INC.
8308 S. Kedzie Ave., Chicago, IL, 60652-3309. Contact: Steven Gilbertz, Pres. - Tel: (312) 737-7800. Advertising and marketing agency specializing in direct response lead generation and franchise marketing materials, public relations, and direct mail for franchise support. Established: 1986.

FIESTA CARTOON MAPS
1003 E. Watson Dr., Tempe, AZ, 85283. Contact: Jack Eddy or Sheri Eddy, Pres./V.P. - Tel: (602) 966-4639 or (800) 541-4963. Advertising business on a cartoon style map. No experience necessary. Training and tools are provided by parent co. Home based business. Full support by parent co. 800 Assistance number. In house production so no equipment or inventory necessary. Established: 1979 - Franchising Since: 1987 - No. of Units: Franchised: 103 - Franchise Fee: $6,495 for territory large enough to complete one map - Royalty: None - Total Inv: Depending upon size of territory starting at $6,495 - Financing: Occasionally.

GREETINGS
Greetings Inc.
P.O. Box 25623, Lexington, KY, 40524. Contact: Larry Kargel, Pres. - Tel: (606) 272-5624. Target market advertising. Established 1984 - Franchising Since: 1989 - No. of Units: Company Owned: 4 - Franchised: 4 - Franchise Fee: $15,000 - Royalty: 5% gross sales - Total Inv: $5,000 operating funds, $6,500 equip. - Financing: Yes, franchise fee only.

HOLE-IN-ONE ADVERTISING
4839 E. Greenway Rd., Ste. 339, Scottsdale, AZ, 85254. Contact: Steve Lawrence, V.P. - Tel: (602) 443-9740. Golf course and bench advertising. Established: 1987 - Franchising Since: 1990 - No. of Units: Company Owned: 2 - Franchised: 20 - Franchise Fee: $3,000 - Royalty: 5% - Financing: Yes.

HOMES & LAND MAGAZINE
Homes & Land Publishing Corporation
1600 Capital Cir., S.W., Tallahassee, FL, 32310. Contact: Lynn Miller, Fran. Sales Coord. - Tel: (800) 277-4357, ext. 199. Pictorial community real estate advertising magazine. Established: 1973 - Franchising Since: 1984 - No. of Units: Company Owned: 2 - Franchised: 212 - Franchise Fee: $20,000 - Royalty: 10.5% of suggested retail page rate - Total Inv: $20,000 initial fee; $25,000 - $75,000 est. work. cap.; $2,500 - $5,000 equip.; $2,600 - $9,000 other - Financing: None.

HOMESTEADER, THE *
Homesteader Enterprises, Inc.
P.O. Box 2824, Framingham, MA, 01701. Contact: Allen Nitschelm, Pres. - Tel: (508) 820-4311. A monthly publication for new homeowners. Help local businesses target market their advertising to one of their best target markets: newcomers to the area! Established: 1990 - Franchising Since: 1995 - No. of Units: Company Owned: 2 - Franchised: 16 - Franchise Fee: $6,000 - Royalty: 10% on received revenue - Total Inv: $9,310 - $28,000 - Financing: No.

INTERNATIONAL DIRECT RESPONSE INC.
900 West Valley Business Center, Ste. 203, Wayne, PA, 19087. Contact: Carolyn Guyer, Sr. Account Mgr. - Tel: (610) 688-6868, Fax: (610) 688-7260. Direct response marketing firm specializing in new customer retention, activation and acquisition programs. Established: 1983.

LOCAL MERCHANT DISPLAY CENTERS
Merchant Advertising Systems, Inc.
4115 Tiverton Rd., Randallstown, MD, 21133-2019. Contact: Don Goldvarg, Pres. - Tel: (410) 655-3201, Fax: (410) 655-0262. Unique display centers for custom-made local merchant signage and promotional literature, installed in major supermarket chains and shopping malls. Established: 1985 - Franchising Since: 1987 - No. of Units: Company Owned: 11 - Franchised: 2 - Franchise Fee: $13,500 - $25,500 - Royalty: 0% (joint venture partnership alternative) - Total Inv: $17,000 - $29,000 incl. start-up costs - Financing: Assistance with indirect financing.

MONEY MAILER
Money Mailer, Inc.
14271 Corporate Dr., Garden Grove, CA, 92643. Contact: Debbie Word, Sales - Tel: (714) 265-4100, Fax: (714) 265-4091. Provide highly targeted advertising services to local and national businesses through a network of 500 franchisees. We have redefined state-of-the-art in design, production and distribution of direct mail. Comprehensive training and support are second to none. Established: 1979 - Franchising Since: 1980 - No. of Units: Franchised: 625 - Franchise Fee: $25,000 - $50,000 - Royalty: varies.

NAMCO SYSTEMS, INC.
4 California Ave., Framingham, MA, 01701-8867. Contact: Mindy Bostwick, Fran. Admin. - Tel: (800) 299-0510. Target market advertising for small businesses on Tel-A-Cover. Franchisee sells ads and franchisor is responsible for administration, artwork, proofing, etc. Established: 1953 - Franchising Since: 1982 - No. of Units: Company Owned: 6- Franchised: 40 - Franchise Fee: $9,900 varies depending on size of territory - Royalty: none - Total Inv: $33,000 incl. work cap. - Financing: No.

NCC PROMOTIONS
620 19th St., Ste. 127, Niagara Falls, NY, 14301. Contact: Nathan Tanner - Tel: (800) 265-6229. Marketing, sales and service of register roll product promotions: Full color advertising for grocery store, mass merchandiser, bank machine and other receipt rolls. Clients range from small business to Fortune 500 companies. Established: 1987 - Franchising Since: 1992 - No. of Units: Company Owned: 2 - Franchised: 21 - Franchise Fee: $2,000 - $5,000 - Royalty: No royalty - shared revenue (up to 43% of gross sales) - Total Inv: $2,500 - $6,000 - Financing: Yes.

ON-TARGET! MARKETING & MEDIA, INC.
2830 North Ave., #C401, Grand Junction, CO, 81501. Contact: Kevin Van Gundy, Pres. - Tel: (970) 242-6030. Provides advertising to businesses through cartoon maps and coupon books. Our trademarked products include Cartoon Cartographics & Calendars plus The Student Super-Saver. Established: 1982 - Licensing Since: 1990 - No. of Units: Company Owned: 2 - Licensed: 3 - License Fee: $4,995 - Royalty: 10.85% of gross sales - Total Inv: approx. $5,000 - $10,000 - Financing: Yes.

PASSPORT GETAWAY MAGAZINE
Passport Publishing Corporation
5343 N. 16th St., Ste. 110, Phoenix, AZ, 85016. Contact: Bob Hamlett, Dir. of Fran. Sales - Tel: (602) 285-1000. Publisher of regional editions of tourist and travel oriented magazines. Established: 1991 - Franchising Since: 1993 - No. of Units: Franchised: 12 - Franchise Fee: $40,000 bimonthly, $60,000 monthly, $70,000 mega markets - Royalty: $14,300 to $14,900 per month or bimonthly - Total Inv: $59,150 - $107,200 - Financing: 50% for the initial franchise fee.

PENNYSAVER
Community Publications of America, Inc.
80 Eighth Ave., New York, NY, 10011. Contact: Allan Horwitz, Pres. - Tel: (212) 243-6800. America's favorite shopping guide, offering advertisers total market coverage of all households and most businesses in the community. Established: 1973 - Franchising Since: 1979 - No. of Units: 25 - Franchise Fee: $29,900 with money-back guarantee - Royalty: $200+ per issue - Total Inv: $29,900 plus $10,000 work cap.- Financing: Yes, with 20% down.

POINTS FOR PROFIT
Southwest Promotional Corporation
P.O. Box 2424, La Mesa, CA, 91943-2424. Contact: Rosilyn Nesler, Pres. - Tel: (619) 588-0664. A proof of purchase advertising and marketing promotion that broadcast stations can add to their spot commercial air time. Promotion attracts major national and local advertisers on noncancellable contracts. Station has exclusive in its market area. Station gets its best spot rates. Promotion now in a number of large and small market areas. Station references available. Established: 1970 - Franchising Since: 1975 - No. of Units: Compa..y Owned: 2 - Franchised: 13 - Franchise Fee: 10% of station's gross sales - Total Inv: Fran. fee covers all - Financing: No.

PREMIUM SHOPPING GUIDE
Dolphin Publications of America, Inc.
1235 Sunset Grove Rd., Fallbrook, CA, 92028. Contact: Bob Neral, Nat'l Mkt. Dir. - Tel: (800) 343-1056, Fax: (619) 728-3145. Direct mail coupon/display magazine. Franchisor does all production. Franchisee provides local marketing. Established: 1984 - Franchising Since: 1992 - No. of Units: Company Owned: 107 - Franchised: 41 - Franchise Fee: $8,900 - Total Inv: $8,900 + $500 startup (misc.) - Financing: Fran. fee only.

PRIME TIME GUIDE & T.V. LISTINGS
Kosdale Corp.
P.O. Box 15406, Phoenix, AZ, 85060-5406. Contact: Roger Shearer, Pres. - Tel: (602) 273-1243. Publishing T.V. guides for hospitality industry. Established: 1968 - Franchising Since: 1975 - No. of Units: Company Owned: 44 - Franchised: 5 - Franchise Fee: $12,500 includes training - Royalty: 5% for furnishing T.V. programming - Total Inv: $50,000 start-up funds - Financing: Partial.

PROFIT-ON-HOLD *
Ad-Comm International
3401 Ridgelake Dr., Ste. 108, Metairie, LA, 70002. Contact: Otto Mehrgut, Pres. - Tel: (504) 832-8000, Fax: (504) 828-2141. On hold advertising. We create the script, install digital reproducing equip. and custom make informational messages while customers remain on hold. Established: 1991 - Franchising Since: 1993 - No. of Units: company Owned: 2 - Franchised: 1 - Franchise Fee: $15,000 - Royalty: 3% adv. - Total Inv: $15,000 fee, $10,000 hardware, $5,000 work. cap. - Financing: No.

Q-PON BOOK, THE
Mid State Mailers Inc.
1827 N. Michigan Ave., Saginaw, MI, 48602. Contact: Dave Birnbaum, Dir. of Market Dev. - Tel: (517) 754-0000, Fax: (517) 754-0898. Direct mail advertising coupon book. All artwork & layout, printing, assembly and mailing services are provided. Unique color format. Established: 1989 - Franchising Since: 1990 - No. of Units: Company Owned: 1 - Franchised: 41 - Franchise Fee: $495 - Royalty: None - Total Inv: Varies - Financing: No.

RECOGNITION EXPRESS
Recognition Express Int'l, Inc.
P.O. Box 713, Bonita, CA, 91908. Contact: Jeff Tino, V.P. Fran Dev. - Tel: (619) 479-2052, Fax: (619) 267-0911. Manufacture and sale of corporate recognition products such as name badges, signage, plaques, awards, and advertising specialties. Established: 1972 - Franchising Since: 1974 - No. of Units: Franchised: 71 - Franchise Fee: $15,000 -

Total Inv: $15,000 fran. fee, $15,000 start-up, $45,000 equip., leasehold, inv, $25,000 work cap. - Royalty: 6% up to $100,000 gross, lower % as sales increase - Financing: Assistance.

RENTAL GUIDE MAGAZINE
Homes & Land Publishing Corporation
1600 Capital Cir., SW, , Tallahassee, FL, 32310. Contact: Lynn Miller, Mktg. Ass't. - Tel: (800) 277-4357, ext. 199. Color community advertising magazine for rental properties and apartment complexes, free to consumers. Franchisee handles advertising, sales and distribution; franchisor offers production, printing, training and marketing support services. Established: 1973 - Franchising Since: 1988 - No. of Units: Company Owned: 2 - Franchised: 28 - Franchise Fee: $20,000 - Royalty: varies 6% - 16% - Total Inv: $44,750 - $105,000 - Financing: No.

RESORT MAPS FRANCHISE, INC.
Rte. 100, Old High School, P.O. Box 726, Waitsfield, VT, 05673. Contact: Chandler W. Weller, V.P. - Tel: (800) 788-5247, (802) 496-6277, Fax: (802) 496-6278. Engaged in the sales, nurturing and support of franchised publishers of business and tourist information maps under the tradename Resort Maps and depends upon and utilizes the business systems generated by Resort Maps, Inc. A five day comprehensive training program will be conducted in the home office in Waitsfield, VT. Established: 1988 - Franchising Since: 1993 - No. of Units: Franchised: 7 - Franchise Fee: $4,950 - Royalty: 10% of gross adv. sales. RMFI produces all ads and final map artwork the first year - Total Inv: $8,550 - $13,650 incl. fran. fee - Financing: No.

RESORT PUBLICATIONS
4839 E. Greenway Rd., Ste. 339, Scottsdale, AZ, 85254. Contact: Sean McKenzie, V.P. - Tel: (602) 443-9740. Advertising in hotel/motel guest directories. Established: 1987 - Franchising Since: 1991 - No. of Units: Company Owned: 8 - Franchised: 82 - Franchise Fee: $5,000 - Royalty: None - Financing: Yes.

ROOFTOP BALLOONS
10770 Rockville Street, Santee, CA, 92071. Contact: Bob Snider, Gen. Mgr. - Tel: (619) 448-1189. Manufacturer of rooftop inflatables used to provide businesses and corporations with advertising, P.O.P. displays and all other promotional applications, indoor and outdoor. We specialize in custom designs conveying a positive image to all products and services. Established: 1979 - Dealer Since: 1980 - Number of Dealers: 50.

RUSSELL JOHNS ASSOCIATES, LTD.
P.O. Box 1510, Clearwater, FL, 34617. Contact: Richard Barbel, V.P. - Tel: 800-237-9851. Publishers representative for classified advertising representing several noted national publications. Produces monthly opportunities sections for franchise advertising. Creates special franchise advertorial sections and supplements for magazines and newspapers. Established: 1968.

STUDENT SUPER-SAVER®
Alternative Media Group
P.O. Box 1952, Grand Junction, CO, 81502. Contact: Kevin Van Gundy, Pres. - Tel: (970) 242-6030. Advertising publications that target high school and college students. Established: 1982 - Franchising Since: 1995 - No. of Units: Company Owned: 2 - Franchise Fee: $9,999 - Royalty: 10% - Total Inv: $25,000 - Financing: Yes.

SUPER ADS INC.
2121 Abell Lane, Sparks, MD, 21152. Contact: F.J. Beste, Pres. - Tel: (410) 771-4443, Fax: (410) 771-4879. Advertising at resort beach locations 5' X 40' electronic message center mounted on 47' boat, computer controlled messages flash to beach dwellers- easy to operate - experience selling advertising helpful. Established: 1978 - Franchising Since: 1980 - No. of Units: Franchised: 21 - Royalty: escalating fee to max. 7% of gross after 3 yrs. - Total Inv: $150,000 (incls. boat, sign, comps. etc.) - Financing: Assistance.

SUPER COUPS
The Mailhouse, Inc.
180 Bodwell St., Avon, MA, 02322. Contact: Glen Liset, V.P. of Mktg. - Tel: (800) 626-2620, Fax: (508) 588-3347. We specialize in 4 color coupons with one of the lowest print and delivery rates in the nation. Our outstanding training, support and service teams help you run a proven high profit business. Established: 1982 - Franchising Since: 1984 - No. of Units: Franchised: 246 - Franchise Fee: $22,900 - Royalty: $148.00 per mailing - Total Inv: $22,900 + $11,000 oper. capital - Financing: No.

TALKING ADS
Talking Ads of America
P.O. Box 14804, Lenexa, KS, 66285-0804. Contact: Arvin Zwick, Pres./Founder - Tel: (913) 492-SAVE, (800) TALK-AD. TA compliment newspaper, radio or TV ads, by allowing user to drastically reduce size & cost of their ads, etc., saving $100's to $1000's. Minimal investment, high profit margins, easy to operate & promote with staggering potential. Call our sample talking ad at (913) 383-7744. Established: 1992 - Franchising Since: 1992 - No. of Units: Company Owned: 1 - Franchise Fee: None - Royalty: None - Total Inv: $295 plus $1,000 - $5,000 work. cap. - Financing: MC/V.

TIME & TEMPERATURE ADVERTISING
2040 Canyon Rd., Birmingham, AL, 35216-1904. Contact: Hal Harris, Jr., Owner - Tel: (205) 979-3000. Provide local telephone number where the public may call to get the exact time and the current temperature. System sales and distributorship opportunities available in certain master territories. Established: 1989 - Franchising Since: 1991 - No. of Units: Company Owned: 3 - Franchised: 1 - Franchise Fee: $3,500 - $15,000 - Royalty: $150 per month - Total Inv: includes TimePro2 equip. - Financing: No.

TRIMARK, INC.
184 Quigley Blvd., New Castle, DE, 19720. Contact: Gilbert Kinch, V.P. of Sales and Mktg. - Tel: 800-TRIMARK (874-6275). Co-op direct mail advertising. Established: 1977 - Franchising Since: 1978 - No. of Units: Company Owned: 3 - Franchised: 31 - Franchise Fee: Single franchise $4,500; Master franchise $19,000 - Royalty: $0.50 per ad per 1M area - Total Inv: $5,000 training fee - Financing: Yes.

TUNE-IN
Tune-In Publications, Inc.
9800 Richmond St., Unit 740, Houston, TX, 77042. Contact: Sandy Adzgery, Editor - Tel: (713) 781-0781. Monthly human interest magazine with emphasis on show business and entertainment. Three formats available. Established: 1982 - Franchising Since: 1984 - No. of Units: 33 - Total Inv: variable.

TV FACTS MAGAZINE
TV Facts of North America
Liberty Square, Danvers, MA, 01923. Contact: Ronald Rubin, Pres. - Tel: (508) 777-9225. Home-based publishing business, including weekly TV magazine, bridal magazine, home-improvement magazine, entertainment magazine et al. No inventory, no experience necessary. Profits are derived from local advertising revenue. Comprehensive training. Established: 1970 - Franchising Since: 1970 - No. of Units: Franchised: 150 - Franchise Fee: $24,500 - Royalty: $60 per wk. 24 page magazine - Total Inv: $24,500.

TV NEWS MAGAZINE
Community Publications of America, Inc.
80 Eighth Ave., New York, NY, 10011. Contact: Allan Horwitz, Pres. - Tel: (212) 243-6800. An award winning free community publication combining the 7-day readership of a TV guide, with the total market coverage of a penny saver, and the efficiencies of scale of a major national publication. The exciting editorial attracts readers, and the excellent response attracts advertisers. Established: 1973 - Franchising Since: 1979- No. of Units: Company Owned: 1 - Franchised: 9 - Franchise Fee: $29,900 with money-back guarantee - Royalty: $150+ per week - Total Inv: $29,900 fran. fee plus $5,000 work. cap. - Financing: Yes, with min. 20% down.

UNISON MARKETING COMMUNICATIONS
Unison Syndications
6312 S. Fiddler's Green Cir., 545 N., Englewood, CO, 80118. Contact: Leigh Umbarger - Tel: (303) 779-3004. Healthcare marketing and advertising syndicated products. Established: 1983 - Franchising Since: 1990 - No. of Units: Company Owned: 1 - Franchised: 1 - Franchise Fee: $45,000 - $75,000 - Royalty: 45% to franchisee, 55% to franchisor (franchisor supplies product) - Total Inv: F.F., $52,000 - $90,500 start-up - Financing: Partial.

UNITED COUPON OF...(LOCATION OF FRANCHISE TERRITORY)
United Coupon Corp.
8380 Alban Rd, Springfield, VA, 22150. Contact: David Heffernan, Dir. of Fran. Dev. - Tel: (703) 644-0200, Fax: (703) 569-1465. Franchisees sell direct mail advertising products and services (primarily co-op coupon advertising) to businesses and other commercial entities. Established: 1981 - Franchising Since: 1982 - No. of Units: Franchised: 73 - Franchise Fee: $18,900 to $21,900 approx., determined by the number of mailable homes in the franchise territory - Royalty: None - Total Inv: $21,755 to $60,300, estimated initial investment (fran. fee plus 3 months' expenses) - Financing: Yes.

VAL-PAK COUPONS
Val-Pak Direct Marketing Systems, Inc.
8605 Largo Lakes Dr., Largo, FL, 34643. Contact: Joseph H. Bourdow, Exec. V.P. - Tel: (800) 237-6266. Nation's largest local co-op mailer distributing over 9 billion coupons in 370 million envelopes annually. Direct mail division of Cox Enterprises, Inc. Established: 1968 - Franchising Since: 1988 - Franchise Fee: $500 - Royalty: None - Total Inv: Varies - Financing: Yes.

WIZARD OF ADS *
One Maritime Plaza, Ste. 700, San Francisco, CA, 94111. Contact: Homer Hobi, Pres. - Tel: (800) 330-4465. Coupon direct mail residential mailings to neighborhoods. A home-based business. Comprehensive training. Ongoing support. Protected franchise territory. Benefit from our experience, and become your own boss. Established: 1995 - Franchising Since: 1995 - Franchise Fee: $11,000 plus $10,000 in pre opening service fee - Royalty: $75. per week - Total Inv: $28,000 - $35,000 - Financing: No.

YELLOW JACKET DIRECT MAIL ADVERTISING
Yellow Jacket Franchise Corporation
23101 Moulton Pky., Ste. 110, Laguna Hills, CA, 92653-1234. Contact: Bob Philpott, Fran. Dir. - Tel: (714) 951-9500. Cooperative direct mail advertising. Established: 1991 - Franchising Since: 1991 - No. of Units: Company Owned: 1 - Franchised: 14 - Franchise Fee: $19,000 - Royalty: $18.00 royalty fee - Total Inv: $25,000: Fran. Fee + $6,000 cash flow - Financing: Yes, to qualified persons.

AUTOMOBILE RENTAL & LEASING

A.I.N. LEASING CORP.
501 Burnside Ave., Inwood, NY, 11696. Contact: Garry Rothbaum, Pres. - Tel: (516) 239-1516. Automobile and equipment lease funding. Established: 1980 - No. of Units: Franchised: 250 - Royalty:1.5% transaction - Total Inv: $25,000 - Financing: No.

AFFORDABLE CAR RENTAL
96 Freneau Ave., #2, Matawan, NJ, 07747. Contact: Charles Vitale, G.M. - Tel: (800) 631-2290. A program designed for new car dealers. Provide comprehensive training, quality insurance and management support for the rental of new and used cars. Established: 1981 - Licensing Since: 1981 - No. of Units: Franchised: 125 - Franchise Fee: $3,500 - $6,000 - Mgt. Fee: $15. - $10. per mo. per car - Financing: On fran. fee only.

AIR BROOK LIMOUSINE, INC.
115 W. Passiac St., Rochelle Park, NJ, 07662. Contact: Ben Zuckerman, Fran. Dir. - Tel: (201) 368-3974. One of Metro New York's largest transportation companies. Sedans;vans;stretch limousines & buses. Established: 1969 - Franchising Since: 1971- No. of Units: Franchised: 83 - Franchise Fee: $7,500 - $12,500 - Royalty: 60/40 royalty, Bonus 80/20 - Total Inv: Fran. fee + $2,000 (security deposit), $1,000 (uniform/maps/2-way radio) - Financing: Yes.

ALLSTAR RENT-A-CAR
Practical Rent-A-Car Systems, Inc.
1500 E. Tropicana Ave., Ste. 123, Las Vegas, NV, 89119. Contact: Elliott Smoler, Donna Posio, Mng. Dir., Admin. Ass't. - Tel: (702) 798-0025, Fax: (702) 798-4739. Car rental business. Established: 1976 - Franchising Since: 1981 - No. of Units: Franchised: 130 - Franchise Fee: $2,500 to $25,000 depending on population of territory - Royalty: $20 per car - Total Inv: $25,000 to $125,000 - Financing: No.

BUDGET RENT A CAR CORPORATION
4225 Naperville Rd., Lisle, IL, 60532-3662. Contact: Larry Lanham, Dir. Fran. Dev. - Tel: (708) 955-1900. Car and truck rental. Established: 1958 - Franchising Since: 1960 - No. of Units: Company Owned: 558 - Franchised: 2,819 - Franchise Fee: $15,000 minimum (varies by population) - Royalty: 5% service fee, 2.5% franchise maintenance, $1,250 credit card fee - Total Inv: varies by location - Financing: None.

DOLLAR RENT A CAR SYSTEMS, INC.
P.O. Box 33167, Tulsa, OK, 74153-1167. Contact: Peter Fritz, Fran. Mgr. - Tel: (918) 669-3000. Car and truck rental. Established: 1966 - Franchising Since: 1966 - No. of Units: Company Owned: 12 - Franchised: 500+ - Franchise Fee: varies, $7,500 min. - Royalty: 9% - Financing: None.

PAYLESS CAR RENTAL SYSTEM, INC.
2350 N. 34th St., N., St. Petersburg, FL, 33713. Contact: Kathleen Gassner, Dir. Fran. Dev. - Tel: (813) 321-6352 Ext. 148. Car rental franchisor, having a worldwide reservation system through major airline computer tie-ins. Established: 1971 - Franchising Since: 1971 - No. of Units: Franchised: 132 - Franchise Fee: $6,000 - $250,000 ($6,000 Suburban; $30,000 - $250,000 Airport) - Royalty: 5% + 3% adv. - Total Inv: $250,000 start up (net worth approx. $500,000) - Financing: None.

PRACTICAL RENT-A-CAR
Practical Rent-A-Car Systems, Inc.
1500 E. Tropicana Ave., Ste. 123, Las Vegas, NV, 89119. Contact: Elliott Smoler, Donna Posio, Mng. Dir., Admin. Ass't. - Tel: (702) 798-0025, Fax: (702) 798-4739. Car & truck rental operations dealing in airport, local, suburban and replacement rentals. Established: 1974 - Franchising Since: 1974 - No. of Units: Franchised: 130 - Franchise Fee: varies by population of area - Royalty: fixed by units - Total Inv: $25,000 - $500,000 - Financing: None.

RENT A VETTE
Rent A Vette International
1025 W. Laurel, Ste. 102, San Diego, CA, 92101. Contact: John Pounds, Pres. - Tel: (800) 627-0808. Automobile rentals, specializing in corvettes and other fine sports cars. We are unique, in-as-much as Rent A Vette is the only sports car rental franchise that specializes in corvettes. Established: 1981 - Franchising Since: 1992 - No. of Units: Company Owned: 2 - Franchised: 1 - Franchise Fee: $27,500 - Royalty: 3% 1st 12 mos, 5% thereafter - Total Inv: $325,000 - $593,500 - Financing: Fran. fee only.

RENT-A-DENT *
Rent A Dent Corp.
P.O. Box 130, Clear Lake, IA, 50428. Contact: Jerry Krause, CEO - Tel: (515) 357-6222. Car rental of good, clean used cars. Established: 1988 - Franchising Since: 1994 - No. of Units: Company Owned: 1 - Franchised: 5 - Franchise Fee: $10,000 - $25,000 - Royalty: $1.00 per rental day - Total Inv: $10 cars @ $2,500 - $5,000 per car - Financing: Yes, for an established business.

RENT-A-WRECK OF AMERICA, INC.
Bundy American Corp.
11460 Cronridge Dr., Ste. 120, Owings Mills, MD, 21117. Contact: Michael Fein - Tel: (800) 421-7253. New and used car, truck and van rental and leasing. Established: 1970 - Franchising Since: 1978 - No. of Units: Franchised: 400 - Franchise Fee: $5,000 to $75,000 - Royalty: 6% per annum, 2% adv. - Total Inv: Depends on whether a stand alone or add on - Financing: Yes.

SENSIBLE CAR RENTAL, INC.
96 Freneau Ave., Matawan, NJ, 07747. Contact: Charles Vitale, Gen. Mgr. - Tel: (800) 367-5159. Offer training, insurance, risk management & management support to a car rental program. Established: 1986 - Franchising Since: 1986 - No. of Units: Franchised: 115 - Franchise Fee: $3,500 to $15,000 - Royalty: $10-$15/car/mo. - Total Inv: Varies according to the number and value of cars in the program - Financing: Yes.

THRIFTY RENT-A-CAR SYSTEM, INC.
5330 E. 31st St., Tulsa, OK, 74135. Contact: Pete Garcia, Dir., U.S. Fran. Sales - Tel: (918) 669-2219, Fax: (918) 669-2861. Thrifty operates in over 50 countries and territories with over 1,100 locations throughout the North and South America, Europe, the Middle East, the Caribbean, Asia and the Pacific and is the fastest growing car rental company in Canada and Australia. Thrifty has a significant presence both in the airport and local car rental markets. Approximately 60% of its business is in the airport market, 40% in the local market. Established: 1950 - Franchising Since: 1962 - No. of Units: Company Owned: 14 - Franchised: over 1,100 - Franchise Fee: $8,500 and up - Royalty: 3% admin., 5% adv. - Total Inv: Varies - Financing: Financing packages can be made available to qualified licensees for major capital expenditures.

TRANSERV, INC.
20905 Mapleridge Ave., Southfield, MI, 48075-5748. Contact: Konnie Kustron, Sr. V.P. - Tel: (810) 827-1160. Luxury sedan ground transportation. Established: 1978 - Franchising Since: 1988 - No. of Units: Company Owned: 1 - Franchised: 35 - Franchise Fee: $2,500 - Royalty: 20% plus $125 wkly. gross sales (minus tips) - Total Inv: fran. fee, $1,000 radio deposit, cellular phone, insurance & vehicle - Financing: Yes.

U-SAVE AUTO RENTAL
U-Save Auto Rental of America Inc.
7525 Connelley Dr., Hanover, MD, 21076. Contact: Tim or Sandy, Fran. Dept. - Tel: (800) 272-USAV, ext. 146 & 147. A business format franchisor of new and used auto rental outlets. Catering to the needs of small towns and the economy minded consumers in urban and suburban areas. Established: 1978 - Franchising Since: 1979 - No. of Units: Company Owned: 1 - Franchised: 500 - Franchise Fee: $3,500 - $20,000 - Royalty: Flat fee per unit $10 to $19 per month - Total Inv: Varies - Financing: Varies.

UGLY DUCKLING RENT-A-CAR
2525 E. Camelback Rd., #510, Phoenix, AZ, 85016. Contact: Gina Burge, Fran. Admin. - Tel: (800) 843-3825, Fax: (602) 852-6696. Used car rentals. Established: 1977 - Franchising Since: 1978 - No. of Units: Franchised: 75 - Franchise Fee: $5,000 - $25,000 - Royalty: 4% - Total Inv: $25,000 - $125,000 - Financing: None.

VACATIONBOUND GLOBAL MOTORHOME TRAVEL
VacationBound, Inc.
3753 Howard Hughes Pkwy., Ste. 200, Las Vegas, NV, 89109. Contact: Dir. of Fran. Dev. - Tel: (702) 892-3797, Fax: (702) 892-3950. VacationBound serves the multi-billion dollar leisure travel industry via motorhome rentals. Special emphasis on rentals for local, domestic and international family vacations, served by locally owned franchise locations utilizing our International Reservations Center. Established: 1994 - Franchising Since: 1994 - No. of Units: Company Owned: 1 - Franchised: 55 (spring '96) - Total Inv: $45,000 - $1,200,000 incl. franchise fee and initial inventory - Financing: Yes, franchisor will assist with financing, especially inventory financing, through third party.

WHEELCHAIR GETAWAYS, INC.
P.O. Box 819, Newtown, PA, 18940-0832. Contact: Robert Jacoby, Gen. Mgr. - Tel: (215) 579-9120. Wheelchair Getaways rents wheelchair and scooter accessible vans to the general public, for the day, the week or longer. Established: 1988 - Franchising Since: 1989 - No. of Units: Company Owned: 3 - Franchised: 45 - Franchise Fee: Start at $15,000 - Royalty: $525/van/year - Total Inv: $70,000 incl. 2 vans - Financing: Yes.

AUTOMOTIVE: LUBRICATION & TUNEUP

ACC-U-TUNE & BRAKE
2510 Old Middlefield Way, Mountain View, CA, 94043. Contact: Bill Linder, Dir. Fran. Dev. - Tel: (415) 968-8863, Fax: (415) 968-1869. Convenient one stop, brakes, tune ups, drive thru oil change and other minor repair services. Established: 1975 - Franchising Since: 1979 - No. of Units: Company Owned: 4 - Franchised: 22 - Franchise Fee: $27,500 - Royalty: 7.5% - Total Inv: $50,000 - $75,000 cash down, total $125,000 - $230,000 - Financing: In CA, OR, WA & NV.

ALL TUNE AND LUBE
ATL International, Inc.
8334 Veteran's Hwy., Millersville, MD, 21108. Contact: Bruce Frazier, Franchise Dev. - Tel: (410) 987-1011. One-Stop tune-up, engine performance and preventive maintenance service center. Other additional services include high tech under-the-hood maintenance and repairs, engine computer components, brakes, shocks, struts and more. Established: 1985 - Franchising Since: 1986 - No. of Units: Company Owned: 1 - Franchised: 194 - Franchise Fee: $22,500 - Total Inv: $119,900 - Financing: Yes.

AUTO-LAB DIAGNOSTIC & TUNE-UP CENTERS
Auto Lab Franchise Mgt. Corp.
1346 W. Columbia Ave., Ste. 209, Battle Creek, MI, 49015. Contact: Daniel J. Kiefer, Pres. - Tel: (616) 966-0500. Engine performance, electrical systems diagnostics and repair as well as general auto service. Established; 1983 - Franchising Since: 1989 - No. of Units: Company Owned: 1 - Franchised: 20 - Franchise Fee: $19,500 - Royalty: 6%, 3% adv. - Total Inv: $45,000 operating, $75,000 equip. plus real estate - Financing: In-house and placement for outside.

ECONO LUBE N' TUNE, INC.
4911 Birch St., Newport Beach, CA, 92660. Contact: David Wisok, Dir. Fran. Sales - Tel: (800) 628-0253 or (714) 852-6630. 10-minute lube, oil and filter, 30 minute tune-up, smog, brakes, transmission service, air conditioning service, etc. Turn-key franchise featuring 5 and 6 bay drive-thru buildings. Established: 1973 - Franchising Since: 1974 - No. of Units: Company Owned: 66 - Franchised: 133 - Franchise Fee: $29,500 - Royalty: 6% + 8% adv. - Total Inv: $65,000+ - Financing: O.A.C.

EXPRESS OIL CHANGE
190 West Valley Ave., Birmingham, AL, 35219. Contact: Julian Bell, Fran. Sales - Tel: (205) 940-6025. Fast automobile maintenance center, designed to provide 4 quality services: 1) 10 min. oil change; 2) 20 min. transmission service; 3) 30 min. tire rotation and balance; 4) 60 min. brake service. Established: 1979 - Franchising Since: 1983 - No. of Units: Company Owned: 11 - Franchised: 33 - Franchise Fee: $10,000 - Royalty: 5% of gross sales paid monthly - Total Inv: cash = $100,000 plus - Total = $385,000 plus - Financing: None.

FLEETMASTERS *
Fleet Service, Inc.
761 Mabury Rd., Ste. 8-C, San Jose, CA, 95133. , Fran. Dir. - Tel: (901) 867-0600. A service business that performs lube and mechanical repairs to vehicles at the clients location. Established: 1994 - Franchising Since: 1995 - No. of Units: Company Owned: 1 - Franchise Fee: $20,000 - Royalty: 4% - Total Inv: $57,000 - $99,000 (Work. Cap, Inven., Equip.). For further information please contact: Consultants America Corp., 12279 US Highway 64. Eads, TN, 38028, Tel: (901) 867-0600, Fax: (901) 867-0010.

GREASE MONKEY
Grease Monkey International, Inc.
216 16th St. Mall, #1100, Denver, CO, 80202-5125. Contact: Michael Brunetti, V.P., Fran. Dev. - Tel: (303) 534-1660 or (800) 364-0352, Fax: (303) 534-2095. Ten minute lube & oil change. Established: 1978 - Franchising Since: 1979 - No. of Units: Company Owned: 30 - Franchised: 183 - Franchise Fee: $28,000 - Royalty: 5% - 1% adv. - Total Inv: $130,000.

GUARANTEED TUNE UP
Guaranteed Tune Up, Inc.
89 Headquarters Plz., North Twr., 14th Fl., Morristown, NJ, 07960. Contact: William Okita, Pres. - Tel: (800) 543-5829, Fax: (201) 993-1757. Although we specialize in automotive tune-ups, we also allow our franchisees to perform all automotive repairs, such as brakes, engine repairs, etc. Thereby increasing sales volume and cash flow. Established: 1984 - Franchising Since: 1980 - No. of Units: Franchised: 5 - Franchise Fee: $15,000 - Royalty: 6% - Total Inv: $96,000 - Financing: Yes, thru third party.

INDY LUBE 10-MINUTE OIL CHANGE
Indy Lube Service Co., Inc.
6515 E. 82nd St., Ste. 209, Indianapolis, IN, 46250-1590. Contact: Jim Yates, Pres. - Tel: (317) 845-9444. Drive-through 10-minute oil change center specializing in fluid maintenance of all passenger vehicles, recreational vehicles, and light industrial trucks. Full service oil change includes a 15-point safety and fluid check. All centers have point-of-sale computers. Established: 1986 - Franchising Since: 1989 - No. of Units: Company Owned: 13 - Franchised: 6 - Franchise Fee: $18,000 - Royalty: 5% of gross sales - Total Inv: $350,000 - $400,000 (bldg., land, etc.) or leased $50,000 - Financing: No.

LUBE WAGON, THE
9430 Mission Blvd., Riverside, CA, 92509-2635. Contact: Ray Teagarden, Pres. - Tel: (909) 685-5531. Portable lube service business on wheels. Established: 1977 - Franchising Since: 1977 - Number of Dealerships: 39 - Total Inv: $12,000 - Financing: No.

LUBEPRO'S
LubePro's International, Inc.
1630 Colonial Pky., Inverness, IL, 60067. Contact: Phil Robinson, Chairman of the Board - Tel: (708) 776-2500 or (800) 654-5823. Automotive quick lubrication and oil change. Established: 1978 - Franchising Since: 1985 - No. of Units: Company Owned: 10 - Franchised: 26 - Franchise Fee: $25,000 - Royalty: 5% - Total Inv: $165,000: $62,000 cash, $60,000 furn., fix, equip., $18,000 inven., plus fran. fee - Financing: No.

MCQUIK'S OILUBE
McQuik's Oilube, Inc.
3861 N. Wheeling Ave., P.O. Box 46, Muncie, IN, 47304. Contact: Alan Jackson, Fran. Dir. - Tel: (317) 282-2183. Quick lubrication, oil change and oil filter change including checking and filling brake, power steering, transmission, differential battery and windshield washer fluids also, courtesy service such as vacuuming and washing windows. Established: 1980 - Franchising Since: 1985 - No. of Units: Company Owned: 33 - Franchised: 53 - Franchise Fee: $15,000 - Total Inv: $125,000 exclusive of land and bldg. - Royalty: 4%+ adv. fee - Financing: No.

MR. LUBE U.S.
M.L.U.S. Inc.
110 Cypress Station Dr., Suite 150, Houston, TX, 77090. Contact: Kevin Giese, Pres. - Tel: (713) 893-2591 or Fax (713) 893-2594. Quick lube centers featuring 18 brands of oil, 25 brands of manufacturers' filters, and a 21 point visual inspection of the vehicle. Features superflo motor oil in bulk. Established: 1987 - Franchising Since: 1988 - No. of Units: Franchised: 16 - Franchise Fee: $25,000 + $10,000 project management fee if Mr. Lube U.S. manages construction - Royalty: 7% of gross sales - Total Inv: $135,000 - $180,000 - Financing: No.

MULTI-TUNE & TIRE
Multi Management Systems, Inc.
2457 Covington Pike, Memphis, TN, 38128. Contact: Glen Whiteman, Pres. - Tel: (901) 386-9600. Auto tuneup and auto repair and tire sales. Established: 1986 - Franchising Since: 1986 - No. of Units: Company Owned: 3 - Franchise Fee: $17,500 - Royalty: 3% - Total Inv: $123,800 - $168,000 - Financing: No.

OIL BUTLER
Oil Butler International, Corp.
1599 Rt. 22 West, Union, NJ, 07083. Contact: Barbara Kowalczyk - Tel: (908) 687-3283. Windshield repair & quick lube - two money-making opportunities in one franchise. Uniquely designed, state-of-the-art, high-tech vehicle, which provides the corporate image and service customers expect from the leader in the field of on-site changes. Fleet employee, and residential market penetration is taught in intensive training program. Service is the key for the 90's. Oil Butler fulfills this need with the best vehicle maintenance service available. Established: 1987 - Franchising Since: 1991 - No. of Units: Company Owned: 1 - Franchised: 42 - Franchise Fee: $3,000 to $7,000 - Royalty: 7% - Total Inv: $9,000 to $15,000: fran. fee + trailer & equip. $4,000 - $8,000 - Financing: Available through outside sources.

OIL CAN HENRY'S QUICK LUBE CENTER
OCH International, Inc.
1200 N.W. Front Ave., Ste. 690, Portland, OR, 97209. Contact: John E. Shepanek, Pres. - Tel: (503) 243-6311, Fax: (503) 228-5227. Quick oil change for automobiles, vans, light trucks and motor homes. Established: 1988 - Franchising Since: 1988 - No. of Units: Company Owned: 1 - Franchised: 26 - Franchise Fee: $25,000 - Royalty: 5.5% - Total Inv: approx. $300,000 for real estate and $75,000 for bus. inv. and starting cap.

OIL CAN VAN, INC.
1640 Cypress Dr., Jupiter, FL, 33469. Contact: Richard Gifford, Pres. - Tel: (407) 575-1531. Mobile lube service. Business opportunity. Established: 1989 - Franchising Since: 1990 - No. of Units: Franchised: 23 - Total Inv: $45,900 equip. & vehicles - Financing: Yes.

OIL EXPRESS®
Oil Express National, Inc.
15 Spinning Wheel Rd., Ste. 428, Hinsdale, IL, 60521. Contact: Dan Barnas, Pres. - Tel: (708) 325-8666, Fax: (708) 325-8683. 10 minute oil change. Established: 1980 - Franchising Since: 1981 - No. of Units: Company Owned: 20 - Franchised: 37 - Franchise Fee: $25,000 - Royalty: 5% gross, 4.5% adv. - Total Inv: $450,000 to $550,000 all inclusive - Financing: Yes, non-direct.

PRECISION TUNE, INC.
P.O. Box 5000, 748 Miller Dr. SE, Leesburg, VA, 22075. Contact: William T. Carroll, V.P. Real Estate and Fran. Dev. - Tel: (703) 777-9095, Fax: (703) 779-0136. America's largest tune-up franchise company which offers customers service in four categories; all aspects of engine performance, quick oil & lube, brakes and optional services such as a/c repair & service and radiator flush and fill. Established: 1975 - Franchising Since: 1977 - No. of Units: 480 - Franchise Fee: $25,000 - Royalty: 7.5% - Total Inv: $140,000 - $186,400 (incl. fran. fee) - Financing: Equipment leasing only.

PROMPTO 10 MINUTE OIL LUBE & FILTER
Prompto System, Inc.
12 Scott Dr., Westbrook, ME, 04107. Contact: Kevin King, Fran. Dir. - Tel: (207) 775-4016. Drive-thru oil & lube specializing in basic service only with limited additional sales. Very competitive consumer pricing with broader customer base. Established: 1984 - Franchising Since: 1985 - No. of Units: Company Owned: 8 - Franchised: 7 - Franchise Fee: $17,500 - Royalty: 5% - Total Inv: $50,000 for inven., work. cap. & fee, land & bldg. are extra - Financing: Assist in preparation of loans only.

Q LUBE
Q Lube, Inc.
1385 West 2200 South, Salt Lake City, UT, 84119. Contact: Rod Fawson, Fran. Sales Manager - Tel: (801) 975-4731. Oil change, lubrication, and fluid maintenance. Established: 1977 - Franchising Since: 1978 - No. of Units: Company Owned: 341 - Franchised: 124 - Franchise Fee: $25,000 - Royalty: 5% - Total Inv: $150,000 - $450,000 - Financing: None.

SPEEDEE OIL CHANGE & TUNE-UP
159 Hwy. 22 E., Madisonville, LA, 70447-1350. Contact: Kevin Bennett, Exec. V.P. - Tel: (504) 845-1919, Fax: (504) 845-1936. Quick oil change, tune-ups, brakes, and other preventive maintenance services. Services performed while the customer waits and no appointment is necessary. Established: 1980 - Franchising Since: 1982 - No. of Units: Company Owned: 8 - Franchised: 223 - Franchise Fee: $30,000 - $40,000 - Royalty: 6%, 8% adv. - Total Inv: $39,000 - $333,000 - Financing: No.

SPEEDY LUBE / QUIK MARTS
Southeast Companies
P.O. Box 1385, Waukesha, WI, 53187. Contact: John Theisen, Owner - Tel: (414) 524-7951, Fax: (414) 524-7950. 10 minute oil changes. Established: 1975 - Franchising Since: 1978 - No. of Units: Company Owned: 20 - Franchised: 14 - Franchise Fee: $20,000 - Royalty: 6%, 2% adv. - Total Inv: $125,000 land, $150,000 bldg., $25,000 equip. or leasing of entire facilities also available - Financing: Yes.

STAR LUBE *
Texaco Refining & Marketing Inc.
1111 Bagby St., Houston, TX, 77002. Contact: Larry McDonough, Project Mgr., Star Lube - Tel: (713) 752-6706. Quick oil change (14 pt. service) drive thru - stay in your car - add on profit center to a Texaco gasoline location. Established: 1990 - Franchising Since: 1994 - No. of Units: Company Owned: 15 - Franchised: 7 - Franchise Fee: $10,000 - Royalty: 0 - franchisee must purchase Texaco products - Total Inv: Building $100,000 to $120,000, Equip. $20,000 to $30,000 - Financing: Yes, 80% 12 yr. amort.

TUNEX AUTOMOTIVE/DIAGNOSTIC SPECIALISTS
Tunex International, Inc.
556 E. 2100 South, Salt Lake City, UT, 84106. Contact: Franchise Sales Dept. - Tel: (801) 486-8133 or (800) HI TUNEX. Diagnostic services and repairs of engine related systems (i.e., ignition, carburetion, fuel injection, emission, computer controls, cooling, air conditioning). For maximum customer satisfaction, we analyze all systems for problems so that customers can make service and repair decisions. Established: 1974 - Franchising Since: 1975 - No. of Units: Company Owned: 5 - Franchised: 15 - Franchise Fee: $19,000 - Royalty: 5%, $750/mth. adv. - Total Inv: $65,000 cash $105,000 - $120,000 - Financing: No.

VALVOLINE INSTANT OIL CHANGE
Valvoline Instant Oil Change Franchising, Inc.
301 E. Main St., Ste. 1200, Lexington, KY, 40507. Contact: Jeff Malicote, Fran. Sales Rep. - Tel: (800) 622-6846. Oil, filter, lube and other fluid maintenance services. Established: 1986 - Franchising Since: 1988 - No. of Units: Company Owned: 340 - Franchised: 65 - Franchise Fee: $25,000 - Royalty: 4,5,6% years 1,2,3 - Total Inv: $74,000 - $125,000 if leasing - Financing: None.

VICTORY LANE QUICK OIL CHANGE
2610 West Liberty, Ann Arbor, MI, 48103. Contact: Derek Oxender, Dir. of Dev. - Tel: (800) 541-0491 or (313) 996-1196. Ten minute quick oil change utilizing state of the art technology with an emphasis on speed, efficiency and customer participation. No previous experience or mechanical skill is necessary. Established: 1980 - Franchising Since: 1987 - No. of Units: Company Owned: 4 - Franchised: 40 - Franchise Fee: $20,000 - Royalty: 6% weekly gross sales - Total Inv: $60,000 - $80,000 with leasing of equip. available - Financing: Franchisee to arrange own financing. Equipment leasing available. We will assist franchisee in arranging financing.

AUTOMOTIVE: MUFFLER SHOPS

CAR-X MUFFLER & BRAKE/SPEEDY MUFFLER KING
Speedy Car-X, Inc.
8430 W. Bryn Mawr Ave., Ste. 400, Chicago, IL, 60631. Contact: Carolyn Vaughn, Mgr., Fran. Admin. - Tel: (312) 693-1000. Installation and repair of exhaust, brakes, front end & suspension systems. Established: 1971 - Franchising Since: 1973 - No. of Units: Company Owned: 260 - Franchised: 116 - Franchise Fee: $18,500 - Royalty: 5% of gross sales - Total Inv: $220,500 - $277,000 - Financing: Third party.

CUSTOM MUFFLER SERVICE CENTER
5664 South Transit Rd., Lockport, NY, 14094. Contact: Daniel Jendrowski, Owner - Tel: (716) 433-1214. Automotive specialty, muffler, brake and tune-up centers. Established: 1981 - Franchising Since: 1988 - No. of Units: Company Owned: 2 - Franchised: 3 - Franchise Fee: varies - Royalty: 8%, 4% adv. -Total Inv: $30,000 min. and up - Financing: Yes.

LEAVERTON AUTO
827 So. 9th, St. Joseph, MO, 64501. Contact: Ronald J. Martin, Pres. - Tel: (816) 279-7483. Automobile mufflers, brakes, shocks, alignment, quick lube. Franchising Since: 1992 - No. of Units: Company Owned: 2 - Franchise Fee: $25,000 - Royalty: 5% - Total Inv: $133,500 - $203,000 includes fee.

LENTZ USA
1001 Riverview Dr., Kalamazoo, MI, 49001. Contact: Gary R. Thomas, Fran. Sales Dir. - Tel: (616) 342-2200. Undercar repair specialists: Mufflers, brakes, suspension, wheel alignments. Established: 1982 - Franchising Since: 1989 - No. of Units: Company Owned: 11 - Franchised: 22 - Franchise Fee: $18,500 - Royalty: 7% - 0% sliding scale - Total Inv: $40,000 equip., $15,000 - $20,000 inven., $10,000 - $20,000 pre-opening - Financing: 3rd party.

MAD HATTER CAR CARE CENTERS, INC. *
1443 South Blvd., Charlotte, NC, 28203. Contact: Jon Sing, Pres. - Tel: (704) 332-7727, Fax: (704) 333-5067. Under car care. Mufflers, brakes, ride control. Franchising Since: 1989 - No. of Units: Franchised: 50 - Franchise Fee: $30,000 - Financing: US, Canada, Mexico.

MEINEKE DISCOUNT MUFFLER SHOPS
Meineke Discount Muffler Shops, Inc.
128 S. Tryon St., Ste. 900, Charlotte, NC, 28202. Contact: Amy Daniel, Fran. Sales Admin. - Tel: (704) 377-8855. Meineke Discount Muffler Shops offer fast, courteous service in the merchandising of automotive exhaust systems, shock absorbers, struts, and brakes. Unique inventory control and group purchasing power enable Meineke dealers to adhere to a Discount Concept and deliver quality service. Established: 1972 - Franchising Since: 1972 - No. of Units: Company Owned: 8 - Franchised: 931 - Franchise Fee: $22,500 - Royalty: 7% + 10% adv. - Total Inv: $127,000 - Financing: 3rd party financing available to qualified individuals.

MERLIN'S MUFFLER AND BRAKE
Merlin's Franchising, Inc.
One North River Lane, Ste. 206, Geneva, IL, 60134. Contact: Mark Hameister, Dir. Fran. Dev. - Tel: (800) 652-9900. An upscale automotive specialty shop providing complete under body automotive services specializing in exhaust, brake, lubrication and suspension. Established: 1975 - Franchising Since: 1975 - No. of Units: Company Owned: 2 - Franchised: 47 - Franchise Fee: $26,000 - $30,000 - Royalty: 4.9% - Total Inv: $180,000 - $185,000 ($45,000 must be cash) - Financing: Through 3rd parties.

MIDAS
Midas International Corp.
225 N. Michigan Ave., Chicago, IL, 60601. Contact: Richard Pope or Mina Chong, Nat'l Dir. Fran. Dev./Ass't. to Dir. of Fran. - Tel: (800) 621-0144. Automotive aftermarket specialists in mufflers, shocks, struts, brakes and front end. Established: 1956 - Franchising Since: 1956 - No. of Units: Company Owned: 130 US; 222 Foreign - Franchised: 1,742 US; 364 Foreign - Franchise Fee: $20,000 - Royalty: 5% + 5% adv. - Total Inv: $254,050 - $357,500 - Financing: 3rd. party.

MITEY INC.
3530 Jefferson Hwy., Jefferson, LA, 70121. Contact: Melissa Wise - Tel: (504) 832-7925. Retail muffler, exhaust and brake shops. Quick automotive oil change and lubrication centers. Established: 1974 - Franchising Since: 1978 - No. of Units: Company Owned: 1 - Franchised: 21 - Franchise Fee: $20,000 - Total Inv: $75,000 - Royalty: Mitey Muffler 7%, Miteyfast 5%.

ROADWAY MUFFLER & BRAKE CENTERS
23193 Sandalfoot Plaza, Boca Raton, FL, 33428. Contact: Joseph Botwinick, Dir Fran. Sales - Tel: (407) 451-0900. Muffler and brake center franchise. Established: 1989 - Franchising Since: 1990 - No. of Units: Company Owned: 2 - Franchise Fee: $15,000 - Royalty: 5%, 5% adv. (incl. 4% spent locally) - Total Inv: $59,200 - $104,000 - Financing: On equipment.

TOP VALUE MUFFLER SHOPS
Top Value Exhaust Systems
36887 Schoolcraft, Livonia, MI, 48150. Contact: Bob Bernhoft, Fran. Mkt. Dev. - Tel: (313) 462-3633. Undercar repair, includes quick & quality repair of exhaust, brake and suspension systems on automobiles and light trucks. Established: 1977 - Franchising Since: 1980 - No. of Units: Company Owned: 10 - Franchised: 39 - Franchise Fee: $15,000 - Royalty: 6%-9% of gross sales based on marketing area - Total Inv: $50,000 start up cash, $85,000 - $100,000 total inv. - Financing: 3rd party financing assistance available through banks, SBA and minority associations.

USA MUFFLER AND BRAKES
USA Automotive Systems
2624 W. Lincoln Hwy., Merrillville, IN, 46410. Contact: James Petsas, V.P., Fran. Dev. - Tel: (219) 769-9441, 1-800-ASK 4 USA. A business system that will operate as a retail automotive service center specializing in the sale, replacement and installation of motor vehicle exhaust systems, mufflers, brakes, shock absorbers, suspension including frontend, emphasizing fast, friendly and convenient services 6 days a week, 9 hours a day. Established: 1987 - Franchising Since: 1989 - No. of Units: Company Owned: 4 - Franchised: 8 - Franchise Fee: $15,000 - Royalty: 5%, 6% adv., 1% warranty fund - Total Inv: $53,600 - $596,250 - Financing: Assistance with loan package preparation for banks & SBA.

WEAR MASTER MUFFLER AND BRAKE CENTERS
Wear Master Company
235 Oakview Dr., Lapeer, MI, 48446. Contact: Brian E. Bedwell, Owner - Tel: (810) 664-4365, Fax: (810) 664-0694. Outlets specializing in the service of automobiles and light trucks for exhaust systems, brakes, shock absorbers and suspension systems in a clean, customer-oriented environment on a while-you-wait basis. (Wear Master® is a federally registered trademark.) Established: 1972 - Franchising Since: 1992 - No. of Units: Company Owned: 4 - Franchised: 12 - Start Costs: $10,000 incl. security deposits, training, etc. - Royalty: 5% royalty/$1,100 a month adv. budget - Total Inv: $80,000 to $150,000 incl. work. cap., inven., signage, start up exp.'s, equip., etc. - Financing: Not directly, except for a few locations company owned.

AUTOMOTIVE: PRODUCTS AND SERVICES

21ST CENTURY AUTOMOTIVE MARKETING
14755 Grover St., Omaha, NE, 68144. Contact: Paul N. Treakle, CEO - Tel: (402) 333-3191 (fax). 21st Century Automotive Marketing has developed a unique system that assists auto dealers in marketing previously owned cars and trucks. This system utilizes a computer generated window sticker that gives an estimated value of the vehicle's worth, plus a wealth of information for the consumer. Helps auto dealers comply with state and federal regulations. Prime territories available nationwide many with existing customer base. Established: 1986 - Franchising Since: January, 1995 - No. of Units: Company Owned: 2 - Franchise Fee: $6,000 - Royalty: 1% adv.- Total Inv: $8,000 - $15,000 incl. fran. fee - Financing: Equip. financing available.

ABRA AUTO BODY & GLASS
6601 Shingle Creek Pkwy., Ste. 200, Minneapolis, MN, 55430. Contact: Rollie Benjamin, Dir. of Fran. - Tel: (800) 536-2334, (612) 561-7220, Fax: (612) 561-7433. One of the finest automotive collision & glass franchises. Operating company and franchised auto body collision & autoglass replacement shops. Support with marketing, business management, equipment & material purchases. Investment opportunities for quality owners & managers. Established: 1984 - Franchising Since: 1987 - No. of Units: Company Owned: 17 - Franchised: 27 - Franchise Fee: $22,500 - Royalty: 5% of sales - Total Inv: $229,000 - $287,500 (assuming building is leased) - Financing: None.

AERO-COLOURS® FRANCHISES
Aero-Colours, Inc.
6971 Washington Ave. S., Ste. 102, Minneapolis, MN, 55439-1508. Contact: James F. Spellmire, Fran. Dev. - Tel: (800) 696-AERO (2376), Fax: (612) 942-0628. Aero-Colours is a mobile air brush touch-up process serving the automotive industry. Vans are fully equipped mobile mixing labs that can custom match colors on-site. Training, support and service to franchises far surpasses any available. Established: 1985 - Franchising Since: 1993 - No. of Units: Company Owned: 4 - Franchised: 31 - Franchise Fee: $25,000 - Royalty: 7% to 4% based on sales - Total Inv: $55,000 min. - Financing: Aero-Colours financial program includes SBA - 8 yrs., Aero-Colours loans - 3yrs., and assistance for conventional bank loans.

AID AUTO STORES, INC.
P. O. Box 281, Westbury, NY, 11590-0281. Contact: Philip Stephen, Pres. - Tel: (516) 338-7889. Retail automotive parts, accessories, tools, chemicals and equipment. Established: 1951 - Franchising Since: 1966 - No. of Units: Company Owned: 4 - Franchised: 88 - Franchise Fee: $400/month - Royalty: $775/month, adv. fee - Total Inv: $135,000 - Financing: No.

AIRCHEK
Otto Cool, Inc.
6600 S.W. 62 Ave., Miami, FL, 33143. Contact: Fran. Mktg. Dept. - Tel: (800) 288-6247 or (305) 661-8963. Automobile air conditioning service & repair center. Established: 1992 - Franchising Since: 1992 - No. of Units: Company Owned: 1 - Franchised: 1 - Franchise Fee: $25,000 - Royalty: 5% - Total Inv: $91,800, initial fran. fee $25,000, initial investment $66,800 - $73,500 - Financing: On inventory by select approved suppliers.

ALTA MERE WINDOW TINTING & AUTO ALARMS *
AMI Franchising Inc.
3201 N.E. Loop 820, #180, Fort Worth, TX, 76137. Contact: Chance Parker, Fran. Dir. - Tel: (817) 232-1833, Fax: (817) 232-5793. Specializing in the professional installation of automotive aftermarket accessories including window tint, auto alarms and cellular. Alta Mere has a proven marketing and production system that allows maximum volume for retail and wholesale accounts. Established: 1986 - Franchising Since: 1993 - No. of Units: Franchised: 57 - Franchise Fee: $20,000 - Royalty: 4% - Total Inv: $76,000 to $120,000 - Financing: 3rd party.

ALTRACOLOR SYSTEMS
Aftermarket Appearance Industries Inc.
P.O. Box 2124, Kenner, LA, 70063. Contact: J.A. Richards, Pres. - Tel: (800) 678-5220, Fax: (504) 454-7233. Mobile automotive paint and plastic repair and touch-up system. Intensive 3 day training at co. hdq. and 1 week in the field. Seeking franchises in all countries. Well established in 20 states. Established: 1988 - Franchising Since: 1991 - No. of Units: Company Owned: 4 - Franchised: 40 - Independents: 70 - Franchise Fee: $9,950 - Royalty: $95 per week - Total Inv: $9,950 fran. fee, $13,500 equip. & paint, $1,750 training - Financing: $13,500 equip. may be financed by company.

AMERICAN BRAKE SERVICE
3715 Northside Pky. N.W., #300-500, Atlanta, GA, 30327-2806. Contact: Marvin Young, Pres. - Tel: (800) 362-7005. Specialists in automotive brake and undercar services, offering individual franchises and area management franchises. Established: 1991 - Franchising Since: 1991 - No. of Units: Franchised: 14 - Franchise Fee: $19,500 - Royalty: 6% - Total Inv: $89,000 - $134,000 - Financing: Third party financing available.

AMERICAN FLUID TECHNOLOGY™ AFT™ MOBILE ON-SITE FLUID RECYCLING SERVICES
A.F. Technologies
239 Littleton Rd., #40, Westford, MA, 01886-3500. Contact: Gerry Hall, Dir. of Training - Tel: (508) 692-6700. Mobile on-site anti-freeze/coolant recycling services approved by General Motors and exceeds all ASTM specifications. Authorized Prestone recycling featuring the exclusive Prestone recycling formula. Established: 1991 - Franchising Since: 1991 - No. of Units: Company Owned: 1 - Franchised: 6 - 37 franchised territories sold - Franchise Fee: $25,000 - Royalty: 10% - Total Inv: $160,000 (equip., machinery, van); $25,000 Fran.Fee = $185,000 - Financing: Yes $35,000 down payment.

APPEARANCE RECONDITIONING CO.
12833 Industrial Park Blvd., Plymouth, MN, 55441. Contact: D. Almen, Pres. - Tel: (612) 559-3292. Services to used car market - reconditioning interiors and vinyls, plastics, cloths and leathers. Established: 1977 - No. of Units: Franchised: 75 - Total Inv: $15,000 - Financing: No.

AUTO ACCENTS, INC.
6550 Pearl Rd., Parma Heights, OH, 44130. Contact: W.E. Poston, V.P. - Tel: (800) 567-3120. Auto Accent is a retail business specializing in the sales and installation of the most in demand automotive add ons such as state of the art stereo equipment, alarms, cellular phones, pagers, custom truck and van accessories, sunroofs, power windows and door locks.

Established: 1985 - Franchising Since: 1994 - No. of Units: Company Owned: 6 - Franchised: 4 - Franchise Fee: $14,900 - Royalty: 5%, 1% adv. - Total Inv: $70,000 - $130,000 - Financing: No.

AUTO AMERICA
Western Auto Supply Company
2107 Grand Ave., Kansas City, MO, 64108. Contact: Chuck Hutchens, V.P. Store Dev. - Tel: (816) 346-4000. Discount automotive superstore featuring tires, batteries, parts, accessories, and service in markets of 30,000 to 50,000 vehicles. Established: 1909 - Franchising Since: 1935 - No. of Units: Company Owned: 370 - Franchised: 15/assoc's 1,100 - Franchise Fee: $25,000 - Royalty: 5% net sales - Total Inv: $400,000 - $550,000 (inven., fix, equip., pre-opening costs, work cap., fran. fee, deposit, grand opening funds) - Financing: No.

AUTO ARTISTRY, INC. *
Auto Artistry, Inc.
500 East North Ave., Chicago, IL, 60188. Contact: Wayne Pyrant, V.P., Fran. Sales - Tel: (800) 669-6413, Fax: (708) 462-6196. Mobile franchise that offers on-site installation and design of automotive aftermarket products: graphics, spoilers, sunroofs & more - to auto dealerships, body shops, and fleet companies. Established: 1994 - Franchising Since: 1995 - No. of Units: Company Owned: 1 - Franchised: 6 - Franchise Fee: $25,000 - Royalty: 7% - Total Inv: $60,500 - $86,500 - Financing: Yes.

AUTO EXAM, INC. *
1901 N. Central Expressway, Ste. 220, Richardson, TX, 75080. Contact: Douglas Keane, Pres. - Tel: (800) 757-EXAM or (214) 690-0550. 'Look before you leap' 112-Pt. mobile used vehicle inspection service. ASE certified technicians. Before you buy, have it inspected. The perfect home business, no mechnical background required. Established: 1991 - Franchising Since: 1995 - No. of Units: Franchised: 4 - Franchise Fee: $5,995 - Royalty: 5%, 3% adv. - Total Inv: $5,995 fran.; $5,000 - $15,000 tools & equip. - Financing: No.

AUTO ONE GLASS & ACCESSORIES
15965 Jeanette St., Southfield, MI, 48075. Contact: Colleen McGaffey - Tel: (810) 557-2784, Fax: (810) 557-7931. Installed products and services which enhance the value of automotive vehicles. Strong retail merchandising programs for auto glass, automotive security systems, cellular phones, car and truck accessories and protection sealants, fabric protection and rust proofing. Established: 1988 - Franchising Since: 1988 - No. of Units: Franchised: 40 - Franchise Fee: $20,000 - Royalty: 5% w/cap - Total Inv: $45,000 - $90,000 - Financing: No.

AUTOLIST
Autolist Corporation
P.O. Box 674, Gulf Breeze, FL, 32562-0674. Contact: Robert Smith, Exec.V.P. - Tel: (904) 932-4431. A used car sales and brokerage dealership franchise opportunity that specializes in selling and locating quality private owner vehicles. Each franchise also offers financing, warranties, and trade-ins. Established: 1988 - Franchising Since: 1988 - No. of Units: Franchised: 15 - Franchise Fee: $6,500 - Royalty: $350 flat - Total Inv: $100,000 - $50,000 cash inv. - Financing: Yes.

BIG O TIRES
Big O Tires, Inc.
11755 E. Peakview Ave., Englewood, CO, 80111. Contact: Nancy LaViolette, Bus. Dev. Coord. - Tel: (800) 622-2446, Fax: (303) 790-0225. Fast growing franchisor of independent retail tire and under-car service centers in North America. Offer 30 years of proven success, site selection assistance, comprehensive training, protected territory, on-going field support, and much more. Established: 1962 - Franchising Since: 1962 - No. of Units: Company Owned: 5 - Franchised: 377 - Franchise Fee: $21,000 - Royalty: 2% gross sales - Total Inv: $300,000 net worth, $100,000 cash - Financing: Equip. leasing.

BRAKE CENTERS OF AMERICA
35 Old Battery Road, Bridgeport, CT, 06605. Contact: Bill Pelletier, Pres. - Tel: (203) 336-1995. Low cost, easy to run automotive brake specialty shop. Brake Centers of America offers it's customers a better job at about 1/2 the price of it's competitors. Established: 1989 - Franchising Since: 1995 - No. of Units: Company Owned: 6 - Franchise Fee: $12,000 - Royalty: 6% - Total Inv: $65,300 complete - Financing: None.

BRAKE SHOP, THE
44899 Centre Ct. #104, Clinton Township, MI, 48038. Contact: Ken Rempel, Dir. of Fran. - Tel: (313) 228-9010 or (800) 866-2725. Automotive brake repair specialists. Established: 1987 - Franchising Since: 1989 - No. of Units: Company Owned: 3 - Franchised: 97 - Franchise Fee: $22,500 - Royalty: 8% - Total Inv: $50,000 - $80,000 depends on location - Financing: Will assist. VetFran sponsor.

BRAKE WORLD
5415 N.W. 15th St., Margate, FL, 33068. Contact: Gerry Hopkins, Pres. - Tel: (305) 973-2810. Automotive centers specializing in brakes, suspension and exhaust. Established: 1970 - Franchising Since: 1976 - No. of Units: Company Owned: 2 - Franchised: 8 - Royalty: $500 or 5% - Approx. Inv: $60,000 - Financing: Yes.

BULLHIDE LINER
Bullhide Liner Corp.
N. 1000 Argonne Rd., Ste. 120, Spokane, WA, 99206. Contact: Ron Grossman, Pres. - Tel: (509) 891-0520, (800) 789-BULL (2855), Fax: (509) 922-3970. Bullhide Liner, as an add-on or stand-alone business, can be your entry into the fast growing truck/auto accessory market. Bullhide is spray-molded directly to the prepared pickup truckbed, forming a rubber-like, nonskid, liner. It protects truckbeds from damage due to rust, abrasion and chemical attack. Established: 1993 - Franchising Since: 1993 - No. of Units: Company Owned: 1 - Franchised: 4 - Franchise Fee: $12,500 - Royalty: 3.5%, .5% adv. on gross sales - Total Inv: $70,000 incl. equip., starting inventory capital $20,000 - Financing: No.

BUMPER-TO-BUMPER
Downey Automotive Warehouse
4105 S. Creek Rd., Chattanooga, TN, 37406. Contact: Jimmy Gorham, Gen. Mgr. - Tel: (615) 622-6274. Retail automotive. Established: 1976 - Franchising Since: 1976 - No. of Units: Company Owned: 21 - Franchised: 155 - Royalty: $300 mth. adv. - Total Inv: $100,000 - Financing: Yes.

CARSTAR AUTOMOTIVE, INC.
8400 W. 110th St., Ste. 200, Overland Park, KS, 66210. Contact: Carol Collis, Fran. Dev. Coord. - Tel: (913) 451-1294. Conversion of existing auto collision repair stores nationwide. Established: 1989 - Franchising Since: 1989 - No. of Units: Company Owned: 1 - Franchised: 360 - Franchise Fee: Varies - Total Inv: Initial fee, percentage of gross revenues - Financing: No.

CHAMPION AUTO STORES
Champion Auto Stores, Inc.
9353 Jefferson Hwy., Maple Grove, MN, 55369-4237. Contact: Mart Wold, Fran. Dir. - Tel: (612) 391-6655. Retail stores featuring auto parts and accessories. The franchisor provides an extensive support system which includes site development, training, accounting, inventory control, purchasing, advertising and more. Established: 1956 - Franchising Since: 1961 - No. of Units: Company Owned: 40 - Franchised: 138 - Franchise Fee: $20,000 - Royalty: 5% gross sales - Total Inv: $175,000 - $255,000 - Financing: 50% equity required, assistance provided in securing financing for the balance.

CLEANCO, INC.
2211 W. County, C2, Roseville, MN, 55113. Contact: James Trapp, Pres. - Tel: (612) 784-2293. Mobile and drive-thru truck washing. Established: 1963 - No. of Units: 16 - Approx. Inv: $20,000 - Royalty: 4% - Financing: Assistance.

COLLISION SHOP, THE
15965 Jeanette St., Southfield, MI, 48075. Contact: Colleen McGaffey - Tel: (810) 557-2784, Fax: (810) 557-7931. Time-proven system for repairing today's vehicles which focuses on body and paint repairs, including unibody repair, metal finishing, two-stage painting system, and detailing. Established: 1991 - Franchising Since: 1993 - No. of Units: Company Owned: 4 - Franchised: 10 - Franchise Fee: $35,000 - Royalty: 6% - Total Inv: $100,000 - $150,000 - Financing: Yes.

COLORS ON PARADE
Total Car Franchising Corporation
3305 Breckinridge Blvd., Ste. 100, Duluth, GA, 30136. Contact: Gaile Brown, Oper. Dir. - Tel: (404) 923-0559, Fax: (404) 923-0559. Offer an appearance technology franchise specializing in a unique paint duplication and repair system for vehicles of all sorts. Paintless dent repair is part of the package. Two to three weeks initial training, on-site training, toll free operations hotline, access to in house technical expertise, national & regional meetings, monthly technical and business updates provided. Established: 1989 - Franchising Since: 1991 - No. of Units: Franchised: 91 - Franchise Fee: $500 - $25,000 - Royalty: 7% - 40% - Total Inv: $31,000 to $110,000 - Financing: Will assist.

COLORWORKS
Colorworks Franchise Group
620 6th Ave. S.W., P.O. Box 1796, Aberdeen, SD, 57402-1796. Contact: Rob Johnson, Pres. - Tel: (800) 719-5888, (605) 225-2003. The Colorworks Franchise Group sells franchised Colorworks stores; paint, body and equipment wholesale specialty outlets serving local market body shops. Established: 1987 - Franchising Since: 1994 - No. of Units: Franchised: 2 - Franchise Fee: $12,000 plus $3,000 pre-opening mktg. fee - Royalty: 2% plus 1% mktg. fund of gross revenue - Total Inv: $114,200 - $195,000 incl. inven. - Financing: No.

CREATIVE COLORS INTERNATIONAL
Creative Colors International, Inc.
5550 W. 175th St., Tinley Park, IL, 60477. Contact: JoAnn Foster, Pres. - Tel: (800) 933-2656. Mobile unit repair, color restoration of leather, fabric, vinyl, and carpeting in the automobile industry as well as the commercial industry. Established: 1980 - Franchising Since: 1991 - No. of Units: Company Owned: 1 - Franchised: 21 - Franchise Fee: $17,000 - Royalty: 6% - Total Inv: $9,950+ - Financing: Yes, available on equipment and supplies ($5,000)

CURTIS SYSTEM - THE ADVANCED AUTOMOTIVE CARE
Haldorn & Mann, Inc./Black Magic Supply
55 Hercules Dr., Colchester, VT, 05446. Contact: Peter Macone, Sales Mgr. - Tel: (800) 334-1497, (802) 655-4121, Fax: (802) 655-4129. Auto detail start-up business systems including: training, marketing, promotional materials, equipment chemical and toll free support. Established: 1987 - Franchising Since: 1988 - No. of Independents: 650+ - Total Inv: Starting at $1,895 U.S. - Financing: No.

CUSTOM AUTO RESTORATION SYSTEMS
479 Interstate Court, Sarasota, FL, 34240. Contact: Bob Wyatt, Pres. - Tel: (800)-736-1307, Fax: (941) 378-3472. Originator of mobile cosmetic reconditioning systems including paint restoration, vinyl & velour repair, glass repair, paintless dent repair & odor removal. Established: 1984 - Franchising Since: 1986 - No. of Units: Company Owned: 1 - Franchised: 982 - Franchise Fee: $995 - $5,495 - Royalty: None - Financing: Visa & MC.

DAN HANNA AUTO WASH
Hanna Auto Wash Franchise, Inc.
2000 S.E. Hanna Harvester Dr., Milwaukee, OR, 97222-7573. Contact: Ron Bottaro, Domestic Dev. - Tel: (503) 659-0361. Automatic drive thru, roll-over and conveyorized car and vehicle washes. Established: 1954 - Franchising Since: 1986 - No. of Units: Company Owned: 32 - Franchised: 9 - Franchise Fee: $24,000 - Royalty: 5% - Total Inv: $350,000 - $1,000,000 - Financing: Yes.

DENT DOCTOR
Dent Doctor, Inc.
7708 Cantrell Road, Little Rock, AR, 72207. Contact: Tom Harris, Franchise Sales Dir. - Tel: (501) 224-0500, Fax: (501) 224-0507. Paintless dent removal, minor dents, door dings and hail damage removed with no painting. Established: 1986 - Franchising Since: 1990 - No. of Units: Company Owned: 4 - Franchised: 23 - Franchise Fee: $29,500 - Royalty: 6% - Total Inv: $40,850 - Financing: None.

DENTPRO *
DentPro Franchise Corp.
45 Quail Ct., Ste. 103, Walnut Creek, CA, 94596. Contact: Mitch Buick, Pres. - Tel: (800) 868-DENT, (510) 944-3323, Fax: (510) 944-1844. Our innovative, on site repair service is made possible by a fleet of specially equipped mobile units. Each truck is a complete repair shop on wheels, with the latest in metal sculpting tools and equipment. The DentPro technicial can repair almost any ding or dent without the need for costly fillers, sanding or repainting. Established: 1991 - Franchising Since: 1993 - No. of Units: Company Owned: 1 - Franchised: 22 - Franchise Fee: $25,000+ - Royalty: 7% - Total Inv: $45,000+ - Financing: Yes.

DETAIL PLUS CAR WASH & AUTO APPEARANCE CENTERS
Detail Plus Systems, Inc.
P.O. Box 20755, Portland, OR, 97294. Contact: R. L. Abraham, Pres. - Tel: (800) 284-0123, (503) 251-2955, Fax: (503) 251-5975. Automatic car wash systems and auto detailing equipment providing washing, engine cleaning, exterior polish & wax, interior shampoo, paint touch up and glass repair. Established: 1980 - Franchising Since: 1982 - No. of Units: Franchised: 200 - Franchise Fee: None - Royalty: None - Total Inv: Car wash - min. $350,000; Detail $5,000 min. - Financing: Lease financing.

DOWNEY'S AUTO STORES / BUMPER TO BUMPER AUTO STORES
A.I. Automotive Corp.
4105 S. Creek Rd., Chattanooga, TN, 37406. Contact: James Gorham, Gen. Mgr./ Sales Mgr. - Tel: (615) 622-6274. Automotive after market parts. Retail/wholesale. Established: 1976 - Franchising Since: 1976 - No. of Units: Company Owned: 34 - Franchised: 130 - Franchise Fee: $300. per mo. advertising - Royalty: none - Total Inv: $150,000 - Financing: Yes.

DR. VINYL
Dr. Vinyl and Associates, Ltd.
13665 E. 42nd Terrace, Independence, MO, 64055. Contact: Tom Buckley, Pres. - Tel: (816) 478-0800. Vinyl, leather and velour, fabric repair & coloring, auto windshield repair, dashboard & hard plastic repair, vinyl striping and protective molding to new & used car dealers. Established: 1972 - Franchising Since: 1980 - No. of Units: Company Owned: 5 - Franchised: 107 - Franchise Fee: $19,500 - Royalty: 4% - 7%, adv. 1% - Total Inv: $35,000 - $40,000 - Financing: Yes.

ENDRUST AUTO APPEARANCE SPECIALISTS
Endrust Industries
1725 Washington Rd., Ste. 205, Pittsburgh, PA, 15241. Contact: Gary B. Griser, V.P. - Tel: (412) 831-1255, Fax: (412) 833-3409. Complete appearance services, plus rustproofing, undercoating, paint sealant, fabric protection, washing, waxing, automotive detailing services etc. Established: 1969 - Total Inv: $30,000 plus working cap. - Financing: No.

EVER VISION INC.
235 Hundersview, Roswell, GA, 30075. Contact: Cheryl Keeter, Pres. - Tel: (404) 594-0974. Manufacturer & distributor of windshield washer fluid. Established: 1992 - Franchising Since: 1992 - No. of Units: Company Owned: 4 - Franchise Fee: $25,000 - Royalty: 6% - Total Inv: approx. $85,000 - Financing: No.

FABRION REPAIR SYSTEMS
Cartex Limited
42816 Mound Rd., Sterling Heights, MI, 48314. Contact: Mr. L. Klukowski, CEO/Pres. - Tel: (313) 739-4330. Offer professional fabric repairs to auto dealerships, lease car companies & auctions. Provide open accounts, all equipment and materials necessary with comprehensive training in the franchise territory. Established: 1981 - Franchising Since: 1988 - No. of Units: Company Owned: 1 - Franchised: 82 - Franchise Fee: (a) $18,500; (b) $15,000; (c) $12,500 - Royalty: (a) $240.; (b) $200.; (c) $160. - Total Inv: $1,000 over cost of fran. fee - Financing: Vet fran. program.

FAST PLATES + PLUS *
245 S. 84th St., Lincoln, NE, 68510. Contact: Mike Ware, Business Dev. Mgr. - Tel: (800) 301-9504 or (402) 484-7100. Processing & mailing new vehicle license plates. Contracted by new car dealers and supported by state dept. of motor vehicles. All contacts established by franchisor for franchisee. Established: 1995 - Franchising Since: 1995 No. of Units: Company Owned: 2 - Franchised: 2 - Franchise Fee: $22,500 base (varies with size of market) - Royalty: 18% service fee - Total Inv: $25,000 - $40,000 (varies with size of market) - Financing: Yes.

FIXX-A-DENT *
Fixx Enterprises Inc.
4959 N. Buford Hwy., Norcross, GA, 30071. Contact: Ron Delxalle, Pres. - Tel: (770) 449-4878. Automotive paintless dent removal service. Established: 1993 - Franchising Since: 1994 - No. of Units: Company Owned: 4 - Franchised: 1 - Franchise Fee: $40,000 - Royalty: 6% gross sales - Total Inv: $60,000 - $70,000 - Financing: Yes.

GAS TANK RENU-USA
12727 Greenfield, Detroit, MI, 48227. Contact: Dan Sullivan, Pres. - Tel: (313) 837-6122. Auto aftermarket. Repair auto and marine fuel tanks. Lifetime warranty. No. of Units: Franchised: 30 - Franchise Fee: depends on geographical population - Royalty: none - Total Inv: from $15,000 - $55,000.

GLASS TECHNOLOGY WINDSHIELD REPAIR
434 Turner Dr., Durango, CO, 81301. Contact: Dan Wanstrath, Pres. - Tel: (800) 441-4527 or (303) 247-9374. Glass repair service for windshields, plate glass and scratch removal. Customers consisting of insurance companies, private car owners, commercial fleet accounts and retail store owners. Established: 1984 - No. of Units: Licensed: 440 - Total Inv: $2,500 equip. & supplies - Financing: No.

GOODYEAR TIRE CENTERS
Goodyear Tire & Rubber Co.
1144 E. Market St., Akron, OH, 44316. Contact: H.M. Harding, Mgr. Fran. Tire Centers - Tel: (216) 796-3467. Tire sales and automotive services. Established: 1898 - Franchising Since: 1968 - No. of Units: Company Owned: 884 - Franchised: 205 - Franchise Fee: $15,000 - Royalty: 3% - Total Inv: $100,000 and up - Financing: Yes.

GUARDIAN INTERLOCK SYSTEMS
110 Marietta Station Walk, Ste. 320, Marietta, GA, 30060. Contact: Don Gilliam, Fran. Rep. - Tel: (404) 499-0499. The Guardian Interlock System connects a breath analyzer to a vehicle's electrical system. Once installed, the driver must pass a breath test before the vehicle will start. Courts use the system as an alternative sentencing for DWI offenders. Established: 1991 - Franchising Since: 1993 - No. of Units: Company Owned: 83 - Franchised: 7 - Franchise Fee: $8,500 and up - Total Inv: fran. fee plus $3,500 equip. - Financing: Partial through third party, if qualified.

IT'S DENTS OR US
7801 W. 63rd. St., Overland Park, KS, 66202. Contact: Jim Crilly, Oper. Mgr. - Tel: (913) 384-6787, Fax: (913) 384-6923. Paintless dent removal. Remove hail damage and every day dents without harming factory paint or drilling excess holes. Established: 1992 - Franchising Since: 1992 - No. of Units: Company Owned: 1 - Franchise Fee: $18,000 - Royalty: $500 - Total Inv: $18,000 - $25,000 - Financing: No.

J.D. BYRIDER SALES
J.D. Byrider Systems
5780 W. 71st St., Indianapolis, IN, 46278. Contact: Ryan P. Devoe, Dir. of Dev. - Tel: (317) 387-2345. Pre-owned car sales and financing. Established: 1979 - Franchising Since: 1989 - No. of Units: Company Owned: 2 - Franchised: 71 - Franchise Fee: $29,000 - Royalty: 4% gross sales, 1% adv. - Total Inv: $500,000 - $1,300,000 - Financing: Yes.

LEMONBUSTERS
5818 Balcones Dr., Ste. 201, Austin, TX, 78731-4278. Contact: John Adams, Franc. Dir. - Tel: (512) 454-5999. Mobile used car pre-purchase inspections. LemonBusters' professional mobile service offers a complete (mechanical, electrical, body & chassis) inspection and report. Individuals and financial institutions are able to know the exact condition before they buy or make loan. Established: 1990 - Franchising Since: 1991 - No. of Units: Company Owned: 18 - Franchise Fee: $30,000 - Royalty: 10% - Total Inv: $65,000 ($30,000 fran. Fee; $35,000 start-up capital, van & equip.) - Financing: No.

MAACO AUTO PAINTING & BODYWORKS
Maaco Enterprises, Inc.
381 Brooks Rd., King of Prussia, PA, 19406. Contact: Linda Kemp, Fran. Dev. Mgr. - Tel: (800) 296-2226. Production auto painting and bodyworks centers. No prior automotive exp. necessary. Management and sales exp. necessary. Four weeks training and on-going operational support. Established: 1972 - Franchising Since: 1972 - No. of Units: Franchised: 465 - Franchise Fee: $30,000 - Royalty: 8% - 9% if late - Total Inv: $184,900 - $55,000 cash - Financing: Third Party.

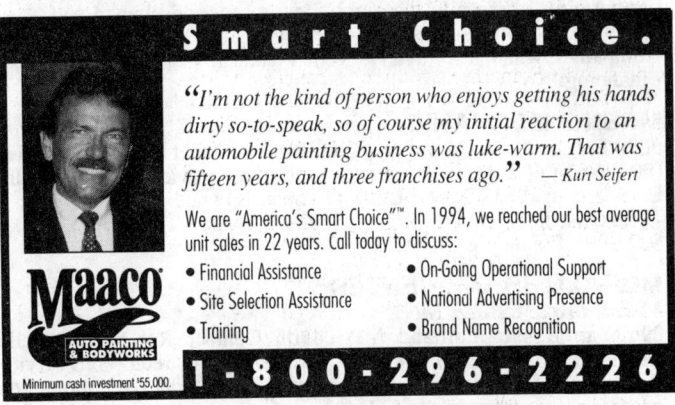

MATCO TOOLS
NMTC, Inc.
4403 Allen Rd., Stow, OH, 44224. Contact: Earl Farr, Dir., Distributor Dev. - Tel: (216) 929-4949. Matco franchised distributors sell world class hand tools and test equipment to professional automotive technicians from mobile showrooms at their place of employment. Established: 1979 - Franchising Since: 1993 - No. of Units: Franchised: 1000+ - Total Inv: $42,500 - Financing: $27,500.

MERMAID CAR WASH
Mermaid Marketing, Inc.
526 Grand Canyon Dr., Madison, WI, 53719. Contact: Peter Aspinwall, Pres. - Tel: (608) 833-9273. A business devoted to total service washing, cleaning, and waxing of cars, vans, pick-up trucks, RV's, motor homes and boats. Established: 1984 - Franchising Since: 1985 - No. of Units: Company Owned: 2 - Franchised: 4 - Franchise Fee: $50,000 - Royalty: 2% gross for 20 yrs.

MIGHTY DISTRIBUTING SYSTEM
Mighty Distributing System of America, Inc.
50 Technology Park, Norcross, GA, 30092. Contact: Ron L. Taylor, V.P. Fran. Dev. - Tel: (770) 448-3900. Sales and distribution of automotive equipment and supplies to service stations and other repair facilities in the automotive aftermarket. Services to franchisees and their customers include inventory control and technical assistance programs. Established: 1963 - Franchising Since: 1970 - No. of Units: Company Owned:14 - Franchised: 178 - Franchise Fee: $15,000+ - Royalty: 5% - Total Inv: $30,000 - $240,000 - Financing: Limited inv. purchasing.

MING AUTO BEAUTY CENTERS
Ming International, Inc.
346 East, 100 South, Salt Lake City, UT, 84111. Contact: Mr. Bill Terry, V.P. Sales - Tel: (801) 521-8799. Exclusive Ming Mirror finish process on automobiles. Other services include rust protection and appearance reconditioning. Established: 1936 - Franchising Since: 1976 - No. of

Units: Company Owned: 2 - Franchised: 35 + Australia and Japan - Franchise Fee: $25,000 - Royalty: 5% - Total Inv: $60,000 - $80,000 - Financing: No.

MIRACLE AUTO PAINTING AND BODY REPAIR
Miracle Auto Painting, Inc.
P.O. Box 56834, Hayward, CA, 94545-6834. Contact: Jim Jordan, Mktg. Dir. - Tel: (510) 887-2211. Auto painting and collision repair. Established: 1953 - Franchising Since: 1964 - No. of Units: Company Owned: 2 - Franchised: 48 - Franchise Fee: $35,000 - Royalty: 5%, 5% adv.- Total Inv: $138,000 - $161,000 - Financing: No.

MOBILE AUTO SYSTEMS
P.O. Box 2094, Dublin, CA, 94568. Contact: Lisa Trujillo, Accts. Mgr. - Tel: (510) 828-2131, Fax: (510) 828-3353. Business manual and consultation services in the mobile automotive oil change and repair business. Established: 1989 - Franchising Since: 1989 - No. of Units: Company Owned: 1 - Royalty: None - Total Inv: $7,000 to $47,000 - Financing: No.

MOBILE MECHANIC
3820 Premier Ave., Memphis, TN, 38118. Contact: Bill Richey - Tel: (901) 867-0600. Mobile (on-site) repair and service of automobiles. Established: 1981 - No. of Units: Company Owned: 2 - Franchised: 23 - Franchise Fee: $5,000 - Royalty: 6% + 1% adv. - Total Inv: $13,500 - $27,000 - Financing: None.

MORALL BRAKE CENTER
Morall Brake Center, Inc.
296 Warren Ave., Portland, ME, 04103. Contact: Robert Tortoriello, Dir. Fran. - Tel: (207) 878-5379. State of the art retail auto service. Brakes and CV joints for all cars and trucks to 1 ton. No appointment necessary - one hour or less. Industries strongest lifetime guarantee. Five weeks training. Established: 1978 - Franchising Since: 1987 - No. of Units: Company Owned: 2 - Franchised: 34 - Franchise Fee: $24,000 - Royalty: 5% + 6% adv. - Total Inv: $100,000 - Financing: Various sources with franchisor assistance.

MOTORWORKS REMANUFACTURED ENGINE INSTALLATION CENTRES
Motorworks, Inc.
4210 Salem St., Philadelphia, PA, 19124. Contact: Richard Robinson, V.P. - Tel: (800)327-9905, (215) 755-3310. Specialize in the removal and installation of remanufactured engines. Consumers are keeping cars longer than ever - cost of new cars is rising. Todays motorists save thousands when they trade their engine, not their car. Established: 1987 - Franchising Since: 1987 - No. of Units: Company Owned: 2 - Franchised: 51 - Franchise Fee: $23,500 - Royalty: 4% + 1% adv. - Total Inv: $55,200 - $89,000 - Financing: Assistance on equipment lease.

NOVUS GLASS REPAIR & REPLACEMENT
Novus Inc.
10425 Hampshire Ave. S., Minneapolis, MN, 55438. Contact: Roger Taylor, Dir. Fran. Sales - Tel: (800) 328-1117. Novus is an international franchise specializing in the repair of cracks & breaks as well as full-service replacement of automotive glass. As a franchise owner, you will be backed by the resources of the Trans America Glass network, highly experienced franchise advisory staff, outstanding training programs & ongoing support. Established: 1972 - Franchising Since: 1985 - No. of Units: Company Owned: 1 - Franchised: 529 - Franchise Fee: $15,000 - $25,000 - Royalty: 9% - Total Inv: $28,195 - $42,195 - Financing: Yes, partial & equipment leasing.

ONE STOP UNDERCAR, INC.
14831 Myford Rd., #A, Tustin, CA, 92680. Contact: Fred Myers, Pres. - Tel: (714) 505-2600. Distribution of automotive undercar parts to all types of automotive repair shops. Established: 1988 - Franchising Since: 1990 - No. of Units: Company Owned: 4 - Franchised: 4 - Franchise Fee: $40,000 - $80,000 - Royalty: 5% of gross sales - Total Inv: $250,000 - $325,000 - Financing: No.

PREVENT-A-CRACK
Prevent-A-Crack, Inc.
3116 E. Shea Blvd., Ste. 247, Phoenix, AZ, 85028. Contact: Gerd D. Linke, Pres. - Tel: (602) 996-4450. Mobile windshield repair business. Established: 1985 - Franchising Since: 1986 - No. of Units: Company Owned: 1 - Franchised: 28 - License Fee: none - Royalty: none - Total Inv: $690. equip. only - Financing: No.

PRO-PAINT REPAIR
Pro-Paint International
1411 Woodbend, Germantown, TN, 38138. , Fran. Dir. - Tel: (901) 867-0600. A business that provides paint repair using a unique paintless refinishing as well as spot touch-ups. Established: 1989 - No. of Units: Company Owned: 1 - Franchise Fee: $15,000 - Royalty: 6% - Total Inv: $22,750 - $60,300 (work. cap., supplies, insurance, equip.) - Financing: Equip.For further information please contact: Consultants America Corp., 12279 US Highway 64. Eads, TN, 38028, Tel: (901) 867-0600, Fax: (901) 867-0010.

PROPAINT PLUS, INC.
25760 1st St., Westlake, OH, 44145. Contact: Jacklyn Nemchik, Pres. - Tel: (800) 72-PAINT (727-2468), Fax: (216) 892-4920. Mobile system bringing a complete refurbishing service to the customer. Services include paint repair, velour, vinyl and leather repairs, paintless dent removal, windshield repair. System includes fully customized truck, all supplies and equipment, computer system, extensive marketing support program, 3 week training program and much more. Established: 1991 - Franchising Since: 1994 - No. of Units: Company Owned: 8 - Franchised: 4 - Franchise Fee: $20,000 - Royalty: 12% declining to 8% - Total Inv: $42,500 total cash needed - Financing: Truck & equip. can be financed to qualified individuals.

RENNSPORT *
Rennsport Franchising Inc.
10390 Alpharetta St., Ste. 620, Roswell, GA, 30075. Contact: Robb Rice, Pres. - Tel: (770) 992-9442. Rennsport shops specialize in the repair, polishing and restoration of alloy wheels. Established: 1995 - Franchising Since: 1995 - No. of Units: Company Owned: 1 - Franchise Fee: $25,000 - Royalty: 6% service fee, 1% nat'l. adv. - Total Inv: $48,000 to $146,500 - Financing: On equipment only.

RUSS AUTO
Russ Auto Inc.
CSS Franchising: 177 Main St., Ste. 103, Fort Lee, NJ, 07024. Contact: Franchise Sales Rep. - Tel: (201) 585-4753. Full auto repair shops using the latest computer diagnostic equipment. Established: 1928 - Franchising Since: 1994 - No. of Units: Company Owned: 1 - Total Inv: $140,000 - $180,000 incl. build-out, equip. & stock - Financing: Yes.

SAF-T AUTO CENTERS
R & R Enterprises, Inc.
121 No. Plains Industrial Rd., Wallingford, CT, 06492. Contact: Richard Bilodeau, Pres. - Tel: (800) 382-7238. Auto repair shop offering steering, suspension, brakes, mufflers, lubrication and minor repairs. Ability, skill and talent to do auto repair is a prerequisite. Established: 1978 - Franchising Since: 1985 - No. of Units: Company Owned: 2 - Franchised: 13 - Franchise Fee: $15,000 - Royalty: $400 per month - Total Inv: $65,000 - Financing: Third party assistance.

SHIP SHAPE CAR WASHES INC. *
3910 Mormon Coulee Rd., La Crosse, WI, 54601. Contact: Sonia Brye, Office Manager - Tel: (608) 788-9995. Complete full service car wash. Established: 1987 - No. of Units: Company Owned: 3.

SIMONIZ EXPRESS DETAIL CENTERS *
Jiffy Shine USA, Inc.
201 Boston Tpke., Bolton, CT, 06043. Contact: Martin Sudy, Pres. - Tel: (860) 646-0172, Fax: (860) 646-4158. Twenty-minute, while you wait, automobile exterior & interior detailing (waxing, polishing, carpet & upholstery shampoo, etc.). Established: 1992 - Franchising Since: 1994 - No. of Units: Company Owned: 4 (by affiliate) - Franchised: 38 - Franchise Fee: $7,995 if in auto bus., $15,995 if not - Royalty: $300 p/m if in auto bus., 4% if not - Total Inv: $13 - $30,000 depending on business - Financing: No.

SNAP-ON-TOOLS CORPORATION
2801 80th, Kenosha, WI, 53141-1410. Contact: Paul Tutskey, Mgr. Fran. Oper. - Tel: (414) 656-5424. Distribution of professional mechanics tools using a mobile van tool showroom. Established: 1920 - Franchising Since: 1991 - No. of Independent Dealers: 650 - Franchises: 2,765 - Franchise Fee: $3,000 - Royalty: $50 per month - Total Inv: $15,600 - $169,000 - Financing: Yes.

SPEEDY AUTO GLASS
9675 S.E., 36th St., Mercer Island, WA, 98040. Contact: Dan Chavis, Dir. Fran. Sales - Tel: (206) 232-9500. Replacement and repair of auto, residential and commercial glass. Also, sliding glass doors, shower doors, mirrors and sunroofs. Established: 1946 - Franchising Since: 1982 (in Canada) - No. of Units: Company Owned: 310 - Franchised: 212 - Franchise Fee: $30,000 for new, $10,000 for conversion - Total Inv: $25,000 for conversion, $140,000 for new - Financing: Assistance.

SPOT-NOT CAR WASHES
RACO Car Wash Systems, Inc.
2011 W. 4th St., Joplin, MO, 64801. Contact: Forrest Uppendahl, V.P. Fran. - Tel: (417) 781-2140 or (800) 682-7629. Coin-operated, self-service and brushless automatic car wash. Parent is oldest continuous manufacturer of high pressure no-touch automatic systems. Established: 1967 - Franchising Since: 1985 - No. of Units: Franchised: 25 - Franchise Fee: $25,000 - Royalty: 5% - Total Inv: $546,000 - $940,000 - Financing: Through contracted lending firms.

SUN SCREEN INTERNATIONAL
1712 S. Valley Mills Dr., Waco, TX, 76711. Contact: Karl Kolm, Owner - Tel: (817) 754-4222. Window tinting, auto and truck accessories, installed aerodynamic kits. Established: 1984 - Franchising Since: 1986 - No. of Units: Company Owned: 1 - Franchised: 3 - Franchise Fee: $15,000+ - Royalty: 7% - Total Inv: $25,000.

SUPERGLASS WINDSHIELD REPAIR
SuperGlass Windshield Repair, Inc.
6090 McDonough Dr., Ste. O, Norcross, GA, 30093. Contact: David Casey, Pres. - Tel: (770) 409-1885. Mobile & fixed windshield repair primarily to commercial fleets, auto dealers & rental. Two week training program, one week in Atlanta, one week in exclusive territory. Established: 1992 - Franchising Since: 1993 - No. of Units: Company Owned: 1 - Franchised: 106 - Franchise Fee: $5,617.06 - Royalty: 3% of gross sales - Total Inv: $9,500 - Financing: 30% financed W.A.C.

SUPPLY MASTER USA®
Master Supply Systems International, Inc.
Box 156, Sparta, NJ, 07871. Contact: Albert T. Owens, Pres. - Tel: (201) 729-5006. Unique mobile distribution of quality maintenance hardware (fasteners/connectors) in quantity packages/assortments to the maintenance professional. This is a home based service industry which can be operated by a male or female on a full or part-time basis. No mechanical skill required. Established: 1982 - Franchising Since: 1990 - No. of Units: Company Owned: 2 mobile units - Franchised: 5 under district review - Franchise Fee: $5,000 - Royalty: 5% + 2% adv. - Total Inv: $15,000 - $35,000 incl. tow unit/mobile vehicle, inven. system, uniforms, fran. fee, training - Financing: Mobile unit/business financing through dealership/bank.

TILDEN FOR BRAKES CARE CARE CENTERS *
1325 Franklin Ave., Garden City, NY, 11530. Contact: Robert Baskind, VP - Tel: (516) 482-2632, Fax: (516) 482-9388. Auto & truck repair & service centers. Established: 1922 - Franchising Since: 1975 - No. of Units: Franchised: 9 - Franchise Fee: $25,000 - Royalty: 5% - Total Inv: $130,000 - $150,000 - Financing: None.

TIRE CENTRES
300 N. Cleveland, Massilon Rd., Ste.200, Akron, OH, 44333-2484. Contact: Fran. Dept. - Tel: (216) 668-8800. Tires and related automotive service merchandise. Established: 1870 - No. of Units: Company Owned: 200 - Franchised: 3,500 - Total Inv: varies as to market, style of business, projected volume, etc.

TRUCK OPTIONS *
On & Off Road Options
5835 University Blvd. W., Jacksonville, FL, 32216. Contact: Michael Balanky, Pres. - Tel: (904) 731-5222. Automotive aftermarket - sell and install aftermarket products for trucks, vans and sport utility vehicles. Established: 1987 - Franchising Since: 1995 - No. of Units: Company Owned: 2 - Franchise Fee: $20,000 - Royalty: 4% gross sales - Total Inv: $175,000 - $280,000 (two concepts available) - Financing: Conventional sources.

TRUCKSTOPS OF AMERICA FRANCHISE SYSTEMS, INC.
Div. of BP Oil Co.
24601 Centre Ridge Rd., Ste. 300, Westlake, OH, 44145. Contact: Charles H. Gregory or Ara A. Bagdasarian, Fran. Dev. Mgr. or Mgr. Franc. - Tel: (800) 872-7496, (216) 808-3000. Full-service interstate truck/travel plazas. Established: 1960 - Franchising Since: 1980 - No. of Units: Company Owned: 38 - Franchised: 5 - Franchise Fee: $100,000 - $150,000 - Royalty: 4¢ gallon fuel sales; 4% non-fuel sales - Total Inv: Conversion $350,000 - $4,000,000; New build. $3,256,000 - $7,657,000 - Financing: None directly; will assist with lender packages and presentations.

TUFFY AUTO SERVICE CENTERS
Tuffy Associates Corp.
1414 Baronial Plaza Dr., Toledo, OH, 43615. Contact: Jim McKay, Fran. Sales - Tel: (800) 228-8339. Retail sales and installation of exhaust systems, brakes, ride control products, steering and front end. Initial training and ongoing field support and advertising support. Established: 1970 - Franchising Since: 1971 - No. of Units: Company Owned: 8 - Franchised: 165 - Franchise Fee: $20,000 - Royalty: 5%, 5% adv. - Total Inv: $190,000 - $210,000 ($80,000 cash).

US-1 AUTOPARTS FRANCHISE CORP.
5 Dakota Dr. #210, Lake Success, NY, 11042. Contact: Reuben Alcalay, C.E.O. - Tel: (516) 358-5100. Automotive discount auto parts supermarket. Established: 1983 - Franchising Since: 1990 - No. of Units: Company Owned: 1 - Franchised: 22 - Franchise Fee: $25,000 - Royalty: 7% - Total Inv: $150,000 - $250,000 - Financing: Yes.

WESTERN AUTO
Western Auto Supply Company
2107 Grand Ave., Kansas City, MO, 64108. Contact: Chuck Hutchens, V.P. Mktg. Dev. - Tel: (816) 346-4000. Retail automotive supplies such as tires, parts, accessories and service supplemented as needed with big ticket home and leisure lines including bicycles, outdoor power equipment, major home appliances and consumer electronics. Established: 1909 - Franchising Since: 1935 - No. of Units: Company Owned: 357 - Franchised: 1,090 - Franchise Fee: none - Royalty: none - Total Inv: $250,000 - $390,000 - Financing: None.

WINZER FRANCHISE COMPANY
Winzer Corp.
10560 Markison Rd., Dallas, TX, 75238. Contact: Diane Vanderbilt - Tel: (214) 341-2122. Distribution of aftermarket repair supplies and fasteners to automotive and trucking dealerships, body shops and independent repair facilities. Established: 1978 - Franchising Since: 1991 - No. of Units: Company Owned: 35 - Franchised: 46 - Franchise Fee: $2,500 - $5,000, depending upon type - Royalty: 10% - 16% of gross sales, depending upon volume - Financing: $5,000 (computer, merchandising, materials) - Financing: Yes.

ZIEBART TIDYCAR
Ziebart International Corp.
1290 E. Maple Rd., Troy, MI, 48083. Contact: Greg Longe, Director/ N.A. Fran. Dev. - Tel: (800) 877-1312, (810) 588-4100, Fax: (810) 588-1444. Car & truck detailing, accessory and protection retail stores. Established: 1954 - Franchising Since: 1963 - No. of Units: Company Owned: 19 - Franchised: 607 - Franchise Fee: $14,000 - $24,000 - Royalty: 5% - 8% - Total Inv: $77,000 - $161,000 - Financing: Yes.

AUTOMOTIVE: TRANSMISSION REPAIR

AAMCO TRANSMISSIONS
AAMCO Transmissions, Inc.
One Presidential Blvd., Bala Cynwyd, PA, 19004. Contact: Gary Gray, Dir. of Fran. Dev. - Tel: (800) 223-8887, Fax: (610) 617-9532. AAMCO is the world's largest chain of transmission specialists with over 32 years of experience as the leader in the transmission industry. Over 40% of AAMCO's franchisees set all time sales records in both 1993 and 1994. Established: 1963 - Franchising Since: 1963 - No. of Units: Company Owned: 4 - Franchised: 652 - Franchise Fee: $30,000 - Royalty: 7% - Minimum Cash: $43,000 - Total Inv: $136,000 - Financing: Assistance in acquiring provided.

AAMCO is the World's Largest Chain of Transmission Specialists with over 33 years of experience as the leader in the transmission industry. AAMCO has been selected the #1 franchise in it's field 14 out of the last 16 years by Entrepreneur Magazine and in the Top 5 of all franchises by Income Opportunities Magazine in 1993 and 1994. Over 40% of AAMCO's franchisees set new all time sales records the last three years in a row.

Tel: (800) 223-8887

AMERICAN TRANSMISSIONS
38701 West 7 Mile Rd., #105, Livonia, MI, 48152-1058. Contact: John Folino, Pres. - Tel: (313) 591-9411. Centers service all types of transmissions, foreign or domestic. Specially trained mechanics are on-site. Established: 1979 - No. of Units: Franchised: 17 - Approx. Inv: $83,000 depending upon location - Financing: Can be arranged through American Transmission.

AMMARK CORPORATION
10 West Main St., Carmel, IN, 46032. Contact: Curtis Butcher, Pres. - Tel: (317) 846-1216. Service, installation and repair of automobile transmissions. Only area franchises available with the right to sub-franchise in that area. Established: 1974 - No. of Units: 28 - Approx. Inv: operating capital of $2,000 per bay plus ability to obtain loan to pay for franchise, parts, equip. and inv. - Financing: Through outside sources.

ATLAS TRANSMISSION *
Transmission USA, div. of Moran Industries, Inc.
4444 West 147th St., Midlothian, IL, 60445. Contact: John Colarossi, V.P. - Tel: (800) 377-9247, (708) 389-5922, Fax: (708) 389-9882. Transmission service, repair and drive line service. Established: 1956 - Franchising Since: 1968 - No. of Units: Franchised: 29 - Franchise Fee: $27,500 - Royalty: 7% of weekly gross sales - Total Inv: $35,000 - $100,000 - Financing: Yes, will assist qualified applicants.

COTTMAN TRANSMISSION CENTERS
Cottman Transmission Systems, Inc.
240 New York Dr., Ft. Washington, PA, 19034. Contact: Mark DiMuzio, Dir. Fran. Dev. - Tel: (800) 394-6116, (215) 643-5885. Repair and service of automatic and standard transmissions. Established: 1962 - Franchising Since: 1964 - No. of Units: Company Owned: 1 - Franchised: 159 - Franchise Fee: $22,500 - Royalty: 7.5% of gross sales - Total Inv: $97,500 - Financing: Yes (assistance).

DIAMOND QUALITY TRANSMISSION CENTERS OF AMERICA, INC.
P.O. Box 6147, Philadelphia, PA, 19115-6147. Contact: Al Gold, Pres. - Tel: (215) 742-8333. Automatic and standard auto & truck transmission service centers. Established: 1949 - Franchising Since: 1963 - No. of Units: Franchised: 5 - Franchise Fee: $35,000 - Financing: With good credit.

DR. NICK'S TRANSMISSIONS
Transmission USA, div. of Moran Industries, Inc.
4444 West 147th St., Midlothian, IL, 60445. Contact: John Colarossi, V.P. - Tel: (800) 377-9247, (708) 389-5922, Fax: (708) 389-9882. Transmission service, repair and drive line service. Established: 1956 - Franchising Since: 1968 - No. of Units: Franchised: 12 - Franchise Fee: $27,500 - Royalty: 7% of weekly gross sales - Total Inv: $35,000 to $100,000 - Financing: Yes, will assist qualified applicants.

DURA-BUILT TRANSMISSIONS
Dura-Built Franchise System, Inc.
777 Campus Commons Rd. #200, Sacramento, CA, 95825. Contact: Jay Byers, Chairman - Tel: (916) 920-2243. Franchisor of transmission repair centers (regional locations only in California and Nevada). Complete training, service and support; nationwide warranty program; patented diagnostic equipment; all inclusive operational software program. Established: 1971 - Franchising Since: 1987 - No. of Units: Company Owned: 2 - Franchised: 11 - Franchise Fee: $20,000 - Royalty: 7% + 3% adv. - Total Inv: $80,000 fee, equip., deposits, work. cap. - Financing: No.

GOODEAL DISCOUNT TRANSMISSIONS
P.O. Box 50, National Park, NJ, 08063. Contact: John Mikulski, Pres. - Tel: (800) 626-8695. Establishing center to rebuild and replace automobile and truck transmissions. Established: 1979 - Franchising Since: 1980 - No. of Units: Franchised: 30 - Franchise Fee: $32,500 - Royalty: $200 wkly. - Total Inv: (inven., equip., signs) $17,000 + $32,500 + work cap. $20,000 - Financing: Will assist.

KENNEDY TRANSMISSION
Kennedy Franchising, Inc.
410 Gateway Blvd., Burnsville, MN, 55337-2559. Contact: Andrew Hammond, Pres. - Tel: (612) 894-7020. Service and repair of automatic & manual transmissions, clutches, transfer cases, differentials, and other driveline components. Established: 1962 - Franchising Since: 1976 - No. of Units: Company Owned: 1 - Franchised: 18 - Franchise Fee: $17,500 - Royalty: 6% - Total Inv: $83,500 - $157,500 - Financing: No.

LEE MYLES TRANSMISSIONS
Lee Myles Corp.
140 Rte. 17 N., Paramus, NJ, 07652. Contact: Mark Savel, Sal Gargone, Dir. of Sales & Mktg. - Tel: (201) 262-0555 or (800) Lee Myles. Auto aftermarket-specialty transmissions. Established: 1947 - Franchising Since: 1964 - No. of Units: Franchised: 77 - Franchise Fee: $25,000 - Royalty: 6% - Total Inv: $98,500 to $127,600.

MR. TRANSMISSION
Transmission USA, div. of Moran Industries, Inc.
4444 West 147th St., Midlothian, IL, 60445. Contact: John Colarossi, V.P. - Tel: (800) 377-9247, (708) 389-5922, Fax: (708) 389-9882. Transmission service, repair and drive line service. Established: 1956 - Franchising Since: 1968 - No. of Units: Franchised: 86 - Franchise Fee: $27,500 - Royalty: 7% of weekly gross sales - Total Inv: $35,000 - $100,000 - Financing: Yes, will assist qualified applicants.

MULTISTATE TRANSMISSIONS
Transmission USA, div. of Moran Industries, Inc.
4444 W. 147th St., Midlothian, IL, 60445. Contact: John Colarossi, V.P. - Tel: (800) 377-9247, (708) 389-5922, Fax: (708) 389-9882. Transmission service, repair and drive line service. Established: 1956 - Franchising Since: 1968 - No. of Units: Franchised: 30 - Franchise Fee: $27,500 - Royalty: 7% of weekly gross sales - Total Inv: $35,000 - $100,000 - Financing: Yes, will assist qualified applicants.

SPEEDY TRANSMISSION CENTERS
Autotech Franchise Systems, Inc.
902 Clint Moore Rd., #216, Boca Raton, FL, 33487. Contact: Dan Hinson, Dir./Fran. Sales - Tel: (407) 995-8282. Repair and replacement of automatic and standard transmissions. Retail, commercial and fleet. Full training provided in sales and management. Technical services provided. Established: 1983 - Franchising Since: 1983 - No. of Units: Franchised: 28 - Franchise Fee: $19,500 - Royalty: 7% - Total Inv: approx. $75,000 incl. equip. and work. cap. - Financing: Equip. financing supplied to qualified applicants.

BEVERAGES

APPLE SIDRA COSCO FLAVORS
Cosco International, Inc.
P.O. Box 8187, Northfield, IL, 60093-8187. Contact: John W. Ullmann, Pres. - Tel: (708) 446-9390. Soft drink franchise, usually dealing with existing soft drink bottlers (Coke, Pepsi, 7-up) who are looking for additional brands or flavors to increase sales. All franchises are outside USA. Established: 1880 - Franchising Since: 1940 - No. of Units: 38 in 23 countries - Approx. Inv: varies.

BIG ORANGE, INC.
7700A W. Fairfield Dr., Pensacola, FL, 32506. Contact: Joseph F. Morgan, Gen. Mgr. - Tel: (904) 455-9685. Orange juice stand franchise. Established: 1980 - Franchising Since: 1980 - No. of Units: Company Owned: 2 - Franchise Fee: $10,000 - Royalty: 6% - Total Inv: $34,000.

BORVIN BEVERAGE
Borvin Beverage Franchise Corp.
1022 King Street, Alexandria, VA, 22314. Contact: Don Mikovch, Pres. - Tel: (703) 683-9463. Wine wholesale and distribution. Established: 1985 - Franchising Since: 1993 - No. of Units: Company Owned: 1 - Franchised: 1 - Franchise Fee: $25,000 - Royalty: 5%, 2% promotion/adv. fee - Financing: $15,000 of fran. fee.

CHEERWINE BOTTLERS
Carolina Beverage Corp.
P.O. Box 697, Salisbury, NC, 28145. Contact: Mark Ritchie, V.P. Sales and Mktg. - Tel: (704) 637-5881. Soft drink franchisor. Established: 1917 - Franchising Since: 1917 - No. of Units: Company Owned: 1 - Franchised: 18 - Approx. Inv: depends on market - Financing: None.

FAT TUESDAY
Fat T, Inc.
701 Metairie Rd., Metairie, LA, 70005. Contact: Judy Oreck, Fran. Coord. - Tel: (504) 831-9415. Distinctive system relating to the operation of retail frozen beverage service businesses. Established: 1993 - Franchising Since: 1993 - No. of Units: Company Owned: 7 - Franchised: 2 - Franchise Fee: $25,000 - Royalty: 6%, 1% adv. - Total Inv: Ranges from $450,000 - $850,000 - Financing: None.

BUILDING PRODUCTS AND SERVICES

ABC SEAMLESS, INC.
ABC Seamless, Inc.
3001 Fiechtner Drive, Fargo, ND, 58103. Contact: Veryl Vik, Fran. Sales Rep. - Tel: (701) 293-5952. Siding, soffit, fascia, gutters, and replacement windows. Established: 1972 - Franchising Since: 1979 - No. of Units: Company Owned: 1 - Franchised: 92 - Franchise Fee: $12,000 - Royalty: 5% declining to 2% - Total Inv: $65,000 trailer & siding machine - Financing: Lease Co.

AFFORDABLE LUXURY HOMES, INC.
Hwy. 224 W., P.O. Box 288, Markle, IN, 46770. Contact: Mr. Cossairt, Pres. - Tel: (219) 758-2141. Sale of highly insulated panelized custom designed homes, energy efficient. Established: 1974 - Franchising Since: 1974 - No. of Units: Franchised: approx. 200 - Total Inv: deposit to cover materials refundable after the first two transactions.

AHRENS CHIMNEY TECH., INC.
2000 Industrial, Sioux Falls, SD, 57104-0230. Contact: Monty Lutz, Sales Mgr. - Tel: (800) 843-4417 or (605) 334-2827. Chimney lining and restoration for residential and commercial masonry chimneys. Established: 1982 - Licensing Since: 1982 - No. of Units: Franchised: 177 - Total Inv: $10,000 - Financing: To qualified applicants.

AIRE SERV HEATING & AIR CONDITIONING
Aire Serv Corporation
1020 University Parks Dr., Waco, TX, 76707. Contact: Matt Michel, V.P. - Tel: (800) 583-2662, Fax: (817) 745-2501. America's Comfort Company, a heating, ventilating and air conditioning franchise creating top-of-the-mind consumer awareness and a national name for service excellence. Established: 1992 - Franchising Since: 1993 - No. of Units: Franchised: 52 - Franchise Fee: $14,000 and up - Royalty: 3% to 6% - Total Inv: $14,000 and up - Financing: Up to 70% of franchise investment, plus 100% working capital and vehicle financing.

AMBIC BUILDING INSPECTION CONSULTANTS
Building Inspection Consultants
1200 Rt. 130, Robbinsville, NJ, 08691. Contact: David Goldstein, Pres. - Tel: (609) 448-3900. Inspections of residential, commercial and industrial buildings including environmental inspections (i.e., radon, lead, water, asbestos, septic); termite inspections & consulting services for prospective buyers & sellers & lenders. Established: 1987 - Franchising Since: 1988 - No. of Units: Franchised: 25 - Franchise Fee: $10,000 - $16,500 - Royalty: 6% on-going support, 3% adv. - Total Inv: $15,000 - $26,500 incl. fran. fee. - Financing: For qualified individuals.

AMERICAN CONCRETE RAISING INC.
918 Fairway Dr., Bensenville, IL, 60106. Contact: John Meyers, Pres. - Tel: (708) 595-5225. Engage in the business of inspecting, evaluating and raising settled concrete by a method of pressure injection and providing such services to businesses, homes, commercial shopping centers, apartment complexes, municipalities, hotels and other related entities following a detailed service plan. Established: 1983 - Franchising Since: 1992 - No. of Units: Company Owned: 1 - Franchised: 3 - Franchise Fee: $15,000 - Royalty: 8% - Total Inv: $42,000 - $66,000 - Financing: No.

AMERICAN DECK & SUNROOM COMPANY *
ADSF Inc.
15 Turtle Creek Rd., Monticello, IL, 61856. Contact: Jim Edward, Dir. - Tel: (217) 762-9740, Fax: (217) 762-7811. Remodeling specialists in screen rooms, sun room & custom designer decks., Established: 1989 - Franchising Since: 1993 - No. of Units: Company Owned: 7 - Franchised: 9 - Franchise Fee: $7,500 - Royalty: Variable by state - Total Inv: Variable by state - Financing: None.

AMERICAN LEAK DETECTION
888 Research Dr., Ste. 100, Palm Springs, CA, 92262. Contact: Sheila Bangs, Fran. Sales - Tel: 1-800-755-6697. Pinpoint detection of water or sewer leaks under concrete slabs of homes, pools, spas, commercial buildings, etc. using electronic equipment manufactured by co. Established: 1974 - Franchising Since: 1984 - No. of Units: Company Owned: 1 - Franchised: 228 - Franchise Fee: $45,000+ - Royalty: 8%-10% gross - Total Inv: $45,000+ fee, $25,000 truck, $3,000 tools - Financing: 50% of franchise fee o.a.c.

AMERICAN LINCOLN HOMES AMERLINK
Contemporary Classic Log Homes by American Lincoln Ltd.
P.O. Box 669, Battleboro, NC, 27809. Contact: Ernie Spoor, V.P. - Tel: (919) 977-2545. Manufacture and marketing of home packages of log, solid timber and conventional wood frame construction. Established: 1982 - Franchising Since: 1986 - No. of Units: Company Owned: 1 - Franchised: 2 - Franchise Fee: $25,000 - Royalty: 5% - Total Inv: $250,000 - Financing: Yes, up to 85%.

AMERISEAL, INC.
3060 Leon Rd., Jacksonville, FL, 32246. Contact: Melvin Carter, Exec.V.P. - Tel: (904) 642-5213. Asphalt pavement maintenance contractors specializing in a spectrum of protective asphalt coatings, asphalt repair, asphalt striping and asphalt crack sealing. Other procedures include thermoplastic road striping. Established: 1987 - Franchising Since: 1987 - No. of Units: Company Owned: 1 - Franchised: 14 - Franchise Fee: $19,500 - Royalty: 5%, 2% adv. - Total Inv: $99,500 incl. $80,000 in equip. and supplies - Financing: No.

VARCON Construction Co. Ltd.
Industrial • Residential • Commercial • Institutional

CUSTOMERS WANTED
Can we build your next franchise store, corporate offices or distribution center? Construction budgets & deadlines are a priority to us.

WE OFFER:
• Turnkey or partial construction
• Project management
• Design and build
• Budget consultations

25 Rutherford Rd. South, Unit 5
Brampton, Ont., L6W 3J3
(800) 581-6729
Tel: (905) 451-7316, Fax: (905) 451-8563

ARCHADECK
U.S. Structures, Inc.
2112 W. Laburnum Ave., Ste. 100, Richmond, VA, 23227. Contact: Julie West, Fran. Dev. - Tel: (804) 353-6999. Largest custom builder of wooden patios, screened porches, gazebos, sunrooms and awnings. Established: 1980 - Franchising Since: 1988 - No. of Units: Franchised: 90 - Franchise Fee: $32,500 - Royalty: 5% - 7% + 1% adv. - Financing: Limited.

ARMSTRONG WORLD INDUSTRIES
P.O. Box 3001, Lancaster, PA, 17604. Contact: Bill Freeman - Tel: (717) 397-0611. Sales of resilient floor material. Established: 1962 - Franchising Since: 1986 - No. of Units: Franchised: 275 - Inv: $8,000 for display - Financing: Yes.

B-DRY SYSTEM
B-Dry System, Inc.
1341 Copley Rd., Akron, OH, 44320. Contact: Carl Rakich, V.P. - Tel: (216) 867-2576 or (800) 321-0985. A basement waterproofing patented system. Established: 1958 - Franchising Since: 1978 - No. of Units: Company Owned: 1 - Franchised: 71 - Franchise Fee: $30,000 - $60,000 - Royalty: 6% - Total Inv: 50% of fran. fee, equip. $15,000, $20,000 adv. - Financing: Yes.

BASEMENT DE-WATERING/SAFE-AIRE INC.
Basement De-Watering Systems, Inc.
162 E. Chestnut St., Canton, IL, 61520. Contact: Fran. Dir. - Tel: (309) 647-0331. The nation's premier company in the fields of basement de-watering and radon gas mitigation. High-profit margins/ low-overhead/ vast market potential/ minimal competition/ protected territories/ patented systems/ EPA proven methods/ year-round installations. Training and support provided. Established: 1978 - Franchising Since: 1986 - No. of Units: Company Owned: 1 - Franchised: 110 - Franchise Fee: $15,900 total fee/ $30,000 required liquid net worth - Total Inv: ranges from $26,000 - $56,000 - Financing: franchisee responsible for total investment. BDW/SA will assist qualified applicants in preparation of loan package.

BATH FITTER
Bath Fitter Franchising Inc.

27 Berard Dr., #2701, South Burlington, VT, 05403-5810. Contact: Linda Brakel, Dir. of Fran. - Tel: (800) 892-2847. Franchisees will sell and install custom-molded acrylic bath tub liners, wall systems and related accessories to commercial, residential and institutional customers in an exclusive geographic territory. Established: 1992 - Franchising Since: 1992 - No. of Units: Company Owned: 2 - Franchised: 23 - Franchise Fee: $12,500 - Royalty: 0% - Total Inv: $26,500 - $48,900 - Financing: No.

BATHCREST
Bathcrest, Inc.
2425 South Progress Dr., Salt Lake City, UT, 84119. Contact: Craig Peterson, V.P. Mktg. & Sales - Tel: (800) 826-6790. Bathroom fixture resurfacing. Saves homeowners up to 80% of conventional replacement. Residential & commercial work. Easy start-up, low overhead, high gross profit & little competition. Now you can easily cash-in on lucrative remodeling business that is growing every year. Established: 1979 - Franchising Since: 1985 - No. of Units: Company Owned: 1 - Franchised: 164 - Franchise Fee: $3,500 - Royalty: None - Total Inv: $24,500 - Financing: Yes, up to 50% based on credit application.

CALIFORNIA CLOSET COMPANY
1700 Montgomery St., #249, San Francisco, CA, 94111. Contact: Jake Brown, V.P. Fran. Dev. - Tel: (415) 433-9999. Custom designed and installed storage systems for both residential and commercial applications. Closet & garage systems, office systems & more. Established: 1978 - Franchising Since: 1982 - No. of Units: Company Owned: 3 - Franchised: 102 - Franchise Fee: $9,000 - $38,000 - Royalty: 6% - Total Inv: $65,000 - $225,000 - Financing: No.

CARROUSEL WOOD PRODUCTS
Carrousel Wood Products Ltd.
1617 Fifth Ave., Arnold, PA, 15068. Contact: Dan Howard, V.P. Sales - Tel: (800) 962-7235. Curved wood products for curved decks, gazebos, bridges, fencing arbors and other items and curved structural components. Established: 1988 - Franchising Since: 1992 - No. of Units: Company Owned: 1 - Franchised: 23 - Franchise Fee: $5,000 - Royalty: 1% - Total Inv: $5,000 - $50,000 - Financing: Yes.

CLASSY CLOSETS ETC.
2001 W Alemeda Dr., Tempe, AZ, 85282-3101., Fran. Dir. - Tel: (602) 967-2200. Manufacture and install custom closets and storage units. Established: 1983 - Franchising Since: 1989 - No. of Units: Franchised: 1 - Franchise Fee: $17,500 - Total Inv: $17,500 - $40,000 - Financing: Yes.

CLOSET FACTORY, THE
Closet Factory Franchise Corp., The
12800 Broadway, Los Angeles, CA, 90061. Contact: David Louy, V.P. & Fran. Dir. - Tel: (310) 516-7000. Design, build & install custom closet & storage systems. Established: 1983 - Franchising Since: 1986 - No. of Units: Company Owned: 1 - Franchised: 29 - Franchise Fee: $39,500 - Royalty: 5 3/4% gross receipts - Total Inv: $185,000 - $195,000 - Financing: May obtain for equipment.

CLOSETS TO GO
Closets To Go, Inc.
9978 SW Arctic Dr., Beaverton, OR, 97005. Contact: Jeff Turner, Fran. Dir. - Tel: (503) 644-7776. A non-manufacturing company that customizes closets and other storage areas for the home and office. Concept allows for the concentration of sales and services by having all products in stock. Established: 1985 - Franchising Since: 1987 - No. of Units: Company Owned: 1 - Franchised: 5 - Franchise Fee: $3,300 - $17,000 - Royalty: 5%, 2% adv. fund - Total Inv: $32,300 - $118,900 - Financing: Yes, indirectly.

CLOSETTEC
Closettec Franchise Corp.
55 Providence Hwy., Norwood, MA, 02062. Contact: David Rogers, Pres. - Tel: (617) 769-9997, Fax: (617) 769-9996. Design, manufacture and install custom closet and storage systems for residential and commercial use. Established: 1985 - Franchising Since: 1986 - No. of Units: Franchised: 34 - Franchise Fee: $30,000 - Royalty: 5.5% - Total Inv: $128,000 to $230,000.

COMPREHENSIVE PAINTING
Comprehensive Franchising Systems, Inc.
4723 N. Academy Blvd., Colorado Springs, CO, 80918. Contact: Michael Cranford, Pres. - Tel: (719) 599-8983, Fax: (719) 599-0471. A residential home painting business which offers customers painting, staining, wallpapering and wood restoration services, which enables franchisees to take advantage of the experience, proven track record and unlimited income potential of an efficiently designed franchise system. Established: 1986 - Franchising Since: 1992 - No. of Units: Company Owned: 1 - Franchised: 2 - Franchise Fee: $6,500 - Royalty: 0.06% - Total Inv: $11,500 - $30,000 - Financing: Yes.

CRITERIUM ENGINEERS
Coast To Coast Engineering Services, Inc.
650 Brighton Ave., Portland, ME, 04102. Contact: Peter Hollander, Dir. of Operations - Tel: (207) 828-1969, Fax: (207) 775-4405. Consulting engineering, specializing in existing buildings, including inspection, evaluation, maintenance planning, insurance investigation, feasibility studies, plan of repair, environmental assessment, and related services. Established: 1957 - Franchising Since: 1958 - No. of Units: Franchised: 67 - Franchise Fee: $22,500 - Royalty: 6%, 1% communications fee - Financing: Yes.

DE/MAR
Large Ltd.
6025 SW Jean Rd., Lake Oswego, OR, 97035. Contact: Cathy Anderson - Tel: (800) 635-3507, (503) 635-1446, Fax (503) 635-9938. Brokers of famous name brand building materials. Established: 1978 - Franchising Since: 1979 - No. of Units: Company Owned: 3 - Franchised: 8 - Franchise Fee: $50,000 - Royalty: 1/2 of 1% of sales monthly - Total Inv: $10,000 in liquid assets when opening - Financing: No.

DORACO
USA Doraco
301 W. Hunting Park Ave., Philadelphia, PA, 19140-2697. Contact: Mr. Fromm, Pres. - Tel: (215) 455-2100. Selling doors and windows to homeowners on an installed basis. Established: 1987- Franchising Since: 1988 - No. of Units: Company Owned: 6 - Franchise Fee: $10,000 - $30,000 - Royalty: 5% to 8% - Total Inv: $25,500 - $85,000 - Financing: Will assist.

ELDORADO STONE CORP.
4190 Tolt Ave., NE, P.O. Box 27, Carnation, WA, 98014. Contact: Phil Pearlman, V.P. Fran. Growth - Tel: (206) 333-6722. Franchisor who licenses the technology to manufacture and distribute lightweight concrete stone veneers and landscape stepstones and pavers through dealer networks and contractor direct. Established: 1969 - Franchising Since: 1969 - No. of Units: Franchised: 32 - Franchise Fee: $9,400 - Royalty: 5% - Total Inv: $35,000 (to Eldorado, incl. fran. fee) plus $65,000 - $175,000 in addition - Financing: No financing available.

ENVIROBATE, INC.
401 N. 3rd St., #200, Minneapolis, MN, 55401. Contact: Jeff Anlauf, Pres. - Tel: (612) 349-9211, (800) 944-8095. Provides environmental services for residential and commercial clients. Services include testing, surveying, inspections and audit abatement of environmental problems. Established: 1989 - Franchising Since: 1991 - No. of Units: Franchised: 3 - Franchise Fee: $25,000 - Royalty: 6% of gross revenues - Total Inv: $35,000 equip. & supplies, $10,000 truck, $20,000 work. cap. - Bank or other sources.

EVER-DRY WATERPROOFING
Ohio State Waterproofing
365 E. Highland Rd., Macedonia, OH, 44056. Contact: Jack Jones, V.P. - Tel: (216) 467-1055. Basement waterproofing and foundation repair. Patented system. Established: 1977 - Franchising Since: 1984 - No. of Units: Company Owned: 2 - Franchised: 16 - Franchise Fee: $18,000 - $60,000 - Royalty: 6% - Total Inv: $60,000 - $100,000 - Financing: To qualified applicants.

FIBRE TECH POOL COATINGS
Fibre Tech, Inc.
2181 34th Way N., Largo, FL, 34641. Contact: Scott Morris, V.P. - Tel: (813) 539-0844. Swimming pool, decorative pond, chemical storage tank refinishing. Established: 1986 - Licensing Since: 1988 - No. of Units: Company Owned: 3 - Licensed: 21 - Royalty: None-must buy resin from us - Total Inv: $3,500 territorial fee includes all promotional material - Financing: No.

FLEAPRUF 365 *
AllerClean Inc.
711 N. Main St., Pleasantville, NJ, 08232. Contact: Charles Rosenberg, Pres. - Tel: (800) 745-5631. Hypo-allergenic pest control services. Established: 1992 - Franchising Since: 1995 - No. of Units: Company Owned: 1 - Franchised: 8 - Franchise Fee: $15,000 - Royalty: 8%, 2% adv. - Total Inv: $35,000 - $75,000 - Financing: None.

FORESIGHT ENGINEERING, INC. *
17 Cook Ave., Box 621, Madison, NJ, 07940. Contact: F. Hammitt, Pres. - Tel: (201) 377-0600. Home and building inspection, radon testing, environmental testing, radon mitigation. Established: 1984 - Franchising Since: 1987 - No. of Units: Company Owned: 1 - Franchised: 6 - Franchise Fee: $15,000 - Royalty: 7% + 2% adv. - Total Inv: No other investment required - Financing: Yes.

FOUR SEASONS SUNROOMS
Four Seasons Marketing Corp.
5005 Veterans Memorial Hwy., Holbrook, NY, 11741. Contact: Tony Russo, V.P. Sales - Tel: (516) 563-4000, Fax:(516) 563-4010. Offer and sell the world's finest line of solariums and sunroom products in maintenance-free aluminum or wood frames with energy efficient glazing options. Established: 1975 - Franchising Since: 1984 - No. of Units: Company Owned: 4 - Franchised: 267 - Franchise Fee: $7,500, $10,000, $15,000 - Total Inv: $12,750 - $62,750 incl. fran. fee - Financing: No.

H.E.L.P. HEAT & ENERGY LOSS PREVENTION
100 St. Mary's Ave., Staten Island, NY, 10305. Contact: Thomas Masucci, Pres. - Tel: (718) 448-3400. An energy consulting business dealing in all forms of auditing/management using highly sensitive infrared equipment. Also, asbestos abatement services. Established: 1980 - Franchising Since: 1980 - No. of Units: Company Owned: 2 - Franchised: 2 - Franchise Fee: $10,000 - Royalty: 5% 1st yr., 8% 2nd yr. - Total Inv: $10,000 - $25,000.

Handyman CONNECTION

HANDYMAN CONNECTION
Mamar, Inc.
230 Northland Blvd., Cincinnati, OH, 45246. Contact: Matt Chimsky, Fran. Dir. - Tel: (800) 466-5530, Fax: (513) 771-6439. Provide small to medium sized home repairs and remodeling services. Bring together the skilled carpenter, painter, plumber, electrician with the public's need for a reliable, guaranteed source for these skills. Established: 1990 - Franchising Since: 1991 - No. of Units: Company Owned: 1 - Franchised: 24 - Franchise Fee: $25,000 - $75,000, based upon population of exclusive city or territory - Royalty: 5% reduce to 4% with incentive program - Total Inv: Fran. fee plus $15,000 to $20,000 start-up costs - Financing: Yes, 50% of the franchise fee financed for 24 months.

HERITAGE LOG HOMES, INC.
Box 610, U.S. Hwy. 321, Gatlinburg, TN, 37738. Contact: Graig Boull, Reg. Sales Mgr. - Tel: (615) 436-9331. Manufacturers of pre-cut, do-it-yourself log home kits for residential and commercial use. Established: 1974 - Franchising Since: 1974 - No. of Units: Company Owned: 1 - Franchised: 30+ - Franchise Fee: purchase of model home - $10,000 average kit price - Total Inv: $50,000 - $100,000 in model and commercial high traffic setting - Financing: None.

HOME RATERS OF...
Home Raters of America, Inc.
512 Green Bay Rd., Highwood, IL, 60040. Contact: Stuart Zwang, Gen. Mgr. - Tel: (800) 572-8377, Fax: (708) 433-3520. Franchising building inspection company by teaching proper inspection methods using proprietary systems to build business and prevent future problems. Established: 1976 - Franchising Since: 1995 - No. of Units: Company Owned: 1 - Franchise Fee: Negotiated - Royalty: Negotiated % of sales - Financing: No.

HOME SERVICES ALLIANCE *
HSA International, Inc.
100 N. Tampa St., Ste. 2610, Tampa, FL, 33602. Contact: Jim Tisony, Pres. - Tel: (813) 226-1800. Home Services Alliance provides property services management for its homeowner members. As the oldest and largest franchised home services network, HSA aggressively manages the process of matching any type of home repair, maintenance or improvement need with quality tradespeople who do the job right and guarantee HSA member satisfaction. Established: 1989 - Franchising Since: 1992 - No. of Units: Company Owned: 4 - Franchised: 32 - Franchise Fee: $15,000 / 100,000 pop. - Royalty: 3% of sales - Total Inv: $35,000 - $100,000 - Financing: Yes.

HOUSE DOCTORS HANDYMAN SERVICE
H.D. Franchising Systems, Inc.
4010 Executive Park, Ste.101, Cincinnati, OH, 45241. Contact: Franchise Dept. - Tel: (513) 563-0200. A Handyman service providing home owners with a low cost, quality repair service. Established: 1994 - Franchising Since: 1994 - No. of Units: Franchised: 10 - Franchise Fee: $10,900 - $22,900 - Royalty: 6% - Total Inv: $3,050 - $12,750 - Financing: Yes.

INSPECTECH *
3201 Danville Blvd., Alamo, CA, 94507. Contact: Ted Torbutt, Fran. Dev. Mgr. - Tel: (800) 773-2832. With Inspectech virtually anyone with the desire to succeed, some mechanical aptitude and good business sense

can be a home inspector. Support includes a full training program, the System 2000™, all computer hardware and software, ongoing marketing and technical assistance. Established: 1990 - Franchising Since: 1993 - No. of Units: Franchised: 100 - Franchise Fee: $7,500 - $21,500 - Royalty: 8% + 2% - Total Inv: $15,000 - $30,000 - Financing: Yes.

INSULATED DRY-ROOF SYSTEM
IDRS, Inc.
152 S.E. 5th Ave., Hillsboro, OR, 97123. Contact: Dick Burns, Nat'l. Fran. Dir. - Tel: (503) 693-1619. Sell and install vinyl roofing with shingle imprint on it: for mobile and manufactured homes, low slope residential & commercial. Lifetime warranty, no experience necessary. Established: 1986 - Franchising Since: 1989 - No. of Units: Franchised: 30 - Franchise Fee: avg. $50,000 (based on territory) - Royalty: 3% of gross sales - Total Inv: $50,000 - $100,000 tools, equip., open. cap. - Financing: Some.

KITCHEN SOLVERS
401 Jay St., La Crosse, WI, 54601. Contact: Dave Woggon, Fran. Dir. - Tel: (608) 784-2855, Fax: (608) 784-2917. Cabinet refacing specialists providing the homeowner with the opportunity to turn their old, worn out kitchens into a new kitchen in 2-4 days and save them up to 50% when compared to replacing. Established: 1982 - Franchising Since: 1984 - No. of Units: Company Owned: 1 - Franchised: 52 - Franchise Fee: $4,995 plus $50 per 1,000 population - Royalty: 5% of gross profit - Total Inv: $16,695 to $26,245 - Financing: No.

KITCHEN TUNE-UP
KTU Worldwide
131 N. Roosevelt, Aberdeen, SD, 57401. Contact: Tony Haglund, S.V.P. - Tel: (800) 333-6385 , Fax: (605) 225-1371. Wood and laminate restoration services along with the sales of replacement hardware and replacement door and drawer fronts. Established: 1986 - Franchising Since: 1988 - No. of Units: - Company Owned: 1 - Franchised: 284 - Franchise Fee: $12,500 - Royalty: 7%, 0% adv. - Total Inv: $19,600 - $29,700 - Financing: No.

KITCHENPRO *
10451 Mill Run Cir., Ste. 400, Owings Mills, MD, 21117-5577. Contact: Franchise Coordinator - Tel: (410) 356-8889. Kitchen and bath design showrooms. Established: 1993 - Franchising Since: 1993 - Franchise Fee: $25,000 - Total Inv: $136,000 to $252,000 incl. fran. fee - Financing: None.

LINC CORPORATION, THE
4 North Shore Center, Pittsburgh, PA, 15212. , V.P. - Tel: (412) 359-2123. Maintenance of mechanical systems in non-residential buildings. Established: 1978 - Franchising Since: 1979 - No. of Units: Franchised: 92 - Franchise Fee: $30,000 - Total Inv: $50,000 - Royalty: graduated scale 4.5% (high) to 1% (low) based on gross revenues.

MAGNUM PIERING
13230 Ferguson Lane, Bridgeton, MO, 63044. Contact: Mark G. Murphy, Pres. - Tel: (314) 291-7437. Company stabilizes and corrects building settlement utilizing patented products & processes. System can be used on residential & commercial structures. Established: 1985 - Franchising Since: 1985 - No. of Units: Franchised: 7 - Franchise Fee: $20,000 - Royalty: 6% gross receipts - Total Inv: $75,000 - $105,000 excl. fran. fee - Financing: None.

MARBLELIFE
Marblelife, Inc.
6900 Haggerty Rd., Ste. 140, Canton, MI, 48187. Contact: Bill Osborne or Ed Williams, Pres. - Tel: (800) 627-4569. Interior marble and stone restoration services. Established: 1989 - Franchising Since: 1989 - No. of Units: Franchised: 34 - Franchise Fee: $25,000 - Royalty: 6%, 2% adv. - Total Inv: $65,000 - $80,000 - Financing: No.

MIRACLE METHOD BATHROOM RESTORATION
Miracle Method of the U.S.
2767 W. Broadway, Los Angeles, CA, 90041-1038. Contact: Richard Crites, Pres. - Tel: (800) 444-8827. You can make worn out, discolored tubs and tile look new again. Replacement of fixtures and tile costs thousands, refinishing them costs only hundreds. Established: 1977 - Franchising Since: 1979 - No. of Units: Franchised: 125 - Franchise Fee: $16,500 - Royalty: 5%-7.5% (on declining scale) - Total Inv: $28,500 - Financing: Third party financing assistance.

MR. ELECTRIC *
1020 N. University Parks Dr., Waco, TX, 76707. Contact: David Brandt, Vice Pres. Sales - Tel: (800) 805-0575. Electrical service and repair for residential and light commercial businesses. Established: 1994 - Franchising Since: 1994 - No. of Units: Franchised: 10 - Franchise Fee: $12,500 per 100,000 population - Royalty: Variable from 6% to 3% - Total Inv: $25,000 - $47,000 depending on size of bus. - Financing: Yes.

MR. ROOTER CORP.
1020 N. University Parks Dr., Waco, TX, 76707. Contact: Robert Tunmire, Pres. - Tel: (817) 755-0055. Full service plumbing and sewer & drain. Established: 1968 - Franchising Since: 1972 - No. of Units: Company Owned: 1 - Franchised: 211 - Franchise Fee: $17,500 per 100,000 population - Royalty: 6% on gross rev. - Total Inv: $25,000 - $100,000 plus depending on area - Financing: To qualified parties.

NATIONAL INTERNATIONAL ROOFING
National International Roofing Corporation
11804 South Route 47, Huntley, IL, 60142. Contact: Christine Grechis, Dir. of Fran. Sales - Tel: (815) 356-1155. Professional roofing contractors specializing in new construction, re-roofing, repair & preventative maintenance and rooftop analysis. Designed as a way for qualified entrepreneurs to build their own business futures. Individual or Master franchises now available to qualified candidates. Established: 1991 - Franchising Since: 1993 - No. of Units: Company Owned: 14 - Franchised: 2 - Franchise Fee: $17,500 ind., $20,000 - $30,000 master - Royalty: 10% ind., 2% master - Total Inv: $28,600 - $38,250 ind., $112,500 - $292,000 master - Financing: Aid in presentation to lenders.

NATURE INDOORS
Nature Indoors, Inc.
3000 Greystone Dr., Semmes, AL, 36575. Contact: William Wyers, V.P. - Tel: (334) 649-7733. Interior landscape, design and maintenance. Established: 1986 - Franchising Since: 1986 - No. of Units: Franchised: 8 - Franchise Fee: $10,000 - $20,000 - Royalty: 5% gross - Total Inv: $30,000+ - Financing: No.

NEWCOMERS OF AMERICA HOME INSPECTION SERVICE, INC. *
210 Wisconsin Ave., Waukesha, WI, 53186. Contact: Jim Jankowski, Dir. of Fran. Sales - Tel: (414) 549-8070, Fax: (414) 549-8065. Home inspection at time of buying a home. Established: 1988 - Franchising Since: 1994 - No. of Units: Company Owned: 13 - Franchised: 70 - Franchise Fee: $16,275 - Royalty: 7% of revenue, 1.5% nat'l. adv. - Financing: On more than one unit.

NOEL LOG HOMES, INC.
Rt. 2 Box 164, Noel, MO, 64854. Contact: Jim Dooley, Pres. - Tel: (417) 475-3183. Log home manufacturer. Established: 1974 - Franchising Since: 1974 - No. of Units: Company Owned: 11 - Franchised: 125 - Franchise Fee: $15,000 - Total Inv: $50,000 - Royalty: 20% - Financing: No.

PAUL W. DAVIS SYSTEMS, INC.
9000 Cypress Green Dr., Jacksonville, FL, 32256-7791. Contact: Dave Kelly, Franchise Director - Tel: (904) 739-9963. Computerized insurance restoration service working with major insurance companies. Established: 1966 - Franchising Since: 1970 - No. of Units: Franchised: 260 - Franchise Fee: $48,500 - Royalty: 3.5% - Total Inv: $65,000 - Financing: Yes.

PERMA CERAM
Perma Ceram Enterprises, Inc.
65 Smithtown Blvd., Smithtown, NY, 11787. Contact: Joseph Tumolo, Pres. - Tel: (516) 724-1205, (800) 645-5039. Bathroom fixture resurfacing in private homes, hotels, motels, apartment houses, hospitals, etc., with our own PORCELAINCOTE. Wherever there is a bathroom there is a need for our service. Established: 1975 - Franchising Since: 1976 - No. of Units: Company Owned: 1 - Franchised: 186 - Total Inv: $24,500

PERMA-GLAZE
Perma-Glaze, Inc.
1638 S. Research Loop Rd., Ste. 160, Tucson, AZ, 85710. Contact: Dale Young, Pres. - Tel: (602)722-9718 or U.S(800)332-7397, Fax: (602)296-4393. Restoration and refinishing of bathroom and kitchen fixtures such as bathtubs, sinks, wall tile, appliances, and shower stalls. Materials to refinish consist of porcelain, fiberglass, acrylic, marble and formica. Established: 1978 - Franchising Since: 1981 - No. of Units: Company Owned: 1 - Franchised: 168 - Franchise Fee: $27,500 - Total Inv: $30,500: ($27,500 + $3,000 start-up) - Financing: No.

PERMA-JACK CO.
9066 Watson Rd., St. Louis, MO, 63126. Contact: Joan Robinson or John Langenbach, Owners - Tel: (314) 843-1957. Stabilizing building foundations with steel piers driven to rock or equal load bearing strata, fast, with no expensive excavation. Established: 1974 - Franchising Since: 1975 - No. of Units: Franchised: 38 - Franchise Fee: 0 - Royalty: 5% - Total Inv: $24,200 - $68,300 - Financing: No.

PERMAFLU
Chimney Relining International, Inc.
P.O. Box 4035, Manchester, NH, 03108. Contact: Clifford Martel, Pres/Nat'l Sales Mgr. - Tel: (603) 668-5195. Offers the strongest poured masonry chimney liner. An acid resistant liner that seals and strengthens cracked or crooked chimneys at substantial savings over demolition and reconstruction without the mess. Established: 1979 - Franchising Since: 1980 - No. of Units: Company Owned: 1 - Franchised: 46 - Total Inv: $6,900 - $14,700 - Financing: Assistance.

POLY-TUB RESTORATION
SPR International
4492 Acworth Industrial Dr., Ste. 102, Acworth, GA, 30101. Contact: Larry Stevens, Pres. - Tel: (770) 966-1331. Restore the beauty to dull, hard to clean tub & tile. No painting, no spraying, no odors, use the same day. Established: 1973 - Franchising Since: 1973 - No. of Units: Company Owned: 1 - Franchised: 75 - Franchise Fee: $5,995 - Royalty: 20% - Financing: None.

POTTY DOCTOR PLUMBING SERVICE
Potty Doctor Franchise Systems
P.O. Box 1426, Lake Worth, FL, 33460. Contact: Mr. Guthrie, Pres. - Tel: (800) 682-4444. Residential plumbing service. Service agreements, faucet and sink repair and replacement, water filtration and conservation. Established: 1992 - Franchising Since: 1993 - No. of Units: Company Owned: 1 - Franchised: 1 - Franchise Fee: $15,000 - $30,000 - Royalty: 6% of gross sales, 2% adv. - Total Inv: Depends on applicant - Financing: None.

PRINCETON ENERGY PARTNERS, INC.
2221 Stackhouse Dr., Yardley, PA, 19067. Contact: David Brown, Pres. - Tel: (215) 493-5737. Market comfort improvement and energy savings to the home owner and new construction markets. Instrumented energy analysis and retrofit service. Established: 1981 - No. of Units: 8 - Approx. Inv: $45,000 - $77,000 - Financing: None.

PROFESSIONAL HOUSE DOCTORS
Professional House Doctors, Inc.
1406 E. 14th St., Des Moines, Iowa, 50316. Contact: Dane J. Shearer, Pres. - Tel: (515) 265-6667. Building science and environment specialists. Established: 1982 - Franchising Since: 1991 - No. of Units: Company Owned: 1 - Franchised: 4 - Franchise Fee: $15,000 - Royalty: 6%, 2% adv. - Total Inv: $22,500 - $15,000 fran. fee - $7,500 equip. & supplies, support, training - Financing: None.

PROHOME *
ProHome Incorporated
7701 E. Kellogg, Ste. 890, Wichita, KS, 67207. Contact: Jack Salmans, Pres./Sales - Tel: (316) 687-6776, Fax: (316) 687-0455. Provides warranty callback service for home builders and services home maintenance plans for homeowners. Established: 1993 - Franchising Since: 1993 - No. of Units: Franchised: 10 - Franchise Fee: $25,000 - $40,000 - Royalty: 6% 1st year, 7% thereafter - Total Inv: fee + $40,000 - $60,000 - Financing: Yes.

PULL-OUT SHELF COMPANY, THE
Pull-Out Shelf Company, Inc.
2701 E. Camelback Rd., Ste. 301, Phoenix, AZ, 85016. Contact: Jeff Smith, Mktg./Fran. Dev. Dir. - Tel: (602) 381-6225, (800) 962-0050, Fax: (602) 468-3117. The Pull-Out Shelf Company has created a unique patented system changing fixed shelves into custom pull-out drawers. A perfect fit for the kitchen, bath, pantry, linen closet or office. Installation is quick and efficient providing more time for marketing and pulling in sales. Established: 1992 - Franchising Since: 1994 - No. of Units: Company Owned: 1 - Franchised: 10 - Franchise Fee: $12,500 - Royalty: 5% of gross sales - Total Inv: $25,000 incl. fran. fee - Financing: Yes.

PUROFIRST
Purofirst International, Inc.
5610 N.W. 12 Ave., #209, Ft. Lauderdale, FL, 33309. Contact: Rory O'Dwyer, V.P. - Tel: (800) 247-9047, (305) 771-3121. Building contractors doing specialty high profit property casualty restoration and reconstruction. Franchisees work directly with insurance companies and owners. Established: 1985 - Franchising Since: 1991 - No. of Units: Franchised: 115 - Franchise Fee: $22,500 - Royalty: 2% - 6% - Financing: 3rd party.

RE-BATH
Re-Bath Corporation
1055 S. Country Club Dr., Bldg. 2, Mesa, AZ, 85210. Contact: David Andow, Dir. of Fran. Dev. - Tel: (800) 426-4573. Unique service business. Sell and install custom-molded acrylic bathtub liners, shower base liners and wall systems. No experience necessary, complete training, exclusive territory. Established: 1979 - Franchising Since: 1991 - No. of Units: Company Owned: 1 - Franchised: 52 - Franchise Fee: $.02 per person with 500,000 population (min.) + $5,000 start-up package - Royalty: Included in cost of product - Total Inv: $27,500 - $51,600 - Financing: No.

RE-SSIDE AMERICA
11002 Park Rd., Fairfax, VA, 22030. Contact: Richard Ressa, Pres. - Tel: (703) 691-4331. Windows, doors, exterior wall products. Established:1976 - Franchising Since: 1989 - No. of Units: Company Owned: 1 - Franchise Fee: $25,000 - Royalty: 7% - Total Inv: $49,800 - Financing: No.

REFACE IT KITCHEN SYSTEMS INC.
P.O. Box 874, Ferndale, WA, 98248. Contact: Ron Good, Pres. - Tel: (360) 384-3546. Refacing kitchens & bathrooms. Each location has a complete shop for custom renovations of cabinets. Established: 1989 - Franchising Since: 1989 - No. of Units: Company Owned: 1 - Franchised: 6 - Franchise Fee: $23,000 - Royalty: 8% reducing to 3% - Total Inv: $55,000 - $100,000 - Financing: No.

RESIDENTIAL BUILDING INSPECTORS
701 Fairway Dr., Clayton, NC, 27520. Contact: Claude Canipe, Pres. - Tel: (919) 553-3959. Home inspection service. Established: 1986 - Franchising Since: 1989 - No. of Units: Franchised: 8 - Franchise Fee: $6,875 - Royalty: 10% - Total Inv: $1,500 - $4,000 start-up + fran. fee.

ROCKY MOUNTAIN LOG HOMES
Montana Sundown, Inc.
1883 Hwy. 93 S., Hamilton, MT, 59840. Contact: Mark Moreland, V.P. Sales. - Tel: (406) 363-5680. Log home manufacturer seeking distributors for home packages, provide 30+ standard plans and support for custom home packages. Established: 1974 - Licensing Since: 1974 - No. of Units: Company Owned: 2 - Licensed: 90 - Franchise Fee: $500 - $3,000 - Total Inv: $75,000.

ROLL-A-WAY STORM AND SECURITY SHUTTERS
Roll-A-Way, Inc.
10601 Oak St., N.E., St. Petersburg, FL, 33716. Contact: Bill Salin, V.P. Fran. Dev. Tel: (813) 576-6044, (800) 683-9505, Ext. 229. Manufacturer of top quality storm and security shutter systems for commercial and residential applications. Franchise entails sales and installation. Professional training and ongoing support. Proven product for over 20 years. Established: 1974 - Franchising Since: 1994 - No. of Units: Company Owned: 5 - Franchised: 9 - Franchise Fee: $6,585 - $18,500 - Royalty: None - Total Inv: $13,365 - $33,950 incl. fee - Financing: None.

ROTO-ROOTER CORP.
300 Ashworth Rd., West Des Moines, IA, 50265. Contact: Paul E. Barkman, Dir. of Int'l. Dev. - Tel: (515) 223-1343. We are seeking serious, financially capable individuals or entities for master license opportunities in plumbing repair, sewer-drain service and related service product opportunities worldwide. Roto-Rooter offers training, advertising, support and over 60 years of industry experience to qualified principals. Established: 1934 - Franchising Since: 1935 - No. of Units: Company Owned: 84 - Franchised: 566 - Franchise Fee: varies - Royalty: per agreement - Total Inv: varies by country - Financing: No.

RYAN HOMES, INC.
100 Ryan Ct., Dept. 500, Pittsburgh, PA, 15205. Contact: Michelle Staulfer, Fran. Dir. - Tel: (412) 276-8000. Offers a variety of building options, each home built to customer's specific order. Franchise offers a market-tested product, expertise in production, administration, marketing and financing. Established: 1948 - Franchising Since: 1978 - Number of Operating Divisions: Company Owned: 26 - Franchised: 8 - Franchise Fee: $10,000 - Royalty: 1% - Total Inv: $50,000 - $200,000 - Financing: Yes.

SERVISTAR CORPORATION
P.O. Box 1510, Butler, PA, 16003. Contact: Donald Belt, V.P. Sales - Tel: (412) 283-4567. A purchasing co-operative. Generally retail hardware, home centers and/or lumber and building supply stores. Established: 1910 - No. of Units: 3,863 - Approx. Inv: $150,000 - Financing: None.

SMOKEY MOUNTAIN HOMES
Smokey Enterprises, Inc.
P.O. Box 549, Maggie Valley, NC, 28751. Contact: Donald Sanders, Prod. Mgr. - Tel: (704) 926-0888. Log home kit mfg. and dist. Established: 1974 - Franchising Since: 1975 - No. of Units: Company Owned: 1 - Franchised: 17 - Franchise Fee: purchase of log home kit used as model - Royalty: 20% basic price - Total Inv: $35,000+ - Financing: No.

SPEED FAB-CRETE CORP.
P.O. Box 15580, Fort Worth, TX, 76119. Contact: David Bloxom Jr., Pres. - Tel: (817) 478-1137. Precast concrete wall panel building system, plant manufactured. Established: 1962 - Licensing Since: 1962 - No. of Units: Licensed: 1- License Fee: $50,000 - Royalty: 1% gross sales monthly.

SPR COUNTERTOP & TUB REPAIR
SPR International Inc.
3398 Sanford Dr., Marietta, GA, 30066. Contact: Ray Johnson, Salesman - Tel: (404) 429-0232, Fax: (404) 424-1494. Repair chips, cracks, burns & holes in fiberglass, acrylic, porcelain, countertops, tubs, sinks, spas, showers. High demand from home builders, manufacturers, hotels & apartments. Established: 1973 - Franchising Since: 1973 - No. of Units: Company Owned: 1 - Franchised: 30 - Franchise Fee: $5,995 - Royalty: 20% - Financing: None.

SURFA SHIELD
Surf-Shield Corp.
3930 Walnut St., Fairfax, VA, 22030. Contact: J. Davis, Pres. - Tel: (703) 591-1700. Home improvement contractors such as roofing, siding, window and door replacement plus porch and patio enclosures and decks. Also provides total operating systems for existing contractors. Established: 1957 - Licensing Since: 1962 - No. of Units: 41 - License Fee: $2,490 - Total Inv: varies - Financing: No.

SURFACE SPECIALISTS
Surface Specialists Systems, Inc.
2362 - 175th Lane N.W., Andover, MN, 55304. Contact: Wayne McClosky, Pres. - Tel: (612) 753-3717. Repair/refinish of plastic laminate, cultured marble, fiberglass & acrylic tubs & spas, porcelain tubs. Skid resistant treatment of tubs, showers & tile floors, in place conversion of tubs to whirlpool units. Warranty work for 34 manufacturers. Excellent opportunity. Established: 1981 - Franchising Since: 1982 - No. of Units: Franchised: 26- Franchise Fee: $14,500 - Royalty: 5% - Total Inv: $20,500: fran. fee + $6,000 oper. cap. - Financing: Partial.

TECHSTAFF
Techstaff, Inc.
One Park Plaza, Ste. 111, Milwaukee, WI, 53224. Contact: Scott Salick, C.E.O. - Tel: (414) 359-4444. Contract engineering services. Established: 1985 - Franchising Since: 1986 - No. of Units: Company Owned: 4 - Franchised: 6 - Franchise Fee: $15,000 - Royalty: 6.9% - Total Inv: $75,000 - Financing: Possibly with prior industry experience.

TIMBERMILL STORAGE BARNS INC.
P.O. Box 218, Sonoma, CA, 95476. Contact: Tom Hoover, Pres. - Tel: (707) 939-1430. Sale and construction of pre-fab small storage buildings. Established: 1985 - Franchising Since: 1986 - No. of Units: 19 - Franchise Fee: $12,000 - Total Inv: additional $6,000 set-up costs - Financing: None.

TOP DRAWER CUSTOM CLOSETS
1705 Lyndale Blvd., Maitland, FL, 32751. Contact: Tania Torruella, Pres. - Tel: (407) 647-8479. Design & installation of custom closets and garages. This is a low overhead business with big profit margins. Established: 1985 - Franchising Since: 1987 - Franchise Fee: $2,900 - Royalty: 0 - Total Inv: $9,000 - $22,000 - Financing: Some available, vendors accept credit cards.

U.S. ROOTER SERVICE
U.S. Rooter Corp.
17023 Batesville Pike, North Little Rock, AR, 72120-1701. Contact: Maxine, Sec./Tres. - Tel: (501) 835-1500. Franchise the use of our name, trademark & patented sewer & drain cleaning equipment. Established: 1965 - Franchising Since: 1968 - No. of Units: Franchised: 10 - Franchise Fee: min. $10,000 - Royalty: Flat fee based on population/tele book coverage - Total Inv: Approx. $30,000, depending on what kind of vehicle franchisee would purchase + supplies, fran. fee etc. - Financing: No.

UNITED STATES SEAMLESS *
2001 1st Ave. N., Fargo, ND, 58102. Contact: David Hedman, Nat'l. Sales Mgr. - Tel: (701) 241-8888, Fax: (701) 241-9999. Marketing program to sell & install seamless steel siding, seamless gutters, soffit, fascia, windows, storm and entry doors, other siding, insulation, accessories, and other products. New construction and existing homes, apartment buildings and commercial buildings. Established: 1991 - Franchising Since: 1991 - No. of Units: Company Owned: 1 - Franchised: 33 - Royalty: Based on number of machines in territory - Total Inv: $52,000 to $94,000 - Financing: Yes.

WALL-FILL WORLDWIDE INC.
P.O. Box 420, Wheaton, IL, 60189. Contact: Ed Lowry, Fran. Dir. - Tel: (708) 871-8740. Construction franchise specializing in maintenance free products. Established: 1928 - Franchising Since: 1987 - Total Inv: $31,250 start up cash. - Financing: Assistance only.

WAYNE'S SCREEN MACHINE
Wayne's Screen Machine Inc.
19636 8th St. E., Sonoma, CA, 95476. Contact: Wayne Wirick, Pres. - Tel: (707) 996-5551, Fax: (707) 996-0139 . Mobile unit for window screens, new screens, rescreens, custom screens & window coverings (blinds). Established: 1986 - Franchising Since: 1988 - No. of Units: Company Owned: 1 - Franchised: 13 - Franchise Fee: $25,000 - Royalty: 5% (Not in effect 3% adv. fee) - Total Inv: $42,083.

WILDERNESS LOG HOMES, INC.
N. 5821 County Rd. S., Plymouth, WI, 53073. Contact: Jim Koepsell, Dealer Co-ord. - Tel: (414) 893-8416. Manufacturer of log home kits. Established: 1972 - Franchising Since: 1973 - No. of Units: Company Owned: 1 - Franchised: 110 - Franchise Fee: $10,000 - Total Inv: $125,000 - Royalty: commission.

WOODWORKERS CLUB, THE *
Woodworkers Club Franchising, Inc.
1919 S. 40th St., Lincoln, NE, 68506. Contact: Jack L. Rediger, Pres. - Tel: (402) 434-5620, Fax: (402) 434-5624. Woodworkers Club is a unique franchising opportunity which allows members access to tools, instruction, and shop-price, all at a fraction of the cost of outfitting their own shops. Call for more information on this rapidly growing concept.

Established: 1994 - Franchising Since: 1995 - No. of Units: Company Owned: 1 - Franchised: 1 - Franchise Fee: $24,000 - Royalty: 5%, 1% adv. - Total Inv: $182,500 to $333,000 - Financing: No.

WORLDWIDE REFINISHING SYSTEMS, INC.
P.O. Box 3146, Waco, TX, 76707-0146. Contact: Charles Wallis, V.P. - Tel: (817) 776-2282 or (800) 583-9900. Recolor or refinish tubs, showers, countertops, fiberglass, porcelain, acrylic, formica, ceramic tile, metal and more. Established: 1970 - Franchising Since: 1988 - No. of Units: Company Owned: 1 - Franchised: 511 - Franchise Fee: $19,500 - Royalty: 5% - Total Inv: $19,500 fran. fee; $6,000 equp.; $2,000 work. cap.; $1,500 travel/lodging; $6,500 van - Financing: No.

BURGLAR & FIRE PREVENTION

CITIZENS AGAINST CRIME
1022 S. Greenville Ave., Allen, TX, 75002. Contact: Barry Layl, Fran. Dir. - Tel: (800) 466-5566. National safety corporation providing crime prevention seminars for business and organizations. Safety products are sold in conjunction with the seminar. Established: 1980 - Franchising Since: 1986 - No. of Units: Company Owned: 1 - Franchised: 45 - Franchise Fee: $22,500 - Royalty: not at this time - Total Inv: $30,000 - $100,000 - Financing: Yes.

DYNAMARK SECURITY CENTERS, INC.
19833 Leitersburg Pike, Hagerstown, MD, 21742. Contact: Marcus Peters, V.P., Dev. - Tel: (800) 342-4243. Residential/light commercial security systems. Established: 1975 - Franchising Since: 1984 - No. of Units: Franchised: 135 - Franchise Fee: $15,000 - Royalty: $100 - Total Inv: $42,000 - $46,000 - Financing: Yes.

FIRE DEFENSE INTERNATIONAL, INC.
3919 Morton St., Jacksonville, FL, 32217. Contact: I.A. LaRusso, Dir. Mktg. - Tel: (904) 731-0244, (800) 554-3028. Guaranteed sales: Sales and service of fire extinguishers, restaurant hood systems, first aid and municipal supplies. Established: 1973 - Franchising Since: 1987 - No. of Units: Company Owned: 29 - Franchised: 7 - Franchise Fee: $18,500 - Royalty: 10% weekly - Total Inv: $38,500 - Financing: Yes, up to $10,000 for qualified applicants.

JADE SECURITY, INC.
137-1/2 Main, New Eagle, PA, 15067. Contact: Dennis Stancoven, Mktg. Agent - Tel: (412) 258-8555. Unarmed security guard service. Established: 1986 - Franchising Since: 1987 - No. of Units: Company Owned: 1 - Franchised: 1 - Franchise Fee: $10,000 - Royalty: 4% - Total Inv: $30,000 - $50,000.

SECURITY ALLIANCE CORP., THE
1865 Miner St., Des Plaines, IL, 60016. Contact: Ron Davis, Pres. - Tel: (708) 298-7300. Security systems for residences and small businesses. A support services group for the independent alarm dealer. Call for fee information.

SONITROL
Sonitrol Corporation
1800 Diagonal Rd., #180, Alexandria, VA, 22314-2840. Contact: Colin Harold, Mkt. Mgr. Dev. - Tel: (703) 684-6606. Sale, installation, monitoring and service of electronic security services. Established: 1960 - Franchising Since: 1963 - No. of Units: Company Owned: 15 - Franchised: 165 - Franchise Fee: $20,000 - $50,000 - Royalty: 2.5% gross - Total Inv: $200,000 - $800,000 - Financing: No.

BUSINESS PRODUCTS AND SERVICES

1-DAY RESUME
3820 Permier Ave., Memphis, TN, 38118. Contact: Bill Richey, Nat'l Sales Dir. - Tel: (901) 867-0600. Complete resume writing and counselling service. Established: 1990 - Franchising Since: 1993 - No. of Units: Company Owned: 1 - Franchised: 15 - Franchise Fee: $10,000 - Royalty: 6% - Total Inv: $40,000 - Financing: Yes.

A CORPORATE A'FAIR, INC. *
1922 Lynn Brook Place, Memphis, TN, 38116. Contact: Norma Martin, Fran. Dir. - Tel: (901) 396-7918, Fax: (901) 398-5081. Full service party planning with emphasis on company picnics, grand openings, open houses, etc. Established: 1973 - Franchising Since: 1993 - No. of Units: Company Owned: 1 - Franchised: 4 - Franchise Fee: $20,000 - Royalty: 6% on gross - - Financing: Yes, to qualified applicants only.

AAA VENDING
P.O. Box 498, Ranson, WV, 25438. Contact: F. Franke, Mktg. Dir. - Tel: (304) 725-1110. Vending sales to business & industry. Established: 1986 - Franchising Since: 1986 - No. of Units: Company Owned: 1 - Franchised: 25 - Franchise Fee: varies - Total Inv: varies - Financing: Yes.

ACCTCORP INTERNATIONAL *
7414 N.E. Hazel Dell Ave., Ste. 209, Vancouver, WA, 98665. Contact: Sue Mattson, Fran. Sales - Tel: (800) 844-4024. Franchising of full service collection agencies. Established: 1955 - Franchising Since: 1994 - No. of Units: Company Owned: 3 - Franchised: 7 - Franchise Fee: $20,000 - Royalty: 8% continuing service and royalty up to 2% adv. - Total Inv: $35,000 - Financing: No.

ADVANCED SALES TRAINING CORP. *
Advanced Sales and Management Courses
927 Eastern Shore Dr., Salisbury, MD, 21801. Contact: Donnie Williams, Fran. Dir. - Tel: (800) 801-7355 (SELL). On-going sales, management and human relation skills training for CEO's, entrepreneurs, sales managers, supervisors, marketing and sales professions and no selling professionals (accountants, doctors, lawyers, etc). Established; 1993 - Franchising Since: 1995 - No. of Units: Company Owned: 1 - Franchise Fee: $20,000 - $25,000 dep. upon territory size - Royalty: 8%, $200/wk. min. paid weekly - Total inv: $25,000 fee, $20,000 equip., office, work. cap. - Financing: No.

ADVENTURES IN ADVERTISING
Adventures in Advertising Franchise, Inc.
2353 - 130th Ave. N.E., Ste. 100, Bellevue, WA, 98005. Contact: Bob Zaffarano, Dir. of Fran. Dev. - Tel: (206) 882-0818, Fax: (206) 882-2225. Providing companies with creative promotional products, ideas, and programs. Established: 1979 - Franchising Since: 1994 - No. of Units: Company Owned: 1 - Franchised: 14 - Franchise Fee: $24,500 - Royalty: 4%-7% - Total Inv: $30,000 start-up, $67,000 total inv. - Financing: No.

AIM MAIL CENTERS
Amailcenter Franchise Corporation
20381 Lake Forest Dr., Ste. B-2, Lake Forest, CA, 92630. Contact: Michael Sawitz, Owner - Tel: (714) 837-4151. Postal and business service centers. Services offered: UPS, packing & shipping, US mail,

international mail, public fax, copies, high speed duplication, rubber stamps, business cards, notary, money order, money transfer. Established: 1985 - Franchising Since: 1989 - No. of Units: Franchised: 26 - Franchise Fee: $17,500 - Royalty: 5% of sales - Total Inv: $55,000 - $75,000 incl. fran. fee - Financing: Yes.

ALPHA LASER CARTRIDGE INC.
600 U.S. Hwy. I, Ormond Beach, FL, 32174. Contact: Al Lynch, Pres. - Tel: (904) 677-1600/677-8903/677-1601. Recycling ribbons, copier cartridges, laser printer cartridges. Sale of laser printers, Brother copiers. Lease/rental of copiers, laser printers, fax machines. Established: 1986 - Franchising Since: 1988 - No. of Units: Company Owned: 2 - Franchise Fee: $5,990 - Royalty: None - Total Inv: $5,990 - Financing: Yes.

AMALISA SERVICES
Dept. AS, Ste. A, P.O.Box 24, Fayetteville, AR, 72702. Contact: Henry Nwauwa, Pres. - Tel: (501) 443-9785. Dealership in sales & leasing of office/business equipment & supplies, printed products and advertising specialties. Licensed and protected territories are available. Established: 1977 - Franchising Since: 1990 - No. of Units: Company Owned: 2 - Franchise Fee: $25. - $500. - Total Inv: $25. - $9,900 - Financing: Yes.

AMC SERVICE MANAGEMENT, CO. *
AMC Service Management International, LLC
10100 W. 87th St., Ste. 207, Overland Park, KS, 66212. Contact: Bill Baughman, V.P. - Tel: (913) 492-8777, Fax: (913) 648-8858. One of Kansas City's fastest growing companies (995% growth in 3 yrs.), finds your customers for you and helps you keep them. Program features nationally recognized and independently certified training, hi-tech communications, computerized marketing and account management. Established: 1990 - Franchising Since: 1995 - No. of Units: Company Owned: 2 - Franchised: 2 - Master Franchise Fee: $9,500 to $120,000 - Service Franchise Fee: $2,750 to $29,400 - Royalty: Masters 5%, Service 5% - Total Inv: $577 to $49,770 in addition to initial fee - Financing: Up to 65% for 5 years.

AMERICA ONE
America One Inc.
2214 University Park Dr., Okemos, MI, 48864. Contact: Joanne Dillman, V.P. - Tel: (517) 349-1988. Establishing agencies for licensed casualty agencies and expanding small independent agencies. Presently available in Michigan only. Established: 1980 - Franchising Since: 1981 - No. of Units: Franchised: 29 - Franchise Fee: $10,000 - Royalty: 15%-2% adv., fee. Total Inv: $11,000 - $20,000 - Financing: No.

AMERICAN LENDERS SERVICE CO.
P.O. Drawer 7238, Odessa, TX, 79760-7238. Contact: Jim Golden, Pres. - Tel: (915) 332-0361. A vehicle and collateral recovery business. Established: 1979 - Franchising Since: 1979 - No. of Units: Company Owned: 2 - Franchised: 125 - Franchise Fee: varies - Royalty: 5% of gross billings - Total Inv: $50,000 - Financing: Yes.

AMERICOUNTS *
3664 Satellite Blvd., Duluth, GA, 30136. Contact: Brenda Hogan/Carol Campbell, Pres./V.P. - Tel: (404) 476-0210, Fax: (404) 476-0147. Marketing research. Tests consumer products such as foods, advertising etc. with the public and collects data to forward to represented companies. Americounts provides the company client base with ready made business. It also provides training and ongoing support. Established: 1995 - Licensing Since: 1995 - No. of Units: Company Owned: 1 - Franchised: 2 - Franchise Fee: $20,000 - Total Inv: $20,000 plus start up costs, start up costs depend upon type of location.

ASSET ONE
Broker One Securities Corp.
1097-C Irongate Lane, Columbus, OH, 43213. Contact: Raymond A. Strohl, Pres. - Tel: (614) 864-1440. Financial and investment planning service. Advice given on budgeting, plans to reduce taxes, and advice given on various investment. Advice given on sources of real estate and business loans and financing and equipment leasing. Asset One affiliates are stockbrokers and commodity brokers. Established: 1989 - Franchising Since: 1989 - No. of Units: Company Owned: 1 - Franchised: 6 - Franchise Fee: Varies - Royalty: Varies, but small - Total Inv: Varies but small - Financing: Not needed.

BARTER EXCHANGE, INC.
1120 S. Capital Of Texas Hwy., #300, Austin, TX, 78746-6460. Contact: Tim Valentine - Tel: (512) 329-7250. Franchised network of trade exchange marketing offices and service centers. Established: 1983 - Franchising Since: 1988 - No. of Units: Company Owned: 3 - Franchised: 17 - Franchise Fee: $60,000 - Royalty: 20% - Total Inv: Training, fee, computer system, supplies - Financing: To qualified applicants.

BRILLIANT IDEAS!
Brilliant Ideas! Inc.
7939 E. Arapahoe Rd., Ste. 250, Englewood, CO, 80112. Contact: Kimberlee Hayward, Pres. - Tel: (303) 741-6196 or (800) 275-9000, Fax: (303) 741-6197. Brilliant Ideas! developed the nation's only step-by-step, simple, comprehensive and logical marketing system which uses only low or no cost ideas. A customized living marketing manual is created and training is provided. Established: 1990 - Franchising Since: 1995 - No. of Units: Company Owned: 1 - Franchised: 2 - Franchise Fee: $7,500 - Royalty: 15%, 1% adv. - Total Inv: $15,000 - Financing: None.

BUSINESS BROKERS HAWAII, INC.
P.O. Box 1810, Kihei, HI, 96753. Contact: Milton Docktor, Pres. - Tel: (808) 879-8833, Fax: (800) 682-3147. Selling business opportunities with a local focus and an International scope. Business appraisals, financing and consultation. Established: 1985 - Franchising Since: 1995 - No. of Units: Company Owned: 2 - Franchise Fee: $250,000 - Royalty: 10% - Total Inv: Complete turnkey office for the Mid-Pacific basin - Financing: Via a joint venture with a $125,000 credit.

BUSINESS CONSULTANTS OF AMERICA
Horizons of America, Inc.
222 Munson Rd., Wolcott, CT, 06716-2708. Contact: Gregg Nolan, Pres. - Tel: (203) 879-4675 or Fax: (203) 879-4178. Franchised offices for business brokerage and consulting. Established: 1951 - Franchising Since: 1973 - No. of Units: 7 - Franchise Fee: $15,000 - Royalty: 5% - Total Inv: $25,000 - $30,000 incl. fran fee - Financing: Assistance.

BUSINESS INFORMATION INTERNATIONAL, INC. *
1116 Poplar Ave., #5, Memphis, TN, 38105. Contact: Deborah Camp, Pres. - Tel: (901) 525-2024. We franchise a system for producing business-to-business directories and databases. Our unique system provides a methodology for compiling, verifying, publishing & selling information on businesses in their community. Established: 1994 - Franchising Since: 1995 - No. of Units: Company Owned: 2 - Franchise Fee: $7,500 to $25,000 based on population size - Royalty: 8%, 2% institutional adv. - Total Inv: Range $55,000 - $95,000.

CA$H PLUS
Ca$h Plus, Inc.
3572 Arlington Ave., #2C, Riverside, CA, 92506-3932. Contact: Mr. John Collins, Int'l Dev. Dir. - Tel: (800) 729-3142, (909) 682-2274. Check cashing and related services. Established: 1985 - Franchising Since: 1988 - No. of Units: Company Owned: 1 - Franchised: 17 - Franchise Fee: $14,500 - Royalty: 6% gross - Total Inv: $40,000 - $60,000 fran. fee incl.

CAREER BLAZER RESUME SERVICES
Career Blazers
590 Fifth Ave., 7th Fl., New York, NY, 10036. Contact: Howard Kane, Exec. V.P. - Tel: (800) 284-3232. Our product/service is consistently utilized by all levels of the working population. Write, format & produce resumes using proven formulas. Provide career services such as cover letter preparation, direct mail & occupational testing. Affiliated with Career Blazers Personnel Services. Established: 1949 - Franchising Since: 1992 - No. of Units: Company Owned: 1 - Franchised: 2 - Franchise Fee: $12,000 - Royalty: 8% of net receipts - Total Inv: $4,750 - $14,750 capital required.

CHECK EXPRESS USA, INC.
Check Express, Inc.
101 E. Kennedy Blvd., Ste. 3800, Tampa, FL, 33602. Contact: Mike Riordon, V.P., Fran. Dev. - Tel: (800) 521-8211. Computerized check cashing and related financial services. Cash all types of checks, Travelers Express money orders, Western Union wire transfer, electronic tax filing, etc. Established: 1982 - Franchising Since: 1988 - No. of Units: Company Owned: 26 - Franchised: 210 - Franchise Fee: $24,500 -

Royalty: 5% of gross, $750 min. - Total Inv: $130,000 (fran fee, $55,500 leasehold & equip., $50,000 for operations) - Financing: Yes, third party leasing - must qualify.

CHECK MART
Convenience Money Centers, Inc
1055 Auraria Pkwy., Ste. 100, Denver, CO, 80204. Contact: Harold G. Arnold, Pres. - Tel: (303) 892-7171. Check cashing and related services. Established: 1983 - Licensor Since: 1985 - No. of Units: Company Owned:7 - Licensed: 9 - Fee: $7,500 - Royalty: 5%- Total Inv: $7,500 fran. fee, $20,000 buildout, 6 mo. oper. exp., $40,000 line of credit - Financing: Yes.

CHECK PATROL
115 W. Kagy Blvd., #G, Bozeman, MT, 59715. Contact: Raul Luciani, Pres. - Tel: (406) 586-7744. Return check recovery. (Recovery of returned checks for merchants issued by customers. A return fee is charged to the check writer.) Established: 1995 - Franchising Since: 1991 - No. of Units: Franchised: 8 - Franchise Fee: $15,000 - Royalty: 6% on gross receipts from fees charged for check recovery - Total Inv: $15,000 fran. fee, $7,000 equip. & supply - Financing: Yes.

CHECKCARE SYSTEMS, INC.
P.O. Box 9636, Columbus, GA, 31908. Contact: Bill Brandon, Fran. Dir. - Tel: (706) 596-1306. Computerized check guarantee agency. Established: 1982 - Franchising Since: 1985 - No. of Units: Company Owned: 1 - Franchised: 60 - Franchise Fee: $12,500 - $45,000 - Royalty: 5% - Total Inv: $78,000 - $128,000 - Financing: Yes.

COLORFAST MARKETING SYSTEMS INC.
9522 Topanga Cyn Blvd., Chatsworth, CA, 91311. Contact: Mike Elk, Pres. - Tel: (818) 407-1881. Manufacturer of photo business cards & promotional material such as magnets, postcards, flyers, folding & rolodex cards & more. Established: 1986 - Franchising Since: 1986 - No. of Units: Franchised: 3,900 - Franchise Fee: $50. - Royalty: Pay to Colorfast our cost - the rest is profit, recommend 100% markup - Total Inv: $50. - Financing: None.

COMMWORLD
Communications World International, Inc.
6025 S. Quebec St., Ste. 300, Englewood, CO, 80111. Contact: Michael Karge, Dir., Fran. Dev. - Tel: (303) 721-8200. Franchisor of interconnect communications companies offering equipment, training and support. Established: 1979 - Franchising Since: 1983 - No. of Units: Company Owned: 4 - Franchised: 60 - Franchise Fee: $7,500 to $12,500 - Royalty:4% to 18% - Financing: Limited.

COMPUTER BUSINESS SERVICES, INC.
CBSI
CBSI Plaza, Sheridan, IN, 46069. Contact: Bob Haverstick, V.P. Adv. - Tel: (317) 758-4415. Provide software, hardware and training material to run over 20 services for your community from your home with a computer. Established: 1981 - Franchise Fee: Starting cost is $3,000 - $15,000 depending upon what program starting - Royalty: None - Financing: Yes, through leasing companies.

CONFIDENTIAL BUSINESS CONNECTION *
Business Connection, Inc.
7939 E. Arapahoe Rd., #250, Englewood, CO, 80112. Contact: Johnny M. Wilson, Pres. - Tel: (303) 771-8251, Fax: (303) 741-6197. Computerized database matching buyers and sellers of businesses and franchises. Established: 1990 - Franchising Since:1994 - No. of Units: Franchised: 2 - Franchise Fee: $15,500 + varies with territory - Royalty; 5% (2%) - Total Inv: $25,000 to $100,000 - Financing: None.

CONTROL-O-FAX
Control-O-Fax Systems, Inc.
3070 W. Airline Hwy., Waterloo, IA, 50703. Contact: Sandy Reicks, Fran. Dir. - Tel: (800) 553-0070. Medical office automation systems. Established: 1969 - Franchising Since: 1971 - No. of Units: Franchised: 58 - Franchise Fee: $20,000 - Total Inv: $40,000 - $70,000 - Financing: 50% of the franchise fee.

CREATIVE ASSET MANAGEMENT™
Creative Asset Management, Inc.
120 Wood Ave. S., #300, Iselin, NJ, 08830. Contact: Christopher G. Kau, Pres. - Tel: (908) 549-0010. Fee based investment advisor service. Franchisee structures diversified investment portfolios for his clients. Works with clients on long term basis. Also works with other professionals i.e., accountants, lawyers, etc. Established: 1982 - Franchising Since: 1988 - No. of Units: Franchised: 40 - Franchise Fee: $17,500 - Royalty: $300/mo. maintenance fee - Total Inv: $17,500 fran. fee - Financing: 1/3 of franchise fee will be considered.

CRESTCOM INTERNATIONAL, LTD.
Crest Group, The
6900 E. Belleview Ave., Englewood, CO, 80111. Contact: Mr. Kelly Krause, Dir. of Mktg. - Tel: (303) 267-8200. Crestcom® franchisees market and conduct video-based management and sales training. The training is a unique combination of video instruction featuring renowned business/management personalities combined with stimulating, hands-on monthly seminars. Crestcom® training is available in 36 countries and 16 languages. Established: 1987 - Franchising Since: 1992 - No. of Units: Company Owned: 3 - Franchised: 72 - Franchise Fee: $35,000 to $52,500 (varies internationally) - Royalty: 1.5% - Total Inv: $44,355 - $71,960 - Financing: Some.

DATABAR INC.
5210 12th St. E., Tacoma, WA, 98424. Contact: Eric Docken, C.E.O. - Tel: (206) 922-9303. Business office products distribution. Established: 1986 - Franchising Since: 1990 - No. of Units: Company Owned: 4 - Franchised: 7 - Franchise Fee: $15,000 - Financing: Yes.

DIRECT OPINIONS™
Direct Opinions Franchising, Inc.
23600 Mercantile Rd., Beachwood, OH, 44122. Contact: Simon Cohen, Dir. of Franc. Dev. - Tel: (216) 831-7979. Telesurveying business specializing in customer satisfaction surveys for retail sales and service, lead qualifying and generation and other related telemarketing services. Utilize a system of home-based contractors to make the actual telephone calls. Reporting and record keeping is accomplished through a proprietary computer software program. Established: 1983 - Franchising Since: 1993 - No. of Units: Company Owned: 1 - Franchised: 1 - Franchise Fee: $5,000+ depending on territory - Royalty: 6% of 1st $100,000 gross revenue; 3% over $100,000 - Total Inv: $24,150 - $49,800 based on $5,000 franchise fee, includes working cap. - Financing: Some.

DIXON COMMERCIAL INVESTIGATORS, INC.
728 Center St., Lewiston, NY, 14092. Contact: E. Dixon, Sr. - Tel: (716) 754-2224. Complete range of credit and collection services. Credit reporting. Territories available by state or province. Established: 1956 - Offering Partnerships Since: 1961 - No. of Units: Company Owned: 5 - Franchised: 2 - Franchise Fee: $5,000 - Total Inv: $10,000 - Royalty: negotiable - Financing: None.

DUN & BRADSTREET RMS FRANCHISE CORP. *
Dun & Bradstreet
One Diamond Hill Road, Murray Hill, NJ, 07974. Contact: Jerry Mayo, Dir., Fran. Sales - Tel: (908) 665-5331. Franchise will solicit clients for Dun & Bradstreet's commercial debt collection and receivable management services (but the franchisee will not perform any of these services). Established: 1995 - Franchising Since: 1995 - No. of Units: Company Owned: 18 - Franchised: 3 - Franchise Fee: $25,000 plus 10% of gross earnings in previous years $36,000 to $46,000 - Royalty: 35% commission for sale of D&B services - Total Inv: $50,000 initial investment required - Financing: No.

E. K. WILLIAMS & CO.
Edwin K. Williams & Co.
1010 N. University Parks Dr., Waco, TX, 76707. Contact: Franchise Director - Tel: (817) 756-2122. A business management service specializing in maximizing small business profits through a network of franchised offices. Provides accounting, tax and business counseling services plus a wide range of computer services. Established: 1935 - Franchising Since: 1947 - No. of Units: Franchised: 226 - Franchise Fee: $25,000 - Royalty: 8%, 6%, 4% mo. - Total Inv: $38,000 - $90,000 - Financing: No.

EQUALITY PLUS TELECOMMUNICATIONS
Equality plus Telecommunications Corp.
26A Barnes Park Rd. N., Wallingford, CT, 06492-1883. Contact: Glenn D. Slovenko, VP Fran. Dev. - Tel: (800) 221-1511, Fax: (203) 949-0097. Sells telecommunications management and long distance services. Established: 1992 - Franchising Since: 1993 - No. of Units: Company Owned: 1 - Franchised: 9 - Franchise Fee: $20,000, Master Franchise - $80,000 - Royalty: 3% adv. - Total Inv: (excluding fran. fee) $3,000 for computer, telephone, fax machine - Financing: None.

EXECUTRAIN
4800 Northpoint Pkwy., Alpharetta, GA, 30202. Contact: Tom Burns, Fran. Sales Rep. - Tel: (404) 667-7700, Fax: (404) 664-2006. Computer training on popular business related software. Established: 1984 - Franchising Since: 1986 - No. of Units: Company Owned: 3 - Franchised: 125 - Franchise Fee: $30,000 U.S., $50,000 Master - Royalty: 9% - 6% sliding scale - Total Inv: $125,000 - $175,000 - Financing: Yes.

EXPRESS POSTAL CENTERS FRANCHISING, INC.
6475 28th St, S.E., Grand Rapids, MI, 49506. Contact: Scott Fenstemacher, V.P. - Tel: (800) 968-6870. Provides the services of the post office, United Parcel Service, Emery, Western Union, etc., all under one roof. A neat, professional and highly efficient business system focused on variable profit centers which complement its strategic business plan and aggressive marketing approach. Established: 1987 - Franchising Since: 1987 - No. of Units: Franchised: 21 - Franchise Fee: $15,000 - Royalty: 3% - Total Inv: $45,000 - $54,000 - Financing: Assistance.

FACTUAL DATA
Factual Data Corp.
P.O. Box 270458, Fort Collins, CO, 80527-0458. Contact: J. Donnan, Pres. - Tel: (303) 226-3600. Services the mortgage and rental industry by furnishing accurate and timely residential mortgage and rental reliance credit reports. Established: 1985 - Franchising Since: 1987 - No. of Units: Company Owned: 11 - Franchised: 10 - Franchise Fee: $120,000 - Total Inv: $120,000 fran. fee, $30,000 cap. - Royalty: sliding scale to 11% - Financing: Yes.

FAX-9
Fax-9 Holding Corp.
1235 Lake Plaza Dr., #127, Colorado Springs, CO, 80906. Contact: Sales Dept. or Rene Boutin, Pres. - Tel: (800) 727-3299, Fax: (719) 579-0952. An international network of public fax stations. Fax-9 will assist in securing an existing retail store (contracts signed with large national chains) which will operate the fax service for a small percentage of the fax revenues. This concept eliminates virtually all monthly overhead. Established: 1988 - Franchising Since: 1988 - No. of Units: Company Owned: 34 - Franchised: 493+ - Franchise Fee: $3,500 - Royalty: $25 a month - Total Inv: $3,500 - Financing: No.

FINDERBINDER™ & SOURCE BOOK™ DIRECTORIES
California Publicom, Inc.
8546 Chevy Chase Dr., La Mesa, CA, 91941-5325. Contact: Gary Beals, C.E.O. - Tel: (619) 463-5050 or (800) 255-2575. These are add-on profit centers to existing small businesses and consulting firms, ideally those in the marketing or communication fields. Established: 1974 - Franchising Since: 1980 - No. of Units: Company Owned: 2 - Franchised: 20 - Franchise Fee: $1,000 - Royalty: 10% - 5% - Total Inv: $8,000 - $12,000 - Financing: No.

FKA AM MARKETING
Business Images Distributing
196 Park Ave., Dalton, MA, 01226. Contact: Tom Reynolds, Owner - Tel: (413) 684-2666. Full color photo business cards and post cards. Established: 1990 - Franchising Since: 1990 - No. of Units: Company Owned: 1 - Franchised: 974 - Franchise Fee: $500 - Financing: No.

FORTH FINANCIAL NETWORK FRANCHISE
Forth Financial Resources, Ltd.
6610 West Broad Street, Richmond, VA, 23230. Contact: John L. Knowles Jr., President - Tel: (804) 289-6700. Financial products and services distribution network which allows franchisees to represent and provide life insurance, health insurance, and annuity products from a number of companies within the insurance industry while receiving such support services as technical, legal, and marketing expertise in the presentation of products offered through the network. Established: 1984 - Franchising Since: 1986 - No. of Units: Company Owned: 1 - Franchised: 26 - Franchise Fee: $15,000 first year; $5,000 each of years 2-10 - Financing: 3rd party financing for qualified individuals, partnerships, or corporations.

FRANKLIN TRAFFIC SERVICE, INC.
5251 Shawnee Rd., P.O. Box 100, Ransomville, NY, 14131. Contact: James R. Golding, Mgr. Franc. Sales - Tel: (716) 731-3131. Hands on traffic managers to small and medium sized businesses. Franchisee sells both traffic management and freight bill payment/audit and associated traffic services in exclusive territory. Established: 1969 - Franchising Since: 1984 - No. of Units: 2 - Franchise Fee: $25,000 - Royalty: varies - Total Inv: varies depending on location - Financing: To qualified applicants.

GENERAL BUSINESS SERVICES, INC.
1010 N. University Parks Dr., Waco, TX, 76707. Contact: Don Dwyer Jr. - Tel: (817) 756-2122. Business counseling, financial management and tax related products and services. Established: 1962 - Franchising Since: 1962 - No. of Units: 400+ - Franchise Fee: $25,000 reserve fund for $5,000 plus 6 months current living expenses - Royalty: 7% gross profits - Total Inv: fee plus six months living expenses - Financing: No.

GILBREATH'S INFORMATION SERVICES, INC.
5272 South Lewis, Ste. 23, Tulsa, OK, 74105. Contact: John Favell, Pres. - Tel: (918) 743-3111. Business training company renting video products. Established: 1986 - Franchising Since: 1986 - No. of Units: Company Owned: 2 - Franchised: 16 - Inv.: $25,000 - Financing: No.

GOFAX PUBLIC PHONE/FAX STATIONS
Continental Telefax
4101 S.W. 73rd Ave., Miami, FL, 33155. Contact: Ralph F. Geronimo, Pres. - Tel: (305) 264-6060, Fax: (305) 264-7312. Package of six Gofax credit card phone/fax stations as a business opportunity. Investor secures own locations or a locater is recommended. Investor receives a check monthly, marketing support and more. Established: 1988 - Franchising Since: 1990 - Total Inv: $29,500 - Financing: Yes.

HANDLE WITH CARE PACKAGING STORE
Packaging Store, Inc., The
5675 DTC Boulevard, #280, Englewood, CO, 80111. Contact: Franchise Sales - Tel: (800) 525-6309. Packaging and shipping. Established: 1980 - Franchising Since: 1984 - No. of Units: Franchised: 331 - Franchise Fee: $19,500 - Royalty: 5% - Total Inv: $40,000 - $50,000 - Financing: Equip. to lease ($20,000) - Financing: N/A.

HEADQUARTERS COMPANIES
1120 6th Ave. #4Fl., New York, NY, 10036-6700. Contact: Robert Arcoro, Dir. of Lic. & Area Planning - Tel: (212) 308-6338. An interactive, nationwide network of professionally staffed executive office centers offering space and communication support services to business executives on a local, regional and national basis. Established: 1967 - Franchising Since: 1978 - No. of Units: Company Owned: 26 - Franchised: 97 - Franchise Fee: $100,000 - Total Inv: $750,000 - Royalty: 6% - Financing: No.

HOUSE OF STENO, INC.
1708 Placer St., Redding, CA, 96001. Contact: Michael Arnold, Pres. - Tel: (916) 241-6051. Complete secretarial service and instant printing. Established: 1962 - Franchising Since: 1978 - No. of Units: 2 - Franchise Fee: varies - Royalty: varies - Total Inv: $50,000.

HQ BUSINESS CENTERS
HQ Network Systems, Inc.
120 Montgomery Street, Ste. 2350, San Francisco, CA, 94104. Contact: Lesley Rice, Dir. of Dev. - Tel: (415) 781-7811, Fax: (415) 781-8034. Provider of offices, administrative services and telecommunications in a shared, corporate environment. Established: 1967 - Franchising Since: 1977 - No. of Units: Franchised: 151 - Franchise Fee: $30,000 to $100,000 - Royalty: 2.35% per month (no adv. fee charged) - Total Inv: $352,000 - $1.5 million - Financing: None.

IMPRESSIONS ON HOLD INTERNATIONAL *
6218 S. Lewis, Ste. 116, Tulsa, OK, 74136. Contact: Brett Bond, Fran. Dev. - Tel: (800) 580-4653. Custom write and produce "on-hold" programming for business phone systems. Franchise owner markets and sells our product on their local level, and corporate produces the work and administrates. Established: 1991 - Franchising Since: 1994 - No. of Units: Franchised: 28 - Franchise Fee: $27,500 - Royalty: 5% on gross sales (4% royalty, 1% adv.) - Financing: No.

INQUIRY PLUS
Inquiry Plus Franchising Corp.
814 Eagle Dr., Bensenville, IL, 60106. Contact: Franchise Dept. - Tel: (708) 595-5059. Providing businesses of all various types of services relating to the processing, fulfillment, tracking and reporting of prospect inquiries. Included but not limited to direct mailing programs, label preparation, premium fulfillment and telemarketing qualification. Established: 1985 - Franchising Since: 1991 - No. of Units: Company Owned: 1 - Franchise Fee: $17,500 - Royalty: (monthly) 8% gross revenues, 4% gross revenues for mktg./promotion (monthly) - Total Initial Inv: $29,000 low - $37,000 high - Financing: None.

INTERNATIONAL MERGERS & ACQUISITIONS
4300 N. Miller Rd., Ste. 230, Scottsdale, AZ, 85251. Contact: Neil D. Lewis, Pres. - Tel: (602) 990-3899, Fax: (602) 990-7480. International affiliation of independent individuals who are professionals in various fields, engaged in the profession of providing M&A services on a confidential basis in the areas of consulting, financing, divestitures, mergers and acquisitions; in essence, a one stop service for corporate needs. Established: 1969 - Franchising Since: 1977 - No. of Units: Franchised: 54 - Franchise Fee: $10,000 - Royalty: $375 per quarter commencing 2nd year - Total Inv: $10,000 + living expenses - Financing: No.

INTERNATIONAL VOICE EXCHANGE (IVX)
2323 Foothill Dr., Salt Lake City, UT, 84109-1489. Contact: D. Bruce Brown, V.P. Fran. Dev. - Tel: (801) 486-9922, Fax: (801) 486-8294. State-of-the-art Voice Messaging and our 1-800+ network allow franchisees to offer cost-effective communications solutions to a wide customer base. Selected territory development franchises also available. Established: 1988 - Franchising Since: 1988 - No. of Units: Company Owned: 1 - Franchised: 10 - Franchise Fee: $9,875 - $75,000 - Royalty: 3% to 8% depending on annual volume - Total Inv: $45,000 - $85,000 - Financing: Yes.

INVENTION SUBMISSION CORP.
903 Liberty Ave., Pittsburgh, PA, 15222. Contact: Peter Geiringer, Dir. Corp. Sales - Tel: (412) 288-1307. Provides services to inventors and new product entrepreneurs. Established: 1984 - Company licenses its services to independent sales agents - No. of Units: approx. 35 - Approx. Inv: up to $10,000 working capital - Financing: No.

ISU INTERNATIONAL
100 Pine St., Ste. 1700, San Francisco, CA, 94111. Contact: Nyla Starr, Fran. Dir. - Tel: (415) 788-9810. Established: 1981 - No. of Units: 120 (conversion franchises only) - Approx. Inv: $10,000 fran. fee - Royalty: $600 monthly service fee.

J. ROBERTS & ASSOCIATES
81 N. Chicago St., Ste. 206, Joliet, IL, 60431. Contact: John Meers, Pres. - Tel: (312) 236-6640 or (815) 722-0683. Financial services. Established: 1965 - Franchising Since: 1984 - No. of Units: 30 - Franchise Fee: $7,300 - Total Inv: $10,000 - Financing: No.

"With Mail Boxes Etc., we've built a solid future for our business and our family."

Doug and Nanette Reetz, Owners
Mail Boxes Etc. #174, 352, 2374
Seattle, Washington

"We're really glad we made the decision to grow with Mail Boxes Etc.® The local support we get plus the support from MBE Headquarters makes all the difference. We've been with MBE about ten years now, and we like the direction we're heading."

Start building your future with Mail Boxes Etc. today. Call 1-800-456-0414 *for more information on franchising opportunities in the U.S. and internationally. In Canada call 1-800-661-MBEC.*

IT'S NOT WHAT WE DO. IT'S HOW WE DO IT.™

Mail Boxes Etc. Franchised Centers are independently owned and operated. ©1995 Mail Boxes Etc.

JAY ROBERTS & ASSOCIATES, INC.
81 N. Chicago St., Joliet, IL, 60431. Contact: John S. Meers, Pres. - Tel: (312) 236-6640. Financial consultants and brokers specializing in government business loans, commercial business and real estate loan and turnaround consulting. Established: 1965 - Franchising Since: 1982 - No. of Units: Company Owned: 2 - Franchised: 31 - Approx. Inv: $17,300 - Financing: None.

KNOWLEDGE DEVELOPMENT CENTERS *
Knowledge Development Centers, Inc.
445 Hutchinson Ave., Ste. 120, Columbus, OH, 43235. Contact: Tony R. Wells, Pres. - Tel: (614) 888-2444, Fax: (614) 888-0411. Rentable training facility franchise. We provide state-of-the-art facilities fully equipped with hardware, software, production and sound equipment. We are utilized by companies such as Oracle, Sybase, Microsoft, Powersoft to host technical classes. Established: 1993 - Franchising Since: 1994 - No. of Units: Company Owned: 1 - Franchised: 2 - Franchise Fee: $25,000 - Royalty: 5%, 1% nat'l. adv. fund - Total Inv: $230,000 - $360,000 - Financing: Limited.

LETTER WRITER, THE
9437 Haggerty, Plymouth, MI, 48170. Contact: Ginny Eades, Owner - Tel: (313) 455-8892. Creative writing, letter writing, medical billing, resume writing and full secretarial. Established: 1981 - Franchising Since: 1985 - No. of Units: Company Owned: 1 - Franchise Fee: $15,000 - Royalty: 2% of mon. gross - Total Inv: $15,000 + $5,000 equip. - Financing: No.

LITE OFFICE
Shellar Corp.
3901 MacArthur Blvd., Ste. 200, Newport Beach, CA, 92660. Contact: Shellie S. Bean, Pres. - Tel: (800) 222-9055, (714) 222-5600. Provides satellite offices and support services for homebased and traveling business people. Be part of the business created to support this exploding market. Established: 1986 - Franchising Since: 1991 - No. of Units: Company Owned: 1 - Franchise Fee: $22,500 - Royalty: 6% of gross, 3% adv. - Total Inv: $89,200 - $242,900 - Financing: Possible.

MAIL BOXES ETC.
6060 Cornerstone Ct. W., San Diego, CA, 92121-3795. Contact: Rick Milner, Nat'l. Sales Mgr. - Tel: (800) 456-0414. World's largest franchisor of postal, business and communications service centers. Offers private mailbox service with 24-hour access and street address; packing/shipping supplies and services via ground/2nd day shipping service/rapid air; fax; photocopies; office supplies; postage sales; money transfers; passport photos; printing etc. Also provides a cost-effective national distribution system for a variety of retail services through such major corporations as Xerox, Toshiba, Nintendo, Panasonic, Thomson Electronics and many more. Established: 1980 - Franchising Since: 1980 - No. of Units: Company Owned: 2 - Franchised: over 2,800 worldwide and master licensees sold in 50 countries - In house financing for qualified buyers (up to 70% estimated start-up costs $93,500 - $137,400 varies by location). Complete training and support.

MAIL BOXES ETC.®

Kenneth C. Sully
Vice President
Franchise Development

6060 Cornerstone Ct. West
San Diego, CA 92121

TEL 619 455-8800
FAX 619 546-7488

MANAGEMENT CONSULTANTS *
Unified Management Corp.
285 Harrington Ave., Warwick, RI, 02888. Contact: W.H. Bonneau, Dir. Human Resources - Tel: (401) 781-5795. We manage corporate & business payrolls as well as workers compensation insurance. Through our system, we are able to save companies 15% to 30% on their workers compensation insurance and as an added benefit, companies do not have to prepay their insurance in advance. Also they save on administration costs. Learn to earn $100,000 a year + more working from home as a consultant. Established: 1993 - No. of Units: Company Owned: 5 - Franchise Fee: $12,500 to $25,000 depending on part or full time.

MANUFACTURING MANAGEMENT ASSOCIATES
1301 W. 22nd St., Ste. 516, Oak Brook, IL, 60521. Contact: Roger E. Dykstra, Pres. - Tel: (708) 575-8700. Systems and operations consulting for small and medium sized manufacturing companies. Established: 1982 - Franchising Since: 1990 - No. of Units: Company Owned: 3 - Franchised: 2 - Total Inv: $14,900 - $79,450 incl. initial fee, office space and equip.

METRO OFFICE SUITES & BUSINESS CENTER AT THE WOODBRIDGE HILTON
120 Wood Ave. S., 3rd Flr., Iselin, NJ, 08830. Contact: Fran Rush, Dir. of Oper. - Tel: (908) 603-7700. Shared offices and business center at Woodbridge Hilton. General services include secretarial, telephones, faxing, photocopying, individual daily, weekly, monthly office or conference room rentals. Established: 1992 - No. of Units: 110; Company Owned: 1 - Franchised: 1.

MOBILE MONETARY SERVICES
Mobile Monetary Services International
148 19th St. N.W., Canton, OH, 44709. Contact: Joseph McClellan, Pres. - Tel: (216) 430-1900. MMS is a nationwide network of payroll check cashing vehicles that arrives at plants, factories, hotels, hospitals and other businesses at break times, lunch hours or after shift to service the payroll needs of the work force. The average amount of time spent per transaction is 20 seconds. Cash up to 300 checks per hour. Established: 1990 - Franchising Since: 1990 - No. of Units: Company Owned: 2 - Franchised: 26 - Franchise Fee: $24,500 - Royalty: 5% - Total Inv: $80,000 - $85,000: van $50,000, fee $24,500, work. cap. $7,500, (additional collateral may be needed by bank, $50,000 - $100,000) - Financing: Vehicle only.

MONEY BROKER ONE
Broker One Securities Corp.
1097-C Irongate Lane, Columbus, OH, 43213. Contact: Raymond A. Strohl, Pres. - Tel: (614) 864-1440. Offering loans and financing to individuals, businesses, and churches for almost any worthwhile project. Offer real estate loans and business loans, and equipment leasing. There is no upper limit on the size of the loans. Also act as a business broker, re: sales of businesses. Established: 1983 - Franchising Since: 1989 - No. of Units: Company Owned: 1 - Franchised: 5 - Franchise Fee: varies, but small - Royalty: None - Total Inv: varies, but small - Financing: Not needed.

MONEY MASTERS
Money Masters Fran. Dev. Corp.
2445 State St., Lafayette, IN, 47905. Contact: Norm Neiburger, Pres. - Tel: (317) 474-9887. We offer training in professional credit counselling and debt management, helping indebted consumers get out of debt without borrowing. Our clients stay with our program longer than anyone else in the industry. Established: 1966 - Franchising Since: 1993 - No. of Units: Company Owned: 3 - Franchised: 1 - Franchise Fee: $10,000 - Royalty: 7.5% of fees - Total Inv: fran. fee plus $5,000 start-up adv. & office furn. - Financing: No.

MR. PAYROLL CORPORATION *
1600 West 7th St., Ste. 800, Ft. Worth, TX, 76102. Contact: John Templer, Jr., V.P. - Tel: (800) 322-3250, (817) 335-7200, Fax: (817) 335-8200. Largest check casher located inside retail businesses in the U.S. Complete turnkey operation. We are the future of check cashing. Excellent opportunity for single unit and multi unit operators. Established: 1990 - Franchising Since: 1991 - No. of Units: Company Owned: 8 - Franchised: 124 - Franchise Fee: $30,000 - Royalty: 5%, 20% usage fee - Total Inv: $35,000 operating capital - Financing: SBA loans for qualified candidates.

NACOMEX USA
118 E. 25th St., #10th, New York, NY, 10010-2915. Contact: Robert Zises, Pres. - Tel: (800) 622-6639. Provide an appraisal, valuation and brokerage service which assists corporations and municipalities to valuate, buy and sell new and used computers and peripherals, and offers related products and services to the public. Established: 1987 - Franchising Since: 1992 - No. of Units: Company Owned: 1 - Franchised: 2 - Franchise Fee: $9,500 - Royalty: 2%, 1% adv. - Total Inv: $34,000 ($5,000 equip., $5,000 adv., $1,000 software, $2,500 legal/acctg., $1,000 travel, $10,000 work. cap.) - Financing: No.

NATIONAL FINANCIAL COMPANY
5477 Clouds Rest St., Mariposa, CA, 95338-9614. Contact: Leonard Vander Bie, Pres. - Tel: (209) 966-3456. Clients seeking business capital will utilize over 15,000 viable sources of capital that have been computerized for clients. Also makes compensating balance deposits in your clients banks to give the banks incentive to do business with clients. Established: 1957 - Franchising Since: 1957 - No. of Units: Company Owned: 1 - Franchised: 640 - Franchise Fee $18,000 - Royalty: None - Total Inv: $18,000 plus $4,500 start up cap. - Financing: No.

NATIONAL TELE-COMMUNICATIONS
300 Broadacres Dr., Bloomfield, NJ, 07003. Contact: Jim Hendricks, Licensee Support - Tel: (201) 338-1200. Local and long distance telephone bill auditors and consultants recommending discounted access to the AT&T, MCI, Sprint networks etc. Established: 1990 - Franchising Since: 1990 - No. of Units: Company Owned: 1 - Franchised: 144 - Franchise Fee: $14,500 - Royalty: None - Total Inv: $14,500 - Financing: No.

NATIONAL TENANT NETWORK
National Tenant Network, Inc.
P.O. Box 1664, Lake Grove, OR, 97035. Contact: Ed Byczynski, Pres. - Tel: (503) 635-1118 or (800) 228-0989, Fax: (503) 635-9392. Residential and commercial tenant performance reporting involving credit analysis and fraud detection as well as local tenant performance. National data base on main frame system accessed by all offices. Established: 1980 - Franchising Since: 1987 - No. of Units: Company Owned: 3 - Franchised: 14 - Franchise Fee: $11,000 - Royalty: 10% - Total Inv: $24,000 ($3,500 mkt. study/$20,500 inv. in operation) - Financing: Varies.

OFFICE ALTERNATIVE, INC., THE
OA Franchise Sales, Inc.
1455 So. Reynolds Rd., Ste. 389, Toledo, OH, 43615. Contact: W.W. Clow, Pres. - Tel: (419) 389-8389. Offer executive level business services to the working public with The Office Alternative retail systems approach. Personalized telephone answering, word processing, laser printing, mail accommodations incl. shipping/receiving, overnites & FAX, conference room, office, desk space, resumes, instant printing and more. Support includes site selection, lease negotiation, start up, training, business and operations, supply and pricing manuals, marketing program. Established: 1983 - Franchising Since: 1986 - No. of Units: Company Owned: 1 - Franchised: 20 - Franchise Fee: $15,000 - Royalty: 5% - Total Inv: $55,000 est. - Financing: Yes, external sources up to $22,000 - $25,000.

OFFICE OASIS *
Office Oasis, Inc.
12 Parmenter Rd., Londonderry, NH, 03053. Contact: Jai Desai, V.P. Fran. - Tel: (603) 432-0900, Fax: (603) 425-1956. Business services and supplies. Established: 1993 - Franchising Since: 1994 - No. of Units: Company Owned: 1 - Franchised: 1 - Franchise Fee: $25,000 - Royalty: 4% + 2% adv. - Total Inv: approx. $150,000.

OFFICE ONE
1097-C Irongate Lane, Columbus, OH, 43213. Contact: Raymond A. Strohl, Pres. - Tel: (614) 864-1440. Subletting office space to professional people, sales reps, and small businesses. Also, the furnishing of various office services. Established: 1989 - Franchising Since: 1989 - No. of Units: Company Owned: 1 - Franchised: 3 - Franchise Fee: varies greatly - Royalty: varies greatly - Total Inv: varies greatly - Financing: No.

ON-HOLD INTERNATIONAL *
5650 Breckenridge Park Dr., Tampa, FL, 33610. Contact: Allen Castleman, V.P. Fran. - Tel: (800) 401-HOLD, (813) 622-7770. Custom message on-hold for telephone and fm broadcast. Established: 1989 - Franchising Since: 1993 - No. of Units: Company Owned: 1 - Franchised: 48 - Franchise Fee: $18,750 to $49,500 - Royalty: 0 - Total Inv: $18,750 to $49,500 - Financing: Yes.

ONE INVESTOR ONE
Broker One Securities Corp.
1097-C Irongate Lane, Columbus, OH, 43213. Contact: Raymond A. Strohl, Pres. - Tel: (614) 864-1440. Stockbroker offering securities, commodities, and managed commodity programs, precious metals, and insurance products. Stocks, bonds, options, mutual funds, limited partnerships, retirement plans, annuities. Established: 1984 - Franchising Since: 1986 - No. of Units: Company Owned: 1 - Franchised: 7 - Franchise Fee: varies - Total Inv: varies - Financing: Not needed.

P.A.S.S. PACKAGING AND SHIPPING SPECIALISTS
3513 103rd St., Ste. 104, Lubbock, TX, 79423. Contact: Marilyn Butler, Myrna Hewett, Mike Gallagher, V.P. Oper., Admin. Ass't. - Tel: (800) 877-8884, Fax: (806) 745-6810. A complete postal, copy, printing, and business communications center. Established: 1981 - Franchising Since: 1988 - No. of Units: Company Owned: 6 - Franchised: 304 - Franchise Fee: $22,500 - Royalty: none - Total Inv: $39,500 - $74,500 - Financing: Yes.

PACKY THE SHIPPER/ PACK 'N SHIP
PNS, Inc.
409 Main St., Racine, WI, 53403. Contact: Lisa Pipik, Dir. Mktg. - Tel: (414) 633-9540. Complete packaging and shipping service centers set up as an addendum to currently existing businesses. Established: 1981 - Franchising Since: 1981 - No. of Units: 1,400 - Total Inv: $495 - Financing: No.

PAK MAIL CENTERS OF AMERICA, INC.
3033 S. Parker Rd., Ste. 1200, Aurora, CO, 80014-2934. Contact: Chuck Prentner, V.P. Fran. Dev. - Tel: (303) 752-3500. Convenience centers offering commercial and residential clients complete packaging, shipping and mail services as well as private mail box rental, fax, copying, printing, and much more. Established: 1983 - Franchising Since: 1984 - No. of Units: Company Owned: 2 - Franchised: 200 - Franchise Fee: $17,500 - Royalty: 5%, 2% adv. - Total Inv: $50,000 - $80,000 build-out, fran. fee - Financing: No.

PARA-LEGAL OFFICE
Transworld Import/Export Corp.
3116 E. Shea #247, Phoenix, AZ, 85028. Contact: G. Linke, V.P. - Tel: (602) 548-9566. Legal document preparation service. Established: 1991 - Franchising Since: 1991 - No. of Units: Company Owned: 1 - Licensed: 9 - License Fee: $1,750 - Royalty: none - Total Inv: Software $1,200 + Lic. $1,750 - Financing: No.

PARCEL PLUS
Parcel Plus, Inc.
2661 Riva Rd., Bldg. 1000, Ste.#1022, Annapolis, MD, 21401. Contact: Don Patch, Dir. of Sales - Tel: (410) 662-5553, Fax: (410) 266-3266. Shipping, packaging, business support and computer services. Established: 1986 - Franchising Since: 1988 - No. of Units: Franchised: 95 - Franchise Fee: $21,500 - Royalty: 4%, 1% nat'l. adv. - Total Inv: $70,000 - $85,000 all inclusive - Financing: None.

PC PARAMEDIC COMPUTER REPAIR *
7035 Beracasa Way, #208, Boca Raton, FL, 33433. Contact: Howard Fellman, Dir. - Tel: (407) 750-7879. Providing emergency computer repair service, either on-site or in-house. Fully turn-key package including training, authorizations & national accounts. Established: 1989 - Franchising Since: 1995 - No. of Units: Company Owned: 1 - Franchise Fee: Call for details - Financing: Yes.

PONY MAIL BOX & BUSINESS CENTER
13110 N.E. 177th Pl., Woodinville, WA, 98072. Contact: R. E. Howell, Pres. - Tel: (800) 767-7668, Fax: (206) 486-6495. Mailing and shipping center handling Fax;UPS-Fed X-Western Union-Private mail boxes-Word processing-Business Cards-Cartons-Mailing materials-Copies-Rubber stamps. Established: 1982 - Franchising Since: 1986 - No. of

Units: Company Owned: 1 - Franchised: 42 - Franchise Fee: $19,950 - Royalty: $3,500 1st yr., $3,000 rest of contract annually - Total Inv: $49,000 - $50,000 incl. fran. fee - Financing: U.S.A.

POSTAL ANNEX
Postal Annex, Inc.
9050 Friars Rd. #400, San Diego, CA, 92108. Contact: David Wilky, Fran. Dev. - Tel: 1-(800) 456-1525, (619) 563-4800. Business services centers. Complete postal services, mailbox rental, electronic communications, high speed Xerox copying, FAX, stationery & office products. Established: 1985 - Franchising Since: 1986 - No. of Units: Franchised: 165 - Franchise Fee: $19,500 - Royalty: 5% of gross receipts. - Total Inv: $65,000 - $70,000 (including franchise fee) - Financing: Leasing assistance available.

POSTNET
PostNet International Franchise Corp.
2501 Green Valley Pky., Ste. 101, Henderson, NV, 89014-2158. Contact: Brian Spindel, V.P. - Tel: (702) 792-7100. Business and communication center offering shipping, packaging, fax, copies, business services and much more. Established: 1985 - Franchising Since: 1992 - No. of Units: Company Owned: 3 - Franchised: 200 - Franchise Fee: $22,500 US - Royalty: 5% - Total Inv: $55,000 - $65,000 US - Financing: Assistance.

PRIORITY MANAGEMENT SYSTEMS, INC.
500-108th Ave. N.E. #1740, Bellevue, WA, 98004. Contact: Ray DePouli, V.P., Fran. Dev. - Tel: (800) 221-9031, Fax: (206) 454-5506. Management training & skills development for individuals and organizations. The purpose: to increase personal and organizational productivity while maintaining a balanced lifestyle. Established: 1981 - Franchising Since: 1984 - No. of Units: Franchised: 302 worldwide - Franchise Fee: $29,500 - Royalty: 9%, 1% adv. - Total Inv: $29,500 fran. fee, $7,500 to $15,000 operating capital - Financing: Yes.

PRIVATE POSTAL CENTERS
Salsbury Industries
1010 E. 62nd St., Los Angeles, CA, 90001. Contact: Brian Fraher, Dir. of Mktg. - Tel: (213) 232-6181. A one-stop postal, communication & business service center. A center is based around mailbox rentals plus the optional services of package wrapping and shipping, faxing, notarizing, photocopying, telephone answering, word processing and/or a host of other service oriented ideas. Established: 1936 - Franchising Since: 1978 - Franchise Fee: Equipment sales only - Total Inv: $15,000 - $20,000.

PRODUCTIVITY POINT INTERNATIONAL
Global Training Network
15 Salt Creek Ln., Ste. 200, Hinsdale, IL, 60521. Contact: Ralph Loberger, V.P., Network Dev. - Tel: (800) 848-0980. Computer training and support for corporate clients. Specialize in needs assessment and customized training solutions. Established: 1982 - Franchising Since: 1990 - No. of Units: Franchised: 94 - Franchise Fee: $30,000 - Royalty: 4% to 8% depending on size - Total Inv: $250,000 to $400,000 - Financing: No.

PROFESSIONAL LEGAL ASSISTANCE ASSOCIATES
4701 Brierley Dr., Ste. 317, Knoxville, TN, 37921. Contact: C.M. Mattox, Dev. Mgr. - Tel: (615) 531-1703. Work with lawyers/clients. $200. hour + exp. possible. Reconstruct, investigate, analyze accidents/injuries, expert witness, law enforcement investigations/analysis, legal/paralegal assistance, write & file wills/divorces/deeds etc. No experience necessary. Start-up & ongoing training/ consultation/ advertising/ marketing assis. avail./operation manual provided. Turnkey operation. Operate in area of your choice. Established: 1963 - Franchising Since: 1986 - No. of Units: Company Owned: 3 - Franchised: 8 - Franchise Fee: $11,900 (partnerships/ joint ventures available/ negotiable) - Royalty: 10% (includes adv.) - Total Inv: F/LF + $2,000 startup and opr. exp. - Financing: Yes, (will consider partial payment & on the job progress payments).

PROFORMA, INC.
4705 Van Epps Rd., Cleveland, OH, 44131. Contact: John Campbell, Dir. Fran. Dev. - Tel: (216) 741-0400, (800) 825-1525. The sale of printed business products such as business forms, commercial printing and advertising specialties to businesses. Established: 1978 - Franchising Since: 1985 - No. of Units: Company Owned: 2 - Franchised: 104 - Franchise Fee: $19,500 - Royalty: 9% + 1% adv. - Total Inv: $23,000 - $25,000 - Financing: Yes.

PROVENTURE
Proventure Business Group, Inc.
P.O. Box 338, Needham Heights, MA, 02194. Contact: William J. Tedoldi, Pres. - Tel: (617) 444-8278, Fax: (617) 444-0565. All-inclusive New England based brokerage, consulting and management company for going businesses (up to $25 million). Also offered is a moderately priced consulting service for new franchise start-ups. Established: 1979 - Franchising Since: 1981 - No. of Units: Company Owned: 4 - Franchised: 5 - Franchise Fee: $10,000 - Royalty: 6% - Total Inv: $35,000 - Financing: No.

RAPIT MAIL & SERVICES INC.
34 Cambridge E., Oxford, NJ, 07863-9762. Contact: Tom Caleca, Pres. - Tel: (800) 724-8935. Postal and business support services emphasizing duplicating & laser technology. Established: 1987 - Licensing Since: 1989 - No. of Units: Company Owned: 1 - Licensed: 25 - License Fee: $18,000 - Total Inv: $60,000: $18,000 service fee, $30,000 build-out, $12,000 work. cap. - Financing: Some.

RENAISSANCE EXECUTIVE FORUMS, INC. *
875 Prospect St., Ste. 302, La Jolla, CA, 92037. Contact: Fran. Dir. - Tel: (619) 551-6600, Fax: (619) 551-8777. Work with the top executive (CEO, President or Business Owner exclusively) facilitating peer review forums that include an interactive instructional curriculum, a focused peer review process and a round table peer review process. Established: 1994 - Franchising Since: 1994 - No. of Units: Franchised: 14 - Franchise Fee: $39,500 - Royalty: 20% - Total Inv: $44,200 to $60,000 - Financing: No.

SANDY HOOK SCIENTIFIC, INC.
P.O. Box 432, Gloucester, MA, 01931-0432. Contact: David Sneed, V.P. Mktg. - Tel: (508) 281-8011. Consulting service whereby a small company can benefit from the use of small computers and/or improved manual systems. Established: 1976 - No. of Units: Company Owned: 7 - Franchised: 5 - Total Inv: $5,000.

SERVICE CENTER
7655 E. Gelding, #A3, Scottsdale, AZ, 85260. Contact: Gerald Zukerman, Pres. - Tel: (800) 729-7424. A low overhead, business management franchise which provides an umbrella under which small independent contractors receive work. Supply office, customers, management functions. Established: 1991 - Franchising Since: 1992 - No. of Units: Company Owned: 2 - Franchised: 13 - Franchise Fee: $25,000 - Royalty: 5.25% - Total Inv: $39,000 - $51,000 - Financing: SBA approved 30% down.

SHIPPING CONNECTION
Shipping Connection, Inc.
820 Simms St., #12, Golden, CO, 80401-4434. Contact: Steve Vogel & Carol B. Green, Brokers, Brokers - Tel: (303) 331-6430 or (800) 880-1995. Retail packaging and shipping centers offering services to business and residential customers. Founded by ex-UPS management personnel who will provide franchisee with 3 weeks training and the latest techniques in packaging and shipping. Established: 1982 - Franchising Since: 1987 - Number of Units: Company Owned: 1 - Franchised: 18 - Franchise Fee: $15,500 - Royalty: 5% gross, 2% adv. - Total Inv: $40,000 - $50,000 - Financing: Equipment can be leased with approved credit.

SHIPPING DEPARTMENT, THE
5880 Siegen Lane, #G, Baton Rouge, LA, 70809. Contact: Robert Hafele, Pres. - Tel: (504) 295-1085. Small household moves worldwide. Established: 1985 - Franchising Since: 1987 - No. of Units: Company Owned: 1 - Franchise Fee: $12,000 - Royalty: 4% + 1% adv. - Total Inv: $2,900 equip., $3,000 work cap., $2,150 inv.

SHRED-IT
Shred-It America, Inc.
7530 Orangewood Ave., Unit 5, Stanton, CA, 90689-3450. Contact: John Prittie, V.P. Dev. - Tel: (714) 894-0917. Mobile paper shredding and recycling serving Fortune 1000 companies, banks, hospitals, medical facilities, high-tech industries, etc. Established: 1989 - Franchising Since: 1992 - No. of Units: Company Owned: 3 - Franchised: 8 - Franchise Fee: $35,000 - Royalty: 5% of gross revenues, 1.5% adv. fund - Total Inv: $350,000 incl. truck, franchise fee & other - Financing: Third party.

STRATEGIC BUSINESS SYSTEMS, INC.
P.O. Box 137, Star Prairie, WI, 54026-0137. Contact: Richard Danielson, CEO - Tel: (715) 248-3289. Founded to provide small businesses with effective, yet affordable, computer management systems for franchises. It's first product, AUTOnet, is designed for the car care industry. Established: 1985.

SUCCESS CENTERS INTERNATIONAL
681 Marshall Rd., Rochester, NY, 14624. Contact: H. Vought - Tel: (716) 247-4485. Business brokers. Established: 1986 - Franchising Since: 1986 - No. of Units: Company Owned: 1 - Franchised: 1 - Approx. Inv: $50,000 - Financing: Yes.

SUNBELT BUSINESS BROKERS *
1 Poston Rd., Ste. 190, Charleston, SC, 29407. Contact: Ed Pendaruis, Pres. - Tel: (800) 771-7866, Fax: (803) 766-8160. List and sell privately owned businesses for a fee. Established: 1978 - Franchising Since: 1993 - No. of Units: Company Owned: 1 - Franchised: 72 - Franchise Fee: $5,000 or $10,000 depends on size of market - Royalty: None, flat fee of $1,500 or $3,000 every 6 mo. - Total Inv: $5,000 to $50,000 - Financing: None.

SUREWAY AIR EXPRESS
Sureway Air Traffic Corp.
24-30 Skillman Ave., Long Island City, NY, 11101. Contact: Steve Dorfman, Co-chairman - Tel: (718) 937-7600. Air express/air courier, sameday, 9a.m. and next day delivery, 24 hours a day, 7 days a week. Established: 1984 - Franchising Since: 1994 - No. of Units: Company Owned: 5 - Franchised: 8 - Franchise Fee: None - Royalty: 10% 1st million, 7% 2nd million, 5% thereafter - Total Inv: $7,000 - $37,500 - Financing: No.

TELECHECK SERVICES, INC.
3025 S. Parker Rd., Aurora, CO, 80014. Contact: Franchise Director - Tel: (800) 525-8999. Personal and business check verification (guaranteed) and credit card verification. Established: 1964 - Franchising Since: 1972 - No. of Units: Company Owned: 10 - Franchised: 76 - Approx. Inv: $350,000 - Royalty: 7% + 1/2% advertising - Financing: Yes.

TRANSMARK GROUP, THE *
Ste. 104, 5333 Commercial Way, Spring Hill, FL, 34606. Contact: Wm. J. Bylsma, Pres. - Tel: (904) 596-4141, Fax: (904) 596-4626. Full service business. Real estate, construction & property management. Corporation is promoted in 14 countries and the northern states. 80% of clients are foreign. Established: 1979 - Franchising Since: 1993 - No. of Units: Company Owned: 1 - Franchised: 4 - Franchise Fee: $50,000 - Royalty: 2% of turnover of constr., 2% over comm. received - Total Inv: $50,000 ($25,000 for office set up, $25,000 for running cost) - Financing: Yes.

TYPING TIGERS
P.O. Box 8, San Marcos, TX, 78667. Contact: Floyd MacKenzie, Manager - Tel: (210) 629-1400. Typesetting and desk top publishing for the small business user. Established: 1987 - Licensed Since: 1988 - No. of Units: Company Owned: 1- Royalty: $300. monthly.

UNITED CHECK CASHING
United Check Cashing Co. Inc.
325 Chestnut St., Ste. 1005, Philadelphia, PA, 19106. Contact: Seth N. Schonberg, Dev. Dir. - Tel: (215) 238-0300, (215) 238-9056. Financial services, i.e., check cashing, money order, wire transfer, bill payments, tax prep., consumer loans, fax, notary copies, photo id's, and other services. Established: 1977 - Franchising Since: 1992 - No. of Units: Company Owned: 1 - Franchised : 43 - Franchise Fee: $19,500 - Royalty: .2% of 1% of check cashing vol. - Total Inv: $40,000 build out, $40,000 cash (invent.) - Financing: Third party.

VALET EXPRESS
Valet Express Franchising Inc.
10151 University Blvd., Ste. 224, Orlando, FL, 32817. Contact: Darrell New, Pres. - Tel: (800) 788-1107. Executive drycleaning delivery service, catering exclusively to professionals and their support staff, at their place of work. Customers receive computerized monthly billing service, personal liaison service, and a 100% satisfaction guarantee on all work, all at no additional charges. Established: 1988 - Franchising Since: 1993 - No. of Units: Company Owned: 1 - Franchised: 7 - Franchise Fee: $9,500 - Royalty: 3.5% of gross monthly billing - Total Inv: $5,000 - $7,000 plus fran. fee - Financing: May finance up to 50% of franchise fee.

VIDEO DATA SERVICES
3136 Winton Rd. S., #304, Rochester, NY, 14623-2928. Contact: Stuart Dizak, Pres. - Tel: (800) 836-9461. Video taping at social occasions, legal, real estate, conventions, etc. Established: 1980 - Franchising Since: 1982 - No. of Units: Company Owned: 1 - Franchised: 272 - Franchise Fee: $19,950 - Royalty: $750/yr. - Financing: No.

VOICE-TEL
Voice-Tel Enterprises, Inc.
Four Commerce Park Square, Ste. 800, 23200 Chagrin Blvd., Cleveland, OH, 44122. Contact: Don Marks, Nadia Gaster, Mgr. Field Oper., Fran. Dev. - Tel: (216) 360-4400. Voice messaging service bureaus, providing the transmission, storage and retrieval of verbal messages through a combination of computer and telephone. Established: 1986 - Franchising Since: 1986 - No. of Units: Company Owned: 7 - Franchised: 124 - Franchise Fee: $29,000 - $105,000 - Royalty: 6% 1st 12 mos., 8% 2nd 12 mos., 10% thereafter - Total Inv: minimum inv. of $175,000 - Financing: Yes, third party.

VOICESMART CORP.
VoiceSmart Corp.
2160 North Central Rd., Fort Lee, NJ, 07024. Contact: Alex Mashinsky, Pres. - Tel: (800) 878 SMART. Voice mail services for business, 900 and 800 numbers, audiotex, voice response. Established: 1988 - Franchising Since: 1988 - No. of Units: Company Owned: 3 - Franchised: 2 - Total Inv: starting at $18,000 USD - Financing: leasing, joint venture.

VR BUSINESS BROKERS
TD Inc.
1151 Dove St. #100, Newport Beach, CA, 92660. Contact: Marci Rossi, Dir. of Fran. Sales - Tel: (800) 377-8722, Fax: (714) 975-1940. Help sellers to sell and buyers to buy small to mid sized businesses. Complete and detailed training and support are provided. VR sells more businesses in the USA than anyone. Established: 1979 - Franchising Since: 1979 - No. of Units: Franchised: 55 - Franchise Fee: $19,750 - Royalty: $250/mo. plus 7.5% for 1st 36 mos., then 4.5% up to 1 million in gross commissions each calendar year - Total Inv: $41,150 approx. incl. fran. fee - Financing: No.

WESTERN APPRAISERS
West App. Inc.
2075 Winchester Blvd., STe. 103, Campbell, CA, 95008-3432. Contact: Lou Celentano, Pres. - Tel: (408) 374-3551. Appraising and evaluating of damage to automobiles, equipment, farm machinery and recreational vehicles. Established: 1960 - Franchising Since: 1975 - Royalty: 7% of gross income - Total Inv: $20,200 - $32,000.

WILLIAM TELL EVENT SPECIALISTS *
P.O. Box 4640, Frisco, CO, 80443. Contact: Bert Bassford, Pres. - Tel: (800) 547-5111. Company offers for sale a variety of products & services to companies that exhibit in trade shows, i.e., exhibits, graphics, presentations, printing, training, etc. Established: 1990 - Franchising

Since: 1994 - No. of Units: Company Owned: 1 - Franchised: 3 - Franchise Fee: $20,000 - Royalty: varies, based on sales - Total Inv: $28,000: $20,000 fran. fee, $8,000 equip. - Financing: Yes.

X-BANKERS CHECK CASHING
X-Bankers Express, Inc.
809 Chapel St., New Haven, CT, 06510-3001. Contact: Robert Swift, Pres. - Tel: (203) 495-8564. Check cashing & financial services. Franchising Since: 1982 - No. of Units: Franchised: 13 - Franchise Fee: $14,500 - Royalty: 3% of gross revenues - Total Inv: $71,500 - $83,000 - Financing: Yes, part of franchise fee.

CARPET, DRAPERY AND UPHOLSTERY CLEANING

A-PRO SERVICES
A-Pro Services Inc.
P.O. Box 132, Harding Hwy., Newfield, NJ, 08344. Contact: Charles A. Simpson, Pres. - Tel: (800) 467-APRO, (609) 205-1000, Fax: (609) 205-1001. Full carpet service: carpet & upholstery dyeing and cleaning, mobile floor covering sales & installations, water restoration, deodorization, carpet repair etc. Established: 1987 - Franchising Since: 1992 - No. of Units: Company Owned: 1 - Franchised: 6 - Franchise Fee: $7,000 - Royalty: $200/mo. - Total Inv: $10,700 - Financing: 0% interest on fran. fee.

AMERICAN ENTERPRISES, INC.
P.O. Box 2374, Kailua - Kona, HI, 96745. Contact: Ray Dille, Pres. - Tel: (808) 329-2001, (800) 247-3001. An extraordinary carpet & UPH cleaning system, that not only makes carpets appear new again, but actually detox's and de-chemicalizes by using a special chemical and rinsing technique used in separation. Rinse-Out® and Thermal Rinse®. Established: 1985 - Franchising Since: 1990 - No. of Units: Company Owned: 1 - Franchise Fee: $14,500 - Royalty: 7% monthly gross - Total Inv: $20,000-$30,000 (fran. fee, $5,000 legal fees, $10,000 equip.) - Financing: Equipment - lease.

CAPITAL CARPET CLEANING
Capital Sales Corp.
535 Indian Lilac Rd., Vero Beach, FL, 32963. Contact: Robert Campbell, Pres. - Tel: (407) 234-3707, Fax: (407) 234-3707. Ultra high powered carpet and upholstery cleaning - guaranteed price! guaranteed service! Established: 1983 - Franchising Since: 1990 - No. of Units: Company Owned: 5 - Franchised: 7 - Franchise Fee: $10,000 or $1,000 + 5% royalty - Royalty: 6% of recorded gross sales - Total Inv: new van $15,000, system $15,000 - Financing: Yes.

CHEM-DRY® CARPET, DRAPERY AND UPHOLSTERY CLEANING
Harris Research Inc.
1530 North 1000 West, Logan, UT, 84321. Contact: Mark S. Coon, Nat'l. Fran. Dir. - Tel: (800) 841-6583, Fax: (801) 755-0021. Ranked number one in our industry. Our patented carbonating process and specialized spotting techniques make Chem-Dry uniquely different. For your low down payment, you receive all necessary equipment, solutions and office supplies to begin your business. Established: 1977 - Franchising Since: 1978 - No. of Units: Franchised: 4,101 - Franchise Fee: $11,000 - Royalty: $180.00/month, no adv. fee - Total Inv: $17,950 - Financing: $4,950 down, $13,000 financed, Finance $13,000 at 0% interest over 56 months, monthly payment $232.14.

COIT DRAPERY AND CARPET CLEANERS
897 Hinckley Rd., Burlingame, CA, 94010. Contact: Nick Granato, Dir. Fran. Relations - Tel: (415) 697-5471 or (800) 243-8797 Ext.121. Drapery, carpet, upholstery and area rug cleaners. Established: 1950 - Franchising Since: 1962 - No. of Units: Company Owned: 12 - Franchised: 46 - Franchise Fee: $9,950+ - Royalty: 5% - Total Inv: varies on size of operation - Financing: Partial, third party.

COLOR YOUR CARPET
C.Y.C., Inc.
2465 Ridgecrest Ave., Orange Park, FL, 32065. Contact: Connie D'Imperio, C.E.O. - Tel: (904) 272-6567 or (800) 321-6567. Features on-site ability to walk on carpet surface within 30 seconds after application. Provides to residential and commercial properties a unique dyeing, cleaning and restoration service on carpets. Dyes are safe, non-toxic and odorless, and are guaranteed colorfast for the life of the carpet. Established: 1987 - Franchising Since: 1987 - No. of Units: Company Owned: 1 - Franchised: 72 in 11 states & 2 countries - Franchise Fee: $15,000 - Royalty: 3% to 5% - Total Inv: $15,000 fran. fee, equip/inv. $5,000, start up $3,000 - $5,000 - Financing: No.

COMPOSIL OF SOUTH TEXAS
CompleteSeal Fabric Protection
P.O. Box 700149, San Antonio, TX, 78270-0149. Contact: Chris Amundsen, Pres. - Tel: (210) 545-3376, Fax: (210) 494-1820. Composil textile protection fluid guards against permanent staining from most water born and oil based solutions. Also guards against mildewing, flame spread, and reduces smoke density. Composil protective seal last for at least two years and is maintained in an alternative less damaging cleaning methods. Established: 1978 - Franchising Since: 1978 - No. of Outlets: Company Owned: 22 - Franchised: 8 - Total Inv: $5,000 - Financing: None.

CONSOL CARPET CLEANING
Consol Carpet Cleaning Franchise Corporation
P.O. Box 630, Stoughton, MA, 02072. Contact: Robert G. Melchionno, V.P. - Tel: (617) 341-0168. Carpet cleaning and floor maintenance. Established: 1977 - Franchising Since: 1988 - No. of Units: Company Owned: 1 - Franchised: 5 - Franchise Fee: $9,500 - $22,500 - Royalty: 7%, 3% adv. - Total Inv: $20,000 - $50,000 - Financing: Partial.

DURACLEAN INTERNATIONAL, INC.
2151 Waukegan Rd., Deerfield, IL, 60015. Contact: Mike Higgins, Dir. of Mktg. - Tel: 1-800-251-7070. Multi-revenue services including: carpet cleaning, uph. & drapery cleaning, ceiling & wall cleaning, fire & water restoration, janitorial services, floor cleaning, ventilation duct cleaning, pressure washing and ultrasonic cleaning can deliver continuous growth. Established: 1930 - Franchising Since: 1945 - No. of Units: Franchised: 536 - Franchise Fee: $5,700 - Royalty: 2-8% - Total Inv: $10,900 and up - Financing: Yes.

FABRI-ZONE CLEANING SYSTEMS
Lew-Port Industrial Park, Balmer Rd., Youngstown, NY, 14174. Contact: David Collier, Pres. - Tel: (716) 754-4383. Carpet cleaning, upholstery cleaning, ceiling cleaning, odour removal, water damage, fire restoration. Established: 1981 - Offering Licenses Since: 1984 - No. of Units: Company Owned: 1 - Licensed: 38 - Fee: $18,660 - Total Inv: $24,000 - Royalty: 5% - Financing: Assistance only.

FIBER SEAL
Fiber Seal, Inc.
10254 Miller Rd., Dallas, TX, 75238. , Fran. Dir. - Tel: (901) 867-0600. A service business providing treatment and cleaning of fabric, upholstery and carpet, using unique techniques. Regional franchises available. Established: 1971 - Franchising Since: 1994 - No. of Units: Company Owned: 1 - Franchise Fee: $10,000 - Royalty: 6% - Total Inv: $11,600 - $28,500 (Working Cap., Inven., Signs, Insur., Training expenses) - Financing: No. For further information please contact: Consultants America Corp., 12279 US Highway 64, Eads, TN, 38028, Tel: (901) 867-0600, Fax: (901) 867-0010.

HEAVEN'S BEST CARPET & UPHOLSTERY CLEANING
M-Co., Inc.
P.O. Box 607, Rexburg, ID, 83440. Contact: Cody Howard, Owner - Tel: (208) 359-1106, Fax: (208) 359-1236. An alternative to the traditional wet saturation carpet cleaning methods. Offers advantages of modern, low-moisture cleaning. Operators receive professional training. Dry in one hour. Established: 1983 - Franchising Since: 1983 - No. of Units: Company Owned: 2 - Franchised: 140 - Franchise Fee: $9,500 - Royalty: $80.00/mo. - Total Inv: $9,500 to $14,500 - Financing: Yes.

KAMEHAMEHA CARPET CLEANERS
American Enterprises Inc.
P.O. Box 2374, Kailua-Kona, HI, 96745. Contact: Ray Dille, Pres. - Tel: (800) 247-3001, (808) 329-2001. Unique carpet & upholstery cleaning system with our own amazing chemical that makes other systems obsolete! Established: 1985 - Franchising Since: 1992 - No. of Units: Company Owned: 1 - Franchise Fee: $14,500 - Royalty: 8% of gross - Total Inv: $5,000 start up costs - Financing: Leasing of equipment.

LANGENWALTER CARPET DYEING
Langenwalter Industries Inc.
1111 S. Richfield Rd., Placentia, CA, 92670-6790. Contact: John, V.P. - Tel: (714) 528-7610. Complete carpet color correction to include sunfading, bleach spots and other discolorations, as well as complete color change. Established: 1975 - Franchising Since: 1980 - No. of Units: Company Owned: 3 - Franchised: 160 - Franchise Fee: $17,750 - Royalty: $143/ mo. - Total Inv: $17,750 - Financing: No.

LASER CHEM ADVANCED CARPET AND UPHOLSTERY DRYCLEANING
Laser Chem International Corp.
7022 So. 400 West, Midvale, UT, 84047. Contact: Michael Jenkins, Pres. - Tel: (800) 272-2741. Highly advanced carpet and upholstery dry cleaning for commercial and residential areas. Dries in minutes, deep & thorough cleaning, protects life of carpet and upholstery. Established: 1978 - Franchising Since: 1990 - No. of Units: Company Owned: 1 - Franchised: 22 - Franchise Fee: $6,975 ($1,000 off if paid in full) - Royalty: $125 per month starting 6 months after purchase - Total Inv: $2,000 - $20,000 for advertising and van (if needed) - Financing: Yes; $4,675 down, $2,300 financed at 0% interest up to 36 months.

MEDICLEAN *
Restorx, Inc.
1135 Braddock Ave., Braddock, PA, 15104. Contact: Judith Zachary, V.P. Sales - Tel: (412) 351-8686, Fax: (412) 351-1394. Carpet cleaning and sanitizing system. Established: 1993 - Franchising Since: 1995 - No. of Units: Company Owned: 1 - Franchise Fee: $5,000 - Royalty: Flat Fee $50 - $250 per week - Total Inv: Fran fee, $10,000 vehicle/equip., $5,000 work. cap. - Financing: Partial.

PROFESSIONAL CARPET SYSTEMS
5182 Old Dixie Hwy., Forest Park, GA, 30050. Contact: Franchise Counselor - Tel: (800) 925-5055, (404) 362-2300. Professional Carpet Systems is the leader in "on-site" carpet redyeing, servicing thousands of apartment complexes, hotels and motels worldwide. Other PCS services include carpet cleaning, rejuvenation, repair, water and flood damage restoration and "guaranteed odor control". PCS has a total carpet care concept. Established: 1978 - Franchising Since: 1981 - No. of Units: Company Owned: 6 - Franchised: 216 - Franchise Fee: $10,000 - Royalty: 6% - Total Inv: $14,700: fran. fee plus $4,700 inven. - Financing: No.

RAINBOW INTERNATIONAL CARPET DYEING AND CLEANING COMPANY, INC.
P.O. Box 3146, Waco, TX, 76707. Contact: John Appel, Pres. - Tel: (800) 583-9100, Fax: (817) 752-0661. Carpet dyeing and cleaning, upholstery and drapery cleaning, carpet repair, odor control, water and fire restoration, ceiling cleaning. Established: 1981 - Franchising Since: 1981 - No. of Units: Company Owned: 1 - Franchised: 1,000 - Franchise Fee: $12,000 - Royalty: 7% - Total Inv: $27,000 - Financing: Yes.

RUG DOCTOR PRO
Rug Doctor LP
2788 N. Larkin Ave., Fresno, CA, 93727. Contact: Art Tosti, Dir. Fran. Dev. - Tel: (800) 678-7844. Carpet, upholstery, drapery, and ceiling cleaning and maintenance. Established: 1971 - Franchising Since: 1987 - No. of Units: Company Owned: 1 - Franchised: 60 - Franchise Fee: $3,500 and up - Royalty: 3% - 6% adv. - Total Inv: $11,000 - $59,000 - Financing: Yes, for equip. only.

STANLEY STEEMER CARPET CLEANER
5500 Stanley Steemer Pkwy., Dublin, OH, 43017. Contact: Philip Ryser, V.P. Gen. Counsel - Tel: (614) 764-2007. Carpet and furniture cleaning. Established: 1947 - Franchising Since: 1972 - No. of Units: Company Owned: 21 - Franchised: 229 - Franchise Fee: $20,000 per 100,000 population - Royalty: 7% gross monthly - Total Inv: varies - Financing: Varies.

STEAM BROTHERS INC.
933 1/2 Basin Ave., Bismarck, ND, 58504. Contact: Adam Leier, Pres. - Tel: (701) 222-1263. Professional cleaning and restoration franchisor. Established: 1977 - Franchising Since: 1983 - No. of Units: Franchised: 17 - Franchise Fee: $14,400 - Royalty: 7% - Total Inv: $14,400 - $30,000 - Financing: Yes.

STEAMATIC
Steamatic, Inc.
1320 South University Dr., Ste. 400, Fort Worth, TX, 76107. Contact: Scott Bevien, Dan Billings, Sr. V.P., Fran. Dev. - Tel: (800) 527-1295. Indoor air control, air duct cleaning, fire & water restoration, odor control, corrosion control, carpet, furniture & drapery cleaning & wood restoration. Established: 1948 - Franchising Since: 1967 - No. of Units: Company Owned: 9 - Franchised: 264 - Franchise Fee: $12,000 - $18,000 - Royalty: 8% down to 5% - Total Inv: Fran. fee + equip. pkg. $27,500 + Oper. Cap. $15,000 - $45,000 - Financing: Yes, of the $27,500 equip. pkg. will finance up to 100% from 1-5 yrs.

CHILDREN'S PRODUCTS AND SERVICES

A CHOICE NANNY
ACN Franchise Systems, Inc.
5110 Ridgefield Rd., Bethesda, MD, 20816. Contact: Jacqueline Clark, Pres. - Tel: (301) 596-9384. Nanny referral business. Franchise fee includes computer system, 1-2 weeks training for 2 people, advertising materials and brochures, start-up, public relations, sample legal contracts and paperwork. Established: 1983 - Franchising Since: 1988 - No. of Units: Company Owned: 2 - Franchised: 14 - Franchise Fee: $24,900 - Royalty: 7.5% - 10% gross sales - Total Inv: $36,000 - $46,000 (incl. fran. fee) - Financing: Yes, thru qualified lenders.

ALPHABETLAND
Child Enrichment Services, Inc.
139 Bergen Ave., Cearny, NJ, 07032. Contact: Russell Rupon, V.P. - Tel: (201) 991-5684. Pre-school, kindergarten and summer camp. Established: 1967 - Franchising Since: 1967 - No. of Units: Company Owned: 1 - Franchised: 9 - Franchise Fee: $20,000 - Royalty: 7% - Total Inv: $65,000.

BABY NEWS CHILDRENS STORES
23521 Foley St., Hayward, CA, 94545. Contact: Roger O'Callaghan, Pres. - Tel: (510) 786-3460. Complete children's stores specializing in juvenile furniture, clothing, preschool toys, safety equipment and accessories. Established: 1962 - No. of Units: Company Owned: 1 - Franchised: 40 - Franchise Fee: $15,000 - Royalty: 1% - Total Inv: $150,000 - $200,000 incl. inven. - Financing: No.

BABY TOWN INC.
1662 Clarkson Rd., Chesterfield, MO, 63017. Contact: Mark Widdicombe, Pres. - Tel: (800) 8BABY 69. Large infant and toddler discount specialty stores, juvenile furniture, accessories and toys. Established: 1990 - Franchising Since: 1993 - No. of Units: Company Owned: 2 - Franchised: 4 - Franchise Fee: $12,500 - Royalty: 3%, 1% adv. - Total Inv: $150,000 - $350,000 - Financing: None.

BABY-TENDA CORP.
123 S. Belmont, Kansas City, MO, 64123. Contact: David Garnett, Gen. Mgr. - Tel: (816) 231-2300. Direct sale of safety equipment for babies. Person should enjoy speaking to expectant couples. Established: 1937 - Franchising Since: 1962 - No. of Units: Company Owned: 8 - Franchised: 56 - Total Inv: $6,800 - Financing: Yes.

BELLINI JUVENILE DESIGNER FURNITURE
Bellini Juvenile Designer Furniture Corp.
1305 Second Ave., New City, NY, 10021. Contact: Irving Freeberg, Mkt. Dir. - Tel: (212) 517-9233. European designer furniture for infants & juveniles - also related accessories. Established: 1982 - Franchising

Since: 1983 - No. of Units: Company Owned: 8 - Franchised: 47 - Franchise Fee: $25,000 - Royalty: 5% - Total Inv: $110,000 - $140,000 plus fran. fee - Financing: None, will assist.

BUILDING BLOCKS, INC. *
1720 Post Rd. E., Ste. 112, Westport, CT, 06880. Contact: Russ Fein, Dir. of Fran. - Tel: (203) 256-4380. Educational and developmental specialty toy stores. Established: 1987 - Franchising Since: 1995 - No. of Units: Company Owned: 14 - Franchise Fee: $25,000 - Royalty: 5%, 1% adv. - Total Inv: $150,000 - $250,000 - Financing: No.

BZIRCUS *
Bzircus Franchise Corporation
53 Water St., Lebanon, NJ, 08833. Contact: Frank Anthony, Exec. VP - Tel: (908) 832-9315. BZIRCUS brings large regional theme park fun into the communities where the more than 50 million US kids and their families live. BZIRCUS features proprietary costumed characters, specialized entertainment, and multiple revenue points: vending and game machines, rides, retail product sales, birthday and group packages, food and drink sales. BZIRCUS is the only franchise to meet the entertainment needs of preschoolers to adults in this $800 million industry. Established: 1995 - Franchising Since: 1995 - No. of Units: Company Owned: 1 - Franchise Fee: $50,000 - Royalty: 8% royalty based on gross sales - Total Inv: $1.7 to $2.2 million - Financing: Assistance provided in sourcing financing options. Internal financing not available.

Frank Anthony
Executive Vice President

Bzircus Franchise Corporation
53 Water Street
Lebanon, NJ 08833
908-832-9315 Fax 908-832-9358

CHILDREN'S ORCHARD
Children's Orchard, Inc.
315 E. Eisenhower Pkwy., Ste. 316, Ann Arbor, MI, 48108. Contact: Walt Hamilton, Pres. - Tel: (313) 994-9199. National franchise of upscale children's resale boutiques. Buy and sell new and nearly new children's clothing, toys and equipment. Comprehensive 15-day training in operations, marketing, management, etc. Unparalleled ongoing support. Established: 1980 - Franchising Since: 1985 - No. of Units: Franchised: 62 - Franchise Fee: $14,500 - $19,500 - Royalty: 6%; then declining scale, 1.5% adv. - Total Inv: $50,000 - $98,000 incl. license fee, work. cap., leasehold, inventory, rent, deposits - Financing: SBA.

COMPUTERTOTS
ECW Corp.
10132 Colvin Run Rd., Great Falls, VA, 22066. Contact: Kevin Scharback, Dir. of Fran. Dev. - Tel: (703) 759-2556, Fax: (703) 759-1938. Computer education classes for young children offered on site at daycare centers, schools, community centers and other sites. Established: 1983 - Franchising Since: 1989 - No. of Units: Franchised: 144 - Franchise Fee: $25,900 - Royalty: 6%, 1% - Total Inv: $31,900 Fran. fee & start up - Financing: No.

EXPLORATIONS
Explorations Franchise Group, Inc.
902 Clint Moore Rd., Ste. 136, Boca Raton, FL, 33487-2846. Contact: Chuck Woolweave, V.P. Fran. - Tel: (407) 998-3435. Children's fitness and entertainment centers featuring proprietary play structures, licensed characters, full-view restaurant, arcade, classes & programs and merchandise. Established: 1993 - Franchising Since: 1994 - No. of Units: Company Owned: 1 - Franchised: 12 - Franchise Fee: $30,000 - Royalty: 5% - Total Inv: $460,000 - Financing: No.

FIT-BY-FIVE
Perkins Fit by Five Inc.
1606 Penfield Rd., Rochester, NY, 14625. Contact: Judith Webster, Program Dir. - Tel: (716) 586-7980. Pre-school physical fitness program for children 2-5 yrs. old. Academics are taught through physical fitness, sports, games, and movement. Can also be incorporated into existing programs. Established: 1969 - Franchising Since: 1991 - No. of Units: Company Owned: 1 - Franchised: 1 - Licensed: 17 - License Fee: $6,000 - Royalty: $2,000 annual renewal fee - Total Inv: $20,000 - Financing: No.

FIZZ KIDS
Fizz Kids of America Franchising, Inc.
576 South Rd., Poughkeepsie, NY, 12601. Contact: Gordon Weiss - Tel: (914) 463-0234, (800) 521-2223. Indoor child soft play centers, offer fun, food, parties & excercise. Established: 1992 - Franchising Since: 1992 - No. of Units: Franchised: 3 - Franchise Fee: $25,000 - Royalty: 6%, 2% adv. - Total Inv: $410,000 - $530,000 incl. buildout & equip. - Financing: Yes. For further franchise information, contact Fizz Kids, (800) 521-2223.

FRENCH TOAST
Lollytgos Ltd.
100 W. 33rd St., Ste. 1012, New York, NY, 10001-2900. Contact: Craig Kalter, V.P. Licensing - Tel: (212) 594-4740. Children's apparel/footwear & accessories. Established: 1955 - Franchising Since: 1990 - No. of Units: 12 Licensed Accessory Mfrs. - Franchise Fee: Negotiable - Royalty: 6% - Total Inv: $250,000 - Financing: None.

FRIDAY NITE LIVE! INC.
1901 N. Central Expy., Ste. 220, Richardson, TX, 75080. Contact: Dale Oakes, Pres. - Tel: (214) 644-2292, Fax: (214) 470-9295. Youth entertainment for ages 9 to 14 one night a week on either Friday or Saturday night from 7:00pm to 11:00pm. Established: 1989 - Franchising Since: 1991 - No. of Units: Company Owned: 1 - Franchised: 32 - Franchise Fee: $7,500 to $10,000 - Royalty: 75¢ per child - Total Inv: $15,000 - Financing: No.

FUNDAZZLE
Little Fun Station, Inc.
500 Newport Ctr. Dr., Ste. 740, Newport Beach, CA, 92660. Contact: Brenda Jones, Corporate Administration - Tel: (714) 640-0857. FunDazzle, where kids learn to play and play to learn, giant indoor children's playground with Kids Gourmet Restaurant, unique children's toys and novelties gift shop, private birthday/celebration party rooms, and Club FunDazzle Children's Educational & Fun Activity & Drop-Off Child-Care Programs. Established: 1991 - Franchising Since: 1994 - No. of Units: Company Owned: 2 - Franchise Fee: $100,000 - Royalty: 5%, 2% adv. - Total Inv: $1,000,000.

FUTUREKIDS, INC.
5777 W. Century Blvd., #1555, Los Angeles, CA, 90045. Contact: Fran. Dev. - Tel: (800) 876-5444, (310) 337-7006, Fax: (310) 337-9346. Computer learning centers for children ages 3-15. Established: 1983 - Franchising Since: 1989 - No. of Units: Company Owned: 1 - Franchised: 435 - Franchise Fee: $26,500 - Royalty: $360 + 10%/mo. - Total Inv: $80,000 - $115,000 - Financing: No.

GODDARD SCHOOL, THE
Carousel Systems
20 Creek Rd., Glen Mills, PA, 19342. Contact: Phil Schumacher, Dir. Center Dev. - Tel: (610) 558-3700, ext. 15. High quality pre-school offering day-care hours - All teachers have 4 year degrees in early childhood or elementary education. Established: 1986 - Franchising

Since: 1988 - No. of Units: Company Owned: 6 - Franchised: 12 - Franchise Fee: $25,000 - Royalty: 7% - Total Inv: $184,000 - Financing: Assistance available.

GYM DANDY FOR TOTS
3290 Tierney Pl., New York, NY, 10465. Contact: Bob Arenholz, V.P. - Tel: (800) 831-6283. Parent-toddler play and party program. Established: 1983 - Franchising Since: 1990 - No. of Units: Company Owned: 1 - Franchised: 9 - Franchise Fee: $22,000 - Royalty: 6%, 2% adv. - Total Inv: $44,000.

GYM ROMPERS
Gym Rompers Franchise, Inc.
1140 City Park Ave., New Orleans, LA, 70119. Contact: Peggy Bolton, Mktg. Dir. - Tel: (504) 833-6380. Children's music/movement/learning program. Established: 1984 - Franchising Since: 1993 - No. of Units: Company Owned: 2 - Franchised: 1 - Franchise Fee: $10,000 - Royalty: 5% gross - Total Inv: $13,000 equip. - Financing: None.

GYMBOREE
The Gymboree Corporation
700 Airport Blvd., Ste. 200, Burlingame, CA, 94010. Contact: Bob Campbell, Dir. Fran. Dev. - Tel: (415) 696-7440. A parent/child play program for ages newborn through 5 years of age. Using custom-designed equipment, sensory integration theory, positive parenting, child development principles and the importance of play. Established: 1976 - Franchising Since: 1978 - No. of Units: Company Owned: 9 - Franchised: 378 - Franchise Fee: $14,000 - $27,000 - Royalty: 6% of gross sales - Total Inv: $50,000 - $60,000 - Financing: None

GYMNASTICS IN MOTION/KANGAROO KIDS, INC.
5728 Maplecrest Rd., Ft. Wayne, IN, 46815-3879. Contact: Mary McGaharan, Pres. - Tel: (219) 485-2524. Classes in gymnastics for kids (18 months and up) and adults, including bars, beams, vaulting, tumbling, mini and full sized trampolines. Established: 1981 - Franchising Since: 1983 - No. of Units: 2 - Franchise Fee: $2,000 - Royalty: 10% gross - Total Inv: $10,000 - Financing: No.

GYMSTERS INC.
6111 Paseo Pueblo Dr., San Jose, CA, 95120-2741. Contact: Lonnie Coppock, Pres. - Tel: (408) 997-6997. The sports skill program that comes to kids at private schools, daycare centers, etc.; specialize in providing physical education instruction for children from two through twelve. Established: 1980 - Franchising Since: 1988 - No. of Units: Company Owned: 1 - Franchised: 8 - Franchise Fee: $12,000 - Royalty: 7%; 3% adv. - Total Inv: $18,000 - $25,000 - Financing: No.

HEAD OVER HEELS
Head Over Heels Franchise System, Inc.
#1 Independence Plaza, Ste. 414, Birmingham, AL, 35209. Contact: Renee O'Neal, Dir. of Fran. Sales - Tel: (205) 879-6305, (800) 850-3547. Head Over Heels is a creative gymnastics program for children ages three and up. Head Over Heels works to develop strength, balance, flexibility and overall body coordination in each child. Established: 1990 - Franchising Since: 1993 - No. of Units: Company Owned: 2 - Franchised: 6 - Franchise Fee: Equal to the aggregate registration fees and the first month's tuition for each student - Royalty: 10% on first 300,000 gross revenues/ 8% on next $200,000 and 6% on anything in excess of $500,000 - Total Inv: $21,000 - $38,000 - Financing: On equipment and computer only.

HIGH TOUCH - HIGH TECH *
High Touch Investment Corp.
7908 Wiles Rd., Coral Springs, FL, 33067. Contact: Daniel Shaw, Pres. & CEO - Tel: (305) 755-2900, Fax: (305) 755-1242. Hands-on science experiences for children serving schools as an in-school field trip. Also science birthday parties for children. Established: 1990 - Franchising Since: 1994 - No. of Units: Company Owned: 2 - Franchised: 10 - Franchise Fee: $50,000 - Royalty: 7% gross sales - Total Inv: $50,000 + $8,000 - $10,000 in start-up costs - Financing: Yes, offer 20-30% financing.

IDENT-A-KID PROGRAM
Ident-A-Kid Services of America
2810 Scherer Dr., Ste. 100, St. Petersburg, FL, 33716. Contact: Robert King, Pres. - Tel: (813) 577-4646. Provides parents with laminated I.D. cards containing child's photograph, fingerprint, and physical description. Marketed through public and private schools as a "parent option" program. Established: 1986 - Franchising Since: 1986 - No. of Units: Company Owned: 1 - Franchised: 170 - Franchise Fee: $12,500 - Royalty: None - Total Inv: $12,500 - Financing: None.

IMAGIMAZE FAMILY FUN CENTERS *
Developing Concepts, Inc.
7710 Chateau, Meadville, PA, 16335. Contact: Tom Nickerson, Pres. - Tel: (814) 724-8300. An Imagimaze Family Fun Center is a business that caters to the booming 2 to 12 year old market with an adult friendly offering of first-class food, soft playground, games, merchandise and party facilities. Established: 1993 - Franchising Since: 1993 - No. of Units: Franchised: 4 - Franchise Fee: $25,000 - Royalty: 5% 1st 3 yrs., 4% yrs. 4-6, 3% yrs. 7-10, 1% nat'l. adv. Total Inv: $362,000 - $537,000 depend. on size - Financing: Source assistance provided.

IMAGINE TOMORROW® *
I To The Future, Ltd.
1095 Mt. Kemble Ave., Morristown, NJ, 07960. Contact: David Dunne, Marketing - Tel: (201) 425-1608, Fax: (201) 425-1618. Multimedia education centers which incorporate the latest computer and communication technology in an academic enrichment program for children. Established: 1991 - Franchising Since: 1994 - No. of Units: Company Owned: 3 - Franchised: 8 - Franchise Fee: $23,000 - Royalty: 10% of monthly gross - Total Inv: $33,000 to $98,000 depending if equip. is leased or purchased, plus fran. fee - Financing: Partial for qualified entrepreneurs.

ISLANDMANIA *
IslandMania Franchise Corp.
520 Falls Watch Cir., Alpharetta, GA, 30202. Contact: Kirk Price, Pres. - Tel: (770) 751-6361. Children's indoor playground. Established: 1995 - Franchising Since: 1995 - No. of Units: Company Owned: 1 - Franchise Fee: $35,000 - Royalty: 8% - Total Inv: $300,000 to $750,000 - Financing: No.

J.W. TUMBLES®, A CHILDREN'S GYM
J.W. Tumbles Licensing Corp.
12750 Carmel Country Rd., #A102, San Diego, CA, 92130-2159. Contact: Melissa Woods, Dir. of Fran. - Tel: (800) 886-2532, (619) 481-5576. A gym just for children 4 months to 9 years of age - classes are packed with challenging non-competitive activities - physical skills, coordination, balance, sports skills and more. Each class is individualized to help children develop a healthy body and good self-esteem. Established: 1985 - Franchising Since: 1993 - No. of Units: Company Owned: 1 - Franchise Fee: $25,000 - Royalty: 5%, 1% adv. first 5 months below 5% - Total Inv: $99,600 (includes fran. fee) - Financing: No.

KANGAKAB INC.
4001 - F Rt. 73 & Lincoln Dr. W., Marlton, NJ, 08053. Contact: David Parkin, V.P. - Tel: (609) 424-5437. Transportation service for kids. Established: 1992 - Franchising Since: 1993 - No. of Units: Company Owned: 1 - Franchised: 7 - Franchise Fee: $18,500 - Royalty: 5% after 6 months - Total Inv: $34,000 - Financing: No.

KID KINGDOM
15965 Jeanette St., Southfield, MI, 48075. Contact: Colleen McGaffey - Tel: (810) 557-2784, Fax: (810) 557-7931. Family physical fitness and fun indoor play park in a safe, clean, climate-controlled supervised environment that stimulates children's imagination and challenges them physically. Kid Kingdom is a place where parents and their children can have hours of fun together. Safe and imaginative play is a concept that will never grow old... Established: 1993 - Franchising Since: 1994 - No. of Units: Company Owned: 1 - Franchised: 4 - Franchise Fee: $30,000 - Royalty: 5% - Total Inv: $400,000 - $650,000 - Financing: Yes.

KID SECURE OF AMERICA
D&K Enterprises Inc.
3216 Commander Dr., Ste. 101, Dept. 17, Carrollton, TX, 75006. Contact: Marketing Dept. - Tel: (214) 248-9100. Finally a business you can be proud of while earning an excellent income. The card contains all

the vital information required in an emergency. Cards sell best through schools, kindergartens, business sponsors and community organizations. Franchising Since: 1987 - No. of Units: Company Owned: 1 - Franchised: 30 in 12 states in 3 countries - Total Inv: $6,995 (complete turn-key package) - Financing: Yes.

KID TO KID *
Kid to Kid Franchise System, Inc.
406 W. South Jordan Pkwy., Ste. 160, South Jordan, UT, 84095. Contact: Brent Sloan, Pres. - Tel: (801) 553-8799, Fax: (801) 553-8793. Retail sale of gently-used children's products sold in upscale stores. Recycling that makes sense! Established: 1992 - Franchising Since: 1994 - No. of Units: Franchised: 9 - Franchise Fee: $20,000 - Royalty: 5% of gross sales, .5% of gross sales mktg. fund - Total Inv: $88,000 - $116,000 depending on location - Financing: None, but will assist.

KID'S KAB
Kid's Kab, Inc.
2701 Troy Center Dr., #291, Troy, MI, 48084-4741. Contact: Gene O'Neil, V.P., Fran. Operations - Tel: (810) 362-8280. Family transportation. Established: 1991 - Franchising Since: 1992 - No. of Units: Company Owned: 1- Franchised: 23 - Franchise Fee: $26,000 - Royalty: 5%, 3% adv. - Total Inv: $43,000 - Financing: No.

KIDDIE ACADEMY LEARNING CENTERS
Kiddie Academy International, Inc.
108 Wheel Rd., Ste. 200, Bel Air, MD, 21015. Contact: Beth Howard, V.P. Fran. Dev. - Tel: (800) 554-3343. Premier developer of Early Learning Centers. We offer advanced, state-of-the-art curriculum for infant through 12 years of age. Established: 1979 - Franchising Since: 1992 - No. of Units: Company Owned: 4 - Franchised: 79 - Franchise Fee: $30,000 - Royalty: 7% (no adv. fund) - Total Inv: $130,000 - $216,000 ($40,000 cash, $45,000 equity needed to meet loan req.) - Financing: Yes.

KIDDING AROUND
Just Kidding, Inc.
728 Center St., P.O .Box 550, Lewiston, NY, 14092-0550. Contact: Celie Grove, Fran. Dir. - Tel: (716) 754-4669. Taxi service for children to school, hockey practice, dance class, etc. Established: 1989 - Franchising Since: 1994 - No. of Units: Company Owned: 1 - Franchised: 5 - Franchise Fee: $25,000 - Royalty: 6%, 1% nat'l. adv. - Total Inv: $100,000 - $210,000 incl. fran. fee - Financing: No.

KIDS AGAIN *
Kids Again, Inc.
11837 Dublin Blvd., Dublin, CA, 94568. Contact: Ken Pfeifer, Dir., Fran. Sales - Tel: (800) 828-0819, (510) 803-0540, Fax: (510) 803-0691. Specialty resale stores for infant/children's apparel, toys, furniture and accessories. Established: 1985 - Franchising Since: 1993 - No. of Units: Company Owned: 1 - Franchise Fee: $18,000 - Royalty: 5% gross sales, 1% adv. - Total Inv: $65,000 to $71,000: $35,000 store set up, $12,000 work. cap., $18,000 fran. fee - Financing: No.

KINDERDANCE INTERNATIONAL
268 N. Babcock St., Ste. A, Melbourne, FL, 32935. Contact: Bernard Friedman, V.P. - Tel: (800) 554-2334. Educational dance, gymnastic and creative movement program taught to pre-school children in child care centers & other viable locations. Established: 1979 - Franchising Since: 1985 - No. of Units: Franchised: 74 - Franchise Fee: $12,000 - $21,000+ - Royalty: 6% - 10% - Total Inv: $2,550 to $5,600 in addition to fran. fee - Financing: Yes.

LITTLE GYM, THE
Little Gym International, Inc., The
8180 N. Hayden Rd., #D-200, Scottsdale, AZ, 85258. Contact: Rick Adams, Exec. V.P. of Fran. Dev. - Tel: (602) 948-2878, (800) 418-2878, Fax: (602) 948-2878. The Little Gym fitness centers for children age 4 months to 12 years offer a unique, integrated approach to child development that not only teaches basic motor skills, gymnastics, sportskill development and karate, but also helps build positive self-esteem and a love for physical exercise. Established: 1976 - Franchising Since: 1992 - No. of Units: Company Owned: 4 - Franchised: 106 - Franchise Fee: $32,500 - Royalty: 8% ff, 1% mktg. - Total Inv: $110,000: fran. fee, $11,000 equip, $61,500 operating cap. - Financing: None.

MONDAY MORNING MOMS
Monday Morning America, Inc.
276 White Oak Ridge Rd., Bridgewater, NJ, 08807-1532. Contact: Warren Schmidt, Pres. - Tel: (908) 526-4884. Family day care management service, recruiting family day care providers into a privately managed network, comprehensively servicing the family day care providers, and marketing the network to parents and employers in need of quality child care. Established: 1981 - Franchising Since: 1990 - No. of Units: Franchised: 5 - Franchise Fee: $9,000 - Royalty: 6% of revenue - Total Inv: $14,000 - $28,000 - Financing: No.

ONCE UPON A CHILD *
Grow Biz International
4200 Dahlberg Dr., Minneapolis, MN, 55422. Contact: Steve Gemlo, V.P., Fran. Dev. - Tel: (612) 520-8500, Fax: (612) 520-8501. Ultra high value retail store that buys and sells new and used brand name children's apparel, furniture and toys. Established: 1985 - Franchising Since: 1993 - No. of Units: Company Owned: 8 - Franchised: 148 - Franchise Fee: $20,000 - Royalty: 5% - Total Inv: $80,000 to $138,000 - Financing: SBA financing available, up to two-thirds of capital.

PEE WEE WORKOUT
Cardiac Carr Co.
34976 Aspenwood Ln., Willoughby, OH, 44094. Contact: Margi Carr, Pres. - Tel: (216) 946-7888. Aerobic fitness program for children. Established: 1986 - Franchising Since: 1987 - No. of Units: Company Owned: 1 - Franchised: 19 - Franchise Fee: $1,500 - Royalty: 10% - Total Inv: $2,000 - Financing: No.

PERSONALIZED BOOKS
D & K Enterprises Inc.
3216 Commander Dr., #101 , Carrollton, TX, 75006-3518. Contact: Thomas Mosey, V.P. - Tel: (214) 248-9100. The creation of a full personalized hard bound, full color childrens book in only 4 minutes. Established: 1987 - Franchising Since: 1988 - No. of Units: Company Owned: 4 - Franchised: 350 - Franchise Fee: $2,495 - Total Inv: $5,000 - Financing: Yes.

PERSONALIZED CHILDREN'S BOOKS
Best Personalized Books, Inc.
4201 Airborne, Dallas, TX, 75248. Contact: Sales Department - Tel: (800) 275-7770, (214) 250-1000. Make money with a computer. Print personalized children's books at home or on location in just 3 minutes. Low start-up, high profit. Distributors receive a lifetime license to produce this patented product. License includes software and technical and marketing support. Also customize invitations, stationery, audio cassettes, business cards and holiday letters. Established: 1991 - Franchising Since: 1991 - No. of Units: Company Owned: 1 - Franchised: 3,000 - Franchise Fee: $1,995 - Royalty: No royalty - Total Inv: $1,995 - Financing: Best Personalized Books will finance Visa, Mastercard or Discover.

PRE-FIT FRANCHISES, INC.
Pre-Fit, Inc.
10340 So. Western Ave., Chicago, IL, 60643. Contact: Latrice Lee, Fran. Dir. - Tel: (312) 233-7771. A mobile preschool fitness program of sports, exercise, and health. Franchisees are trained to market schools and conduct on-site physical education classes for children two through six years of age. Franchisees also receive uniforms and start-up equipment. Established: 1987 - Franchising Since: 1992 - No. of Units: Company Owned: 1 - Franchised: 31 - Franchise Fee: $6,500 - Royalty: 10% - Total Inv: $7,000 - $7,500.

PRECIOUS PLACES
Precious Places, Ltd.
8321 Linden Oaks Court, Lorton, VA, 22079. Contact: Gary Hobar, V.P. Mktg. & Fran. - Tel: (800) 937-6880 or (703) 690-0854. Shop-at-home service for decorating children's rooms. Established: 1989 - Franchising Since: 1993 - No. of Units: Company Owned: 1 - Franchised: 3 - Franchise Fee: $9,000 - Royalty: 7% - Total Inv: $2,720 - $8,800 + fran. fee - Financing: No.

PROMISES FULFILLED
Promises Marketing Int'l.
2060 Whalen Ave., Merrick, NY, 11566. Contact: Louise Levine, V.P. - Tel: (516) 623-2424, Fax: (516) 623-2424. Child's Wonderland. Everything personalized with child's name. Custom orders filled. Artwork to coordinate with child's room. Place where childrens' dreams come true. Training available. Established: 1982 - Franchising Since: 1988 - No. of Units: Franchised: 8 - Franchise Fee: $25,000 - Royalty: 5% - Total Inv: $125,000 - Financing: Will assist.

RAINBOWLAND, INC.
1210 New Haven Rd., Naugatuck, CT, 06770. Contact: Joseph B. Goetschius Jr., Pres. - Tel: (203) 729-0013. A corporate, commercial, or domestic day care and nursery school operating under the franchisor's trademark Rainbowland and according to the franchisor's methods and systems of operation. Established: 1984 - Franchising Since: 1990 - No. of Units: Company Owned: 1 - Franchise Fee: Domestic-$7,500, Commercial-$18,000, Corporate-$25,000 - Royalty: 5% net gross sales - Estimated Total Inv: $26,080 - $183,895 including franc. fee - Financing: no franchisor financing; will provide financing assistance.

ROMP AROUND
Romp Around Fun Centers, Inc.
215 Rt. 22 E., Green Brook, NJ, 08812. Contact: Shelley Davimos, COO - Tel: (908) 752-1818 Ext. 24. Childrens indoor play center. 10,000 - 12,000 sq. ft. rec. Includes climbing apparatus, ballpits, slides. Much of business is in birthday parties. Established: 1993 - Franchising Since: 1994 - No. of Units: Company Owned: 2 - Franchised: 1 - Franchise Fee: $35,000 - Royalty: 7% + 4% adv. - Total Inv: $402,000 - $729,000 - Financing: No.

SAFE-T-CHILD
Safe-T-Child, Inc.
401 Friday Mountain Rd., Austin, TX, 78737. Contact: Dennis Wagner, V.P. - Tel: (512) 288-2882. Proven business offers a child safety service that helps keeps children safe in the 90's. Provides an exceptional opportunity for emotional satisfaction and profit. The Safe-T-Child program is easily marketed through child cares, schools, churches and community organizations. Immediate Response I.D. card and nationally acclaimed educational products for parent and child. Card contains vital information that is often overlooked. Established: 1987 - Franchising Since: 1992 - No. of Units: Company Owned: 1 - Franchised: 80 - Franchise Fee: $12,900 - Royalty: None - Total Inv: $15,000 incl. fran. fee - Financing: None.

SIMPLICITY SEWING & CRAFT CENTER
Simplicity Sewing & Craft Centers Int'l.
815 N. Red Rock Rd., #10, St. George, UT, 84770. Contact: Carolyn Curtis, Owner - Tel: (801) 628-7505, Fax: (801) 628-7985. Simplicity Sewing & Craft Centers - teaching sewing to kids thru adults. Courses in clothing apparel to home decor. Established: 1989 - Licensing Since: 1991 - No. of Units: Licensed: 615 - License Fee: $299 - Royalty: 10%, $100 per mo. - Total Inv: $299 to join (license) less than $1,000 - Financing: No.

SITTERS ON SITE
SOS Sales, Inc.
210 Abbott Rd. #44, East Lansing, MI, 48823-4348. Contact: Karen Kayes, Legal Counsel - Tel: (860) 721-1411. Child and senior care placement and referral agency. Complete system computerized and training provided. Established: 1987 - Franchising Since: 1991 - No. of Units: Franchised: 3 - Franchise Fee: $10,000 - Royalty: $50. monthly service fee - Total Inv: $15,700: (fran. fee, $5,200 start-up, $500. work cap.) - Financing: Yes.

TODDLIN' TIME
Toddlin' Time, Inc.
8084 Station Rd., Manassas, VA, 22111-2558. Contact: Tanya Wallace, Pres. - Tel: (703) 361-2945. Parent/toddler playgym. Established: 1990 - Franchising Since: 1992 - No. of Units: Franchised: 14 - Franchise Fee: $5,000 - Royalty: Annual membership $450 ($100 for adv.) - Financing: No.

TOY TRADERS *
Toy Traders Franchise, Inc.
4334 Leland St., Chevy Chase, MD, 20007. Contact: Nancy Schwartz, Mktg. Dir. - Tel: (301) 718-6188. Secondhand toy store where people can sell outgrown toys and buy "good as new" ones at half of the original retail price. Established: 1980 - Franchising Since: 1995 - No. of Units: Company Owned: 3 - Franchise Fee: $20,000 - Royalty: 5%, 1.5% adv. - Total Inv: $50,000 incl. fran. fee - Financing: No.

TUTOR TIME CHILD CARE LEARNING CENTERS
Tutor Time Child Care Systems, Inc.
4517 NW 31st Ave., Ft. Lauderdale, FL, 33309. Contact: Linda Weissman, Dir., Public Relations - Tel: (800) 275-1235, Fax: (305) 730-7550. Child care franchise, chosen by NASA to be their exclusive child care providers at Kennedy Space Center. Tutor Time's beautiful state of the art facilities offer top quality child care and a high tech curriculum. Rated the #1 child care franchise three years running. Established: 1979 - Franchising Since: 1990 - No. of Units: Company Owned: 7 - Franchised: 228 - Franchise Fee: $32,000 - $63,000 for multiple commitment - Royalty: 5% plus 1% regional adv. & 1% national adv. - Total Inv: $175,000 - $200,000 incl. work. cap. - Financing: Yes.

USA BABY
Baby's Room USA, Inc.
857 N. Larch Ave., Elmhurst, IL, 60126. Contact: Janet Hughes, Fran. Coord. - Tel: (708) 832-9880, Fax: (708) 832-0139. Juvenile and children's furniture and accessories. Established: 1975 - Franchising Since: 1986 - No. of Units: Company Owned: 9 - Franchised: 46 - Franchise Fee: $7,500 - $16,500 - Royalty: 3% - Total Inv: $200,000 - $250,000 - Financing: None.

CLEANING PRODUCTS AND SERVICES

A-1 WINDOW CLEANING *
727 Main St., Niagara Falls, NY, 14301. Contact: Vincent Agnello, Fran. Cons. - Legal - Tel: (716) 285-2533. Residential and commercial window cleaning. A 1-800 number call in for service. Regional territory. Established: 1995 - No. of Units: Company Owned: 1 - Franchise Fee: $34,500 incl. truck, equip. & uniform - Royalty: 10% plus 2% adv. - Financing: Assistance.

A-1 WINDOW RESIDENTIAL & COMMERCIAL CLEANING *
5 Colombia Dr., Ste. 176, Niagara Falls, NY, 14305. Contact: Wm. Siarto, Fran. Dev. - Tel: (905) 356-4242, Fax: (905) 356-9373. Corporate identity residential & commercial cleaning for single person or group seeking corporate identity and marketing. Established: 1996 - Franchising Since: 1996 - Franchise Fee: State Master franchise $25,000, Single Franchise: $1,000 - Royalty: 10%, 3% adv. - Total Inv: $200 - Financing: No.

ACOUSTIC CLEAN
Tangible Research & Development Corp.
2901 Wayzata Blvd., Minneapolis, MN, 55405. Contact: Gordon Hamilton, Pres. - Tel: (612) 374-1105, Fax: (612) 374-4840. One of the oldest, largest, and most reputable firms in the ceiling cleaning industry, giant mist, low pressure tank system with a 20 year unmatched history of perfection in cleaning all types of soiling on walls and ceilings. Low overhead, high margin of profit: Over 400 dealers worldwide have been trained. Established: 1978 - Franchising Since: 1985 - No. of Units: Company Owned: 1 - Franchised: International - Financing: Lease purchase.

AIRE-MASTER OF AMERICA
Aire-Master of America, Inc.
Hwy. CC, P.O. Box 2310, Nixa, MO, 65714. Contact: David Burton, Fran. Dir. - Tel: (417) 725-2691. Restroom deodorizing and disinfecting, deodorizing for all rooms. Established: 1958 - Franchising Since: 1976 - No. of Units: Company Owned: 5 - Franchised: 50 - Franchise Fee: $15,000 - Royalty: 5% of monthly sales and service gross - Total Inv: $30,000 start up cash, $30,000 - $75,000 total inv. - Financing: 50% of franchise fee to qualified applicants.

AMERICAN AIR CARE, INC.
4751 Lydell Rd., Cheverly, MD, 20781. Contact: Eric Moreno, V.P. Operations - Tel: (301) 772-2000. Professional commercial & residential air duct cleaning. Established: 1961 - Franchising Since: 1990 - No. of Units: Company Owned: 1 - Franchised: 2 - Franchise Fee: $25,500 - Royalty: 7% - 10% - Total Inv: $108,000 - $180,000 - Financing: 3rd Party financing to qualified individuals.

AMERICAN GRAFFITI *
International American Graffiti Franchising Corp.
10331 IH 35 North, San Antonio, TX, 78217. Contact: Andrew Taylor, Pres. - Tel: (210) 653-3535. Graffiti removal. Established: 1992 - Franchising Since: 1995 - No. of Units: Franchised: 6 - Franchise Fee: $15,000 - Royalty: 7% of gross sales - Total Inv: $30,000 to $60,000: fran. fee, $15,000 equip., $15,000 vehicle, start up cost - Financing: Yes.

AMERICAN RESTORATION SERVICES
American Exterior Cleaning Corp.
2061 Monongahela Ave., Pittsburgh, PA, 15218. Contact: Russell K. Case, Pres. - Tel: (800) 245-1617. An international company specializing in exterior and interior cleaning systems. These systems, which use exclusive spray-on/rinse-off formulas, are clean, fast, and environmentally safe. Established: 1970 - Franchising Since: 1976 - No. of Units: Company Owned: 1 - Franchised: 255 in 26 states in 5 countries - Franchise Fee: $12,500 - Royalty: $1,500 renewal fee, $300.00 advertising fee - Total Inv: $22,500 (includes fran. fee) - Financing: Partial financing available through leasing company.

AMERICAN ROOF-BRITE
SPR International, Inc.
3398 Sanford Dr., Marietta, GA, 30066. Contact: Larry Stevens, Pres. - Tel: (404) 429-0232. Clean ugly, stained asphalt roofing shingles. Used by asphalt shingle manufacturers. High demand business, little or no competition. Established: 1990 - Franchising Since: 1990 - No. of Units: Company Owned: 1 - Franchised: 27 - Franchise Fee: $5,995 - Financing: None.

ANAGO INTERNATIONAL, INC., ANAGO OF DETROIT, INC.
Anago International, Inc.
1515 University Dr., Ste. 226, Coral Springs, FL, 33071. Contact: David E. Povlitz, Pres. - Tel: (305) 341-3768, (305) 341-3331. Commercial cleaning franchisor. Start your business with as little as $1,000 down payment and 0 - $10,000 per month in annual contracts, excellent training program. Master franchises avail. in your area, nice profit potential. Established: 1989 - Franchising Since: 1991 - No. of Units: Company Owned: 2 - Franchised: 65 - Franchise Fee: $5,400 - $18,950 plus - Royalty: 10% - Financing: $5,400 - $18,950+.

BLACK MAGIC PRESSURE WASHING *
Haldorn & Mann, Inc.
55 Hercules Dr., Colchester, VT, 05446. Contact: Max Pelleria, V.P. - Tel: (800) 334-1497, (802) 655-4121, Fax: (802) 655-4129. Commercial restaurant duct cleaning. We provide training, marketing aids, equipment and chemical for the pressure washing of restaurant kitchen exhaust ducts. Established; 1987 - Franchising Since: 1988 - No. of Independents: 250+ - Total Inv: $7,480 - Financing: Some.

BRITE SITE
4616 W. Fullerton, Chicago, IL, 60639-1896. Contact: Andreas Vassilos, Pres. - Tel: (312) 772-7300. Providing cleaning services to retailers in defined territories. Established: 1971 - Franchising Since: 1992 - No. of Units: Company Owned: 2 - Franchise Fee: $20,000 - Royalty: 10% - Total Inv: $5,000 - $10,000 work. cap. + fran. fee; balance vehicles & equip. - Total Inv: $37,000 - $75,000 - Financing: No.

BUCKET BRIGADE, INC.
2043 Creekside Dr., Wheaton, IL, 60187. Contact: Patricia Sebastian, Pres. - Tel: (708) 462-1149. Team home cleaning services and management. Established: 1979 - Franchising Since: 1982 - No. of Units: Company Owned: 1 - Franchised: 9 - Franchise Fee: $4,500-$6,500 - Total Inv: $5,300 - Royalty: 10% gross receipts.

BUILDING SERVICE AND MAINTENANCE
Servpro Industries
575 Airport Blvd. P.O. Box 1978, Gallatin, TN, 37066. Contact: Richard Isaacson, V.P. Mktg. - Tel: (615) 451-0200. Complete commercial cleaning services including janitorial, carpet, hard floor, window and ceiling cleaning, etc. Established: 1967 - Franchising Since: 1969 - No. of Units: Franchised: 40 - Franchise Fee: $12,000 - Royalty: 7% - 4% - Total Inv: $19,500 - Financing: Yes.

BUSY BEE MAID SERVICE INC.
3820 Premier Ave., Memphis, TN, 38118. Contact: Bill Richey - Tel: (901) 867-0600. Operate a residential home cleaning service. Established: 1990 - Royalty: 5% - Total Inv: $7,400 - $10,000.

CEILING CLEAN
D.P.L. Enterprises, Inc.
5115 S. Industrial Rd., Ste. 506, Las Vegas, NV, 89118. Contact: Richard Papaleo, Pres. - Tel: (702) 736-4063. Manufacture and distribute acoustic ceiling cleaning equipment and chemicals. Established: 1978 - Franchising Since: 1978 - No. of Units: Company Owned: 1 - Dealers: 305 - Total Inv: $12,500 - Financing: Yes.

CEILING DOCTOR
Ceiling Doctor Inc.
5151 Beltline Rd., Ste. 950, Dallas, TX, 75240. Contact: Rob Forrest, Chairman - Tel: (214) 702-8046. Specialty cleaning of commercial buildings. The role as the franchisee is that of a manager and a supervisor with employees doing the actual cleaning. Established: 1984 - Franchising Since: 1986 - No. of Units: Company Owned: 1 - Franchised: 105 - Franchise Fee: $10,000 - Royalty: 8% - Total Inv: $19,500 - Financing: No.

CEILTECH CEILING CLEANING
Ceiltech
825 Gatepark Dr. #3, Daytona Beach, FL, 32114. Contact: Charles Werz, V.P. - Tel: (800) 662-9299, Fax: (904) 239-9712. Manufacturer of acoustical ceiling and wall cleaning equipment featuring an exclusive nontoxic, nonflammable detergent based solution. Electrical sprayer backed by 10 year warrantee. Established: 1986 - Licensing Since: 1987 - No. of Units: Company Owned: 1 - Licensed: 1,043 - Total Inv: $5,995 to $7,995 - Financing: Leasing to qualified applicants, visa, amex, mc.

CHEMSTATION
ChemStation International
3400 Encrete Lane, Dayton, OH, 45439. Contact: Kip Knowles, Dir. of Operations - Tel: (513) 294-8265, Fax: (513) 294-5360. ChemStation is a service which manufacturers, sells, and distributes custom formulated industrial detergents by a containerless delivery system. Established: 1965 - Franchising Since: 1982 - No. of Units: Company Owned: 4 - Franchised: 27 - Franchise Fee: $25,000 - Royalty: 4%, 1% adv. - Total Inv: $150,000 equip. & inven., $150,000 work. cap., $25,000 fran. fee - Financing: For equity.

CLASSY MAIDS
Classy Maids USA, Inc.
P.O. Box 160879, Altamonte Springs, FL, 32716-0879. Contact: William Olday, Pres. - Tel: (800) 445-5238, Fax: (407) 862-4221. Multi-cleaning services franchise. Team cleaning. Professional image. Computer

management software available. Auto decals, equipment & supplies to get started is included in franc. fee. Complete training program customized to your needs. Low fees. Established: 1980 - Franchising Since: 1985 - No. of Units: Franchised: 7 - Franchise Fee: $2,900 - Royalty: 6% on total sales - Total Inv: $500+ (insurance start-up), $750 (grand opening), $500 (misc.) - Financing: Yes. 50% of franchise fee.

CLEANNET USA
9861 Broken Land Pkwy., Ste. 208, Columbia, MD, 21046. Contact: Dennis Urner, Sr. V.P. - Tel: (410) 720-6444. Commercial office cleaning and other commercial facilities - full service. Established: 1987 - Franchising Since: 1988 - No. of Units: Company Owned: 3 - Franchised: 886 - Franchise Fee: $2,950 to $32,000 - Royalty: 3% - Total Inv: $1,800 - $25,000 - Financing: Yes @ 9%.

CLENTECH ACOUSTIC CLEAN *
Tangible Research & Development Corp.
2901 Wayzata Blvd., Minneapolis, MN, 55405. Contact: Gordon Hamilton, Pres. - Tel: (612) 374-1105, Fax: (612) 374-4840. Acoustic ceiling and wall cleaning. Established: 1978 - Franchising Since: 1985 - No. of Units: Company Owned: 1 - Franchised: International.

COTTAGECARE
6323 W. 110th St., Overland Park, KS, 66211. Contact: Jacqueline M. Hall, Dir., Fran. Mktg. - Tel: (913) 469-8778. Housecleaning service - big business approach. Only 125 "Jumbo" (large demographically defined) territories in U.S. Highly interactive franchisor. We do all marketing, even to the extent of signing up and initially scheduling new customers through our corporate headquarter's telemarketing staff. Established: 1988 - Franchising Since: 1989 - No. of Units: Company Owned: 4 - Franchised: 16 - Franchise Fee: $15,500 - Royalty: 5.5% - Total Inv: $50,000 - $75,000: fran. fee, $24,000 mktg., balance for work. cap - Financing: Yes, franchise fee only.

COUSTIC-GLO
Coustic-Glo International, Inc.
7111 Ohms Lane, Minneapolis, MN, 55439. Contact: Scott Smith, V.P. - Tel: (612) 835-1338 . Ceiling & wall restoration, resurfacing and sanitation. Patented products clean, restore and/or change color. Regrid all ceilings while restoring acoustical/firerating. Also clean wall and retint vinyl wall coverings. 90% savings to property, 80% GMP to franchisee. Established: 1978 - Franchising Since: 1982 - No. of Units: Company Owned: 1 - Franchised: 196 - Franchise Fee: $12,000 - Royalty: 5%, 1% adv. - Total Inv: $12,000 - $15,000 - Financing: Limited.

COVERALL CLEANING CONCEPTS
Coverall North America, Inc.
3111 Camino Del Rio North, Ste. 950, San Diego, CA, 92108. Contact: Ken Sully, V.P. of Fran. Dev. - Tel: (800) 537-3371. Complete turnkey business includes training, equipment & supplies, and customer accounts. Services provided to franchisees include training, billing & collections, equipment leasing, insurance and volume purchasing discounts. Established: 1985 - Franchising Since: 1985 - No. of Units: Franchised: 3,500+ system-wide - Franchise Fee: $3,250 - $33,600 (9 different levels to choose from) - Royalty: 5% monthly - Total Inv: $3,600 - $37,100 - Financing: Partial, downpayment required, balance financed.

CUSTOM MAID, INC.
Cam Systems Inc.
14500 W. 8 Mile Rd., Ste. 301, Oak Park, MI, 48237. Contact: Shenell C. Toliver, Off. Mgr. - Tel: (810) 967-4002. Maid service for both domestic and commercial applications in the marketplace. A proven, time-tested system dedicated to the old fashioned tradition of quality maid service. An extensive training and support program with computerized or manual operations and management system. Established: 1982 - Franchising Since: 1987 - No. of Units: Company Owned: 1 - Franchised: 1 - Franchise Fee: $12,500 - Royalty: 8%, 1%-3% adv. - Total Inv: $28,000 - Financing: Limited.

DAYS EASE, INC.
473 Charing Cross, Grand Blanc, MI, 48439. Contact: Sally Tartoni, Pres. - Tel: (810) 694-3895. House cleaning service. Established: 1976 - Franchising Since: 1977 - No. of Units: Company Owned: 2 - Franchised: 3 - Franchise Fee: $7,500 - Total Inv: $10,000 - Royalty: 2% + 1% adv. - Financing: No.

DELTA JANITORIAL SYSTEMS, INC. *
2621 W. Airport Frwy. #210, Irving, TX, 75062. Contact: Rhona Springfield, Pres. - Tel: (214) 256-6475, Fax: (214) 256-4194. Janitorial broker. Established: 1975 - Franchising Since: 1981 - No. of Units: Franchised: 120 - Franchise Fee: $3,000 - Royalty: 6% admin., 4% royalty - Total Inv: $3,000 fran., $4,000 contracts, $500 supplies - Financing: Yes.

DIAL A MAID
D. M. Coughlin, Inc.
823 Oakdale Rd., Johnson City, NY, 13790. Contact: Dennis Coughlin, Sr., Pres. - Tel: (607) 798-8865. Maid service handling both residential and small commercial accounts. The team cleaning concept is employed, along with systems and procedures that have been developed for both quality and cost control. Established: 1983 - Franchising Since: 1986 - No. of Units: Company Owned: 1 - Franchised: 3 - Franchise Fee: $5,000 - $9,500 - Royalty: 6% + 2% adv. - Total Inv: $14,000 - $21,000 - Financing: None.

DRAIN TECH, INC.
540 Robeson St., Reading , PA, 19601. Contact: Eugene Tobolski, Pres. - Tel: (610) 372-8541. Plumbing contractor, sewer and drain cleaning, also general plumbing, repair and installation. Established: 1990 - Franchising Since: 1990 - No. of Units: Company Owned: 1 - Franchised: 2 - Franchise Fee: $15,000 - $25,000 - Royalty: varies 3% - 6% depending on program chosen - Total Inv: $10,000 - $25,000 - Financing: Yes.

DUCTBUSTERS
29160 U.S. Hwy. 19 N., Clearwater, FL, 34621. Contact: Erin Hill, Dir. of Mktg. - Tel: (813) 787-7087. Air conditioning duct cleaning, service, repair and installation. Established: 1985 - Franchising Since: 1992 - No. of Units: Company Owned: 1 - Franchised: 6 - Franchise Fee: $15,500 - Royalty: 7% of sales - Total Inv (excl. fran. fee): $20,000+ - Financing: No.

E.P.I.C. SYSTEMS, INC. *
4424 Vogel Rd., Ste. 204, Evansville, IN, 47715. Contact: Kenneth Godeice, V.P., Dev. - Tel: (812) 473-0442, Fax: (812) 473-0448. Commercial janitorial maintenance services, retail firm care & carpet cleaning programs. Established: 1993 - Franchising Since: 1994 - No. of Units: Company Owned: 1 - Franchised: 2 - Franchise Fee: $15,300 - Royalty: 8% on 1st $600,000, 4% on 2nd $600,000 - Total Inv: Excluding fran. fee $10,800 - $25,000 - Financing: Yes.

HANDYMAN HOUSE CALLS, INC.
640 Northland Rd., Ste. 33, Forest Park, OH, 45240. Contact: Alan Arend, Pres. - Tel: (513) 825-3863. Handyman, odd job repair service. Established: 1985 - Franchising Since: 1986 - Franchise Fee: $6,250 - Total Inv: varies - Financing: Yes.

HOME CLEANING CENTERS OF AMERICA
1111 W. 95th St., Overland Pk., KS, 66214. Contact: Mike Calhoon, Pres. - Tel: (800) 767-1118. Primarily a residential home cleaning service with secondary emphasis on carpet, window, and small office cleaning. Established: 1981 - Franchising Since: 1984 - No. of Units: Franchised: 26 - Franchise Fee: $16,500- Royalty: 5% - 4.5% - Total Inv: Fran. fee plus $1,800 equip., $5,000 - $10,000 work. cap. - Financing: No.

HOWE CEILING CLEANING
7100 Timberline Rd., Black Hawk, SD, 57718. Contact: Michael Howe, Owner - Tel: (605) 787-5249. How to manual, listing suppliers, and techniques in ceiling cleaning (manual $14.95). Established: 1986 - Franchising Since: 1988 - No. of Units: Company Owned: 1 - Franchised: 1 - Franchise Fee: How to manual for $14.95 - Total Inv: $500. Smart Shopping - Financing: No.

HYDRO-CHEM SYSTEMS, INC. (EST. 1971) *
5550 Clay Ave., S.W., Grand Rapids, MI, 49548. Contact: John Teague, V.P. HCS Franchise,Inc. - Tel: (800) 666-1992. Chemical sales and delivery as well as pressure washer sales and service. Specializing in truck fleet wash chemicals and equipment as well as industrial degreasers and floor cleaners. Also large selection of cleaning accessories, equipment accessories, and specialty cleaners. Comprehensive training at HCS and in franchise territory. Exclusive area or territory. New 1995 franchise

opportunity. Territories located in Michigan and Ohio. Franchise Fee: $20,000 - Royalty: 5% - Total Inv: $36,000 to $79,000, depends on vehicle, equip., and tools already owned by franchisee - Financing: Negotiable.

I HAVE A WONDERFUL MAID
SPR International, Inc.
3398 Sanford Dr., Marietta, GA, 30066. Contact: Larry Stevens, Pres. - Tel: (404) 424-4003. Unique, up-scale maid service for private homes, covering all aspects of general housecleaning. High demand business. No cleaning crews used. Private independent maids used. Established: 1992 - Franchising Since: 1993 - No. of Units: Company Owned: 1 - Franchised: 4 - Franchise Fee: $5,995 - Royalty: 5% - Financing: None.

INTERNATIONAL CLEANING SERVICES
659 Henderson Dr., Ste. H, Cartersville, GA, 30120. Contact: Tammy Spivey, Sales Mgr. - Tel: (404) 387-2455, Fax: (404) 606-0638. The alternative to franchising in the maid service industry. You can own a maid service without all the complicated contracts and ongoing fees associated with a franchise. Included are manuals, forms, videos, etc. Established: 1977 - Offering Offices Since: 1982 - No. of Units: Company Owned: 2 - Offices: 197 - Total Inv: $6,990 - Financing: Yes.

JAN-PRO *
Jan-Pro Cleaning Systems
845 North Main St., Unit 4, Providence, RI, 02904. , Fran. Dir. - Tel: (901) 867-0600. A janitorial and building maintenance service. Established: 1991 - No. of Units: Franchised: 188 - Franchise Fee: $2,800 - $44,000 - Royalty: 8% - Total Inv: $3,150 - $46,500 (Equip., Supplies, Floor buffing Machine and Work. Cap.) - Financing: Yes. For further information please contact: Consultants America Corp., 12279 US Highway 64. Eads, TN, 38028, Tel: (901) 867-0600, Fax: (901) 867-0010.

JANI-KING INTERNATIONAL, INC.
4950 Keller Springs Road, Ste. 190, Dallas, TX, 75248. Contact: Jerry L. Crawford, Pres. - Jani-King Franchising Inc. - Tel: (214) 991-0900. World's largest commercial cleaning franchisor with 26 years experience. Federally registered trademark #1399797. Most programs include a specified amount of initial business, depending on the area and plan purchased. Professional training & continuous support while franchises provide commercial cleaning services on a long-term contract basis. The program has proven itself many times over & produces 100's of successful business people every year. Established: 1969 - Franchising Since: 1974 - No. of Units: Company Owned: 33 - Franchised: 4,484 - Franchise Fee: $6,500 - $32,000+ - Royalty: 10% on gross for unit franchise and 7% on gross for associate depending on area and plan purchased - Total Inv. (excluding franchise fee): $2,400 - $23,500+ - Financing: Jani-King will finance some of the total investment depending on location desired.

The World Leader In Commercial Cleaning

Become part of the largest commercial cleaning franchisor in the world. With over 4,400 franchises worldwide and 26 years of experience, Jani-King offers you a tremendous business opportunity.

FOR MORE INFORMATION CALL: 1-800-552-5264

JANTIZE AMERICA INC.
15449 Middlebelt, Livonia, MI, 48154. Contact: Jerry Grabowski, V.P. - Tel: (800) 968-9182. Commercial office and residential cleaning. Established: 1985 - Franchising Since: 1989 - No. of Units: Company Owned: 1 - Franchised: 17 - Franchise Fee: $3,200 - $16,000 - Royalty: 9% varies to 6% - Financing: 50%.

MAID BRIGADE SERVICES
Maid Brigade Systems, Inc.
850 Indian Trail, Atlanta, GA, 30247. Contact: Don M. Hay, Pres. - Tel: (800) 722-MAID. Residential maid service offering outstanding training & support at the lowest price. Established: 1979 - Franchising Since: 1980 - No. of Units: Company Owned: 5 - Franchised: 240 - Franchise Fee: $8,500 - Royalty: 3% - 7% - Total Inv: $35,000 - Financing: No.

MAID EASY
43 Orchard Lane, Glastonbury, CT, 06033. Contact: Patricia Brubaker, Fran. Dev. - Tel: (203) 659-2953. Professional & streamlined maid service system available with heavy emphasis on business, marketing & personnel. Maid Easy seeks only those who love working with people & who impart a professional image. Established: 1981 - Franchising Since: 1987 - No. of Units: Company Owned: 1 - Franchised: 2 - Franchise Fee: $5,000 - Total Inv: $11,000 - Financing: No.

MAID TO PERFECTION
7133 Rutherford Rd., Baltimore, MD, 21244. Contact: Gloria Goldstraw, V.P. - Tel: (800) 648-6243, Fax: (410) 944-6469. An upscale maid service which offers both residential and commercial cleaning. Our formatted system makes service easy to sell and, by combining both residential and commercial cleaning, MTP franchisees benefit from two separate multi-billion dollar industries. Established: 1980 - Franchising Since: 1990 - No. of Units: Company Owned: 3 - Franchised: 48 + 148 under contract - Franchise Fee: $8,995 - Royalty: 7%, 5% on sales in excess of $500,000; 4% on select commercial contracts - Total Inv: $24,920 (incl. fran. fee, all packages, licenses, insurances, add'l. funds for 3 months) to $39,545 - Financing: Up to $10,000 of total inv., 100% for add'l. territory.

MAIDS AHOY! *
Maids Ahoy, Inc.
1240 E, 800 N, Orem, UT, 84057. Contact: Wendy Peck, Pres. - Tel: (801) 221-7049. Residential maid service. Maids Ahoy! uses its distinct nautical theme to set itself from the rest. Maids Ahoy! franchisees are also proud of their professional service. Established: 1993 - Franchising Since: 1994 - No. of Units: Company Owned: 23 master sold - Franchised: 7 operating - Total Inv: $25,500 - Financing: None.

MAIDS, THE
Maids International, The
4820 Dodge St., Omaha, NE, 68132. Contact: Rick Spalding, Exec. Dir. Reg. Services - Tel: (800) 843-6243. Residential cleaning service. Established: 1980 - Franchising Since: 1981 - No. of Units: Franchised: 244 - Franchise Fee: $17,500 - Royalty: 5.5% - 7%, adv. 8% - Total Inv: $27,500 - $32,500, $17,500 fran. fee - Financing: up to 50%.

MASTER STROKE
142 Shore Dr., #H, Peabody, MA, 01960-3028. Contact: Alex Kulpa, Owner - Tel: (508) 532-8485. Residential window cleaning. Established: 1986 - Franchising Since: 1987 - No. of Units: Company Owned: 1 - Franchised: 15 - Franchise Fee: $5,000 - Royalty: 6% - Total Inv: $7,500 - Financing: Yes.

MCMAID, INC.
10 West Kinzie St., Chicago, IL, 60610. Contact: Cynthia Okon, Gen. Mgr. - Tel: (312) 321-6250. Maid service utilizing team cleaning. Established: 1975 - Franchising Since: 1986 - No. of Units: Company Owned: 4 - Franchised: 10 - Franchise Fee: $10,000 and up, depending on size of territory - Royalty: 6% of sales - Total Inv: $17,400 - $50,000 - Financing: No.

MERRY MAIDS
860 Ridge Lake Blvd., Memphis, TN, 38120. Contact: Jon Nelson, Franchise Sales Manager - Tel: (800) 798-8000. Provides a comprehensive five-day training program at its headquarters and continuous follow-up assistance through Merry Maids support staff of 38 full-time employees, 21 regional coordinators, regional meetings and workshops, a national

convention, newsletters and a modem bulletin board. Established: 1980 - Franchising Since: 1981 - No. of Units: Company Owned: 1 - Franchised: 675 - Franchise Fee: $11,500 - $19,500 - Royalty: 7% - Total Inv: Fran. Fee + working capital of $8,500 - $15,000 - Financing: Up to $10,500 of fran. fee.

MINI MAID
Mini Services Company, Inc., The
1341 Canton Rd., #C-1, Marietta, GA, 30066. Contact: Thomas E. Gelarden, Pres. - Tel: (404) 421-1588. Team residential cleaning business. Established: 1973 - Franchising Since: 1976 - No. of Units: Franchised: 87 - Franchise Fee: $12,500 - Royalty: 6% 1st $100,000, 5% next $100,000, 4% next $100,000, 3% next $100,000+ - Total Inv: $19,000 - $25,000 - Financing: None.

MOLLY MAID
Molly Maid Inc.
540 Avis Dr., Ann Arbor, MI, 48108. Contact: Paul M. Wiljanen, VP of Sales & Mktg. - Tel: (800) MM-MOLLY. Customers choose Molly Maid for their professional image and proven results world-wide. Have been rated as one of the 500 fastest-growing companies for 3 years. Proven system with over 3.5 million cleanings performed. Established: 1979 - Franchising Since: 1979 - No. of Units: Franchised: 327 - Franchise Fee: $14,900 - Royalty: 6%/5%/4%/3% - Total Inv: $14,900 fran. fee, $2,000 initial pkg. fee, $10,000 - $15,000 work. cap. - Financing: None.

NATIONAL CHEMICALS AND SERVICES INC.
257 N. West Ave., Ste. 203, Elmhurst, IL, 60126. Contact: Rusty D. Buck, Mgr. - Tel: (708) 832-8407. Washroom sanitation service. Established: 1964 - Franchising Since: 1968 - No. of Units: Company Owned: 1 - Franchised: 25 - Franchise Fee: $7,500 - Total Inv: $1,000 work. cap. - Financing: No.

NATIONAL HYGIENE SERVICE *
National Hygiene Franchise Corp.
P.O. Box 533, 691 N. Church Rd., Elmhurst, IL, 60126. Contact: Mr. Gus DeBuck, G.M. - Tel: (708) 832-8407, Fax: (708) 832-8474. Service & clean washrooms in business places. Route type of work. Established: 1964 - Franchising Since: 1968 - 1995 - No. of Units: Company Owned; 10 - Franchised: 24 - Franchise Fee: $9,500 - Royalty: 1/3 of weekly gross - Total Inv: $10,950 - $33,500 - Financing: None.

NATIONAL MAINTENANCE CONTRACTORS
National Maintenance Franchise Corp.
1801-130th Ave., N.E., Bellevue, WA, 98005. Contact: Lyle Graddon, Pres. - Tel: (800) 347-7844. Janitorial franchise business actively looking for master and unit franchisees in major metropolitan markets. Established: 1970 - Franchising Since: 1973 - No. of Units: Company Owned: 2 - Franchised: 300 - Franchise Fee: $2,000 - $5,000 unit, $50,000 - $100,000 master - Royalty: 20% unit, 3% - 4% master - Financing: Yes.

O.P.E.N. CLEANING SYSTEMS
2398 E. Camelback Rd., Ste. 740, Phoenix, AZ, 85016. Contact: Eric Goldmann, V.P. - Tel: (800) 777-6736. Selling commercial cleaning franchises. Each franchisee is guaranteed the initial customers accounts and receives training equipment and constant support from the franchisor. Established: 1983 - Franchising Since: 1983 - No. of Units: Company Owned: 3 - Franchised: 500 - Franchise Fee: $3,400 - $30,000 - Royalty:10% - Total Inv: $4,000 - $34,000 - Financing: Yes.

OMEX
OMEX International, Inc.
3905 Hartzdale Dr., Camp Hill, PA, 17011. Contact: Stephen Thomas, Dir. of Fran. - Tel: (800) 827-6639. Commercial contract cleaning. Established: 1979 - Franchising Since: 1991 - No. of Units: Company Owned: 1 - Franchised: 4 - Franchise Fee: $15,000 - Royalty: 4% - Total Inv: $58,000 with franchise fee - Financing: None.

PRECISION POWERWASH 2000
Clean Machine Powerwash Inc.
P.O. Box 463, West Springfield, MA, 01090. Contact: Mark Kraver, Pres. - Tel: (413) 734-4384. Cleaning of exterior of homes, buildings and truck fleets. Established: 1974 - Franchising Since: 1993 - No. of Units: Company Owned: 6 - Franchised: 3 master - Franchise Fee: $13,500 - Royalty: 5% - $100,000, 4% 2nd $100,000 - Total Inv: $13,500 fran. fee; $12,000 equip.; $650 lease vehicle; $5,000 adv.; $5,000 work. cap.; $5,000 misc. - Financing: Yes.

PRO-TOUCH
100 E 20th St., Kansas City, MO, 64108. Contact: Rick Oddo, Owner - Tel: (816) 842-1515. Commercial office cleaning franchise including janitorial, carpet cleaning and window washing. Low overhead and high margins are the reasons to get into this business. Established: 1959 - Franchising Since: 1990 - No. of Units: Company Owned: 1 - Franchised: 1 - Franchise Fee: $6,500 - Royalty: 8%: to $5,000, 7%: $5,000 - $10,000, 6%: $10,000 - $20,000, 5%: above $20,000 - Total Inv: $6,500 fran. fee, $2,500 equip., $5,000 work cap. - Financing: $3,000 of fran. fee.

PROFORCE USA - COMMERCIAL CLEANING SYSTEMS, INC.
1950 Old Gallows Rd., Ste. 420, Vienna, VA, 22182. Contact: John Zsidisin, V.P. Fran. Dev. - Tel: (703) 556-4424, Fax: (703) 556-6728. Franchisor of cleaning services for offices & a variety of commercial facilities. Established: 1992 - Franchising Since: 1992 - No. of Units: Company Owned: 5 - Franchised: 221 - Franchise Fee: from $1,250 to $23,000 - Royalty: 3% per month - Total Inv: from $2,900 to $31,500 - Financing: Yes.

RACS INTERNATIONAL INC.
Racs International
931 E 86th St., Se. 208, Indianapolis, IN, 46240. Contact: Chuck Morrison, Pres. - Tel: (317) 259-7227. Commercial cleaning services. Established: 1990 - Franchising Since: 1991 - No. of Units: Company Owned: 7 - Franchised: 22 - Franchise Fee: $15.00 - Royalty: 10% - Total Inv: $25 - $14,000 - Financing: Yes.

REMODELING CONTRACTING & CLEANING SERVICE, INC. *
9530 James A. Reed Rd., Kansas City, MO, 64134. Contact: Bill Sutter, V.P. Mktg. - Tel: (816) 767-8818, 1-800-761-7227. Fire, water and storm structural/cleaning restoration - residential and commercial. Established: 1974 - Franchising Since: 1991 - No. of Units: Franchised: 8 - Franchise Fee: $20,000 - Royalty: 5% - Total Inv: $50,000 - $90,000 - Financing: Yes.

RESTORX, INC.
1135 Braddock Ave., Braddock, PA, 15104. Contact: Tom Cordina, Gen. Mgr. - Tel: (412) 351-8686, Fax: (412) 351-1394. Restoration of fire and water damaged property. Established: 1982 - Franchising Since: 1982 - No. of Units: Company Owned: 1 - Franchised: 40 - Franchise Fee: $5,000 - $20,000 - Royalty: flat fee $150. - $275. weekly - Total Inv: fran. fee, $25,000 vehicle/equip., $15,000 work. cap. - Financing: Partial.

SCRUBWAY INC. *
P.O. Box 80642, Valley Forge, PA, 19484. Contact: Joe DeWitt, Nat'l. Fran. Dir. - Tel: (800) 355-3000, Fax: (610) 650-8269. Public restroom hygiene service. Established: 1994 - Franchising Since: 1995 - No. of Units: Company Owned: 1 - Franchised: 2 - Franchise Fee: $36,000 to $80,000 - Royalty: 6% - Total Inv: $47,850 to $104,000 - Financing: Yes, in house.

SERV U-1ST
Serv U-1, Inc.
10175 S.W. Barbur Blvd., Bldg. B. Ste. 100 BA, Portland, OR, 97219. Contact: Bob Rosenkranz, Pres. - Tel: (503) 244-7628. Janitorial maintenance business serving commercial and industrial clients. Low investment with ongoing training in financial control, procuring clients, production and management. Regional may provide accounts. Established: 1988 - Franchising: 1988 - No. of Units: Franchised: 11 - Franchise Fee: $3,300 - Royalty : 12% of 1st, $3,000 gross/m, 3% of total gross/m. - Total Inv. varies - Financing: Yes.

SERVICE ONE JANITORIAL
Service One Commercial Cleaning Systems, Inc.
5104 N. Orange Blossom Tr., Ste. 224, Orlando, FL, 32810. Contact: Stephen L. Rathel, Pres. - Tel: (407) 293-7645, (800) 522-7111. Janitorial. Established: 1985 - Franchising Since: 1985 - No. of Units: Franchised: 80+.

SERVICE-MAID INDUSTRIES, INC.
2255 S. Wadsworth Blvd., Ste. 202, Lakewood, CO, 80227. Contact: Don Lekawa, V.P. - Tel: (303) 988-9000. Marketing janitorial franchises. Complete operation includes equipment, training and optional accounts. Established: 1973 - Franchising Since: 1979 - No. of Units: Company Owned: 4 - Franchised: 6 - Total Inv: $38,000 - $90,000 - Royalty: 9% royalty plus 1% advertising fee - Financing: No.

SERVICE-TECH CLEANING
Service-Tech Corporation
21012 Aurora Rd, Warrensville Hts., OH, 44146-1010. Contact: Alan Sutton, Pres. - Tel: (800) 992-9302. Offering extensive line of services which include: air duct cleaning, kitchen exhaust, pressure washing and vacuum cleaning, plus more to hospitals, restaurants, schools, homes and industrial and commercial customers. Established: 1960 - Franchising Since: 1988 - No. of Units: Company Owned: 5 - Franchised: 3 - Franchise Fee: $19,000 - Royalty: 4% - 6% plus 1% adv. - Total Inv: $49,000 ($19,000 fran. fee, $30,000 equip., training etc.) - Financing: None.

SERVICEMASTER
The ServiceMaster Company
860 Ridge Lake Blvd., Memphis, TN, 38122. Contact: Dan Kellow, V.P. Market Expansion - Tel: (901) 527-0444. Residential & commercial cleaning. Established: 1947 - Franchising Since: 1952 - No. of Units: Franchised: 4,306 - Franchise Fee: $8,700 - $19,700; $1,000 - $4,000 experience discount - Royalty: 4% - 10% + adv. royalty 5% - 1% - Total Inv: $16,600 - $29,900 - Financing: 70%.

SERVPRO INDUSTRIES, INC.
575 Airport Rd., P.O. Box 1978, Gallatin, TN, 37066. Contact: Michelle, Advertising Assistant - Tel: (615) 451-0200. A complete cleaning and restoration business, specializing in insurance disaster restoration; carpet, upholstery and drapery cleaning; deodorizing; carpet dyeing; soil protecting and most other cleaning functions in residential, retail and commercial establishments. Established: 1967 - Franchising Since: 1969 - No. of Units: Franchised: 850 - Franchise Fee: $36,000 - Royalty: 7%-10% - Total Inv: varies - Financing: Yes.

SHINE-A-BLIND
P.O. Box 7, St. Clair, MI, 48079. Contact: Dan Griffin, Pres. - Tel: (810) 329-8600. Manufacture and distribute ultrasonic mini-blind cleaning equipment. International network of 315 members. Established: 1988 - Franchising since: 1988 - No. of Units: Company Owned: 2 - Franchised: 300+ - Franchise Fee: $1,000 - Royalty: $100. per month - Total Inv: $15,000 - Financing: Yes.

SPARKLE WASH
Sparkle International Inc.
26851 Richmond Rd., Cleveland, OH, 44146. Contact: Sales Dept. - Tel: (800) 321-0770 or (216) 464-4212. International network of mobile power cleaning and restoration franchises. Mobile power cleaning services are provided utilizing Sparkle Wash developed patented mobile power cleaning equipment and marketing programs. Services include: washing, restoration, masonry cleaning and sealing, paint and graffiti removal, wood cleaning/sealing, etc. Established: 1965 - Franchising Since: 1967 - No. of Units: Company Owned: 1 - Franchised: 215 - Franchise Fee: $10,000+ - Royalty: 5% - 3%, no adv. fee - Financing: Yes.

SPARKLING MAID
Sparkling Maid, Inc.
7936 E. Arapahoe Ct., Englewood, CO, 80112. Contact: Eileen T. Martin, Pres. - Tel: (303) 770-6059, Fax: (303) 843-0276. Housecleaning and contracts for moveouts in apartment complexes. Established: 1979 - Franchising Since: 1983 - No. of Units: Franchised: 5 - Franchise Fee: $7,000 - Royalty: $200/mo. - Total Inv: $7,000 fran. fee, $7,000 start-up - Financing: Yes.

SWISHER HYGIENE FRANCHISE CORPORATION
Swisher International
6849 Fairview Rd., Charlotte, NC, 28210. Contact: Bruce Mullan, V.P. Sales - Tel: (800) 444-4138, Fax: (800) 444-4565. Restroom hygiene service and related products. Established: 1983 - Franchising Since: 1990 - No. of Units: Company Owned: 2 - Franchised: 91 - Franchise Fee: $35,000 - $75,000 (population based) - Royalty: 6%, 2% adv. - Total Inv: $75,000 - $115,000 - Financing: Percentage available to qualified candidates.

TANGIBLE RESEARCH & DEVELOPMENT CORP. *
2901 Wayzata Blvd., Minneapolis, MN, 55405. Contact: Gordon Hamilton, Pres. - Tel: (612) 374-1105. One of the oldest, largest, and most reputable firms in the ceiling cleaning industry, giant mist, low pressure tank system with a 20 year unmatched history of perfection in cleaning all types of soiling on walls and ceilings. Low overhead, high margin of profit: Over 400 dealers worldwide have been trained. Established: 1978 - No. of Units: Company Owned: 1 - Franchised: Foreign Only - Total Inv: $5,900+.

TEAM WORKS CLEANING SERVICES *
CSS Franchising
177 Main St., Fort Lee, NJ, 07024. Contact: Fran. Rep. - Tel: (201) 585-4753. Professional commercial cleaning franchise - no charge for contracts - no limits on income. Don't be fooled by the "big guys". Established: 1986 - Franchising Since: 1993 - No. of Units: Company Owned: 1 - Franchised: 5 - Franchise Fee: $10,000 - Royalty: Adjustable - Total Inv: $20,000 - Financing: Yes.

TEAM-WORKS
Lip-N-Lor's Enterprises, Inc.
101 Rt. 130 S., Washington Bldg., #3, Cinnaminson, NJ, 08077. Contact: Lori Lippincott, Pres. - Tel: (800) 854-7912, Fax: (609) 829-5474. Providing quality commercial building maintenance services since 1986. We specialize in the total care concept and provide janitorial services, floor cleaning, carpet cleaning, landscape design and maintenance, snow removal and specialty services to commercial establishments. Established: 1986 - Franchising Since: 1994 - No. of Units: Company Owned: 1 - Franchised: 1 - Franchise Fee: $19,500 - Royalty: 7% - Total Inv: $22,500 - Financing: No.

TOWER CLEANING SYSTEMS *
P.O. Box 80642, Valley Forge, PA, 19484. Contact: J.C. DeWitt, Nat'l. Fran. Dir. - Tel: (800) 67-TOWER, (610) 650-9000, Fax: (610) 650-8269. Office cleaning services. Established: 1988 - Franchising Since: 1990 - No. of Units: Franchised: 1,150 - Franchise Fee: $4,000 to $33,600 - Royalty: 3% - Total Inv: $4,000 to $33,600 - Financing: In house.

TOWN AND COUNTRY OFFICE & CARPET CARE SYSTEMS
2850 San Ramon Valley Blvd., Ste. B208, San Ramon, CA, 94583. Contact: Ted Prince, Pres. - Tel: (510) 867-3850. Janitorial and carpet care. Established: 1971 - Franchising Since: 1986 - No. of Units: Franchised: 86 - Franchise Fee: $1,500. - Royalty: $75. per month - Total Inv: $2,900. - $10,000. - Financing: Yes.

TRIAD EQUIPMENT MAINTENANCE SYSTEMS, INC. *
500 W. Michigan Ave., P.O. Box 1108, Jackson, MI, 49201. Contact: Dave Faunce, Nat'l. & Reg'l. Account Mgr. - Tel: (800)468-7423. A Conversion franchise focused on cleaning and power equipment service centers. Providing computer software, training and complete service systems. Established: 1990 - Franchising Since: 1990 - No. of Units: Franchised: 13 - Franchise Fee: $25,000 - Royalty: 5% gross revenue - Total Inv: $34,500 to $79,260 - Financing: No.

VALUE LINE MAINTENANCE SYS.
Western Maintenance Co.
P.O. Box 6450, Great Falls, MT, 59401. Contact: Jerry McAllister - Tel: (406) 761-4471. Flexible cleaning programs for supermarkets and other large retail outlets. Established: 1959 - No. of Units: 32 - Franchise Fee: $30,000 - Royalty: 10% - Total Inv: $50,800 - Financing: Yes.

WASH ON WHEELS
5401 S. Bryant Ave., Sanford, FL, 32773. Contact: Jim Good, Pres. - Tel: (407) 321-4010. WOW is a general purpose mobile wash cleaning service addressing all surface dirt: indoor and/or outdoor directed at the residential, commercial and industrial marketplace. The chemicals, training, customized software and continuing franchise development

program support growth and success. Established: 1964 - Franchising Since: 1986 - No. of Units: Franchised: 142 - Franchise Fee: $7,500 - Royalty: $80/mo. - Total Inv: $14,500 - $60,000 - Financing: Yes.

WEST SANITATION SERVICES, INC.
3882 Del Amo Blvd., #602, Torrence, CA, 90503. Contact: Graham Emery, Pres. - Tel: (310) 793-4242. Aerowest and Westair odor control and washroom sanitation services. Established: As West Chemical Products 1880, as West Sanitation 1984 - Franchising Since: 1980 - Number of Routes: Franchised: 27 - Franchise Fee: $2,000 plus 40% of annualized route value - Total Inv: less than $10,000 - Royalty: 35% - 40% incl. fee for full admin./bus service provided by franchisor - Financing: Yes, 80% of pymt. based on annualized route value.

CONSUMER BUYING SERVICES

SHOPPING SERVICE OF AMERICA
Shopping Delivery Service of America
2 Halsey Dr., Ste. 110, Wilmington, DE, 19807. Contact: Marc A. Falcone, Pres./CEO - Tel: (302) 429-6985 (also Fax). Shopping Delivery Service of America provides guaranteed contracts with a variety of businesses in franchisee's immediate area. Also offers specialized services that guarantee success. Advertising support is provided by SDS. Earning potential is limited only by individual's motivation. Established: 1990 - Franchising Since: 1992 - No. of Units: Company Owned: 1 - Franchised: 3 - Franchise Fee: $10,000 - $15,000 - Royalty: 2% - Total Inv: $15,000 - $20,000.

UNITED CONSUMERS CLUB
United Consumers Club Franchising Corp.
8450 Broadway, Merrillville, IN, 46410. Contact: Richard Cofoid, Fran. Dev. Mgr. - Tel: (800) 827-6400, Fax: (219) 755-6208. Hundreds of thousands of consumers have already joined UCC. Their membership allows them to purchase directly from more than 700 manufacturers - NO MARK-UP, NO MIDDLEMAN, NO KIDDING! Our franchisees enroll and service members through our time-tested marketing system with the support of more than 130 specialists at the UCC Corporate Support Center. Established: 1971 - Franchising Since: 1972 - No. of Units: Company Owned: 7 - Franchised: 86 - Franchise Fee: $55,000 - Total Inv: $115,000 - Financing: Partial financing ($40,000) of initial fran. fee.

UNIWAY MANAGEMENT CORP.
277 Southfield Pkwy., Ste. 170, Forest Park, GA, 30050. Contact: Robert C. Hardy, Pres./CEO - Tel: (404) 363-6200. Buying service - Uniway members have access to over 600 major manufacturers, furniture, appliances, carpet and other merchandise for in and around the home. Members and/or merchandise through Uniway at Uniway's cost. Established: 1972 - No. of Units: Company Owned: 2 - Franchised: 14 - Franchise Fee: $25,000 - $50,000 - Royalty; 11% on membership gross sales - Total Inv: $75,000 to $100,000 - Financing: N/A.

DISTRIBUTORS

AGI SOFTWARE
Amerasia Group, Inc.
P.O. Box 53114, Indianapolis, IN, 46253. Contact: Ben Yanto Jr., Pres. - Tel: (317) 299-8827. Specializing in shareware and public domain programs for IBM, Apple, Commodore and Mac computers. The economy software store. Established: 1987 - Distributing Since: 1989 - No. of Units: Company Owned: 2 - Distributed: 6 - Franchise Fee: $500 - Royalty: none - Total Inv: $2,000 + fran. fee - Financing: $500 down, $2,500 payable in 10 months.

ALLENTOWN VINYL INC.
Box 20102, Lehigh Valley, PA, 18002-0102. Contact: Charles Jamo, Mgr. - Tel: (610) 432-7457. Computerized sign manufacturing and plastic repair. Established: 1972 - Offering Distributorships Since: 1973 - No. of Units: 295 - Inv: $199.

ALOE SHOPPE
Nature's Choice
1301 West Copans Rd., Pompano Beach, FL, 33064. Contact: Tedd Vurraro, Pres. - Tel: (305) 968-2155, Fax: (305) 979-6309. Carts and kiosks in major shopping malls. Established: 1980 - Offering Distributorships Since: 1982 - No. of Units: Company Owned: 1 - Total Inv: $9,995 - Financing: No.

AMAVEND VENDING SYSTEMS
Dept. Av., Ste. A, P.O. Box 24, Fayetteville, AR, 72702. Contact: Henry K.U.A. Nwauwa, Pres. - Tel: (501) 443-6791. Vending & amusement machines. Business opportunity & distributorships for individuals and companies. Guaranteed financing with our secured lease program. Publisher of the guides to coin-operated businesses. Established: 1987 - Franchising Since: 1989 - No. of Units: Company Owned: 2 - Franchise Fee: none - Royalty: 0% for independent units, 5% for licensed units - Total Inv: $6,000 (min.) - Financing: Yes, guaranteed financing (secured lease), regular leasing program available.

AMERICAN NAME-JEWELRY
Lasting Impressions, Inc.
P.O. Box 22065-Dept. FA, Lake Buena Vista, FL, 32830. Contact: B. Manning, Sales Mgr. - Tel: (407) 876-0341, Fax: (407) 649-6435. Easy to make custom-made bead jewelry. Unlimited market with profits to 1000%. No special jewelry training needed. Free color catalog and details available. Established:1991 - Distributing Since: 1991 - No. of Units: Company Owned: 1 - Distributed: 100+ - Royalty: n/a - Total Inv: $299.00 for complete starter kit - Financing: Visa, MC, Amex, Optima, C.O.D.

AMI PIZZA WHOLESALE *
914 Cantrell Ave., Nashville, TN, 37215. Contact: Don Hunt, CEO - Tel: (615) 385-5699. A wholesale pizza distributorship that provides a fresh dough pizza program. Established: Started in pizza wholesale business in 1962.

AQUAPURA CORPORATION, THE
24 Desiree Dr., Greenwich, CT, 06830. Contact: James Iorio, Pres. - Tel: (203) 661-6064. Manufacture and sell home water purifiers direct to the consumer and commercial end users through independent distributors. Established: 1976 - Offering Distributorships Since: 1979 - Number of Distributors: 18 - Inv: $4,500.

ASUKA CORPORATION
7800 River Rd., N. Bergen, NJ, 07047. Contact: Roy Kanda, Pres. - Tel: (201) 861-5450. Direct importer of pearl oysters from its own factory in Japan. Distribute throughout the USA and other countries. Pearl home parties, fairs, jewelry stores, etc. are main outlets. Established: 1979 - Offering Distributorships Since: 1979 - Total Inv: $2,500 - $3,000 - Financing: No.

AUTHENTIC LOG HOMES CORP.
P.O. Box 1288, Laramie, WY, 82070. Contact: Sue Benson, Customer Services - Tel: (307) 742-3786. Manufacturing and sale of precut log home kits.

AUTO VALET
7110 Blondo St., Omaha, NE, 68104. Contact: Paul Riddle - Tel: (402) 553-4122. Offers detailing of cars, window tinting, sun roofs, paint sealant, running boards, etc. Established: 1971 - Franchising Since: 1984 - No. of Units: 9 - Franchise Fee: $5,500 - Total Inv: $20,000 - Financing: No.

AVANTI VENDING MACHINES
P.O. Box 493441, Redding, CA, 96049-3441. Contact: Phil Scrima, Pres. - Tel: (800) 541-7943, (916) 244-8070. Sell full line vending machines. (Also, small machines, counter tops, etc.) Snacks, soft drink, hot bev., cold food etc. Established: 1974 - Financing: Yes.

BAR-MASTER INTERNATIONAL
940 Venice Blvd, Los Angeles, CA, 90015. Contact: Paul Nye, Distributorship Sales - Tel: (213) 746-9835. Manufacture soft drink and liquor dispensers and market them through local distributors. Established: 1952.

BEAUTY BY SPECTOR, INC.
Dept. FADQ-96, McKeesport, PA, 15134-0502. Contact: Myer Spector, Pres. - Tel: (412) 673-3259. Internationally known fashion authority offers dealerships in Men's Hairpieces, Women's Wigs, Women's Intimate and Fashion Wear, and continental-designed Fine and Fashion Jewelry. These dealerships, successfully field-tested for over 3 decades, offer a high return with little or no investment. The firm was established in 1958, and began offering dealerships in 1967. Dealerships are available for a token fee of only $29.95. Dealers can use M/C or Visa to purchase the dealership, as well as to purchase replacement inventory.

BIG MIKE'S FROZEN DESSERT BLENDING MACHINE
Big Mike's Flavors Unlimited
48 Westminster Crt., New Rochelle, NY, 10801. Contact: Bill Reichert, Fran. Dev. - Tel: (800) 424-MIKE. Company grants a product distribution franchise for the Big Mike's Frozen Dessert Blending Machine. Unlimited flavor capacity, no wastage, easy clean-up. Home-based business. Established: 1992 - Franchising Since: 1993 - No. of Units: Company Owned: 1 - Franchise Fee: $29,990 - Royalty: None - Total Inv: $39,990 - $41,490 - Financing: None.

BLACK MAGIC CHIMNEY SWEEPS, INT'L. *
Haldorn & Mann, Inc./Black Magic Supply
55 Hercules Dr., Colchester, VT, 05446. Contact: Max Pelleria, V.P. - Tel: (800) 334-1497, (802) 655-4121, Fax: (802) 655-4129. Training and equipment to get started in the business of chimney sweeping and flue technology. Established: 1978 - Total Inv: $2,500 - Financing: No.

BOSCO JEWELERS INC.
6344 Linn Ave., N.E., Albuquerque, NM, 87108. Contact: Robert, Patty, Sheri - Tel: (800) 545-6262. Jewelry wholesale, mostly Southwestern, sales booklets provided and displays are available. Fast order processing through our toll free 800 number. Established: 1979 - Distributing Since: 1979 - No. of Units: Company Owned: 1 - Distributorships: 2,900 - Total Inv: $375 starting inventory recommended - Financing: Visa/MC.

BURKE AND ASSOCIATES
9927 Galway, Dallas, TX, 75218. Contact: George Burke, Pres. - Tel: (214) 328-9064. Multi level sales of various products by mail order. Established: 1985 - Franchising Since: 1985 - Total Inv: $250.00 - Financing: No.

BUTLER LEARNING SYSTEMS
Butler Associates Inc.
1325 W. Dorothy Lane, Dayton, OH, 45409. Contact: Bob Butler, V.P. - Tel: (513) 298-7462. Audio visual training program for supervisors, managers, all workers and sales professionals. Sell programs and/or hold seminars for all organizations. Established: 1959 - Distributing Since: 1975 - No. of Units: Company Owned: 1 - Distributed: 55 - Fee: inventory - under $500 - Royalty: 10% - Approx. Inv: $10,000 for working cap. - Financing: No.

BUTTONS BY BOBBY
P.O. Box 588, Bloomfield, NJ, 07003. Contact: Bobby Dennis, Pres. - Tel: (201) 677-0565. Produces novelties; buttons, t-shirts, keychains, mirrors, etc. for promotional, private, business, fundraising, etc. purposes. They offer exclusive area distributorships to qualified persons. Distributors run it as their own business as to format, pricing, etc. The company specializes in short run novelties; will ship to distributor or drop-ship to ultimate consumer. Established: 1982 - Offering Distributorships Since: 1986 - Number of Distributors: 3 - Fee: $895 (with annual renewal fees of $100) - Total Inv: $895 for distributorship; $100 annual renewal fee - Financing: None.

CADILLAC PLASTIC
143 Indusco Court, Troy, MI, 48007. Contact: Rachael Dolson, Mktg. Mgr. - Tel: (810) 583-1200. Plastic Distributor. Established: 1943 - No. of Units: Company Owned: 147 world wide.

CANCORP
465 - A Ash Rd., Kalispell, MT, 59901. Contact: Mary Kratz, Exec. V.P. - Tel: (406) 257-8015, Fax; (406) 257-8018. Complete set-up to go into your own Gift Canning business and make up to 300% profit. Established: 1979 - Franchising Since: 1979 - No. of Units: Franchised: 2,614 - Total Inv: $216.60 - $1,087.20 - Financing: Visa, M/C, Amex., Discover.

CHEM-MARK INTERNATIONAL
635 E. Chapman Ave., P.O. Box 1126, Orange, CA, 92666. Contact: Darol Carlson, Pres. - Tel: (714) 633-8560. Food service equipment. Low energy dishwashing machine, bar glass brushes, swing-mark valves, chemicals, air cleaners. Established: 1959 - Distributing Since: 1964 - No. of Units: Company Owned: 1 - Distributorships: 83 - Total Inv: under $10,000 - Royalty: 25 cents per month per Swing-mark valve - Financing: No.

CHISHOLM TRAIL BUILDERS
P.O. Box 335, San Marcos, TX, 78667. Contact: Floyd MacKenzie, Treasurer - Tel: (210) 629-1400 or Fax: (512) 353-5333. Country and rustic homes, performed and partially factory built modular homes. Established: 1986 - Distributing Since: 1987 - No. of Units Company Owned: 1- Royalty: $300 month fixed fee -Total Inv: approx. $20,000 cost of home - Financing: No.

CLEAN-AIRE INTERNATIONAL, INC.
2223 Handley Ederville Rd., Ft. Worth, TX, 76118. Contact: Bob Allen, V.P. - Tel: (817) 589-7873, Fax: (817) 595-0240. Televised duct cleaning service. Join in the growing demand for cleaner indoor air from businesses and residential customers. Established: 1981 - Distributing Since: 1987 - No. of Units: Company Owned: 1- Distributed: 152 - Fee: $18,850 - Financing: Leasing.

CLOSET CLASSICS
Windquest (formerly Laminations, Inc.)
3311 Windquest Dr., Holland, MI, 49424. Contact: Randy Tallman, Nat'l. Sales Mgr. - Tel: (800) 562-4257, (616) 399-3311. Distributors sell and install custom closet systems using standard components supplied by Closet Classics. System is well engineered, fully adjustable, and of premium quality construction. All materials provided. Established: 1984 - Offering Distributorships Since: 1986 - No. of Units: Distributed: 120 - Total Inv: $10,000 - $20,000 - Financing: No.

COASTAL CHOCOLATE CO.
Chocolate Group, The
600 Commercial Ave., Carlstadt, NJ, 07072. Contact: Franchise Dir./Pres. - Tel: (201) 438-8784. Chocolate soft drinks. Established: 1974.

COLOR-PRO
Tech Systems Inc.
66 Marion St., Boston, MA, 02128. Contact: Ronald Stoll, V.P., Mktg. - Tel: (617) 561-0400 or (800) 447-6646. These full color printing systems produce sublimation transfers for T-shirts, caps, jackets, bumper stickers, pennants, metal, plastic, wood, leather, and most other materials. This opportunity puts you in a 3 billion dollar industry for ad specialities, premium incentives, imprinted sportswear, awards/trophy, non-profit organizations, signage, and custom gift items. Training in Los

Angeles, Boston and Chicago. Established: 1987 - Distributing Since: 1988 - No. of Units: Company Owned: 12 - Distributed: 622 - Royalty: none - Total Inv: $3,550 cash on lease with option to buy equipment - Financing: Yes.

COLOR/MATCH
AAA Dye and Chemicals Co.
1872 Del Amo Blvd., Ste. C, Torrance, CA, 90501. Contact: Shannon David, Mktg. Dir. - Tel: (310) 618-1165. Carpet dyeing, restoration of original color or new color conversions. Training with manual, on-site and video. Support after training with technical assistance, marketing and co-op advertising. Established: 1979 - Offering Distributorships Since: 1984 - Total Inv: $1,000 - $25,000 - Financing: Yes.

CREDIT PLUS CARD
American Security Financial Corp.
4132 Shoreline Dr., Ste. J, Earth City, MO, 63045-1237. Contact: John Weigel, Pres - Tel: (314) 344-1111. Provide consumers with Credit Plus card which includes an initial $2,500 credit line, $100 merchandise check, everyone is approved, no credit rejects. Dealers earn $50 per card issued. Established: 1977 - Offering Since: 1977 - No. of Units: 851 - Inv: $1,000 - Financing: Yes.

CURBMATE CORP.
111 E. 5600 S., #322, Salt Lake City, UT, 84107. Contact: Larry Rose, Pres. - Tel: (801) 262-7509. Produces continuous concrete landscape edging for lawns and flower beds. Excellent cash flow business. No experience necessary. Established: 1983 - Distributing Since: 1983 - No. of Units: Distributed: 700 - Fee: $5,495 for the curbmate machine - Financing: Leasing.

D.J. GILL ASSOCIATES, INC.
P.O. Box 591, 1595 Imperial Way, Unit 114, Thorofare, NJ, 08086-0591. Contact: Don Gill, Pres. - Tel: (609) 384-0440. Sales & distribution of all types of vending machines. Coin-operated snacks, soda, bulk, etc., and non-coin-operated such as popcorn carts, etc. Established: 1981 - Franchising Since: 1986 - No. of Units: Company Owned: 3 - Franchised: 15,000+ - Franchise Fee: None - Royalty: None - Total Inv: $950. - $25,000 - Financing: None.

DELCO CLEANING SYSTEMS
Rahsco Manufacturing Co, Inc.
2513 Warfield, Ft. Worth, TX, 76106. Contact: Robert Hinderliter, Pres - Tel: (800) 433-2113. Mobile power wash operation. Clean cars, trucks, heavy equipment, exterior building restoration, kitchen vent hoods, airplanes and more. Video tape training, seminars, and schools. Established: 1973 - Total Inv: $1,000 - $15,000 - Financing: No.

DURASTILL, INC.
4200 Burmingham Rd., N.E., Kansas City, MO, 64117. Contact: Joyce Giovagnoli, V.P. - Tel: (816) 454-5260 or Fax: (816) 452-7581. Premier manufacturer of water distillation systems for the home for solving today's serious drinking water problems, such as lead and hundreds of other contaminants in drinking water. Established: 1969 - Offering Distributorships Since: 1979 - No. of Units: Distributors: 37 - Total Inv: average $5,000 - Financing: None.

DYNAMIC DEVELOPMENT ASSOCIATES
Bridle Lane, PO Box 18, Media, PA, 19063. Contact: Bill Eggert, Pres. - Tel: (215) 565-3860. Market and conduct popular, professional growth seminars. This business includes income opportunities in four areas: Conduct public seminars, run programs in-house for organization, train corporate trainers, sell materials and sponsor new training consultants. Established: 1969 - Fee: $495 - Total Inv: less than $1,000 - Financing: No.

ELECTRON PURE LTD.
P.O. Box 886, Madison, AL, 35758-0886. Contact: Lou Rife, Dist. Dir. - Tel: (205) 430-0876. Offers an electronic copper/silver system that eliminates chlorine in swimming pools and spas. An industrial application that prevents scaling in cooling towers, boilers, and ice machines. Video presentation, operations & marketing manual & professional training program. Established: 1988 - Distributing Since: 1990 - No. of Units: Distributed: 65 US, 4 Foreign - Total Inv: $14,800. - Financing: No.

END-A-FLAT TIRE SAFETY SEALANT
Endrust Industries
1725 Washington Rd., Ste. 205, Pittsburgh, PA, 15241. Contact: Gary B. Griser, V.P. - Tel: (412) 831-1255, Fax: (412) 833-3409. Distributorships available, can be operated from home or office. Sales of tire sealant for cars, trucks, fleets, off road vehicles, golf carts etc. Flat tire preventive. Established: 1982 - Total Inv: $5,000 - $10,000 - Financing: No.

ENERGY AUTOMATION SYSTEM, INC.
114 Canfield Place, Ste. A-8, Hendersonville, TN, 37075. Contact: Joseph Merlo, Pres. - Tel: (615) 822-7250. Dealers provide a complete, passive turn-key system of products that will reduce a businesses electric bill by 20 - 30%. Established: 1978 - Distributing Since: 1985 - No. of Units: Company Owned: 1 - Distributed: 70 - Fee: $12,500 - $23,500 includes demonstration equipment, training, inventory - Financing: Yes, if applicant already owns an established business.

ENERGY PRODUCTS, INC.
300 Harris Ave., Sacramento, CA, 95838. Contact: E. W. Jones, Pres. - Tel: (916) 925-3065. Produce coatings for roofs, decks and vertical walls, as well as other types of coatings for various applications, commercial and residential. Established: 1981 - Total Inv: $25,000 material - Financing: Yes.

EUROPEAN BODY WRAP INTERNATIONAL
P.O. Box 1578, Whitney, TX, 76692-1578. Contact: Richard Kelly, V.P. - Tel: (817) 694-4500. Body wrap, immediate inch loss. Great with toning tables, tanning, spas, beauty shops, etc. Also, high fiber diet cookies in 9 flavors and more. Established: 1977 - Franchising Since: 1979 - No. of Units: Company Owned: 1 - Franchised: 2,761 - Franchise Fee: $595 - $5,000 - Royalty: none - Total Inv: varies - Financing: No.

FORD GUM & MACHINE COMPANY
Newton & Hoag Ave., Akron, NY, 14001. Contact: George Stege, V.P. - Tel: (716) 542-4561. Bulk vending operators. Company provides product and equipment. Machines sponsored by local charities. Established: 1934 - Offering Distributorships Since: 1939 - Number of Distributors: 187.

GATEWAY APPAREL
8500 Valcour, St. Louis, MO, 63123-0990. Contact: Bill Rizzo, New Acct's Mgr. - Tel: (314) 638-1500. Distributor of name brand off price women's clothing (Jr. & Ms). Established: 1970 - Distributing Since: 1970 - No. of Units: Company Owned: 190 - Total Inv: $30,000 min. - Financing: None.

GOLD MEDAL PRODUCTS *
2001 Dalton Ave., Cincinnati, OH, 45214. Contact: Gary Wood, Nat'l. Sales Mgr. - Tel: (513) 381-1313, Fax: (513) 381-1570. Gold Medal is a full line concession manufacturer and distributor with dealers throughout the world. The products produced include popcorn machines, cotton candy machines, nacho equipment, snokone and shave ice equipment, hot dog cookers, pizza/pretzel equipment and much more. Established: 1931 - No. of Units: Company Owned: 8.

GOLFOMAT CORP.
7401-K Fullerton Rd., Springfield, VA, 22153. Contact: Arthur Angelos, Pres. - Tel: (703) 549-3400. Computerized golf courses for indoor use. Permits full 18 holes of real golf on any of 7 golf courses. A foursome takes 2 1/2 hours for 18 holes. Established: 1977 - Approx. Inv: $175,000.

HAPPY & HEALTHY PRODUCTS INC.
1600 S. Dixie Hwy., #2AB, Boca Raton, FL, 33432. Contact: Mary Galinat, Dir. of Fran. Rel. - Tel: (407) 367-0739. Distributorship for the sale of frozen fruit bars through dedicated freezers in a retail location as well as in retailers own freezers. Established: 1991 - Franchising Since: 1993 - No. of Distributors: 95 - Fee: $12,800 - $17,800 - Total Inv: $18,422 - $40,161 - Financing: No.

HI-SHOTS AERIAL PHOTOGRAPHY LTD.
1040 Airport Rd., Salem, IL, 67881. Contact: R.B. Jones, V.P. Personnel - Tel: (618) 548-6691, Fax: (618) 548-6250. Manufacturer & marketer of low level aerial photography systems as a low overhead, high profit business opportunity, including a full training, service and support

network of over 125 worldwide affiliates. Established: 1989 - No. of Units: Company Owned: 2 - Affiliates: 125 - Total Inv: $19,500 - Financing: No.

HUB COMMUNICATIONS LTD. *
66 Marion St., Boston, MA, 02128. Contact: Ron Stoll, V.P. - Tel: (800) 447-6646, (617) 561-0400, Fax: (617) 569-2164. Coin operated public telephones. Smart phones, durable, and call back800 service. Earn $ every time someone makes a call! Established: 1978 - Franchising Since: 1984 - No. of Units: Company Owned: 37 - Franchised: 11,000 phones - Franchise Fee: None - Total Inv: $1,700+ - Financing: Lease, if qualified.

IMAGE IN TIME
Martek Ltd.
Box 15160, Charlotte, NC, 28211. Contact: Paul Muckler, Mgr. - Tel: (704) 764-7213. Dealership that allows novel and personalized clocks to be made from business cards, photos, and logos. Established: 1980 - Distributing Since: 1990 - No. of Units: Company Owned: 1 - Distributed: 11 - Total Inv: $3,995 - Financing: No.

INDEPENDENT LIGHTING FRANCHISE CORP.
873 Seahawk Cir., Virginia Beach, VA, 23452. Contact: Chris Carpenter, Pres. - Tel: (804) 468-5448. Light bulb producers specializing in showing businesses (commercial, industrial, institutional) how to save money in all light bulb replacement needs, material, labor, and energy. Established: 1983 - Franchising Since: 1991 - No. of Units: Company Owned: 30 - Franchise Fee: $22,500 - Royalty: 7.5% gross sales - Total Inv: indiv. fran. invest. $38,650 - $52,350, conversion fran. invest. $22,875 - $31,175 - Financing: No.

INKY DEW, LLC
7297 University Ave., La Mesa, CA, 91941-5927. Contact: Eileen Cummings, Pres. - Tel: (619) 465-9339. Turn-key operation packages sold to re-ink and reload computer, cash register and calculator ribbons. Also, refill inkjet cartridges. Established: 1988 - Licensing Since: 1988 - No. of Units: Company Owned: 1 - Licensed: 60+ worldwide - Total Inv: $2,000 entry level or $10,000 comprehensive pkg. - Financing: Visa, MC, Discover.

INNOVATIVE MOVING STYTEMS, INC.
P.O. Box 181, Oostburg, WI, 53070. Contact: Elmer Hazen, Sales Mgr. - Tel: (414) 564-6272, (800) 619-0625, Fax: (414) 564-2322. Manufacture and distribute material handling equipment. Main product is the Lectro Truck, a battery powered stair climbing hand truck for powering loads up or down stairs, from trucks, docks, semis, etc. Established: 1973 - No. of Units: Distributors: 8 - Dealers: 144 - Total Inv: $5,000 for inv. and training.

INTERNATIONAL ENTERTAINMENT SYSTEMS (IES)
United Ventures, Inc.
P.O. Box 180, 4501 N. Route 12, Richmond, IL, 60071. Contact: A.H. Shambaugh, Sales Mgr. - Tel: (815) 675-2277. Motion picture equipment and film rental to commercial accounts. Also manufacture large screen television projection systems for outright sale or lease purchase basis to: restaurants, pubs, taverns, bowling centers, hotels, motels, discos, pizza parlors, night clubs, private clubs, etc. Established: 1971 - Offering Dealerships Since: 1973 - No. of Units: Company Owned: 1 - Dealers: 143 - Total Inv: $10,000 TV inventory, $4,500 movie equipt. & films - Financing: Two plans; manufacturer to dealer and dealer to dealer's customer.

JET, INC.
750 Alpha Dr., Cleveland, OH, 44143. Contact: Sales Dept. - Tel: (216) 442-9008. Manufacturer of home and commercial wastewater treatment systems, pressure dosing systems, JET-CHLOR Tablet Chlorinators, JET-CHLOR, CHLOR-AWAY, BIO JET-7 and Air Seal Diffusers. Established: 1955 - Offering Distributorships Since: 1957 - Royalty: Varies with product - Total Inv: $10,000 for wastewater treatment systems. None for other products - Financing: No.

JEWELRY-BY-THE-INCH
Lasting Impressions, Inc.
P.O. Box 22065, Dept. IF, Lake Buena Vista, FL, 32830. Contact: Bruce Manning, Sales Mgr. - Tel: (407) 876-0341, Fax: (407) 649-6435. Gold-layered chain made into custom jewelry including neck, wrist, waist and ankle chains. Also, crystal by-the-inch, rainbows, charms, etc. Free details and color catalogue available. Established: 1980 - Franchising Since: 1980 - No. of Units: Company Owned: 1 - Distributed: 1200+ - Total Inv: $399. for start-up kit - Financing : Visa, M.C., Amex. or ship C.O.D.

JOB BANK USA
F & A, Inc.
P.O. Box 200248, Denver, CO, 80220-0248. Contact: Gary Franklin, CEO - Tel: (303) 388-8486, Fax: (303) 355-4213. Job Bank USA is a computerized data base company which provides recruiting, outplacement and career advancement services. It is now establishing distributorships. Established: 1990 - Total Inv: $45.

K & N MOBILE DISTRIBUTION SYSTEMS
4909 Rondo Dr., Ft. Worth, TX, 76106. Contact: Curtis Nelson, Pres. - Tel: (817) 626-2885. Mobile distribution of electrical supplies, wholesale. Established: 1972 - Franchising Since: 1987 - No. of Units: Company Owned: 8 - Franchised: 23 - Franchise Fee: $23,500 - Royalty: 13% - Total Inv: $22,400 - $82,300 - Financing: Yes.

KEMPER INTERNATIONAL INC.
20438 N.E. 15th Court, Miami, FL, 33179. Contact: Bob Kemper Sr., V.P. - Tel: (800) 749-3345 or (305) 653-3333. Provide unique valuable services and supplies in making slippery floors non slip even when wet. Flame retardants, mold mildew control. Established: 1990 - Dealerships Since: 1992 - No. of Units: Company Owned: 1 - Dealerships: 10 - Total Inv: $7,900 - Financing: Yes.

KUSTOM CARDS INTERNATIONAL, INC.
219 Walnut Ave., P.O. Box 590, Vinton, VA, 24179. Contact: Kathrine Barnette, Pres. - Tel: (800) 344-7728. Distributors market company's unusual product line to businesses and individuals in their areas. Products include unique full color magnetic business cards, photo mag shots™, full color business cards, Ad Shots™ and various other photographic products. Established: 1986 - Licensing Since: 1986 - No. of Units: Company Owned: 1 - Licensed: 237 - License Fee: $125. for business start up kit - Total Inv: $125. - Financing: No.

LAW ENFORCEMENT ASSOCIATES
P.O. Box 639, Youngsville, NC, 27596-0639. Contact: Paul Feldman, V.P. Sales - Tel: (919) 554-4700. Mfg. and distribute security and police equipment (lie detectors, de-bugging equipment, bomb detection, etc.), Established: 1972 - Approx. Inv: $5,000.

LIL' ORBITS MINI DONUTS
Lil' Orbits Inc.
2850 Vicksburg Ln., Minneapolis, MN, 55447. Contact: Sales Dept. - Tel: (612) 559-7505, Fax: (612) 559-7545. Manufacturer fast food equipment such as automatic mini-donut, pancake, crepe and soft serve machines for special events and permanent locations. Established: 1974 - Franchising Since: 1977 - No. of Units: Franchised: 15,000 - Franchise Fee: None - Royalty: None - Total Inv: Avg. turn-key investment $5,500 - Financing: Lease financing to qualified applicants.

LION SECURITY PRODUCTS *
2611 Ulysses St. N.E., Minneapolis, MN, 55418. Contact: Sal DeLeo, CEO - Tel: (612) 789-7657. Manufacturer of personal security alarms. Sporting safety devices. Home & car alarms. Seeking independent dealers & distributors worldwide. Full turn-key support. Established: 1991 - No .of Units: Company Owned: 1 - Total Inv: $50 and up - Financing: No.

LOSURDO'S RESTAURANT
Losurdo's Foods, Inc.
20 Owens Rd., Hackensack, NJ, 07601. Contact: Mike Losurdo, Sr., Pres./C.E.O. - Tel: (201) 343-6680. Italian family restaurant. Established: l959 - No. of Units: Distributorships: 3.

MAC TOOLS, INC.
P.O. Box 370, S. Fayette St., Washington Court House, OH, 43160. Contact: Rick Cote, V.P. Sales - Tel: (614) 755-7000. Carrying complete inventory of over 8000 items, sockets, wrenches, chisels, screwdrivers, tool boxes, pneumatic tools and specialty items selling directly to mechanics and light industry. Established: 1938 - Offering

Distributorships Since: 1938 - No. of Units: 1,600 - Approx. Inv: $30,000 plus initial investment for tool truck, business supplies and back up capital - Financing: On initial inventory for qualified applicants.

MACPHERSON MEISTERGRAM
3517 West Wendover Ave., Greensboro, NC, 27407. Contact: Billie Steed, Mktg. Svcs. Supervisor - Tel: (910) 294-5165, Fax: (910) 855-0106. Opportunity to enter the growing personalization industry. Choose either computerized monogram/embroidery or engraving. Training, supplies and technical support. Established: 1932 - Distributing Since: 1932 - Total Inv: $25,000 embroidery/monogram, $10,000 engraving - Financing: Outside leasing.

MAR-KAL PRODUCTS CORP.
105 Walnut St., Montclair, NJ, 07042. Contact: Hans Schmid, Pres. - Tel: (201) 783-7155. Manufacturing decals and signs. Established: 1962 - Offering Distributorships Since: 1977 - No. of Units: 5 - Fee: $50,000 - Total Inv: $54,000.

MARKETING SERVICES BY VECTRA, INC.
3990 Business Park Drive, Columbus, OH, 43204-5008. Contact: Duane Hickerson, Principal - Tel: (614) 351-6868. Print and distribute marketing materials for franchise organizations. Provide printing, couponing, direct mail, warehousing and fulfillment services worldwide. Established: 1982.

MESSAGE ON HOLD NETWORK, THE
Digital Message Systems, Corp.
2502 N. Rocky Point, Ste. 1000, Tampa, FL, 33607-1446. Contact: J.B. Seligman, Pres. - Tel: (800) 526-5355. Provides on-hold programming for business telephone systems. Companies promote their products/services to their callers on-hold. Program includes digital equipment, recording studios, customer in-house financing and technical support. Established: 1984 - Dealerships Since: 1991 - No. of Dealerships: 110 - Dealership Fee: $24,995, $29,995 - Royalty: none - Total Inv: Non-exclusive license agreements by county territories per business listings - Financing: None.

MONEY STRETCHERS
Media Marketing
6799 Parma Park, Cleveland, OH, 44130. Contact: Joan Gallagher, Pres. - Tel: (216) 842-9080. Full color direct mail advertising business opportunity. Established: 1981 - Offering Distributorships Since: 1982 Company Owned: 1 - No. of Units: 18 - Total Inv: $495 - Financing: Not available.

MONOGRAMS TO GO, INC.
14200 E. Alameda Ave., Aurora, CO, 80012. Contact: Marlena Krueger, Pres. - Tel: (303) 366-8812. Retail embroidery and monogramming outlet, customer merchandise monogrammed or gift item in store. Established: 1985 - Distributing Since: 1985 - No. of Units: Company Owned: 1 - Distributed: 2 - Fee: $15,000 - Total Inv: $18,000 - $35,000 - Financing: Up to individual.

MOTOR KOTE, INC.
1386 E. Clinton Trail, Charlotte, MI, 48813. Contact: Dr. David Persell, Pres. - Tel: (517) 543-3552; Fax (517) 543-3178. Manufactures and distributes MotorKote 100 engine wear protector. Four times more concentrated than the brand leaders. Available in 1 can to 55 gallon drum sizes sold worldwide. Test machines available. Established: 1991 - Total Inv: minimum cash requirement - Financing: No.

MOUNTAIN MAN NUT & FRUIT CO.
P.O. Box 160, 10338 S. Progress Way, Parker, CO, 80134. Contact: David Conner, Pres. - Tel: (303) 841-4041. Distribution of nuts, dried fruits, chocolates, and trail mixes. Established: 1977 - Distributing Since: 1978 - No. of Units: Company Owned: 4 - Distributors: 275 - Fee: $3,500 - Total Inv: $6,000 - Financing: Not necessary.

MOUNTAIN MARKETING
P.O. Box 18, Cottageville, WV, 25239. Contact: Glen A. Durst, Owner - Tel: (304) 372-2902. Network marketing business allows you to build a lucrative monthly income from home, part-time or full-time. No ceiling on income. No employees necessary. No territorial restrictions. Minimal overhead. No experience necessary. Free professional consultation. Income is residual. Established: 1981 - Total Inv: Business can usually be launched for less than $150 - Financing: Not necessary.

MR. CHECKOUT DISTRIBUTORS
Mr. Checkout Distributors, Inc.
1650 S.W. 22nd Ave., Boca Raton, FL, 33486. Contact: Bob Goldstein, Pres. - Tel: (800) 367-0076. Wholesale route distributors of general merchandise & health and beauty aids (GM/HBA) to convenience stores and marts. Established: 1989 - No. of Distributors: 70 - Fee: $17,900 plus inven. - Royalty: None - Total Inv: $25,000 complete - Financing: None.

NANETTE CREATIONS
6119 Pierce St., Hollywood, FL, 33024-7943. Contact: E. Foley, Mktg. Dir. - Tel: (305) 966-1530. Distributorship for jewelry and related women's products including giftware and novelty items. Company supplies bookkeeping system, products, location and racks. Established: 1981 - Approx. Inv: $4,000 minimum - Financing: None.

NATIONAL ASSOCIATION OF BUSINESS LEADERS
36 Four Seasons, Dept. 318, Chesterfield, MO, 63017. Contact: Ron German, Nat'l. Mktg. Dir. - Tel: (314) 344-0920. Professional association of small business owners. Benefits include: $10,000 line of credit, D & B rating, discounts on business products and services. Local chapter franchises available. Established: 1989 - Franchising Since: 1994 - No. of Units: Company Owned: 1 - Franchised: 2 - Franchise Fee: $2,000 - Total Inv: $2,000 and up, depending on market size - Financing: Yes.

NATIONAL PROTECTIVE ASSOCIATION
1515 W. Sharp Ave., Ste. 22, Spokane, WA, 99201. Contact: John L. Van Dyke, Exec. Dir./Owner - Tel: (509) 326-1974, Fax: (509) 326-1974. Wholesale distribution of self-defense sprays, personal alarms, wireless entry alarms and security decals. Exclusive distributor of "The Equalizer" line of pepper defense sprays, Fed. Trademark #1,884,838. Company subsidized classified advertising program available to mail order distributors. Established: 1990 - Independent Dealerships Since: 1991 - No. of Units: Company Owned: 1 - Distributors: 1,350 - Total Inv: Inventory Only, no min. purchase req'd. - Financing: No.

NATIONAL SURVIVAL GAME
NSG, Inc.
P.O. Box 1439, New London, NH, 03257. Contact: Jack Iacopino, Sales Director - Tel: (603) 763-3299. Paintball adventure games. NSG invented the paintball game in 1981, and has remained the leader in its rapid growth rate. NSG products are the #1 selling paintguns in the world. Established: 1981 - Distributorships Since: 1981 - Total Inv: $2,995.

NATIONWIDE MARKETING
P.O. Box 498, Ranson, WV, 25438. Contact: F. Franke, Dealer - Tel: (304) 725-1110. Sales and distribution of energy conservation products. May be handled by mail order. Established: 1988 - Franchising Since: 1988 - No. of Units Company Owned: 1- Franchise Fee: $200.00 - Total Inv: $200.00 - Financing Available: No.

NESS STUDIOS
83 Scarcliffe Dr., Malverne, NY, 11565. Contact: Howard Ness, Owner/Dir. - Tel: (516) 593-2410. Hand-painted oil portraits on canvas from any photo. We ask for agents to sell our work. Anyone can sell our paintings and make big profits. Established: 1967 - Distributing Since: 1967 - Franchise Fee: $5 for agent kit - Royalty: 40% commissions - Financing: $5 for dealer/distributor/agent kit.

NIAGARA CYCLO MASSAGE
Niagara Of America Inc.
P.O. Box 156, Lowell, NC, 28098-0156. Contact: John J. Luptak, Mktg. Mgr., Corp. Sec. - Tel: (704) 824-5288. Manufacturer and distributor of massage products for home, office and professional use. Direct sales to home and exhibit selling. Products include reclining lounge chair, adjustable beds, portable massage units, office chairs, lift chairs. Established: 1949 - Offering Distributorships Since: 1951 - Number of Distributors: 120 international - Inv: $10,000 to $50,000 depending upon population and territory - Financing: No.

NU-CONCEPT BODY WRAP, INC.
603 Cleveland St., Elyria, OH, 44035. Contact: Dennis Doman, V.P. - Tel: (216) 365-7378. Distributor of solution concentrate used in European Body Wraps. Established: 1981 - Fee: $5,000 - Total Inv: $5,000 fee plus $2,500 setup.

O'BRIEN BUDD, INC.
3620 Swenson, St. Charles, IL, 60174. Contact: Lucille Pontecorvo, Franc. Sales Dir. - Tel: (708) 584-9200. A business form distributor & product distribution center. Established: 1911 - Franchising Since: 1990 - Franchise Fee: $7,500-$17,500 - Royalty: 1% adv., 9% gross for servicing - Total Inv: $13,500 - $49,750.

OLYMPIC GOLD SPORTING GOODS
4 Freemans Bridge Rd., Schenectady, NY, 12302. Contact: H. Goldstock or Mike Kausch, Pres. - Tel: (518) 382-2030. Distributorship for sports equipment to schools, teams, leagues, etc. No inventory necessary. Established: 1980 - Offering Distributorships Since: 1980 - No. of Distributors: 255 - Approx. Inv: $4,000 - Financing: No.

ORIENTAL FURNITURE WAREHOUSE
Pacific Trade Resources, Inc.
9030 W. Sahara Ave. #132, Las Vegas, NV, 89117-5826. Contact: Lydia M. Hawkins, Pres. - Tel: (702) 255-2222. Direct importers of Asian Arts, crafts and furniture. Using retail promotional sales. Established: 1977 - Offering Since: 1981 - No. of Distributors: 35.

PARCOM TECHNOLOGIES, INC.
1945 Palomar Oaks Way, Ste. C, Carlsbad, CA, 92009. Contact: Neal Anstadt, Pres. - Tel: (619) 931-8385, (800) 395-7781. Franchise software and system design point of sale, accounting, royalty reporting and tracking, home office or regional office systems for product sale and royalty gathering. Will customize for franchisor. Established: 1985 - Total Inv: priced economically - Financing: Yes.

PARKWAY MACHINE CORP.
1930 Green Spring Dr., Timonium, MD, 21093-0277. Contact: Steve Kovens, Oper. Mgr. - Tel: (410) 252-1020. Manufacture & sales of bulk vending machines & merchandise. Established: 1944 - Total Inv: $1,000 - Financing: Yes.

PETROLON SLICK 50
Scientia Corp.
1187 Brittmoore Rd., Houston, TX, 77043. Contact: David Dillingham, C.E.O. - Tel: (713) 932-9954. Direct marketing of automotive aftermarket products including Slick 50, a PTFE engine treatment. National distribution through a network of independent distributors. Established: 1978 - Approx. Inv: $5,500.

PHOTO ADVERTISING INDUSTRIES INC.
262 S. Coconut Lane, Miami Beach, FL, 33139. Contact: Rick Dronsky, Pres. - Tel: (305) 673-3686. Turn-key photography kits, focused on the selling of photo-key ring (photographs in key rings) to customers of restaurants, clubs, etc. while they are dining. Established: 1981 - Licensing Since: 1985 - No. of Units: Company Owned: 6 - Licensed: 9 - License Fee: $3,500 - Total Inv: $3,500 - Financing: No.

PIZZA HOUSE PIZZA *
Hunt Brothers, Inc.
914 Cantrail Ave., Nashville, TN, 37215. Contact: Fran. Dir. - Tel: (901) 867-0600. A pizza distributorship business that provides fresh baked pizza within an established business, such as convenience stores, etc. Established: 1990 - No. of Units: Franchised: 7 - Franchise Fee: $56,250 to $150,000 - Royalty: 3% - Financing: Equipment.

POPCORN PLUS
Pacific Products
4277 Transport St., Ventura, CA, 93003. Contact: A. Glickman, Pres. - Tel: (805) 658-7369, Fax: (805) 658-1458. Retail sales of gourmet multi-flavored popcorn & allied food & gift products. Established: 1984 - Franchising Since: 1985 - No. of Outlets: 600 - Total Inv: $25,000 - $40,000 - Financing: No.

PREMIER PUBLISHERS, INC. *
2778 SE Loop 820, Ft. Worth, TX, 76140-1017. Contact: Neal Michaels, Pres. - Tel: (817) 293-7030. Publisher & wholesale distributor to the mall trade of financial, self-improvement and instructional books, manuals and tapes. Provide books for resale, sales aids to assist distributors in sales procurement, and personalized assistance via telephone or mail. Established: 1971 - Franchising Since: 1976.

PRO-LITE, INC.
3505 Cadillac Ave., Ste. D, Costa Mesa, CA, 92626-1430z. Contact: Wayne Lin, Sales Mgr. - Tel: (714) 668-9988. New invented outdoor L.E.D. (Low Energy Maintenance) electronic information displays, single color and multicolor. Established: 1986 - Distributing Since: 1986 - No. of Units: Distributed: 350 - Fee: $10,000 - Total Inv: $10,000 - Financing: Yes.

PROFESSIONAL WAY CORP.
27173 Grand River, Detroit, MI, 48240. Contact: Rich Gaden, V.P. Sales - Tel: (313) 535-9380. Dental products mfg. selling direct to dentists. No. of Units: Company Owned: 2 - Franchised: 12 - Approx. Inv: $10,000 - Financing: None.

PROFIT ASSOCIATES *
P.O. Box 538, Watertown, CT, 06795. Contact: Brian Owens, Sales - Tel: (860) 274-1219. 1,000+ self-help books & tapes drop-shipped (50% profit) or purchase in quantity (up to 80% profit). Use color catalog, b/w catalog, and/or 80+ camera-ready circulars. Your worldwide customers can order by credit cards through our company. Established: 1974 - Distributorships Since: 1975 - No. of Units: Company Owned: 1 - Distributors: 175+ - Total Inv: Start-up kit (manual, catalog samples, and 80+ sample circulars - $20.00) - Financing: None.

PROSOURCE WHOLESALE FLOORCOVER
2458 Old Dorsett Rd., #102, Maryland Heights, MO, 63043-0423. Contact: Rick Newborn, V.P. - Tel: (314) 291-0000. Floorcoverings to the trade (wholesale). Established: 1990 - Franchising Since: 1991 - No. of Units: Company Owned: 1 - Franchised: 40 - Franchise Fee: $32,500 - Total Inv: $150,000 - Financing: No.

PTR TUB & TILE RESTORATION
SPR International Inc.
3398 Sanford Dr., Marietta, GA, 30066. Contact: Larry Stevens, Pres. - Tel: (800) 34 MR. TUB. Restore the original look to ugly, worn tub & tile, no odors, no paint, no spraying, ready to use same day. Used by major hotel chains. Cannot chip, crack or peel. Lifetime warranty. Established: 1973 - Franchising Since: 1973 - No. of Units: Company Owned: 1 - Franchised: 34 - Franchise Fee: $5,995 - Royalty: 20% chemical fee - Financing: None.

R & S INDUSTRIES CORP.
8255 Brentwood Industrial Dr., St. Louis, MO, 63144-2814. Contact: Ronald B. Schwartz, Pres. - Tel: (314) 781-5400. Manufacture Miracle Polishing Cloth and sell it at wholesale to independent distributors. Established: 1965 - Franchising Since: 1965 - Total Inv: $243.36 min. - Financing: No.

RENT-A-ROBOT
I. Robotics, Inc.
66 Marion St., Boston, MA, 02128. Contact: Tom Anderson, V.P. - Tel: (617) 561-0400, (800) 447-6646. Utilizing a proven marketing plan, the owner rents robots for promotion and entertainment. Robots are used for product introductions, store openings, trade shows, corporate good will events, parties, parades, etc. Complete equipment, training, marketing material and national referral for rentals included. Established: 1981 - Offering Distributorships Since: 1983 - No. of Units: Company Owned: 11 - Distributors: 166 - Royalty: none - Total Inv: $5,700 - $15,000 - Financing: Yes, leasing and financing.

RICHMOND SALES INC.
Dept. F.A.D., 42 Power Rd., Pawtucket, RI, 02860. Contact: Raymond Pacia, Pres. - Tel: (401) 722-7110. Fashion jewelry. Established: 1959.

RIDEABLE BICYCLE REPLICAS INC.
2329 Eagle, Alameda, CA, 94501. Contact: Mel Barron, Pres. - Tel: (510) 769-0980. Bicycle rickshaw (pedicab). Established: 1974 - No. of Units: Company Owned: 6 - Distributed: 7 - Total Inv: $5,500 - 2 units - Financing: No.

ROJOS POPCORN CO.
RoJo's U.S.A., Inc.
241 McHenry St., Burlington, WI, 53105-1827. Contact: Jim Bortmess, Pres. - Tel: (414) 763-9434. Wholesale popcorn to retail outlets. Established: 1982 - Offering Distributorships Since: 1983 - No. of Units: Company Owned: 1 - Franchised: 20 - Total Inv: $7,000 - $20,000 - Financing: No.

ROMANCO PUBLISHERS
2842 Ridge Rd., P.O. Box 324, Lansing, IL, 60438-0324. Contact: Operators, Data Entry Personnel - Tel: (800) 699-6099, ext. 20543. Mortgage reduction and auditing requires no previous experience in loan acceleration or auditing. We train you and/or your agent network. Just call the toll free number 24 hours a day and ask for your free information package now. Established: 1988 - Franchising Since: 1988 - No. of Units: Franchised: Several hundred - Total Inv: can start for less than $1,000 - Financing: None.

RX SURGICAL SERVICES
525 Lisbon Ave., Rio Rancho, NM, 87124. Contact: Ozzie Martin, Owner - Tel: (505) 892-9520. Sharpening and repair of surgical instruments on hospital site via mobile truck. Established: 1983 - Franchising Since: 1983 - No. of Units: Company Owned: 1 - Franchised: 6 - Total Inv: $75,000.

SAS TAX PAC DISTRIBUTORS
22865 Lakeforth, El Toro, CA, 92630. Contact: Davest Adams, Sales Mgr. - Tel: (714) 586-0522. Sales distributors for quality tax preparation product. No tax prep license required. Established: 1981 - Offering Distributorships Since: 1984 - No. of Units: 1 - Approx. Inv: $10,000 inventory.

SELECTIVE BOOKS INC.
Box 1140, Clearwater, FL, 34617. Contact: Lee Howard, Pres. - Tel: (813) 447-0100. Mail order book selling. We publish manuals, books and trade directories which are sold by mail order dealers in US and abroad. Up to 1,000% profit to registered dealers. Established: 1969 - No. of Units: Company Owned: 1 - Independent Dealers: 175 - Registered dealer fee: $124.95 - Total Inv: Dealership fee plus capital necessary for advertising and mailing expenses - Financing: None.

SENSOMATIC SAVER SYSTEM DEALERS
Sensormatic Electronics Corp.
500 N.W. 12th Ave., Deerfield Beach, FL, 33442. Contact: Bob Clucas, Senior Sales Dept. - Tel: (305) 427-9700. Distribution of anti-shoplifting equipment and closed circuit TV. Established: 1968 - Offering Distributorships Since: 1987 - No. of Units: Company Owned: 64 - Distributors: 48 - Total Inv: $5,495 for an area of 1 million people plus $600 tools - Financing: Yes to qualified applicants.

SMALL BUSINESS CLUB
2014 N. Saginaw Rd., Ste. #110, P.O. Box 2440, Midland, MI, 48640. Contact: Dale W. Woys, Mktg. Dir. - Tel: (517) 839-1069. For a small yearly fee, members receive the clubs monthly newsletter as well as services for: Logo preparation, typesetting, media & list selection, ad preparation, military marketing service, mailing list service, database dev. & main., wholesale printing, publicity releases prepared, and a number of other services for the small business person. Established: 1990 - Franchising Since: 1990 - No. of Units: Company Owned: 1 - Franchised: 275 - Franchise Fee: below $100. - Royalty: None - Total Inv: below $100. - Financing: Visa/MC.

SMOKEETER ELECTRONIC AIR CLEANERS & INDOOR AIR QUALITY SYSTEMS
United Air Specialists, Inc.
4440 Creek Rd., Cincinnati, OH, 45242. Contact: Lynne Eagan, Mktg. Dir. - Tel: (800) 551-5401. Sales and service of leading brand name air cleaners. Protected territory with a large number of prospects in each. Advertising support available. Established: 1966 - Offering Distributorships Since: 1967 - Number of Distributors: 58 - Total Inv: $30,000.

SOLID/FLUE CHIMNEY SYSTEMS, INC.
4937 Starr St., S.E., Grand Rapids, MI, 49546-6350. Contact: Doug La Fleur, Pres. - Tel: (616) 940-8809. Chimney lining and restoration. Established: 1980 - Offering Dealerships Since: 1989 - No. of Dealerships: 25 - Fee: $9,800 - Total Inv: $40,000.

SPR DETAIL MAGIC
SPR International, Inc.
4492 Acworth Industrial Dr., Ste. 102, Acworth, GA, 30101. Contact: Larry Stevens, Pres. - Tel: (770) 966-1331. Complete line of auto detail products, easy to use. Established: 1990 - Franchising Since: 1990 - No. of Units: Company Owned: 1 - Franchised: 75 - Franchise Fee: $995. - Royalty: None - Financing: No.

TEMPACO
Tempaco, Inc.
1701 Alden Rd., Orlando, FL, 32803. Contact: Chuck Clark or Lori Gibbs, President and Assistant - Tel: (407) 898-3456, Fax: (407) 898-7316. Wholesale parts and controls for heating, air conditioning, refrigeration, steam and process hot water; and control systems. Established: 1946 - Franchising Since: 1972 - No. of Units: Company Owned: 5 - Franchised: 16 - Franchise Fee: $25,000 single system - Royalty: 50/50 split of gross - Total Inv: $25,000 single unit - Financing: Multi-unit and Vetfran.

TIMBER LOG BUILDING SYSTEMS
639 Old Hartford Rd., Colchester, CT, 06415. Contact: Tony Koenig, Owner - Tel: (203) 537-2394 or (800) 533-5906. Sales and construction of precut log homes and commercial log structures. Established: 1975 - Offering Distributorships Since: 1976 - No. of Units: Company Owned: 2 - Distributors: 30 - Total Inv: $100,000 - $150,000 (cost of model home and operational expenses) - Financing: No.

TOM'S FOOD, INC.
900 8th St., Columbus, GA, 31902. Contact: Charles Gosa, Dir. Fran. Dev. - Tel: (706) 323-2721. Snack foods under Tom's brand name. Distribution in 46 states. Established: 1925 - Franchising Since: 1985 - No. of Units: Company Owned: 20 - Franchised: 439 - Franchise Fee: varies with size (min. $7,500 for single route) - Total Inv: varies with size of business - Financing: Yes, for qualified applicants.

TOTAL SHAVING SOLUTION, THE
Total Solutions, Inc.
2400 S.W. Jefferson Ave., Peoria, IL, 61605-3650. Contact: Linda Crotz, Admin. - Tel: (309) 637-0600. The 'Total Shaving Solution' is a 100% natural and 100% guaranteed shaving discovery that provides the closest, most comfortable shave available to mankind for both men or women. Eliminates nicks, razor burn & cuts. Replacements for foams, creams, gels & soaps. Can shave with 3 drops! Established: 1988 - Offering dealerships Since: 1988 - Total Inv: $490 - Financing: N/A.

TRANSWORLD INDUSTRIES
2961 W. Glenlord Rd., Stevensville, MI, 49127. Contact: Mktg. Dept. - Tel: (616) 429-8706, Fax: (616) 426-1760. KDF-Carbosyl Water filtration products for the domestic-foreign markets - Distributors - manufacturers of a complete line of quality water treatment products - water filters - water softeners for commercial, industrial and residential needs. No franchise to buy, no sales quota, no inventory investment, guaranteed exclusive territory, no start up costs! You only order what you have sold. Established: 1968 - No. of Units: Company Owned: 2,653 distributors - Total Inv: $140.00 for 4 colored sample counter top filters - Financing: Local banks.

ULTRA BOND, INC.
3696 Beatty Dr., Riverside, CA, 92506-2423. Contact: Richard Campfield, Pres. - Tel: (800) 347-2820, (909) 782-0991. Specializing in windshield repair, stone damage and long cracks. The original long crack repair inventor. Patents pending. Established: 1989 - No. of Units: Company Owned: 1 - Distributed: 225 - Fee: $1,850 - $4,850 - Total Inv: $1,850 - $4,850 - Financing: Yes.

UNCO INDUSTRIES, INC.
7802 Old Spring St., Racine, WI, 53406. Contact: Tom Chapman, Pres. - Tel: (414) 886-2665, Fax: (414) 886-2296. Manufacturer of nightcrawlers and organic fertilizers. Established: 1980 - No. of Units: Company Owned: 1 - Dealership Fee: $3,490 - Total Inv: depends on level of production - Financing: Partial.

VACUFLO - CENTRAL VACUUM CLEANING SYSTEMS
H-P Products, Inc.
512 W. Gorgas St., Louisville, OH, 44641. Contact: Bud Kirkpatrick, Dir./Mktg. - Tel: (216) 875-5556. Vacuum cleaning business. Designed for installation in residential and commercial applications in new and existing construction markets. Marketing assistance includes factory training, co-op funds, communications program for print ads, radio, T.V., trade shows, vehicle graphics. Distributorships available. Established: 1948 - No. of Units: Company Owned: 1 - Distributors: 300+ - Total Inv: $5,000+ - Financing: No, but net 30 days with approved credit on equipment.

VENDOR$ CHOICE™, THE
D.J. Gill Associates Inc.
P.O. Box 591, 1595 Imperial Way, Unit 114, Thorofare, NJ, 08086-0591. Contact: Lory Gill, V.P. - Tel: (609) 384-0440, Fax: (609)384-0044. Set up and design of all types of vending routes as well as sales & service. Established: 1981 - Franchising Since: 1986 - No. of Units: Company Owned: 3 - Franchised: 15,000 plus.

VITAMIN POWER
Vitamin Power Incorporated
Box 0818 E2, Freeport, NY, 11520 - 0818. Contact: Bob Edwards, Dir. of Marketing - Tel: (516) 378-0900. Producers of over 350 health and fitness nutritional products including body-building, dieting, skin-care and functionalized nutritional purposes. Effective sales support material available. Established: 1975 - No. of Independent Distributors: 10,000.

WASCOMAT OF AMERICA
461 Doughty Blvd., Inwood, NY, 11096. Contact: Jack McCloy, Cont. - Tel: (516) 371-4400. Coin operated laundry centers. Total Inv: Variable.

WAT-A-HEATER WATER PRE-HEATING SYSTEM
Watsco Inc.
1943 Oakley, Topeka, KS, 66604. Contact: Chris Waters, Sales Mgr. - Tel: (913) 233-8881. Established dealers to distribute a retro-fit unit that attaches to a customer's existing gas fired water heater. The system increases hot water capacities by twice the norm, while saving on the consumer's gas water heating bill by more than 50%. Established: 1985 - Offering Distributorships Since: 1988 - No. of Units: Company Owned: 1 - Distributors: 2 - Total Inv: $1,000 inventory - Financing: No.

WESTROCK ICE CREAM
1565-D Fifth Industrial Court, Bayshore, NY, 11706. Contact: Stephen Kronrad, Pres. - Tel: (516) 666-5252. Mobile vending of ice cream, candy, soda and hot dogs from a moped-powered vending vehicle or expand to a master distribution center with 25 vehicles. Established: 1971 - Offering Distributorships Since: 1971 - No. of Units: Company Owned: 80 - Distributors: 500 - Total Inv: starting at $1,495 - Financing: On trucks only.

WIMBERLEY HOMES
P.O. Box 335, San Marcos, TX, 78667. Contact: Floyd MacKenzie, Treasurer - Tel: (210) 629-1400 or Fax: (512) 353-5333. Construction of homes under $50,000. Modular and pre-constructed at factory. Established: 1987 - Licensed Since: 1988 - No. of Units: 1 - Royalty: $300/mthly. - Total Inv: cost of home - Financing: No.

WORLD OF WARES
Creative Ventures Corp.
P.O. Box 4713, Albany, GA, 31706-4713. Contact: Melvin James, Jr., Pres. - Tel: (912) 431-0825. Specialty merchandise, business advertising specialties. Established: 1980 - Total Inv: $25. refundable - Financing: No.

WORLDWIDE PRODUCTS - REHEATER LTD.
3666 N. Miller Rd., Ste. 101, Scottsdale, AZ, 85251. Contact: Michael E. Slominski, Principal/Owner - Tel: (602) 945-0393. Product marketing and manufacturing company offering distributorships in the USA. Overseas markets also available on exclusive basis. Portable, re-usable instant heat packs is the main product line. Seven U.S patents. Medical and sports applications. Established: 1985 - Franchising Since: 1990 - No. of Units: Franchised: 102 - Franchise Fee: $12,000 with 75% in product - Total Inv: All additional orders at dist. costs.

WORM WAREHOUSE
Flynn Rd., Burke, NY, 12917. Contact: Conrad Kruger, Owner - Tel: (518) 483-7687 or (800) 535-2248. Live bait packaging and distribution. Includes worms, night crawlers, fish, crayfish and insects. Established: 1970 - Distributing Since: 1991 - No. of Units: Company Owned: 2 - Total Inv: $5,000 - Financing: No.

WRITE-1 CORPORATION
415 Route 18, Ste. 111, East Brunswick, NJ, 08816. Contact: Allan A. Paulvin, Pres. - Tel: (908) 238-4327. Imprinted advertising specialty items. Established: 1990 - Franchising Since: 1991 - No. of Units: Company Owned: 1 - Franchised: 1 - Franchise Fee: $500 - Royalty: $150 - $300 yearly maintenance fees.

YAMAHA MOTOR CORP., USA
6555 Katella Ave., Cypress, CA, 90630. Contact: John Donaldson, Legal Dept. - Tel: (714) 761-7300. Distributor Yamaha motorized products. Established: 1966 - Offering Distributorships Since: 1966 - Approx. Inv: $30,000 - $100,000 - Financing: Inventory

YELLOWSTONE LOG HOMES
280 N. Yellowstone Hwy., Rigby, ID, 83442. Contact: Lynn Youngstrom, Owner - Tel: (208) 745-8108. Manufactures logs for homes. Machined to a uniform size. Established: 1962 - No. of Units: 1 - Inv: $4,000 - Financing: No.

EMPLOYMENT & PERSONNEL

A-1 EMPLOYMENT SERVICES
1 Woodbridge Center, Woodbridge, NJ, 07095. Contact: Tom Greene, Pres. - Tel: (908) 855-8585 or (908) 855-0898. Two franchises are available: Apoxiforce is a temporary employment service; Plusmates is a permanent employment service. Involving recruitment & placement of professional & clerical personnel. Franchising available only in the states of NJ, NY, PA & CT. Established: 1960 - Franchising Since: 1962 - No. of Units: Company Owned: 6 - Franchise Fee: $15,000 - Royalty: 6-7%- assist in payroll funding, billing & collection - Total Inv: $25,000 - $30,000 - Financing: can be made available.

ACCOUNTANTS INC.
Accountants Inc. Services
111 Anza Blvd., Ste. 400, Burlingame, CA, 94010. Contact: William McPherson, Fran. Dev. Mgr. - Tel: (415) 579-1111, Fax: (415) 579-1927. Personnel services company specializing in temporary and permanent staffing of accounting and finance positions. Established: 1986 - Franchising Since: 1994 - No. of Units: Company Owned: 14 - Franchised: 5 - Franchise Fee: $30,000 - Royalty: 8%-10% - Total Inv: $73,000 - $95,000 additional working capital requirements - Financing: 100% temporary payroll and accounts receivable.

ADIA PERSONNEL SERVICES
Adia Services, Inc.
100 Redwood Shores Pkwy., Redwood City, CA, 94065. Contact: Barbara Richardson, Franc. Dev. - Tel: (800) 827-8928. Full service temporary help and full-time placement service providing skilled clerical, secretarial, word processing, technical, and light industrial personnel. Established: 1957 - Franchising Since: 1976 - No. of Units: Company Owned: 157 - Franchised: 133 - Franchise Fee: $17,500 - Royalty: varies according to hours billed in a calendar year - Total Inv: $90,380 - $159,830 incl. fran. fee - Financing: on specific computer equip. hardware; temporary payroll.

ALLAN & PARTNERS
625 Stanwix St., Pittsburgh, PA, 15222. Contact: Allan Hyman - Tel: (412) 391-9400. Executive marketing out-placement, resume services to corporate and private sector clients. Established: 1972 - Franchising Since: 1984 - No. of Units: 2 - Approx. Inv: $25,000 - Financing: None.

ATWORK
Atwork Personnel Services
1470 Main St., White Pine, TN, 37890. Contact: John Hall, CEO - Tel: (615) 674-7666, Fax: (615) 674-8780. Temporary staffing. Established: 1990 - Franchising Since: 1992 - No. of Units: Franchised: 30 - Franchise Fee: $1.00 - Royalty: 8% - Total Inv: $15,000 - $25,000 office set-up - Financing: Funding of payroll.

BURNETT PERSONNEL SERVICES
Burnett Companies Consolidated
9800 Richmond St., Ste. 800, Houston, TX, 77042. Contact: Debbie D'Ambrosio or Sue Burnett, Fran. Mgr/Sr. V.P. - Tel: (713) 977-4777. Personnel business. Permanent and temporary help service. Established: 1974 - Franchising Since: 1990 - No. of Units: Company Owned: 11 - Franchised: 1 - Franchise Fee: $15,000 - Total Inv: $15,000 - Financing: Yes.

CAREER ADVANCEMENT SCIENCES
101 N. Meadows Dr., #112, Wexford, PA, 15090-8368. Contact: Richard D. Hindman, Pres. - Tel: (412) 934-9080. Executive marketing, corporate outplacement and professional resume preparation services. Appoint qualified agents in major markets to represent firm. Training provided. A centralized support center produces all services sold. A unique opportunity with great profit potential and virtually no risk. Established: 1962 - Licensing Since: 1989 - No. of Units: Company Owned: 4 - Licensed: 14 - Total Inv: $3,000 - $5,000 for working capital only.

CAREER BLAZERS STAFFING SERVICES
590 Fifth Ave., 7th Fl., New York, NY, 10036. Contact: Howard Kane, Exec. V.P. - Tel: (800) 284-3232. Full service employment organization specializing in permanent and temporary personnel. Focus is on administrative support through middle management. Established: 1949 - Franchising Since: 1987 - No. of Units: Company Owned: 4 - Franchised/Licensed: 8 - Franchise Fee: $15,000 to $18,000 - Royalty: varies with gross billings - Total Inv: $90,000 to $120,000 capital required - Financing: Full financing of temporary payroll includes all mandatory payroll expenses, accounts receivable, credit & collections support.

CAREERS U.S.A., INC.
1825 JFK Blvd., Philadelphia, PA, 19103. Contact: George Ounjian, Pres. - Tel: (800) 822-8300. Temporary and permanent personnel services. General office support, telemarketing, data entry, computer operations, word processing. Light industrial. Established: 1981 - Franchising Since: 1987 - No. of Units: Company Owned: 13 - Franchised: 5 - Franchise Fee: $15,000 (1/2 of which may be financed) - Royalty: percentage of profit - Total Inv: $84,500 - $99,500 (fran. fee, training, equip., work cap.) - Financing: From lending institutions if qualified.

CHECKMATE *
Checkmate Systems, Inc.
P.O. Box 32034, Charleston, SC, 29417. Contact: Ed Arrington, V.P. Mktg. - Tel: (803) 763-9393. Employee leasing. Established: 1992 - Franchising Since: 1993 - No. of Units: Franchised: 15 - Franchise Fee: $19,500 - Royalty: 7.5% of gross fees received - Total Inv: $40,400 to $51,000 - Financing: None.

COMPUTEMP, INC.
4401 N. Federal Hwy., Ste. 202, Boca Raton, FL, 33431. Contact: Leo Gordon, V.P. Mkt. Dev. - Tel: (407) 362-9104, Fax: (407) 367-9802. National temp staffing service, specializing in tech. support in the data processing industry. Established: 1984 - Franchising Since: 1991 - No. of Units: Company Owned: 6 - Franchised: 8 - Franchise Fee: $30,000 - Royalty: 7% of gross sales - Total Inv: $124,000 - $175,000 ($30,000 fee, $30,000 - $40,000 start-up, $50,000 - $100,000 op. cap.) - Financing: Accounts receivable.

DR. PERSONNEL
Dr. Personnel, Inc.
9785 S. Chanteclair Ct., Highlands Ranch, CO, 80126. Contact: George M. Fornnarino, Pres. - Tel: (303) 791-7643. Placement service providing paramedical and paradental personnel to the health care industry. Established: 1976 - Franchising Since: 1977 - No. of Units: Franchised: 14 - Franchise Fee: $10,000 - $15,000 - Royalty: 2% gr. sales - Total Inv: $30,000 - $35,000.

DUNHILL PERSONNEL SYSTEM, INC.
1000 Woodbury Rd., Woodbury, NY, 11797. Contact: Joe Melillo, Sales Coord. - Tel: (516) 364-8800. An international company offering three different franchises in the personnel service industry. The Professional Search franchise recruits and searches for management and professional personnel; the Office Personnel franchise specializes in high demand office personnel and the Temporary Service franchise contracts out office or light industrial staff on short- or long-term assignments. Established: 1952 - Franchising Since: 1961 - No. of Units: Company Owned:18 - Franchised: 260- Franchise Fee: $10,000 - $25,000 - Royalty: 7% on perm., 4% on temp. - Total Inv: $50,000 - $125,000 - Financing: Partial.

DYNAMIC TEMPORARY SERVICES, INC.
3535 Piedmont Rd. NE, Atlanta, GA, 30305-4603. Contact: Mark Guyette - Tel: (800) 765-6342. Temporary help service specializing in providing office automation and personnel to major businesses. Special programs include cross-training for temp. employees, on-the-job reference aids, client service, and an OA Specialist in each office and a legal staffing program. Established: 1974 - Franchising Since: 1987 - No. of Units: Company Owned: 1 - Franchised: 6 - Royalty: commission plus bonus - Total Inv: $60,000 - $90,000 - Financing: No.

EXPRESS PERSONNEL SERVICES
Express Services, Inc.
6300 N.W. Expressway, Oklahoma City, OK, 73132. Contact: Fran. Dept. - Tel: (800) 652-6400. Employment staffing company with temporary, permanent placement & executive search divisions. Established: 1983 - Franchising Since: 1985 - No. of Units: Franchised: 253 - Franchise Fee: $3,000 - $5,000 - Royalty: 6% - 9% - Total Inv: $14,500 to $17,500 initial fees; total investment range $80,000 to $120,000 - Financing: 100% temporary payroll financing.

F-O-R-T-U-N-E PERSONNEL CONSULTANTS
Fortune Franchise Corp.
1155 Avenue of the Americas, 15th Flr., New York, NY, 10036-2711. Contact: H. Pete Erbe, Jr., Dir., Fran. Sales - Tel: (800) 886-7839. Middle management and executive recruiting. Established: 1959 - Franchising Since: 1973 - No. of Units: Franchised: 65 - Franchise Fee: $35,000 - Royalty: 7%, 1% adv. - Total Inv: $62,850 - $75,600 - Financing: 1/3 of franchise fee.

FIRSTAFF, INC.
3800 W. 80th St. #1155, Bloomington, MN, 55431-4426. Contact: James Ginther, Pres. - Tel: (612) 896-3999. First modern franchise exclusively in the office support marketplace for permanent and temporary personnel. A full compliment of support services are provided including: computerized market analysis, site assistance, comprehensive training, pre-opening services and more. Established: 1967 - Franchising Since: 1990 - No. of Units: Company Owned: 6 - Franchised: 3 - Franchise Fee $20,000 - $50,000 (depending on pop. size) - Royalty: 7%, 1% adv. - Total Inv: $115,000 - $200,000 - Financing: Yes.

FLEX-TEAM
Flex Team, Inc.
265 South Main St., Akron, OH, 44308. Contact: Sanford Rose, Pres. - Tel: (216) 762-3838. A full temporary service business offering rapid response for client requirements for personnel categories including clerical, light industrial, medical, technical, and food service. Also offers a lease to hire option to its clients. Established: 1985 - Franchising Since: 1990 - No. of Units: Company Owned: 2 - Franchise Fee: $15,000 - Royalty: 6% - Total Inv: $25,000 - $75,000 - Financing: Yes.

FORTUNE FRANCHISE CORPORATION *
1155 Avenue of Americas, 15th Flr., New York, NY, 10036. Contact: H. Pete Erbe, Jr., Dir. of Sales - Tel: (800) 886-7839, Fax: (212) 302-2422. Executive recruiting industry placing mid-management professionals on a contingency and/or retainer basis. Opportunity to expand into interim recruitment business as Alternastaff. Extablished: 1959 - Franchising Since: 1974 - No. of Units: Franchised: 72 - Franchise Fee: $36,000 - Royalty: 7% royalty and 1% adv. - Total Inv: $30,000 - $50,000+ fran. fee - Financing: 50% for fran. fee for qualified candidates.

FRIEND OF THE FAMILY
Merlin Services Corp.
10825 Stroup Rd., Roswell, GA, 30075-2215. Contact: Judi Merlin, Pres. - Tel: (404) 643-3000, Fax: (404) 643-3020. Booking agency for child care, elder care and other staff. Established: 1984 - Franchising Since: 1990 - No. of Units: Company Owned: 1 - Licensed: 5 - License Fee: $9,500 - Total Inv: $35,000 - $70,000 - Financing: No.

HAMILTON-RYKER COMPANY, THE
P.O. Box 1068, Martin, TN, 38237. Contact: Pam Thompson, Fran. Mgr. - Tel: (901) 587-3195 or (800) 554-4726. Temporary and permanent employment service. Established: 1971 - Franchising Since: 1990 - No. of Units: Company Owned: 14 - Franchised: 1 - Franchise Fee: $15,000 - Royalty: 7% - Total Inv: $60,000 - $100,000 - Financing: Yes.

HEALTH FORCE, INC.
Career Employment Services
177 Crossways Park Dr., Woodbury, NY, 11797. Contact: Pat Hiller, Dir. of Fran. Dev. - Tel: (800) 967-1001. Temporary nursing service which specializes in home care and staffing. Payroll funding, fully computerized, become involved in one of the fastest growing industries. Established: 1975 - Franchising Since: 1982 - No. of Units: Company Owned: 19 - Franchised: 45 - Franchise Fee: $39,500 - Royalty: 12.5% - 8.5% of gross sales - Total Inv: $100,000 - $125,000 - Financing: Half of franchise fee.

HEALTHCARE RECRUITERS INT'L
5430 LBJ Freeway, Ste. 1600, Dallas, TX, 75240. Contact: Frank Cooksey, Pres. - Tel: (800) 634-1839 or (214) 770 2020. Recruiting medical sales, sales management and marketing personnel throughout the U.S. and Canada, utilizing our exclusive registered client candidate referral system. Established: 1983 - Franchising Since: 1985 - No. of Units: 35 - Franchise Fee: $25,000+ - Royalty: 10% - Total Inv: additional $25,000+ $50,000 work cap - Financing: Yes.

HOPE CAREER CENTERS
Helping Others Pursue Education
2735 S. Newton St., Denver, CO, 80236. Contact: Manning A. Mann, Exec. Dir. - Tel: (303) 934-1018, Fax: (303) 934-1112. Hope offers a business of helping others providing education and financial help including scholarships, funding assistance, career planning, college planning, corporate reimbursement programs for displaced workers, undergraduates, veterans, college bound students, disadvantaged citizens, and people wanting career change for home entrepreneurs. Established: 1985 - Franchising Since: 1989 - No. of Units: Company Owned: 1 - Franchised: 700 plus - Franchise Fee: $659. - Royalty: None - Total Inv: $659. - Financing: Yes.

HOSTESS HELPER
20 Whittlesey Rd., Newton Centre, MA, 02159-2622. Contact: Ellen Hochberger, Owner/Mgr. - Tel: (617) 244-7465. Hostess Helper is a temporary waitstaff and party planning service. Established: 1973 - Franchising Since: 1990 - No. of Units: Company Owned: 1 - Franchise Fee: $10,000 - Royalty: 7% - Total Inv: $10,000 - $17,000 - Financing: None.

INTERIM HEALTHCARE
Interim Services, Inc.
2050 Spectrum Blvd., Ft. Lauderdale, FL, 33309. Contact: Gigi Garcia, Dir. Mktg. Dev. - Tel: (800) 840-6568. One of the largest providers of nurses and para-professionals in home health care as well as hospitals and nursing homes. Established: 1946 - Franchising Since: 1956 - No. of Units: Company Owned: 98 - Franchised: 290 - Franchise Fee: $5,000 - Royalty: 5% to 8% of sales - Total Inv: $125,000, start-up & operating expenses - Financing: Payroll funding and invoicing by franchisor.

INTERIM PERSONNEL
Interim Services Inc.
2050 Spectrum Blvd., Ft. Lauderdale, FL, 33309. Contact: John J. Marquez, Dir., Market Dev. - Tel: (305) 938-7600. Temporary and full-time employee staffing services. Office clerical, light industrial, marketing support, telemarketing, para-technical, data processing, word processing. Company is a wholly owned subsidiary of H & R Block, the income tax company. Established: 1946 - Franchising Since: 1956 - No. of Units: Company Owned: 158 - Franchised: 190 - Franchise Fee: $5,000 - Royalty: Gross Profit Split - 75% to licensee - Total Inv: $50,000 - $100,000 working cap. - Financing: Temporary employee payroll, taxes and insurance.

LABOR FINDERS / OFFICE FORCE *
Labor Finders International, Inc.
3910 RCA Blvd., #1001, Palm Beach Gardens, FL, 33410. Contact: Jeff Burnett, CFO - Tel: (407) 627-6507, Fax: (407) 627-6556. Temporary personnel - industrial, construction, semi-skilled & skilled trades. Office/clerical occupations. Established: 1975 - Franchising Since: 1979 - No. of Units: Franchised: 91 - Franchise Fee: $5,000 - Royalty: 4% sales - Total Inv: $60,000 work. cap., $5,000 fran. fee - Financing: Third party.

LABOR WORLD
Outsource International
8000 N. Federal Hwy., Boca Raton, FL, 33487. Contact: Ed Secaul, Dir., Fran. Dev. - Tel: (407) 997-5000, ext. 236. Temporary industrial personnel. Rated in top 7% of Inc. 500 for 2 consecutive years. Territories available nationwide. Established: 1974 - Franchising Since: 1984 - No. of Units: Company Owned: 21 - Franchised: 83 - Franchise Fee: $20,000 - Royalty: Declining percentage of gross profit - Total Inv: $100,000 - Financing: None.

LINK STAFFING SERVICES
Personnel Concepts, Inc.
One West Loop South, Ste. 590, Houston, TX, 77027. Contact: Ike Steele, V.P. Fran. - Tel: (713) 622-7488. A temporary staffing company addressing the various needs of business and industry. Established: 1980 - Franchising Since: 1994 - No. of Units: Company Owned: 8 - Franchised: 3 - Franchise Fee: $15,000 - Royalty: Percentage of gross margin varies - Total Inv: $95,000 - $155,000 - Financing: Link finances the temporary payroll and receivables.

LLOYD PERSONNEL SYSTEMS, INC.
445 Broadhollow Rd., Ste. 120, Melville, NY, 11747. Contact: Merrill Banks, Pres. - Tel: (516) 777-7600. Place personnel in temporary or permanent employment.

MANAGEMENT RECRUITERS / SALES CONSULTANTS
Management Recruiters International, Inc.
1127 Euclid Ave., Ste. 1400, Cleveland, OH, 44115-1638. Contact: Robert A. Angell, V.P. Fran. Mktg. - Tel: (216) 696-1122, (800) 875-4000, Fax: (216) 696-3221. Complete range of recruitment and human resource services including: permanent executive, mid-management, professional, marketing, sales management, and sales placement both on a contingency and retainer basis; interim professional and sales staffing; video-conferencing; permanent and temporary office support personnel; and outplacement. Established: 1957 - Franchising Since; 1965 - No. of Units: Company Owned: 45 - Franchised: 572 - Franchise Fee: US $40,000, CAN $45,000 - Royalty: US 7%, .5% adv., CAN 7%, 1% adv. - Total Inv: US $70,000 to $100,000, CAN $95,000 to $120,000 - Financing: None.

MANPOWER TEMPORARY SERVICES
5301 N. Ironwood Rd., , Milwaukee, WI, 53201. Contact: John Simon , Fran. Dir. - Tel: (414) 961-1000. Temporary help service. Established: 1948 - Franchising Since: 1954 - No. of Units: Company Owned: 573 - Franchised: 447 - Franchise Fee: $50,000 min. - Total Inv: varies - Financing: No.

NAT'L RESTAURANT SEARCH, INC.
910 West Lake St., #108, Roselle, IL, 60172-3352. Contact: John W. Chitvanni, Pres. - Tel: (708) 924-1800. Executive search for key executives and presidents. Handle search assignments in the areas of operations, franchise sales and development, real estate and construction, marketing, finance and human resources. Established: 1981.

NORRELL TEMPORARY SERVICES
3535 Piedmont Rd., N.E., Atlanta, GA, 30305. Contact: Mark Guyette, V.P. Fran Dev. - Tel: (404) 240-3476, Fax: (404) 240-3084. Meets client personnel needs by providing quality temporary help in the areas of clerical, secretarial, office automation and light industry. Established: 1961 - Franchising Since: 1966 - No. of Units: Company Owned: 130 - Franchised: 114 - Royalty: 60% to 40% GM$ (Varies) - Total Inv: $60,000 - $95,000 - Financing: To current owners & associates.

PERSONNEL NETWORK, THE - PERSONET *
PersoNet, Inc.
P.O. Box 4923, Palm Harbor, FL, 34685-0223. Contact: Bob Riley, Pres. - Tel: (813) 372-2996. Temporary & permanent placement, employment, staffing services and human resources consulting services. Established: 1994 - Franchising Since: 1995 - No. of Units: Franchised: 3 - Franchise Fee: $12,000 or $15,000 - Royalty: 6% of gross sales - Total Inv: $12,000 or $15,000 fran. fee, $15,000 first year work. cap. - Financing: Yes.

PRO-TEM, FLEX-STAFF
JBS, Inc.
214 N. Main St., #202, Natick, MA, 01760-1131. Contact: Giles A. Powers, Pres. - Tel: (508) 650-0035. We offer a low-cost franchise opportunity, which is restricted to individuals having a minimum of two years of successful hands-on management experience in the staffing industry. Established: 1970 - Franchising Since: 1975 - No. of Units: Company Owned: 1 - Franchised: 11 - Franchise Fee: $1,000 - Royalty: varies by market - Total Inv: $25,000 - $60,000 - Financing: Partial working capital financing.

PROFESSIONAL DYNAMETRIC PROGRAMS/PDP, INC.
400 W. Hwy. 24, Ste. 201, Box 5289, Woodland Park, CO, 80866. Contact: Bruce M. Hubby, Pres. - Tel: (719) 687-6074. A business to business franchise. Interface with corporate decision makers and CEO's. Sell, train, consult and service large and small businesses in comprehensive management programs for: hiring, motivating, stress managing and evaluating performances. Established: 1978 - Franchising Since: 1980 - No. of Units: Franchised: 28 - Franchise Fee: $29,500 - Royalty: 10% - Total Inv: $5,000 - $10,000 work cap. + fran. fee - Financing: $15,000 down, 1 yr. zero interest note on balance.

PROFILES - SECURITY & PERSONNEL RISK ASSESSMENTS
Profiles
P.O. Box 880461, San Diego, CA, 92168. Contact: Phil Sprague, Pres. - Tel: (619) 280-3486, Fax: (619) 234-9340. Accurate assessments about an applicant's or employee's past and their potential capabilities. Attitudes, security risk, alcohol or drug abuse, psychological adjustment, theft investigations. Evaluations of clerks, vehicle drivers, supervisors, managers, and executives. No one can match our price or provide employers with as many methods for answering this very import question - Asset or Liability? Make money by providing this valuable answer. Established: 1982 - Franchising Since: 1986 - No. of Units: Company Owned: 1 - Franchised: 13 - Franchise Fee: $1,000 - Royalty: $3.50 per test - Total Inv: $1,500 to $15,000 - Financing: Varies.

REGIONAL NETWORK OF PERSONNEL CONSULTANTS, THE
Murphy Management Corporation
211 W. 22nd St., Ste. 221, Oak Brook, IL, 60521. Contact: Wm Murphy, Pres. - Tel: (708) 571-1088. Local area network of existing private employment agencies/search/recruiting firms sharing job orders, job order information and placements. Established: 1984 - Franchising Since: 1985 - No. of Units: Company Owned: 3 - Franchised: 8 - Total Inv: $5,000 plus additional $5,000 for computer equipment - Financing: None.

REMEDY STAFFING SERVICES
RemedyTemp, Inc.
32122 Camino Capistrano, San Juan Capistrano, CA, 92675. Contact: Gerry Rhydderch, V.P. Fran. Dev. - Tel: (800) 722-8367. Full service staffing business providing both temporary & full time positions in office, clerical, legal, accounting, admin, office automation & light industrial areas. The only staffing co. with validated behavioral testing. Established: 1965 - Franchising Since: 1987 - No. of Units: Company Owned: 70 - Franchised: 81 - Franchise Fee: $17,000 - Royalty: Varies depending on hours billed - Total Inv: $55,000 (incl. fee) cash, $50,000 work. cap. - Financing: Not thru co.

RETAIL RECRUITERS
Retail Recruiters International, Inc.
3820 Premier Ave., Memphis, TN, 38118. Contact: Bill Richey, Fran. Dir. - Tel: (901) 867-0600. Personnel search and recruiting. The placing of job candidates with client companies on a local and national level serving many specialists including executive search, retail, medical, sales and marketing, clerical, data processing, accounting and finance, banking and insurance, legal, food and hospitality and others. Established: 1975 - Franchising Since: 1976 - No. of Units: Company Owned: 1 - Franchised: 17 - Franchise Fee: $25,000 - Royalty: 7% + 1% adv.

RETIREE SKILLS, INC.
1475 W. Prince Rd., Tucson, AZ, 85705. Contact: Bob Rheinhart, Pres. - Tel: (602) 888-8310. Temporary help service specializing in the "over 50" worker, both men and women. In business over 17 years in Tucson. Over 200 job skills listed. Furnishing skilled, experienced and dependable workers to both business and industry. Established: 1978 - Franchising Since: 1989 - No. of Units: Company Owned: 1 - Franchise Fee: $9,500 - $15,000 depending on area - Royalty: 4% - Total Inv: $15,000 fran. fee, total approx. $30,000 - Financing: No. Franchising discontinued temporary.

ROCKPORT INSTITUTE
10124 Lakewood Dr., Rockville, MD, 20850. Contact: Susan Ayars, Train. Mgr. - Tel: (301) 279-2383. Aptitude testing/career consulting to help adults and young people choose the best career direction. Some licensees consult with organizations in personnel selection and human resource development. Established: 1981 - Franchising Since: 1989 - No. of Units: Company Owned: 1 - Franchised: 32 - Franchise Fee: $2,880 - Royalty: $100 per testing unit, no percentage royalty - Total Inv: $5,000 (fran. fee plus office expenses) - Financing: No.

ROTH YOUNG PERSONNEL SERVICES, INC.
Winston Franchise Corp.
535 Fifth Ave., New York, NY, 10017. Contact: William Beck, Pres. - Tel: (212) 557-4900. Franchise sales of executive recruiting. Established: 1962 - Franchising Since: 1964 - No. of Units: Company Owned: 18 - Franchised: 18 - Franchise Fee: $35,000 up-front cash - Royalty: 3% to 8% - Total Inv: $50,000 - Financing: No.

RUSSOLI TEMPS
Grey Fox Ltd.
P.O. Box 1961, Allentown, PA, 18105. Contact: H.A. Russoli, Pres. - Tel: (610) 432-8430. Provide temporary employees to companies in the following fields: clerical, light industrial, accounting, home companion care, data processing and technical. Established: 1981 - Franchising Since: 1986 - No. of Units: Company Owned: 1 - Franchised: 10 - Franchise Fee: $14,000 - Royalty: 5% to $700,000 billings, 4.5% $700,000 - $1,000,000, 4% over $1,000,000 - Financing: No.

SANFORD ROSE ASSOCIATES
SRA International, Inc.
265 S. Main St., Akron, OH, 44308. Contact: Doug Eilertson, V.P. - Tel: (800) 731-7724 Fax: (216) 762-1007. SRA International, Inc. operates the Sanford Rose Associates Executive Search System, a franchise network of highly motivated men and women who have left their jobs in corporate America for the challenges and rewards of private business ownership. As top-flight recruiters of professional, managerial and executive talent, they continue to make full use of their corporate skills while gaining the opportunity for personal and financial independence. Established: 1959 - Franchising Since: 1970 - No. of Units: Franchised: 50 - Franchise Fee: $32,000 - Royalty: 7% - 3% - Total Inv: $45,000 - $60,000 - Financing: Yes.

SCIENTIFIC SEARCH ASSOCIATES, INC.
260 Park Valley Dr., Coppell, TX, 75019-2924. Contact: Ric J. Favors, V.P., Fran. Opers. - Tel: (800) 772-2329, (214) 304-3938, Fax: (214) 484-1579. Contingency and retained personnel recruitment services for technology driven and scientific industries. Established: 1990 - Franchising Since: 1994 - Franchise Fee: $20,000 - Royalty: 8% decreasing to 6% in yr. 5 - Total Inv: $25,000 to $35,000 - Suggest

additional 6 mo. living expenses on hand - In home office start up approved, no initial requirement to hire staff, complete training, systems and support, location flexibility. Partial financing considered.

SNELLING PERSONNEL SERVICES
Snelling and Snelling, Inc.
12801 N. Central Expy., Ste. 700, Dallas, TX, 75243. Contact: Robert O. Snelling, Sr. /Brian G. Dailey, Chairman/Sr.V.P. Fran. Dev. - Tel: (800) 766-5556. Full-service permanent placement and temporary help franchise. Fully computerized. Specialities include, but are not limited to, sales and marketing, accounting and finance, data processing, engineering, health care and office support. Established: 1951 - Franchising Since: 1956 - No. of Units: Franchised: 265 - Franchise Fee: $5,000 - Royalty: 7% permanent, 7.5% - 8.5% temporary - Total Inv: $22,000 - $126,000 - Financing: Temporary payroll funding provided. Master franchises available.

STAFF BUILDERS HOME HEALTH CARE
1983 Marcus Ave., Lake Success, NY, 11042. Contact: Ed Teixeira, Sr. VP Fran. - Tel: (800) 444-4633. Franchisees provide home health care services to patients in the home. Services include skilled and non-skilled nursing. Established: 1961 - Franchising Since: 1987 - No. of Units: Company Owned: 20 - Franchised: 140 - Franchise Fee: $29,500 - Royalty: variable - Total Inv: $100,000 - $130,000.

SULLIVAN & COGLIANO
230 Second Avenue, Waltham, MA, 02154. Contact: Herb Cogliano, V.P. - Tel: (617) 890-7890. Temporary help and permanent placement firm. Providing office and light industrial personnel services for all types of businesses. Established: 1966 - Franchising Since: 1989 - No. of Units Company Owned: 8 - Franchise Fee: $25,000 - $30,000 - Royalty: 40% of the gross margin - Total Inv: $50,000 - $90,000 - Financing: Payroll and Accounts Receivable.

TALENT TREE PERSONNEL SERVICES
9703 Richmond Ave., Houston, TX, 77042. Contact: Judy Bishop, Mgr. Fran. Dev. - Tel: (800) 827-8733 or (713) 789-1818. A national temporary service with $200 million in revenues, 135 offices and 15 yrs. experience. Established: 1976 - Franchising Since: 1990 - No. of Units: Company Owned: 135 - Franchised: 7 - Franchise Fee: $10,000 - Royalty: varies - Total Inv: $75,000 - $125,000 (start-up & oper. cap.) - Financing: Partial for industry experienced people.

TEMPS & CO.
MSI International
245 Peachtree Center Ave., Ste. 2500 Marquis One Tower, Atlanta, GA, 30303. Contact: Guy Storey, Dir. of Fran. Dev. - Tel: (404) 659-5236, (800) 438-6086. Staffing services company specializing in office automation, technical and light industrial personnel. Our unique office automation and technical departments provide an outstanding service to our customers. Established: 1968 - Franchising Since: 1988 - No. of Units: Company Owned: 15 - Franchised: 14 - Franchise Fee: $12,500 - Royalty: 7.5% of sales or 40% of gross profit, whichever is greater - Total Inv: $60,000 - $100,000 (incl. fran. fee) - Financing: 100% temporary payroll and accounts receivable financing.

TIME TEMPORARY SERVICES
Time Services, Inc.
6422 Lima Rd., Fort Wayne, IN, 46818. Contact: Thomas C. Ward, COO - Tel: (219) 489-2020. Clerical, industrial, technical temporary help. Plant staff, staffing services. Established: 1981 - Franchising Since: 1984 - No. of Units: Company Owned: 10 - Franchised: 4 - Franchise Fee: Negotiable - Royalty: Franchisee 60%, franchisor 40% - Total Inv: $80,000+ - Financing: Negotiable.

TIMS MANAGEMENT SYSTEMS, INC.
2940 N. Swan Rd., Ste. 212, Tucson, AZ, 85712-1255. Contact: Thomas Hendrickson, CEO - Tel: (602) 721-1636. A program giving franchisors the opportunity to place the right person in the position where personality, motivation and goals can be integrated right into the job. Established: 1972.

TODAYS TEMPORARY
18111 Preston Rd., Ste. 700, Dallas, TX, 75252. Contact: Janis Domino, Franchise Development - Tel: (800) 822-7868 or (214) 380-9380. Provides temporary help services to large and small companies. Emphasis is on providing skilled clerical personnel whose skills have been tested and references thoroughly checked. Established: 1982 - Franchising Since: 1983 - No. of Units: Company Owned: 58 - Franchised: 29 - Franchise Fee: Varies - Royalty: Varies - Total Inv: $90,000 - $145,000 - Financing: finances 100% of temp. employees' payroll and accounts receivables. Also, 50% of local advertising on pre-approved programs.

TRC STAFFING SERVICES, INC.
100 Ashford Ctr. N. #500, Atlanta, GA, 30338. Contact: Michael Baer, V.P. Fran. - Tel: (404) 392-1411. Provides a full service temporary help franchise program. Skill classifications filled by TRC are clerical, secretarial, word and data processing, accounting, computer related activities and light industrial. Established: 1980 - Franchising Since: 1984 - No. of Units: Company Owned: 30 - Franchised: 22 - Royalty: varies - Total Inv: $75,000 - $125,000 - Financing: Yes.

UNIFORCE STAFFING SERVICES
1335 Jericho Turnpike, New Hyde Park, NY, 11040. Contact: Rosemary Maniscalco, Pres. - Tel: (516) 437-3300. Uniforce Temporary Services grants exclusive licenses to operate offices which provide temporary personnel with a large variety of skills to employers in business, industry, and government. Also, provide personnel in general/automated office, MIS, marketing, records management, hospitality, legal, technical and light industrial categories. Established: 1961 - Franchising Since: 1964 - No. of Units: Company Owned: 78 - Franchised: 9 - Franchise Fee: $15,000 - Royalty: 45% - Total Inv: $15,000, plus $75,000 - $100,000 - Financing: N/A.

V.I.P. COMPANION-CARE, INC.
4914 W. Genesee St., Camillus, NY, 13031. Contact: Gordon Buck, Pres. - Tel: (315) 468-5500. A professional service providing care and companionship to the elderly in their own home as an alternative to institutionalization. Established: 1984 - Franchising Since: 1988 - No. of Units: Company Owned: 1 - Franchised: 1 - Franchise Fee: $25,000 - Royalty: 7%, 1/2% adv.- Total Inv: $125,000 - $175,000 - Financing: Affiliated with financing company.

WESTERN MEDICAL SERVICES
Western Staff Services, Inc.
301 Lennon Lane, Walnut Creek, CA, 94598. Contact: A. Terry Slocum, Pres., Fran. Div. - Tel: (800) 872-8367. Full service home health agency (staffing, home care). Western offers exclusive territories, comprehensive training, Medicare certification, JCAHO accreditation, Medicare and non-Medicare billing, cost reporting services, computerized caregiver payroll, A/R financing, managed care national contracts, professional risk management, credit and legal expertise and more. Established: 1967 - Franchising Since: 1975 - No. of Units: Company Owned: 18 plus 1 recruiting - Franchised: 14 - Franchise Fee: $30,000 - $40,000 - Royalty: 8% - Total Inv: $130,000 min. - Financing: Payroll and receivables; Assistance with franchise fee available for qualified applicants with home health agency experience.

WESTERN STAFF SERVICES
Western Staff Services, Inc.
301 Lennon Lane, Walnut Creek, CA, 94598. Contact: A. Terry Slocum, Pres., Fran. Div. - Tel: (800) 872-8367. Full-service international staffing service. Provide: computerized temporary payroll and accounts receivable financing; two week training; QWIZ testing and tutorial software; office automation resources for scheduling and retrieval; and professional expertise for risk management, legal, credit, and information services. Handle all invoicing and insurance coverage for the temporaries. Franchises available in select cities. Established: 1948 - Franchising Since: 1957 - No. of Units: Company Owned: 179 + 7 recruiting - Franchised: 127 - Franchise Fee: $10,000 - $50,000 - Royalty: 8% - Total Inv: $50,000 - $100,000 - Financing: Payroll and receivables; assistance with franchise fee financing available for qualified applicants.

ENTERTAINMENT

AFTER THE GOLD RUSH, INC.
Entertainment Concepts, Ltd.
6464 Greenbriar Dr., Englewood, CO, 80111. Contact: Rob or Dennis Muck, Mktg. Dir. - Tel: (303) 740-7331. Quality entertainment centers offering a modern versatile entertainment format. Established: 1972 - Licensing Since: 1978 - No. of Units: 5 - Inv: varies with location and size of facility.

AMACADE AMUSEMENT & ENTERTAINMENT CENTERS
Ste. A, Block AA-1, P.O. Box 24, Fayetteville, AR, 72702. Contact: Henry Nwauwa, Pres. - Tel: (501) 443-6791. Family amusement/ entertainment and fun centers featuring various games, rides, and other forms of family entertainment. Children's entertainment for malls. Billiard & game rooms, game parks. Established: 1988 - Franchising Since: 1990 - No. of Units: Company Owned: 4 - Franchise Fee: $500. - $50,000 - Royalty: 5% - 15% (Amacade interest in each center) - Total Inv: $50,000 - $20,000,000 - Financing: Yes.

AMERICAN DARTERS ASSOCIATION, INC.
1000 Lake St. Louis Blvd., Ste. 310, Lake St. Louis, MO, 63367. Contact: Glenn Remick, Pres. - Tel: (314) 625-8621. Sell Anheuser-Busch Bud Light Dart League sponsored franchises. Established: 1991 - Franchising Since: 1991 - No. of Units: Franchised: 75 - Franchise Fee: starting at $1,000 - based on area population - Financing: No.

AMERICAN MOBILE SOUND
AMS Franchise Corp.
5266 Hollister #105, Santa Barbara, CA, 93111. Contact: Tad Clark, Fran. Dev. Coord. - Tel: (805) 681-8132, Fax: (805) 681-8134. Professional mobile disc jockey service, providing MC's and amplified music for any occasion. Established: 1991 - Franchising Since: 1994 - No. of Units: Franchised: 8 - Franchise Fee: $6,000 - $15,000 - Royalty: 7%, no adv. royalty - Total Inv: $16,106+ depending on units purchased & territory.

BLACK FILMMAKERS ASSOCIATION *
Promotions Etcetera, Inc.
230 - I Rimview Dr., Colorado Springs, CO, 80919. Contact: Judith Fluker, Exec. Dir. - Tel: (719) 593-7537. Filmmaker's association promoting young black/minority film students and non-professional filmmakers. Film festivals, networking, film projects and award programs/scholarships. Established: 1994 - Franchising Since: 1995 - No. of Units: Company Owned: 2 - Franchise Fee: $3,000 - $7,000 per year depending on location - Royalty: None - Total Inv: $7,000 - Financing: Nationwide.

BLUE NOTE INTERNATIONAL
131 West 3rd St., New York, NY, 10012. Contact: Sal Haries, Pres. - Tel: (212) 475-0049, Fax: (212) 529-1038, e-mail: bluenote@panix.com. Internationally renown jazz club, restaurant and café. Established: 1981 - Licensing Since: 1987 - No. of Units: Company Owned: 1 - Licensed: 5 - Management Service Fee: $100,000 plus Licensing Fee: $200,000 - Royalty: 10% - Total Inv: $2,000,000 to $2,500,000 - Financing: No.

CASI
Creative Amusement Services Inc.
6 Executive Plz., Yonkers, NY, 10701-6801. Contact: Dept. AL-46 - Tel: (914) 376-7400 or (800) 842-5580. Print virtually any name on a variety of custom art backgrounds that show mountains, icebergs, tropical scenes, sports themes and more. Printed with the name is the place of origin, meaning and a list of flattering personality traits. The backgrounds can be inserted into wood, paper and lucite frames or made into mugs, keychains, ceramic plates, buttons and more. You can also attach a photo to the art background or create greeting cards, poems, or motivational quotations. Established: 1977 - Total Inv: $3,500 - $9,995.

COMPLETE MUSIC
7877 L St., #3, Omaha, NE, 68127-1808. Contact: G. E. Maas, Pres. - Tel: (402) 391-4847 or (800) 843-3866. Disc jockey entertainment, providing dance music for over 1,000,000 people each year. The uniqueness of this business allows owners to use their skills in management to hire and book their own Complete Music trained D.J.'s for all types of special events. Established: 1972 - Franchising Since: 1981 - No. of Units: Company Owned: 94 - Franchised: 1 - Franchise Fee: $9,500 - Royalty: 8% - Total Inv: $9,500 fran. fee; $6,000 train. & supp.; $3,000 equip. - Financing: Partial on franchise fee only.

FUN SERVICES
Div. of Ace Novelty Co. Inc.
13434 N.E. 16th St., Bellevue, WA, 98005. Contact: Jay Hoult, Business Development - Tel: (800) 759-1223, or direct (615) 254-FUNS. FUN SERVICES provides a wide range of Fun and fund raising programs. They include the original "Santa's Secret Shop" program, the "Fun Fair" school carnival program, and several special event and company picnic programs. Fun Services provides the experience, training and equipment for a wide variety of events. Established: 1970 - Franchising Since: 1970 - No. of Units: Franchised: 90 - Franchise Fee: $25,000 & up - Royalty: $150/mo. & up - Financing: Possibly.

Jay Hoult
Director of Business Development

13434 N.E. 16th St.
Bellevue, WA, 98005
(206) 644-1820

Div. of Ace Novelty Co., Inc.
(206) 644-5282 FAX
(800) 759-1223

GLAMOUR GIRL AND BOY BEAUTY CONTESTS
12808 Sidney Rd., Dover, FL, 33527. Contact: Olga Knight, Director - Tel: (813) 689-4308. Beauty pageants for boys and girls, young men and women. Established: 1960 - Franchising Since: 1990 - No. of Units: Company Owned: 51 - Franchise Fee: $4,000 - Total Inv: $4,000 per state - Financing: Yes, at 6%.

HAUNTED HAYRIDES ™ *
Hauntrepreneurs, Ltd.
135 Old Cove Rd., #210, Liverpool, WY, 13090. Contact: Matthew Jacob, Pres. - Tel: (315) 453-6009, Fax: (315) 453-3820. Sell & service Haunted Hayrides, Halloween themed seasonal event. Established: 1985 - Franchising Since: 1987 - No. of Units: Franchised: 21 - Franchise Fee: $5,000 to $15,000 - Royalty: 10%-6% - Total Inv: $50,000 to $90,000.

MARTY WOLF GAME CO.
2120 "G" S. Highland Dr., Las Vegas, NV, 89102. Contact: Marty Wolf, Owner - Tel: (702) 385-2963. Casino party rental business - Casino equipment rental or turnkey "Las Vega Nite" parties for fundraisers, theme or fun parties. Start up package includes: Full size blackjack tables (6); Craps table (1); Roulette table (1) in assemble kit form with all additional required supplies & accessories plus owners manual & training tapes. Established: 1970 - No. of Units: Company Owned: 1 - Total Inv: $6,000-equip. & teaching material - Financing: No.

MISS ARISTA PAGEANT, U.S.A. *
Promotions Etcetera, Inc.
230 - I Rimview Dr., Colorado Springs, CO, 80919. Contact: Judith Fluker, Exec. Dir. - Tel: (719) 447-8719 / 593-7537. Scholarship program. Entertainment competitions for men, women and children promoting education in the performing arts. Non-profit organizations. Established: 1981 - Franchising Since: 1993 - No. of Units: Company Owned: 3 states & 20+ cities - Franchised: 3 states - Franchise Fee: $10,000 - $30,000 depending on location, size of territory and state - Royalty: up to 3% - Total Inv: varies - Financing: California, Colorado and Tennessee.

MUZAK
2901 Third Ave., Ste. 400, Seattle, WA, 98121. Contact: Jack Craig, V.P. - Tel: (800) 331-3340 or (206) 633-3000. Producer and distributor of programmed music service to business subscribers. Franchise owned operations install and service sound systems to deliver music and other communication services. Established: 1934 - Licensing Since: 1934 - No. of Units: Company Owned: 35 - Licensed: 138 - Approx. Inv: $250,000 - Royalty: 10% of mthly. subscriber billing plus a mthly. market fee.

PARTY ANIMALS
Party Animals, Inc.
180 Allen Rd., Ste. 204, Atlanta, GA, 30328. Contact: Cheryl Carter, Pres. - Tel: (404) 303-7789. Full service family entertainment providing costumed characters for special events, grand openings, holidays, birthday parties and much more. Established: 1987 - Franchising Since: 1992 - No. of Units: Franchised: 17 - Franchise Fee: $12,500 - Royalty: 6% 1st 100,000 in sales then 5% down to 4% - Total Inv: $12,500 fee, $3,500 costumes, additional $3,000 - $5,000 for office, etc. - Financing: Yes.

POCO-LOCO WESTERN TOWNS, INC.
Sunshine Properties Int'l Inc.
7700 W. Fairfield Dr., Pensacola, FL, 32506. Contact: Joseph Morgan, G.M. - Tel: (904) 455-9685, Fax: (904) 458-0096. Amusement parks with western theme. Will also joint venture. Established: 1978 - Franchising Since: 1988 - No. of Units: Company Owned: 3 - Total Inv: $300,000 - $500,000 - Financing: Arranged.

RIPLEY'S BELIEVE IT OR NOT
Ripley's Attractions Inc.
5728 Major Blvd., Ste. 700, Orlando, FL, 32819. Contact: Sylvia Matiko, Fran. Dev. - Tel: (407) 345-8010. Walk through tourist attractions featuring the odd, the unusual and the unbelievable. Established: 1962 - Franchising Since: 1990 - No. of Units: Company Owned: 6 - Franchised: 14 - Franchise Fee: $30,000 U.S. - Royalty: 15% of gross admissions - Total Inv: varies with size of museum and market - Financing: None.

RODENTVELT RACEWAY
1402 W. Danby Rd., Newfield, NY, 14867. Contact: Robert Tottey, Pres. - Tel: (607) 564-7834. Thoroughbred gerbil racing as entertainment for taverns, clubs, private parties, conventions and fundraisers. Established: 1987 - Franchising Since: 1990 - No. of Units: Company Owned: 5 - Franchised: 2 - Franchise Fee: $3,500 - Royalty: $4,000 - Total Inv: $7,500 - Financing: Yes.

SINGING MACHINE COMPANY INC., THE
6350 E. Rogers Cir., Boca Raton, FL, 33487-2623. Contact: Gene Settler, Pres. - Tel: (800) 451-3692, (954) 968-8006. Recording booths, portable and stationary - Karaoke hardware and software products. Established: 1982 - Franchising Since: 1985 - No. of Units: Company Owned: 2 - Franchised: 38 - Franchise Fee: dependent on location - Total Inv: $10,000 - $12,000 - Financing: Yes.

SOUNDSATION ENTERTAINMENT
21515 Chagrin Blvd., Cleveland, OH, 44122. Contact: Mark Cheplowitz, Pres. - Tel: (216) 561-5700, Fax: (216) 561-3600. Live entertainment such as bands, DJ's and specialty acts. Also produce shows, grand openings, ground breakings. Established: 1980 - Franchising Since: 1994 - No. of Units: Company Owned: 1 - Franchised: 1 - Franchise Fee: $25,000 - Royalty: 3.5% - Total Inv: $40,000 - $67,000 - Financing: No.

VIRTROPOLIS *
Virtropolis Corporation, The
100 Smith Ranch Rd., Ste. 301, San Rafael, CA, 94903. Contact: Will Pemble, CEO - Tel: (800) 492-8177. Virtual Reality Entertainment, merchandise and food/beverage concession in retail environment along with virtual reality rental service for special events. Established: 1995 - Franchising Since: 1995 - No. of Units: Company Owned: 1 - Franchise Fee: $26,000 - Royalty: 7%, 3% co-op. - Total Inv: $237,000 to $315,000 (approx. $160,000 in VR equip.) - Financing: No.

FOOD: CONVENIENCE STORES, SPECIALTY SHOPS, AND SUPERMARKETS

6 TWELVE CONVENIENT MART
77 S. Washington St., #207, Rockville, MD, 20850-2335. Contact: Aris Mardirossian, Pres./CEO - Tel: (301) 840-8559. Convenience stores. Established: 1984 - Franchising Since: 1985 - No. of Units: Company Owned: 10 - Franchised: 29 - Franchise Fee: $30,000 - Royalty: 5%, 2% adv. - Total Inv: $300,000 - Financing: Yes.

7-ELEVEN FOOD STORES
Southland Corp., The
2711 N. Haskell Ave., Dallas, TX, 75204. , For franchise information, - Tel: (800) 255-0711. Convenience store - retail grocery. Established: 1927 - Franchising Since: 1964 - No. of Units: Company Owned: 2,543 - Franchised: 2,957 - Franchise Fee: $0 - $145,000 - Royalty: gross profit split - Total Inv: $12,500 - $162,000 - Financing: Yes.

A & M FOOD STORES, INC.
450, S. Old Dixie Hwy, #8, Jupiter, FL, 33458. Contact: Ashok G. Patel, V.P. - Tel: (407) 747-4384. Convenience stores franchise having 60 stores, located in South Florida. Established: 1980 - Franchising Since: 1981 - No. of Units: Company Owned: 60 - Franchise Fee: $40,000 max. - Royalty: $900 per month or 3% of gross revenue - Total Inv: $50,000 per store - Financing: No.

ALWAYS OPEN
Always Open Franchise Corp.
1130 S. Wabash Ave., Chicago, IL, 60605. Contact: George Slowinski, Pres. - Tel: (312) 408-0333. 2,500 sq. ft. market with branded fast food programs such as Subway, gasoline retailing and name brand groceries. Established: 1988 - Franchising Since: 1992 - No. of Units: Franchised: 8 - Franchise Fee: $10,000 - Royalty: 4% of sales - Total Inv: to start $60,000 - $120,000 - Financing: No.

AMERICANDY
U.S.A Candy, Inc.
1401 Lexington Rd., Louisville, KY, 40206. Contact: Omar Tatum, Pres./Founder - Tel: (502) 583-1776, Fax: (502) 583-1776. Offers a deliciously unique candy store / packaging plant that creatively displays/ markets 50 gourmet chocolates representing each state in the U.S.A. Exclusive franchise, distributor and dealer rights available. Tour America through candy. Established: 1990 - Franchising Since: 1990 - No. of Units: Company Owned: 1 - Franchise Fee: $25,000 - Royalty: 6% - Total Inv: $125,000 - Financing: Yes.

APRAT MART
3820 Premier Ave., Memphis, TN, 38118. Contact: Bill Richey - Tel: (901) 867-0600. Operating a convenience store offering food & related convenience items & video tape rentals, video machines and dry cleaning services within a highrise or village type apartment complex. Established: 1989 - Franchising Since: 1990 - No. of Units: Company Owned: 3 - Royalty: 2.5% - Total Inv: $50,900 - Financing: Yes.

BOARDWALK PEANUT SHOPPE, THE
Boardwalk Franchise Corp.
10th Street & Boardwalk, Box 749, Ocean City, NJ, 08226. Contact: Leo Yeager, III, Pres. - Tel: (609) 399-3359. Retail nut and candy shop. Established: 1971 - Franchising Since: 1988 - No. of Units: Company Owned: 3 - Franchised: 4 - Franchise Fee: $12,000 - Royalty: 5% - Total Inv: $45,500 - $90,000 depending on leasehold - Financing: No.

BON APPETIT INTERNATIONAL GOURMET FOODS, INC.
616 S. Roosevelt, Boise, ID, 83705. Contact: Mick Chandler, Pres. - Tel: (208) 345-0475, (800) 493-3513. In home gourmet food sales. Franchises available in Northwest only at this time. Our systematic approach on getting and keeping customers is second to none. Established: 1978 - Franchising Since: 1994 - No. of Units: Franchised: 3 - Franchise Fee: $25,000 - Royalty: 6% on gross sales - Total Inv: $25,000 fee, $5,000 inven., $17,000 van, $3,000 misc. - Financing: 25% plus van.

BOURBON STREET CANDY CO.
Ste. 287, 266 N. Elmwood Ave., Buffalo, NY, 14222. Contact: Blaine McGrath, Beth Hughes, Owners - Tel: (800) 949-5115. A dynamic selection of confectionary items geared to impulse buying, self serve system. Established: 1990 - Franchising Since: 1991 - No. of Units: Company Owned: 1 - Franchised: 25 - Franchise Fee: $20,000 - Royalty: 5% - Total Inv: $65,150 to $163,000.

BREAD & CHEESE CUPBOARD
7 Timberlea Lane, Cape May Court House, NJ, 08210. Contact: Sue Wilson, Pres. - Tel: (609) 967-5335. Gourmet shop that bakes 56 varieties of breads, full line of gourmet foods, coffee, pastas, crackers, etc. Also, sandwiches, and over 100 international cheeses. Established: 1975 - Franchising/Licensing Since: 1980 - No. of Units: Company Owned: 2 - Franchise Fee: $15,000 + $10,000 training fee - Royalty: 7% - Total Inv: $225,000 turn-key operation - Financing: No.

CANDY BLOSSOMS
Candy Blossoms, Inc.
7511 Lemont Rd., Darien, IL, 60561. Contact: Sam Norton, V.P. - Tel: (708) 985-9406. Candy bouquet resembling floral arrangement but using an assortment of hard candy and chocolate bars. Established: 1991 - Franchising Since: 1992 - No. of Units: Company Owned: 1 - Franchised: 16 - Franchise Fee: $15,000 - Royalty: 5%, 2% adv. - Total Inv: $50,000 supplies & fixtures plus fran. fee of $15,000 - Financing: None.

CANDY BOUQUET *
Candy Bouquet International, Inc.
5909 "R" St., Little Rock, AR, 72207. Contact: Margaret McEntire, Pres. - Tel: (501) 666-4770, Fax: (501) 664-6018. Retail business selling floral type arrangements made of candy. Established: 1989 - Franchising Since: 1993 - No. of Units: Company Owned: 1 - Franchised: 63 - Franchise Fee: $4,500 and up - Royalty: 0% - Total Inv: $7,200 and up - Financing: No.

CANDY HQTRS
Candy Headquarters, Inc.
40 Twenty-Fourth St., Lower Level, Pittsburgh, PA, 15222. Contact: Mark R. Lando, Pres. - Tel: (412) 456-7811. Bulk candy, help yourself retail store. Established: 1991 - Franchising Since: 1993 - No. of Units: Company Owned: 5 - Franchised: 31 - Franchise Fee: $30,000 - Royalty: 6% - Total Inv: $125,000 - $200,000 - Financing: No.

CANDYLAND
CandyMen Inc.
40 24th St., #502, Pittsburgh, PA, 15222-4643. Contact: Mark R. Lando, Pres. - Tel: (412) 687-4441. Help yourself bulk candy with over 280 different flavors. No popcorn, coffee beans, or nuts, so stores have less waste and less square footage than most of their competitors. Established: 1991 - Franchising Since: 1992 - No. of Units: Company Owned: 4 - Franchised: 6 - Franchise Fee: $30,000 - Royalty: 6% - Total Inv: $125,000 - $200,000 depending on leaseholds - Financing: No.

CANTEEN CORP.
P.O. Box 818, Fairforest, SC, 29336. Contact: Don Schafer, V.P. Fran. Rel. - Tel: (803) 587-9510. Food service and vending machines. Established: 1930 - No. of Units: Company Owned: 63 - Franchised: 78 - Inv: varies.

CASEY'S GENERAL STORES, INC.
P.O. Box 3001, 1 Convenience Blvd., Ankeny, IA, 50021. Contact: Deb Syverson, Accounting - Tel: (515) 965-6100. Convenience Stores. Not presently offering franchises.

CATERINA'S
Caterina's Franchise Company, Inc.
415 Avenida Pico, Ste. N2, San Clemente, CA, 92672. Contact: Len Pieri, Sales Mgr. - Tel: (800) 901-7285. Upscale candy, chocolates and gift items. Also, store baked cookies, gourmet coffee and yogurt. Year round sales, extensive training and support. Established: 1990 - Franchising Since: 1993 - No. of Units: Company Owned: 1 - Franchised: 3 - Franchise Fee: $19,000 - Royalty: 5% - Total Inv: $129,900 - $211,500 ($50,000 liquid) - Financing: OAC.

CLUB SANDWICH
Club Sandwich Franchising, Inc.
107 Cherry St., New Canaan, CT, 06840. Contact: Diane DeVito, Ex. V.P. - Tel: (203) 966-4053. Gourmet sandwich shop. Established: 1986. Franchising Since: 1990. No. of Units: Franchised: 1 - Franchise Fee: $25,000 - Royalty: 5% wkly, 1% adv. - Total Inv: $130,000: $60,000 equip, $25,000 imp, fran fee.

CONVENIENT FOOD MART
Convenient Food Mart Inc.
31225 Bainbridge Rd., Cleveland, OH, 44139. Contact: Franchise Dir. - Tel: (216) 519-1550. C-store offering deli, bakery, food to go and gasoline programs. Established: 1958 - Franchising Since: 1959 - No. of Units: Company Owned: 7 - Franchised: 382 - Franchise Fee: $18,000 - Royalty: 5% incl. adv., support, accounting - Total Inv: Min. invest. $65,000 - Financing: Franchise owner has ability to build equity in business and may seek financing through third-party lending sources.

CUB FOODS
421 S. Third St., P.O.Box 9, Stillwater, MN, 55082. Contact: Chuck Tryon, Fran. Dir. - Tel: (612) 439-7200. Convenience stores.

DAIRY MART CONVENIENCE STORES
Dairy Mart Convenience Stores, Inc.
1 Vision Dr., Enfield, CT, 06082. Contact: Franchise Dept. - Tel: (203) 741-4444. Convenience stores with fast food, deli and gasoline programs. Operating in 11 states. Established: 1958 - Franchising Since: 1962 - No. of Units: Company Owned: 668 - Franchised: 322 - Franchise Fee: $10,000 - Royalty: 9% - 16% - Total Inv: $50,000: fran. fee $10,000, location fee $10,000, inventory $28,000, operating cap. $2,000 - Financing: Only on the balance of the inventory to qualified candidates.

EXPRESS MART CONVENIENT STORES
Petr-All Petroleum Corp.
6567 Kinne Rd., DeWitt, NY, 13214. Contact: Mark Maher, Dir. of Fran. - Tel: (315) 446-0125, Fax: (315) 446-1355. Gas station, convenience store with emphasis on fast food. Seeking master franchisees and development agents. Established: 1975 - Franchising Since: 1989 - No. of Units: Company Owned: 33 - Franchised: 5 - Franchise Fee: $15,000 first unit, $7,000 thereafter - Royalty: 3%, 1% adv. - Financing: Third party assistance.

FILTERFRESH
378 University Ave., Westwood, MA, 01772. Contact: Steve Smith, Fran. Dir. - Tel: (800) 332-6771. Hi-tech office coffee service using patented coffee/computer and gourmet coffee. Established: 1987 - Franchising Since: 1987 - No. of Units: Company Owned: 7 - Franchised: 41 - Franchise Fee: $24,500 - Royalty: 5%, 2% adv. - Total Inv: full franchise $200,000 work. cap., $250,000 financing - Financing: Yes joint venture franchise $50,000 - $100,000.

FIRE GLAZED HAM BY THE SWISS COLONY
Swiss Colony Stores Inc.
1112 Seventh Ave., Monroe, WI, 53566. Contact: Gene Curran, Exec. Dir. - Tel: (608) 328-8803. Specializing in spiral sliced honey glazed ham and turkey, Swiss Colony products and a unique upscale cafe all in one retail store. Established: 1963 - Franchising Since: 1993 - No. of Units: Company Owned: 2 - Franchised: 17 - Franchise Fee: $20,000 year round - Royalty: 4% of gross sales - Total Inv: $150,000 - Financing: No.

FOOD-N-FUEL
Food-N-Fuel, Inc.
4366 Round Lake Rd. W., Arden Hills, MN, 55112. Contact: Edward Bird, Gen. Mgr. - Tel: (612) 633-7863. Retail grocery and gasoline. Established: 1978 - Franchising Since: 1979 - No. of Units: Company Owned: 27 - Franchised: 79 - Franchise Fee: $10,000 - Royalty: 3.5% of sales, no fee on gas sales - Total Inv: $350,000-$600,000.

FUDGE CO., THE
103 Belvedere Ave., Charlevoix, MI, 49720. Contact: R.L. Hoffman, Pres. - Tel: (616) 547-4612. Retail fudge store. An important part of the operation is cooking in large copper kettles and creaming (forming) done on large marble slabs. Only natural ingredients are used and combined with the showmanship of making fudge provide a unique, enjoyable and profitable retail operation. Each store requires 400 - 600

sq. ft. Company provides all equip., franchisee leases or purchases its own building, with guidance from Fudge Co. Established: 1978 - Franchising Since: 1981 - No. of Units: Franchised: 5 - Franchise Fee: $12,500 - Royalty: 3% - Total Inv: $25,000 - $50,000 - Financing: No.

GOURMET SPECIALTY GOURMET *
OK Food Management USA Corp.
5 Colombia Dr., Ste. 176, Niagara Falls, NY, 14305-1275. Contact: William Siarto, Fran. Dev. - Tel: (905) 356-4242, Fax: (905) 356-9373. Domestic & import specialties food lines also preparation of gift baskets. Established: 1996 - Franchising Since: 1996 - No. of Units: Company Owned: 1 - Franchise Fee: $2,900 - Royalty: $50/mo., 3% adv. - Financing: No.

HAM SUPREME SHOPS
Ham Supreme Shops, Inc.
P.O. Box 07009, Detroit, MI, 48207. Contact: Don Bonanno or Robert Hetu, Pres. / Fran. Coordinator - Tel: (313) 259-HAMS or (800) 783-HAMS. National franchise featuring private labeled supreme spiral sliced fire glazed hams - sold whole or half, whole smoked turkeys, BBQ ribs, hickory smoked and Canadian style bacons. Six outstanding overstuffed sandwiches and party trays. Complete deli with homemade soup & baked beans. Established: 1986 - Licensing Since: 1986 - Number of Units: Company Owned: 1 - Licensed: 11 - Franchise Fee: $20,000 - Royalty: 5% of gross, 2% adv. spent locally - Total Inv: Initial inv: $142,000 - $208,000 plus leasehold improv: $15,000 - $45,000 - Financing: None.

HEAVENLY HAM
Paradise Foods, Inc.
20 Mansell Ct., Ste. 500, Roswell, GA, 30076-4814. Contact: R.H. (Hutch) Hodgson, Pres. - Tel: (404) 993-2232. Retail stores selling honey-spiced glazed, spiral sliced, fully baked, whole and half hams, plus smoked turkey, barbecued ribs, bacon, and other food related items. Established: 1984 - Franchising Since: 1984 - No. of Units: Company Owned: 1 - Franchised: 120 - Franchise Fee: $25,000 - Royalty: 5%, 1% adv. - Total Inv: $132,000 - $184,000 inc. franc. fee - Financing: No.

HICKORY FARMS
Hickory Farms, Inc.
1505 Holland Rd., P.O. Box 219, Maumee, OH, 43537. Contact: Miss Sandy Schott, Fran. Dir. - Tel: (419) 893-7611. Specialty food retailing. Established: 1959 - Franchising Since: 1960- No. of Units: Company Owned: 135 - Franchised: 95 - Franchise Fee: $20,000 - Royalty: 6%, 2% nat'l adv. - Total Inv: $160,000 - $200,000 - Financing: No.

JACKPOT FOOD MART
Jackpot Convenience Stores, Inc.
P.O. Box 24447, Seattle, WA, 98124. Contact: Steve Gray, Fran. Mgr. - Tel: (206) 286-6436. Jackpot Convenience Stores, Inc. has active franchises in Washington, Oregon, California, Nevada and Idaho. JCSI provides franchisees with a wide array of services, including training and marketing programs. Established: 1990 - Franchising Since: 1990 - No. of Units: Company Owned: 2 - Franchised: 136 - Franchise Fee: $5,000 - Royalty: .5% fran. royalty - Total Inv: minimum $48,000 - Financing: No.

JERKY HUT
Jerky Hut International, Inc.
Hamlet Rt. 934, Seaside , OR, 97138. Contact: Stephen Risch, Pres./ Franchise Sales - Tel: (800) 223-5759, Fax: (503) 738-0715. Business to business route sales - retail sales of Jerky Hut products, fairs, shows and events, wholesale route & fund raising, mail order. Established: 1991 - Franchising Since: 1991 - No. of Units: Company Owned: 1 - Franchised: 8 - Franchise Fee: $15,000 - Royalty: 5% gross sales, 1% adv. - Total Inv: fran. fee plus $28,000 van, $7,000 equip., $5,000 - $10,000 work. cap., $5,000 - $10,000 start up inventory - Financing: Yes, 50% of franchise fee O.A.C.

JOHNNY QUIK FOOD STORES, INC.
5794 E. Shields Ave., #102, Fresno, CA, 93727-7820. Contact: Ernie Beal, V.P. - Tel: (209) 291-7136. Convenience stores with gas and fast food program. Established: 1985 - Licensing Since: 1985 - No. of Units: Franchised: 22 - Franchise Fee: $35,000 - Royalty: 2 1/2%/mth -1/4 of 1% goes to advertising - Total Inv: $35,000 franc. fee, $250,000 equip. - Financing: Some for equipment.

JR. FOOD MART
J.F.M., Inc.
440 N. Mill St., Jackson, MS, 39207. Contact: Joe Arancio, V.P. of Bus. Dev. - Tel: (601) 944-0873, Fax: (601) 354-3543. Convenience food marts - multiple profit centers. Self serve gasoline, convenience grocery and branded fast service restaurant. Established: 1920 - Franchising Since: 1920 - Franchise Fee: $20,000 single unit and $35,000 non-exclusive territory - Royalty: 2% single unit and 1.5% territory - Total Inv: Single unit: $75,000 and assets of $100,000+, Territory: $150,000 and assets of $250,000+ - Financing: Assistance available.

JUICE WORLD *
1238 Grand Ave., Arroyo Grande, CA, 93420. Contact: Michael Fullam, Pres. - Tel: (805) 481-9596. Healthy fast food alternative juice and smoothie bar. Established: 1995 - Franchising Since: 1995 - No. of Units: Company Owned: 3 - Franchised: 4 - Franchise Fee: $20,000 - Royalty: 6%, 2% - Total Inv: $114,000 - $210,000 - Financing: No.

KELLY'S COFFEE & FUDGE FACTORY
Kelly's Specialty Group, Inc.
1081 Westwood Blvd., Ste. 218, Los Angeles, CA, 90024. Contact: Stuart Benson, Chairman - Tel: (800) 853-5597 or (310) 277-5801. Franchisor of coffee & candy, muffins, cinnamon rolls, bagels, stores. Established: 1983 - Franchising Since: 1985 - Number of Units: Company Owned: 1 - Franchised: 17 - Franchise Fee: $25,000 - Royalty: 6% - Total Inv: $75,000 - $100,000 - Financing: Yes.

KILWIN'S CHOCOLATES AND ICE CREAM
Kilwin's Chocolates Franchise
355 N. Division Rd., Petoskey, MI, 49770. Contact: Don McCarty, V.P. - Tel: (616) 347-3800. Old fashioned confectionary shoppes featuring quality hand made chocolates, fudge, and Kilwin's own premium ice creams. Established: 1947 - Franchising Since: 1981 - No. of Units: Franchised: 25 - Franchise Fee: $20,000 - Royalty: 5% gross - Total Inv: $100,000 - $165,000 - Financing: No.

KRON CHOCOLATIER
821 17th St., Altoona, PA, 16601. Contact: Deborah Forgione, Fran. Dir. - Tel: (814) 941-2200. Chocolate as molded chocolate products. Established: 1974 - Franchising Since: 1976 - No. of Units: Franchised: 8 - Franchise Fee: $25,000 - $75,000 - Royalty: to be negotiated - Total Inv: $120,000 - Financing: No.

L.A. SMOOTHIE HEALTHMART AND CAFE
L.A. Smoothie Franchises, Inc.
3001 Division St., Ste. 140, Metairie, LA, 70002. Contact: Albert Gardes, C.O.O. - Tel: (800) 643-3910. Specialty retail/restaurant aimed at today's health conscious lifestyle. The franchise system has 2 main concepts, stores serving 21 all natural smoothies, health foods, guilt-free goodies, along with vitamins and supplements. The carts dispense prepacked smoothies and guilt-free goodies. Established: 1991 - Franchising Since: 1992 - No. of Units: Franchised: 22 - Franchise Fee: $15,000 per store or $9,000 per cart - Royalty: 5% royalty-store, 3% adv. -store; 0%-cart - Total Inv: $57,500-store/ $19,900-cart - Financing: 0 on store/ up to 100% on cart.

LIL' PEACH
101 Billerica Ave., N. Billerica, MA, 01862. Contact: Kevin M. Lydon, Dir. of Fran. - Tel: (617) 721-0000, Fax: (508) 663-9622. Operates convenience stores in the state of Massachusetts. Offer a turn-key operation, complete site selection, full training and excellent follow-up. Services provided include sales/marketing assistance, loss prevention assistance, operational follow-up, payroll and accounting. Established: 1971 - Franchising Since: 1974 - No. of Units: Company Owned: 3 - Franchised: 61 - Franchise Fee: $5,000 - $25,000 - Royalty: 15.5% average - Total Inv: $50,000 - $60,000 fran. fee/security deposit/ inventory - Financing: Yes.

MAISON DU POPCORN
188 Washington St., Norwich, CT, 66360. Contact: Bill or Louise, Pres. and V.P. - Tel: (203) 886-0360. Gourmet popcorn in 28 flavors, shaved ice and hot pretzels. Established: 1984 - Franchising Since: 1987 - No. of Units: Company Owned: 2 - Franchised: 11 - Franchise Fee: $20,000 - Royalty: 6% of net sales - Total Inv: approx. $110,000: $20,000 fran.

fee, $60,000 - $70,000 for building of store in shopping center and much less if standing building. $15,000 for equip., $5,000 capital, $10,000 misc.

MR. BULKY TREATS & GIFTS
Mr. Bulky Treats & Gifts Limited Partnership
755 W. Big Beaver, Ste. 1600, Troy, MI, 48084. Contact: Bob Anders, Dir. of Fran. Dev. - Tel: (810) 244-9000. Upscale retail centers located in major malls coast to coast. Offering self service merchandise centers featuring a dazzling array of quality mouthwatering domestic and international candies and snacks sold by the ounce or pound. Stores also merchandise a wide selection of gifts and treats, over 1,000 individually selected items from around the world. Established: 1984 - Franchising Since: 1984 - No. of Units: Company Owned: 119 - Franchised: 92 - Franchise Fee: $45,000 - Royalty: 6% weekly, based on gross revenues - Total Inv: $206,000 - $275,000 - Financing: No.

NUTMEG PANTRY SUPERETTE
Nutmeg Pantry Inc.
P.O. Box 948, Middlebury, CT, 06762. Contact: Al Lussier III, V.P. Oper. - Tel: (203) 758-2421. Convenience stores most with self service gas. Established: 1975 - Franchising Since: 1978 - No. of Units: Company Owned: 5 - Franchised: 6 - Franchise Fee: $45,000 - Royalty: 9 - 12% of sales - Total Inv: fee plus $35,000 inv, $15,000 small oper. equip. - Financing: Thru banks.

OKY-DOKY FOODS
TFM, Co.
1250 Iowa St., Box 300, Dubuque, IA, 52004. Contact: J. F. Thompson, Pres. - Tel: (319) 556-8050, ext. 22. Convenience stores. Established: 1928 - Franchising Since: 1964 - No. of Units: Company Owned: 10 - Franchised: 6 - Franchise Fee: None - Royalty: 3% - Total Inv: inventory only, lease equipment - Financing: Depends.

OLD FASHIONED EGG CREAM CO. INC. *
Original Egg Cream Co.
4270 N.W. 19th Ave., Ste. D, Pompano Beach, FL, 33064. Contact: Mark Streisfeld, Pres. - Tel: (305) 969-1632. An idea based on fond memories of enjoying a frosty egg cream with a pretzel rod. Also serve bakery confections. One is the Charlotte Russe and another is the Old Fashioned Cookie On A Sick, along with our Old Fashioned Gourmet Fountain Sodas. All served from a beautiful self-contained mobile wood and brass cart. Well received at malls, business centers, sports complexes and other locations where people meet. Established: 1994 - Franchising Since: 1995 - No. of Units: Company Owned: 2 - Franchised: 3 - Franchise Fee: $10,000 - $15,000 - Royalty: 5% (10% at stadiums) - Total Inv: $10,000 - $15,000 + $20,000 - $25,000 (other invest. & open. costs) - Financing: None.

PERFECT PRETZEL, THE
Perfect Pretzel, Inc.
4 Garden Rd., Little Silver, NJ, 07739. Contact: Ronald S. Hari, Dir. of Fran. - Tel: (908) 741-7347. Fresh baked pretzels hand rolled with 10 different flavors. Established: 1992 - Franchising Since: 1992 - No. of Units: Company Owned: 2 - Franchised: 1 - Franchise Fee: $6,000 - Royalty: 5% of gross - Total Inv: $65,000: $30,000 construction, $10,000 equip., $6,000 fee, $19,000 lease - Financing: Will assist.

PIGGLY WIGGLY
Piggly Wiggly Corporation
1991 Corporate Ave., Memphis, TN, 38132. Contact: Lee Bryson, Exec. V.P. - Tel: (901) 395-8215. Retail supermarkets. Established: 1916 - Franchising Since: 1919 - No. of Units: Franchised: 811 - Total Inv: varies.

QUICKWAY CONVENIENCE STORES *
Quickway, Inc.
44 Grand St., Sidney, NY, 13838. Contact: Tom Mirabito Jr., V.P., Mktg. - Tel: (607) 561-2700. Convenience store & gasoline station. Established: 1992 - Franchising Since: 1992 - No. of Units: Company Owned: 38 - Franchised: 3 - Franchise Fee: $7,500 - Royalty: 3% gross inside sales plus gas supply contract - Total Inv: $400,000 to $850,000 - Financing: No.

QUIK STOP MARKETS
Quik Stop Markets, Inc.
4567 Enterprise St., Fremont, CA, 94537. Contact: Larry Kranich, Pres. - Tel: (510) 657-8500. 24-hour convenience market with self-serve gasoline in most locations. Established: 1965 - Franchising Since: 1966 - No. of Units: Franchised: 117 - Franchise Fee: $25,000 - $70,000 - Royalty: min. of 15% to max. of 17% of net sales - Total Inv: $55,000 - $100,000 - Financing: Yes.

RALPH ROTTEN'S NUT POUND
Global Nuts & Fruits, Inc.
4314 Merrick Rd., Massapequa, NY, 11758-6019. Contact: Robert Baskind, Pres. - Tel: (516) 482-2632. Franchised retail stores trading under name Ralph Rotten's Nut Pound, that sell nuts, dried fruit, candies chocolates, yogurt & related gift items to the general public & the business community. Established: 1982 - Franchising Since: 1986 - No. of Units: Franchised: 25 - Franchise Fee: $15,000 - Royalty: 5% of monthly gross sales - Total Inv: Turnkey Fee $65,000 complete stocked store - Financing: Yes, 10%.

ROCKY MOUNTAIN CHOCOLATE FACTORY, INC.
265 Turner Dr., Durango, CO, 81301. Contact: Franklin E. Crail, Pres. - Tel: (303) 259-0554. Fast food. Established: 1982 - No. of Units: Company Owned: 3 - Franchised: 68.

ROYAL APPLES *
Royal Apples, Inc.
1500 E. Beltline S.E., Ste. 160, Grand Rapids, MI, 49506. Contact: Tim Klein, Pres. - Tel: (616) 940-2744. Market the Nutrimatic-602 fruit vending machine as a franchise. Also offer quarterly newsletter, 1-800 hot line, training, parts for machine, insurance, and location finding services. Established: 1992 - Franchising Since: 1995 - No. of Units: Franchised: 1 - Franchise Fee: None - Royalty: 5% - Total Inv: $3,950 cost of machine, complete - Financing: No.

STUCKEY'S
Stuckey's Corporation
4601 Willard Ave., Chevy Chase, MD, 20815-4641. Contact: Walter S. Tellegen, CEO - Franchising - Tel: (301) 913-9800, ext. 23. The sale of candy, gifts, fast food items as well as gasoline. Established: 1933 - No. of Units: Franchised: 100 - Franchise Fee: $2,500 - Royalty: 5% of inside sales, with a ceiling of approx. $9,000 - Total Inv: $28,000 - $135,000 for a conversion.

SUGAR CREEK STORES INC.
760 Brooks Ave., Rochester, NY, 14619. Contact: Thomas Giannone, Prop.Mgr. - Tel: (716) 436-2691. Convenience stores with self serve fuel operations. Established: 1982 - Franchising Since: 1989 - No. of Units: Company Owned: 102 - Franchised: 5 - Franchise Fee: $15,000 - Royalty: 4.5%, 1 adv. - Total Inv: $297,140 - $475,280 - Financing: No.

SWEET CITY
Sweet City International, Inc.
1604 Hilltop W., Ste. 204, Virginia Beach, VA, 23451. Contact: Joseph L. Caffrey, Dir. of Fran. Dev. - Tel: (804) 422-3061. Visually stunning, mall based retail candy store. Each store carries 500-700 different confections in bulk. Established: 1991 - Franchising Since: 1992 - No. of Units: Company Owned: 1 - Franchised: 9 - Franchise Fee: $20,000 - Royalty: 6% - Total Inv: $60,000 - $135,000 - Financing: Assistance is available.

SWISS COLONY SEASONALS
Swiss Colony Stores Inc.
1112 Seventh Ave., Monroe, WI, 53566. Contact: Gene Curran, V.P. - Tel: (608) 328-8803. Holiday locations featuring Swiss Colony gifts and specialty foods, located in shopping malls around the country. Established: 1963 - Franchising Since: 1963 - No. of Units: Company Owned: 8 - Franchised: 110 - Franchise Fee: $500 per location per year - Royalty: 4% of gross sales - Total Inv: $20,000 - $60,000 - Financing: No.

TINDER BOX AND TINDER BOX GOURMET CAFE
Tinder Box International, Inc.
3 Bala Plaza E., Ste. 102, Bala Cynwyd, PA, 19004. Contact: Fred Haas, Dir. of Fran. Sales - Tel: (800) 846-3372, (610) 668-4220, Fax: (610) 668-4266. 1. Tinder Box Classic: Specialty tobacco and collectable

stores; 2. Tinder Box Gourmet Cafe: Combination coffee cafe and tobacco shoppe; 3. Tinder Box Gourmet Coffee Cart: Low cost coffee cart. Established: 1928 - Franchising Since: 1963 - No. of Units: Franchised: 105 - Franchise Fee: Store Fee $25,000; Cart lic. fee $10,000 - Royalty: Store 4%; Cart 6% - Total Inv: Classic: $150,000 - $175,000; Gourmet Cafe: $175,000 - $250,000; Gourmet Coffee Cart: $25,000 - $30,000 - Club Tinder Box Int'l: $175,000 - $250,000; Gourmet Coffee To Go - a mobile coffee trailer: $35,000.

TROPIK SUN FRUIT & NUT
Diversifoods, Inc.
37 Sherwood Ter., #101, Lake Bluff, IL, 60044. Contact: Barbara J. Wellard, Pres. - Tel: (708) 234-3407, Fax: (708) 234-3856. Featuring fun munchies, nuts, candy, popcorn, fudge, drinks and giftware. Established: 1980 - Franchising Since: 1980 - No. of Units: Company Owned: 11 - Franchised: 70 - Franchise Fee: $20,000 - Royalty: 6% (no adv.) - Total Inv: $55,000 kiosk - $100,000 in-line - Financing: Yes, assistance in obtaining.

WHITE HEN PANTRY
660 Industrial Dr., Elmhurst, IL, 60126. Contact: Brian Doyle, Fran. Mgr. - Tel: (708) 833-3100. A convenience store specializing in fresh deli sandwiches, bakery and produce. Stores are open 24hrs. and 365 days a yr. Established: 1965 - Franchising Since: 1965 - No. of Units: Company Owned: 4 - Franchised: 340 - Franchise Fee: $20,000 - Total Pre-Opening Inv: $56,800 - Financing: Yes.

ZIP FOOD STORES
1200 W. 15th St., Gary, IN, 46407. Contact: E.T. Eskilson, Pres. - Tel: (219) 885-6101. Food convenience stores. Established: 1970 - No. of Units: 10 - Franchise Fee: $8,000 - Total Inv: $30,000 - Financing: Possible.

FOOD: DONUT, BAKERY AND COFFEE SHOPS

AHH-SOME GOURMET COFFEE INC.
724 E. Industrial Park Dr., #1, Manchester, NH, 03109-5629. Contact: Daniel A. Laufer, Pres. - Tel: (603) 624-7600. Gourmet coffee, espresso based beverages, gift baskets, office coffee service. Established: 1992 - Franchising Since: 1993 - No. of Units: Company Owned: 0 - Franchised: 3 - Franchise Fee: $15,500 - Royalty: 5%, 2% adv. - Total Inv: $75,000 - $150,000 - Financing: No.

ALL MY MUFFINS
AMM Licensing Inc.
P.O. Box 852, Hillside, IL, 60162. Contact: Paul Bernstein, V.P. - Tel: (708) 415-0324. Gourmet muffins, soups, salads. Over 250 different types of muffins baked from scratch in each store. Established: 1984 - Franchising Since: 1985 - No. of Units: Franchised: 3 - Franchise Fee: $20,000 - Royalty: 6%, 2% adv. - Total Inv: $99,000-$175,000 - Financing: No.

AU BON PAIN
19 Fid Kennedy Ave., Boston, MA, 02210. Contact: Mr. Shaich, C.E.O. - Tel: (617) 423-2100. Bakery/cafe. Established: 1981 - No. of Units: Company Owned: 115 - Franchised: 30.

AUNTIE ANNE'S HAND-ROLLED SOFT PRETZELS
Auntie Anne's Inc.
160-A Route 41, P.O. Box 529, Gap, PA, 17527. Contact: Dave Hood, Dir. of Fran. - Tel: (717) 442-4766. Unique soft pretzel shops, selling a variety of specialty flavored pretzels, assorted dips and great fresh-squeezed lemonade. Product is made fresh, in customer's full view. Established: 1988 - Franchising Since: 1989 - No. of Units: Company Owned: 13 - Franchised: 240 - Franchise Fee: $28,000 - Royalty: 5%, 1% adv. fund - Total Inv: $130,000 - $194,000 incl. - Financing: No.

BAGEL BUILDERS FAMOUS OVEN FRESH BAGELS
Specialty Bakeries, Inc.
1263 Glen Ave., Ste. 220, Moorestown, NJ, 08057-1139. Contact: R. Florentino, Pres. - Tel: (609) 840-0800. Bagel bakery and salad cafe featuring our famous award winning bagels, gourmet cream cheese spreads, deli & grilled specialties, gourmet coffee, eggs, omelets & more. Established: 1984 - Franchising Since: 1992 - No. of Units: Company Owned: 6 - Franchised: 16 - Franchise Fee: $25,000 - Royalty: 4% - Total Inv: $165,000 - $240,000 - Financing: To qualified applicants.

BAGELS ARE FOREVER!
Centrix Group, The
P.O. Box 7169, Boston, MA, 02269. Contact: Leo F. Meady, Pres. - Tel: (619) 984-0405. Retail bagel shops. Turn-key package for inexperienced persons. Eat-in/take-out. May add muffins, deli meats, soups, sandwiches etc. Recommend that bagels be made from scratch, on premises. May use the name "Bagels are Forever", or choose any other name. Established: 1994 - Franchise Fee: Included in package price - Royalty: None - Total Inv: $95,000 to $145,000 - Financing: About one-half total cost, from third party sources.

BARISTA BRAVA COFFEE *
1150 17th St., Washington, DC, 20036. Contact: Ronniann Silver, Exec. V.P. Fran. Dev. - Tel: (202) 331-0962, Fax: (202) 331-0964. Coffee and Espresso Bar adapted to the fast pace of urban life serving a wide variety of brewed coffee and espresso based drinks, freshly baked pastries, muffins, filled croissants, and light sandwiches & salads. Established: 1992 - Franchising Since: 1995 - No. of Units: Company Owned: 4 - Franchised: 1 - Franchise Fee: $25,000 for unit #1, $15,000 thereafter with upfront commitment - Royalty: 5%, 1% nat'l. adv. - Total Inv: Lease neg./legal/acct. permits, lic. $3,750 to $10,000; Construction, FFE, Inven. $102,000 to $183,000; Grand opening, work. cap. $40,000 to $50,000 - Financing: No.

BEST BAGELS IN TOWN
480-19 Patchogue - Holbrook Rd., Holbrook, NY, 11741. Contact: Jay Squatriglia, Pres. - Tel: (516) 472-4104, Fax: (516) 472-4105. Retail bagel bakery restaurant. Established: 1988 - Franchising Since: 1988 - No. of Units: Company Owned: 2 - Franchised: 19 - Franchise Fee: $15,000 - Royalty: 4% gross sales - Total Inv: $135,000 - $190,000 excl. fran. fee - Financing: Assistance.

BIG APPLE BAGELS
BAB Systems, Inc.
8501 W. Higgins Rd., Ste. 320, Chicago, IL, 60631. Contact: Tom Ryan, Dir. of Fran. Dev. - Tel: (312) 380-6100. Retail sales of made from scratch bagels in 16 varieties, 16 varieties of cream cheeses, deli sandwiches, gourmet coffee, fresh juices, desserts. Established: 1992 - Franchising Since: 1993 - No. of Units: Company Owned: 2 - Franchised: 96 - Franchise Fee: $18,500 - Royalty: 5% of sales + 2% mktg. - Total Inv: $150,000 - $160,000 - Financing: No.

BIG CITY BAGELS *
151 Kalmus Dr., #C-100, Costa Mesa, CA, 92626. Contact: Michael Reynolds, V.P. - Tel: (800) 88-BAGEL, Fax: (714) 434-1641. Bagel bakery cafe featuring fresh baked authentic N.Y. style bagels, fresh varietal cream cheeses, salads, sandwiches and gourmet coffees. Established: 1992 - Franchising Since: 1993 - No. of Units: Company Owned: 1 - Franchised: 10 - Franchise Fee: $30,000 - Royalty: 4% - Total Inv: $250,000 to $300,000 - Financing: Through outside sources.

BIG SKY BREAD COMPANY
455 Delta Ave., #204, Cincinnati, OH, 45226. Contact: Harold Tieger, C.E.O. - Tel: (800) 536-5050. Whole grain retail bread bakery featuring breads, cookies, muffins, rolls & gourmet coffee. Established: 1990 - Franchising Since: 1992 - No. of Units: Company Owned: 5 - Franchised: 18 - Franchise Fee: Varies - Royalty: Sliding scale based on volume - Total Inv: $150,000 - Financing: No.

BIXBY'S BAGEL CO. *
Bixby's Food Systems, Inc.
8000 W. 78th St., #110, Edina, MN, 55439. Contact: Al Freed, V.P. Fran. Dev. - Tel: (612) 947-9905, Fax: (612) 947-9923. Bagel restaurant/bakery. Bagels, cream cheeses, bagel sandwiches (meat condiments etc.), espresso and specialty coffees, salads, soups & desserts. Merchandise - gift baskets. Established: 1994 - Franchising Since: 1994 - No. of Units: Company Owned: 2 - Franchised: 12 - Franchise Fee: $25,000 - Royalty: 4% of sales - Total Inv: $125,000 equip., $75,000 to $100,000 build out - Financing: SBA.

BLUE CHIP COOKIES
Blue Chip Franchises Corp.
100 First St., San Francisco, CA, 94105. Contact: Matt Nader, Pres. - Tel: (415) 546-3840, Fax: (415) 546-9717. Fresh baked cookies, muffins and brownies. Established: 1983 - Franchising Since: 1985 - No. of Units: Company Owned: 7 - Franchised: 34 - Franchise Fee: $29,500 - Royalty: 4% - Total Inv: $117,000 - $190,000 - Financing: Yes.

BONJOUR BAGEL CAFE
Fast Trak Development Company, Inc.
225 S. Lake Ave., Ste. 273, Pasadena, CA, 91101-3005. Contact: Stephan A. Metz, Pres. - Tel: (818) 304-9023, Fax: (818) 304-0391. An ambient, upscale bagel bakery cafe that offers a wide variety of freshly baked bagels, wholesome bagel sandwiches, delicious soups and salads, fresh juices and beverages, specialty baked goods, and a complete selection of aromatic, gourmet coffees. Established: 1992 - Franchising Since: 1993 - No. of Units: Company Owned: 1 - Franchised: 17 - Franchise Fee: $35,000 - Royalty: 5% - Total Inv: $275,000 - $385,000 - Financing: No.

BREADSMITH
2632 N. Downer Ave., Milwaukee, WI, 53211. Contact: Marc Cayle, Dir. of Dev. - Tel: (414) 962-1965. Retail traditional European bread bakery featuring a variety of award-winning hearth breads and rolls. Open bakery concept allows customers to view the baking process. Established: 1993 - Franchising Since: 1993 - No. of Units: Company Owned: 4 - Franchised: 9 - Franchise Fee: $25,000 - Royalty: 7% gross sales - Total Inv: $155,000 - $215,000 (incl. fran. fee) - Financing: Will assist with business plan for third party.

BREADSOUL CAFE
Breadsoul Franchise, Inc.
118 East 60, New York, NY, 10022. Contact: Dori Evans, Pres. - Tel: (212) 832-7495. Specializes in coffee, cappuccino, imported bread dough baked in stores, gourmet sandwiches and pastries. Take-out, upscale country decor. Established: 1990 - Franchising Since: 1993 - No. of Units: Company Owned: 4 - Franchised: 1 - Franchise Fee: $10,000 - Royalty: $200 - $300/wk., no percentage - Total Inv: $75,000 - $138,000 - Financing: Not at this time.

BREWSTER'S COFFEE
Brewster's Coffee Franchise Company
430 Lake Cook Rd., Ste. B, Deerfield, IL, 60015. Contact: Peter Grumhaus Jr., Dir. of Fran. - Tel: (708) 940-0020. Operator and franchisor of full service and drive-thru coffee stores, featuring the freshest coffee available anywhere. Established: 1994 - Franchising Since: 1994 - No. of Units: Company Owned: 6 - Franchised: 3 - Franchise Fee: $10,000 - $20,000 - Royalty: 6% of sales, plus adv. fee of up to 3% - Total Inv: $85,000 - $200,000 - Financing: Franchisor will assist in obtaining leasing.

A FRESH APPROACH TO SPECIALTY COFFEE.

♦

For more information, you can reach us at:
Brewsters™ Coffee Company
430 Lake Cook Rd, Suite B
Deerfield, IL 60015
708-940-830   fax 940-8326

BRUEGGER'S BAGEL BAKERY
Bruegger Franchise Corp.
159 Bank St., Burlington, VT, 05402. Contact: Mary Bunting - Tel: (802) 862-4700, Fax: (802) 865-9739. Fresh bagel bakery. Established: 1982 - Franchising Since: 1993 - No. of Units: Company Owned: 29 - Franchised: 154 - Franchise Fee: $20,000 - $25,000 per unit - Royalty: 5% - Total Inv: $200,000 - $600,000 - Financing: Yes.

CHESAPEAKE BAGEL BAKERY
1360 Beverly Rd., Ste. 104, McLean, VA, 22101. Contact: Dan Rowe, Dir. Fran. Dev. - Tel: (703) 893-0166, Fax: (703) 893-0168. Full - scratch bagel bakery restaurant cafe/coffee house. Oldest & largest chain in country. Established: 1981 - Franchising Since: 1984 - No. of Units: Company Owned: 8 - Franchised: 135 - Franchise Fee: $22,500 - Royalty: 4% - Total Inv: $300,000 - Financing: Third party.

CINDY'S CINNAMON ROLLS
1432 So. Mission Ste. A, Fallbrook, CA, 92028. Contact: Tom Harris, Pres. - Tel: (619) 723-1121 or (800) HOT-ROLL. Specialty bakery - major malls only - bake from scratch all day. Established: 1985 - Franchising Since: 1986 - No. of Units: Franchised: 40 - Franchise Fee: $25,000 - Royalty: 5% - Total Inv: $62,000 - $102,000 - excluding franc. fee - Financing: no.

COFFEE BEANERY LTD., THE
P.O. Box 310349, Flint, MI, 48531-0349. Contact: Franchise Development - Tel: (800) 728-2326, ext. 151. Gourmet coffee units that specialize in providing superior products. Currently looking for highly motivated individuals that are willing to learn and be the best at operating carts, cafes, mall stores, kiosks, and street fronts. Established: 1976 - Franchising Since: 1985 - No. of Units: Company Owned: 32 - Franchised: 165 - Franchise Fee: $10,000 - $25,000 - Royalty: 6%, 2% adv. - Total Inv: $54,000 - $250,000 - Financing: Third party leasing.

COOKIE BOUQUET/COOKIES BY DESIGN
Cookie Bouquet Franchising Corp.
6757 Arapaho Rd., Ste. 761, Dallas, TX, 75248. Contact: David Patterson, Fran. Mktg. - Tel: (214) 239-7474 or (800) 945-2665. Gift bakery specializing in cookie arrangements and gourmet cookies. The cookie arrangements are created for special events, holidays, corporate logos, centerpieces, etc. A wonderfully delicious alternative to flowers and balloons. Established: 1983 - Franchising Since: 1987 - No. of Units: Company Owned: 1 - Franchised: 108 - Franchise Fee: $18,500 - Royalty: 6% - Total Inv: $50,000 - $100,000 - Financing: No.

COOKIE MUG, THE
Cookie Mug Inc., The
2010 Edinboro Rd., Erie, PA, 16509. Contact: Mr. Hugill, Pres. - Tel: (800) 455-0440 or (814) 866-6847. Gourmet cookie bouquet delivery service. Established: 1989 - Franchising Since: 1993 - No. of Units: Company Owned: 1 - Franchised: 1 - Franchise Fee: $10,000 - Royalty: 5%, 0% adv. - Total Inv: $52,800 - (incl. fran. fee) - Financing: None at present.

COOKIES IN BLOOM
Cookies In Bloom, Inc.
5429 N. MacArthur Blvd., Irving, TX, 75038. Contact: Mary Pinac, V.P. - Tel: (214) 518-1749. Cookie gift shop, specializing in hand decorated cookie arrangements. The cookies come in over 200 shapes and the bases are constantly being upgraded with new styles and motifs. Established: 1988 - Franchising Since: 1992 - No. of Units: Franchised: 5 - Franchise Fee: $9,500 - Royalty: 7% with 2% refunded upon proof of advertising - Total Inv: $35,000 - $65,000 - Financing: 50% of franchise fee.

DAWN DONUT SYSTEMS, INC.
G-4300 W. Pierson Rd., Flint, MI, 48504. Contact: Franchise Director - Tel: (810) 733-0760. Donuts, baked goods and beverages. Most new units have gasoline and a convenience store. Established: 1956 - Franchising Since: 1956 - No. of Units: Company Owned: 13 - Franchised: 48 - Franchise Fee: $20,000 - Royalty: 4.5% - Total Inv: varies - Financing: on certain unit developments or franchising of company operated shops.

DAYLIGHT DONUTS
Daylight Corporation
P.O. Box 580818, Tulsa, OK, 74158-0818. Contact: Jim Perrymore, Sales Mgr. - Tel: (918) 438-0800. Full line donut & pastry retail shops. Established: 1954 - Franchising Since: 1954 - No. of Units: Company Owned: 2 - Franchised: 135 - Total Inv: $25,000 equip., $3,000 inventory, $10,000 approx. remodel - Financing: 70% of equip.

DONUT INN
Donut Inn, Inc.
22120 Clarendon St., Ste. 110, Woodland Hills, CA, 91367-6315. Contact: Steve Blum, Dir. of Franc. Mktg. and Sales - Tel: (818) 888-2220. Upscale donut, pastry, muffin and bagel shoppes. Considered fastest growing franchise of its kind in CA. Registered in 37 states and overseas. Training and manuals provided. No experience required. Established: 1975 - No. of Units: Company Owned: 2 - Franchised: 32 - Capital Required: $45,000 - $65,000 - Royalty: 5.5%, 3% adv. - Total Inv: $95,000 - $145,000 - Financing: assistance.

DONUT MAN, THE
American Food Lines, Inc.
5418 Mayview, Minnetonka, MN, 55345. Contact: Mike Lebine, Sales Mgr. - Tel: (612) 930-9999. Mini donut equipment and concession trailers. Established: 1977 - Franchising Since: 1977 - No. of Units: Franchised: 1000 + - Approx. Initial Inv: $3,500 - Total Inv: $3,500 - $15,000 - Financing: yes.

DONUTLAND
Donutland USA Ltd.
5265 Rockwell Dr., N.E., Cedar Rapids, IA, 52402. Contact: Gary Kent, Fran. Dir. - Tel: (319) 395-9636. Bakery & donut shop with deli. Established: 1963 - Franchising Since: 1964 - No. of Units: Franchised: 14 - Franchise Fee: $25,000 - Royalty: 4.5% - Total Inv: $135,000 - $160,000 - Financing: No.

DUNKIN' DONUTS INC.
Hovanian Commerce Blvd., 112 N. Center Drive, North Brunswick, NJ, 08902. Contact: Franchise Dept. - Tel: (908) 422-7000. Franchised coffee and donut shops featuring drive-in and walk-in units. Retail selling of more than 55 varieties of donuts along with coffee and soft drinks. Established: 1950 - Franchising Since: 1955 - No. of Units: Company Owned: 2 - Franchised: 2,900 - Franchise Fee: $40,000 producing unit, $10,000 satellite - Royalty: 4.9% royalty fees, 5% adv. - Total Inv: total cost for real estate dev., equip., signs, fran. fee. Shop ranges from $130,000 - $600,000 depending on area of country & type of real estate dev. - Financing: No.

EXPRESSO TERMINI *
1611 N. Federal Hwy., Ft. Lauderdale, FL, 33305. Contact: Laura Scoble, Pres., Expresso Termini Fran. Group - Tel: (305) 568-6828. Initially began as gourmet drive-thru concept and has expanded to include coffee bars as well as satellite units within specified areas. Established: 1993 - Franchising Since: 1994 - No. of Units: Company Owned: 3 - Franchised: 1 - Franchise Fee: $22,500 - Royalty: $250 per week - Total Inv: $59,500 to $108,000 - Financing: None.

GLORIA JEAN'S GOURMET COFFEES
2255 Glades Rd., Boca Raton, FL, 33431. Contact: Cecil Johnson, V.P., Fran. - Tel: (407) 995-2601. Retail gourmet coffee, tea, coffee & espresso makers, grinders, accessories, fresh brewed coffees, exclusive gift packages. Established: 1979 - Franchising Since: 1986 - No. of Units: Company Owned: 25 - Franchised: 210 - Franchise Fee: $25,000 - Royalty: 6% of monthly gross sales - Total Inv: $210,600 to $319,500 - Financing: Assistance in seeking 3rd party financing.

GOURMET CUP COFFEE
Gourmet Cup of America, Inc.
11 N. Skokie Hwy., Ste. 205, Lake Bluff, IL, 60044. Contact: Fran. Dev. Dept. - Tel: (708) 735-0200, Fax: (708) 735-0244. Gourmet Cup Coffee is America's premier specialty coffee franchise. Currently we have over 145 franchised and corporate owned stores in operation or under contract in six states and eight Canadian provinces. With GCC, franchisees learn to generate maximum revenue from a product that half of all Americans use every day. Established: 1985 - Franchising Since: 1985 - No. of Units: Company Owned: 1 - Franchised: 144 - Franchise Fee: $15,000 GCC store, $12,000 kiosk or drive-thru, $9,500 for cart - Royalty: 1% 1st yr., 3% 2nd yr., 5.5% yrs. 3-10, .5% adv. - Total Inv: $100,000 to $300,000 - Financing: Third party lending sources available for equip. leasing and SBA loan programs. Ongoing evaluation of other potential lenders. Standard business plan for franchisee's use and loan application assistance.

GREAT AMERICAN COOKIE COMPANY
4685 Frederick Dr., S.W., Atlanta, GA, 30336. Contact: Jim Squire, Senior V.P. - Tel: (800) 336-2447. Four hundred retail cookie stores located in major malls throughout the U.S. Specializing in fresh baked cookies, special event decorated jumbo cookies, brownies, and frozen beverages. Established: 1977 - Franchising Since: 1978 - Franchise Fee: $25,000 - Royalty: 7% includes in store advertising and point of purchase material - Total Inv: Average $170,000 incl. fran. fee - Financing: None.

GREAT HARVEST BREAD CO.
Great Harvest Franchising
28 S. Montana St., Dillon, MT, 59725. Contact: John Poundstone, Fran. Dev. - Tel: (406) 683-6842, Fax: (406) 683-5537. Premium bread bakery, specializing in whole wheat breads. Established: 1976 - Franchising Since: 1978 - No. of Units: Franchised: 94 - Franchise Fee: $24,000 - Royalty: 7% of monthly gross sales - Total Inv: $103,000 - $225,000 (incl. initial fee) - Financing: Help with financing proposals.

GRETEL'S PRETZELS
Restaurant Systems International
1000 South Ave., Staten Island, NY, 10314. Contact: Raymond Habib, Dir., Fran. Sales - Tel: (718) 494-8888. Fresh baked hand-rolled pretzels, combined with a delicious blend of frosty fruit shakes. Established: 1993 - Franchising Since: 1993 - No. of Units: Company Owned: 1 - Franchised: 6 - Franchise Fee: $20,000 - Royalty: 5% - Total Inv: $150,000 - Financing: Yes, indirect.

HOT SAM PRETZEL BAKERY *
Hot Sam Franchise Development, Inc.
5885 Grant Ave., Cleveland, OH, 44125 . Contact: M. Winick, Fran. Sales Mgr. - Tel: (800) 4HOTSAM ext. 4221, (216) 883-9700. Freshly baked soft Bavarian and hand rolled, hand twisted sweet dough pretzels with a variety of toppings; fresh-squeezed lemonade and other beverages. Established: 1967 - Franchising Since: 1994 - No. of Units: Company Owned: 140 - Franchise Fee: $22,500 - Royalty: 6% of gross sales - Total Inv: $148,950 - $199,950 (incl. fran. fee) - Financing: No.

HOUSE OF COFFEE INC.
4 Garden Rd., Little Silver, NJ, 07739. Contact: Ronald S. Hari, Dir. Franc. - Tel: (908) 741-7347. Coffee house/cafe. Coffee franchise that roasts it's own coffee, serving coffee & pastries in a coffee house atmosphere. Established: 1988 - Franchising Since: 1989 - No. of Units: Company Owned: 2 - Franchised: 3 - Franchise Fee: $20,000 - Royalty: 5% - Total Inv: Franc. Fee + $60,000 constr., $50,000 equip. - Financing: Assistance.

IKE'S DELI & BAKERY INC. *
3000 Sunrise Blvd., Ste. 6, Rancho Cordova, CA, 95670. Contact: Abe Bandak, Pres. - Tel: (916) 635-9808, Fax: (916) 635-5073. Bakery & deli. Established: 1985 - Franchising Since: 1993 - No. of Units: Company Owned: 1 - Franchised: 1 - Franchise Fee: $10,000 - Royalty: $500 up to $5,000, 3% thereafter - Total Inv: $60,000 - Financing: None.

INCREDIBLE CHOCOLATE CHIP COOKIE COMPANY
I.C.C.C.C.
640 Lower Poplar St., P.O Box 6375, Macon, GA, 31208. Contact: Ted Senters, Pres. - Tel: (912) 742-8455. Fast Food - ice cream/yogurt/ cookies. Established:1980 - No. of Units: Company Owned: 10 - Franchised: 2.

JAVA CENTRALE
Java Centrale, Inc.
1610 Arden Way, Ste. 299, Sacramento, CA, 95815. Contact: Karl Thompson, Dir., Fran. Dev. - Tel: (916) 568-2310. Gourmet coffee cafe franchise company offering 40 fine roasted coffees by the pound, fresh brewed and specialty coffee beverages, breakfast pastries, deli sandwiches and fancy desserts all served in a relaxed atmosphere. Established: 1992 - Franchising Since: 1992 - No. of Units: Company Owned: 1 -

Franchised: 120 (under contract) - Franchise Fee: $25,000 - Royalty: 6% of gross sales - Total Inv: $175,000 - $250,000 - Financing: Corporation will assist in third party financing.

JOLLY PIRATE ENTERPRISES
3923 E. Broad St., Columbus, OH, 43213. Contact: Robert W. Maloney, Dev. Dir. - Tel: (614) 235-4501. Donut and coffee shop open 24 hrs. catering to the general public featuring fresh hand cut donuts and complimentary beverages. Established: 1961 - Franchising Since: 1970 - No. of Units: Company Owned: 6 - Franchised: 18 - Royalty: 4%, adv. 3% - Total Inv: $300,000.

KRISPY KREME DOUGHNUT CORP.
P.O. Box 83, Winston-Salem, NC, 27102. Contact: Scott Livengood, Pres. - Tel: (910) 725-2981. Established: 1937. No. of Units: Company Owned: 75 - Franchised: 75.

LE CROISSANT SHOP
Blue Mill Enterprises Corp.
227 West 40th St., New York, NY, 10018. Contact: J. Pelletier, V.P. - Tel: (212) 719-5940. French café bakery. Established: 1981 - Franchising Since: 1984 - No. of Units: Company Owned: 3 - Franchised: 23 - Franchise Fee: $22,500 - Royalty: 5% - Total Inv: $300,000 - Financing: None.

LOX OF BAGELS
24412 Hawthorne Blvd., Torrance, CA, 90505. Contact: Ted Taylor, V.P. - Tel: (310) 539-3582, (800) 879-6927. Since 1986, we have built our reputation on marketing great tasting bagels, cream cheeses, deli sandwiches, bagel chips and gourmet coffees in Southern California. We also show you how to make pizzas and various breads. In fact, our bagel chips are sold nationally in food stores in over 40 states under our trademark "King David's Bagel Chips". Call "Toll Free" at 1-800-879-6927 for more information about this exciting opportunity. Established: 1986 - No. of Units: Company Owned: 3 - Franchised: 2 - Franchise Fee: $24,500 - Royalty: No Royalty - Total Inv: $125,000 - $150,000.

Ted Taylor
Vice President

24412 Hawthorne Blvd.   (800) 879-6927
Torrance, CA, 90505   (310) 539-7494 Fax

MICHEL'S BAKERY & CAFE
17 W 705 Butterfield Rd., Ste. E, Oakbrook, IL, 60181-4363. Contact: Robert Tischler, V.P. Corp. Dev. - Tel: (708) 629-0821, Fax: (708) 629-0823. Retail stores located in malls, strip centers and office complexes offering muffins, cinnamon rolls, cookies & treats along with a deli offering a unique array of sandwiches, soups and salads. Established: 1988 - Franchising Since: 1991 - No. of Units: Company Owned: 1 - Franchised: 8 - Franchise Fee: $25,000 - Royalty: 6% sales - Total Inv: $120,000 - $175,000 - Financing: None.

MOXIE JAVA
Moxie Java International
199 E. 52nd., Boise, ID, 83714. Contact: Todd Sternfeld, Fran. Dir. - Tel: (800) 659-6963, (208) 322-7773. Sell licenses for Moxie Java Systems which consist of carts, kiosks & cafes that serve exceptional espresso beverages. Established: 1989 - Franchising Since: 1991 - No. of Units: Company Owned: 4 - Franchised: 17 - Franchise Fee: $3,500, $15,500 - Royalty: 5% power branding & ongoing support, .5% research & dev. - Total Inv: $26,000+/-, $70,000 +/-, $112,000 +/-, - Financing: No, but have ongoing relations with local bank.

MRS. FIELDS COOKIES
Mrs. Fields Inc.
462 West Bearcat Dr., Salt Lake City, UT, 84115. Contact: Keith Gerson, Sen. V.P. Fran. & Licensing. - Tel: (801) 463-2000. Cookie and bakery segment leader offering its recipe for success. Reknown for commitment to quality and service, qualified franchisees will share in national brand recognition, award winning operating systems and products, expert technical and operations assistance, training etc. Established: 1977 - Franchising Since: 1990 - No. of Units: Company Owned: 345 - Franchised: 262 - Franchise Fee: New stores: $25,000 - Royalty: 6% - Total Inv: $35,000 - $250,000 for existing company owned stores - Financing: Assistance in securing third party financing.

MRS. POWELL'S BAKERY EATERY
Mrs. Powell's Inc.
1911 Roselawn Ave., Ste. 3, Monroe, LA, 71201. Contact: P. Teixeira, Mktg. Mgr. - Tel: (318) 329-9565. High quality bakery goods specializing in cinnamon rolls, muffins, and variety coffees, deli sandwiches and gourmet salads. Satellite store concept reduces capital costs for retail development and maximizes production capabilities of producing store kitchens. Established: 1984 - Franchising Since: 1984 - No. of Units: Franchised: 31 - Franchise Fee: $25,000 - Royalty: 5%, 2% adv. - Total Inv: $112,000 - $190,000 (Total investment/incl. fran. fee) - Financing: Third party.

MUFFIN TIN, THE
AMT Inc.
P.O. Box 202, Helena St., Alden, MI, 49612. Contact: Jane Van Etten, Pres. - Tel: (616) 331-6808. Specialty bakery: muffins, cookies, scones, coffee/teas. Established: 1987 - Franchising Since: 1994 - No. of Units: Company Owned: 2 - Franchise Fee: $20,000 - Royalty: 10%, 10% adv. - Total Inv: $50,000 - $80,000 - Financing: None.

MY FAVORITE MUFFIN
My Favorite Muffin Too, Inc.
155 N. Main St., New City, NY, 10956-3850. Contact: Stacey Sheinbaum, Mkt. Dir. - Tel: (201) 871-0370 or (800) 332-2229. Specialty bakery offering, muffins, muffin gift baskets, gourmet coffee & related items. Established: 1987 - Franchising Since: 1987 - No. of Units: Company Owned: 3 - Franchised: 47 - Franchise Fee: $25,000 - Royalty: 5% - Total Inv: $145,500 - $311,000 (excl. fran. fee) - Financing: None, will assist.

MY MOTHER'S DELICACIES™ CAFE *
My Mother's Delicacies, Inc.
501 South Washington Ave., Scranton, PA, 18505. Contact: Ms. Ronni Grossman or Susan Herlands, Dir. of Fran. Dev./Pres. - Tel: (717) 343-5266 Ext. 6. A unique, upscale cafe for people who savor the highest quality, delicious Old World flavor of baked delicacies, 'The Way Mother Used to Make Them'. Featuring Rugala, a cresent-shaped, hand rolled taste bud treasure, and much more. Established: 1988 - Franchising Since: 1995 - No. of Units: Company Owned: 1 National Distributor = Parent Co. - Franchise Fee: Rugala only bakery $15,000; Full line bakery $25,000 - Royalty: 6% gross sales - Total Inv: Rugala only bakery - $94,900 - $129,800; Full line bakery - $185,100 - $251,200 (Some working cap. will be required) - Financing: No.

NEW ENGLAND PASTRY MILL
The Gendron Corp.
3275 Hillmont Cir., Orlando, FL, 32817. Contact: Jess Gendron, Pres. - Tel: (407) 679-6700. Retail cookie shops with gifts, juices, cookie accessories & products. Established: 1992 - Franchising Since: 1993 - Franchise Fee: $15,000 - Royalty: 5% - Total Inv: Turnkey $150,000 - $225,000 - Financing: Not at this time.

OK COFFEE TIME *
5 Colombia Dr., Ste. 176, Niagara Falls, NY, 14305-1275. Contact: William Siarto, Fran. Dev. - Tel: (905) 356-4242, Fax: (905) 356-9373. Level 1: Basic entry of existing coffee shops looking for strong corporate identity; Level 2: Quality coffee, light lunch & dessert - food court, hospital, univeristy, office bldg., military base etc.; Level 3: Coffee, donuts, muffins, sandwiches, salads, soups and sweet baked goods.

Established: 1995 - Franchising Since: 1996 - No. of Units: Company Owned: 1 - Franchise Fee: Level 1: $2,900; Level 2: $5,900; Level 3: $10,500 - Royalty: Level 1: $50/mo., $25 adv.; Level 2: 5%, 2% adv.; Level 3: 5% plus 2% adv. - Total Inv: Level 1: $2,900; Level 2: $39,000 avg. turnkey; Level 3: $70,000 to $98,000 kiosk locations, $98,000 to $133,000 satellite store, $133,000 to $168,000 full producing - Financing: Arranged through financial institutions.

P.J.'S COFFEE AND TEA *
P.J.'s USA, Inc.
500 N. Hagen Ave., New Orleans, LA, 70119. Contact: Lisa Amoss, V.P., Dev. - Tel: (504) 486-2827, Fax: (504) 486-2345. Specialty coffee and tea café and retail sales, accepting applications for territories in the southeastern and southwestern United States. Established: 1978 - Franchising Since: 1987 - No. of Units: Company Owned: 4 - Franchised: 13 - Franchise Fee: $16,000 - Royalty: 5% of gross sales - Total Inv: approx. $120,000 to $150,000 incl. fran. fee - Financing: No.

PARADISE BAKERY & CAFE
Paradise Bakery, Inc.
115 S. Acacia Ave., Solana Beach, CA, 92075. Contact: Roberta Alford, Fran. Coord. - Tel: (619) 755-8281, Ext. 182. Bakeries and bakery cafes serving delicious freshly baked cookies, muffins, healthy soups, salads and sandwiches. Established: 1976 - Franchising Since: 1985 - No. of Units: Company Owned: 6 - Franchised: 43 - Franchise Fee: $20,000 limited menu bakery, $25,000 bakery cafe - Royalty: 4% of gross sales due monthly - Total Inv: $160,000 - $315,000 - Financing: No.

PENNSYLVANIA PRETZEL FRANCHISE CORPORATION *
295 Greenwich St., New York, NY, 10007. Contact: Franchise Dept. - Tel: (212) 587-5938, (800) 346-0775, Fax: (212) 587-5938. Sells hand rolled fresh soft pretzels/espresso bar. Established: 1993 - Franchising Since: 1994 - No. of Units: Company Owned: 2 - Franchised: 1 - Franchise Fee: $15,000 - Royalty: 6% - Total Inv: $100,000 - Financing: Some.

PEPPERIDGE FARM, INC.
P.O. Box 5500, Norwalk, CT, 06851. Contact: C.P. Davis, Dir. Sales Admin. - Tel: (203) 846-7000. Direct store delivery of bakery (bread, rolls, dry stuffing mix), biscuits and snack crackers to retail stores. Established: 1937 - Franchising Since: 1941 - No. of Units: 2,000 - Approx. Inv: varies - Financing: Yes.

PHILLY'S FAMOUS SOFT PRETZEL CO. INC.
2000 W. Glades Rd., Ste. 200, Boca Raton, FL, 33431. Contact: Hank Lotman, Pres. - Tel: (407) 338-5575, (800) 262-1567. Gourmet flavored soft pretzel distribution. Established: 1992 - Franchising Since: 1992 - No. of Units: Franchised: 33 - Franchise Fee: $14,900 and up - Royalty: None - Total Inv: fee plus $10,000 work. cap. (recommended) - Financing: Possibly.

PRETZEL TIME
Pretzel Time, Inc.
2101 Lehman St., Lebanon, PA, 17046. Contact: Anthony M. Shamoun, Fran. Coord. - Tel: (717) 270-9456. Retail sales of fresh dough, hand-rolled soft pretzels with a variety of toppings, as well as a variety of soft beverages. Where available, dual concept PretzelTime and TCBY Yogurt thru Pretzel Time's association as master franchisee. For TCBY exclusive in mall environments. Established: 1991 - Franchising Since: 1992 - No. of Units: Company Owned: 3 - Franchised: 179 - Royalty: 7%, 1% nat'l adv. - Total Inv: $70,000 bldg., $30,000 equip. - Financing: No.

PRETZEL TWISTER, THE
2706 Horseshoe Dr. S., Ste. 112, Naples, FL, 33942-6154. Contact: Keith Johnson, Pres. - Tel: (813) 643-2075. Hand rolled and twisted soft gourmet pretzels and hand squeezed lemonade. Established: 1991 - Franchising Since: 1993 - No. of Units: Company Owned: 2 - Franchised: 6 - Franchise Fee: $10,000 - Royalty: 4% + 1% adv. - Total Inv: $86,000 - $112,500.

PRETZEL WORLD
Pretzel World Inc.
CSS Franchising: 177 Main St., Ste. 103, Fort Lee, NJ, 07024. Contact: Franchise Sales Rep. - Tel: (201) 585-4753. Hand made fresh baked pretzels in 16 flavors all 100% fat free. Stores set in malls, airports, store front locations. Established: 1994 - Franchising Since: 1994 - No. of Units: Company Owned: 1 - Franchise Fee: $9,500 - Royalty: 6% of gross - Total Inv: $60,000 - $100,000 incl. build-out, equip. and stock - Financing: Yes.

PRETZELMAKER
Pretzelmaker, Inc.
1050 17th St., Ste. 1400, Denver, CO, 80265. Contact: Bill Naylor, Fran. Dir. - Tel: (303) 573-4800. Fresh, hand rolled pretzels, cooked moments before customers request, with a variety of 12 - 15 different toppings to meet each individuals taste. Established: 1991 - Franchising Since: 1992 - No. of Units: Franchised: 86 - Franchise Fee: $12,500 - Royalty: 5% gross sales, 2% adv. - Total Inv: $49,500 to $105,500 - Financing: No.

PRETZELS PLUS *
Pretzels Plus, Inc.
13 Carlisle St., Hanover, PA, 17331. Contact: Jonathan Bankert, Dir. of Fran. - Tel: (800) 559-7927, Fax: (717) 633-5078. Sales of soft, hand rolled pretzels, sandwiches on our famous pretzel roll, soups, pretzel dogs, sodas, and other beverages. Seeking mall locations in the eastern United States. Established: 1991 - Franchising Since: 1992 - No. of Units: Franchised: 20 - Franchise Fee: $12,000 - Royalty: 3% of sales, no ad fund fee/percentage - Total Inv: $50,000 - $70,000 depending on site - Financing: N/A.

QUIKAVA *
190 Old Derby St., Ste. 304, Hingham, Ma, 02043. Contact: Gerry Pelissier, V.P. - Tel: (617) 749-4242. We have combined two of the hottest trends in foodservice today, gourmet coffees and drive-thru convenience. We serve over 30 gourmet/specialty coffees and fresh baked goods, from a free standing modular double drive-thru 500 sq. ft. bldg. This wholly-owned subsidiary of the Chock Full o' Nuts Corp., a 60 year old coffee roaster listed on the NYSE, is seeking experienced business principals to become multi-unit Quikava franchise operators throughout the U.S. Established: 1990 - Franchising Since: 1993 - No. of Units: Company Owned: 3 - Franchised: 8 - Franchise Fee: $20,000 - Royalty: 5% gross yr. 1, 5.5% yr. 2+ - Financing: None.

SEATTLE'S BEST COFFEE
1321 2nd Ave., Ste. 200, Seattle, WA, 98111. Contact: Tom Reid, Dir. of Fran. Sales - Tel: (800) 722-3190, Fax: (206) 624-3262. Specialty coffee cafes featuring a variety of coffee products from North America's premier coffee roaster. Other food items as well as coffee related products. Established: 1979 - Franchising Since: 1984 - No. of Units: Company Owned: 11 - Franchised: 43 - Franchise Fee: $25,000 - Royalty: 6% - Total Inv: $275,000 - $325,000 - Financing: Assistance.

SOUTHERN MAID DONUT SHOP
3615 Cavalier Dr., Garland, TX, 750427599. Contact: D. Franklin, Lon Hargrove, V.P., Pres. - Tel: (214) 272-6425, Fax: (214) 276-3549. Manufacturer of donut mixes. Established: 1937 - Franchising Since: 1939 - No. of Units: 80 - Franchise Fee: $5,000 - Total Inv: $50,000.

STAN EVANS BAKERY
Stan Evans Bakeries, Inc.
2280 W. Henderson Rd., Ste. 208, Columbus, OH, 43220. Contact: Stan Evans, Pres. - Tel: (614) 459-1251. Bakeries of stone ground whole wheat breads, rolls, and sweets. All natural ingredients. No oils, shortening, milk products, egg products or coloring. Established: 1987 - Franchising Since: 1993 - No. of Units: Company Owned: 4 - Franchised: 1 - Franchise Fee: $25,000 - Royalty: 6%, 1% adv. - Total Inv: $125,000 - $150,000 - Financing: No.

T.J. CINNAMONS BAKERY
T.J. Cinnamons, Inc.
135 Seaview Dr., Secaucus, NJ, 07094. Contact: Vincent Loccisano, Sales Dir. - Tel: (201) 422-0910, Fax: (201) 422-0858. An upscale gourmet cinnamon roll bakery featuring "Hot From The Oven" original and "Sticky Bun" rolls, as well as cinnamon breads, muffins, cookies, and other fresh baked items. Also, coffee, tea and soft drinks. Bakeries are located in shopping malls, community and specialty shopping

centers. Established: 1984 - Franchising Since: 1986 - No. of Units: Company Owned: 1 - Franchised: 59 - Franchise Fee: $17,500 - Royalty: 5% gross monthly - Total Inv: $120,000, 50% buildout, 50% equip. - Financing: Yes, through sources.

THE MILL
800 P Street, Lincoln, NE, 68508. Contact: Joe Field, Bus. Dev. Mgr. - Tel: (800) 301-9504. Retail sale of various flavors of gourmet coffee by the cup or pound, custom roasting and other related coffee items. Established: 1975 - Franchising Since: 1993 - No. of Units: Company Owned: 1 - Franchise Fee: $20,000 - Royalty: 5%, 2% adv. - Total Inv: $107,650 to $241,250 - Financing: Will assist.

VIE DE FRANCE BAKERY/CAFÉ
Vie de France Yamazaki, Inc.
8201 Greensboro Dr., Ste. 1200, McLean, VA, 22102. Contact: Gary Cohen, Supervisor, Fran. Oper. - Tel: (703) 442-9205. Bakery/cafe featuring fresh baked breads, croissants, muffins, danish & cookies, freshly prepared salads, sandwiches & soups, served cafeteria style. Established: 1972 - Franchising Since: 1985 - No. of Units: Company Owned: 34 - Franchised: 3 - Franchise Fee: $25,000 - Royalty: 5%, 1% adv. - Total Inv: between $400,000 and $1,000,000, depending upon concept - Financing: No. Not presently selling franchises, but planning to franchise again in the near future.

WHOLE DONUT, THE
894 New Britain Ave., Hartford, CT, 06106. Contact: Frank Gencarelli, Pres. - Tel: (203) 953-3569. Donut and coffee, muffins, brownies, cookies, croissants, soups, sandwiches. Franchising in CT only. Franchising Since: 1984 - No. of Units: Company Owned: 12 - Franchised: 28 - Franchise Fee: $25,000 - Royalty: 5% plus 2% for national adv. - Total Inv: $135,000 - $175,000.

FOOD: ICE CREAM AND YOGURT

2001 FLAVORS PLUS POTATOES
2001 Flavors of America
8920 Independence Ave., Canoga Park, CA, 91304-1740. Contact: Mike Whitman, Pres. - Tel: (818) 341-9910 or (800) 2001-352. Yogurt, ice cream, smoothies, salads, sandwiches, soups & stuffed potato creations. Established: 1983 - Franchising Since: 1993 - No. of Units: Company Owned: 1 - Franchised: 10 - Franchise Fee: $15,000 - Royalty: 5%, 2% adv. - Total Inv: turnkey: $125,000 - $135,000 complete - Financing: Some.

ABBOTT'S FROZEN CUSTARD, INC.
4791 Lake Ave., Rochester, NY, 14612. Contact: Jack Perry, Dir. Fran. Dev. - Tel: (716) 865-7400, Fax: (716) 865-6034. Abbott's Frozen Custard is an ice cream business offering to sell the franchisee the right to operate one or more retail frozen custard (and related products) stands where the public may purchase frozen custard, frozen yogurt, sherbert, soft drinks, and other desserts and related food products. Established: 1903 - Franchising Since: 1954 - No. of Units: Company Owned: 6 - Franchised: 18 - Franchise Fee: $24,500 - Royalty: 5.5%, 2% adv. - Total Inv: $60,000 equip., $24,500 fee, $25,000 leasehold improv. & signs - Financing: No.

ALL AMERICAN FROZEN YOGURT AND ICE CREAM SHOPS
All American Frozen Yogurt Co., Inc., The
812 SW Washington St., Ste. 1110, Portland, OR, 97205-3215. Contact: C.R. Duffie Jr., Pres. - Tel: (503) 224-6199, Fax: (503) 224-5042. Frozen yogurt and ice cream shops located in the regional enclosed shopping malls. Established: 1986 - Franchising Since: 1988 - No. of Units: Company Owned: 1 - Franchised: 18 - Franchise Fee: $13,200 - $20,000 - Royalty: 5% adv. - 1% - Total Inv: $90,000 - $135,000 - Financing: Assistance only.

BAHAMA BUCK'S ORIGINAL SHAVED ICE COMPANY
Bahama Buck's Franchise Corporation
1741 W. University Ste. #148, Tempe, AZ, 85281. Contact: Eric Lee, Blake Buchanan, Treas./Pres. - Tel: (602) 894-4408. Serve gourmet Hawaiian shaved ice, tropical drinks, and fresh squeezed 100% natural lemonades & limeades in a fun tropical atmosphere. Established: 1989 - Franchising Since: 1993 - No. of Units: Company Owned: 2 - Franchised: 2 - Franchise Fee: $10,000 - Royalty: 5% of gross sales - Total Inv: $46,000 - $115,000 - Financing: No.

BANANAS
Restaurant Systems International
1000 South Ave., Staten Island, NY, 10314-3403. Contact: Raymond Habib, Dir., Fran. Sales - Tel: (718) 494-8888, Fax: (718) 494-8776. A popular blend of fruit, fruit juice and ice in five tropical flavors. Established: 1976 - Franchising Since: 1981 - No. of Units: Company Owned: 7 - Franchised: 104 - Franchise Fee: $20,000 - Royalty: 5% - Total Inv: $150,000 - Financing: Indirect.

BASKIN-ROBBINS '31' ICE CREAM AND YOGURT
31 Baskin Robbins Place, Glendale, CA, 91201. Contact: Bill Grimm, Dir. of Franchise Development - Tel: (818) 956-0031. Ice cream stores. Established: 1948 - Franchising Since: 1948 - No. of Units: Company Owned: 29 - Franchised: over 3,557 - Inv: $142,500 - $187,500 - Financing: Yes.

BEN & JERRY'S
Ben & Jerry's Homemade, Inc.
Route 100, P.O. Box 240, Waterbury, VT, 05676. Contact: Bruce Bowman, Dir. Retail Oper. - Tel: (802) 244-6957. Super premium ice cream parlor and scoop shops, featuring 34 flavors, sundaes, fountain sodas, ice cream cakes and freshly baked cookies and brownies. Established: 1978 - Franchising Since: 1981 - No. of Units: Company Owned: 4 - Franchised: 85 - Franchise Fee: $25,000 - Royalty: 4% monthly fee used for adv. - Total Inv: $175,000 - $200,000 - Financing: None.

BLOMMER'S ICE CREAM/SAM'S SUBS/OLLIE'S OVENS
Biss, Inc.
5900 N. Port Washington Rd., Milwaukee, WI, 53217. Contact: Peter Blommer, Pres. - Tel: (414) 291-7833. Side by side ice cream and sub units placed in food courts in major regional malls. Established: 1988 - Franchising Since: 1989 - No. of Units: Company Owned: 6 - Franchised: 2 - Franchise Fee: $23,500 - Royalty: 4% of sales - Total Inv: $40,000 - $160,000 - Financing: No.

BOY BLUE OF AMERICA, INC.
14260 W. Greenfield Ave., Ste. 103, Brookfield, WI, 53005. Contact: Earl J. Phillips, Fran. Dir. - Tel: (414) 785-1850. Soft serve ice cream, frozen yogurt and lite sandwiches. Established: 1963 - Franchising Since: 1970 - No. of Units: Franchised: 12 - Franchise Fee: $10,000 - Royalty: 5% + 1.5% adv. - Total Inv: $75,000 - $90,000/ $50,000 cash - Financing: Assist in securing.

BRESLER'S ICE CREAM AND YOGURT SHOPS
Bresler's Industries, Inc.
999 E. Touhy Ave., Des Plaines, IL, 60018. Contact: Howard B. Marks, V.P., Dir. of Fran. Dev. - Tel: (800) 535-3333. Multi flavor specialty ice cream, yogurt and treat shop. Single & multi-unit opportunities. Established: 1929 - Franchising Since: 1963 - No. of Units: Company Owned: 5 - Franchised: 250 - Franchise Fee: $15,000 - Royalty: 6%, 3% adv. - Total Inv: $136,000 - $160,000 - Financing: Will assist in acquiring third party financing.

BRIDGEMAN'S, THE ORIGINAL ICE CREAM RESTAURANTS, BRIDGEMAN'S DIPPING STATIONS, BRIDGEMAN'S SODA FOUNTAINS
Bridgeman's Restaurants, Inc.
5700 Smetana Dr., #110, Minnetonka, MN, 55343. Contact: Mary McKee, Fran. Dev. - Tel: (800) 297-5050. Bridgeman's franchises are available in 4 forms: 1) Full service, family style restaurant featuring our famous ice cream specialty treats and American style cuisine. 2) Dip Shoppe, good in food court setting, offering ice cream treats along with a limited sandwich menu. 3) Soda Fountain, ice cream treats in other retail areas. 4) Dip Station, ice cream for cones. Established: 1936 - Franchising Since: 1967 - No. of Units: Company Owned: 5 - Franchised: 27 - Franchise Fee: $750 for rural dip stations to $25,000 for urban restaurants - Royalty: 2% on gross sales, 2% adv. - Total Inv: minimum $7,000 to $350,000 for full restaurant - Financing: None.

BRODY'S YOGURT CO.
106 N.W. 33 Ct., Gainesville, FL, 32607. Contact: John Chambers, Dir. of Franc. Sales - Tel: (904) 377-0774. Retail frozen yogurt stores. Established: 1983 - Franchising Since: 1984 - No. of Units: Company Owned: 9 - Franchised: 12 - Franchise Fee: $10,000 - Royalty: 4% gross sales monthly - Total Inv: $70,000 - $125,000 - Financing: No.

BRUSTERS ICE CREAM *
1445 Market St., Bridgewater, PA, 15009. Contact: Bruce Reed, Pres. - Tel: (412) 774-4250. Premium ice cream stores, which are open year 'round and feature ice cream, sherbert, yogurt, Italian ices made fresh daily in each store. Also feature homemade waffle cones, ice cream cakes & pies and novelties (ice cream sandwiches, shakes, sundaes, etc.). Established: 1989 - Franchising Since: 1993 - No. of Units: Company Owned: 3 - Franchised: 7 - Franchise Fee: $30,000 - Royalty: 5% on net sales - Total Inv: $400,000 - $600,000 land/bldg./equip. - Financing: No.

CARVEL ICE CREAM BAKERY
Carvel Corp.
20 Batterson Park Rd., Farmington, CT, 06032. Contact: R. Wayne King, Dir. Distribution Planning - Tel: (203) 677-6811. Positioned to provide high quality, custom ice cream desserts and novelties professionally prepared from scratch, on premises. In addition to full-service retail outlets, branch unit opportunities include kiosks, mini-stores and vending carts, as well as participation in a Branded Freezer Program in supermarkets and convenience stores. Established: 1934 - Franchising Since: 1947 - No. of Units: Company Owned: 20 - Franchised: 508 - Franchise Fee: $10,000 - Royalty: $1.41/gallon, min. 8,000 gallons = $11,280 - Total Inv: $175,000 - $205,000: $10,000 license fee; $75,000 equip.; $60,000 - $90,000 renovations; $30,000 start-up - Financing: Third party.

CONES & COFFEE
Cones & Coffee Inc.
CSS Franchising: 177 Main St., Ste. 103, Ft. Lee, NJ, 07024. Contact: Franchise Rep. - Tel: (201) 585-4753. Stationary carts feature pastry, gourmet ice cream & coffee. Mall based or in line units. Established: 1994 - Franchising Since: 1994 - No. of Units: Company Owned: 2 - Franchised: 1 - Franchise Fee: $7,950 - Royalty: 5% on sales - Total Inv: $25,000 - $40,000 incl. build out - Financing: Yes.

CULVER'S FROZEN YOGURTS
Culver Franchising Systems, Inc.
827 Water St., Sauk City, WI, 53583. Contact: Craig Culver, Pres. - Tel: (608) 643-7980. Fast service specialty restaurant featuring butterburgers and frozen custard. Established: 1984 - Franchising Since: 1988 - No. of Units: Company Owned: 3 - Franchised: 1 - Franchise Fee: $13,500 - Royalty: 3.5%, 1% adv - Total Inv: $200,000 - $700,000 - Financing: Some.

DOUBLE RAINBOW CAFE
Double Rainbow Gourmet Ice Creams Inc.
275 S. Van Ness Ave., San Francisco, CA, 94103. Contact: Michael Sachar, Pres. - Tel: (415) 861-5858. Gourmet ice creams and dessert cafe. Additionally, some locations offer frozen yogurt, custom made ice cream cakes and gourmet filled sandwiches. Established: 1976 - Franchising Since: 1982 - No. of Units: Company Owned: 3 - Licensed: 29 - License Fee: None - Royalty: None - Total Inv: $100,000 - $200,000 - Financing: No.

EMACK & BOLIO'S
P.O. Box 703, Brookline Village, MA, 02147. Contact: Bob Rook, Pres. - Tel: (617) 739-7995. Company provides training & manuals. Company sells super premium ice creams & hard no fat yogurts. Yogurts are low calorie & come in outrageous flavours. Established: 1975 - Franchising Since: 1977 - No. of Units: Franchised: 30 - Total Inv: $35,000 - $75,000 - Financing: No.

ESKIMO PIE CORP.
901 Moorefield Park Dr., Richmond, VA, 23236-3660. Contact: David Clark, Pres. - Tel: (804) 560-8400. Franchise sales for hand dipped ice cream carts. Established: 1990 - Franchising Since: 1991 - Franchise Fee: TBD - Royalty: TBD - Total Inv: TBD.

EVERYTHING YOGURT & SALAD CAFE
Restaurant Systems International
1000 South Ave., Staten Island, NY, 10314. Contact: Raymond Habib, Dir. Sales - Tel: (718) 494-8888, Fax: (718) 494-8776. A unique combination of freshly made salads, soups & sandwiches with a full line of frozen yogurt sundaes and shakes. Established: 1976 - Franchising Since: 1981 - No. of Units: Company Owned: 9 - Franchised: 112 - Franchise Fee: $25,000 - Royalty: 5% - Total Inv: $250,000 - $275,000 - Financing: Yes.

GELATO AMARE
11504 Hyde Place, Raleigh, NC, 27614. Contact: John Franklin, Pres. - Tel: (919) 847-4435. Retail stores serving homemade super premium Italian style low fat ice cream, no fat yogurt, espresso, cappuccino, pastries, light salads and sandwiches. Established: 1983 - Franchising Since:1986- No. of Units: Company Owned: 1 - Franchised: 4 - Franchise Fee: $18,900 1st store, $7,000 each addit'l store - Royalty: 5% of sales - Total Inv: $150,000 - $200,000 - Financing: Will assist.

GORIN'S HOMEMADE, INC.
158 Oak St., Avondale Estates, GA, 30002. Contact: Michael Philips, Dir., Fran. Dev. - Tel: (404) 292-0043. Homemade gourmet ice cream, hard yogurt, soft yogurt, sherbert, sorbet. Plus full line of salads, sandwiches, roll ups, drinks. Operate as diner, in line units, mall food courts & strip centers. Established: 1980 - Franchising Since: 1980 - No. of Units: Company Owned: 3 - Franchised: 38 - Franchise Fee: $21,500 - Royalty: 5% + 2% adv. - Total Inv: $150,000 - $200,000 - Financing: No.

HAAGEN-DAZS
Haagen-Dazs Shoppe Company, Inc., The
Glenpointe Centre East, Teaneck, NJ, 07666. Contact: Development Dept. - Tel: (201) 692-0900. Ice cream and frozen dessert shop. Established: 1961 - Franchising Since: 1978 - No. of Units: Company Owned: 3 - Franchised: 235 - Franchise Fee: $35,000 - Royalty: $1.16/gallon - Total Inv: approx. $200,000 - Financing: No.

HEIDI'S FROGEN YOZURT SHOPPE
Heidi's Frogen Yozurt Shoppes, Inc.
4175 Veterans Hwy., Ronkonkoma, NY, 11779. Contact: Anthony Parete, V.P. Dev. - Tel: (516) 585-0900. Frozen Yogurt Shoppes. Established: 1983- Franchising Since: 1984 - No. of Units: Company Owned: 4 - Franchised: 63 - Franchise Fee: $25,000 - Royalty: 4% - Total Inv: $175,000 - Financing: No.

HELEN HUTCHLEYS *
Helen Hutchleys Inc.
P.O. Box 80995, Stn. C, Canton, OH, 44708-0995. Contact: Kenneth W. Esber, Reg. Fran. Mgr. - Tel: (216) 477-4515 ext. 721. Ice cream and candy stores. Hand dipped old fashioned ice cream with a complete line of homestyle gourmet chocolates and hundreds of other candies. Established: 1963 - Franchising Since: 1965 - No. of Units: Franchised: 7 - Franchise Fee: $10,000 - Royalty: 4% - Total Inv: $76,000 to $175,000 - Financing: No.

HIGH WHEELER RESTAURANT & ICE CREAM PARLOUR
High Wheeler Inc., The
P.O. Box 141, Kalamazoo, MI, 49004-0141. Contact: Roger W. Buchholtz, Pres. - Tel: (616) 345-0950. Large turn-of-the-century family restaurant & ice cream parlors featuring extensive ice cream creation menu and over 45 flavors of ice cream, yogurts, and fat free frozen desserts, gourmet hamburgers, salad bar, and complete breakfast, lunch and dinner menus featuring many healthy heart offerings. Established: 1975 - Franchising Since: 1985 - No. of Units: Company Owned: 2 - Franchised: 2 - Franchise Fee: $35,000 - $250,000 - Royalty: 4% - Total Inv: $100,000 - $1,000,000 - Financing: Counsel and referrals.

HILLARY'S GOURMET ICE CREAM & YOGURT PARLORS
Hillary's Gourmet Ice Cream Co.
P.O. Box 571, Newtown Square, PA, 19073-0571. Contact: Mr. Lammers, V.P. Fran. Relations - Tel: (610) 356-3200. A leader in the gourmet ice cream parlor field since 1976. Striking glass block and neon designs

highlight current parlors. Established: 1976 - Franchising Since: 1979 - No. of Units: Franchised: 45 - Franchise Fee: $25,000 - Royalty: 4% gross sales - Total Inv: $125,000 - $175,000 - Financing: Yes.

HOGI YOGI SANDWICHES AND FROZEN YOGURT *
Hogi Yogi Franchising Corporation
71 South State St., Orem, Ut, 84058. Contact: Dan Waters, Dir. of Fran. - Tel: (800) 653-4581. Unique combination of fresh, custom-made sandwiches and custom-blended frozen yogurt under one roof. Complete initial training and thorough continual support provided. Firm commitment to the success of each individual franchisee. Established: 1989 - Franchising Since: 1992 - No. of Units: Company Owned: 2 - Franchised: 58 - Franchise Fee: $15,000 - Royalty: 6% of net sales plus 2% of net sales for adv. - Total Inv: $90,000 - $160,000+ including fran. fee - Financing: Total investment required.

HURDY GURDY INTERNATIONAL *
450 Fairway Dr., Ste. 107, Deerfield Beach, FL, 33441. Contact: Timothy Mayer, Mktg./Promotions/Sales - Tel: (305) 481-8834, Fax: (305) 481-8856. Old world carts with mechanical monkeys and interactive barrol organs. Serving gourmet sorbet that tastes great and has a whole vitamin package. Established: 1991 - Franchising Since: 1992 - No. of Units: Company Owned: 10 - Franchised: 50 - Franchise Fee: $15,000 - Royalty: None - Total Inv: $15,000 turnkey operation - Financing: No.

I CAN'T BELIEVE IT'S YOGURT
The Brice Group
3361 Boyington, Suite 200, Carrollton, TX, 75006. Contact: Franchise Sales - Tel: (800) 269-4374. One of the world's leading brands of frozen yogurt. Can be combined with gourmet coffee and bakery modules. Established: 1977 - Franchising Since: 1983 - No. of Units: Company Owned: 2 - Franchised: 252 - Franchise Fee: $15,000 - Royalty: 5%, 2% adv. - Total Inv: average inv. $150,000 - Financing: None.

ICE CREAM CHURN
Ice Cream Churn Inc.
204 Hwy. 49, P.O. Box 1569, Byron, GA, 31008. Contact: Dayle Parker, VP Sales - Tel: (912) 956-5880, Fax: (912) 956-1864. Franchise offers an add-on concept for existing businesses such as deli's, bakeries, convenience stores and restaurants. Also have mall kiosks, trailer units and drive-thru units available. Established: 1973 - Franchising Since: 1978 - No. of Units: Franchised: 515 - Franchise Fee: $5,000 - Royalty: $1.40 per gallon of ice cream & yogurt - Total Inv: $5,000 fran. fee, $10,000 equip. and signs - Financing: Yes.

ICE CREAM & YOGURT CLUB, THE
Ice Cream Club, Inc., The
1580 High Ridge Rd., Boynton Beach, FL, 33426. Contact: Richard Draper, Pres. - Tel: (407) 731-3331. Retail ice cream and yogurt shops. Better income areas and upscale locations sought. Premium products and attractive decor. Established: 1982 - Franchising Since: 1984 - No. of Units: Company Owned: 3 - Franchised: 14 - Franchise Fee: $20,000 - Total Inv: $87,000 incl. fran. fee - Financing: Equip. lease programs.

ISLAND FREEZE FRANCHISE SYSTEMS, INC.
P.O. Box 10883, Honolulu, HI, 96816. Contact: Catherine Richman, V.P. - Tel: (808) 922-0030. Sale of Dolewhip non-dairy soft serve. Established: 1986 - Franchising Since: 1989 - No. of Units: Company Owned: 3 - Franchised: 2 - Franchise Fee: $18,500 - Royalty: 5% plus 1% national adv. Each unit must spend 2% themselves for local adv. - Total Inv: $39,500 to $114,000 all incl. - Financing: No.

JULIE ANN'S FROZEN CUSTARD *
Julie Ann's Corporation
831 Broadway, Crystal Lake, IL, 60014. Contact: Peter Wisniewski, Pres., CEO - Tel: (815) 459-9193, Fax: (815) 459-9195. Retail fast food outlets or frozen custard dessert products & steamed food products. Established: 1985 - Franchising Since: 1995 - No. of Units: Company Owned: 1 - Franchised: 1 - Franchise Fee: $20,000 - Royalty: 3% - Total Inv: $181,000 to $280,000 - Financing: No.

KOHR BROS. FROZEN CUSTARD *
Kohr Bros., Inc.
2115 Berkmar Dr., Charlottesville, VA, 22901. Contact: Bradley D. Kohr, Director of Franchising - Tel: (804) 975-1500. Kohr Bros. Frozen Custard stores, famous on the seaside boardwalks of America since the

Roaring 20's, can now be found in prestigious malls. Call today to find out if you qualify to own a rewarding and enjoyable Kohr Bros. Frozen Custard franchise. We are now awarding both individual and multiple unit franchises. The smiles on our customers' faces tell us everyday, "The Original still tastes the best!" Established: 1919 - Franchising Since: 1994 - No. of Units: Company Owned: 9 - Franchised: 3 operating, 14 under contract - Franchise Fee: $22,500 - Royalty: 5% of gross sales - Total Inv: $100,900 to $286,500 - Financing: None.

LARRY'S ICE CREAM AND YOGURT PARLOURS
Larry's Industries, Inc.
999 E. Touhy Ave., Des Plaines, IL, 60018. Contact: Howard B. Marks, V.P., Dir. of Fran. Dev. - Tel: (800) 424-6285. Multi-flavor specialty ice cream, yogurt and treat parlour. Single and multi-unit opportunities. Established: 1983 - Franchising Since: 1983 - No. of Units: Company Owned: 2 - Franchised: 35 - Franchise Fee: $15,000 - Royalty: 3%, 3% adv. - Total Inv: $127,000 - $149,000 - Financing: assist in third party financing.

LEE'S ICE CREAM
Mary-Lee Co., Inc.
1125 De Soto Rd., Baltimore, MD, 21223. Contact: Scott Garfield, V.P.; Dir. of Fran. - Tel: (410) 525-2224. Offer a super-premium gourmet ice cream in addition to a line of cookies, pastries, brownies and other desserts. Prime locations available for franchises in the Mid-Atlantic. Established: 1979 - Franchising Since: 1985 - No. of Units: Company Owned: 3 - Franchised: 10 - Franchise Fee: $30,000 - Royalty: none - Total Inv: $150,000 - $190,000 (fran. fee, equip., const.) - Financing: No.

LIC'S
Lloyd's Ice Cream, Inc.
11 N.W. 5th St., Evansville, IN, 47708-1601. Contact: Don Smith, Pres. - Tel: (812) 424-3066. Ice cream, yogurt, and sandwiches. Regional - IN, IL, KY, TN. Established: 1950 - Franchising Since: 1988- No. of Units: Company Owned: 9 - Franchised: 2 - Franchise Fee: $10,000 - Royalty: 4% - Total Inv: $100,000 - $125,000 - Financing: No.

LOARD'S ICE CREAM & CANDIES
2000 Wayne Ave., San Leandro, CA, 94577. Contact: Russell B. Falyards, Pres. - Tel: (510) 351-4131. Fast food/ice cream restaurant. Established: 1950 - No. of Units: Company Owned: 9 - Franchised: 13.

LOVE'S YOGURT
Love's Group
1830 Techny Court, Northbrook, IL, 60062. Contact: Marsha Silverstein, V.P. - Tel: (708) 480-9200. Offers a unique soft-serve frozen yogurt and salad bar concept. The emphasis is toward healthy, quality foods with salads prepared daily, in addition to soups, chili, baked potatoes with toppings, and freshly-baked muffins. Personalized service is our specialty. Established: 1987 - Franchising Since: 1988 - No. of Units: Company Owned: 3 - Franchised: 5 - Franchise Fee: $20,000 - Royalty: 4%, 2% adv. - Total Inv: $160,000 - $200,000 - Financing: No, indirect assistance.

MARBLE SLAB CREAMERY
Marble Slab Creamery, Inc.
3100 S. Gessner, Ste. 305, Houston, TX, 77063. Contact: Ronald Hankamer, Jr., Dir. of Fran. Dev. - Tel: (713) 780-3601, Fax: (713) 780-0264. Retail ice cream stores featuring super-premium ice cream, daily baked cones, fresh frozen yogurt, pies, cakes, homemade cookies and brownies. Ice cream is custom designed for customer on frozen marble slabs and made daily in the store. Established: 1983 - Franchising Since: 1984 - No. of Units: Company Owned: 1 - Franchised: 41 - Franchise Fee: $19,000 - $25,000 - Royalty: 5% first yr., 6% after - Total Inv: $137,275 - $158,275 - Financing: No.

MISTER SOFTEE, INC.
P.O. Box 313, Runnemede, NJ, 08078. Contact: James Conway, Gen. Mgr. - Tel: (609) 939-4103. Mobile soft ice cream trucks. Established: 1956 - No. of Units: 724 - Franchise Fee: $20,000 - Total Inv: additional $2,000 start up, licenses, supplies, etc.

NATURALLY YOGURT & SPEEDSTER'S CAFE'S
NY Corp.
P.O. Box 511, San Ramon, CA, 94583-0511. Contact: Shell Feinberg, V.P. - Tel: (510) 743-9234, Fax: (510) 743-8825. A quality, fresh frozen yogurt operation. Clean high-tech graphics in a unique presentation offering a wide range of toppings, sundaes, shakes, smoothies, and other specialty items. Speedster's offers fresh salads, homemade soups, baked potatoes, and a complete yogurt presentation. Established: 1983 - Franchising Since: 1984 - No. of Units: Franchised: 3 - Franchise Fee: $20,000 - Royalty: 0-5% - Total Inv: $155,000 - $225,000 - Financing: No.

NEW ORLEANS SNOWBALLS, INC.
11 Carriage Square, Boone, NC, 28607. Contact: Monty Joynes, Pres. - Tel: (704) 262-3952 or (800) 854-0915. Snow-like shaved ice and fresh-made syrups made into snowballs and snowshakes. Famous for snowballs with cream. Also hot beverage products. Established: 1985 - Licensing Since: 1986 - No. of Units: Company Owned: 2 - Licensed: 110 - Fee: $5,295 (includes 2 days training and ice shaving equip.) - Total Inv: equip., initial supplies, training - Financing: No.

PERKITS YOGURT SHOPS
P.O. Box 2862, Cleveland, TN, 37320. Contact: Dir. of Sales - Tel: (615) 559-9505. Frozen yogurt shops. Established: 1985 - Franchising Since: 1986 - No. of Units: Company Owned: 1 - Franchised: 31 - Franchise Fee: $15,000 - Royalty: 2%, 1% adv. - Total Inv: $60,000 - $90,000.

RAINBOW SNOW, INC.
9075 South 1300 E., Sandy, UT, 84107. Contact: Michael Romriell, Fran. Dir. - Tel: (801) 553-7223. Shaved ice - with up to 37 plus flavors. Complete building package including equipment, buildings & supplies. Established: 1980 - Franchising Since: 1981 - No. of Units: Company Owned: 15 - Franchised: 87 - Franchise Fee: $1000 down - Total Inv: $19,500.

RITA'S WATER ICE & RITA'S ITALIAN ICES
Rita's Water Ice Franchise Corp.
1251 Byberry Rd., Unit #1, Philadelphia, PA, 19116. Contact: Stephen J. Izzi, Fran. Dir. - Tel: 1-800-677-RITA, Fax: (215) 698-9860. Retail sale of Italian Ices and frozen soft serve custard. Established: 1984 - Franchising Since: 1989 - No. of Units: Company Owned: 1 - Franchised: 72 - Franchise Fee: $20,000 - Royalty: 6.5% of gross sales - Total Inv: $72,000 - $127,000 - Financing: No.

ROBIN ROSE ICE CREAM & CHOCOLATE
Robin Rose America, Inc.
215 Rose Ave., Venice, CA, 90291. Contact: Robin Rose, Pres. - Tel: (310) 392-4921. Retail sales of gourmet ice cream, chocolate, non-fat yogurt, beverages, with possibly baked goods. Established: 1981 - Licensing Since: 1985 - No. of Units: Company Owned: 3 - Licensed: 3 - Total Inv: store build-out + equip. ranges from $50,000 - $95,000 - Financing: No.

SCOOPERS ICE CREAM
Scoopers Ice Cream Inc.
22 Woodrow Ave., Youngstown, OH, 44512. Contact: Norman Hughes, Pres. - Tel: (216) 758-3857. Retail old fashioned ice cream stores. Made fresh daily. Established: 1980 - Franchising Since: 1991 - No. of Units: Company Owned: 2 - Franchised: 6 - Franchise Fee: $15,000 - Royalty: 5% - Total Inv: $50,000: $35,000 equip. + fran. fee - Financing: No.

SHOW PLACE ICE CREAM PARLOURS *
Show Place Franchising Corp.
202 Centre St., Beach Haven, NJ, 08008. Contact: Anne Lombardo, Fran. Dev. - Tel: (800) 835-2567, (609) 492-2639. A unique blend of family entertainment and premium ice cream. Customers perform for the desserts and each seating culminates in a Broadway Revue by The Show Place Singing Waiters. Ranked top ten ice cream parlour for families in America by Child Magazine and received "Vacationers Choice Award" for Best Ice Cream Shop. Seasonal/year round locations available, full support package. Established: 1975 - Franchising Since: 1995 - No. of Units: Franchised: 1 - Franchise Fee: $20,000 - Royalty: 5% gross - Total Inv: $190,000+ - Financing: No.

STEVE'S ICE CREAM
Steve's Homemade Ice Cream, Inc.
P.O. Box 1223, Ronkonkoma, NY, 11779. Contact: Anthony S. Parete, V.P. Dev. - Tel: (516) 737-9700. Super-premium ice cream stores also serving Heidi's yogurt and David's cookies. No. of Units: Franchised:19 - Franchise Fee: $25,000 - Royalty: 6% - Total Inv: $225,000 - Financing: No.

SUNSPLASH *
7345 N. Via Paseo Del Sur., #630, Scottsdale, AZ, 85258. Contact: James Marek, Pres. - Tel: (602) 998-4426, Fax: (215) 698-9860. Juice bar specializing in the sale of fresh fruit smoothies, fresh squeezed juices, and baked goods. Established; 1994 - Franchising Since: 1995 - No. of Units: Company Owned: 2 - Franchised: 1 - Franchise Fee: $15,000 - Royalty: 5% - Total Inv: $100,000 - Financing: No.

TASTEE-FREEZ
Tastee-Freez International
48380 Van Dyke Ave., Utica, MI, 48317-3270. Contact: James Brasier, Pres. - Tel: (810) 739-5520. Fast food/soft serve ice cream. Established: 1950 - Franchising Since: 1950 - No. of Units: Franchised: 300 - Franchise Fee: $10,000 - Royalty: 4% & 1% - Total Inv: Estimated: low $145,000, high $530,000 - Financing: No.

TCBY
1100 TCBY Tower, 425 West Capitol Ave, Little Rock, AR, 72201. Contact: Fran. Sales Dept. - Tel: (501) 688-8229. Own brand of distinctive frozen yogurt that is served in a variety of special desserts. Attractive decor and successful marketing programs enhance repeat business. Established: 1981 - Franchising Since: 1982 - No. of Units: Company Owned: 103 - Franchised: 1000 - Franchise Fee: $20,000 - Total Inv: $93,000 - $177,000 - Financing: Not on initial store.

TOPSY'S POPCORN & ICE CREAM SHOPPE
221 W. 74 Terrace, Kansas City, MO, 64114. Contact: Robert Ramm, Pres. - Tel: (816) 523-5555. Shoppes retail quality gourmet popcorn, ice cream and related confection food items. No. of Units: Company

Owned: 5 - Franchised: 8 - Franchise Fee: $20,000 - Royalty: 5% + 3% adv. - Total Inv: $100,000 - $130,000 - Financing: Yes, through local lenders.

WE LOVE YOGURT & DELI
We Love Yogurt Franchise, Inc.
3000 Old Canton Rd., Ste. 500, Jackson, MS, 39216. Contact: John Stermer, Fran. Dev. Dir. - Tel: (800) 780-1860. Fun and happy place for the whole family, offering gourmet soft serve yogurt, ice cream, deli sandwiches, soups, salad bars and speciality beverages for a healthy all day business. Established: 1985 - Franchising Since: 1995 - No. of Units: Company Owned: 3 - Franchise Fee: $15,000 - Royalty: 6%, 2.5% adv. - Total Inv: $150,000 total; $60,000 liquid - Financing: Not from franchisor.

WHITE MOUNTAIN CREAMERY
Entrecept, Inc.
1576 Bardstown Rd., Louisville, KY, 40205. Contact: Charles Ducas, V.P. - Tel: (502) 456-1841, Fax: (502) 456-2056. Unique concept featuring on site production of award-winning super premium ice cream, yogurt and bakery goods. Come grow with us - we offer three fast-moving product lines under 1 room. Established: 1982 - Franchising Since: 1983 - No. of Units: Company Owned: 5 - Franchised: 31 (1 under dev.) - Franchise Fee: $20,000 - Royalty: 4%, 1% adv. - Total Inv: $107,000 - $150,000 - Financing: No.

YOGURT & SUCH
Yogurt & Such Franchise Systems Inc.
438 Woodbury Rd., Plainview, NY, 11803. Contact: Bill Reichert, Fran. Dev. - Tel: (800) YOG-SUCH (964-7824), (516) 785-7552. America's healthy fast food restaurants featuring frozen nonfat yogurt and dietary desserts along with a full menu of natural, healthy food such as soups, sandwiches, pasta, salads and beverages. Seeking unit and multi-unit franchisees (area developers). Established: 1982 - Franchising Since: 1989 - No. of Units: Company Owned: 5 - Franchised: 7 - Franchise Fee: $25,000 - Royalty: 5% + 1% adv. - Total Inv: $169,325 to $248,750 complete turnkey - Financing: Will assist.

YOGURTERIA
Yogurteria Franchise Corp.
2465 Hempstead Tpk., E. Meadow, NY, 11554. Contact: Dominic Maggiure, Pres. - Tel: (516) 829-7480. Yogurt and salad restaurant seating 36 to 48. Established: 1987 - Franchising Since: 1993 - No. of Units: Company Owned: 1 - Franchised: 7 - Franchise Fee: $15,000 - Royalty: 5% of gross sales - Total Inv: $150,000 - Financing: To qualified individuals.

YUMMY YOGURT, INC.
1010 17th NW St., Washington, DC, 20036. Contact: Abi Soltani, Pres. - Tel: (202) 659-9858. Fast food and ice cream. Established: 1976 - No. of Units: 7 - Approx. Inv: $25,000 plus.

ZACK'S FAMOUS FROZEN YOGURT, INC.
4400 Silas Creek Pkwy., #302, Winston Salem, NC, 27104-3823. Contact: Sherri England, V.P. - Tel: (910) 768-9446. A chain of up-scale, leading edge fun food outlets with frozen yogurt as the primary menu item. Established: 1977 - Franchising Since: 1978 - No. of Units: Franchised: 54.

FOOD: RESTAURANTS AND QUICK SERVICE

1 POTATO 2, INC.
7000 Bass Lake Rd., #200, Crystal, MN, 55428-3858. Contact: Connie Martin, Fran. Admin. - Tel: (612) 537-3833. Fast food restaurant chain with a unique menu concept featuring baked potato entrees with a variety of toppings, and fresh cut fries. Established: 1977 - Franchising Since: 1984 - No. of Units: Company Owned: 28 - Franchised: 44 - Franchise Fee: $20,000 - Royalty: 4.5% - Total Inv: $95,000 - $160,000 - Financing: Negotiable.

256 OPERATING ASSOCIATES
625 Amherst St., Nashua, NH, 03063. Contact: William R. Crowder, Pres. - Tel: (603) 598-3738. Fast food restaurant. No. of Units: Franchised: 13.

A & W RESTAURANTS
A & W Restaurants, Inc.
17197 N. Laurel Park Dr., Ste. 500, Livonia, MI, 48152. Contact: Fran. Sales Dept. - Tel: (313) 462-0029 or (800) 222-2337. Quick service restaurant featuring world famous A&W Root Beer, hamburgers, hot dogs and coney dogs, grilled chicken sandwiches, french fries & onion rings. Various configurations for food courts & in-lines in malls to free-standing building. Conversions also considered. Established: 1919 - Franchising Since: 1925 - No. of Units: Company Owned: 10 - Franchised: 684 - Franchise Fee: $20,000 - Royalty: 4% gross sales monthly - Total Inv: $150,000 - $400,000 - Financing: No direct financial assistance.

ABBY'S PIZZA INNS
Broughton & Harrell Corp.
1960 River Rd., Eugene, OR, 97404. Contact: Craig Heath, Operations - Tel: (503) 689-0019. Family style pizza restaurants offering pizza, salad bar and pocket bread sandwiches. Established: 1964 - Franchising Since: 1967 - No. of Units: Company Owned: 15 - Franchised: 8.

ABERDEEN BARNS
A.B. Franchise Corp.
2018 Holiday Dr., Charlottesville, VA, 22901. Contact: Terry Spathos, Pres. - Tel: (804) 296-9906. Dinnerhouse - American. Established: 1965. No. of Units: Company Owned: 2 - Franchised: 2

AJ TEXAS HOTS
AJ Texas Hots Fast Food Franchise
824 Foote Ave., Jamestown, NY, 14701. Contact: Samuel G. Colera, Pres. - Tel: (716) 484-9646. Fast food specializing in a unique Texas Hot (hot dog), and burgers. Also fish, chicken, ham & cheese sandwiches, fries and onion rings. Drive Thru - 1st in Chauto Cnty. Established: 1968 - Franchising Since: 1994 - No. of Units: Company Owned: 1 - Franchised: working on 2 - Franchise Fee: $25,000 - Royalty: $300 per mo. 1st yr, $400 per mo. 2nd yr, $500 per mo. after - Total Inv: $100,000 incl. fran. fee, equip., leasehold improv. - Financing: None.

AL'S BAR-B-QUE INC.
22 W. 140 North Ave., Glen Ellyn, IL, 60137. Contact: Terry Pacelli, Pres. - Tel: (708) 858-9090. Fast food and sandwiches. Includes beef, Italian sausage, hot dogs, fries, and drinks. Established: 1939 - Franchising Since: 1984 - No. of Units: Franchised: 7 - Franchise Fee: $20,000 - Royalty: 4% + 2% adv. - Total Inv: $45,000 - $60,000, decor $50,000 - Financing: No.

AL'S DINER
Al's Diner Inc.
17600 Torrence Ave., Lansing, IL, 60438. Contact: Al Gull, Pres. - Tel: (708) 418-1950. A 1950 style diner catering to all age groups, beautifully decorated, 50's music, fun atmosphere, quality food at reasonable prices. Established: 1986 - Franchising Since: 1990 - No. of Units: Company Owned: 3 - Franchised: 2 - Franchise Fee: $15,000 - Royalty: 3 1/2% first year, 4% thereafter - Total Inv: $196,000 - $340,000, depending on site - Financing: possible bank financing.

ALL-V'S SUBMARINE SANDWICH SHOPPES
P.O. Box 4426, Highlands Ranch, CO, 80126-0400. Contact: Kenneth Cox, Pres. - Tel: (303) 791-0333. Submarine sandwich shoppes offering a variety of 44 hot and cold sandwiches from steak and cheese, vegetarian, mushroom and egg to eggplant parmesan. Each sandwich is freshly prepared for the individual customer. Established: 1973 - Franchising Since: 1974 - No. of Units: 5 - Franchise Fee: $16,000 - Royalty: 3% + 3% adv. - Total Inv: $100,000 - $175,000 - Financing: No.

AMECI PIZZA AND PASTA
Ameci In & Out, Inc.
6603 C Independence Ave., Canoga Park, CA, 91303. Contact: Nick Andrisano, Pres.-CEO - Tel: (818) 712-0110. Selling quality food at inexpensive prices. More than just pizza, Italian fast food. Take-out, delivery, pick-up. Established: 1984 - Franchising Since: 1986 - No. of Units: Company Owned: 3 - Franchised: 37 - Franchise Fee: $25,000 -

Royalty: 4% weekly - Total Inv: $185,000: $25,000 Fran. Fee, $85,000 equip., $60,000 build.outs, $15,000 inven.-lease deposit, work. cap. - Financing: None.

ANDY'S RESTAURANT
Andy's of America
11521 W. Markham, Little Rock, AR, 72211. Contact: Garland Street, Chairman/Pres. - Tel: (501) 221-1020. Fast Food - hamburgers. Established: 1978 - No. of Units: Company Owned: 14 - Franchised: 3.

ANGELO'S PIZZA, INC. *
100 - 7th Ave. S., S. St. Paul, MN, 55075. Contact: John Burbank, Owner (Pres.) - Tel: (612) 450-1270. Small restaurant, family owned, serve pizzas and other Italian dishes. All food is homemade and of the highest quality. Established: 1971 - Franchising Since: 1979 - No. of Units: Company Owned: 1 - Franchised: 4 - Franchise Fee: $15,000 initially (no franchise fee) - Royalty: None - Financing: No.

ANGILO'S PIZZA
911 Church Street, Cincinnati, OH, 45215. Contact: Steven Jones, V.P. Dir. Franc. - Tel: (513) 563-9320. Fast food - pizza. Established: 1959 - No. of Units: Franchised: 48.

APPLEBEE'S NEIGHBORHOOD GRILL & BAR/RIO BRAVO CANTINA
Applebee's International, Inc.
4551 W. 107th St., #100, Overland Park, KS, 66207. Contact: Larry Bader, Gilbert Simon, U.S. Franchising, Int'l. Franchising - Tel: (913) 967-4000, Fax: (913) 341-4970. Developer, operator, and franchisor of restaurants under the trademark Applebee's Neighborhood Grill & Bar and Rio Bravo Mexican Cantinas. Established: 1983 - Franchising Since: 1983 - No. of Units: Company Owned: 118 - Franchised: 487 - Franchise Fee: Applebee's $35,000 in USA, $40,000 int'l. - Royalty: Applebee's 4% of each calendar month's gross sales, 5% international - Total Inv: Applebee's $1.7 - $3.1 million - Financing: No.

ARABICA CAFES INC. *
4208 Prospect Ave., Cleveland, OH, 44103. Contact: Marvin Schwartz, Exec. V.P. - Tel: (216) 361-8787. Coffeehouse restaurant. Established: 1976 - Licensing Since: 1990 - Franchising Since: 1995 - No. of Units: Company Owned: 3 - Licensed: 9 - Franchise Fee: $22,500 - Royalty: 4% plus 1.5% adv. - Total Inv: $150,000 to $240,000 - Financing: No.

ARBY'S, INC.
P.O. Box 407008, Ft. Lauderdale, FL, 33340. Contact: Mr. Anthony G. Foster, V.P., Fran. - Tel: (305) 351-5100. Fast food restaurants specializing in roast beef. Established: 1964 - Franchising Since: 1965 - No. of Units: Company Owned: 218 - Franchised: 2,102 - Franchise Fee: $25,000 - $37,500 - Royalty: 4% - Total Inv: $525,000 - $850,000 - Financing: No.

ARCTIC CIRCLE RESTAURANTS, INC.
411 W. 7200 S., Ste. 200, Midvale, UT, 84047. Contact: Paul Hallman, V.P. Franchising - Tel: (801) 561-3620. Fast food specializing in hamburgers, shakes, etc. Established: 1950 - Franchising Since: 1954 - No. of Units: Company Owned: 44 - Franchised: 65 - Franchise Fee: $20,000 - Royalty: 3% - Total Inv: Bldg. $180,000, Equip. $140,000 - Financing: No.

ARMAND'S CHICAGO PIZZERIA; ARMAND'S PIZZA EXPRESS *
Armand's Restaurant Franchising
47569 Hidden Cone Ct., Ste. B, Sterling, VA, 20165. Contact: Cal Everett, Corporate General Manager - Tel: (202) 363-6268, Fax: (703) 450-7383. Casual theme pizza restaurant specializing in Chicago style deep-dish pizza. Winner of 15 best pizza awards. Three concepts to choose from: restaurant & bar; express delivery; cafe. Established: 1973 - Franchising Since: 1984 - No. of Units: Company Owned: 4 - Franchised: 6 - Franchise Fee: $15,000 - Royalty: 4%, 1% adv. - Total Inv: $150,000 to $275,000 - Financing: No.

ARNI'S INC. *
Arni's Franchising Inc.
2415 N. 18th St., Lafayette, IN, 47906. Contact: Bradley Cohen, Dir. of Fran. Srvcs. - Tel: (317) 742-7455. Family style restaurant specializing in pizza, salads, sandwiches, some pasta. Operations consist of dine in

CUSTOMERS WANTED
Can we build your next franchise store, corporate offices or distribution center? Construction budgets & deadlines are a priority to us.

WE OFFER:
- Turnkey or partial construction
- Project management
- Design and build
- Budget consultations

25 Rutherford Rd. South, Unit 5
Brampton, Ont., L6W 3J3
(800) 581-6729
Tel: (905) 451-7316, Fax: (905) 451-8563

and carry out. Some have bars. Unique decors. Established: 1965 - Franchising Since: 1991 - No. of Units: Company Owned: 7 - Franchised: 3 - Franchise Fee: $7,500 to $20,000 - Royalty: 4%.

ARTHUR TREACHER'S FISH & CHIPS
Arthur Treacher's, Inc.
7400 Baymeadows Way, Jacksonville, FL, 32256. Contact: Michael Proulx, Dir. Fran. Dev. - Tel: (904) 739-1200. Fast food seafood restaurant chain serving English style fish & chips, chicken, shrimp, clams, hushpuppies, coleslaw and beverages. Established: 1969 - Franchising Since: 1970 - No. of Units: Company Owned: 30 - Franchised: 130 - Franchise Fee: $19,500 - Royalty: 6%, 3% adv. - Total Inv: $74,000 - $150,000 - Financing: No.

AURELIO'S PIZZA, INC.
18162 Harwood Ave., Homewood, IL, 60430. Contact: Mr. Aurelio, Pres. - Tel: (708) 798-8050. Pizzerias, limited menu, pasta, salads, sandwiches, dessert. Dine-in, carry-out and delivery. Established: 1959 - Franchising Since: 1978 - No. of Units: Company Owned: 4 - Franchised: 24 - Franchise Fee: $20,000 - Royalty: 3% - Total Inv: $100,000-$2,200,000 (location and services offered).

AUTO DINER, INC.
3820 Premier Ave., Memphis, TN, 38118. Contact: Bill Richey, Fran. Dir. - Tel: (901) 867-0600. Franchise utilized to offer hot fried foods through the Auto Diner's fried foods electronic vending machines which are to be located in existing businesses, factories, office buildings and schools. Established: 1989 - Franchising Since: 1989 - Franchise Fee: $20,000 - Royalty: 3% + 1% adv. - Total Inv: fee $20,000/Auto Diners $350 ea./working cap. $3,000 - $10,000/inv. $380/equip. $2,800/misc. $700/training $16,000 - Financing: Yes.

BACK YARD BURGERS
Back Yard Burgers, Inc.
2768 Colony Park Dr., Memphis, TN, 38118. Contact: Barry Pitts, Dir., Fran. Dev. - Tel: (901) 367-0888. Fresh 1/3 lb. charbroiled hamburgers, chicken, sandwiches and other food of gourmet quality in a double drive-thru format. A unique concept, well placed for success in the nineties and the century ahead. Established: 1987 - Franchising Since: 1988 - No. of Units: Company Owned: 30 - Franchised: 42 - Franchise Fee: $25,000 - Royalty: 4% of wkly. sales, 2% local adv., 1% nat'l adv. - Total Inv: $350,000 - $595,000 - Financing: No.

BAGEL CONNECTION, THE
Bagel Franchise Systems, Inc.
1408 Whalley Ave., New Haven, CT, 06515. Contact: Mark Merrill, Fran. Sales Agent - Tel: (203) 387-0595, Fax: (203) 387-6611. A 20-70 seat fast food restaurant serving 26 varieties of bagels, 20 sandwiches, appetizers, salads, desserts, gourmet coffees and more. Stores may vary in size from 1,000 to 2,500 sq. ft. Established: 1983 - Franchising Since: 1991 - No. of Units: Company Owned: 2 - Franchised: 8 - Franchise Fee: $30,000 - Royalty: 1% 1st 6 mo., 2% 2nd 6 mo., 3% 3rd 6 mo., 4% thereafter - Total Inv: $104,000 - $200,000 - Financing: Yes.

BAGEL SHOPPE, INC., THE
11406 Reisterstown Rd., Owings Mills, MD, 21117. Contact: Gary VanHoven, Pres. - Tel: (410) 356-7200. Fast food restaurant. Established: 1965 - No. of Units: Company Owned: 4 - Franchised: 3.

BAGELSMITH RESTAURANTS & FOOD STORES
Bagelsmith Franchising Company, Inc.
37 Van Syckel Rd., Hampton, NJ, 08827. Contact: Wayne Smith, Pres. - Tel: (908) 730-8600. What makes us special is, of course, our Bagelsmith Bagel. But we are also famous for our delicatessen, featuring only high quality products. Whether in our restaurants or in our convenience food stores, we provide our customers with high quality products and friendly knowledgeable service, in a clean, pleasant, family-oriented environment. Established: 1979 - Franchising Since: 1982 - No. of Units: Company Owned: 2 - Franchised: 22 - Franchise Fee: $25,000 - Royalty: Under 500,000 - 1%; $500,000 - $599,999 - 1.5%; $600,000 - $699,999 - 2%; $700,000 - $999,999 - 3%; Over $1,000,000 - 2% - Total Inv: $185,000 - $225,000 - Financing: No.

BAIN'S DELI
Bain's Deli Franchise Associates
555 E. North Ln., #6050, Conshohocken, PA, 19428-2233. Contact: Mr. Ross P. Lederer, V.P. - Tel: (800) 969-1910. Shopping center deli chain. Established: 1910 - Franchising Since: 1990 - No. of Units: Company Owned: 42 - Franchised: 48 - Franchise Fee: $25,000 - Royalty: 5% with an additional 1% adv. - Total Inv: $134,000 - $188,000.

BALDINOS GIANT JERSEY SUBS, INC.
760 Elaine St., Hinesville, GA, 31313. Contact: William Baer, Pres. - Tel: (912) 368-2822. Freshest Subs in Town - Sandwich chain with a variety of hot and cold subs, sliced fresh as ordered. Also in store baking, and grilled steak subs. Multi production lines for faster service. Established: 1975 - Franchising Since: 1985 - No. of Units: Company Owned: 6 - Franchised: 15 - Franchise Fee: $10,000 - Royalty: 4.5% + .5% adv. - Total Inv: $70,000 (equip. fix), $25,000 - $40,000 (leasehold, improvements) - Total pkg. $100,000 - $150,000 - Financing: N/A

BARBEQUE COUNTRY JAMBOREE RESTAURANT *
Barbeque Country Franchising
10208 Wendove Dr., Vienna, VA, 22181. Contact: George, Sales Mgr. - Tel: (703) 281-4384. Restaurants featuring smoked ribs beef, pork, chicken and sausage. Open pit barbeques. Established: 1989 - Franchising Since: 1994 - No. of Units: Company Owned: 3 - Franchised: 3 - Franchise Fee: $10,000 - Royalty: 5%, 2% adv. - Total Inv: $110,000 - $190,000 - Financing: No.

BASSETT'S ORIGINAL TURKEY
Bassett Management Co., Inc.
212 Haddon Ave., Westmont, NJ, 08108. Contact: Rick Obrzut, CEO - Tel: (609) 869-9180, Fax: (609) 869-9125. Quick service restaurant featuring fresh roasted turkey sandwiches and platters. Established: 1983 - Franchising Since: 1989 - No. of Units: Company Owned: 2 - Franchised: 88 - Franchise Fee: $25,000 - Royalty: 5%, 1% adv. - Total Inv: $221,100 - $298,250 food court, $257,225 - $431,250 non-food court - Financing: No.

BATES BURGERS, INC. *
43410 Grand River, Novi, MI, 48375. Contact: Gary Bates, Owner - Tel: (810) 349-3083. Sit down and carry-out "Bag of Burgers". High volume slider type hamburger business with proven record of high quality and success. Established: 1985 - Franchising Since: 1994 - No. of Units: Company Owned: 3 - Franchise Fee: $10,000 - Royalty: 6% of gross sales - Total Inv: $20,000 to $150,000 - Financing: Possible financing available.

BEEFSTEAK CHARLIE'S
Bombay Palace Restaurants, Inc.
236 W. 48th St., New York, NY, 10036-1424. Contact: Scott J. Kriger, Sr. V.P. Oper. - Tel: (212) 563-7440. Full service family restaurants serving steaks, BBQ ribs, chicken and seafood. Also featuring unlimited shrimp and salad bar with beer, wine, soda or sangria with your meal. Established: 1978 - Franchising Since: 1985 - No. of Units: Company Owned: 8 - Franchised: 8 - Franchise Fee: $25,000 - Royalty: 5% - Total Inv: $250,000+ - Financing: No.

BEN FRANKS
525 E. Bayshore Blvd., Redwood City, CA, 94063-2717. Contact: Franchise Dir./Pres. - Tel: (415) 367-1300. Hot dogs. Established: 1979 - Franchising Since: 1985 - No. of Units: Company Owned: 7 - Franchised: 2 - Royalty: 5% + 1.5% adv. - Approx. Inv: $138,000 - Financing: Yes.

BENIHANA OF TOKYO
Benihana, Inc.
8685 N.W. 53rd Terrace, Miami, FL, 33166. Contact: Michael W. Kata, V.P. - Tel: (305) 593-0770, Fax: (305) 592-6371. Benihana is an award winning Japanese steakhouse chain featuring teppanyaki cooking. Each guest's meal is prepared right before their eyes by an entertaining chef who introduces all ingredients before he masterfully cooks. Menu includes steak, chicken and seafood. Established: 1963 - Franchising Since: 1970 - No. of Units: Company Owned: 38 - Franchised: 14 - Franchise Fee: $50,000 - Royalty: 6%, .5% adv. - Total Inv: $1,200,000 - $1,800,000 - Financing: No.

BENNETT'S BAR-B-QUE
6551 S. Revere Pky. #285, Englewood, CO, 80111. Contact: Jim Silbaugh, V.P. Mktg. - Tel: (303) 792-3088, Fax: (303) 792-5801. Casual theme dinner house restaurant serving real hickory smoked bar-b-que and hickory grilled steaks. Established: 1985 - Franchising Since: 1989 - No. of Units: Company owned: 5 - Franchised: 12 - Franchise Fee: $35,000 - Royalty: 3.5%, 1% adv. - Total Inv: $485,000 low to $1,000,000 high - Financing: No.

BERGSON'S ICE CREAM & FOOD SHOPS
206 Boston Tpke., P.O. Box 1086, Westboro, MA, 01581. Contact: Eric Pearson, Pres. - Tel: (508) 366-9254. Dinner house/fast food. Established: 1962 - No. of Units: Company Owned: 16 - Franchised: 2.

BETWEEN ROUNDS BAGEL DELI & BAKERY
Between Rounds Franchise Corp.
19A John Fitch Blvd., South Windsor, CT, 06074. Contact: Jerry Puiia, Pres. - Tel: (203) 291-0323. Bagel/deli/bakery. Sit down, take out and catering. Established: 1990 - Franchising Since: 1992 - No. of Units: Company Owned: 3 - Franchised: 2 - Franchise Fee: $15,000 - Royalty: 4% - Total Inv: $139,400 - $180,000 - Financing: No.

BIG BOY FAMILY RESTAURANTS
Elias Brothers Restaurants, Inc.
4199 Marcy Dr., Warren, MI, 48091. Contact: Ron Johnston, Sr. V.P. - Tel: (810) 755-8114. Full service family restaurant, featuring wide menu selection at breakfast, lunch and dinner. Established: 1936 - Franchising Since: 1952 - No. of Units: Company Owned: 129 - Franchised: 817 - Franchise Fee: $25,000 - Royalty: 3%, 3% adv. - Total Inv: $450,000 - $1.4 million - Financing: None offered. Will refer qualified franchisees to lenders.

BIG ED'S HAMBURGER
12235 N. Pennsylvania Ave., #240, Oklahoma City, OK, 73120-7810. Contact: Ed Thomas, Pres. - Tel: (405) 720-2889. Fast food. Established: 1974 - No. of Units: Company Owned: 4 - Franchised: 12.

BIG FRANK'S CHICAGO STYLE HOT DOGS
5502 Kirby Dr., Houston, TX, 77005. Contact: Mr. Israel Justiniano, Pres. - Tel: (713) 664-3647. Gourmet hot dogs and chili. Established: 1985 - Franchising Since: 1987 - No. of Units: Company Owned: 3 - Franchise Fee: varies - Financing: Yes.

BIG TOWN HERO SANDWICHES
Big Town Hero Franchising Inc.
412 Southwest Second St., Portland, OR, 97204. Contact: Jim Jeter, Dir. of Fran. - Tel: (503) 220-0481. Submarine sandwiches, soups & salads. Fresh baked bread from scratch, never use day old. Low start-up, low fees. Family type atmosphere with all our franchisees. Established: 1982 - Franchising Since: 1990 - No. of Units: Franchised: 13 - Franchise Fee: $15,000 - Royalty: 5% of sales + $50/month adv. - Total Inv: $36,000 up to $80,900 - Financing: None directly, assistance available.

BILL'S SANDWICH SHOPS
2425 Wilmington Rd., New Castle, PA, 16105. Contact: William K. Papazekos, Pres. - Tel: (412) 654-7573. Fast food restaurants with 55-85 seats specializing in hot dogs with special hot chili sauce, subs, steak

sandwiches, gyros, and french fries. Established: 1973 - No. of Units: Company Owned: 3 - Franchise Fee: $10,000 - Royalty: 3% of gross sales, 3% adv. - Total Inv: $60,000 equip., $70,000 improv. (May vary) - Financing: No.

BJ'S KOUNTRY KITCHEN
4325 N. Golden St. Blvd. #102, Fresno, CA, 93722. Contact: Judy Williams, Pres. - Tel: (209) 275-1981. Family restaurant. Established: 1981 - No. of Units: Company Owned: 1 - Franchised: 9.

BLIMPIE SUBS & SALADS
Blimpie International, Inc.
1775 The Exchange, Ste. 600, Atlanta, GA, 30339. Contact: Dennis G. Fuller, V.P. - Tel: (800) 447-6256, Fax: (404) 980-9176. National submarine sandwich and salad restaurant chain. Established: 1964 - Franchising Since: 1970 - No. of Units: Franchised: 1150 - Franchise Fee: $18,000 - Royalty: 6%, 3% adv. - Total Inv: $90,000 - $120,000 - Financing: Thru 3rd party sources.

BOARDWALK FRIES, INC.
8901 Hermann Dr., Columbia, MD, 21045. Contact: Jack Csicsek, V.P. Fran. & Leasing - Tel: (410) 720-6003. Fresh cut gourmet french fries. Established: 1981 - Franchising Since: 1983 - No. of Units: Company Owned: 5 - Franchised: 57 - Franchise Fee: $20,000 - Royalty: 7% - Total Inv: $99,000 - $170,000 - Financing: No.

BOBBY RUBINO'S PLACE FOR RIBS
Bobby Rubino's USA, Inc.
1990 E. Sunrise Blvd., Ft. Lauderdale, FL, 33304. Contact: Kay Ferrara, Dir of Fran. Oper. - Tel: (305) 763-1478, Fax: (305) 467-1192. Casual, full service restaurant offering barbecued ribs & chicken, steaks, seafood, salads and more in an inviting, comfortable atmosphere. Full liquor service. Established: 1978 - Franchising Since: 1982 - No. of Units: Company Owned: 14 - Franchise Fee: $35,000 - Royalty: 4% - Total Inv: $400,000 - $594,000 - Financing: None.

BOJANGLES' FAMOUS CHICKEN 'N BISCUITS®
Bojangles' Restaurants, Inc.
9600-H Southern Pine Blvd., Charlotte, NC, 28273. Contact: David Maisel, V.P. Fran. Dev. - Tel: (704) 527-2675, Fax: (704) 523-6676. Fast service chicken and biscuits restaurant. Established: 1977 - Franchising Since: 1978 - No. of Units: Company Owned: 103 - Franchised: 108 - Franchise Fee: $20,000; $15,000 - Royalty: 4% gross sales - Financing: No.

BOMBAY PALACE RESTAURANTS
236 W. 48th St., New York, NY, 10036-1424. Contact: Scott J. Kriger, Sr. V.P./Dir of Ops. - Tel: (212) 563-7440. Full service family restaurants featuring all you can eat shrimp and salad bars. Also, beverages such as beer, wine, soda or sangria with entrees. Established: 1978 - Franchising Since: 1985 - No. of Units: Company Owned: 8 - Franchised: 8 - Franchise Fee: $25,000 - Royalty: 5% - Total Inv: $250,000 plus - Financing: No.

BONANZA RESTAURANTS
Metromedia Steakhouses, Inc.
12404 Park Central Drive, Dallas, TX, 75251. Contact: Kenneth Myres, Dir. of Fran. Dev. - Tel: (214) 404-5000. Moderately priced, self service family restaurants generally seating 150 - 280 persons and offering a standardized menu consisting of steak, chicken and seafood dinners. Established: 1963 - Franchising Since: 1963 - No. of Units: Company Owned: 2 - Franchised: 605 - Franchise Fee: $30,000 - Royalty: 4.8% + 1% adv. - Total Inv: $850,000 - $1,000,000 (initial cash required $150,000 - $175,000) - Financing: No.

BOSTON BEANERY RESTAURANT & TAVERN
Boston Beanery Restaurants, Inc.
265 High St., Ste. 600, Morgantown, WV, 26505. Contact: Steven Jones, V.P. Admin. - Tel: (304) 292-2035. American casual theme restaurants specializing in sandwiches and dinners. Value oriented, large portions, unique menu, plus full bar with 1890's Boston theme. Flexible sites, low investments, full training and design services are featured. Established: 1983 - Franchising Since: 1988 - No. of Units: Company Owned: 2 - Franchised: 3 - Franchise Fee: $20,000 - Royalty: 5.5% gross sales - Total Inv: equip + fix ($250,000 - $375,000), inven.($8,500 - $17,500), work cap. & pre-paid exps.($20,000 - $35,000) - Financing: None.

BOSTON MARKET
14103 Denver W. Pkwy., Golden, CO, 80401. Contact: Tom Beck, V.P. Fran. - Tel: (303) 278-9500. Stores offer the flavor and wholesomeness of home cooking through retail format. The menu consists of chicken roasted on brick-fire rotisseries for better flavor and less fat. The vegetables, soups, and salads are prepared daily. The perfect solution without sacrificing quality for convenience. Established: 1988 - Franchising Since: 1989 - No. of Units: Company Owned: 46 - Franchised: 519 - Franchise Fee: $30,000 - Royalty: 4% - Total Inv: $191,600 - $466,500 incl. fran fee - Financing: May finance a portion of investment for qualified franchisees.

BOWINCAL INTERNATIONAL INC.
421 Virginia St., W., Charleston, WV, 25302. Contact: Franchise Dir./Pres. - Tel: (304) 345-8843. Old fashioned hot dogs, specialty sandwiches, soft serve dairy treats and soft drinks. Established: 1974 - No. of Units: 14 - Franchise Fee: $20,000-$25,000 - Total Inv: $40,000-$65,000.

BOX LUNCH, INC.
Sandwich Specialists, Inc.
50 Briar Lane, Wellfleet, MA, 02667. Contact: Owen MacNutt, Pres. - Tel: (508) 349-3509. We franchise Rollwich sandwich shops. Rollwiches are rolled pita sandwiches of a very high quality to the broad lunch market. We have 8 units on Cape Cod and 1 in Portland, ME. Established: 1977 - Franchising Since: 1990 - No. of Units: Franchised: 9 - Franchise Fee: $15,000 - Royalty: 4.5%, 2% adv. - Total Inv: $75,000: $30,000 build-out, $25,000 equip., $5,000 grand open., $15,000 fran. fee - Financing: Limited.

BOXIES CAFE
Brice Group, The
3361 Boyington Dr., Ste. 200, Carrollton, TX, 75006. Contact: Franchise Sales - Tel: (800) 269-4374, Fax: (214) 788-4788. Upscale, quick service restaurant offering branded modules, such as I Can't Believe It's Yogurt, Java Coast fine coffees, Boxies gourmet soups, salads, and sandwiches, Dough-Re-Me bakery, and retail items. Established: 1994 - Franchising Since: 1994 - No. of Units: Franchised: 7 - Franchise Fee: $20,000 - Royalty: 5%, 2% mktg. - Total Inv: $190,000 - $260,000 - Financing: None.

BOZ HOT DOGS
770 East 142nd St., Dolton, IL, 60419. Contact: Don Hart, Pres. - Tel: (312) 468-3647. Fast foods specializing in hot dogs and sausage, mostly carry out but some locations have sit down. Established: 1969 - Franchising Since: 1973 - No. of Units: Company Owned: 5 - Franchised: 29 - Franchise Fee: $5,000 - $10,000 - Royalty: 3-5% - Total Inv: min. $50,000.

BREADEAUX PIZZA, INC.
23rd & Frederick, P.O. Box 6158, St. Joseph, MO, 64506. Contact: Director Fran. Dev. - Tel: (800) 835-6534, Fax: (816) 364-3739. Eat in and carry out and/or delivery. Provides training and assistance for all phases of operation including location, construction, floor plans, accounting and marketing. Established: 1985 - Franchising Since: 1985 - No. of Units: Company Owned: 2 - Franchised: 77 plus 1 international - Franchise Fee: $15,000 - Royalty: 5%, 3% ad. fund - Total Inv: $75,000 - $169,000 - Financing: No.

BROADWAY
Broadway Pizza
2025 West River Rd., Minneapolis, MN, 55411. Contact: Eddie Peck, Pres. - Tel: (612) 529-7745. Family restaurant specializing in pizza. Established: 1960 - No. of Units: Company Owned: 4 - Franchised: 4.

BROWN'S CHICKEN & PASTA
Brown's Chicken & Pasta, Inc.
2809 Butterfield Rd., Oak Brook, IL, 60521. Contact: Robert Pyrce, Dir., Fran. Dev. - Tel: (708) 571-5300, Fax: (708) 571-5378. Fast food restaurant specializing in fried chicken cooked to order pasta 7 Italian dishes, numerous side dishes, sandwiches & salads. Professional 8 week training program with on going seminars and numerous store visits & support. Established: 1960 - Franchising Since: 1964 - No. of Units: Company Owned: 25 - Franchised: 82 - Franchise Fee: $25,000 per unit for exclusive territory - Royalty: 5% (reduced royalty 1st 5 years) - Total Inv: $150,000 (strip center); $650,000 (freestanding building) - Financing: Various sources but not direct from franchisor.

BUBBA'S BREAKAWAY
Bubba's Breakaway Franchise Systems Inc.
202 Highwood Rd., South Glastonbury, CT, 06073-2910. Contact: Ron Jordon, Pres. - Tel: (814) 237-4616. Sub sandwich and cheesesteak delivery operation specializing in 29 minute free delivery. Established: 1981 - Franchising Since: 1984 - No. of Units: Company Owned: 6 - Franchised: 14 - Franchise Fee: $18,500 single, $13,500 multi-unit - Royalty: 5% single, 4.5% multi-unit - Total Inv: $60,000-$80,000 incl. fran. fee, equip., leaseholds, etc. - Financing: No.

BUCK'S PIZZA *
P.O. Box 405, 204 W. Long Ave., DuBois, PA, 15801. Contact: Neil Shindledecker, Dir. of Fran. Sales - Tel: (814) 371-3076. Retail carry-out / delivery pizza shop. Menu items inc. pizza, baked hoagies, strombolis. $250/mo. flat fee royalty, not a percentage of gross sales!! $75,000 total startup. Established: 1994 - Franchising Since: 1994 - No. of Units: Franchised: 3 - Franchise Fee: $10,000 - Royalty: $250/mo. flat fee - Total Inv: $75,000: $10,000 fran. fee, $6,000 unit dev., $40,000 equip., $19,000 work. cap, remodeling, inventory, deposits - Financing: Assist franchisee with bus. plan.

BUDDY'S BAR-B-Q, INC. *
5806 Kingston Pike, Knoxville, TN, 37919. Contact: Todd Wolf, V.P. Fran. - Tel: (423) 558-9253. Upscale fast food barbeque. Dine or drive thru. All meats are smoked on site at each location. Established: 1972 - Franchising Since: 1992 - No. of Units: Company Owned: 9 - Franchised: 4 - Franchise Fee: $30,000 - Royalty: 4% + .25% adv. - total Inv: $486,500 - $992,500 lease vs. purchase land & build. - Financing: No.

BUFFALO PHIL'S *
Phil's Food Service
2124-B 7th St., Tuscaloosa, AL, 35401. Contact: Robert Head, V.P. - Tel: (205) 345-2891, Fax: (205) 345-2822. Sit down, semi fast food, Buffalo wings, chicken fingers, sandwiches, burgers, salads, soups, bar in some stores, bar is optional. Established: 1980 - Franchising Since; 1994 - No. of Units: Company Owned: 1 - Franchised: 5 - Franchise Fee: $20,000 - Royalty: 5% - Total Inv: $250,000 to $350,000 - Financing: No.

BUFFALO WILD WINGS & WECK
bw-3 Franchise Systems Inc.
2634 Vine St., Cincinnati, OH, 45219. Contact: Art Bowman, Fran. Sales Dir. - Tel: (513) 943-9293. bw-3 is the leader among food service establishments offering Buffalo wings. Their secret sauce recipe results in the best Buffalo wings in the country. bw-3 prefers to locate near college campuses and areas of heavy pedestrian traffic. Established: 1982 - Franchising Since: 1991 - No. of Units: Company Owned: 12 - Franchised: 34 - Franchise Fee: $19,500 - Royalty: 5%, 3% adv. - Total Inv: $225,000 - $400,000 - Financing: No.

BUFFALO'S CAFE
Buffalo's Franchise Concepts Inc.
2937 Cobb Pkwy., N.W., Atlanta, GA, 30339-3116. Contact: Kevin Culkin, Dir. of Fran. - Tel: (404) 916-1617, Fax: (404) 916-1696. Casual, old west style neighborhood restaurant. A limited menu specializing in Buffalo style chicken wings and all fresh food concept. Established: 1985 - Franchising Since: 1990 - No. of Units: Company Owned: 1 - Franchised: 33 - Franchise Fee: $25,000 - Royalty: 5% of gross sales - Total Inv: $300,000 - $350,000 total turnkey incl. fran. fee - Financing: SBA approved franchisor.

BULLETS *
Bullets Corp. of America, Inc.
9201 Forest Hill Ave., Ste. 109, Richmond, VA, 23235. Contact: Bruce Budny, V.P. - Tel: (804) 330-0837, Fax: (804) 330-5405. Restaurant chain that serves flame-broiled hamburger and chicken, Oscar Mayer hot dogs, fries, shakes, and barbecue in a variety of outlets - double drive thrus, traditional single drive thru restaurants, c-store express drive thrus and diners, kiosks for office buildings, schools, stadiums, etc. Established: 1990 - Franchising Since: 1993 - No. of Units: Company Owned: 7 - Franchised: 9 - Franchise Fee: $25,000 DDT or free standing restaurant, $20,000 c-store express - Royalty: 4% DDT/freestanding, 6% C-store express, 1% nat'l. adv., 3% local advertising (all royalties based on net sales) - Total Inv: varies on concept, $56,700 to $531,500 - Financing: No.

BURGER KING CORPORATION
P.O. Box 520783 (GMF), Miami, FL, 33157. Contact: James Lyons, V.P. Franchising - Tel: (800) 394-0940. Highly recognized, worldwide brand with over 7,547 points of distribution. New, lower cost facility design and flexible ownership guidelines continue to make Burger King an attractive franchise investment. Established: 1954 - Franchising Since: 1954 - No. of Units: Company Owned: 794 - Franchised: 6,753 - Franchise Fee: $40,000 - Royalty: 3.5% mthly. gross sales - Total Inv: $135,500 - $1,264,000 (excl. real estate) - Financing: Yes.

BUSCEMI'S PIZZA & SUB SHOPPES
Buscemi's International
30362 Gratiot Ave., Roseville, MI, 48066. Contact: Anthony Buscemi, Pres., C.E.O. - Tel: (810) 296-5560, Fax: (810) 296-3366. Buscemis Party Shoppes, beer, wine, liquor, pizza square sicilian, Italian submarine sandwiches, grocery deli - carry out only. Buscemis Pizza & Subs shops pizza, subs, salads, pasta - dine in, carry out, delivery. Established: 1955 - Franchising Since: 1972- No. of Units: Company Owned: 4 - Franchised: 14 - Franchise Fee: $50,000 master terr. ($15,000 for individual units) - Royalty: 4% + 2% adv. - Total Inv: $100,000-$170,000.

CAFE BRESLERS
Cafe International, Inc.
999 E. Touhy Ave., Des Plaines, IL, 60018. Contact: Howard B. Marks, V.P. Fran. Dev. - Tel: (800) 535-3333, (708) 298-1100. Quick service cafe featuring health/lite fare, located in high traffic business areas. Menu features salads, sandwiches, pasta, ice cream and yogurt, all from our no-cooking kitchen. Established: 1992 - Franchising Since: 1992 - No. of Units: Company Owned: 2 - Franchised: 5 - Franchise Fee: $25,000 - Royalty: 5%, 2% adv. - Total Inv: $200,000 - $300,000 - Financing: Will assist in acquiring third party financing.

CAFE ON MAIN
Infrangibles, Inc.
1621 Washington St., Blair, NE, 68008. Contact: Franchise Consortium - Tel: (800) 301-9504. Specialty restaurant, specializing in homemade soups, salads and sandwiches. Designed to be an indoor street cafe. Established: 1986 - Franchising Since: 1993 - No. of Units: Company Owned: 1 - Franchise Fee: $19,500 - Total Inv: $108,250 to $183,000 - Financing: Will assist in locating financing.

CAFFE CLASSICO
190 Hubbell St., #103, San Francisco, CA, 94107. Contact: Tom Heffernan, Dir. of Dev. - Tel: (415) 621-7998. European style cafe, featuring high quality coffees, sandwiches, salads, espresso and award winning gelato (Italian Ice Cream). Established: 1976 - Franchising Since: 1982 - No. of Units: Company Owned: 1- Franchised: 30 - Franchise Fee: $25,000 - Royalty: 5% - Total Inv: $131,000 - $220,000 includes franc. fee - Financing: Available.

CAMI'S THE SEAFOOD PLACE
Cami Restaurant Corp.
6272 S. Dixie Hwy., South Miami, FL, 33143. Contact: Linda Biciocchi, Fran. Consultant - Tel: (305) 942-9524. Serve fresh seafood and delicious pasta quickly and at budget prices. Prior restaurant experience and business experience is preferred. Offer complete training programs and manuals. Single unit or area development franchises are available. Established: 1986 - Franchising Since: 1992 - No. of Units: Company Owned: 3 - Franchise Fee: $30,000 - Royalty: 3.5% - Total Inv: $361,000 - $496,000 - Financing: None.

CAP'N TACO
California Restaurant Systems Inc.
P.O. Box 415, North Olmsted, OH, 44070-0415. Contact: Raymond Brown, Dir. Fran. Sales - Tel: (216) 676-9100. Mexican fast food with full service dining rooms and theme atmosphere. Featuring margaritas, draft beer, special activities, newsletters, and customer flying club devoted to social activities. Established: 1976 - Franchising Since: 1987 - No. of Units: Company Owned: 2 - Franchised: 2 - Franchise Fee: $15,000 - Royalty: 5%, 2% combined adv., 1% indiv. adv. - Total Inv: $80,000 - $125,000 - Financing: Assistance.

CAPERS COMPANY
4908 W. Nassau St., Tampa, FL, 33607. Contact: Joseph Casper, Pres. - Tel: (813) 287-2231. Fast food restaurant. Established: 1958 - No. of Units: Franchised: 27.

CAPT'N NEMO'S
Capt'n Nemo's Franchise Systems, Inc.
7367 N. Clark St., Chicago, IL, 60626. Contact: Steve Ragusi, Exec. V.P. - Tel: (312) 973-0570. Restaurant operation which specializes in homemade soups and quality submarine sandwiches served quickly. A unique system which is simple to operate and easy to control. Established: 1971 - Franchising Since: 1988 - No. of Units: Company Owned: 2 - Franchised: 1 - Franchise Fee: $14,000 - Royalty: 5% + 2% to co-op nat'l adv. - Total Inv: $99,960 - Financing: Assistance provided.

CAPTAIN D'S SEAFOOD
Shoney's, Inc.
1717 Elm Hill Pike, Ste. A10, Nashville, TN, 37210. Contact: Tom Davis, Dir. of Fran. - Tel: (615) 391-5201. Quick service dine in or take out seafood restaurant. Serving broiled, baked and fried fish, shrimp, and crab entrees, as well as chicken, specialty salads, a wide choice of vegetables and desserts. Established: 1969 - Franchising Since: 1969 - No. of Units: Company Owned: 352 - Franchised: 293 - Franchise Fee: $12,500 - Royalty: 3% - Total Inv: $559,000 - $783,000 (average) - Financing: Sources are available.

CAPTAIN TONY'S PIZZA & PASTA EMPORIUM
1945 E. Ridge Road, Ste. 103, Rochester, NY, 14622. Contact: Michael Martella, Pres. - Tel: (716) 467-2250. Pizza and pasta. Take-out and delivery or full dining. Established: 1974 - Franchising Since: 1987 - No. of Units: Franchised: 14 - Franchise Fee: $9,500 for take-out/delivery, $15,000 dine-in - Royalty: $100 - $400.

CARBONE & SONS
680 E. Seventh St., St. Paul, MN, 55106. Contact: Tom Carbone, Dir. Fran. Dev. - Tel: (612) 771-5553. Family pizza restaurants. Established: 1953 - Franchising Since: 1963 - No. of Units: Company Owned: 3 - Franchised: 16 - Franchise Fee: $10,000 - Royalty: 4% + 1% adv. - Total Inv: $175,000 - $450,000 - Financing: No.

CARL'S JR. RESTAURANTS
Carl Karcher Enterprises, Inc.
1200 N. Harbor Blvd., Anaheim, CA, 92803. Contact: Connie Codon, Fran. Admin. Mgr. - Tel: (714) 490-3682, Fax: (714) 520-4485. Quick service restaurants featuring charbroiled hamburgers and chicken sandwiches. Established: 1941 - Franchising Since: 1984 - No. of Units: Company Owned: 390 - Franchised: 236 - Franchise Fee: $35,000 - Royalty: 4% - Total Inv: $1,011,500 to $1,787,500: fran. fee, equip., signs, work. cap., training, start-up supplies - Financing: No.

CARROWS RESTAURANT
CFC Franchising Company
18831 Von Karman Avenue, Irvine, CA, 92715. Contact: Kevin Relyea, Pres. - Tel: (714) 757-7900. Family restaurant featuring breakfast, lunch and dinner twenty four hours a day with a $5.50 check average. Emphasis on a distinctive western style of family dining at value oriented prices. Established: 1969 - Franchising Since: 1992 - No. of Units: Company Owned: 120 - Franchise Fee: $35,000 - Royalty: 3.5%, 2.5% adv. - Total Inv: $1,100,000 - $1,500,000, on build to suits, $300,000 - $900,000 on remodels; turn-key negotiable - Financing: No.

CARTER INVESTMENT CO.
28851 N. Main St., Ste. 1, P.O. Box 2010, Daphne, AL, 36526. Contact: Mike Carter, Pres. - Tel: (334) 626-5811. Fast food restaurant. No. of Units: Franchised: 27.

CASA MIA RESTAURANTS
716 Plum St. SE, Olympia, WA, 98501. Contact: Robert Knudson, V.P. - Tel: (206) 352-0440. Family style Italian restaurant and pizzeria. Established: 1952 - Franchising Since: 1989 - No. of Units: Company Owned: 3 - Franchised: 1 - Franchise Fee: $18,500 - Royalty: 5% - Total Inv: $43,000-$50,000 - Financing: No.

CASA OLE RESTAURANT & CANTINAS
1135 Edgebrook Dr., Houston, TX, 77034-1803. Contact: Pat Morris, Pres. - Tel: (713) 943-7574. Dinnerhouse - Mexican. Established: 1973 - No. of Units: Company Owned: 19 - Franchised: 17.

CASSANO'S PIZZA & SUBS
Cassano's, Inc.
1700 E. Stroop Rd., Kettering, OH, 45429. Contact: Tim Sayer, Sr. V.P. - Tel: (513) 294-8400, ext. 205. Retail sale of pizza and subs. Eat-in, carry-out and delivery. Established: 1953 - Franchising Since: 1957 - No. of Units: Company Owned: 44 - Franchised: 12 - Franchise Fee: $10,000 - Royalty: 4%, .5% prod. fee - Total Inv: $150,000 avg. - Financing: No.

CATFISH KITCHEN
CKC
3820 Premier Ave., Memphis, TN, 38118. Contact: Bill Richey, Sales - Tel: (901) 867-0600. Full service restaurant. Special recipe catfish. Unique decor. Established: 1987 - Franchising Since: 1990 - No. of Units: Company Owned: 1 - Franchise Fee: $25,000 - Royalty: 6% - Total Inv: $80,000 - Financing: No.

CENTRAL PARK
Central Park USA, Inc.
300 High St., Chattanooga, TN, 37403. Contact: Lauri White, Fran. Sales Admin. - Tel: (615) 267-6575, Fax: (615) 267-4361. Double drive through hamburgers. Established: 1982 - Franchising Since: 1986 - No. of Units: Company Owned: 22 - Franchised: 56 - Franchise Fee: $20,000 - Royalty: 4% on total gross volume, 2% nat'l. adv. on total gross volume - Total Inv: $300,000 - $350,000 - Financing: No.

CHARLEY'S STEAKERY
Gosh Enterprises, Inc.
6610 Busch Blvd., #100, Columbus, OH, 43229. Contact: Mark Hardcastle, Nat'l. Dev. Dir. - Tel: (614) 847-8100. Fresh grilled subs, featuring award-winning Philly cheesesteak, hand cut fries, made to order salads, fresh squeezed lemonade. Established: 1986 - Franchising Since: 1991 - No. of Units: Company Owned: 5 - Franchised: 36 - Franchise Fee: $19,500 - Royalty: 5% - Total Inv: $99,000 - $150,000 - Financing: Will assist with finding financing.

CHARLIE'S CHICKEN
Charlie's Chicken of America
3325 West Okmulgee, Muskogee, OK, 74401. Contact: Vim Harris, Darren Kilpatrick, Fran. Dir. - Tel: (918) 687-8741. A restaurant that offers "The Best Fried Chicken" and related items in the world. Established: 1978 - No. of Units: Company Owned: 2 - Franchised: 16 - Franchise Fee: $25,000 - Royalty: 4% - Total Inv: $300,000 to $600,000 excl. property - Financing: No.

CHECKERS DRIVE-IN RESTAURANTS, INC.
P.O. Box 1079, Clearwater, FL, 34617. Contact: Jeff Christiansen, Fran. Sales - Tel: (800) 275-3628 or (813) 298-2120; Fax (813) 461-1341. Double drive-thru, hamburgers, french fries, hot dogs, chicken, colas and shakes. Established: 1985 - Franchising Since: 1988 - No. of Units: 500 - Franchise Fee: $30,000 - Royalty: 4% - Total Inv: $475,000 - $600,000 - Financing: 3rd party.

CHECKERS PIZZA
Checkers Pizza, Inc.
659 West Main Rd., Middletown, RI, 02840. Contact: David A. Haag, Pres. - Tel: (401) 849-8890. Freshly made pizza prepared entirely on premises. Sit down/take out/delivery. Established: 1985 - Franchising Since: 1992 - No. of Units: Company Owned: 3 - Franchised: 2 - Franchise Fee: $10,000 - Royalty: 3% - Financing: Assistance available.

CHEEBURGER CHEEBURGER
Cheeburger Cheeburger Restaurants Inc.
2413 Periwinkle Way, Sanibel, FL, 33957. Contact: Bill Connery, President - Tel: (941) 472-0550, Fax: (941) 472-5620. Full service restaurant specializing in gourmet cheeseburgers. Established: 1986 - Franchising Since: 1990 - No. of Units: Company Owned: 1 - Franchised: 4 - Franchise Fee: $13,500 - Royalty: 4.5% gross sales - Total Inv: $125,000 - $170,000.

CHEESE VILLA
ISCO, Ltd.
414 Walnut #508, Cincinnati, OH, 45202-3903. Contact: Carl Perin, Pres. - Tel: (513) 579-0023. Limited menu non-cooking restaurants located in downtown high density, high traffic office buildings and commercial locations. Established: 1975 - Franchising Since: 1975 - No. of Units: Company Owned: 3 - Franchised: 8 - Franchise Fee: $12,500 - Royalty: 5% of gross sales - Total Inv: $80,000 - $175,000 depending upon locations - Financing: No.

CHEF'S FRIED CHICKEN
Chef's Fried Chicken, Inc.
20 Audubon Oaks Blvd., Lafayette, LA, 70506. Contact: Lee Shelton, Pres. - Tel: (318) 233-1621. Fast food outlet specializing in chicken and seafood by cajun method. Established: 1971 - Franchising Since: 1974 - No. of Units: Franchised: 8 - Franchise Fee: $20,000 - Royalty: 4%, 2% adv. - Total Inv: $50,000 - $60,000 equip. - Financing: Some construction financing.

CHEF'S TAKEOUT
111 North Victory Blvd., Burbank, CA, 91502. Contact: Tom Hanson Sr., Owner - Tel: (818) 841-2203, Fax: (818) 845-9115. Hand carving real food. Established: 1985 - No. of Units: Company Owned: 2 - Total Inv: $180,000 - Financing: No.

CHIC CHICK *
Chic Chick, Inc.
7 Penn Plaza, New York, NY, 10001. Contact: Frank Coppa Jr., Pres. - Tel: (800) 511-2442, Fax: (212) 714-1287. Flame roasted chicken. Established: 1991 - Franchising Since: 1991 - No. of Units: Franchised: 7 - Franchise Fee: $10,000 - Royalty: 5%, 3% adv. - Total Inv: $150,000 to $225,000 - Financing: Equipment leasing.

CHICAGO'S PIZZA
Chicago's Pizza Franchises
1111 N. Broadway, Greenfield, IN, 46140. Contact: R.L. McDonald, CEO - Tel: (317) 462-9878. Pizza, sandwiches, inside dining/carry out/drive-thru. Established: 1979 - Franchising Since: 1980 - No. of Units: Franchised: 10 - Franchise Fee: $10,000 - Royalty: 4%, 2% adv. - Total Inv: $75,000 - $350,000 - Financing: None.

CHICKEN CHARLIES *
P.O. Box 4451, Northbrook, IL, 60062. Contact: Alan Kray, Pres. - Tel: (708) 272-0125, Fax: (708) 559-9095. Upscale fast food grilled chicken, grilled chicken sandwiches, salads. Established: 1989 - Franchising Since: 1994 - No. of Units: Company Owned: 2 - Franchised: 1 - Franchise Fee: $17,500 - Royalty: 5% of gross sales - Total Inv: $200,000 to $225,000 build-out & capital.

CHICKS NATURAL
Chicks Natural, Inc.
11494 Sorrento Valley Rd., San Diego, CA, 92121-1318. Contact: Randy White, Pres. - Tel: (619) 793-0310. Restaurant chain - rotisserie chicken. Established: 1985 - Franchising Since: 1989 - No. of Units: Company Owned: 3 - Franchised: 6 - Franchise Fee: $25,000 - Royalty: 4% - Total Inv: Approximately $200,000 ($25,000 franchise fee) - Financing: No.

CHICO'S *
P.O. Box 890144, Temecula, CA, 92589-0144. Contact: Terry Shores, Pres. - Tel: (800) 772-4426. Fresh, authentic, healthy, fast Mexican food. "Dinner house quality in a fast food setting." Established: 1993 - Franchising since: 1994 - No. of Units: Company Onwed: 1 - Franchised: 90 - Franchise Fee: $25,000 - Royalty: 5%, 2% - Total Inv: $150,000 - $300,000 - Financing: No.

CHILI COMPANY, THE
2121 Freeman Ave., Cincinnati, OH, 45214-1820. Contact: Pete Poulos, Pres. - Tel: (513) 741-9555. Full service restaurants, open 24 hours, breakfast available all day. Established: 1978 - No. of Units: Company Owned: 1 - Franchised: 14 - Approx. Inv: $165,000 + land & building.

CHILI'S, OTB, SPAGGEDDIES, GRADY'S, COZYMEL'S, RAMANO'S MAC GRILL
Brinker Int'l.
6820 LBJ Freeway #200, Dallas, TX, 75240. Contact: Norman Abdallah, V.P. Fran. - Tel: (214) 980-9917, Fax: (214) 770-5580. Casual dining, family dinnerhouse with liquor. Southwestern decor, specializing in ribs, chicken, burgers, steaks, and a variety of entree salads. Established: 1975 - Franchising Since: 1986 - No. of Units: Company Owned: 470 - Franchised: 128 - Franchise Fee, Royalty & Total Inv: depends on concept - Financing: No.

CHUBBY'S DINER
Chubby's Food Service, Inc.
11638 Fair Oaks Blvd., #210, Fair Oaks, CA, 95628. Contact: Mr. Kris Edwards, V.P. Fran. Sales - Tel: (916) 966-7773, Fax: (916) 863-6778. A 1950's style restaurant. Established: 1990 - Franchising Since: 1991 - No. of Units: Franchised: 56 - Franchise Fee: $12,000 + $1,000 adv. fee - Royalty: 6% of net sales wkly. - Total Inv: varies - Financing: No.

CHURCHS CHICKEN
America's Favorite Chicken Co.
Six Concourse Pkwy., Ste. 1700, Atlanta, GA, 30328. Contact: Elizabeth Smith, Mktg. Comm. Coord. - Tel: (800) 848-8248. World's second-largest quick service chicken company. Features southern fried chicken, mash potatoes, corn, biscuits, and other side items. Established: 1952 - Franchising Since: 1964 - No. of Units: Company Owned: 593 - Franchised: 604 - Franchise Fee: $10,000 dev. fee; $15,000 fran. fee - Royalty: .5% gross revenue - Total Inv: Traditional $214,800 to $290,600; Alternative $147,300 to $270,600 - Financing: N/A.

CICI'S PIZZA
CiCi Enterprises, Inc.
1620 Rafe St., #114, Carrollton, TX, 75006-6642. Contact: Steve Berkman, Fran. Dir. - Tel: (214) 466-2424. CiCi's offers an all-you-can-eat buffet featuring pizza, pasta, salad bar and dessert for only $2.99 at lunch and dinner, 7 days a week. Operated from approximately 4,000 sq. ft. and seating 180, CiCi's is everyone's favorite family restaurant wherever it opens. Established: 1984 - Franchising Since: 1988 - No. of Units: Company Owned: 15 - Franchised: 85 - Franchise Fee: $25,000 - Royalty: 4% of gross sales - Total Inv: $320,000 - Financing: SBA guaranteed loans for qualified buyers.

CLARKE'S CHARCOAL BROILER
Clarke's Franchising, Inc.
1563 Begen Ave., Mountain View, CA, 94040. Contact: James P. Blach, Pres. - Tel: (415) 967-0851. Specializing in 1/3 lb. Clarkesburgers done over charcoal B-B-Q style, using fresh meat, along with other great items such as B-B-Q baby back ribs (pork). Great milk shakes made with real ice cream, thick and flavorful, including our peanut butter shake. With beer & wine for those that like it. Just a great place. Established: 1944 - Franchising Since: 1993 - No. of Units: Company Owned: 1 - Franchised: 2 - Franchise Fee: $27,000 - Royalty: 6%/wk. - Total Inv: $130,000 - $180,000 depending on size - Financing: SBA & other.

CLUCK-U-CHICKEN
Cluck-U-Chicken, Inc.
1 Executive Dr., Monmouth Junction, NJ, 08852. Contact: Bob Atex, V.P. Fran. Sales - Tel: (908) 821-6063, Fax: (908) 821-4281. Retail food service, chicken, chicken wing specialty. Established: 1985 - Franchising Since: 1991 - No. of Units: Franchised: 20 - Franchise Fee: $20,000 - Royalty: 4% of weekly sales - Total Inv: $150,000 - $230,000 (excl. fran. fee) - Financing: Through SBA.

COCK OF THE WALK
CWI Incorporated
Mobile, AL, 27709-4181. Contact: Mike Rickles, Franc. Dir. - Tel: (334) 626-2322. Specialty catfish family restaurant. Established: 1977 - Franchising Since: 1980 - No. of Units: Company Owned: 1 - Franchised: 7 - Franchise Fee: $25,000 - Royalty: 3-4% - Total Inv: $600,000 - Financing: No.

COLUMBIA STEAK HOUSE
Penn Brothers Enterprises Inc.
261 Midand Dr., Lexington, KY, 40508. Contact: Gary D. Penn, V.P. - Tel: (606) 231-0008. Steak house restaurants. Established: 1948 - Franchising Since: 1982 - No. of Units: Company Owned: 3 - Franchised: 3 - Franchise Fee: $20,000 plus training fees, time & travel - Royalty: 4% - Total Inv: varies - Financing: No.

CONEY'S EXPRESS
Coney's Corp.
102 Dunlap, P.O. Box 1137, Batesville, MS, 38606. Contact: Robert Crites, Fran. Sales Dir. - Tel: (601) 563-5822. Featuring all beef hot dogs and sausage and Coney Snow. Established: 1991 - Franchising Since: 1994 - No. of Units: Company Owned: 1 - Franchised: 4 - Franchise Fee: $3,500 - Royalty: 6%, 2% adv. - Total Inv: $12,400 - $38,100 - Financing: None.

CONGRESS ROTISSERIE
10 Columbus Blvd., Hartford, CT, 06106. Contact: Marge Morrissey, Dir. of Mktg. - Tel: (860) 549-2211. Made-to-order specialty sandwiches, healthful rotisserie chicken, a variety of homemade soups, salads, hot vegetables and freshly baked breads & pastries. Proprietary dressings including honey mustard & balsamic vinaigrette also are customer favorites. Established: 1986 - Franchising Since: 1992 - No. of Units: Company Owned: 5 - Franchised: 8 - Franchise Fee: $20,000 satellite store, $25,000 full production facility - Royalty: 6% gross receipts - Total Inv: $150,000 - $225,000 excluding leasehold improv. & fran. fee - Financing: No.

CONNECTICUT RESTAURANT GROUP, INC.
285 Riverside Ave., Westport, CT, 06880-4806., Fran. Dir. - Tel: (203) 222-1000. Retail restaurant & bar. Established: 1978 - Franchising Since: 1988 - No. of Units: Company Owned: 10 - Franchised: 3 - Royalty: 5.75% of sales.

COOPER'S TURKEY PLACE *
CTP International, Inc.
P.O. Box 547, Oakwood, OH, 45873. Contact: Rudy Hampton, V.P./Dir. of Fran. - Tel: (614) 837-9034. Homestyle restaurant with limited menu focusing on turkey based items with counter service in a farm-style atmosphere - Just Like Grandma's. Established: 1992 - Franchising Since: 1994 - No. of Units: Company Owned: 2 - Franchised: 1 - Franchise Fee: $20,000 - Royalty: 5% of gross sales - Total Inv: $60,000 to $125,000 liquidity - Financing: Will Assist.

CORN DOG 7
Corn Dog 7, Inc.
Hwy 161, Corn Dog Lane; P.O. Box 907, Hughes Springs, TX, 75656. Contact: Mike Wellborn, V.P. - Tel: (903) 639-3575, Fax: (903) 639-3647. Retail sales of fast food in shopping malls. Specializing in corn dogs, and fresh lemonade. Established: 1978 - Franchising Since: 1982 - No. of Units: Company Owned: 31 - Franchised: 50 - Franchise Fee: $5,000 - Royalty: 5% of net sales - Total Inv: $50,000 leas. improve.; $30,000 equip.; $5,000 fran. fee - Financing: No.

COTTAGE INN PIZZA
3001 Plymouth Rd., Ste. 201, Ann Arbor, MI, 48105-3205. Contact: Jeffrey H. Wong, Dir. of Fran. - Tel: (313) 663-2470, Fax: (313) 747-7177. Pizza delivery company. Established: 1948 - Franchising Since: 1982 - No. of Units: Company Owned: 8 - Franchised: 12 - Franchise Fee: $15,000 - Royalty: 5%, 3% adv. - Total Inv: $85,000 - $130,000 - Financing: No.

COUCH'S CORNER BARBECUE
Couch's Corner BBQ Franchising Systems, Inc.
5323 - 37 East Nettleton, Jonesboro, AR, 72401., Fran. Dir. - Tel: (901) 867-0600. B-B-Q restaurant. Established: 1970 - Franchising Since: 1978 - No. of Units: Company Owned: 3 - Franchise Fee: $15,000 - Royalty: 4% - Total Inv: $163,000 - $178,000 (equip., work. cap., lease inven.) - Financing: Financable equipment. For further information please contact: Consultants America Corp., 12279 US Highway 64. Eads, TN, 38028, Tel: (901) 867-0600, Fax: (901) 867-0010.

COUNTRY KITCHEN RESTAURANTS
Country Hospitality Corp.
P.O. Box 59159, Carlson Pkwy., Minneapolis, MN, 55459-8203. Contact: Lynette McKee or Harry Stillwell, Director of Development - Tel: (612) 449-1300. Franchised restaurant (family dining). Established: 1939 - Franchising Since: 1965 - No. of Units: Franchised: 245 - Franchise Fee: $25,000 - Royalty: 4% - Total Inv: $250,000 - Financing: Assist in sourcing.

COUSINS SUBS
Cousin's Subs Systems, Inc.
N83 W13400 Leon Rd., Menomonee Falls, WI, 53051. Contact: D.K. Kilby, V.P. - Tel: (414) 253-7700. Uniquely developed, volume oriented, submarine sandwich operation with over 20 yrs experience. Quality, fast service in an upscale decor. "Better Bread-Better Subs" slogan results from bread baked fresh daily. Hot and cold subs, soups, and salads from free standing and in-line locations. Some with pick-up windows. Established: 1972 - Franchising Since: 1985 - No. of Units: Company Owned: 39 - Franchised: 178 - Franchise Fee: $10,000 - Royalty: 6% to $750,000, 5% next $250,000, 4% over $1,000,000 - Total Inv: $60,000 equip., $55,000 leaseholds, $25,000 misc. - Financing: Yes, 3rd party, SBA/bank relationship, national accounts.

COWBOY CHICKEN
Brice Group, The
3361 Boyington, Ste. 200, Carrollton, TX, 75006. Contact: Franchise Sales Dept. - Tel: (800) 269-4374. Rotisserie chicken concept with healthy and delicious side dishes. Established: 1981 - Franchising Since: 1994 - No. of Units: Company Owned: 2 - Franchise Fee: $15,000 - Royalty: 5%, 2% adv. - Total Inv: $120,000 - $150,000 - Financing: None.

COZZOLI'S PIZZA
Cozzoli's Pizza Systems, Inc.
Bay Pt. Twr., #1400, 4770 Biscayne Blvd., Miami, FL, 33137. Contact: John Cozzoli, Pres. - Tel: (305) 358-5086. Fast Food Pizza. Established: 1953 - No. of Units: Company Owned: 26 - Franchised: 26.

CREATIVE CROISSANTS
St. Clair Development Corp.
2712 Transportation Ave., #F, National City, CA, 91950. Contact: Sayed Ali, Pres. - Tel: (619) 474-3388. Bakery and cafe featuring soups, salads, and sandwiches. Established: 1981 - Franchising Since: 1988 - No. of Units: Company Owned: 3 - Franchised: 37 - Franchise Fee: $17,500 - Royalty: 4.5%, 2% mktg/adv. - Total Inv: $95,000 - $125,000 - Financing: No.

D'ANGELO SANDWICH SHOPS
D'Angelo's Sandwich Shops, Inc.
321 Manley St., West Bridgewater, MA, 02379. Contact: Roy A. Jemison, V.P. Gen. Mgr. - Tel: (508) 583-2116. Upscale 2,000 sq. ft. sandwich shop with approximately 50 seats featuring subs, pitas, salads and soup. Menu includes grilled items and Healthy D'Lite sandwiches for adults and kids. Established: 1967 - Franchising Since: 1988 - No. of Units: Company Owned: 150 - Franchised: 50 - Franchise Fee: $25,000 - Royalty: 5.2% - License Royalty: 7.0% - Presently licensing to colleges, airports, hospitals, business & industry, arenas, etc.

DADDY-O'S EXPRESS DRIVE-THRU
G.D. Ritzy's Inc.
P.O. Box 20576, Columbus, OH, 43220. Contact: Richard Einhorn, V.P. Fran. - Tel: (614) 486-1224. A 50's style double drive-thru offering a limited menu at very low prices. Established: 1979 - Franchising Since: 1983 - No. of Units: Company Owned: 16 - Franchised: 34 - Franchise Fee: $10,000 - Royalty: 3.5% - Total Inv: $150,000 - Financing: None.

DAIRY BELLE FREEZE DEVELOPMENT CO., INC.
832 N. Hillview Dr., Milpitas, CA, 95035. Contact: Steven Goodere, Exec. V.P. - Tel: (408) 263-2612. Fast food restaurant featuring soft-serve products, hamburgers, fries, specialty sandwiches, etc. Established:

1957 - No. of Units: 16 - Franchise Fee: $12,500 new, $6,250 existing - Royalty: $4.5%, 2.% adv. - Total Inv: $130,000 - $253,100 - Financing: None.

DAIRY QUEEN
Interstate Dairy Queen Corp.
4601 Willard Ave., Chevy Chase, MD, 20815. Contact: Walt Tellegen, Pres. - Tel: (301) 913-5923. Specialists in twining with fuel centers. Fast food/treat franchisor on interstate highways. Established: 1977 - Franchising Since: 1977 - No. of Units: Company Owned: 2 - Franchised: 108 - Franchise Fee: $25,000 - Royalty: 4% or 6% - Total Inv: varies with building - Financing: No.

DAIRY QUEEN, KARMELKORN SHOPPES, ORANGE JULIUS
7505 Metro Blvd., Minneapolis, MN, 55439-3042. Contact: Eric Lavanger, V.P. Fran. Dev. - Tel: (612) 830-0200. Established: 1929 - Franchising Since: 1929 - Franchise Fee: $30,000 - Royalty: 6% - Total Inv: $75,000 - $120,000 - Financing: Yes.

DAMON'S, THE PLACE FOR RIBS/DAMON'S CLUBHOUSE
Damon's International Inc.
4645 Executive Dr., Columbus, OH, 43220. Contact: Shannon R. Foust, V.P. of Dev. - Tel: (614) 442-7900. A casual theme full service restaurant specializing in BBQ ribs and prime rib together with the signature item onion loaf. The Clubhouse is known for its sports theme dining room with the same great menu. Established: 1979 - Franchising Since: 1982 - No. of Units: Company Owned: 18 - Franchised: 68 - Franchise Fee: $50,000 - Royalty: 4%, .5% nat'l. adv. - Total Inv: $500,000 - $1,500,000 - Financing: No.

DEL TACO
Del Taco, Inc.
1800 W. Katella Ave., Orange, CA, 92667-3449. Contact: Franchise Dev., - Tel: (714) 540-8914. A quick-service Mexican/American restaurant chain that originated in Southern California over a quarter century ago. Established: 1964 - Franchising Since: 1967 - No. of Units: Company Owned: 193 - Franchised: 80 - Franchise Fee: $25,000 (multi-unit) - Royalty: 5% - Total Inv: Varies - Financing: No.

DENNY'S INC.
Flagstar
203 E. Main St., Spartanburg, SC, 29319. Contact: Ted Liner/Vaughn Berg/ Ellen Lanford/Shelley Barton/Frank Ferguson, Regional Directors - Tel: (803) 597-8000. Family service restaurant offering a wide variety of food items. 24 hour operation. Established: 1953 - Franchising Since: 1984 - No. of Units: Company Owned: 976 - Franchised: 482 - Franchise Fee: $35,000 - Royalty: 4% + 2% adv.- Total Inv: $1,400,000 incl. land, bldg., site improv., equip., sign, inven. - Minimum Net Worth Req.: $750,000, cash & liquid assets of $250,000 - Financing: No.

DER WEINERSCHNITZEL
Galardi Group Franchise Corp.
4440 Von Karman, Ste. 150, Newport Beach, CA, 92660. Contact: Frank Coyle, Fran. Sales Mgr. - Tel: (800) 426-0036. Fast food restaurant chain featuring hot dogs, hamburgers and breakfast items. Established: 1961 - Franchising Since: 1965 - No. of Units: Franchised: 340 - Franchise Fee: $10,000 to $30,000 - Royalty; 5% fran. fee, 1% nat'l. adv., 4% local adv. - Total Inv: $250,000 to $800,000 - Financing: No.

DESI'S FAMOUS PIZZA *
D.F.P. Franchising Inc.
438 Hazie Ave., Ste. 200, Wilkes-Barre, PA, 18702. Contact: Debbie Desiderio, Pres. - Tel: 1-800-694-DESI (3374). Serve delicious, secret recipe pizza, wings, ribs and other items in a restaurant designed for broad market appeal and computer-efficient operations. Dine-in, pick-up or delivery of all menu items. Desi's Famous Pizza franchisees enjoy complete training, volume buying power, extensive marketing support and much more. Call for franchise information. Established: 1989 - Franchising Since: 1995 - No. of Units: Company Owned: 5 - Franchise Fee: $15,000 - Royalty: 5% and 4% adv. - Total Inv: Prototype A: $69,625 - $175,660; Prototype B: $84,575 - $227,000 - Financing: No.

DIAMOND DAVE'S TACO CO.
Diamond Dave's Taco Co., Inc.
201 S. Clinton St. #281, Iowa City, IA, 52240-4011. Contact: Stanley J. White, Pres. - Tel: (319) 337-7690. Mexican/American restaurant featuring full service dining with a bar. Established: 1979 - Franchising Since: 1981 - No. of Units: Company Owned: 4 - Franchised: 31 - Franchise Fee: $15,000 - Royalty: 4% + 1% adv. - Total Inv: $122,200 - $250,000 - Financing: None.

DIXON'S FAMOUS CHILI
Dixon's Chili, Inc.
9105 E. Hwy. 40, Independence, MO, 64055. Contact: Terry Steffes, Owner - Tel: (816) 861-7308. Established: 1919 - No. of Units: Company Owned: 1 - Franchised: 2.

DOLLY'S PIZZA *
Dolly's Pizza Franchising Corp.
45049 Pontiac Trail, Novi, MI, 48377. Contact: Robert Lewis, C.E.O. - Tel: (810) 669-3579. Pizza carry out, delivery, limited seating. Dolly's Pizza was voted best in Michigan by the Michigan Rest. Assoc. Menu: Pizza, subs, salads, breadsticks, pasta. Established: 1964 - Franchising Since: 1993 - No. of Units: Company Owned: 3 - Franchised: 8 - Franchise Fee: $9,500 - Royalty: 3% year 1, 4% thereafter, 1%-4% adv.

DOMINO'S PIZZA
Domino's Pizza, Inc
30 Frank Lloyd Wright Dr., Ann Arbor, MI, 48106. Contact: Paul Skinner, Dir. of Dev. - Tel: (313) 930-3900. Pizza delivery. Established: 1960 - Franchising Since: 1967 - No. of Units: Company Owned: 1,200 - Franchised: 4,400 - Franchise Fee: $10,000 - Royalty: 5.5% of net sales - Total Inv: $150,000: $100,000 equip./leaseholds; $50,000 fees/work. cap. - Financing: No.

DON RICARDO'S MEXICAN RESTAURANT
9225 Alabama Ave. #A, Chatsworth, CA, 91311. Contact: Victor Sampson, Pres. - Tel: (818) 709-7477. Mexican restaurant. Established: 1974 - No. of Units: Company Owned: 5 - Franchise Fee: $25,000 - Royalty: 3% mgmt., 1% adv. - Total Inv: build. $550,000, FF&E $425,000.

DONATOS PIZZA, INC.
935 Taylor Station Rd., Blacklick, OH, 43004-9538. Contact: Kevin King, V.P. of Fran. - Tel: (614) 864-2444. Retail outlet specializing in the sale of pizza and other products and featuring carry-out dine-in and delivery services. Established: 1963 - Franchising Since: 1991 - No. of Units: Company Owned: 35 - Franchised: 3 - Franchise Fee: $15,000 - Royalty: 4% of net sales - Total Inv: $250,000 - $350,000: $110,000 equip., $75,000 leasehold, $50,000 work cap. - Financing: None.

DUCHESS WORLDWIDE, INC.
125 Bruce Ave., Stratford, CT, 06497. Contact: Bernard Levin, Pres. - Tel: (203) 375-7199. Menu runs the gamut from breakfast to fried chicken, with hamburgers, hot dogs, and deli sandwiches in between. Developing in CT first. Established: over 30 years - Franchising Since: 1989 - No. of Units: Company Owned: 11 - Franchise Fee: $25,000 - Royalty: 4% - Total Inv: varies depending on the area - Financing: No.

EAST OF CHICAGO PIZZA COMPANY, INC. *
318 West Walton, Willard, PH, 44890. Contact: Eric Ludewig, Asst. Dir. of Oper. - Tel: (419) 935-3033. A strong union of franchised and corporate owned units specializing in pan pizza and related products. Established: 1990 - Franchising Since: 1991 - No. of Units: Company Owned: 1 - Franchised: 48 - Franchise Fee: $16,000 - Royalty: 5% of gross sales, plus 2% of sales mktg. fee - Total Inv: Varies - Financing: No.

EDWARDO'S NATURAL PIZZA RESTAURANT
Bravo Restaurants, Inc.
205 W. Wacker Dr., Ste. 1400, Chicago, IL, 60606-1213. Contact: Don Scatena, V.P. Franchising - Tel: (800) 344-5455. Upscale family restaurant specializing in the award winning, unique 'Chicago style' stuffed pizza. Also serves thin crust pizza, pasta, salads, desserts and liquor. Complete support system which includes eight week training school in Chicago. Requires previous restaurant experience. Group purchasing power. Established: 1978. National franchise rollout: 1991

- No. of Units: Company Owned: 13 - Franchised: 11 - Franchise Fee: $25,000 - Royalty: 5% - Total Inv: $277,000 - $560,000 - Financing: None.

EL CHICO
El Chico Restaurants, Inc.
12200 Stemmons Freeway, Ste. 100, Dallas, TX, 75234. Contact: Elizabeth Clark, Fran. Admin. - Tel: (214) 241-5500. Full-service, family Mexican restaurants. Established: 1940 - Franchising Since: 1969 - No. of Units: Company Owned: 56 - Franchised: 29 - Franchise Fee: $35,000 - Royalty: 4% + 1% marketing fee - Total Inv: $1,000,000 - Financing: No.

EL POLLO LOCO
Denny's Inc.
P.O. Box 15390, Irvine, CA, 92713-5390. Contact: Mr. Dave Anderson, VP Franchising - Tel: (714) 251-5000. Fast food serving chicken. Established: 1980 - No. of Units: Company Owned: 125 - Franchised: 125.

EL TACO RESTAURANTS
7870 E. Florence, Downey, CA, 90240. Contact: J. Toogood, Pres. - Tel: (310) 692-5400. Mexican fast food. Established: 1958 - Franchising Since: 1978 - No. of Units: Company Owned: 3 - Franchised: 27 - Franchise Fee: $75,000 - Royalty: 5% - Total Inv: $150,000.

ELLIOTTS' OFF BROADWAY DELI, INC.
Individual
404 Royal Glen Ct., Oak Brook, IL, 60521-1541. Contact: Franchise Dir./Pres. - Tel: (708) 571-9191. Offering pizza, breakfast and desserts, sandwiches, soups, bagels, lunch and dinner with daily specials. Basically self-serve. Established: 1988 - Franchising Since: 1988 - No. of Units: Company Owned: 1 - Franchised: 12 - Franchise Fee: $12,500 - Royalty: 4%, 1% adv. - Total Inv: $50,000 - $100,000 - Financing: No.

ELMER'S PANCAKE & STEAK HOUSE
11802 S.E. Stark, Portland, OR, 97216. Contact: Anita Goldberg, Fran. Dir. - Tel: (503) 252-1485. Full service upscale family restaurant serving breakfast, lunch and dinner. Everything on menu served all day. Established: 1960 - Franchising Since: 1966 - No. of Units: Company Owned: 11 - Franchised: 17 - Franchise Fee: $25,000 - Royalty: 4% - Total Inv: $200,000 min. equity capital + ability to finance equip. pkg. etc. - Financing: No.

EMPRESS CHILI
Empress Food Products, Inc.
Nine W. Office Center, 2200 Fletcher Ave., Fort Lee, NJ, 07024. Contact: J. Kiradjieff, Pres. - Tel: (513) 771-1441. Processing and making of chili for restaurants and chain stores. (Super Markets). Established: 1959 - Franchising Since: 1960 - No. of Units: 100% franchised.

ENTREES ON TRAYS
3 Lombardy Terrace, Ft. Worth, TX, 76132. Contact: Don Shipe, Founder-Owner - Tel: (817) 735-8558. Dinner delivery service serving the finer restaurants of Ft. Worth with chef uniformed drivers. Operated from home. Established: 1986 - Franchising Since: 1987 - No. of Units: Company Owned: 1 - Lic. Agree: 14 - License Fee: $8,750 incl. all equip. except radios - Royalty: 0 - Total Inv: approx. $10,500 incl. radios - Financing: None.

ERBERT & GERBERT'S SUBS & CLUBS
Erbert & Gerbert & Friends, Inc.
408 Riverside Ave., Eau Claire, WI, 54703. Contact: Kevin Schippers, Pres. - Tel: (800) 283-5241. Gourmet sandwich shops that specialize in delivering fresh, delicious sandwiches to homes and businesses. Erbert & Gerbert's has earned the reputation of being the place where people send their friends. Established: 1988 - Franchising Since: 1992 - No. of Units: Company Owned: 1 - Franchised: 10 - Franchise Fee: $9,500 - Royalty: 6.5% - Total Inv: $72,600 - $143,900 - Financing: No.

ERIK'S DELICAFE FRANCHISES INC.
365 Coral St., Santa Cruz, CA, 95060. Contact: Pam Gruen, Franc. Dir. - Tel: (408) 458-1818. Limited service restaurant. Soups, salads & sandwiches. Western theme oriented setting. (No preservatives).

Established: 1973 - Franchising Since: 1986 - No. of Units: Company Owned: 10 - Franchised: 13 - Franchise Fee - $20,000 - Royalty: 5% - Total Inv: $126,000 - $157,000 - Financing: No.

FAJITA WILLIE'S CAFE & CANTINA
Frijoles Restaurants, Inc.
14960 Northwest Freeway, Houston, TX, 77040. Contact: John Barnes, Pres. - Tel: (713) 466-5925. Fajita Willie's operates and controls a comprehensive restaurant system for the retailing of a menu of uniform and quality food products in a fast, efficient, clean and comfortable atmosphere. Established: 1985 - Franchising Since: 1987 - No. of Units: Company Owned: 1 - Franchised: 1 - Franchise Fee: $25,000 - Royalty: 4% - Total Inv: $300,000 - $350,000 - Financing: None.

FAMILY RESTAURANTS
2450 White Rd., P.O. Box 19609, Irvine, CA, 92714. Contact: M. Casey, Pres. - Tel: (714) 863-6400. Dinnerhouse. Established: 1954 - No. of Units: Company Owned: 183 - Franchised: 4.

FAMILY STEAK HOUSES OF FLORIDA
2113 Florida Blvd., Neptune Beach, FL, 32266. Contact: Lewis Christman, Pres./CEO - Tel: (904) 249-4197. Family restaurant. Established: 1982 - No. of Units: Franchised: 25.

FAMOUS DILL BURGER, THE
Famous Dill Burger, Inc., The
3535 First Ave., S. E., Cedar Rapids, Iowa, 52402. Contact: Terry Hanson, Pres. - Tel: (319) 364-7029. Quality homestyle fast food made from scratch. Established: 1984 - Franchising Since: 1989 - No. of Units: - Franchised: 1 - Franchise Fee: $16,000 - Total Inv: $60,000 - $150,000.

FARO'S PIZZA *
Faro's Franchise Systems
2153 Wealthy St., #321, Grand Rapids, MI, 49506. Contact: Sharon White, V.P. - Tel: (616) 451-9288, Fax: (616) 451-9395. We franchise pizza stores. Established: 1992 - Franchising Since: 1993 - No. of Units: Franchised: 9 - Franchise Fee: $10,000 - Royalty: 4%, 3% ad fund - Total Inv: $91,000 - $134,500 - Financing: Not provided by company.

FAT BOYS BAR-B-Q
Fat Boys' Bar-B-Q Franchise Systems, Inc.
1550 W. King St., Cocoa, FL, 32926. Contact: Glenn Summers, Pres., C.E.O. - Tel: (407) 636-1000. A family restaurant specializing in wood-cooked barbeque beef, pork, chicken, and ribs. Steaks and seafood are also available. Image unit seats 167 with banquet room option, serving breakfast, lunch and dinner seven days a week. Franchisor provides training program of 400 hours conducted at corp headquarters and in several operational units and assist in operation of restaurant. Established: 1958 - Franchising Since: 1968 - No. of Units: Franchised: 22 - Franchise Fee: $35,000 - Royalty: 4%, 1% adv. - Total Inv: $750,000 for build., land, and equip.

FATBURGER
Fatburger North America, Inc.
1218 3rd Street Promenade, Santa Monica, CA, 90401. Contact: Glen Hutloff, C.O.O. - Tel: (310) 319-1850, Fax: (310) 319-1863. Quick service restaurant. Established: 1952 - Franchising Since: 1990 - No. of Units: Company Owned: 13 - Franchised: 12 - Franchise Fee: $30,000 - Royalty: 5%, 3% adv. - Total Inv: $225,000 to $585,000 - Financing: No.

FIGARO'S FRESH-TO-BAKE-PIZZA
Figaro's Italian Pizza Inc.
P.O. Box 12575, Salem, OR, 97309-0575. Contact: Ken Robertson, Pres. - Tel: (503) 371-9318. Prepare fresh pizza in stores for the consumer to take home and bake. Established: 1981 - Franchising Since: 1986 - No. of Units: Company Owned: 2 - Franchised: 40 - Franchise Fee: $18,500 - Royalty: 5%, 1% adv. - Total Inv: $90,000 - $110,000 - Financing: Yes, depending on area.

FIREGRILL *
America's Steak Experts, Inc.
1401 17th St., Ste. 800, Denver, CO, 80202-1246. Contact: James Bishop, V.P. Fran. Dev. - Tel: (303) 293-0200, (303) 293-0299. The Firegrill restaurant is a casual dining steakhouse, accenting the innovative and delicious food is the unique Southwestern 'Dine Under The Stars'

decor. Established: 1992 - Franchising since: 1993 - No. of Units: Franchised: 3 - Franchise Fee: $25,000 - royalty: 4%, 1.5% adv. - Total Inv: $801,500 - $1,057,000 with ground lease - Financing: No.

FIREHOUSE SUBS *
10131-9 San Jose Blvd., Jacksonville, FL, 32257. Contact: Robin Sorensen, Pres. - Tel: (904) 886-2179. Firehouse Subs is a quality sub shop offering the finest in sub sandwiches. It takes advantage of popular sentiment for firemen by placing fire fighting artifacts throughout the restaurant. Established: 1994 - Franchising Since: 1995 - No. of Units: Company Owned: 2 - Franchised: 2 - Franchise Fee: $10,000 - Royalty: 4%, 0-3% mktg. - Total Inv: $50,000: fran. fee plus $40,000 for FF&E - Financing: No.

FLAMERS CHARBROILED HAMBURGERS
Flamers Corporation
8761 Perimeter Park Blvd., #201, Jacksonville, FL, 32216-6398. Contact: Farzin Darabi, Pres. - Tel: (904) 641-7171. Fresh gourmet quality charbroiled hamburgers and chicken. Established: 1987 - Franchising Since: 1988 - Franchise Fee: $25,000 - Royalty: 5% of net sales - Total Inv: $175,000.

FLUKY'S
1768 W. Devon Ave., Chicago, IL, 60660. Contact: Jack Drexler - Tel: (312) 761-1101. Top quality hot dog establishment. Established: 1928 - Franchising Since: 1980 - No. of Units: Company Owned: 3 - Franchised: 2 - Franchise Fee: $25,000 - Royalty: 5% - Total Inv: $324,500 incl. leasehold improvements - Financing: No.

FMS MANAGEMENT SYSTEMS, INC.
2655 N.E. 189th St., North Miami Beach, FL, 33180. Contact: Carlos Diaz, V.P. Finance and Admin. - Tel: (305) 931-5454. International House of Pancakes franchising in the state of Florida. Established: 1963 - Franchising Since: 1963 - No. of Units: Company Owned: 50 - Franchised: 40 - Franchise Fee: varies upon location - Royalty: varies upon location - Total Inv: varies upon location - Financing: assistance.

FONTANO'S SUBS *
Fontano's Subs Franchise System Inc.
1058 W. Polk St., Chicago, IL, 60607. Contact: Fontano Family, Owners - Tel: (312) 421-4474. Deli/sub sandwiches. Family style store. Established: 1935 - Franchising Since: 1995 - No. of Units: Company Owned; 2 - Franchised: 3 - Franchise Fee: $12,500 stores 1 to 5, $15,000 stores 6 to 10 - Royalty: 5%, 2% adv. - Total Inv: $90,000 to $150,000 - Financing: No.

FOODEE'S PIZZA *
Foodee's Inc.
100 Memorial St., Franklin, NH, 03235. Contact: Tom Gagnon, Franchise Licensing - Tel: (603) 934-2928, Fax: (603) 934-3017. International and specialty pizzas, using old bread recipes for crusts and international pastas. Winner "Best Pizza In New England" by WBZ Radio Boston, MA. Established: 1985 - Franchising Since: 1987 - No. of Units: Franchised: 12 - Franchise Fee: $15,000 full size store, $6,000 Foodee's Jr. - Royalty: 5% for full size, 5%-6% depending on sales for Foodee's Jr. - Total Inv: Full Size: $173,400 to $460,500 - Foodee's Jr.: $56,500 to $120,250 - Financing: None.

FOSTERS FREEZE/FOSTERS FREEZE JR.
Fosters Freeze International, Inc.
3701 S. Higuera St., Ste. 102, San Luis Obispo, CA, 93401-7452. Contact: Dennis Poletti, Dir. Fran. Lic. - Tel: (805) 781-6100. Fosters Freeze Int'l is the franchisor of Fosters Freeze. Fast food chain offers a full fountain with limited menu and designed to go into strip shopping centers, and some free standing, smaller drive-thru restaurant models. Established: 1946 - Franchising Since: 1946 - No. of Units: Company Owned: 1 - Franchised: 163 - Franchise Fee: $40,000 Fosters Freeze - $25,000 Fosters Freeze Jr. - Royalty: 4% gross sales - Total Inv: approx. $160,000 - Financing: Assistance in the location of financing available through corp. office.

FOUR STAR PIZZA
P.O. Box W, Claysville, PA, 15323. Contact: Ed Cotton, Dir., Fran. - Tel: (800) 628-3398, Fax: (412) 484-9235. Free home delivery of fresh made (nothing is frozen!) pizza, subs and other products. Focus is on product & profit! Established: 1981 - Franchising Since: 1985 - No. of Units: Company Owned: 7 - Franchised: 30 - Franchise Fee: $9,000 - Royalty: 5% total - Total Inv: $60,000.

FOX'S PIZZA DEN
3243 Old Frankstown Rd., Pittsburgh, PA, 15239. Contact: James Fox - Tel: (412) 733-7888. Pizza restaurants. Established: 1971 - Franchising Since: 1974 - No. of Units: Franchised: 140 - Franchise Fee: $8,000 - Royalty: $200 monthly - Total Inv: $50,000 - Financing: No.

FRANK & STEIN DOGS & DRAFTS
Caldwell Enterprises, Inc.
1630 Braeborn Dr., Ste. A, Salem, VA, 24153. Contact: C. Gregory Caldwell, Pres. - Tel: (540) 389-8435. Fast food restaurant; selling gourmet style hot dogs and sausages as well as full menu options selling hamburgers and other items, featuring draft beer through on-counter brass beer towers. Units in major retail shopping centers and airport food courts. Established: 1985 - Franchising Since: 1986 - No. of Units: Company Owned: 3 - Franchised: 32 - Franchise Fee: $20,000 - Royalty: 4% of sales, 1% adv. - Total Inv: $20,000 fee, $50,000 equip., $90,000 constr. - Financing: Equip. leasing pkgs.

FRANKFURTER RESTAURANTS, THE
Frankfurter USA, Inc., The
226 S. Orcas St., Seattle, WA, 98108. Contact: Stan Moffett, V.P. - Tel: (206) 763-9669. Retail specialty food service. Featuring uniquely seasoned old world sausages on a french roll, fresh squeezed lemonade and fresh baked cookies. Franchising Since: 1990 - No. of Units: Company Owned: 12 - Franchise Fee: $15,000 - Royalty: 5% sales - Financing: No.

FRANKIE'S FAMILY RESTAURANTS
643 Lakewood Rd., Waterbury, CT, 06704. Contact: Frank Caiazzo, Pres. - Tel: (203) 756-2935. Fast food restaurants. Established: 1938 - Franchising Since: 1978 - No. of Units: Company Owned: 3 - Franchised: 4 - Franchise Fee: $23,500 - Royalty: 3% - Total Inv: fee plus $60,000 for equip. - Financing: No.

FRIDAY'S FRONT ROW SPORTS GRILL *
7540 LBJ Fwy., Ste. 100, Dallas, TX, 75251. Contact: Wallace Doolin, Pres. & CEO - Tel: (214) 450-5775. Casual theme, full service restaurants. Initial Fee: $150,000 - Royalty: 4% gross food plus 5% non-food sales - Adv./Mktg. Fee: Capped at 4% gross sales - Outside U.S. - Franchise Fee: $150,000 - Consulting Fee: $250,000 - Royalty Fee: 4% gross sales plus 5% merchandise sales.

FRONT PAGE CAFE
Front Page, Inc.
1101 S. Caraway, Jonesboro, AR, 72401. , Fran. Dir. - Tel: (901) 867-0600. A cafe-style restaurant that would appeal to all ages. Established: 1989 - No. of Units: Company Owned: 1 - Franchise Fee: $20,000 - Royalty: 5% - Total Inv: $57,400 - $184,000 (Work. Cap., Equip., Inven., Lease, Leasehold Impro., Uniforms). For further information please contact: Consultants America Corp., 12279 US Highway 64. Eads, TN, 38028, Tel: (901) 867-0600, Fax: (901) 867-0010.

FRULLATI CAFE *
Frullati Franchise Systems, Inc.
5720 LBJ Fwy., Ste. 370, Dallas, TX, 75240. Contact: Benjamin C. Litalien, Pres. - Tel: (800) 289-8291. Experience a fresh break from the ordinary...food court locations in shopping malls featuring a healthful, lite-fare menu of salads, sandwiches, soups, fresh baked goods and our signature line of "fruit smoothies". Established: 1985 - Franchising Since: 1994 - No. of Units: Company Owned: 15 - Franchised: 8 - Franchise Fee: $20,000 - Royalty: 6% - Total Inv: $150,000 - $250,000 - Financing: No.

FUDDRUCKERS
One Corporate Pl., 55 Ferncroft Rd., Danvers, MA, 01923. Contact: Bill Freeman - Tel: (508) 774-9115. Upscale hamburger casual family restaurant featuring 1/2 and 1/3 lb. burgers, chicken, fish and hot dog sandwiches and salads. On premise butcher shop & bakery to insure freshness. Full produce bar to do your own thing. Established: 1980 - Franchising Since: 1983 - No. of Units: Company Owned: 63 - Franchised: 77 - Franchise Fee: $50,000 - Royalty: 5% mthly. sales - Financing: No.

FUN TIME PIZZA - WORLD OF ENTERTAINMENT *
Funtime International
4809 Cole Ave., Ste. #330, Dallas, TX, 75205. Contact: Jeana Clary, VP-Franchise Dev. - Tel: (214) 740-0000, Fax: (214) 740-0011. Most spectacular family entertainment center ever built. Great pizza, unbelievable games, plus a fully capable international staff to assist you in growing your business. Established: 1987 - Franchising since: 1992 - No. of Units: Company Owned: 2- Franchised: 42 - Franchise Fee: Single store $30,000/Master License $300,000 avg. - Royalty: 4%-6% depending on no. of units - Total Inv: $800,000 - $1.6 million USD based on store size - Financing: Partial financing on equip. pack. available based on credit.

GALLUCCI'S PIZZERIA, INC.
Gallucci's International, Inc.
2845 N.W. Hwy 101, Lincoln City, OR, 97367. Contact: Sharon Gallucci Wright, CEO - Tel: (503) 994-3411. Pizzeria that seats 230 people. Beer, wine, 30 item salad bar, frozen yogurt, chicken & JoJo potatoes, chicken strips, 6 sizes of pizza, soup, sandwiches, nachos. Birthday party packages. Three giant screen TV's. Established: 1974 - Franchising Since: 1989 - No. of Units: Company Owned: 1 - Franchised - 1 - Franchise Fee: $25,000 - Royalty: 5% (to franchise co. from gross) + 1% advertising/mktg. - Total Inv: $100,350 - $175,000 depending on size of operation - Financing: No.

GEPPETTO'S PIZZA & RIBS
3314 Warren Rd., Cleveland, OH, 44111. Contact: Michael O'Malley, Pres. - Tel: (216) 941-1120. Delivery or take-out of pizza & ribs. Established: 1979 - Franchising Since: 1986 - No. of Units: Company Owned: 2 - Franchised: 1 - Franchise Fee: $15,000 - Royalty: 5% + 1% adv. - Total Inv: $110,000 - Financing: No.

GIFF'S SUB SHOP
Giff's Sub Shop Franchise System Inc.
634 Eglin Pky. N.E., Ft. Walton Beach, FL, 32547. Contact: Rick Arnette, Dir. of Oper. - Tel: (904) 863-9011. Submarine sandwiches, specializing in steak subs. Each sub is custom made. Established: 1977 - Franchising Since: 1985 - No. of Units: Company Owned: 1 - Franchised: 6 - Franchise Fee: $10,500 - Royalty: 4%, 2% adv. - Total Inv: $25,000 - $30,000 depending on renovation required - Financing: None.

GIOVANNI'S PIZZA *
Giovanni's Pizza Inc.
715 Greenup Ave., Ashland, KY, 41101. Contact: Dave Grant - Tel: (800) 955-9055, (606) 325-9743. Pickup, delivery & full service pizza restaurants serving pizza, pasta, salads & sandwiches. Locations: OH, KY, WV, VA, NC, TN. Established: 1964 - Franchising Since: 1969 - No. of Units: Franchised: 100 - Franchise Fee: $3,000 - Royalty: 3% - Total Inv: Equip. $30,000 to $60,000 - Financing: No.

GODFATHER'S PIZZA
Godfather's Pizza, Inc.
9140 W. Dodge Rd., #300, Omaha, NE, 68114. Contact: Bruce N. Cannon, V.P. of Fran., R.E. & Constr. - Tel: (402) 391-1452. Pizza restaurant chain featuring dine-in, carry-out and delivery. Established: 1973 - Franchising Since: 1974 - No. of Units: Company Owned: 148 - Franchised: 376 - Franchise Fee: $7,500 - $15,000 - Royalty: 3% service + 2% royalty - Total Inv: $72,000 - $291,000 - Financing: No.

GOLD COAST DOGS *
Gold Coast Dogs Franchise Systems, Inc.
401 N. Michigan Ave., 26th Fl., Chicago, IL, 60611. Contact: Paul or Barry, Co-Owners - Tel: (312) 836-1896. Upscale fast food. The most popular hot dog restaurant in Chicago, written up numerous times and have won several awards. Established: 1985 - Franchising Since: 1994 - No. of Units: Company Owned: 7 - Franchised: 2 - Franchise Fee: $17,500 - Royalty: 4.5% - Total Inv: $150,000 to $200,000 - Financing: No.

GOLD STAR CHILI
Gold Star Chili, Inc.
5204 Beechmont Ave., Cincinnati, OH, 45230. Contact: Raymond P. Peterson, V.P./Fran. Dir. - Tel: (513) 231-4541. Chili and hot dogs. Established: 1965 - Franchising Since: 1965 - No. of Units: Company Owned: 9 - Franchised: 91 - Franchise Fee: $10,000 - Royalty: N/A - Total Inv: $120,000 - $175,000 - Financing: None.

GOLDEN CHICKEN FRANCHISES
3810 West National Ave., Milwaukee, WI, 53215. Contact: Marliss Bloom, Pres. - Tel: (414) 384-3160. Fast food specializing in chicken, pizza and seafood. Both carryout and home delivery. Established: 1959 - No. of Units: Company Owned: 6 - Franchised: 6 - Franchise Fee: varies - Total Inv: $30,000 - Financing: No.

GOLDEN CORRAL FAMILY STEAKHOUSE
Golden Corral Corp.
5151 Glenwood Ave., Raleigh, NC, 27612. Contact: Peter J. Charland, V.P. Fran. Dev. - Tel: (919) 881-4647. Family style steak house featuring steaks, chicken & seafood entrees, golden choice buffet (salad bar & hot items) in-store bakery, dessert bar. Established: 1973 - Franchising Since: 1986 - No. of Units: Company Owned: 375 - Franchised: 106 - Franchise Fee: $40,000 - Royalty: 4% gross sales mtly. - Total Inv: $1,800,000 - $2,300,000 ($500,000 equip., balance land & bldg.) - Financing: No.

GOLDEN FRIED CHICKEN
Golden Franchising Corporation
11488 Luna Rd., Dallas, TX, 75234. Contact: Victor F. Erwin, Exec. V.P. - Tel: (214) 831-0911, Fax: (214) 831-0401. Fast food chicken retail. Established: 1967 - Franchising Since: 1972 - No. of Units: Company Owned: 6 - Franchised: 99 - Franchise Fee: $10,000 - Royalty: 4%, .5% adv. - Financing: No direct financial assistance but guidance to potential sources available.

GOLDIE'S PATIO GRILL
8332 E. 73rd. St. S., Tulsa, OK, 74133. Contact: Richard Harkey, Fran. Dir. - Tel: (918) 254-8100. Charbroiled 1/3 and 2/3 pound burgers cooked to order, seasoned with secret spices. Full waitress service, casual patio theme. Established: 1962 - Franchising Since: 1985 - No. of Units: Company Owned: 7- Franchised: 10 - Franchise Fee: $15,000 - Royalty: 4% - Total Inv: $100,000+ - Financing: No.

GRANDY'S, INC.
997 Grandy's Lane, Lewisville, TX, 75067. Contact: Brian Hunt, Fran. Dir. - Tel: (214) 317-8025. Chain of restaurants positioned at the quality end of fast food. It serves three full meal segments consisting of a full country breakfast; lunch and dinner centers around fried chicken, grilled chicken sandwiches with a variety of vegetables, salads and fresh baked products. Established: 1973 - Franchising Since: 1977 - No. of Units: Company Owned: 112 - Franchised: 52 - Franchise Fee: $30,000 - Royalty: 4%, .8% adv.- Total Inv: $850,000 - $1,700,000.

GRANNY FEEL GOOD'S NATURAL FOOD
111 N.W. 1st St., Miami, FL, 33128. Contact: Irving Fields, Pres. - Tel: (305) 358-6233. Restaurant featuring natural food products. Established: 1969 - Franchising Since: 1984 - No. of Units: Company Owned: 3 - Franchised: 1 - Franchise Fee: $10,000 - Royalty: 5% gross - Total Inv: $150,000 - Financing: No.

GREAT AMERICAN BAGEL, THE *
The Great American Bagel, Inc.,
519 N. Cass Ave., Westmont, IL, 60559. Contact: Pat Ross, Dir. Fran. - Tel: (708) 963-3393, Fax: (708) 963-7799. Bagel bakery/deli offering 20 varieties of bagels, baked fresh from scratch on premises, 19 different homemade cream cheese spreads, made to order deli sandwiches & more. Established: 1987 - Franchising Since: 1994 - No. of Units: Company Owned: 12- Franchised: 13 - Franchise Fee: $20,000 - Royalty: 4% of gross sales- Total Inv: $183,500 - $280,500.

GREAT OUTDOOR SUB SHOPS, INC.
6306-B Greenville Ave., Dallas, TX, 75206. Contact: Gail Voelcker, Pres. - Tel: (214) 373-8259. Top of the line deli/sub shop, serving subs, salads, ice cream in a refreshing atmosphere. Bread baked daily on site. Established: 1973 - Franchising Since: 1994 - No. of Units: Company Owned: 9 - Franchise Fee: $25,000 - Royalty: 4%, 3% adv. - Total Inv:

approx. $175,000 (fran. fee, $80,000 construction, $5,000 signage, menus, $40,000 equip., $8,000 inven., $10,000 furn./fix., $7,000 operating cap., opening labor) - Financing: SBA.

GREAT STEAK & FRY CO., THE
Nicar Franchising, Inc.
222 High St., Ste. 300, Hamilton, OH, 45011. Contact: Nick Lanni, Pres. - Tel: (513) 896-9695. Up-scale, quick food concept located in regional shopping malls and mixed-use projects. Established: 1980 - Franchising Since: 1984 - No. of Units: Company Owned: 18 - Franchised: 96 - Franchise Fee: $20,000 - Royalty: 5% of net sales - Total Inv: $150,000 - $180,000 - Financing: No.

GREAT WRAPS!
158 Oak St., Avondale Estates, GA, 30002. Contact: Michael Philips, Dir. of Fran. Dev. - Tel: (404) 299-5081. Fast food Mediterranean concept. Pita bread sandwiches wrapped around grilled chicken, beef and vegetable combinations. Also offering salads, fries and soft drinks. Established: 1974 - Franchising Since: 1981 - No. of Units: Company Owned: 3 - Franchised: 51 - Franchise Fee: $25,000 - Royalty: 5%, 2% adv. - Total Inv: $225,000 turn key - Financing: Thru 3rd party.

GREEK'S PIZZERIA
1600 University Ave., Muncie, IN, 47303. Contact: Chris Karamesines, Planning & Dev. - Tel: (317) 284-5655 or (800) 453-6786. Casual dining with the availability of a new 'Patent Pending' amusement concept. Carry-out & free delivery is avail. Specialties are New York style & Chicago deep dish pizzas, calzones, pastas, gyros, subs, and imported & domestic beers & wines. Established: 1969 - Franchising Since: 1978 - No. of Units: Company Owned: 34 - Franchised: 20 - Franchise Fee: $16,500 - Royalty: 7% wkly. sales - Total Inv: Limited dining $88,500, full dining $258,000 - Financing: Consultation offered, bank, lease sources & financing on 2nd units avail. to qualified applicants.

GRINDERS AND SUCH RESTAURANTS
Grinders & Such, Inc.
805 E. Lincolnway, Minerva, OH, 44657-1211. Contact: Dennis Hosterman, V.P. Operations - Tel: (216) 868-6100. Full service family restaurant featuring gourmet sandwiches, homemade soups and desserts in a casual dining theme designed by Morris Nathanson Group. Established: 1978 - Franchising Since: 1982 in Ohio only - No. of Units: Company Owned: 2 - Franchised: 2 - Franchise Fee: $25,000 - Royalty: 4% + 1% adv. - Total Inv: $400,000 + land & bldg. - Financing: No.

GROUND ROUND RESTAURANTS
Ground Round Inc., The
P.O. Box 9078, Braintree, MA, 02184-9078. Contact: Ed Daly, Dir. of Fran. Dev. - Tel: (617) 380-3116. Full service family restaurant, casual theme, variety of menu offerings, sandwiches, seafood, appetizers, steaks, ribs, chicken, burgers. Alcoholic beverages available. Established: 1969 - Franchising Since: 1970 - No. of Units: Company Owned: 155 - Franchised: 47 - Franchise Fee: $40,000 - Royalty: 3%, 2% mktg. - Total Inv: Conversions $300,000 - $600,000; Ground Up $1,300,000 - Financing: No. Through referral - outside source.

H.M.S. BROWN BAGGERS
H.M.S. Franchising, Inc.
1228 P, Lincoln, NE, 68508. Contact: Franchise Consortium - Tel: (800) 301-9504. Sandwich retail shop, bakery and delivery; specializing in homemade bread. Established: 1988 - Franchising Since: 1992 - No. of Units: Company Owned: 3 - Franchised: 1 - Franchise Fee: $20,000 - Total Inv: $69,375 - $125,000 - Financing: Will provide assistance in locating financing.

HAPPI HOUSE
Happi House Franchising Corp.
2901 Moorepark Ave., #255, San Jose, CA, 95128. Contact: Carlo Besio, Pres. - Tel: (408) 244-0665. Japanese fast food. Established: 1975 - Franchising Since: 1990 - No. of Units: Company Owned: 6 - Franchise Fee: $25,000 - Royalty: 4% 1st yr., 5% every other yr. - Total Inv: $192,000 - $235,000 incl. franc. fee - Financing: No.

HAPPY CHEF SYSTEMS, INC.
500 S. Front St., Ste. 103, P.O. Box 3328, Mankato, MN, 56002-3328. Contact: Thomas Frederick, Pres. - Tel: (507) 345-4571. Family Restaurant. Established: 1963 - No. of Units: Company Owned: 48 - Franchised: 6.

HAPPY JOE'S PIZZA & ICE CREAM PARLORS, INC.
2705 Commerce Dr., Bettendorf, IA, 52722. Contact: Larry Whitty, Fran. Mktg. Dir. - Tel: (319) 332-8811. Pizza and ice cream in family atmosphere. Large or small communities. Advertising materials available. Single delivery unit also available. Established: 1972 - Franchising Since: 1973- No. of Units: Company Owned: 18 - Franchised: 65 - Franchise Fee: $10,000 - Royalty: 6% - Total Inv: $150,000 - Financing: No.

HAPPY STEAK, THE
Dynaco, Inc.
2246 E. Date Ave., Fresno, CA, 93706. Contact: Orlando Bathauer, Fran. Dir. - Tel: (209) 485-8520. Low budget family steak house. Established: 1969 - Franchising Since: 1970 - No. of Units: Company Owned: 3 - Franchised: 32 - Franchise Fee: $35,000 - Royalty: 4% + 1% admin. fee - Total Inv: $300,000 - Financing: Depends.

HARDEE'S FOOD SYSTEMS, INC.
1233 Hardee's Blvd., Rocky Mount, NC, 27804. Contact: Debbie Arrington, Dir. Corp. Dev. - Tel: (919) 977-2000. Hardee's is America's third largest fast food hamburger chain, with about 4000 restaurants. Established: 1960 - Franchising Since: 1961 - No. of Units: Company Owned: 892 - Franchised: 2359 - Franchise Fee: $15,000 - Royalty: 3.5% yrs 1-5, 4% yrs 6-20 - Total Inv: $699,000 - $1,740,000 - Financing: Hardee's will assist in securing financing.

HARTZ KRISPY CHICKEN
Hartzog, Inc.
14441 Cornerstone Village Dr., Ste. 200, Houston, TX, 77014. Contact: George N. Samaras, Pres./CEO - Tel: (713) 583-0020. Retail fast food chicken restaurant. Established: 1972 - Franchising Since: 1975 - No. of Units: Company Owned: 10 - Franchised: 36 - Royalty: 4% + 2% adv. fee - Approx. Inv: $425,000 per store.

HEID'S OF LIVERPOOL
Heid's Development Co.
P.O. Box 711, 130 Atlanta Ave., Cohasset, MA, 02025. Contact: Ron Blain, Pres. - Tel: (617) 383-6383. Quick serve limited menu consisting of a 100 year old recipe frank (hot dog), coney sausage, Philly cheese-steak sandwichs, ice cream & beverages. Established: 1917 - Franchising Since: 1993 - No. of Units: Franchised: 6 - Franchise Fee: $25,000 (20 year agreement) - Royalty: 5%, 2% adv. - Total Inv: $150,000 - $350,000 complete.

HENNING'S FISH HOUSE
Henning's Fish House Ltd.
1885 Allison Park Dr. PO Box 632, Richland Center, WI, 53581. Contact: Gary Henning, Pres. - Tel: (608) 647-6557. Family restaurant, carry-out or dine-in, seafood, steak and ribs. Established: 1973 - Franchising Since: 1990 - No. of Units: Company Owned: 2 - Franchise Fee: $7,500 - Royalty: 5% - Total Inv: $57,500: $50,000 equip. & $7,500 fran. fee - Financing: No.

HONEY DEW DONUTS
Honey Dew Associates
2 Taunton St., Plainville, MA, 02762. Contact: Richard Bowen, Pres. - Tel: (508) 699-4426. Family Restaurant. Established: 1973 - No. of Units: Company Owned: 2 - Franchised: 28.

HOOTERS OF AMERICA, INC.
1815 T Exchange, Atlanta, GA, 30339. Contact: Kay Sassi, Fran. Sales Mgr. - Tel: (404) 951-2040. Casual, full-service dining. Limited menu featuring chicken wings, seafood, hamburgers & sandwiches. Beer & wine. Established: 1983 - Franchising Since: 1988 - No. of Units: Company Owned: 30 - Franchised: 78 - Franchise Fee: $75,000 - Royalty: 6% gross sales, 1% nat'l adv. - Total Inv: ($2.5 million available capital) $500,000 approx. cost per unit - Financing: No.

HOT DOG CHARLIE ENTERPRISES
626 2nd Ave., Troy, NY, 12182. Contact: John Fentekes, Pres. - Tel: (518) 235-2485. Specialize in mini hot dogs, fish fries on hot dog roll and Italian sausage torpedo. Established: 1922 - Franchising Since: 1987 - No. of Units: Company Owned: 4 - Franchised: 1 - Franchise Fee: $20,000 - Royalty: 5% - Total Inv: $100,000 - $200,000 - Financing: No.

HOT STUFF PIZZA, SMASH HIT SUBS, CINNAMON STREET BAKERY *
Orion Food Systems
2930 W. Maple, P.O. Box 780, Sioux Falls, SD, 57101. Contact: Tom Kaspar, V.P., Fran. Dev. - Tel: (605) 336-6961, Fax: (605) 336-0141. Franchised branded fast food developed specifically for the convenience store & other non-traditional fast food outlets. Established: 1982 - Franchising Since: 1994 - No. of Units: Company Owned: 7 - Franchised: 408 - Licensed: 524 - Franchise Fee: None - Royalty: None, product based franchise vs. business format - Total Inv: Approx. $25,000 per concept.

HOULIHAN'S *
Houlihan's Restaurant Group
2 Brush Creek Blvd., Kansas City, MO, 64112. Contact: Andrew Gunkler, V.P., Fran. - Tel: (800) 753-3675, (816) 756-2200. Houlihan's is the one casual dining restaurant and bar with a varied menu catering to adults. Established: 1972 - Franchising Since: 1994 - No. of Units: Company Owned: 95 - Franchised: 3 - Franchise Fee: $40,000 - Royalty: 4% gross revenues monthly, 1% local adv., 0.5% production, up to 3% promotions - Total Inv: $1,400,000 to $2,000,000 - Financing: Yes, using third party vendors.

HOWARD JOHNSON'S RESTAURANTS
Franchise Associates Inc.
541 Main St., Ste. 320, So. Weymouth, MA, 02190-1845. Contact: Arthur Barrett, Pres. - Tel: (617) 337-7940, Fax: (617) 337-1777. National restaurants with expanded menus ranging from snack items to full course dinners popularly priced. Take-out service is also available. Most locations serve alcoholic beverages and many have salad bars. Restaurants are usually open 24 hours, or 18 hours a day at least. Established: 1986 - Franchising Since: 1986 - No. of Units: Company Owned: 22 - Franchised: 80 - Franchise Fee: $10,000 - Royalty: 2% gross food and beverage.

HUBB'S
Hubb's Development, Inc.
1535 N. Cogswell St., #A-3, Rockledge, FL, 32955. Contact: Robert Linder, V.P. Corp. Dev. - Tel: (407) 639-5080. Restaurant ("The Home of Colossal Sandwiches") specializing in imported beers from around the world. Each unit has 39 taps for draft beer and over 200 bottled brands. "Hubbs...where you always meet a friend." Established: 1982 - Franchising Since: 1992 - No. of Units: Company Owned: 5 - Franchised: 3 (incl. 1 under const.) - Franchise Fee: $50,000 - Royalty: $500/mo. 1st yr; $750/mo. 2nd yr; $1,000 /mo. 3rd yr and thereafter, $400/mo. adv. - Total Inv: $350,000 - $450,000 - Financing: No.

HUDDLE HOUSE RESTAURANT
Huddle House, Inc.
2969 E. Ponce de Leon Ave., Decatur, GA, 30030. Contact: John McCormack, V.P. Real Estate/ Fran. - Tel: (404) 377-5700, Fax: (404) 377-0497. Restaurant-open 24 hours. Breakfast oriented. Full service with broad based menu. Established: 1964 - Franchising Since: 1964 - No. of Units: Company Owned: 7 - Franchised: 267 - Franchise Fee: $15,000 - Royalty: 4% - Total Inv: $370,000 - $470,000 for total project - Financing: HHI does not provide financing.

HUDSON'S GRILL
Hudson's Grill of America, Inc.
16970 Dallas Pkwy., Ste. 402, Dallas, TX, 75248. Contact: Thomas A. Sacco, Sr. V.P. Oper. & Fran. Dev. - Tel: (214) 931-9237. Casual dining, lunch and dinner full-service restaurants with full bar. Flirt with the 50's decor. Concept focuses on excellent food value, friendly service and commitment to quality. Established: 1985 - Franchising Since: 1990 - No. of Units: Franchised: 17 - Franchise Fee: $25,000 - Royalty: 4% sales, 1% adv. - Total Inv: $125,000 start-up cash, $250,000 total inv. required - Financing: No.

HUNGRY HOWIE'S PIZZA & SUBS, INC.
30300 Stephenson Hwy., Madison Heights, MI, 48071. Contact: Tony Noga, Dir. of Franc. Dev. - Tel: (800) 624-8122 or (810) 414-3300, Fax: (810) 414-3301. Flavored Crust (™) Pizza. Carry-out/delivery. Menu offerings include eight varieties of the original Flavored Crust Pizza, salads and subs. Established: 1973 - Franchising Since: 1982 - No. of Units: Franchised: 300 - Franchise Fee: $9,500 - Royalty: 1st year-3%; 2nd year-4%; 3rd year-5% - Total Inv: $70,000 - $90,000.

HUNTINGTON RESTAURANT
817 Delaware St., Berkeley, CA, 94710-2064. Contact: Charles Thomas, Pres. - Tel: (510) 528-9074. Fast food restaurant. No. of Units: Franchised: 4.

INTERNATIONAL HOUSE OF PANCAKES RESTAURANTS
IHOP, Inc.
525 N. Brand Blvd., 3rd Flr., Glendale, CA, 91203. Contact: Anna Ulvan, V.P. Fran. - Tel: (818) 240-6055. Full service family restaurants featuring breakfast, lunch and dinner. Established: 1958 - Franchising Since: 1960 - No. of Units: Company Owned: 61 - Franchised: 429 - Franchise Fee: $50,000 - $600,000 - Royalty: 4.5% - Total Inv: varies - Financing: No.

INTERNATIONAL POULTRY COMPANY
IPC Franchising Corp.
1133 Madison Ave., New York, NY, 10025. Contact: Greg Steinhauser, Franchise Dir. - Tel: (212) 879-3600, Fax: (212) 879-3921. Quick service restaurant featuring chicken, turkey, other poultry items, award-winning soups, salads and pastas. Eat-in, take-out, catering, and delivery available. Established: 1988 - Franchising Since: 1993 - No. of Units: Company Owned: 1 - Franchised: 3 - Franchise Fee: $25,000 - Royalty: 4.5% royalty & service fee, 5.5% adv. - Total Inv: $250,000 - $350,000 total package based on leased bldg. - Financing: Work with several lending institutions.

IRVINGS FOR RED HOT LOVERS
Irvings Franchise Systems
436 W. Frontage Rd., #2, Northfield, IL, 60043-3076. Contact: Irving Greensphan or Andrew Greensphan, Pres./C.E.O. - Tel: (708) 446-2855. The Hot Dog Store and a Whole Lot More Specialty is hot dogs, charbroiled burgers, chicken sandwiches and our original cheddar fry. Fast service, quality food, & a clean environment has made us the top dog. Established: 1975 - Franchising Since: 1989 - No. of Units: Company Owned: 3 - Franchised: 9 - Franchise Fee: $20,000 - Royalty: 4%, 3% adv. - Total Inv: $160,000, including equip., decor, opening inventory etc. - Financing: Yes-local banks or SBA approved.

ITALIAN EXPRESS FRANCHISE CORP.
1051 Essington Rd., Ste. 270, Joliet, IL, 60435. Contact: Hass Aslami, Pres. - Tel: (815) 729-4494, Fax: (815) 729-4508. Pizza, delivery, carry-out, and dine-in. Offering pan style & thin crust pizza, garlic bread and soft beverages. Established: 1986 - Franchising Since: 1989 - No. of Units: Franchised: 47 - Franchise Fee: $18,500 - Royalty: 5% + 2% adv - Total Inv: $32,000 - $122,000 - Financing: No.

ITALIAN OVEN, THE
Italian Oven, Inc.
11 Lloyd Ave., Latrobe, PA, 15650. Contact: Jeffrey Fields, V.P. Fran. - Tel: (412) 537-5380. Full service, sit-down, family-oriented, neighborhood Italian restaurant. Established: 1989 - Franchising Since: 1990 - No. of Units: Company Owned: 9 - Franchised: 44 - Franchise Fee: $39,500 - Royalty: 4% of gross sales, 3.5% total adv. - Total Inv: Multiple units: $400,000 - $800,000 per store - Financing: None.

ITALIAN PLACE, THE
Gledhill Enterprises
1718 N. University Pkwy., Provo, UT, 84604. Contact: Robert Gledhill, Pres. - Tel: (801) 377-5007. Sandwiches, pizzas. Established: 1971 - No. of Units: Company Owned: 1 - Franchised: 3 - Franchise Fee: $25,000 - $40,000 - Total Inv: $80,000 - $120,000 per unit.

ITALIANNI'S *
7540 LBJ Fwy., Ste. 100, Dallas, TX, 75251. Contact: Wallace Doolin, Pres. & CEO - Tel: (214) 450-5775. Casual theme, full service restaurants. Initial Fee: $50,000 per store - Royalty: 4% gross sales - Adv./Mktg. Fee: Capped at 4% gross sales - Outside U.S.- Franchise Fee: $100,000 - Consulting Fee: $150,000 - Royalty Fee: 4% gross sales.

ITALO'S PIZZA SHOP, INC.
3560 Middlebranch Rd., N.E., Canton, OH, 44705. Contact: Italo Ventura, Pres. - Tel: (216) 455-7443, Fax: (216) 455-7443. Carry-out pizza & Italian dishes(pasta, subs, chicken), delivery optional. Personal service with emphasis on quality and value. Established: 1966 - Franchising Since: 1975 - No. of Units: Company Owned: 3 - Franchised: 10 - Franchise Fee: $12,000 - Royalty: 5% gross - Total Inv: $75,000 to $150,000 - Financing: Franchisee must provide own financing.

IZZY'S PIZZA RESTAURANTS
Covalt Enterprises, Inc.
110 Third Ave., S.E., Albany, OR, 97321. Contact: Bill Arant, Pres. - Tel: (503) 926-8693. Restaurants serving pizza, chicken, sandwiches, hot buffet and salad bar. Established: 1970 - Franchising Since: 1983 - No. of Units: Company Owned: 12 - Franchised 12 - Franchise Fee: $35,000 - Royalty: 4% - Total Inv: $100,000+ - Financing: No.

J.P. LEE'S INTERNATIONAL
7 Broad St., Red Bank, NJ, 07701. Contact: Gerald A. Marks, Officer/Owner - Tel: (908) 747-7100. Oriental stir fry cuisine where the customer is the chef and selects vegetables, meats and sauces to suit his or her own taste preferences. Low fat and calories make J.P. Lee's the inexpensive alternative in the casual dining field. Established: 1990 - Franchising Since: 1990 - No. of Units: Company Owned: 1 - Franchised: 3 - Franchise Fee: $30,000 - Royalty: 6%, 3% adv. - Total Inv: $175,000 - $235,000 - Financing: No.

JACK IN THE BOX
Foodmaker, Inc.
9330 Balboa Ave., San Diego, CA, 92123. Contact: Jerry Prinds, Dir., Fran. Dev. - Tel: (619) 571-2121, Fax: (619) 571-2101. Upscale version of quick service. Established: 1951 - Franchising Since: 1982 - No. of Units: Company Owned: 626 - Franchised: 384 - Franchise Fee: $25,000 - Royalty: 2%(2yrs), 4% thereafter - Total Inv: $574,625 - $801,625, exclusive of land - Financing: Access to Nat'l lenders.

JAKE'S PIZZA
Jake's Pizza International
16 W. Official Rd., Addison, IL, 60101. Contact: James J. Banks, Pres./CEO - Tel: (708) 543-0022. Specialize in the sale of premium thin crust, pan and stuffed pizza. Eat in, pick up and delivery service is provided. Each store is designed with an open display kitchen, open to the customers view. Established: 1961 - Franchising Since: 1965 - No. of Units: Company Owned: 3 - Franchised: 53 - Franchise Fee: $15,000 - Royalty: 5%, 2% adv. - Total Inv: $110,000 - Financing: No.

JANUZZI'S PIZZA & SUBS
Januzzi Franchising Inc.
325 Park View Circle, Wilkes-Barre, PA, 18702. Contact: John Januzzi, Partner - Tel: (717) 823-8857. Pizza delivery chain. Menu includes 10 varieties of subs, hot chicken wings, and five pasta dinners. Salads also available. Eat in, take out or delivery of complete menu. Established: 1973 - Franchising Since: 1976 - No. of Units: Company Owned: 3 - Franchised: 11 - Franchise Fee: $2,500 - Royalty: 6% + 3% adv. - Total Inv: $59,900 - Financing: 40% total inv. required down.

JB'S RESTAURANTS
Summit Family Restaurants, Inc.
440 Lawndale Dr., Salt Lake City, UT, 84115. Contact: George Gehling, Sr. V.P. - Tel: (801) 463-5520, Fax: (801) 463-5585. A leading family restaurant company in 8 western states. Offers a variety of menu selections at breakfast, lunch and dinner centered around all you can eat fresh food buffet. A full range of franchise support services is provided. Established: 1961 - Franchising Since: 1990 - No. of Units: Company Owned: 80 - Franchised: 24 - Franchise Fee: $35,000 - Royalty: 4%, 3.5% adv.

JERRY'S SUBS AND PIZZA
Jerry's Systems, Inc.
15942 Shady Grove Rd., Gaithersburg, MD, 20877. Contact: Larry Feierstein, Dir. Fran. Dev. - Tel: (301) 921-8777. This mid-Atlantic based franchise, famous for overstuffed sub sandwiches and fresh dough pizza, offers self service dining in upscale, high volume, high traffic locations. Established: 1954 - Franchising Since: 1981 - No. of Units: Company Owned: 1 - Franchised: 82 - Franchise Fee: $25,000 - Royalty: 5% + 3% adv. - Total Inv: $150,000 - $225,000 - Financing: Qualifies for SBA financing.

JERSEY MIKE'S SUBMARINES
Jersey Mike's Franchise Systems Inc.
2517 Rt. 35, Bldg. H, Ste. #102, Manasquan, NJ, 08736. Contact: Peter Cancro, Pres. - Tel: (908) 528-7676. Submarine sandwich and salad restaurant serving a large variety of hot and cold subs and salads. Established: 1956 - Franchising Since: 1987 - No. of Units: Company Owned: 5 - Franchised: 24 - Franchise Fee: $14,500 - Royalty: 5% gross + 2.5% adv. - Total Inv: $47,000 - $127,000 - Financing: No.

JIMBOY'S TACOS
1485 Response Rd., #110, Sacramento, CA, 95815. Contact: George Heath, V.P. - Tel: (916) 564-8226 or (800) 248-8226. Mexican food. Established: 1954 - Franchising Since: 1965 - No. of Units: 25 - Franchise Fee: $18,000 - Royalty: 3.5% + 3% adv. - Total Inv: $150,000 - $185,000 - Financing: No.

JIMMY JOHN'S
1500 Executive Dr., Elgin, IL, 60123. Contact: Linda Kelley, Pres. - Tel: (708) 888-7221. Gourmet sandwich shops. Established: 1983 - Franchising Since: 1993 - No. of Units: Company Owned: 11 - Franchised: 9 - Franchise Fee: $25,000 - Royalty: Call for additional information.

JOHNNY APPLESEED RESTAURANTS
537 Warrenton Rd., Fredericksburg, VA, 22405. Contact: Ashton Trice, Fran. Dir. - Tel: (703) 899-3602. Full service family oriented restaurant serving breakfast, lunch and dinner. Established: 1973 - Franchising Since: 1986 - No. of Units: 3 - Franchise Fee: $25,000 - Royalty: 3% 1st yr., 4% thereafter - Total Inv: $600,000 - $1,000,000 - Financing: Yes, on franchise fee.

JOHNNY ROCKETS
1888 Century Park E. Ste. 224, Los Angeles, CA, 90067. Contact: Rober Host, Fran. Dir. - Tel: (310) 556-8811. Hamburger fast food. Established: 1985 - Franchising Since: 1987 - No. of Units: Company Owned: 4 - Franchised: 23 - Royalty: 5% gross - Total Inv: $350,000 - $450,000 - Financing: No.

JON SMITH SUBS
Jon Smith Enterprises, Inc.
3900 Woodlake Blvd., Ste. 206, Lake Worth, FL, 33463. - Tel: (407) 964-6113, Fax: (407) 964-9822. A high-quality alternative to the sub shop concept. Prepares all products in own kitchens and specializes in marinated sirloin steak subs. Committed to serving the absolutely highest quality subs. Established: 1988 - Franchising Since: 1992 - No. of Units: Company Owned: 7 - Franchised: 4 - Franchise Fee: $12,000 - Royalty - 6%, 3% reg. adv., 1% local adv. - Total Inv: $89,000 - $128,000 - Financing: Available for purchase of company stores only.

JRECK SUBS, INC.
P.O. Box 6, Watertown, NY, 13601. Contact: Peter Whitmore, Fran. Dir. - Tel: (315) 782-0760. Fast food establishment serving submarine sandwiches and beverages. Established: 1969 - Franchising Since: 1974 - No. of Units: Franchised: 54 - Franchise Fee: $10,000 - Royalty: 5% + 2% adv. - Total Inv: $40,000 - $200,000 - Financing: No.

JUICY LUCY'S DRIVE-THRU
Juicy Lucy's, Inc.
2235 1st St., Suite 206, Ft. Myers, FL, 33901. Contact: Suzanne Grady, Pres. - Tel: (813) 332-0022. Double drive-thru restaurant with emphasis on quality products. Fresh pattied hamburgers, hand cut chicken breasts, pork loins, and BBQ pork prepared from scratch. Breakfast menu consists of various fresh egg sandwiches made to order. Established: 1988 - Franchising Since: 1990 - No. of Units: Company Owned: 6 - Franchised: 7 - Franchise Fee: $25,000 - Royalty: 5% wkly gross - Total Inv: $325,000 - $375,000 plus land - Financing: No.

JULIO'S
Julio's Enterprises
13035 Arbor St., Omaha, NE, 68144. Contact: Jerry Aquila, Fran. Dir. - Tel: (402) 330-1360. Tex/Mex restaurant. Established: 1977 - Franchising Since: 1985 - No. of Units: Company Owned: 3 - Franchised: 5 - Franchise Fee: $15,000 - Royalty: 4% - Total Inv: $225,000 - Financing: No.

K-BOB'S STEAKHOUSES
K-Bob's Capital Resource Group, Ltd.
1601 Randolph SE, Ste. 220, Albuquerque, NM, 87106. Contact: Louis Gray, Dir. of Dev. - Tel: (505) 242-8403, Fax: (505) 764-0492. Steakhouse chain catering to small communities with an emphasis on affordable, yet quality food - "A good steak at an honest price®". Established: 1966 - Franchising Since: 1975 - No. of Units: Company Owned: 6 - Franchised: 35 - Franchise Fee: $25,000 - Royalty: 3% - Total Inv: Land/bldg. - $500,000, equip. $200,000 - Financing: Yes, depends on qualification of franchisee.

KATIE MCGUIRE'S, INC.
17682 Sampson Lane, Huntington Beach, CA, 92647. Contact: Kaye Bass, Pres. - Tel: (714) 852-1249. Fast food. Established: 1983 - No. of Units: Franchised: 20.

KENNY ROGERS ROASTERS *
Roasters Corp.
899 W. Cypress Creek Rd., Ft. Lauderdale, FL, 33309. Contact: Andrew S. Howard, Sr. V.P. of Franchising - Tel: (305) 938-0330. Restaurant. Established: 1991 - Franchising Since: 1991 - No. of Units: Company Owned: 29 - Franchised: 203 - Franchise Fee: $29,500 - Royalty: 4.5% - Total Inv: $347,500 for building, equipment and sign costs; $8,000 opening inven., $10,000 security deposit, $20,000 misc. expenses, $5,000 grand opening, plus fran. fee, legal or accounting costs.

KETTLE RESTAURANTS, INC.
P.O. Box 2964, Houston, TX, 77252. Contact: George Harris, Dir. of Fran. - Tel: (713) 524-3464. Full menu restaurant, open 24 hours daily. Established: 1968 - Franchising Since: 1973 - No. of Units: Company Owned: 93 - Franchised: 93 - Royalty: 5% - Approx Initial Inv: $20,000 - Total Inv: $84,000 - Financing: No.

KFC
KFC Corporation
1441 Gardiner Lane, P.O. Box 32070, Louisville, KY, 40232. Contact: Walter Simon, V.P. Bus. Dev. - Tel: (502) 456-8300 or 456-8904. Quick service restaurants. Established: 1952 - Franchising Since: 1953 - No. of Units: Company Owned: 1250 - Franchised: 5,650 - Franchise Fee: $20,000 - Royalty: 4% - Total Inv: $722,000 - $1,122,000 - Financing: Financial sources avail.

KRUMBLY BURGER INC.
1452 Whispering Creek Dr., Ballwin, MO, 63021. Contact: Jack Baker, Pres. - Tel: (314) 225-2993. Specially designed cooker. 92% fat free burgers. Use existing locations. Investment under $90,000. Complete training. Established: 1987 - Franchising Since: 1987 - No. of Units: Franchised: 2 - Franchise Fee: $10,000 - Royalty: 5% - No royalties first two years - Financing: None.

KRYSTAL COMPANY, THE
One Union Square, Chattanooga, TN, 37402. Contact: Tom Adams, Director - Tel: (615) 757-1577. Full size restaurants and double drive-thru's. Both feature the unique Krystal Burger which is prepared on a grill and topped with steamed onions to give its one of a kind, mouth watering flavor. Established: 1932 - Franchising Since: 1989 - No. of Units: Company Owned: 255 - Franchised: 68 - Franchise Fee: $32,500 - Royalty: 4.5% - Total Inv: $600,000 - $900,000 - Financing: No.

LA CASITA RESTAURANTS
2006 Madison, Memphis, TN, 38104. Contact: Robert Chapman, Pres. - Tel: (901) 726-6221. Full service Mexican restaurant. No. of Units: Company Owned: 2.

LA PIZZA LOCA
Crazy Pizza Inc.
7920 Orangethorpe Ave., Buena Park, CA, 90620. Contact: Tony Tavantzis, V.P. Fran. Dev. - Tel: (714) 670-0934. Hispanic pizza delivery company. Unique Latin flavored pizzas. Fast, free delivery. Targeted to the rapidly growing Hispanic market in the west, southwest, and southeast U.S. Established: 1986 - Franchising Since: 1991 - No. of Units: Company Owned: 32 - Franchised: 25 - Franchise Fee: $20,000 - Royalty: 5% of net total sales - Total Inv: $125,000 - Financing: None.

LA SALSA
La Salsa Holding Co.
11601 Santa Monica Blvd., Los Angeles, CA, 90025. Contact: Larry Sarokin, V.P. Fran. Dev. - Tel: (310) 575-4233, Fax: (310) 575-4940. Fresh Mexican grill QSR's serving tacos al carbon, gourmet burritos & fresh salsas. Established: 1979 - Franchising Since: 1989 - No. of Units: Company Owned: 25 - Franchised: 25 - Franchise Fee: $29,500 per unit - Royalty: 5%, 1% nat'l. mktg. fund - Total Inv: minimum 3 units @ $29,500 + $200,000 build-out per unit - Financing: No.

LA SENORITA MEXICAN RESTAURANTS *
604 S. Garfield Ave., Traverse City, MI, 49686. Contact: Kenneth Kleinrichert, Pres. - Tel: (616) 947-8889, Fax: (616) 947-8137. Mexican food and beverages. Family-style casual dining. Established: 1980 - Franchising Since: 1991 - No. of Units: Company Owned: 4 - Franchised: 4 - Franchise Fee: $20,000 - Royalty: 5% fran. fee, 3% adv. - Total Inv: $526,000 to $843,000 - Financing: Various sources of financing available. Franchisor can assist.

LAMPPOST PIZZA
Lamppost Franchise Corporation
3002 Dow #320, Tustin, CA, 92680. Contact: Tom Barro, Pres. - Tel: (714) 731-6171, Fax: (714) 731-0951. Family restaurant with emphasis on sports include satellite antenna and wide screen t.v.'s. Established: 1976 - Franchising Since: 1981 - No. of Units: Company Owned: 5 -

Franchised: 47 - Franchise Fee: $20,000 - Royalty: 4%, 1.5% adv. - Total Inv: $275,000: fran. fee, equip., fixtures, leasehold improv. - Financing: No.

LAROSA'S PIZZERIAS
2334 Boudinot Ave., Cincinnati, OH, 45238-3417. Contact: Stewart Smetts, Fran. Dir. - Tel: (513) 347-5660. Family style Italian restaurant. Established: 1954 - Franchising Since: 1967 - No. of Units: Company Owned: 4 - Franchised: 40+ - Franchise Fee: $24,000 - Total Inv: $95,000 - $275,000 - Financing: No.

LARRY'S GIANT SUBS®
8616 Baymeadows Rd., Jacksonville, FL, 32256. Contact: Larry Raikes, Pres. - Tel: (904) 739-2498, Fax: (904) 739-2509. Upscale NY style submarine sandwich shop featuring 50 varieties of subs and numerous salads. Easy operation, no experience necessary, non-cooking environment, low royalty, full training in corporate shop, affordable. Established: 1982 - Franchising Since: 1985 - No. of Units: Company Owned: 2 - Franchised: 39 - Franchise Fee: $15,000 - Royalty: 5%, 2% adv. - Total Inv: equip. $35,000, $25,000 to $30,000 improvements - Financing: Phoenix leasing.

LASORDA'S DUGOUT, INC. *
10875 Gulf Blvd., Treasure Island, FL, 33706. Contact: Hal Pippin, V.P. Sales & Mktg. - Tel: (813) 360-6562. Lasorda's Dugout Inc. is America's Healthy Deli™, featuring 97% fat free meats & cheeses, fresh baked bread & bakery goods, bearing the name of Tommy Lasorda - baseball's favorite Ambassador. Established: 1994 - Franchising Since: 1995 - No. of Units: Company Owned: 2 - Franchised: 3 - Franchise Fee: $25,000 - Royalty: 6% - Total Inv: Equip. $25,000, Buildout & Cap. $25,000 - Financing: N/A.

LE PEEP RESTAURANTS, INC.
4 West Dry Creek Circle, Ste.201, Littleton, CO, 80120. Contact: Anthony E. Doyle, Exec. V.P. - Tel: (303) 730-6300. Unique upscale full service specialty restaurant with specialized breakfast/lunch concept that has evolved into the combined breakfast/lunch/dinner operation. We are the result of 20 years of listening to our customers. Established: 1982 - No. of Units: Company Owned: 25 - Licensed: 35 - Total Inv: $100,000 - $300,000 - Financing: No.

LEDO PIZZA *
Ledo Pizza Systems, Inc.
6011 Greenbelt Rd., College Park, MD, 20740. Contact: Kathleen, Office Mgr. - Tel: (301) 474-7551. Franchise pizza & sub shops in MO, DC, VA and PA. 5 stores opened this year. Established: 1989 - Franchising Since: 1989 - No. of Units: Franchised: 35 - Franchise Fee: $20,000 - Royalty: 5%, 1% adv. fund - Total Inv: $60,000 - $275,000 - Financing: No.

LETTUCE LEAF
Retrac Corporation
11 Claycrest Crt., St. Charles, MO, 63304. Contact: Kristine Krekeler or Jerome Carter, Owners - Tel: (314) 928-1451. Food service business with entree salads as well as homemade, high quality soups, dressings, quiches, gourmet sandwiches, bakery items, beverages and other food products prepared according to a unique and confidential recipe and method of production. Facilities have inside seating as well as carry-out capacity. Prices of food range from $4.50 - $6.95 per entree. Established: 1989 - Franchising Since: 1991 - No. of Units: Company Owned: 1 - Franchise Fee: $10,000 - Royalty: 5% gross sales, 2% gross sales for adv. - Total Inv: fran. fee, $20,000 - $100,000 leasehold, $10,000 - $50,000 equip., $10,000 - $50,000 furn. & fix. - Financing: Negotiable.

LINDA'S FLAME ROASTED CHICKEN *
11 Commerce Dr., Cranford, NJ, 07016. Contact: Keith Emerson, V.P. Fran. - Tel: (800) 546-3221, Fax: (908) 276-0552. Flame roasted, open hearth, rotisserie chicken, turkey and fabulous side dishes served to hungry, impatient customers who want "home-made" quality at fast food prices. Established: 1991 - Franchising Since: 1995 - No. of Units: Company Owned: 5 - Franchised: 3 - Franchise Fee: $25,000 - Royalty: 5% of net sales - Total Inv: $250,000 to $468,000 - Financing: 70% financing available through approved lenders.

LITTLE CAESAR'S PIZZA
2211 Woodward Ave., Fox Office Ctr., Detroit, MI, 48201. Contact: John Lafferty, Dir. Fran. Sales - Tel: (313) 983-6000. Pizza carry-out stores, pizza stations, parlors and family restaurants. Established: 1959 - Franchising Since: 1962 - No. of Units: Company Owned: 650 - Franchised: 1,950 - Franchise Fee: $15,000 - Royalty: 5% + 6% adv. - Total Inv: $175,000 - Financing: Yes, approx. $125,000 per store.

LITTLE CHEF ENTERPRISES
1616 S. Saginaw, Midland, MI, 48640. , Pres. - Tel: (517) 631-3660. Family restaurant. Established: 1973 - No. of Units: Franchised: 4.

LITTLE KING INC.
11811 "I" Street, Omaha, NE, 68137. Contact: Syd Wertheim, Pres. - Tel: (402) 330-8019. Submarine/deli style sandwich and pizza optional. Emphasis is on fresh fast food, with products prepared from the freshest ingredients in full view of customer. Bread baked fresh on premises. Established: 1968 - Franchising Since: 1978 - No. of Units: Company Owned: 6 - Franchised: 44 - Franchise Fee: $7,500/$1,500 additional units - Royalty: 6% - Total Inv: $60,000 - $75,000 - Financing: None.

LITTLE KING OF TOPEKA
4308 Pennsylvia Ct., Topeka, KS, 66609. Contact: Leslie Richling, Pres. - Tel: (913) 233-3323. Fast food restaurant. Established: 1980 - No. of Units: Franchised: 3.

LIZIO'S SPAGHETTI VENDORS
Spaghetti Vendors Franchise System Inc.
7601 E. Gray Rd., Scottsdale, AZ, 85260. Contact: Patrick Lizio, Pres. - Tel: (602) 951-1883. A fresh pasta & sauce restaurant with a large selection of salads. Established: 1987 - Franchising Since: 1991 - No. of Units: Company Owned: 1 - Franchised: 5 - Franchise Fee: $17,500 - Royalty: 5% gross sales - Total Inv: $120,000 to $150,000 complete package - Financing: No.

LONG JOHN SILVER'S SEAFOOD SHOPPES
101 Jerrico Dr., Lexington, KY, 40509. Contact: John Ramsey, Dir. Fran. Sales - Tel: (606) 263-6000. Quick service fish and seafood restaurants with a variety of fish, shrimp, chicken and salad meals served in a warm, friendly environment. Established: 1969 - Franchising Since: 1970 - No. of Units: Company Owned: 1,004 - Franchised: 481 - Franchise Fee: $20,000 - Royalty: 4% - Total Inv: $300,000 in liquid assets required for qualification - Financing: No.

LONGBRANCH STEAKHOUSE & SALOON *
105 Deercreek Rd., M-204, Deerfield Beach, FL, 33442. Contact: Bill Manseau, V.P. - Tel: (305) 360-9927. A casual western style family steakhouse restaurant. Established: 1990 - Franchising Since: 1995 - No. of Units: Company Owned: 2 - Franchise Fee: $50,000 - Royalty: 4% of weekly gross sales - Total Inv: $450,000 to $1,200,000 - Financing: 40% of master franchise fee.

MACAYO MEXICAN RESTAURANTS
4001 N. Central, Phoenix, AZ, 85012. Contact: Stephen Johnson, Pres. - Tel: (602) 264-6141. Full service Mexican restaurants with lounges. Established: 1945 - Franchising Since: 1987 - No. of Units: Company Owned: 12 - Franchise Fee: $45,000 - Royalty: 4% - Total Inv: $600,000 - $1,800,000 - Financing: None.

MACRI'S DELI FRANCHISE, INC.
6910 N. Gumwood Rd., Unit 34, Granger, IN, 46530. Contact: Margy Macri, V.P. - Tel: (219) 271-0061. Deals with a variety of deli items such as sandwiches and soups.

MAGIC WOK
N.S. & T.
2060 W. Laskey Rd., Toledo, OH, 43613. Contact: Sutas Pipatjarasqit, Pres. - Tel: (419) 471-0696. Chinese fast food. Established: 1983 - Franchising Since: 1991 - No. of Units: Company Owned: 6 - Franchised: 20 - Franchise Fee: $12,500 - Royalty: 5% - Total Inv: $94,900 - $149,500 - Financing: No.

MAJOR MAGIC'S ALL STAR PIZZA REVUE INC.
Clinton Township, MI, 48035. Contact: Robert Rashid, Pres. - Tel: (810) 792-6933. Pizza entertainment restaurants seating 750 persons and averaging 16,000 sq. ft. with animated robot shows. Established: 1981 -

Franchising Since: 1982 - No. of Units: Company Owned: 6 - Franchised: 1 - Franchise Fee: $25,000 - Royalty: 6.5% - Total Inv: $850,000 - Financing: No.

MAMA LENA'S SPAGHETTI EXPRESS *
Mama Lena's Spaghetti Express, Inc.
5993 Bartlett Ctr., Bartlett, TN, 38134. Contact: Fran. Dir. - Tel: (901) 867-0600. Specialized carry-out and delivery fast food business providing spaghetti and other Italian specialties. Established: 1989 - Franchising Since: 1993 - No. of Units: Company Owned: 3 - Franchise Fee: $15,000 - Royalty: 5% - Total Inv: $47,200 to $84,700.

MAMA ROSA'S PIZZA
177 John Sims Pkwy, Valparaiso, FL, 32580. Contact: Buddy Lewis, Owner - Tel: (904) 897-4949. Fast Food Pizza. Established: 1974 - No. of Units: Company Owned: 2 - Franchised: 6.

MAMMA ILARDO'S PIZZERIA
9505 Reisterstown Rd. #100-N, Owings Mills, MD, 21117. Contact: John A. Filipiak, V.P. Oper. & Dev. - Tel: (410) 356-1405, Fax: (410) 356-9668. By the slice pizzeria; food court, in-line, non traditional locations. Other menu items: sandwiches, calzones, salads, pasta. Established: 1976 - Franchising Since: 1989 - No. of Units: Company Owned: 8 - Franchised: 25 - Franchise Fee: $25,000 - Royalty: 5% mktg. - Total Inv: Up to $220,000 incl. fran. fee, equip., construction, soft costs - Financing: Third party.

MANCHU WOK
S.C. Food Services Inc.
400 Fairway Dr., Unit 106, Deerfield Beach, FL, 33441. Contact: Tom Bryant, Dir. Fran. - Tel: (305) 481-9555, Fax: (305) 481-9670. Largest Oriental quick service restaurant chain in North America operating primarily in shopping mall food courts. Established: 1981 - Franchising Since: 1981 - Number of Units: Company Owned: 146/US, 110/CND - Franchised: 120 - Franchise Fee: $30,000 - Royalty: 6%, 2% adv. - Total Inv: approx. $275,000 - Financing: Yes.

MANHATTAN BAGEL CO.
Manhattan Bagel Co., Inc.
246 Industrial Way W., Eatontown, NJ, 07724. Contact: Daniel Levy, C.F.O. - Tel: (908) 544-0155, Fax: (908) 544-1315. Franchisor of bagel bakery and deli. Established: 1987 - Franchising Since: 1988 - No. of Units: Company Owned: 19 - Franchised: 200 (sold & operating) - Franchise Fee: $30,000 - Royalty: 5% - Total Inv: $210,000 ($30,000 fran. fee, $80,000 const., $80,000 equip., $20,000 misc.) - Financing: 2 sources, Stephens & SBA.

MARCO'S PIZZA
Marco's Inc.
5254 Monroe St., Toledo, OH, 43623. Contact: Ken Switzer, V.P. of Admin. - Tel: (419) 885-4844. Offer premium quality pizza and hot submarine sandwiches, cheesebread and salads for carryout and delivery. Their emphasis on high quality, excellent service and tremendous value has enabled Marco's Pizza to become the leading pizza company in their major markets. Seeking experienced food service operators. Established: 1978 - Franchising Since: 1979 - No of Units: Company Owned: 25 - Franchised: 70 - Franchise Fee: $8,000 to $12,000 - Royalty: 4.5% - 5%, 1% adv. - Total Inv: $90,000 - $125,000 incl. equip. of $60,000 - $65,000 - Financing: Assistance.

MARK PI'S CHINA GATE/MARK PI'S FEAST OF THE DRAGON/ MARK PI'S EXPRESS
Mark Pi's Franchise Corp.
3120 Valleyview Dr., Columbus, OH, 43204. Contact: Mark Pi Jr., Fran. Dev. - Tel: (614) 276-0901. Franchisor of Chinese fast food, casual dining buffet and gourmet restaurants featuring Szechuan, Mandarin and Hunan cuisine cooked in an open kitchen with no M.S.G. Established: 1978 - Franchising Since: 1992 - No. of Units: Franchised: 68 - Franchise Fee: Express $20,000; China Gate/Feast of the Dragon $30,000 - Royalty: (Express: 4%; China Gate & Feast of the Dragon: 0 - $150,000 2%, $150,000 - $200,000 3%, $200,000 up 2%; - Total Inv: Express: $100,000 - $500,000; China Gate/Feast of the Dragon: $200,000 - $1,000,000 - Financing: No.

MARKET STREET BUFFET & BAKERY
Western Sizzlin, Inc.
P.O. Box 291509, Nashville, TN, 37229. Contact: Eva Schram, Dir. of Dev. - Tel: (800) 247-8325. Buffet concept featuring six hot and cold buffet bars and display bakery. Established: 1992 - Franchising Since: 1992 - No. of Units: Company Owned: 1 - Franchised: 12 - Franchise Fee: $25,000 - Royalty: 2%, .5% adv. - Total Inv: $500,000 - Financing: Will assist.

MARY ANN'S GOLDEN FRIED CHICKEN
450 Stockton, Jacksonville, FL, 32204. Contact: Vincent Desalvo, Sr., Owner - Tel: (904) 389-1606. Fast food featuring chicken. Established: 1967. No. of Units: Company Owned: 1 - Franchised: 2.

MARY'S PIZZA SHACK
18360 Sonoma Hwy., Boyes Hot Springs, CA, 95416. Contact: Cullen Williamson, Pres. - Tel: (707) 938-3602, Fax: (707) 938-5976. Full service pizza and Italian restaurant, serving lunch and dinner in a casual atmosphere. Established: 1959 - Franchising Since: 1990 - No. of Units: Company Owned: 9 - Franchised: 3 - Franchise Fee: $30,000 - Royalty: 5%, 3% adv. - Total Inv: $150,000 leasehold imp., $170,000 F.F. &E, $46,000 soft cost, $50,000 work. cap. - Financing: No.

MASH HOAGIES/MASH SUBS & SALADS
Mash Hoagies Inc.
3164 Lk. Washington Rd., Melbourne, FL, 32934. Contact: Alan Lee, Pres. - Tel: (407) 242-2066. Sub/sandwich/salad franchise. Established: 1982 - Franchising Since: 1982 - No. of Units: Franchised: 17 - Franchise Fee: $7,500 - Royalty: 3%, 2% adv. - Total Inv: Approx. $50,000 ($30,000 leasehold improv., $15,000 equip., $7,500 fran. fee) - Financing: Fran. fee may be financed, equipment leasing available.

MAURICE'S GOURMET BARBEQUE/PIGGIE PARK RESTAURANTS
Piggie Park Enterprises, Inc.
P.O. Box 6847, West Columbia, SC, 29171. - Tel: (803) 791-5887. Specialize in gourmet barbeque with a mustard base barbeque sauce. Considered a mini dinner house with an in-house corporate test kitchen, which delivers barbequed items and hamburgers with a fast food style. Offer financial stability with 50 years plus experience in the barbeque business. Established: 1951 - Franchising Since: 1991 - No. of Units: Company Owned: 7 - Franchised: 1 - Franchise Fee: initial fee $33,500: ($5,000 dev. & $28,500 fran. fee) - Royalty: 5%, 2% adv., 1% company opt. adv. fee - Total Inv: facility bldg. & equip. $325,000 & land costs - Financing: None.

MAVERICK FAMILY STEAK HOUSE
1104 West Reynolds, Springfield, IL, 62702. Contact: Russ Ruby, Pres. - Tel: (217) 787-4660. Semi-cafeteria style steak house. Established: 1983 - No. of Units: 4 - Approx. Inv: $100,000 - $150,000 - Financing: None.

MAX'S DELI & RESTAURANT
Deli Corporation of America, Inc.
4930 W. Oakton St., Skokie, IL, 60077. Contact: Dean Stellas, Dir. of Dev. - Tel: (708) 982-9600. Delicatessen/restaurant. Established: 1989 - Franchising Since: 1994 - No. of Units: Company Owned: 2 - Franchised: 1 - Franchise Fee: $20,000.

MAZZIO'S PIZZA
Mazzio's Corporation
4441 S. 72nd E. Ave., Tulsa, OK, 74145-4692. Contact: Mark Long, Mgr. of Brand Dev./Licensing - Tel: (918) 663-8880. Upscale Italian restaurant featuring 3 types of pizza along with excellent pasta, calzone rings, sandwiches and salad. There is an emphasis on an attractive decor and surroundings along with a distinctive exterior. Delivery is available from an existing dine-in unit. Established: 1961 - Franchising Since: 1966 - No. of Units: Company Owned: 80 - Franchised: 123 - Franchise Fee: $20,000 - Royalty: 3%, Adv. 1% - Total Inv: $309,000 - $606,000: with out real estate; $684,000 - $976,000: with real estate - Financing: No.

MCDONALD'S
McDonald's Corp.
One McDonald's Plaza, Oak Brook, IL, 60521. Contact: Franchising Dept. - Tel: (708) 575-6196. McDonald's is the world's leading food service retailer in the global consumer marketplace, with over 15,000 restaurants in 83 countries. Eighty-four percent of the McDonald's restaurant businesses in the U.S. are locally owned and operated by independent entrepreneurs. Established: 1955 - Franchising Since: 1955 - No. of Units: Company Owned: 4,300 - Franchised: 11,083 - Franchise Fee: $45,000 initial fee, $15,000 security deposit - Royalty: Service fee of 4% of monthly sales plus the greater of: a) monthly base rent, or b) percentage rent that is a least 8.5% of monthly sales - Total Inv: New restaurant costs range from $423,000 to $651,000, excl. fran. fee - Financing: None.

MEALS TO YOU *
15965 Jeanette St., Southfield, MI, 48075. Contact: Ms. Colleen McGaffey - Tel: (810) 557-2784, Fax; (810) 557-7931. Meal delivery to businesses, hotels and homes. Upscale delivery of meals from a variety of local restaurants. Highly sophisticated computer system runs this low-cost opportunity in the growing market of meal delivery. Established: 1989 - Franchising Since: 1991 - No. of Units: Company Owned: 1 - Franchised: 4 - Franchise Fee: $10,000 - Royalty: 4% - Total Inv: $30,000 - $35,000 - Financing: No.

MELLOW MUSHROOM
Home Grown Industries
695 North Ave., N.E., Atlanta, GA, 30308. Contact: Marc Weinstein, Fran. Dir. - Tel: (404) 524-6133. Pizza and sandwich restaurant. Established: 1974 - Franchising Since: 1987 - No. of Units: Company Owned: 1 - Franchised: 12 - Franchise Fee: $25,000 - Royalty: 5%, 1% adv. - Total Inv: $75,000 - $85,000.

MELTING POT RESTAURANT, THE
Melting Pot Restaurants, Inc., The
8406 G. Benjamin Rd., Tampa, FL, 33634. Contact: Robert P. Johnson, Pres. Fran. Sales - Tel: (813) 881-0055. Fondue restaurant features creamy cheese fondues, meat and vegetable fondues in oil or broth, chocolate fondue desserts and an array of fine wines. Established: 1975 - Franchising Since: 1984 - No. of Units: Company Owned: 4 - Franchised: 19 - Franchise Fee: $12,540 - Royalty: 4% on gross - Total Inv: fran. fee & $89,000 - $150,000 dev. costs. - Financing: No.

MIAMI SUBS
Miami Subs Corporation
6300 N.W. 31st. Ave., Ft. Lauderdale, FL, 33309. Contact: Donald L. Perlyn, Exec. V.P. Fran. - Tel: (305) 973-0000. Quick service restaurant concept featuring fresh food cooked-to-order, providing a diverse menu with exceptional quality and moderately priced items designed to encourage frequent visits. Our lively, bright, distinctive decors create both a daytime and evening appeal. Established: 1983 - Franchising Since: 1986 - No. of Units: Company Owned: 29 - Franchised: 132 - Franchise Fee: $25,000 - Royalty: 4%, 1% adv. - Total Inv: $275,000 ($175,000 equip. & $100,000 constr. cost) - Financing: Offer equip. financing to qualified franchisees through an independent company.

MICKEY FINN'S SPORTS CAFE
Castle Rose, Inc.
2211 Peoples Rd., Ste. A, Bellevue, NE, 68005. Contact: Roy G. Breeling, Pres. - Tel: (402) 341-2424, Fax: (402) 292-9712. Casual sports bar and restaurant with sandwiches, appetizers and light entrees. Established: 1981 - Franchising Since: 1988 - No. of Units: Company Owned: 1 - Franchised: 4 - Franchise Fee: $15,000 - Royalty: 5% - Total Inv: $175,000 to $225,000 - Financing: Assistance only.

MIKE ANDERSON'S SEAFOOD RESTAURANTS
Mike Anderson's Seafood Restaurant Consulting, Inc.
2830 Canal St., New Orleans, LA, 70119. Contact: Richard Williams, Co-Owner - Tel: (504) 821-2258, Fax: (504) 822-7943. Casual, family priced seafood restaurant specializing in high quality, fresh Louisiana seafood. High volume establishment with attention to detail. Maintain excellent reputation with customers. Established: 1975 - Franchising Since: 1986 - No. of Units: Company Owned: 4 - Franchised: 1 - Franchise Fee: $75,000 - Royalty: 2% - 4% - Financing: No.

MIKE SCHMIDT'S PHILADELPHIA HOAGIES
Three Neshaminy Interplex, Suite 301, Trevose, PA, 19053. Contact: Richard Speeney, Pres. - Tel: (215) 245-2234. Hoagie & steak restaurant. Established: 1990 - Franchising Since: 1991 - No. of Units: Franchised: 6 - Franchise Fee: $12,500 - Royalty: 6% - Total Inv: $74,500 - $125,900 - Financing: No.

MINUTE MAN
Minute Man of America
P.O. Box 828, Little Rock, AR, 72203. Contact: James L. Hansen, Owner - Tel: (501) 565-8271. Charbroiled hamburgers and Mexican food. Established: 1949 - Franchising Since: 1965 - No. of Units: Franchised: 2 - Franchise Fee: $7,500 - Royalty: 3% sales - Total Inv: $75,000.

MOBILE CHEF
Augies, Inc.
1900 W. County Rd. C., St. Paul, MN, 55113. Contact: Ray Augustine, Pres. - Tel: (612) 633-5308. Industrial catering lunch trucks. Established: 1957 - Franchising Since: 1977 - No. of Units: Company Owned: 3 - Franchised: 55 - Approx. Inv: $20,000.

MOE'S ITALIAN SANDWICHES *
Moestogo Corp.
160 Winnicutt Rd., Stratham, NH, 03885. Contact: Mary Jane Keane, V.P. - Tel: (800) 588-6637. Fast food - specialty Italian sandwiches and soups. Established: 1958 - Franchising Since: 1993 - No. of Units: Company Owned: 2 - Franchised: 14 - Franchise Fee: $12,500 - Royalty: 5%, 2% adv. - Total Inv: $41,000 - $77,000 - Financing: No.

MOM'S BAKE AT HOME PIZZA
4457-59 Main St., Philadelphia, PA, 19127. Contact: Glen Bair, Pres. - Tel: (215) 482-1044. Company manufactures fresh handmade shells and supplies sauce and cheese to franchisees. Established: 1960 - Franchising Since: 1961 - No. of Units: 19 - Approx. Inv: $38,000 - Financing: No.

MOM'S FAMILY FAVOURITE U BAKE PIZZA
Moma's Family Favorite Inc.
3401 Paxford Rd., Richmond, VA, 23234-4314. Contact: Mr. Gerald L. Daly, V.P. - Tel: (804) 271-7522. Pizzas created to customer's specifications in less than 5 min. and taken home. Established: 1988 - Franchising Since: 1988 - No. of Units: Company Owned: 12 - Franchised: 7 - Franchise Fee: $15,000 - Royalty: 5% per week - Total Inv: $50,000 - $65,000 - Financing: No.

MOUNTAIN MIKE'S PIZZA
Q&S Management
3841 N. Freeway Blvd., Ste. 290, Sacramento, CA, 95834-1948. Contact: Tom Stanger, Dir. Operations - Tel: (800) 982-MIKE (6453), (916) 929-3946. Family style sit-down pizza restaurant with a relaxed, casual atmosphere featuring a unique thick crust pizza with mountains of toppings. Other menu items include oven-baked sandwiches, hamburgers, salad, a limited pasta line and beverages. All items can be taken out and most locations deliver. No-frills franchise with low investment in order to max. the return. Established: 1978 - Franchising Since: 1979 - No. of Units: Company Owned: 1 - Franchised: 79 - Franchise Fee: $15,000 - Royalty: 5% of gross sales minus sales tax and discount coupons vs. $1,000. - Total Inv: $112,400 - $209,000 opens the door - Financing: Yes.

MR. BURGER, INC.
Div. of Blankenship Enterprises
5625 Fulton, P.O. Box 8248, Amarillo, TX, 79114-8248. Contact: Norman Blankenship, Pres. - Tel: (806) 355-9936. A fast food hamburger restaurant specializing in hamburgers, onion rings, chicken, snack items and feature drinks. Building features two drive-up windows and a seating capacity for up to 72 people. Established: 1969 - Franchising Since: 1972 - No. of Units: Company Owned: 27 - Franchised: 40 - Franchise Fee: $10,000 - Royalty: 3% monthly gross - Total Inv: $170,000-$270,000.

MR. CONEY
Coney America Corporation
214 Downing St., Pottsville, PA, 17901. Contact: Mickey Palles, Pres. - Tel: (717) 622-2754. Famous Coney Island chili dogs and hamburgers, plus more. Established: 1917 - Franchising Since: 1987 - No. of Units:

Company Owned: 4 - Franchised: 3 - Franchise Fee: $15,000 - Royalty: 3%, 2% adv. - Total Inv: variable, depending on size & location - Financing: Partial.

MR. GATTI'S, INC.
P.O. Box 1522, 44 Sidney Baker, Kerrville, TX, 78028. Contact: Joel Longtin, Exec. VP, Franchising - Tel: (210) 792-5700. Pizza restaurants with salads, submarine sandwiches, pasta. Established: 1969 - No. of Units: Company Owned: 109 - Franchised: 174 - Franchise Fee: $20,000 - Total Inv: $315,000 - $500,000 - Financing: None.

MR. GOODCENTS SUBS & PASTAS
Mr. Goodcents Franchise Systems, Inc.
16210 W. 110th St., Lenexa, KS, 66219. Contact: Bruce A. Hatcher, Dir. Fran. Dev. - Tel: (800) 648-CENT, Fax: (913) 888-8477. Quick service subs & pasta restaurant. No food experience needed. A small business that works. Complete training program and ongoing support. Established: 1989 - Franchising Since: 1990 - No. of Units: Company Owned: 5 - Franchised: 71 - Franchise Fee: $12,500 - Royalty: 5% mthly gross, 2.5% adv. - Total Inv: $82,000 - $159,000 (incl. fran. fee) - Financing: No.

MR. HERO
Restaurant Developers Corp.
5755 Granger Rd., Ste. 200, Independence, OH, 44131-1410. Contact: Wm. Plautz, Fran. Dir. - Tel: (216) 398-1101 or (800) 837-9599. Fast food featuring the philly style cheesesteak sandwich, romanburger, crisp salads, cheesecake and french fries. Established: 1965 - Franchising Since: 1970 - No. of Units: Company Owned: 21 - Franchised: 130 - Franchise Fee: $21,500 - Royalty: 5% + 2%-6% adv. - Total Inv: $165,000 - $185,000 ($50,000 cash required) - Financing: No.

MR. HOT DOG
Shan Investment Co.
811 N. Euclid, Bay City, MI, 48706. Contact: Harry Stumpus, G.M. - Tel: (517) 684-6590. Fast Food. Established: 1961. No. of Units: Company Owned: 1 - Franchised: 3

MR. JIM'S PIZZA
555 Republic Dr., Ste. 319, Plano, TX, 75074. Contact: Chris Bowman, Exec. Dir. - Tel: (214) 423-4405, Fax: (214) 423-4269. Pizza carry-out and delivery. Established: 1975 - Franchising Since: 1981 - No. of Units: Company Owned: 2 - Franchised: 60 - Franchise Fee: $10,000 - Royalty: 4% - Total Inv: $50,000 - $75,000 - Financing: None.

MR. STEAKS
America's Steak Experts, Inc.
1401 17th St., Ste. 800, Denver, CO, 80202-1246. Contact: James Bishop, V.P. Fran. Dev. - Tel: (303) 293-0200, Fax: (303) 293-0299. Mr. Steak is a family oriented steakhouse with the accent on value, service, and great food. Established: 1962 - Franchising Since: 1962 - No. of Units: Franchised: 16 - Franchise Fee: $25,000 - Royalty: 3% - Total Inv: $750,000 - $900,000 - Financing: No.

MR. SUBB
Mr. Subb Franchise Corp.
601 Columbia St., Cohoes, NY, 12047-3801. Contact: Gary Sheehan, Dir. of Fran. - Tel: (518) 783-0276. Subbmarine sandwich restaurant featuring soups, salads, & subbs. Primarily take-out. Normally located in strip malls and some regional malls. Established: 1978 - Franchising Since: 1994 - No. of Units: Company Owned: 21 - Franchised: 8 - Franchise Fee: $15,000 - Royalty: 6%, 2% adv. - Total Inv: $15,000 fran. fee, $52,000 equip., $42,000 leasehold, $15,100 work. cap. - Financing: Not at present, but Marine Midland gives preferential treatment to NY applicants.

MR. SUBMARINE OF BERWYN INC.
18 W. Jackson, Chicago, IL, 60602. Contact: Gus Tzoumas, Pres. - Tel: (312) 461-9383. Fast food restaurants. Established: 1975 - No. of Units: Company Owned: 2 - Franchised: 23.

MRS. MARTY'S DELI RESTAURANT
2520 Parke Lane, Broomall, PA, 19008. Contact: Mel Messinger, Fran. Dir. - Tel: (610) 359-1996. Full service restaurant in an old fashioned family atmosphere where the food is fresh and the prices are affordable. Established: 1984 - Franchising Since: 1992 - No. of Units: Company Owned: 1 - Franchise Fee: $60,000 - Royalty: 4% of sales - Total Inv: $310,000 - Financing: No.

MRS. SPOON'S FRESH BURGERS/ICE CREAM
415 Hawthorne Lane, Charlotte, NC, 28204. Contact: Jerry Bardin, Pres. - Tel: (910) 256-6031. Specializing in homemade ice cream, fresh meat burgers, hot dogs and deli sandwiches. Established: 1929 - Franchising Since: 1982 - No. of Units: 2 - Franchise Fee: $5,000 - Royalty: 2% - Total Inv: $35,000.

MY FRIEND'S PLACE
MFP Franchise Systems, Inc.
106 Hammond Dr., Atlanta, GA, 30328. Contact: Rosalind Katz, V.P. - Tel: (404) 843-2803. Retail restaurant specializing in sandwiches, salads, soups, and homemade desserts. Established: 1980 - Franchising Since: 1990 - No. of Units: Company Owned: 2 - Franchised: 9 - Franchise Fee: $15,000 - Royalty: flat fee, wkly, mos. 1-12: $150 per. wk, mos. 13-60: $200 per wk., etc. - Total Inv: $57,000 - $107,000 plus work cap. - Financing: No.

MY PIE - UNIQUE PIZZA IN THE PAN
P.O. Box 9033, Winnetka, IL, 60093-9033. Contact: Lawrence Aronson, Pres. - Tel: (708) 835-1312, Fax: (708) 835-0877. High quality Chicago-style pizza and related items. Established: 1971 - Franchising Since: 1976 - No. of Units: Company Owned: 5 - Franchised: 2 - Franchise Fee: $20,000 - Royalty: 5% - Total Inv: $100,000 - $250,000 - Financing: No.

NACHO NANA'S
Nacho Nana's International
1220 South Alma School Rd. #101, Meza, AZ, 85210. Contact: Robert L. Plait, Pres. - Tel: (602) 644-1340. New concept in Mexican fast food serving authentic Mexican food in an attractive Mexican setting. Most affordable Mexican fast food franchise available. Established: 1993 - Franchising Since: 1993 - No. of Units: Company Owned: 1 - Franchise Fee: $15,000 - Royalty: 5%, 2% adv. - Total Inv: $42,200 - $104,400 - Financing: None.

NATHAN'S
Nathan's Famous, Inc.
1400 Old Country Rd., Westbury, NY, 11590. Contact: Carl Paley, Sr. V.P. - Tel: (516) 338-8500, Fax: (516) 338-7220. Fast food restaurants offering flexible prototypes (11) and menu variety featuring Nathan's Famous hot dogs & fresh crincle cut french fries. Established: 1916 - Franchising Since: 1989 - No. of Units: Company Owned: 21 - Franchised: 182 - Franchise Fee: $30,000 full restaurant, $15,000 kiosk, modular, Cart - Royalty: 4.5% - Total Inv: ranging from $20,000 - $600,000.

Mr. Subb

Gary P. Sheehan
Director of Franchising

Mr. Subb Franchise Corp (518) 783-0276
601 Columbia Street (800) 267-7822
Cohoes, NY 12047-3801 Fax: (518) 783-0294

NATURE'S TABLE
Nature's Table Systems, Inc.
233 W. 47th St., Kansas City, MO, 64112. Contact: Jason Gilchnst, Fran. Agent - Tel: (816) 531-8898. Healthy and sensible foods restaurant for the enclosed regional mall food courts. Established: 1977 - Franchising Since: 1987 - No. of Units: Company Owned: 6 - Franchised: 18 - Franchise Fee: $25,000 - Royalty: 5% - Total Inv: $101,800 - $185,500 - Financing: None.

NATURE'S WAY CAFE
Nature's Way Franchising Group, Inc.
800 Lake Ave., Lake Worth, FL, 33460. Contact: Karen Spina, Sales Dir. - Tel: (407) 533-9100. Healthy eateries serving lunch - breakfast in some locations. Established: 1979 - Franchising Since: 1987 - No. of Units: Company Owned: 1 - Franchised: 13 - Franchise Fee: $20,000 - Royalty: 4%, 3% adv. - Total Inv: $100,000 min. - Financing: No.

NEUBAUER RESTAURANTS CORP.
2900 Grand Ave., Fort Smith, AR, 72901. Contact: John J. Neubauer, Pres. - Tel: (501) 783-8880. Fast food restaurants. Established: 1977 - No. of Units: Franchised: 5.

NEW ENGLAND PIZZA
New England Food, Inc.
1543 Church St., Philadelphia, PA, 19124. Contact: Demetrios Malitas, Pres. - Tel: (215) 288-1727. Fast food pizza. Established: l959 - No. of Units: Company Owned: 2 - Franchised: 2.

NEW TOWNE DINER *
Captain's Cottage Franchise, Inc.
200 Broadhollow Rd., Ste. 207, Melville, NY, 11747. Contact: Chris Levano, V.P. Dev. - Tel: (516) 271-0221, Fax: (516) 271-0449. A contemporary version of an original old town American diner. Menu features breakfast, lunch, full-course dinners and a bakery. Restaurants are open extended hours 7 days/wk. Established: 1994 - Franchising Since: 1994 - No. of Units: Franchised: 1 - Franchise Fee: $35,000 - Royalty: 5% on-going, .5% local adv., 1% nat'l. adv. - Total inv: $450,000 to $1,400,000 (includes fees) - Financing: No.

NU-WAY WEINERS
Nu-Way Weiners, Inc.
428 Cotton Ave., Macon, GA, 31201-2720. Contact: Spyros Dermatas, Pres. - Tel: (912) 743-6593. Fast food restaurant chain specializing in hotdogs and hamburgers. Established: 1916 - Franchising Since: 1968 - No. of Units: Company Owned: 6 - Franchised: 3 - Franchise Fee: $10,000 - Royalty: 2% - Total Inv: $95,000 - Financing: None.

NUMERO UNO
Numero Uno Franchise Corp. Gelet Enterprises, Inc.
15414 Cabrito Ave., Ste. A, Van Nuys, CA, 91406. Contact: Dan Rouse, V.P. Operations - Tel: (818) 788-0007. Full-service Italian restaurant with emphasis on deep dish pizza, thin crust pizza, pastas, salads, sandwiches, variety of wines, beers and desserts. Established: 1973 - Franchising Since: 1975 - No. of Units: Company Owned: 7 - Franchised: 54 - Franchise Fee: $25,000 - Royalty: 10% incl. adv. - Total Inv: $175,000 - $250,000 - Financing: No.

O. T. HODGE CHILI PARLORS
Eirten's Parlors, Inc.
1800 Market St., St. Louis Union Station, MO, 63103. Contact: Larry Rugg, Owner - Tel: (314) 421-9938. Fast food sit down diner motif featuring chili. Established: 1904 - Franchising Since: 1985 - No. of Units: Company Owned: 1 - Franchised: 3 - Royalty: 5% - Inv: $100,000 - $200,000 - Financing: No.

OK FOOD MANAGEMENT US CORP. *
727 Main St., Niagara Falls, NY, 14301. Contact: Vincent Agnello, Fran. Cons. - Legal - Tel: (716) 285-2533. Hot dog vending cart. Optional: Master franchise available in state area. Established: 1995 - No. of Units: Company Owned: 1 - Franchise Fee: $14,900 includes cart - renewable every 5 years - Royalty: $50 per month plus 2.5% adv. - Financing: Assistance.

OK SUBMARINE CORPORATION *
727 Main St., Niagara Falls, NY, 14301. Contact: Vincent Agnello, Fran. Cons. - Legal - Tel: (716) 285-2533. Submarine sandwich chain and salads. Bread baked fresh daily. Optional steak and fries. Operating in US and Canada. Established: 1995 - No. of Units: Company Owned: 1 - Franchised: 5 - Franchise Fee: $10,000 - Royalty: 6% plus 2.5% adv. - Total Inv: $52,000 - $98,000 with grill and friers and sit down/drive thru optional $98,000 to $150,000 - Financing: Assistance.

OLD STYLE HAMBURGERS
3820 Premier Ave., Memphis, TN, 38118. Contact: Franchise Dir./Pres. - Tel: (901) 867-0600. Fast food double drive thru, inexpensive items. Established: 1987 - Franchising Since: 1987 - No. of Units: Company Owned: 2 - Franchised: 60 - Franchise Fee: $10,000 - Royalty: 5% + 1% adv. - Total Inv: $100,000 - Financing: Yes.

OLIVE'S GOURMET PIZZA
Olive Industries Ltd., Inc.
3249 Scott St., San Francisco, CA, 94123. Contact: Craig Cooper, Pres. - Tel: (415) 567-4488. Gourmet pizza operation using award-winning cornmeal crust and sauces, blended from secret recipies and made according to exacting standards. In addition to pizza, the Olive's menu features pasta, sandwiches, salads, desserts and other Italian food items. Sit-down, take-out and delivery services are offered. Established: 1985 - Franchising Since: 1989 - No. of Units: Company Owned: 2 - Franchise Fee: $10,000 - Royalty: 5% of gross - Total Inv: $75,000 - $190,000 incl. fran. fee - Financing: Traditional lending institutions.

OLIVER'S PIZZA INC.
35418 Jefferson Ave., Mt. Clemens, MI, 48045. Contact: Joseph Hayes - Tel: (313) 790-0770. Carry out and delivery pizza, subs and salads. Both round and square pizzas. Established: 1983 - Franchising Since: 1986 - No. of Units: Franchised: 30 - Franchise Fee: $15,000 - Royalty: 5% gross + 3% adv. - Total Inv: $80,000 ($7,500 fran. fee, $25,000 - leasehold impro. $35,000 - equip. package, $12,500 work. cap.) - Financing: Third party.

OREAN THE HEALTH EXPRESS
817 N. Lake Ave., Pasadena, CA, 91104-4561. Contact: Orean Thomas, Pres. - Tel: (818) 794-0861. The first fast food vegetarian restaurant. Established: 1984 - Franchising Since: 1990 - No. of Units: Company Owned: 1 - Franchise Fee: $25,000 - Royalty: 6% - Financing: None.

ORIGINAL GINO'S EAST OF CHICAGO, THE
Gino's East Restaurant Corp.
205 W. Wacker Dr., Ste. 1800, Chicago, IL, 60606. Contact: William Bronner, V.P. Fran. - Tel: (312) 346-5455, Fax: (312) 346-2115. Full service restaurant featuring Chicago-style deep dish pizza since 1966. Franchising Since: 1992 - No. of Units: Franchised: 7 - Franchise Fee: 35,000 - Royalty: 5% - Total Inv: $600,000 ($250,000 equip., $250,000 build out, $100,000 capital) - Financing: No.

ORIGINAL HAMBURGER STAND
4440 Von Karman Ave., Ste. 150, Newport Beach, CA, 92660. Contact: Frank Coyle, Mgr., Fran. Sales - Tel: (714) 752-5800, (800) 764-9353, Ext. 609. Fast food hamburgers. No. of Units: Company Owned: 18 - Franchised: 39.

ORIGINAL PANCAKE HOUSE, THE
8601 S.W. 24th Ave., Portland, OR, 97219. Contact: Ann Highet - Tel: (503) 246-1049, Fax: (503) 245-2396. Family Restaurant. Established: 1953 - No. of Units: Company Owned: 1 - Franchised: 54.

ORIGINAL PITA SUB SHOP
4063 17 Mile Rd., Sterling Hts., MI, 48310. Contact: Mazen, Owner - Tel: (810) 264-5480. Sub shop, sales of subs, salads, soups, soft drinks. Established: 1986 - Franchising Since: 1990 - No. of Units: Company Owned: 1 - Franchised: 1 - Franchise Fee: $15,000 - Royalty: 4% of gross sales - Total Inv: $80,000 - Financing: No.

ORIGINAL TACO CABANA MEXICAN PATIO CAFE, THE
Taco Cabana, Inc.
262 Losoya St., #330, San Antonio, TX, 78205-2684. Contact: James Eliasberg, Sr. V.P. & General Counsel - Tel: (210) 231-8226. 24 hour retail Mexican fast food, patio dining with drive-through service. Established: 1978 - Franchising Since: 1987 - No. of Units: Company Owned: 36 - Franchised: 16 - Franchise Fee: $50,000 per store; 3 store min. - Royalty: 4% of gross - Total Inv: $800,000 - $1,200,000 - Financing: None by franchisor.

OTTOMANELLI'S CAFE FRANCHISING CORP.
1549 York Ave., New York, NY, 10028. Contact: Nicolo Ottomanelli, Chairman - Tel: (212) 772-8423. Italian/American cafe, featuring pasta, pizza, burger & ribs. Catering to families and others who appreciated good quality food at a moderate price. Established: 1988 - Franchising Since: 1989 - No. of Units: Company Owned: 4 - Franchised: 14 - Franchise Fee: $19,540 - Royalty: 3.5%, 1% adv. - Total Inv: $150,000 - $475,000.

OYSTER KRACKER, THE
7515 Greenville Bank Tower, Ste. 300, Dallas, TX, 75231. Contact: William Hensley, Pres. - Tel: (214) 691-3452. Fast service, casual, quality seafood restaurant. Established: 1984 - Franchising Since: 1986 - No. of Units: Company Owned: 3 - Franchised: 4 - Total Inv: $250,000 - Financing: None.

PADOW'S DELI SHOPS *
4925 W. Broad St., Ste. 407, Richmond, VA, 23230. Contact: Sidney Padow, Pres. - Tel: (800) 344-4267. Deli sandwiches, boxed lunches, party platters, corporate catering. 2 types of franchises. Both include the above, but Hams & Deli includes mail order hams, peanuts and gifts. Established: 1994 - Franchising Since: 1995 - No. of Units: Company Owned: 3 - Franchised: 1 - Franchise Fee: $15,000 Deli Shop, $25,000 Hams & Deli - Royalty: 7% of gross sales - Total Inv: $110,000 Deli Shop, $185,000 Hams & Deli format - Financing: No.

PANCAKE COTTAGE FAMILY RESTAURANTS
Captain's Cottage Franchise Inc.
200 Broadhollow Rd., Ste. 207, Melville, NY, 11747. Contact: Chris Levano, V.P. Fran. Dev. - Tel: (516) 271-0221. Full-service family restaurant, offering breakfast, lunch, full-course dinners and dessert menu. Established: 1964 - Franchising Since: 1967 - No. of Units: Franchised: 20 - Franchise Fee: $35,000 - Royalty: 5%, .5% local adv., 1% Nat. fund - Total Inv: $350,000 - $600,000 - Financing: Guidance available.

PANCAKES-A-PLENTY *
773 Independence Dr., Ste. 52-3, Palatine, IL, 60074. Contact: A. Bailey, Pres. - Tel: (708) 776-8882. Established catering and fund raising company has several franchises immediately available in the Chicago area. We offer: 1 person operation, part or full time, 4 wks. free training, complete support, financing to qualified individuals. Pancake breakfast catering to schools (elementary, secondary and high schools), churches, men's and women's groups and companies for whom we do picnics with varied menus for the latter. Established: 1971 - Franchising Since: 1993 - No. of Units: Company Owned: 5 - Franchise Fee: $25,000 - Royalty: 10% monthly sales - Total Inv: Van $25,000 + equip. and initial supplies - Financing: No, or possibly SBA.

PANCHERO'S MEXICAN GRILL *
Panchero's Franchise Corporation
P.O. Box 1786, Iowa City, IA, 52244-1786. Contact: Franchise Rep. - Tel: (319) 351-4551. Made-to-order, authentic Mexican food prepared in an exciting and fun-to-watch display cooking area. Established: 1992 - Franchising Since: 1995 - No. of Units: Company Owned: 7 - Franchise Fee: $25,000 - Royalty: 5% - Total Inv: $122,500 - $350,000 - Financing: No.

PANDA EXPRESS
Panda Systems, Inc.
899 El Centro St., South Pasadena, CA, 91030. Contact: John Su, Dir. of Licensing - Tel: (818) 799-9898. Gourmet Chinese food services. Established: 1988 - Franchising Since: 1989 - No. of Units: Company Owned/Affiliate: 52 - Franchise Fee: $28,500 - Royalty: 6%, 1% adv. - Financing: None.

PAPA JOHN'S PIZZA
Papa John's International, Inc.
11492 Bluegrass Pkwy., Louisville, KY, 40299. Contact: Tom Ragan, V.P. of Fran. Dev. - Tel: (502) 266-5200, Fax: (502) 263-7352. Pizza delivery and carry-out. Established: 1985 - Franchising Since: 1986 - No. of Units: Company Owned: 169 - Franchised: 560 - Franchise Fee: $20,000 - Royalty: 4% of net sales - Total Inv: $120,000 to $170,000 - Financing: None.

PAPA MURPHY'S INTERNATIONAL, INC.
775 Baywood Dr., #316, Petaluma, CA, 94954-5500. Contact: Bob Graham; Jerry Kenney, V.P. Dev. & Purch.; V.P. Oper. & Training - Tel: (707) 769-1200, Fax: (707) 769-8100. High quality pizzas made from scratch for customers to bake at home. Pricing reflects great value to the customer. Established: Murphy's 1984, Papa Aldos 1981 - Franchising Since: Murphy's 1986, Papa Aldos 1982 - No. of Units: Company Owned: 5 - Franchised: 200 - Franchise Fee: $17,500 - Royalty: 5% - Total Inv: $77,000: leasehold $20,000, fix. & equip. $22,000, signs $3,000, inven. $3,500, dep. $1,800, insur. $1,200, adv. $3,000, work cap. $5,000 - Financing: None.

PAPA ROMANO'S
45355 Helm St., Plymouth, MI, 48170-6024. Contact: Dan Morelli, V.P. - Tel: (313) 416-9500. Delivery/carryout pizzeria. (Some units offer dine-in). Established: 1970 - No. of Units: Company Owned: 6 - Franchised: 50 - Franchise Fee: $20,000 - Royalty: 6% - Total Inv: $155,000: $5,000 adv., $70,000 equip., $20,000 fran. fee, $60,000 buildout - Financing: Yes.

PAPA'S PIZZA TO-GO
2825 Breckinridge Blvd., #140, Duluth, GA, 30136. Contact: Ken White, V.P. - Tel: (404) 279-1450. Pizza operations, also selling subs, riblets and wings. Established: 1986 - Franchising Since: 1987 - No. of Units: Company Owned: 15 - Franchised: 55 - Franchise Fee: $8,500 - Royalty: 5% of sales - Total Inv: $110,000 - $135,000 - Financing: Sources provided.

PAPACHINO'S RISTORANTE & PIZZA RESTAURANTS
Papachino's Franchise Corp., Inc.
2650 Via De La Valle, Del Mar, CA, 92014-1909. Contact: Stephen Slamon, V.P. - Tel: (619) 453-9595. Full service Italian restaurant offering full menu of fine Italian food including pizza, pasta, sandwiches, veal, chicken and beverages. Established: 1977 - Franchising Since: 1988 - No. of Units: Company Owned: 2 - Franchised: 3 - Franchise Fee: $25,000 - Royalty: 2% - Total Inv: $100,000 - $350,000 - Financing: No.

PASQUALE'S PIZZA & PASTA
983 Yeager Pkwy., Pelham, AL, 35124. Contact: Millard L. Deason, Pres. - Tel: (205) 664-1839. Pizza, pasta and sandwiches. Established: 1952 - Franchising Since: 1952 - No. of Units: Franchised: 37 - Franchise Fee: $5,000 - Royalty: 5% - Total Inv: $126,500 - $180,000 - Financing: Limited financing avail.

PASTA EXPRESS *
Pasta Express Systems, Inc.
c/o Jim Morris & Assoc., 1650 E. Battlefield Rd., Springfield, MO, 65804. Contact: Jeff Craine, Fran. Coord. - Tel: (417) 887-0501. Quick service Italian restaurant specializing in quality made-to-order pastas, soups, salads and sandwiches. Served in a novel, casual atmosphere or prepared for take out, delivery or catering. Training includes 4 weeks at company store, 2 weeks+ on location. Established: 1982 - Franchising Since: 1993 - No. of Units: Company Owned: 3 - Franchised: 1 - Franchise Fee: $20,000 - Royalty: 4% of gross, 2% promotional fund - Total Inv: $50,000 - $100,000 start-up cash, $75,000 - $350,000 total inv. - Financing: No.

PASTA TO GO
15965 Jeanette St., Southfield, MI, 48075. Contact: Colleen McGaffey - Tel: (810) 557-2784, Fax: (810) 557-7931. Italian fast food dine-in and carry-out. Gourmet home cooked. Pasta to Go provides full-line catering for graduations, birthdays, etc. Competitive pricing allows Pasta to Go to expand sales in a segment of the market that is generally much higher. Pasta to Go is for people on the go who still want good,

healthy Italian food. Established: 1987 - Franchising Since: 1990 - No. of Units: Company Owned: 1 - Franchised: 77 - Franchise Fee: $15,000 - Royalty: 5% - Total Inv: $75,000 - Financing: Yes.

PAUL REVERE'S PIZZA
Paul Revere's Pizza Int'l., Ltd.
1570-42nd St. NE., Cedar Rapids, IA, 52402. Contact: Larry Schuster or Tom Mueller, Pres./Executive V.P. - Tel: (319) 395-9113, Fax: (319) 395-9115. Pizza delivery and carry-out. Established: 1975 - Franchising Since: 1981 - No. of Units: Company Owned: 5 - Franchised: 44 - Franchise Fee: $10,000 - Royalty: 4% -gross sales - Total Inv: $35,000 - Financing: None.

PEDRO'S TACOS
Pedro's Tacos of California, Inc.
31721 Camino Capistrano, San Juan Capistrano, CA, 92675-2653. Contact: Ed McNary, Owner/Operator - Tel: (714) 489-7752 (and Fax). Drive-thru, limited Mexican value priced menu. Established: 1985 - Franchising Since: 1992 - No. of Units: Company Owned: 2 - Franchised: 1 - Franchise Fee: $15,000 - Royalty: 4% net sales - Total Inv: $110,000 if new unit, not incl. land and bldg. - Financing: Partial available.

PEGGY LAWTON KITCHENS, INC.
P.O. Box 33, East Walpole, MA, 02032-0033. Contact: William Wolf, V.P./G.M. - Tel: (800) 843-7325. Eastern seaboard areas licensed for development. Route selling portion packaged snacks to other businesses. Sales repeat weekly. High quality line. Established: 1949 - Licensing Since: 1979 - Number of Licensees: 2 - Approx. Inv: $40,000 - License Fee: flat $2,500 yr.

PENGUIN POINT
Penguin Point Franchise Systems, Inc.
2691 U.S. 30 E., P.O. Box 975, Warsaw, IN, 46581. Contact: W.E. Stouder Jr., Pres. - Tel: (219) 267-3107. Quick serve, drive thru, chicken burgers, specialty sandwiches, catering. Established: 1961 - Franchising Since: 1995 - No. of Units: Company Owned: 15 - Franchise Fee: $15,000 - Royalty: 4% continuing service fee, 1% adv. - Total Inv: $435,000 - $605,000 - Financing: None.

PENN STATION
Penn Station, Inc.
8276 Beechmont Ave., Cincinnati, OH, 45255. Contact: Jeff Osterfeld, Pres. - Tel: (513) 474-5957, Fax: (513) 474-7116. Retail sale of Philadelphia style cheese steaks, fresh cut fries & fresh squeezed lemonade. Established: 1985 - Franchising Since: 1988 - No. of Units: Franchised: 25 - Franchise Fee: $17,500 - Royalty: 6% of net sales - Total Inv: $142,000 - $266,000 - Financing: No.

PEPE'S MEXICAN RESTAURANTS
PePe's, Incorporated
1325 W. 15th St., Chicago, IL, 60608. Contact: Edwin Ptak, Fran. Dir. - Tel: (312) 733-2500. Mexican family dining restaurant. Offering a full menu of authentic Mexican specialties, beer, wine, and liquor. Established: 1967 - Franchising Since: 1967 - No. of Units: Company Owned: 1 - Franchised: 53 - Franchise Fee: $15,000 - Royalty: 4% (3% adv. fee) - Total Inv: $175,000 - $350,000 - Financing: No.

PERKINS FAMILY RESTAURANT & BAKERY
Perkins Restaurants Operating Company, L.P.
6075 Poplar Ave., Ste. 800, Memphis, TN, 38119. Contact: Robert J. Winters, Sr. Dir. Fran. Dev. - Tel: (800) 877-7375. Family-style restaurants which serve a wide variety of high quality, moderately priced breakfast, lunch and dinner entrees. Generally open 24 hours a day, 7 days a week. Established: 1958 - Franchising Since: 1958 - No. of Units: Company Owned: 138 - Franchised: 309 - Franchise Fee: $35,000 for first and second restaurants, $25,000 addt'l restaurants - Royalty: 4% of gross sales - Total Inv: $1,074,361 - $2,023,025.

PETER PIPER PIZZA
Peter Piper Inc.
2036 E. Camelback Rd., Phoenix, AZ, 85016. Contact: Mike Cullen, Dir. Fran. - Tel: (602) 995-1975. Safe, casual, family fun pizza restaurants serving quality products at value pricing. Families, parties & groups enjoy our prizes, games, rides & videos. We always treat kids special.

Established: 1972 - Franchising Since: 1976 - No. of Units: Company Owned: 27 - Franchised: 73 - Franchise Fee: $25,000 domestic - Royalty: 5% - Total Inv: $700,000 - Financing: Referrals to sources.

PHIL'S FOOD SERVICE, INC. *
2124 B 7th St., Tuscaloosa, AL, 35401. Contact: Robert S. Head Jr., V.P. Fran. - Tel: (205) 345-2898. Buffalo wings, sandwiches, salads, sit-down, take-out, drive-thru, beer & wine sold. Established: 1982 - Franchising Since: 1994 - No. of Units: Company Owned: 1 - Franchised: 4 - Franchise Fee: $20,000 - Royalty: 5%, 1% adv. local, 1% adv. nat'l. - Total Inv: $225,000 - $275,000 - Financing: Various sources.

PHILADELPHIA BAR & GRILL
Castle Rose, Inc.
2211 Peoples Rd., Ste. A, Bellevue, NE, 68005. Contact: Roy G. Breeling, Pres. - Tel: (402) 341-2424, Fax: (402) 292-9712. Casual family restaurant and bar featuring Philly Steak Sandwiches and other lite entrees. Established: 1981 - Franchising Since: 1985 - No. of Units: Franchised: 8 - Franchise Fee: $15,000 - Royalty: 5% - Total Inv: $175,000 to $225,000 - Financing: Assistance only.

PHILLY CONNECTION
Philly Franchising Co., The
120 Interstate N. Parkway E., #112, Atlanta, GA, 30339-2103. Contact: Raymond Gaspart, Pres./Franchising - Tel: (800) 886-8826 or (770) 952-6152. Specialty sandwich restaurant - Philadelphia Cheesesteak sandwich, hoagies, salads and related restaurant items. Dine-in, take-out and delivery. Lunch/dinner, strip center locations, high quality, prepared to order menu items. Established: 1984 - Franchising Since: 1987 - No. of Units: Franchised: 43 - Franchise Fee: $20,000 - Royalty: 5%, 2% local co-op fund - Total Inv: $20,000 fee, $55,000 construction, $40,000 equip./fixtures/misc. - Financing: Assist with 3rd party sources.

PHILLY'S FINEST
Philly's Finest, Inc.
P.O. Box 12926, Tucson, AZ, 85732-2926. Contact: Steve Goumas, Pres. - Tel: (602) 323-1776. Franchises Philly's Finest restaurants. Owner of company stores. Established: 1984 - Franchising Since: 1985 - No. of Units: Company Owned: 2 - Franchised: 14 - Franchise Fee: $20,000 - Royalty: 4% net sales - Total Inv: $100,000 - Financing: Limited.

PICASSO'S PIZZA EXPRESS
2714 Sheridan Dr., Buffalo, NY, 14150. Contact: Franco Kroese, Fran. Dir. - Tel: (716) 833-5633. Offering pizza, wings, salads, and sandwiches. Also take-out and delivery. Established: 1990 - Franchising Since: 1991 - No. of Units: Company Owned: 17 - Franchised: 1 - Franchise Fee: $15,000 - Royalty: 5%, 2% adv.

PICCADILLY CIRCUS PIZZA
Land Mark Products
1009 Okoboji Ave., Milford, IA, 51351. Contact: Jerry Ryker, Gen. Mgr. - Tel: (800) 338-4340. Fast food pizza, carry out and delivery, convenience store kiosk, non-traditional kiosk. Established: 1977 - Franchising Since: 1977 - No. of Units: Franchised: 475 - Total Inv: Avg. kiosk $17,000 to $22,000 - Financing: Yes.

PICCOLO'S PIZZA
421 N. I St., Madera, CA, 93637. Contact: Stephen L. Frazier, Pres. - Tel: (209) 673-0435. Take 'n bake pizza. Established: 1983 - Franchising Since: 1985 - No. of Units: Company Owned: 6 - Franchised: 16 - Franchise Fee: $7,500 - Royalty: 3.5% - Total Inv: $65,000 - $70,000 - Financing: No.

PIETRO'S PIZZA PARLORS
317 E. Kettleman Ln., Lodi, CA, 95240. Contact: Jim Murdaca, Pres. - Tel: (209) 368-0613. Restaurant. Established: 1958 - Franchising Since: 1971 - No. of Units: Company Owned: 2 - Franchised: 9 - Approx. Inv: $200,000 - Financing: No.

PIG-N-OUT *
M&S Enterprises
Route 2, Box 1, Camden, TN, 38320. , Fran. Dir. - Tel: (901) 867-0600. A barbeque restaurant. Established: 1992 - No. of Units: Company Owned: 1 - Franchise Fee: $15,000 - Royalty: 5% - Total Inv: $72,500 - $133,000 (Work. Cap., Inven., Lease, Leasehold Improv., Signs, Equip., Fixtures). For further information please contact: Consultants America Corp., 12279 US Highway 64. Eads, TN, 38028, Tel: (901) 867-0600, Fax: (901) 867-0010.

PIZZA COLORE *
Pizza Colóre Franchising, Inc.
1550 Larimer St., #312, Denver, CO, 80202. Contact: Tamyra Wallace, Dir. of Fran. Dev. - Tel: (303) 291-0609. European style specialty pizzeria cafe. Established: 1992 - Franchising Since: 1992 - No. of Units: Company Owned: 5 - Franchised: 7 - Franchise Fee: $15,000 - Royalty: 5% - Total Inv: $153,400 to $258,500 (includes fran. fee) - Financing: Yes.

PIZZA DEPOT
Pizza Depot Inc.
3722 Wheatsheaf Rd., Huntington Valley, PA, 19006. Contact: Fred Malitas, Pres. - Tel: (215) 947-8716. Pizzas, subs & steaks. Established: 1985 - Franchising Since: 1986 - No. of Units: Company Owned: 4 - Franchised: 4 - Franchise Fee: $7,500 - Royalty: 4% - Total Inv: $140,000 - $190,000 - Financing: No.

PIZZA FACTORY, INC
We Toss'em, They're Awesome Pizza Factory
49430 Road 426, (P.O. Box 989), Oakhurst, CA, 93644. Contact: Ron Willey, V.P. - Tel: (209) 683-3377. Family style restaurant serving pizza, pasta, and sandwiches. Handmade dough tossed the old fashioned way. Established: 1979 - Franchising Since: 1984 - No. of Units: Company Owned: 3 - Franchised: 80 - Franchise Fee: $20,000, $2,500 training fee - Royalty: 3%, 1% adv. - Total Inv: $100,000 - $170,000 incld. fran fee - Financing: No.

PIZZA HUT, INC.
P.O. Box 428, Wichita, KS, 67201. Contact: Scott Mackey, VP Fran. - Tel: (316) 681-9805. Pizza restaurants. Established: 1958.

PIZZA INN
Pizza Inn, Inc.
5050 Quorum Dr., #500, Dallas, TX, 75240. Contact: Lynda Hallo, VP Fran. Sales - Tel: (214) 701-9955. Family style, pizza restaurant chain offering carry-out, delivery, dine-in and buffet. Established: 1961 - Franchising Since: 1961 - No. of Units: Company Owned: 8 - Franchised: 423 - Franchise Fee: $20,000 full service inn, $7,500 delivery/take-out - Royalty: 4% - Total Inv: $113,000 - $179,000 for a carryout/delivery & $194,500 - $535,500 for a full service inn - Financing: No.

PIZZA JOE'S
Pizza Joe's, Inc.
PO Box 8157, New Castle, PA, 16107-8157. Contact: Joe Seminara, Pres. - Tel: (412) 652-8838. Fast Food - Pizza. Established: 1981 - No. of Units: Company Owned: 5 - Franchised: 17.

PIZZA MAN - HE DELIVERS
El Centro Foods, Inc.
6930-1/2 Tujunga Ave., North Hollywood, CA, 91605. Contact: Robert Ohanian, Pres. - Tel: (818) 766-4395. Established: 1971- Franchising Since: 1978 - No. of Units: Company Owned: 3 - Franchised: 62 - Franchise Fee: $25,000 - Royalty: 4% - Total Inv: $110,000 - Financing: Yes, up to 40% of O.A.C.

PIZZA PIPELINE, THE
Pizza Pipeline Inc., The
418 W. Sharp, Spokane, WA, 99201. Contact: Gene J. Boik, V.P. - Tel: (509) 326-1977. A delivery and carry out pizza business offering 25 different items and assorted sauces along with salads, Tricky Stix®, sub sandwiches and chicken wings. Established: 1988 - Franchising Since: 1990 - No. of Units: Company Owned: 5 - Franchised: 5 - Franchise Fee: $5,000 - Royalty: 3% of gross corporate fee, 1% of gross nat'l. adv. - Total Inv: $120,000 - $250,000 - Financing: None.

PIZZA PIT
Pizza Pit Investment Enterprises, Inc.
4253 Argosy Crt., Madison, WI, 53714. Contact: Kerry Cook, V.P. - Tel: (608) 221-6777. Free home delivery and carry-out of handcrafted pizzas and specialty sandwiches. Units are also adaptable to inside seating with prepared salads and pizza by the slice. Also, catering and food court.

Established: 1969 - Franchising Since: 1982 - No. of Units: Company Owned: 10 - Franchised: 25 - Franchise Fee: $16,000 - $17,500 - Total Inv: $109,000 - $237,000 - Royalty: 4.5%, 1% adv. - Financing: None.

PIZZA RANCH
1112 Main, Box 823, Hull, IA, 51239. Contact: Lawrence M. Vander Esch, Pres. - Tel: (712) 439-1150, (800) 321-3401. Pizza, chicken, salad bar, buffet and sandwiches. Established: 1981 - Franchising Since: 1984 - No. of Units: Company Owned: 6 - Franchised: 72 - Franchise Fee: $10,000 - Royalty: 3% - Total Inv: $50,000 - $100,000 equip., $2,000 - $4,000 inven., $5,000 misc., $3,000 - $5,000 signs, $5,000 - $10,000 working cap. - Financing: Not directly, but will assist in arranging.

PIZZA, U.S.A.
Pizza USA Franchise Corp.
2201 W. Sample Rd., Bldg. 9, #1B, Pompano Beach, FL, 33073. Contact: Ray Nevin, Pres. - Tel: (305) 972-5625, Fax: (305) 978-6406. Sale of Italian specialty items including pizza, calzone, pasta, salad. Specialize in mall food courts. Also offer "Express" and "Cafe" formats. Established: 1982 - Franchising Since: 1994 - No. of Units: Company Owned: 11 - Franchised: 10 - Franchise Fee: $25,000 - Royalty: 5%, .25% admin. fee, 2.5% adv. - Total Inv: varies $170,000 to $250,000 - Financing: No.

PIZZAS BY MARCHELLONI
Italian Express Franchise Corp.
1051 Essington Rd., Ste. 270, Joliet, IL, 60435. Contact: Hass Aslami, Pres. - Tel: (815) 729-4494. Pizza delivery, carry-out or dine-in. Strong local restaurant marketing. Featuring pan pizza, thin pizza, garlic bread and soft drinks. Established: 1986 - Franchising Since: 1989 - No. of Units: Franchised: 50 - Franchise Fee: $18,500 - Royalty: 5% + 2% adv. - Total Inv: $32,000 - $112,000. Financing: None.

PIZZERIA UNO
UNO Restaurants Corp.
100 Charles Park Rd., W. Roxbury, MA, 02132. Contact: William Gallucci, V.P. Fran. Dev. - Tel: (617) 323-9200; (800) 442-8667. Casual theme restaurant specializing in Chicago-style deep dish pizza. Established: 1943 - Franchising Since: 1979 - Franchise Fee: $50,000 - Royalty: 5% of sales - Financing: 2nd units only.

PIZZETTI'S PIZZA *
Mazzio's Corporation
4441 So. 72nd E. Ave., Tulsa, OK, 74145-4692. Contact: Mark Long, Mgr., Brand Dev./Lic. - Tel: (981) 663-8880, Fax: (918) 641-1236. Pizzetti's Pizza is a high volume pizza restaurant that features an all you can eat buffet with a wide variety of pizza, pasta, dessert pizza, cinnamon sticks and salad. Ordering from a menu is available along with carry-out. Pizzetti's are spacious, attractive facilities that are very customer oriented. Established: 1993 - Franchising Since: 1995 - No. of Units: Company Owned: 8 - Franchised: 1 - Franchise Fee: $25,000 - Royalty: 4%, 1% adv. - Total Inv: $370,000 to $535,000 without real estate, $770,000 to $1,135,000 with real estate - Financing: No.

PLUS 1 PIZZA
R.D.F. Developments, Inc.
1354 Clark Street, P.O. Box 516, Cambridge, OH, 43725-0516. Contact: Robert Fettes, Sr., Pres. - Tel: (614) 432-6066. Carry-out and delivery pizza business selling pizzas 2 for 1. Established: 1977 - Franchising Since: 1988 - No. of Units: Company Owned: 11 - Franchised: 3 - Franchise Fee: $20,000 - Royalty: 5%, 2% adv. fee - Total Inv: $34,900 - $89,900 - Financing: Assistance with lenders and bank presentation.

POFOLKS
P.O. Box 10, Mount Sterling, KY, 40353-0010. Contact: Martha Dickens, V.P. Fran. - Tel: (606) 498-2200. A full-service restaurant serving home-style meals in large portions, priced moderately, in a rustic country setting. Beverages (non-alcoholic) are served in mason jars, country music plays in the background, and the extensive menu is written in traditional country idioms. Established: 1975 - Franchising Since: 1978 - No. of Units: Company Owned: 70 - Franchised: 69 - Franchise Fee: $25,000 - Royalty: 2.5% - Total Inv: $650,000 - $900,000 - Financing: No.

POLLO TROPICAL
Pollo Tropical, Inc.
7300 N. Kendall Dr., 8th Floor, Miami, FL, 33156. Contact: Daniel W. O'Grady, VP, Fran. Dev. - Tel: (305) 670-POYO (7696), Fax: (305) 670-6403. Quick service flame grilled chicken with Caribbean and traditional side dishes served in a festive and inviting atmosphere. Established: 1988 - Franchising Since: 1993 - No. of Units: Company Owned: 35 - Franchised: 5 - Franchise Fee: $40,000 - Royalty: 4% - Total Inv: $700,000 to $800,000 building & equip. - Financing: No.

PONDEROSA
Metromedia Restaurant Group
12404 Park Center Dr., Dallas, TX, 75251. Contact: Edward J. Day, Dir. Fran. Sales - Tel: (800) 543-9670, (214) 404-5000. America's Family Steakhouse, a modified full-service, affordable family steakhouse restaurant, open 7 days a week for lunch and dinner. Menu features approximately 10 beef entrees, 4 seafood entrees, 3 chicken entrees and the Grand Buffet. Established: 1965 - Franchising Since: 1966 - No. of Units: Company Owned: 347 - Franchised: 360 domestic, 37 international - Franchise Fee: $30,000 - Royalty: 4.8%, 4% adv. - Total Inv: $1,210,000 - Financing: Assists in identifying sources.

POPEYES FRIED CHICKEN & BISCUITS
America's Favorite Chicken Co.
Six Concourse Pkwy., Ste. 1700, Atlanta, GA, 30328. Contact: Elizabeth Smith, Mktg. Comm. Coord. - Tel: (770) 353-3000. World's second largest quick service chicken company featuring buttermilk biscuits, seafood specialties, onion rings, battered french fries and more. Established: 1972 - Franchising Since: 1977 - No. of Units: Company Owned: 114 - Franchised: 799 - Franchise Fee: $10,000 dev. per unit; $15,000 fran. fee - Royalty: .5% of gross revenue - Total Inv: Traditional $214,800 to $290,600; Alternative $147,300 to $270,600 - Financing: N/A.

PORT OF SUBS
Port of Subs, Inc.
5365 Mae Anne Ave., #A-29, Reno, NV, 89523. Contact: Pat Larsen, Pres. - Tel: (702) 747-0555. Up-scale fresh-sliced submarine sandwiches served on custom rolls baked on premises, salads, party platters, breakfast sandwiches and pastries. Established: 1975 - Franchising Since: 1986 - No. of Units: Company Owned: 14 - Franchised: 59 - Franchise Fee: $16,000 - Royalty: 5.5% of net sales - Total Inv: $127,000-$165,000 - Financing: No.

POTATO SACK, THE
Potato Sack Franchise Corp.
201 Monroeville Mall, Monroeville, PA, 15146. Contact: Buzz Pasquini, Dir. of Fran. Oper. - Tel: (800) 828-3770, Fax: (412) 373-4497. Regional mall food court operation specializing in baked potatoes, fresh cut french fries and potato skins with a wide variety of gourmet toppings. Established: 1980 - Franchising Since: 1993 - No. of Units: Company Owned: 6 - Franchised: 2 - Franchise Fee: $20,000 - Royalty: 5%, 1% adv. - Total Inv: $150,000 - $225,000 - Financing: None.

POTTS' HOT DOGS
P.O. Box 08195, Ft. Myers, FL, 33908. Contact: William Potts, Pres. - Tel: (813) 466-7747. Retail sales of mainly hot dogs. Established: 1984 - Franchising Since: 1984 - No. of Units: Company Owned: 5 - Franchised: 4 - Franchise Fee: $15,000 - Royalty: 4% gross sales - Total Inv: $20,000 equip., $10,000 operating, $15,000 fran. fee - Financing: No.

POUR LA FRANCE!
650 S. Cherry, #1200, Denver, CO, 80222. Contact: John Bennett, Pres. - Tel: (303) 322-1298. Retail French style cafes featuring sandwiches, baked goods and French pastries as well as two wholesale bakeries. Established: 1980 - Franchising Since: 1988 - No. of Units: Company Owned: 7 - Franchised: 2 - Franchise Fee: $15,000 - Royalty: 4% - Total Inv: $250,000 turn-key - Financing: No.

PRAIRIE HOUSE RESTAURANT
65 Hassan St. S., Hutchinson, MN, 55350. Contact: Curtis Bradford, Pres. - Tel: (612) 587-4417. Family restaurant. Established: 1976 - No. of Units: Company Owned: 7 - Franchised: 5.

PUDGIE'S FAMOUS CHICKEN
333 Earl Ovington Blvd., #604, Uniondale, NY, 11553. Contact: Alan Guinn, V.P. Fran. Sales - Tel: (800) 992-4425, Fax: (516) 222-8044. Known for convenience and service, Pudgie's offers sit down, take-out, and delivery options. Serving our skinless fried chicken, with accompanying side items. State of the art training and continuous field support. Intensive marketing & advertising support. Established: 1981 - Franchising Since: 1989 - Franchise Fee: $30,000 - Royalty: 5% of net sales - Total Inv: $165,000 - $195,000 - Financing: Available through third party financing sources.

PUDGIE'S PIZZA & SUBS
Pudgie's Pizza Franchising, Inc.
520-530 North Main St., Elmira, NY, 14901. Contact: F.J. Cleary, Pres.. Pizza, subs, wings. Family run since 1963. All products made fresh daily on site. Take out, pick up window or delivery. Self serve dining room. Established: 1963 - Franchising Since: 1969 - No. of Units: Franchised: 34 - Royalty: 4%.

PUDLEY'S
390 El Camino, Belmont, CA, 94002. Contact: Richard Mazzoni, Pres. - Tel: (415) 593-1144. An exciting concept featuring a unique western atmosphere specializing in a large variety of hamburgers, sandwiches, salad wagon, beer and wine bar and video games. Established: 1980 - Franchising Since: 1983 - No. of Units: 2 - Royalty: 1% min., 2% max. - Approx. Inv: $100,000 - Financing: No.

QUIJAS ENTERPRISES
2214 E. 11th St., East Davenport, IA, 52803. Contact: Marilyn Quijas, Owner - Tel: (319) 322-0668. Fast food restaurants. Established: 1973 - No. of Units: Company Owned: 2- Franchised: 7.

QUIZNO'S CLASSIC SUBS
The Quizno's Corp.
7555 E. Hampden Ave., #601, Denver, CO, 80231. Contact: Scott Adams, Nat'l. Fran. Dev. Mgr. - Tel: (303) 368-9424. Upscale Italian deli-style restaurant specializing in made-to-order oven-baked sub sandwiches, hot pastas, salads & soups. Established: 1981 - Franchising Since: 1983 - No. of Units: Company Owned: 1 - Franchised: 57 - Franchise Fee: $20,000 - Royalty: 5%, 3% adv. - Total Inv: $160,000 - $200,000 incl. FF (turn key) - Financing: No.

R.J. GATOR'S RAW BAR & SEA GRILLE
R.J. Gator's Inc.
609 N. Hepburn Ave. #103, Jupiter, FL, 33458. Contact: Reginald Timoteo, Pres. - Tel: (407) 575-0326. Fun, casual restaurants. Established: 1986 - Franchising Since: 1991 - No. of Units: Company Owned: 3 - Franchised: 3 - Franchise Fee: $30,000 - Royalty: 5% of gross - Total Inv: $480,000: equip. & improv. $400,000, startup & supplies $50,000, franc. fee.

RALLY'S INC.
10002 Shelbyville Rd., Ste. 150, Louisville, KY, 40223. Contact: Jody Hermann, Dir. of Fran. - Tel: (502) 245-8900. Double drive-thru hamburger (fast food) limited menu with outside patio area. Established: 1985 - Franchising Since; 1986 - No. of Units: Company Owned: 170 - Franchised: 254 - Franchise Fee: $20,000 per store - Royalty: 4% sales, 4% adv. - Total Inv: $360,000 for build., equip. & site prep. costs - Financing: None.

RAMS HORN RESTAURANTS INC.
24225 W. Nine Mile, Ste. 214, Southfield, MI, 48034. Contact: E. Kasapis, Partner - Tel: (810) 350-3430. Family restaurants. Established: 1967 - No. of Units: Company Owned: 8 - Franchised: 16.

RANCH *1
*Ranch *1 Group, The*
CSS Franchising: 177 Main St., Ste. 103, Fort Lee, NJ, 07024. Contact: Franchise Sales Rep. - Tel: (201) 585-4753. Bistro style grilled chicken specialties combined with the speed and value of traditional fast food restaurants. Established: 1991 - Franchising Since: 1994 - No. of Units: Company Owned: 3 - Franchised: 31 sold - Franchise Fee: $18,000 - Royalty: 5% of gross - Total Inv: $150,000 incl. build-out, equip., stock - Financing: Yes.

RED BOY PIZZA
Red Boy Pizza Franchising Corp.
1000 5th Ave., San Rafael, CA, 94901. Contact: Kathleen Forstner, Fran. Dir. - Tel: (415) 459-4271. Upscale in house service. Emphasis on pizza, homemade soup, spaghetti sauce and an outstanding blue cheese dressing. Take-out and delivery units. Family oriented. No video machines or juke boxes. Established: 1970 - Franchising Since : 1988 - No. of Units: Company Owned: 1 - Franchised: 8 - Franchise Fee: $25,000 - Royalty: 5%, 1% adv. - Total Inv: varies - Financing: No.

RED HOT & BLUE
1600 Wilson Blvd., Arlington, VA, 22209. Contact: Bob Friedman, Pres. - Tel: (703) 276-8833. Serve Memphis-style barbeque, featuring ribs, pork shoulder & chicken. The casual theme restaurant also features blues music & the walls are covered with blues memorabilia. Established: 1988 - Franchising Since: 1990 - No. of Units: Company Owned: 3 - Franchised: 15 - Franchise Fee: $20,000 - Royalty: 5% - Total Inv: $500,000 - Financing: No.

RED ROBIN BURGER & SPIRITS EMPORIUM
Red Robin International, Inc.
28 Executive Park, #200, Irvine, CA, 92714. Contact: Madison Jobe, V.P./Director - Tel: (714) 756-2121. Full service, casual dining restaurants offering high quality, moderately priced food and alcoholic beverages in an attractive, informal setting that is decorated to entertain. Established: 1969 - Franchising Since: 1979 - No. of Units: Company Owned: 47 - Franchised: 79 - Franchise Fee: $35,000 per restaurant - Royalty: 4%, 0.5% adv. - Total Inv: $1,000,000 - $3,500,000 - Financing: Outside financing available.

RENZIOS INC.
701 W. Hampden, Ste. B109, Englewood, CO, 80110. Contact: Bill Brinstead, Fran. Dir. - Tel: (303) 781-3441, (800) 892-3441. Greek fast food offering a unique and highly professional restaurant appearance and format, serving primarily Greek fast food. Established: 1979 - Franchising Since: 1989 - No. of Units: Company Owned: 8 - Franchised: 4 - Franchise Fee: $18,000 - Royalty: 5% + 2% adv. - Total Inv: $50,000 - $90,000 varies upon location - Financing: Assistance.

RICHY'S RESTAURANTS *
1400 King St., Ste. B, Bellingham, WA, 98226. Contact: Ron Hildebrand, Sr. V.P. - Tel: (800) 7Rickys. Family restaurant chain. Established: 1979 - Franchising Since: 1987 - No. of Units: Company Owned: 5 - Franchised: 25 - Franchise Fee: $40,000 - Royalty: 3%, 2.5% adv. - Total Inv: $150,000 - $475,000.

RICKSHAW CHINESE FOOD
Rickshaw Restaurants, Inc.
1230 El Camino Real, Ste. D4, San Bruno, CA, 94066. Contact: Anna Laveria May, Dir. - Tel: (415) 952-8666. Chinese fast-food restaurants specializing in freshly prepared Chinese food. A good portion of our business focuses on take-out meals. Established: 1981 - Franchising Since: 1992 - No. of Units: Company Owned: 4 - Franchised: 4- Franchise Fee: $14,000 - Royalty: 4% of gross sales, up to 3% of gross sales for adv. - Total Inv: $78,000 - $96,000 start-up cash; $153,000 - $193,000 total inv. - Financing: May offer up to 50% financing of initial fran. fee and can refer franchisees to equipment leasing companies and for select existing company-owned stores we may consider financing for qualified prospects.

RICKY'S RESTAURANTS *
1400 King St., Ste. B., Bellingham, WA, 98226. Contact: Ron Hildebrand, Sr. V.P. - Tel: (800) 7Rickys. Family restaurant chain. Established: 1979 - Franchising Since: 1987 - No. of Units: Company Owned: 5 - Franchised: 25 - Franchise Fee: $40,000 - Royalty: 3%, 2.5% adv. - Total Inv: $150,000 - $475,000.

ROCCO RACCOON'S INDOOR PLAYGROUNDS *
Rocco Raccoon's Indoor Playgrounds Inc.
27 Minard St., Lockport, NY, 14094. Contact: Mr. Varlis, Franchise Dept. - Tel: (716) 434-7553. Canadian Inquiries: 12-111 Fourth Ave., Ste. 350, Ridley Square, St. Catharines, ON, L2S 3P5, Tel: (905) 984-5115. Contact: Mr. Varlis, Franchise Dept. We specialize in opening Fun Family Play Centers with Indoor supervised play areas, with a full menu (including pizza), gift shops, skill testing games and animated characters. Established: 1994 - Franchising Since: 1994 - Franchise Fee: $40,000 - Royalty: 3% of gross annual sales - Total Inv: $500,000 to $850,000 - Financing: Reality, comp., acct., admin., complete training program and ongoing support. "Where Kids Of All Ages Have Fun."™ Our concept welcomes those who are looking for this fastest growing industry sweeping North America.

ROCKY ROCOCO PAN STYLE PIZZA
P.O. Box 207, Oconomowoc, WI, 53066. Contact: Tom Hester, Pres. - Tel: (414) 569-5580. Pizza restaurants. Established: 1974 - Franchising Since: 182 - No. of Units: Company Owned: 12 - Franchised: 38 - Franchise Fee: $35,000 territorial only - Royalty: 3.5% - Total Inv: $700,000 per restaurant - Financing: No.

ROGER CLEMENS FLAME ROASTED CHICKEN
Celebrity Sports Assoc.
1525 Mineral Spring Ave., North Providence, RI, 02904. Contact: Anthony Manzo, Pres. - Tel: (401) 353-5585. Rotisserie chicken, fast food of the 90's, multi-unit chain. Established: 1991 - Franchising Since: 1993 - No. of Units: Company Owned: 1 - Franchised: 4 - Franchise Fee: $30,000 - Royalty: 4.5% - Total Inv: $150,000 - $200,000.

ROLLO POLLO
4801 Sherburn Lane, Ste. 215, Louisville, KY, 40207. Contact: Rick Jeffrey, Pres. - Tel: (502) 896-6181, Fax: (502) 896-1534. Rotisserie chicken. Established: 1991 - Franchising Since: 1992 - No. of Units: Company Owned: 1 - Franchised: 1 - Franchise Fee: $15,000 - Royalty: 4% - Total Inv: $250,000 - Financing: No.

RON'S PIZZA DELIVERY/RON'S PIZZA HOUSE/A & R PIZZA
18 N 12th St., Miamisburg, OH, 45342. Contact: Rollin Holp/Tim Holp, Pres./Fran. Oper. - Tel: (513) 866-6221. Family restaurant. Established: 1961 - No. of Units: Company Owned: 4 - Franchised: 6.

RONZIO PIZZA
Pizzeria Management Systems, Inc.
194 Waterman St., Providence, RI, 02906. Contact: Julian Angelone, Gen. Mgr. - Tel: (401) 751-4470. Pizza and sandwich shops with primary focus on the delivery of high quality hand tossed pizzas. Established: 1986 - Franchising Since: 1992 - No. of Units: Franchised: 17 - Franchise Fee: $10,000 - Royalty: 4% of gross sales, 1% adv. - Total Inv: $76,000 - $106,000 - Financing: No.

ROSATI'S PIZZA
Rosati's Franchise Systems, Inc.
33 W. Higgins Rd., Ste. 1010, S. Barrington, IL, 60010. Contact: Ron Stockman, Pres. & CEO - Tel: (800) 210-1322. Rosati's Pizza restaurants specialize in the sale of pizza and other menu items for carry-out and delivery and utilize distinctive trade secret recipes, fresh ingredients and methods of preparing food. Established: 1964 - Franchising Since: 1988 - No. of Units: Company Owned: 37 - Franchised: 24 - Franchise Fee: $15,000 - Royalty: 5% gross sales - Total Inv: $110,000 to $170,000 equip., leasehold improvements, inventory, promotional expense, work. cap. & franchise fee - Financing: None.

ROUND TABLE PIZZA
Round Table Franchise Corp.
655 Montgomery St., 7th Floor, Ste. 700, San Francisco, CA, 94111. Contact: Jake Brown, Dir. Fran. Sales - Tel: (800) 866-5866. Family style pizza restaurant that provides the public with quality pizza and related food products. Established: 1959 - Franchising Since: 1962 - No. of Units: Franchised: 560 - Franchise Fee: $25,000 - Royalty: 8%-4% fran. fee & 4% adv. fee - Total Inv: $300,000-$100,000 cash and $200,000 equity - Financing: We offer third party lending to qualified franchisees.

ROUND THE CORNER RESTAURANTS, INC.
8620 Wolff Ct., #330, Westminster, CO, 80030-3690. Contact: Boyd Hoback, Pres. - Tel: (303) 427-1415. Family restaurants. No. of Units: Company Owned: 13 - Franchised: 7.

ROYAL GUARD FISH & CHIPS
4 Apple Tree Dr., Stamford, CT, 06906. Contact: Henry R. Parent, Pres. - Tel: (203) 324-1225. Family restaurants. Established: 1970 - No. of Units: Company Owned: 2 - Franchised: 4.

RUBY'S DINER
Ruby's Franchise Systems, Inc.
110 Newport Center Dr., Ste. 110, Newport Beach, CA, 92660. Contact: Doug Cavanaugh, Pres. & CEO - Tel: (714) 644-7829. Full serve restaurant. Established: 1982 - Franchising Since: 1988 - No. of Units: Company Owned: 10 - Franchised: 5 - Franchise Fee: $40,000 - Royalty: 5%, 1% adv., 2% self directed adv. - Total Inv: $300,000 - $800,000 depending on location - Financing: None.

RUDOLPH'S BAR-B-Q
1933 Lindale Ave. S., Minneapolis, MN, 55403. Contact: Franchise Director - Tel: (612) 871-8855. Family Restaurant. Established: 1975. No. of Units: Company Owned: 3 - Franchised: 2.

RUNZA DRIVE INN RESTAURANTS
5931 S. 58th Ste. C & D, Lincoln, NE, 68516. Contact: Ron Owens, Dir. of Fran. - Tel: (402) 423-2394. Fast food restaurant featuring unique Runza sandwiches, and homemade onion rings. Our food is top quality. Franchising Since: 1979 - No. of Units: Company Owned: 20 - Franchised: 35 - Franchise Fee: $22,000 - Royalty: 5%, 1.5% - Total Inv: $150,000 - $675,000.

RYAN'S FAMILY STEAK HOUSE
405 Lancaster Ave., P.O. Box 100, Greer, SC, 29652. Contact: Amy Austin, Fran. Dir. - Tel: (803) 879-1000. Family restaurant. Established: 1977 - No. of Units: Company Owned: 104 - Franchised: 28.

SALADALLEY RESTAURANTS, INC.
41 St. James Pl., Ardmore, PA, 19003. Contact: Michael Cullina, Pres. - Tel: (610) 642-0453. Restaurant. Established: 1978 - Franchising Since: 1986 - No. of Units: Company Owned: 5 - Franchised: 2 - Franchise Fee: $25,000 - Royalty: 4% + 2% adv. - Total Inv: $300,000: $200,000 B.I., $75,000 R.E., fran. fee - Financing: No.

SALVATORE SCALLOPINI
Scallopini Ventures
27190 Dequinore, Warren, MI, 48092. Contact: Lawrence or Sarina Bongiovanni, Pres./V.P. - Tel: (810) 573-8960. Full-service restaurant with liquor, and authentic Italian fare. Specialize in homemade pasta. Carry-out from menu available. Also catering service. Established: 1983 - Franchising Since: 1988 - No. of Units: Company Owned: 5 - Franchised: 6 - Franchise fee: $25,000 - Royalty: 4% - Total Inv: $275,000 - $525,000 - Financing: No.

SAM'S HOT DOGS *
Sam's Hot Dogs, Inc.
P.O. Box 539, Waynesboro, VA, 22980. Contact: Frank Lucente, Pres. - Tel: (703) 949-6186, Fax: (703) 949-6186. Fast food restaurant. Established: 1988 - Franchising Since: 1990 - No. of Units: Franchised: 18 - Franchise Fee: $4,000 - Royalty: 4% gross sales - Total Inv: $18,000 - $25,000.

SAM'S ITALIAN FOODS
268 Main St., Lewiston, ME, 04240. Contact: Gerald Clement, Pres. - Tel: (207) 782-2550. Dinnerhouse - Fast food. Established: 1969 - No. of Units: Company Owned: 5 - Franchised: 10.

SAMMI'S DELI
Sammi's Deli Inc.
114 Wilton Hill Rd., Columbia, SC, 29212. Contact: Sam, Pres. - Tel: (803) 256-7762. Fast food operation. Special philly steak gyro subs with concentration on free delivery. Established: 1984 - Franchising Since: 1990 - No. of Units: Company Owned: 1 - Franchised: 4 - Franchise Fee: $9,500 - Royalty: $350 a mon. or 5% whichever is higher - Total Inv: $60,000 - $80,000 - Financing: No.

SAMUEL MANCINO'S ITALIAN EATERY *
Nu-Ventures Inc.
1595 W. Centre St., Ste. 101, Portage, MI, 49002. Contact: Sam Mancino, Pres. - Tel: (616) 527-6800, Fax: (616) 327-6807. Italian eatery serving Italian grinders, pizza's, pastas & appetizers. Established: 1992 - Franchising Since: 1994 - No. of Units: Franchised: 12 - Franchise Fee: $40,000 First Store $10,000 each additional - Royalty: 4% - Total Inv: $175,000 - $225,000 - Financing: None.

SANDY'S ASSOCIATES, INC.
1503 N. Boeke Rd., Evansville, IN, 47711. Contact: Joseph H. Harrison, Pres. - Tel: (812) 477-5569. Fast food restaurants. Established: 1963 - No. of Units: Franchised: 16.

SBARRO THE ITALIAN EATERY
Sbarro, Inc.
763 Larkfield Rd., Commack, NY, 11725. Contact: Gennaro A. Sbarro, V.P. Fran. - Tel: (516) 864-0200. Fast food Italian restaurants. Established: 1959 - Franchising Since: 1977 - No. of Units: Company Owned: 480 - Franchised: 150 - Franchise Fee: $35,000 - Royalty: 5%, 1% adv. - Min. Start Up Cost: $224,000 - Financing: None.

SCHLOTZSKY'S DELI RESTAURANT
Schlotzsky's Inc.
200 W. Fourth St., Austin, TX, 78701. Contact: Mr. Kelly Arnold, V.P. Fran. Dev. - Tel: (512) 469-7500, Fax: (512) 477-2897. Bakery/deli/restaurant. Deli sandwiches served on Schlotzsky's unique proprietary bread, sourdough crust pizzas, soups, salads, desserts, gourmet coffees, and specialty breakfast items. Established: 1971 - Franchising Since: 1977 - No. of Units: Company Owned: 2 - Franchised: 400 - Franchise Fee: $20,000 - Royalty: 6%, 1% mktg. fund - Total Inv: $200,000 - $300,000 - Financing: Yes.

SCHOOP'S HAMBURGERS
Schoop's Hamburgers, Inc.
215 Ridge Rd., Munster, IN, 46321. Contact: Mark Schoop, Pres. - Tel: (219) 836-6233. Fast Food/Hamburgers. Established: 1948 - No. of Units: Franchised: 17.

SCOTTO PIZZA
1895 Greentree Rd., Cherry Hill, NJ, 08003. Contact: John Harty, Fran. Dir. - Tel: (609) 424-4260. Pizza. Established: 1975 - Franchising Since: 1975 - Franchise Fee: $30,000 - $50,000 - Royalty: 7% - Total Inv: $60,000 - $150,000 - Financing: Yes.

SERGIO'S MEXICAN RESTAURANT
16 Broadway, Ste. 212, Fargo, ND, 58102. Contact: Russell Maring, Dir. of Fran. Sales - Tel: (701) 237-5151. Mexican restaurants planned for growth in secondary markets of 40,000 to 150,000 population. Established: 1981 - Franchising Since: 1985 - No. of Units: Company Owned: 4 - Franchised: 5 - Franchise Fee: $25,000 - $37,500 - Royalty: 2% to 4% - Total Inv: $150,000 - Financing: No.

SHAKEY'S PIZZA RESTAURANTS
Shakey's, Inc.
651 Gateway Blvd. #950, S. San Francisco, CA, 94080-7025. Contact: Greg Krupski, Fran. Dev. - Tel: (800) 444-9268, (415) 873-0640. Family pizza restaurant featuring pizza, salad bar, chicken, mojo-potatoes, and pasta. Also offer expanded lunch display. Established: 1954 - Franchising Since: 1958 - No. of Units: Company Owned: 20 - Franchised: 371 - Franchise Fee: $25,000 - Royalty: 4.5%, 2% nat'l adv. fund - Total Inv: $350,000 - $500,000 - Financing: By local sources or equip. leasing comp.

SHARI'S MANAGEMENT CORP. DBA SHARI'S RESTAURANTS
8205 SW Creekside Pl. #D, Beaverton, OR, 97008. Contact: Tom Gibbons, Dir. of Real Estate - Tel: (503) 641-6338. 24 hr. family style restaurant. Established: 1978 - No. of Units: Company Owned: 50 - Franchised: 10.

SHOOTERS ON THE WATER
Shooters International, Inc.
3033 N.E. 32nd Ave., Fort Lauderdale, FL, 33308. Contact: Melvin Burge, V.P. of Dev. - Tel: (954) 566-3044, Fax: (954) 566-2953. Upscale waterfront cafe and bar. Both indoor & patio dining, boat docking. Established: 1982 - Franchising Since: 1985 - No. of Units: Company Owned: 1 - Franchised: 6 - Franchise Fee: $75,000 - Royalty: 4% gross - Total Inv: $1,200,000 - $1,600,000 - Financing: No.

SHOWBIZ PIZZA PLACE AND CHUCK E. CHEESE'S
Showbiz Pizza Time, Inc.
4441 W. Airport Freeway, Irving, TX, 75062. Contact: Mickey Dire, Exec. V.P./Dir. Fran. Dev. - Tel: (214) 258-8507. Family-oriented restaurants featuring pizza and other food and beverages. Entertainment at the restaurant, by three dimensional computer-controlled animated characters, a kiddie and skill game area w/coin and/or token operated games, rides and the sale of novelty products. Established: 1980 - Franchising Since: 1981 - No. of Units: Company Owned: 135 - Franchised: 127 - Franchise Fee: $25,000 - Royalty: 3.8% +3.3% adv. - Total Inv: $750,000 - $1,000,000 turn-key - Financing: No.

SICILY'S, THE PIZZA PLACE, INC./SICILY'S PIZZA JR.
4635 S. Sherwood Forest Blvd., Baton Rouge, LA, 70816. Contact: Don Dogu, Pres. - Tel: (504) 291-7284. Quality pizza, lasagna and sandwiches, salad bar, beer, wine, wine coolers, served in an upscale dining atmosphere. Table service. Established: 1975 - Franchising Since: 1984 - No. of Units: Company Owned: 1 - Franchised: 12 - Franchise Fee: $10,000 - Royalty: 4% - Total Inv: approx. $125,000 for full service.

SIMPLE SIMON'S PIZZA *
J&H Foods
6650 S. Lewis, Tulsa, OK, 74136. Contact: Todd Miller, Fran. Dir. - Tel: (918) 496-1272. A full service and non-traditional pizza company that specializes in small markets and rural areas. Emphasis is on quality and a great price - value relationship for customers. Established: 1985 - Franchising Since: 1987 - No. of Units: Company Owned: 80 - Franchised: 30 - Franchise Fee: $15,000 - Royalty: 3%, 1% adv. - Total Inv: $60,000 to $120,000 - Financing: No.

SIR GEORGE'S ROYAL BUFFET
Kronan Corp.
7855 S. River Pkwy., #105, Tempe, AZ, 85284-1825. Contact: David Kronwald, Pres. - Tel: (602) 838-1101. Family Restaurant. Established: 1981 - No. of Units: Company Owned: 8 - Franchised: 10.

SIR PIZZA
SP United, Inc.
1500 W. Cypress Creek Rd., Ste. 512, Ft. Lauderdale, FL, 33309. Contact: Michael Al-Omari, Pres. - Tel: (305) 351-0121. Specializing in pizza, pasta, sandwiches, salads, full service, take out and delivery. Established: 1958 - Franchising Since: 1966 - No. of Units: Company Owned: 26 - Franchised: 79 - Franchise Fee: $15,000 - Royalty: 5% - Total Inv: $131,000: (leasehold $55,000, equip. $52,000, inven/training $9,000) - Financing: Yes.

SIRLOIN STOCKADE FAMILY RESTAURANTS
Sirloin Stockade International, Inc.
2908 North Plum, Hutchinson, KS, 67502. Contact: Judy Froese, Dir. Fran. Dev. - Tel: (316) 669-9372, Fax: (316) 669-0531. Featuring a selection of top quality steaks, chicken and fish; self-service salad, hot food buffet, and display bakery - at affordable prices. Restaurants seat 300 - 400 guests; approx. 10,000 sq. ft. bldg; requires 1.5+ acres of land. Eight weeks training, recipes, manuals provided. Established: 1984 - Franchising Since: 1984 - No. of Units: Company Owned: 8 - Franchised: 75 - Franchise Fee: $15,000 in USA - Royalty: 3% in USA + 1% mktg. fund - Total Inv: $1,200,000 to $2,260,000: land, bldg, equip. - Financing: None.

SIZZLER
Sizzler Restaurants International, Inc.
P.O. Box 92092, Los Angeles, CA, 90009. Contact: James Collins, Chairman - Tel: (310) 827-2300. Specializing in steaks, seafood and salads. Established: 1954 - No. of Units: Company Owned: 265 - Franchised: 430.

SIZZLER SANTA CLARA, INC.
5353 B. Almaden Expy., San Jose, CA, 95118. Contact: O. Printy, Pres. - Tel: (408) 267-2242. Family restaurants. Established: 1971 - No. of Units: Franchised: 10.

SIZZLIN' QUICK HAMBURGERS, INC.
9442 Capital of Texas Hwy. N., Arboretum Plz. One, Ste. 785, Austin, TX, 78759. Contact: Stephen Hatch, Pres. - Tel: (512) 343-8493. Established: 1991 - Franchising Since: 1992 - No. of Units: Company Owned: 2 - Franchised: 6 - Franchise Fee: $25,000 - Royalty: 4% of gross - Total Inv: $350,000 - $500,000 - Financing: Not through corporation.

SLACK'S HOAGIE SHACK
CSS Franchising: 177 Main St., Ste. 103, Ft. Lee, NJ, 07024. Contact: Franchise Rep. - Tel: (201) 585-4753. Full menu Hoagie shop featuring Philia's Original Cheese Steak. All sports motif, in line units. Established: 1988 - Franchising Since: 1993 - No. of Units: Company Owned: 2 - Franchised: 1 - Franchise Fee: $20,000 - Royalty: 5%, 3% adv. - Total Inv: $120,000 - $140,000 incl. build-out and all equip. - Financing: Yes.

SOBIK'S SUBS
SBK Franchise Systems, Inc.
807 S. Orlando Ave., Ste. H, Winter Park, FL, 32789. Contact: Beth Mendez, Dir. Marketing - Tel: (800) 323 INFO (4636). Fast service restaurant serving sandwiches, subs, salads, spaghetti. Stress high quality, fast services, simplicity of operation. Established: 1969 - Franchising Since: 1981 - No. of Units: Company Owned: 10 - Franchised: 50 - Franchise Fee: $10,000 - Royalty: 5%, 4% adv. - Total Inv: $50,000 - $110,000 - Financing: Some.

SONIC DRIVE-IN RESTAURANTS
Sonic Industries Inc.
101 Park Ave., Ste. 1400, Oklahoma City, OK, 73102. Contact: Ms. J. Archer, Dir. Fran. Mktg. - Tel: (405) 232-4334. Drive-in restaurant fast food menu featuring hamburgers, hot dogs, french fries, onion rings, soft drinks & dessert products. Established: 1948 - Franchising Since: 1973 - No. of Units: Company Owned: 93 - Franchised: 1,262 - Franchise Fee: $15,000 - Royalty: scaled to 4% - Total Inv: $300,000 - $500,000 - Financing: Available through outside sources.

SONNY'S REAL PIT BAR-B-QUE, INC.
Sonny's Franchise Co.
2605 Maitland Center Pky #C, Maitland, FL, 32751. Contact: Jane Damron, Fran. Coord. - Tel: (407) 660-8888. Sonny's Real Pit Bar BQ offers franchises for full service barbeque restaurants. Family dining with a salad bar, childrens menu, variety of lunch specials and diet plates. Take-out and catering service also available. Established: 1969 - No. of Units: Company Owned: 8 - Franchised: 75- Franchise Fee: $25,000 - Royalty: 2.5%, 1% adv. - Financing: No.

SOUPER SALAD, INC.
5460 Weslayan St., Houston, TX, 77005-1050. Contact: Ray Barshick, Pres. - Tel: (713) 660-8950. Cafeteria - American style. Established: 1978 - No. of Units: Company Owned: 27 - Franchised: 9.

SOUTHERN MANAGEMENT ASSOC.
324 S.W. 16th St., Belle Glade, FL, 33430. Contact: Charles F. Royal, Pres. - Tel: (407) 996-6581. Fast food restaurants. No. of Units: Franchised: 8.

SPAD'S PIZZA, INC.
2420 East Grand River, P.O. Box 239, Williamston, MI, 48895. Contact: Mark Tithof, Dir. of Mktg. - Tel: (517) 655-3944. Pizza by the slice drive-thru only. The concept was developed by Frank R. Spadafore in 1991 to capture the untapped niche of pizza by the slice drive-thru market. Established: 1991 - Franchising Since: 1992 - No. of Units: Company Owned: 1 - Franchised: 14 - Franchise Fee: $15,000 - Royalty: 4% of gross sales - Total Inv: $225,000 - $250,000 not including land - Financing: None at the present time.

SPAGHETTI JACK'S *
Stoico Food Services, Inc.
1861 N. Rock Rd., Ste. 202, Wichita, KS, 67206. Contact: Louis Stoico Jr., Founder - Tel: (800) 454-2199, (316) 683-7766. Quick-service casual Italian dining with an extensive menu of classic Italian favorites that are "always fast, fresh & affordable." Established: 1991 - Franchising Since: 1993 - No. of Units: Company Owned: 5 - Franchised: 6 - Franchise Fee: $25,000 - Royalty: 5% - Total Inv: $300,000 to $400,000 - Financing: No.

SPAGHETTI SHOP, THE
917 C Street, Ste. A, Charleston, IL, 61920. Contact: James Teaters, CEO - Tel: (217) 348-1535. Provide authentic, fresh cooked Italian food, served quickly and inexpensively. We have low start up and operating cost, allowing for tremendous potential. Food experience is not necessary but highly recommended. Established: 1985 - Franchising Since: 1987 - No. of Units: Company Owned: 1 - Franchised: 40 - Franchise Fee: $20,000 - Royalty: 5%, 3% adv. - Total Inv: $200,000 - $600,000 - Financing: Outside only.

SPINNER'S PIZZA & SUBS
10606 Shady Tr., #109, Dallas, TX, 75220. Contact: Bob Kogler, VP, Fran. - Tel: (214) 902-9011. Pizza and sub delivery and take out featuring the finest ingredients to make delicious pizza. Established: 1984 - Franchising Since: 1986 - No. of Units: Company Owned: 5 - Franchised: 25 - Franchise Fee: $15,000 - Royalty: 4% + 2% adv. - Total Inv: $40,000 equip., $15,000 fee, $10,000 work cap., $15,000 other - Financing: None.

SPOONER'S SNAPPY TOMATO PIZZA COMPANY
12115 Maddison Pike, Independence, KY, 41051. Contact: Steve Markovich, Dir. of Mktg. - Tel: (606) 363-0940. Carry out - dine-in and delivery pizzeria. Established: 1978 - Franchising Since: 1980 - No. of Units: Company Owned: 1 - Franchised: 42 - Franchise Fee: $15,000 - Royalty: 5%, 2% adv. - Total Inv: fran. fee plus $40,000 equip., $15,000 renovations - Financing: None, we will help in acquiring equipment packages.

STEAK & EGGER
5838 W. 26th St., Cicero, IL, 60650. Contact: Terrance Carr, Pres. - Tel: (708) 652-5522. Fast Food. Established: l965 - No. of Units: Company Owned: 1 - Franchised: 6.

STEAK ESCAPE, THE
Escape Enterprises Inc.
222 Neilston St., Columbus, OH, 43215-2636. Contact: Gary S. Jensen, Dir. of Fran. Sales - Tel: (614) 224-0300. Grilled sandwiches, freshly cut fries and fresh lemonade. All fresh ingredients. Nutritional food prepared to order in full view of customers. Established: 1982 - Franchising Since: 1983 - No. of Units: Company Owned: 11 - Franchised: 105 - Franchise Fee: $20,000 - Royalty: 6%, .5% mktg. - Total Inv: $169,000 to $253,500 - Financing: No.

STEAK & HOAGIE SHOP, THE
T & P Hoagie Systems, Inc.
2620 N. Sharon Amity Rd., Charlotte, NC, 28205. Contact: Tom Pappas, Pres. - Tel: (704) 568-7352. Fast food steak & deli sandwich shops. Established: 1979 - Franchising Since: 1987 - No. of Units: Company Owned: 3 - Franchised: 15 - Franchise Fee: $8,500 - Royalty: 4%, 3% adv. - Total Inv: $45,000 - $50,000 - Financing: 30% of total inv.

STEAK 'N SHAKE
Steak N Shake, Inc.
36 S. Pennsylvania St., Ste. 500, Indianapolis, IN, 46204. Contact: James Richmond, V.P. - Tel: (317) 633-4100. Unique restaurant concept serving quick-seared steak-burgers, thin french fries, genuine chili and hand dipped milk shakes. Steak N Shake offers full waitress service with food served on china as well as drive thru and take out service, in a casual environment reminiscent of the 50's. Established: 1934 - Franchising Since: 1939 - No. of Units: Company Owned: 131 - Franchised: 29 - Franchise Fee: $30,000 per location - Royalty: 4%, 5% adv. - Total Inv: $1,105,000 - $1,930,000 ($250,000 - $600,000 land; $420,000 - $635,000 site improv. bldg.; $315,000 - $360,000 equip.; $120,000 - $335,000 other) - Financing: No.

STEAK-OUT
Steak-Out Franchising, Inc.
8210 Stephanie Dr., Huntsville, AL, 35802. Contact: Emily Williams, Dir. of Licensing - Tel: (205) 883-2300. Specialize in the home and office delivery of char-broiled steaks, burgers and chicken. Established: 1986 - Franchising Since: 1987 - No. of Units: Franchised: 64 - Franchise Fee: $21,500 - Royalty: 4%, 2% Adv. - Total Inv: $175,250 - $249,000 (initial fee included in estimate) - Financing: No.

STEAKS TO GO *
Steaks To Go Franchise Co.
1475 Terrell Mill Rd., #112, Marietta, GA, 30067. Contact: Daniel O'Konta, C.O.O. - Tel: (770) 929-6024. Home and office delivery of charbroiled steaks, chicken and sandwiches. Established: 1990 - Franchising Since: 1995 - No. of Units: Franchised: 3 - Franchise Fee: $15,500 - Royalty: 3% - Total Inv: $100,000 to $150,000 - Financing: Assistance.

STEWART'S DRIVE-IN
Stewart's Restaurants, Inc.
114 W. Atlantic Ave., Clementon, NJ, 08021. Contact: Michael W. Fessler, Pres. - Tel: (609) 346-1300. Fast food restaurants featuring draft mugs of cold root beer, hot dogs, hamburgers, etc. Established: 1924 - Franchising Since: 1925 - No. of Units: Franchised: 51 - Franchise Fee: $15,000 - Royalty: 4% - Total Inv: approx. $135,000 - $175,000 without property - Financing: Assistance.

STONE CRAB INN
P.O. Box 557, Washington, PA, 15301-0557. Contact: James Deleo, Fran. Dir. - Tel: (412) 225-5991. Full menu seafood restaurant. Established: 1982 - No. of Units: 4 - Total Inv: $500,000 - Financing: Assistance through venture capital.

STOUT & CO.
109 Wheeler Exec. Center, Augusta, GA, 30909. Contact: Merrill L. Stout, Pres. - Tel: (706) 733-1484. Fast food restaurants. No. of Units: Franchised: 7.

STRAW HAT PIZZA
Straw Hat Cooperative Corporation
6400 Village Parkway, Dublin, CA, 94568. Contact: Jack Wood, Pres./C.E.O. - Tel: (510) 829-1500. Eat-in, take-out, or delivery of pizza, salads, sandwiches, spaghetti, beer, wine and soft drinks. Also gourmet pizzas, kids meals, cartoons & old-time movies. Group parties, birthdays, sports sponsorships, school programs & community fundraisers. Established: 1969 - Franchising Since: 1970 - No. of Units: Franchised: 65 - Franchise Fee: $10,000 - Royalty: Administrative 1.25%; Mktg. .5% - Total Inv: $50,000 - $500,000 - Financing: No.

STRINGS ITALIAN CAFE
Strings Franchises Inc.
11344 Coloma Rd. #545, Gold River, CA, 95670. Contact: Terry Odneal, Dir. Fran. Sales - Tel: (916) 635-3990, Fax: (916) 631-0775. Full service, casual restaurant. Menu focus on variety of pasta entrees, pizza, salads, desserts, espresso. Central kitchen/commissary provides most of product requirements. Established: 1987 - Franchising Since: 1989 - No. of Units: Company Owned: 4 - Franchised: 25 - Franchise Fee: $37,500 - Royalty: 5% - Total Inv: $265,000 - $350,000 (w/o fran. fee) - Financing: No.

STUFF 'N TURKEY
Stuff'n Turkey, Inc.
155 N. Main St., New City, NY, 10956. Contact: John Sterns, Sales Mgr. - Tel: (914) 638-4111. Specialty deli offering freshly roasted turkey dishes, sandwiches and related specialties. Established: 1986 - Franchising Since: 1987 - No. of Units: Company Owned: 7 - Franchised: 14 - Franchise Fee: $25,000 - Royalty: 5% - Total Inv: $138,000 - $168,000 plus fran. fee - Financing: None, will assist.

STUFT PIZZA FRANCHISE CORP.
Stuft Pizza Franchise Corp.
1040 Calle Cordillera, #103, San Clemente, CA, 92673. Contact: Jack Bertram, Pres. - Tel: (714) 361-2522, Fax: (714) 361-2501. Franchisor. Established: 1976 - Franchising Since: 1985 - No. of Units: Company Owned: 2 - Franchised: 32 - Franchise Fee: $15,000 to $25,000 - Royalty: 3% - Total Inv: $100,000 - $300,000 - Financing: No.

SUB SHOPS
Seawest Sub Shops, Inc.
1 Lake Bellevue Dr., Ste. 201, Bellevue, WA, 98005. Contact: Mitchell Day, Pres. - Tel: (206) 453-5216. Specialty submarine sandwiches, soups, salads. Established: 1980 - Franchising Since: 1986 - No. of Units: Company Owned: 7 - Franchised: 90 - Franchise Fee: $10,000 for new franchises; $5,000 for additional - Royalty: 5% of sales - Total Inv: $27,000 - $77,000 - Financing: 3rd party.

SUB STATION II
Sub Station II, Inc.
425 North Main St., Sumter, SC, 29150. Contact: Susan H. Vaden, V.P. Fran. - Tel: (803) 773-4711. Sandwich shops offer a variety of over 25 submarine sandwiches, developing an efficient method of preparing each sandwich to the customer's specifications. Emphasis on high quality food and cleanliness. Established: 1975 - Franchising Since: 1976 - No. of Units: Company Owned: 3 - Franchised: 97 - Franchise Fee: $10,500 - Royalty: 4% - Total Inv: $75,000 - Financing: Assistance.

SUB & STUFF SANDWICH SHOP
Stoico Food Services, Inc.
1861 N. Rock Rd., Ste. 202, Wichita, KS, 67206. Contact: Louis Stoico, Jr., Founder - Tel: (316) 683-7766, Fax: (316) 683-6194. Specialty submarine sandwich operation featuring a unique variety of subs, burgers, fries & more. Specialized preparation allows for made-to-order sandwiches on fresh baked bread, served quickly. Established: 1977 - Franchising Since: 1979 - No. of Units: Company Owned: 14 - Franchised: 1 - Franchise Fee: $15,000 - Royalty: 6%, 1% nat'l. adv. - Total Inv: $125,000 to $150,000 - Financing: No.

SUBWAY SANDWICHES AND SALADS
Doctor's Associates, Inc.
325 Bic Dr., Milford, CT, 06460. Contact: Fran. Sales Dept. - Tel: (800) 888-4848. Submarine sandwich chain, operating in all 50 States and 29 countries including Canada. Bread baked fresh daily in every store. Established: 1965 - Franchising Since: 1974 - No. of Units: Company Owned: 1 - Franchised: 11,200 - Franchise Fee: $10,000 - Royalty: 8% + 2.5% adv. - Total Inv: $65,720 - $150,700 - Financing: Equipment leasing to qualified candidates.

SUNQUEST SYSTEMS
7102 Lakeview Pkwy, West Dr., Indianapolis, IN, 46268. Contact: Elbert Cobb, Chairman - Tel: (317) 299-3391. Established: 1965 - No. of Units: Company Owned: 6 - Franchised: 34.

SUNSHINE CAFE RESTAURANTS *
SunQuest Systems, Inc.
7102 Lakeview Pkwy. W.Dr., Indianapolis, IN, 46268. Contact: E.M. Cobb, Chairman - Tel: (317) 299-3391, Fax: (317) 299-3390. Full service casual dining restaurant offering a complete menu of freshly prepared items in breakfast, lunch and dinner segments. Units accommodate 120 to 150 guests. Established: 1986 - Franchising Since: 1975 - No. of Units: Company Owned: 3 - Franchised: 12 - Franchise Fee: $25,000 - Royalty: 4% franchise royalty, 3% adv. - Total Inv: $100,000 (conversion) to $1.1 million new construction - Financing: No.

SUPER KING CATFISH
Super King Catfish, Inc.
3820 Premier Ave., Memphis, TN, 38118. Contact: Bill Richey, Dir. - Tel: (901) 867-0600. Full service restaurant offering limited menu of catfish and related products. Established: 1987 - Franchising Since: 1992 - No. of Units: Company Owned: 2 - Franchise Fee: $20,000 - Royalty: 4.5% - Total inv: $97,000 - $174,000 - Financing: No.

SUPREME PRODUCTS INC.
605 East Loop 340, P.O. Box 154308, Waco, TX, 76715-0308. Contact: Pat Hood, Pres. - Tel: (817) 799-4941. Mobile food and drink vending business operated from trailer & pushcart. Established: 1966 - Number of Operators: 300+ - Inv: $2,595+ - Financing: None.

T.G.I. FRIDAY'S RESTAURANTS
Friday's Hospitality Worldwide
7540 LBJ Fwy., Ste. 100, Dallas, TX, 75251. Contact: Wallace Doolin, Pres. & CEO - Tel: (214) 450-5775. Casual theme, full service restaurants. Established: 1965 - Franchising Since: 1970 - No. of Units: Company

Owned: 149 - Franchised: 24 - Initial Fee: $75,000 for 1st restaurant, $65,000 for 2nd and $50,000 for 3rd and each thereafter for first five years - Royalty: 4% gross sales - Adv./Mktg. Fee: Capped at 4% gross sales - Outside U.S.- Franchise Fee: $100,000 - Consulting Fee: $350,000 - Royalty Fee: 4% gross sales.

TACO BELL CORP.
17901 Von Karman, Irvine, CA, 92714. Contact: Anna Rubene, Franchise Dept. - Tel: (714) 863-4500. Mexican style fast food restaurants. Established: 1962 - Franchising Since: 1964 - No. of Units: Company Owned: 1,232 - Franchised: 1,035 - Franchise Fee: $35,000 - Royalty: 5.5% weekly - Total Inv: $750,000 average costs including land, bldg. & equip. - Financing: Through outside approved financing companies.

TACO CASA
Taco Casa International, Ltd.
P.O. Box 4542, Topeka, KS, 66604. Contact: James F. Reiter, Pres. - Tel: (913) 267-2548. Fast food Mexican restaurants. Established: 1963 - Franchising Since: 1976 - No. of Units: Company Owned: 1 - Franchised: 20 - Franchise Fee: $15,000 - Royalty: 4% - Financing: No.

TACO GRANDE
P.O. Box 780066, Wichita, KS, 67278. Contact: John Wylie, Pres. - Tel: (316) 744-0200. Limited-menu Mexican restaurant featuring drive-thru service. Recipes are authentic Mexican recipes. Successful operation for over 34 years. Offer excellent products, training and a cost efficient and labor-saving building design. Established: 1960 - Franchising Since: 1966 - No. of Units: Company Owned: 10 - Franchised: 9 - Franchise Fee: $20,000 - Royalty: 3% - Total Inv: $250,000 - $450,000 - Financing: No.

TACO HUT *
Taco Hut America Inc.
2014 Rangeline, Joplin, MO, 68804. Contact: John P. Gray, Pres. - Tel: (417) 781-4781. Mexican food cooked fresh on each location. 23 years in business. Three franchisees in Kansas. Family owned. We operate four restaurants in Missouri lease two others. We don't fry anything. We steam or braise food. Established: 1972 - Franchising Since: 1989 - No. of Units: Company Owned: 4 - Franchised: 3 - Franchise Fee: $15,000 - Royalty: 3% gross sales less sales tax - Total Inv: Net worth $150,000 plus $135,000 typical investment plus $25,000 to $35,000 for expenses - Financing: No.

TACO JOHN'S
Taco John's International, Inc.
808 W. 20th St., P.O. Box 1589, Cheyenne, WY, 82003. Contact: Dave Ulve, V.P. Fran. Dev. - Tel: (307) 635-0101. Mexican fast food. Established: 1969 - Franchising Since: 1969 - No. of Units: Company Owned: 12 - Franchised: 436 - Franchise Fee: $19,500 - Royalty: 4% - Total Inv: $100,000 - $450,000 plus land - Financing: No.

TACO LOCO
Taco Concepts, Inc.
349-B West Tremont Ave., Charlotte, NC, 28203. Contact: Curtis Rudolph, Pres. - Tel: (704) 375-9450. Mexican restaurant. Established: 1984 - Franchising Since: 1991 - No. of Units: Franchised: 3 - Franchise Fee: $15,000 - Royalty: 4% of net sales, 3% adv. - Total Inv: equip. $33,000, leasehold $35,000 - $40,000, misc. $5,000 - $7,000 - Financing: Yes.

TACO MAKER, THE
Taco Maker, Inc., The
P.O. Box 9519, Ogden, UT, 84409-0519. Contact: Gil L. Craig, V.P. Sales - Tel: (801) 621-7486. International Mexican fast food specializing in fast, friendly service and a complete menu with made-from-scratch and fresh ingredients. Centralized purchasing, corporate marketing and promotional support, and progressive store design provides for the most comprehensive and fun investment opportunity. Established: 1978 - Franchising Since: 1978 - No. of Units: Franchised: 85 - Franchise Fee: $22,500 - Royalty: 5%, 3% adv. - Total Inv: $185,000 - $500,000 - Financing: No.

TACO MAYO
Taco Mayo Franchise Systems, Inc.
10405 Greenbriar Pl., Oklahoma City, OK, 73159. Contact: Kurt Dinnes, V.P. Real Est. & Dev. - Tel: (405) 691-8226, Fax: (405) 691-2572. Quick service restaurant featuring Tex-Mex favorites like tacos, burritos, nachos and salads. Established: 1978 - Franchising Since: 1980 - No. of Units: Company Owned: 30 - Franchised: 60 - Franchise Fee: $15,000 - Royalty: 3.5% - Total Inv: $75,000 (liquid), $200,000 (net worth) - Financing: No.

TACO TICO, INC.
260 N. Rock Rd., #220, Wichita, KS, 67206-2240. Contact: Larry Seger, Dir. of Lic. - Tel: (316) 688-4492. Mexican style fast food. Established: 1967 - Franchising Since: 1968 - No. of Units: Company Owned: 72 - Franchised: 42 - Franchise Fee: $10,000 - Royalty: 4% gross - Total Inv: $120,000 excl. real estate - Financing: No.

TACO TIME
Taco Time International
3880 W. 11th Ave., Eugene, OR, 97402. Contact: Jim Thomas, Sr. V.P. Fran. Dev. - Tel: (503) 687-8222. Taco Time is a dynamic leader in the Mexican fast food business. Outstanding food products feature quality fresh ingredients, and exciting menu items. Established: 1959 - Franchising Since: 1961 - No. of Units: Company Owned: 7 - Franchised: 309 - Franchise Fee: $18,000 - single unit - Royalty: 5% of gross sales - Total Inv: $129,500 to $229,500 excl. real estate and leasehold improv. - Financing: No - packaging assistance, options available.

TACO TREAT
Taco Treat Inc.
1316 Central Ave., Great Falls, MT, 59401. Contact: Jack Deck, V.P. - Tel: (406) 727-7582. Fast food (Mexican). Established: 1960 - Franchising Since: 1980 - No. of Units: Company Owned: 4 - Franchised: 3 - Franchise Fee: $10,000 - $15,000 - Royalty: 3%, no adv. fee - Financing: Open.

TACO VIA
Taco Via Franchise Systems Inc.
8603 E. 81st St., Kansas City, MO, 64138-1545. Contact: Robert Throneberry, Pres. - Tel: (816) 474-0679. Fast Mexican food. Established: 1968 - Franchising Since: 1972 - No. of Units: Company Owned: 1 - Franchised: 19 - Franchise Fee: $25,000 - Royalty: 4% - Total Inv: $78,000 - $187,000 - Financing: No.

TACO VIVA
321 North University Dr., Plantation, FL, 33324. Contact: Joe Ronselli, Franchise Director - Tel: (407) 370-1942. Mexican fast food with operations in food courts, major centers and malls, plus free-standing units with or without drive-thru. Established: 1968 - Franchising Since: 1988 - No. of Units: 58 - Franchise Fee: $18,500 - Royalty: 4% + 3% adv.- Total Inv: $120,000 courts, $250,000 free-standing - Financing: None.

TAKEOUT TAXI
Takeout Taxi Franchising Systems, Inc.
1175 Herndon Pkwy., Ste. 150, Herndon, VA, 22070. Contact: Kari Popek, Fran. Sales - Tel: (703) 689-4800. Multiple restaurant delivery service. Established: 1987 - Franchising Since: 1991 - No. of Units: Franchised: 63 - Franchise Fee: $5,000 - Royalty: 4% of gross sales - Total Inv: min. $71,000 - $91,000 min. net worth requirement $250,000 - Financing: No.

TASTY TACOS
T.T. Foods, Inc.
1420 E. Grand Ave., Des Moines, IA, 50316. Contact: Rich Mosqueda, Pres. - Tel: (515) 262-3940. Restaurants offering Mexican quick service food. Established: 1961 - Franchising Since: 1991 - No. of Units: Company Owned: 5 - Franchised: 1 - Franchise Fee: $7,500 - Royalty: 4% monthly - Total Inv: $30,000 - $45,000 plus fran. fee.

TEXAS LOOSEY'S CHILI PARLOR AND SALOON
River-Diego Inv. Corp.
P.O. Box 1697, Temecula, CA, 92390. Contact: Ron Walton, Pres. - Tel: (909) 677-3345. Restaurant and Lounge. Established: 1982 - Franchising Since: 1986 - No. of Units: Company Owned: 5 - Franchised: 2 - Franchise Fee: $30,000 - Royalty: 5% + 2% adv. - Total Inv: $450,000 - $500,000 - Financing: None.

THUNDERCLOUD SUBS
Cumulus Inc.
1102 W. 6th St., Austin, TX, 78703. Contact: David Cohen, Fran. Dir. - Tel: (512) 479-8805, Fax: (512) 479-8806. Prepares fresh submarine sandwiches, salads, soups, and other complimentary items. A unique atmosphere different from other fast food restaurants. Occupies 800 sq. ft. to 1,500 sq. ft. in a retail strip center or free-standing site. Full seating, limited seating, drive-thru, or drive-thru only. Established: 1975 - Franchising Since: 1981 - No. of Units: Company Owned: 7 - Franchised: 25 - Franchise Fee: $10,000 - Royalty: 4% gross sales - Total Inv: $55,000 - $75,000 - Financing: No.

TIPPY'S TACO HOUSE
Locklier Co., Inc.
P.O. Box 2253, McKinney, TX, 75070. Contact: W.L. Locklier - Tel: (214) 547-0888. An eating establishment featuring Mexican-style food specialties. Established: 1958 - Franchising Since: 1968 - No. of Units: Franchised: 15 - Franchise Fee: $20,000 - Royalty: 3% - Total Inv: $100,000 to $140,000 - Financing: Assistance in applying for loan.

TOGO'S EATERY
M.T.C. Management, Inc.
900 E. Campbell Ave., Ste. #1, Campbell, CA, 95008. Contact: Valerie Evans, Fran. Coord. - Tel: (408) 377-1754, Fax: (408) 377-4130. A high quality, fast service, specialty sandwich restaurant. Established: 1972 - Franchising Since: 1977 - No. of Units: Company Owned: 11 - Franchised: 163 - Franchise Fee: $12,500 - $40,000 - Royalty: 5% of sales - Total Inv: $180,000 - $200,000 (does not incl. fran. fee) - Financing: No.

TOM & JERRY'S BURGERS & BEER
Tom & Jerry's, Inc.
1110 Austin St., McAllen, TX, 78501. Contact: Jerry L. Pace, Pres. - Tel: (210) 687-7703. Restaurant and bar with casual dining featuring burgers, fajitas, chicken and hot dogs which are all charbroiled. Established: 1976 - No. of Units: Company Owned: 4 - Franchise Fee: $25,000 - Royalty: 5%.

TONY ROMA'S, A PLACE FOR RIBS
Roma Corporation
9304 Forest Ln., Ste. 200, Dallas, TX, 75243-8953. Contact: Larry Zimmerman, V.P. of Dev. - Tel: (214) 343-7800. Dinnerhouse specializing in BBQ ribs and chicken along with famous onion ring loaf. A special niche in the industry with great price/value relationship, high quality food products and full service bar. Also offering take-out and delivery. Established: 1972 - Franchising Since: 1979 - No. of Units: Company Owned: 17 - Franchised: 130 - Franchise Fee: $50,000 - Royalty: 4% + .5% adv. - Total Inv: $750,000 (liq. assets of $300,000) - Financing: No.

TOWN PUMP FOOD STORES, INC.
600 S. Main, Butte, MT, 59701. Contact: Thomas Kenneally, Pres. - Tel: (406) 782-9121. Family Restaurant/Fast Food. No. of Units: Company Owned: 30 - Franchised: 30.

TRANS/PACIFIC RESTAURANTS, INC.
17320 Red Hill Ave., Ste. 150, Irvine, CA, 92714. Contact: Ronald F. Higgins, Chairman, CEO - Tel: (714) 250-0331. Family restaurants. Established: 1948 - No. of Units: Company Owned: 46 - Franchised: 10.

TROTTER'S BARBECUE
Trotter's Corp.
2857 S. Campbell Ave., Springfield, MO, 65807-3630. Contact: Jon Garnier, Fran. Dir. - Tel: (417) 889-9044. Barbecue restaurant with full service menu, as well as an award winning food bar with recipes made from scratch. All stores have drive-thru service and adult beverages. Established: 1976 - Franchising Since: 1989 - No. of Units: Company Owned: 3 - Franchised: 4 - Franchise Fee: $50,000 - Royalty: 4% of net sales - Total Inv: bldg. approx. $850,000, $290,000, F.F.E. - Financing: No.

TUBBY'S SUB SHOPS
Tubby's Sub Shops, Inc.
6029 East 14 Mile Rd., Sterling Heights, MI, 48312. Contact: Amy B. Jones, V.P., Fran. Dev. - Tel: (800) 752-0644. Submarine sandwich shop featuring 28 specialty sandwiches. All sandwiches are made to order and 80% of the menu offers hot sandwiches. Established: 1968 - Franchising Since: 1978 - No. of Units: Company Owned: 2 - Franchised: 65 - Franchise Fee: $15,000 - Royalty: 4% - Total Inv: $100,000 - $254,000 including franchise fee - Financing: Third party.

TUMBLEWEED MEXICAN RESTAURANT
1900 Mellwood Ave., Louisville, KY, 40206. Contact: Jack Butorac, Fran. Dir. - Tel: (502) 893-0323. Mexican family restaurant. Established: 1976 - No. of Units: Company Owned: 3 - Franchised: 3.

UNCLE TONY'S PIZZA & PASTA RESTAURANTS
Uncle Tony's International, Inc.
27 Airport Plaza, 1800 Post Road, Warwick, RI, 02886. Contact: Edward A. Carosi, Pres. - Tel: (401) 738-1321, Fax: (401) 732-1936. Family style Italian restaurant featuring pizza & pasta, beer & wine. Established: 1970 - Franchising Since: 1976 - No. of Units: Company Owned: 3 - Franchised: 7 - Franchise Fee: $35,000 - Royalty: 4%, 3% adv. - Total Inv: $500,000 to $600,000 total turnkey package - Financing: Will assist.

UNO RESTAURANT CORP.
100 Charles Park Rd., West Roxbury, MA, 02132. Contact: Craig Miller, Pres. - Tel: (617) 323-9200. Dinnerhouse. Established: 1978 - Franchising Since: 1979 - No. of Units: Company Owned: 25 - Franchised: 47.

UPPER KRUST
1919 N. Main St., Dayton, OH, 45405. Contact: Douglas Goudy, V.P. Dir. Fran. Dev. - Tel: (513) 277-7200. Fast Food - Sandwich. Established: 1970 - No. of Units: Company Owned: 3 - Franchised: 1.

VALENTINO'S INC.
P.O. Box 83089, Lincoln, NE, 68501-3089. Contact: Anthony Messineo, Jr., Pres. - Tel: (402) 434-9350. Family restaurants. Established: 1957 - No. of Units: Company Owned: 19 - Franchised: 25.

VARSITY, THE
61 North Ave. N.W., Atlanta, GA, 30308. Contact: NAncy Simms, Pres. - Tel: (404) 881-1706. Fast food restaurants. Established: 1928 - No. of Units: Company Owned: 2 - Franchised: 1.

VERN'S DOG HOUSE, INC.
1257 NYS Rte. 96N, Waterloo, NY, 13165. Contact: Jane Shaffer, C.E.O. - Tel: (315) 539-3379. A franchise program unique in its simplicity. German style hot dogs on a fresh bread roll, with your choice of 6 hot toppings (self serve) for one low price. Salt potatoes, homemade macaroni salad, tossed salad, and self serve beverages. Seasonal operation with outside seating under tent and umbrellas. Established: 1985 - Franchising Since: 1988 - No. of Units: Company Owned: 5 - Franchised: 2 - Franchise Fee: $10,000 - Royalty: 3% gross and 1% gross for adv. - Total Inv: $69,000 - $99,000 - Financing: Negotiable.

VILLA PIZZA
Villa Enterprises Management Ltd., Inc.
17 Elm St., Morristown, NJ, 07960. Contact: Adam Torine, Dir. of Mktg. - Tel: (201) 285-4800, Fax: (201) 285-5252. Quick service pizza and Italian food restaurant primarily located in large regional shopping malls & outlet centers either in a food court or in-line location. Large tantalizing food displays offer a wide variety to customers. Established: 1964 - Franchising Since: 1994 - No. of Units: Company Owned: 91 - Franchised: 2 - Franchise Fee: $29,000 - Royalty: 4.5%, 1.5% adv./mktg. - Total Inv: $200,000 - $400,000 - Financing: Franchisor assistance.

VILLAGE INN RESTAURANTS
VICORP
400 W. 48th Ave., Denver, CO, 80216. Contact: Maxine Crogle, Mgr. Oper. Adm. - Tel: (303) 296-2121, (800) 800-3644. Mid-scale family restaurants serving all day. Established: 1958 - Franchising Since: 1961 - No. of Units: Company Owned: 105 - Franchised: 107 - Franchise Fee: $30,000 - Total Inv: $700,000 - $1,800,000 - Financing: No.

VISTA RESTAURANTS
P.O. Box 399, Manhattan, KS, 66502. Contact: Bradley Streeter, Pres. - Tel: (913) 537-0100. Fast food restaurant specializing in prepared to order quality hamburgers and dairy items. Established: 1964 - Franchising Since: 1967 - No. of Units: 7 - Franchise Fee: $20,000 - Royalty: 3% + 1% adv. fund - Total Inv: $500,000 - Financing: Possible.

WAFFLETOWN U.S.A. LTD.
2113 Pleasure House Rd., Virginia Beach, VA, 23455. Contact: George - Tel: (804) 460-2460. Waffle, pancake, omelette, sandwich, salad, sit-down restaurant. Established: 1981 - Franchising Since: 1981 - No. of Units: Franchised: 4 - Franchise Fee: $15,000 - Royalty: 3% - Total Inv: $90,000 - $150,000 - Financing: None.

WALT'S ROAST BEEF INT'L, INC.
680 Reservoir, Cranston, RI, 02910. Contact: Raymond Perotta, Pres. - Tel: (401) 785-2530. Roast beef sandwiches. Established: 1951 - Franchising Since: 1960 - No. of Units: Company Owned: 2 - Franchised: 4 - Approx. Inv: $30,000 - Financing: No.

WARD'S FOOD SYSTEMS, INC.
P.O. Box 870, Hattiesburg, MS, 39403. Contact: Kenneth R. Hrdlica, Pres. - Tel: (800) 748-9273, (601) 268-9273. Fast food restaurant chain featuring chili-burgers, chili-dogs, and frosted mugs of homemade rootbeer. Menu is complimented by full breakfast line and a variety of sandwiches, fries and beverages. Established: 1984 - Franchising Since: 1985 - No. of Units: 46 - Franchise Fee: $15,000 - Royalty: 3% - Total Inv: $275,000 - $325,000 - Financing: None.

WAREHOUSE RESTAURANT
Burtson Corporation
4499 Admiralty Way, Marina Del Rey, CA, 90292. Contact: Franchise Dir. - Tel: (310) 823-5451. Full dinner house food and beverages (liquor) seafood and steak dishes. Entertainment, no dancing. Established: 1970 - Franchising Since: 1980 - No. of Units: Company Owned: 3 - Franchised: 1 - Franchise Fee: $30,000 - Royalty: 3% - Total Inv: $200,000.

WENDY'S
Wendy's International, Inc.
4288 W. Dublin Granville Rd., Dublin, OH, 43017. Contact: Barbara Langsdon, Nat'l Sales Dir. - Tel: (614) 764-3100. Fast food restaurants. Established: 1969 - Franchising Since: 1972 - No. of Units: Company Owned: 983 - Franchised: 2,454 - Franchise Fee: $25,000 TAF - Royalty: 4%, 4% adv. - Total Inv: bldg. $525,000, equip. $200,000, land-variable - Financing: Yes, sale lease back program.

WESTERN SIZZLIN
Western Sizzlin, Inc.
P.O. Box 2091509, Nashville, TN, 37229. Contact: Eva Schram, Fran. Dir. - Tel: (800) 247-8325, (615) 251-0023. Family styled steakhouse featuring buffet bars & bakery, also serving seafood & chicken. Established: 1962 - Franchising Since: 1966 - No. of Units: Company Owned: 1 - Franchised: 320 - Franchise Fee: $25,000 - Royalty: 3%, .5% adv. - Total Inv: $825,000 - Financing: Will assist.

WESTERN STEER FAMILY RESTAURANTS
WSMP, Inc.
WSMP Dr., P.O. Box 399, Claremont, NC, 28610. Contact: Kenneth L. Moser, V.P. Fran. - Tel: (704) 459-7626. Economy family steakhouse with full steak menu, some chicken, full salad and hot food bar. Established: 1967 - Franchising Since: 1970 - No. of Units: Company Owned: 31 - Franchised: 105 - Franchise Fee: $25,000 - Royalty: 3% gross sales - Total Inv: $800,000 - $1,200,000 - Financing: No.

WHATABURGER
Whataburger, Inc.
4600 Parkdale Dr., Corpus Christi, TX, 78411. Contact: Fran. Dev. Dept. - Tel: (512) 878-0650. Fast food restaurant, high quality made to order hamburgers and breakfast. Most units opened 24 hrs. Established: 1950 - Franchising Since: 1953 - No. of Units: Company Owned: 278 - Franchised: 166 - Franchise Fee: $15,000 - Royalty: 5% gross monthly sales - Total Inv: $500,000 - $800,000 - Financing: No.

WHITE HORSE LTD.
1110 Palmyra Dr., Fort Mill, SC, 29715. Contact: Wm. Mathias, Pres. - Tel: (803) 548-1389. Theme restaurants. Established: 1970 - Franchising Since: 1976 - No. of Units: Company Owned: 1 - Franchised: 5 - Franchise Fee: $10,000 - Royalty: 3% - 4% - Total Inv: $30,000 - $150,000 based on location - Financing: No.

WIENER KING SYSTEMS, INC.
1201 Bushkill St., Easton, PA, 18042. Contact: Richard Dennis, Pres. - Tel: (610) 252-3313. Fast food restaurant specializing in hot dogs, chili and hamburgers. Established: 1970 - Franchising Since: 1973 - No. of Units: Franchised: 17 - Franchise Fee: $15,000 - Royalty: 3% - Total Inv: $350,000 - $500,000 - Financing: No.

WIENERSCHNITZEL
Galardi Group, Inc.
4440 Von Karmen Ave., Newport Beach, CA, 92660. Contact: Mr. Frank Coyle, Fran. Sales Mgr. - Tel: (800) 764-9353, ext. 609. Nation's largest hot dog fast food chain in the nation. Other menu items include hamburgers, fries, soft drinks and breakfast. Established: 1961 - Franchising Since: 1965 - No. of Units: Franchised: 348 - Franchise Fee: 5% of sales - Royalty: 5% of sales for local adv., 1% of sales for nat'l. adv. - Total Inv: $150,000 to $350,000 bldg., $45,000 to $150,000 equip., plus land - Financing: No.

WIFE SAVER
P.O. Box 14515, Augusta, GA, 30919. Contact: Chris Cunningham, Pres. - Tel: (706) 798-5897. Fast food delivery. Established: 1965 - Franchising Since: 1965 - No. of Units: Company Owned: 3 - Franchised: 6 - Approx. Inv: $375,000 - Financing: No.

WING WAGON
Wing-It of Watertown, Inc.
71 Public Square, Watertown, NY, 13601. Contact: Charles G. Wert, Pres. - Tel: (315) 788-4580. Fast food specializing in Buffalo style chicken wings with 7 different sauces. Also pizza and various side dishes. Established: 1982 - Franchising Since: 1989 - No. of Units: Company Owned: 1 - Franchised: 2 - Franchise Fee: $10,000 - Royalty: $100/week for 6 mths, $150 thereafter (flat rate) - Total Inv: $65,000 - $95,000 - Financing: No.

WINGS TO GO
Wings To Go, Inc.
1256 S. Little Creek Rd., Dover, DE, 19901. Contact: Eric Weaver, Fran. Coord. - Tel: (302) 734-5512, (302) 734-5812. Retail restaurants, specializing in authentic Buffalo style chicken wings. Established: 1985 - Franchising Since: 1989 - No. of Units: Company Owned: 2 - Franchised: 45 - Franchise Fee: $15,000 - Royalty: 4%, 2% regional adv. - Total Inv: $50,000 - $76,500 - Financing: Not at this time.

WOK ON THE RUN
W.O.T.R. Franchising, Inc.
140 N. 8th., Ste. 340, Lincoln, NE, 68508. Contact: Franchise Consortium - Tel: (800) 301-9504. Fast food Chinese restaurant specializing in delivery and drive-thru. Established: 1986 - Franchising Since: 1992 - No. of Units: Company Owned: 6 - Franchised: 3 - Franchise Fee: $20,000 - Total Inv: $70,200 - $111,300 - Financing: Will provide assistance in location of financing.

WOODY'S BAR-B-Q
Woody's Bar-B-Q Franchise Sales, Inc.
1626 Atlantic University Cir., Jacksonville, FL, 32207. Contact: Bill Moon, V.P. Fran. Dev. - Tel: (904) 724-1976, Fax: (904) 721-9321. Full service Bar-B-Q restaurant. Featuring pork ribs, baby back ribs, beef, pork, and chicken plus famous desserts. Established: 1980 - Franchising

Since: 1989 - No. of Units: Company Owned: 10 - Franchised: 22 - Franchise Fee: $25,000 - Royalty: 3%,1% adv. - Total Inv: $150,000 - Financing: Yes, S.B.A.

WRY ENTERPRISES INC.
1807 7th St. N.W., Rochester, MN, 55901. Contact: Ron Yanish, Pres. - Tel: (507) 282-3090. Family restaurants. Established: 1982 - No. of Units: Franchised: 5.

YASIN'S FAST SUPREME
Yasin's Franchise Systems Inc.
1300 Simpson Rd. N.W., Atlanta, GA, 30314. Contact: Ken Coggins, Pres. - Tel: (404) 758-4158. Quick serve seafood. Established: 1987 - Franchising Since: 1992 - No. of Units: Company Owned: 6 - Franchised: 2 - Franchise Fee: $15,000 - Royalty: 4%, 1.5% adv. - Total Inv: $95,000 equip., $50,000 to $80,000 leaseholds, $25,000 misc., Total : $200,000 - Financing: No.

YAYA'S FLAME BROILED CHICKEN
C.S.C. Inc.
521 S. Dort, Flint, MI, 48503. Contact: John Chinonis, Pres. - Tel: (810) 235-6550. Dine in and take out flame broiled chicken marinated in YAYA's marinate mix. Established: 1985 - Franchising Since: 1988 - No. of Units: Company Owned: 1 - Franchised: 19 - Franchise Fee: $15,000 - Royalty: 4% - Total Inv: $200,000 - $275,000 - Financing: No.

YOUNG MANAGEMENT COMPANY
1617 S. Beacon Blvd., Grand Haven, MI, 49417. Contact: Dick Young, Pres. - Tel: (616) 846-7200. Fast food restaurants. No. of Units: Franchised: 3.

ZANIE'S COMEDY SHOWPLACE
1548 N. Wells, Chicago, IL, 60610. Contact: Rick Uchwat, Owner - Tel: (312) 337-6134. Dinnerhouse. Established: 1982 - No. of Units: Company Owned: 3 - Franchised: 1.

ZEPPE'S PIZZERIA *
JTC Management, Inc.
10 Alpha Park, Highland Heights, OH, 44143. Contact: Joseph T. Ciresi, Pres. - Tel: (216) 442-9898. Zeppe's specializes in pizza, pasta, subs, salads, and wings. Zeppe's offers 10 different types of pizza from traditional to gourmet; 17 different subs; 6 different salads, 9 types of pasta dinners, plus Zeppe's famous wings with 6 flavors of sauce to choose from. Established: 1987 - Franchising Since: 1990 - No. of Units: Company Owned: 12 - Franchised: 19 - Franchise Fee: $15,000 - Royalty: 5% - Total Inv: approx. $150,000 - Financing: Upon review of financials.

ZUZU HANDMADE MEXICAN FOOD RESTAURANTS
ZuZu Franchising Corp.
2651 N. Harwood, Ste. 100, Dallas, TX, 75201. Contact: Vick Pryor, Fran. Coordinator - Tel: (800) 824-8830, (214) 922-8226. Authentic, handmade Mexican food, served in a quick, casual atmosphere. Established: 1989 - Franchising Since: 1992 - No. of Units: Company Owned: 4 - Franchised: 120 - Franchise Fee: $25,000 - Royalty: 4.5%, 4% adv. - Total Inv: $135,000 - $275,000 - Financing: No, but will assist in obtaining outside financing.

FRANCHISE CONSULTANTS AND FRANCHISE SERVICES

AAA FRANCHISE FINDERS *
Franchise Foundations, division of
540 Pacific Ave., San Francisco, CA, 94133. Contact: Terry Murphy, Fran. Counselor - Tel: (800) 942-4402, Fax: (707) 942-0444. A public interest organization that helps individuals evaluate the franchise option by developing a Personal Profile to see if franchising is right for them. In-depth research and reporting on any franchise company is provided so intelligent decisions can be made before funds are invested. Established: 1980 - No. of Units: Company Owned: 2.

ABX - ASSOCIATES BUSINESS XCHANGE
American Business Group, Inc.
12221 Merit Dr., Ste. 950, Dallas, TX, 75251. Contact: Don McIver BCB, CBI, Senior Associate - Tel: (214) 233-3300. Franchise brokers, business opportunity brokers and consultants. Established: 1969.

ADVANCED FRANCHISING WORLDWIDE
7100 E. Lincoln Dr., Ste. B-123, Scottsdale, AZ, 85253-4434. Contact: Chris Wright, Brook Carey, Pres., CEO - Tel: (602) 443-0432, Fax: (602) 991-1418. Business expansion assistance through franchising, branching, dealerships, distributorships, agents and more. Marketing of new business concept. Hands on development of prototype for pre-expansion entrepreneurs. Emphasis on creative, affordable solutions. Offices worldwide. Established: 1979.

ALEXANDER & ALEXANDER OF MINNESOTA, INC.
4000 Olson Memorial Parkway, Minneapolis, MN, 55422. Contact: Jim Walters, A.V.P. - Tel: (800) 328-0592 or (612) 520-3000. Providing and administering sponsored national insurance programs for franchisors with over 100 units. Programs include property, casualty, workers compensation, auto, group health, accident and life insurance. Established: 1963.

ALLAN COHEN & ASSOC., INC.
P.O. Box 1722, Hallandale, FL, 33008-1722. Contact: Allan Cohen, Pres. - Tel: (305) 454-7216. Marketing and management consultants to retailers, hotels, restaurants, distributors and manufacturers of consumer goods and services in Canada and the U.S. Established: 1967.

ALTAMAR GROUP LTD.
6810 S. Cedar, Ste. 2B, Lansing, MI, 48911. Contact: Raymond Damas, Pres. - Tel: (517) 694-0400. This experienced group of franchise professionals offers all of the development services required to franchise a business, including feasibility studies, business plans, raising capital, patent and trademark protection, operating and training manuals, marketing materials, and franchise marketing. The group also investigates and evaluates franchises being purchased by franchisees. Established: 1979.

AMERICAN FRANCHISEE ASSOCIATION
53 W. Jackson Blvd., #205, Chicago, IL, 60604. Contact: Susan P. Kezios, Pres./Founder - Tel: (312) 431-0545. The American Franchisee Association (AFA), is a large franchisee trade association, representing over 14,000 franchised outlets nationwide. AFA works to better the climate for franchising allowing both the franchisees and franchisors to prosper, but not at the other's expense. Established: 1992.

AMERIDIAL INC., FRANCHISE SERVICES *
4535 Strausser St. N.W., N. Canton, OH, 44720. Contact: Steve Trifelos, Sales & Mktg. Mgr. - Tel: (800) 445-7128. For Franchisors: We provide lead generation telemarketing service as a value added service passed on to franchisees. For Franchisee: We ensure immediate start-up business activity through lead generation telemarketing. Long & proven track record. Seven phoning centers.

ANDREX CONSULTING SERVICES
199 Heywood Ct., Matawan, NJ, 07747. Contact: Ed Possumato, Pres. - Tel: (800) 959-2515, Fax: (908) 290-1545. Consulting services: All areas, UFOC updates, franchise agreement revisions, business plans, operations and training manuals. Established: 1989.

ARRIBA FRANCHISE MARKETING, INC.
3522 Charlotte St., Pittsburgh, PA, 15201. Contact: Mark Lando, Pres. - Tel: (412) 687-3725. Franchise consulting specialists with national accounts such as Stride-Rite, Athlete's Foot, Hotlicks, Candyland, General Nutrition Centers, etc. Works with both franchisor and franchisee. Established: 1989.

ARTHUR ANDERSEN & CO.
33 W. Monroe St., 12th Fl., Chicago, IL, 60603. Contact: Leonard N. Swartz, Worldwide Man. Dir. Fran. Serv. - Tel: (312) 931-1907. An international professional services firm with over 325 offices in 75 countries providing service in the areas of franchise consulting, auditing, tax and financial planning, appraisals and valuation, info systems, management consulting, small business advisory services and litigation support. Established: 1913.

Judge us by the companies we keep

Getting top quality goods, services and support is easy if you know who to call. The Franchisee CounseLine℠, LegaLine℠ and FinanciaLine℠ are powerful referral networks for AAFD members.
Call us today for details: (800) 733-9858

The American Association of Franchisees & Dealers

A national non-profit trade association
Bringing fairness to franchising

1420 Kettner Blvd., Suite 415, San Diego, California 92101
Mail: P.O. Box 81887, San Diego, CA 92138-1887
Internet: http://www.servint.com/aafd
E-mail: aafd@aol

(800) 733-9858

Here is just a sample of the many outstanding companies providing high quality products and services and <u>discounts</u> to AAFD members.

- NDC Check Service
- Mutual of Omaha
- Bank of America
- IBM
- Sprint
- Avis Rent A Car
- Franchise Network
- Connex International
- NEBS Business Forms
- Lantel Systems Solutions
- Luce, Smith & Scott Insurance

ASGAT AGENCY, INC.
15965 Jeanette, Southfield, MI, 48075. Contact: Marc Lichtenstein - Tel: (810) 557-2784. Franchise development, marketing, sales, and business consulting. Established: 1973.

BABCOCK & SCHMID ASSOCIATES, INC.
P.O. Box 808, Bath, OH, 44210-0808. Contact: Bill Babcock, Owner - Tel: (216) 666-8826. Provide corporate identification design, package design, prototype facility design and product design. Clients include Goodyear, Pizza Hut, Sherwin Williams, Midas International, Ponderosa, KFC, Stouffers, T.J. Cinnamons & Bob Evans Farms.

BENCHMARK GROUP
121 W. Walnut St., Rogers, AR, 72756. Contact: Jim Parks, Dir. of Mktg. - Tel: (800) 321-8721. Architectural/Engineering firm specializing in prototypical designs for retail stores, restaurants, and automotive centers. Licensed in 48 states. Experience in producing construction documents to meet specific local building code requirements. Established: 1978.

BLAKE GROUP, INC., THE
425 SW Madison Ave., Ste. J, Corvallis, OR, 97333. Contact: Gary Blake, Pres. - Tel: (503) 758-7224, Fax: (503) 758-7449. The Blake Group is a micro-market information consultancy specializing in development of the franchise growth and support strategies through utilization of information technology. Established: 1989.

BOTTOM LINE CONSULTANTS
1500 Cedarbluff Dr., Richmond, VA, 23233. Contact: Richard L. Russakoff, Pres. - Tel: (804) 741-5771. Franchise consulting, speaking and training. Complete customized programs for franchisors/franchisees on increasing profitability of others, complete re-sale programs, mediation, speeches and seminars to train, inspire and innovate.

BROWNING GROUP, THE
734 Crossbrook Dr., Moraga, CA, 94556. Contact: Wm. Mulcahy, Exec. V.P. - Tel: (415) 635-3878. Developer of business expansion programs and strategies. Services include all areas of marketing support required to expand business operations or improve business performance - specializes in retail and service business program. Established: 1980.

BUSINESS AMERICA
Business America Associates, Inc.
2120 Greentree Rd., Pittsburgh, PA, 15220-1406. Contact: Thomas Atkins, Pres. - Tel: (412) 833-1910. Complete line of business and franchise brokerage. Confidential handling of businesses and buyers.

Commissions earned on sales of businesses or acceptance of licensee on franchises. Established: 1984 - Franchising Since: 1985 - No. of Units Franchised: 4 - Franchise Fee: $4,995 - Royalty: none - Total Inv: $10,000 equip., $4,995 fran. fee, $5,000 misc.- Financing: No.

BUSINESS EXPANSIONS INTERNATIONAL
210 S. Anita Ave., Los Angeles, CA, 90049. Contact: Aaron Rothenberg, Pres. - Tel: (310) 476-5262, Fax: (310) 478-1876. Since 1981, have structured & established franchise systems in Canada, Australia, Singapore, Malaysia, Manila, Japan & South Africa. Trade missions from France, Norway, Sweden, Poland & Sakhalin (Russia) etc. Instructor: UCLA ext. (12 yrs), USC Pepperdine, U of Hawaii. ALL FACETS: Business plans, surveys, S.O.P., training, financials, prospectus, franchise contracts, prospect kits, advertising, P.R., pert chart, legalities, signage, field counselling.

CAPITAL FUNDING SERVICES
P.O. Box 424, Waco, TX, 76703. Contact: Denis M. Hanley, Pres. - Tel: (817) 744-6950. Provide franchise start-up SBA financing in all states. From $40,000 up, for 5 to 25 year terms. Established: 1988.

CAPTEC FINANCIAL GROUP, INC.
24 Frank Lloyd Wright, Lobby L 4th Flr., P.O. Box 544, Ann Arbor, MI, 48106-0544. Contact: William McPherson, V.P. - Tel: (313) 994-5505. Nationwide supplier of capital to franchisors and franchisees. Service provided through creative leasing programs and mortgage financing designed to assist in the easy rapid expansion of operations.

CASH CONNECTION
11902 S.E. Stark St., Portland, OR, 97216-3764. Contact: Steve Hanson - Tel: (503) 255-2274. Franchisor Consultant.

CENTER FOR BUSINESS REGENERATION, INC.
3305 Buckridge Blvd., Ste. 100, Duluth, GA, 30136-4932. Contact: Timothy Galfas, II, Pres. - Tel: (770) 923-0220. Specialists in business turnarounds and dispute resolution for franchised outlets of all sorts. Focus is on the franchisee, the business and creating situation wherein the profits and or cash flow will be sufficient to the needs of the business. Develop effective alternatives to legal actions in working with distressed franchisees. Provide workshops, seminars and toll free management helpline. Provide creative ways to promote stalled out mature franchisors and help young franchisors get on track they need. Established: 1990.

CHECKERS SIMON & ROSNER
111 N. Orange Ave., Ste. 1250, Orlando, FL, 32801. Contact: Henry M. Cairo, Partner - Tel: (312) 346-4242. Franchise consulting, accounting, tax planning, systems work, and business counseling. Established: 1930.

CHUNOWITZ, TEITELBAUM & BAERSON, LTD., CERTIFIED PUBLIC ACCOUNTANTS
401 Huehl Rd. , Northbrook, IL, 60062. Contact: Martin Magida - Tel: (708) 498-9620. Personal and timely service throughout the country and the Virgin Islands. Over twenty years of franchise accounting, tax planning, cash flow analysis, appraisals and valuations, personal financial planning and litigation support. Established: 1973.

COLEMAN-GARVIN REALTY, INC.
P.O. Box 7345, Charlottesville, VA, 22906. Contact: Lee Garvin, CCIM, CRE, GRI/Pres - Tel: (804) 973-1481. Commercial real estate site selection, and consulting service. Complete demographic reports, feasibility studies, aerials and other pertinent data. Established: 1964.

COMPANY CORPORATION, THE
Three Christina Centre, 201 N. Walnut St., Wilmington, DE, 19801. Contact: Alison Deprisco, Dir. of Mktg. - Tel: (302) 575-0440. Provider of incorporation services in all 50 states, without legal fees. Specialize in Delaware corporations, but can incorporate in any state, for as little as $45 plus state filing fees. Established: 1972.

COMPREHENSIVE FRANCHISING, INC.
FPI
2465 Ridgecrest Ave., Orange Park, FL, 32065. Contact: Connie D'Imperio, Pres. - Tel: (800) 321-6567 or (904) 272-6567. Import and export of master and regional, foreign and domestic franchises worldwide, global introductions, full service international documentation packaging, recruits candidates to purchase regional and master territories in all markets. Complete monitoring, profit and control for overseas expansion. Established: 1988.

CONCEPTUAL EDGE, THE
2102 Business Center Dr. #130, Irvine, CA, 92715. Contact: John Collins, Pres. - Tel: (714) 474-1764. Franchise development and consulting firm. Concept, structure, operations and marketing assistance. Feasibility studies, strategic planning, financial projections, legal documentation, operations manuals, problem solving, marketing and sales materials. Introductions to Japanese market. Established in 1980.

CONNEX INTERNATIONAL, INC.
68 Main St., Danbury, CT, 06810. Contact: Michelle Yanik, Public Relations Co-ordinator - Tel: (800) 426-6639. Connex is the main supplier of audio teleconference services to a large majority of franchise corporations, as well as to the International Franchise Assoc. Connex provides bridging capabilities that allow companies to link multiple locations - domestically or internationally - by telephone for conference calls. Connex also provides consulting services to corporations on audio conferencing, user training, video conferences, etc. Established: 1980.

CONSULTANTS, THE
Franchise Consultants, Inc.
Oliver's Corner, P.O. Box 403, Essex, CT, 06426-0403. Contact: Theron Kearney, Sr. Fran. Consultant - Tel: (203) 767-9009. Complete franchise development services including legal documentation, operations manuals and promotional packages. Site locating and equipment financing. Franchise sales and franchisor consulting. Twenty plus yrs. experience. No. of Units: Company Owned: 8.

CRONER COMPANY, THE
1028 Sir Francis Drake Blvd., Kentfield, CA, 94904. - Tel: (415) 485-5532. Management consultants specializing in compensation including executive and management incentives, organizational planning and design and facilitation of business and strategic planning. Established: 1978.

CSS FRANCHISE NETWORK
Creative Sales Solutions
177 Main St., Ste. 103, Ft. Lee, NJ, 07024. Contact: Franchise Rep. - Tel: (201) 585-4753. Franchise development & sales network, offering franchisors rapid expansion through aggressive marketing & screening of franchise applicants. Established: 1991 - No. of Units: Company Owned: 2 - Branch Offices: 2 - Franchise Fee: $10,000 - Royalty: $250. per month service fee - Total Inv: $20,000 - $25,000 office set-up - Financing: Yes.

CSS FRANCHISING NETWORK *
Creative Sales Solutions, Inc.
177 Main St., Ste. 103, Fort Lee, NJ, 07024. Contact: Gary Occhiogrosso, Franchise Rep. - Tel: (201) 585-4753. The only franchise consulting firm that specializes in sales. The actual franchise sales process is our priority. We have sold over 500 franchises for our clients. EAch office is part of the overall marketing strategy with four separate income streams. Established: 1991 - Franchising Since: 1995 - No. of Units: Company Owned: 1 - Franchised: 2 - Franchise Fee: $9,500 - Royalty: flat fee as low as $1,500 per year - Total Inv: $15,000 to $25,000 (office, work. cap., adv.) - Financing: Yes, SBA.

DAMAS & ASSOCIATES
6810 S. Cedar St., Ste. 2B, Lansing, MI, 48911. Contact: Raymond J. Damas, Pres. - Tel: (517) 694-0910 or (800) 443-2627. For over 12 yrs., has been investigating and evaluating franchises which persons are considering purchasing, and has been developing successful businesses into franchises. Includes feasibility studies, business plans, raising capital, patent and trademark protection, operating and training manuals, marketing materials, and franchise marketing. Established: 1979.

DEAN CONSULTANTS
17300 17th St., Ste. J-204, Tustin, CA, 92680. Contact: Paul Wilmoth, Pres. - Tel: (714) 739-4614. Franchisor Consultant.

DEMOMETRICS CORP.
1117 White St., Ann Arbor, MI, 48104. Contact: Charles Hammerslough, Pres. - Tel: (313) 747-7097. Marketing and site selection consultants. We create and develop market potential reports and evaluate franchise encroachment. Established: 1992.

DEUTSCH GROUP, THE
4509 Candleberry Ave., Seal Beach, CA, 90740-3026. Contact: Barry J. Deutsch, Pres. - Tel: (310) 431-1785, Fax: (310) 431-4306. The Deutsch Group offers all of the franchise development services required to franchise a business, including feasibility studies and analysis, strategic planning, direction, all legal documentation, sales kits, development of operational marketing and training manuals, business plan development and going public. Established: 1970.

DR. JOHN A. BERGER & ASSOCIATES
2021 Midwest Rd., Ste. 300, Oak Brook, IL, 60521. Contact: Franchise Dir./Pres. - Tel: (708) 953-8638. Human resource consultants to franchisors/franchisees. Management, recruiting and hiring programs, training programs compensation programs, turnover reduction programs; productivity improvement programs; team building; strategic planning.

ELDORADO BANK
2730 E. Chapman Ave., Orange, CA, 92669. Contact: Robert W. Tompkins, V.P. - Tel: (714) 288-1974. Specializes in financing (SBA loans) for new expanding franchises from 7 - 25 yrs. - $75,000 & up. Ninety percent real estate loans for acquisition and /or construction of owner-occupied commercial buildings. Established: 1972.

ENTREPRENEUR EXPO, THE
SC Promotions, Inc.
6890 S. Tucson Way, Ste. 112, Englewood, CO, 80112. Contact: Shael Buchen, Pres. - Tel: (303) 799-9700. Promotes business opportunity and franchise shows across the U.S. and Canada. Established: 1988. North America's largest privately held promoter of business opportunity & franchise shows.

ENTREPRENEUR'S SOURCE, THE *
211 Schrafft's Dr., Waterbury, CT, 06705. Contact: Terry Powell, Pres. - Tel: (800) 289-0086. Franchise Consultants with 10 offices & 11 years experience. Find the franchise that meets your unique needs through our exclusive Franchise Finders Profile Matching System. "Your success is our only business." Established: 1984 - No. of Units: Company Owned: 2 -Associates: 8.

STOP
Making Money for Someone Else
Take control of your future as the owner of your own successful Franchise Consulting Firm. The Entrepreneur's Source guarantees your success by matching your clients to the RIGHT Franchise with our exclusive Franchise Finders Profile Match. Bring over 10 years experience to your new business day one. Call for details 1-800-289-0086

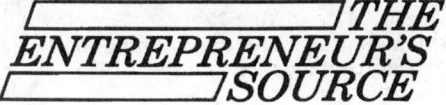

EQUIFAX MARKETING DECISION SYSTEMS
5375 Mira Sorrento Pl., Ste.400, San Diego, CA, 92121-3804. Contact: Steve Nye, Pres. - Tel: (619) 622-0800. Marketing research firm specializing in locational research of forecasting sales for proposed retailers and development of computer systems to forecast sale. Established: 1971.

ERNST & YOUNG
1221 McKinney St. #2400, Houston, TX, 77010-2007. Contact: Dan Reese, Principal - Tel: (713) 750-1500. Consists of 450 offices worldwide. Provides finance, accounting and tax assistance to help franchisors deal with business problems of growing up. Established: 1903.

F.C.I.A.
Franchise Consultants International Association
5147 South Angela Rd., Memphis, TN, 38117. Contact: W.C. Richey - Tel: (901) 682-2951, Fax: (901) 867-0010. An organization of professional consultants who specialize in sales, advertising, development, seminars, training, education, supply supervision, support and management involved with the franchise industry. Established: 1986.

FHG INTERNATIONAL INC. *
1825 Ponce de Leon Blvd., Coral Gables, FL, 33134. Contact: Peter Gaffe, Dir. - Tel: (305) 460-3583. Management consulting firm specializing in foodservice, retail and hospitality franchising including: business plan development, cross border strategies, litigation support, arbitration. Established: 1984.

FIRST CHOICE FRANCHISE SERVICES INC.
6465 Millcreek Dr., Ste. 205, Mississauga, ON, Canada, L5N 5R3. Contact: George Kostopoulos, Pres. - Tel: (905) 567-4180 or (800) 387-8335. A full service franchise development and marketing company that specializes in the promotion and sale of quality franchise concepts regionally, nationally and internationally. Our qualified franchise specialists, with extensive sales and marketing background can ensure successful expansion of your concept. Established: 1988. (See our ad on page 106.)

FRANCHISE ACQUISITION DIVESTMENT CONSULTANTS LTD.
2535 Glenview Rd., Glenview, IL, 60025-2714. Contact: Ron Owens, Pres. - Tel: (708) 998-0767. Specializing in re-sale of fast food franchises. Consultants to prospective franchisees and sellers of franchised restaurants. Established: 1988.

FRANCHISE ARCHITECTS, THE
3 Metawa Lane, Riverwoods, IL, 60015. Contact: Craig S. Slavin, Pres. - Tel: (708) 808-0870. Established: 1979. Franchise consulting firm specializing in the design of custom expansion programs. Our proprietery Franchise Architecture process is well tested and the basis for the expansion programs for hundreds of worldwide companies in over 40 industries and 4 continents. Development program includes all operations, marketing, advertising, sales, financial, organizational structure, human resource, staffing and compliance issues and franchise sales and marketing assistance.

FRANCHISE ASSOCIATES
2212 Aralia St., Newport Beach, CA, 92660. Contact: Sidney Nadler, Sr. Partner - Tel: (714) 759-0055. Senior franchisor executives and franchise company founders evaluate and validate concepts, prepare registrations, marketing and sales programs and offer prospective franchisee's investigative procedures and guidelines for purchase decisions. Established: 1975 - No. of Units: Company Owned: 1.

FRANCHISE ASSOCIATES, THE
541 Main St., South Weymouth, MA, 02269-9102. Contact: Franchise Dir./Pres. - Tel: (617) 337-7940. Franchisor/Franchisee Consultant.

Thinking of new territories? Think Canada!

Canada is hot for new franchise concepts. And First Choice Franchise Services will help you successfully break into the Canadian marketplace.

First Choice Franchise Services is a full-service franchise development and marketing company that specializes in the promotion and sale of quality franchise concepts regionally, nationally and internationally. Our service retains the flavor and effectiveness of an in-house franchise division, but at a much lower cost and risk to the franchisor.

Our goal is to provide you with results that count—closed sales. Our qualified franchise specialists, with extensive sales and marketing experience, will guide you through the process of successfully expanding into Canada.

For more information call, or write to: George Kostopoulos, President
1-800-387-8335

6465 Millcreek Drive,
Suite 205,
Mississauga, Ontario,
Canada, L5N 5R3

FIRST CHOICE FRANCHISE SERVICES INC.®

Member of The Canadian Franchise Association

FRANCHISE AXIS
Franchise Profiles International
2465 Ridgecrest Ave., Orange Park, FL, 32065. Contact: Connie B. D'Imperio, Pres. - Tel: (904) 272-6567 or (800) 321-6567. Marketing and research service for franchisors that recruits and screens potential candidates for master franchise areas. Established: 1988.

FRANCHISE BROKER NETWORK OF ILLINOIS
190 Big Peninsula Rd., Elgin, IL, 60123-1506. Contact: Roger Baldwin, Pres. - Tel: (708) 622-9988. National network of independent offices that help prospective franchisees select the best business opportunity to match their desires, skills, and budget. The buyer pays no fees for our assistance, all fees are paid by the sellers. We can also help obtain a location, financing, and find legal or other professional help. Established: 1990.

FRANCHISE BUILDERS
185 Pine St. Ste.818, Manchester, CT, 06040-5882. Contact: Mark Merrill, Pres. - Tel: (203) 647-7542, Fax: (203) 646-6544. Turn your business into a franchise. Financing also available. Established: 1987.

FRANCHISE BUSINESS INTERNATIONAL
5310 Zelzah, #305, Encino, CA, 91316. Contact: Lou Gurnick, Pres. - Tel: (818) 705-3222. Structuring franchise systems U.S.A., expansion into Europe, Mexico, Canada and Asia. Also every phase of franchise therapy for ailing companies. Established: 1954. Clients include: Midas, Int'l. House of Pancakes, Computerland, Casablancas, Domino's, Capt. Tonys Pizza, Futurekids etc. Former chairman of the International Committee of the I.F.A. and Board of Directors; member of the American Arbitration Association etc. Franchise instructor, UCLA.

FRANCHISE BUSINESS SYSTEMS INC.
4200 Dahlberg Dr., Minneapolis, MN, 55422. Contact: Ron Olson, Pres. - Tel: (612) 520-8500. Consulting firm with emphasis on sales and managing of franchises. Established: 1986.

FRANCHISE CENTRE™, THE(DBA)
Donald J. Foltz & Associates, Inc.
5555 DTC Pkwy., Tower C, Ste 3210, Englewood, CO, 80111. Contact: Jon S. Brynestad, Exec. V.P. - Tel: (303) 220-0147, Fax: (303) 220-1048. Franchise development and general franchisor consulting since 1970 experience in franchising as a successful franchisor and consultant. Competitive charges for feasibility study, operations manuals, full legal documentation, trademark registration, marketing plans, franchisee relations. Franchise experience since 1958.

FRANCHISE CONSORTIUM, LTD.
245 S. 84th, Ste. 210, Lincoln, NE, 68510. Contact: J. Field, Pres. - Tel: (800) 301-9504. Franchise consulting firm specializing in the development of franchise systems. Services include: preparation of legal documents, operating and sales manuals, marketing and sales of units and system management. Established: 1990.

FRANCHISE CONSULTING GROUP, THE
1888 Century Park E. #1900, Los Angeles, CA, 90067-1723. Contact: Edward Kushell, Pres. - Tel: (520) 552-2901, Fax: (520) 886-4459. Consultants specializing in new and existing franchise development and expansion, alternate business strategies, and expert witness litigation services. Includes: feasibility analysis, business plan evaluation, capital sourcing, international acquisition and expansion and financial projections; development and implementation of advertising, marketing, communications and service/support programs; design and production of sales and marketing brochures, operations, training and sales manuals, and collateral materials. Established: 1978.

FRANCHISE CONSULTING SERVICES
Business Opportunities of America, Inc.
2666 N. First Ave., Ste. B, Tucson, AZ, 85719. Contact: Richard Beuzekom, Pres. - Tel: (520) 622-9392, Fax: (520) 886-4459. A Franchising/Multi-Unit specialist in consulting and/or marketing from start-ups to existing operations. Established: 1975.

TO GROW OR NOT TO GROW?

Deciding whether franchising is the "right" way for your company to grow is difficult because it requires special know-how and background.

That's where we come in. **FRANCHISE DEVELOPMENTS** has the expertise and methods to help you decide if you should franchise - and is fully capable of then helping to develop a successful franchise program for your business. Some of the services we offer are:

* Conducting Feasibility Studies
* Developing Franchise Agreements
* Preparing Disclosure Statements (UFOC or FTC)
* Creating Franchise Brochures
* Building Franchise Support Programs
* Developing Operations Manuals and Training Formats
* Designing Forms, Systems, Controls and Procedures
* Structuring Franchise Relationships
* Finding Sources of Financing
* Recruiting, Qualifying and Selecting Franchisees

For a survey or exploratory review contact:

Franchise Developments Inc.

4730 CENTRE AVENUE, PITTSBURGH, PENNSYLVANIA 15213
412/687-8484   FAX # 412/687-0541

FRANCHISE DEVELOPERS *
1919 South 40th St., Ste. 202, Lincoln, NE, 68506-5248. Contact: Jack L. Rediger, Pres. - Tel: (800) 865-2378. If your concept is worthy of franchising, it's worth a call to Franchise Developers. Complete franchise development services including: In-house legal, marketing, sales, and support. Experience with superior customer service. Excellent references. Established: 1994.

FRANCHISE DEVELOPMENT INTERNATIONAL, INC.
2103 N.W. 45th Ave., Coconut Creek, FL, 33066. Contact: Linda D. Biciocchi, Pres. - Tel: (305) 942-9424. Franchise/marketing consulting firm specializing in small successful businesses looking to expand through franchising. Principals are a group of qualified professionals in the areas of law, marketing, operations, finance, advertising, purchasing, and real estate. Established: 1991.

FRANCHISE DEVELOPMENTS, INC.
4730 Centre Avenue, Pittsburgh, PA, 15213. Contact: Kenneth Franklin, Pres. - Tel: (412) 687-8484, Fax: (412) 687-0541. Specializing in designing and implementing a total franchise development program. Package includes legal documents, manuals, training programs, system design, support program, sales plan & recruitment brochure. Established: 1970.

FRANCHISE FOUNDATIONS *
540 Pacific Ave., San Francisco, CA, 94133. Contact: Kevin Murphy, Dir. of Oper. - Tel: (800) 942-4402, Fax: (707) 442-0444. Management consulting firm specializing in franchise planning, development & implementation. Services include feasibility studies, legal documentation & registration, business plans, operations documentation, training curriculum development & public relations. Established: 1980 - No. of Units: Company Owned: 2.

FRANCHISE GROUP, THE
401 N. Michigan Ave., Suite 2600, Chicago, IL, 60611-4240. Contact: Gerald Shadlen, Pres. - Tel: (312) 245-1622. Specializing in providing franchise program development, consulting and implementation services to emerging and established franchisors. Services include: feasibility studies, financing arrangements, management systems and procedures review, franchise offering analysis/review, marketing, operations manual preparation, legal documentation and general management consulting. Established: 1989.

FRANCHISE LEARNING & CONSULTING CENTER LTD.
20 Lattingtown Rd., Glen Cove, NY, 11542. Contact: Robert E. Kushell - Tel: (516) 759-3380. Consultants to prospective franchisees and franchisors, individual counseling, educational services, seminar activities. Established: 1980.

FRANCHISE MARKETING NETWORK
1643 Lazy Trail Dr., Chico, CA, 95926. Contact: Stanton I. Parker, Mktg. Dir. - Tel: (916) 894-6734, Fax: (916) 893-9720. Specialists in West Coast market penetration for new franchisor consulting for (scared seeker) franchisee. Franchising Since: 1986 - No. of Units: Company Owned: 1.

FRANCHISE MASTERS
1000 Shelard Pky., #320, Minneapolis, MN, 55426-4919. Contact: John A. Campbell, Pres. - Tel: (800) 328-4158. Feasibility, potential, development, legal, marketing and sales services to new and existing franchisors nationally and in Canada. Locations in Minneapolis, San Francisco, Los Angeles and Tampa/St. Petersburg. Established: 1981.

FRANCHISE NETWORK INTERNATIONAL (DBA)
Trans Pacific Investment Corp.
1314 S. King St., #407, Honolulu, Hawaii, 96814. Contact: Mr. J.J. Reyes, Managing Dir. - Tel: (808) 593-9065, Fax: (808) 593-9165. Sale of U.S. franchising companies and operating franchises to Asian investors, consultant to M & A Depts. of foreign banks on U.S. franchise acquisition and intermediary services for international franchise licensing agreement. Established: 1986.

FRANCHISE OPPORTUNITIES, INC.
Artek, Inc.
6754 Gretchen Pl. N., Saint Paul, MN, 55128-3137. Contact: Richard Gahler, Pres. - Tel: (612) 777-4829. Represent franchisors in a marketing capacity. Consultations involving new and existing businesses plus sales and marketing. Franchise offering circulars and brochures, sales kits, advertising, attorney referral, real estate and franchise agreements. Established: 1983.

FRANCHISE PERFORMANCE PARTNERS
1 Northfield Plz., Ste. 300, Northfield, IL, 60093-1284. Contact: Harold Krieger, Sr. Partner - Tel: (708) 441-2672. Design and develop franchise systems. Redesign existing franchise systems that need to work better. Plan and implement programs that will reduce tension and will improve franchisor/franchisee relationship. Also contact: Robert Jacob, Sr. Partner, 770 Menlo Ave., Ste. 101, Menlo Park, CA, 94025-5119, Tel: (415) 325-0553.

FRANCHISE RECRUITERS LTD. SM
3500 Innsbruck, Lincolnshire Country Club, Village of Crete, IL, 60417. Contact: Jerry Wilkerson, Formen/Exec. V.P./Dir at IFA - Tel: (708)757-5595, (800)334-6257, Fax:(708)758-8222. Nineteen years of franchise experience. An international executive search corporation dedicated exclusively to franchising. Unconditional one year guarantee. Excellent client references. Placement of experienced franchise professionals in sales, operations, executive, marketing, training, finance, legal and international development. Established: 1984. Also: Offices in Canada.

FRANCHISE RESOURCE DEVELOPMENT CORP.
3572 W. Brocker Rd., Ste. 201, Metamora, MI, 48455-9330. Contact: Frank H. Migliore, Pres. - Tel: (810) 797-2275, Fax: (810) 797-2276. Assist both franchisor and franchisee in development of sales, marketing, master, regional and single unit development. International contacts for franchisor expansion. Financing opportunities for growth capital and single unit financing. Established: 1990.

FRANCHISE SALES CENTER
1255 Dorothy Rd., Crownsville, MD, 21032. Contact: George M. Palmer, Dir. - Tel: Voice mail (301) 913-1791. The center works in a franchise sales capacity only. Directed toward the Mid-Atlantic states, the center represents a select group of franchisors looking to establish themselves in the Washington, DC/Baltimore markets. Established: 1982.

FRANCHISE SEARCH, INC.
20 Lattingtown Rd., Glen Cove, NY, 11542. Contact: Doug T. Kushell, Pres. - Tel: (516) 671-6447, Fax: (516)-671-1989. Established the first executive search firm specializing exclusively in franchising. Represents only franchisor clients and places only professional franchise management candidates in franchise sales, operations, training, marketing, financial, real estate, construction, legal and international development and CEO's. There are specially designed sales programs available for new franchisors. Established: 1983.

FRANCHISE STORES INTERNATIONAL
12279 U.S. Highway 64, Eads, TN, 38028-9314. Contact: W.C. Richey, Pres. - Tel: (901) 867-0600. License to represent, exclusively, numerous franchises, dealerships, distributorships; licenses for sale in assigned territory. Established: 1976 - No. of Units: Company Owned: 1 - Franchised: 54 - Franchise Fee: $2,500 - Royalty: 5% - Total Inv: $20,000 - Financing: None.

FRANCHISE SYSTEMS CORPORATION
44 Cocoanut Row, #T-5, Palm Beach, FL, 33480-4005. Contact: Tom Feltenstein, Senior Principal - Tel: (407)-655-9207. Assisting start up and existing franchisors with their franchising programme, corporate marketing, franchise marketing plans, sales and compliances, human resources and training, trade area marketing programs. Established: 1989.

FRANCHISING BOARD, LTD., THE
6727 Lemai, Lincolnwood, IL, 60646. Contact: Norman D. Axelrad, Pres. - Tel: (708) 673-7114. Franchise business/legal consulting. Established: 1983.

FRANCHISING BUSINESS CONCEPTS, LTD.
6253 N. Fair Oaks Pl., Boise, ID, 83703. Contact: Bob Schmellick, Owner - Tel: (208) 853-0126, Fax: (208) 853-0127. Consultant to franchisors for development of sales and marketing programs to sell the franchise to the franchisee. Established: 1983 - Franchising Since: 1974.

FRANCHISING WORKS, INC.
P.O. Box 100, Dousman, WI, 53118. Contact: Frederick Welk, Principal - Tel: (414) 965-2212. System development for franchisors.

FRANCHISINTERNATIONAL, INC.
4730 Centre Ave., Pittsburgh, PA, 15213. Contact: Gisela Claper, Pres. - Tel: (412) 687-2760. Franchise consultants & brokers with special focus on the Latin American market - Brazil, Chile, Argentina, Peru and Mexico. Established: 1991.

FRANCORP, INC.
20200 Governors Dr., Olympia Fields, IL, 60461. Contact: Client Services Dept. - Tel: (800) 877-1103, (708) 481-2900. Francorp, Inc., is a management consulting firm specializing in franchise development. Francorp consultants have provided full development programs including feasibility studies, business plans, legal documents, operations manuals, and marketing materials for more than 600 clients since 1976. Francorp also provides post-development services for established franchisors including lead generation programs, franchise brochures, videotapes, international brokerage, public relations, and expert witness services. Offices in New York, Chicago, Los Angeles, Naples FL, Buenos Aires, La Plata, Mexico City, Santiago, Montevideo & Tokyo.

FRANDATA
Frandata Corp.
1155 Connecticut Ave. N.W., Ste. 275, Washington, DC, 20036. Contact: Jeffrey E. Kolton, Pres. - Tel: (202) 659-8640. Information specialist to the franchise industry, providing research, consulting, and document retrieval. Established: 1989.

FRANWAY INTERNATIONAL *
Business Opportunities of America, Inc.
2666 N. 1st Ave., Ste. B, Tucson, AZ, 85719. Contact: R.A. Beuzekom, Pres. - Tel: (520) 622-9685, Fax: (520) 886-4459. An international franchise marketing company. Established: 1994.

GENERAL ELECTRIC CREDIT CORP.
44 Old Ridgebury Rd., Danbury, CT, 06810-5105. Contact: Tom Ade, Mgr. Fran. Financing - Tel: (203) 796-8500. Financial services organization. Franchise Financing.

HAYES GROUP, INC., THE
715 Twining Rd., Ste. 100A, Dresher, PA, 19025. Contact: Robyn Axner, Dir. of Public Relations - Tel: (215) 887-7800, Fax: (215) 887-1028. Firm is engaged in the development, marketing and promotions of franchised businesses nationally and internationally. Established: 1986. Offices in Philadelphia, PA and Dallas, TX.

ICN
8855 Atlanta Ave., Ste. 356, Huntington Beach, CA, 92714. Contact: Robert Martin, Dir. - Tel: (714) 753-3312. A national and international network of consultants in over 200 specialities working with small to Fortune 500 companies. Established: 1974 - No. of Units: Company Owned: 400+ - Franchise Fee: Independent - Total Inv: $2,000 - $8,000 - Financing: None.

IMPAC FRANCHISING *
8249 N. First Dr., Phoenix, AZ, 85021. Contact: Jon Eberenz, CEO - Tel: (602) 997-5671. Comprehensive consulting in franchise development, operations, finance, sales and marketing. Specializing in long term planning and implementation of growth and profit strategies for established and emerging companies nationally and internationally. Practical solutions from experienced advisors. Established: 1981.

IMTEC (INTERNATIONAL MANAGEMENT TECHNOLOGY CORPORATION)
One Dock St., Stamford, CT, 06902. Contact: Joseph A. Lev, Pres. - Tel: (203) 964-9619, Fax: (203) 356-1557. Arrange tie-ups between U.S. companies and companies in the Far East etc. International management consulting firm. Established: 1982.

INTERNATIONAL BOARD OF DIRECTORS
3 Riverway, Ste. 1285, Houston, TX, 77056. Contact: Craig S. Rice, Pres. - Tel: (713) 850-8371, (800) 851-8371. IBD is a full service consulting firm specializing in facilitating entry or expansion of U.S. franchises into Mexico. Established: 1985.

INTERNATIONAL FRANCHISE ASSOCIATION
1350 New York Ave., N.W., Ste.900, Washington, DC, 20005. Contact: Don DeBolt, President - Tel: (202) 628-8000.

INTERNATIONAL FRANCHISE DEVELOPMENT
23611 Chagrin Blvd., #101, Beachwood, OH, 44122. Contact: Jerry Libava, Pres. - Tel: (216) 831-2610, Fax: (216) 464-1802. Franchise development with a focus on marketing. Our team can handle all aspects of franchising including legal documents, brochures and manuals. We are a member of Franchise Network, The Franchise Matchmakers. Established: 1990.

IRV H. KAUFMAN & ASSOCIATES
145 Manor Dr., Deerfield, IL, 60015. Contact: Irv H. Kaufman, Owner/Operator - Tel: (708) 945-0145, Fax: (708) 945-0740. Franchise sales/Marketing broker/Consultant. Established: 1964 - Franchising Since: 1964 - Financing: Yes.

J.C.M. CONSULTING
132 Pierpont Ave., # 205, Salt Lake City, UT, 84101. Contact: Clyde Johnson, Pres. - Tel: (801) 322-3700. Employee selection and development. Phase II Honesty and drug profiling, personality profiling, performance evaluation program. Established: 1984.

KANALY TRUST COMPANY
4550 Post Oak Place Blvd., Houston, TX, 77027. Contact: E. Deane Kanaly, Chairman & C.E.O. - Tel: (713) 626-9483. Exclusive private trust company with national and international clientelle, is the acknowledged leader in providing custom sophisticated financial services on a fees only basis. Offer Master Retirement & Plans to franchisors and franchisees.

KEMP STRATEGIES
2800 Farview Lane, Minneapolis, MN, 55356. Contact: Linda Kemp, Owner - Tel: (612) 476-0232. Specializes in developing training strategies for rapidly growing franchisees and franchisors. Works with franchisors to design and develop new training, re-design their current training programs, as well as focus on needs of seasoned franchisees. Established: 1989.

KOACH ENTERPRISES, INC.
5529 N. 18th St., Arlington, VA, 22205. Contact: Joseph L. Koach, C.E.O. - Tel: (703) 241-8361, Fax: (703) 241-8623. Franchise Developer/Franchise Consultant. Former president of the International Franchise Association. Established: 1981.

KUSHELL ASSOCIATES, INC.
Franchise Advisors Worldwide
20 Lattingtown Rd., Glen Cove, NY, 11542. Contact: Robert E. Kushell, Pres. - Tel: (516) 759-3380, Fax: (516) 671-1989. Our Consulting Group advises multinational and entrepreneurial companies on how to develop franchise programs. We assist established franchisors with growth, marketing and sales strategies. We have offices in Brazil, Chile, Argentina, Uruguay, Taiwan, Saudi Arabia and South Africa and find Master partners for U.S. franchisors.

LAMY GROUP, LTD., THE
650 Poydras St., Ste. 2245, New Orleans, LA, 70130. Contact: Kenneth S. Lamy - Tel: (504) 525-9914 or 1-(800) 999-LAMY . Management consulting firm comprised of CPA's and MBA's specializing in retail sales, compliance, royalty payments and specialty examinations for franchisors throughout North America. Established: 1989 - Franchising Since: 1989 - No. of Units: Company Owned: 1.

LARUE MARKETING CONSULTANTS
P.O. Box 11223, Pompano Beach, FL, 33061. Contact: Robert F. LaRue, Pres. - Tel: (305) 781-4478, (908) 981-1711, Fax: (305) 783-0097. Counsel and service to established and prospective franchisors. Feasibility studies. Marketing strategies and plans. Concept development and refinement. Marketing analysis and research. Evaluation of alternative channels of distribution. Sales/marketing theme development. Marketing communication plans and programs. Merchandising strategies. Competitive analysis. Area potential forecasts. Training programs. In-the-field monitoring of program execution. Materials for closing of sales to franchisees. Established: 1968.

MANAGEMENT 2000
Gappa & Kirkham, Inc.
10445 Westoffice, Houston, TX, 77042. Contact: Bob Gappa, Pres. - Tel: (713) 952-3177, Fax: (713) 952-3830. Products & services include: Complete program for "start-up" companies; How to "Close More Franchise Sales"; How to get your franchisees to use business plans; Convention speeches; Strategic planning; Customer acquisition/retention strategies; Strategies to build average unit volumes; How to improve the effectiveness of your field consultants; Customer services strategies; Prospect profiling; Franchisee attitude survey; Improving the effectiveness of your area developers; and more. Established: 1981.

MANAGEMENT ACTION PROGRAMS
5722 N. Seventh St., Ste. 207, Phoenix, AZ, 85014. Contact: Jack Eberenz, Senior Consultant - Tel: (602) 279-7700. Consultants specializing in developing and managing franchise companies. Maximize return on investment through better operations and successful franchisees. Achieve high growth without losing control of quality. Established: 1960 - No. of Units: Company Owned: 12.

MAP
5727 N. 7th St., Ste. 207, Phoenix, AZ, 85014. Contact: Jack Eberenz, Senior Consultant - Tel: (602) 297-7700, Fax: (602) 279-6990. 35 years of dedication to helping our clients meet their goals. Our clients have national and international success because MAP helps in implementation to get results. Established: 1960.

MARKET TARGET RESEARCH
4004 Stags Leap Way, Paso Robles, CA, 93446-8725. Contact: Greg Shipley, Pres. - Tel: (805) 239-8714 or (800) 727-5911, Fax: (805) 239-0517. Franchise investigation, business plan/disclosure statement preparation, site analysis, business valuation/appraisal, deal structuring, and funding. Established: 1983 - Total Inv: ranging between $650 - $13,500 & 8% of funding - Financing: Venture Funding and Bank Negotiations.

MARKETING CONSULTANTS OF AMERICA 'MCA'
Consultants of America Professional Corp.
3820 Premier Ave., Memphis, TN, 38118. Contact: Bill Richey, CEO - Tel: (901) 867-0600. Franchisor consulting, managing, financing, logistics, structuring and re-structuring, documentation, registration, manuals, site location, sales, training, advertising and sales material preparation. International. Principals in franchising since 1947. Established: 1976 - Franchising Since: 1976 - No. of Units: Company Owned: 1 - Franchised: 54 - Franchise Fee: $10,000 - $400,000 - Royalty: none - Total Inv: $25,000 - $500,000 - Financing: Yes.

MARKETING RESOURCES GROUP
71-58 Austin St., Suite 101, Forest Hills, NY, 11375. Contact: Franchise Marketing Dept. - Tel: (718) 261-8882. Franchise sales. Franchise development. Franchise marketing and consulting. We help business expand through franchising and grow through marketing. Advertising and public relations systems and services developed and implemented.

MARSHALL GROUP, THE
1000 South Main St., Ste. 687, Salinas, CA, 93901. Contact: Lois Marshall, Pres./Founder - Tel: (408) 484-1144. Executive search corporation serving franchisors nationally and internationally. Offices in the United States and Canada. Competitive rates, one year guarantee. Exceptional references. Established: 1968.

MCGROW CONSULTING
62 Derby St., #8, Hingham, MA, 02043. Contact: Jack McBirney, Pres. - Tel: (617) 740-2211 or (800) 358-8011. Full range of services assisting companies to become franchisors. Established: 1981. This firm has many success stories.

MONEY STORE INVESTMENT CORPORATION, THE
6200 Canoga Ave., #303, Woodland Hills, CA, 91367-2402. Contact: Ann Sisneros, Asst. V.P. Fran. Finance - Tel: (818) 906-2999. Lender of SBA guaranteed, long term business loans, loans for working capital, equipment and real estate. Established: 1967.

MOORE BUSINESS FORMS & SYSTEMS DIVISION
275 N. Field Dr., Lake Forest, IL, 60081. Contact: Don V. Booty, Mgr. Fran. Sales - Tel: (708) 205-0770. Multinational organization providing business information management solutions designed to enhance the efficiency and profitability of franchise operation. Established: 1885.

NATIONAL ASSOCIATION OF FRANCHISE COMPANIES
Nafco
6119 Pierce St., Hollywood, FL, 33024. Contact: Ed Foley, Exec. Dir. - Tel: (305) 966-1530. Marketing services for new franchisors with development of franchise theme and collateral sales and marketing materials. Also involved in taking companies public and writing business plans. Consulting services also available. Established: 1969.

NATIONAL CONSULTANT REFERRALS, INC. *
Powerbase, Inc.
8445 Camino Santa Fe, #207, San Diego, CA, 92121. Contact: Carl Kline, CEO - Tel: (800) 434-5200, Fax: (619) 552-0854. Need an expert? No charge referral service. See our ad in AT&T 800 Directory under Consultant Referrals. Go to http://www.referrals.com on internet. Established: 1979 - Franchising Since: 1994 - No. of Units: Company Owned: 1 - Franchise Fee: $25,000 - Royalty: 8%, 2% nat'l. adv. fund - Total Inv: Need 3 to 6 months operating capital - Financing: None.

NATIONAL COOPERATIVE BANK
1401 Eye St. NW, #700, Washington, DC, 20005-2204. Contact: Stanley Dreyer, V.P.Dev. - Tel: (202) 336-7618. Provides commercial, leasing and development banking services to franchise co-operatives, as well as consultation on employee stock ownership plans (ESOP) and the formation of cooperatives within the franchising system. Established: 1980 - Financing: For co-operatives.

NATIONAL FRANCHISE ASSOCIATES
3473 Satellite Blvd., Ste. 201, Duluth, GA, 30136-4658. Contact: Stephen S. Raines, Pres. - Tel: (404) 873-6200. Full service consulting and developmental firm with expertise in feasibility studies, franchise agreement and disclosure documents, advertising and public relations, operations and training manuals, videos, franchise selling program and insurance risk management programs. Established: 1981 - No. of Offices: 3.

NATIONAL FRANCHISE CONSULTANTS
Wrights Square, 140 Helens Ave., #200, Highlands, NC, 28741. Contact: Steve Ruttenberg, Pres. - Tel: (704) 743-1000. Franchise consulting, full service, specializes in franchise development and franchise sales. Established: 1986 - No. of Offices: 2.

NATIONAL FRANCHISE SALES *
7699 Ninth St., Ste. 104, Buena Park, CA, 90621. Contact: Paul Wilmoth, V.P., Fran. Div. - Tel: (714) 739-4446, Fax: (714) 523-8908. Selling of new and existing franchises for both franchisors and franchisees. Established: 1977.

NATIONWIDE FRANCHISE MARKETING SERVICES *
12806 Midway Rd., Ste. 2024, Dallas, TX, 75244-6384. Contact: Marvin J. Migdol, Pres. - Tel: (214) 661-0167. Consulting firm specializing in all areas of franchise development. Serves as consultants to individuals who are contemplating the purchase of a franchise/distributorship. Conducts feasibility studies, disclosure statements & agreements, marketing plans & research, public relations and advertising programs plus financing. Established: 1971.

NEXUS - CONSULTANTS TO MANAGEMENT
P.O. Box 1531, Novato, CA, 94948. Contact: Dr. J.H. Carbone, Ph.D., Owner - Tel: (415) 897-4400, Fax: (415) 898-2252, Modem: (415) 898-2252, e-mail: JimNexus@aol.com. Management consulting since 1962. We consult to owners, boards, and CEOs during firm's cycle. Services offered: merger and acquisition, franchising, alternative dispute resolution, executive counseling, family businesses, managerial seminars and workshops. Statewide network, 30 years' California consulting. Many business plans don't sustain investor's burden of proof justifying franchising. We help "ready-fire-aim" clients decide whether franchise or another business form. Represent franchisor starting or strengthening western region business. Turnkey franchise consulting, planning, feasibility study, site selection, statutory filing, strategy, marketing. Don't bring us your problems, bring us your solutions - we'll tell you how good they are.

NICHOL & COMPANY PUBLIC RELATIONS
245 Fifth Ave., Room 2204, New York, NY, 10016-8781. Contact: Betsy Nichol, Pres. - Tel: (212) 889-6401. A public relations firm that specializes in serving the marketing communications and advertising needs of franchised businesses. Established: 1981.

PACIFIC FUNDING GROUP, INC.
4615 First St., #230, Pleasanton, CA, 94566-7367. Contact: Theresa Golden, Pres. - Tel: (510) 484-1711. A leading lender in franchise financing. Established: 1986.

PATTER MARKETING SERVICES
International Marketing Systems, Inc.
3077 E. Commercial Blvd., Ste. #200, Fort Lauderdale, FL, 33308. Contact: Patrick Terhune, Chairman/CEO - Tel: (305) 351-0663 or Fax: 351-0665. Consultants in the restaurant industry. Established: 1989.

PERFORMANCE GROUP LTD.
P.O. Box 437, Barrington, IL, 60011. Contact: Jim Burns, Pres. - Tel: (708) 526-9298. Consulting services and contract management for both new and seasoned franchisors. Specialists in franchise program development, marketing and retail location acquisition. Established: 1979.

PERFORMANCE Marketing Strategists inc.

PERFORMANCE MARKETING STRATEGISTS INC. *
165 EAB Plz., W. Twr., 6th Fl., Uniondale, NY, 11556-0165. Contact: Henry Weber, Pres. - Tel: (516) 522-2574, Fax: (516) 522-2845. Franchise sales "out source" and consulting firm. Consulting relationships with Century 21 Real Estate Corp., The Coffee Beanery Ltd., U-Save Auto Rental, Comprehensive Business Services. No. of Units: Company Owned: 2.

NATIONAL FRANCHISE SALES
7966 Ninth St., Ste. 104
Buena Park, CA, 90621
Contact: Paul Wilmoth
Tel: (714) 739-4446   Fax: (714) 739-4806

Now in its 18th year. We have both new and existing franchises available. With offices in Calif., Minnesota, and Florida.

R.C. KNOX AND COMPANY, INC.
1 Goodwin Sq., Hartford, CT, 06103-4305. Contact: Mike O'Hara, Fran. Insurance Mgr. - Tel: (203) 524-7600. Provides all forms of insurance services to companies who are franchisors. Programs take advantage of the group buying power of many businesses and pass the savings on to the franchise owners. Established: 1893.

RAGER AND ASSOCIATES
10933 Crabapple Rd., Roswell, GA, 30075. Contact: Les Rager, Partner - Tel: (404) 973-1135. Franchise consultants providing assistance for the development, financing and marketing of a franchise expansion effort. Established: 1979.

RETAIL TECHNOLOGIES INTERNATIONAL *
4800 Manzanita Ave., Ste. 1, Carmichael, CA, 95608. Contact: Nate Jessup, V.P., Mktg. - Tel: (800) 233-0793. Developer of Retail Pro®, the world leader in PC based point-of-sale inventory control software for retail industry. We have the solution to standardizing franchise operations. Established: 1986.

RG PARTNERS, INC.
245 N. Ocean Blvd., Ste. 201, Deerfield Beach, FL, 33441. Contact: Scott Richards, Pres. - Tel: (305) 428-1100. A full service Real Estate Firm specializing in site selection and consulting. Specific services include demographic analysis, market studies, lease negotiations, construction management, operational management.

RJF FINANCIAL SERVICES, INC.
13014 N. Dale Mabry, Ste.#215, Tampa, FL, 33618. Contact: Richard J. Franco, Pres. - Tel: (813) 968-1914. Financial services working with newly formed businesses and entrepreneurs to establish sound business practices, financial planning and employee benefit programs.

ROBERT J. BAER MARKETING
64 Niuiki Cir., Honolulu, HI, 96821-2318. Contact: Robert J. Baer, Pres. - Tel: (808) 373-8877. Active consulting firm whose dedicated purposes are to consult on marketing practices with special emphasis on franchising. Robert Baer also taught a course on franchising at the Hawaii Pacific University. Also, the founder of TeleCheck Services and Certified Franchise Exec. Established: 1985 - Franchising Since: 1967.

SANDERSON & ASSOCIATES
2310 Skokie Blvd., Ste. 204, Highland Park, IL, 60035. Contact: Rhonda Sanderson, Pres. - Tel: (708) 432-2370. Currently the premier company in franchise publicity with emphasis on highest quality media placements and personal service. Established: 1985.

SANWA BUSINESS CREDIT CORPORATION
One South Waker Drive, Chicago, IL, 60606. Contact: John Henkel - Tel: (312) 853-1369. A subsidiary of Sanwa Bank Ltd., one of the world's 5 largest banks. Over 25 yrs. experience in finance programs and provides full service financing for franchisees and franchisors.

SIEGEL BUSINESS SERVICES, INC.
1 Bala Plaza, Ste. 621, Bala Cynwyd, PA, 19004. Contact: Bernard Siegel, Pres. - Tel: (610) 668-9780. Business broker which sells franchises for both new and re-sales. Established: 1983. Maintains a national brokerage network.

SINGER, LEWAK, GREENBAUM, & GOLDSTEIN
10960 Wilshire Blvd., Ste. 1100, Los Angeles, CA, 90024. - Tel: (310) 477-3924. CPA's and management consultants to franchises. Established: 1959.

SOL ABRAMS, PUBLIC RELATIONS AND MARKETING CONSULTANTS
331 Webster Dr., New Milford, NJ, 07646. Contact: Sol Abrams, Pres. - Tel: (201) 262-4111. Public relations, publicity, marketing, communications, counsel and service. They provide franchisors and franchisees with professional, personalized, customized, creative counsel and service to increase their sales, incomes, images, publicity, profits and prestige. Established: 1943 - Practicing 52 years.

SPECTRUM WEST FRANCHISE SALES & MARKETING CONSULTANTS
4711 N.E. 50th, Seattle, WA, 98105. Contact: J.W. Smith, Pres. - Tel: (206) 524-5958, Fax: (206) 524-7826. Marketing and consulting for international franchise expansion. Working with all aspects of taking a franchise overseas to Japan, Asia & Australasia including: cultural aspect, advertising, sales & marketing, training, strategic planning.

STORE PACK, INC.
15247 East Skelly Dr., Tulsa, OK, 74116. Contact: Phil Ashmore, Pres. - Tel: (918) 437-9335, (800) 536-3774. Retail store interior design & supplies & central point distributors for franchise. Established: 1990.

STRATEGIC BUSINESS DEVELOPMENT CORP.
23 Townsend Sq., Oyster Bay, NY, 11771-2333. Contact: Martin Lund, Pres. - Tel: (516) 624-7100, (800) 200-7232. Specialists in franchise consulting, sales and development. Assist start-up and existing franchisors with their franchise development and national roll-out. Develop the entire program from concept to reality. Established: 1992.

STRATEGIC CREATIVE SERVICES
7 Summitt Ave., Bronxville, NY, 10708. Contact: Peter M. Johnson, Pres. - Tel: (914) 771-9260. Providing franchisors with advertising without wasting money on an advertising agency. Established: 1990.

TARGET BUSINESS CONSULTANTS, INC.
11956 Bernardo Plaza, #533, San Diego, CA, 92128. Contact: Frank Bellanova, VP - Tel: (619) 592-9250. Franchise planning and development. Assisting franchisors in the formulation of the franchise and in its marketing sales.

THIRTEEN-ONE, INC.
2221 Westcreek Ln. 15F, Houston, TX, 77027. Contact: Andrew H. Cohen, Pres. - Tel: (713) 622-7209. Franchise consulting & sales. Also assists prospective franchisees in evaluating franchises. Experienced in re-sales and start up as well as established franchises. Established: 1980.

TKO REAL ESTATE ADVISORY GROUP
P.O. Box 2630, Mercerville, NJ, 08690-0630. Contact: Ted Kraus - Tel: (609) 587-6200. Provides consulting on turn-around management or real estate for franchisors and franchisees. Established: 1978.

TORRENCE ENTERPRISES (BROKER)
483 N. Mulford Rd., #3, Rockford, IL, 61107. Contact: John Torrence, Fran. Dir. - Tel: (815) 399-4410. Business Brokers - assist in franchising opportunities as well as real estate.

TOWNSEND, O'LEARY, SUMAN AND MCKEE, INC.
23282 Mill Creek Dr. #300, Laguna Hills, CA, 92653-1676. Contact: Ray Townsend, Chairman - Tel: (714) 855-7870. 19 yrs experience in franchise, advertising and marketing specialized in working with all levels of franchise companies to produce motivational image advertising and effective franchise sales material and field services presentations and organizational consultations.

UNITED FRANCHISE CONSULTANTS
3955 Ellenita Ave., Tarzana, CA, 91356-5413. Contact: Annette Sunshine, Pres. - Tel: (818) 705-8555, Fax: (818) 705-3860. Franchise industry search specialist. Exclusively recruit and place personnel within the franchise industry. Our network of proven recruiters and search specialists seek and profile the most qualified professionals. Established: 1978.

UNIVERSAL TRAINING
255 Revere Dr., Northbrook, IL, 60062. Contact: Consultant - Tel: (708) 498-7467. Design and develop custom

VARCON Construction Co. Ltd.
Industrial • Residential • Commercial • Institutional

CUSTOMERS WANTED
Can we build your next franchise store, corporate offices or distribution center? Construction budgets & deadlines are a priority to us.

WE OFFER:
• Turnkey or partial construction
• Project management
• Design and build
• Budget consultations

25 Rutherford Rd. South, Unit 5
Brampton, Ont., L6W 3J3
(800) 581-6729
Tel: (905) 451-7316, Fax: (905) 451-8563

training programs, operation manuals, policy and procedure manuals for franchisors to train their franchisees. Established: 1968.

UPLAND & ASSOCIATES
1100 Industrial Rd., #3, San Carlos, CA, 94070. Contact: Debbie Upland, Owner - Tel: (415) 592-7333. Insurance broker developing programs for franchisees for business liability, workers compensation, medical & dental. Established: 1980.

VENTURE MARKETING ASSOC.
800 Palisade Ave., #907, Fort Lee, NJ, 07024-4111. Contact: S. Altshuler, Pres. - Tel: (800) 342-7311. Provides a wide range of services to franchisors including preliminary planning, franchise agreements, disclosures, manuals, internal controls, lead generation programs, program revitalization, program evaluation. Established: 1976.

VIKING MANAGEMENT CORPORATION
360 Fern Gln., La Jolla, CA, 92037-5317. Contact: Gordon Jonnson, Pres. - Tel: (619) 454-1606. Consulting firm serving franchisors and franchiees. Established: 1978.

VIS CONSULTANTS, INC.
2195 W. 211th St., Sheridan, IN, 46069. Contact: Saul Lemke, Pres. - Tel: (317) 758-0755. Specialize in franchise development from feasibility studies to operations and training manuals and legal documents. We can even train you to sell your package. Substantial experience in launching franchises. We can do it cost effectively for you. Established: 1983.

WOMEN IN FRANCHISING, INC.
53 W. Jackson Blvd., Ste. 205, Chicago, IL, 60604. Contact: Pam Smith, Dir. of Operations - Tel: (312) 431-1467 or (800) 222-4943. Association for women interested or active in franchising. Quarterly newsletter, one-day conferences held nationally to educate women and minorities about franchise business ownership. Corporate memberships for franchisors interested in marketing to women. Established: 1987.

WORLD FRANCHISE CONSULTANTS
25820 Southfield Rd., Ste. 201, Southfield, MI, 48075-1828. Contact: Geoffrey Stebbins - Tel: (810) 559-1415. Research, screening, consulting, and referrals to the franchise of your choice. Established: 1973.

WRITERS' BLOC, THE
666 Baker St., Ste. 269, Costa Mesa, CA, 92626-4407. Contact: Linda Reitman, Dir. - Tel: 1-800-600-3862. Full-service documentation specialists offering the following to franchisors: Turnkey operations manual packages, training guides, custom forms, brochures and information kits, and more. Combining a decade of writing experience with first-hand knowledge of running a retail shop, The Writers' Bloc provides customized documentation that is detailed, reader-friendly, and visually appealing. Established: 1984.

FRANCHISE CONSULTANTS - LEGAL

ABRAHAM, PRESSMAN & BAUER, PC
1818 Market St., 35th Floor, Philadelphia, PA, 19103. Contact: Arthur L. Pressman, Sr. Partner - Tel: (215) 569-9798. Offices also located at: 2000 Pennsylvania Ave. N.W., Ste. 5500, Washington, DC, 20006, Contact: Andrew P. Loewinger, Of Counsel, Tel: (202) 887-1587. Represents franchisors in litigation and regulatory matters. Established: 1973.

ACCURATE LEGAL OPINIONS
Kevin Brendan Murphy, A Prof. Corp.
540 Pacific Ave., San Francisco, CA, 94133. Contact: Kevin Murphy, Sr. Fran. Counsel - Tel: (415) 956-1800, Fax: (707) 942-0444. Law firm that specializes in providing expert opinions, including testimony in arbitration and litigation matters, on all aspects of franchisor-franchisee relationships as well as custom and practice in the franchise industry. Established: 1980 - No. of Units: Company Owned: 2.

ANNE L. KLEINDIENST *
Jennings, Strouss & Salmon, P.L.C.
2 N. Central Ave., Phoenix, AZ, 85004. Contact: Anne L. Kleindienst - Tel: (602) 262-5950. Attorney engaged in practice of franchise law.

ARMSTRONG, TEASDALE, SCHLAFLY & DAVIS *
1700 City Center Sq., 1100 Main, Kansas City, MO, 64105. Contact: Edward R. Spalty - Tel: (816) 221-3420. Franchise consultant - legal. Established: 1883 - Franchising Since: 1975.

ARNOLD COHEN
2424 N. Federal Highway, Ste. 314, Boca Raton, FL, 33431. - Tel: (407) 750-6706. Law office also located at 1101 Stewart Avenue, Garden City, NY, 11530 - Tel: (516) 741-7771.

Arnold Cohen
ATTORNEY AT LAW

LAKE WYMAN PLAZA
SUITE 314
2424 NORTH FEDERAL HIGHWAY
BOCA RATON, FLORIDA 33431

TELEPHONE (407) 750-6706
FAX (407) 750-7143

BARBIER & BARBIER
19251 Mack Ave., #200, Grosse Pointe, MI, 48236-2800. Contact: Ralph Barbier, Pres. - Tel: (313) 882-9500. Law Firm. Established: 1967.

BARTKO, TARRANT & MILLER
900 Front St., Ste. 300, San Francisco, CA, 94111. Contact: Charles G. Miller, Kim Lambert & Mary Beth Trice, Attorneys - Tel: (415) 956-1900. Law firm which specializes in domestic and international franchise and distribution law and franchise litigation.

BECKETT & STEINKAMP, ATTORNEYS AT LAW
1400 Commerce Trust Building, 922 Walnut, Kansas City, MO, 64106. Contact: Attorney - Tel: (816) 474-9500. Deal with franchising.

BRIGGS AND MORGAN, PROFESSIONAL ASSOCIATION
80 So. 8th St., 2400 IDS Center, Minneapolis, MN, 55402. Contact: Andrew C. Selden, Attorney - Tel: (612) 334-8485, Fax: (612) 334-8650. Law Firm. Established: 1883.

BROWN & STADFELD
66 Long Wharf, Boston, MA, 02110-3610. Contact: Harold Brown or Seth Stadfeld - Tel: (617) 720-4200, Fax: (617) 720-0240. Harold Brown has represented both franchisors and groups of franchisees. He is a founding member of the ABA Forum Committee on Franchising and has served on its council for six years. He has served on the Industry Sub-Committee of NASAA, has written numerous books and articles on franchising and has lectured widely on the subject. Seth Stadfeld has extensive experience representing franchisors and franchisees both in transaction work and litigation. He has written many articles and been a frequent speaker on franchise-related topics at legal and industry conferences for the ABA Forum Committee on Franchising, the International Franchise Association, state and local bar associations. Attorney L. Michael Hankes also has substantial experience handling franchise litigation, arbitration and mediation.

BROWNSTEIN & ZEIDMAN
1401 New York Avenue, N.W., Ste. 900, Washington, D.C., 20005-2102. Contact: Philip Zeidman, Founding Principal - Tel: (202) 879-5700. General Counsel to the International Franchise Association, the firm specializes in franchising. Represents hundreds of franchisors (counseling, negotiating, drafting, registration, litigation) both domestically and internationally. Established: 1968.

Advice for smart franchisees:
Practice Safe Franchising

Ask about our special membership package for franchise buyers, including the AAFD's *Road Map to Selecting a Franchise* plus discounts for legal and financial consultations. All for just $60. Mention this ad and save another $10.

Let us read you your rights:

The AAFD developed the Franchisee Bill of Rights and works to promote awareness and acceptance of it in the franchise industry and the public.
- The right to an equity in the franchise business
- The right to engage in a trade or business
- The right to trademark protection
- The right to market protection
- The right to continuing support
- The right to marketing assistance
- The right to local dispute resolution
- The right to initial and ongoing training
- The right to associate with other franchisees
- The right to full disclosure from the franchisor
- The reasonable right to renew the franchise
- The right not to face termination, unless for cause
- The right to representation and access to the franchisor
- The right to a franchisor's loyalty, good faith and due care
- The reciprocal right to terminate the franchise for cause

Look before you leap —

Getting qualified legal, financial, management and marketing guidance for your franchise is easy if you know who to call: The Franchisee LegaLine℠, FinanciaLine℠ and CounseLine℠, powerful member benefits of the AAFD.
Call us today for details: (800) 733-9858

The American Association of Franchisees and Dealers

Bringing fairness to franchising.
A national non-profit trade association can help you make a wise franchise investment.

1420 Kettner Blvd., Suite 415, San Diego, CA 92101
Mail: P.O. Box 81887, San Diego, CA 92138-1887
Internet: http://www.servint.com/aafd
E-mail: aafd@aol   **(800) 733-9858**

BRUCE S. SCHAEFFER, ESQ.
404 Park Ave. S., 16th Flr., New York, NY, 10016. Contact: Bruce S. Schaeffer, Attorney - Tel: (212) 689-0400. Legal, financial and tax counseling for the franchise community. Established: 1975.

BUCHANAN INGERSOLL, P.C.
600 Grant Street, 58th Floor, Pittsburgh, PA, 15219. Contact: President - Tel: (412) 562-8800. The Franchising Group is part of a full service law firm, dedicated to high quality, innovative, cost effective legal services. Has assisted both national and regional franchisors and franchisees.

BUNDY & MORRILL, INC., P.S.
10655 NE 4th., Ste 700, Bellevue, WA, 98004-5022. Contact: Howard E. Bundy - Tel: (206) 455-4441. Franchise attorneys.

CARTER & TANI
402 E. Roosevelt Rd., Ste. 206, Wheaton, IL, 60187. Contact: Doris Adkins Carter or Christine K. Tani, Partner - Tel: (708) 668-2135. Law firm concentrating in franchise law; assisting start-up franchisees and franchisors. Established: 1977.

CHESTER E. BACHELLER, ESQ.
Holland & Knight
P.O. Box 3542, St. Petersburg, FL, 33731-3542. Contact: Chester E. Bacheller, Attorney - Tel: (813) 896-7171. Legal representation of franchisors and franchisees. Established: 1985 - Franchising Since: 1985.

CROWE & DUNLEVY *
321 S. Boston, 500 Kennedy Bldg., Tulsa, OK, 74103-3313. Contact: Kathy Taylor, Shareholder/Director - Tel: (918) 592-9833. Attorney specializing in franchise & distribution law, securities, corporate and international law. Formerly vice president & general counsel of Thrifty Car Rental and Dollar Rent A Car. Year Firm Organized: 1981 - Practicing: 1984.

DAVEY LAW CORPORATION
8001 Irvine Center Dr., Ste. 1550, Irvine, CA, 92718. Contact: Gerard P. Davey, Pres. - Tel: (714) 453-8001. Law practice specializing in franchise law matters. Established: 1974 - Franchising Since: 1977.

DAVID E. HOLMES
697 Higuera St., Ste. C, San Luis Obispo, CA, 93401. Contact: David Holmes, Attorney - Tel: (805) 547-0697. Domestic and international franchise law, concentrating on the structuring and development of new & established franchise systems, drafting of documents for registration & legal compliance and international expansion. Established: 1975.

DOUGHERTY & ASSOCIATES
541 Main St., S. Weymouth, MA, 02190. Contact: John Dougherty, Attorney - Tel: (617) 337-5894. Franchise, real estate and commercial law representing franchisors and franchisees. Established: 1986.

DYKEMA, GOSSETT, SPENCER, GOODNOW & TRIGG
35th Floor, 400 Renaissance Center, Detroit, MI, 48243. Contact: D. Richard McDonald, Assoc. Attorney - Tel: (313) 568-6866. Law firm representing many franchisors from the Great Lake Region.

EDWARD M. DOLSON *
Smith, Gill, Fisher & Butts
One Kansas City Pl., 35th Fl., Kansas City, MO, 64105. Contact: Edward M. Dolson, Partner - Tel: (816) 474-7400. Law firm. Franchising Since: 1971.

FELDMAN, WALDMAN & KLINE
235 Montgomery St., Ste. 2700, San Francisco, CA, 94104. Contact: Kenneth A. Freed, Chairman Fran. Practice Group - Tel: (415) 981-1300. A full service law firm experienced in franchise law, including disclosure and registration matters, preparation of franchise related agreements, intellectual property protection, franchise litigation and dispute resolution and business planning. Established: 1958.

FOSTER, PEPPER & SHEFELMAN
1111 3rd Ave., Ste. 3400, Seattle, WA, 98101. Contact: William C. Erxleben, Partner - Tel: (206) 447-4400. Emphasis on commercial matters. Legal counsel available for franchisors and franchisees. Established: 1921.

FOUNTAIN RHOADES, P.C.
421 S.W. Sixth Ave., Portland, OR, 97204. Contact: Jay Fountain, Shareholder - Tel: (503) 223-6113, Fax: (503) 274-7718. Law firm specializing in business, corporate, franchising, general consulting. Established: 1986.

FRANCHISE LAW TEAM
30021 Tomas, Ste. 260, Rancho Santa Margarita, CA, 92688. Contact: Robin Day Glenn, J.D., L.L.M. - Tel: (714) 459-7474, Fax: (714) 459-7772. Law firm specializing in domestic and international business law. Established: 1985 - In Practice Since: 1975.

FRANKIE FOOK-LUN LEUNG, ATTORNEY AT LAW
Lewis D'Amato Brisbois & Bisgaard
221 No. Figueroa St., Ste. 1200, Los Angeles, CA, 90012. Contact: Frankie Leung, Partner - Tel: (213) 680-5119. Advise American franchisors to expand business overseas. Established: 1970 - No. of Units: Company Owned: 7.

GILBERT E. HISCOTT, ESQ.
25 South Shore Dr., Toms River, NJ, 08753. Contact: Gilbert Hiscott, Attorney - Tel: (908) 255-8885. Law practice specializing in distributorship and franchise law. Established: 1979.

GILROY, CRAMER, MCLAUGHLIN & GELSON, P.C.
Monmouth Shores Corp. Park, 1305 Campus Pkwy., P.O.Box 1110, Wall, NJ, 07719. Contact: Roger J. McLaughlin - Tel: (908) 919-1155. Represent franchisors and purchasers of franchises in all aspects of franchise law. Established: 1978.

GRAHAM & DUNN
1420 Fifth Ave., Ste. 3300, Seattle, WA, 98101. Contact: Gary R. Duvall, Franchise Attorney - Tel: (206) 624-8300. Franchise law, including regional, national and international franchise systems, compliance, registration, document preparation, dispute resolution and litigation. Particular emphasis on Northwest and Pacific Rim subfranchising and joint ventures. Established 1977.

GREENBERG TRAURIG *
1300 Connecticut Ave., #1000, Washington, DC, 20036. Contact: Andrew J. Sherman, Shareholder - Tel: (202) 331-3130, Fax: (202) 331-3101. Franchise, licensing and distribution attorney.

GREGORY J. ELLIS, ESQ.
1301 W. 22nd St., #407, Oak Brook, IL, 60521-2013. Contact: Gregory J. Ellis, Attorney - Tel: (708) 572-1175. Law firm concentrating in franchise law and related litigation providing full range of legal services to franchisors and franchisees.

GUNSTER, YOAKLEY, VALDES-FAULI & STEWART P.A.
500 E. Broward Blvd., Ste. 1400, Ft. Lauderdale, FL, 33394. Contact: Michael G. Platner, Chairman/Fran. Practice Group - Tel: (305) 462-2000. Franchise Practice Group consists of experienced attorneys from diverse technical backgrounds, all relating to franchising and the distribution of products and services. The firm is a full service law firm with over 115+ lawyers in South Florida. Established: 1924.

HAROLD L. KESTENBAUM, ESQ.
170 Old Country Rd., Mineola, NY, 11501. Contact: Harold L. Kestenbaum, Attorney At Law - Tel: (516) 873-6161. Full service law firm specializing in all aspects of franchise law, including franchisee representation. Established: 1977.

HARRY A. HALKOWICH *
Murtaugh, Miller, Meyer & Nelson
3200 Park Center Dr., 9th Fl., Costa Mesa, CA, 92668. Contact: Harry Halkowich, Partner - Tel: (714) 513-6800. Legal services to franchisors and franchisees. Established: 1975.

HELEN ROWE
Rowe & Associates
550 West "C" Street, Ste. 800, San Diego, CA, 92101-3573. Contact: Helen Rowe, Attorney - Tel: (619) 233-1900, Fax: (619) 238-1616. Franchise attorney.

HESSIAN, MCKASY & SODERBERG, P.A.
4700 IDS Center, Minneapolis, MN, 55402. Contact: Susan Rester Miles, Esq., Attorney - Tel: (612) 330-3000. Law firm providing advice on pre-purchase contract issues and representation in dispute resolutions to individual franchisees and franchisee trade groups. Established: 1972.

HOPPER AND KANOUFF, P.C. *
1610 Wynkoop St., Ste. 200, Denver, CO, 80202. Contact: Kim I. McCullough, Attorney At Law - Tel: (303) 892-6000. Attorneys specializing in franchise law.

HOWARD & HOWARD ATTORNEYS *
Pinehurst Office Ctr., Ste 101, 1400 N. Woodward Ave., Bloomfield Hills, MI, 48304-2856. Contact: Sally Lee Foley, Attorney - Tel: (810) 645-1483, Direct Dial: (810) 433-7365, Fax: (810) 645-1568. Franchise Attorneys. Established: 1869.

HOWARD & HOWARD
ATTORNEYS

Sally Lee Foley
Direct Dial: (810) 433-7365

The Pinehurst Office Center, Ste. 101
1400 North Woodward Avenue
Bloomfield Hills, MI 48304-2856

Phone: (810) 645-1483
Fax: (810) 645-1568

Kalamazoo, MI	Lansing, MI	Peoria, IL
(616) 382-1483	(517) 485-1483	(309) 672-1483

J. MICHAEL DADY & ASSOCIATES, P.A. *
4000 IDS Center, 80 S. Eighth St., Minneapolis, MN, 55402. Contact: J. Michael Dady, Sr. Partner - Tel: (612) 359-9000. Representing franchisees, dealers and distributors nationwide in a variety of legal disputes. Mr. Dady is listed in Best Lawyers in America. Established: 1994 - Franchising Representation Since: 1975.

JAMES A. MEANEY *
Thompson, Hine & Flory
10 W. Broad St., Columbus, OH, 43215-3435. Contact: James A. Meaney, Partner - Tel: (614) 469-3289. Franchise Consultant - Legal. Representation on all franchising matters. Established: 1911.

JOHN L. HAY *
201 N. Central Ave., Ste. 3300, Phoenix, AZ, 85073. Contact: John L. Hay, Lawyer - Tel: (602) 257-7468. Lawyer. Established: 1964 - Advising Franchisors Since: 1976.

JOHN MOHR, ATTORNEY AT LAW
7545 Winding Way, Tipp City, OH, 45371. Contact: John R. Mohr, Attorney - Tel: (513) 667-4960, Fax: (513) 667-7050. Franchise law, real estate development and finance, and general business planning. Prior experience with national franchisor. Over 15 years experience in franchising.

KEESAL, YOUNG & LOGAN
Catalina Landing, 310 Golden Shore, P.O. Box1730, Long Beach, CA, 90801-1730. Contact: Stephen C. Clifford, Attorney - Tel: (213) 436-9051. Experienced commercial and franchise legal counsel providing litigation, registration, disclosure. Offices in Los Angeles - Orange County and San Francisco. Established: 1971.

KENNEDY A. BROOKS
#1 Embarcadero Ctr., 26th Fl., #2600, San Francisco, CA, 94111. Contact: Kennedy A. Brooks - Tel: (415) 398-3344. Law firm representing franchisors and franchisees in the full range of legal services. Prior experience as in-house counsel for major franchisors gives special insight to operating concerns of franchised and other distribution businesses. Special expertise in computer products and other high-tech distribution. Kennedy A. Brooks has been admitted to practice law since 1977. Established: 1987.

KENNETH F. DARROW, PA
9200 S. Dadeland Blvd., #412, Miami, FL, 33156-2703. Contact: Kenneth F. Darrow, Principal - Tel: (305) 670-1710. Law firm providing all aspects of representation to franchisors and franchisees. Over 15 years of experience in the franchise field. In practice over 25 years.

KENNETH P. ROBERTS
Kenneth P. Roberts, A Prof. Law Corp.
6355 Topanga Canyon Blvd., Ste. 403, Woodland Hills, CA, 91367. Contact: Ken Roberts, Attorney - Tel: (818) 888-3553. Law Office emphasizing practice in representation of franchisors and franchisees including registration and litigation. Established:1977.

KLEIN, HEISLER & KLARREICH P.C.
1 Penn Plaza, New York, NY, 10119-0142. Contact: Carl S. Klein - Tel: (212) 736-6076. Associates representing franchisors. Established: 1950.

KRASSENSTEIN & SAUER PROFESSIONAL CORP.
7500 Brooktree Dr., Wexford, PA, 15090. Contact: Juliet B. Krassenstein/ Claire J. Sauer, Attorneys - Tel: (412) 935-6227, Fax: (412) 935-0742. High quality, cost-effective legal services, representing franchisors and franchisees on a national and local basis; contract drafting and negotiation; franchise and business opportunity registration and compliance. Established: 1992.

LARKIN, HOFFMAN, DALY & LINDGREN, LTD.
7900 Xerxes Ave., South, Ste. 1500, Minneapolis, MN, 55431. Contact: Charles S. Modell, Esq. - Tel: (612) 835-3800. Full service law firm, providing specialized services to franchisors, including registration of disclosure documents, negotiations with franchisees, mergers and acquisitions, regulatory compliance, lobbying and litigation services. Established: 1958.

LAW OFFICE OF KENNETH G. PROTONENTIS, P.A.
1591 Gulf Boulevard, Penthouse 2, Clearwater, FL, 34630-2922. Contact: Kenneth G. Protonentis, Attorney - Tel: (813) 596-3435, Fax: (813) 596-2076. Legal practice limited to franchise, intellectual property, corp. and gen. business matters.

LEWIS & TRATTNER
1150 18th St., NW, Ste. 875, Washington, DC, 20036-3816. Contact: Warren L. Lewis, Partner - Tel: (800) 333-2540. Lewis & Trattner is a law firm that represents established and start-up franchisors, subfranchisors, licensors, licensees and other organizations with counseling and litigation needs in the franchise, licensing, trademark, copyright, unfair competition and antitrust fields.

LOCKE PURNELL RAIN HARRELL
2200 Ross Ave., Ste. 2200, Dallas, TX, 75201-6776. Contact: Joyce Mazero, Fran. Dir./Dist. Law - Tel: (214) 740-8000. Established: 1893.

MACKALL, CROUNSE & MOORE, PLC
1400 AT&T Tower, 901 Marquette Ave., Minneapolis, MN, 55402-2859. Contact: G. Thomas MacIntosh II, Attorney At Law. Mackall, Crounse & Moore, PLC represents international and domestic franchisors, master franchisors, manufacturers and distributors throughout the free world in (i) planning, structuring and restructuring franchise, distribution and dealer business concepts and programs; (ii) complying with franchise, distribution, business opportunity and related business laws and regulations; (iii) franchise and dealer litigation; (iv) private placements and public offerings; (v) real estate development, licensing and financing; (vi) mergers and acquisitions; (vii) tax and business planning; (viii) executive compensation and employment law; (ix) registration and protection of service marks, trademarks and copyrights, and (x) software protection and computer law. Established: 1918.

MCGUIRE, WOODS, BATTLE & BOOTHE
8280 Greensboro Drive, McLean, VA, 22102. Contact: Business Dept. - Tel: (703) 712-5000. Counsels franchisees through franchise agreement negotiations, establish appropriate business entities, and assist with tax, real estate, employment and general corporate matters. Guide franchisors through preparation of offering circulars and franchise agreements. Established: 1892.

MERCHANT, GOULD, SMITH, EDELL, WELTER & SCHMIDT, P.A.
3100 Norwest Center, 90 South 7th Street, Minneapolis, MN, 55402. Contact: John L. Beard, Assistant V.P. - Tel: (612) 332-5300. Specializes in intellectual property law, including trademark, patent, copyright and unfair competition matter, as well as, licensing, trade secrets and computer law.

PAUL, HASTINGS, JANOFSKY & WALKER
600 Peachtree St. N.E., Ste. 2400, Atlanta, GA, 30308-2222. Contact: Richard M. Asbill, Partner - Tel: (404) 815-2400, Fax: (404) 815-2424. Full service, eight-office firm specializing in domestic/international franchising, distribution, trade regulation, international trade, real estate, securities, venture capital, employment law, tax and litigation.

PEAR SPERLING EGGAN & MUSKOVITZ, P.C.
24 Frank Lloyd Wright Drive, Ann Arbor, MI, 48105. Contact: Paul R. Fransway, Attorney - Tel: (313) 665-4441. Complete legal administration services for franchisors including disclosure/registration, negotiation and litigation management. Established: 1969.

PETER I. HOPPENFELD
100 Mamaroneck Ave., Mamaroneck, NY, 10543. - Tel: (914) 698-3440. Law firm involved in franchising & distribution. Extensive experience in domestic & international franchising as well as issues relating to direct sales, infomercials, seminar sales, licensing & technology issues. Established: 1989.

PHILLIPS, NIZER, BENJAMIN, KRIM & BALLON
666 Fifth Ave., New York, NY, 10103. Contact: Jonathan R. Tillem, Partner - Tel: (212) 977-9700, Fax: (212) 262-5152. Full service law firm with special depts., in franchising, corporate, labor, litigation, entertainment, trust and estate specialties. Established: 1927.

PILLSBURY, MADISON & SUTRO
725 S. Figueroa St., Los Angeles, CA, 90017. Contact: Blase P. Dillingham, Partner - Tel: (213) 488-7437. Full service law firm including all aspects of state and federal franchise disclosure, registration and enforcement law, preparation of franchise-related agreements, trademark and service mark protection and related litigation, securities, taxation, environmental and anti-trust laws.

PITEGOFF, OCKO & HARRINGTON
81 Main St., #205, White Plains, NY, 10601-1711. Contact: Thomas M. Pitegoff, Partner - Tel: (914) 686-4800. A business-oriented national and international law firm with special expertise in franchise law, representing franchisors in contract and disclosure statement drafting, trademark protection, registration, sales compliance, and dispute resolution. The firm also represents franchisees and master franchisees. Established: 1992.

QUINN, KULLY & MORROW
520 South Grand Ave., 8th Floor, Los Angeles, CA, 90071. Contact: Richard C. Smith, Attorney - Tel: (213) 622-0300. Emphasizing franchisor representation, including registration, corporate franchise documents, real estate and litigation. Established: 1967.

REED, SMITH, SHAW & MCCLAY
1301 K. Street, N.W. Ste. 1100, East Power, Washington, DC, 20005. Contact: John F. Dienelt, Partner - Tel: (202) 414-9218. Represents franchising companies, in regard to anti-trust, contractual, litigation, registration and disclosure and termination issues. Offices: Pittsburgh, Philadelphia, Harrisburg (PA) and McLean, Virginia. Established: before 1900.

REVA S. BAUCH, ATTORNEY AT LAW
1414 W. Barry Ave., Chicago, IL, 60659. Contact: Reva S. Bauch, Attorney - Tel: (312) 248-6630. Franchise/distrib. - protection/defense. Litigation, contracts and evaluations. Established: 1991.

REX. P. CORNELISON, III, ATTORNEY AT LAW, P.C.
11285 Elkins Rd., Ste. J-7, Roswell, GA, 30076. Contact: Rex Cornelison, Attorney/Pres. - Tel: (770) 475-8874. Franchise Attorney. Established: 1986.

ROBIN C. CARTER, ATTORNEY AT LAW, P.C. *
1760 E. River, #119, Tucson, AZ, 85718. Contact: Robin Carter, Attorney - Tel: (520) 577-5146. Law firm with emphases in business, real estate, estate planning and governmental matters. Established: 1994 - Lawyering Since: 1973.

ROGER J. MCLAUGHLIN, ESQ.
2130 Hwy. 35, Bldg. B, Ste. 222, Sea Girt, NJ, 08750. Contact: Franchise Dir./Pres. - Tel: (201) 449-1133. Deals in franchise law.

RONALD N. ROSENWASSER, P.A.
One Boca Place, Ste. 234 West, 2255 Glades Rd., Boca Raton, FL, 33431. Contact: Ronald N. Rosenwasser, Pres. - Tel: (407) 241-7777, Fax: (407) 241-5811. All aspects of franchising/licensing and distribution law, including development of domestic and international programs, review and preparation of disclosure statements and agreements, state and federal agency negotiations, business structuring and financing, wide-ranging transactional expertise, and litigation support. Services include trademark protection, lease negotiations, acquisitions and sales, joint ventures, computer law, and general commercial representation. Founding member and vice-chairman of Florida Franchise Law Committee. AV rating (highest) from Martindale-Hubbell International Legal Directory. Established: 1986.

RUDNICK & WOLFE
101 E. Kennedy Blvd., Ste. 2000, Tampa, FL, 33602. Contact: David A. Beyer, Partner - Tel: (813) 229-2111. Full service commercial law firm specializing in franchise distribution, trademark and intellectual property, business finance and securities, merger and acquisition, real estate development, finance and leasing, litigation, arbitration and alternate dispute resolution. Established: 1936.

SCHNADER, HARRISON, SEGAL & LEWIS
330 Madison Ave., New York, NY, 10017. Contact: Michael Garner, Partner - Tel: (212) 973-8022, Fax: (212) 972-8798. Law firm specializing in franchise and distribution matters. Represents franchisors and franchisees in all aspects of franchising. Established: 1935.

SEMET, LICKSTEIN, MORGENSTERN, BERGER, FRIEND, BROOKE & GORDON, P.A.
1201 Alhambra Circle, Ste. 1200, Coral Gables, FL, 33134. Contact: Ronald Peter Roman, Attorney - Tel: (305) 444-1400, Fax: (305) 444-2768. Law firm providing franchise representation to franchisors including registration and disclosure, both domestically and internationally, as well as trademark and trade regulation legal advice and litigation of franchise and business opportunity disputes.

SEVERSON & WERSON
1 Embarcadero Ctr., Ste. 2600, San Francisco, CA, 94111. Contact: Franchise Attorney - Tel: (415) 398-3344. Law firm involved in entire cycle of business life with group specializing in the franchise area. Counsel franchisors in areas of capital information, intellectual property, registration and compliance, operations, and trial work and other forms of dispute resolution. Established: 1945.

SHAPIRO, ROSENFELD & CLOSE
2029 Century Park East, #2600, Los Angeles, CA, 90067. Contact: Rochelle B. Spandorf, Partner - Tel: (310) 277-1818, Fax: (310) 201-4776. Full service business and litigation practise emphasizing franchise law. Represents franchise clients in disclosure/registration regulatory matters, business planning, domestic and international expansion and dispute resolution and litigation in all courts. Established: 1975.

SHEFSKY FROELICH & DEVINE LTD.
444 N. Michigan Ave., Ste. 2400, Chicago, IL, 60611. Contact: Gary Levenstein, Partner in charge of Franchising - Tel: (312) 836-4080. Law firm specializing in franchising, distribution, securities law, corporate law, real estate, employee benefits, estate planning, health care laws, tax and litigation. Established: 1970.

SILVER FREEDMAN & TAFF *
1100 New York Ave., N.W., Ste. 700E, Washington, DC, 20005. Contact: Lucretia Lawson, Office Admin. - Tel: (202) 414-6100. Legal and strategic planning services for early stage and growing franchisors. Established: 1970.

SMITH & UNDERWOOD, P.C.
2 Lincoln Ctr., 5420 LBJ Fwy., Ste. 600, Dallas, TX, 75240. Contact: William J. Underwood Jr. - Tel: (214) 661-5114. Full service law firm, provides legal counsel to franchisors and franchisees. Established: 1980.

STEIN & KAHAN, A LAW CORPORATION
1299 Ocean Ave., 4 Flr., Santa Monica, CA, 90401. Contact: Robert L. Kahan, Partner - Tel: (310) 458-6900. Law Firm. Established: 1976.

STEVEN A. CHASE, ATTORNEY AT LAW
Lincoln Ctr. Twr., 10260 S.W. Greenburg Rd., Ste. 400, Portland, OR, 97223. Contact: Steven Chase, Owner - Tel: (503) 293-3594. A law firm practicing general business and corporation law, with emphasis on trademark, copyright and franchise law. The practice serves both franchisees and franchisors.

STEVEN S. RAAB LAW OFFICE
2033 Walnut St., Philadelphia, PA, 19103. Contact: Steven S. Raab - Tel: (215) 977-8333, Fax: (215) 972-8150. Franchise legal services, including UFOC review and contract negotiations. Established: 1979.

STRASBURGER & PRICE
901 Main Street, 4300 NCNB Plaza, Dallas, TX, 75202. Contact: John Vernon, Partner - Tel: (214) 651-4757. Civil practise law firm, encompasses preparation and registration of domestic and international franchise programs consultation on franchise operational matters and litigation arising out of the franchise relationship.

THELEN, MARRIN, JOHNSON & BRIDGES
2 Embarcodero Ctr., Ste. 2100, San Francisco, CA, 94111-3995. Contact: R. Jonas, R.L. Meyer or K. Costello, Partners - Tel: (415) 392-6320. Law firm with specialties in franchising, antitrust, other distribution systems.

THOMAS, BALLENGER, VOGELMAN & TURNER, P.C.
124 S. Royal St., Alexandria, VA, 22314. Contact: John M. Ballenger, Attorney - Tel: (703) 836-3400, Fax: (703) 836-3549. Law firm engaged in practice of franchise law (among other fields of law). Established: 1982 - Franchise Law Since: 1985 - No. of Units: Company Owned: 1 - Fee: $150@ hr.

THOMPSON & NIGHT, P.C.
1700 Pacific Ave., Ste. 3300, Dallas, TX, 75201. Contact: Gayle Cannon, Attorney - Tel: (214) 969-1550, Fax: (214) 934-6567. Broad range legal services to franchisors and franchisees. Emphasizing contracts and disclosure statement drafting for start up franchisors, contract analysis/negotiations for prospective franchisees, and litigation relating to franchise and distribution law.

VLOCK & BROWN
230 Park Ave., Ste. 2525, New York, NY, 10169-0076. Contact: Stephen Vlock or Virginia R. Brown, Lawyers - Tel: (212) 557-5157, Fax: (212) 661-2153. Law firm.

WELTY & BLAIR
Welty & Blair P.C.
2111 Wilson Blvd., Ste. 550, Arlington, VA, 22201-3057. Contact: Anita K. Blair, Attorney at Law - Tel: (703) 276-0114, Fax: (703) 522-9107. Legal services relating to franchising registration and disclosure, franchisor/franchisee relations, protection of proprietary marks and information, marketing and advertising, contract enforcement and administration, dispute resolution, multi-unit and three-tiered franchising, and international franchising. Participated in revision of UFOC Guidelines as member of NASAA Franchise Advisory Committee.

WILLIAMS, MULLEN, CHRISTIAN & DOBBINS
1021 E. Cary St., 2 James Center, Richmond, VA, 23219. Contact: Sandy T. Tucker, Attorney, Head of Fran. Group - Tel: (804) 643-1991. Provides services to franchisors and franchisees in all areas of franchising,

including state & federal registration & disclosure, contract drafting & review, intellectual property, litigation, government regulation & international expansion. Established: 1909.

FURNITURE REFINISHING AND REPAIR

BIX FURNITURE STRIPPING
6 Clark Cir., P.O. Box 309, Bethel, CT, 06801. Contact: Rick White, Sales Mgr. - Tel: (800) 243-6670 or (203) 743-3263. Furniture stripping and refinishing service. Utilizes Flo-on and Immersion stripping systems featuring built-in ventilation. Removing compounds are non-flammable, non-caustic and do not discolor wood. Established: 1958 - Offering Licenses Since: 1963 - No. of Units Licensed: 200 of 600 shops serviced - Approx. Inv: $6,000 - $15,000 - Financing: None.

DIP 'N STRIP, INC.
2141 S. Platte River Dr., Denver, CO, 80223. Contact: E. Roger Schuyler, Pres. - Tel: (303) 781-8300. Furniture stripping, providing the household community, antique dealers, furniture refinishers, industrial and commercial accounts in the removal of finishes from wood and metal. Established: 1970 - Franchising Since: 1972 - No. of Units: Company Owned: 1 - Franchised: 253 - Franchise Fee: None - Royalty: 6% of which 3% returned for co-op advertising - Total Inv: $12,500.

FURNITURE MEDIC
277 Southfield Pkwy., Ste. 130, Forest Park, GA, 30050. , Franchise Counselor - Tel: (404) 361-9933, (800) 877-9933. Furniture Medic is a furniture restoration & repair service franchise with an unlimited market. Manufacturers, hotels, restaurants, office buildings, furniture retailers, as well as the residential market & many others have a need for furniture restoration. Furniture Medic is committed to research & development & uses the latest technological advancements to repair furniture on site at a cost that is much less than refinishing or replacement. Established: 1992 - Franchising Since: 1993 - No. of Units: Franchised: 255 - Franchise Fee: $8,000 - Royalty: $210/mo., $20/mo. advertising - Total Inv: fran. fee plus $3,500 inven. & supplies - Financing: No.

GUARDSMAN WOODPRO
Guardsman Products, Inc.
P.O. Box 88010, Grand Rapids, MI, 49518. Contact: Tony Ziegler, Dir. of Fran. Oper. - Tel: (800) 253-3957, Ext. 864. Guardsman WoodPro is a mobile, on-site, wood touch-up and repair service. Franchisees service residential and commercial clients, as well as kitchen cabinet refurbishing. Established: 1915 - Franchising Since: 1993 - No. of Units: Company Owned: 1 - Franchised: 6 - Franchise Fee: $18,000 - Royalty: sliding scale (6%-10%) - Total Inv: $21,000 ($18,000 fran. fee, $3,000 misc. costs) - Financing: Third party.

LEATHER SOLUTION, THE
18 Johnson Pl., Baldwin, NY, 11510. Contact: R.J. Daly, Pres. - Tel: (800) 468-5852. Leather repair, reconditioning furniture, clothing, auto, aircraft. Established: 1989 - Franchising Since: 1992 - No. of Units: Company Owned: 1 - Franchised: 12 - Franchise Fee: $12,500 min., $25,000 avg. - Royalty: 7%, 2% adv. - Total Inv: $35,000 - $65,000 - Financing: No.

MINUTEMAN FURNITURE RESTORATION
P.O. Box 8, Waterloo, WI, 53594-0008. Contact: Chad Friedli, Josh Trucks - Tel: (800) 773-1776. Provides a complete range of equipment, supplies, and products for the furniture restoration and wood furnishing industry. Complete turn-key business packages available. Established: 1970 - Total Inv: $2,000 - $15,000 - Financing: Yes.

PROFUSION SYSTEMS
Profusion Systems Inc.
7808 Cherry Creek South Dr., #115, Denver, CO, 80231-5230. Contact: David Lowe, Fran. Dir. - Tel: (303) 337-1949 or (800) 777-3873. Plastic, leather, vinyl, laminate, porcelain repair. Established: 1980 - Franchising Since: 1982 - No. of Units: Company Owned: 3 - Franchised: 210 - Franchise Fee: $20,500 - Royalty: 6% - Total Inv: $10,500 training, $10,000 territory (min.).

SPR CHIP REPAIR
SPR International Inc.
4492 Acworth Industrial Dr., Ste. 102, Acworth, GA, 30101. Contact: Larry Stevens, Pres. - Tel: (770) 966-1331. Repair chips, cracks, burns, holes, porcelain, fiber glass, acrylic and cultured marble. National accounts. Established: 1973 - No. of Units: Company Owned: 1 - Franchised: 18 - Franchise Fee: $995. - Royalty: 20% chemical fee - Financing: None.

GREETING SERVICES

AMERICAN SINGING TELEGRAMS
557 E. Twain Ave., Las Vegas, NV, 89109-4925. Contact: Marty Shadin, Pres. - Tel: (702) 737-0688. The business is sold as a kit containing costumes, songs & supplies and act - descriptions, enabling one to start out of the home or add on to an existing business. Over 200 telegram act combinations for every occasion, birthdays, anniversaries, etc. Established: 1978 - Offering Opportunities Since: 1987 - Total Inv: $4,000.

BALLOON BOUQUETS
Balloon Bouquets, Inc.
69 Kilburn Rd., Belmont, MA, 02178. Contact: Joseph Del Vecchio, V. P. - Tel: (800) 424-2323. Balloon deliveries and decorating. Established: 1977 - Franchising Since: 1979 - No. of Units: Franchised: 15 - Franchise Fee: $5,000 - Royalty: 5% + 3% adv. - Total Inv: $20,000 for supplies, advertising, vans.

BALLOONS + BEARS
D.F.S., Inc.
901 Douglas Ave., Ste. 204, Orlando, FL, 32714. Contact: Thad Bentley, Dir. of Sales - Tel: (800) 771-BEAR, (407) 869-7422, Fax: (407) 869-0580. Department store for gifts, including balloons, teddy bears, gift baskets, & fresh flowers. Established: 1989 - Franchising Since: 1993 - No. of Units: Company Owned: 2 - Franchised: 25 - Franchise Fee: $19,500 - Royalty: 6% - Total Inv: $45,000 to $55,000 excl. fran. fee - Financing: Third party financing.

CARD SENDERS
Boverie Investments, Inc.
2800 Eubank Blvd. N.E., Albuquerque, NM, 87112. Contact: Robert Boverie, Pres. - Tel: (800) 843-6055, Fax: (505) 271-9893. Personalized mailings for businesses & professionals to their customers, patients, and employees. Established: 1985 - Franchising Since: 1987 - No. of Units: Company Owned: 1 - Franchised: 85 - Franchise Fee: $5,900 to $7,500 - Royalty: None - Total Inv: approx. $10,000 - Financing: Some.

DIAL-A-GIFT
Dial-A-Gift, Inc.
2265 E. 4800 South, Salt Lake City, UT, 84117. Contact: Franchise Dept. - Tel: (801) 278-0413. International gift wire service similar floral networks in mall stores, strip center stores and holiday gift kiosks in malls. Established: 1980 - Franchising Since: 1984 - No. of Units: Network over 4,000 locations - No. of Units: Franchised: 50, Dealers 8,000 - Franchise Fee: $10,000 - Royalty: 4% - Total Inv: $15,000 - $50,000 - Financing: Yes, for kiosks and equip.

PAPYRUS
Papyrus Franchise Corp.
954 60th St., Oakland, CA, 94608. Contact: Kathleen A. Low, Dir. of Fran. Dev. - Tel: (510) 428-0166. A Papyrus store offers the finest in greeting cards, paper accessories, gifts and custom printed and engraved invitations, announcements and stationery. An exciting alternative to the traditional card store. Established: 1973 - Franchising Since: 1988 - No. of Units: Company Owned: 21 - Franchised: 59 - Franchise Fee: $29,500 - Royalty: 6% - Total Inv: $163,000 - $317,500 - Financing: Third party.

SIGNED, SEALED AND REMEMBERED
Signature Enterprises
P.O. Box 68324, Tucson, AZ, 85737-8324. Contact: Ann Poyas, Pres. - Tel: (602) 797-2313. Greeting card and gift sending service. Established: 1988 - Franchising Since: 1988 - No. of Units: Company Owned: 1 - Franchised: 2 - Franchise Fee: $5,000 - Royalty: 6%, 2% adv. - Total Inv: fran. fee + $9,500 to $16,500 - Financing: None.

STORK NEWS OF AMERICA, INC.
5075 Morganton Rd., Ste. 12A, Fayetteville, NC, 28314. Contact: John Nelson, Fran. Dir. - Tel: (910) 868-3065. New born announcement service. Large stork in the front yard of new parents, grandparents plus many assorted announcement retail gifts for pre/post-birth celebration. Established: 1983 - Franchising Since: 1985 - No. of Units: Company Owned: 1 - Franchised: 80 - Franchise Fee: $5,000 - Royalty: annual fee based on exclusive territory - Total Inv: $5,000 - $7,000 - Financing: No.

WELCOME HOST
Welcome Host of America, Inc.
13953 Perkins Rd., Baton Rouge, LA, 70810-3438. Contact: Sing Van Cleave, Fran. Dir. - Tel: (504) 769-3000, (800) 962-5431. Direct mail welcoming service aimed at new residents and movers, parents of new babies, newlyweds. Established: 1987 - Franchising Since: 1992 - No. of Units: Company Owned: 3 - Franchised: 3 - Franchise Fee: $6,000 - $8,000 - Royalty: 6% - Total Inv: $8,000 - $12,000 incl. fran. fee - Financing: On franchise fee only.

YARD CARDS®, INC.
2940 West Main St., Belleville, IL, 62223-6614. Contact: Michael Hoepfinger, Pres. - Tel: (618) 233-0491. Service business that rents and places 8' tall greeting cards for all occasions and sells 3' tall greeting cards. Established: 1983 - Franchising Since: 1986 - No. of Units: Company Owned: 1 - Franchised: 11 - Franchise Fee: min. $1,000, based on population - Royalty: 5% of gross sales - Total Inv: $4,000 - $35,000 - Financing: No.

HAIRSTYLING & COSMETICS

ACCENT HAIR SALON
Accent Hair Salons, Inc.
211 S. Main St. Ste. 720, Dayton, OH, 45402. Contact: Claude Patmon, Pres. & CEO. - Tel: (513) 461-0394. The choice for total black hair care, featuring convenient walk-in service, prompt service, attractive mall location, affordable prices and a full range of black hair care products. A carefully-planned salon system designed with today's black woman in mind. Established: 1981 - Franchising Since: 1987 - Number of Units: Company Owned: 2 - Franchised: 7 - Franchise Fee: $20,000 - Royalty: 5% Franchise - Total Inv: $100,000 - $200,000 ($30,000 - $40,000 cash invest. $20,000 fran. fee) - Financing: Assistance.

ALOETTE COSMETICS, INC.
1301 Wrights ln., E., West Chester, PA, 19380. Contact: Jim Reid, Dir. of Fran. Oper. - Tel: (610) 692-0600. Direct sales of skin care products and cosmetics by the companies marketing system at home shows. Established: 1978 - Franchising Since: 1978 - No. of Units: 72 USA, 27 Canada, 3 U.K., 5 Australia, 1 New Zealand, 1 Latin America, 1 Bahamas - Franchise Fee: $50,000 of which $10,000 at time of agreement and balance financed - Total Inv: $66,000 incl. initial purchase of stock - Royalty: 5%.

AMERICUTS FAMILY BARBER SHOP *
Americuts Franchise Systems, Inc.
41 Durant Ave., Ste. 103, Bethel, CT, 06801. Contact: Michael Perrone, Pres. - Tel: (203) 792-9955 or (800) 718-CUTS, Fax: (203) 792-3990. Family barber shops that emphasize on children, with a creative playscape environment with old fashioned services. Established: 1989 - Franchising Since: 1995 - No. of Units: Company Owned: 1 - Franchise Fee: $19,500 - Royalty: 6%, 4% adv. - Total Inv: $31,600 - $118,000 - Financing: Yes.

BOCA BEAUTY CLUB
Boca Beauty Club Franchise, Inc.
8221 Glades Rd., Boca Raton, FL, 33434. Contact: Ruth Mandel or David Playter, Owner/Oper. Mgr. - Tel: (407) 487-1191. Full service beauty salon operating on a club basis. Based upon high volume. The average club enrolls fifty new members per week. Established: 1990 - Franchising Since: 1991 - No. of Units: Company Owned: 2 - Franchised: 8 - Franchise Fee: $25,000 - Royalty: 5%, 1% mktg. - Total Inv: $75,000 - $100,000 incl. fee - Financing: Yes, assist in loan placement.

BODY SHOP, THE
Buth-Na-Bodhaige
45 Horsehill Road, Cedar Knolls, NJ, 07927. Contact: Troy Berry, Fran. & Real Est. Mgr. - Tel: (201) 984-9200. International skin and hair care business which places a strong emphasis upon the principles of the business as well as the profits. Established: 1988 - Franchising Since: 1990 - No. of Units: Company Owned: 24 - Franchised: 111 - Franchise Fee: $40,000 - Royalty: no royalty for the first three years, 3% in yr. 4, 5% in yr. 5 and for each ensuing year of the agreement - Financing: No.

CAROL BLOCK, LTD.
1403 S. Belden St., McHenry, IL, 60050. Contact: Neal E. Rohr, C.E.O. - Tel: (800) HAIRLES, (815) 344-0488, Fax: (815) 344-2503. Permanent hair removal. Xenon light, lease machines out. Established: 1937 - Franchising Since: 1986 - No. of Units: Company Owned: 13 - Franchised: 4 - Franchise Fee: $3,000 - Royalty: 20% - Total Inv: $10,000 - Financing: None.

CITY LOOKS SALONS INTERNATIONAL
Barbers, Hairstyling For Men & Women, Inc., The
300 Industrial Blvd., N.E., Minneapolis, MN, 55413. Contact: Julie Wollcat, Real Est. Mgr. - Tel: (612) 331-8500. Full service, upscale hair care salon offering a broad range of hair care services and products in tasteful, comfortable surroundings, filling a need for clients who place a strong emphasis on full-service, personalized hair care. Established: 1963 - Franchising Since: 1967 - No. of Units: Company Owned: 1 - Franchised: 61 - Franchise Fee: $19,500 - Royalty: 4%, 4% adv. - Total Inv: $59,000 to $125,000 - Financing: Counseling available.

COMMAND PERFORMANCE STYLING SALONS *
Performance Salon Systems, Inc.
P.O. Box 3000-266, Georgetown, TX, 78627. Contact: Denise Hiebner - Tel: (512) 869-1201. Full service styling salons, in regional malls or larger strip centers. Comprehensive stylist educational certification program. Established: 1976 - Franchising Since: 1976 - No. of Units: Company Owned: 12 - Franchised: 140 - Franchise Fee: $25,000 - Royalty: 6% - Total Inv: $75,000 to $150,000.

COST CUTTERS FAMILY HAIR CARE
Barbers, Hairstyling for Men & Women, Inc., The
300 Industrial Blvd., N.E., Minneapolis, MN, 55413. Contact: Julie Wollcat, Real Estate Manager - Tel: (612) 331-8500, Fax: (612) 331-2821. Value priced, family hair care salon with over 600 salons nationwide. Established: 1982 - Franchising Since: Parent company since 1967 - No. of Units: Company Owned: 5 - Franchised: 607 - Franchise Fee: $19,500 - Royalty: 6%, 4% adv. - Total Inv: $62,000 - $110,000 - Financing: Equipment leasing and financing through 3rd party vendor.

EASY HAIR
2635 Sandy Plains Rd., Marietta, GA, 30066. Contact: Terry Castle, Pres. - Tel: (404) 977-6820. Full service, value priced, high volume family hair care center offering a full range of services including cuts, perms and various coloring techniques and an entire line of specially formulated hair care products. Established: 1984 - Franchising Since: 1986 - No. of Units: Franchised: 7 - Franchise Fee: $20,000 - Royalty: 5% gross sales +2% adv. - Total Inv: $85,000-$110,000 - Financing: None.

ELEGANT IMAGES
Elegant Images Franchise Corp.
1019 Wilson Dr., Baltimore, MD, 21223. - Tel: (612) 832-4314. Complete makeover & photography studio. Established: 1989 - Franchising Since: 1991 - No. of Units: Company Owned: 5 - Franchised: 9 - Franchise Fee: $25,000 - Royalty: 5% - Total Inv: $136,000 - $215,000 plus fran. fee - Financing: None, will assist.

ELIZABETH GRADY, FACE FIRST
200 Boston Ave., #3500, Medford, MA, 02155. Contact: John P. Walsh, Exec. Pres. - Tel: (617) 391-9380. Esthetic salon chain consisting of salon services and personal line of skincare and make-up products.

Established: 1974 - Franchising Since: 1982 - No. of Units: Company Owned: 9 - Franchised: 13 - Franchise Fee: $25,000 - Royalty: 6% mnth. gross - Total Inv: $90,000-$130,000 - Financing: Corporate financing to qualified individuals.

ENCORE NAILS
Encore Nails, LLC
7939 Arapahoe Rd., Ste. 250, Englewood, CO, 80112. Contact: Johnny Wilson, Pres. - Tel: (303) 771-8251. Upscale studio offering unique proprietary products for the beautification and maintenance of nails and hands. Established: 1989 - Franchising Since: 1994 - No. of Units: Company Owned: 1 - Franchised: 1 - Franchise Fee: $5,500 - $15,500 - Royalty: 5%, 1% adv. - Total Inv: $19,400 - Financing: No.

FAMILY HAIRCUT STORE
Rancar Corporation
3045 Main St., Glastonbury, CT, 06033. Contact: Randy Givens - Tel: (203) 659-1430. Family oriented haircare facility. Offer quality services at a price for the value conscious shopper. Established: 1985 - Franchising Since: 1987 - No. of Units: Company Owned: 4 - Franchised: 22 - Franchise Fee: $23,000 - Royalty: 6% - Total Inv: $60,000 - $99,000 - Financing: Advice.

FANTASTIC SAM'S, THE ORIGINAL FAMILY HAIRCUTTERS
Fantastic Sam's International, Inc.
5101 E. La Palma, Ste. 100, Anaheim, CA, 92807. Contact: Richard Williams, Pres. - Tel: (714) 779-3910. Franchisor of family-oriented hair care salons. Established: 1974 - Franchising Since: 1976 - No. of Units: Company Owned: 7 - Franchised: 1323 - Franchise Fee: $25,000 - Royalty: $160.12 weekly license fee; $74.11 weekly adv. fee - Total Inv: including initial license fee, the total range is $58,745 - $123,043 - Financing: Yes.

GOUBAUD
Fern Laboratories, Inc.
280 Smith St., Farmingdale, NY, 11735. Contact: Emil Backstrom, Pres. - Tel: (516) 420-8000. Skin care and cosmetics. Established: 1946 - Franchising Since: 1946 - No. of Units: Company Owned: 1 - Franchised: 25 - Royalty: products sold at discount - Financing: No.

GREAT CLIPS
Great Clips, Inc.
3800 West 80th St., Ste. 400, Minneapolis, MN, 55431-4419. Contact: Danielle Steele, Franc. Dev. Coor. - Tel: (612) 893-9088 or (800) 999-5959, Fax: (612) 844-3443. Low cost quality haircare for the entire family. Excellent training provided for franchisees and their staff, innovative advertising and promotion campaigns. Established: 1982 - Franchising Since: 1983 - No. of Units: Franchised: 592 - Franchise Fee: $17,500 - Royalty: 6% service fee, 5% adv. - Total Inv: $80,650 - $120,400 - Financing: No.

GREAT CUTS
Landa Corporation
463 Salem St., Medford, MA, 02155-3336. Contact: Mr. Monroe Windgate, Pres. - Tel: (617)393-5451. Company provides haircutting services and retail hair care products to men, women and children. Established: 1983 - Franchising Since: 1985 - No. of Units: Company Owned: 8 - Franchised: 5 - Franchise Fee: $16,500 - Royalty: 10% continuing service fee + 5% adv. fund - Total Inv: approx. $120,000 - Financing: No, but will offer assistance in this area.

GREAT EXPECTATIONS PRECISION HAIRCUTTERS
CutCo Industries, Inc.
125 S. Service Rd., P.O. Box 265, Jericho, NY, 11753. Contact: Don Vonliebermann, Pres. - Tel: (516) 334-8400 or (800) 992-0139. Full service hair care salon serving 18 to 50 year old image and fashion conscious clientele. Salons offer contemporary hair care services including precision haircutting, perms and coloring. Franchise package offers a modern, attractively designed salon, operational support, advertising material training, grand opening and on-going assistance. Established: 1955 - Franchising Since: 1961 - No. of Units: Company Owned: 28 - Franchised: 157 - Franchise Fee: $20,000 - Royalty: 6% - Total Inv: $83,000 - $176,500 - Financing: To qualified applicants.

HAIR N' THINGS INC.
21655 Coolidge Hwy., Oak Park, MI, 48237. Contact: Gregory J. Reed, Esq., Legal Advisor - Tel: (f810) 546-0229. Beauty salon, unisex hair. Established: 1978 - Franchising Since: 1989 - No. of Units: Company Owned: 3 - Franchise Fee: $15,000 - Royalty: 6% - Total Inv: $57,000 $68,000 - Financing: Assistance.

HAIR REPLACEMENT CENTERS INT. INC. *
12100 Wilshire Blvd., #900, Los Angeles, CA, 90025. Contact: Scott Bernhardt, V.P. Fran. Opers. - Tel: (310) 820-0730. Non-surgical hair replacement. Established: 1971 - Franchising Since: 1994 - No. of Units: Company Owned: 12 - Franchise Fee: $25,000 - Royalty: 6% on gross sales/20% on adv. fund - Total Inv: $50,000 - $125,000 - Financing: Outside.

HAIR REPLACEMENT SYSTEMS / HRS
Hair Associates, Inc.
400 S. Dixie Hwy., Hallandale, FL, 33009. Contact: Kevin Maggs, Fran. Oper. - Tel: (800) 327-7971. Sales and service of non-surgical men's and women's hair replacement procedures. Established: 1969 - Franchising Since: 1980 - No. of Units: Franchised: 41 - Franchise Fee: $9,500 plus $1,000 for each 100,000 of population - Royalty: 5% of gross plus 1% adv. fee - Total Inv: $60,000 for small areas to $150,000 for large - Financing: No.

HAIRCRAFTERS
CutCo Industries, Inc.
125 S. Service Rd., P.O. Box 265, Jericho, NY, 11753. Contact: Don von Liebermann, Pres. - Tel: (516)334-8400 or (800) 992-0139. Full service hair care salon serving the entire family. Franchise package offers a modern, attractively designed salon, operational support, advertising material, training, grand opening and on-going assistance. Established: 1955 - Franchising Since: 1961 - No. of Units: Company Owned: 20 - Franchised: 295 - Franchise Fee: $20,000 - Royalty: 6% - Total Inv: $73,000 - $131,500 - Financing: To qualified applicants.

HAIRLINES FRANCHISE SYSTEMS, INC.
656 E. Golf Rd., Arlington Heights, IL, 60005. Contact: Paul V. Finamore, Pres. - Tel: (708) 593-7900, Fax: (708) 593-7955. Manufacture, sales and service of hair replacements, hair additions and hair pieces. Established: 1989 - Franchising Since: 1992 - No. of Units: Company Owned: 4 - Franchised: 1 - Franchise Fee: $35,000 - Royalty: 8% - Total Inv: $35,000 fran. fee plus $70,000 for furniture, fixtures, supplies and working capital = $105,000 est. total - Financing: No, however, the SBA has approved our franchise agreement.

INVISIONS
Invisions International Corp.
18000 Horizon Way, #800, Mt. Laurel, NJ, 08054-4309. Contact: Timothy Leogrande, Dir. of Franc. Dev. - Tel: (609) 273-9800. Hair replacement products and services for men and women. Established: 1987 - Franchising Since: 1990 - No. of Units: Company Owned: 6 - Franchised: 8 - Franchise Fee: $35,000 - Royalty: 12%, 3% adv. - Total Inv: $147,500 - $191,500 - Financing: No.

KEY WEST ALOE
Key West Cosmetic & Fragrance Factory
P.O. Box 1079, Key West, FL, 33041. Contact: Michael J. Miarecki, Mktg. Dir.. Manufacturer and distributor of over 300 unique and high quality Aloe based cosmetics, haircare, suntan, bath, men's products, as well as unusual and extensive fragrance line. Established: 1971 - Franchising Since: 1975 - No. of Units: Company Owned: 5 - Licensed: 16 - Franchise Fee: $7,500 - Royalty: none - Total Inv: $15,000 inven., $7,500 lic. fee + costs of lease & fix. - Financing: No.

LEMON TREE A UNISEX HAIRCUTTING ESTABLISHMENT, THE
Joan M. Cables La Femmina Beauty Salons, Inc.
3301 Hempstead Turnpike, Levittown, NY, 11756. Contact: John L. Wagner, V.P. - Tel: (516) 735-2828, (800) 345-9156. Meeting the haircare needs of all people servicing the entire family at low affordable prices. Name brand quality products and hours from early morning to late evening. Established: 1976 - Franchising Since: 1976 - No. of Units: Franchised: 75 - Franchise Fee: $10,000 - Royalty: 6% of weekly gross

- Total Inv: $37,500 - $70,600 - Financing: Franchisor may assist in obtaining for fee and equipment, may agree to finance 1/2 of franchisee's purchase of equipment and fee.

LORD'S AND LADY'S HAIR SALONS
450 Belgrade Ave., W. Roxbury, MA, 02132. Contact: Michael M. Barsamian, Pres. - Tel: (617) 323-4714. Hair styling full service for men and women. Established: 1972 - Franchising Since: 1979 - No. of Units: Company Owned: 16 - Franchised: 12 - Franchise Fee: $25,000 - Royalty: 6% - Total Inv: $125,000-$175,000 - Financing: No.

MEN'S HAIR NOW
MHN Franchising, Inc.
111-17 Queens Blvd., Forest Hills, NY, 11375. Contact: Theron Kearney, Fran. Dir. - Tel: (800) 299-0510. Hair replacement. Established: 1970 - Franchising Since: 1994 - No. of Units: Company Owned: 3 - Franchise Fee: $25,000 - $200,000 depending on size of exclusive territory - Royalty: 6% - Total Inv: $115,000 - $340,000 - Financing: No.

MERLE NORMAN COSMETICS, INC.
9130 Bellanca Ave., Los Angeles, CA, 90045. Contact: Marvin Landon, V.P. Studio Dev. - Tel: (800) 421-6648. Merle Norman cosmetics, a manufacturer of state-of-the-art, scientifically developed cosmetic products, distributes exclusively through 2,000 plus independently owned Studios, primarily in the U.S. and Canada. Established: 1931 - Franchising Since: 1989 - No. of Units: Franchised: 2,165 - Franchise Fee: None - Royalty: None - Total Inv: Product inventory $6,300 to $18,000 plus leasehold improvements - Financing: Assistance in obtaining financing.

NECTAR USA, INC.
4164 A Innslake Dr., Richmond (Glen Allen), VA, 23060. Contact: Steve Goff, Dir. of Fran. Dev. - Tel: (804) 527-4356. All natural, cruelty free skin care shops. Master franchises available. Established: 1981 - Franchising Since: 1993 - No. of Units: Franchised: 335 - Franchise Fee: $25,000 - Royalty: 8%, 2% adv. - Total Inv: $182,000 to $317,500 - Financing: Assistance.

NO APPOINTMENT FAMILY HAIRCUTTERS, INC.
14637 North Cave Creek, Phoenix, AZ, 85022. Contact: Ray Burke, Pres. - Tel: (602) 256-6000. High volume family haircare centers offering an a la carte price menu and professional grooming products to the consumer. Established: 1980 - Franchising Since: 1982 - No. of Units: Company Owned: 26 - Franchised: 30 - Franchise Fee: $25,000 - Royalty: 6% - Total Inv: $70,000-$85,000 - Financing: Thru buyers own bank.

POTIONS & LOTIONS
Body & Soul, Inc.
P.O. Box 26952, Phoenix, AZ, 85068-6952. Contact: Sharon Muir, Pres. - Tel: (602) 944-6642, Fax: (602) 395-9518. Offering natural, cruelty-free American made body care products and perfumes. Choose from over 200 fragrances. Can custom-scent their lotions, oils, soaps, haircare, and massage products. Established: 1974 - Franchising Since: 1989 - No. of Units: Company Owned: 8 - Franchised: 4 - Franchise Fee: $15,000 - Royalty: 0 - Total Inv: $75,000 - $200,000 - Financing: No.

PRO CUTS
Hawkin's Pro-Cuts, Inc.
500 Grapevine Hwy., Ste. 400, Hurst, TX, 76054-2708. Contact: Don Stone, Pres. - Tel: (817) 788-8000. Professional haircuts for the whole family at affordable prices. Exhibits a friendly yet professional atmosphere. Franchisees are provided with support in all phases of the operation as well as on going training for employees. Established: 1982 - Franchising Since: 1984 - No. of Units: Company Owned: 22 - Franchised: 73 - Franchise Fee: $25,000 - $10,000 - Royalty: 6%, 5% adv. - Total Inv: $65,000-$85,000 - Financing: Existing franchisees.

SNIP N' CLIP HAIRCUT SHOPS
SNC Franchise Corp.
7910 Quivira Rd., Lenexa, KS, 66215-2733. Contact: Ron Mitchell, Pres., CEO - Tel: (913) 438-1200 or (800) 622-6804. Family haircut shops in 14 states in strip centers, budget priced, no appointment, open 7 days & nights. Established: 1976 - Franchising Since: 1986 - No. of Units: Company Owned: 37 - Franchised: 42 - Franchise Fee: $10,000 - Royalty: 5% gross sales, 1% adv. - Total Inv: $10,000 fran. fee, $31,750 for turnkey shop, all equip. & decor & supplies & trained staff complete to open - Financing: Leasing available ($25,000) if qualified.

OPERATING & FRANCHISING FAMILY HAIRCUT SHOPS

Ron Mitchell, President

SNIP N' CLIP HAIRCUT SHOPS, INC.

Executive Offices
7910 Quivira Road • Lenexa, KS 66215
(913) 438-1200 • (800) 622-6804 • FAX (913) 438-3456

SPORT CLIPS *
Performance Salon Systems, Inc.
P.O. Box 3000 - 266, Georgetown, TX, 78627. Contact: Kevin Hogan - Tel: (713) 952-3177, Fax: (713) 952-3830. Haircuts - only sports-themed salons targeted to men of all ages. sold in "six packs" only. New concept, available for the first time in October, 1995. Established: 1993 - Franchising Since: 1995 - No. of Units: Company Owned: 2 - Franchise Fee: $100,000 (for a "six pack") - Royalty; Weekly fee plus 5% of sales - Total Inv: $100,000 fran. fee + $400,000 equip. & build-out - Financing: Equip. leasing for about 50% of equip./build-out costs.

SUPERCUTS
1094 Hertel Ave., Buffalo, NY, 14216. Contact: Tom Franciose, Pres. - Tel: (716) 875-2545. Provide volume services in haircutting, shampoos, style drys and perms at affordable prices with many convenient locations. Established: 1982 - Franchising Since: 1985 - No. of Units: 12 - Franchise Fee: $10,000 U.S. - Royalty: 4% + 5% advertising market fund - Total Inv: $35,000-$39,000 US (including franchise fee).

SYD SIMONS COSMETICS, INC.
2 East Oak St., Ste. 3804, Chicago, IL, 60611. Contact: Jerry Weitzel, Pres. - Tel: (312) 943-2333. Makeup and skin care products and related services and accessories. Established: 1936 - Licensing Since: 1974 - No. of Units: Company Owned: 1 - Licensed: 6 - Approx. Inv: $40,000 - $60,000 plus $15,000 - $25,000 working capital - Financing: no, Licensor will assist in obtaining local financing.

THIRD DIMENSION CUTS, INC.
8015 Broadway, Everett, WA, 98203. Contact: Jeff Wilmot, Pres. - Tel: (206) 355-2247. Haircuts, perms and coloring for men, women and children. Competitive pricing. Franchisees are provided with on-going support for new locations, hiring, training, advertising/marketing, educational classes, retail product inventory. Established: 1979 - Franchising Since: 1982 - No. of Units: Company Owned: 37 - Franchised: 13 - Franchise Fee: $15,000 - Total Inv: $67,000 - $125,000 - Royalty: 5% + 1.5% adv.

TRADE SECRET
Trade Secret, Inc.
130 Henry Street, Dousman, WI, 53118. Contact: Bryan Patzkowski, Fran. Sales - Tel: (414) 965-2196 or (800) 462-6092. Mall-based retail concept specializing in "salon-only" hair care products. Trade Secret presents an exciting retail product environment to shoppers, while operating a compact, yet full service salon. Established: 1982 - Franchising Since: 1988 - No. of Units: Company Owned: 104 - Franchised: 68 - Franchise Fee: $27,500 - Royalty: 6.5% - discounted for timely payment - Total Inv: $117,000 - $197,000 incl. fran. fee - Financing: No.

VOLPE NAILS, INC.
1747 Independence Blvd., Ste. E6, Sarasota, FL, 34234-2146. Contact: Gary Donson, V.P. - Tel: (941) 358-0940. Sale of nail care franchises. Specializing in sculptured acrylic nails, natural nail care & quality nail care products. Established: 1980 - Franchising Since: 1989 - No. of Units: Company Owned: 1 - Franchised: 53 - Franchise Fee: $4,000, $8,000, $12,000 - Royalty: 4% of gross - Total Inv: $14,000 - $103,000 (fran. fee, equip and inven. $6,500 - $41,300 & work. cap. $3,800 - $50,000) - Financing: No.

WE CARE HAIR
We Care Hair Development
7327 W. 90th St., Bridgeview, IL, 60453. Contact: Ronald Andersen, Franchise Sales Dir. - Tel: (800) 676-5264, Fax: (708) 598-8037. We Care Hair incorporates three revenue centers under one roof: 1) Professional beauty supply retail center; 2) Tanning center; 3) Hair care services center. Each center is marketed and advertised independently. Centers are cross-promoted within store. Established: 1985 - Franchising Since: 1990 - No. of Units: Company Owned: 6 - Franchised: 153 - Franchise Fee: $10,000 - Royalty: 8% - Total Inv: $80,000 - $140,000 depending on store size & # of tanning units - Financing: Yes.

HEALTH AIDS AND SERVICES

ACC SOLUTIONS, INC. *
1000 Abernathy Rd., Ste. 1040, Atlanta, GA, 30328. Contact: W. Surman, Pres. - Tel: (404) 481-7272. Medical billing & practice management software licensing to become a reseller and billing center. No. of Units; Licensed: 300+ - License Fee: $6,900 - Royalty: None - Total Inv: $10,000+.

ADDRA MEDICAL, INC.
2231 N. Winton Ave., Speedway, IN, 46224. Contact: Hugh W. Craig, Distributor - Tel: (317) 241-4900. Fantastic unlimited ground floor distributorship opportunity. New exciting health drink that is sweeping the country. Big successful multiple level marketing people are joining us. Why? Because they can sponsor doctors and our company provides $957 in products on consignment to the doctor. This is truly a great money maker. You market to people who need our two great products and they repeat monthly. Established: 1993 - Total Inv: $245.50 or send $10 for VCR video/audio cassette/product sample and marketing plan. Royalty: Up to 45% override.

AFTCO ASSOCIATES
AFTCO Associates, Ltd.
600 Houze Way, Suite 12D, Roswell, GA, 30076. Contact: Alan Thornburg, Pres. - Tel: (404) 992-0924. Medical/dental consulting business buying, selling, merging and consolidating healthcare practices throughout the US and Canada. Established: 1968 - Franchising Since: 1986 - No. of Units: Company Owned: 3 - Franchised: 36 - Franchise Fee: $25,000+ - Royalty: 10% - Total Inv: $50,000 - Financing: Yes, up to 50% of franchise fee.

AMERICA'S DOCTORS OF OPTOMETRY
200 South St., Tracy, MN, 56175. Contact: Charles R. Patterson, C.E.O. - Tel: (507) 629-3361. Develop and distribute a marketing program for professional services of members of A.D.O., Inc. Established: 1980 - Franchising Since: 1980 - No. of Units: 150 - Approx. Inv: $3,000 - Financing: No.

AMERICAN MEDICAL WEIGHT ASSOCIATION
N & J Medical Corp.
P.O. Box 1323, Medina, OH, 44258-1323. Contact: Norbert Meadows, Fran. Dir. - Tel: (216) 225-4240 or (800) 321-9517. Weight loss program. Total systems provided with thorough training for franchisee with grand opening assistance. A professional weight loss business combining exclusive "Diet Plus" product line and service. Established: 1981 - Franchising Since: 1985 - No. of Units: Franchised: 28 - Franchise Fee: $15,500 - Royalty: 7% - Total Inv: $60,000- Financing: No.

AMERICAN NURSING CARE
8044 Montgomery Rd., #505, Cincinnati, OH, 45236. Contact: Tom Karpinski, Pres. - Tel: (513) 984-9989. Temporary staffing and private duty nursing. Franchising Since: 1982 - No. of Units: 6 - Approx. Inv: $30,000-$40,000.

AMERICAN PHYSICAL REHABILITATION NETWORK
APRN, Inc.
4050 Talmadge Rd.,P.O. Box 8864, Toledo, OH, 43623. Contact: Harvey Bowes, C.F.O. - Tel: (419) 474-0507 or (800) 331-3058. A total system for management and operation of free-standing physical therapy clinics. Established: 1957 - Franchising Since: 1987 - No. of Units: 6 - Franchise Fee: $25,000 - Royalty: 7% + 1% adv. - Total Inv: $232,632 - Financing: No, will assist with feasibility and may consider partnership.

AMERICAN VISION CENTERS, INC.
90 John St., New York, NY, 10038. Contact: Seth Poppel, Pres. - Tel: (800) 232-5558, (212) 385-1000. Provide full-service, quality eyecare and eyewear at value-oriented prices. AVC franchisees must be an optometrist, optician or experienced optical store manager. Established: 1977 - Franchising Since: 1979 - No. of Units: Franchised: 55 - Franchise Fee: $10,000 - Royalty: 8.5% of gross sales - Total Inv: $75,000 - $225,000 - Financing: Direct and 3rd party avail. for up to 90% of total investment.

AMERICARE DENTAL CENTERS, U.S.A.
Americare Dental System
P.O. Box 35365, Phoenix, AZ, 85069-5365. Contact: Bernard Serbin, Pres. - Tel: (602) 548-9178. Dental delivery systems and offices. Established: 1983 - Franchising Since: 1985 - No. of Units: Company Owned: 5 - Franchise Fee: $10,000-Royalty: 7% adv. + 3% use of name - Total Inv: $150,000-$200,000 min.- Financing: External.

AMIGO MOBILITY CENTER
Mobility Center, Inc.
6693 Dixie Hwy., Bridgeport, MI, 48722. Contact: Richard Zimmer, Fran. Oper. & Sales Mgr. - Tel: (800) 821-2710. A retail sales and service outlet carrying products for mobility impaired individuals or anyone with walking difficulties. Established: 1968 - Franchising Since: 1984 - No. of Units: Company Owned: 6 - Franchised : 19 - Franchise Fee: $20,000+ - Royalty: 5% decreasing + 1% adv. - Total Inv: $68,000 - $80,000 - Financing: Will assist in making a presentation to a lender.

BE SOME BODY
Cheryl Lents Exercise Dance, Inc.
23150 Sandalfoot Plaza Dr., Boca Raton, FL, 33428. Contact: Gary - Tel: (407) 487-0988. Aerobic exercise & dance franchises. Established: 1979 - Franchising Since: 1981 - No. of Units: Company Owned: 2 - Franchised: 5 - Franchise Fee: $15,000 - Total Inv: $17,500 - Royalty: 8%.

BENEFICIAL HEALTH & BEAUTY, INC.
Beneficial International
1780 W. 500 So., Salt Lake City, UT, 84104. Contact: Linda T. Nelson, Ph.D., Pres. - Tel: (800) 367-0990. Urban health and beauty spas using products unsurpassed for quality and effectiveness. Total health and beauty care at local

outlets. Established: 1981 - Franchising Since: 1990 - No. of Units: Franchised: 23 - Franchise Fee: $15,000 - Royalty: 3%, 4% adv. - Total Inv: F.F., $14,500 product & equip., lease space costs - Financing: No.

BETTER BACK STORE
Thomas Blantz Enterprises Inc.
7939 E. Arapahoe Rd., #140, Greenwood Village, CO, 80112. Contact: Kerri Thomas, Pres. - Tel: (303) 773-BACK or (800) 501-BACK. Retail stores selling products for back care. Training and support provided by franchisor. Established: 1981 - Franchising Since: 1992 - No. of Units: Company Owned: 1 - Franchised: 4 - Franchise Fee: $15,000 - Royalty: 4.5% gross royalty - Total Inv: $90,000 to $135,000 - Financing: No.

BETTER BIRTH FOUNDATION
739 Main St., Ste. D, Stone Mountain, GA, 30083. Contact: Dir. of Mktg. - Tel: (404) 469-8870. Childbirth educational service, certification program for R.N.'s which includes early pregnancy nutrition, C.B. preparation, refresher, post-partum infant massage, infant CPR, etc. Established: 1981 - Franchising Since: 1983 - No. of Units: Company Owned: 5 - Franchised: 3 - Franchise Fee: $5,000 - Royalty: 7% + 1% adv. - Total Inv: $5,000 F. Fee + $800 cert. fee + $400 workbook, min. invest. needed. - Financing: No.

BEVERLY HILLS WEIGHT LOSS CLINIC
Beverly Hills International, Inc.
200 Highpoint Ave., Ste. B-5, Portsmouth, RI, 02871. Contact: Ralph Cutillo, Pres. - Tel: (401) 683-6620. Weight loss clinics. Franchising Since: 1989 - No. of Units: Franchised: 44 - Franchise Fee: $15,000 - Royalty: 8% of weekly gross - Total Inv: fran. fee, buildout, clinic supplies - Financing: No.

BIOGIME SKIN CARE CENTERS
Entourage International, Inc.
1665 Townhurst, #100, Houston, TX, 77043. Contact: John Riemann, Pres. - Tel: (800) 338-8783. Natural skin care specialty store. Established: 1983 - Franchising Since: 1991 - No. of Units: Company Owned: 7 - Franchised: 10 - Franchise Fee: $15,000 - Royalty: 2% - Total Inv: $78,000 - $123,000 - Financing: No.

BODYCUES
St. Elizabeth Corp., The
601 Edwin Moses Blvd., Dayton, OH, 45408. Contact: Franchise Dir./Pres. - Tel: (513) 229-6000. Home health parties for women. Franchising Since: 1986 - No. of Units: 13 - Inv: $18,000.

BODYLOG INC.
120 Kisco Ave., Mt. Kisco, NY, 10549. Contact: Jerald Greenberg - Tel: (914) 241-7121, (800) 233-2911, Fax: (914) 241-7043. Our dealers and affiliates place our patented fitness evaluation machine in health clubs, stores, malls, schools, etc. (facilities). These facilities are offered free use of the machine provided they place them in locations easily available to the public. The public takes the test free. We sell ads on the machine to local merchants as well as data from the machine. Established: 1984 - Franchising Since: 1989 - No. of Units: Franchised: 28 - Franchise Fee: dealer $295, affiliate $7,900 master affiliate $10,900.

CALLANETICS
Callanetics Franchise Corporation
22 W. 38th St., 12th Flr., New York, NY, 10018-6204. Contact: Aletha Zens, Mktg. Mgr. - Tel: (212) 765-2900. Body shaping studios featuring the callanetics exercise program which tones and shapes the body, producing measurable results quickly. Established: 1990 - Franchising Since: 1990 - No. of Units: Company Owned: 1 - Franchised: 31 - Franchise Fee: $15,800 - Royalty: 12%, 4% - Total Inv: $27,000 - $42,000 - Financing: No.

CALORIE SHOP WEIGHT LOSS CENTERS OF AMERICA, INC.
395 Springside Dr., Akron, OH, 44333. Contact: Steve Sandler, Fran. Dev. - Tel: (216) 666-7952. Supervised weight reduction business, offering the consumer a comprehensive program utilizing individual treatment, pre-planned meals, personal care, counseling and weight maintenance. Established: 1992 - Franchising Since: 1993 - No. of Units: Company Owned: 4 - Franchised: 33 - Franchise Fee: $9,500 - Royalty: Varies - Total Inv: $40,000 - $100,000 - Financing: No.

CHALL-AIDE MEDICAL PRODUCTS
Rt. 15 - P.O. Box 965, Sparta, NJ, 07871. Contact: Mr. Roger Day Jr., V.P. - Tel: (201) 383-0700. Offering the market the right product at the right time. Medical kits and products as well. Established: 1975.

CHART REHABILITATION
Chart Corporation
P.O. Box 5978, Incline Village, NV, 89450. Contact: Harry Flagg - Tel: (702) 831-5896. Physical rehabilitation centers. Established: 1979 - Franchising Since: 1983 - No. of Units: Franchised: 15 - Franchise Fee: $65,000 - Royalty: 8% + 1% adv. - Total Inv: $375,000 - $425,500 - Financing: No.

CLAFLIN HOME HEALTH CENTERS, INC.
486 Silver Spring St., Providence, RI, 02904. Contact: Richard Westlake, Pres. - Tel: (401) 331-0154. Free standing retail stores offering health care equipment and supplies. Established: 1817 - Franchising Since: 1982 - No. of Units: 5 - Franchise Fee: $25,000 - Royalty: 5% net receipts - Total Inv: $150,000 - $200,000 - Financing: Assistance.

COMP-U-MED SYSTEMS, INC.
1230 W. Rosecrans Ave., Ste. 1000, Manhattan Beach, CA, 90266. Contact: Ed Zalewski, Mgr. Fran. Sales - Tel: (310) 643-5106. Medical equipment leasing. Established: 1973 - Franchising Since: 1978 - No. of Units: - Franchised: 1,211 - Total Inv: $7,000 - $36,000.

CONSUMER DENTAL NETWORK
ConsumerHealth, Inc.
1401 Dove St., Ste. 290, Newport Beach, CA, 92660. Contact: Bob Milunas, V.P. - Tel: (714) 752-8522. Operation of well advertised and promoted dental centers delivering complete spectrum of dental services, general dentistry, prosthetics, periodontics, endodontics, orthodontics and oral surgery within a large, modern multi-operatory facility operating greater than conventional hours and days. Established: 1979 - Franchising Since: 1983 - No. of Units: Company Owned: 16 - Franchised: 4 - Franchise Fee: $15,000 - Royalty: 6% gross - Total Inv: $160,000.

D.O.C OPTICAL
D.O.C Optics Corp.
19800 West Eight Mile Rd., Southfield, MI, 48075. Contact: Charles M. Males, Sr. V.P. & Fran. Dir. - Tel: (810) 354-7100 Ext. 2279. Retail optical business. Established: 1961 - Franchising Since: 1986 - No. of Units: Company Owned: 52 - Franchised: 63 - Franchise Fee: $12,500 - Royalty: based on sales - Total Inv: varies

DENTAL STORE, THE
Dental Store, Ltd. The
1010 Grove Mall, Elk Grove Village, IL, 60007-3775. Contact: Dr. Neil H. Shulkin, Pres. - Tel: (708)439-5440, (800)437-5440 US & CAN.. A license (exclusive, territorial) for the use of 'The Dental Store' registered trademarks in the operation of pre-existing dental offices. Established: 1986 - Licensing Since: 1992 - No. of Units: Company Owned: 1 - Franchised: 3 - Franchise Fee: $2,500 - Royalty: 1.5% - Total Inv: License fee only - Financing: One year financing available.

DERMACULTURE CLINIC
1936 W. 135th St., Gardena, CA, 90249. Contact: Donald James, Pres. - Tel: (310) 538-1300. Skin care franchises. Offering a unique skin care therapy. The product line includes cleansers, astringents, moisturizers, etc. Established: 1937 - Franchising Since: 1937 - No. of Units: 110.

DIET CENTER
Diet Center Inc.
395 Springside Dr., Akron, OH, 44333-4512. Contact: Denis Kline, V.P. Fran. Dev. - Tel: (800) 333-2581. A counseling based program built around 3 key points. 1) Determine level of body fat; 2) Counsel client how to eat real, rather than pre-packaged foods; 3) Behavior modification. Established: 1972 - Franchising Since: 1973 - No. of Units: Franchised: 1,100 - Franchise Fee: $12,000 - $18,000 - Royalty: 8% up to $150,000, 7% beyond - Total Inv: $33,000 - $53,000 - Financing: Yes, to qualified applicants.

DIET LIGHT WEIGHT LOSS SYSTEM
300 Market St., Ste. 101, Lebanon, OR, 97355. Contact: Kathy Bengtson, Pres. - Tel: (503) 259-3573, (800) 248-7712, Fax: (503) 259-3506. Weight loss counseling on an individual basis with portion controlled meals, and lifetime maintenance. Established: 1983 - Franchising Since:

1988 - No. of Units: Company Owned: 10 - Franchised: 5 - Franchise Fee: $15,000 - Royalty: None - Total Inv: $25,000 ($15,000 fran. fee, $5,000 inven., $5,000 signs, furnishings) - Financing: Yes.

DIET WORKSHOP
One University Office Park, 29 Sawyer Rd., Waltham, MA, 02154. Contact: Lois L. Lindauer, Founder & Nat'l. Dir. - Tel: (617) 893-1007. Weight reduction and control. Established: 1965 - Franchising Since: 1967 - No. of Units: Company Owned: 36 - Franchised: 62 - Franchise Fee: $12,500.

E-Z TAN TANNING SALONS
E-Z Tan Franchise Systems, Inc.
21073 Powerline Rd., #63, Boca Raton, FL, 33433. Contact: Donna Barnett, Dir. - Tel: (407) 479-2105. Professional tanning salons featuring the latest in technology. Also features retail swimming apparel, tanning accessories, lotions & general outdoor related merchandise. Established: 1986 - Franchising Since: 1992 - No. of Units: Company Owned: 7 - Franchise Fee: $15,000 - Royalty: 6% + 1% adv. national, 5% local - Total Inv: $60,000 - $80,000 - Financing: Yes.

EMSAR
Equipment Management Services & Repair
1032 W. Main St., Wilmington, OH, 45177. Contact: David Gamble, Pres. - Tel: (513) 383-1052. Servicing medical equipment. Established: 1993 - Franchising Since: 1993 - No. of Units: Franchised: 22 - Franchise Fee: $15,280 - Royalty: 15% - Financing: No.

EUROPEAN TAN SPA, INC.
5002 Main Street, Downers Grove, IL, 60515. Contact: Sandra H. Lindholm, Pres. - Tel: (708) 963-2626. Indoor tanning salon featuring J.K. Soltran tan beds, complete insurance package, logo promotion, in a definer/territory. Established: 1982 - Franchising Since: 1983 - No. of Units: Company Owned: 3 - Franchised: 90 - Franchise Fee: $5,000 - Royalty: 40¢ per running/operating hours on each tanning bed - Total Inv: fran. fee plus number of tanning beds - Financing: No.

EYEGLASS EMPORIUM
8120 Georgia St., Merrillville, IN, 46410. Contact: Don Stewart, Dir. of Fran. - Tel: (219) 736-1366. Retail optical stores - eye exams, frame and glass adjustments. Established: 1979 - Franchising Since: 1990 - No. of Units: Company Owned: 9 - Franchise Fee: $20,000 for 1st store, $15,000 subsequent - Royalty: 8% - Total Inv: Exam store (no lab) $136,000, with lab $288,000 - Financing: No.

EYESUPPLY EYEWEAR & EYECARE CENTERS
1111 Route 110, 3rd Fl., E. Farmingdale, NY, 11735. Contact: Keith Orlean, Pres. - Tel: (516) 420-4383. High fashion discount retail eyecare franchising company. Established: 1985 - Franchising Since: 1989 - No. of Units: Company Owned: 2 - Franchised: 13 - Franchise Fee: $15,000 - Royalty: 7%, 3% regional & 3% local adv. - Total Inv: $149,000 - $199,000 incl. fran. fee - Financing: Yes.

FASTSERV MEDICAL
Fastserv Central
9523 Alta Mesa Rd., Wilton, CA, 95693. Contact: Mike Donnell - Tel: (916) 687-8930, Fax: (916) 687-8932. Maintenance and repair of medical equipment, home health equipment, personal mobility items. Company provides warranty service for many manufacturers. Established: 1989 - Franchising Since: 1992 - No. of Units: Company Owned: 2 - Franchised: 68 - Franchise Fee: $20,000 min. ($1,000/10,000 population) - Royalty: 5.6% to 12% - Total Inv: $60,000 to $140,000 - Financing: None.

FIRST OPTOMETRY EYECARE CENTERS, INC.
32600 Gratiot, Roseville, MI, 48066. Contact: D. Borsand, C.E.O. - Tel: (810) 296-7800. Sale of vision care services and optical products (contact lenses and eyeglasses). Established: 1980 - Franchising Since: 1981 - No. of Units: Company Owned: 22 - Franchised: 18 - Franchise Fee: $10,000 - Total Inv: $10,000 - $100,000 - Royalty: 7% - Financing: Yes.

FIRSTAT NURSING SERVICES
Firstat of America
1645 Palm Beach Lakes Blvd., Ste. 480, West Palm Beach, FL, 33401. Contact: Dennis R. Allen, V.P. - Tel: (800) 845-7828, Fax: (407) 684-9008. Home health care services and supplemental staffing for medical facilities. Established: 1990 - Franchising Since: 1990 - No. of Units: Company Owned: 1 - Franchised: 23 opened, 16 scheduled to open - Franchise Fee: $25,000 - $50,000 depending on market - Royalty: .05 private pay, .03 medicare - Total Inv: $200,000 - Financing: None.

FITNESS ON WHEELS
Fitness On Wheels, Inc.
1185 S. Milwaukee, Denver, CO, 80210. Contact: Jeff Hopley, CEO - Tel: (303) 778-8060. Mobile gym business offering personal fitness instruction in home or office. Established: 1987 - Franchising Since: 1991 - No. of Units: Company Owned: 1 - Franchised: 2 - Franchise Fee: $10,000 - Royalty: 7%, 1% adv. - Total Inv: $17,500 - $20,000 - Financing: No.

FORM-YOU 3 WEIGHT LOSS CENTERS
Form-You-3 International, Inc.
4790 Douglas Cir., N.W., Canton, OH, 44718-36—. Contact: Ken Massey, Regional VP of Fran. - Tel: (800) 525-6315. Weight loss counseling and sales of related weight loss products. Established: 1982 - Franchising Since: 1984 - No. of Units: Company Owned: 2 - Franchised: 150 - Franchise Fee: $7,900 - Royalty: 5%, 1% adv. - Total Inv: $20,000 - $25,000.

GENERAL NUTRITION CENTER
GNC Franchising, Inc.
921 Penn Ave., Pittsburgh, PA, 15237. Contact: Dir. of Franchising - Tel: (800) 766-7099, (412) 288-2043, Fax: (412) 288-2033. GNC is the leading retailer of vitamins, minerals, herbs and sports nutrition products. We hold the greatest share of the nutritional supplement market and are uniquely positioned to capitalize on the accelerating trend toward self-care. Established: 1935 - Franchising Since: 1988 - No. of Units: Company Owned: 1,509 - Franchised: 809 - Franchise Fee: $25,000 - Royalty: 6% - Total Inv: $25,000 fee, $30,000 inven., $30,000 fixtures, $25,000 construction - Financing: Direct & third party assistance.

GREAT EARTH VITAMIN STORES
11726 San Vicente Blvd., Ste. 360, Los Angeles, CA, 90049-5046. Contact: Chris Barr, Dir. of Fran. Sales - Tel: (800) 374-7328, (310) 571-0571. Sale of vitamins and nutritional supplements. Established: 1970 - Franchising Since: 1972 - No. of Units: Company Owned: 3 - Franchised: 130 - Franchise Fee: $22,500 - Royalty: 6% on all sales - Total Inv: $70,000 - $80,000 - Financing: Yes.

HEALTH MART
Fox Meyer Health Corp.
1220 Senlac Dr., Carrollton, TX, 75006. Contact: John Kogut, Pres. - Tel: (214) 446-4800. Full-line, community-based drug stores. Established: 1980 - Franchising Since: 1982 - No. of Units: 650 - Total Inv: varies - Financing: No.

HEALTH SYSTEMS PLUS WELLNESS & WEIGHT MANAGEMENT
P.O. Box 1150, Orem, Utah, 84059. Contact: Arthur E. Hansen, Dir. Fran. Sales - Tel: (801) 225-2739. Wellness & Weight Management Co. is one of the most sophisticated & comprehensive programs available. Program includes: individualized nutritional programs; body composition; fitness advisor; personal activity program; medical risk analysis; optional full food. Established: 1990 - Franchising Since: 1990 - No. of Units: Company Owned: 1 - Franchised: 53 - Franchise Fee: $9,000 - Royalty: 6% (4% to Corp; 2% to Field reps.) - Total Inv: $27,000 - $61,000 - Financing: No.

HEALTHMART, INC.
1220 Senlac Dr., Carrollton, TX, 75006. Contact: John Kogut, Pres. - Tel: (214) 446-4800. Health services. Full-line, community based drug stores. Established: 1980 - Franchising Since: 1982 - No. of Units: 720 - Total Inv: varies - Financing: No.

HEMORRHOID CLINICS OF AMERICA
22000 Greenfield Rd., Oak Park, MI, 48237. Contact: Max M. Ali, M.D. - Tel: (801) 967-4140. The clinic provides out-patient non-operative treatment of hemorrhoids and other minor anorectal ailments. Cryogenics, banding and laser are the common methods employed currently at the clinics. No hospitalization is required. Training is available to physicians in the procedures utilized at the clinics. Managerial assistance is available. Established: 1984 - No. of Units: 2 - Financing: Partial.

HOLLYWOOD WEIGHT LOSS CLINICS
P.O. Box 1070, College Station, Fredericksburg, VA, 22402. Contact: Rita Liming, Pres. - Tel: (540) 891-7494. Weight loss centers. Established: 1989 - Franchising Since: 1990 - No. of Units: Company Owned: 2 - Franchised: 44 - Franchise Fee: $5,000 - Royalty: 8% of gross revenue - Total Inv: $8,500 - $45,000 - Financing: Yes, 50% down, balance upon opening.

HOME INSTEAD SENIOR CARE *
Home Instead, Inc.
1104 S. 76th Ave., Omaha, NE, 68114. Contact: Paul R. Hogan, Pres. - Tel: (402) 391-2555. Our name says it all! We offer a franchise to provide affordable, professional non-medical care for elderly people who need assistance, supervision, light housework and/or companionship to remain in their homes. Established: 1994 - Franchising Since: 1995 - No. of Units: Company Owned: 1 - Franchised: 6 - Franchise Fee: $7,500 - Royalty: 5% - Total Inv: $13,500 - $18,500 (incl. fran. fee) - Financing: None.

INCHES-A-WEIGH
P.O. Box 59346, Birmingham, AL, 35259. Contact: Ken Giglio, Fran. Dev. - Tel: (800) 241-8663. Weight loss/figure correction centers for ladies only. Real foods & positive motivation through onsite exercise. Established: 1986 - Franchising Since: 1991 - No. of Units: Company Owned: 5 - Franchised: 12 - Franchise Fee: $29,500 - Royalty: 4% - Total Inv: $40,000 - $50,000 - Financing: Yes.

JACKI'S, INC.
P.O. Box 289, DeLand, FL, 32721-0289. Contact: Neil A. Sorensen, Chairman - Tel: (904) 738-3292. Franchisees market and sell a comprehensive system of aerobics and resistance training exercise classes along with other fitness-related products & services. Established: 1990 - Franchising Since: 1990 - No. of Units: Franchised: 738 - Franchise Fee: $500 - Royalty: $300 per quarter - Total Inv: approx. $1,950 - $3,900 first year - Financing: None.

JAZZERCISE
2808 Roosevelt St., Carlsbad, CA, 92008. Contact: Joann Kocyk, Instructor Training Coord. - Tel: (619) 434-2101. Worldwide dance-fitness franchise offering a wide variety of fitness classes & formats. Established: 1977 - Franchising Since: 1983 - No. of Units: Franchised: 4,748 - Franchise Fee: $325 foreign; $650 U.S. - Royalty: 20% of gross - Total Inv: Ranges between $1,360 - $16,850.

JENNY CRAIG WEIGHT LOSS CENTERS
Jenny Craig International Inc.
445 Marine View Ave. Ste. 300, Del Mar, CA, 92014. Contact: Susan Liesegang, Dir. of Fran. Dev. - Tel: (619) 259-7000, Ext. 371. Weight loss centers. Established: 1983 - Franchising Since: 1986 - No. of Units: Company Owned: 524 - Franchised: 191 - Franchise Fee: $50,000 - Royalty: 7% - Total Inv: $152,500 to $295,500 incl. fran. fee - Financing: None.

JOSLIN DIABETES AFFILIATED CENTERS *
Joslin Diabetes Center, Inc.
1 Joslin Place, Boston, MA, 02215. Contact: Raymond Capers, Exec. Dir. - Tel: (617) 732-2666, Fax: (617) 732-2562. Works with leading health care facilities to establish regional diabetes treatment centers of excellence that annually, on average, achieve significant growth, improved health outcomes, and attract payors. Established: 1898 - Franchising Since: 1987 - No. of Units: Company Owned: 7 - Franchised: 17 - Franchise Fee: Negotiable - Royalty: Negotiable - Total Inv: Proprietary.

LADY OF AMERICA
2400 E. Commercial Blvd., Ste. 808, Ft. Lauderdale, FL, 33308. Contact: Mr. Bill Landman, Nat'l. Fran. Dir. - Tel: 1-800-833-5239, Fax: (305) 492-1187. Ladies only fitness centers specializing in aerobics. Full service with equipment and cardiovascular machinery. Established: 1983 - Franchising Since: 1984 - No. of Units: Company Owned: 4 - Franchised: 110 - Franchise Fee: $35,000 - Royalty: 10% - Total Inv: $100,000 - Financing: On equipment.

LEAN LINE, INC. THIN LIFE CENTERS FRANCHISE CORP.
151 New World Way, S. Plainfield, NJ, 07080. Contact: Lorraine Wurtzel, V.P. - Tel: (908) 757-7677. Weight reduction club that utilizes a nutritionally-balanced diet with behavior modification. Moderately priced for popular appeal. Established: 1968 - Franchising Since: 1968 - No. of Units: Company Owned: 8 - Franchised: 3 Lean Line, 2 Thin Life - Approx. Inv: $5,000 - $15,500 - Royalty: 10% gross.

LIFE TRENDS WEIGHT LOSS & TONING CENTERS
P.O. Box 266, Independence, MO, 64051-0266. Contact: Glen E. Henson, V.P. - Tel: (816) 795-7171. Exercise salons featuring life trend toning tables, combined with tanning beds. Many salons add isokinetic exercise equipment which include toning exercises that the toning tables do not provide and many add herbal body wraps. Also provide nutrition weight loss programs. Help with all phases of the operation, as our most successful salons have diversified with services that appeal to the female market. Established: 1973 - No. of Units: Franchised: 300 - Total Inv: min. of $15,000 start up cost-$2,500., total cost of equip. & start up costs approx. $20,000 - $25,000.

LORRAINE'S TROPI-TAN *
Tropi-Tan, Inc.
G-4290 Miller Rd., Flint, MI, 48507. Contact: Vince Lorraine, Pres./Owner - Tel: (313) 230-0090. Indoor suntanning salon & related services - retail clothing. Established: 1979 - Franchising Since: 1984 - No. of Units: Company Owned: 5 - Franchised: 3 - Franchise Fee: $7,000 - Royalty: $3,500, $3,500 adv. - Total Inv: $60,000 to $250,000 - Financing: None.

MEDICAL INSURA FORM SERVICE
9465 Western Plz., Apt. 3, Omaha, NE, 68114-2547. Contact: Pat LeClair, Fran. Dir. - Tel: (402) 397-5667. A business that co-ordinates and processes all medicare and medical insurance forms. Medical reimbursement consultants. Established: 1980 - No. of Units: 2 - Approx. Inv: $35,000 - $40,000 - Financing: None.

MEDICAP PHARMACY
Medicap Pharmacies Inc.
4700 Westown Pkwy., #300, West Des Moines, IA, 50266-6730. Contact: Calvin C. James, V.P. Fran. Dev. - Tel: (800) 445-2244, Fax: (515) 224-8415. Small professional pharmacies 90% prescription with 10% health related non-prescription products. Convenient locations, competitive prices and personal service offered by these stores. Low overhead along with sound business principles. Buying power and aggressive modern advertising campaigns help to increase profitability. Established: 1971 - Franchising Since: 1974 - No. of Units: Franchised: 127, 24 under development - Franchise Fee: $15,000 for new store, $8,500 for conversion store - Royalty: New store 4% plus 1% adv., conv. store 2% of base receipts plus 1% adv. and 4% on growth - Total Inv: New store $140,000 - $167,000; conv. $25,000 - $80,000 - Financing: Assistance.

MEDICINE SHOPPE, THE
Medicine Shoppe International Inc., The
1100 N. Lindbergh Blvd., St. Louis, MO, 63132. Contact: Mike Eicher, V.P. Fran. Dev. - Tel: (314) 993-6000. Retail prescription and health centers. Emphasis on the counselling pharmacist/manager being an integral part of screenings and delivery in the market area. Approx. 90% prescription and 10% non-prescription ethical medicines and Medicine Shoppe brand products. Established: 1970 - Franchising Since: 1971 - No. of Units: 1100 - Franchise Fee: $18,000 - Royalty: 5.5% - Total Inv: $93,000 - Financing: Yes.

MEDIPOWER
P.O. Box 335, San Marcos, TX, 78667. Contact: F. MacKenzie, Sales Mgr. - Tel: (210) 629-1400 or Fax: (512) 353-5333. Supplying computer services to doctors, clinics and laboratories. Established: 1983 - Franchising Since: 1985 - No. of Units: 3 - Total Inv: $10,000 - Royalty: $300/month - Financing: No.

MERIDIAN REGULATORY ACUPUNCTURE
3820 Premier Ave., Memphis, TN, 38118. Contact: Franchise Dir./Pres. - Tel: (901) 867-0600. Acupuncture medical clinic designed to be added to a present physicians practice. Established: 1978 - Franchising Since: 1990 - No. of Units: Company Owned: 1 - Franchise Fee: $25,000 - Royalty: 5% - Total Inv: $26,000 - $933,000 - Financing: No.

MIRACLE-EAR
4101 Dahlberg Dr., Minneapolis, MN, 55422. Contact: Jim Darland, Dir. Fran. Lic. - Tel: (800) 234-7714. Manufacturer of hearing instruments. Established: 1948 - Franchising Since: 1984 - No. of Units: Company Owned: 13 - Franchised: 1,009 - Franchise Fee: $20,000 + $4,000/ 100,000 population - Royalty: approx. 3% of retail cost - Total Inv: $75,000 - $150,000 - Financing: after initial unit.

MONFRIED OPTICAL, KINDY OPTICAL, DULING OPTICAL
D & K Optical
4415 Poplar Level Rd., Louisville, KY, 40233. , V.P. Fran. - Tel: (502) 459-6722. Retail optical stores. Sell eyeglass frames, lenses, contacts. Also provide eye exams. Franchising Since: 1986 - No. of Units: Company Owned: 36 - Franchised: 115 - Franchise Fee: $5,000 - Royalty: 7% - Total Inv: $25,000 - $250,000 - Financing: Yes.

NURSEFINDERS
1200 Copeland Rd., Arlington, TX, 76011. Contact: Ed McGuinness, V.P. Fran. - Tel: (800) 445-0459. National provider of nursing services to health care industry. Special emphasis on rapidly growing home health care market. Also provide supplemental staffing to hospitals, nursing homes etc. Established: 1974 - Franchising Since: 1978 - No. of Units: Company Owned: 47 - Franchised: 53 - Franchise Fee: $19,500 - Royalty: 7% - Total Inv: $110,000 - $145,000 - Financing: Partial financing available to qualified prospects.

NUTRI/SYSTEM WEIGHT LOSS CENTERS
410 Horsham Rd., Horsham, PA, 19044-2014. Contact: Fran. Dept. - Tel: (215) 442-5300. Multi-disciplined weight-loss program. Established: 1971 - Franchising Since: 1976 - No. of Units: Company Owned: 149 - Franchised: 890 - Franchise Fee: $13,000 up - Royalty: 7% - Total Inv: $60,000 + fee - Financing: No.

NUVISION OPTICAL
NuVision, Inc.
2284 S. Ballenger Hwy., Flint, MI, 48503. Contact: Joanne Holmquist, Mgr., Fran. Oper. - Tel: (810) 767-0900. Provide complete optical services with retail sales of optical products. Many locations with one hour service and also has own manufacturing lab. Established: 1949 - Franchising Since: 1983 - No. of Units: Company Owned: 130 - Franchised: 48 - Franchise Fee: $15,000 - Royalty: 8.5% plus adv. fee of 7% - Total Inv: $60,000 - $500,000 - Financing: Yes.

O.P.T.I.O.N. CARE, INC.
100 Corporate N. Ste. 212, Bannockburn, IL, 60015. Contact: Jeff Mayhew, Fran. Dir. - Tel: (708) 615-1690. Home I.V. and nutritional services.

O2 EMERGENCY MEDICAL CARE SERVICE
5950 Pine Tree Dr., West Bloomfield, MI, 48322. Contact: Donald Stern, Pres. - Tel: (810) 661-0581. Program to all businesses of portable oxygen units (emergency), first aid kits, basic first aid and CPR. Training classes to employees. Established: 1986 - Franchising Since: 1989 - No. of Units: Company Owned: 1 - Franchised: 16 - Franchise Fee: varies depending on territory - Royalty: varies - Total Inv: up to $35,000 - Financing: Yes through third party leasing companies.

OPTION CARE
Option Care, Inc.
100 Corporate N., Ste. 212, Bannockburn, IL, 60015. Contact: Jeff Mayhew, Fran. Sales Mgr. - Tel: (708) 615-1690. Established: 1979 - Franchising Since: 1984 - No. of Units: Company Owned: 10 - Franchised: 180 - Franchise Fee: $2,500 - $35,000 - Royalty: 9% $1 M, 7% $2M, 5% over $2M per year.

OUR WEIGH
3340 Poplar, Ste. 136, Memphis, TN, 38111. Contact: Helen K. Seale, Owner - Tel: (901) 458-7546. A unique weight control group consisting of thirty minute meetings, behavior modification, exercise and most important, a nutritional diet that allows members to eat only foods they like. First in the field to introduce "food rewards", free weekly weigh in upon reaching desired weight. Established: 1974 - Franchising Since: 1974 - No. of Units: Company Owned: 8 - Franchised: 4 - Franchise Fee: $1,500 - Total Inv: $1,500 - Financing: No.

OXYGEN THERAPY INSTITUTE, INC.
11880 Belden Ct., Livonia, MI, 48150-1459. Contact: Marge Skrobola, Pres. - Tel: (313) 522-2700. Manufacturer of portable emergency oxygen equipment. Established: 1968 - Franchising Since: 1968 - No. of Units: Company Owned: 1 - Franchised: 46.

PARCOURSE LTD.
P.O. Box 38, Orinda, CA, 94563. Contact: Richard Cunningham, Pres. - Tel: (800) 227-3323, (415) 546-0808, (800) 624-5091. The manufacturer and marketing of parcourse fitness systems (indoor and outdoor exercise equipment). Franchising overseas only. Established: 1973.

PEAK PERFORMERS *
Peak Performers Franchise Corp.
34020 W. Seven Mile, #102, Livonia, MI, 48152. Contact: Phillip Stark, Pres. - Tel: (810) 477-5777, Fax: (810) 477-7032. Dentistry's first on call human resource dept. Temporary & contract staffing, direct placement, temp-hire consulting, personnel manual services exclusively for dentistry. Established: 1991 - Franchising Since: 1994 - No. of Units: Company Owned: 2 - Franchised: 1 - Franchise Fee: $22,500 - Royalty; 6% gross rev., 1% adv. - Total Inv: $60,000 to $100,000 - Financing: N/A.

PEARLE VISION
Pearle, Inc.
2534 Royal Lane, Dallas, TX, 75229. Contact: Deno Scoular, Fran. Sales Mgr. - Tel: (800) PEARLE-1. Optical retailer. Established: 1960 - Franchising Since: 1981 - No. of Units: Company Owned: 327 - Franchised: 361 - Franchise Fee: $30,000 - Royalty: 7.5% - Total Inv: $134,950 - $2,472,750 - Financing: Yes.

PERMANENT WEIGHT CONTROL CENTER
Permanent, Inc.
P.O. Box 1144, Orange, CT, 06477. Contact: Christina Toomey, Admin. Assist - Tel: (203) 891-0544. Weight loss center. Established: 1980 - Franchising Since: 1987 - No. of Units Company Owned: 8 - Franchised: 9 - Franchise Fee: $20,000 - Royalty: 7% 1st yr., 5% thereafter - Total Inv: $35-$40,000 - Financing: Yes, to qualified applicants.

PHYSICIAN DISPENSING SYSTEMS, INC.
24 N. Cliffe Dr., Wilmington, DE, 19809. Contact: Mel Messinger, Dir. of Fran. - Tel: (800) 992-0243 or (302) 792-1049. Marketing and placement of the rx-direct medication management system to physicians, which will enable the physician to dispense medications to their patients. Established: 1992 - Franchising Since: 1993 - Franchise Fee: $79,990 - Royalty: None - Total Inv: $79,990 - Financing: No.

PHYSICIANS WEIGHT LOSS CENTERS
PWLC of America, Inc.
395 Springside Dr., Akron, OH, 44333-2496. Contact: Dennis K. Brown, Dir. of Dev. - Tel: (216) 666-7952. With over 1 million clients served we are the only weight loss franchise that bridges the gap between expensive hospital "liquid only" programs and the "do it yourself" weight loss. We offer medically supervised programs and foods that work. Established: 1979 - Franchising Since: 1979 - No. of Units: Franchised: 105 - Franchise Fee: $15,000 - Royalty: 3.5% to 5.5% - Total Inv: $45,000 - $106,500 - Financing: None.

PILDES OPTICAL
Pildes Management Corp.
160 Le Grand Ave., Northvale, NJ, 07647. Contact: Daniel Pildes, Pres. - Tel: (201) 930-8896. Retail optical services. Store locations primarily greater metropolitan area. Established: 1982 - Franchising Since: 1982 - No. of Units: Company Owned: 1 - Franchised: 13 - Franchise Fee: $7,500 - Royalty: 8% gross - Total Inv: $100,000 to $300,000 - Financing: Purchase money mortgage.

PROCARE VISION CENTERS INC.
926 North 21 St., Newark, OH, 43055. Contact: Eva Pound-Bickle, Ph.D., Vice Pres. - Tel: (614) 366-7011. Retail eye and vision care franchises only sold to licensed eye care professionals. Established: 1981 - Franchising Since: 1985 - No. of Units: Company Owned: 1- Franchised: 19 -Franchise Fee: $8,000 - Royalty: 5%, 1% adv.- Approx. Total Inv: $125,000 - Financing: Through financial institutions.

PROFESSIONAL SITTER SERVICE
3820 Premier Ave., Memphis, TN, 38118. Contact: Franchise Dir./Pres. - Tel: (901) 867-0600. In home care by nurses and nurses aids for the sick, handicapped and the elderly. Established: 1987-Franchising Since: 1989-No. of Units Company Owned: 2-Franchise Fee: $10,000- Royalty:5%-Total Inv: $29,000 to $13,650-Financing: No.

RCI, INC.
P.O. Box 367, Central Village, CT, 06332. Contact: Ralph Campagna, Pres. - Tel: (203) 564-4018. Hearing aids in Montgomery Ward and other major retail stores. Established: 1961.

READING GLASSES TO GO
9131 King Arthur Dr., Dallas, TX, 75247. Contact: Robert Granoff, Pres. - Tel: (214) 631-6082. Retail stores selling only non prescription, custom made reading glasses. Priced from $16.00 - $49.00. Established: 1987 - Franchising Since: 1992 - No. of Units: Company Owned: 8 - Franchised: 4 - Franchise Fee: $19,000 - Royalty: .06% - Total Inv: $71,900 - $102,900 (incl. fran. fee) - Financing: No.

RELAX THE BACK STORE
Relax the Back Franchising Co.
3355 Bee Caves Rd., #7-705, Austin, TX, 78746-6673. Contact: Vern Stewart, C.O.O. - Tel: (800) 451-5168. Specialty retail stores offering products for relief and prevention of back pain and discomfort. Established: 1984 - Franchising Since: 1989 - No. of Units: Company Owned: 1 - Franchised: 29 - Franchise Fee: $19,500 - Royalty: 4%, 1% adv. - Total Inv: $75,000+ - Financing: N/A.

RESPOND FIRST AID SYSTEMS
P.O. Box 39925, Denver, CO, 80239. Contact: Tom Gray, Pres. - Tel: (303) 371-6800. Selling first aid cabinets and supplies, safety equipment and emergency care training classes to the industrial and office markets. Operating from customized, fully-stocked vans. Established: 1984 - Distributing Since: 1984 - No. of Units: Company Owned: 36 - Distributors: 36 - Total Inv: $25,000 - Financing: No.

ROBBINS' RETIREMENT COMMUNITIES *
430 South 600 West, Sontaquin, UT, 84655. Contact: Liz Christensen, Office Administrator - Tel: (801) 754-3231, Fax: (801) 754-3233. Franchise elderly care residential communities. Established: 1989 - Franchising Since: 1994 - No. of Units: Company Owned: 2 - Franchise Fee: 8% of dev. fee - Royalty: 5% of monthly gross - Financing: we provide a financial pkg. and will do a presentation.

SANVITA PROGRAMS
Medela, Inc.
P.O. Box 660, McHenry, IL, 60051-0660. Contact: Rona Cohen, Program Mgr. - Tel: (800) 435-5557. Selling and implementing maternal and child health programs in corporations through work/family, wellness or benefit departments. Established: 1992 - Franchising Since: 1992 - No. of Units: Franchised: 80 - Royalty: 12% of gross revenues - Total Inv: $750 for training, $38/mo. for 24 months for marketing support - Financing: No.

SINGER/SPECS DISCOUNT VISION CENTERS
Singer Specs., Inc.
1235 Westlakes Dr., Ste. 160, Berwyn, PA, 19312. Contact: Alan Singer, Pres. - Tel: (610) 695-0999. Full service optical retail outlets. Established: 1946 - Franchising Since: 1986 - No. of Units: Company Owned: 7 - Franchised: 29 - Franchise Fee: $15,000 - Royalty: 7%, 4% adv. - Total Inv: $65,000 - $184,500 - Financing: Financing available for total investment.

SITE FOR SORE EYES
10 Peninsula Blvd., Lynbrook, NY, 11563. Contact: Robert Greenberg, Pres. - Tel: (516) 887-2100. Retail - one hour optical service. Established: 1979 - Franchising Since: 1986 - No. of Units: Company Owned: 11 - Franchised: 10 - Franchise Fee: $25,000 - Royalty: 10% + 4% adv. - Total Inv: $175,000 - $250,000 - Financing: referral only.

SLENDER CENTER
6515 Grand Teton Plaza, Madison, WI, 53719. Contact: Martin Plotkin, Pres. - Tel: (608) 833-1477. Weight loss consultation educational program. One-on-one using real food. Programs for men, women, adolescents, nursing mothers & vegetarians. Educational materials include cookbook, tape, affirmation card deck set. Established: 1979 - Franchising Since: 1981 - No. of Units: Company Owned: 1 - Franchised: 16 - Franchise Fee: $12,000 - $27,000 - Royalty: 6% - Total Inv: $12,000 - $27,000 fran. fee + $12,000 - $30,000 start up - Financing: None.

SMOOTHIE KING
Smoothie King Franchises
2400 Veterans Blvd., Ste. 110, Kenner, LA, 70062. Contact: Richard Leveille Jr., V.P. Fran. Sales - Tel: (504) 467-4006, Fax: (504) 469-1274. Frozen nutritional fruit drinks, vitamin and protein supplements, and all the latest trends in sports nutrition. Established: 1973- Franchising Since: 1988- No. of Units: Company Owned: 3 - Franchised: 65 - Franchise Fee: $20,000 - Royalty: 5% + 3% adv. - Total Inv: $90,500 - $198,500, $50,000 cash - Financing: Through lending companies for qualified individuals.

STERLING OPTICAL CORP.
10 Peninsula Blvd., Lynbrook, NY, 11563-2464. Contact: Jerry Darnell, VP Fran. - Tel: (516) 887-2100. Provides quality eyewear and optometric services to the public at convenient retail locations. Established: 1912 - Franchising Since: 1987 - No. of Units: Company Owned: 110 - Franchised: 100 - Franchise Fee: $20,000 - Royalty: 8% - Total Inv: $200,000 - $500,000 - Financing: No.

STOP SMOKING PLAN
P.O. Box 232, E. Amherst, NY, 14051. Contact: Ricki Nixon, Owner, Pres. - Tel: (716) 688-4573. Offer a business opportunity to teach a 10 day smoking cessation program & sell an at-home kit. All necessary supplies & training manual with phone contact for set up provided. Established: 1981 - Franchising Since: 1987 - No. of Units: Company Owned: 1 - Franchised: 11 - Franchise Fee: $1,500 - Royalty: None - Financing: No.

TEXAS STATE OPTICAL
TSO, Inc.
4925 W. Cardinal Dr., Beaumont, TX, 77705. Contact: Keith R. Albright, Exec. V.P. - Tel: (409) 842-4113, Fax: (409) 842-3522. Franchised professional optical practice / retail optical dispensary. Established: 1934 - Franchising Since: 1972 - No. of Units: Company Owned: 2 - Franchised: 153 - Franchise Fee: Varies - Royalty: 4% - Total Inv: $92,500 - $438,500 - Financing: No.

THE RIGHT WAY BY POLLY
416 New London Rd., Newark, DE, 19711. Contact: Polly Grimaldi, Pres. - Tel: (302) 454-1970, Fax: (302) 731-5524. A business designed to augment a physician's existing practice by offering the patient lifestyle changes in addition to conventional medical treatments. A comprehensive program based on nutrition, exercise and stress management giving the physician the opportunity to increase both services and revenues. Established: 1984 - Franchising Since: 1994 - No. of Units: Company Owned: 1 - Franchised: 1 - Franchise Fee: $25,000 - Royalty: 10% of monthly gross revenue with a min. of $200 - Total Inv: $25,000 initial fee, $1,850 initial inven., $6,000 security deposit - Financing: No.

ULTIMATE TAN, THE
New Business Inv Corp.
408 Warren Ave., Ste. AA, Normal, IL, 61761. Contact: Lawrence Pritts, Pres. - Tel: (309) 888-9988. Tanning salons. Established: 1984 - No. of Units: Company Owned: 4 - Franchised: 1 - Franchise Fee: $20,000 - Royalty: 8% weekly - Total Inv: $100,000 - $125,000 - Financing: Yes.

WOMEN'S HEALTH BOUTIQUE
Women's Health Boutique Franchise System, Inc.
315 S. Fredonia, Longview, TX, 75601. Contact: Vicki D. Jones, CEO - Tel: (903) 236-0886. Health-related products and services for women: mastectomy, maternity, wigs, personal care, nutrition and wellness, in a beautiful, boutique setting. Established: 1991 - Franchising Since: 1993 - No. of Units: Franchised: 6 - Franchise Fee: $25,000 to $35,000 - Royalty: 5% - Total Inv: $122,500 to $191,500 includes fran. fee, start-up costs, training cost, inventory, working capital - Financing: No, except assistance in loan package preparation.

WOMEN'S WORKOUT WORLD
16015 Harlem Ave., Tinley Park, IL, 60477-1631. Contact: Shari Whiley, CEO - Tel: (708) 429-7766. Offering a unique exercise program for women at an affordable price. The program offers state-of-the-art exercise equipment, weight loss and continuous exercise classes within a modern health club setting. Established: 1969 - Franchising Since: 1986 - No. of Units: Company Owned: 15 - Franchised: 12 - Franchise Fee: $35,000 - Royalty: 10% - Total Inv: $150,000-$225,000 - Financing: None.

HOME FURNISHINGS

3 DAY BLINDS
2220 E. Cerritos Ave., Anaheim, CA, 92806. Contact: Jeff de Boer, Dir. of Fran. Sales - Tel: (800) 800-3329 Ext. 333. One of the largest custom window covering retail chains worldwide. 129 stores currently operating. Retail store location and shop at home service maximizes your business. Computerized ordering system, training & complete support provided. Established: 1984 - Franchising Since: 1993 - No. of Units: Company Owned: 129 - Franchise Fee: $20,000 - Royalty: varies - Total Inv: w/ fran. fee - $68,500 - $108,500 - Financing: No.

A SHADE BETTER, INC. *
3615 Superior Ave., Cleveland, OH, 44114. Contact: Wendy Beerbower, Exec. V.P. - Tel: (800) 722-8676. Distinctive retail stores selling beautiful lamp shades, lamps and accessories. Franchisees will also have the opportunity to develop and service the wholesale market in their exclusive territory. A Shade Better, Inc. has combined streamlined operating systems, efficient distribution and high profile marketing techniques. And we've put them together with support from a management team bolstered by 20 years in the industry. Established: 1989 - Franchising Since: 1994 - No. of Units: Company Owned: 5 - Franchised: 7 - Franchise Fee: $35,000 - Royalty: 6% - Total Inv: $115,500 - $147,000 inc. fran. fee & inven. - Financing: No.

A WORLD OF DECORATING
World of Decorating, Inc.
4731 W. Atlantic Ave., #21, Delray Beach, FL, 33445-3866. Contact: Jay Terrez, Fran. Dir. - Tel: (407) 637-8319, Fax: (407) 637-8428. Unique operation allows franchisee to offer all types of decorating products such as window treatments, floor coverings, wallpaper, furnishings, accessories etc. Franchisee purchases with nat'l. discount prices but has mom & pop overhead. Can operate from Van with home base or open Retail Center. Master Franchises avail. Established: 1993 - Franchising Since: 1994 - No. of Units: Franchised: 8 - Franchise Fee: $12,500 & $19,500 - Royalty: 5% of gross sales - Total Inv: $12,500 fran. fee for Van franchise + $3,000 working capital; $19,500 fee for retail center + approx. $30,000 for build out & working capital.

ABOFF'S
410 New York Ave., Huntington, NY, 11743. Contact: Michael Aboff, V.P. - Tel: (516) 427-2000. Paint and wallpaper. Established: 1928 - Franchising Since: 1970 - No. of Units: 12 - Approx. Inv: $15,000.

AMERICA'S CARPET GALLERY
Magic Marketing, Inc.
4395 Electric Rd., Roanoke, VA, 24014. Contact: Sands Woody, Pres. - Tel: (800) 344-7557 or (703) 772-1729. Retail floor covering and home decorating stores catering to middle-to upper income households. Established: 1986 - Franchising Since: 1992 - No. of Units: Company Owned: 4 - Franchised: 12 - Franchise Fee: $15,000 - Royalty: 2% - 4% depending on sales - Total Inv: $85,000 - $185,000 depending on store size and location - Financing: No.

ART SOURCE AND DESIGN
Decorative Arts, Inc.
200 E. Hill Street, Oklahoma City, OK, 73105. , Fran. Dir. - Tel: (901) 867-0600. Manufacturer of framed wall decor. Established: 1985 - Franchising Since: 1992 - No. of Units: Company Owned: 1 - Franchise Fee: $25,000 - Royalty: 6% - Total Inv: $90,150 - $146,000 (Working Cap., Inven., Equip., Real Estate and Re-Dec.) - Financing: No.

ATTIC LTD, THE
7211 Charles Way, Peoria, IL, 61614. Contact: Jim M. Tedford , Fran. Dir. - Tel: (309) 692-6109. Retail store selling pre-owned home furnishings on consignment. Established: 1980 - Franchising since: 1991 - No. of Units: Company Owned: 1 - Franchise Fee: $15,000 - Royalty: 10% of commissions (approx. 4% - 5% of sales) - Total Inv: $15,000 fran. fee, $5,000 adv., $5,000 cash, $8,000 other - Financing: None.

BUDGET BLINDS, INC.
3176 Pullman St., Ste. 110, Costa Mesa, CA, 92626. Contact: Vince Paglia, Pres. - Tel: (800) 420-5374. Window coverings. Established: 1992 - Franchising Since: 1994 - No. of Units: Company Owned: 1 - Franchised: 63 - Franchise Fee: $12,950 - Royalty: 5% - Total Inv: $20,000 includes $3,600 adv. and work. cap. - Financing: Yes.

CARPET NETWORK
109 Gaither Dr., Ste. 302, Mt. Laurel, NJ, 08054. Contact: Kenneth Sacks, V.P. - Tel: (800) 428-1067, Fax: (609) 273-0160. Mobile floor covering & window treatment business that brings over 3,000 choices directly to the home or business. Extensive training, 24 hour support. Buy direct from major mills, large exclusive territories. Established: 1991 - Franchising Since: 1992 - No. of Units: Company Owned: 1 - Franchised: 40 - Franchise Fee: starting from $15,500 - Royalty: 5% of gross sales - Total Inv: start-up $3,400 plus van and work. cap. - Financing: No.

CERTA PROPAINTERS LTD.
P.O. Box 718, Valley Forge, PA, 19482-0718. Contact: Charlie Chase, Pres. - Tel: (610) 983-9411. Painting (interior & exterior), wallpaper, decorative finishes such as rag rolling, sponge painting, polychrome products etc. Established: 1991 - Franchising Since: 1991 - No. of Units: Franchised: 35 - Franchise Fee: $15,000 - Royalty: $1,000 per month - Total Inv: $22,000; fran. fee plus $7,000 capital investment - Financing: Yes.

COLOR TILE & CARPET
Color Tile, Inc.
515 Houston, Ft. Worth, TX, 76102. Contact: Gary T. Lomax, Sr. V.P. Franchise - Tel: (800) 688-8063. Retail flooring, window and wall coverings. Established: 1953 - Franchising Since: 1989 - No. of Units: Company Owned: 673 - Franchised: 200 - Franchise Fee: $25,500 - Royalty: 4.25% on-going support; 9% advertising/merchandising/distribution - Total Inv: Fran. fee plus $60,000 inven., $48,000 fixtures - Financing: Friendly lenders.

CONSIGN & DESIGN FURNISHINGS
Consign & Design Franchise Corp.
1826 W. Broadway Rd., Ste. #3, Mesa, AZ, 85202. Contact: Marcus Curtis, Pres. - Tel: (602) 461-0400. Home furnishings retailer dealing in new and gently used home furnishings, accessories, art and antiques from model homes, new liquidations, estates and fine homes. Established: 1979 - Franchising Since: 1993 - No. of Units: Company Owned: 5 - Franchise Fee: $24,000 - Royalty: 2% - Total. Inv: $70,000 - 130,000 - Financing: No.

DECOR-AT-YOUR-DOOR INTERNATIONAL *
Deco Home Stores, Inc.
3200 East Hwy. 50, Ste. 7, Camino, CA, 95709. Contact: Norman McGee, Pres. - Tel: (800) 936-3326, Fax: (916) 644-6073. One of the best franchises in America. Blinds & carpet business, selling from a custom mobile showcase to your customers at great prices. Royalty only $50 mo. or 2%, no quotas, no renewal charge, no transfer charge. No experience necessary, we train you, great part or full time job. Established: 1983 -

Franchising Since: 1995 - No. of Units: Franchised: 7 - Franchise Fee: $2,500 - Royalty: $50/mo. or 2% - Total Inv: $2,500 fee plus $6,400 - Total from $8,900 - Financing: No.

DECORATING DEN
Decorating Den Systems, Inc.
7910 Woodmont Ave., Bethesda, MD, 20814. Contact: Marc Kiekenapp, Dir. of Fran. Mktg. - Tel: (800) 428-1366. Full service interior decorating franchise business. Provides affordable, shop-at-home decorating service. Decorator brings thousands of samples to your home or office. Free consultation. Established: 1969 - Franchising Since: 1970 - No. of Units: Franchised: 1,000 - Franchise Fee: $9,900 - $23,900 - Royalty: 7% to 15% - Total Inv: $18,530 - $55,130 (includes start up costs) - Financing: Yes.

DECOWALL
5413 Rhea Ave., Tarzana, CA, 91356. Contact: Arni Heiderich, Pres. - Tel: (818) 884-6322. Service of applying wallpaper designs with design-embossed paint rollers in 1, 2 or 3 colors. Hundreds of design and color combinations possible. Established: 1972 - Franchising Since: 1974 - No. of Units: Company Owned: 2 - Franchised: 200 - Total Inv: $5,950 equip., manual, sales aids, training - Financing: Yes.

EURO-WALL STYLES
Rol-A-Decor
10022 Iroquois St., Apple Valley, CA, 92308. Contact: Martin Logan, Owner - Tel: (619) 247-1900. Design wall printing (European). The wallpaper look with paint. Home decorating. Established: 1979.

EXPRESSIONS CUSTOM FURNITURE
Expressions In Fabrics, Ltd.
1921 Petra Lane, Placentia, CA, 92670. Contact: Bobby McKnight - Tel: (714) 577-8400. Manufacturer of custom upholstered furniture/access. sales. Established: 1978 - Franchising Since: 1983 - No. of Units: Company Owned: 15 - Franchised: 61 - Franchise Fee: $30,000 - Royalty: 3.5% of gross sales of business - Total Inv: $241,500 to $362,000 - Financing: Franchisee must secure financing.

FLOOR COVERINGS INTERNATIONAL
5182 Old Dixie Highway, Forest Park, GA, 30050. Contact: Franchise Counselor - Tel: (800) 955-4324, (404) 361-5047. Floor Coverings International is a mobile floor covering retailer that brings the carpet store to the customer's front door. FCI's mobile service concept means that there are no high overhead costs. Our CarpetVan is loaded with a store full of colorful, name brand styles that customers coordinate with their existing decor and lighting. Established: 1985 - Franchising Since: 1988 - No. of Units: Franchised: 330 - Franchise Fee: $14,000 - $29,000 - Royalty: 5%, 2% ad. fund - Total Inv: $18,500 to $34,500: fran. fee plus $4,500 - $5,500 start up costs - Financing: No.

FURNITURE WEEKEND
Furniture Weekend Franchising, Inc.
21 W. Main St., Malone, NY, 12953. Contact: Larry Kriff, Pres. - Tel: (518) 483-1328 or (800) 562-1606. Retail furniture store, open only Fri, Sat, Sun. Simplified business system, proven to eliminate most problems normally associated with the retail furniture business. Training and ongoing support provided. Established: 1982 - Franchising Since: 1990 - No. of Units: Company Owned: 2 - Franchised: 7 - Franchise Fee: $15,000 ($10,000 conversion) - Royalty: 5%, 1% adv. - Total Inv: $89,000 - $145,500 incl. fran. fee - Financing: No.

HOUSE OF BLINDS & MORE
House Of Blinds & More Franchise Corp.
23300 W. 8 Mile Rd., Southfield, MI, 48034. Contact: Barry Balbes, Pres. - Tel: (810) 357-4710. Fabrication, installation and sale of custom window treatment products such as mini-blinds, vertical blinds, shutters, shades, draperies. Established: 1959 - Franchising Since: 1993 - No. of Units: Company Owned: 14 - Franchised: 4 - Franchise Fee: $15,000 - Royalty: 0 - 5% - Total Inv: $53,600 - $116,300 - Financing: Yes, $10,000 of franchise fee.

INTERNATIONAL HOME MARKETING SYSTEMS, INC.
1450 Mitchell Blvd., Schaumburg, IL, 60193. Contact: John Belltramo, Fran. Dir. - Tel: (708) 980-2400. Consumer club - memberships for home furnishings. Established: 1972 - Franchising Since: 1986 - No. of Units: Company Owned: 3 - Franchised: 3 - Franchise Fee: $25,000 - $37,500 - Financing: No.

MOUNTAIN COMFORT FURNISHINGS
Mountain Comfort Furnishings, Inc.
507 Summit Blvd., Frisco, CO, 80443. Contact: Mr. Bill Jarski, Owner - Tel: (303) 668-3661. Home furnishings featuring solid woods such as oak and pine. Upholstered custom and specialty casual mountain contemporary. Established: 1985 - Franchising Since: 1990 - No. of Units: Company Owned: 2 - Franchised: 2 - Franchise Fee: $22,500 - Royalty: 5%, mktg. fund 1.5% - Total Inv: $120,655 - $158,555 - Financing: Yes. when available.

NAKED FURNITURE
Summit-Naked Furniture, Inc.
P.O. Box F, 1157 Lackawanna Trail, Clarks Summit, PA, 18411. Contact: Bruce C. MacGowan, President - Tel: (800) 352-2522. Home furnishings retailer featuring custom-finished and ready-to-finish real wood furniture. Established: 1972 - Franchising Since: 1976 - No. of Units: Company Owned: 3 - Franchised: 40 - Franchise Fee: $19,500 - Royalty: 4%, 0% adv. - Total Inv: $143,000 - $245,000 with $75,500 - $122,500 in available cash - Financing: $30,000 - $40,000.

NORWALK - THE FURNITURE IDEA
100 Furniture Pkwy., Norwalk, OH, 44857. Contact: Bob Young, V.P., Fran. - Tel: (419) 668-4461, (800) 806-8786, Fax: (419) 663-0021. Custom upholstered furniture specialty stores. Offers consumers choice of 2,000 fabrics and leathers available on any of 500 styles with delivery in just 35 days. Franchising Since: 1987 - No. of Units: Company Owned: 7 - Franchised: 43 - Franchise Fee: $35,000 - Royalty: 0 - Initial Inv: $250,000 - Financing: Third party affiliation.

RAINBOW CARPET COLOR CENTERS
Rainbow Carpet Centers Inc.
P.O. Box 4085, Dalton, GA, 30719-1085. Contact: Nick Howard, Chairman/Partner - Tel: (706) 278-4063. Marketing company offering exclusive license agreements to home furnishings retailers or to new businesses. Established: 1991 - Licensing Since: 1992 - No. of Units: Licensed: 50 - License Fee: $5,000.

ROCHE-BOBOIS U.S.A. LTD.
183 Madison Ave., New York, NY, 10016. Contact: Michael Lerner, Pres. - Tel: (212) 889-5304. Exclusive high-fashion contemporary retail furniture. Established: 1974 - Franchising Since: 1974 - No. of Units: 24 - Franchise Fee: $20,000 - Royalty: 6% - Total Inv: $350,000 - $400,000.

SIESTA SLEEP SHOPS INC.
661 Falmouth Rd., Apt. 117R, Mashpee, MA, 02649-3323. Contact: Manuel Glickman, Owner - Tel: (617) 344-4888. Bedding, mattresses and items related to beds. No sleep sofas or upholstered furniture. Limited to the Massachusetts area. Established: 1955 - Licensing Since: 1960 - No. of Units: Company Owned: 7 - Licensed: 5 - Franchise Fee: $5,000 - Total Inv: $20,000 - $40,000 - Royalty: 5% - Financing: yes.

SLUMBERLAND INTERNATIONAL
3060 Centerville Rd., Little Canada, MN, 55117. Contact: Ken Larson, Pres. - Tel: (612) 482-7500. Specialty retailer of quality home furnishings. Established: 1968 - Franchising Since: 1968 - No. of Units: Company Owned: 13 - Franchised: 23 - Franchise Fee: $15,000 - Royalty: 3% - Total Inv: varies - Financing: No.

STELLARVISION/STARROOMS
Startech Inc.
5812 E. Burnside St., Portland, OR, 97215. Contact: Jim Stotler, Pres. - Tel: (503) 231-9243, Fax: (503) 233-8982. Home decorating. Paints starry skies - glows in the dark - bedrooms. Established: 1984 - Franchising Since: 1986 - No. of Units: Company Owned: 2 - Franchised: 14 - Franchise Fee: $4,800 - Royalty: None - Total Inv: $6,800 - Financing: No.

UNIVERSITY PAINTERS
University Painters, Inc.
2111 Eisenhower Ave., #300, Alexandria, VA, 22314. Contact: David R. Zier, V.P. - Tel: (800) 390-4848, (703) 548-6336. Franchisor of residential house painting franchises. Franchises are owned primarily by college student business owners for a one to three year period. Established: 1990 - Franchising Since: 1991 - No. of Units: Franchised: 90 - Franchise Fee: Varies - Royalty: Varies - Total Inv: Under $2,000 - Financing: Yes.

WALLPAPERS TO GO
Wallpapers To Go, Inc.
16825 North Chase Dr., Ste. 900, Houston, TX, 77060. Contact: Darlete Brents, Coord., Fran. Dev. - Tel: (800) 843-7094, (713) 874-0800. Large national chain of in-stock wallcoverings, special order wallcoverings, window treatments, fabrics, paint supplies & decorative accessories. Stores designed, stocked & merchandised to appeal to growing do-it-yourself market. Established: 1986 - Franchising Since: 1986 - No. of Units: Company Owned: 13 - Franchised: 65 - Franchise Fee: $25,000 - Royalty: 8% - Total Inv: $122,000 - $133,500 - Financing: Assistance in securing financing.

WATERBED EMPORIUM
Waterbed Emporium Franchising Co.
7120 Krick Rd., Walton Hills, OH, 44146-4418. Contact: Bruce Davis, V.P. Oper. - Tel: (216) 786-8800. Retail waterbeds and bedroom furniture. Established: 1987 - Franchising Since: 1989 - No. of Units: Company Owned: 1 - Franchised: 21 - Franchise Fee: $18,000 - Royalty: 3% of wholesale purchases - Approx. Inv: $76,950 - $141,800 - Financing: Help secure financing.

WINDO VANGO *
Owners' Alliance, Inc.
P.O. Box 805, Fogelsville, PA, 18051. Contact: Franchise Dev. - Tel: (800) 75-VANGO. Home-based window covering franchise using vans to deliver the highest quality products and service directly to customers' homes. Established: 1993 - Franchising Since: 1994 - No. of Units: Franchised: 27 - Franchise Fee: $12,750 - Royalty: 4% declining with volume - Total Inv: $9,000 to $14,000 plus fran. fee - Financing: No.

WINDOW WORKS
Window Works International, Inc.
6321 Bury Dr., Ste. 2, Eden Prairie, MN, 55346. Contact: Ed Johnson, V.P. of Operations - Tel: (612) 934-5665. Window Works is a retail store that sells & installs custom draperies, shutters & blinds. Established: 1978 - Franchising Since: 1979 - No. of Units: Franchised: 18 - Franchise Fee: $17,500 - Royalty: 4%, 1% adv. - Total Inv: $65,000 - $95,000 - Financing: Yes-up to 70%.

HOUSE/PET SITTING SERVICES

CRITTER CARE
8261 Summa, #F, Baton Rouge, LA, 70809. Contact: Stan Bumgarner, Pres. - Tel: (504) 769-4160, Fax: (504) 769-4268. Professional in-home pet care service, plant and homecare. Product sales home-based. Continual training and support provided. Established: 1980 - Franchising Since: 1984 - No. of Units: Franchised: 17 - Franchise Fee: $8,500 - Royalty: 5% + 2% adv. - Total Inv: $4,000 - $10,000 start up cost - Financing: No.

HOMEWATCH INTERNATIONAL, INC.
2865 S. Colorado Blvd., Ste. 319, Denver, CO, 80222. Contact: Paul Sauer, Pres. - Tel: (303) 758-7290 or (800) 777-9770. Customers know they can rely on Homewatch Professionals to care for all their household & property needs. One phone call does it all. Home services include: elderly care service, business and vacation services and a broad range of maintenance/repair services. Established: 1973 - Franchising Since: 1986 - No. of Units: Company Owned: 4 - Franchised: 26 - Franchise Fee: $18,500 - Royalty: 5% - Total Inv: $5,000 + fran. fee - Financing: X multi units (other considerations).

PET NANNY®
Pet Nanny of America, Inc.
1000 Long Blvd., Ste. 9, Lansing, MI, 48911. Contact: Rebecca Brevitz, Pres. - Tel: (517) 694-4400, Fax: (517) 694-5113. Professional, personalized in-home pet care. Franchisees are trained via vet-developed video program plus training by corporate executives covering all aspects of business operations. Extensive supplies. Established: 1983 - Franchising Since: 1986 - No. of Units: Company Owned: 1 - Franchised: 18 - Franchise Fee: $8,700 - Royalty: 5% or $25/week minimum - Total Inv: Fran. fee + additional from $1,500 - $4,500 - Financing: In-house to qualified applicants covering up to 75% of initial franchise fee.

PET-TENDERS®
Pet-Tenders® International, Inc.
P.O. Box 23622, San Diego, CA, 92193. Contact: Cheryl Dagostaro, Pres. - Tel: (619) 298-3033. In-home pet/housesitting service. Established: 1983 - Franchising Since: 1990 - No. of Units: Company Owned: 1 - Franchised: 4 - Franchise Fee: $8,500 - Royalty: 5%, 2% adv. - Total Inv: $10,500 - $13,900 - Financing: Qualified applicants.

PETS ARE INN
Pets Are Inn, Inc.
7723 Tanglewood Ct., Ste. 150, Minneapolis, MN, 55439. Contact: Jim Platt, CEO - Tel: (800) 248-7387, Fax: (612) 941-4919. Pet boarding in private "host families". Established: 1982 - Franchising Since: 1986 - No. of Units: Franchised: 50 - Franchise Fee: $15,000 - Royalty: 10% - Total Inv: $20,000 - $25,000 (fran. fee, supplies, computer & software) - Financing: Yes.

POOCH PROTECTORS®
P.O. Box 550, Lewiston, NY, 14092-0550. Contact: Zack Williams, V.P. - Tel: (716) 754-4669. Professional, bonded pet & house nanny. Established: 1990 - Franchising Since: 1991 - No. of Units: Company Owned: 1 - Franchised: 8 - Franchise Fee: $7,000 - $10,000 - Royalty: 5%, 2% adv. - Total Inv: $21,000 - $30,000 - Financing: No.

SITTERS UNLIMITED
23015 Del Lago Dr., #D2-118, Laguna Hills, CA, 92653. Contact: Sharon Gastel, Owner - Tel: (800) 328-1191. Childcare, elderly companion care, home and pet care services on both a temporary and permanent basis. Convention services available. Established: 1979 - Franchising Since: 1983 - No. of Units: Company Owned: 1 - Franchised: 10 - Franchise Fee: $8,000 - $15,000 - Royalty: 5% - 4% - Total Inv: $8,000 - $15,000 + work. cap. - Financing: Yes.

LAUNDRY & DRY CLEANING

APPARELMASTER, INC.
P.O. Box 62687, Cincinnati, OH, 45262. Contact: George Beetz, Mgr./ Fran. Sales - Tel: (513) 772-7721. System enabling drycleaners/launderers to diversify into industrial uniform rental. Established: 1971 - Franchising Since: 1971 - No. of Units: Company Owned: 1 - Franchised: 215 - Franchise Fee; $17,000 - $12,800 - Royalty: 5% down to 0.5% - Total Inv: $25,000 - Financing: No.

AWC COMMERCIAL WINDOW COVERINGS
AWC Commercial Window Coverings, Inc.
825 W. Williamson Ave., Fullerton, CA, 92632. Contact: Jim Wells, V.P. - Tel: (714) 879-3880, (800) 252-2280. Mobile dry cleaning services, provided on location to commercial customers; including sales, installation and repair of all types of window coverings. Utilizing the customer base, references and reputation of the franchisor developed over the last thirty years. Nationwide contracts are transferred to franchisees. Established: 1963 - Franchising Since: 1992 - No. of Units:

Company Owned: 4 - Franchised: 5 - Franchise Fee: $35,000 - Royalty: 5% to 12.5%, 2.5% adv. - Total Inv: $122,520 - $202,350 - Financing: Yes, equipment lease, 3rd party.

COACHMAN DRY CLEANING & LAUNDRY
1 Tower Bridge, Ste. 800, W. Conshohocken, PA, 19428. Contact: Delores Schmitzel, C.O.O. - Tel: (800) 841-8484. Pick up and delivery service of dry cleaning at people's homes and/or offices. Established: 1991 - Franchising Since: 1993 - No. of Units: Franchised: 24 - Franchise Fee: $4,500 - Royalty: varies, 1% adv. - Total Inv: $29,000 - Financing: Yes.

COMET CLEANERS
Jack Godfrey & Sons, Inc.
406 West Division, Arlington, TX, 76011. Contact: Jack Godfrey, Jr., V.P. - Tel: (817) 461-3555. Drycleaning and professional laundry equipment sales and installation. Initial assistance, guidance and support is offered in every phase of your Comet operation including management, advertising, and promotion. Up to two weeks of training at a local plant with follow up. Assistance in site selection. Professional store design. Established: 1947 - Franchising Since: 1967 - No. of Units: Company Owned: 13 - Franchised: 285 - Franchise Fee: $10,000 initially; $1,000 year thereafter - Royalty: 0 - Total Inv: $150,000 - $200,000 - Financing: Yes.

DRY CLEANING STATION
1000 Shelard Pky., Ste. 320, Minneapolis, MN, 55426-4919. Contact: John Campbell, C.E.O. - Tel: (800) 655-8134 or (612) 541-0832. Discount dry cleaning stores located in high drive-by traffic locations in medium to larger cities. Full franchising services available. Established: 1987 - Franchising Since: 1990 - No. of Units: Company Owned: 3 - Franchised: 21- Franchise Fee: $15,000 - Royalty: 5% - Total Inv: $170,000 - $270,000 - Financing: $105,000 - $200,000 thru leasing of equipment.

DRY CLEANING WORLD & LAUNDRY WORLD
World Franchises, Inc.
3760 Fishcreek Rd., Stow, OH, 44224-4379. Contact: Jerry Freeman, Sec. & Assist. Training Dir. - Tel: (216) 673-9806. Dry cleaning and laundry services. Also offering coin laundry. Established: 1987 - Franchising Since: 1988 - No. of Units: Company Owned: 2 - Franchise Fee: $25,000 - Royalty: payable wkly., shall be equal to the greater of 5% of the total gross sales for the week or $100 - Total Inv: The est. initial investment required including the initial fran. fee may range from a low of $90,000 to a high of $405,000.

DRYCLEAN-USA
Dryclean-USA Franchise Company
1875 W. Commercial Blvd., #140, Fort Lauderdale, FL, 33309-3067. Contact: Jorge Salvat, Dir. of Operations - Tel: (305) 493-6700. Dryclean USA is part of Johnson Cleaners, the largest dry cleaning company in the world. A master franchise program was established in 1992, offering exclusive development territories in the US and worldwide. Established: 1976 - Franchising Since: 1977 - No. of Units: 281 - Royalty: 5% gross sales - Total Inv: $99,500 - $250,000 - Financing: Assistance.

EAGLE CLEANERS
Great American Cleaners Inc.
1750 University Dr., Ste. 111, Coral Springs, FL, 33071. Contact: Art Savard, Sr. V.P. - Tel: (800) 275-9751. Drycleaning and laundry using state of the art, EPA approved equipment and stylish designs in an industry with history of high profitability...training, field operations and marketing support...turnkey. Established: 1991 - Franchising Since: 1993 - No. of Units: Company Owned: 1 - Franchised: 31 - Franchise Fee: $10,000 - Royalty: $75/wk. yr. 1; $125/wk yr. 2; $175/wk. thereafter - Total Inv: $114,900 plus fran. fee - Financing: Financing and leasing packages.

HARVEY WASHBANGERS®
Harvey Washbangers® Franchise Corporation
110 29th Ave. N., Nashville, TN, 37203. Contact: David Harvey, Fran. Dev. - Tel: (615) 322-1270. A high tech blend of laundry, restaurant and bar facilities. Award-winning menu and friendly atmosphere make a comfortable, neighborhood place that people come back to again and again. Established: 1986 - Franchising Since: 1994 - No. of Units: Company Owned: 1 - Franchise Fee: $20,000 - Royalty: 5% of gross sales, 2% adv. - Total Inv: Equip. $210,000; Leasehold Inv. $123,000; Working cap. $120,600 - Financing: Third party leasing avail. on laundry equip.

HIS & HERS IRONING SERVICE
Mairs, Inc.
P.O. Box 480066, Kansas City, MO, 64148-0066. Contact: Kenneth Mairs, V.P. - Tel: (816) 941-8383. Ironing and laundry featuring pick-up and delivery. Serving commercial and residential customers. Established: 1983 - Franchising Since: 1985 - No. of Units: Company Owned: 1 - Franchised: 1 - Franchise Fee: $10,000 - Royalty: 5% + 2% adv. - Total Inv: additional $10,000-$25,000 start-up capital - Financing: No.

JIM DANDY CLEANERS
Jim Dandy International, Inc.
13273 Ventura Blvd., Ste. 101, Studio City, CA, 91604-1840. Contact: Mary Ann Leiker, Site Locator - Tel: (800) 635-0516. Retail discount dry cleaning stores with on going support in all areas. Established: 1985 - Licensing Since: 1990 - No. of Units: Company Owned: 1 - Licensed: 18 - Total Inv: $195,000 - Financing: $135,000.

MAYTAG HOMESTYLE LAUNDRIES
Amerivend Corp.
4101 S.W. 73rd. Ave., Miami, FL, 33155. Contact: R. Geronimo, Regional Sales Mgr. - Tel: (800) 780-WASH, Fax: (305) 264-7312. Since 1959, 1000 coin laundry & dry cleaning stores have been built. Established: 1959 - Franchising Since: 1961 - No. of Units: Company Owned: 1 - Franchised: over 1,000 - Franchise Fee: None - Royalty: None - Total Inv: Equip. $100,000 - $150,000 - , leasehold $65,000, impact fees $20,000 - $50,000 - Financing: Yes 5-7 years lease/purchase. We export equipment and expertise too.

MR. WISE CLEANERS
Drycleaning Systems International Inc.
6004 Anaheim, Ste. A, Albuquerque, NM, 87113. Contact: Gene Wise, Pres. - Tel: (505) 828-0771. Drycleaning franchisor, sales and services. Established: 1985 - Franchising Since: 1985 - No. of Units: Franchised: 9 - Franchise Fee: $25,000 - Royalty: 4% - Total Inv: equip. & install. $175,000 - Financing: None.

ONE HOUR MARTINIZING DRY CLEANING
Martin Franchises Inc.
2005 Ross Ave., Cincinnati, OH, 45212-2099. , Dev. Director - Tel: (513) 351-6211 or(800) 827-0207. Complete start-up assistance, comprehensive training program, location/site assistance with NDS computerized demographics capabilities, grand opening marketing package and on-going local store and marketwide promotional programs, field and operations assistance. Established: 1949 - Franchising Since: 1949 - No. of Units: 823 in 42 states and 17 countries - Franchise Fee: $25,000 - Royalty: 4% monthly gross sales, .5% - 4% monthly gross sales - advertising - Total Inv: Low as $146,500 - Financing: Assistance.

ONE PRICE DRY CLEANERS
Olympus One Price Dry Cleaning, Inc.
5100 W. Copans Rd., Ste. 410, Margate, FL, 33063. Contact: Irv Rosenblatt, Pres. - Tel: (305) 974-6800, (800) 367-1276. Dry cleaning stores, all garments cleaned for same price. Volume generating dry cleaning plants due to low one price. Established: 1985 - Franchising Since: 1985 - No. of Units: Company Owned: 6 - Franchised: 32 - Franchise Fee: None - Total Inv: $124,900 - $159,900 - Financing: Yes.

PRESSED 4 TIME
Pressed 4 Time, Inc.
124 Boston Post Rd., Sudbury, MA, 01776-2406. Contact: James Markson, Pres. - Tel: (800) 423-8711. Mobile dry cleaning services, utilizing specially marked delivery vehicles. Established: 1987 - Franchising Since: 1989 - No. of Units: Company Owned: 1 - Franchised: 67 - Franchise Fee: $9,500 - Royalty: Varies $300/mo. per van or 3.5% of sales, whichever is greater - Total Inv: $11,900 to $17,200 - Financing: None.

SIP 'N SPIN *
Sip 'N Spin Franchise Inc.
207 W. 10th, Hays, KS, 67601. Contact: Kris, Pres. - Tel: (913) 625-9292. Full service laundry, full service bar & grill, full service salon. Established: 1994 - Franchising Since: 1995 - No. of Units: Company Owned: 1 - Franchise Fee: $25,000 - Royalty: 5% gross, 1% adv. - Total Inv: $25,000 fee, $225,000 investment - Financing: Yes.

STAR CLEANERS, INC.
5858 Central Ave., 1st Floor, St. Petersburg, FL, 33707. , President - Tel: (813) 572-4892. Upscale, full service dry cleaning. Established: 1990 - Franchising Since: 1991 - No. of Units: Franchised: 7 - Franchise Fee: $20,000 - Royalty: $145/wk., $45/wk. adv. - Total Inv: $189,000 - Financing: Lease-finance.

SUNDAY BEST!
P.O. Box 7169, Boston, MA, 02269. Contact: Thomas Gilmore, Sales Mgr. - Tel: (617) 984-0405. Company dedicated to putting inexperienced men and women in dry cleaning business (U.S., Canada, Mexico). Turnkey package includes sites, permits, store design, installation of equip., training, initial sales promotions. Owners may choose any name, or they may join Sunday Best! Owners Cooperative. Established: 1991 - Franchise Fee: None - Total Inv: Complete plants from $125,000 - Financing: Yes, usually two-thirds of total inv.

LAWN, GARDEN CARE AND FLORISTS

ALLEN'S FLOWERS & PLANTS
Allen's Flowers, Inc.
18500 Sherman Way, Reseda, CA, 91335. Contact: Ben or Nace Goldman, Pres./V.P. - Tel: (818) 996-2603. High volume and visibility retail flower shops located in high density corners. With an emphasis on cash and carry trade. Turn-key operation. Established: 1978 - Franchising Since: 1980 - No. of Units: Company Owned: 2 - Franchised: 5 - Franchise Fee: $50,000 - Royalty: 6%-10%- Total Inv: $125,000 depending on location - Financing: Yes.

AMERICAN WHOLESALE FLORAL
8601 Georgia Ave., Ste. 905, Silver Spring, MD, 70910. Contact: Michael Politz, Chairman - Tel: (301) 231-9088. Wholesale florist to trade and open to the public. Established: 1987 - Franchising Since: 1993 - No. of Units: Company Owned: 3 - Franchised: 3 - Franchise Fee: $15,000 - Royalty: 5% gross, 1.5% adv. fund - Total Inv: approx. $50,000 - Financing: No.

BUNING THE FLORIST
3860 W. Commercial Blvd., Ft. Lauderdale, FL, 33309. Contact: Franchise Dir. - Tel: (305) 731-1776. Florist. Established: 1956 - Franchising Since: 1972 - No. of Units: Company Owned: 25 - Franchised: 4 - Franchise Fee: $15,000 - Royalty: $300/mo 1st yr., 3.6% 2nd yr. - Total Inv: $45,000 - Financing: No.

CONROY'S FLOWERS
6621 E. Pacific Coast Highway, Ste.280, Long Beach, CA, 90803. Contact: Barry Kurtz, E.V.P. - Tel: (310) 594-4484. Full service florists and mass merchandisers of cut flowers. The stores are approximately 2,500 sq. ft. and located on high exposure signalized intersections. Conroy's performs real estate site acquisition; 4 week training in Southern CA; coordinates initial set-up and grand opening; provides complete computerized accounting services; coordinates and manages advertising programs. Established: 1960 - Franchising Since: 1974 - No. of Units: Franchised: 94 - Franchise Fee: $75,000 - Royalty: 7.75% - Total Inv: $250,000 - $300,000 - Financing: No.

CUT ONLY *
15965 Jeanette St., Southfield, MI, 48075. Contact: Colleen McGaffey - Tel: (810) 557-2784, Fax: (810) 557-7931. Customer controlled lawn care. Offers home owners dependable, quality workmanship, customer selected service options and low prices, Combines 20 years of lawn care knowledge with a unique and original marketing tool. Established; 1973 - No. of Units: Company Owned: 1 - Franchise Fee: $15,000 - Royalty; $2,000 - Total Inv: $35,000 - Financing: Yes, small business loan.

EMERALD GREEN LAWN CARE
Emerald Green, Inc.
46258 Carlynn Dr., Cincinnati, OH, 45241-2202. Contact: Jim Miller, Gen. Man. - Tel: (513) 489-7322. Lawn and landscape maintenance. Established: 1984 - Franchising Since: 1985 - No. of Units: Company Owned: 3 - Franchised: 15 - Franchise Fee: $8,500 to $25,000 - Royalty: % of gross sales - Total Inv: $15,000 to $40,000.

FASGRAS INTERNATIONAL, INC.
13751 Travilah Rd., Rockville, MD, 20850. Contact: Mark Johnson, Dir. Fran. - Tel: (301) 424-7333. A patented pre-germination seed system of hydro seeding which can establish a lawn in 3 to 5 days that is mowable in 14. This is a product franchise sold to existing landscapers, hydroseeders, and lawn care businesses. Established: 1967 - Franchising Since: 1981 - No. of Units: Company Owned: 2 - Franchised: 5 - Franchise Fee: $6,000 - Royalty: none - Total Inv: $9,000 - $30,000 - Financing: No.

FLORIDA TROPICALS
3820 Premier Ave., Memphis, TN, 38118. Contact: Bill Richey - Tel: (901) 867-0600. Retail store offering cut and live flowers and plants, but specializes in roses. Established: 1983 - Franchising Since: 1990 - No. of Units: Company Owned: 9 - Franchise Fee: $15,000 - Royalty: 6% - Total Inv: $77,880 - $117,100 - Financing: no.

FLOWERAMA
Flowerama of America, Inc.
3165 West Airline Hwy., Waterloo, IA, 50703. Contact: Robert Whitt, Dir. of Mktg. - Tel: (319) 291-6004. Retail floral and gift shops. Established: 1966 - Franchising Since: 1971 - No. of Units: Company Owned: 18 - Franchised: 42 - Franchise Fee: $30,000 - Royalty: 5% - Total Inv: $100,000 - $500,000 - Financing: Assistance in securing local financing.

FOLIAGE DESIGN SYSTEMS
Foliage Design Systems Franchise Co.
1553 S.E. Fort King St., Ocala, FL, 34471. Contact: John S. Hagood, Pres. - Tel: (904) 629-7351, or (800) 933-7351, Fax: (904) 629-0355. Interior plant design, installation & maintenance; sale & lease programs & short-term rentals. Established: 1971 - Franchising Since: 1980 - No. of Units: Company Owned: 6 - Franchised: 40 - Franchise Fee: $20,000 - $100,000 - Royalty: 6% - Total Initial Inv: $35,000 - $150,000 - Financing: No.

JOHNSON HYDRO SEEDING CORP.
Fas Gras International, Inc.
13751 Travilah Rd., Rockville, MD, 20850. Contact: Mark Johnson, Fran. Dir. - Tel: (301) 340-0805. Specializing in installing new lawns through a new, patent pending process. Established: 1967 - Franchising Since: 1980 - No. of Units: Company Owned: 6 - Franchised: 4 - Franchise Fee: $19,500 - Royalty: 6% starting 90 days after opening + 2% adv. - Total Inv: $100,000 - $167,000 - Financing: No direct assistance.

LAWN DOCTOR
Lawn Doctor, Inc.
142 Highway #34, Box 401, Holmdel, NJ, 07733. Contact: Edward L. Reid, Nat'l. Sales Dir. - Tel: (800) 631-5660. Automated lawn care and tree & shrub care service. All natural and regular fertilization plus control applications using exclusive Turf Tamer equipment manufactured and used only by Lawn Doctor; supplemented by a broad range of cultural care practices utilizing Integrated Pest Management to develop the health and beauty of turf and landscape areas with environmentally balanced care. Established: 1967 - Franchising Since: 1968 - No. of Units: Company Owned: 0 - Franchised: 306 - Royalty: 10% - Total Inv: $35,500 - Financing: Yes.(See our ad on page 132.)

Work From Home...
JOIN AMERICA'S #1 LAWN CARE FRANCHISE

Over a billion sq. ft. of America's landscape receives lawn, tree, & shrub nutrition-protection-enhancement services from 300+ Lawn Doctor owners from many backgrounds. Come grow with us...
- 28 Years of Success
- Exclusive, Patented Equipment
- Complete Training & Support
- No Experience Needed
- Protected Territories
- Financing Available

Call Today!
LAWN ✱ DOCTOR INC
800-631-5660
Dept. 161

LIQUI-GREEN LAWN CARE CORP.
9601 North Allen Rd., Peoria, IL, 61615. Contact: C.M. Dailey, Dir. - Tel: (309) 243-5211. Lawn and tree care. Established: 1953 - Franchising Since: 1971 - No. of Units: Company Owned: 1 - Franchised: 25 - Franchise Fee: $5,000 - Royalty: $6,000 annually - Total Inv: Option 1 $20,900 - Option 2 $23,900 - Financing: Lease for qualified buyers.

LIVING GREEN
307 Powell Ave. #A, Healdsburg, CA, 95448-3417. Contact: Frank Bramante, Pres. - Tel: (707) 571-8300. Hydroponic growing systems and supplies. Specialty nutrients. Established: 1977 - Franchising Since: 1985 - No. of Units: Company Owned: 30 - Franchised: 65 -Total Inv: $12,500 - $25,000 - Financing: Yes.

MR. TREES
Mr. Trees Franchise Corp.
343 San Anselmo Ave., San Anselmo, CA, 94960. Contact: Tripp Curtis, Fran. Sales Dir. - Tel: (415) 485-1180. Environmentally sound tree and shrub care franchise. Established: 1983 - Franchising Since: 1993 - No. of Units: Company Owned: 1 - Franchised: 1 - Franchise Fee: $28,500 - Royalty: 6% of gross revenue - Total Inv: $28,500 fran. fee, $60,000 - $72,000 start up - Financing: None.

NATURALAWN OF AMERICA
141 W. Patrick St., Frederick, MD, 21701. Contact: Randy Loeb, Fran. Dev. Mgr. - Tel: (800) 989-5440, Fax: (301) 846-0320. Providing an alternative to pesticides and harsh chemicals through an organic/biological based lawn care service serving commercial and residential customers. Established: 1987 - Franchising Since: 1989 - No. of Units: Company Owned: 3 - Franchised: 26 - Franchise Fee: $29,500 - Royalty: 7% - 9%, no adv. fee - Total Inv: $29,500 fran. fee; $20,000 start-up cap.; $40,000 - $60,000 line of credit - Financing: Third party sources.

NICE 'N GREEN FRANCHISE SYSTEMS *
Nice 'N Green Franchise Systems, Inc.
682 Phelps Ave., Romeoville, IL, 60441. Contact: James Mello, Agronomist - Tel: (708) 963-2171. Professional lawn and tree care services, both residential and commercial. Established: 1963 - Franchising Since: 1995 - Franchise Fee: $19,500 - Royalty: 8.5%, 1% adv. - Total Inv: $50,000 - $70,000 - Financing: No.

NITRO-GREEN PROFESSIONAL LAWN & TREE CARE
Nitro-Green Corp.
2791-F North Texas St., Ste.300, Fairfield, CA, 94533. Contact: Roger Albrecht, Pres. - Tel: (800) 982-5296. Automated professional lawn and tree care services. Fertilizing, insect control, disease control, weed control. Established: 1977 - Franchising Since: 1979 - No. of Units: Company Owned: 2 - Franchised: 41 - Franchise Fee: $17,400 - Royalty: 7% - Total Inv: $40,000 - $50,000 - Financing: On equip.

PARKER INTERIOR PLANTSCAPE
1325 Terrill Rd., Scotch Plains, NJ, 07076. Contact: Rich Parker - Tel: (908) 322-5552. Sell, lease or rent, live, artificial or preserved plants, trees, flowers, containers, etc. to offices, malls, and atriums etc. Established: 1959 - Franchising Since: 1985 - No. of Units: Company Owned: 1 - Franchised: 1 - Franchise Fee: $35,000 - Total Inv: $35,000 - Financing: No.

SERVICEMASTER LAWNCARE
Servicemaster Company, LP, The
855 Ridge Lake Blvd., Memphis, TN, 38120-9792. Contact: Bob Morris, Dir. Mkt. Expansion - Tel: (800) 228-2814. Professional lawn care for residential and commercial accounts. Established: 1948 - Franchising Since: 1985 - No. of Units: Franchised: 186 - Franchise Fee: $17,000 - Royalty: 8% of gross - Total Inv: fran. fee, equip, and supplies $7,500 - $24,500 service sales - Financing: Yes, up to $16,300.

SHARP-N-LUBE
Ray Enterprises Inc.
3245 St. Rt. 589, Casstown, OH, 45312. Contact: Stan Ray, Pres. & CEO - Tel: (800) 842-2782. Mobile lawn equipment service business (We go where you mow.). Established: 1989 - Franchising Since: 1993 - No. of Units: Company Owned: 1 - Franchised: 4 - Franchise Fee: $7,900 - Royalty: 3.5% - 5% with 1% adv. rebate - Total Inv: $23,800 to $25,800 - Financing: No.

SHE'S FLORISTS
She's Flowers Inc.
494 Alley St., Pasadena, CA, 91107. Contact: Helen Shih, Pres. - Tel: (818) 796-3685. Full service retail florist shop. Completely computerized communication networking operation. Established: 1979 - Franchising Since: 1986 - No. of Units: Company Owned: 2 - Franchised: 7 - Franchise Fee: $20,000 - Royalty: 5.5% gross sales - Total Inv: $103,000 - $156,500 - Financing: Yes.

SILK PLANT FOREST
5639 Brookshire Blvd., Charlotte, NC, 28216. Contact: David Elden, Dir. of Fran. - Tel: (704) 399-4445, Fax: (704) 399-0140. A specialty retailer of artificial silk plants, trees, floral arrangements and other related home furnishings. The operations of the stores also include commercial service. The manufacturing company has a central design center which constantly develops new products, the individual store can provide custom arrangements, professional decorating, installation and consulting to businesses. Established: 1987 - Franchising Since: 1993 - No. of Units: Company Owned: 10 - Franchise Fee: $25,000 - Royalty: 5% sales, 2% adv. - Total Inv: $80,000 - $110,000 - Financing: No.

SPRING-GREEN LAWN CARE
Spring-Green Lawn Care Corp.
11927 Spaulding School Dr., Plainfield, IL, 60544. Contact: Bill Ticknor, Mktg. Mgr. - Tel: (815) 436-8777. Professional lawn, tree and shrub care services for residential and commercial customers. Primary focus is on highly efficient customer oriented services including fertilization, weed control and aeration. Established: 1977 - Franchising Since: 1977 - No. of Units: Company Owned: 4 - Franchised: 110 - Franchise Fee: $12,900 - Royalty: 6% to 9% - Total Inv: $30,000 - Financing: No.

SUPERLAWNS
Super Industries, Inc.
P.O. Box 5677, Rockville, MD, 20855. Contact: Ron Miller, Fran. Dir. - Tel: (301) 948-8181. Profitable concept of lawn care performed with automated equipment, seeding, aerating, fertilizing, etc. No mowing, low overhead and low labor costs. Renewal factor of 70% or better and excellent annual growth for this recession proof business. Established: 1976 - Franchising Since: 1976 - No. of Units: Company Owned: 2 - Franchised: 21 - Franchise Fee: $17,500 - Royalty: 10% first $150,000 annually, then 5% - Total Inv: $62,000 ($17,000 fran. fee/$32,000 equip./$12,500 work cap.) - Financing: Assistance.

TERRA SYSTEMS *
Terra Systems Franchise Corp.
1515 Cliffwood Pl., Charlotte, NC, 28203. Contact: Kevin Robke, Pres. - Tel: (704) 342-0310. We provide a natural organic turf and shrub care service. Granular turf fertilization & plant health care / coupled with integrated pest management. Established: 1991 - Franchising Since: 1993 - No. of Units: Company Owned: 1- Franchised: 2 - Franchise Fee: $22,500 - Royalty: 7% of gross, reported quarterly - Total Inv: fran. fee with approx. $20,000 per yr. living expenses.

U.S. LAWNS, INC.
369 Mears Blvd., Oldsmar, FL, 34677-3048. Contact: Todd Moershen, Pres. - Tel: (813) 855-9002. Professional and commercial landscape maintenance. Established: 1987 - Franchising Since: 1987 - No. of Units: Franchised: 16 - Franchise Fee: $15,000 - $40,000 - Royalty: 4%, 2% adv. - Total Inv. $25,000 - $40,000 - Financing: No.

WESLEY BERRY FLOWERS
Future Corporation
6677 Orchard Lake Rd., W. Bloomfield, MI, 48322-3404. Contact: Wesley Berry Jr., Fran. Dir. - Tel: (810) 851-2881. Retail flower shop offering a full line of flowers, plants and associated gift items. Established: 1946 - Franchising Since: 1985 - No. of Units: Company Owned: 2 - Franchised: 16 - Franchise Fee: $20,000 - Royalty: 5% - Total Inv: fee plus $25,000 equip., $7,000 opening inventory - Financing: Limited.

MOTELS, HOTELS AND CAMPGROUNDS

AMERICINN MOTEL
AmericInn International, Inc.
18202 Minnetonka Blvd., Deephaven, MN, 55391. Contact: Jon Kennedy, V.P., Fran. Dev. - Tel: (612) 476-9020. Upscale limited service motel chain with quality construction and furnishings. Established: 1979 - Franchising Since: 1987 - No. of Units: Franchised: 35 - Franchise Fee: $20,000 - Royalty: 4.5% - Financing: No.

BEST INNS OF AMERICA
1205 Skyline Dr., Rt. #3, Box 1719, Marion, IL, 62959-7719. Contact: Bob Brewer, Pres. - Tel: (618) 997-5454. Limited service up-scale motels and suites. Established: 1968 - Franchising Since: 1982 - No. of Units: Company Owned: 15 - Franchised: 17 - Franchise Fee: $10,000 - Royalty: 5% mgmt. fee, if applicable - Total Inv: approx. $20,000 - $43,000 (excl. of land & soft costs) - Financing: No.

BEST WESTERN
Best Western International, Inc.
6201 N. 24th Parkway, Phoenix, AZ, 85016. Contact: Nancy Vaughan, Dir., Corp. Comm. - Tel: (602) 957-5751, Fax: (602) 957-5505. Best Western International, Inc. is the world's largest single hotel brand with more than 3,400 hotels in 60 countries throughout North America, Europe, South America, Asia, Africa, the Middle East and the South Pacific. All Best Western hotels are independently owned & operated. Established: 1946 - No. of Units: Company Owned: 281,789 - Franchise Fee: (Entrance fee) $32,000 for 100 rooms; $42,000 for 200 rooms - Annual Dues: $3,096 for 100 rooms - Membership fee: $23,634 - Reservation fee: $12,045 first year - Total Inv: Varies according to size - Financing: No.

BUDGET HOST INNS
Budget Host International
3607 Pioneer Pkwy. W., P.O. Box 14341, Arlington, TX, 76094. Contact: Ray Sawyer, Pres. - Tel: (817) 861-6088, Fax: (817) 861-6089. A referral chain of affiliated independent inns, providing full chain services. Prospective affiliates must have a lodging facility either in operation or under construction. Established: 1976 - Franchising Since: 1976 - No. of Units: Franchised: 178 - Franchise Fee: $3,500 - Royalty: $50 per room per year; reservations, $30 per unit per year (approx.) - Total Inv: $8,000 and up depending on number of rooms.

BUDGETEL INNS
Marcus Corp.
250 E. Wisconsin Ave., #1750, Milwaukee, WI, 53202. Contact: G. Edward Wilson, V.P. - Tel: (414) 274-0376, Fax: (414) 272-3270. Economy lodging chain with 80-100 rooms operating in 27 states. Established: 1974 - Franchising Since: 1986 - No. of Units: Company Owned: 84 - Franchised: 26 - Franchise Fee: $25,000 - Royalty: 5%, 1% adv., 1% reserv. - Total Inv: $300,000 to $800,000 - Financing: No.

CAMPTOWN U.S.A.
R.F.D. #2, Box 56, Brimfield, MA, 01010. Contact: George N. Van Fleet, Pres. - Tel: (413) 245-9525. Complete marketing and financial services to membership camping franchise. Established: 1986 - Franchising Since: 1986 - No. of Units: 1 - Franchise Fee: $20,000 - Royalty: 12% - Total Inv: $63,500 - Financing: Yes.

CARLSON HOSPITALITY WORLDWIDE
Carlson Pky., P.O. Box 59159, Minneapolis, MN, 55459-8204. Contact: James Olson, Sr. V.P. Dev. - Tel: (612) 540-5335, Fax: (612) 449-3400. Carlson Hospitality Worldwide operates, manages and franchises a number of key global brands including: Radisson Hospitality Worldwide (Radisson Hotels Worldwide, Radisson Seven Seas Cruises), Friday's Hospitality Worldwide (T.G.I. Friday's, Italiani's and Friday's Front Row Sports Grill) and Country Hospitality Worldwide (Country Inns & Suites By Carlson, and Country Kitchen). Established: Radisson, 1983; Country Inns & Suites, 1987 - Hotels: 371, Rooms: 83,849 - Total Inv: Review UFOC - Financing: N/A.

CLARION INNS
Choice Hotels International
10750 Columbia Pike, Silver Spring, MD, 20901. Contact: Jeffrey T. Williams, Sr. V.P. - Tel: (800) 547-0007, (301) 593-5600. Franchisor of inns, hotels, suites, and resorts. Established: 1941 - Franchising Since: 1941 - No. of Units: Company Owned: 12 - Franchised: 2,821 - Franchise Fee: $35,000 - Royalty: 3% of GRR.

CLUBHOUSE INNS OF AMERICA, INC.
11230 College Blvd. #130, Overland Park, KS, 66210. Contact: David H. Aull, Pres. - Tel: (913) 451-1300. Very high-quality, garden style hotel with a club-like atmosphere; sized from 120-148 rooms and suites. Features full complete breakfast and cocktails. 1993 systemwide occupancy 73.9%. Established: 1984 - Franchising Since: 1984 - No. of Units: Company Owned: 11 - Franchised: 8 - Franchise Fee: $25,000 - Royalty: 4% + 1.5% - Total Inv: approx. $6,000,000 - Financing: From financial lending institutions.

COMFORT INNS
Choice Hotels International
10750 Columbia Pike, Silver Spring, MD, 20901. Contact: Jeffrey T. Williams, Sr. V.P. - Tel: (800) 547-0007, (301) 593-5600. Franchisor of inns, hotels, suites, and resorts. No. of Units: Company Owned: 12 - Franchised: 2,821 - Franchise Fee: $35,000 - Royalty: 4% of GRR.

COMPRI HOTEL
DOUBLEtree Hotels Corp.
410 N. 44th St., #700, Phoenix, AZ, 85008. Contact: Shelley Berro, Mgr. Fran. Adm. - Tel: (602) 220-6666. Franchisor of limited service, mid-market hotel products. Established: 1984 - Franchising Since: 1984 - No. of Units: Company Owned: 5 - Franchised: 20 - Franchise Fee: $30,000 - Royalty: 3% gross room revenue - Total Inv: $10,000,000 - $15,000,000 - Financing: No.

CONDOTELS
Condotels International, Inc.
2703 Hwy. 17 S, N. Myrtle Beach, SC, 29582. Contact: Tom Taylor, Owner - Tel: (800) 852-6636 US; (800) 845-0631 CAN.. Franchisees act as rental manager for condo owners. Operates much like a hotel franchisor except that the lodging provided is condos rather than hotel rooms. Established: 1982 - Franchising Since: 1989 - No. of Units: Franchised: 7 - Franchise Fee: $25,000 - $75,000 - Royalty: 4% - Total Inv: $45,000 - $193,000 - Financing: No.

COUNTRY HEARTH INN
BAC Franchising Inc.
4243 Dunwoody Club Dr., Ste. 200, Dunwoody, GA, 30350. Contact: Larry Owens, Dir. of Operations - Tel: (404) 393-2662. Hotel franchise sales. Established: 1994 - Franchising Since: 1994 - No. of Units: Franchised: 6- Franchise Fee: The greater of $20,000 or $250 per guest room - Royalty: 4%, Reservation Fee: 1%, Marketing Fee: 1.5% - Total Inv: $526,000 - $683,000 (does not include property or construction costs) - Financing: No.

COUNTRY INN & SUITES BY CARLSON
P.O. Box 59159, Minneapolis, MN, 55459-8203. Contact: Nancy Johnson, V.P., Lodging Development - Tel: (612) 449-1326. Franchise limited-service lodging properties. Established: 1987 - Franchising Since: 1987 - No. of Units: Company Owned: 2 - Franchised: 53 - Franchise Fee: $25,000 - Royalty: Continuing fee, 2% yr. 1, 3% yr. 2-15, Mktg. fee: 2% yr. 1, 3% yr. 2-15 - Total Inv: $988,750 (100 room Inn), $1,106,250 (100 Suites) - Financing: Introduction.

DAYS INNS OF AMERICA
Hospitality Franchise Systems
339 Jefferson Rd., Parsippany, NJ, 07054. Contact: Roger Bloss, V.P. - Tel: (201) 428-9700. Hotels and motels in 31 states and Canada. Established: 1970 - Franchising Since: 1970 - No. of Units: Company Owned: 2 - Franchised: 900 - Franchise Fee: $26,000 or $300 per room - Total Inv: varies - Royalty: 5%-1.5% adv. fee plus reservation fees.

ECONO LODGES OF AMERICA, INC.
Choice Hotels International
10750 Columbia Pike, Silver Spring, MD, 20901. Contact: Jeffrey T. Williams, Sr. V.P. - Tel: (800) 547-0007, (301) 593-5600. Franchisor of inns, hotels, suites, and resorts. Established: 1941 - Franchising Since: 1941 - No. of Units: Company Owned: 12 - Franchised: 2,821 - Franchise Fee: $25,000 - Royalty: 4% of GRR.

ECONOMY LODGING SYSTEMS, INC.
26650 Emery Pkwy., Cleveland, OH, 44128. Contact: Carrie Lencewicz, Fran. Dev. - Tel: (216) 464-2118. Franchise, manage & develop limited-service lodging facilities nationwide. Established: 1991 - Franchising Since: 1991 - No. of Units: Company Owned: 12 - Franchised: 185 - Franchise Fee: $15,000 or $150/room, whichever is greater - Royalty: 4%, 2% mktg., 2% reservations - Total Inv: $15,000 downpayment - Financing: Not presently.

EMBASSY SUITES HOTELS
Embassy Suites, Inc.
850 Ridgelake, Ste. 400, Memphis, TN, 38120. Contact: Phil Cordell, Dir. Fran. Oper. - Tel: (901) 680-7200. Hotel chain. Established: 1983 - Franchising Since: 1984 - No. of Units: Company Owned: 55 - Franchised: 47.

FAMILY INNS OF AMERICA
P.O. Box 10, Pigeon Forge, TN, 37868-0010. Contact: Harold Foshie, Controller - Tel: (615) 453-1240 . Deluxe budget motels. Established: 1968 - Franchising Since: 1972 - No. of Units: Company Owned: 8 - Franchised: 20 - Franchise Fee: $15,000 - $25,000 - Royalty: 3% room sales - Total Inv: $100,000 - $250,000 - Financing: Through lending institutions.

FORTE HOTELS, INC.
1973 Friendship Dr., El Cajon, CA, 92020. Contact: Chris Cullen, V.P. Comm. & Promo. - Tel: (619) 448-1884. Lodging/hospitality. Established: 1935 - Franchising Since: 1966 - No. of Units: Company Owned: 140 - Franchised: 291 - Franchise Fee: $30,000 + - Royalty: 4%, 4% adv. - Total Inv: varies - Financing: No.

HAMPTON INN HOTELS
850 Ridgelake Blvd., Ste. 300, Memphis, TN, 38120. Contact: Pat Ferguson, V.P., Fran. - Tel: (901) 374-5000. One of the fastest growing moderately-priced chains. Development opportunities exist with our standard prototype, our modified prototype designed for communities of 75,000 people or less, and conversions. Hampton Inn is a division of The Promus Companies Inc. Established: 1983 - Franchising Since: 1984 - No. of Units: Company Owned: 15 - Franchised: 302 - Franchise Fee: $300 per room (min. $35,000) - Royalty: 4%; Mktg./reserv. - Total Inv: $2,500,000 - $7,000,000.

HAWTHORN SUITES
400 Fifth Ave., Waltham, MA, 02154. Contact: Paul T. White; John J. Lyons, Exec. V.P.; Sen. V.P. - Tel: (617) 290-0175. All-suite hotels. Established: 1986 - Franchising Since: 1986 - No. of Units: Company Owned/Managed: 4 - Franchised: 13.

HILTON HOTELS
9336 Civic Center Dr., Beverly Hills, CA, 90210. Contact: James Abrahamson, Fran. Dept. - Tel: (213) 278-4321. Hotels and inns. Established: 1965 - Franchising Since: 1965 - No. of Units: Franchised: 223 - Franchise Fee: $250 1st 100 rooms, $150 per room thereafter - Royalty: 5% room sales - Total Inv: $60,000 - $75,000 per room - Financing: No.

HOLIDAY INNS, INC.
3 Ravinia Dr., #2000, Atlanta, GA, 30346. Contact: Bryan Langton, CEO - Tel: (404) 604-2000. National hotel chain. Established: 1953 - Franchising Since: 1954 - No. of Units: 1,700.

HOMEWOOD SUITES HOTELS
Homewood Suites, Inc.
850 Ridgelake Blvd., #300, Memphis, TN, 38120. Contact: David C. Sullivan, Sr. V.P., Operations/Dvt. - Tel: (901) 374-5000. Chain of extended-stay, all suite hotels geared to today's business travel market. Offer guests a 100% satisfaction guarantee. Homewood Suites is a division of The Promus Companies Inc. Established: 1989 - Franchising Since: 1989 - No. of Units: Company Owned: 8 - Franchised: 16 - Franchise fee: $300 per guest suite with min. $35,000 - Royalty: 4%; mktg./reservations - Total Inv: $3,000,000 - $8,000,000.

HOWARD JOHNSON FRANCHISE SYSTEMS
Hospitality Franchise Systems
339 Jefferson Rd., Parsippany, NJ, 07054. Contact: John Osborne, Exec. V.P. Fran. Sales - Tel: (201) 428-9700. Hotels, lodges, resorts and Ho Jo Inns in the U.S., Canada, and Mexico. Established: 1925 - Franchising Since: 1954 - No. of Units: Franchised: 450 - Franchise Fee: $30,000 min. or $300 per room - Royalty: 5%, 1% adv., 1.5% reserv. fee - Financing: No.

IBIS
Sphere North America Corp.
2 Overhill Rd., Ste. 420, Scarsdale, NY, 10583. Contact: Michael Flaxman, Fran. Dir. - Tel: (914) 472-0370. Hotel development and management company. Established: 1981 - Franchising Since: 1982 - No. of Units: Company Owned: 1 - Franchised: 2 - Franchise Fee: $20,000 - Royalty: 3% mgmt. fee, 1.5% mktg. fee - Total Inv: $5,500,000.

INNSUITES HOTELS
Hospitality Corporation International
1651 W. Baseline Rd., Tempe, AZ, 85283. Contact: Mona Adams, Trademark License Dir. - Tel: (602) 820-2030, Fax: (602) 491-1008. Studio and 2-room suite hotels. Established: 1980 - Franchising Since: 1986 - No. of Units: Company Owned: 8 - Franchised: 6 - Franchise Fee: Zero to $15,000 - Royalty: 1.5% of gross or percent of reservations sent - Total Inv: Conversion and new - Financing: N/A.

KAMPGROUNDS OF AMERICA, INC.
550 North 31st Tw. III, 4th Flr., Billings, MT, 59101. Contact: David Johnson, V.P. Licensing - Tel: (406) 248-7444 . Campgrounds for recreational vehicles, investment opportunities to purchase existing KOA campgrounds, new franchise territories and conversion of independent campgrounds to KOA status. Established: 1962 - Franchising Since: 1962 - No. of Units: Company Owned: 11 - Franchised: 546 - Franchise Fee: $20,000 - Royalty: 2% adv. + 8% royalty fee - Total Inv: $85,000 minimum start up - Financing: None.

KNIGHTS INN, KNIGHTS COURT
Hospitality Franchise Systems, Inc.
339 Jefferson Rd., Parsippany, NJ, 07054. Contact: Remesh Gokal, Pres. - Tel: (201) 428-9700. Franchise and develop limited, service hotels/motels nationwide. Established: 1991 - Franchising since: 1992 - No. of Units: Company Owned: 22 - Franchised: 185 - Franchise Fee: $150/room - Royalty: 4% Marketing 2% Reservation 2% - Financing: Yes.

LEES INN
Lees Inns Of America, Inc.
130 N. State St., P.O. Box 86, North Vernon, IN, 47265. Contact: Henry E. Marsolais, V.P. Franchising - Tel: (812) 346-5072. Hotel/Motel. Franchisor for partnerships or joint ventures only. Builder/developer. Franchisor is an equity investor in each franchise. Franchisor performs as general managing partner of each franchise. Established: 1985 - Franchising Since: 1987 - No. of units: Company Owned: 17 - Franchise Fee: $35,000 - $45,000 - Royalty: 7% royalty/reservation fee - Total Inv: $6,000,000 for 120 rooms - Financing: Negotiable.

MARRIOTT CORP.
HD. QTRS. Mail Center, #1 Marriott Dr., Washington, DC, 20058. Contact: Fran Dept. - Tel: (301) 380-9000. Hotel chain.

MASTER HOSTS INNS & RESORTS / RED CARPET INN / SCOTTISH INNS / PASSPORT INN / DOWNTOWNER INNS
Hospitality International, Inc.
1726 Montreal Cir., Tucker, GA, 30084. Contact: Don Deaton, Wanda Overby, Pres., Fran. Coord. - Tel: (404) 270-1180, Fax: (404) 270-1077. Hotel franchisor of nearly 350 franchised properties in 35 states, the Bahamas, Canada and South America. "State of the Art" 24 hr. reservation center, group sales & marketing, housekeeping & mgmt. training, creative services, reasonable fees & a genuine interest in franchisee's success. Established; 1982 - franchising Since: 1982 - No. of Units: Franchised: 347 - Franchise Fee: $100/rm. or $10,000 min. for Scottish, Passport and Downtowner Inns; $150/rm. or $15,000 min. for Red Carpet, Master Hosts Inns & Resorts - Royalty: 3.5% to 4.5% - Total Inv: Varies with chain and conversion vs. new construction - Financing: Will assist franchisee in locating financing.

MICROTEL
1 Airport Way, Ste. 200, Rochester, NY, 14624. Contact: E. Anthony Wilson, Chairman of the Board/CEO - Tel: (716) 436-6000. Franchising of the Microtel Limited Service Hotel. Established: 1987 - Franchising Since: 1988 - No. of Units: Franchised: 25 - Franchise Fee: $250 per room or $25,000 whichever is greater - Royalty: 2 1/2-3 1/2% gross room revenue - Total Inv: 100 rms. $2.2 - $3.0 million dollars - Financing: By franchisee.

MIDWAY MOTOR LODGES
1025 S. Moorland Rd., Brookfield, WI, 53005. Contact: Peyton A. Muehlmeier, Pres. - Tel: (414) 782-7411. Motor lodges, restaurants, showroom lounges. Established: 1963 - No. of Units: Company Owned: 11 - Franchised: 2 - Franchise Fee: $300/room - Royalty: 3% + 1% adv. - Total Inv: 20% - 30% of total project - Financing: Yes.

NATIONAL 9 INNS, SUITES, MOTELS
2285 S. Main St., Salt Lake City, UT, 84115. Contact: Kevin Howell, V.P. Oper. - Tel: (801) 466-9826. Franchising existing properties, enabling them to compete with larger franchises. Established: 1984 - Franchising Since: 1984 - No. of Units: Company Owned: 7 - Franchised: 169 - Franchise Fee: $3,500 - Royalty: $5 monthly per room - Total Inv: $3,500 f.f., $5,000 r.f., $3,500 sign - Financing: OAC.

NENDELS CORPORATION
520 Pike St., Ste. 1515, Seattle, WA, 98101. Contact: Gary Maisel, V.P. Dev. - Tel: (206) 623-4832. Hotel inns and resorts franchise company. Established: 1934 - Franchising Since: 1986 - No. of Units: Company Owned: 35 - Franchised: 50 - Franchise Fee: $100/room ($10,000 min) - Royalty: 2% + 10 cents/room/day reservations fee + - 50 cents/room/day mktg. - Financing: No.

QUALITY INNS
Choice Hotels International
10750 Columbia Pike, Silver Spring, MD, 20901. Contact: Jeffrey T. Williams, Sr. V.P. - Tel: (800) 547-0007. Franchisor of inns, hotels, suites, and resorts. Established: 1941 - Franchising Since: 1941 - No. of Units: Company Owned: 12 - Franchised: 2,821 - Franchise Fee: $35,000 - Royalty: 4% of GRR.

RADISSON HOTELS WORLDWIDE
Carlson Pky., P.O. Box 59159, Minneapolis, MN, 55459-8204. Contact: T. Peter Blyth, Pres. of Dev. - Tel: (612) 540-5335, Fax: (612) 449-3400. Radisson Hotels International caters to the upscale business travel and leisure destination markets. Radisson offers five hotel products plazas, hotels, suites, inns and resorts. Established: 1983 - Initial Fee: $30,000 - Royalty Fee: 4% gross room sales - Adv./Mktg. Fee: 3.5% gross room sales - Reservation Fee: Included in Adv/Mktg. fees - Locations Outside of the U.S.: Initial Fee: $200 per room with a min. of $40,000 - royalty: 4% gross room rev. - Adv./Mktg. Fees: 2.5% gross room sales - Reservation Fee: $11 per reservation booked through the Radisson system.

RAMADA FRANCHISE SYSTEMS
Hospitality Franchise System
339 Jefferson Rd., Parsippany, NJ, 07054. Contact: John Osborne, Exec. V.P. Fran. Sales - Tel: (201) 428-9700. Hotels, Inns and resorts throughout the United States. Established: 1954 - Franchising Since: 1990 - No. of Units: Franchised: 550 - Franchise Fee: $30,000 or $300 per room - Royalty: 4%, 4.5% adv./reserv. - Financing: None.

RESIDENCE INNS BY MARRIOTT, THE
1 Marriott Dr., Dept. 851.07, Washington, D.C., 20058. Contact: Gerald J. O'Neill, V.P. Fran. Dev. - Tel: (301) 380-3853. Extended stay all-suite hotels featuring sleeping quarters, living rooms, fireplaces, fully equipped kitchens and breakfast bars, recreational facilities and swimming pools. Established: 1985 - Franchising Since: 1985 (when system was purchased from Brock Residence Inns, Inc.) - No. of Units: Company Owned: 30 - Franchised: 88 - Franchise Fee: $50,000 or $400/suite (whichever is greater) - Total Inv: $3,400,000 - $5,600,000 (for a 64-suite Inn) - Royalty: 4% gross sales - Financing: Advisory assistance only.

RODEWAY INNS INTERNATIONAL
Choice Hotels International
10750 Columbia Pike, Silver Spring, MD, 20901. Contact: Jeffrey T. Williams, Sr. V.P. - Tel: (800) 547-0007. Franchisor of inns, hotels, suites, and resorts. Established: 1941 - Franchising Since: 1941 - No. of Units: Company Owned: 21 - Franchised: 2,821 - Franchise Fee: $25,000 - Royalty: 3% of GRR.

SELECT INNS FRANCHISING INC.
9801 Dupont Ave S., Ste. 190, Bloomington, MN, 55431. Contact: Scott Timmington, Pres. - Tel: (612) 881-6255. Motel Franchising. Established: 1976 - Franchising Since: 1991 - No. of Units: Company Owned: 10 - Franchised: 3 - Franchise Fee: 3.5% - Royalty: included in fran. fee - Total Inv: $150 per room (min. $9,000, max. 15,000) initial fee - Financing: No.

SHERATON HOTELS AND INNS
ITT Sheraton Corp.
Sixty State St., Boston, MA, 02109. Contact: Mike Getto, V.P. Dir. of Fran. Sales - Tel: (617) 367-3600, (770) 857-2000. Inns with a minimum of 100 rooms, together with restaurant, meeting rooms, swimming pool and lounge. Established: 1962 - Franchising Since: 1962 - No. of Units: 344 worldwide - Franchise Fee: planned property, $30,000 - Royalty: 5% gross room sales - Total Inv: varies - Financing: no.

SIGNATURE INNS *
Signature Inns, Inc.
250 E. 96th St., Ste. 450, Indianapolis, IN, 46240. Contact: Patrick Taylor, Exec. Dir., Fran. & Dev. - Tel: (317) 581-1111. Hotel chain nationally recognized as an industry leader in the mid-priced segment offering friendly and consistent services in especially clean rooms. Established: 1978 - Franchising Since: 1981 - No. of Units: Franchised: 23 - Franchise Fee: greater of $25,000 or $200 per room - Royalty: 4%, 3.5% reservation & mktg. - Total Inv: Varies per hotel - Financing: Will assist, but not provide.

SLEEP INNS
Choice Hotels International
10750 Columbia Pike, Silver Spring, MD, 20901. Contact: Jeffrey T. Williams, Sr. V.P. - Tel: (800) 547-0007. Inns, hotels, suites and resorts. Established: 1941 - Franchising Since: 1941 - No. of Units: Company Owned: 12 - Franchised: 2,821 - Franchise Fee: $35,000 - Royalty: 4% of GRR.

STUDIO PLUS
Studio Plus of America Inc.
1999 Richmond Rd., Ste. 4, Lexington, KY, 40502. Contact: Benjamin A. Keam, V.P. - Tel: (606) 269-1999. Economical extended stay lodging facilities. Studio Plus offers furnished designer studios by the week for less. Established: 1985 - Franchising Since: 1990 - No. of Units: Company Owned: 16 - Franchise Fee: $35,000 or $500 per studio, whichever is higher - Royalty: 5% of gross revenue - Total Inv: $1.7 - $1.85 million exclusive of land.

SUBURBAN LODGE *
Suburban Lodges of America, Inc.
120 Interstate North Parkway East, Ste. 120, Atlanta, GA, 30339. Contact: Dan J. Berman, Pres., Fran. - Tel: (770) 951-9511. Franchise, own, develop and operate economy extended stay motels. Established: 1986 - Franchising Since: 1991 - No. of Units: Company Owned: 4 - Franchised: 13 - Franchise Fee: $25,000 or $190 per room, whichever is greater - Royalty: 3% gross revenues, 1% reservation/referral, 1% adv. - Total Inv: $3,350,000 (125 rooms) ($7-800,000 equity) - Financing: Lender introduction and loan package assistance.

SUPER 8 MOTELS
Hospitality Franchise Systems
1910 8th Ave. N.E., Aberdeen, SD, 0705457401. Contact: Marge Meyer, Fran. Sales - Tel: (605) 225-2272, Fax: (605) 229-8900. Franchise economy motels. Operate extensive franchise services, supply and management division. Established: 1973 - Franchising Since: 1976 - No. of Units: Company Owned: 52 - Franchised: 862 - Franchise Fee: $20,000 - Royalty: 4% + 3% adv. - Financing: Assistance in loan preparation.

TRAVELODGE
Forte Hotels, Inc.
1973 Friendship Dr., El Cajon, CA, 92020. - Tel: (619) 448-1884. Travelodge is a brand of economy lodging for accommodations owned and operated by the most profitable hotel and catering company in the world. Franchises are available in all lodging segments. Established: 1935 - Franchising Since: 1966 - No. of Units: Company Owned: 50 - Franchised: 300 - Franchise Fee: $30,000 or $300/room, whichever is greater - Royalty: 4% - Financing: No.

WILSON HOTEL MANAGEMENT CO. INC.
Kemmons Wilson
1629 Winchester Rd., Memphis, TN, 38116. Contact: Geo. Glover, Pres. - Tel: (901) 346-8800. Luxury budget and full service - 110 rooms - 5 story interior corrider - ranging from $30 to $49 per day. Established: 1987 - No. of Units: Company Owned: 30 - Franchise Fee: 1% adv. assess - 1% reservation - Royalty: 4% - Total Inv: $7,000,000 - Financing: No.

WOODFIN SUITES
12707 High Bluff Dr., #200, San Diego, CA, 92130-2037. Contact: Samuel Hardage, Chairman - Tel: (619) 793-4100. All-suite hotel concept. Established: 1985 - No. of Units: Company Owned: 5 - Franchised: 1 - Franchise Fee: $300/suite (min. $30,000) - Royalty: 4% sales - Total Inv: $46,850/suite excluding land - Financing: Assist.

YOGI BEAR'S JELLYSTONE PARK CAMP-RESORTS
Leisure Systems, Inc.
6201 Kellogg Ave., Cincinnati, OH, 45228. Contact: Rob Schutter, Pres./COO - Tel: (513) 232-6800, or (800) 626-3720. Vacation leisure resort/campground. Established: 1969 - Franchising Since: 1969 - No. of Units: Franchised: 75 - Franchise Fee: $18,000 - Royalty: 6% + 1% adv. Total Inv: - varies widely - Financing: No.

PET PRODUCTS AND SERVICES

CANINE COUNSELORS
Canine Counselors Inc.
1660 Southern Blvd., West Palm Beach, FL, 33406. Contact: Bob Ward, Dir. of Fran. Promotions - Tel: (407) 640-3970. Professional animal behavior and on-site dog training company offering all levels of training services on a contract basis, specializing in correcting destructive behavior. Established: 1975 - Franchising Since: 1987 - No. of Units: Company Owned: 3 - Franchised: 4 - Franchise Fee: $19,000 - Royalty: 7% of gross, 2% nat'l. adv. contribution - Total Inv: $33,500 - $39,500 - Financing: Yes.

DOG WASH
Southwest Pet, Inc.
5724 S.W. Green Oaks Blvd., Arlington, TX, 76017. Contact: Fran. Dir. - Tel: (817) 561-1801. A do-it-yourself pet care center that offers affordable pet care and vaccinations. Established: 1972 - Franchising Since: 1988 - No. of Units: Company Owned: 1 - Franchised: 1 - Franchise Fee: $17,500 - Royalty: 5.5% - Total Inv: fee, $20,000 equip./fixtures - Financing: No.

LAUND-UR-MUTT *
Pet Pioneers, Inc.
8854 S. Edgewood St., Highlands Ranch, CO, 80126. Contact: Scott Southworth, Pres. - Tel: (303) 470-1540. The premier self-service dog wash. We franchise the finest facilities where people can come and wash their pets themselves. Our custom stainless steel tubs and software, along with our exclusive system make it easy for the customer and store owner alike. Established: 1992 - Franchising Since: 1994 - No. of Units: Franchised: 3 - Franchise Fee: $5,000 - Royalty: 5% of gross revenue per mo. - Total Inv: $40,000 incl. all fees, equip. and improvements - Financing: Assistance through lending process, i.e., documents.

PET PALS
Pet Pals Inc.
7939 E. Arapahoe Rd., Ste. 250, Englewood, CO, 80112. Contact: Johnny M. Wilson, Pres. - Tel: (303) 771-8251. Retail store offering proprietary products in foods, toys and accessories for pets. Established: 1988 - Franchising Since: 1993 - No. of Units: Company Owned: 8 - Franchise Fee: $17,500 - Royalty: 6%, 1% adv. - Total Inv: $94,000 - Financing: Yes.

PETLAND
Petland, Inc.
195 N. Hickory St., Chillicothe, OH, 45601. Contact: Drew Musser, Fran. Dev. Assoc. - Tel: (614) 775-2464, Fax: (614) 775-2575. Full service retail pet stores carrying pets and pet supplies, specializing in innovative pet care, housing, and customer education. Established: 1967 - Franchising Since: 1972 - No. of Units: Company Owned: 1 - Franchised: 141 - Franchise Fee: $25,000 - Royalty: 4.5% paid twice a month - Total Inv: $125,000-$450,000 based on size of the store - Financing: No, but will assist.

SAFARI ANIMAL CARE CENTERS
2450 East Main St., Ste. D, League City, TX, 77573. Contact: Cheryl Garner, Fran. Dir. - Tel: (713) 332-1873. Veterinary hospital, pet shop, grooming and boarding. Established: 1984 - Franchising Since: 1985 - No. of Units: Company Owned: 1 - Franchise Fee: $30,000 - Approx. Inv: $200,000 - $300,000 - Financing: No.

SHAKE A PAW PUPPIES
International Franchising
CSS Franchising: 177 Main St., Ste. 103, Fort Lee, NJ, 07024. Contact: Franchise Sales Rep. - Tel: (201) 585-4753. Retail puppy boutique featuring only purebred puppies, never from puppy mills in an animal friendly environment. Stores also carry a full line of puppy supplies. Established: 1989 - Franchising Since: 1989 - No. of Units: Franchised: 20 - Franchise Fee: $30,000 - Royalty: 5% of gross - Total Inv: $130,000 incl. build-out, equip. and stock - Financing: Yes.

SHAMPOO CHEZ
Shampoo Chez, Inc.
1380 Soquel Ave., Santa Cruz, CA, 95062. Contact: Anne Singer, Pres. - Tel: (408) 427-2284. Self service dog wash with unique features of convenience and service. Offers waist-high tubs, professional blow dryers, towels, brushes, and water-proof aprons for the owners. Grooming services for dogs and cats are also available. Also carry line of pet food, supplies and private label pet health care products. Established: 1983 - Franchising Since: 1988 - No. of Units: Company Owned: 1 - Franchised: 2 - Franchise Fee: $15,000 - Royalty: 3.5% - 5% gross - Total Inv: $60,000 - $77,000 - Financing: No.

SKEETER'S GROOMING FACILITY
728 Center St., P.O. Box 550, Lewiston, NY, 14092-0550. Contact: E.S. Anderson, Pres. - Tel: (716) 754-4669. Professional dog grooming facilities and supplies. Established: 1991 - Franchising Since: 1991 - No. of Units: Company Owned: 1 - Franchised: 3 - Franchise Fee: $10,000 - Royalty: 5%, 2% adv. - Total Inv: approx. $15,000 - $20,000 - Financing: No.

THREE DOG BAKERY *
Three Dog Bakery, Inc.
1700 Holmes, Kansas City, MO, 64108. Contact: Jason Gilchnst, Fran. Agent - Tel: (816) 531-8898. Unique retail bakery serving wholesome treats for dogs. Established: 1990 - Franchising Since: 1995 - No. of Units: Company Owned: 3 - Franchise Fee: $25,000 - Royalty: 5% - Total Inv: $150,000 - $220,000 - Financing: None.

PHOTO, FRAMING AND ART

1 HOUR PHOTO
Watch What Develops Franchise Concepts, Inc.
P.O. Box 3777, Youngstown, OH, 44513-3777. Contact: Cathy Clagett, Exec. Asst. - Tel: (216) 758-0982. One hour mini-labs. Established: 1980 - Franchising Since: 1980 - No. of Units: Company Owned: 4 - Franchised: 27 - Franchise Fee: $45,000 - Royalty: 6% - Total Inv: $220,000-$280,000 - Financing: None.

ACTION SPORTS PHOTOS
Chromatech Laboratories Inc.
4526 N.W. 1st, Oklahoma City, OK, 73127. Contact: Gary L. Fearnow, Pres. - Tel: (405) 942-7007. Photography business specializing in action photos and team photos. Package is complete including all business materials, cameras, photographic supplies and training. 3 packages available. Established: 1985 - Franchising Since: 1992 - No. of Units: 2 - Franchise Fee: $9,000 - $13,650 - Total Inv: $14,560 to $40,058 - Financing: No.

AMERICAN FAST PHOTO & CAMERA
157 South Pine St., Spartanburg, SC, 29302. Contact: Mr. Nixon, Dir. of Dev. - Tel: (803) 585-2391. Full service photo imaging center and portrait studio. Established: 1984 - Franchising Since: 1984 - No. of Units: Franchised: 21 - Franchise Fee: $27,500 - Royalty: 6% + 2% to advertising - Total Inv: $165,000 - Financing: Yes, equip.

ART AVENUE
Original Oil Paintings Franchise Corp.
242 Great Northern Mall, North Olmsted, OH, 44070. Contact: Paul Sykes, Pres. - Tel: (216) 734-2645. A unique and exciting marketing concept featuring hand-painted, high quality decorative art works, framed and unframed. Offers original oil paintings, prints, posters and custom framing services in a choice of a kiosk and/or in-line mall location. Established: 1988 - No. of Units: Company Owned: 2 - Franchised: 3 - Franchise Fee: $15,000 - Financing: No.

BAVARIAN WAX ART
6380 Euclid Rd., Cincinnati, OH, 45236. Contact: Robert Young, Dir. - Tel: (513) 793-5151 or 793-9789. A special form of statues, wall plaques and Christmas ornaments, utilizing special casting wax from Germany to create beautiful and lasting decorative sculpture for home and office. Finely detailed, hand finished. Established: 1981 - Franchising Since: 1986 - No. of Units: Company Owned: 4 - Franchised: 12 - Franchise Fee: $995 - Total Inv: $1,995 - Financing: None.

CAR'S THE STAR FRANCHISE SYSTEMS
420 W. 7th St., Kansas City, MO, 64105. Contact: Phillip L. Schroeder, Pres. - Tel: (816) 474-1959. Auto art/gift gallery in upscale malls selling all car art and car related gifts. In celebration of the automobile. The car is really the star at Car's The Star®. Established: 1988 - Franchising Since: 1992 - No. of Units: Company Owned: 1 - Franchise Fee: $25,000 - Royalty: 5% - Total Inv: $350,000: store buildout, inventory, fee, working capital - Financing: No.

COLOR COMPUTER PORTRAITS
Tech Systems, Inc.
66 Marion St., Boston, MA, 02128. Contact: R. Stoll, V.P. - Tel: (617) 561-0400, (800) 447-6646. Capture faces live or from photos (in color) produce transfers for T-shirts, mugs, buttons, caps, wall hangings, posters and pillowcases. Operate at fairs, carnivals, malls, indoor or out. Established: 1977 - No. of Units: Company Owned: 8 - Outlets: 4,720 - Total Inv: $3,500 - $14,000 - Financing: Lease programs available.

CONTEMPO PORTRAITS
CP Enterprises Inc.
1235 S. Gilbert St., Ste. 16, Mesa, AZ, 85204. Contact: Patrick Silard, Pres. - Tel: (602) 926-2216. Contemporary portrait studio offering a whole new concept in portraiture. Established: 1987 - Franchising Since: 1993 - Franchise Fee: $25,000 - Royalty: 7%, 1% adv. - Total Inv: $65,000 plus fran. fee - Financing: Will assist.

CREATIVE DISPLAY OF FLORIDA, INC.
Sunshine Properties Inc.
7700 W. Fairfield Dr., Pensacola, FL, 32506. Contact: Joseph Morgan, G.M. - Tel: (904) 455-9685, Fax: (904) 458-0096. Manufacturer of art sculptures anything the human mind can conjure. Cows, bells, horses, fountains, fish, serpents, shoes, boots, sandles, etc. Established: 1960 - Franchising Since: 1960 - No. of Units: Company Owned: 4 - Franchise Fee: purchase of display unit - Total Inv: $25,000 - Financing: Case by case.

CYGNUS SYSTEMS INC.
3416 S. Dixon Rd., Kokomo, IN, 46902-4812. Contact: Craig Swartz, Fran. Dir. - Tel: (317) 453-7077. Computer portrait systems that produces prints that transfer by a heating process. Established: 1974 - No. of Units: 150 - Total Inv: $15,900 - Financing: Yes.

DECK THE WALLS
P.O. Box 1187, Houston, TX, 77251-1187. Contact: Steve Lowrey, Sr. V.P. - Tel: (713) 775-5200, Fax: (713) 775-5250. The nation's largest retailer of art and custom framing. Stores offer prints, posters and frames that compliment today's decorating styles. Inviting decor and emphasis on personal service make shopping at Deck The Walls a quality experience. Established: 1979 - Franchising Since: 1980 - No. of Units: Company Owned: 2 - Franchised: 191 - Franchise Fee: $35,000 - Royalty: 6% monthly - Total Inv: $165,000 - $210,000 - Financing: 3rd party.

DIVERSIFIED ARTS
15 Palmer Rd., Box 603, Waterford, CT, 06385. Contact: Joseph Abrahms, Pres. - Tel: (860) 443-5173. Consignment of oil paintings, part-time, requires 4 days per mth. Established: 1971 - Franchising Since: 1971 - No. of Units: Company Owned: 4 - Franchised: 5 - Inv: $6,500 - Financing: None.

FASTFRAME
Fastframe USA, Inc.
1200 Lawrence Dr., #300, Newbury Park, CA, 91320. Contact: Brian J. Harper, CEO - Tel: (800) 521-3726, (805) 498-4463. Custom picture framing service & art gallery. Established: 1986 - Franchising Since: 1987 - No. of Units: Company Owned: 3 - Franchised: 145 - Franchise Fee: $25,000 - Royalty: 7.5%, 3% adv. - Total Inv: $125,000 min. - Financing: Equip. leasing.

FINE ART RENTALS
Fine Art Rentals Franchising Inc.
24321 La Hermosa Ave., Laguna Niguel, CA, 92677. Contact: Steve Smith, So.CA Mgr. - Tel: (714) 831-0222. Have rented quality art work to business and professional offices for 31 yrs. Oldest and largest art rental service in CA, now offering a limited number of exclusive franchise territories. Included in fran. fee is 100 tastefully framed original serigraphs, watercolors, etchings and other limited edition works, complete training program, support of a parent company. Established: 1959 - Franchising Since: 1987 - No. of Units: Company Owned: 1 - Franchised: 3 - Franchise Fee: $30,000 - Royalty: 5% gross rentals per mth. - Total Inv: $30,000 - Financing: No.

FRAME IT YOURSELF
55 W. Main St., Ramsey, NJ, 07446. Contact: Scott Bower, Pres. - Tel: (201) 327-4220. Do it yourself picture framing. Established: 1976 - Franchising Since: 1976 - No. of Units: Company Owned: 1 - Franchised: 16 - Franchise Fee: $10,000 - Royalty: 4% - Total Inv: $40,000 - Financing: No.

FRAME & SAVE
Frame King, Inc.
27 Spiral Dr., Florence, KY, 41042-1357. Contact: Chuck Karlosky, Pres. - Tel: (606) 341-1210. Do it yourself and custom picture framing. No. of Units: Company Owned: 5 - Franchised: 35 - Franchise Fee: $10,000 - Royalty: 3% gross - Total Inv: $40,000 - Financing: No.

GALLERY 92 INC.
P.O. Box 4315, S. Daytona, FL, 32121. Contact: Tim Papadeas, V.P. - Tel: (904) 788-6633. Dealerships offer a vast selection of popular posters and fine art prints. Both laminated, ready to hang and in paper form only. Truly unique liquid glass process manufactured exclusively by Gallery 92. Established: 1985 - Licensing Since: 1987 - No. of Units: Company Owned: 2 - Licensed: 3 - Inv: $39,000 - $69,000 - Financing: None.

GLAMOUR SHOTS LICENSING, INC. *
1300 Metropolitan Ave., Oklahoma City, OK, 73108. Contact: Kim McElroy, Fran. Sales Mgr. - Tel: (405) 947-8747, ext. 323. Retail customers are treated to a complete makeover and personal photo session, then they view their proofs instantly on a color video monitor and place their orders for professional finished portraits instantly. The customer receives their portraits in about a week. Established: 1988 - Franchising Since: 1992 - No. of Units: Company Owned: 3 - Franchised: 308 - Franchise Fee: $15,000 - Royalty: None, franchisor meets their color lab needs and charges wholesale pricing for these services - Total Inv: $208,982 (incl. fran. fee and $75,000 in work. cap.) - Financing: Leasing options available for photographic & computer equipment.

GREAT FRAME UP SYSTEM, INC., THE
9335 Belmont Ave., Franklin Park, IL, 60131. Contact: Michael Kohn, Consumer Mktg. & Fran. Sales - Tel: (312) 671-2530 or (800) 553-7263. Completely inventoried and equipped retail stores specializing in high volume sales of quality picture frames. All necessary materials and equipment are provided for each customer's framing needs on a do-it-yourself or custom basis and offers absolute minimum prices. Turn-key operation with 5 weeks training provided. Established: 1970 - Franchising Since: 1975 - No. of Units: Franchised: 135 - Franchise Fee: $25,000 - Royalty: 6% + 2% adv. - Total Inv: $140,000 - Financing: Indirectly.

HOT LOOKS HIGH FASHION PORTRAITS
Hot Looks International, Inc.
724 Old York Rd., Jenkintown, PA, 19046. Contact: Barry Fineman, Pres. - Tel: (800) 92-LOOKS. Rapidly growing specialty chain featuring high fashion glamour photography, cosmetic makeovers plus wedding and special event photography and videos. Established: 1968 - Franchising Since: 1992 - No. of Units: Company Owned: 6 - Franchised: 3 - Franchise Fee: $19,500 - Royalty: 7%, 1% adv. - Total Inv: $70,000 - $120,000 - Financing: No.

KENNEDY STUDIOS, INC.
140 Tremont St., Boston, MA, 02111. Contact: Kevin Richard, G.M. - Tel: (617) 542-0868. Art gallery carrying limited edition prints and posters offering custom framing. Unique arrangement with franchisor which is also an art publishing company supplying images to the new franchise territory. Established: 1973 - Franchising Since: 1983 - No. of Units: Company Owned: 15 - Franchised: 38 - Franchise Fee: $15,000 - $25,000 - Royalty: 3%, (no ad fee) - Total Inv: $45,000 - $100,000 work cap., fran. fee incl. - Financing: No.

MAK'N WAVES, INC.
419 Main St. #19, Huntington Beach, CA, 92648. Contact: Peter Schuorer, Pres. - Tel: (714) 962-7010. Giant wave photography props used for amusements, promotions and marketing tourist industry. Established: 1987 - No. of Units: Company Owned: 3 - Franchised: 24 - Total Inv: $14,900. - Financing: No.

MALIBU GALLERY *
Malibu Gallery Franchise, Inc.
1919 South 40th St., Ste. 202, Lincoln, NE, 68506-5248. Contact: Jack L. Rediger, Pres., Franchise Developers - Tel: (402) 434-5624,.Fax: (402) 434-5620. Are you looking for a clean, professional and enjoyable environment? Malibu Gallery offers both custom framing services and an art gallery in a franchise opportunity. Simple to learn and very rewarding. You owe it to your future to check out what Malibu has to offer you. Established: 1986 - Franchising Since: 1995 - No. of Units: Company Owned: 3 - Franchised: 1 - Franchise Fee: $15,000 - Royalty: 6% of sales, 2% adv. - Total Inv: $49,000 - $132,000 - Financing: None.

MILFORD HEIRLOOM INC.
403 New Haven Ave., Milford, CT, 06460-6649. Contact: Dennis Brown, Pres. - Tel: (203) 877-8334. Manufacturer of photoglazing equipment wholesaler of china plates and novelties to entrepreneurs who wish to start a photo plate business. Established: 1982 - No. of Units: Company Owned: 1 - Dealers: 594 - Total Inv: $4,995 - $6,995 package price.

ONE HOUR MOTO PHOTO & PORTRAIT STUDIO®
Moto Photo, Inc.
4444 Lake Center Dr., Dayton, OH, 45426. Contact: V.P. Fran. Sales - Tel: (513) 854-6686 or (800) 733-6686. Photo stores featuring on-site one hour photo processing and portrait studios. Services include enlargements, reprints, video transfer and other imaging services. Offers full support services in real estate, design & construction, training, marketing and business management. Established: 1981 - Franchising Since: 1982 - No. of Units: Company Owned: 61 - Franchised: 371 - Franchise Fee: $35,000 1st store, $20,000 add. store - Royalty: 6% - Total Inv: $170,000: ($75,000 cash) - Financing: Yes.

PHOTO DRIVE-UP FRANCHISING, INC. *
Photo Drive-Up, Inc.
1900 Camden Ave., San Jose, CA, 95124. Contact: David Lopez, Nat'l. V.P. Fran. - Tel: (800) 835-9772. Three distinct services combined under one roof: 1 hour photo, new release video rentals, copy center. Established: 1976 - Franchising Since: 1994 - No. of Units: Company Owned: 25 - Franchised: 1 - Franchise Fee: $23,500 - Royalty: 5%, 2% adv. - Total Inv: $100,000 liquid, $175,000 lease - Financing: Leasing assistance.

PORTRAIT MASTERS
Portrait Masters, Inc.
114 High Country Dr., Cary, NC, 27513. Contact: Ken Bedford, Fran. Dir. - Tel: (800) 926-8654. Franchisees bring new level of portrait quality to daycares, youth sports and other group-oriented functions. Franchise includes all top quality professional equipment such as Hasselbaad® camera and training in franchised territory. Franchises are renewable at no cost. Established: 1989 - Franchising Since: 1992 - No. of Units: Company Owned: 4 - Franchised: 2 - Franchise Fee: $20,000 - Royalty: No franchise royalties - Total Inv: $2,000 - $9,000 (excl. fran. fee) - Financing: Assistance in locating financing provided.

RPL SUPPLIES INC.
280 Midland Ave., Saddle Brook, NJ, 07662. Contact: Lawrence Milazzo, Pres. - Tel: (201) 794-8400. Ceramic photo mugs and computer portraits. Sell both equipment and all of the supplies. Established: 1982- No. of Units: Franchised: 3,164 - Franchise Fee: None - Royalty: None - Total Inv: $5,160 - $17,500 - Financing: None.

SNAP SHOTS
Martek Ltd.
Box 15160, Dept. IFNS, Charlotte, NC, 28211. Contact: Paul T. Muckler, Mgr. - Tel: (704) 364-7213. A complete promotional color portrait photography business that provides full color, glamour portraits. Established: 1990 - Licensing Since: 1993 - No. of Units: 11 - Total Inv: $1,995 - Financing: No.

SPORTS SECTION, THE
3120 B. Medlock Bridge Rd., Norcross, GA, 30071. Contact: Joe Lindenmayer, Fran. Sales Mgr. - Tel: (800) 321-9127 or (404) 416-6604. Childrens sports photography. No photography experience required. Business minded people with sales and/or marketing experience helpful. Fun, flexible franchise. Established: 1983 - Franchising Since: 1984 - No. of Units: Company Owned: 2 - Franchised: 109 - Franchise Fee: Plan 1) $29,500 2) $19,500 3) $29,500 Rural $9,900 - Total Inv: Fran. fee plus $3,000 equip. - Financing: Yes, only plan I.

SURF FOTO
1030 Vale View Dr., Vista, CA, 92083. Contact: Rick Ireton, Pres. - Tel: (619) 945-0452. Creator of the original award winning giant wave photography prop. Offers would be fair/party goers an instant photo surfing in the tube section of a pounding 10" - 12" wave. No photo

experience necessary, lots of fun to operate. Established: 1986 - No. of Units: Company Owned: 2 - Licensed: 6 - Fee: $15,000 - Total Inv: $15,000 wave $2,000 trailer $1,000 bamboo surf shack & 2 picture kiosks - Financing: No.

TRADING FACES
Jackson Digital Imaging Corp.
3660 Cinder Lane, Las Vegas, NV, 89103. Contact: Nick Freeman, Mktg. Dir. - Tel: (800) 584-8181, Fax: (702) 871-8595. Instant portraits featuring state-of-the-art computer enhancement. Small space, easy operation and high profit make this "No Royalty" fun business opportunity the best value. Featured @ Caesar's Forum Shop & MGM Grand Casino. Established: 1987 - No. of Units: Company Owned: 3 - Licensed: 130 worldwide - Total Inv: $50,000 to $200,000 (equip.) - Financing: 36 to 60 month equip. lease.

PRINTING AND COPYING SERVICES

ALPHAGRAPHICS® PRINTSHOPS OF THE FUTURE
AlphaGraphics, Inc.
3760 N. Commerce Dr., Ste. 100, Tucson, AZ, 85705. Contact: Tom Camplese, V.P., Fran. Dev. - Tel: (602) 293-9200. AlphaGraphics® high-tech rapid-response printing stores offer a complete line of reprographic services, which include high-speed duplicating, single and multi-color printing, desktop design and publishing, custom presentation materials and an electronic communications network that transmits digital camera-ready text and graphics in minutes to AG stores worldwide. Established: 1970 - Franchising Since: 1980 - No. of Units: Company Owned: 1 - Franchised: over 330 (nat'l & int'l) - Franchise Fee: $25,900 - Royalty: 3% - 8% - Total Inv: $228,700 - $413,900 - Financing: SBA, local bank, 3rd party leasing.

AMERICAN SPEEDY PRINTING CENTERS
American Speedy Printing Centers, Inc.
1800 West Maple, Troy, MI, 48084. Contact: Dirk Nelson, Dir. of Dev. - Tel: (810) 614-3700, Fax: (810) 614-3719. 2-4 color printing, copying, desktop publishing & color copying. Established: 1976 - Franchising Since: 1977 - No. of Units: Franchised: 450 - Franchise Fee: $19,500 - Royalty: 6% - 3.6% - Total Inv: $198,000 - $202,000 new center - Financing: Yes.

AMERICAN WHOLESALE THERMOGRAPHERS, INC.
12715 Telge Rd., P.O. Box 777, Cypress, TX, 77429-0777. Contact: Kevin Camp, Pres. - Tel: (800) 942-9526 (US) or (713) 373-9142 (TX). Provides thermographed printing on a wholesale basis to printers, office supply stores, card and gift shops. Specializes in business cards, stationery, announcements and wedding invitations. Established: 1980 - Franchising Since: 1981 - No. of Units: 22 - Franchise Fee: $30,000 - Royalty: 5% - Total Inv: $211,353 to $221,353 plus $60,000 working capital. Financing Options Available: Ask about our interest free financing for franchise fee.

BCT (BUSINESS CARDS TOMORROW)
Business Cards Tomorrow, Inc.
3000 NE 30th Pl., 5th Flr., Fort Lauderdale, FL, 33306. Contact: Joseph Musso, Dir., Fran. Dev. - Tel: (800) 627-9998 ext. 305, Fax: (305) 565-0742. Wholesale printing franchise specializing in next-day delivery of thermographed and offset printed products and rubber stamps. Our extensive wholesale product line includes business cards, letterhead, envelopes, announcements, stationery and rubber stamps. Established: 1975 - Franchising Since: 1977 - No. of Units: Company Owned: 3 - Franchised: 97 - Franchise Fee: $35,000 - Royalty: 6% - Total Inv: $35,000 fran. fee, $50,000 inven., $175,000 equip. plus work. cap. - Financing: Third party outsourced.

BCX PRINTING
BXC Printing Centers Inc.
613 E. Indian School Rd., Phoenix, AZ, 85012. Contact: Gene Cufone, Pres. - Tel: (602) 241-1231. Full service printing specializing in thermography and raised printing. Established: 1979 - Franchising Since: 1982 - No. of Units: Company Owned: 1 - Franchised: 7 - Franchise Fee: $25,000 - Royalty: 5% + 2% adv. - Total Inv: additional $85,000 plus work cap. - Financing: Yes.

BUDGET PRINTING CENTERS
4133 Presidential, Ste. #1, Lafayette Hill, PA, 19444. Contact: L. Stevens, Pres. - Tel: (800) 836-5215, (215) 836-5215. A business opportunity with support ongoing. Established: 1976 - Franchising Since: 1950 - Total Inv: $79,900 with more than ample equipment - Financing: Yes.

D & K ENTERPRISES INC.
3216 Commander Dr. #101, Dept. 17, Carrollton, TX, 75006-2518. Contact: Mktg. Department - Tel: (214) 248-9100. This proven home-based business allows you to print personalized books in only 4 minutes. We have over 36 titles to choose from including children's books, grown-up books and licensed books. Personalized tapes and stationery also available. Established: 1987 - No. of Units: 1300 in 50 states & in 15 countries - Franchise Fee: $2,475 - Financing: Yes.

FRANKLIN'S PRINTING, DIGITAL IMAGING & COPYING
Franklin's Systems, Inc.
1117 Perimiter Center W., Ste. W-101, Atlanta, GA, 30338. Contact: Anthony Roselli, Fran. Dev. - Tel: (800) 554-5699, Fax: (770) 396-9648. Franklin's is the modern version of the Quick Printer. What makes Franklin's different is our leadership position in being able to accept digital images from customers, producing upscale commercial printing, volume hi-speed copying and color copying with connectivity. Start owners from day one with outside sales rep trained in using a proven system of targeting volume repeat corporate accounts. Established: 1971 - Franchising Since: 1977 - No. of Units: Franchised: 75 - Franchise Fee: $25,000 - Royalty: 5% - Total Inv: $225,398, incl. $65,000 work. cap. & FF - Financing: Assistance in preparation of package & presentation to lending institutions.

INFORM
Inform International Inc.
2408 Felts Ave., Nashville, TN, 37211. , Fran. Dir. - Tel: (901) 867-0600. Provides full-service printing able to handle entire range of printing requirements by using their in-house print shop and selected business form manufacturers. Established: 1988 - No. of Units: Company Owned: 1 - Franchise Fee: $25,000 - Royalty: 4% - Total Inv: $142,000 - $215,050 (work. cap., inven., rent, equip., lease) - Financing: Equip. For further information please contact: Consultants America Corp., 12279 US Highway 64. Eads, TN, 38028, Tel: (901) 867-0600, Fax: (901) 867-0010.

INK WELL, THE
Ink Well of America, Inc., The
P.O. Box 777, Cypress, TX, 77429-0777. Contact: La Donna Meadows, V.P. ICED (Parent Co.) - Tel: (800) 942-9526 (US) or (713) 373-9142 (TX). Printing and related services. Established: 1972 - Franchising Since: 1981 - No. of Units: Franchised: 48 - Franchise Fee: $25,000 - Royalty: 4%-6%, 2.5% adv. - Total Inv: $166,500 to $174,100, plus $65,000 working capital - Minimum Cash: $42,300 to $75,600 - Financing: Yes.

INSTY-PRINTS
Insty-Prints, Inc.
15155 Technology Dr., Eden Prairie, MN, 55344-2273. Contact: David Oswald, V.P. - Tel: (800) 779-1000. Provides high quality printing and copying services. Emphasis on fast, convenient service in a friendly, professional atmosphere. Established: 1965 - Franchising Since: 1967 - No. of Units: Franchised: 300 - Franchise Fee: $36,000 - Royalty: 4.5% thereafter 2% ad. - Total Inv: $200,000 - Financing: Yes, partial.

JACK'S COPY CENTER
Xerographic Copy Centers Franchising
6903 Atlantic Blvd., Jacksonville, FL, 32211. Contact: David Matchett, V.P. - Tel: (904) 721-8074. The company provides high speed, high quality copy services to businesses and consumers. By concentrating its efforts on duplication and related services, franchisees provide a needed service to those customers requiring large amounts of copying. Established: 1984 - Franchising Since: 1984 - No. of Units: Company Owned: 6 - Franchised: 1 - Franchise Fee: $15,000 - $35,000 - Total Inv: $40,000 - $75,000 - Royalty: 5% - Financing: Yes.

JET PRESS - BIZWIZ
391 Broadway, Ste. 205, Box 860, Everett, MA, 02149. Contact: Marshall Nanis, C.E.O./Mktg. Dir. - Tel: (617) 394-0820. Help franchisee establish instant business card business. Established: 1990 - Franchising Since: 1990 - No. of Units: Company Owned: 2- Franchised: 2 - Total Inv: $4,995 - Financing: Yes.

KOPY RITE
Kopy Graphics International, Inc.
6119 Pierce St., Hollywood, FL, 33024. Contact: E. Foley, Sr. V.P. - Tel: (305) 966-1530. Copy services with off premises full printing capability using high tech transmission and computers. Can be operated by one person. Also includes mail boxes, office supplies and graphic services. Established: 1987 - Franchising Since: 1988 - No. of Units: Company Owned: 1 - Franchised: 2 - Franchise Fee: $5,000 - Royalty: 5% plus 2% adv. - Total Inv: $22,000 + includes fee - Financing: Possibly.

KWIK KOPY CORPORATION
One Kwik-Kopy Lane, Cypress, TX, 77429-0777. Contact: Ladonna Meadows, V.P., ICED (Parent Co.) - Tel: (800) 231-1304 (US) or (713) 373-3535 (TX). Centers offer complete printing, copying & related services primarily to the business community. Kwik Kopy is in its 28th year helping men & women start their own business & stay in business. Kwik Kopy owners have access to the support and resources of the largest printing franchisor in the world. Established: 1967 - Franchising Since: 1967 - No. of Units: Franchised: 880 - Franchise Fee: $25,000 - Royalty: 4,6 or 8% - Total Inv: Min. cash $42,300 to $75,600 - Est. total pkg. $166,500 - $174,500 - Financing options available. Ask about interest-free financing for franchise fee.

LASER PRODUCT CONSULTANTS
1075 Bellevue Way N.E., Ste. 501, Bellevue, WA, 98004. Contact: Jamie Fields, Sales Mgr. - Tel: (800) 878-7008, Fax: (206) 462-1163. Laser cartridge recycling and printer repair. Established: 1987 - Franchising Since: 1988 - No. of Units: Franchised: 1,700 - Total Inv: $695. manuals, videos & tech. support.

LAZERQUICK COPIES
Graphic Information Systems, Inc.
27375 SW Parkway Ave., Wilsonville, OR, 97070. Contact: Michael Hart, Dir. of Fran. - Tel: (800) 477-2679. Computer oriented, full service printing, copying and graphic imaging centers, employing the latest in traditional and digital graphic imaging technologies. Established: 1968 - Franchising Since: 1990 - No. of Units: Company Owned: 34 - Franchised: 11 - Franchise Fee: $20,000 - Royalty: 5% 1st 5 yrs., 2.5% of increased sales yrs. 6-20 - Total Inv: $136,000 - $212,100 incl. fran. fee, work. cap. and all furn. fixtures and inven. - Financing: None directly, assistance in business plan preparation and securing 3rd party financing.

MINUTEMAN PRESS & INTERNATIONAL MINUTE PRESS
Minuteman Press International
1640 New Highway, Farmingdale, NY, 11735. Contact: Nick Gimpel, Senior V.P. - Tel: (516) 249-1370. Full service printing and graphics centers filling the niche between the small insty print shop and the large commercial printer. Multi-color printing primarily geared to the commercial/business sector. Established: 1973 - Franchising Since: 1975 - No. of Units: Franchised: 854 - Franchise Fee: $44,500 - Royalty: 6% - Total Inv: $102,000 - $170,000 - Financing: Various financing programs available.

NOVA MEDIA MULTI MEDIA PRESUME SHOP™
Nova Media Inc.
1724 N. State , Big Rapids, MI, 49307. Contact: Tom Rundquist, Mktg. Mgr. - Tel: (616) 796-7539, Fax: (616) 796-0486. Multi Media Resume and other multi media presentation development and design that combines audio, including music & voice, graphics, photo & other images on a computer, writing to CD ROM Disks (multi-media format) for printers, resume counselors, employment agencies and placement companies plus recording studios. Established: 1981 - No. of Units: Company Owned: 1 - Dealership Fee: $15,000 - Royalty: 5% - Total Inv: $44,000 - $73,000 incl. equip. & work. cap. - Financing: Yes, plus leasing.

PIP PRINTING
27001 Agoura Rd., Ste. 200, Agoura Hills , CA, 91301. Contact: Jaime Vane, Mgr., Bus. Dev. - Tel: (818) 880-3800, Fax: (818) 880-3857. PIP Printing provides a full range of business communications services from initial concept to finished printed product. Established: 1965 - Franchising Since: 1968 - No. of Units: Franchised: 658 - Franchise Fee: $40,000 - Royalty: Sliding scale 7% - 1% - Total Inv: $172,200 - $271,200 - Financing: Third party.

PRINTHOUSE EXPRESS, THE
PrintHouse Express, Inc.
222 Catoctin Cir., SE #102, Leesburg, VA, 22075-3700. Contact: Tom Galloway, Pres. - Tel: (703) 777-2567. Established: 1986 - Franchising Since: 1986 - No. of Units: Company Owned: 1 - Franchised: 20 - Franchise Fee: $42,000 - Royalty: 6% - 3.5% (declines as vol. goes up) - Total Inv: $42,000 fran. fee, $80,000 equip., $40,000 work cap.- Financing: $17,000 fran. fee, 100% ($80,000) equip.

PRINTING ONE *
Printing One Corporation
855 Downtowner Blvd., Mobile, AL, 36609. Contact: Sharon Prescott, Dir. of Mktg. - Tel: (334) 343-1572, Fax: (334) 343-1962. Printing franchise emphasizing marketing & customer service. Franchisor privides centralized production facility. Owners devote majority of their time to developing a strong customer base. Established: 1990 - Franchising Since: 1990 - No. of Units: Franchised: 7 - Franchise Fee: $25,000 - Royalty: 5% - Total Inv: $33,000 to open, plus $24,000 oper. cap. - Financing: $5,000 of franchise fee deferred. Corporate will finance that amount only.

QUIK PRINT
3445 N. Webb Rd., Wichita, KS, 67226. Contact: Jerry K. Ewy, V.P. - Tel: (316) 636-5666. Printing, copying and related business services. Established: 1963 - Franchising Since: 1967 - No. of Units: Company Owned: 69 - Franchised: 142 - Franchise Fee: $35,000 - Royalty: 5% - Total Inv: $80,000 equip, $35,000 fran. fee - Financing: Assistance with SBA loan.

SCREEN PRINTING USA
Screen Printing USA, Inc.
534 W. Shawnee Ave., Plymouth, PA, 18651. Contact: Russ Ownes, Pres. - Tel: (717) 779-5175. Silk screen printing with state-of-the-art equipment for T-shirts, signs, posters, metal, + ASI, wood, hats, jackets, etc. Established: 1989 - Franchising Since: 1989 - No. of Units: Company Owned: 1 - Franchised: 30, 2 in Canada - Franchise Fee: $25,000 - Royalty: 6% - Total Inv: $48,000 - Financing: Yes.

SIGNAL GRAPHICS PRINTING
SAMPA Corp.
6789 S. Yosemite, Englewood, CO, 80112. Contact: Bob Orban, Dir. of Fran. Dev. - Tel: (800) 852-6336, (303) 779-6789. Full service, quality printing centers catering to the business printing market. Comprehensive training, a proven system of operations, and state-of-the-art equipment package can help newcomers to the field quickly dominate their marketplace. On-going franchise support is a specialty, with management and technical help from headquarters on call. Established: 1974 - Franchising Since: 1982 - No. of Units: Franchised: 46 - Franchise Fee: $18,000 - Royalty: 5% declining to 0% based on gross sales - Total Inv: $181,300 - ($45,000 work cap., $104,300 equip., $10,000 start-up fee, $4,000 direct mail fee, $18,000 fran. fee) - Financing: Yes, SBA and 3rd party leasing programs.

SIR SPEEDY PRINTING CENTERS
Sir Speedy, Inc.
23131 Verdugo Dr., Laguna Hills, CA, 92653. Contact: Dave Collins, V.P. - Tel: (800) 854-3321, Fax: (714) 472-3444. Printing, copying, digital network services provided to businesses and individuals. We are the small business communications network. Established: 1968 - Franchising Since: 1968 - No. of Units: Franchised: 800 - Franchise Fee: $17,500 - Royalty: 4% first yr., 6% thereafter - Total Inv: $17,500 fee; $32,500 start-up; $110,000 equip. - Financing: Yes.

SMALL CITY BUSINESS JOURNALS INC.
110 Merchants Row, Rutland, VT, 05701. Contact: Richard S. Rohe, Pres. - Tel: (802) 775-9500. Newspaper business journal. Established: 1986 - Franchising Since: 1986 - No.of Units: Company Owned: 4 - Franchised: 1 - Franchise Fee: $30,000 - Royalty: 7% of gross sales - Total Inv: $100,000 ($30M fee/bal. equip-capital) - Financing: Yes.

UNITED PRINTING UNLIMITED
United Printing Unlimited Inc.
P.O. Box 2020, Davenport, IA, 52809. Contact: Jack Swat, G.M. - Tel: (319) 386-2351. Full service printing centers. Complete support, 3 wks. training, covering all aspects of printing and business. Established: 1985 - Franchising Since: 1986 - No. of Units: Company Owned: 2 - Franchised: 13 - Franchise Fee: $25,000 - Royalty: 5% of gross profit - Total Inv: $25,000 fee, $75,000 equip. - Financing: Yes, 90%.

REAL ESTATE SERVICES

4-SALE HOTLINE
Primark International, Inc.
14 Inverness Dr. E., Ste. E-200, Englewood, CO, 80112. Contact: Chris Petty, Dir., Fran. Sales - Tel: (303) 790-4373. Telephone accessed information assisting real estate agents in increasing sales and gaining listings. Established: 1991 - Franchising Since: 1993 - No. of Units: Company Owned: 5 - Franchised: 10 - Franchise Fee: $15,000 - $25,000 (depending on size of territory) - Royalty: 7%, 1% adv.- Total Inv: $71,500 - $118,500 - Financing: Third party lease available.

ADVANTAGE RADON CONTROL CENTERS
804 Second St. Pike, Southampton, PA, 18966. Contact: Barton Ecksel, C.O.O. - Tel: (215) 953-9200. Offers a franchisee the opportunity to tap into the growing market of home and business owners seeking a safer environment. Our centers provide radon detection, testing and reduction services. Customer-oriented, spotting and solving radon problems quickly and efficiently. Comprehensive two-week training and support package is included, which qualifies you for EPA listing and state certification. Established: 1984 - Franchising Since: 1990 - No. of Units: Company Owned: 1 - Franchise Fee: $17,500 - Royalty: 8% - Financing: Will assist.

ALLIED BROKERS
AB BROKERS
3003 Hopyard Rd., #A, Pleasanton, CA, 94588. Contact: Gary Luperine, V.P. - Tel: (510) 846-8116. Real estate. Established: 1966 - Franchising Since: 1967 - No. of Units: 18 - Franchise Fee: $4,500 - Total Inv: additional $300/mo and 2% over-ride/salespersons - Financing: No.

AMERICA'S CHOICE® CANADA'S CHOICE®
Preferred Realty Concepts, Inc.
646 N. French Rd., Amherst, NY, 14228. Contact: Kathy Akey, Pres. - Tel: (716) 691-0596 or (800) 831-2493 (US/Canada). Owner-assisted Real Estate Marketing. No license needed. Full service owner assisted marketing-owner shows home. Full franchisee training and support. High profit per unit. Established: 1991 - Franchising Since: 1993 - No. of Units: Company Owned: 1 - Franchised: 17 units, 1 state - Franchise Fee: $5,000 - option 1; $13,000 - option 2 State/Province options available - Royalty: 10%, 1% nat'l. adv. - Financing: Yes (options 2 & state/province option).

AMERICAN BROKERS NETWORK, INC.
167 South River Rd., Bedford, NH, 03110-6920. Contact: Ronald P. Boufford, Pres. - Tel: (603) 622-4637. Real estate referrals through a system utilizing inactive licenses to generate leads from within participating brokers community. Established: 1982 - Franchising Since: 1982 - No. of Units: 1 - Approx. Inv: $6,300 plus work inv.- Financing: No.

AMERISPEC HOME INSPECTION SERVICE, INC.
1855 W. Katella Ave., Ste. 330, Orange, CA, 92667. Contact: Gale Sherwood, Dir. of Fran. Recruitment - Tel: (800) 426-2270 or (714) 744-8360, Fax: (714) 744-4602. One of the largest home inspection franchises in both the U.S. and Canada, ranked #1 in our industry for the last two years. We provide exclusive locations, extensive training, and regionally based on-going support. Established: 1987 - Franchising Since: 1988 - No. of Units: Franchised: 262 - Franchise Fee: $11,900 - $22,900 - Royalty: 7%, 3% nat'l adv. - Total Inv: $20,000 - $55,000 - Financing: Up to 50% of initial franchise fee for standard territories.

ARTHUR RUTENBERG HOMES, INC.
13922 58th St. N., Clearwater, FL, 34620. Contact: Raja Jaghab, Sr. V.P. - Tel: (813) 536-5900. Franchisor provides format for residential building business including copyrighted plans, software for sales, purchasing, job cost control, accounting, financial statements and business management. Franchisee sells homes from furnished models and uses Arthur Rutenberg Homes trade name. Established: 1980 - Franchising Since: 1980 - No. of Units: Franchised: 35 - Franchise Fee: $60,000 - Royalty: 3.5% - Total Inv: $250,000 to $350,000 incl. initial fran. fee - Financing: No.

BETTER HOMES AND GARDENS REAL ESTATE
Meredith Corporation
2000 Grand Ave., Des Moines, IA, 50312. Contact: Scott Hale, Mktg. Dir. - Tel: (800) 274-7653. Franchising of real estate companies in all 50 states with a full-service support system. Established: 1977 - Franchising Since: 1978 - No. of Units: Company Owned: 2 - Franchised: 680 - Franchise Fee: $11,000 and up - Royalty: from 6% - Total Inv: varies - Financing: Deferred payment plan for one year.

BETTER HOMES REALTY
Better Homes Realty, Inc.
1556 Parkside Dr., Walnut Creek, CA, 94596-8181. Contact: Florence Stevens, V.P. of Operations - Tel: (510) 937-9001, (800) 642-4428. Real estate franchisor of independently owned and operated offices. Established: 1964 - Franchising Since: 1964 - No. of Units: Franchised: 48 - Franchise Fee: $9,950 - Royalty: 6% royalty/service per transaction - Total Inv: $9,950 for existing brokerages; up to $40,000 start-up - Financing: $4,000 down payment; franchisor may agree on deferred payment.

BRICKKICKER HOME INSPECTION *
Ronlen Enterprises, Inc.
1200 Iroquois Dr., Naperville, IL, 60563. Contact: Ron Ewald, Pres. - Tel: (800) 821-1820. Home and building inspections. Established: 1989 - Franchising Since: 1995 - No. of Units: Company Owned: 2 - Franchised: 71 - Franchise Fee: $4,950 - $13,950 - Royalty: 6% of gross - Total Inv: $9,400 - $24,900 - Financing: 50% of fran. fee.

BUY OWNER INTERNATIONAL
5757 N. Andrews Way, Ft. Lauderdale, FL, 33309. Contact: Scott A. Eckert, Pres. - Tel: (305) 771-7777. A real estate advertising service where sellers pay an up front advertising fee to appear on our computer matching system, TV show, and magazine. Buyers receive free information of properties that meet their requirements. Established: 1984 - No. of Units: Company Owned: 1 - Franchised: 5 - Franchise Fee: $25,000 - Royalty: 5% - Total Inv: $75,000 - $300,000.

BUYER'S AGENT, INC., THE
2014 Exeter Rd., Germantown, TN, 38138. Contact: Andrea Morgan, Fran. Coord. - Tel: (901) 758-1141. Franchisees represent buyers exclusively, in real estate transactions. Established: 1988 - Franchising Since: 1988 - No. of Units: Franchised: 43 - Franchise Fee: $14,900 - Royalty: 5%, 1% adv. - Total Inv: $20,000 - $50,000 - Financing: None offered.

BUYER'S RESOURCE REAL ESTATE
6950 E. Belleview Ave., #100, Englewood, CO, 80111. Contact: Richard Hogue, Pres. - Tel: (800) 359-4092. The nation's largest exclusive buyer brokerage franchise system, offering support in training, management & extensive corporate/consumer referrals. Established: 1989 - Franchising Since: 1989 - No. of Units: Franchised: 95 - Franchise Fee: $14,000 metro, 9,500 rural/resort - Royalty: 5% monthly gross, 2% adv. - Total Inv: $20,000 - $40,000 - Financing: No.

BY OWNER REALITY NETWORK
By Owner, Inc.
Appleway Sq. Mall, 501 W. Appleway, Coeur d'Alene, ID, 83814. Contact: Ann Wall, V.P. - Tel: (208) 667-6184, Fax: (208) 664-4539. Discount and full service real estate centers. Established: 1985 -

Franchising Since: 1986 - No. of Units: Company Owned: 1 - Franchised: 6 - Franchise Fee: $16,500 - Royalty: 10% incl. adv. - Total Inv: Fran. fee plus $14,850 start-up - Financing: No.

CASTLETON *
Castleton Home Corp., Inc.
1960 Congressional Dr., St. Louis, MO, 63146. Contact: Linda Eise, V.P. Sales & Mktg. - Tel: (314) 567-1500, (800) 908-0706. Service to provide a central professional resource for employers & individuals who require quality, cost effective, turnkey temporary housing due to relocation, project assignment or disaster/fire etc. Established: 1987 - Franchising Since: 1994 - No. of Units: Company Owned: 2 - Franchised: 1 - Franchise Fee: $20,000 - Royalty: 6% if less than $83,000 gross rev. per month; 5% if between $83,000 - $125,000 per month; 4% if exceeding $125,000 per month - Total Inv: $50,000 - $110,000 - Financing: Not directly, but will assist in developing a business plan for financial sources.

CENTURY 21 REAL ESTATE
Century 21 Real Estate Corp.
2601 S.E. Main St., Irvine, CA, 92713-9564. Contact: Duane Mora, V.P., Fran. Sales - Tel: (714) 553-2100, (800) 826-8083. Provides a marketing support system for independently owned and operated real estate brokerage offices, offering international advertising, VIP referral system, residential & commercial sales training, national accounts center, client follow-up and other real estate-related services. Established: 1971 - Franchising Since: 1972 - No. of Units: Franchised: 6,081 - Franchise Fee: $15,000 - $30,000 (varies regionally) - Royalty: 6% - Total Inv: varies regionally - Financing: Some financing available; varies regionally.

COLDWELL BANKER RESIDENTIAL AFFILIATES
27271 Las Ramblas, Mission Viejo, CA, 92691. Contact: Darlene Aut, 1st V.P., Fran. Dev. - Tel: (714) 367-1800. National real estate affiliations of existing, selected high quality brokerage firms. Established: 1982 - Franchising Since: 1982 - No. of Units: Franchised: 1,845 - Total Inv: $14,600 to $55,400.

COMREAL INTERNATIONAL, INC.
8725 N.W. 18th Terr., Ste. 105, Miami, FL, 33172. Contact: Stephen H. Smith, Pres. - Tel: (305) 591-3044. Independently owned commercial real estate offices. Established: 1984 - No. of Units: 6 - Total Inv: $400,000 - Financing: None.

CORPORATE HOUSING SERVICES
CHS Holdings Inc.
6135 Mt. Moriah, Ste. 102, Memphis, TN, 38115. Contact: Buddy Carnett & Larry Paylor - Tel: (901) 363-2615. Service provides unique solution for provision of living arrangements for people who are relocating. Established: 1987 - Franchising Since: 1993 - No. of Units: Company Owned: 1 - Franchised: 1 - Franchise Fee: $25,000 - Royalty: 5% monthly - Total Inv: $46,500 to $74,000 - Financing: None available.

ERA MID-AMERICA LTD.
P.O. Box 636, Marshfield, WI, 54449. Contact: Ken Shong, Pres. - Tel: (715) 384-8070. Regional master for real estate. Established: 1984 - Franchising Since: 1971 - No. of Units: Franchised: 19 - Franchise Fee: Varies - Royalty: Monthly - Total Inv: Varies - Financing: Yes.

ERA® - (NAME OF FRANCHISE)
Electronic Realty Associates, L.P.
4900 College Blvd., Overland Park, KS, 66211. Contact: Mike Storen, Sr. V.P. Fran. Sales - Tel: (913) 491-1000. Electronic Realty Associates, L.P. is a real estate franchisor providing related products and services to its franchisees. ERA franchises provide real estate services. Established: 1971 - Franchising Since: 1972 - No. of Units: Franchised: 2,486 - Franchise Fee: $18,900 - Royalty: Flat fee, not based on percent of sales - Total Inv: Variable - Financing: Yes.

H.O.M.E.
P.O. Box 290837, Port Orange, FL, 32129. Contact: M.V. Biro, Dir. - Tel: (904) 767-7523. Instant property information listing network. For Sale By Owner publishing area magazine. Established: 1990 - Franchising Since: 1993 - Franchise Fee: $500 - Royalty: 5% of gross - Total Inv: $2,000 - Financing: No.

HELP-U-SELL REAL ESTATE
102 W. 500 S., #600, Salt Lake City, UT, 84101. Contact: Michael David, Nat'l. Sales Mgr. - Tel: (800) 366-1177. Full service real estate company that offers sellers a menu of services to choose from which could potentially save them money. In addition, buyers are given assistance in purchasing Help-U-Sell listings as well as multiple listing properties. Established: 1976 - Franchising Since: 1978 - No. of Units: Franchised: 315 - Franchise Fee: $295 per 1,000 population - $4,500 min. - Royalty: 8.5% or monthly set fee in some areas - Total Inv: Varies - Financing: Yes.

HER REAL ESTATE INC.
Her Realtors
4656 Executive Dr., Columbus, OH, 43220. Contact: Karen Workman, Pres. - Tel: (614) 457-7400. Real Estate franchise. Established: 1976 - Franchising Since: 1981 - No. of Units: Company Owned: 23 - Franchised: 12 - Franchise Fee: $2,500 - $80,000 - Royalty: 5%, 1% adv. - Total Inv: $6,800 - $23,000 - Financing: Yes.

HOME MARKETING SPECIALISTS, INC. /THE NO-COMMISSION REAL ESTATE EXPERTS
HMS Franchise, Inc.
26222 Telegraph Rd., #300, Southfield, MI, 48034. Contact: J.R. Paine, Chairman - Tel: (810) 353-7170. Helps homeowners sell their own home by providing them with essential professional, technical and legal assistance. HMS charges a flat fee and does not charge a commission. Established: 1986 - Franchising Since: 1987 - No. of Units: Company Owned: 2 - Franchised: 2 - Franchise Fee: $8,900 - Royalty: 6.5% mo. - Total Inv: $30,000 (fee plus $21,000 office set up costs) - Financing: Yes.

HOMEBUYERS' ASSISTANCE PROGRAM, INC.
4725 Parkwick Dr., Columbus, OH, 43228. Contact: Mark Schell, Mgr. - Tel: (614) 276-5577. The services appeal to qualified home buyers presently renting due to the lack of a down payment. The service is marketing as an add-on program for existing real estate companies or builders. - Established: 1990 - Franchising Since: 1993 - No. of Units: Company Owned: 1 - Franchise Fee: $500 - $15,000 - Royalty: 1% - Total Inv: Varies - Financing: No.

HOMEOWNERS CONCEPT, INC.
611 North Mayfair Rd., Wauwatosa, WI, 53226. Contact: J. Michael Phillips, Pres. - Tel: (414) 258-7778. Unique concept in marketing and selling real estate for a small flat fee. The homeowner shows their own home and Homeowners Concept provides everything else that the traditional brokerage offers. Established: 1982 - Franchising Since: 1985 - No. of Units: Franchised: 34 - Franchise Fee: $15,000 - Royalty: 5% monthly gross income, whichever is less - Total Inv: $45,500 - $52,750 - Financing: No.

HOMETEAM INSPECTION SERVICE, THE
4010 Executive Park Dr., #420, Cincinnati, OH, 45241. Contact: Franchise Dept. - Tel: (800) 598-5297, Fax: (513) 563-7614. A Home Inspection Service that emphasizes marketing and ongoing support. As one of our franchisees said, "With our marketing, image and value to our customers, I found that my competition was doing nothing but helping me build my business. People were so accustomed to the 'typical inspection', they just couldn't believe how different we are." Established: 1991 - Franchising Since: 1992 - No. of Units: Franchised: 193 - Franchise Fee: $11,900 - $22,900 - Royalty: 6%, 3% nat'l. adv. - Total Inv: $16,450 to $37,550 incl. fran. fee - Financing: Yes, up to 50% of franchise fee.

HOUSEMASTER - "THE HOME INSPECTION PROFESSIONALS"
421 W. Union Ave, Bound Brook, NJ, 08805. Contact: John Granito, Dir. of Fran. Sales - Tel: (800) 526-3939, Fax: (908) 469-7405. Home inspection and environmental testing. Established: 1971 - Franchising

Since: 1979 - No. of Units: Franchised: 179 - Franchise Fee: $5,000 - $26,000 - Royalty: 7.5%, 2.5% adv. - Total Inv: $12,050 - $62,500 - Financing: No.

INVIRO
"good for a change"
REAL ESRATES 'IN' CROWD™

191 University, # 240, Denver, CO, 80206. Contact: William Krings, Owner - Tel: (800) 571-2044, Fax: (303) 744-0230. Real estate marketing franchise for brokerage management and marketing, associates, collective image advertising, referral system, conversion. Established: 1984 - Franchising Since: 1993 - Franchise Fee: from $5,000 dependent on area - Royalty: Sliding scale based on income: 2% - 4% - Total Inv: conversion: from $10,000, new to $50,000 - Financing: No.

IOWA REALTY MEMBERS
Iowa Realty Company, Inc.
3501 Westown Parkway, W. Des Moines, IA, 50265. Contact: Jack MacWilliams, V.P. - Tel: (515) 224-6222. Franchising real estate companies. Established: 1952 - Franchising Since: 1978 - No. of Units: Company Owned: 27 - Franchised: 60 - Franchise Fee: $4,500 - Total Inv: $2,500 signs, tapes, printed material - Royalty: 5% - Financing: Yes.

KEY ASSOCIATES, INC.
P.O. Box 495, Rockport, IN, 47635. Contact: Don Schultz, Pres. - Tel: (812) 649-9716. Real estate membership. Established: 1977 - Licensing Since: 1977 - No. of Units: Licensed: 45 - Fee: $5,000 - Royalty: flat fee - Total Inv: $7,000 incl. fran. fee - Financing: No.

MJB INTERNATIONAL REAL ESTATE
200 W. Imperial Hwy., Brea, CA, 92621. Contact: Jerome J. Kolb, Pres. - Tel: (714) 990-9000. Real estate resales. Established: 1977 - Franchising Since: 1977 - No. of Units: Company Owned: 17 - Franchised: 119 - Franchise Fee: $5,700 - Total Inv: $8,000 - Royalty: 5.5% - Financing: None.

MSA NATIONWIDE FIELD SERVICE *
19 Thompson St., East Haven, CT, 06473. Contact: J.D. Raffone, Pres. - Tel: (800) 767-3004, Fax: (203) 468-2587. Property inspection and preservation for banks, mortgage companies, and insurance companies. Established: 1979 - Franchising Since; 1986 - No. of Units: Company Owned: 1 - Franchised: 1 - Franchise Fee: $26,500 - Royalty: 2.5% to 15% varies - Total Inv: $26,500 avg. - Financing: No.

NATIONAL PROPERTY INSPECTIONS
11620 Arbor St., Ste. 100, Omaha, NE, 68144. Contact: Julie Erickson, Dir. of Mktg. - Tel: (800) 333-9807. Residential & commercial property inspection. Exclusive territories, expansion encouraged, two week training program, financial assistance, step by step business plan and savy marketing program. National referral network. Established 1987 - Franchising Since: 1987 - No. of Units: Company Owned: 70 - Franchised: 70 - Franchise Fee: $10,000 to $17,000 - Royalty: 8% - Total Inv: $17,000 - Financing: 50% of franchise fee.

NATIONAL REAL ESTATE SERVICE, INC.
P.O. Box 45828, Salt Lake City, UT, 84145-0828. Contact: Mike Desmarteau, V.P. Fran. Sales - Tel: (800) 654-7653, Fax: (619) 277-5352. Our real estate franchise system offers a total marketing system that integrates your office computer in assembling and disseminating marketing data through our House by Mouse® electronic listing catalog, printed monthly listing catalogs, a wide variety of personalized marketing tools for real estate agents, plus exposure of listings on the Internet World Wide Web. Established: 1955 - Franchising Since: 1966 - No. of Units: 400 (U.S. and Canada). Monthly fees for agents. Franchise Fee: $9,500.

PRUDENTIAL REAL ESTATE AFFILIATES, INC., THE
3200 Park Center Drive Ste. l400, Costa Mesa, CA, 92626. Contact: Franchise Dir./Pres. - Tel: (714) 966-9600. Real Estate Services.

RE/MAX
Re/Max International, Inc.
5445 D.T.C. Pkwy., Ste. 1200, Englewood, CO, 80111. Contact: Bob Harple, Mktg. Dir. - Tel: (303) 770-5531. An international real estate network of independent member offices located throughout the U.S. and Canada. The concept is based upon a fair exchange: the highest possible compensation for the sales associate in return for shared common overhead expenses. Established: 1973 - Franchising Since: 1977 - No. of Units: 1,711 - Franchise Fee: $15,500 - $25,000 - Royalty: varies - Total Inv: varies - Financing: Yes.

REAL ESTATE ONE LICENSING CO.
3922 E. M72, P.O. Box 3171, Acme, MI, 49610. Contact: Gary L. Pownall, Pres. - Tel: (616) 938-4444. Full service support system for real estate companies. Appropriate for new or existing businesses. Established: 1972 - Franchising Since: 1972 - No. of Units: Company Owned: 61 - Franchised: 40 - Franchise Fee: $9,800 - Royalty: 5% - Financing: Yes.

REALTY 500
4600 Kietzke Lane, Bldg. M, Ste. 247, Reno, NV, 89502. Contact: Mark N. Ashworth, C.E.O. - Tel: (702) 689-8545, Fax: (702) 689-8546. Complete real estate sales operation. We do conversion & start up, and continuing support. Agent training and continuing education. Discounts on retail supplies, services & staff support at corporate level. Established: 1979 - Franchising Since: 1979 - No. of Units: Franchised: 14 - Franchise Fee: Call for quote - Royalty: 5% of gross commissions - Total Inv: $5,000 to $10,000 depending on office size and location - Financing: Yes.

REALTY EXECUTIVES
Realty Executives International, Inc.
4427 North 36th St., #100, Phoenix, AZ, 85018. Contact: William A. Powers, Chief Oper. Officer - Tel: (800) 733-9327 or (602) 957-0747. Originator of the 100% Commission Concept in real estate, which attracts the top producing agents in the industry and ends the revolving door syndrome that is so common with traditional brokerages. Established: 1965 - Franchising Since: 1973 - No. of Units: Franchised: 357 - Franchise Fee: $15,000 - Royalty: $25 - $35/agent/month - Total Inv: $15,000 - $100,000 - Financing: Yes.

REALTY ONE
Realty One Corp.
7310 Potomac Dr., Boise, ID, 83704. Contact: David Dildine, Pres. - Tel: (208) 322-2700. Full service real estate franchise company offering a new and proven concept to the small broker providing a large office image and support system featuring maximum income and minimum overhead. Established: 1985 - Franchising Since: 1987 - No. of Units: Franchised: 2 - Franchise Fee: $15,000 - Royalty: Per agent monthly fee - Total Inv: $50,000 - $100,000 - Financing: None.

REALTY WORLD CORP.
18500 Von Karman Ave., Ste. 100, Irvine, CA, 92715. Contact: Franchise Director - Tel: (714) 251-0200. Real estate services to unaffiliated real estate brokers. Established: 1974 - Franchising Since: 1974 - No. of Units: 1,500 - Approx. Inv: $20,000 - $30,000 - Royalty: 3%-6% - Financing: Yes.

RED CARPET KEIM REAL ESTATE
29201 Telegraph Rd., Southfield, MI, 48034-7647. Contact: Jim Batcha, V.P. - Tel: (810) 799-9300. Broker owned franchising company providing services to its members in recruiting, advertising, relocation, education & management. Established: 1958 - Franchising Since: 1969 - No. of Units: Franchised: 79 - Franchise Fee: $5,000 - Royalty: Flat fee declining - Total Inv: $5,000 - $80,000 - Financing: No.

REMERICA
Remerica Real Estate Corp.
44523 Ann Arbor Rd., Plymouth, MI, 48170. Contact: James Courtney, Pres. - Tel: 1-800-REMERICA. Real estate franchises. Established: 1989 - Franchising Since: 1990 - No. of Units: Franchised: 20 - Franchise Fee: $5,000 - Royalty: 6% to $30,000, 0% thereafter, 2% adv. to $6,000, 0% thereafter - Financing: None.

RENTAL NETWORK
130 N. Butte, Ste. A, Willows, CA, 95988. Contact: Roger Memmott, V.P. - Tel: (916) 934-8827. Computer matching renters to available properties. Established: 1986 - Franchising Since: 1988 - No. of Units: Company Owned: 1 - Franchised: 7 - Franchise Fee: $25,000 - Royalty: 10% of gross income - Total Inv: $25,000 fran. fee, $15,000 cap. invest. - Financing: No.

ROOM-MATE REFERRAL SERVICE CENTERS & ROOM-MATE REGISTRY
Room-Mate Referral Service Center, Inc.
P.O. Box 890575, Oklahoma City, OK, 73189-0575. Contact: Florence S. Cook, C.E.O. - Tel: (405) 692-0947. A service company that handles the placement of persons as roommates for economic and a variety of other needs. Established: 1979 - Franchising Since: 1984 - No. of Units: Company Owned: 1 - Franchised: 6 - Franchise Fee: $3,000 - $10,000 - Royalty: 5% plus 2% adv. - Total Inv: $5,000 - $15,000 incl. fee - Financing: Yes.

SALE BY OWNER SYSTEMS
2851 S. Parker Rd., Ste. 100, Aurora, CO, 80014. Contact: Phyllis Tasler, Franchisor - Tel: (303) 755-8180, Fax: (303) 755-8142. Marketing and support to sell homes without the use of a real estate agent. Services provided: market analysis, advertising, professional signage, buyers qualification and computerized loan origination. Established: 1992 - Franchising Since: 1994 - No. of Units: Franchised: 2 - Franchise Fee: $15,000 - Royalty: 6%, 2% adv. - Total Inv: fran. fee plus $11,000 - $30,000 - Financing: No.

SEARS REALTY PROFESSIONALS HAS A DREAM HOME FOR YOU CALL AND START PACKING™
A Dream Home For You Corp.
2231 N. Winton Ave., Speedway, IN, 46224. Contact: Hugh Craig, Pres. - Tel: (317) 241-4900. Fantastic real estate franchise brand name, that is affordable for real estate brokers. Our signs are reflective at night from car lights. Free regional vice president district. Established: 1993 - Total Inv: Only $495 compared to $17,500 to $30,000 - Royalty: Can earn $36,000 to $360,000 per year continued service commissions. Can also market Sears Home Warranty Copyright 1993 ADHFY. A resume please.

SELL YOUR OWN HOME
Sell Your Own Home of America
P.O. Box 14804, Lenexa, KS, 66285-0804. Contact: Arvin Zwick, Pres./Founder - Tel: (913) 492-SAVE. Offering a broad range of real estate products and services at discount prices. Unique services include: Talking Home, By Owner Referral Network, nationally recognized How To manual, and much more. The SYOH programs and value are unequalled. Established: 1987 - Franchising Since: 1992 - No. of Units: Company Owned: 1- Franchise Fee: None - Royalty: None - Total Inv: $495. plus working capital - Financing: MC/V.

TRANEX RESIDENTIAL LENDING NETWORK *
24450 Evergreen, Ste. 100, Southfield, MI, 48075-5586. Contact: Mark Tisdel, Dir. of Fran. - Tel: (800) 655-5144. Franchise opportunity for existing residential lenders and interested entrepreneurs. Tranex proven methods of originating and processing loans increases productivity while creating operational efficiencies. Established: 1994 - Franchising Since: 1994 - No. of Units: Company Owned: 1 - Franchised: 6 - Franchise Fee: $15,000 - Royalty: 12.5 basis points (1/8%) of closed loans, monthly - Total Inv: Initial fee, phone line, business cards, letterhead - Financing: Yes.

WORLD INSPECTION NETWORK
World Inspection Network International, Inc.
2701 First Ave., Ste. 340, Seattle, WA, 98121-1123. Contact: Dianne Knapp - Tel: (800) 967-8127, Fax: (206) 441-3655. Professional home based business providing inspection services to sellers, buyers, real estate professionals, lenders and homeowners. As America's leader in the home inspection and environmental screening services, World Inspection Network provides franchisees the most aggressive marketing approach and unique business operating system available. We have a comprehensive 2 week training program that includes inspection marketing and business development, conducting the inspection, and operational procedures for managing your own franchise. Established: 1987 - Franchising Since: 1993 - No. of Units: Franchised: 16 - Franchise Fee: $8,900 - $16,900 - Royalty: 7%, 2% adv. - Total Inv: $13,785 - $25,479 - Financing: Yes, fran. fee.

RENTAL SERVICES

AARON'S RENTAL PURCHASE
309 E. Paces Ferry Rd. N.E., Atlanta, GA, 30305-2377. Contact: Todd Evans, Dir., Fran. Dev. - Tel: (800) 551-6015 or (404) 240-6500. One of the nation's largest publicly held furniture, electronics and appliance rental and sales chains. Established: 1955 - Franchising Since: 1992 - No. of Units: Company Owned: 95 - Franchised: 26 - Franchise Fee: $35,000 - Royalty: 5% gross revenue - Total Inv: $116,950 - $267,900 - Financing: Inventory financing available.

AL'S FORMAL WEAR
Al's Formal Wear, Inc.
P.O. Box 379, Bedford, TX, 76095. Contact: Allen Bodzy, V.P./G.M. - Tel: (817) 355-4444. Tuxedo rental and sales. Established: 1952 - Franchising Since: 1989 - No. of Units: Company Owned: 49 - Franchised: 5 - Franchise Fee: $15,000 - Royalty: Yrs. 1-2 (6%) gross vol., Yrs. 3-10 (10%) gross vol. - Total Inv: $81,000-$137,000 (area fran fee, store fran fee, leasehold, inv, equip, supplies, work cap.) - Financing: No.

APARTMENT SEARCH
Apartment Search International
7900 Xerxes Ave. S., Ste. 2250, Bloomington, MN, 55431. Contact: John Appert, Exec. V.P. - Tel: (612) 830-0509. You're probably aware of how a travel agency or a real estate brokerage firm works. Imagine a similar type of business helping renters find apartments, and you'll have a basic understanding of Apartment Search. The properties are listed with Apartment Search as a form of advertising. The service is paid for by the apartment owner, and is free to renters. Established: 1967 - Franchising Since: 1992 - No. of Units: Company Owned: 18 - Franchise Fee: $40,000 - Royalty: 15% - Total Inv: $85,040 - $135,010 - Financing: Available through private sources for furniture, fixtures and equipment.

APARTMENT SELECTOR
6060 N. Central Exp., #464, Dallas, TX, 75205. Contact: Kendall A. Laughlin, Pres. - Tel: (214) 361-4420, Fax: (214) 361-8677. Free service to renters, apartment owners pay us fee for locating residents. Established: 1959 - Franchising Since: 1982 - No. of Units: Franchised: 20 - Franchise Fee: $2,500 - Royalty: 5% of cash deposits - Total Inv: $15,000 - Financing: None.

BABY'S AWAY
Baby's Away International, Inc.
846 South Vance St., Ste. B, Lakewood, CO, 80226. Contact: Michael Hendler, Steve Hoodecheck, V.P. - Tel: (303) 936-7151, Fax: (303) 727-8828. Rental of baby and children's supplies including, but not limited to, cribs, high chairs, strollers, toys, etc. Established: 1990 - Franchising Since: 1993 - No. of Units: Company Owned: 12 - Franchised: 11 - Franchise Fee: $7,000 - Royalty: 9% plus 5% nat'l. adv. - Total Inv: $13,000 - $18,000 - Financing: Yes.

COLORTYME
1231 Greenway Dr., #900, Irving, TX, 75038-2531. Contact: Ray Orgera, Dir. Fran. Dev. - Tel: (214) 675-9291, (800) 411-8963, Fax: (214) 417-5435. Appliance/television video furniture rentals. Established: 1978 - Franchising Since: 1981 - No. of Units: Company Owned: 8 - Franchised: 331 - Franchise Fee: $25,000 - Royalty: 4%-3%, nat. adv. $250./mth.- Total Inv: $254,616 - $466,480 - Financing: No.

CONDOMINIUM TRAVEL ASSOCIATES, INC.
2001 W. Main St., Ste. 140, Stamford, CT, 06902. Contact: Richard Fisher, Pres. - Tel: (203) 975-7714. Business Opportunity: Condo vacation rental business; home or storefront; part-time or full-time. Includes quality product inventory source, sales training program, marketing plan, educational trips and seminars, and national convention. Established: 1989 - Franchising Since: 1989 - Franchise Fee: $495. first yr. initial member. fee ($250.00 annual renewal fee) - Royalty: none - Total Inv: start-up approx. $2,500 - Financing: None.

GINGISS FORMALWEAR CENTERS
Gingiss International, Inc.
2101 Executive Dr., Addison, IL, 60101-1482. Contact: Jerry Sutlin, Dir. of Fran. Dev. - Tel: (800) 621-7125. The rental and sales of men's formal wear and related accessories. Major shopping center location in 36 states. Established: 1936 - Franchising Since: 1968 - No. of Units: Company Owned: 41 - Franchised: 201 - Franchise Fee: $15,000 - Royalty: 1996=.5%, 1997=.5%, 1998=2.5%, 1999=4.5%, the year 2000 and thereafter=6% - Total Inv: $65,000 inven., $25,000 - $100,000 constr., $8,000 equip. - Financing: Yes.

INACOMP COMPUTER CENTERS
1393 Wheaton Ave. #500, Troy, MI, 48083-1965. Contact: Gail Durkin, Pres. - Tel: (810) 528-5180. A franchise opportunity specializing in short term rentals of personal computers and peripherals; IBM, Apple, Compaq Hewlitt Packard, and a wide variety of peripherals. Established: 1984 - Franchising Since: 1990 - No. of Units: Company Owned: 5 - Franchise Fee: $25,000 - Royalty: 7%, 2% adv. - Total Inv: $40,000 - $170,000 - Financing: Guidance available.

MILITARY RENT-ALL, INC.
United Business Group, Inc.
10351 Santa Monica Blvd., Ste. 430, Los Angeles, CA, 90025. Contact: Matt Feinstein, VP, Fran. Dev. - Tel: (310) 552-2280 or (800) 669-2221. Furniture and appliance rental stores near military bases. Established: 1969 - Franchising Since: 1988 - No. of Units: Company Owned: 1 - Franchised: 14 - Franchise Fee: $20,000 - Royalty: 6% on revenues - Total Inv: $100,000 - $150,000 - Financing: Yes.

NATION-WIDE GENERAL RENTAL CENTERS, INC.
5510 Hwy. #9, North, Alpharetta, GA, 30201. Contact: Ike Goodvin, Pres. - Tel: (800) 227-1643 or (404) 664-7765, Fax: (404) 664-0052. A full line rental center including items for the contractor, do-it-yourself homeowner, such as baby equipment, camping supplies, contractors equipment and tools, invalid needs, lawn and yard tools, mechanics tools, painters equipment, moving needs, party and banquet needs, plumbers tools, sanding machines, household equipment. Established: 1976 - Franchising Since: 1976 - No. of Units: Franchised: 209 - Total Inv: $112,500, cash $40,000 balance of $68,500 can be bank financed - Financing: Assistance available for growth inventory.

PRESIDENT TUXEDO
32185 Hollingsworth, Warren, MI, 48092. Contact: Michael A. Sbrocca, V.P. - Tel: (810) 264-0600. Rentals and sales of men's and women's formalwear and accessories. Established: 1970 - Franchising Since: 1984 - No. of Units: Company Owned: 16 - Franchised: 5 - Franchise Fee: $18,000 - Royalty: 7% - Total Inv: $115,000 - Financing: Yes.

RENT-A-CENTER STORES
8200 E. Rent-A-Center Dr., Wichita, KS, 67226. Contact: Jill Whitemore, Dir. Fran. Dev. - Tel: (316) 636-7368. Rental of household durable goods. Established: 1973 - Franchising Since: 1984 - No. of Units: Company Owned: 265 - Franchised: 157 - Franchise Fee: $25,000 - Royalty: varies - Total Inv: $400,000 per store - Financing: No in-house.

RENTAL REFERRAL PROS
JJB Enterprises
6040-A Six Forks Rd., Ste. 407, Raleigh, NC, 27609. Contact: Stuart Trauberman, Pres. - Tel: (919) 821-7368. Rental listing service. Established: 1991 - Franchising Since: 1991 - No. of Units: Company Owned: 4 - Franchise Fee: $5,000-negotiable - Royalty, Total Inv. and Financing are negotiable.

RENTALAND
Rentaland, Inc.
P.O. Box 5261, Lake Wylie, SC, 29710. Contact: R. J. Guiney, Pres. - Tel: (803) 831-0702. Party rental centers. Exclusive territory by county. High class merchandise of silver, china, linens, flatware, tables, tents, chairs. Established: 1982 - Franchising Since: 1987 - No. of Units: Franchised: 7 - Franchise Fee: $18,000 - Royalty: 5% gross revenue - Total Inv: F.F. $18,000, $100,000 inven., $20,000 fix., $15,000 op. cap. - Financing: $100,000, based on credit qualifications.

SERVISTAR
American Hardware Supply Co.
P.O. Box 1510, Butler, PA, 16003. Contact: Don Belt, V.P. Mktg. - Tel: (412) 283-4567. Complete hardware and lumber supplies with full retail and support systems. Established: 1910 - No. of Units: 3,800.

TALKING BOOK WORLD *
Talking Book Inc.
6692 Orchard Lake Rd., W. Bloomfield, MI, 48322. Contact: Richard Simtob, Pres. - Tel: (810) 737-7171. Audio book store - rentals and sales of audio books in a retail strip center. Established: 1993 - Franchising Since: 1995 - No. of Units: Company Owned: 1 - Franchise Fee: $20,000 development, training, site selection & territory - Royalty: 5% of gross revenues, 1% NH adv. fund - Total Inv: $40,000 inven., $20,000 fee, $15,000 signs & fixtures, $5,000 misc. $5,000 work. cap., $5,000 deposit - Financing: No.

VIP BOAT CLUB
VIP Boat Clubs of Florida Inc.
P.O. Box 1344, Dunedin, FL, 34697. Contact: Frank Reinke, Pres. - Tel: (800) 352-2169, (813) 734-5969. Boat rental in beautiful locations, relaxed lifestyle, with special programs, operations manual, volume prices for insurance, boats & equipment, ongoing support. Established: 1990 - Franchising Since: 1992 - No. of Units: Company Owned: 1 - Franchised: 1 - Franchise Fee: $500 license + expenses + $25/hr for initial training - Royalty: Annual license $500 + expenses + $25/hr support - Total Inv: $60,000 fixed assets; $15,000 oper. cap.; $5,000 license, training & materials; plus varying expenses - Financing: None.

RETAIL

14 KARAT PLUM, THE
Plum International, Inc.
46-022 Alaloa St., #205, Kaneohe, HI, 96744. Contact: Sandy Gottesman, V.P. - Tel: (808) 247-1127. A fine 14 karat gold gift boutique. Established: 1984 - Franchising Since: 1989 - No. of Units: Company Owned: 1 - Franchise Fee: $25,000 - Royalty: 7%, 1% adv. - Total Inv: $165,000 - $225,000 incls. inven. - Financing: No.

A.J. BARNES BICYCLE EXPRESS
Bicycle Franchisors, Inc.
2505 Boca Raton Blvd. NW, Boca Raton, FL, 33431. Contact: Franchise Director - Tel: (901) 867-0600. Retail business specializing in bicycle sales, service, assessories, clothing and rental. Established: 1990 - Franchising Since: 1991 - No. of Units: Franchised: 7 - Franchise Fee: $15,000 - Royalty: 6% - Total Inv: $52,500 - $95,000 (Work. Cap., Inven., Lease, Leasehold Improv., Equip., and Misc.) - Financing: No. For further information please contact: Consultants America Corp., 12279 US Highway 64. Eads, TN, 38028, Tel: (901) 867-0600, Fax: (901) 867-0010.

A NOVEL IDEA BOOKSTORE
Professional Recycled Booksellers Association
168 Great Rd., Rt. 2A, Acton, MA, 01720. Contact: Annie Adams, Pres. - Tel: (508) 263-3158. Recycled paperback bookstores in an upscale atmosphere. Strong new childrens' book section. Greeting cards, bookmarks, CD's & tapes. Established: 1990 - No. of Units: Company Owned: 3 (members 38 in 12 states & Canada) - Franchise Fee: $5,000 - Total Inv: $36,000 - $52,000 - Financing: No.

ABBEY CARPET CO.
3434 Marconi Ave., #A, Sacramento, CA, 95821-6234. Contact: Phil Gutierrez, Pres. - Tel: (916) 974-7080. Retail carpet specialty store franchising to people already in the retail carpet business. Established: 1967 - No. of Units: approx. 130 - Approx. Inv: $2,500 - $5,000 - Financing: Possible.

ACCESSORIES FOR HER
P.O. Box 21261, Fort Lauderdale, FL, 33335-1261. Contact: Bill Henry, Consultant - Tel: (305) 764-7942. We offer earrings and other jewelry accessories at unbelievable savings. Our 216 earring displays are exceptionally profitable in retail stores. For those interested in an accessory boutique - 500 to 1,000 sq. ft. is required and all inventory is guaranteed to sell. Established: 1975 - Total Inv: $4,950 plus.

ACE HARDWARE, ACE HARDWARE HOME CENTER
2200 Kensington Court, Oakbrook, IL, 60521. Contact: Dan Miller, Nat'l Sales Mgr. - Tel: (708) 990-6630 or (708) 932-1000. Nationally branded and private label merchandise at low cost. Established: 1924 - Franchising Since: 1924 - No. of Units: 4,900 - Total Inv: $100,000 - $200,000 - Financing: No, but marketing plan available.

AGWAY, INC.
P.O. Box 4746, Syracuse, NY, 13221. Contact: Dave Menapace, Dir. of Reps. - Tel: (315) 449-7061. Farm, home and garden supplies. Established: 1964 - No. of Units: Company Owned: 265 - Franchised: 370 - Total Inv: varies.

AL'S POTTERY, CHINA & SILVER
Al's Pottery Franchise Systems
5684 Mayfield Rd., Lyndhurst, OH, 44124. Contact: Ellen Lippman, Pres. - Tel: (216) 473-1450 (ext.20). Giftware, china, collectibles & gourmet housewares retail primarily aimed at the bridal market. A truly recession resistant business addressing upscale consumers. Established: 1977 - Franchising Since: 1993 - No. of Units: Company Owned: 1 - Franchise Fee: $25,000-format A; $40,000-format B - Royalty: 5% - Total Inv: $235,000 (low) - $498,000 (high) - Financing: No, applicant must see their own lending institution.

ALMOST HEAVEN, LTD.
Rt. 5-I, Renick, WV, 24966. Contact: Art Glick, V.P. Sales - Tel: (304) 497-3163 or Fax: (304) 497-2698. World's leading manufacturer of hot tubs, spas, saunas, steamrooms and whirlpool baths. Established: 1976 - Franchising Since: 1978 - No. of Units: Franchised: 1,983 - Total Inv: $5,000 - $10,000 - Financing: Yes.

AMERICAN HERITAGE SHUTTERS
American Heritage Shutters Inc.
2345 Dunn Ave., Memphis, TN, 38114. Contact: W. Thomas Crutcher; Ralph Quick, Pres.; VP Mktg./Fran. Dev. - Tel: (901) 743-2800, (800) 541-1186 or Fax: (901) 744-8356. Custom interior and exterior shutters. Established: 1972 - Franchising Since: 1983 - No. of Units: Franchised: 11 - Franchise Fee: $7,500 - Royalty: 5%, 1% adv. - Financing: Negotiable.

ASHLEY AVERY'S COLLECTABLES
16825 Northchase, #910, Houston, TX, 77060. Contact: Ann Nance, Fran. Dev. - Tel: (713) 775-5290. At Ashley Avery's Collectables you will find upscale proven products from the best known names in the collectables industry. Our stores are located in regional malls & offer both an attractive free standing boutique or an elegant in line store. Established: 1990 - Franchising Since: 1990 - No. of Units: Franchised: 5 - Franchise Fee: $20,000/$25,000 - Royalty: 6%, 2% adv. - Total Inv: $92,000 - $250,000 - Financing: 3rd party.

ATLANTIC MOWER PARTS & SUPPLIES, INC.
13421 S.W. 14th Place, Ft. Lauderdale, FL, 33325. Contact: Robert J. Bettelli, Pres. - Tel: (305) 474-4942. Supplier of lawn mower parts. Established: 1978 - Franchising Since: 1987 - No. of Units: Franchised: 14 - Franchise Fee: $15,900 - Royalty: 5% - Total Inv: $45,000 + - Financing: None.

AUSTIN HARDWOODS
2119 Goodrich, Austin, TX, 78704. Contact: Carl Lasner, Pres. - Tel: (512) 442-4001. Retail and wholesale of fine woods. Established: 1972 - Franchising Since: 1977.

BARBECUES GALORE
15041 Bake Pkwy., Ste. A, Irvine, CA, 92718. Contact: Sydney Selati, Chairman - Tel: (714) 581-1753. Chain of stores specializing in barbecue equipment, fireplace and hearth products and related accessories. Established: 1980 - Franchising Since: 1987 - No. of Units: Company Owned: 21 - Franchised: 6 - Franchise Fee: $25,000 - Royalty: 3% on first $1 million and 5% thereafter - Total Inv: Approx. $250,000 incl. approx. $100,000 of inven. - Financing: Sources can be introduced.

BATTERIES PLUS - AMERICA'S BATTERY STORES
625 Walnut Ridge Dr., Hartland, WI, 53029. Contact: Terry Carstenn, Fran. Dev. - Tel: (800) 274-9155. Retailer and distributor of "1,000's of batteries for 1,000's of items." Established: 1988 - Franchising Since: 1992 - No. of Units: Company Owned: 14 - Franchised: 33 operational, 78 under development - Franchise Fee: $22,500 - Royalty: 3% years 1-10, - Total Inv: Fran. fee plus $40,000 fixt. & equip., $55,000 inven., $2,500 prepaid expenses, $12,000 initial adv., $20,000 work. cap. - Financing: Guidance only.

BEADWORKS
Beadworks International, Inc.
149 Water Street, Norwalk, CT, 06854. Contact: Stephen Sammons, Pres. - Tel: (203) 852-9108. Retailing beads and related products to general consumers for making their own jewelry and accessories. Established: 1989 - Franchising Since: 1991 - No. of Units: Company Owned: 3 - Franchised: 6 - Franchise Fee: $15,000 - Royalty: 5% - Total Inv: $110,000 - $160,000 - Financing: No.

BEN FRANKLIN CRAFTS
Ben Franklin Stores Inc.
500 E. North Ave., Carol Stream, IL, 60188. Contact: Wayne Pyrant, V.P. Fran. Sales - Tel: (800) 669-6413. The franchisee operates a general merchandise or craft retail business with the advantages of chain-store buying, merchandising and promotional expertise, with a nationwide reputation for professional service to the public. Established: 1877 - Franchising Since: 1927 - No. of Units: Franchised: 913 - Franchise Fee: $30,000 initial fee - Royalty: 2.5% - Total Inv: $250,000 - $1,000,000 - Financing: yes.

BIG BOB'S USED CARPET SHOPS
Big Bob's Used Carpet Shops of America, Inc.
112 N. Clairborne Ave., Olathe, KS, 66062. Contact: David Elyachar, Pres. - Tel: (913) 782-1991. Big Bob's Used Carpet Shop sells twice cleaned and professionally sanitized used carpet and new carpet at the entry level price point in a warehouse atmosphere. Our operation captures a unique niche in the market that is virtually untapped and has proven successful in a variety of metro areas greater than 250,000 people throughout North America. Established: 1984 - Licensing Since: 1989 - Franchising Since: 1993 - No. of Units: Company Owned: 4 - Franchised: 20 - Franchise Fee: $7,500 - Royalty: 1%-5% sliding scale based on gross sales - Total Inv: $60,000 - $100,000 turn key - Financing: No.

BIGHORN SHEEPSKIN CO.
4810 E. U.S. Highway 90 E, San Antonio, TX, 78219-0596. Contact: Ian Whitaker, Pres. - Tel: (210) 661-4118. Temporary retail locations (kiosks, carts & temp. in-line stores) selling specialty sheepskin products during November & December. Established: 1984 - Franchising Since: 1986 - No. of Units: Company Owned: 14 - Franchised: 82 - Total Inv: $5,000-$10,000, $1,000 equip. rental fee, $2,500 wall rent, $750.00 misc. expenses - Financing: Yes.

BIKER'S DREAM SUPERSTORES
1420 Village Way, Santa Ana, CA, 92705. Contact: Jim Kenefick, Fran. Dir. - Tel: (714) 835-8464. Sale of Harley Davidson motorcycles, accessories, clothing, custom bikes. Established: 1990 - Franchising Since: 1993 - No. of Units: Company Owned: 1 - Franchised: 12 - Franchise Fee: $15,000 - Royalty: 5% + 2% adv. - Total Inv: $150,000 turnkey - 4,000 sq. ft. bldg.

BLACKBERRY COTTAGE
P.O. Box 20927, Albuquerque, NM, 87154-0927. Contact: Owen, Fran. Dir. - Tel: (505) 292-3323. Sale of dolls plush animals. (collector & everyday) toys and games. Established: 1987 - Franchising Since: 1988 - No. of Units: Company Owned: 1 - Franchised: 5 - Franchise Fee: $18,500 - Royalty: 6% - Total Inv: $130,000 - $170,000 - Financing: No.

BOOK RACK
Book Rack Franchising Corp.
2715 E. Commercial Blvd., Ft. Lauderdale, FL, 33308. Contact: Fred Darnell, Pres. - Tel: (305) 771-4310. Used and new paperback books. Established: 1963 - Franchising Since: 1966 - No. of Units: Company Owned: 1 - Franchised: 266 - Franchise Fee: $6,000 - Royalty: $75 per month - Total Inv: $18,000 to $33,000 - Financing: None.

BUTTERFIELD'S ETC.®
Butterfields Development, Inc.
1040 William Hilton Pky., Circle Bldg., Hilton Head, SC, 29928. Contact: Jim Lunceford, Pres. - Tel: (803) 842-6000, Fax: (803) 842-6999. Retail gourmet kitchen store located in upscale malls. Our merchandise mix includes high quality cookware, largest assortment of kitchen gadgets, cookbooks, decorative ceramics, linens, cutlery and fresh roasted coffee beans. Established: 1979 - Franchising Since: 1986 - No. of Units: Franchised: 22 - Franchise Fee: $20,000 declining to $14,000 - Royalty: 5% declining to 4% - Total Inv: $135,000 to over $200,000 - Financing: No, assist with SBA and proforma.

CALIDO CHILE TRADERS
Calido Chile Traders Systems Inc.
233 W. 47th St., Kansas City, MO, 64112. Contact: Jason Gilchnst, Fran. Agent - Tel: (816) 531-8898. Southwestern-style retail store which carries salsas, spices, and cookware. Established: 1993 - Franchising Since: 1994 - No. of Units: Company Owned: 4 - Franchised: 24 - Franchise Fee: $25,000 - Royalty: 5% - Total Inv: $125,850 - $194,300 - Financing: None.

CANDLEMAN
Candleman Corp.
1021 Industrial Pk. Rd., P.O. Box 731, Brainerd, MN, 56401. Contact: Sara Wise, V.P. - Tel: (218) 829-0592, (800) 328-3453, Fax: (218) 825-2449. Upscale retail candle store located in high traffic shopping malls offering candles, candle holders and related accessories. Established: 1991 - Franchising Since: 1992 - No. of Units: Company Owned: 2 - Franchised: 56 - Franchise Fee: $25,000 - Royalty: 6% - Total Inv: $150,000 - $200,000 - Financing: Indirect financial assistance.

CANDY EXPRESS
Candy Express Franchising, Inc.
10480 Little Patuxent Pkwy., #320, Columbia, MD, 21044-3506. Contact: Joel Rosenberg, Pres. - Tel: (410) 964-5500. Specialty retail candy stores located in regional shopping centers. Self serve format that is easy to operate & profitable. Franchisor offers total turnkey including site selection, lease negotiation, store design & construction, training and grand opening. Established: 1988 - Franchising Since: 1990 - No. of Units: Company Owned: 6 - Franchised: 55 - Franchise Fee: $25,000 - Royalty: 6% gross sales per wk., 1% adv. fee - Total Inv: $175,000 - Financing: Yes.

CARPETERIA
Carpeteria, Inc.
25322 Rye Canyon Rd., Valencia, CA, 91355. Contact: Craig Bruce, V.P. Fran. - Tel: (805) 295-1000, Fax: (805) 294-1167. Retail floor and window coverings business operating from a network of inventory stores, sample showrooms and shop at home vans. Established: 1960 - Franchising Since: 1972 - No. of Units: Company Owned: 31 stores, 10 vans - Franchised: 38 stores, 12 vans - Franchise Fee: $25,000 - $100,000 - Royalty: 5% adv. - Total Inv: $100,000 - $500,000 - Financing: Yes, fran. fee.

CARTOON CLASSICS
3069 N. Mall Rd., #B, Knoxville, TN, 37924-2072. Contact: Lisa Sands, Owner/Pres. - Tel: (615) 521-9434. Sells licensed Cartoon Merchandise from Mickey Mouse, Bugs Bunny to Underdog. The shops also carry classic merchandise that features the likes of Elvis, Marilyn Monroe, James Dean, the 3 Stooges and more. Established: 1992 - Franchising Since: 1994 - No. of Units: Company Owned: 7.

CASWELL-MASSEY
121 Fieldcrest Ave., Edison, NJ, 08818. Contact: Mary Gardner, - Tel: (908) 225-2181. Founded in 1752, Caswell-Massey is a nationwide chain of retail stores offering high quality fragrance and personal care items. We provide operations and training support. Established: 1752 - Franchising Since: 1976 - No. of Units: Company Owned: 21 - Licensed: 5 - Total Inv: $75,000 - $170,000 inventory and store set-up - Financing: no.

CATHOLIC STORE *
3441 S. Broadway, Englewood, CO, 80110. Contact: Michael Cyrus, Pres - Tel: (800) 776-4569, Fax: (303) 789-2754. Catholic bible, book and gift store. Established: 1981 - Franchising Since: 1994 - No. of Units: Company Owned: 1 - Franchised: 1 - Franchise Fee: $15,500 - Royalty: 4%, 1% adv. - Total Inv: $120,000 - $170,000 - Financing: Assistance provided.

CD WAREHOUSE *
Compact Discs International, Ltd.
1710 Firman Dr., Ste. 300, Richardson, TX, 75081. Contact: David G. Smith, V.P., Fran. Sales - Tel: (214) 437-3559. CD Warehouse is a rapidly expanding chain of retail stores that sell new and used compact discs. Our innovative P.O.S. computer system allows you to operate a store, buying and selling pre-owned compact discs, without any prior music knowledge. Established: 1990 - Franchising Since: 1992 - No. of Units: Company Owned: 1 - Franchised: 94 - Franchise Fee: $6,000 - Royalty: 5% of gross sales - Total Inv: $47,000 - $60,000 - Financing: None.

CHESAPEAKE KNIFE & TOOL
9385-G Gerwig Ln., Columbia, MD, 21046. Contact: Sarah Herman, Mktg. Dir. - Tel: (410) 720-5114. Retail sales of cutlery, knives, and collectibles. Established: 1980 - Franchising Since: 1993 - No. of Units: Company Owned: 12 - Franchised: 6 - Franchise Fee: $25,000 - Royalty: 6% - Total Inv: $160,000 - $250,000 - Financing: Work with lending institutions.

CLASSIC CHINA *
Classic China Franchising, Inc.
870 Colt Rd., Ste. 2653, Richardson, TX, 75080. , Franchising Dir. - Tel: (901) 867-0600. Retail store selling china, silver, crystal and other gift items including bridal registry services and wedding stationary. Established: 1988 - No. of Units: Company Owned: 1 - Franchised: 3 - Franchise Fee $20,000 - Royalty: 2% - 4% - Total Inv: $141,500 - $175,000 (real estate, office equip. and furn., inven., work. cap.). For further information please contact: Consultants America Corp., 12279 US Highway 64. Eads, TN, 38028, Tel: (901) 867-0600, Fax: (901) 867-0010.

COAST TO COAST HARDWARE
Coast to Coast Stores, Inc.
501 South Cherry St., Ste. 100, Denver, CO, 80222. , Dir. Fran. - Tel: (901) 867-0600. Retail store specializing in automotive, electrical hardware, appliances, furniture, housewares, gifts, lawn, farm & garden paints, plumbing, sporting goods, toys, and wheels. Established: 1990 - No. of Units: Franchised: 843 - Franchise Fee: $6,000 - Royalty: variable percentage - Total Inv: $236,500 - $720,500 (train., equip., inven., real

estate, and misc.) - Financing: Yes. For further information please contact: Consultants America Corp., 12279 US Highway 64. Eads, TN, 38028, Tel: (901) 867-0600, Fax: (901) 867-0010.

CONNOISSEUR, THE
Connoisseur Franchise Corp.
201 Torrence Blvd., Redondo Beach, CA, 90277. Contact: Sandy French, Pres. - Tel: (310) 374-9768, Fax: (310) 372-9097. Personalized gifts. Established: 1975 - Franchising Since: 1995 - No. of Units: Company Owned: 1 - Franchised: 2 - Franchise Fee: $29,500 - Royalty: 6% - Total Inv: $100,000 approx. - Financing: No.

COUNTRY CLUTTER
Country Visions
3333 Vaca Valley Pkwy., #900, Vacaville, CA, 95688. Contact: Ken Petersen, Partner - Tel: (800) 425-8883. A charming country store for gifts, collectibles and home decor. A unique business that offers old fashioned quality, selection and customer service. A complete franchise program that is professionally designed, computerized and planned to sell a perfected blend of country merchandise made up of primarily American manufacturers and crafters. Rich arrangements and displays of textures, colors and aromas make shopping at Country Clutter a true sensory delight. Established: 1991 - Franchising Since: 1992 - No. of Units: Franchised: 17 - Franchise Fee: $25,000 - Royalty: 4% - Total Inv: $158,000 to $258,000 - Financing: Will assist.

CRAFTERS BOUTIQUE *
Diana Crafters, Ltd.
1600 Deer Park Ave., Deer Park, NY, 11729. Contact: Diana, Pres. - Tel: (516) 825-2275, Fax: (516) 825-2280. A unique retail store where no inventory is required. Local artisans and crafters rent display-space in your beautifully designed showroom. Established: 1994 - Franchising Since: 1994 - No. of Units: Company Owned: 1 - Franchised: 1 - Franchise Fee: $15,000 - Royalty: $2,400 per yr. paid quarterly - Total Inv: $50,000: Fran. Fee + $35,000 capital - Financing: 3rd party.

CRAZY BENZY'S FRANCHISE CORP. *
23 S. Telegraph Rd., Pontiac, MI, 48341-1568. Contact: Stefan London, V.P. - Tel: (810) 335-2100. Retailer of hand, air & power tools for mechanics & woodworkers. Established: 1981 - Franchising Since: 1987 - No. of Units: 3 - Franchised: 6 - Franchise Fee: $14,900 - Royalty: 3.9% of net revenue - Total Inv: $190,000 for turn-key operation - Financing: Yes.

CROWN TROPHY, INC.
1 Odell Plaza, Yonkers, NY, 10701. Contact: Chuck Weisenfeld, Pres. - Tel: (914) 963-0005. Manufacture and assemble all types of awards. All engraving done on premises. Established: 1978 - Franchising Since: 1985 - No. of Units: Company Owned: 2 - Franchised: 28 - Franchise Fee: $15,000 - Royalty: 4% - Total Inv: $75,000.

DAN'S FAN CITY
Dan's Fan City, Inc.
300 Dunbar Ave., Oldsmar, FL, 34677. Contact: Howard Christians, Pres. - Tel: (813) 855-7384. Ceiling fan specialty retailer. Established: 1979 - Franchising Since: 1989 - No. of Units: Company Owned: 26 - Franchised: 46 - Franchise Fee: $10,000 - Royalty: none - Total Inv: $41,100: lic. fee $10,000, real estate $1,300, lease & deposits $1,300, lease improv. $1,000, equip. $1,000, inven. $12,650, insur. $1,000, training $1,000, grand open adv. $5,000, work cap. $5,000, signage $1,500, permits & lic. $100, office equip. & supplies $250 - Financing: No.

DIAMONTRIGUE
Diamonflair Corp.
7701 Broadway, #1, San Antonio, TX, 78209. Contact: Phylis Rosberg, Pres. - Tel: (210) 828-1394. First class salon approach. Simulated diamond jewellery in 14 karat gold. Established: 1971 - Franchising Since: 1978 - No. of Units: Company Owned: 2 - Franchised: 6 - Inv: $90,000 - $100,000 - Royalty: 2% gross + 1% adv. - Financing: yes.

DISC GO ROUND *
Grow Biz International
4200 Dahlberg Dr., Minneapolis, MN, 55422. Contact: Steve Gemlo, V.P., Fran. Dev. - Tel: (612) 520-8500, Fax: (612) 520-8501. Retail music CD store that buys, sells and trades used and new CD's, CD-Rom, and accessories. Established: 1990 - Franchising Since: 1994 - No. of Units: Company Owned: 2 - Franchised: 182 - Franchise Fee: $20,000 - Royalty: 5% - Total Inv: $80,000 to $105,000 - Financing: SBA financing available, up to two-thirds of capital.

DISCOUNT PARTY WAREHOUSE
Concord Franchise Corp.
538 Larkfield Rd., E. Northport, NY, 11731. Contact: Ed Rosenberg - Tel: (516) 368-5200. Retail and wholesale of party supplies, balloons and greeting cards at greatly discounted prices. Our stores are a warehouse concept with a large assortment of merchandise and special attention paid to customer service. Established: 1986 - Franchising Since: 1986 - No. of Units: Company Owned: 22 - Franchised: 14 - Franchise Fee: $25,000 - Royalty: 5% - Total Inv: $250,000: $25,000 fee, $150,000 merchandise, $25,000 computer, $25,000 store fixtures, $25,000 other - Financing: None.

DONNA JEAN'S UNIQUE COUNTRY GIFTS *
1919 South 40th St., Ste. 202, Lincoln, NE, 68506-5248. Contact: Jack L. Rediger, Pres., Franchise Developers - Tel: (402) 434-5624, Fax: (402) 434-5620. Do something for yourself! Own your very own Donna Jean's Unique Country Gifts store. Be a part of an exciting growth store. Complete support and training to get you started and keep you going. Volume buying. Low investment. High returns. Established: 1989 - Franchising Since: 1995 - No. of Units: Company Owned: 10 - Franchised: 1 - Franchise Fee: $20,000 - Royalty: 7%, 1% adv. - Total Inv: $59,300 - $196,700 - Financing: None.

DRAPERY FACTORY, THE
80 Tanforan Ave., Ste. 10, South San Francisco, CA, 94080. Contact: Vic Brown, Fran. Dir. - Tel: (415) 583-1300 or (800) 637-2731. Custom window coverings, custom drapery, blinds and bedspreads. Established: 1980 - Franchising Since: 1988 - Number of Units: Franchised: 27 - Franchise Fee: $25,000 - Royalty: 6% - Total Inv: $50,000-$60,000 - Financing: Yes.

DRUG CASTLE FRANCHISES, INC.
810 E. High St., Springfield, OH, 45505. Contact: Rich Brown, V.P. - Tel: (513) 323-4243. Deep discount drug stores combining drug store items with household food and sundry items. High volume, low margin. Established: 1982 - Franchising Since: 1984 - No. of Units Franchised: 11 - Franchise Fee: $27,500 - Total Inv: $722,000 - $1,100,000 - Royalty: 1% - 2% - Financing: No.

DRUG EMPORIUM, INC.
155 Hidden Ravines Dr., Powell, OH, 43065. Contact: Pat Hiller, V.P. Fran. - Tel: (614) 548-7080. Deep discount drug store selling primarily health and beauty aids, cosmetics and greeting cards with an in-house pharmacy. Established: 1977 - No. of Units: Company Owned: 114 - Franchised: 104 - Inv: $600,000 equity capital with $300,000 line of credit per store, franchise fee $25,000 first store, $10,000 each additional store - Royalty: scale 1% - 1.25%.

EASYRIDERS FRANCHISING INC.
5055 Chesebro Rd., Agoura Hills, CA, 91301. Contact: Ed Geise, Fran. Sales Associate - Tel: (818) 879-6114, Fax: (818) 879-6124. Full service parts and accessories aftermarket store specializing in Harley-Davidsons. Established: 1993 - Franchising Since: 1994 - No. of Units: Company Owned: 3 - Franchised: 17 - Franchise Fee: $15,000 - Royalty: 3% - Total Inv: $261,500 - $488,000 - Financing: No.

EXQUISITE CRAFTS
Exquisite Crafts, Inc.
108 Gleneida Ave., Carmel, NY, 10512. Contact: Marianne Montagna, Pres. - Tel: (914) 245-5112. A special craft supply store offering over 30 different departments, as well as workshops and quality finished crafts and designs. Customer service is a strong point in selling needlecrafts, candy, art supplies, flowers, children's crafts and doll-house miniatures. Established: 1972 - Franchising Since: 1989 - No. of Units: Company Owned: 1 - Franchise Fee: $10,000 - Royalty: 4% of gross sales - Total Inv: $42,000 - $58,505 - Financing: No.

FIELD OF DREAMS
42620 Caroline Ct., Palm Desert, CA, 92211-5144. Contact: Lou Novak, Nat'l Fran. Sales - Tel: (619) 776-1010. Sports celebrity personality gift store in regional mall locations. Exclusive and limited

edition sports celebrity personality autographs and signed sports memorabilia (baseballs, footballs, jerseys, baseball cards etc.). Established: 1990 - Franchising Since: 1991 - No. of Units: Franchised: 20 - Franchise Fee: $19,000 - $32,500 - Royalty: 6%, 3% adv./mktg. - Total Inv: $50,000 - $240,000 - Financing: Will assist with SBA, etc.

FLOORS TO GO
2333 Arden Way, Sacramento, CA, 95825. Contact: Jake Kimmel, Owner - Tel: (916) 920-2070. Retail floor covering. Group together floor dealers in key areas. Together they combine their advertising thusly lowering their adv. cost by 95%. Also they are able to save between 10% - 25% on purchasing. Established: 1976 - Franchising Since: 1990 - No. of Units: Franchised: 15 - Franchise Fee: $1,500/month - Financing: None.

FOUR EVERGREEN SILK PLANT STORES *
Everlasting Expressions
511 S. Airport Rd., Bismarck, ND, 58504. Contact: Mike Dolbec, Pres. - Tel: (701) 224-8301. Retail silk plant stores, in home & commercial decorating service. Established: 1989 - Franchising Since: 1994 - No. of Units: Company Owned: 1 - Franchise Fee: $15,000 - Royalty: 400/mo. - Total Inv: $40,000 - buyer gets $40,000 worth of retail product - Financing: No.

FUNCTION JUNCTION
Simian Commercial
P.O. Box 6064, Leawood, KS, 66206. Contact: Laura Stewart, Admin. Dir. - Tel: (816) 471-6000. Retail lifestyle housewares. Established: 1976 - Franchising Since: 1982 - No. of Units: Company Owned: 10 - Franchised: 3 - Franchise Fee: varies - Total Inv: $150,000 - $200,000.

GAME PLAYER
Game Player Franchising Inc.
1919 South 40th St., Ste. 202, Lincoln, NE, 68508. Contact: Franchise Developers - Tel: (800) 865-2378. Exciting new industry. Retail sales and exchange of new and pre-played video games. Established: 1993 - Franchising Since: 1993 - No. of Units: Company Owned: 2 - Franchise Fee: $16,500 - Total Inv: $45,650 - $77,400 - Financing: Will provide assistance in locating financing.

GENDRON GIFTS
The Gendron Corp.
3275 Hillmont Cir., Orlando, FL, 32817. Contact: Jess Gendron, Pres. - Tel: (407) 679-6700. Retail gift shop with humor & hilarious items, mall locations. Established: 1992 - Franchising Since: 1993 - Franchise Fee: $10,000 - Royalty: 5% - Total Inv: Const. & products turnkey $180,000 - $210,000 - Financing: Not at this time.

GEORGIA CARPET OUTLETS
GCO, Inc.
7061 Halcyon Summit Dr., Montgomery, AL, 36117. Contact: Dick McAdams, Pres. - Tel: (334) 279-8345. Franchisor for cash and carry retail carpet/floor covering outlets. Established: 1988 - Franchising Since: 1989 - No. of Units: Company Owned: 3 - Franchised: 20 - Franchise Fee: $20,000 - Royalty: 5% for first $500,000 gross sales during each yr., 3% on gross sales in excess of $500,000 during such yr. - Total Inv: $188,700 - $481,500 - Financing: No.

GOLF USA
Golf USA, Inc.
1801 South Broadway, Edmond, OK, 73013. Contact: Jim Gould or Steve Mace, Fran. Dept. - Tel: (800) 488-1107, Fax: (405) 340-8716. Sale of franchise for discount retail golf equipment and accessories stores. Established: 1986 - Franchising Since: 1989 - No. of Units: Company Owned: 1 - Franchised: 107 - Franchise Fee: $30,000 - $40,000 - Royalty: 2% gross sales, 1% coop. adv. fund - Total Inv: $138,300 - $277,500 - Financing: Franchisee's responsibility with assistance from franchisor.

H20 +
676 N. Michigan Ave., Ste. 3900, Chicago, IL, 60611. Contact: Liz Walfers, Fran. Mgr. - Tel: (312) 642-1100, Fax: (312) 642-9207. Retailer of innovative cosmetic, bath, skincare and fragrance products. Established: 1989 - Franchising Since: 1993 - No. of Units: Company Owned: 57 - Franchised: 9 - Franchise Fee: $28,000 - Royalty: 4% yr. 1, 5% yr. 2, 5.5% yrs. 3-10 - Total Inv: $250,000 - $280,000 - Financing: None.

HAPPI-NAMES
Happi-Stores, Inc.
6645 Poplar Ave., Germantown, TN, 38138-0641. Contact: J. Richard Holley, Pres. - Tel: (901) 758-0034. Personalized gift store. Established: 1982 - No. of Units: 9 - Approx. Inv: $30,000 - Financing: None.

HAT ZONE, THE *
Hat Zone Franchising Co. Ltd., The
130 Independence Ctr., Independence, MO, 64057. Contact: Roger Johnson, V.P. - Tel: (816) 795-1077. Specialty retail store featuring the largest & best selection of hats ranging from fashion hats to baseball. Established: 1993 - Franchising Since: 1995 - No. of Units: Company Owned: 6 - Franchise Fee: $25,000 - Royalty: 6% - Total Inv: $87,370 to $234,300 - Financing: None.

HYCITE CORPORATION
Royal Prestiges
333 Holtzman Rd., Madison, WI, 53713. Contact: Peter O. Johnson, Pres. - Tel: (608) 273-3373. Complete line of cookware, cutlery, china, stonewear, casual and formal crystal and premium items for direct sales industry, together with financial package, sales promotion and incentive program. Established: 1961 - No. of Units: Company Owned: 3 - Franchised: 68 - Approx. Initial Inv: $500-$1,000 - Approx. Total Inv: $3,000 -$5,000.

ILLUSIONS REPLICA JEWELRY
Illusions Jewelry Company
30 Wall St., Asheville, NC, 28801. Contact: Carol C. Hensley, New Store & Product Dev. - Tel: (704) 252-3289. Sales of replica jewelry & other related products. Established: 1989 - No. of Units: Company Owned: 3 - Total Inv: opening inven. $25,000 - $30,000 inventory wholesale; $8,000 - $11,000 cases; $10,000 - $15,000 upfitting location - Financing: No.

ISLAND WATER SPORTS
Island Water Sports Franchise Group Inc.
1985 NE 2nd St., Deerfield Bch., FL, 33441-3799. Contact: Gregory Dooley, Dir. of Operations - Tel: (305) 427-5665. Retail surf apparel store that also sells water sporting goods equipment according to area. Stores also sell skateboards. Established: 1979 - Licensing Since: 1989 - No. of Units: Company Owned: 25 (3 co-owned) - Franchised: 1 - Franchise Fee: $25,000 - Total Approx. Inv: $125,000 - Financing: Assistance only.

JEANNE PIAUBERT COSMETICS, LTD. *
11845 Olympic Blvd., Ste. 900, Los Angeles, CA, 90064. Contact: Mary Leix - Tel: (800) 888-9932. Retail skin & bodycare products with facial & body service offered in upscale malls. Established: 1995 - Franchising Since: 1995 - No. of Units: Company Owned: 1 - Franchise Fee: $35,000 - Royalty: 3% gross, 2% adv. - Total Inv: $275,000 to $325,000 - Financing: No.

JOHN SIMMONS
STS, Inc.
36 W. Calhoun, Memphis, TN, 38103. Contact: Frances Cianciolo, Pres. - Tel: (901) 526-5567. Retail gift shops. Established: 1970 - Franchising Since: 1970 - No. of Units: Company Owned: 1 - Franchised: 1 - Franchise Fee: $15,000 - Royalty: 3.5% - Total Inv: $110,000 - $185,000 - Financing: No.

JOHN T'S UNIQUE GIFTS *
1018 Garden St., Ste. 206, Santa Barbara, CA, 93101. Contact: George Antonaros, Pres. - Tel: (800) 782-8988, (805) 564-6948, Fax: (805) 564-6953. Games, gifts, cigars & gobacco products retail sales. Established: 1967 - Franchising Since: 1991 - No. of Units: Company Owned: 5 - Franchised: 1 - Franchise Fee: $10,000 - Royalty: 5% - Total Inv: $125,000 to $215,000 - Financing: No.

JUST-A-BUCK
155 N. Main St., New City, NY, 10596. Contact: Stacey Sheinbaum, Mktg. Dir. - Tel: (800) 332-2229. Diverse selection of unique merchandise for Just-A-Buck. Retail operation that caters to the ever-evolving low price point marketplace. Established: 1980 - Franchising Since: 1992 -

No. of Units: Company Owned: 8 - Franchised: 3 - Franchise Fee: $25,000 - Royalty: 3% - Total Inv: $183,650 - $264,900 (incl. fran. fee) - Financing: Assistance, not direct.

KIDS TEAM
Kids Franchise Corp.
8466 Colorado St., Merrillville, IN, 46410. Contact: Kevin Schmidt, Pres. - Tel: (219) 947-4115. Retailer of children's licensed sports apparel featuring professional and collegiate apparel in sizes ranging from infant to youth size 20. Established: 1972 - Franchising Since: 1993 - No. of Units: Company Owned: 2 - Franchised: 1 - Franchise Fee: $10,000 - Royalty: 4% - Total Inv: $60,500 - $138,500 - Financing: None.

KING KOIL BEDQUARTERS
King Koil Sleep Products
770 Transfer Rd., Ste. 13, St. Paul, MN, 55114. Contact: Dave Powers, V.P. Sales/Mktg. - Tel: (800) 888-6070, Fax: (612) 646-8864. Sleep shop mattress retail strategy. Free standing or business expansion of furniture or appliance operation - or electronics store expansion. Established: 1898 - Franchising Since: 1982 - No. of Units: Franchised: over 100 - Total Inv: Upon request - Financing: N/A.

LEMSTONE BOOKS
Lemstone, Inc.
1123 Wheaton Oaks Ct., Wheaton, IL, 60187. Contact: Mr. Jim Doyle, Sales Mgr. - Tel: (708) 682-1400. Christian book/gift/music stores in regional malls. Established: 1982 - Franchising Since: 1982 - No. of Units: Company Owned: 1 - Franchised: 57 - Franchise Fee: $30,000 - Royalty: 4% + 1% adv. fund contribution - Total Inv: $150,000 - $185,000 - Financing: No.

LITTLE PROFESSOR BOOK CENTER / LITTLE PROFESSOR BOOK COMPANY
Little Professor Book Centers, Inc.
130 South First St., #300, Ann Arbor, MI, 48104. Contact: Christi Shaw, Fran. Dev. - Tel: (800) 899-6232. Full-line, full-service community book stores carrying a complete selection of books, magazines and book related sidelines. Franchisor provides complete assistance and counsel needed to open and operate a book store from site selection to store opening, through the life of the agreement. Established: 1961 - Franchising Since: 1969 - No. of Units: Franchised: 108 - Franchise Fee: $34,000 - Royalty: 3% + .5% adv. - Total Inv: $285,000 ($110,000 cash) - Financing: Indirect financing available thru national lenders.

LOCKS & KEYS, INC. *
378 Washington St., Woburn, MA, 01801. Contact: John, Manager - Tel: (617) 935-9999, Fax: (617) WEL-COME (935-2663). Key making, key chains and gift center, engraving etc. Established: 1976 - Franchising Since: 1986 - No. of Units: Company Owned: 1 - Franchised: 1.

LOGOS AND LABELS
Wickenhauser, Inc.
145 St. Louis Union Station, St. Louis, MO, 63103. Contact: Matt Wickenhauser, Pres. - Tel: (314) 621-0702. A unique specialty retail store that offers a variety of merchandise bearing world and nationally known trademarks such as Coca-Cola, Budweiser and Pepsi-Cola. Stores are located in major retail centers. Established: 1986 - Franchising Since: 1987 - No. of Units: Company Owned: 2 - Franchised: 2 - Franchise Fee: $10,000 - Royalty: 5% plus 2% adv. - Total Inv: $75,000 - $125,000 - Financing: No.

M.G.M. LIQUOR WAREHOUSE
M.G.M. International
1124 Larpenteur Ave., W., St. Paul, MN, 55113. Contact: Jackie Jorgenson, Fran. Dir. - Tel: (612) 487-1006. Retail, off-sale liquor stores, 5,000-8,000 sq. ft. Established: 1970 - Franchising Since: 1979 - No. of Units: Company Owned: 2 - Franchised: 27 - Franchise Fee: $25,000 - $50,000 - Total Inv: $250,000 - Royalty: varies - Financing: No.

MISTER MONEY - USA *
234 Walnut St., Fort Collins, CO, 80524. Contact: Tim Lanham, Fran. Dev. - Tel: (970) 493-0574. Franchisees provide loan funds to customers. Under one program, franchisees operate a loan store. It loans money and accepts collateral as security. If a customer defaults, franchisee moves all the merchandise through Mister Money - USA, receives cash plus profit and loans out money again. Under another arrangement, franchisee keeps items to sell at retail. Opportunities exist in large and small markets and multiple unit growth. Established: 1976 - Franchising Since: 1995 - No. of Units: Company Owned: 15 - Franchise Fee: $21,500 - $24,500 - Royalty: 8% - Total Inv: Plan A: $64,000 (fee $21,500; start up $27,500; loan funds $15,000), Plan B: $128,000 (fee $24,500; start up $43,500; loan funds $30,000; inventory $30,000) - Financing: Partial support of pawn loans.

MOLE HOLE, THE
1201 Third St., S., Naples, FL, 33940. Contact: Jack D. Harris, Pres. - Tel: (813) 262-5115. Gallery with high quality gifts, household accessories, professional handcrafted gifts and art items. Established: 1964 - Franchising Since: 1968 - No. of Units: Company Owned: 1 - Franchised: 125 - Approx. Inv: $75,000 - $100,000.

MUNCHABLE BOUQUET *
Candy Magic, Inc.
7634 Morgan Ave. S., Richfield, MN, 55423. Contact: Thomas Lee, Pres. - Tel: (612) 869-1006. We design & sell floral-looking bouquets made with edible products such as candy, gourmet coffees, teas and biscuits. Established: 1991 - Franchising Since: 1994 - No. of Units: Company Owned: 1 - Franchised: 1 - Franchise Fee: $7,500 - Royalty: 6% - Total Inv: $40,000 - $55,000 - Financing: No.

MUSIC GO ROUND *
Grow Biz International
4200 Dahlberg Dr., Minneapolis, MN, 55422. Contact: Steve Gemlo, V.P., Fran. Dev. - Tel: (612) 520-8500, Fax: (612) 520-8501. Retail music stores that buy, sell, trade and consign used and new musical instruments and equipment. Established: 1986 - Franchising Since: 1994 - No. of Units: Company Owned: 3 - Franchised: 10 - Franchise Fee: $20,000 - Royalty: 3% - Total Inv: $145,000 to $200,000 - Financing: SBA financing available, up to two-thirds of capital.

MY VERY OWN CLOCK
D&K Enterprises Inc.
3216 Commander Dr., Ste. 101, Dept. 17, Carrollton, TX, 75006. Contact: Marketing Dept. - Tel: (214) 248-9100. The gift of time will last forever when its personalized. Home-based or on location opportunity with unlimited income potential. These personalized clocks make great gifts for weddings, birthdays, holidays or for any gift giving occasion. Franchising Since: 1987 - No. of Units: Company Owned: 1 - Franchised: 18 in 6 states in 4 countries - Total Inv: $2,495 - Financing: Yes.

NATIONALITIES
Nationalities Franchising Inc.
7561 Dodge, Ste. 1, Omaha, NE, 68114. Contact: Mike Ware, Bus. Dev. Mgr. - Tel: (800) 301-9504. RRetail T-shirts and accessories for all nationalities. Established: 1989 - Franchising Since: 1993 - No. of Units: Company Owned: 23 - Franchised: 8 - Franchise Fee: $3,000 - $20,000 - Royalty: 1% - 5%, 1% adv. - Total Inv: $12,875 - $128,500 - Financing: No.

NATURE OF THINGS STORE, THE
NOTS, Inc.
10700 W. Venture, Franklin, WI, 53132. Contact: Marsha Radaj, Pres. - Tel: (414) 529-2192, Fax: (414) 529-2253. Retail sales of science & nature related gift & education items. Established: 1989 - Franchising Since: 1991 - No. of Units: Company Owned: 2 - Franchised: 13 - Franchise Fee: $25,000 - Royalty: 5% net sales - Total Inv: $125,000 - $250,000 depends on size of store and leasehold improvements - Financing: No.

NATURE'S 10 *
P.O. Box 890, North Sioux City, SD, 57049. Contact: Brian Gunderson, Pres. - Tel: (800) 610-8610. A unique, friendly retail store selling diamonds and fine jewelry. Conversion of existing stores invited. Established: 1993 - Franchising Since: 1995 - No. of Units: Company Owned: 1 - Franchise Fee: $27,000 - Total Inv: $50,000 - $150,000 existing store; $350,000 - $650,000 new store - Financing: No.

OFFICE 1 SUPERSTORE *
Office 1 Superstore, International
P.O. Box 5093, 125 Apaquogue Rd., East Hampton, NY, 11937. Contact: Mark Baccash, Pres., CEO - Tel: (516) 324-2857, Fax: (516) 324-0963. Office products retail stores - offer only master franchises outside the United States. Established: 1989 - Franchising Since: 1990 - No. of Units: Company Owned: 34 - Franchised: 45 - Franchise Fee: Master fee to de determined - Royalty: To be determined - Total Inv: over $1 million - Financing: No.

ONE ACCORD, INC.
14435 N. 7 th St. #204, Phoenix, AZ, 85022. Contact: G. Linke, V.P. - Tel: (602) 375-1023. Christian bookstore. Established: 1991 - Franchising Since: 1991 - Franchise Fee: $25,000 - Royalty: 2%, .5% adv. - Total Inv: $25,000 fee, $150,000 inventory, $75,000 working capital - Financing: No.

ONE STOP KITCHEN SHOP
Latonia Sales & Supply Co.
19 Montgomery Dr., Erlanger, KY, 41018. Contact: Geo. Weidner, Mgr. - Tel: (606) 341-1800. Retail outlets sell Weidner kitchens. Established: 1972 - Franchising Since: 1978 - No. of Units: 3 - Franchise Fee: $2,000 - Royalty: 3% adv. - Total Inv: $20,000 - Financing: No.

PAPER BY DESIGN
PBD International, Inc.
11401 Pines Blvd., #594, Pembroke Pines, FL, 33026. Contact: Barry Dreyer, pres. - Tel: (305) 437-7576. With over 900 styles to choose from, we custom print invitations and announcements while you wait. Established: 1992 - Franchising Since: 1994 - No. of Units: Company Owned: 2 - Franchise Fee: $20,000 - Royalty: 5%, 1.5% adv. - Total Inv: $75,000 - $175,000 - Financing: No.

PAPER FIRST AND PARTY
Paper First Franchising, Inc.
6900 Folger Dr., Charlotte, NC, 28270. Contact: Melvin W. Frank, Pres. - Tel: (704) 364-1785, Fax: (704) 366-0334. Party and paper stores selling to public and commercial accounts in a festive wholesale environment. Established: 1980 - Franchising Since: 1988 - No. of Units: Franchised: 68 - Franchise Fee: $2,500 to $15,000 - Royalty: .5% to 2.5% or flat mo. fee of $200 to $1,500 - Total Inv: $160,000: 70% inventory @ cost/ 30% fix./equip. - Financing: No.

PAPER FIRST/PAPERTOWN
Paper First Franchising, Inc.
4420 Monroe Rd., Charlotte, NC, 28205. Contact: Melvin W. Frank, Owner - Tel: (704) 342-5815. Paper products, party supplies and janitorial supplies. Established: l980 - Franchising Since: l988 - No. of Units: Company Owned: 1 - Franchised: 68 - Franchise Fee: $15,000 - Royalty: downscale from 2.5% to .5% - Total Inv: $85,000 - $120,000 incl. fran. fee - Financing: Assistance.

PAPER WAREHOUSE
7630 Excelsior Blvd., Minneapolis, MN, 55426. Contact: Jan Pithey, Dir. of Fran. Sales - Tel: (800) 229-1792. Retail party stores. Three store profiles: 4,000 and 6,500 and 8,500 square feet. Established: 1983 - Franchising Since: 1987 - No. of Units: Company Owned: 50 - Franchised: 45 - Franchise Fee: $19,000 - $25,000 - Royalty: 4% - Total Inv: $149,100 - $464,500 - Financing: No.

PARTY CITY
Party City Corp.
400 Commons Way, Rockaway, NJ, 07866. Contact: Valerie Szymaniak, Dir. of Fran. Sales - Tel: (800) 883-2100. Deep discount party supply superstore. 6,000 - 10,000 sq. ft. Established: 1986 - Franchising Since: 1987 - No. of Units: Company Owned: 12 - Franchised: 115 - Franchise Fee: $30,000 - Royalty: 4% - Total Inv: $290,000 min. investment - Financing: Assistance in securing financing.

PARTY FAIR FRANCHISING CO.
Franchise Store, The (c/o)
The Dover Mall, Rte. 166& 37, Toms River, NJ, 08753-2206. Contact: Marvin Levy, Owner - Tel: (908) 286-2727. One-stop party supply store. Attractive, well designed retail locations offering the consumer selection, quality and value. Established: 1983 - Franchising Since: 1987 - No. of Units: Company Owned: 4 - Franchised: 16 - Franchise Fee: $24,000 - Royalty: 5% - Total Inv: $80,000 - $120,000 - Financing: Yes.

PARTY LAND
5215 Militia Hill Rd., Plymouth Meeting, PA, 19462. Contact: John Barry, V.P., Sales - Tel: (800) 778-9563, Fax: (610) 941-6301. World's largest international party supply retail chain. Established: 1986 - Franchising Since: 1988 - No. of Units: Company Owned: 1 - Franchised: 100+ - Franchise Fee: $25,000 - Royalty: 5%, 4% adv. - Total Inv: $149,000 to $229,000 - Financing: No.

PERSONALIZED DREAM SCENES *
Nightshift International, Inc.
3200 S. Andrews Ave., #105, Ft. Lauderdale, FL, 33316. Contact: Fred Delibero, V.P. - Tel: (305) 763-8005. Computer generated personalized artwork depicting people's dreams & ambitions through sports, leisure activities & occupations. Retailed at mall kiosks, theme parks & special attractions nationwide. Established: 1994 - Franchising Since: 1994 - No. of Units: Company Owned: 1 - Franchised; 18 - Franchise Fee: $5,000 - Royalty: None - Total Inv: $10,900 - $14,900 - Financing: No.

PINCH A PENNY, INC.
Porpoise Pool & Patio
14480 62nd St., N. or Box 6025, Clearwater, FL, 34618. Contact: Fred Thomas, Pres. - Tel: (813) 531-8913. Retail pool and patio supply store. Established: 1975 - Franchising Since: 1976 - No. of Units Company Owned: 2 - Franchised: 86 - Franchise Fee: $15,000 - $250,000 - Total Inv: $100,000 - $500,000 - Royalty: 10% - Financing: negotiable.

PRECIOUS IMAGE JEWELERS
6004 University Ave., Cedar Falls, IA, 50613. Contact: Dave Cutler, Pres. - Tel: (319) 277-0717. Fine gold & diamond & colored gemstone jewelry complete from lease, const., training & start up. Multi-option contracts from 0% no royalty, hire as consultant basis or standard royalty relationship, inline mall or kiosk or free standing locations. Established: 1988 - Franchising Since: 1990 - No. of Units: Company Owned: 1 - Franchised: 1 - Franchise Fee: $35,000 - $55,000 or /$25,000 - Royalty: 0% or /6% - Total Inv: Variable inventory from $75,000 - $350,000 - Financing: Yes.

PRO IMAGE, THE
563 W. 500 S., Ste. 330, Bountiful, UT, 84010. Contact: Kent Sulser, Sales & Leasing Dir. - Tel: (801) 292-8777. A chain of sports fan souvenir stores featuring licensed and logo products from the NFL, NBA, NCAA, NHL, and Major League Baseball. Established: 1985 - Franchising Since: 1985 - No. of Units: Company Owned: 1 - Franchised: 210 - Franchise Fee: $19,500 - Royalty: 4% - Total Inv: $112,000 - $222,500 - Financing: No.

RE-SELL-IT SHOPS, INC.
3316 Governor Dr., San Diego, CA, 92122. Contact: Florence Kalanquin, Pres. - Tel: (619) 455-1010. Two types of consignment stores. One sells furniture, china, art, antiques, sporting goods, almost anything that one uses in their home; and a boutique that features clothing and accessories. Established: 1979 - Franchising Since: 1983 - No. of Units: Company Owned: 1 - Franchised: 2 - Franchise Fee: $9,500 - Royalty: 4% + 1% nat'l adv. - Total Inv: $20,000 - $25,000 including franchise fee - Financing: Yes.

RECORD SWAP *
18061 Dixie Hwy., Homewood, IL, 60430. Contact: Ted Diener, VP - Tel: (708) 798-0251. Specializing in new and used CD's, cassettes, and records. Must enjoy music and be customer service oriented. Willing to work retail hours. Established: 1977 - Franchising Since: 1994 - No. of Units: Company Owned: 4 - Franchised: 1 - Franchise Fee: $15,000 - Royalty: 6%, 2% adv. of gross - Total Inv: $150,000 - $250,000 - Financing: No.

REDDING'S BESTSELLER AUDIOBOOKS
Bestseller Retail Group, Int'l.
Drawer 7729, Phoenix, AZ, 85011. Contact: Edward Richards, C.E.O. - Tel: (602) BESTSELLER. Retail audiobook superstore sale and rental. Established: 1989 - Franchising Since: 1991 - No. of Units: Company Owned: 1 - Franchised: 2 - Franchise Fee: $32,500 - Royalty: 5% - Total Inv: $125,000 - $300,000 turnkey - Financing: No.

ROCS CARDS AND GIFTS
Recycled Paper Greetings
3636 N. Broadway, Chicago, IL, 60613. Contact: Mort Baron, Sr. V.P. - Tel: (312) 348-6410, (800) 777-3331. Fun & exciting card & gift stores. Established: 1984 - No. of Units: Company Owned: 3 - Licensed: 90 - Total Inv: $100,000 - $150,000 - Financing: No.

ROLLING PIN KITCHEN EMPORIUM
Aropi Inc.
4624 Winters Chapel Rd., Bldg. B, Atlanta, GA, 30360. Contact: Glenn Kaas, Pres. - Tel: (404) 457-2600. Retail kitchen utensils and accessories for the homemaker and gourmet. Established: 1978 - Franchising Since: 1982 - No. of Units: Company Owned: 9 - Franchised: 20 - Royalty: 5% gross + .5% adv. - Total Inv: $200,000 - $240,000 - Financing: No.

ROSE VALENTI FRAGRANCES
Rose Valenti, Inc.
CSS Franchising: 177 Main St., Ste. 103, Fort Lee, NJ, 07024. Contact: Fran. Sales Rep. - Tel: (201) 585-4753. Mall based designer perfume, cosmetic and accessory shops. Retail location can be either kiosk or store front in regional and super regional malls. Established: 1981 - Franchising Since: 1993 - No. of Units: Company Owned: 7 - Franchised: 1 - Franchise Fee: $20,000 - Total Inv: $70,000 - $100,000 incl. build-out, equip. and stock - Financing: Yes.

SCANDIA DOWN SHOPS
Scandia Down Corp.
500 Company Store Rd., La Crosse, WI, 54601. Contact: Jeff Potts, Pres. - Tel: (608) 785-7755. High quality down comforters, pillows, linens, wool sleeper pads, and designer brass beds, and a variety of other bedroom accessories. Established: 1970 - Franchising Since: 1980 - No. of Units: Company Owned: 6 - Franchised: 77 - Franchise Fee: $25,000 - Royalty: 6% gross sales + 2% adv. - Total Inv: $167,050 to $338,000 - Financing: none.

SCIENCE SHOP, INC., THE
148 Archer St., San Jose, CA, 95112. Contact: Rudy Yannitte, Pres. - Tel: (408) 453-5616, Fax: (408) 453-5691. Retail scientific equipment. A complete line of chemicals and lab equipment as well as scientific kits for schools and colleges. Established: 1978 - No. of Units: 2 - License Fee: $25,000 - Total Inv: $150,000.

SGO DESIGNER GLASS OF...
Stained Glass Overlay, Inc.
1827 North Case St., Orange, CA, 92665. Contact: Susan L. Pope, V.P./GM - Tel: (714) 974-6124, Fax: (714) 974-6529. SGO is a rapidly growing international franchise company, featuring the unique process of manufacturing solid, seamless, one piece decorative or beveled glass products in any design. Established: 1974 - Franchising since: 1981 - No. of Units: Franchised: 332 - Franchise Fee: $34,000 - Royalty: 5% + 2% adv. - Total Inv: $34,000FF, $8,000 start up pkg., $3,000 training. Additional capital required $10,000 - $30,000 studio set up - Financing: No.

SMOKERS EXPRESS
2260 Scott Lake Rd., Waterford, MI, 48328. Contact: Jay or Gary Greenspan, Owners - Tel: (810) 674-1100, Fax: (810) 674-2953. Retail cigarette outlet. Established: 1992 - Franchising Since: 1994 - No. of Units: Company Owned: 6 - Franchised: 2 - Franchise Fee: $12,500 - Total Inv: $75,000 - $150,000 inventory/fixtures - Financing: Yes, if franchisee is credit worthy.

SNYDER DRUG STORES, INC.
14525 Highway #7, Minnetonka, MN, 55345. Contact: Bill Vidmar, Fran. Dir. - Tel: (612) 935-5441. Wholesaler of health and beauty aids, drugs and general merchandise. Established: 1928 - No. of Units: 105 - Approx. Inv: $300,000.

SPORT IT
Sport It, Inc.
4196 Corporate Sq., Naples, FL, 33942. Contact: Ron Eastman, Pres. - Tel: (800) 762-6869. Home based business offering competitively priced brand name sporting goods and apparel. Established: 1984 - Franchising Since: 1984 - No. of Units: Franchised: 461 Franchise Fee: $1,500 - Royalty: $25 per month - Total Inv: $1,500 - Financing: Visa/Mastercard/Discover.

SPORTS FANTASY MARKETING, INC.
P.O. Box 1380, Columbus, GA, 31902-0980. Contact: Franchise Director - Tel: (706) 322-3665. Specialty retail store selling authentic licensed sports apparel and novelties. Established: 1986 - Franchising Since: 1986 - No. of Units: Company Owned: 28 - Franchised: 10 - Franchise Fee: $15,000 - Royalty: 5% - Total Inv: $115,000 - $130,000 - Financing: no.

SPORTSLIFE ENTERPRISES
80 Weston St., Hartford, CT, 06120. Contact: Ted Nevins, Pres. - Tel: (203) 251-6148, (800) 909-5433. Sporting goods, pro-college team apparel- retail. Home-based business. Established: 1992 - Franchising Since: 1992 - No. of Units: Franchised: 500 - Franchise Fee: $895 - Total Inv: $895 - 30 mo. - Financing: Yes.

SPRING CREST DRAPERY CENTERS
Spring Crest Company, Inc.
190 Arovista Ave., Brea, CA, 92621-3829. Contact: Jack W. Long, Pres. - Tel: (714) 529-9993. Custom window fashions, including exclusive products. Established: 1955 - Franchising Since: 1968 - No. of Units: Franchised: 148 - Franchise Fee: $15,000 - Royalty: 3% - 5% - Total Inv: $65,000.

STAR VALLEY INSTALLATIONS
Cazier Enterprises
2253 Linda St., Saginaw, MI, 48603. Contact: Monty Cazier, Owner - Tel: (517) 776-0733. Franchisee will be provided with the products and training to install flagpoles, mailboxes, landscape lighting, and much more. Established: 1987 - Franchising Since: 1992 - No. of Units: Company Owned: 1 - Franchise Fee: $3,000 - Royalty: 8%, no advertising fee - Total Inv: $3,000 initial package plus $3,000 - $5,000 misc. expenses - Financing: None.

STARLOG - THE COMIC & SCIENCE FICTION UNIVERSE
Starlog Franchise Corp.
10855 U.S. Hwy. 19 North, Clearwater, FL, 34624. Contact: Mark Savel, Dir. of Fran. Dev. - Tel: 1-800-STARLOG, Fax: (813) 573-2466. Retailer of over 500 different comic books, science fiction and supernatural magazines, books, games, toys, videos, compact discs, apparel, jewelry, pins, trading cards, jokes, tricks, candy and related mdse. licensed under names "Star Trek", "Star Wars", "Marvel Comics" and "DC Comics". Carts & kiosks. Established: 1992 - Franchising Since: 1993 - No. of Units: Company Owned: 7 - Franchised: 2 - Franchise Fee: $30,000 - Royalty: Based on gross receipts: 6% first $400,000, 4.5% $400,001 - $800,000, 3% $800,001+; Ad Fund Royalties: 2% 1st $400,000, 1.5% $400,001 - $800,000, 1% $800,001+ - Total Inv: $225,000 - $300,000 - Financing: Third party.

STREET CORNER NEWS *
McColla Enterprises, Ltd.
2945 S.W. Wanamaker Rd., Topeka, KS, 66614. Contact: Peter Lacolla, C.E.O. - Tel: (913) 272-8529. Retail newsstand/convenience store outlets generally located in large regional shopping malls. Established; 1988 - Franchising Since: 1995 - No. of Units: Company Owned: 7 - Franchise Fee: $15,000 - Royalty: 4.5% - Total Inv: $75,000 to $125,000 - Financing: No.

SUCCESSORIES
Celex
919 Springer Drive, Lombard, IL, 60148. Contact: Terry Keenan, Dir. of Fran. Sales - Tel: (800) 621-1423 ext. 5071. Specialty retailer of motivation gift and award products for personal and business use. Established: 1985 - Franchising Since: 1992 - No. of Units: Company Owned: 36 - Franchised: 34 - Franchise Fee: $25,000 - Royalty: 2% - Total Inv: fran. fee $25,000, set-up (excl. fee) $85,000 - $150,000 - Financing: No.

SUN SHADE OPTIQUE
International Sun Shade, Inc.
843 Racquet Lane, Boulder, CO, 80303-2972. Contact: Wallis Arnold, Pres. - Tel: (303) 289-8740. Sunglass specialty boutiques that carry the widest selection of quality famous brand name sunglasses of any boutique of its kind. Established: 1987 - Franchising Since: 1988 - No.

of Units: Company Owned: 4 - Franchised: 12 - Franchise Fee: $15,000 - Royalty: 5% + 2% adv. - Total Inv: $70,000 - $117,000 turn-key - Financing: yes.

SUNGLASS BOUTIQUE
Eyewear House, The
P.O. Box 21023, Columbia, SC, 29221-1023. Contact: Dean Faulkenberry, Pres. - Tel: (904) 942-2334. Retail sunglass stores. Established: 1985 - Franchising Since: 1994 - No. of Units: Company Owned: 8 - Franchise Fee: $4,000 - Royalty: $200/wk. - Total Inv: $35,000 - $75,000 - Financing: No.

THE CAR PHONE STORE
Automotive Technologies, Inc.
1807 Berlin Turnpike, Wethersfield, CT, 06109. Contact: Susan Suhr, Dir. of Bus. Dev. - Tel: (203) 571-7600, Fax: (203) 257-1818. Retail sales, service and installation of cellular telephones and other wireless communications products and services. Established: 1988 - Franchising Since: 1989 - No.of Units: Company Owned: 2 - Franchised: 40 - Franchise Fee: $25,000 - Royalty: percentage of activation commissions and residuals - Total Inv: $86,900 - $124,750 - Financing: Yes.

TREASURE CACHE, THE
CSS Franchising: 177 Main St., Ste. 103, Fort Lee, NJ, 07024. Contact: Franchise Sales Rep. - Tel: (201) 585-4753. Mall based retail arts and crafts showroom. Store owners rent shelf space to local artisans and crafters and sell their work to consumers from showrooms featured in regional malls. Established: 1992 - Franchising Since: 1992 - No. of Units: Franchised: 31 - Royalty: 6% of shelf rental, 2% of product sales - Total Inv: $45,000 - $65,000 incl. build-out, equip., & fran. fee - Financing: Yes.

TRUSTWORTHY HARDWARE STORES
Emery Waterhouse Co., The
P.O. Box 659, Rand Rd., Portland, ME, 04104. Contact: Steve Frawley, Pres. - Tel: (207) 775-2371. Retail hardware stores. Established: 1840 - Franchising Since: 1963 - No. of Units: Company Owned: 20 - Franchised: 160 - Franchise Fee: $60,000 - Total Inv: $120,000.

VICTORIAN PAPERS' - LEGACY
Victorian Papers
1819 Baltimore, Kansas City, MO, 64108. Contact: Julie Capen, Fran. Dir. - Tel: (816) 471-7808. Turn of the century themed card and gift shop offering elegant correspondence papers, antique reproduction gifts and replica jewelry, nostalgic toys and books. The daughter of a successful mail order company. Established: 1987 - Franchising Since: 1994 - No. of Units: Company Owned: 2 - Franchise Fee: $175,000+ - Royalty: 5% - Total Inv: $25,000 (initial inves.), $85,000 constr. - Financing: No.

WATCH GALLERY
5075 Westhemier, Ste. 850, Houston, TX, 77056. Contact: Steven Shoeman, Pres. - Tel: (713) 439-0003. Watch & jewelry franchise. Established: 1989 - Franchising Since: 1994 - No. of Units: Company Owned:3 - Franchise Fee: $25,000 - Royalty: 6% - Total Inv: $75,000: $25,000 fran. fee, $25,000 inven., $15,000 fixtures, $10,000 misc. - Financing: No.

WATER MART
Water Mart Inc.
1854 S. MacDonald Dr., Mesa, AZ, 85210. Contact: Harry McKee, CEO - Tel: (800) 800-8580, (602) 844-0123, Fax: (602) 844-5601. Full service retail water stores featuring purified water and hundreds of water related products. Extensive training provided. Established: 1990 - Franchising Since: 1991 - No. of Units: Company Owned: 2 - Franchised: 31 - Franchise Fee: $10,000 - Royalty: 5% gross - Financing: Yes, partial.

WHISKEY DUST
526 Hudson St., New York, NY, 10014. Contact: Mervin Bendewald, Owner - Tel: (212) 691-5576. Vintage western apparel and western oddities. Established: 1989.

WICKS 'N' STICKS
Wicks 'N' Sticks, Inc.
16825 Northchase Dr., #900, Houston, TX, 77060. Contact: Deborah Sondock, Denise Hudson, Pres., Fran. Dev. - Tel: (800)231-6337, (713) 874-0800. Large retailer of candles, fragrancing and related home decorative products. We offer outstanding name recognition, comprehensive training and extensive merchandising support. Established: 1968 - Franchising Since: 1968 - No. of Units: Franchised: 196 - Franchise Fee: $25,000 - Royalty: 6% - Total Inv: $120,500 - $183,000: Inv./supplies $42,500 - $55,000; Fixtures $15,000 - $25,000; leasehold improv. $25,000 - $50,000; work. cap. $10,000 - $20,000; travel/living while training $500 - $3,000; architects fee $2,500 - $5,000 - Financing: Assistance in securing financing.

WILD BIRD CENTERS
Wild Bird Centers of America, Inc.
7687 MacArthur Blvd., Cabin John, MD, 20818. Contact: George Petrides or Howard Margolis, Pres., Fran. Dev. Officer - Tel: (800) 945-3247. Specialty retail stores which supply and educate backyard bird watchers. Products include bird seed, feeders, houses, baths, binoculars, and gifts. Home office publishes custom editions of educational newsletter for each store, and assists in the development of educational programs. Established: 1985 - Franchising Since: 1989 - No. of Units: Franchised: 76 - Franchise Fee: $18,500 - Royalty: 3% first yr., 4.5% thereafter - Total Inv: $59,800 - $83,150 incl. fran. fee - Financing: No.

WILD BIRD CROSSING
Wild Bird Centers of America, Inc.
7687 MacArthur Blvd., Cabin John, MD, 20818. Contact: George Petrides / Howard Margolis, Pres. / Fran. Dev. Officer - Tel: (800) 945-3247. Specialty retail stores which supply and educate backyard bird watchers. Products include bird seed, feeders, houses, baths, binoculars, and gifts. Home office assists in publishing of newsletter and in the development of educational programs. Established: 1994 - Franchising Since: 1989 - No. of Units: Franchised: 17 - Franchise Fee: $9,500 - Royalty: 3% 1st year, 4.5% thereafter - Total Inv: $48,550 - $68,550 incl. fran. fee - Total Inv: None.

WILD BIRD MARKETPLACE
AF&G Supply Inc.
710 West Main, New Holland, PA, 17557. Contact: John F. Gardner, Pres. - Tel: (800) 851-2711. Retail specialty store, serving the needs of the birder, the gardener and the Naturalist. Established: 1988 - Franchising Since: 1990 - No. of Units: Franchised: 29 - Franchise Fee: $15,000 - Royalty: 4% on gross sales - Total Inv: $75,000 - $95,000 - Financing: No.

WILD BIRDS UNLIMITED
Wild Birds Unlimited, Inc.
11711 N. College Ave., Ste. 146, Carmel, IN, 46032. Contact: Paul E. Pickett, Dir. Fran. Sales - Tel: (800) 326-4928, Fax: (317) 571-7110. Large group of retail stores catering to the backyard birdfeeding and nature enthusiast. Stores provide birdseed, feeders, houses, optics and nature-related gifts. Franchisees are provided a support system which includes site selection assistance, extensive training, customer flyers, group purchasing programs, proprietary products, field support, advertising and marketing assistance, and on-going business planning. Established: 1981 - Franchising Since: 1983 - No. of Units: Franchised: 200 - Franchise Fee: $18,000 - Royalty: 4% of gross sales - Total Inv: $76,000-$131,000 - Financing: No.

WINDOW WORLD INTERNATIONAL
1020 N. University Parks Dr., Waco, TX, 76707. Contact: Bob Phillips, Pres. - Tel: (800) 583-2133. Sale and installation of window coverings and related services such as blind cleaning, alarms & tinting. Established: 1992 - Franchising Since: 1992 - No. of Units: Franchised: 5 - Franchise Fee: $27,500 - Royalty: 5% - Total Inv: approx. $35,000 - Financing: Yes.

WINDOWEAR
Windowear Inc.
1437 S. State College Blvd., Anaheim, CA, 92806. Contact: Jim Nichols, V.P. Franc. Sales - Tel: (800) 559-2546, Fax: (714) 778-6070. Home based mobile window covering sales and installation company. Established: 1989- Franchising Since: 1991 - No. of Units: Company Owned: 1 - Franchised: 5 - Franchise Fee: $12,500 - Royalty: 5% of monthly gross sales - Total Inv: $2,000 + Fran. fee - Financing: Yes.

RETAIL: CLOTHING AND SHOES

13-BELOW
Traditions, Ltd.
2169 Telegraph Rd., Bloomfield Hills, MI, 48302. Contact: Franchise Consortium - Tel: (800) 301-9504. Ladies clothing and fashion accessories retail stores. Everything is priced at $12.97 or less. Established: 1979 - Franchising Since: 1994 - No. of Units: Company owned: 18 - Franchise Fee: $20,000 - Royalty: 5% - Total Inv: $45,000 to $95,000 (incl. fran. fee) - Financing: No.

À JAMAIS INC.
4196 Corporate Sq., Naples, FL, 33942. Contact: Julie Eastman, Pres. - Tel: (800) IN STYLE. à jamais is a home-based franchise. Franchisees market women's custom casual wear, accessories, and image consultations. Established: 1994 - Franchising Since: 1994 - Franchise Fee: $1,500 - Royalty: $30 per month - Total Inv: $1,500 - Financing: No.

A REAL NEW YORK BARGAIN
A Real New York Bargain Franchise Corp.
469 7th Ave., New York, NY, 10018. Contact: Larry Salinas, Pres. - Tel: (212) 736-7600, Fax: (212) 736-0624. Men's and women's sportswear, domestic & imports at one low price point. Established: 1989 - Franchising Since: 1992 - No. of Units: Company Owned: 8 - Franchised: 8 - Franchise Fee: $40,000 - Royalty: 3% of purchases + 50¢ per unit - Total Inv: $125,000 - $200,000 - Financing: No.

A'GACI
Twigland Fashions Inc.
3201 Cherry Ridge, Ste. 205, San Antonio, TX, 78230. Contact: David Won, V.P. - Tel: (210) 377-3393. Fashion store specializing in very feminine clothes for the woman who enjoys being sexy and attractive. A'gaci has a distinctly designer look, though its prices are in the moderate to upper range. Established: 1972 - Franchising Since: 1985 - No. of Units: Company Owned: 18 - Franchised: 11 - Franchise Fee: $50,000 - Royalty: 5% - Total Inv: $191,000 - $231,000 - Financing: No.

ANGELICA UNIFORMS GROUP
700 Rosedale Ave., St. Louis, MO, 63112. Contact: Thomas T. Marxer, V.P. Nat'l Acc'ts - Tel: (314) 889-1111. Designers and manufacturers of image apparel and custom designed uniform programs. Established: 1878.

ATHLETE'S FOOT, THE
Athlete's Foot Group Inc., The
1950 Vaughn Rd., Kennesaw, GA, 30144. Contact: Russell Smith, Dir. of Fran. Sales - Tel: (800) 524-6444 or (404) 514-4721, Fax: (404) 514-4903. The industry's #1 franchisor in athletic footwear. We offer the availability to top brand inventory to include special make-up inventory which is exclusive to The Athlete's Foot. Established: 1972 - Franchising Since: 1973 - No. of Units: Company Owned: 282 - Franchised: 386 - Franchise Fee: $25,000 - Royalty: 5% , 1% nat'l. adv. - Total Inv: $125,000 - $300,000; fran. fee, build-out, inven. & capital - Financing: Third party.

ATHLETIC ATTIC MARKETING, INC.
18 N.W. 33rd Ct., Gainesville, FL, 32607. Contact: Jack Thompson, Dir. Fran. Sales/Leasing - Tel: (904) 377-5289. Specialists in athletic footwear and apparel. Small amount of hard goods (raquets, weights, balls, etc). Franchising Since: 1974 - No. of Units: Company Owned: 17 - Franchised: 143 - Franchise Fee: $50,000 (fran. fee $7,500) - Royalty: 3% - Total Inv: $150,000 - Financing: no.

ATHLETIC LADY
Athletic Attic Marketing, Inc.
18 N.W. 33rd Ct., Gainesville, FL, 32607. Contact: Jack Thompson, Dir. Fran. Sales/Leasing - Tel: (904) 377-5289. Sports specialty store catering to active woman of the 90's. Carries activewear, dancewear, aerobicwear, swimwear and athletic shoes. Established: 1980 - Franchising Since: 1981 - No. of Units: Company Owned: 3 - Franchised: 4 - Franchise Fee: $50,000 ($7,500 fran. fee) - Total Inv: $150,000 - Royalty: 3% - Financing: No.

BAGS & SHOES
P.O. Box 21261, Ft. Lauderdale, FL, 33335-1261. Contact: W.H. Bonneau, Pres. - Tel: (305) 764-7942. Offers over 3,000 current designer & brand name fashions & shoes & bags & accessories at 25% to 75% savings. Site selection, lease negotiation, design, construction, fixturing, merchandising, computerization, training and all inventory is guaranteed to sell. Established: 1980 - No. of Units: Franchised: 137 - Franchise Fee: $5,000 per $25,000 of investment - Royalty: None - Total Inv: $50,000 - $150,000 - Financing: No.

FASHION, LTD.
Box 21261, Ft. Lauderdale, FL, 33335-1261. Contact: W.H. Bonneau, Pres. - Tel: (305) 764-7942. Designer and brand name clothes at savings of up to 70%. Current season styles that are all guaranteed to sell. We set up stores in high traffic malls and shopping centers. Site selection, design, layout, fixturing, merchandising, computerization, and training at your location in your city. Established: 1985 - Franchising Since: 1985 - Franchise Fee: $5,000 - $20,000 - Total Inv: $25,000 - $100,000 - Financing: No.

FASHIONS UNDER $10
1036 E. Sibley, Dolton, IL, 60419. Contact: Stephen Tepper, V.P. - Tel: (708) 849-8722. Name brand men's and ladies fashions for under $10. Complete assistance for site selection, stocking, training personnel, store operations and advertising. Franchises are available to people purchasing a minimum of 5 units. Established: 1987 - Franchising Since: 1988 - No. of Units: Company Owned: 14 - Franchised: 9 - Franchise Fee: $27,500 - Royalty: 4% average - Total Inv: $75,000 - $100,000 - Financing: No.

FINE THREADS
Fine Threads, Inc.
2660 N.E. University Village Mall, Seattle, WA, 98105. Contact: Garry Davidson, Pres. - Tel: (206) 525-5888. Better boys and young mens clothing and sportwear. One stop shopping from underwear to suit. Depth of selection with service oriented. Established: 1982 - Franchising Since: 1990 - No. of Units: Company Owned: 1 - Franchise Fee: $20,000 - Royalty: 6% - Total Inv: $150,000-$200,000 - Financing: No.

FLEET FEET SPORTS/FLEET FEET TRIATHLETE
Fleet Feet, Inc.
2407 J. St., Sacramento, CA, 95816. Contact: Sally Edwards, Tom Raynor, Founder, Pres. - Tel: (916) 557-1000. Retail footwear, apparel stores. Owners must be involved in a sporting way of life. Established: 1976 - Franchising Since: 1979 - No. of Units: Company Owned: 2 - Franchised: 37 - Franchise Fee: $17,500 - Royalty: 4% - 2% - Total Inv: $117,500 - $177,500 - Financing: SBA.

HER PLACE
Her Place Franchising, Inc.
Amigoland Mall, 301 Mexico Blvd., Brownsville, TX, 78520. Contact: Joe Field - Tel: (800) 301-9504. Women's accessories and apparel retail store. Established: 1984 - Franchising Since: 1994 - No. of Units: Company Owned: 6 - Franchise Fee: $20,000 - Royalty: 5%, 1% adv. - Financing: No.

JOS. A. BANK CLOTHIERS
500 Hanover Pike, Hampstead, MD, 21074. Contact: Daniel Randolph, E.V.P. - Tel: (410) 239-5777. Men's classic clothier. Established: 1905 - Franchising Since: 1991 - No. of Units: Company Owned: 74 - Franchised: 7.

KALI'S BOUTIQUE
Kali's Cottons Inc.
443 J E/W Frandor Mall, Lansing, MI, 48910. Contact: Lynn, Owner/Pres. - Tel: (517) 337-4445. Natural fiber women's boutique carrying jewellery, accessories, gifts. Established: 1984 - Franchising Since: 1993 - No. of Units: Company Owned: 2 - Franchised: 1 - Franchise Fee: $13,000 to $15,000 depending on location - Royalty: 4% of gross sales.

KRUG'S BIG & TALL
Oversize Clothing Franchise Corp.
155 North Main St., New City, NY, 10596. Contact: Stacey Sheinbaum, Mkt. Dir. - Tel: (201) 871-0370 or (800) 332-2229. Men's specialty retail store featuring big & tall sizes. Established: 1988 - Franchising

Since: 1992 - No. of Units: Company Owned: 4 - Franchise Fee: $18,500 - Royalty: 5% - Total Inv: $209,300 - $483,300 plus fran. fee - Financing: None, will assist.

LEOTARDI EXERCISEWEAR
12120 S.W. 131st Ave., Miami, FL, 33186. Contact: Cinda Steiner, Pres. - Tel: (305) 254-1677. Retail sale of dance fitness and aerobic apparel. Established: 1982 - Franchising Since: 1990 - No. of Units: Company Owned: 1 - Franchised: 2 - Franchise Fee: $7,500 - Royalty: $500/per mo. - Total Inv: $10,000 - $50,000 - Financing: Assessed individually.

MERLE HARMON'S FAN FAIR
Fan Fair Corp.
12425 Knoll Rd., Elm Grove, WI, 53122. Contact: Keith Harmon, V.P. Mktg. - Tel: (414) 784-8884. Franchisor of retail licensed sports apparel stores. Established: 1977 - Franchising Since: 1982 - No. of Units: Company Owned: 20 - Franchised: 59 - Franchise Fee: $25,000 - Royalty: 4%, 5% - Total Inv: $133,500 - $181,000: fran. fee, invent., fix, equip., leasehold, work cap., initial training & transportation - Financing: No.

RED WING SHOES
314 Main St., Red Wing, MN, 55066. Contact: Mr. Arnie Skyberg, Reg. Mgr. - Tel: (612) 388-8211. Casual and work shoes. Established: 1976 - No. of Units: Company Owned: 2 - Franchised: 4.

SHOE FIXERS
1884 Breton Rd., S.E., Grand Rapids, MI, 49506. Contact: Colleen McGaffey - Tel: (810) 557-2784. Retail shoe repair services, sales of shoe related merchandise. Established: 1970 - Franchising Since: 1987 - No. of Units: Company Owned: 64 - Franchised: 36 - Franchise Fee: $25,000 - Royalty: 5% - Total Inv: $50,000 - $100,000 - Financing: equipment leasing.

SHOES FOR HER/SHOES FOR HIM
P.O .Box 21261, Fort Lauderdale, FL, 33335-1261. Contact: W.H. Bonneau, Pres. - Tel: (305) 764-7942. Designer and name brand bags, shoes, belts, briefcases and accessories at affordable prices. Complete program, site selection, lease negotiation, design, construction, fixturing, inventory, one week on-site training, hiring of personnel, computer programming, grand opening, advertising and continued management support. Established: 1985 - Franchising Since: 1987 - No. of Units: 74 - Franchise Fee: $20,000 - Total Inv: $100,000 - $250,000 - Financing: None.

SPORT SHOE, THE *
Sport Shoe Marketing, Inc.
1770 Corporate Dr., Ste. 500, Norcross, GA, 30093. Contact: Jim Duren, Dir. of Fran. - Tel: (770) 279-7494. Athletic shoe store - selling athletic foot wear, apparel and accessories. Established: 1974 - Franchising Since: 1989 - No. of Units: Company Owned: 19 - Franchised: 4 - Franchise Fee: $25,000 - Royalty: 4% of gross sales - Total Inv: $300,000 - Financing: No.

T-SHIRTS PLUS
Plus Companies, The
P.O. Box 20608, Waco, TX, 76702-0608. Contact: David Byrd, Pres. - Tel: (817) 776-8872. Franchise retail specialty chain offering the very best in imprinted sportswear & customized activewear. Located in regional malls. Established: 1972 - Franchising Since: 1973 - No. of Units: Franchised: 111, Projected expansion 15 stores in 1996 - Franchise Fee: $35,000 - Royalty: 6% of sales for first 2 yrs, then flat rate of $1,323/mth. adjusted annually - Total Inv: $111,700 - $213,800: Fran. fee+ $22,000 - $35,000 inven; $12,000 - $17,000 equip.; $29,000 - $83,000 constr.; $1,000 - $2,000 train.; $2,700 - $18,000 init. rent - $10,000 - $15,000 work. cap. - Financing: SBA.

UNDER WARES FOR HIM
210 E. 58th St., New York, NY, 10022. Contact: Ron Lee, Pres. - Tel: (212) 838-1200, (800) 237-8641. Largest selection of men's underwear, robes, p.j.'s, hose, swimwear, work-out wear etc. Established: 1984 - Franchising Since: 1992 - No. of Units: Company Owned: 1 - Franchised: 1 - Franchise Fee: $25,000 - Royalty: 6% - Total Inv: $125,000 - Financing: No.

WALK & JOG/WALK & ATHLETIC FOOTWEAR
P.O. Box 21261, Ft. Lauderdale, FL, 33335-1261. Contact: W.H. Bonneau - Tel: (305) 764-7942. Offering over a 100 designer brand name footwear and accessories with 25% to 70% savings. We will design a store to fit your budget. All inventory is guaranteed to sell in 90 days. Established: 1987 - Franchising Since: 1988 - No. of Units: Franchised: 37 - Franchise Fee: $5,000 plus.

RETAIL: COMPUTER, ELECTRONICS AND VIDEO

20/20 VIDEO
1901 S. Pontius Ave., Los Angeles, CA, 90025. Contact: Morris Shab - Tel: (310) 829-2020. Retail video chain which sells and rents video software and hardware. Established: 1981 - Franchising Since: 1985 - No. of Units: Company Owned: 12 - Franchised: 8 - Franchise Fee: $15,000 - Royalty: 4% - Total Inv: $210,000 - Financing: No.

AIRBORNE FOR MEN *
Airborne For Men Ltd.
1060 Park Ave., Cranston, RI, 02910. Contact: Jay Radin, Dir. of Franchising - Tel: (401) 942-7876. General retailer, men's casual wear and accessories, a full line of adult theme videos, magazines and novelty items. Established: 1994 - Franchising Since: 1994 - No. of Units: Company Owned: 3 - Franchised: 1 - Franchise Fee: $30,000 - Royalty: 5% - 8% (5% less than $10,000/wk.; 6% $10,000 - $14,999/wk.; 7% $15,000 - $19,999/wk.; 8% $20,000 and up/wk.) - Total Inv: $165,000 - $230,000 - Financing: No.

AMERICAN VIDEO INC.
10444 Bluegrass Parkway, Louisville, KY, 40299. Contact: Ben McCaskill, Pres. - Tel: (502) 499-0072, Fax: (502) 499-9683. Established: 1981 - No. of Units: 1 - Franchise Fee: $35,000-$40,000 - Total Inv: $75,000-$190,000 - Financing: Will co-ordinate.

BOOMERANG *
Boomerang Gameware
4986 Park Ave., Memphis, TN, 38117. , Fran. Dir. - Tel: (901) 867-0600. Retail store specializing in the exchange, rental and sale of video games, computer games, discs and programs. Established: 1995 - Franchising Since: 1995 - Franchise Fee: $25,000 - Royalty: 6% - Total Inv: $69,400 - $433,500 (Inven., Real Estate, Re-Dec, Equip., and Working Cap.). For further information please contact: Consultants America Corp., 12279 US Highway 64. Eads, TN, 38028, Tel: (901) 867-0600, Fax: (901) 867-0010.

COMPUTER MAINTENANCE SERVICE
P.O. Box 335, San Marcos, TX, 78667. Contact: Floyd MacKenzie, G.M. - Tel: (210) 629-1400, Fax: (512) 353-5333. Repair, maintenance and service of the personal computer market and peripherals. Established: 1987 - Franchising Since: 1988 - No. of Units: 1 - Royalty: $300 monthly - Total Inv: $10,000 + tools - Financing: No.

COMPUTER POWER SUPPLY
1050 Ocean Ave., Sea Bright, NJ, 07760-. Contact: Willard C. Somers, Pres. - Tel: (908) 842-9100 . License computer and software operations and sales. Franchising Since: 1992 - Total Inv: $50,000 - Financing: Assistance.

COMPUTER RENAISSANCE *
Grow Biz International
4200 Dahlberg Dr., Minneapolis, MN, 55422. Contact: Steve Gemlo, V.P., Fran. Dev. - Tel: (612) 520-8500, Fax: (612) 520-8501. Retail computer stores that buy, sell and trade used and new computer equipment. Established: 1988 - Franchising Since: 1993 - No. of Units: Company Owned: 5 - Franchised: 38 - Franchise Fee: $25,000 - Royalty: 3% - Total Inv: $128,700 to $193,500 - Financing: SBA financing available, up to two-thirds of capital.

COMPUTERLAND
Merisel F.A.B.
5964 West Las Positas Blvd., Pleasanton, CA, 94566 . Contact: Mark Russell, Market Dev. - Tel: (510) 734-4600. Full service computer resellers. Franchises provide hardware, software, service, training and consulting to a customer base of small, medium and large businesses. Established: 1976 - Franchising Since: 1977 - No. of Units: Franchised: 250 nationally - Franchise Fee: MSA<100,000=$15,000; MSA 100,000-$350,000 = $22,500; MSA> 350,000 = $30,000 - Royalty: .75% on gross revenue, mark-up on purchases determined by volume - Financing: Partial financing of franchise fee available.

CURTIS MATHES HOME ENTERTAINMENT CENTERS
10911 Petal St., Dallas, TX, 75238-2424. Contact: Jodi, Fran. Sales - Tel: (214) 503-8880. Centers sell, rent and lease a broad line of high quality electronic home entertainment products carrying extended warranties. The stores also offer video movie rental clubs, satellite antenna systems and complete service capability. Established: 1920 - Franchising Since: 1982 - No. of Units: Franchised: 610 - Franchise Fee: $25,000 - Total Inv: $125,000 - Financing: Indirectly through 3rd party sources.

CYBER EXCHANGE *
2686 East Main St., St. Charles, IL, 60174. Contact: Dr. Robert Drwer-Bishop, Dir. of Fran. - Tel: (800) 520-7311. New and used computers, software, computer upgrades and CD Rom rentals. Resale stores maximizing unique position in 90 Billion a year market. Fun to run for those who like customers & computers. Established: 1993 - Franchising Since: 1995 - No. of Units: Company Owned: 3 - Franchised: 12 - Franchise Fee: $10,000 first site, $7,500 additional - Royalty: 5%, 1% adv. - Total Inv: $41,000 to $70,000 (store, stock, software, computers) - Financing: SBA loan help up to 100K.

GREAT VIDEO SHOPPE, INC., THE *
1898 Techny Ct., Northbrook, IL, 60062. Contact: Bill Vanderweele, V.P. - Tel: (708) 272-6662. Leases movies to grocery chains, convenient stores, work places, colleges, hospitals, hotels, apartment buildings. Established: 1992 - Franchise Fee: none - Total Inv: none - Financing: Company pays 8% commission trial on all accounts refer. to lease program.

INACOM CORP.
Valmont Industries, Inc.
9300 Underwood Ave., Omaha, NE, 68114-2685. Contact: Brad Queck, Mgr. - Tel: (402) 392-2700. Sale of IBM and Compaq personal computers, peripherals, software, training and classes. Established: 1981 - Franchising Since: 1982 - No. of Units: Company Owned: 51 - Franchised: 75 - Franchise Fee: $20,000 - Total Inv: $150,000-$250,000 - Royalty: 8%.

INTERNATIONAL VIDEO YEARBOOKS, INC.
25 Century Blvd, Ste. 507, Nashville, TN, 37214. Contact: Jim McCarthy, Pres. - Tel: (615) 889-3700. Students shoot videos throughout the course of the yr. Franchisee edits and sells as yearbooks. Established: 1988 - Franchising Since: 1988 - No. of Units: Franchised: 17 - Franchise Fee: $30,000 - Royalty: 10% - Total Inv: $40,000 - Financing: On equipment.

LASER CHARGE, INC.
2113 Wells Branch Pky., Ste. 6000, Austin, TX, 78728-6971. Contact: Steve Morgan, Fran. Dir. - Tel: (512) 836-6000. License individuals to recharge toner cartridges for laser printers, copiers at half the cost of new ones. Established: 1986 - Franchising Since: 1987 - No. of Units: Company Owned: 1 - Franchised: 1200+ - Franchise Fee: $4,900-$6,900 - Total Inv: $4,900-$6,900 - Financing: None.

LASERQUIPT
Laserquipt International ltd.
10300 Bren Road E., Minnetonka, MN , 55343. Contact: Franchising Dept. - Tel: (612) 931-9925, Fax: (612) 931-9940. Independent service organization that provides service and supplies for laser printer users. In addition, we sell, rent, and lease laser printers. Established; 1989 - Franchising Since: 1995 - No. of Units: Company Owned: 1 - Franchised: 2 - Franchise Fee: $35,000 - Royalty: 10% - Total Inv: $35,000 fran. fee, $20,000 inven., $40,000 capital - Financing: None.

MARBLES MUSIC & VIDEO
United Business Group, Inc.
10351 Santa Monica Blvd., #430, Los Angeles, CA, 90025-6908. Contact: Matt Feinstein, VP Fran. Dev. - Tel: (310) 552-2280 or (800) 669-2221. Video movies, CD's, tapes, laser discs, video games and related merchandise. Established: 1988 - Franchising Since: 1991 - No. of Units: Franchised: 12 - Franchise Fee: $20,000 - Royalty: 6% of revenues, incl. adv. - Total Inv: $100,000 - $200,000 - Financing: Yes.

MARTING RADIO DIAGNOSTIC SERVICES
Marting Franchise Corp.
504 S. Egbert St., Monona, IA, 52159. Contact: Elmer L. Marting, Pres. - Tel: (319) 539-2640. Mobile two-way radio systems sales and service. Established: 1979 - Franchising Since: 1979 - No. of Units: 2 - Franchised: 2 pending - Franchise Fee: $23,500 - Royalty: 7.5% - Total Inv: $35,000 - $75,000 - Financing: Pending.

MEGA VIDEO, INC.
3820 Premier Ave., Memphis, TN, 38118. Contact: Bill Richey - Tel: (901) 867-0600. A wholesale/retail movie rental sales business. Established: 1989 - Franchising Since: 1989 - No. of Units: Company Owned: 3 - Franchise Fee: $25,000 - Royalty: 5% - Total Inv: $166,000 - $322,900 - Financing: No.

MICROAGE COMPUTER CENTERS
MicroAge, Inc.
2308 South 55th St., Tempe, AZ, 85282. Contact: Richard Lawson, Pres. - Tel: (602) 968-3168. Microcomputer reseller/dealer network focused on the sales and support of information technology products and services, including microcomputer systems, workstations, networking and telecommunications equipment, software and related products and services. Established: 1976 - Franchising Since: 1980 - No. of Units: Company Owned: 6 - Franchised: 385 - Franchise Fee: None - Royalty: None - Total Inv: $250,000 - $500,000 - Financing: None.

MOVIE EXCHANGE
3820 Premier Ave., Memphis, TN, 38118. Contact: Bill Richey, Dir. - Tel: (901) 867-0600. Video tape rentals. Established: 1989 - Franchising Since: 1989 - No. of Units: Company Owned: 2 - Franchise Fee: $10,000 - Royalty: 5% - Total Inv: $15,300 - $20,600 - Financing: No.

MOVIE WAREHOUSE
Movie Warehouse Management, Inc.
450 Southland Dr., Ste. E, Lexington, KY, 40503. Contact: Ed Houlihan, Pres. - Tel: (606) 276-0014, Fax: (606) 276-1377. Video rental and sales. Established: 1987 - Franchising Since: 1987 - No. of Units: Company Owned: 4 - Franchised: 44 - Franchise Fee: $20,000 - Royalty: 5% rentals; 2% sales - Total Inv: $180,000 - $250,000 - Financing: No.

MR. CD-ROM *
Mr. CD-ROM Stores, Inc.
17770 Preston Rd., Camelot Pl., Dallas, TX, 75252. Contact: Mike Schlosser, V.P. of Fran. - Tel: (800) 528-7822. Retail sales of CD-ROM computer software. Established: 1994 - Franchising Since: 1995 - No. of Units: Company Owned: 1 - Franchise Fee: $20,000 - Royalty: 4% service fee, 2% market/adv. - Total Inv: Turnkey store set up $35,000, inventory $60,000 - Financing: No.

MR. MOVIES
7625 Parklawn Ave., #200, Edina, MN, 55435-5123. Contact: Teri Stark, Dir. of Fran. Oper. - Tel: (612) 835-3321. Video sales and rental outlets featuring a "neighborhood superstore" concept. Professionally decorated, computerized, up-to-date store design set Mr. Movies apart from other video retailers. Established: 1985 - Franchising Since: 1985 - No. of Units: Franchised: 90 - Franchise Fee: $19,500 - Royalty: 4% + 4% adv - Total Inv: $200,000 - $260,000 - Financing: No.

PALMER VIDEO
Palmer Video Corp.
1767 Morris Ave., Union, NJ, 07083. Contact: Gert Elster, Fran. Coord. - Tel: (908) 686-3030. Sale and rental of video cassettes and related accessories. Established: 1981 - Franchising Since: 1983 - No. of Units: Company Owned: 32 - Franchised: 41 - Franchise Fee: $39,000 - Royalty: 5% - Total Inv: $250,000 - Financing: No.

PARALLAX PRODUCTIONS
4264 Westroads Dr., West Palm Beach, FL, 33407. Contact: David Schain, Producer - Tel: (407) 842-7788, Fax: (407) 842-4566. Film & video production & post production facility. Producing broadcast quality videos for franchises; training videos; corporate & industrials; T.V. commercials. Established: 1986.

PCR - PERSONAL COMPUTER RENTALS, INC.
2557 Route #130, Cranbury, NJ, 08512. Contact: Mark Brown, Sales Mgr. - Tel: (609) 395-0550 or (800) 727-7079. Business oriented microcomputer rental center providing hardware and peripheral equipment to the business sector. Established: 1983 - Franchising Since: 1984 - No. of Units: Company Owned: 1 - Franchised: 50 - Franchise Fee: $25,500 - Royalty: 7% + 1% nat'l adv. fund - Financing: Franchisor provides comprehensive business plan to assist in financing.

PLANET INTERNET LOGON CENTER *
Planet Internet Corporation
Ste. 118, 620-19th St., Niagara Falls, NY, 14301. Contact: John Clarke, V.P. & G.M. - Tel: (905) 358-0688, Fax: (905) 358-0511. Logon centers are high profile centers designed for the sale of Internet on line time. Computers peripherals, software and internet applications, as well as conducting learning seminars for business and personal use of the Internet to make money. Established: 1995 - Franchising Since: 1995 - No. of Units: Company Owned: 1 - Franchise Fee: $15,000 - Royalty: None, no advertising - Total Inv: $75,000 to $100,000 - Financing: Yes.

RADIO SHACK
Tandy Corporation
1600 One Tandy Center, Ft. Worth, TX, 76102. Contact: Robert Owens, V.P. - Tel: (817) 390-3381. Retail consumer electronics. Established: 1922 - No. of Units: Company Owned: 4,835 - Franchised: 2,246.

RED GIRAFFE VIDEO
American Video, Inc.
10444 Bluegrass Parkway, Louisville, KY, 40299. Contact: Ben McCaskill, Fran. Dir. - Tel: (502) 499-0072. Fax: (502) 499-9683. Video rental super stores. Established: 1986 - No. of Units: Company Owned: 18 - Franchised: 1.

SECOND SOURCE COMPUTER CENTERS
307 Newark Shopping Ctr., Newark, DE, 19711-7303. Contact: Scott Oglum, Pres. - Tel: (302) 737-4473. Sale of new and used computers. Save up to 70% when buying used products. Established: 1988 - Franchising Since: 1991 - No. of Units: Company Owned: 1 - Franchised: 6 - Franchise Fee: $15,000 - Royalty: 5% of gross sales - Total Inv: $59,000 - $71,000.

SOFTWARE CITY
26 W. Forest Ave., Englewood, NJ, 07631. Contact: S. Altshuler, Pres. - Tel: (201) 569-8900. Offer computers, software and peripherals to business accounts, school systems and government agencies. Established: 1980 - Franchising Since: 1982 - No. of Units: - Franchised: 35 - Franchise Fee: $15,000 - Royalty: 2% up to $1 million in sales; 1% on sales over $1 million; 1/2% adv. - Total Inv: $50,000 for sales office; $200,000 for retail store.

TODAYS COMPUTERS BUSINESS CENTERS
Intelligent Electronics
411 Eagleview Blvd., Exton, PA, 19341. Contact: Joe de Simone, Dir. Fran. - Tel: (610) 458-5700. For already successful businesses who have an existing customer base and solid reputation under their own name and the opportunity to set up a company within their company. Established: 1982 - Franchising Since: 1984 - No. of Units: 96 - Franchise Fee: $5,000 - Total Inv: $50,000 - $250,000 - Financing: No.

VCR DOCTOR
Doctor Video Technology, Inc.
909 N. Hayden Rd., Scottsdale, AZ, 85257. Contact: Ken Hollowell, V.P., Mktg. - Tel: (602) 945-7648. Repairs of VCRs and camcorders. Established: 1990 - Franchising Since: 1994 - No. of Units: Company Owned: 5 - Franchised: 45 - Franchise Fee: $15,000 - Royalty: 10% - Total Inv: $10,000 incl. equip., inven., rent, leasehold improvements - Financing: None.

VIDE-O-GO TAPE LEARNING CENTERS OF AMERICA
Vide-O-Go, Inc.
P.O. Box 2994, Princeton, NJ, 08543-2994. Contact: Dean Stevens, CEO - Tel: (609) 716-1989. Retail/distributor of "How-To" audio and video cassette learning programs. Established: 1989 - Franchising Since: 1992 - No. of Units: Franchised: 2 - Franchise Fee: $10,500 - Royalty: $250/mo. + 2% - Total Inv: $63,000 - $111,000 - Financing: N/A.

VIDEO BIZ, INC.
224 N Nova Rd., Ormond Beach, FL, 32174. Contact: Steve Edson, Owner - Tel: (904) 672-0851. Sale of video movie stores. Established: 1978 - Franchising Since: 1983 - No. of Units: Company Owned: 12 - Licensed: 350 - Franchise Fee: $15,000 - Total Inv: $75,000 - $150,000 - Financing: None.

VIDEO EDITOR
5975 Roswell Rd., Ste. 355, Atlanta, GA, 30328. Contact: Fran. Dept. - Tel: (404) 256-4108. Do it yourself full service video post production facility. Services available are editing, equipment rentals, video duplications, film, slide and photo transfers. Established: 1985 - Franchising Since: 1989 - No. of Units: 3 - Franchise Fee: $19,500 - Royalty: 9% - Total Inv: $130,000 - Financing: No.

VIDEO GALAXY FRANCHISE, INC.
101 West St., Rockville, CT, 06066. Contact: Bill Corbin, Nat'l Fran Dir. - Tel: (203) 871-7831. Rental and sale of videos and miscellaneous related items. Established: 1981 - Franchising Since: 1985 - No. of Units: Company Owned: 3 - Franchised: 40 - Franchise Fee: $20,000 - Royalty: 5% - Total Inv: $175,000 ($75,000 min. cash) - Financing: None.

VIDEO GAME SWAPPERS
Video Game Swappers, Inc.
4632 Georgetown Pl., Ste. D, Stockton, CA, 95207. Contact: Gloria Pres. - Tel: (209) 474-1052. We buy, sell and trade new and used home video game systems and games. Established: 1990 - Franchising Since: 1994 - No. of Units: Company Owned: 6 - Franchised: 3 - Franchise Fee: $10,000 - Royalty: 5% on annual gross sales - Total Inv: $32,000 - $72,000 - Financing: No.

VIDEO GAMER
15965 Jeanette St., Southfield, MI, 48075. Contact: Colleen McGaffey - Tel: (810) 557-2784, Fax: (810) 557-7931. Video Gamer sells, resells, and buys used/new video games and equipment. Video Gamer offers a wide variety of games and equipment you may also rent and play before taking the game home. Established: 1988 - Franchising Since: 1993 - No. of Units: Company Owned: 2 - Franchised: 2 - Franchise Fee: $16,000 - Royalty: 5% - Total Inv: $77,000 - $96,000 - Financing: Yes.

VIDEO STOP
Video Stop Unlimited Inc.
3303 E. Memorial Dr., Muncie, IN, 47302. Contact: Fran. Dir. - Tel: (317) 288-7800 or (317) 282-2863. Video and Nintendo game rental. VCR and nintendo system rental. Video sell-thru. Family oriented video rental with full line of video rental. Play area for children. Arcade room for adolescents. Established: 1988 - Franchising Since: 1990 - No. of

Units: Company Owned: 3 - Franchise Fee: $17,500 - Royalty: 5% - Total Inv: video software-$50,000; computers-$10,000; improvements are determined on location; display- $30,000 - $40,000; misc.- $5,000 - $15,000 - Financing: No.

VIDEO THRILLS FAMILY ENTERTAINMENT *
125 Rt. 526, Allentown, NJ, 08501. Contact: Sam Schreiber, Pres. - Tel: (800) 55-THRILL. Video retail sales and rentals. Established: 1991 - Franchising Since: 1995 - No. of Units: Company Owned: 12 - Franchise Fee: $25,000 - Royalty: $300. per week 1st five years; $400. 2nd five years - Total Inv: $91,000 - $158,600.

VIDEO UPDATE
Video Update, Inc.
287 E. 6th St., St. Paul, MN, 55101. Contact: John Bedard, Pres. - Tel: (612) 222-0006. Franchisor of video superstores. Twelve years of experience has resulted in the development of a superior management program and site selection ability. Video Update provides the knowledge and material for a turnkey operation. Established: 1982 - Franchising Since: 1983 - No. of Units: Company Owned: 108 - Franchised: 25 - Franchise Fee: $29,500 - Royalty: 5% and 1% adv. - Total Inv: $250,000 and up - Financing: Will assemble business plan/limited financing.

VIDEOGENICS
35660 Harper, Mt. Clemens, MI, 48043. Contact: Franchise Dir./Pres. - Tel: (810) 773-8340. Video stores and videotaping services. Established: 1983 - Franchising Since: 1984 - No. of Units: 32 - Franchise Fee: $7,500 - $15,000 - Total Inv: $17,000 - $70,000 - Royalty: 4% + 2% adv. - Financing: no.

WEST COAST ENTERTAINMENT
9990 Global Rd., Philadelphia, PA, 19115. Contact: Sandy DeVine, Dir. of Fran. Sales - Tel: (800) 433-5171. Full scale video rental and sales outlets. Established: 1983 - Franchising Since : 1985 - No. of Units: Franchised: 516 - Franchise Fee: $25,000 initial, $5,000 each additional - Royalty: 5%, 2% adv. - Total Inv: $225,000 - Financing: No.

WIZ TECHNOLOGY INC. *
Worldwide Information Services Inc.
Box 21261, Ft. Lauderdale, FL, 33335-1261. Contact: W.H. Bonneau, Pres. - Tel: (305) 764-7942. Affordable software publisher that provides software for everyone. Games are 66%, education 25% and home and business represent 9% of the market share. Developers of the $5.00 software store and $9.95 Rainbow Educational Line. CD Rom is the specialty market today. Offer affordable and unconditionally guaranteed products to sell. Established: 1989 - No. of units: Company Owned: 1 - Total Inv: $8,000 and up - Financing: No.

SCHOOLS AND TEACHING

ABC PHONETIC READING SCHOOL INC.
Phx. Ed. Franchise Sys. Inc.
4530 N. Central, #200, Phoenix, AZ, 85012. Contact: John Cahal, Pres. - Tel: (800) 538-7323. Tutoring. Established: 1986 - Franchising Since: 1993 - No. of Units: Company Owned: 10 - Franchised: 1 - Franchise Fee: $10,000 - Royalty: 10% gross, 2% adv. - Total Inv: $32,500 to $51,350 - Financing: No.

ACADEMY OF LEARNING
5 Bank St., Ste. 202, Attleboro, MA, 02703-2351. Contact: Lloyd Dove, C.O.O. - Tel: (800) 750-TYPE, (508) 222-0000. State of the art computer and business skills training. Unique, self paced Integrated Learning System. Established: 1987 - Franchising Since: 1987 - No. of Units: Company Owned: 2 - Franchised: 118 - Franchise Fee: $35,000 - Total Inv: $112,600 - $147,800 - Financing: No.

AMERICAN INSTITUTE OF SMALL BUSINESS
7515 Wayzata Blvd., Minneapolis, MN, 55426. Contact: Max Fallek, Pres. - Tel: (800) 328-2906. Provides educational materials including books, software, and videos on small business and entrepreneurship. Provides seminars on small business start up and operation and consulting services to small business. Established: 1986 - Franchising Since: 1990 - No. of Units: Company Owned: 2 - Franchised: 4 - Franchise Fee: $2,000 - Total Inv: $10,000 to $15,000 - Financing: Yes.

AMRON SCHOOL OF THE FINE ARTS
John & Joe Fashions, Inc.
1315 Medlin Rd., Monroe, NC, 28112. Contact: Norma Williams, Pres. - Tel: (704) 283-4290. A franchise sales system set up to teach modeling, acting, cosmetics, and photography for model and actor portfolios and book. Established: 1979 - Franchising Since: 1990 - No. of Units: Company Owned: 4 - Franchise Fee: $15,000 - Royalty: based on a sliding scale of income - Total Inv: $5,000 office equip., and $15,000 fran. fee - Financing: Owner financing at 8% interest.

ATHENEUM LEARNING CORP. OF AMERICA
500 - 108th Ave. N.E., Ste. 1740, Bellevue, WA, 98004. Contact: Fran. Mktg. Dept. - Tel: (800) 221-9031. International training & development organization providing training programs designed to lead corporate success into the 21st century. Established: 1991 - Franchising Since: 1991 - No. of Units: Franchised: 46 - Franchise Fee: $29,500 - Royalty: 25% of gross revenue, includes all training materials - Total Inv: $29,500, $7,000 - $15,000 operating capital - Financing: Yes.

BARBIZON INTERNATIONAL, INC.
1900 Glades Rd., Ste. 300, Boca Raton, FL, 33431. Contact: Barry B. Wolff, Pres. - Tel: (407) 362-8883. Courses in modeling, fashion and acting. Established: 1939 - Franchising Since: 1968 - No. of Units: Franchised: 75 - Franchise Fee: $35,000 - Total Inv: $50,000 - Financing: portion of franchise fee.

BOSTON BARTENDERS SCHOOL OF AMERICA
Boston Bartenders School Associates Inc.
31 Grove St., Wilbraham, MA, 02095. Contact: Bill Green, C.O.O., Exec. V.P., Founder - Tel: (800) 357-3210, Fax: (413) 596-4630. Bartender training school. Established: 1968 - Franchising Since: 1994 - No. of Units: Company Owned: 8 - Franchise Fee: $5,000 to $6,999 - Royalty: 10% to 12% - Total Inv: $21,799 - Financing: Yes.

CAREER BLAZERS LEARNING CENTERS
590 Fifth Ave., New York, NY, 10036 . Contact: Howard Kane, Exec. V.P. - Tel: (800) 284-3232. Computer training schools designed to cater to the adult learner. We teach you all that you'll ever need to know about how to successfully operate a profitable business school. Established: 1949 - Franchising Since: 1994 - No. of Units: Company Owned: 5 - Franchised/Licensed: 120 - Franchise Fee: $25,000 - Royalty: 9%-12% - Total Inv: $90,000 - $150,000 not incl. fran. fee.

CLEANING CONSULTANT SERVICES, INC.
P.O. Box 1273, Seattle, WA, 98111. Contact: Wm. R. Griffin, Pres. - Tel: (800) 622-4221, Fax: (206) 622-6876. Licensees act as local small business consultants to the cleaning industry and frequently operate certified vocational training programs, temporary employment services, and a small business centers. They also sponsor seminars and handle local consulting projects and sell line of related books, publications, software and training videos on cleaning, maintenance and self-employment. Established: 1973 - Franchising Since: 1981 - No. of Units: Company Owned: 3 - Franchised: 2 - Franchise Fee: $2,500 - Total Inv: up to $7,500 - Financing: Partial.

COMPREHEND! COMPUTER EDUCATION CENTERS *
COMPrehend! Franchise Corp.
3200 N. 29th Ave., Hollywood, FL, 33020-1313. Contact: Dean Snow, Pres. - Tel: (954) 921-6040, (800) 601-5876. Personal computer education centers designed to increase the productivity among corporate and individual computer users/owners. Established: 1991 - Franchising Since: 1995 - No. of Units: Company Owned: 1 - Franchise Fee: $30,000 - Royalty: 6.5% of gross rev., local adv. up to 2% of gross rev., adv. fund 3% of gross rev. - Total Inv: $192,500 to $297,100 - Financing: No.

COMPUQUEST EDUCATIONAL SERVICES
6161 Busch Blvd., Ste. 100, Columbus, OH, 43229. Contact: Stan Gebhardt, Pres. - Tel: (614) 888-5437. Computer education for children ages 3 1/2 and older, SAT/ACT prep course, and adult computer literacy curriculum. Established: 1991 - Franchising Since: 1991 - No. of Units: Franchised: 75 - Franchise Fee: $3,250 to $22,500 - Royalty: 10%, no advertising royalty - Financing: Yes.

ECHOLS INTERNATIONAL TRAVEL/TRAINING COURSES/INTERNATIONAL TRAVEL TRAINING COURSES, INC.
676 N. Saint Clair St. #1950, Chicago, IL, 60611. Contact: Evelyn Echols, Pres. - Tel: (312) 943-5500. Training personnel for all facets of the travel industry including airlines. Established: 1962 - Franchising Since: 1972 - No. of Units: Company Owned: 2 - Franchised: 2 - Franchise Fee: $50,000 - Total Inv: $125,000 - Royalty: 10% first 5 yrs., 7% thereafter.

EDUCATIONAL RESOURCE CENTERS OF AMERICA
315 Mizner Blvd., Boca Raton, FL, 33432. Contact: Elaine Wyner, Pres. - Tel: (407) 391-2033. Tutorial services, college & school, counseling, test preparation, educational consulting. Established: 1986 - Franchising Since: 1987 - No. of Units: Company Owned: 1 - Franchised: 13 - Franchise Fee: $8,500 - Royalty: 6% - Total Inv: $12,500+ - Financing: No.

ELS INTERNATIONAL (ELSI)
ELS Educational Services
5761 Buckingham Parkway, Culver City, CA, 90230. Contact: Terry Cooper, Pres. - Tel: (310) 642-0982. English as a second language schools. Franchises are sold internationally, USA schools are company-owned. Established: 1956 - Franchising Since: 1978 - No. of Units: Company Owned: 22 - Franchised: 52 - Franchise Fee: $30,000 - Royalty: 3% - Total Inv: $150,000 - $300,000 (excl. fran./train.fees) - Financing: None.

FOURTH R, THE
Fourth R. Inc.
1715 Market St., Ste. 103, Kirkland, WA, 98033. Contact: Robert McCauley, Fran. Sales Dir. - Tel: (800) 821-8653 or (206) 823-0336. An exciting variety of computer classes and services to children and their families to help them meet their ever-changing computer education needs. The program teaches a wide range of computer skills, as well as traditional skills for lifelong learning. The Fourth R attracts an enthusiastic following among parents, schools, youth clubs, and national chains of childcare providers. Established: 1991 - Franchising Since: 1992 - No. of Units: Franchised: 87 - Franchise Fee: $19,000 - Royalty: $120 + 5% thereafter - Total Inv: $42,000 - Financing: For multiple franchises.

GWYNNE LEARNING ACADEMY
Gwynne Systems, Inc.
1432 W. Emerald Ave., Unit 735, Mesa, AZ, 85202-3220. Contact: Penny Gwynne, Treasurer - Tel: (602) 644-1434. Video-based educational courses. Established: 1981 - Franchising Since: 1992 - No. of Units: Company Owned: 1 - Franchised: 13 - Franchise Fee: $45,000 - Royalty: 7% - Total Inv: $9,800 - $14,000 plus fran. fee - Financing: Yes.

HONORS LEARNING CENTER, THE
5959 Shallowford Rd., Ste. 517, Chattanooga, TN, 37421. Contact: Gary Miller, Pres. - Tel: (423) 892-1800. Academic testing & education services. The Honors Learning Center is an educational facility offering academic testing and individualized programs for grades K-12. Remedial and enrichment programs during after-school hours. Established: 1987 - Franchising Since: 1992 - No. of Units: Company Owned: 1 - Franchised: 1 - Franchise Fee: $15,000 - Royalty: 8% - Total Inv: $44,340 - $78,720 (not incl. work. cap.) - Financing: None.

HUNTINGTON LEARNING CENTER, THE
Huntington Learning Centers, Inc.
496 Kinderkamack Rd., Oradell, NJ, 07649. Contact: Helen Trent, Nat'l. Dir. Fran. Dev. - Tel: (201) 261-8400. As the oldest learning center franchisor in the U.S., we offer a unique combination of educational programs and proven support systems known as the Huntington System. Through this system you can help students of all ages achieve academic success by improving their basic skills and SAT entrance exam scores. Established: 1977 - Franchising Since: 1986 - No. of Units: Company Owned: 17 - Franchised: 84 - Franchise Fee: $31,000 - Royalty: 6% first 12 months, then 8% royalty; 2% adv. - Total Inv: $107,000 - $135,000 - Financing: 50% of the initial franchise fee.

INTERNATIONAL BARTENDING INSTITUTE
P.O. Box 866, Osprey, FL, 34229. Contact: Mr. Haren, Chairman of the Board - Tel: (813) 966-2111. Trade schools teaching bartending and mixology. Established: 1977 - Franchising Since: 1977 - No. of Units: Franchised: 32 - Franchise Fee: $2,000 - $5,000 - Total Inv: $25,000 - $30,000 - Financing: None.

J.L. HAMMETT CO.
P.O. Box 859057, Braintree, MA, 02185-9057. Contact: Vince Botti, Dir. - Tel: (617) 848-1000. J.L. Hammett Co. is a supplier of educational and early learning material. The product line has been supplemented to include office supplies and craft products. Established: 1863 - Franchising Since: 1986 - No. of Units: Company Owned: 31 - Franchised: 38 - Franchise Fee: $25,000 - Royalty: 6% + 1% adv. - Total Inv: $96,000 - $216,500 excld. fran. fee - Financing: No.

JOHN CASABLANCAS MODELING AND CAREER CENTERS
Model Merchandising International, L.P.
111 East 22nd St., New York, NY, 10010. Contact: Charyn K. Parker, Dir. of Fran. Dev. - Tel: (212) 420-0655, Fax: (212) 473-2725. John Casablancas, Chairman of the Board of Elite Model Management Corp., Inc., incorporates his modeling and personal development knowledge in Board of Education approved curriculum. Established: 1979 - Franchising Since: 1979 - No. of Units: Franchised: 50 - Franchise Fee: $15,000 - $35,000 - Royalty: 7% + 3% Co-Op. Adv. - Total Inv: $58,000 - $122,000.

JOHN ROBERT POWERS FINISHING, MODELING, AND CAREER SCHOOLS
John Robert Powers School System, Inc.
175 Andover Street, Danvers, MA, 01923. Contact: Richard S. Ciummei, Barbara J. Tyler, Pres., Exec. V.P. - Tel: (800) 262-2954 or (508) 777-8677. Schools specializing in training for men and women in self-improvement, modelling, executive grooming, drama, fashion merchandising, interior design, etc. Established: 1923 - Franchising Since: 1950 - No. of Units: Company Owned: 1 - Franchised: 63 - Franchise Fee: $10,000 - $30,000 - Royalty: 10% on cash collected plus $150/mo. adv fee - Total Inv: $50,000 - $75,000 depending on territory - Financing: 50% of fran. fee.

KIP MCGRATH EDUCATION CENTERS
Forever Learning, Inc.
6465 Wayzata Blvd., Ste. 940, St. Louis Park, MN, 55426. Contact: James Sullivan, Pres. - Tel: (612) 593-1443. Master franchises now available in all areas of USA and Canada. We offer supplemental tutoring to students of all ages in reading, spelling, English, math and study skills. Our goal is to help students achieve their academic goals, build self confidence & provide a learning base for future academic success through private, affordable, individualized instruction. Established: 1992 - Franchising Since: 1992 - No. of Units: Franchised: 9 - Franchise Fee: $10,400 - Royalty: $3,750 annual base plus 3% of gross - Total Inv: $27,000: fran. fee, leasehold imp., work. cap. - Financing: Bank financing if qualified.

KUMON EDUCATIONAL INSTITUTE INC.
2200 Fletcher Ave., Fort Lee, NJ, 07024. , Dir. of Mktg. - Tel: (201) 947-0707. Franchisor of after-school supplemental math centers. Established: 1958 - Franchising Since: 1958 (in Japan) - No. of Units: Company Owned: 4 U.S. - Franchised: 400 - Franchise Fee: $150 - Royalty: 40% of student tuition - 50% of enrollment fee - Financing: No.

LASER PROFESSOR LEARNING CENTERS
Laser Professor Franchising Corp.
2200 Space Park Dr., Ste. 200, Houston, TX, 77058-3698. Contact: Tina Mathis - Tel: (713) 333-5550. Individual training using most advanced hi-tech combination of laser and computer technology. Established: 1986 - Franchising Since: 1990 - No. of Units: Franchised: 2 - Franchise Fee: $20,000 - Royalty: $900/mth. - Total Inv: $130,000 ($85,000 for computers & laser) - Financing: Yes.

LEADERSHIP MANAGEMENT, INC.
4567 Lakeshore Drive, Waco, TX, 76710. Contact: Tony Stigliano - Tel: (800) 365-7437. LMI offers leadership and management development franchises. LMI is one of the world's largest producers of management, executive and leadership development programs in the areas of time

management, personal organization, planning, delegation and goal setting. LMI franchises operate in three major markets: corporate America, small to medium size companies; and continuing adult education. Established: 1965 - Franchising Since: 1966 - No. of Units: Franchised: 552 - Franchise Fee: $30,000 - Royalty: nil - Total Inv: $30,000+ - Financing: Yes.

LEARNRIGHT®
LearnRight Corporation
1315 W. College Ave., Ste. 301, State College, PA, 16801. Contact: Cynthia A. Minter, Pres. - Tel: (800) 876-3450. One-on-one supplemental education schools dedicated to teaching people of all ages how to become more effective learners. We offer dynamic entrepreneurs, investors & educators a unique & exciting franchise opportunity. Established: 1978 - Franchising Since: 1993 - No. of Units: Company Owned: 1 - Franchised: 2 - Franchise Fee: $30,000 - Royalty: 6% - Total Inv: $75,000 - $95,000 - Financing: Will assist franchisee in obtaining 3rd party financing.

NEW HORIZONS COMPUTER LEARNING CENTER
New Horizons Franchising, Inc.
1231 E. Dyer Rd., Ste. 140, Santa Ana, CA, 92705. Contact: Dean Gaston, Dir. Fran. Sales, NA - Tel: (714) 438-9491, Fax: (714) 241-7836. A complete PC, Macintosh, Windows NT, Novell, Unix and Sun training company for businesses and individuals. Franchise locations throughout the world. Established: 1982 - Franchising Since: 1992 - No. of Units: Company Owned: 3 - Franchised: 93 - Franchise Fee: $30,000 - Royalty: Continuing 5% of gross rev., Adv. 1% of gross rev. - Total Inv: $300,000 liquid assets - Financing: 50% of the franchise fee.

PC PROFESSOR COMPUTER TRAINING WORKSHOPS *
7035 Beracasa Way, #208, Boca Raton, FL, 33433. Contact: Howard Fellman, Dir. - Tel: (407) 750-7879. Provides quality, personalized computer training in a relaxed, hands-on manner. Our formula works! Includes thorough training package and software authorizations. Established: 1989 - Franchising Since: 1995 - No. of Units: Company Owned: 1 - Franchised: 1 - Franchise Fee: call for details - Financing: Yes.

PRIMROSE SCHOOL
Primrose School Franchising, Co.
199 S. Erwin St., Cartersville, GA, 30120-3560. Contact: Jo Kirchner, Exec. V.P. - Tel: (770) 606-9600 or (800) 745-0677. Quality educational childcare with proven curriculum and lesson plans for infants through kindergarten. Comprehensive operations manual, thorough training, ongoing support from professional staff. Established: 1982 - Franchising Since: 1989 - No. of Units: Company Owned: 1 - Franchised: 49 - Franchise Fee: $48,500 - Royalty: 7%, 1% adv./dev. - Approx. Total Inv: $900,000 ($150,000) - Financing: Assistance available.

PRINCETON REVIEW, THE
Princeton Review Management Corp., The
2315 Broadway, New York, NY, 10024. Contact: Linda Nessim, Dir. of Mktg. - Tel: (212) 874-8282. Offers courses and tutoring programs for standardized tests. These include the SAT, The College Board Achievements, The ACT, GRE, GMAT and the LSAT. Established: 1981- Franchising Since: 1985 - No. of Units: Company Owned: 4 - Franchised: 37 - Franchise Fee: differs for each location - Royalty: differs for each location - Total Inv: differs for each location.

SANDLER SYSTEMS INC.
10411 Stevenson Rd., Stevenson, MD, 21152. Contact: Phil Goodwin, Fran. Dir. - Tel: (800) 669-3537, Fax: (410) 358-7854. Sales, management and human relations training company. Our target market is small to medium size businesses. Established: 1967 - Franchising Since: 1983 - No. of Units: Franchised: 165 - Franchise Fee: $30,000 - Royalty: None - Financing: Minimal.

SLEEPING GIANT WITHIN, THE *
Sleeping Giant Within, Inc., The
3697 Hwy. C, Leslie, MO, 63056. Contact: Henry Hubenthal, Pres. - Tel: (800) 205-7439. Leadership, management & human development training specialist. Established: 1990 - Franchising Since: 1995 - No. of Units: Company Owned: 14 - Franchised: 1 - Franchise Fee: $25,000 - Royalty: 8% gross sales - Total Inv: $25,000 fran. fee - Financing: Yes.

SYLVAN LEARNING CENTERS
Sylvan Learning Systems, Inc.
9135 Guilford Rd., Columbia, MD, 21046. Contact: Flo Schell, Dir. Fran. System Dev. - Tel: (800) 284-8214. Leading provider of supplemental education to children and adults. Individualized programs in reading, mathematics, writing, study skills, SAT/ACT prep. Instruction by certified teachers. Established: 1979 - Franchising Since: 1980 - No. of Units: Company Owned: 26 - Franchised: 540 - Franchise Fee: $29,000 - $39,000 - Royalty: 8%/9%, - Total Inv: Cash $66,060 - $94,500; Total: $76,060 - $137,500 - Financing: In some instances.

TRAVEL PROFESSIONALS INSTITUTE
10172 Linn Station Rd., Louisville, KY, 40223. Contact: John E. Boyce, Dir. of Fran. Sales - Tel: (800) 626-2469, (502) 423-9900. Franchise travel schools, teaching travel as a vocation for students. Established: 1989 - Franchising Since: 1990 - No. of Units: Company Owned: 1 - Franchised: 5 - Franchise Fee: $17,500 - Royalty: 7% - Total Inv: $51,000 - Financing: No.

TRAVEL TRADE SCHOOL, THE
7921 Southpark Plaza #105, Littleton, CO, 80120. Contact: Adonna L. Hipple, Pres. - Tel: (303) 795-1825. Total computer training for the travel industry. Established: 1975 - Franchising Since: 1980 - No. of Units: Company Owned: 1 - Franchised: 5 - Franchise Fee: $35,000 - Royalty: 7% gross - Total Inv: additional $15,000 - Financing: No.

U.S. SCHOOL OF PROFESSIONAL PAPERHANGING, INC.
16490 Timberlakes Dr., Ste. 203, Ft. Myers, FL, 33908. Contact: Meryl O'Rourke, V.P. - Tel: (941) 489-4621. Accredited post secondary proprietary trade school. Established: 1973 - Franchising Since: 1991 - Franchise Fee: $15,000 - Financing: No.

SIGN PRODUCTS & SERVICES

AMERICAN SIGN SHOPS
All American Signs Shops Inc.
208 Snow Ave., Raleigh, NC, 27603. Contact: Mark Richie, Pres. - Tel: (919) 833-9200 or (800) 966-2700. Retail sign shop manufacturing and sales of small signs through automated equipment. Established: 1984 - Franchising Since: 1987 - No. of Units: Franchised: 36 - Franchise Fee: $15,000 - Royalty: 6% - Total Inv: $55,000 + working capital - Financing: Equipment.

ASI SIGN SYSTEMS, INC.
3890 W. Northwest Highway, Ste. 102, Dallas, TX, 75220. Contact: Lance Utterback, Pres. - Tel: (800) ASI-SPEC. ASI Sign Systems, North America's largest architectural sign company, has maintained undisputed industry leadership for over 20 years by providing our affiliates with the very best in professional marketing, training, business development and on-going support programs. These services, along with ASI's commitment to innovative product development, premium quality and competitive pricing have made the name ASI Sign Systems synonymous with the architectural sign industry. Franchising Since: 1978 - No. of Units: Franchised: 34 - Franchise Fee: $35,000+, depending on territory - Royalty: 5%, 1% adv. - Total Inv. (excl. fran. fee): $145,000 - $200,000 - Financing: Up to 1/2 of fee portion.

FASTSIGNS
American Fastsigns, Inc.
2550 Midway Road, Ste. 150, Carrollton, TX, 75006. Contact: Randy Marshall, Dir. of Fran. Dev. - Tel: (800) 827-7446. Computer-generated vinyl signs and graphics. Retail stores produce signs and graphics for businesses. Unique systems include fully-documented operating procedures; order-based POS with mktg. support; proven sales and marketing techniques; ongoing business consultation; national accounts program. Established: 1985 - Franchising Since: 1986 - No. of Units: Company Owned: 1 - Franchised: 285 - Franchise Fee: $20,000 - Royalty: 6% to franchisor; 2% to National Ad Council - Total Inv: Approx. $100,000 plus work. cap. - Financing: Yes.

FASTSIGNS®
For A Quality Sign That's Right. On Time.

The #1 business-to-business sign franchise since 1992.
-Entrepreneur Magazine
-Success Magazine

JOIN THE WINNING TEAM! 800•827•7446

MAIN EVENT LAWN SIGN INC.
911 E. Brookwood Dr., Arlington Heights, IL, 60004. Contact: Denise Paine, Pres. - Tel: (708) 670-7777. Announcement lawn sign rentals for new baby, birthdays, anniversaries and all other special events. Purchase our plastic signs or make your own with our templates & instructions. Established: 1986 - Franchising Since: 1988 - No. of Units: Company Owned: 1 - Franchised: 49 - Royalty: None - Total Inv: $299. & up - Financing: No.

OUTDOOR FUN SIGNS
138 River Corner Rd., Conestoga, PA, 17516. Contact: Diane Shiffer, Owner - Tel: (717) 872-6916. Rental of all occasions lawn signs. Established: 1986 - Franchising Since: 1989 - No. of Units: Company Owned: 1 - Franchised: 1 - Franchise Fee: $15,000 includes all start-up costs - Royalty: $500/year 1st 5 years - Total Inv: $15,000 all signs & office supplies for 1st year - Financing: No.

SIGN BIZ, INC.
10 Corporate Park., #130, Irvine, CA, 92714. Contact: Sherry Suffens, Nat'l. Sales Dir. - Tel: (800) 633-5580;Outside US (714)263-0400. Computer-aided business-to-business sign stores, independently owned. Store owners use high-tech equipment to create text, logos, and custom graphics. These sign business owners receive exclusive territories, full training, marketing support, conventions, hot lines & deep discounts. Established: 1989 - Sold Since: 1990 - No. of Units: Franchised: 109 - Franchise Fee: none - Royalty: none - Total Inv: $57,000 pkg. + $20,000 start-up (est.) + $20,000 work. cap. (est.).

SIGN EXPRESS
Sign Express, Inc.
6 Clarke Circle, P.O. Box 309, Bethel, CT, 06801. Contact: Laurie Wright, Fran. Dir. - Tel: (800) 525-SIGN or (203) 791-0004. Computerized sign making serving other businesses. Complete training in all sign making, vehicle lettering, site signs, corporate signage systems, etc. Business package includes equipment, supplies and training. Offering franchises internationally, and licensing nationally. Established: 1986 - Franchising Since: 1988 - No. of Units: Franchised: 82 - Franchise Fee: $20,000 - Royalty: 5% - Total Inv: $38,000 - $51,000 includes fran. fee. - Financing: Equipment leasing available.

SIGN IT QUICK
Sign It Quick International, Inc.
3155 Savannah Hwy., Charleston, SC, 29414. Contact: Frank Au Coin, Pres. - Tel: (803) 763-3155. Regular and super sign stores. Menu ranges from basic signs to awnings & more elaborate, depending on type of shop. Best marketing & promotion programs. Owner & president was awarded Small Business Person of the Year, South Carolina, 1994. Established: 1987 - Franchising Since: 1988 - No. of Units: Company Owned: 1 - Franchised: 6 - Franchise Fee: $15,500 - Royalty: 5% gross sales (excluding media trades), 1% adv. 1st yr., 2% thereafter - Total Inv: approx. $125,000.

SIGNS BY TOMORROW
6460 Dobbin Rd., Columbia, MD, 21045. Contact: Robert Nunn, Franchise Director - Tel: (410) 992-7192 or (800) 336-4610. Computerized one day retail sign business. Established: 1986 - Franchising Since: 1987 - No. of Units: Company Owned: 3 - Franchised: 40 - Franchise Fee: $17,500 - Royalty: 5%/3% - Total Inv: $80,000 - $100,000, $50,000 cash to start - Financing: Yes.

SIGNS FIRST
Monotag Corp.
813 Ridge Lake Blvd., Ste. 390, Memphis, TN, 38120. Contact: James Warr, C.E.O. - Tel: (800) 852-2163. Computerized sign shop in a retail store, producing computer designed & cut vinyl lettering & graphics for personal, professional, and commercial needs. Established: 1966 - Franchising Since: 1989 - No. of Units: Franchised: 37 - Franchise Fee: $15,000 - Royalty: 6% - Total Inv: $23,000 with leasing, $82,000 maximum without leasing - Financing: Franchisor will assist with leasing, SBA, or bank financing.

SIGNS & MORE IN 24
Signs & More In 24, Inc.
1739 St. Mary's Ave., Parkersburg, WV, 26101. Contact: Bruce Bronski, Pres. - Tel: (800) 358-2358, (304) 424-7446, Fax: (304) 422-7449. 24 hour signs, awnings, electrical, architectural. Established: 1990 - Franchising Since: 1992 - No. of Units: Company Owned: 1 - Franchised: 3 - Franchise Fee: $13,000 - Royalty: 4% - 6% - Total Inv: $45,000 - $75,000 - Financing: Assistance.

SIGNS NOW
Signs Now Corporation
4900 Manatee Ave. W., Ste. 201, Bradenton, FL, 34209. Contact: Terry Demarest, Dir. of Fran. Sales - Tel: (800) 356-3373, (813) 747-7747, Fax: (813) 747-5074. Computer-generated quick sign industry, founded in 1983. Only company with 21 experienced in-field Regional Managers. Retail stores produce signs & graphics for businesses. Unique systems include fully documented operating procedures; order based POS w/ mktg. support; proven sales & mktg. techniques; nat'l. acts program; nat'l. group discount program; computer bulletin board w/100s of clip art & logos; regular store visits & regional meetings; annual internal rally. Established: 1983 - Franchising Since: 1986 - No. of Units: Franchised: 150 in 34 states in 3 countries - Franchise Fee: $19,800 - Royalty: 5% - Total Inv: $50,620 - $96,150 - Financing: Total leasing available.

SIGNWORLD
P.O. Box 1359, Kona, HI, 96745. Contact: Ken Kindt, Pres. - Tel: (800) 545-2777, Fax: (808) 329-8852. Full service sign companies. Established: 1988 - Offering Business Opportunities Since: 1988 - No. of Business Opportunities: 80 - Total Inv: $60,000 - equip., supplies, training, protected territory, site selection, store design & ongoing support - Financing: Yes, up to $45,000 (75%).

SPEEDY SIGN* A*RAMA, USA, INC.
Speedy Sign A Rama, USA, Inc.
1601 Belvedere Rd., #402E, West Palm Beach, FL, 33406-1541. Contact: Bill Luce, Dir. of Fran. Dev. - Tel: (407) 640-5570 or (800) 286-8671. A full service sign business in a retail format that combines modern technology and computerized, copyrighted software and our proven marketing program. Established: 1986 - Franchising Since: 1986 - No. of Units: Franchised: 225 - Franchise Fee: $32,500 - Royalty: 6% - Approx. Total Inv: $90,000 - $120,000 - Financing: Financing Available.

TSW THE SIGN WASHERS
4278 Pacific Hwy., Bellingham, WA, 98226. Contact: Doug Wilson, Pres. - Tel: (360) 647-8545, Fax: (360) 647-8545. Awning maintenance and repair. Primarily the new generation of Backlite Awning. Also graphics application and removal. Established: 1985 - Franchising Since: 1985 - No. of Units: Company Owned: 2 - Franchised: 14 - Franchise Fee: $22,500 - Royalty: 7% - Total Inv: Equip. & vehicle $15,000 - $7,500 - fee - Financing: Yes.

VAC SET SIGN SHOP
Universal Products Co.
108 N. Archer St., Norton, KS, 67654. Contact: R. L. Eldridge, Mgr. of Sales - Tel: (913) 877-3816. Complete sign shop package for making plastic signs of all kinds for indoor and outdoor use. Established: 1941 - Franchising Since: 1958 - Total Inv: $1,995. - Financing: No.

SPORTS AND RECREATION

AIR BOINGO INC.
5660 S. Meadow Lane, #141, Ogden, UT, 84403. Contact: Kent Singleton, Pres. - Tel: (801) 392-7450. Sell franchise of a steel bungee jumping tower. Established: 1991 - Franchising Since: 1991 - No. of Units: Company Owned: 4 - Franchised: 10 - Franchise Fee: $40,000 - Royalty: 5% of gross revenues - Total Inv: $229,800 - $372,750 - Financing: None.

AMATEUR BOWLERS TOUR
Amateur Bowlers Tour, Inc.
6422 Industry Way, Westminster, CA, 92683-3601. Contact: Ken Daleiden, Pres. - Tel: (714) 898-7874, or 3822. Membership bowling tournament club. Conduct bowling tournaments on regular weekly basis for members with minimum guaranteed prize funds. Established: 1977 - Franchising Since: 1987 - No. of Units: Franchised: 25 - Franchise Fee: $60,000 - Royalty: 25¢ on the first $11 initial expenses + .10 each additional $1 expenses - Total Inv: $85,527 to $94,700 - Financing: ABT will finance some of the total investment depending on location.

AMERICAN POOLPLAYERS ASSOCIATION
1000 Lake St. Louis Blvd., Ste. 325, Lake St. Louis, MO, 63367. Contact: Mr. John Jackel, Fran. Dev. Mgr. - Tel: (800) 372-2536. Franchisees run a national network of amateur pool leagues utilizing a unique handicapping system. No knowledge of pool is required. Complete training and on-going marketing experience is provided. Protected territories. Operate from your home. Work full-time or part-time. Sponsored by Anheuser-Busch since 1980. Established: 1981 - Franchising Since: 1982 - No. of Units: Franchised: 216 - Franchise Fee: varies - Royalty: 20% - Total Inv: $11,500 - Financing: Yes.

AMUSEMENT PRODUCTS, LLC
Pacer Go-Karts
5954 Brainerd Rd., Chattanooga, TN, 37421. Contact: Bill Wilcox, Sales Mgr. - Tel: (615) 892-7265. Manufacture commercial go-karts for go-kart tracks & family entertainment centers. Over 10 styles to choose from. Established: 1975 - Franchising Since: 1975 - No. of Units: Company Owned: 4 - Franchised: 504 - Total Inv: $100,000 - Financing: No.

BABBITT BASEBALL CAMPS *
Babbitt Baseball Camps, Inc.
14801 Perrywood Dr., Burtonsville, MD, 20866. Contact: Todd Babbitt, V.P. - Tel: (800) 253-3014. Instructional baseball camps for youth. Established: 1983 - Franchising Since: 1995 - No. of Units: Company Owned: 50 - Franchised: 8 - Franchise Fee: $1,000 - Royalty: $15 per camper, $1 nat'l. adv. per camper - Total Inv: $3,000 to $5,000 - Financing: No.

BIKE LINE
Paoli Bike & Sports
1035 Andrew Dr., West Chester, PA, 19380. Contact: Terri Kelly, Admin. Ass't. - Tel: (800) 537-2654, Fax: (610) 429-4295. Bicycle & fitness equipment sales & service. Established: 1983 - Franchising Since: 1991 - No. of Units: Company Owned: 24 - Franchised: 45 - Franchise Fee: $24,500 - Royalty: 4%, 1% nat'l adv. - Total Inv: $115,500 - $157,500 - Financing: No, help with obtaining funds from third party sources.

BUD LIGHT DART LEAGUE
American Darters Association, Inc.
1000 Lake St. Louis Blvd., Ste. 325, Lake St. Louis, MO, 63367. Contact: Glenn Remick, Pres. - Tel: (314) 625-8621. Amateur dart league management system, unique with its copyrighted handicap system. Allowing players of all abilities to compete effectively. National tournaments, national discounts and quarterly publication attract players. Established: 1991 - Franchising Since: 1991 - No. of Units: Franchised: 67 - Franchise Fee: Based on population - Royalty: $3.00 per team or 20% of basic weekly fee - Total Inv: Estimated $1,50 plus fran. fee.

CAROLE RIGGS HARRIS
Carole Riggs Dance Studios
116 Bateman Bridge Rd., Forest, VA, 24551. Contact: Carole Harris, Pres. - Tel: (804)525-7070. Instructional system, largely aimed at children and young adults which offers to the public the teaching of dance, motor development skills, modeling, karate and musical programs. Established: 1966 - No. of Units: 3 - Approx. Inv: $19,900 - Financing: None.

CASEY'S SPORTS *
Casey's Sports Cards & Collectibles
1919 S. 40th St., Ste. 202, Lincoln, NE, 68506. Contact: Jack L. Rediger, Pres., Franchise Developers - Tel: (402) 434-5620, Fax: (402) 435-3624. If you enjoy sports cards and collectibles, then quit looking! Casey's Sports allows you the buying power you may thought was not

possible in this industry. With 1000's of items to choose from your sports fans will keep coming back for more. Established: 1990 - Franchising Since: 1995 - No. of Units: Company Owned: 1 - Franchised: 1.

CLUB NAUTICO INTERNATIONAL POWERBOAT RENTALS
Adventurent, Inc.
850 N.E. 3rd St., #204, Dania, FL, 33004-0402. Contact: Gina A. Durnak, Exec. V.P. - Tel: (305) 927-9800. Powerboat rental operation. Franchisee maintains fleet and rents powerboats to the general public, and to members of an international boating club. Club Nautico Centers are located throughout the U.S., Caribbean, Mexico and in Asia. Established: 1984 - Franchising Since: 1986 - No. of Units: Company Owned: 7 - Franchised: 45 - Franchise Fee: $5,000 - Royalty: 5% + 2% adv. - Total Inv: $220,000 - $262,000 which includes 6 month working cap. & fran. fee - Financing: None.

COLLEGE PROSPECTS OF AMERICA®, INC.
12682 College Prospects Dr., P.O. Box 269, Logan, OH, 43138. Contact: Tracy L. Jackson, Pres. - Tel: (614) 385-6624. National and international athletic recruiting organization that furnishes in-depth reports on outstanding high school athletes to all colleges where the student could compete, both athletically and academically. This massive exposure maximizes the students' chances to get an offer to play their sport on the college level. Franchises are currently in 47 states and 6 foreign countries. Established: 1986 - Franchising Since: 1989 - No. of Units: Franchised: 175 - Franchise Fee: $0.60/high school student in franchise area - Financing: Some possible.

CONTINENTAL INDOOR SOCCER LEAGUE
16027 Ventura Blvd., #605, Encino, CA, 91436. Contact: Jorge Ragde, V.P. Oper. - Tel: (818) 906-7627, Fax: (818) 906-7693. 15 team professional indoor soccer league in markets throughout the United States and Mexico. Established: 1993 - Franchising Since: 1991 - No. of Units: Company Owned: 1 - Franchised: 15 - Franchise Fee: $1,000,000 per team - Financing: No.

FORMACOURSE
SGD Company
P.O. Box 8410, Akron, OH, 44320. Contact: Donald Nelson, Chairman - Tel: (216) 239-2828. An 18 hole Formacourse provides unique hole designs with low initial cost. Formacourse can be installed on areas of 10,000 square feet or larger. Formacourse includes pre-positioned pressure treated lumber for sideboards to insure low maintenance. Established: 1964 - Franchising Since: 1989 - No. of Units: Franchised: 7 - Franchise Fee: Built into basic construction package - Royalty: None - Total Inv: 50M - 95M plus land - Financing: None.

GAMES TO GO
1101 1st Ave. N., Moorhead, MN, 56560-2201. Contact: Bill Schwankl - Tel: (218) 236-6828. Basketballs answer to mini golf indoor or outdoor, unique hoop designs with robotic shot blockers. Income generated from rentals, paid plays, sponsorships. Established: 1989 - No. of Units: Company Owned: 3 - Royalty: none - Total Inv: $7,900 - $30,000 - Financing: Yes.

GOLDEN BEAR GOLF CENTERS, INC.
Golden Bear International
11780 U.S. Hwy. #1, N. Palm Beach, FL, 33408. Contact: Mike Kelly, Dir. of Bus. Dev. - Tel: (407) 626-3900, Fax: (407) 626-4104. Golf teaching, practice and entertainment facilities featuring golf instructional programs by the Nicklaus/Flick Golf School. The facilities include a clubhouse with proshop & food service; a practice range designed by Nicklaus Design; short game practice area; fully landscaped miniature golf. Established: 1992 - Franchising Since: 1993 - No. of Units: Franchised: 15 - Franchise Fee: $35,000 per facility - Royalty: 5% gross revenue practice range, miniature golf, batting cage, 3% of food & beverage merchandise - Total Inv: $1,500,000 to $2,500,000 facility - Financing: No.

GRAND SLAM U.S.A.
ATEC Grand Slam U.S.A.
11320 Trade Center Dr., Ste. C, Rancho Cordova, CA, 95742. Contact: Bruce Carlyle, Exec. V.P. of Sales - Tel: (800) 775-2607 or (916) 851-8330, Fax: (916) 851-1899. Offers fully automated, patented modular coin-operated batting cages (baseball/softball) as a franchise opportunity. Stores include retail sales from pro shops, lessons and camps from the training academy, birthday parties, Slam Ball basketball, and other profit centers. Established: 1976 - Franchising Since: 1984 - No. of Units: Company Owned: 1 - Franchised: 90 - Franchise Fee: $15,000 - Royalty: 3.5% gross revenues - Total Inv: $150,000 - $250,000 (depending on size of franchise) - Financing: Referrals only.

GREAT GOLF LEARNING CENTERS
26 Springdale Rd., Cherry Hill, NJ, 08003. Contact: Raabe Kemp - Tel: (609) 751-4653. Golf training for beginners and experienced golfers using a patented training device, one-on-one instruction and videotaping. Year round indoor facility. Established: 1989 - Franchising Since: 1991 - No. of Units: Company Owned: 2 - Franchised: 15 - Franchise Fee: $24,500 - Royalty: 6% gross sales - Total Inv: $80,000 - $150,000 depending on size of facility.

GROVE RECREATIONS INC.
Hwy. 544 Socastee Area, P.O. Box 2435, Myrtle Beach, SC, 29578-2435. Contact: Charles H. Grove, Pres. - Tel: (803) 236-4733, Fax: (803) 236-0336. Designer/builder of exquisitely beautiful and elaborate miniature golf courses - themed with a great deal of mounding/contours, waterfalls, lakes, streambeds, bridges, tunnel systems, lush landscaping, and very unique playable holes. Established: 1977 - Franchising Since: 1977 - No. of Units: Company Owned: 4 - Franchised: 15 - Franchise Fee: negotiable - Total Inv: $250,000 - $400,000 - Financing: Grove Recreations will work with the client to help secure same.

INTERNATIONAL GOLF
International Golf Enterprises Inc.
9101 N. Thornydale, Tucson, AZ, 85742. Contact: Sheila White, Executive Admin. - Tel: (520) 744-1840. Off-course golf retail shops. May be complemented with ski or tennis. Established: 1974 - Franchising Since: 1978 - No. of Units: Company Owned: 6 - Franchised: 55 - Franchise Fee: $42,000 - Royalty: 2% - Total Inv: $250,000 ($42,000 Fran. fee, $150,000 inven., remainder start-up costs) - Financing: No.

JUGS RANGE-PRO
Amusement Products LLC
5954 Brainerd Rd., Chattanooga, TN, 37421. Contact: E.K. Dutch Magrath III, V.P. - Tel: (615) 892-7264, Fax: (615) 855-0432. Commercial batting cage for indoor or outdoor use, using softball or baseball. Established: 1977 - No. of Units: Company Owned: 5 - Franchised: 85 - Franchise Fee: none - Total Inv: $25,000 - $95,000 - Financing: None.

LAS VEGAS DISCOUNT GOLF & TENNIS
Saint Andrews Golf Corp.
5325 S. Valley View Blvd., Ste. 10, Las Vegas, NV, 89118. Contact: Tom Rojas, V.P. Sales & Mktg. - Tel: (800) 873-5110, (702) 798-7777, Fax; (702) 798-6847. Specialty retailers in golf & tennis equipment, repair and other services. Established: 1974 - Franchising Since: 1984 - No. of Units: Company Owned: 4 - Franchised: 60 - Franchise Fee: $40,000 - Royalty: 3%, 3% adv. - Total Inv: $350,000 includes inventory, fixtures, fran. fee, signage, computer system - Financing: Assistance available.

LOMMA GOLF
Lomma Enterprises, Inc.
1120 S. Washington Ave., Scranton, PA, 18505. Contact: Gary Knight, Ex. V.P. - Tel: (717) 346-5559, Fax: (717) 346-5580. Lomma Golf is the world's oldest & largest designer and builder of prefab, portable miniature golf courses, indoors and outdoors. Also a complete line of upscale concrete courses including mountains, waterfalls, ponds, caves, themes, etc. Established: 1963 - Each Lomma Golf is individually owned. Total Inv: from $5,900 to $100,000 - Financing: Some.

LUYE AQUAFIT INTERNATIONAL, INC.
310 East 23rd St., New York, NY, 10010. Contact: Mitch Bogage, Exec. V.P. - Tel: (212) 505-2400. Offer professional, complete, safe and fun cardiovascular and musculoskeletal water aerobics workouts suitable for almost everyone regardless of age, level of fitness, physical capabilities and swimming ability. Other offerings include fitness evaluation, youth and adult swimming classes, workout gear and related products. Established: 1984 - No. of Units: Company Owned: 1 - Franchised: 12 - Franchise Fee: $20,000 - Royalty: 8%, 2% adv. - Financing: Training and operations support.

MAC BIRDIE GOLF GIFTS
Mac Birdie Golf Gifts, Inc.
5250 W. 73rd St., Ste. I, Minneapolis, MN, 55439. Contact: Scott Hage, Dir., Fran. Operations - Tel: (800) 343-1033. Marketer of golf gifts including exclusive Mac Birdie apparel supported by accessories, novelty and executive gifts. Gifts marketed through temporary retail outlets, mail order and limited wholesale. Established: 1989 - Franchising Since: 1993 - No. of Units: Company Owned: 5 - Franchise Fee: $5,000 - $50,000 - Royalty: 5% - Total Inv: $35,000 - $85,000.

MICRO-REALITY INDOOR STOCK CAR RACING
183 N. Main St., Cumberland, IA, 50843. Contact: Keith Namanny, Pres. - Tel: (712) 774-2577. A portable, expandable banked oval speedway complete with 4 cars that you actually drive from your remote racin' station console perfect for bars, corporate events, car shows, fairs & festivals. Use indoors or out. Established: 1993 - Franchising Since: 1994 - No. of Units: Company Owned: 3 - Franchised: 78 - Franchise Fee: $15,000 - Royalty: $495 annually - Total Inv: $15,000 - Financing: Leasing available.

MINI-GOLF, INC.
202FA Bridge St., Jessup, PA, 18434. Contact: Joseph J. Rogari, V.P./Mktg. - Tel: (717) 489-8623. Manufacturer of indoor or outdoor pre-fabricated miniature golf courses. Easy to set up. Layout to scale tailor made for any area or price range. Immediate installation. Established: 1981- No. of Units: Franchised: 1,647 - Total Inv: $5,900 - $27,900 - Financing: None.

NATIONAL COLLEGE RECRUITING ASSOC. INC.
22900 Ventura Blvd., Woodland Hills, CA, 91364. Contact: Jack Wright, V.P. Mktg. - Tel: (818) 225-7500. College athletic recruiting service for high school athletes & we publish a college football and basketball recruiting magazine (Bluechip Illustrated). Established: 1982 - Franchising Since: 1992 - No. of Units: Company Owned: 1 - Franchised: 42 - Franchise Fee: $10,000 avg. - Financing: Yes.

NEVADA BOB'S DISCOUNT GOLF
Nevada Bob's Pros Shop, Inc.
3311 E. Flamingo, Las Vegas, NV, 89121. Contact: Bob Hulley, Fran. Dir. - Tel: (702) 451-3333 or (800) 348-2627. Selling discount golf equip. in an attractive atmosphere, specializing in top of the line golf clubs, golf bags and accessories from MacGregor, Spalding, Prima, Mizuno, Dunlop, etc. Also professional advice on all golf equipment by our professional staff. Established: 1974 - Franchising Since: 1978 - No. of Units: Company Owned: 7 - Franchised: 303 - Franchise Fee: $37,500/$47,500/$57,500 based on population - Royalty: 2% of gross sales monthly - Total Inv: $288,000: $35,000 leaseholds, $180,000 inventory - Financing: No.

ON TARGET GOLF CENTERS *
On Target, Inc.
501 Airport Rd., Bentonville, AR, 72712. Contact: Tom Sheely, Pres. - Tel: (800) 264-1316, Fax: (501) 273-1316. An On Target Golf Center is a standard range with the addition of the unique & patented game of On Target (4 large, 2,300 sq.ft., tents at 70, 100, 130 and 160 yards), electronic signals. Established: 1993 - Franchising Since: 1994 - No. of Units: Franchised: 4 - Franchise Fee: $5,000 to $9,500 - Royalty: 5% of game revenue - Total Inv: $150,000 to $250,000 (plus land) - Financing: No.

OUTDOOR CONNECTION
1001 E. Cliff Rd., Burnsville, MN, 55337. Contact: Robert Laddusaw, Pres. - Tel: (612) 890-0407, Fax: (612) 890-8133. Represent over 70 lodges/outfitters. Market fishing & hunting trips to potential customers. Be paid commission for each trip. Operates much like a travel agency specializing in fishing & hunting trips. Established: 1988 - Franchising Since: 1989 - No. of Units: Company Owned: 1 - Franchised: 50 - Franchise Fee: $5,800 - Royalty: 1% - 4%, 1% adv. - Total Inv: start up costs excluding fran. fee $900 - $4,100 - Financing: All U.S.

PARA-SAILING UNLIMITED, INC. *
288 E. 4600 S., Ogden, UT, 84405. Contact: Kent Singleton, Pres. - Tel: (801) 392-7450, Fax: (801) 392-1130. Manufacturer of para-sailing equipment for boats and over-land para-sailing that is new to industry with patent pending equipment. Established: 1993.

PLAY IT AGAIN SPORTS
Grow Biz International
4200 Dahlberg Dr., Minneapolis, MN, 55422. Contact: Steve Gemlo, V.P., Fran. Dev. - Tel: (612) 520-8500, Fax: (612) 520-8501. Retail sporting goods stores that offer tremendous savings on high quality used and new sports equipment with the best brand names. Established: 1983 - Franchising Since: 1988 - No. of Units: Company Owned: 4 - Franchised: 583 - Franchise Fee: $25,000 - Royalty: 5% - Total Inv: $127,000 to $180,000 - Financing: SBA financing available - up to two-thirds of capital.

POOL CLEAR *
Pool Clear Franchise Corp.
2810 Winnequan, P.O. Box 59124, Dallas, TX, 75229. , Fran. Dir. - Tel: (901) 867-0600. A service business specializing in swimming pool servicing using special techniques, equipment, processes, standards and specifications. Established: 1988 - Franchising Since: 1994 - No. of Units: company Owned: 1 - Franchise Fee: $10,000 - Royalty: 10% - Total Inv: $31,600 - $37,450 (vehicles, equip., work. cap., inven. and supplies, misc.). For further information please contact: Consultants America Corp., 12279 US Highway 64. Eads, TN, 38028, Tel: (901) 867-0600, Fax: (901) 867-0010.

PRO GOLF DISCOUNT
Pro Golf of America, Inc.
32751 Middlebelt Rd., Farmington Hill, MI, 48334-1726. Contact: Steve Gossard, V.P. of Fran. Dev. - Tel: (800) 776-4653. Retail golf shops offering a complete inventory of professional golf equipment, clothing and accessories. Owners benefit from our buying power, national advertising, comprehensive training and access to every major brand. That's why we're America's favorite golf store. Established: 1961 - Franchising Since: 1972 - No. of Units: Franchised: 164 - Franchise Fee: $47,500 - Royalty: 2.5% of sales - Total Inv: $350,000+ - Financing: No.

PUTT-PUTT® GOLF & GAMES
Putt-Putt® Golf Courses of America, Inc.
P.O. Box 35237, Fayetteville, NC, 28303. Contact: Scott Anderson, Nat'l Fran. Dir. - Tel: (910) 485-7131, Fax: (910) 485-1122. Uniquely designed miniature golf courses testing the player's skill, not luck. Established: 1954 - Franchising Since: 1955 - No. of Units: Company Owned: 10 - Franchised: 265 - Franchise Fee: $25,000 - Royalty: Golf 3% service fee, 2% adv.; Other attractions 2% service fee, 1% adv. - Total Inv: $100,000 - $3 million - Financing: On a limited basis.

QUINZI'S GOLF DOCTOR SHOPS, INC.
2472 Gulf to Bay Blvd., Clearwater, FL, 34625. Contact: Mark Quinzi, Mgr. - Tel: (813) 797-2129. Golf teaching, lessons under with 7 nets. Club fitting center, fit & manufacture custom clubs. Retail golf shop with miscellaneous merchandise & exclusive Golf Doctor Products. Established: 1980 - Franchising Since: 1994 - No. of Units: Company Owned: 1 - Franchise Fee: $38,500 - Royalty: 3% of gross sales - Total Inv: $130,000: leasehold imp. $15,000; fixt. & equip. $9,000; oper. exp. $6,500; travel $1,000; inven. $50,000; work. cap. $10,000; fran. fee $38,500 - Financing: No.

ROGER DUNN GOLF SHOPS *
RDGS Franchise Corporation
2985 Lasuen St., Carmel, CA, 93923. Contact: Peter Tonti, Dir. of Franchise Opps. - Tel: (800) 600-9806. Off course discount retailer. Custom fitting with the Pinseeker Game Improvement System. Established: 1983 - Franchising Since: 1983 - No. of Units: Company Owned: 8 - Franchised: 17 - Franchise Fee: $45,000 - Royalty: 3%, 1% co-op ad fee - Total Inv: $275,500 - $610,500 - Financing: 3rd party.

RYAN'S SOCCER INTERNATIONAL, INC.
101E. Alex Bell Rd., #110, Centerville, OH, 45459. Contact: Robert H. Ryan, Pres. - Tel: (513) 434-7687. Sporting goods retail, specializing in soccer/volleyball/rugby. Respected highly in the industry. Modern, high-traffic type operation. Original store currently grossing over $750,000. Established: 1979 - Franchising Since: 1983 - No. of Units: 3 - Franchise Fee: $12,500 - Royalty: 3% - Total Inv: $65,000 - $90,000 - Financing: SBA possibility.

SAN JUAN POOLS *
San Juan Products
2302 Lasso Ln., Lakeland, FL, 33801. Contact: George Sullivan, Pres. - Tel: (941)666-3020, Fax: (941) 665-5211. Sales & installation of one piece, fiberglass swimming pools & spas. Established: 1992 - Franchising Since: 1995 - No. of Units: Franchised: 32 - Franchise Fee: $50,000 - Total Inv: $125,000 - store & equipment - Financing: limited.

SCORECARD PLUS
B.V. Paragon, Inc.
4150 Belden Village St., N.W., Ste. 303, Canton, OH, 44718. Contact: Ed Kalail, V.P. - Tel: (216) 493-9900. A combination scorecard and full-color yardage book which replaces the traditional cardboard scorecard at public and semi-private golf courses throughout the US. The books also include advertising which allows businesses to target the golfer and it decreases the cost of the program to the golf course. Established: 1990 - Franchising Since: 1992 - No. of Units: Company Owned: 3 - Franchised: 10 - Franchise Fee: $22,500 - Royalty: 8% of gross revenues - Total Inv: $59,000 - $80,000 - Financing: On everything except the fran. fee.

SCUBA NETWORK
Scuba Network Stores
10 Bayview Ave., Lawrence, NY, 11559. Contact: Steve D'Apuzzo, Pres. - Tel: (516) 371-5075. Scuba lessons, equipment, dives, tours. Established: 1989 - Franchising Since: 1989 - No. of Units: Company Owned: 5 - Franchised: 5 - Franchise Fee: $15,000 - Royalty: 7% - Total Inv: $80,000 - $120,000 - Financing: No.

SIR GOONY MINIATURE GOLF
Golf Players Inc.
5954 Brainerd Rd., Chattanooga, TN, 37421. Contact: E.K. "Dutch" Magrath III, V.P. - Tel: (615) 892-7264, Fax: (615) 855-0432. Miniature golf courses utilizing large and colourful figures. Established: 1960 - No. of Units: Company Owned: 5 - Franchised: 44 - Total Inv: $49,680 - Financing: No.

SPORTSMAN'S CLUB OF AMERICA
Sportsman's Club International
30 West Stauffer Lane, Murray, UT, 84107. Contact: Steve Putnam, Owner - Tel: (801) 262-2911. Hunting, fishing, travel club, teaching outdoor skills in boating, snowmobiling, hiking, river running, photography, gold panning, and survival skills. Dealership will be selling family memberships plus yearly dues. Established: 1969 - Franchise Fee: Just purchase memberships at discount for resale - 70% to dealership 30% to international office - Financing: Possible.

SUNSHINE PROPERTIES INT'L. INC.
7700 W. Fairfield Dr., Pensacola, FL, 32506. Contact: Joseph Morgan, G.M. - Tel: (904) 455-9685, Fax: (904) 458-0096. Planning, manufacture of art figures and installation of miniature golf courses. Established: 1960 - Franchising Since: 1960 - No. of Units: Company Owned: 3 - Franchise Fee: varies - Total Inv: $65,000 - $350,000 - Financing: J/V, Individual.

TEAM GOLF *
1776 Woodstead Ct., Ste. 213, The Woodlands, TX, 77380. Contact: Bob Heme, V.P., Fran. Dev.. Corporate turnkey golf and special events. Established: 1993 - Franchising Since: 1994 - No. of Units: Company Owned: 1 - Franchised: 4 - Franchise Fee: $9,500 to $15,000 - Royalty: % of gross profit, varies depending on event - Financing: No.

THEMED PUTTING COURSES
Grove Recreations, Inc.
P.O. Box 2435, Highway 544, Myrtle Beach, SC, 29578-2435. Contact: Charles H. Grove, Pres. - Tel: (803) 236-4733. Designer/builders of miniature golf courses with waterfalls, caves, props and lush landscaping. Established: 1975 - Franchising Since: 1977 - No. of Units: Company Owned: 3 - Franchised: 5 - Total Inv: $300,000-$350,000 - Financing: Will help with financial info.

ULTRAZONE, INC.
2880 E. Flamingo Rd., Ste. E, Las Vegas, NV, 89121-5223. Contact: Drew Pawlak, V.P., Dev. - Tel: (702) 734-3617. Ultrazone, the ultimate laser adventure is the most exciting investment in franchising's newest industry, live-action laser games. An American company offering the most advanced laser game technology on the planet, backed by 7 years of research & development and operations. Ultrazone offers franchise owners service & support unequaled in the industry. No. of Units: Company Owned: 1 - Franchised: 4 - Franchise Fee: $15,000 - Royalty: 5% of gross or $2,000 per mo. - Total Inv: $320,000 - $480,000 - Financing: No.

UNITED STUDIOS OF SELF DEFENSE *
United Studios of Self Defense, Inc.
26826 Vista Terrace, Bldg. 18, Lake Forest, CA, 92630. Contact: Jim Holzer, Creative Affairs/Media - Tel: (714) 588-7925. A chain of martial arts' studios teaching a modern system of karate/kung-fu with more than 108 locations nationwide and a membership of more than 30,000. America's self defense leader and largest franchised martial arts studio organization. Established: 1968 - Franchising Since: 1988 - No. of Units: Franchised: 108 - Franchise Fee: $27,000 - Royalty: 5% of total gross sales - Total Inv: $110,000: fran. fee plus $83,000 set-up/operations costs - Financing: None.

WASHINGTON GOLF CENTER
Worldwide Washington Golf Center, Inc.
2625 Shirlington Rd., Arlington, VA, 22206. Contact: Joe McOwen, Dir. of Fran. - Tel: (703) 979-7888, Fax: (703) 521-5440. Retail supplier of discount golf equipment. Established: 1978 - Franchising Since: 1992 - No. of Units: Franchised: 4 - Franchise Fee: Range: $45,000 - $80,000 - Royalty: 2% of gross sales plus 1% adv. - Total Inv: Range: $500,000 - $800,000 - Financing: No.

WORLD GYM
World Gym Licensing, Ltd.
2210 Main St., Santa Monica, CA, 90405. Contact: Mike Uretz, Pres. - Tel: (310) 450-0080. License fitness centers & gyms & allied products & accessories. Established: 1985 - Franchising Since: 1985 - No. of Units: Franchised: 200 - Franchise Fee: $25,000 1st 3 years - Total Inv: $500,000 - $1,200,000.

WORLD ROBOTIC BOXING ASSOCIATION
183 N. Main St., Cumberland, IA, 50843. Contact: Keith Namanny, Pres. - Tel: (712) 774-2577. Sports and entertainment promotions, corporate events, special events, traffic building event, colleges, bars, military. Established: 1986 - Franchising Since: 1987 - No. of Units: Company Owned: 1 - Franchised: 183 - Franchise Fee: $7,500 - Royalty: $495. annual renewal fee - Total Inv: $7,500 for turn-key pkg. - Financing: No.

TRAVEL

ADMIRAL OF THE FLEET CRUISE CENTERS
Cruise Centers of America
3430 Pacific Ave. S.E., Ste. A-5, Olympia, WA, 98501. Contact: Bob Lovely, CEO - Tel: (206) 866-7447. Specialized travel agency selling cruises only. Established: 1983 - Franchising Since: 1986 - No. of Units: Company Owned: 4 - Franchised: 3 - Franchise Fee: $25,000 - Royalty: 5% of gross margin - Total Inv: $75,000 - $125,000 - Financing: No.

BTI AMERICAS PARTNER GROUP
70 East Lake St., Ste. 1100, Chicago, IL, 60601. Contact: Evelyn Engert, V.P./ G.M. - Tel: (312) 782-6870. Conversion franchise or existing travel agencies specializing in corporate travel management. Established: 1985 - Franchising Since: 1991 - No. of Units: Company Owned: 581 - Franchised: 189 - Franchise Fee: $6,000 headquarters + $1,500 per branch - Royalty: $6,495 - $26,675 estimate - Financing: No.

CONCEPT INDEPENDENT TRAVEL AGENCY (CITA)
3820 Premier Ave., Memphis, TN, 38118. Contact: Bill Richey, Dir. - Tel: (901) 867-0600. Providing a unique travel agency concept to existing travel businesses and to new travel agencies. Established: 1991 - Franchising Since: 1991 - No. of Units: Company Owned: 1 - Franchised: 1 - Franchise Fee: $5,000 - $50,000 - Royalty: $50.00 per week - Total Inv: $6,000 - $88,800 - Financing: Yes.

CRUISE HOLIDAYS
Cruise Holidays International, Inc.
9665 Chesapeake Dr., Ste. 401, San Diego, CA, 92193. Contact: Fran. Dev. Dept. - Tel: (619) 279-4780, Fax: (619) 279-4788. Cruise only travel agency. Cruise into business with the largest franchisor of cruise only agencies. Cruises are the fastest growing segment of leisure travel and the most profitable. Established: 1984 - Franchising Since: 1984 - No. of Units: Franchised: 186 - Franchise Fee: $29,500 - Royalty: either .6%, .75% or 1% or minimum of $525.50 - Total Inv: $100,000 - $120,000 incl. fran. fee - Financing: No.

CRUISE LINES RESERVATION CENTER
9229 Kaufman Pl., Brooklyn, NY, 11236. Contact: Bernard Korn, Pres. - Tel: (718) 763-4259. Cruise and travel agency. Established: 1989 - Franchising Since: 1990 - No. of Units: Company Owned: 10 - Franchise Fee: $500. - Royalty: 1% gross sales - Total Inv: $2,000 - $5,000.

CRUISE SHOPPE LTD., THE
Cruise Shoppes America, Ltd.
701 Metairie Rd., #1A-208, Metairie, LA, 70005. Contact: Gary P. Brown, V.P. - Tel: (504) 833-0340. Cruise only travel agencies. Established: 1984 - Franchising Since: 1986 - No. of Units: Company Owned: 1 - Franchised: 32 - Franchise Fee: $22,500 - Royalty: 1% of cruise sales - Total Inv: $10,000 start-up, $50,000 work cap.

EMPRESS TRAVEL FRANCHISE CORP.
Travel Impressions
465 Smith Street, Farmingdale, NY, 11735. Contact: Franchise Director - Tel: (516) 845-7000, (800) 284-0013. Travel agencies. Established: 1956 - Franchising Since: 1974 - No. of Units: Company Owned: 11 - Franchised: 70 - Franchise Fee: $20,000 (incl. working capital) - Total Inv: $50,000 - Royalty: 1.5% - Financing: No.

FIRST DISCOUNT TRAVEL & DISCOUNT TRAVEL
First Discount Travel
1040 Crown Pointe Pkwy., Ste. 425, Atlanta, GA, 30338. Contact: Elizabeth Yancey, Pres. - Tel: (404) 394-0202. Full service travel agencies. Established: 1988 - Franchising Since: 1989 - No. of Units: Franchised: 37 - Franchise Fee: $29,500 - Royalty: $500 per month - Total Inv: $29,500 plus $35,000 work. cap. - Financing: Short term only.

GALAXSEA CRUISES
GalaxSea Associates Inc.
1400 E. Oakland Pk. Blvd., #103, Ft. Lauderdale, FL, 33334. Contact: Bill Morris, Exec. V.P. - Tel: (305) 564-7072. Crusie only travel franchise network with programs in place that help franchisees corner the cruise market - a $50 billion industry. Franchise owners can take advantage of the most rapidly growing profitable segment of the travel industry, and enjoy an exciting lifestyle. Extensive product and sales training, monthly marketing strategies, and volume buying power are a part of the GalaxSea system. Established: 1988 - Franchising Since: 1989 - No. of Units: Company Owned: 1 - Franchised: 54 - Franchise Fee: $25,000 - Royalty: 1% gross sales - Total Inv: $80,000 - $120,000 - Financing: For franchise fee only.

INTERNATIONAL TOURS, INC.
5810 E. Skelly Dr. #1800, Tulsa, OK, 74135. Contact: Roger Jared, Fran. Dir. - Tel: (918) 665-2300. Full service retail travel agencies. Established: 1968 - Franchising Since: 1970 - No. of Units: Company Owned: 3 - Franchised: 278 - Franchise Fee: $28,000 - Royalty: less than 1% - Total Inv: $75,000 - $95,000 - Financing: No.

KIRBY TOURS
Kirby Tours, Inc.
2451 S. Telegraph Rd., Dearborn, MI, 48124. Contact: Shakil A. Khan, Pres. - Tel: (313) 278-2224. Sightseeing tours, airport shuttle service, bus/van/limo charters & convention & meeting planning. Established: 1919 - Franchising Since: 1993 - No. of Units: Company Owned: 5 - Franchise Fee: $15,000 - Royalty: 5%, 5% adv. - Total Inv: $25,000 min. - Financing: Yes.

SUMMIT TRAVEL
Summit Travel Group, Inc.
865 N.W. 4 1/2 St., Winston Salem, NC, 27101. Contact: Richard, Mng. - Tel: (910) 723-1119, (800) 7-SUMMIT. Home based travel business. Complete training and materials necessary to own and operate a successful air, cruise and tour business. Established: 1993 - Franchising Since: 1993 - No. of Units: Company Owned: 1 - Franchised: 100+ - Franchise Fee: $5,875 - Royalty: 0 - Total Inv: $5,875 - Financing: N/A.

TIX TRAVEL & TICKET AGENCY
48 Burd St., Nyack, NY, 10960. - Tel: 1-(800)-2-OWN-TIX Ext. 417. Full service travel agency plus best seats to sold out concerts, sports & theatre worldwide. Operate from home, store or office. Established: 1982 - Franchising Since: 1990 - No. of Units: Franchised: 225 - Franchise Fee: $3,495 - Financing: Major credit cards.

TO HAWAII ONLY
To Hawaii Only Franchise, Inc.
535 Anton Blvd., Ste. 160, Costa Mesa, CA, 92626. Contact: Arie Zukerman, V.P. Oper. - Tel: (714) 966-8209. One destination travel service to Hawaii only. Sales of vacation packages by experts. The retail market. The offices are decorated specially as Hawaiian unique setting. Established: 1988 - Franchising Since: 1989 - No. of Units: Company Owned: 1 - Franchised: 2 - Franchise Fee: $15,000 - Royalty: 1% of the first $500,000 revenue per quarter, 4% of additional revenue - Total Inv: $15,000 fran. fee/$80,000 turn-key set up/$50,000 - Financing: None.

TPI TRAVEL SERVICES
Travel Pros Inc.
3030 N. Rocky Point Dr. W., #100, Tampa, FL, 33607. Contact: Beinhard Benet, Pres. - Tel: (813) 281-5670. Full service travel agency. Can be run from home or office. We provide reservations, software, training and support. Established: 1987 - Franchising Since: 1987 - No. of Units: Company Owned: 1 - Franchised: 385 - Franchise Fee: $5,995 - $15,000 - Royalty: $135 - Total Inv: $10,000 - $50,000 - Financing: No.

TRAVEL AGENTS INTERNATIONAL
Travel Agents International, Inc.
9887 Fourth St. N., St. Petersburg, FL, 33702. Contact: Lori Langenhahn, Fran. Coordinator - Tel: (800) 678-8241, (813) 576-7435, Fax: (813) 579-0529. The package establishes a professional look, uniform and integrated system and quality control program. It translates to a strong support system for the franchisee and professional level travel services for the public. Established: 1980 - Franchising Since: 1982 - No. of Units: Company Owned: 3 - Franchised: 373 - Franchise Fee: $29,950 - Royalty: $500 per mth. - Total Inv: $130,000 incl. work. cap.- Financing: Yes.

TRAVEL CENTER LTD.
3820 Premier Ave., Memphis, TN, 38118. Contact: Bill Richey - Tel: (901) 867-0600. Concept to operate a travel agency. Established: 1987 - Franchising Since: 1990 - No. of Units: Company Owned: 3 - Franchise Fee: $20,000 - Royalty: $75 - $125 per week - Total Inv: $40,550 - $153,000 - Financing: no.

TRAVEL NETWORK
Travel Network Ltd.
560 Sylvan Ave., Englewood Cliffs, NJ, 07632. Contact: Michael Y. Brent or Stephanie Abrams, Pres./V.P. - Tel: (800) TRAVNET or (201) 567-8500. Travel agency. Full service to vacation, cruise, groups, and business travelers. Completely computerized. Intensive marketing, training, support services. Total start-up and on-going assistance. Established: 1982 - Franchising Since: 1982 - No. of Units: Company Owned: 1 - Franchised: 378 - Franchise Fee: $29,900 - Royalty: Flat service fee: $350/mo. 1st yr, $550/mo. 2nd yr, $750/mo. 3rd yr - Total Inv: $15,000 turn-key, fran fee, $40,000 work cap. - Financing: Yes.

TRAVEL PROFESSIONALS INTERNATIONAL
Travel Professionals International, Inc.
10172 Linn Station Rd., Louisville, KY, 40223. Contact: John Boyce, V.P., Fran. Dev. - Tel: (800) 626-2469, Fax: (502) 423-9914. Franchisor of full service travel agencies. Established: 1982 - Franchising Since: 1983 - No. of Units: Company Owned: 1 - Franchised: 79 - Franchise Fee: $33,000 - Royalty: 5% - Total Inv: $110,000 to $150,000 - Financing: No.

TRAVEL SUCCESS
116 E. Howard Ave., Decatur, GA, 30030. Contact: Carol Campbell, Pres. - Tel: (404) 373-5515. Specialists in start up and support for full service travel agencies. ARC/CRS, seminar training/support and more.

Established: 1990 - No. of Units: 8 set up - Consulting Fee: $8,000 - Royalty: None - Total Inv: Our retainer $8,000/cost of bond/applications and furnishings, approximately $10,000: Total start up: $20,000 - $25,000. In home agency $1,995 complete.

TRAVELHOST TRAVEL AGENCY
Travelhost Agencies, Inc.
10701 N. Stemmons Fwy., Dallas, TX, 75220-2419. Contact: Tamela A. Gustafson, V.P. Fran. Sales - Tel: (214) 691-1163. Travel agency turn-key franchise includes: Complete int. furnishings, computer equip., signage and adv. materials along with comprehensive sales and operations training and an array of on-going support programs. Established:1988 - Franchising Since:1988 - No. of Units: Company Owned: 1 - Franchised: 30 - Franchise Fee: $50,000 - Royalty: flat fee of $175 /wk - Total Inv: fran. fee if paid in installments, $42,900 if paid in cash - Financing: Yes.

TRAVELPLEX
WSE Franchising Inc., dba TravelPlex International
655 Metro Place S., Ste.250, Dublin, OH, 43017. Contact: Darryl Waren, Pres. - Tel: (614) 766-6315. Retail travel agency franchise organization, specializing in business and vacation travel arrangements. This unique franchise has been created by working agency owners - managers. A comprehensive training program is provided for all staff levels. TravelPlex provides recruitment services and productive office procedures. Franchisees receive: sales and marketing programs, operational support and effective networking with member agencies. Established: 1984 - Franchising Since: 1989 - No. of Units: Franchised: 15 - Franchise Fee: $30,900 - Royalty: $400 per month - Total Inv: $70,000 - $100,000 - Financing: Yes, portion of fran. fee.

WATER TREATMENT

ASTRO-PURE WATER PURIFIERS
3025 SW 2nd Ave., Ft. Lauderdale, FL, 33315-3309. Contact: R.L. Stefl, Pres. - Tel: (305) 832-0630. Complete line of water treatment equipment, purifiers, filters, decalcifiers, reverse osmosis, iron filters, chemical feed equipment. Sizes for portable, point-of-use, central, commercial and industrial. Established: 1971 - Franchising Since: 1981 - Total Inv: 10,000 inventory.

BYOB WATER STORE, THE
1288 W. Main #103, Lewisville, TX, 75067. Contact: Richard L. Cure, Pres. - Tel: (214) 219-1551. A retail store concept which refines its own product water. The product is sold to the customer in his own bottle. Other sales items include dispensers, coolers, bottles, etc. Established: 1984 - Licensing Since: 1985 - No. of Units: Licensed: 9 - Inv: $48,000+.

CULLIGAN INTERNATIONAL CO.
One Culligan Parkway, Northbrook, IL, 60062. Contact: Kenneth E. Wood, Dir. Mkt. Dev. - Tel: (708) 205-5823. Water conditioning equipment. Franchisee sells, leases, maintains and repairs water conditioning equipment for domestic, commercial and industrial consumers and distributes and sells bottled water and drinking water appliances. Established: 1936 - Franchising Since: 1939 - No. of Units: Company Owned: 20 - Franchised: 750 - Royalty: varies - Total Inv: $103,000 - $224,500 - Financing: None.

ECOWATER SYSTEMS
Ecowater Systems, Inc.
P.O. Box 64420, St. Paul, MN, 55164. Contact: Jerry Johnson, Mktg. Ser. Admin. - Tel: (612) 731-7447. Manufacturer of water treatment equipment for residential, commercial and industrial softening and drinking water systems. Established: 1945 - Franchising Since: 1950 - No. of Units: Franchised: 1,000 - Franchise Fee: none - Royalty: none - Total Inv: $50,000 - $100,000 - Financing: None.

HOME ENVIRONMENT CENTER FRANCHISE, INC. *
Environmental Health Services
9199 Central Ave. N.E., Blaine, MN, 55434. Contact: Don Jamieson, Fran. Dir. - Tel: (612) 780-9043. ATR & water purification units & service in a retail sore plus a retail water store. Network marketing and air purification products. Established: 1995 - Franchising Since: 1995 - No. of Units: Company Owned: 2 - Franchise Fee: $25,000 - Royalty: 2% avg. - Total Inv: $120,000 - Financing: None.

NATURAL CANADIAN SPRING WATER *
OK Food Management USA Corp.
5 Colombia Dr., Niagara Falls, NY, 14365-1375. Contact: Vincent Agnello, Fran. Legal Cons. - Tel: (716) 285-2533, Fax: (905) 356-9373. Canadian Natural Spring Water delivery bottled or tanker shipments, towns, city, schools, hospitals, food processors or farm service bulk delivery. Optional water treatment equipment for residential & commercial. Established: 1996 - Franchising Since: 1996 - No. of Units: Company Owned: 1 - Franchise Fee: $4,900 including product for start-up - Royalty: $50/mo., $25 adv. - Total Inv: $4,900 - Financing: No.

RAINBORN, INC. *
702 S. Thornton Ave., Ste. C, P.O. Box 2766, Dalton, GA, 30722. Contact: Greg Greene, Pres. - Tel: (706) 277-7779 or 1-800-360-5537. Manufactures the RainBorn Point-of-Use Drinking Water Purification System which replaces the bottle on standard bottle water coolers. Patented technology makes tap water up to 99.99% pure. Designed for convenience, can be manually filled or plumbed in. Produces three types of water to drink: two mineralized and one purified. This product is marketed in the U.S. exclusively through franchises. Established: 1993 - Franchising Since: 1994 - No. of Units: Franchised: 3 - Franchise Fee: $15,000 - Royalty: 10% - Total Inv: $46,000 - $54,000 initial investment (incl. fran. fee $100,000 required) - Financing: No.

RAINSOFT WATER CONDITIONING
2080 East Lunt Ave., Elk Grove Village, IL, 60007. Contact: David Cole, Pres. - Tel: (708) 894-8200. Sales & rentals of water purification equipment for homes, businesses, light industry & municipalities from $299-$200,000. Established: 1953 - Franchising Since: 1963 - No. of Units: 250 - Approx. Inv: $10,000 - $25,000 dependent on market size - Financing: Assistance in gaining retail financing.

RAYNE CORPORATION
P.O. Box 90, Santa Barbara, CA, 93102. Contact: Robert E. Denne, V.P. Gen. Mgr. - Tel: (805) 569-0075. Water conditioning and water filtration for domestic and light commercial applications. Established: 1930 - Franchising Since: 1951 - No. of Units: Company Owned: 6 - Franchised: 34 - Approx. Inv: $20,000+ - Financing: No.

UNITED WORTH HYDROCHEM CORP.
413 E. Magnolia, P.O. Box 366, Ft. Worth, TX, 76101. Contact: Roy Coleman, Pres. - Tel: (817) 332-8146. Chemical water treatment of commercial and industrial water systems (boilers, heat exchangers, cooling towers, etc.). Established: 1957 - Franchising Since: 1960 - No. of Units: Company Owned: 2 - Franchised: 100 - Franchise Fee: $500 - Royalty: purchase contract - Total Inv: $1,000 - Financing: No.

WATER RESOURCES INTERNATIONAL
2800 E. Chambers St., Phoenix, AR, 85040. Contact: Chris Bower, Exec. V.P. - Tel: (602) 268-2580. Manufacturing and distribution of water treatment and water purification equipment, both residential and commercial to it's nationwide network of franchisees who retail to the public. Established: 1966 - Franchising Since: 1990 - No. of Units: Company Owned: 1 - Franchised: 35 - Franchise Fee: $15,000 - Royalty: 1% - Total Inv: $38,000 - Financing: No.

WATER SYSTEMS *
Water Systems Management Corp.
2550-2 Midway, Dallas, TX, 75006. , Fran. Dir. - Tel: (901) 867-0600. Water machine distribution business providing water making and filtering systems, as well as parts & service. Established: 1994 - Franchising Since: 1994 - No. of Units: Company Owned: 1 - Franchise Fee: $10,000 - Royalty: 5% - Total Inv: $15,500 - $54,500 (Inven., Signs, Lease, Permits, Leasehold Improv. and Insur.). For further information please contact: Consultants America Corp., 12279 US Highway 64. Eads, TN, 38028, Tel: (901) 867-0600, Fax: (901) 867-0010.

WATERCARE CORPORATION
P.O. Box 1717, Manitowoc, WI, 54221-1717. Contact: Wm. Granger, Mktg. - Tel: (414) 682-6823. Retail, sale, rental and lease of water conditioning equipment for residential, institutional, commercial and industrial. Established: 1946 - Franchising Since: 1967 - No. of Units: Company Owned: 2 - Franchised: 135 - Franchise Fee: $10,000-$15,000 - Approx. Inv: varies.

WATERCHEF WATER CENTER *
WaterChef Franchising, Inc.
6625 N. Scottsdale Rd., #2, Scottsdale, AZ, 85250-4421. Contact: Kelly Rude, Dir. of Fran. Dev. - Tel: (602) 991-4534. Franchisor of water retail store selling pure water, water appliances, water filtration and purification equipment, water treatment equipment and related products, services and accessories. Established: 1994 - Franchising Since: 1994 - No. of Units: Company Owned: 1 - Franchised: 1 - Franchise Fee: $19,750 - Royalty: 5% of gross sales - Total Inv: $82,950 to $106,225 - Financing: No.

WEDDING RELATED SERVICES

A WONDERFUL WEDDING *
Thomason Enterprises, Inc.
1854 Wallace School Rd., Ste. B, Charleston, SC, 29407. Contact: Ken Thomason, Pres. - Tel: (803) 556-1500. Home-based business producing semi-annual bridal publication and annual bridal show in the $32 billion wedding industry. Established: 1993 - Franchising Since: 1995 - No. of Units: Company Owned: 1 - Franchise Fee: $20,000 - Royalty: 10% of gross sales - Total Inv: $5,000 to $10,000 - Financing: No.

BRIDE'S DAY MAGAZINE
Bride's Day Franchise Corp.
750 Hamburg Tpk., Ste. 208, Pompton Lakes, NJ, 07442. Contact: David A. Gay, Publisher - Tel: (201) 835-6551. Free community bridal magazine designed to assist brides-to-be with planning while offering quality, affordable, local exposure to wedding related businesses in a given area. Established: 1987 - Franchising Since: 1990 - No. of Units: Company Owned: 2 - Franchised: 8 - Franchise Fee: $14,900 - Royalty: 6% - Total Inv: $5,000 in work cap. - Financing: Yes.

DISCOUNT BRIDAL SERVICE INC.
7162 Ambassador Rd., Baltimore, MD, 21244. Contact: Kim Strauss, V.P. Sales - Tel: (410) 298-3910, (800) 874-8794, Fax: (410) 298-2286. Retail men's and ladies bridal attire. Established: 1970 - Franchising Since: 1985 - No. of Units: Company Owned: 1 - Franchised: 400-500 - Total Inv: $395,00 for seminar, $500 adv. - Financing: No.

DEAN R. BRUZA
Director of Franchising

27857 Orchard Lake Road
Farmington Hills, MI 48334
810 • 489 • 1144

LITTLE WEDDING CHAPEL, THE *
Wedding Belles, Inc.
27857 Orchard Lake Rd., Farmington Hills, MI, 48334. Contact: Dean Bruza, Dir. of Fran. - Tel: (810) 489-1144. World's only wedding chapel franchise. We have created an entirely new segment in the wedding industry by providing an elegant and romantic setting that offers value and convenience to the consumer. Our franchisees have experienced a tremendous rate of return on their investment while working in an enjoyable and rewarding business. We provide our franchisees with all the important design, operational and administrative procedures necessary as well as an exclusive territory. Established: 1989 - Franchising Since: 1990 - No. of Units: Company Owned: 1 - Franchised: 2 - Franchise Fee: $16,500 - Royalty: 6% gross sales - Total Inv: $90,900 - $158,900 (not inc. fran. fee) - Financing: None.

VIDEO 5000
211 East 43rd St., New York, NY, 10017. Contact: Don Sheff, Pres. - Tel: (212) 867-8800. A nationwide franchise for professional photographers and videographers specializing in weddings and other special anniversaries. The franchisees are given a protected area, training in videography, promotional support, and an editing outlet for their tapes in NYC. Established: 1988 - Franchising Since: 1988 - No. of Units: Franchised: 50 - Franchise Fee: $2,500 - Royalty: None

WEDDING EXPRESSIONS
2120 N. Woodlawn St. #364, Wichita, KS, 67208. Contact: Steve Watson, V.P. - Tel: (316) 681-0121. Full service bridal retailer (gowns, bridesmaid dresses, mothers dresses, tuxedos, cake, flowers, photography, invitations, candelabra rental, accessories). Established: 1982 - Franchising Since: 1988 - No. of Units: Company Owned: 1 - Franchised: 7 - Franchise Fee: $12,000 - $16,000 - Royalty: 3 1/2 + 1/2 adv. - Total Inv: $75,000 - $150,000 - Financing: business bank.

WEDDING GOWN SPECIALISTS RESTORATION LABS
Websco, Inc.
48 King St., #D, Roswell, GA, 30075-4414. Contact: Gary Webster, Founder - Tel: (800) 543-8987. Restores discolored and stained wedding, christening and debutante gowns to true color. Established: 1987 - Licensing Since: 1987 - No. of Units: 1 - Franchised: 84 in 8 countries - Franchise Fee: $1,000+ - Royalty: 20% annual renewal - Financing: No.

WEDDING GUIDE, THE
International Publishing Services, Inc.
P.O. Box 1169, Arvada, CO, 80001-1169. Contact: Yvonne Pearce, Pres. - Tel: (303) 456-2810. Internationally published Bridal magazine, customized for each city/area. Reaches over 1 million engaged couples annually at the beginning of their planning and purchasing cycle. Variety of marketing options, including monthly lists of engaged couples. Exclusive territory, training and complete publishing support services. Established: 1985 - Franchising Since: 1989 - No. of Units: Company Owned: 2 - Franchised: 71(US), 15 (UK) - Franchise Fee: $15,000 - $35,000 - Royalty: 8% of net sales - Total Inv: $1,500 - $2,500 start-up plus fran. fee - Financing: Yes, down payment required, balance financed for qualified applicants.

WEDDING PAGES, THE
Wedding Information Network, Inc.
11106 Mockingbird Dr., Omaha, NE, 68137. Contact: Doug Russell, V.P.-Marketing - Tel: (800) 843-4983, Fax: (402) 331-2887. Complete databased bridal marketing system designed to locate brides 8-10 months before their wedding. It involves sales and marketing to wedding professionals. Established: 1982 - Franchising Since: 1987 - No. of Units: Company Owned: 35 - Franchised: 53 - Franchise Fee: $15,000 - Royalty: 10% - Total Inv: $25,000 - $50,000 work. cap. - Financing: None.

MISCELLANEOUS

AD COM EXPRESS
R.F.F. Enterprises, Inc.
Box 39048, Minneapolis, MN, 55439. Contact: Ward Peterson, Dir. Mktg. Sales. - Tel: (612) 829-1331. National network of overnight small package air express, pick-up and delivery stations offering multi-level personalized services. Established: 1979 - Franchising Since: 1981 - No. of Units: Company Owned: 3 - Franchised: 21 - Franchise Fee: $10,000 - Total Inv: $30,000 - Royalty: 8%.

AG-MART
Ag-Mart, Inc.
P.O. Box 370, Hwy. 377S., Brownwood, TX, 76804. Contact: John D. Harkey, Pres. - Tel: (915) 643-3636. The plant and animal folks lawn and garden, animal health, horse care and pet supplies. Established: 1988 - Franchising Since: 1989 - No. of Units: Company Owned: 5 - Franchised: 3 - Franchise Fee: $19,600 - Royalty: 3% 1st yr. 5% after - Total Inv: $100,000.

Franchise with the first name in language services

Be the first to get in on:
- A recognized brand name in languages that's second to none
- A hot, ground floor opportunity
- The exploding demand for English and language instruction worldwide, as well as translation and publishing products
- A complete support system
  - A company that's been in business 117 years and that is still growing
  - A proven business with 322 company centers worldwide

Sound interesting? Call or fax Frank Garton at Berlitz Franchising Corporation today for a video and brochure. Find out how exciting and rewarding owning your own Berlitz Language Center can be!

1-800-626-6419 U.S. Only
1-609-497-9945 Outside U.S.
1-609-683-9074 FAX

*offering by prospectus only.

Berlitz®
Helping the World Communicate
Instruction
Translation
Publishing

AIT FREIGHT SYSTEMS, INC.
210 Mittel Dr., Wood Dale, IL, 60191. Contact: Herb Cohan, Sr. V.P. - Tel: (708) 766-8300, Fax: (708) 766-0305. Air freight forwarder, domestic & international. Established: 1979 - Franchising Since: 1988 - No. of Units: Company Owned: 2 - Franchised: 17 - Franchise Fee: $6,000 - Royalty: 12.75% domestic and 32% international - Total Inv: $18,000 - $25,000 - Financing: On initial franchise fee only.

ALTERNATIVE VIRTUAL MALL *
P.O. Box 562, Mystic Islands, NJ, 08087. Contact: Thomas Clay, Corp. Mgr. - Tel: (609) 294-2120, Fax: (609) 294-2120. A virtual mall for the Internet. Franchise fee includes everything to get started, the web page design, products, service provider, support, etc. The Internet is hot and you can get involved instantly. Established: 1993 - Franchising Since: 1995 - No. of Units: Company Owned: 1 - Franchised: 3 - Franchise Fee: $2,000 - Royalty: Profit sharing on products - Total Inv: $2,000 + $200 monthly for service provider - Financing: Yes.

AMERICAN LEAD CONSULTANTS *
American Lead Consultants, Inc.
Three Bala Plz. E., Bala Cynwyd, PA, 19004. Contact: Mike Flannery, Dir., Fran. Dev. - Tel: (800) 441-5323. Residential lead inspection for paint, water and soil. Established: 1993 - Franchising Since: 1994 - No. of Units: Company Owned: 1 - Franchised: 5 - Franchise Fee: $10,000 - $25,000 - Royalty: 9%, 6% adv. - Total Inv: $35,000 - $75,000 - Financing: None.

AMERICAN SECURITY FINANCE
4132 Shoreline Dr. Ste. J, St. Louis, MO, 63045. Contact: John Weigel, Mktg. Dir. - Tel: (314) 344-1111. We provide customer financing for credit reject installment finance and revolving credit customers. Dealer financing. Established: 1976 - Franchising Since: 1976 - No. of Units: Company Owned: 1 - Franchised: 1,400 - Total Inv: $192.50 - Financing: Yes.

ARMOLOY CORP., THE
1325 Sycamore Ave., DeKalb, IL, 60115. Contact: Jerome F. Bejbl, Pres. - Tel: (815) 758-6657, Fax: (815) 758-0268. Precision hard, thin, dense chromiom alloy coating for the metals to increase wear life, reduce friction and enhance corrosion resistance. Established: 1957 - Franchising Since: 1978 - No. of Units: Company Owned: 2 - Franchised: 9 - Franchise Fee: From $50,000 - Total Inv: $250,000-$350,000 - Royalty: 7% gross sales - Financing: No.

ARTECH WINDOW TINTING & AUTO SECURITY
BDL Enterprises, Inc.
P.O. Box 1849, Hurst, TX, 76053. Contact: Michelle Flowers, Fran. Coordinator - Tel: (800) 278-3240, Fax: (817) 268-6228. Automotive, commercial & residential window tinting, auto security, sunroofs and truck accessories. Established: 1981 - Franchising Since: 1989 - No. of Units: Franchised: 18 - Franchise Fee: $20,000 - Royalty: $100/week - Total Inv: $67,000 - $99,000 - Financing: Assistance Available.

AUTO DRIVEAWAY CO.
310 S. Michigan Ave., Chicago, IL, 60604. Contact: Mike Kowalchik, V.P. - Tel: (312) 939-3600. Transporting automobiles, trucks and motor homes via driveaway or truckaway. Established: 1952 - Licensing Since: 1954 - No. of Units: Company Owned: 4 - Licensed: 88 - Franchise Security Deposit: $5,000 - Total Inv: $10,000 - Royalty: varies - Financing: No.

BALLOON WRAP, INC.
18032 Lemon Dr., #C-144, Yorba Linda, CA, 92686-1186. Contact: Les Wigger, Pres. - Tel: (714) 993-2295. Sell Balloon Wrap machines that allow you to put gift & novelty items into balloons. Sold as business opportunities. A lifetime license is granted to operate under our patent and a lifetime of free consulting to aid in sales and marketing for the new entrepreneur. Established: 1988 - Franchising Since: 1988 - No. of Units Sold: 2,000 - Total Inv: $1,500 for equip., $300 - $800 for start-up and supplies - Financing: No.

BATH GENIE, INC.
1 Brigham St., Marlborough, MA, 01752-3140. Contact: John Foley, Pres. - Tel: (508) 481-8338. Porcelain repair and resurfacing. Established: 1974 - Franchising Since: 1984 - No. of Units: Company Owned: 1 - Franchised: 26 - Total Inv: $24,500 - Financing: No.

BERLITZ FRANCHISING CORP. *
Berlitz International, Inc.
293 Wall St., Princeton, NJ, 08540. Contact: Frank J. Garton, V.P. Fran. Worldwide - Tel: (609) 497-9945. Worlds largest provider of language instruction and translation services with 117 years of experience. Other businesses: Interpretation Services, Publishing Products, Self-Teaching Language and Travel Guides. Also Dictionaries. Established: 1878 - Franchising Since: 1995 - No. of Units: Company Owned: 323 - Franchise Fee: $30,000 - Royalty: 10% - Total Inv: $150,000-$300,000 - Financing: None.

Frank J. Garton
Vice President
Worldwide Franchising

Berlitz International, Inc.
Research Park
293 Wall Street
Princeton, NJ 08540
Tel: 609.497.9945
　　　800.626.6419 (USA only)
Fax: 609.683.9074

BIRDS OVER AMERICA
3926 Innsbrook Dr., Memphis, TN, 38115. , Fran. Dir. - Tel: (901) 867-0600. The release of live homing pigeons at special events or occasions. Established: 1984 - Franchising Since: 1991 - No. of Units: Company Owned: 1 - Franchise Fee: $10,000 - Royalty: 7% - Total Inv: $16,635 - $26,050 (work. cap., inven., printing, insurance, trailer, release cages, supplies).For further information please contact: Consultants America Corp., 12279 US Highway 64. Eads, TN, 38028, Tel: (901) 867-0600, Fax: (901) 867-0010.

BLACKSTONE DETECTIVE AGENCY
P.O. Box 14021, Norfolk, VA, 23518. Contact: Mr. P. Miller, Pres. - Tel: (804) 588-6354. All types of investigation. Established: 1957 - Financing: Yes.

BLADERUNNER MOBILE SHARPENING SYSTEMS *
Vann Mann Corp.
6431 Orr Rd., Charlotte, NC, 28213. Contact: David Skinner, Pres. - Tel: (800) 742-7754, Fax: (704) 598-7111. A mobile sharpening service for construction, commercial, domestic, industrial and medical markets. Features extensive training, exclusive territories and patented equipment. Established: 1988 - Franchising Since: 1995 - No. of Units: Company Owned: 2 - Total Inv: $10,000 to $60,000 - Financing: Lease company references.

BOOK SHELF, THE
Quality Marketing Associates, Inc.
Ste. 284, 6278 N. Federal Hwy., Ft. Lauderdale, FL, 33308-1916. Contact: W.B. Chappie, Pres. - Tel: (305) 785-2891. Servicing paperback book shelves in hotels, motels, resorts, marinas, etc. Established: 1990 - Total Inv: $25,000 and up - Financing: No.

BOX BROS. CORP.
7050 Owensmouth Ave., #200, Canoga Park, CA, 91303. Contact: Mark S. Frydman, Pres. - Tel: (818) 713-8530. Discount box and packaging store. Stock and sell over 100 different varieties of stock and moving boxes. In addition, also ship any item to any destination domestically and internationally. Work with over 12 different common carriers and movers. Have a special niche with small moves that movers do not service. Established: 1985 - Franchising Since: 1989 - No. of Units: Company Owned: 7 - Franchised: 2 - Franchise Fee: $15,000 - Royalty: 5% weekly, 2% adv. - Total Inv: $27,900 min. - $39,900 max. - Financing: Yes.

BUDGET PEST CONTROL
Parker Pest Control, Inc.
3616 Lake Rd., Ponca City, OK, 74604. Contact: Brad Parker, V.P./G.M. - Tel: (405) 762-6614. Residential & commercial pest control using patented equipment. Established: 1963 - Franchising Since: 1986 - No. of Units: Company Owned: 7 - Franchised: 5 - Franchise Fee: $25,000 - Royalty: 8% 1st $100,000, 6% 2nd $100,000, 4% 3rd $100,000 - Total Inv: $65,000 - Financing: Partial.

CALCULATED COUPLES
Innovations In Corporations, Inc.
3370 N. Hayden Rd., Ste. 123-296, Scottsdale, AZ, 85251. Contact: David E. Gorman, Pres. - Tel: (800) 44-MATCH . Singles matchmaking party business. All cash business, part time or full time. Nationwide. Established: 1983 - Franchising Since: 1987 - No. of Units: Company Owned: 6 - Franchised: 6 - Franchise Fee: $5,000 - $8,000 dep. on territory - Royalty: $100/mo. - Total Inv: $5,100 - $10,000 - Financing: No.

CELLULAND, INC.
5784 Mimar Rd., San Diego, CA, 92122. Contact: Jackie Mann, V.P. - Tel: (619) 450-1900. Retail cellular car phone sales and service centers offering a wide selection of cellular phones, products, installations, customer service, warranty work, number activations and other communications products. Established: 1985 - Franchising Since: 1986 - No. of Units: Company Owned: 2 - Franchised: 24 - Franchise Fee: $25,000 - Royalty: 5% - Total Inv: $80,000 cash - Financing: No.

COBBLESTONE QUALITY SHOE REPAIR
Cobblestone Franchising, Inc.
5944 Luther Ln., Ste. 402, Dallas, TX, 75225. Contact: Jack Brent, V.P. - Tel: (214) 696-4436. Shoe & boot repair and recrafting, luggage repair, dye work, sell shoe care products. Established: 1988 - Franchising Since: 1989 - No. of Units: Company Owned: 35 - Franchised: 80 - Franchise Fee: $13,900 - Royalty: 6% gross sales, 1% nat'l. adv. fund - Total Inv: approx. $50,000 furniture, fixtures, equip., etc.

COLOR SPECIALTIES, INC.
6405 Cedar Ave., S., Richfield, MN, 55423. Contact: H. O. Toupin, CEO - Tel: (612) 861-1555. Reconditioning, repairing, refinishing of auto interiors, boat interiors, furniture, commercial and restaurant. Service business that is completely mobile. Established: 1976 - Franchising Since: 1977 - No. of Units: Company Owned: 2 - Franchised: 571 - Total Inv: $18,600, equip., chemicals, supplies, training - Financing: No.

COLOR-GLO
CGI, Inc.
7111 Ohms Lane, Minneapolis, MN, 55439. Contact: Scott Smith, Mktg. - Tel: (612) 835-1338. Total fabric care & restoration serving the automotive, aircraft, commercial furniture and restaurant furniture market. Established: 1972 - Franchising Since: 1983 - No. of Units: Company Owned: 3 - Franchised: 100 - Franchise Fee: $25,000 - Royalty: 4% - Total Inv: $25,000 - $40,000 - Financing: Yes.

CORNERSTONE FUELS
Cornerstone Fuels International, Inc.
515 Eaton St., St. Paul, MN, 55107. Contact: Mike Lewis, V.P. - Tel: (612) 831-0114. Sale of franchise to pump self serve fuel on airports for aircraft. Established: 1989 - Franchising Since: 1993 - No. of Units: Company Owned: 8 - Franchised: 6 - Franchise Fee: $5,000 - Royalty: flow fee 11¢ - 25¢ per gallon based on volume - Total Inv: Varies by site - Financing: Yes.

CRATERS & FREIGHTERS
Craters & Freighters Franchise Company
11871 E. 33rd Ave., #D, Aurora, CO, 80010. Contact: Dianna S. Nordyke, Fran. Dir. - Tel: (303) 361-6600, (800) 945-5682. Specialty freight handling for art galleries, frame shops, antique stores, estate liquidators, designers and a host of other upscale clients. Established:

1990 - Franchising Since: 1992 - No. of Units: Company Owned: 1 - Franchised: 11 - Franchise Fee: $15,000 - Royalty: 5%, 1% adv. - Total Inv: $14,300 to $18,410 w/o fran. fee - Financing: None.

CRITTER CONTROL *
640 Starkweather, Plymouth, MI, 48170 . Contact: Kevin Clark, Pres. - Tel: (313) 453-6300, Fax: (313)453-6395. Wildlife management and animal pest control services. Established: 1983 - Franchising Since: 1988 - No. of Units: Company Owned: 41 - Franchised: 50 - Franchise Fee: $2,000 - $18,000 - Royalty: 6% - 16% plus 2% adv. - Total Inv: $8,250 - $43,750 - Financing: N/A.

CUSTOM CASE SUPPLY CO.
9329 De Soto Ave., Dept. 783, Chatsworth, CA, 91311. Contact: Joanne Schmickel - Tel: (818) 882-5121. Direct sales, mail order. Build custom cases for salesmen. Established: 1945 - Inv: $9.95 to start. Training and support provided.

DCAP INSURANCE
CSS Franchising: 177 Main St., Ste. 103, Fort Lee, NY, 07024. Contact: Franchise Rep. - Tel: (201) 585-4753. Full service insurance office offering low cost auto insurance. Established: 1981 - Franchising Since: 1994 - No. of Units: Company Owned: 20 - Franchised: 10 - Franchise Fee: $15,000 - Royalty: $1,500 per month - Total Inv: $40,000 for conversion or $80,000 for start-up - Financing: Yes.

DIAL-A-TILE
1604 Hwy. 35, Box 71, Oakhurst, NJ, 07755. Contact: Robert Ballack, Pres. - Tel: (908) 517-0575. Mobile shop at home ceramic tile showroom. Established: 1990 - Franchising Since: 1991 - No. of Units: Company Owned: 3 - Franchise Fee: $20,000 - Total Inv: $40,000 - $50,000 - Financing: Will assist.

DRAPERY WORKS, THE
Drapery Works Systems, Ltd.
4640 Western Ave., Lisle, IL, 60532. Contact: Sheila Muehling, Pres./Owner - Tel: (708) 963-2820. Mobile custom drapery and soft bedding, accessories business. Established: 1978 - Franchising Since: 1993 - No. of Units: Company Owned: 1 - Franchise Fee: $7,500 - Royalty: 5% of gross sales, 2% nat'l adv. - Total Inv: $27,100 - $50,550 - Financing: Referrals only.

ELECTRO MAGIC
D.L.M.
4301 Aurora Ave. N., Seattle, WA, 98103. Contact: Donald L. Midkiff, Pres. - Tel: (206) 521-3376. On-site electrostatic refinishing of metal (office furniture, appliances, lockers, etc.). Program includes all equipment and one week of schooling in Seattle for all facets of starting such a business. Established: 1956 - Franchising Since: 1989 - No. of Units: Company Owned: 1 - Franchise Fee: $19,800 - Financing: No.

ENECON
Enecon Corporation
125 Baylis Rd., Ste. 190, Melville, NY, 11747-3800. Contact: Andrew A. Janczak, Pres. - Tel: (800) 854-1374, (516) 755-0022. Repair and protection products for fluid flow systems performance enhancement. Appoints exclusive distributors. Established: 1990 - No. of Units: Franchised: 15 - Total Inv: $25,000 (min.) start-up inventory & training - Financing: No.

ENERGY MISER WINDOWS
340 W. 4th Ave., Conshohocken, PA, 19428. Contact: Jerry Freid, Pres. - Tel: (215) 834-7283. Energy Miser offers an efficient low cost method to reduce energy cost, and noise infiltration in homes, commercial buildings and historic properties. Included along with the exclusive Energy Miser product line is proven training in marketing, sales and installation developed by Richard Kaller, a nationally recognized speaker and authority. Established: 1964 - Franchising Since: 1991 - No. of Units: Company Owned: 1 - Franchise Fee: $25,000 includes training - Royalty: 8% - Total Inv: $60,000 - Financing: Yes.

ENVIRONMENTAL AIR SERVICES
Environmental Air Services, Inc.
10351 Santa Monica Blvd., Ste. 212, Los Angeles, CA, 90025. Contact: Ronald Dorfman, Gen. Mgr. - Tel: (800) 583-3828. Indoor environmental health improvement services including indoor air assessment, consulting, air testing, filter, air washing, smoke & spot removal, air conveyance system decontamination. Residential, commercial, insurance. Established: 1992 - Franchising Since: 1993 - No. of Units: Company Owned: 1 - Franchised: 30 - Franchise Fee: $15,000 - Royalty: 7% - Total Inv: $15,000 fran. fee, $17,000 equip. - Financing: Yes.

ENVIRONMENTAL BIOTECH, INC.
4404 N. Tamiami Trl., Sarasota, FL, 34234-3864. Contact: Franchise Development - Tel: (941) 358-9112. Environmental waste remediation. EBI seeks solutions to environmental problems. We have over 200 strains of bacteria in our library to remediate lipid grease and oil, sugar, starch, gelatin and blood waste. Research and development is ongoing. In less that 3 yrs we have over 80 franchisees servicing a vast number of end-users with single and multiple installations in the US, Canada, Mexico, expanding into New Zealand, United Kingdom, Spain, Portugal, Japan, U.A.E., Australia, Columbia, Venezuela, Panama & Indonesia. Established: 1991 - Franchising Since: 1991 - No. of Units: Company Owned: 1 Franchised: 80 - Franchise Fee: $50,000 - Total Inv: $120,000 - Financing: No.

FAST-FIX JEWELRY REPAIRS
Jewelry Repair Enterprises, Inc.
1501 Decker Ave., Ste. 107, Stuart, FL, 34994. Contact: Bob Goldstein, CEO - Tel: (407) 221-9207. Jewelry and watch repair centers located in high traffic areas of major regional shopping malls. Now in twelve states. Established: 1984 - Franchising Since: 1987 - No. of Units: Company Owned: 3 - Franchised: 51 - Franchise Fee: $15,000 - Royalty: 5% of gross sales - Total Inv: $74,000 ($15,000 fran. fee, kiosk $35,000, equip. $10,000, inventory $13,000, training $1,000) - Financing: SBA loan assistance.

FORTUNE PRACTICE MANAGEMENT
9191 Towne Centre Dr., #500, San Diego, CA, 92122. Contact: Brad, Dir. of Sales - Tel: (800) 628-1052. Our franchisees consult with health care practitioners in the business and management areas of their practices. Established: 1990 - Franchising Since: 1990 - No. of Units: Franchised: 40 - Franchise Fee: $60,000 - Royalty: 15% - Total Inv: $60,000 - $114,000 - Financing: Yes, up to 75% of fran. fee.

GLASS MAGNUM
5855 S.W. 152nd , Beaverton, OR, 97007. Contact: John Podpah, Pres. - Tel: (503) 641-6926, (503) 641-9393. Glass and crystal reconstruction, bullet proof glass repair, crack repair in windshields, water spot removal, scratch removal in plate glass and windshields, and foreign matter removal from glass. Established: 1982 - Franchising Since: 1990 - No. of Units: Company Owned: 1 - Franchised: 13 - Franchise Fee: $5,000 basic, $10,000 master - Royalty: 1% adv., 1% R&D, 1% admin., 1% corp., 2% to master - Total Inv: $31,500 ins., $5,000 franchise, $10,000 master - Financing: Yes, 50%.

HAKKY INSTANT SHOE REPAIR
Hakky, Inc.
1739 Sands Place, Ste. F, Marietta, GA, 30067. Contact: Patrick Harper, Exec. Mgr. - Tel: (404) 956-8651. European instant shoe repair. Established: 1983 - Franchising Since: 1989 - No. of Units: Company Owned: 1 - Franchised: 72 - Franchise Fee: $9,000 - $12,500 - Royalty: 4%, 1% adv. - Total Inv: $40,000 - $100,000 - Financing: Assistance.

HEEL QUIK! HEEL/SEW QUIK!
Heel Quik!, Inc.
6425 Powers Ferry Rd., Ste. 250, Atlanta, GA, 30339. Contact: Andrea Laiosa, Fran. Coordinator - Tel: (770) 951-9440. Footwear life extension clinics, clothing alterations and monogramming. Established: 1984 - Franchising Since: 1985 - No. of Units: Company Owned: 2 - Franchised: 516 - Franchise Fee: $2,500 - $17,500 - Royalty: 4% sales - Total Inv: $6,000 - $135,500 - Financing: Yes.

HELP U MOVE
3820 Premier Ave., Memphis, TN, 38118. Contact: Bill Richey, Dir. - Tel: (901) 867-0600. Complete planning and moving company. Established: 1991 - Franchising Since: 1991 - No. of Units: Company Owned: 1 - Franchise Fee: $15,000 - $25,000 - Royalty: 5% - Total Inv: $25,000 - $45,000 - Financing: No.

HISTORICAL RESEARCH CENTER, INC., THE
Historical Research Center International, Inc., The
632 S. Military Tr., Deerfield Beach, FL, 33442. Contact: Pat Kelsey, Fran. Dir. - Tel: (305) 421-8713. Specialty retailer of family name histories and a unique line of heraldic (coat-of-arms) products. Established: 1988 - Franchising Since: 1992 - No. of Units: Company Owned: 62 - Franchised: 419 - Franchise Fee: $7,000 - Royalty: Varies - cost of goods 25% - Total Inv: $10,000 - $50,000 - Financing: Yes.

HOBBYTOWN USA
Hobbytown Unlimited
6301 S. 58th St., Lincoln, NE, 68516-3676. Contact: Timothy Whaley, Fran. Sales Mgr. - Tel: (402) 434-5052, Fax: (402) 434-5055. Hobby retail: radio-controlled vehicles, strategy games, train and railroad accessories, models, rockets, kites, sports cards and more. Established: 1969 - Franchising Since: 1985 - No. of Units: Company Owned: 3 - Franchised: 105 - Franchise Fee: $19,500 - Royalty: 3.5% - Total Inv: from $45,000 liquid to $250,000 capitalized - Financing: Sources provided.

HOST HELPERS
1633 Westwood Blvd., Ste. 210, Los Angeles, CA, 90024. Contact: Peter Siegel, Pres. - Tel: (213) 478-7799. A party personnel and party planning network. Established: 1981 - Franchising Since: 1986 - No. of Units: 2 - Franchise Fee: $10,000 - Total Inv: $15,000 - Financing: No.

HOT N' FAST
Consultants America Corp.
3820 Premier Ave., Memphis, TN, 38118. Contact: Bill Richey, Dir. - Tel: (901) 867-0600. Electronic food cooking and serving equipment. Established: 1992 - Franchising Since: 1992 - No. of Units: Company Owned: 1 - Franchise Fee: $10,000 - $100,000 for area - Royalty: 6% - Total Inv: $20,000 - $600,000 - Financing: Yes.

I'M SMART
D.W.I. Alternatives
P.O. Box 252, Syracuse, NY, 13201. Contact: Martin Yenawine, Pres. - Tel: (315) 471-4145. Risk management program - sales and services organization for dispatch service for impaired drivers. Established: 1982 - No. of Units: Company Owned: 1 - Franchised: 1 - Total Inv: varies.

IMAGES IN TIME
Martek Ltd.
P.O. Box 15160 (Dept. IFN), Charlotte, NC, 28211. Contact: Paul Muckler, Pres. - Tel: (704) 364-7213. Make and market a variety of clocks. Good family oriented business. Established: 1980 - Franchising Since: 1991 - No. of Units: Company Owned: 1 - Franchised: 6 - Total Inv: $495 - Financing: No.

INTERNATIONAL TELEVISION PRODUCTIONS, INC. *
448 East, 6400 South, Ste. 210, Murray, UT, 84107. Contact: Jim Goodro, V.P. Sales - Tel: (800) 231-0048. Full service video production company with a network of executive producers and production staff in strategic markets in the USA and Canada. Established: 1984 - Franchising Since: 1994 - No. of Units: Company Owned: 1 - Franchised: 14 - Franchise Fee: $28,500 - Royalty: 5% of gross profit (markup) - Total Inv: $39,000 - $46,000 - Financing: No.

IVY GATE FURNITURE ASSEMBLY
Ivy Gate Assembly
509 E. Campbell Ave., Campbell, CA, 95008. Contact: John Keith, Sales & Mktg. Mgr. - Tel: (800) 794-7856. Assembly services for consumers, retailers and manufacturers of ready-to-assemble furniture products. Established: 1992 - Franchising Since: 1994 - No. of Units: Company Owned: 2 - Franchise Fee: $10,000 - Royalty: 10% of gross sales weekly - Total Inv: $46,300 - $47,000 - Financing: None.

JET-BLACK SEALCOATING & REPAIR
Jet-Black International, Inc.
9033 Lyndale Ave. So., Bloomington, MN, 55420. Contact: Doug Hoiland, Fran. Dev. - Tel: (612) 888-4444, Fax: (612) 888-7050. Blacktop driveway maintenance service (sealcoating, hot crack filling, heat treat oil spots, and patching). Established: 1988 - Franchising Since: 1992 - No. of Units: Company Owned: 1 - Franchised; 7 - Franchise Fee: $6,500 - Royalty: 8% - Total Inv: $25,000 incl. fran. fee - Financing: Will help assist in finding best financing.

JEWELRY REPAIR ENTERPRISES
1501 Decker Ave. #107, Stuart, FL, 34994. Contact: Bob Goldstein, Corp. Sales Mgr. - Tel: (407) 221-9207. Jewelry & watch repairs while you wait. Located in major malls in United States. Established: 1984 - Franchising Since: 1987 - No. of Units: Company Owned: 3 - Franchised: 43 - Franchise Fee: $13,000 - Royalty: 5% on gross sales - Total Inv: $69,000 - Financing: No.

JUST REMINISCING *
Just Reminiscing, Inc.
5373 South Hayne Circle, Memphis, TN, 38119. , Fran. Dir. - Tel: (901) 867-0600. A video recording business which specializes in the production of video memories. Established: 1993 - No. of Units: Company Owned: 1 - Franchise Fee: $5,000 - Royalty: $50. per week - Total Inv: $5,600 - $12,000 (Inven., Signs, Equip.). For further information please contact: Consultants America Corp., 12279 US Highway 64. Eads, TN, 38028, Tel: (901) 867-0600, Fax: (901) 867-0010.

JUSTICE NETWORK, THE *
Justice Network Franchise Corp, The
86 Timber Creek, Ste. 2, Cordova, TN, 38018. Contact: Paul Ross, C.E.O. - Tel: (901) 755-6170, Fax: (901) 755-6358. Provider of alternatives to jail, offering supervision of criminal offenders. Established: 1990 - Franchising Since: 1994 - No. of Units: Company Owned: 1 - Franchised: 6 - Franchise Fee: $20,000 - Royalty: 5% - Total Inv: $32,100 - $65,000 - Financing: No.

KEEP THE CHANGE! *
KTC International, Inc.
2819 Northwood Blvd., Orlando, FL, 32803. Contact: Scott duPont, Pres. - Tel: (407) 629-2273, Fax: (407) 629-4354. Retail sales of pre-paid phone cards and accessories. Established: 1993 - Franchising Since: 1995 - No. of Units: Company Owned: 2 - Franchise Fee: $25,000 - Royalty: 4% - Total Inv: $25,000 to $55,000 - Financing: N/A.

KNOCKOUT PEST CONTROL INC.
Knockout Inspections
1009 Front St., Uniondale, NY, 11553. Contact: A. Katz, Pres. - Tel: (516) 489-7817. Pest control inspections. Established: 1975 - Franchising Since: 1993 - No. of Units: Company Owned: 1 - Franchised: 2 - Franchise Fee: $15,000 - Royalty: 10%, 2% adv. - Total Inv: $10,000 - Financing: No.

KOTT KOATINGS INC.
27161 Burbank, Foothill Ranch, CA, 92610. Contact: John M. Kott - Tel: (714) 770-5055. Porcelain & fiberglass refinishing on location of tub, sinks, tile, counters, showers & fiberglass. Established: 1955 - Franchising Since: 1973 - No. of Units: Company Owned: 1 - Franchised: 400 - Franchise Fee: $19,995 - Total Inv: $19,995 - Financing: O.A.C.

LASERQUEST
162 Terry Rd., Smithtown, NY, 11787. Contact: Jerry Seddon, CEO - Tel: (516) 361-8791, Fax: (516) 265-6623. Mobile in-office laser rentals on per patient fee basis. Established: 1970 - Franchising Since: 1953 - No. of Units: Company Owned: 1 - Franchise Fee: $25,000 - Royalty: 10% - Total Inv: $110,000 (lasers, van, equip.) - Financing: No.

LEROS POINT TO POINT
Leros Associates, Inc.
861 Franklin Ave., Thornwood, NY, 10594. Contact: Lonnie Lehrer, Pres. - Tel: (914) 747-2300. Luxury sedan ground transportation service catering to the executive and corporate traveler. Established: 1980 - Franchising Since: 1988 - No. of Units: Company Owned: 1 - Franchised: 5 - Franchise Fee: $10,000 - $16,000 - Royalty: 6%, 1/2% adv. - Total Inv: $90,000 - $110,000.

LIFESAFE SECURITY
3820 Premier Ave., Memphis, TN, 38118. Contact: Bill Richey, Dir. - Tel: (901) 867-0600. Emergency response system using electronic equipment at a central monitoring station. Established: 1990 - Franchising Since: 1990 - No. of Units: Company Owned: 1 - Franchise Fee: $20,000 - Royalty: 6% - Total Inv: $22,600 - Financing: No.

LOGAN FARMS HONEY GLAZED HAMS
Logan Farms, Inc.
10001 Westheimer, Houston, TX, 77042. Contact: Pink Logan, Pres. - Tel: (713) 781-3773. Retail gourmet meats. Established: 1984 - Franchising Since: 1985 - No. of Units: Company Owned: 2 - Franchised: 7 - Franchise Fee: $15,000 - Royalty: 3% - Total Inv: $250,000 - Financing: No.

MAGIS FUND RAISING SPECIALISTS, INC.
845 Heathermoor Lane, #400, Perrysburg, OH, 43551. Contact: Richard W. Waring, Pres. - Tel: (419) 244-6711. $100 million plus raised for non-profits through capital, annual & endowment campaigns. Leadership training. Fund raising audits, money back guarantee. Try it for 24 months! Established: 1991 - Franchising Since: 1991 - No. of Units: Company Owned: 2 - Franchised: 4 - Franchise Fee: $7,500 - Royalty: 8%, 2% adv. - Total Inv: $25,000 - Financing: Yes.

MANDY'S MATCHING SERVICE
Mandy's Matching Development Corp.
6500 Jericho Tpke., Ste. 206A, Commack, NY, 11725. Contact: Paul Schlanger, Pres. - Tel: (800) 626-3971. Personal matching service for people looking for serious relationships and/or marriage. Established: 1987 - Franchising Since: 1991 - No. of Units: Franchised: 4 - Franchise Fee: $15,000 - Royalty: 7% - Total Inv: $43,000 - $56,000 inclusive of fran. fee & work. cap. - Financing: A portion of the fran. fee may be financed.

MARBLE RENEWAL
SVI Inc.
6805-H W. 12th St., Little Rock, AR, 72204. Contact: Gary Perritt, CEO - Tel: (501) 663-2080, Fax: (501) 663-2401. Marble, hardwood and other stone restoration and maintenance. Exclusive chemicals and processes. International network of trained professionals. Established: 1988 - Franchising Since: 1989 - No. of Units: Company Owned: 1 - Franchised: 17 - Franchise Fee: $5,000 - $75,000 - Royalty: 5% - 8% of gross revenues - Total Inv: $25,000 - $132,000 - Financing: Partial.

MARTEK LTD.
P.O. Box 15160, Dept. IF, Charlotte, NC, 28211. Contact: Paul Muckler, Pres. - Tel: (704) 364-7213. Produce & market a variety of clocks including photo - business card - logo & novelty clocks. Established: 1980 - Franchising Since: 1991 - No. of Units: Company Owned: 1 - Franchised: 6 - Franchise Fee: $1,995 - Royalty: none - Total Inv: $495 - $3,995 - Financing: No.

MELCO EMBROIDERY SYSTEMS
1575 W. 124th Ave., Denver, CO, 80234. Contact: Doug Hunley, Dir. Advertising - Tel: (303) 457-1234. Manufacturer & supplier of computerized personalization equipment & supplies: embroidery, chenille, and digitizing, scanning & editing of designs, for entrepreneurs who want to start their own businesses in home, retail store, or wholesale shop. Established: 1972 - Total Inv: from $10,000 up for equipment - Financing: Lease purchase plans available.

MICROWAVE CLINIC
50 Budney Rd., Newington, CT, 06111. Contact: Renate Hoffman, Pres. - Tel: (203) 665-7599. Microwave oven service center. Established: 1987 - Franchising Since: 1990 - No. of Units: Company Owned: 2 - Franchised: 7 - Franchise Fee: $15,000 (subject to change) - Royalty: 6% gross sales - Total Inv: $15,000 + fran. fee. - Financing: No.

MILLION AIR INTERLINK, INC.
4300 Westgrove, Dallas, TX, 75248. Contact: Lou Pepper, Pres. - Tel: (214) 248-1600. Independently owned, fixed base operations.

MOBILE CONTAINER SERVICE
Mobile Container Service, Inc.
12279 Highway 64, Eads, TN, 38028. Contact: Consultant America Corp., Fran. Dir. - Tel: (901) 867-0600. A business specializing in refurbishing, repainting, and refinishing waste, recycling, trash dumpsters and containers. Established: 1983 - Franchising Since: 1991 - No. of Units: Company Owned: 1 - Franchised: 8 - Franchise Fee: $18,000 - Total Inv: $35,800 - $55,000 (Equip., Inven. and supplies, Truck, Work. Cap.) - Royalty: 6%.

MONITORNET *
1075 Bellevue Way NE #501, Bellevue, WA, 98004. Contact: Kevin Asher, Sales Manager - Tel: (206) 814-2425, Fax: (206) 462-1163. Monitor repair center. Established: 1993 - Franchising Since: 1995 - Franchise Fee: $3,900.

NATGO, INC. *
15965 Jeanette St., Southfield, MI, 48075. Contact: Ms. Colleen McGaffey - Tel: (810) 557-2784, Fax: (810) 557-7931. If you are a marina or current business owner and are looking for an extra product line, Natgo Inc. invites you to join them in an exciting new adventure as natural gas, the fuel of the future, is introduced into American boats and automobiles through innovative technology. Established: 1993 - Franchising Since: 1993 - No. of Units: Franchised: 1 - Franchise Fee: $25,000 - Royalty: 7% - Total Inv: $230,000 to $1,000,000 - Financing: No.

NATIONAL AUTO/TRUCKSTOPS INC.
3100 West End, Ste. 200, Nashville, TN, 37203-1349. Contact: Paul Kohler, Dir., Fran. Dev. - Tel: (615) 783-2725, (800) 688-1276. Full service interstate travel plazas. Established: 1950 - Franchising Since: 1993 - No. of Units: Company Owned: 97 - Franchised: 105 - Franchise Fee: $80,000 - Royalty: Variable - Financing: Yes.

NATIONAL LEAK DETECTION INC.
P.O. Box 3191, Palos Verdes Estates, CA, 90274. Contact: Jeri Honda, Mktg. Dir. - Tel: (800) 444-9421, Fax: (310) 328-3342. Detection of hidden underground water and gas leaks utilizing sonar and ultrasonic field testing equipment. Specializing in spas, pools, fountains, ponds, slab leaks, leaks in walls, domestic water supply systems, irrigation systems and roof leaks. Exclusive product only available to franchisees called AQUA 2000. Established: 1979 - Franchising Since: 1990 - No. of Units: Company Owned: 20 - Franchised: 32 - Franchise Fee: from $15,000 - Royalty: 8% - Total Inv: $30,000 - Financing: Yes.

NATIONAL MAIL ORDER ASSOCIATION, L.L.C. *
2807 Polk St. N.E., Minneapolis, MN, 55418. Contact: John Schulte, Chief Manager - Tel: (612) 788-1673, Fax: (612) 788-1147, E-mail NMOA@aol.com. Provides help to small & medium sized businesses in the use of direct mail and mail order marketing. Publishes Mail Order Digest and Washington Newsletter. Also operates "Mail Order Connection", a computer BBS for members to communicate worldwide.

NATIONAL PROPERTY REGISTRY
NPR Services, Inc.
P.O. Box 72376, Marietta, GA, 30007-2376. Contact: Robert J. Heller, Pres., CEO - Tel: (770) 971-5200, Fax: (770) 977-7810. Video inventory record service for business and home owners, safekeeping and records retrieval. Established: 1993 - Franchising Since: 1994 - No. of Units: Franchised: 8 - Franchise Fee: $1,995 which includes all training and materials.

NATIONAL TRADE EXCHANGE
P.O. Box 180325, Dallas, TX, 75218-0325. Contact: George Burke, Pres. - Tel: (214) 320-8227. Barter and trading among businesses using computerized network select and approve. Established: 1981 - Franchising Since: 1983 - Franchise Fee: $5,000 - Total Inv: $5,000 - Financing: Yes.

NATURE'S REFLECTIONS *
Nature's Reflections Inc.
3375 Buckinghammock Trail, Vero Beach, FL, 32960. Contact: Diane K. Condit or Robert D.S. Condit, Pres./ Secre./Treas. - Tel: (407) 778-8343, Fax: (407) 778-8343. Established: 1995 - Franchising Since: 1995 - No. of Units: Franchised: 1 - Franchise Fee: $15,000 - Royalty: 5% - Total Inv: low-$60,000; high-$120,000.

NAUT-A-CARE *
Naut-A-Care Franchising, Inc.
610 Newport Center Dr., Ste. 700, Newport Beach, CA, 92660-6463. Contact: Vince Paglia, Pres. - Tel: (800) 423-1110, Fax: (714) 760-9551. Complete marine services provided by specially equipped service boats for commercial and pleasure yachts. Oil changes, bilge cleaning, engine repair, exterior and interior cleaning. Established: 1991 - Franchising Since: 1995 - No. of Units: Company Owned: 1 - Franchise Fee: $25,000 - Royalty; $500 or 6% gross to $10,000, 5% to $16,000, 4% over $16,000 - Total Inv: $51,200 to $90,300 w/one or two boats - Financing: Outside.

NEWCHOICES RELATIONSHIP CENTER
NewChoices Franchise Marketing, Inc.
1610 Wynkoop, Ste. 120, Denver, CO, 80202. Contact: C. Lea Osborn, CEO - Tel: (303) 571-1001. Relationship education and personal introduction service. This is America's only psychologically based personal introduction service. Introductions are arranged over lunch by NewChoices, with NewChoices making all the arrangements. Established: 1992 - Franchising Since: 1995 - No. of Units: Company Owned: 1 - Franchise Fee: $35,000 to $85,000 on location - Royalty: 7% + 2% adv. - Total Inv: $32,000 to $85,000 for working capital for rent, security deposits, furniture, equipment, etc. - Financing: No.

NIX CHECK CASHING *
Thomas Nix Distributor, Inc.
17019 Kingsview Ave., Carson, CA, 90746. Contact: Bob Levin, V.P. of Fran. Sales - Tel: (800) 325-1718, Fax: (310) 538-0131. Full range of financial services: Check cashing, money orders, Western union, utility payments, A&M services, transit passes, fax, copies, phone debit cards, lotto etc. Established: 1966 - Franchising Since: 1992 - No. of Units: Company Owned: 65 - Franchised: 15 - Franchise Fee: $19,000 - Royalty: 6%, 2.5% adv, 2% processing fee - Total Inv: $79,000, fran. fee, equip. $50,000, work. cap. $50,000 - Financing: Yes.

OK FOOD MANAGEMENT US CORP. *
727 Main St., Niagara Falls, NY, 14301. Contact: Vincent Agnello, Fran. Cons., Legal - Tel: (716) 285-2533. Corporate identity import & export products. Established: 1995 - Franchising Since: 1996 - No. of Units: Company Owned: 1 - Franchise Fee: $2,000 - Royalty: 7%, no adv. - Total Inv: $1,000 - Financing: No.

PAINTER ONE CORP.
38083 W. Spaulding, Ste. 202, Willoughby, OH, 44094-6142. Contact: Michelle A. Morgan, Exec. Dir. - Tel: (216) 975-4884. Franchisor for painting company owners - individual companies in the paint contracting business. Franchisees receive exclusive Painter One pricing nationwide from the Sherwin Williams Co. and the Glidden Company on paints and related products, plus the Painter One method of business operations and much more. Established: 1994 - Franchising Since: 1994 - No. of Units: Franchised: 5 - Franchise Fee: $150 (introductory offer) - Royalty: $50 per month - Total Inv: $150 fran. fee and up to $250 materials fee - Financing: None.

PARAGRAVE CORP.
1455 West Center St., Orem, UT, 84057. Contact: Lou Jensen, Gen. Mgr. - Tel: (800) 624-7415, (801) 225-8300. Ultra high speed engraving system that turns even non-artists into engraving professionals. Established: 1983 - No. of Dealers: 4000+ - Franchise Fee: None - Royalty: None - Total Inv: $2,999 - Financing: None.

PEARTREE HOME MARKETING
Peartree Home Marketing Consultants
3820 Premier Ave., Memphis, TN, 38118. Contact: Bill Richey, Dir. - Tel: (901) 867-0600. System for home marketing for homeowners which includes methods, techniques for inventory, operation control, bookkeeping, advertising. Established: 1986 - Franchising Since: 1991 - No. of Units: Company Owned: 1 - Franchise Fee: $15,000 - Royalty: 8% - Total Inv: $20,700 - $33,000 - Financing: No.

PILOT AIR FREIGHT CORP.
Rte. 352, P.O. Box 97, Lima, PA, 19037. Contact: Richard Morris, C.O.O. - Tel: (215) 565-8100. Air freight forwarding - buying space aboard air carriers and selling the service at retail. Established: 1970 - Franchising Since: 1979 - No. of Units: Company Owned: 2 - Franchised: 58 - Franchise Fee: $10,000 - $30,000 - Total Inv: $25,000 - $50,000 - Royalty: 13% gross - Financing: No.

PLAINS REFRIGERANT RECLAIM OF (NAME OF CITY)
Plains Refrigerant Reclaim Corp.
14500 Canyon Drive, Amarillo, TX, 79119. Contact: Mank Gollihar, Pres. - Tel: (806) 622-0484. Service to the HVAC/REF industry. We recover reclaim and repackage refrigerants of all commonly used refrigerants. We save the contractor or end user 20% to 50% of the cost of wholesale refrigerants. EPA certified. Established: 1989 - Franchising Since: 1994 - No. of Units: Company Owned: 1 - Franchised: 1 - Franchise Fee: $25,000, $75,000 for equip. etc. - Royalty: 10% of actual processing of refrigerant through our reclaim machine. All other activity is not accessed - Total Inv: $25,000 initial fee for legal fees, training, etc., $75,000 for machinery and installation, etc. - Financing: None.

PLUMBING M.D. *
Fast Aid Franchise Corp.
P.O. Box 982, Winters, CA, 95694. Contact: Mike Farias, Pres. - Tel: (916) 658-8483. Plumbing service and repair, sewer and drain cleaning. Established: 1984 - Franchising Since: 1995 - No. of Units: Franchised: 1 - Franchise Fee: $10,000 to $15,000 - Royalty: 7% - Total Inv: $15,000 to $50,000 - Financing: No.

PROFESSIONAL POLISH JANITORIAL MAINTENANCE/LAWN MAINTENANCE
Professional Polish Inc.
5450 E. Loop 820 S., Fort Worth, TX, 76119. Contact: Sid Cavanaugh, Pres. - Tel: (800) 255-0488, Fax: (817) 561-6193. Commercial cleaning services, lawn maintenance and light building maintenance. Established: 1982 - Franchising Since: 1986 - No. of Units: Company Owned: 1 - Franchised: 31 - Franchise Fee: $25,000 - $45,000 - Royalty: Local 15%, Master passes 5% to corporation - Total Inv: $15,500 local, $250,000 Master - Financing: Yes.

PROPERTY DAMAGE APPRAISERS
Property Damage Appraisers, Inc.
6100 Southwest Blvd., Ste. 200, Ft. Worth, TX, 76109. Contact: Rick Cutler, Dir. Training and Dev. - Tel: (800) 749-7324. Provide automobile and property appraisals for insurance companies and self-insureds. Automobile damage appraising experience a prerequisite. National marketing support and ongoing management assistance. Established: 1963 - Franchising Since: 1963 - No. of Units: Franchised: 231 - Royalty: 15% - Total Inv: $9,250 - $23,450 start up costs.

PROTOCOL
1370 Mendota Hts. Rd., Mendota Hts., MN, 55120. Contact: Brett McKay, V.P. - Tel: (800) 227-5336. Manufacture four models of personal product vending machines that can dispense any combination of more than 30 products, i.e., condoms, aspirins, tampons, fragrances, etc. Established: 1987 - Franchising Since: 1987 - No. of Units: Franchised: 18,000 - Franchise Fee: None - Royalty: None - Total Inv: $10,000 equip. & products - Financing: Yes, lease program following initial investment.

PYTHON'S
Python's Inc.
P.O. Box 6025, St. Cloud, MN, 56302. Contact: Dan Huschke, Pres. - Tel: (612) 253-9553, Fax: (612) 253-9314. Stand alone, for-profit recycling, redemption or buy back centers where individuals can sell all their recyclables and benefit from a unique community based marketing program. Established: 1976 - Franchising Since: 1989 - No. of Units: Company Owned: 6 - Franchised: 3 - Franchise Fee: $25,000 - Royalty: varies - Total Inv: $115,500 - $669,500 - Financing: None.

RICH PLAN
Rich Plan Corp.
4981 Commercial Dr., Yorkville, NY, 13495. Contact: R. Bruce Evans, Chairman - Tel: (800) 243-1358. Each franchisee provides its customers with various food analysis services and offers a line of high quality, prepackaged, perishable frozen food items ordered from a price list, food guide or menu planner and delivered directly to the customer at home. A franchisee also markets freezers and cookware for use by its customers. Established: 1946 - Franchising Since: 1952 - No. of Units: Franchised: 19 - Franchise Fee: $10,000 - Royalty: $10 each new customer for 100 each month, $5 on 101st and each thereafter each month - Total Inv: $25,000 - $50,000: $10,000 fran. fee, $15,000 inven. - Financing: None.

ROHR'S RESTAURANT SERVICE
Rohr's Restaurant Franchising, Inc.
Route 1, Box 83, Quinter, KS, 67752. , Fran. Dir. - Tel: (901) 867-0600. A restaurant servicing business specializing in cleaning and servicing of exhaust systems. Established: 1987 - No. of Units: Franchised: 4 - Franchise Fee: $10,000 - Royalty: 5% - Total inv: $21,700 - $43,000 (Work. Cap., Equip., Van, Insur., Deposits, Misc.) - Financing: Financeable Equip. For further information please contact: Consultants America Corp., 12279 US Highway 64. Eads, TN, 38028, Tel: (901) 867-0600, Fax: (901) 867-0010.

SALSBURY
1010 E. 62nd St., Los Angeles, CA, 90001. Contact: Brian Fraher, Dir. of Mktg. - Tel: (213) 232-6181. Manufacturer of mailboxes for private mail/postal centers that offer mailbox rentals. Established: 1936 - Total Inv: $500 - $5,000 - Financing: No.

SCM
W140 N5946 Lilly Rd., Menomonie Falls, WI, 53051. Contact: Customer Service - Tel: (800) 755-0261, Fax: (414) 251-7895. Hi-tech custom engraving and sandblasting equipment and supplies. Established: 1988 - Franchise Fee: $999 to $2,495 - Royalty: None - Total Inv: $2,495 - Financing: Yes.

SEAGA MANUFACTURING CORPORATION
15 W. Market, P.O. Box 47, Shannon, IL, 61078. Contact: Bill Heid, Sales Mgr. - Tel: (815) 864-2600. Manufacturer and supplier of vending equipment (specifically Super Vend 2000, Super Snack 900C, Super Snack 1800, Super Snack 2700, Super Bite, and Double Play.) Established: 1987 - Financing: Yes.

SEALMASTER
2520 S. Campbell St., Sandusky, OH, 44870. Contact: Roger D. Auker, Dir., Fran. Dev. - Tel: (800) 395-7325, Fax: (419) 626-5477. Manufacture and supply Sealmaster Pavement Maintenance Products and Equipment. Established: 1963 - Franchising Since: 1993 - No. of Units: Company Owned: 7 - Franchised: 9 - Franchise Fee: $35,000 - Royalty: 5% - Total Inv: $225,000 - $450,000 - Financing: Possible on start-up equip.

SERVING BY IRVING, INC.
233 Broadway, Ste. 1036, New York, NY, 10279. Contact: Irving Botwinick, Dir. Mktg. - Tel: (212) 233-3346. Professional process servers. Established: 1976 - Franchising Since: 1990 - No. of Units: Company Owned: 1 - Franchised: 4 - Franchise Fee: $85,000 - Royalty: 7%, 2% adv. - Financing: No.

SHOESMITH/SHOEFIXERS
1884 Breton Rd. S.E., #201, Grand Rapids, MI, 49506. Contact: Judd Freedman, Sales Mgr. - Tel: (800) 335-5894, (616) 453-4754. Instant shoe repair & shoe care. Established: 1987 - Franchising Since: 1987 - No. of Units: Franchised: 45 - Franchise Fee: $12,500 - Royalty: 5% - Total Inv: $32,000 - $90,000 (excl. fran. fee) - Financing: None - will assist.

SIGNATURE ANALYSIS
D&K Enterprises Inc.
3216 Commander Dr., Ste. 101, Dept. 17, Carrollton, TX, 75006. Contact: Marketing Dept. - Tel: (214) 248-9100. Provide a unique and fun product for all ages. A computerized printout of ones true personality traits according to their signature. Franchising Since: 1987 - No. of Units: Company Owned: 1 - Franchised: 32 in 13 states in 2 countries - Total Inv: $4,995. (turn-key package) - Financing: Yes.

SLIDE SHOTS INC. *
498 N. Kings Hwy., Ste. 110, Cherry Hill, NJ, 08034. Contact: Frank Lepore, C.F.O - Tel: (800) 7-SLIDES, Fax: (609) 482-5471. Computer graphics producing 35 mm slides, overheads, brochures and multi-media to the business world. Also we output from customer supplied computer file (diskettes etc.). Established: 1989 - Franchising Since: 1994 - No. of Units: Franchised: 1 - Franchise Fee: $25,000 - Royalty: 7% of net sales - Total Inv: $30,000 equip. & software, $25,000 fee, $25,000 oper. cap.

SPECIAL SELECTIONS
4955 Bitterbush Dr., Boise, ID, 83703. Contact: Roxanne Overton, Owner - Tel: (208) 343-3629. Personal and corporate gift buying service. This is a challenging, fun business that finds gifts for any occasion with 8,000 sources. Established: 1988 - Licensing Since: 1989 - No. of Units: Company Owned: 1 - Licensed: 12 - License Fee: $500.00 - Total Inv: $1,000 - Financing: No.

SPEEDY KEYS
Speedy Keys, Inc.
1815 J & C Blvd., Naples, FL, 33942. Contact: Richard Paganes, Pres. - Tel: (800) 590-3211. Mobile locksmith franchise. Established: 1980 - Franchising Since: 1993 - No. of Units: Company Owned: 1 - Franchised: 3 - Franchise Fee: $7,500 - Royalty: 5% - Total Inv: $14,500 cash needed - Financing: Yes, GMAC will lease van.

STARVING STUDENTS
P.O. Box 351206, Los Angeles, CA, 90035. Contact: E.H. Margalith, Pres. - Tel: (310) 854-4464. Moving. Established: 1973 - Franchising Since: 1982 - No. of Units: Company Owned: 4 - Licensed: 1 - Partnerships: 9 - Franchise Fee: $15,000 - Total Inv: $25,000 - Royalty: $500/mo per truck.

SUGARLOAF CREATIONS, INC.
4870 Sterling Dr., Boulder, CO, 80301. Contact: Randall Fagundo, V.P. - Tel: (303) 444-2559. Amusement crane vending business. Established: 1987 - Franchising Since: 1990 - No. of Units: Company Owned: 2 - Franchised: 40 - Franchise Fee: $5,000 - $60,000 - Royalty: 2.5% - 5% - Total Inv: $26,150 - $210,000 - Financing: No.

SURFACE DOCTOR
5182 Old Dixie Hwy., Forest Park, GA, 30050. Contact: Franchise Counselor - Tel: (404) 362-2868, (800) 735-5055. Surface restoration and refinishing service for tile, countertops, metal appliances, bathtubs, sinks, cultured marble and more. Many markets need Surface Doctor's service including apartments, hotels, homes, restaurants, hospitals, etc. Surface Doctor uses the latest resurfacing technology to restore surfaces for a fraction of the cost of replacement. Established: 1994 - Franchising Since: 1994 - No. of Units: Company Owned: 2 - Franchised: 84 - Franchise Fee: $9,800 - Royalty: $175/mo., $25/mo. ad. fund - Total Inv: fran. fee plus $4,000 inven. - Financing: No.

SWING SYNC
Business Golf Assc.
4711 NE 50th, Seattle, WA, 98105. Contact: James W. Smith, Pres. - Tel: (206) 524-5958, Fax: (206) 524-7826. Swing Sync licenses their system of custom golf club manufacturing. Service includes sales, marketing, custom fitting, club making and promotion. Established: 1985 - Franchising Since: 1985 - No. of Units: Company Owned: 2 - Franchised: 10 - Franchise Fee: $5,000 - $15,000 depends on territory - Royalty: 2% adv. fund - Total Inv: $5,000 - $15,000 - Financing: No.

T & G CRAFTS
597 Rock St., New Braunfels, TX, 78130. Contact: Geraldine Well, Mgr. - Tel: (210) 629-6469. Specialty name plaques. Established: 1992 - Licensing Since: 1992 - No. of Units: 1 - Total Inv: Cost of plaques at wholesale - Financing: No.

TERMINIX INTERNATIONAL
Terminix International Co. L.P.
860 Ridge Lake Blvd., Memphis, TN, 38120. Contact: John Greelan, Dir., Fran. Recruit. & Placement - Tel: (800) 654-7848 or (901) 766-1351. Residential and commercial termite and pest control service. Established: 1927 - Franchising Since: 1927 - No. of Units: Company Owned: 317 - Franchised: 222 - Franchise Fee: $25,000 - $50,000 - Royalty: 7%, up to 2% nat'l adv. - Total Inv: $75,000 - $105,000 - Financing: Yes, with approved credit, up to 70% of initial fran. fee.

THEE CHIMNEY SWEEP, INC.
36 Vernon Rd., N.E., Rome, GA, 30161. Contact: Garry Trotter - Tel: (706) 232-5261. Chimney cleaning and sales of wood heaters, chimney relining and accessories.

THERMAL-ATION
1638 S. Research Loop Rd., Ste. 160, Tucson, AZ, 85710. Contact: Dale R. Young, Pres. - Tel: (602) 722-9718. A revolutionary ceramic latex coating formulated to significantly reduce problems related to heat/cold transfer, work related injuries and energy conservation. Established: 1992 - Franchising Since: 1993 - No. of Units: Franchised: 3 - Franchise Fee: $27,500 - Royalty: None - Total Inv: $27,500 plus $2,000 - $3,000 working capital - Financing: No.

TOGETHER DATING SERVICE
Together Development Corp.
1811 West Dickerson St., Ste. 17, Boseman, MT, 59715. Contact: Chet Tomasiewicz - Tel: (406) 585-5883. Personal introduction. Established: 1974 - Franchising Since: 1981 - No. of Units: Company Owned: 17 - Franchised: over 85 - Royalty: varies around 7% - Total Inv: negotiable - Financing: Negotiable.

TRADE LABOR
P.O. Box 70661, Nashville, TN, 37207. Contact: Jim Shafer, Pres. - Tel: (615) 824-2825. Unique barter exchange business. Established: 1991 - Franchising Since: 1991 - No. of Units: Company Owned: 1 - Franchised: 4 - Franchise Fee: $999 - Royalty: 5% per quarter, $100 min. - Financing: If necessary.

TROPI-TAN, INC.
Lorraine's Tropi-Tan, Inc.
5152 Commerce Rd., Flint, MI, 48507. Contact: Vince Lorraine, Pres. - Tel: (810) 230-0090, Fax: (810) 230-0090. Indoor suntanning salon & related retail sales (clothing, lotions). Established: 1979 - Franchising Since: 1985 - No. of Units: Company Owned: 7 - Franchised: 3 - Franchise Fee: $7,000 - Royalty: 4%, 3.5% adv. - Total Inv: $60,000 - $250,000 - Financing: None.

TWO MEN AND A TRUCK
1915 E. Michigan Ave., Lansing, MI, 48912. Contact: Melanie Bergeron, Pres. - Tel: (800) 345-1070. Local movers moving household & commercial goods at an hourly rate. Established: 1984 - Franchising Since: 1989 - No. of Units: Company Owned: 1 - Franchised: 30 - Franchise Fee: $17,950 - Royalty: 4% gross - Total Inv: 1% gross - Financing: No.

UNISHIPPERS ASSOCIATION INC.
2595 E. 3300 S., Salt Lake City, UT, 84109-2727. Contact: Brad Keyser, Fran. Sales Mgr. - Tel: (800) 999-8721. Discount on overnight air express. Airborne handles the pick-up and delivery. You handle the marketing and billing and maintain a profit margin on each shipment. Established: 1987 - Franchising Since: 1987 - No. of Units: Franchised: 154 - Franchise Fee: $12,500 - Royalty: 6% of gross sales - Total Inv: 1 1/2 to 2 times the franchise fee - Financing: None.

VALDCO T-SHIRTS
3047 W. Berteau, P.O. Box 18170, Dept. FAD, Chicago, IL, 60618-0170. Contact: Rafael Valderrama or Pat Sawiaki, Communications Mgr., Owner - Tel: (312) 267-7037. Silk screening of all imprintables (t-shirts, caps, poly bags, sweats, signs, flags, banners, P.O.P.'s). Established: 1982 - Franchising Since: 1982 - No. of Units: Company Owned: 4 - Franchised: 2 - Franchise Fee: varies - Total Inv: varies - Financing: No.

WATSCO, INC.
1943 Oakley, Topeka, KS, 66604. Contact: Larry G. Waters, Pres. - Tel: (913) 233-8881. Waste heat water heaters; Hard-cooked egg processing and distributing. Both programs are only offered to existing compatible businesses. Established: 1970 - Franchising Since: 1972 - No. of Units: Company Owned: 1 - Franchised: 12 - Franchise Fee: $5,000 - Royalty: 1 cent/dozen for Wat-a-Egg, 3% for Wat-a-Heater - Financing: None.

WESTLAND OF (NAME OF TERRITORY)
Westland Services Corporation
1700 West Park Drive, Westborough, MA, 01581-3915. Contact: Philip G. Haddad, Peter Abdelmaseh, Pres., Mktg. Cons. - Tel: (508) 836-2600, (800) 622-0772. Westland is awarding franchises for exclusive territories to market & sell beautification & maintenance services for individual family cemetery plots anywhere in the U.S. and soon the world - for a one time fee with services performed for 25 years (shorter term contracts also available). Established: 1987 - Franchising Since: 1994 - No. of Units: Company Owned: 1 - Franchise Fee: From $19,000 to $57,000 (average territory cost $25-$30K) - Royalty: None - Total Inv: From $50,000 to $140,000 (office, equipment, furnishings incl.) - Financing: Assistance available.

WORLD CLASS PARKING *
WCP Franchising Inc.
77 Brant Ave., Clark, NJ, 07066. Contact: Gerald Eicke, V.P. - Tel: (908) 381-2525. Valet parking and parking management. Established: 1991 - Franchising Since: 1995 - No. of Units: Franchised: 15 - Franchise Fee: $39,500 - Royalty: $50/wk. to a cap of $150/wk. after 3 years - Total Inv: $38,500 total / turnkey - Financing: No.

WORLDWIDE INFORMATION SERVICES, INC.
Box 21261, Ft. Lauderdale, FL, 33335-1261. Contact: W.H. Bonneau, Pres. - Tel: (305) 764-7942. Become an information consultant, gateway to 1,000's of data sources from credit, criminals, motor vehicle and many more. Attorneys, private investigators, human resources, realtors and individuals who are seeking to find someone or check the background of the one you love before marriage. Established: 1990 - No. of Units: Company Owned: 1 - Total Inv: $12,500 - Financing: No.

WOVENHEARTS® *
Heartland Retirement Services, Inc.
309 W. Washington Ave., Ste. 345, Madison, WI, 53703. Contact: Doug Hennig, Pres. - Tel: (800) 430-0658. WovenHearts Residential Assisted Living was designed to address a crucial need of the fastest growing age segment of the U.S. population, the elderly. WovenHearts provides assistance for older adults, helping them to maintain independence in their home communities. WovenHearts offers investors an opportunity to "Do Well By Doing Good". Established: 1993 - Franchising Since: 1994 - No. of Units: Company Owned: 8 - Franchised: 3 - Franchise Fee: $50,000 - Royalty: 6% of gross monthly receipts - Total Inv: $700,000 inclusive - Financing: No.

YACHT SALES DEALERSHIP
Majestic Yachts Inc.
1831 NE 38th St., Apt. 402, Fort Lauderdale, FL, 33308-6203. Contact: Ray Tankersley, Pres. - Tel: (305) 537-3334. Yacht sales 46 to 75ft. Established: 1985 - Franchising Since: 1985 - No. of Units: Franchised: 6 - Franchise Fee: Buy 46 yacht approx. $400,000 - Total Inv: 46 ft. motoryacht less 20% - Financing: 0 down 15 to 20 years amortization.

CANADIAN LISTINGS

ACCOUNTING AND TAX SERVICES

A+ FINANCIAL SERVICES LTD. *
344 Burland Ave., Winnipeg, MB, R2N 2R5. Contact: Denis Brunet, Pres. - Tel: (204) 256-2151, Fax: (204) 942-8294. Financial Services.

BRIEF ROTFARB WYNBERG CAPPE
3845 Bathurst St., Ste. 402, Willowdale, ON, M3H 3N2. Contact: M. Rotfarb, Partner - Tel: (416) 635-9080, Fax: (416) 635-0462, E-Mail: rotfarb@inforamp.net. Chartered Accountants - Comptables Agréés - services include preparation of business plans, financing proposals, exploring business opportunities and accounting and tax planning services. Established: 1980 - No. of Units: One head office.

CEN-TA GROUP
201 - 935 Marine Dr., N. Vancouver, BC, V7P 1S3. Contact: David G.T. Ingram, Pres. - Tel: (604) 980-0321. Income tax preparation, real estate and property management advisory services, tax counseling. Established: 1969 - Franchising Since: 1970 - No. of Units: Company Owned: 7 - Franchised: 12 - Total Inv: $25,000 approx.

COMPREHENSIVE BUSINESS SERVICES
Comprehensive Business Services of Canada
8500 Leslie St., Ste. 520, Thornhill, ON, L3T 7M8. Contact: Leo G. Lauzen, Sr., Pres. - Tel: (905) 771-1200, Fax: (905) 771-9060. Accountants (designation of CA, CMA, CPA, or CGA required) provide monthly accounting, tax and business consultation services to business clients. The Comprehensive Marketing Team can deliver $75,000 in repetitive annualized (monthly) client fees. Currently processing over 20,000 monthly business clients in North America. Established: 1949 (US), 1991 (CAN) - Franchising Since: 1963 (US), 1991 (CAN) - No.

of Units: Franchised: 40 - Franchise Fee: $54,500 - Royalty: 9%, 2% adv. - Total Inv: $20,000 plus marketing services optional - Financing: Assistance provided.

DELOITTE & TOUCHE
Ste. 1700, 5140 Yonge St., North York, ON, M2N 6L7. Contact: Allen D. Bossin, Chairperson-Metro Toronto Retail Sector Committee - Tel: (416) 512-3477. Also contact: Rajiv Mathur, Senior Manager - Franchise Services - Tel: (416) 512-3460, Telecopier: (416) 229-2524. Chartered accountants and management consultants to the retail industry. Established: pre 1900.

Allen D. Bossin (416) 512-3477 - *Chairperson*
Metro Toronto Retail Sector Committee

Rajiv Mathur (416) 512-3460 - *Senior Manager*
Franchise Services

Chartered Accountants
Management Consultants

Deloitte & Touche

North York City Centre,
5140 Yonge St. Suite 1700, North York, ON

E. K. WILLIAMS & CO. LTD.
EKW Systems
Ste. 200, 15047 Marine Dr., White Rock, BC, V4B 1C5. Contact: Wayne Deane-Freeman, Pres. - Tel: (604) 535-7070, Fax: (604) 535-2881. Manual and computerized bookkeeping, accounting and tax preparation systems for small to medium sized businesses (industry specific). Financial and operational management consulting and training services. Established: 1968 - Franchising Since: 1969 - No. of Units: 29 - Franchise Fee: $10,000 - $25,000 - Royalty: 8% - 3% of sales - Total Inv: $25,000 - $500,000 (depending on established client list and volume of business) - Financing: Yes, 50% of franchise fee; up to 50% of client list.

H & R BLOCK CANADA, INC.
Ste. 200, 340 Midpark Way S.E., Calgary, AB, T2X 1P1. Contact: Arthur Arnott, Franc. Dir. - Tel: (403) 254-8689. Preparation of individual tax returns and related services. Established: 1955 - Franchising Since: 1962 - No. of Units: Company Owned: 487 - Franchised: 384 - Approx. Inv: varies - Royalty: 50/30 with items furnished by the company for operating the franchise.

INVESTORS GROUP FINANCIAL SERVICES INC.
Main Floor, 33 Yonge St., Toronto, ON, M5E 1G4. Contact: Ken Beck, Reg. Mgr. - Tel: (416) 860-1668. Financial planning and tax planning. Wealth creation strategies. Established: 1894 - Franchising Since: 1940 - No. of Units: Franchised: 85 - Franchise Fee: $1,000 - Total Inv: $1,000 - Financing: No.

LGC
LGC Corp.
110 Hannover Dr., St. Catharines, ON, L2W 1A6. Contact: Ron Robertson, Fran. Coord. - Tel: (800) 361-8805, (905) 687-7366. Our unique system provides the direction, marketing, support and technical backup you need to build the right client base and run a profitable accounting and tax practice. Established: 1978 - Franchising Since: 1990 - No. of Units: Franchised: 93 - Franchise Fee: $40,000 - Royalty: 10% to 4% - Total Inv: $40,000 plus $5,000 work. cap. - Financing: Yes.

MONEY TIME ACCOUNTING & TAX OFFICES *
Money Time, Inc.
33 King St. W., Ste. 204, Bolton, ON, L7E 1C7. Contact: M.M. Giammattolo, Pres. - Tel: (905) 857-5823. Offering professional & personalized accounting, tax, financial & consulting services to clients at affordable fees. Established: 1995 - Franchising Since: 1995 - No. of Units: Company Owned: 1 - Franchise Fee: $19,500 - Royalty: 5%, 0% adv. - Total Inv: $10,000 to $20,000 - Financing: No.

ORENSTEIN & PARTNERS CHARTERED ACCOUNTANTS
595 Bay St., Ste. 300, Toronto, ON, M5G 2C2. Contact: Dennis Epstein, Partner - Tel: (416) 596-1711. A full service accounting and audit firm servicing entrepreneurial clients; assisting clients to explore business opportunities; planning for profits and assisting financial needs. Business Advisors.

PADGETT BUSINESS SERVICES
Padgett Business Services of Canada, Ltd.
5580 Kennedy Rd., Ste. 2, Mississauga, ON, L4Z 2A9. Contact: John Higgins, Dir. Fran. Dev. - Tel: (905) 890-5777. Small business - accounting, consulting, and tax. Established: 1966 - Franchising Since: 1975 - No. of Units: Franchised: 340 - Franchise Fee: $34,500 - Royalty: 9% - Total Inv: $50,000 - Financing: Assistance.

PARTNERS IN SMALL BUSINESS *
5225 Orbitor Dr., Unit 10, Mississauga, ON, L4W 4Y8. Contact: Ian W. Bold, Dir., Bus. Dev. - Tel: (905) 602-6408. Accounting and business services. Business planning, financial planning services. Corporate and personal income tax preparation. Credit management services. Business management systems. Established: 1991 - Franchising Since: 1992 - No. of Units: Franchised: 12 - Franchise Fee: from $14,500 to $40,000 full concept - Royalty: 8% services, 4% office products - Total Inv: $50,000 - Financing: Yes.

U & R TAX SERVICES LTD.
1345 Pembina Hwy., Winnipeg, MB, R3T 2B6. Contact: Dan Gagnon, Franc. Dir. - Tel: (204) 949-3636. Income tax preparation. Tax refunds. Income tax & bookkeeping courses (in class & correspondence). Established: 1972 - Franchising Since: 1973 - No. of Units: Company Owned: 25 - Franchised: 41 - Franchise Fee: $2,500 - $7,500 - Royalty: 2% - 40% - Total Inv: $5,000 - $10,000 - Financing: No.

ADVERTISING/PUBLISHING SERVICES

BADGE MAKER, LE BADGE
Canadian Badge Maker Ltd., The
2806 West King Edward Ave., Vancouver, BC, V6L 1T9. Contact: Paul McCrea, Pres. - Tel: (604) 733-4323. Manufacturers of badges, award plaques & personalized corporate recognition products. Established: 1978 - Franchising Since: 1978 - No. of Units: Franchised: 16 - Franchise Fee: $25,000 incl. fee, inven., training & all equip. - Royalty: 6%, 2% adv. - Total Inv: $25,000 - Financing: 50%.

BINGO BUGLE NEWSPAPER
P.O. Box 158, 26 Hale Road, Brampton, ON, L6W 3M1. Contact: Dawna Beatty, Master Fran. - Tel: (905) 457-3627, Fax: (905) 457-1479. Publish your own bingo newspaper - you provide local stories, we provide editorial from a staff of 14 writers. Established: 1979 (US), 1991 (CAN) - Franchising Since: 1991 - No. of Units: Company Owned: 2 - Franchised: 6 - Franchise Fee: $6,000 to $8,000 - Royalty: 8% monthly maintenance - Total Inv: $20,000 to $30,000 (incl. computer & training) - Financing: N/A.

DIGIAD *
Digital Advertising, Inc.
67 Kyla Cres., Markham, ON, L3S 2Y4. Contact: Mr. William Curry, Pres. - Tel: (905) 477-5989, Fax: (905) 477-5035. Provide Internet advertising, marketing and sales. Full marketing and sales support programs. Never touch a computer. Proven money maker. Give us a call today. We succeed when you succeed. Established: 1995 - Franchising Since: 1995 - No. of Units: Company Owned: 1 - Franchised: 3 - Franchise Fee: $13,999 - Royalty: 3%, 4% adv. - Total Inv: $13,999 turnkey package included - Financing: Yes.

FLYER NETWORK
Flyer Network, Inc.
8 Glengrove Circle, St. Catharines, ON, L2G 2Y9. Contact: Alan Beech, Adv. Mgr. - Tel: (905) 688-0743. Direct mail advertising, printing and distribution system to consumers. High profit, no overhead, work from home. Established: 1985 - Franchising Since: 1989 - No. of Units: Company Owned: 1 - Franchised: 7 - Franchise Fee: $10,000 - $22,000 - Royalty: 4% - Total Inv: $10,000 - $22,000 - Financing: Available.

GOOD NEWS ADVERTISING & MAILING INC.
36C Stoffel Dr., Rexdale, ON, M9W 1A8. Contact: Thom Tyson, Fran. Dir. - Tel: (416) 248-5555, Fax: (416) 248-5558. Bulk mailing of direct response advertising. Established: 1984 - Franchising Since: 1989 - No. of Units: Company Owned: 2 - Franchised: 27 - Total Inv: from $7,500 depending on size of area - Financing: No.

NCC PROMOTIONS
425 Britannia Rd. E., Ste. 124, Mississauga, ON, L4Z 3E7. Contact: David Shoniker - Tel: (800) 265-2312. Marketing, sales and service of register roll product promotions: Full colour advertising for grocery store, mass merchandiser, bank machine and other receipt rolls. Clients range from small business to Fortune 500 companies. Established: 1987 - Franchising Since: 1992 - No. of Units: Company Owned: 2 - Franchised: 21 - Franchise Fee: $2,100 - $5,000 - Royalty: No royalties - shared revenues (up to 43% of gross sales) - Total Inv: est. $2,500 - $6,000 incl. fees - Financing: Yes.

SENIORS CHOICE NEWSMAGAZINE, THE
Egress Enterprises Inc.
1476 Latta Rd., R.R. 2, Kelowna, BC, V1Y 7R1. Contact: Joel A. Rickard, Publisher - Tel: (604) 765-6065. A free monthly newsmagazine intertwining senior centres-adult communities and the general senior public with a current event-informative lifestyles publication with a proven powerful cornerstone format. Established: 1989 - Franchising Since: 1992 - No. of Units: Company Owned: 3 (5 BC areas now open) - Franchise Fee: $25,000 and up depending on territory - Royalty: 5%, 3% adv./promotion - Total Inv: $25,000 - $150,000 dep. on area - Financing: Some.

TAKE-A-CARD
Take-A-Card Ontario
200 Jane St., Toronto, ON, M6S 3Y9. Contact: Gary Brown, Gen. Mgr. - Tel: (416) 462-4747. Display advertising system provides an outlet for small businesses to advertise their services. Established: 1993 - Franchising Since: 1994 - No. of Units: Company Owned: 5 - Franchised: 4 - Franchise Fee: $15,000 - Royalty: 5% - Total Inv: $20,000.

TILL-TAPE ADS®
T.T. Ads Marketing Inc.
#727, 1489 Marine Dr., West Vancouver, BC, V7T 1B8. Contact: R.E. (Bob) Peterson, Owner/Mgr - Tel: (604) 925-2063, Fax: (604) 925-1363. Sell & print advertisements on cash register receipt tapes used by major grocery stores. Established: 1981 - Franchising Since: 1984 - No. of Units: Company Owned: 1 - Franchised: 6 - Franchise Fee: Min. $10,000 - Royalty: No royalty, shared revenues - Total Inv: $10,000 per 10 programs first year of five, plus $1,000 per program in excess - Financing: Yes.

TODAY'S SENIORS NEWSPAPER
467 Speers Rd., Oakville, ON, L6K 3S4. Contact: Don Wall, Fran. Dir. - Tel: (800) 387-7682. Monthly newspaper for people 50 plus. Established: 1985 - Franchising Since: 1991 - No. of Units: Company Owned: 3 - Franchised: 3 - Franchise Fee: from $25,000 depending on size of market - Royalty: 4% of revenue - Total Inv: $50,000 + $50,000 working cap. - Financing: No.

AUTOMOBILE RENTAL & LEASING

ASSOCIATED CANADIAN CAR RENTAL OPERATORS (A.C.C.R.O.)
385 Fairway Rd. S., Unit #6, Kitchener, ON, N2C 2N9. Contact: Sid Kenmir, Gen Mgr. - Tel: (519) 893-3700. Help for car rental operators. Rental supplies and forms-rental fleet insurance - rental info meetings - rental software programmes - P.A.I. and cargo protection - loss prevention - provincial and federal lobbyist - rental procedure consultant. Established: 1986 - Recruiting Since: 1986 - No. of Units: Member Owned: 110 - No joining fee: small monthly fee.

AVIS CAR & TRUCK RENTAL
Aviscar, Inc.
1 Convair Dr. E., Etobicoke, ON, M9W 6Z9. Contact: Doug Jacques, Nat'l. Fran. Mgr. - Tel: (416) 213-4273, Fax: (416) 213-8515. Car & light truck rental. Established: 1946 - No. of Units: Company Owned: 53 - Franchised: 134 - Franchise Fee: varies - Royalty: 3% admin., 5% nat'l. adv. - Total Inv: avg. inv. of $125,000 - Financing: No.

BUDGET RENT A CAR OF CANADA LTD.
185 The West Mall, Ste. 900, Etobicoke, ON, M9C 5L5. Contact: Ron Groves, Mgr., License Div. - Tel: (416) 622-3366. Rental of cars and trucks. Established: 1962 - Franchising Since: 1962 - No. of Units: 375 - Franchise Fee: $15,000 ($500,000 credit line) - Royalty: 10% gross revenue - Total Inv: Varies.

BYWAYS RENT A CAR
Byways Automotive Group Ltd.
2156 Barrington St., Halifax, NS, B3K 2W4. Contact: Ed Malloy, Fran. Sales - Tel: (902) 429-0092 or (800) 668-4233. Daily car & truck rental. Market specialist, volume purchasing programs for fleet, insurance, supplies, advertising etc. Established: 1980 - Franchising Since: 1992 - No. of Units: Company Owned: 4 - Franchised: 10 - Franchise Fee: $1 - Royalty: 2.5% + admin. fee - Region/Area: master franchise rights available - Financing: No.

DISCOUNT CAR AND TRUCK RENTALS
Discount Car & Truck Rentals Ltd.
3000 Langstaff Rd., Ste. 16, Concord, ON, L4K 4R7. Contact: John Stanaitis, Dir. of Fran. Oper. - Tel: (905) 738-0123, ext. 225. Car and truck rental. Established: 1980 - Franchising Since: 1984 - No. of Units: Company Owned: 30 - Franchised: 145 - Franchise Fee: varies market to market - Royalty: Canada 8%, U.S.A. 6% - Total Inv: varies - Financing: Yes.

DOLLAR RENT A CAR
Dollar Rent A Car (Canada) Ltd.
1580 Yonge St., Toronto, ON, M4T 1Z8. Contact: Richard Pett, Dir. of Fran. - Tel: (416) 969-1190. One of the largest international car rental companies. Franchisee programs cover fleet purchase, insurance, administration, marketing and training. Established: 1969/1966(US) - Franchising Since: 1990/1966(US) - No. of Units: Company Owned: 6 - Franchised: 19 - Franchise Fee: $25,000 min. - Royalty: 7%, 2% nat'l adv. - Total Inv: varies - Financing: No.

HERTZ CANADA LTD.
5403 Eglinton Ave. West, Etobicoke, ON, M9C 5K6. Contact: Geno Diraddo, Dir. of Mktg. & Sales - Tel: (416) 620-9600. Car and truck, leasing and rental. Established: 1960 - No. of Units: 170.

HOJ CAR AND TRUCK RENTALS/LEASING
HOJ Franchise Systems
434 Steeles Ave. W., Thornhill, ON, L4J 6X6. Contact: Bob Mauro, Dir. of Fran. - Tel: (416) 465-7368, 1-800-387-4926. Short term vehicle rental (car and trucks). Also long term retail leasing. Established: 1966 - Franchising Since: 1984 - No. of Units: Franchised: 43 - Franchise Fee: $10,000 - $50,000 - Royalty: 6%, 2% adv. - Total Inv: $80,000 - $150,000 - Financing: Fleet financing.

PHOENIX CAR & TRUCK RENTALS
2499 Dufferin St., Toronto, ON, M6B 3R3. Contact: Howard Wolfe, Pres. - Tel: (416) 785-3139. Car and truck rentals. Also insurance replacement specialists. Established: 1987 - Franchising Since: 1988 - No. of Units: Company Owned: 4 - Franchised: 8 - Franchise Fee: varied - Royalty: 5%, adv. varied - Total Inv: $65,000 min. cash required - Financing: Assistance.

RENT-A-WRECK
Practicar Systems, Inc.
400 -1509 Centre St. S.W., Calgary, AB, T2G 2E6. Contact: Tony Sansotta, V.P. - Tel: (403) 269-2262, Fax: (403) 269-2265. Rent, lease, sell used vehicles. Established: 1976 - Franchising Since: 1978 - No. of Units: Company Owned: 1 - Franchised: 76 - Franchise Fee: $10,000 - $30,000 - Royalty: 6%, 4% adv. - Total Inv: Varies - Financing: No.

A.D. (Tony) SANSOTTA
VICE PRESIDENT
OPERATIONS AND MARKETING

FORSETH MANAGMENT INC.

400, 1509 Centre Street S.W.　　Tel: (403) 269-2262
Calgary, Alberta T2G 2E6　　Fax: (403) 269-2265

THRIFTY CAR RENTAL
Thrifty Canada, Ltd.
6050 Indian Line, Mississauga, ON, L4V 1G5. Contact: Jonathan Ison, Sr. Dir., Market Dev. - Tel: (905) 612-1881, Fax: (905) 612-1893. Short term car and truck rentals. Full service franchisor providing licensees with fleet, insurance program reservation system, local marketing plus national marketing featuring Wayne Gretzky. Established: U.S. 1950, CDN. 1986 - Franchising Since: 1950 - No. of Units: Company Owned: 34 (CDN) - Franchised: 125 (CDN) - Franchise Fee: $15,000 - $250,000 - Royalty: 5% admin., 3% adv. - Total Inv: $50,000 - $300,000 - Financing: Vehicle acquisition only.

Thrifty Canada, Ltd.
6050 Indian Line
Mississauga, Ontario
L4V 1G5
(905) 612-1881
1-800-667-5925
Fax (905) 612-1893
Out of Town Reservations:
1-800-FOR-CARS

Jonathan S. Ison
Senior Director,
Market Development

TILDEN RENT-A-CAR SYSTEMS LTD.
250 Bloor St., E, Ste. 1300, Toronto, ON, M4W 1E6. Contact: Vince Bunyan, V.P. Central Oper. - Tel: (416) 922-2600, Ext. 228. Automobile rental. Established: 1924 - Franchising Since: 1960 - No. of Units: Company Owned: 55 - Franchised: 345 - Royalty: 8% cars, 4% trucks.

AUTOMOTIVE: LUBRICATION & TUNE UP

GREASE PIT, THE
3485 Harvester Rd., Unit 4, Burlington, ON, L7N 3T3. Contact: M.M. Giammattolo, Pres. - Tel: (905) 634-LUBE (5823). 15 minute fast lube and oil change service. Established: 1989 - Franchising Since: 1991 - No. of Units: Company Owned: 4 - Franchise Fee: $19,500 - Royalty: 5%, 0% adv. - Total Inv: $30,000 - $65,000.

LUBE FACTORY, THE
Lube Factory International Inc., The
1180 Stellar Dr., Unit 10, Newmarket, ON, L3Y 7B9. Contact: J. Petrie, V.P. Corp. Dev. - Tel: (905) 898-3590. Drive thru oil change centres for automobiles & light trucks. Established: 1980 - Franchising Since: 1983 - No. of Units: Company Owned: 2 - Franchised: 14 - Franchise Fee: $20,000 - Royalty: 7% of gross sales - Total Inv: $135,000 - $150,000 - Financing: Yes.

MINIT-TUNE & BRAKE AUTO CENTRES
Minit-Tune International Corp.
398 W. Fifth Avenue, Vancouver, BC, V5Y 1J5. Contact: Roy A. Shand, Pres. - Tel: (604) 873-5551. Tune-ups, lube/oil/filter, brakes and minor engine repairs. Established: 1976 - Franchising Since: 1976 - No. of Units: Franchised: 57 - Franchise Fee: $20,000 - Royalty: 5% service fee + 5% adv. - Total Inv: $95,000, fran. fee plus $50,000 equip. - Financing: On equipment.

MR. LUBE
Mr. Lube, a division of Imperial Oil
210-111 Brunel Road, Mississauga, ON, L4Z 1X3. Contact: Jeff Weinman, Coord. of Fran. Dev. - Tel: (905) 890-5500. Engaged in the fast oil which offers 10 minute service and fluid maintenance of vehicles. No appointment, a selection of 18 brands of oil in multiple bay, open pit, drive thru centres offering a 21 point courtesy inspection. Established: 1976 - Franchising Since: 1978 - No. of Units: Company Owned: 32 - Franchised: 54 - Franchise Fee: $35,000 - Royalty: 7% paid weekly - Total Inv: $185,000 turn-key (incl. $35,000 fran. fee) - Financing: Letter of comfort on bank financing.

PREMIUM PLUS MOBILE OIL CHANGE INC.
Lubrichek Industries, Inc.
100 - 7382 Winston St., Burnaby, BC, V5A 2G9. Contact: John Craine, Dir., Dealer Dev. - Tel: (604) 420-3435, Fax: (604) 420-5221. Mobile oil change and lubrication service catering to the general public as well as commercial and fleets. A 21 point safety check and a wide variety of related products are available from the fully equipped store/van. Established: 1994 - Franchising Since: 1994 - No. of Units: Company Owned: 3 - Franchised: 11 - Franchise Fee: $19,500 - Royalty: approx. 5% of gross sales - Total Inv: $29,500 + $3,000 op. cap. - Financing: Yes to qualified.

QUAKER STATE MINIT-LUBE
Minit-Lube Ontario Inc.
130 Dearborn Place, Waterloo, ON, N2J 4N5. Contact: Joanne Lewis, Fran. Dir. - Tel: (519) 886-0561. Franchising Since: 1977 - No. of Units: Company Owned: 4 - Franchised: 15 - Franchise Fee: $25,000 - Royalty: 5% - Total Inv: $145,000 - Financing: Yes.

AUTOMOTIVE: MUFFLER SHOPS

CARLINE MUFFLERS & MORE
Div. of Walker Exhausts
500 Conestoga Blvd., Cambridge, ON, N1R 5T7. Contact: Glen J. Richstone, Div. Mgr. - Tel: (519) 621-3360 or (800) 265-8686. Retail automotive undercar specialists in exhaust, shocks and brakes. Established: 1981 - Franchising Since: 1981 - No. of Units: Franchised: 97 - Approx. Inv: $40,000 - Financing: Inven., equip., & signage.

MIDAS MUFFLER SHOP
Midas (Canada), Inc.
105 Commander Blvd., Agincourt, ON, M1S 3X8. Contact: Dan Hopkins, Dir. Realty - Tel: (416) 291-4261. Exhaust, brake, suspension and front end specialists. Established: 1960 - Franchising Since: 1958 - No. of Units: Company Owned: 35 - Franchised: 207 - Franchise Fee: $25,000 - Royalty: 5% - Total Inv: $225,000.

MINUTE MUFFLER AND BRAKE
Muffler House Canada Ltd.
1600 - 3rd Ave., S., Lethbridge, AB, T1J 0L2. Contact: R. Sloan, V.P. Sales & Mktg. - Tel: (403) 329-1020. Retail exhaust, brake & shock absorber business. Great emphasis on customer service, quality and more than competitive prices. Established: 1968 - Franchising Since: 1977 - No. of Units: Company Owned: 4 - Franchised: 122 - Franchise Fee: $5,000 - $25,000 - Royalty: 0% of sales, 4% of purchase price - Total Inv: $120,000 - $150,000 on average - Financing: Protections, 5 year business plans etc.

MONSIEUR MUFFLER
Div. Autostock Inc.
8288 Boul Pie IX, Montreal, PQ, H1Z 3T6. Contact: Normand Paquette or Yvon Jutras, V.P./Fran. Dir. - Tel: (514) 593-8000. Mufflers, brakes, alignment, tires, shocks sales and installation. Established: 1956 - Franchising Since: 1976 - No. of Units: Company Owned: 16 - Franchised: 65 - Franchise Fee: $10,000 - Royalty: 5% & 2% - Total Inv: $300,000 - $500,000 - Financing: Yes.

OCTO FREINS SILENCIEUX, OCTO BRAKES MUFFLERS
Autostock, Inc.
8288 Blvd., Pie IX, Montreal, PQ, H1Z 3T6. Contact: Daniel Montmarquette, General Manager - Tel: (514) 593-3809, (800) 363-7131 ext. 809, Fax: (514) 326-8118. Specialist in repairing brakes, mufflers, shock absorbers, front-end and under the car repairs. Established: 1971 - Franchising Since: 1971 - No. of Units: Franchised: 48 - Financing: Bank.

SPEEDY MUFFLER KING CANADA LTD.
Speedy Muffler King Inc.
365 Bloor St. East, Toronto, ON, M4W 3M7. Contact: S. Noble, Dir. - Tel: (416) 961-1133 or (800) 387-1410. Established: 1956 - Franchising Since: 1990 - No. of Units: Company Owned: 150 - Franchised: 5 - Franchise Fee: $20,000 - Royalty: 5%, 5% adv. - Total Inv: approx. $180,000 - Financing: Through chartered banks.

THRUWAY MUFFLERCENTRE
Maremont Exhaust Products
3600A Lakeshore Blvd. W., Etobicoke, ON, M8W 4Y8. Contact: Sandy Bragg, Franchise Dev. - Tel: (416) 255-9555. Muffler specialty shop, independently owned and operated coast to coast, offering a lifetime guarantee, nationwide. Established: 1954 - Franchising Since: 1976 - No. of Units: Associated: 90 - Development Fee: $5,995 - Royalty: None - Total Inv: $50,000 cash - Financing: Balance by bank financing.

AUTOMOTIVE: PRODUCTS AND SERVICES

ACTIVE TIRE & AUTO CENTRES, INC.
580 Evans Ave., Toronto, ON, M8W 2W1. Contact: Ralph Chiodo, Michael Claener, Pres., Exec. V.P. & G.M. - Tel: (416) 255-5581. Tire sales, automotive services and repair. Member of ACF. Established: 1982 - Franchising Since: 1983 - No. of Units: Company Owned: 4 - Franchised: 15 - Franchise Fee: $25,000 - Royalty: 5% gross sales - Total Inv: $105,000 - Financing: No.

APPLE AUTO GLASS LTD.
360 Applewood Cres., Concord, ON, L4K 4V2. Contact: Calvin Hughes, Pres. - Tel: (905) 669-7800, Fax: (905) 669-7821. Auto glass and upholstery. Established: 1983 - Franchising Since: 1983 - No. of Units: Franchised: 125.

APPLE POLISHING SYSTEMS
Apple Polishing Systems Canada Inc.
60 Marycroft Ave., Ste. 7 & 8, Woodbridge, ON, L4L 5Y5. Contact: K.C. Schertenberg Jr., Dir. of Operations - Tel: (905) 850-2001. Mobile paint rejuvenation, restoration and protective finishes for automotive, marine, aviation and other painted surfaces. Established: 1978 - Offering Dealerships Since: 1978 - No. of Units: Company Owned: 1 - No. of Dealerships: 100 in Canada, 6,000+ in the U.S. - Dealership Fee: $3,465 includes all training, technical, marketing, business management and ongoing support - Total Inv: Minimum $7,980 and up includes taxes - Financing: Financial assistance is available.

AUTO APPEARANCE CENTRE
Auto Appearance Centre Ltd.
304 Stafford Dr. N., Lethbridge, AB, T1H 2A6. Contact: Mary Jane Billingsley, Partner - Tel: (403) 320-7805, Fax: (403) 328-6766. Automotive detailing, shampoos, shines, windshield repair and replacement, pinstriping, (total line) moulding, vinyl repair and dyeing, undercoating, rustproofing, and window tinting. Training included. Established: 1987 - Franchising Since: 1988 - No. of Units: Company Owned: 1 - Franchise Fee: $20,000 - Royalty: 4%, 1% adv. - Total Inv: $40,000 - Financing: No.

AUTOMAX
7025 Ontario St. E., Montreal, PQ, H1N 2B3. Contact: Bencit Bouchard, Mktg. Coord. - Programs - Tel: (514) 256-5031, Fax: (514) 256-8469. Jobber/retailer of automotive accessories and parts. Franchising Since: 1989 - No. of Units: 28.

AUTOPRO REPAIR CENTRE
UAP Inc.
7025 Ontario St., E., Montreal, PQ, H1N 2B3. Contact: Denis Bellemore, Nat'l. Dir. - Tel: (514) 256-5031, Fax: (514) 256-5497. A perfect add-on program on under-the-car specialties for a regular service station or independent repair shop. Offers marketing and advertising assistance along with lifetime warranties in brakes, mufflers, suspensions, front-end and front wheel drive parts. UAP Inc. Established: 1926 - Franchising Since: 1983 - No. of Units: Franchised: 600 - Franchise Fee: $4,995 - Adv: $1,800 adv. fee per year - Total Inv: $8,000 - $10,000 - Financing: No.

BUDGET BRAKE & MUFFLER
Ste. 422 - 4940 Canada Way, Burnaby, BC, V5G 4K7. Contact: W. Swanson or L. Vance, Pres/Oper. Mgr. - Tel: (604) 294-6114, Fax: (604) 294-1648. Retail automotive service. Brake & muffler specialists. Established: 1969 - Franchising Since: 1972 - No. of Units: Company Owned: 2 - Franchised: 23 - Franchise Fee: $25,000 - Total Min. Inv: $115,000 equip, $40,000 inv., $10,000 leasehold - Royalty: 4%, 4% adv. - Financing: Thru financial institutions.

CALIFORNIA CUSTOM CLEANING
64 Craiglee Dr., Scarborough, ON, M1N 2M3. Contact: Rick Meloff, Owner/Operator - Tel: (416) 267-1339. Auto-truck-marine-aircraft and awning cleaning & polishing. Complete mobile service. Established: 1987 - No. of Units: Company Owned: 1.

CAP-IT LIGHT TRUCK IMPROVEMENT CENTRES (CAP-IT ACCESSORY CENTRES)
Cap-It Franchise International, Inc.
P.O. Box 8000, Unit 527, Abbotsford, BC, V2S 6H1. Contact: Henry Funk, Pres. - Tel: (604) 850-1202. Retail/wholesale, 8,000 light truck accessories & truck caps. Serving the retail public and the automotive jobber market. Established: 1973 - Franchising Since: 1990 - No. of Units: Company Owned: 1 - Franchised: 7 - Franchise Fee: $25,000 - Royalty: 5%, 2% nat. adv. - Total Inv: $210,000 - Financing: No.

CERTIGARD CAR REPAIR (PETRO-CANADA)
111-5th Ave. S.W., Calgary, AB, T2P 3E3. Contact: Steven Keith, Mgr., Certigard Dev. - Tel: (403) 296-4259. Certigard is a one-stop convenience car repair concept with a nationwide franchise network of service bay outlets supported by Petro-Canada. Established: 1973 - Franchising Since: 1987 - No. of Units: Company Owned: 2 - Franchised: 146 - Franchise Fee: $16,000 - Royalty: 5% of gross sales, 2% adv. - Total Inv: $125,000 ($65,000 cash) - Financing: No, but assistance is provided.

OIL GARD CANADA LTD.

- Annually Applied Automotive Rust Prevention
- Exclusive "Classic" Drip and "Formula II" No Drip
- Add to existing auto operations or free standing specialty shop
- No Royalties and Full Training
- Investments start at $5,000.00
- Over Sixty locations and Growing

MASTER LICENSEES REQUIRED FOR QUEBEC, MARITIMES, CENTRAL WEST AND BRITISH COLUMBIA

CONTACT: NATIONAL OFFICE AT 4056 Meadowbrook Drive, Suite #101 London, Ont. N6L 1E1
(519) 652-9944 OR 1-800-887-2304

"BECAUSE RUST NEVER SLEEPS"™

COAST TO COAST COLLISION CENTRES *
Coast To Coast Franchise Services Inc.
120 King Edward St. E., Winnipeg, MB, R3R 0N8. Contact: Terry Smith, Pres. - Tel: (204) 788-0080, Fax: (204) 788-4355. Conversion franchising of existing body shops. Established: 1990 - Franchising Since: 1990 - No. of Units: Company Owned: 11 - Franchised: 16 - Franchise Fee: $5,000 - Royalty: 1% - Total Inv: Varies - Financing: No.

COBRA CAR PROTECTION CENTRES
1075 Queensway Ave. E., Unit #12, Mississauga, ON, L4Y 4C8. Contact: Sven Sverdrup, Pres. - Tel: (905) 273-7878. Automotive appearance services & accessories, featuring Protectoil rustproofing and related services and Cobra Truck Accessories. Established: 1989 - Franchising Since: 1992 - No. of Units: Company Owned: 1 - Franchised: 3 - Franchise Fee: $12,500 - Royalty: None - Total Inv: franc. fee plus $30,000 equip. & inven., $7,500 leaseholds - Financing: Yes.

CRESTLINE VENTURES CORPORATION
802-57th St. E, Saskatoon, SK, S7K 5Z1. Contact: Ken Sawatsky, Pres. - Tel: (306) 934-5875. Ambulance, rescue vehicle and paratransit bus sales. Established: 1975 - Franchising Since: 1991 - No. of Units: Company Owned: 4 - Franchise Fee: $30,000 - Royalty: average 1.2% of sales - Total Inv: $150,000 - $590,000 - Financing: No.

FIRESTONE TIRE AND AUTOMOTIVE CENTRES
5770 Hurontario St., Ste. 400, Mississauga, ON, L5R 3G5. Contact: Jim West, Mgr. Admin. - Tel: (905) 890-1990. Sale of tires and automotive service to the public. Established: 1919 - Franchising Since: 1974 - No. of Units: 115 - Approx. Inv: $100,000 - Financing: Yes.

GOODTURN RIDE CENTRES
Goodturn Management, Inc.
2345 Barton St. East, Hamilton, ON, L8E 2W8. Contact: Don McLaughlin, Pres. - Tel: (905) 573-2224. Under car care specialists. Quality workmanship at fair prices. Experts in brakes, alignments, shocks, tires, exhaust, steering and frame straightening. Original inventor of lifetime warranty on brakes and mufflers. Established: 1978 - Franchising Since: 1990 - No. of Units: Company Owned: 1 - Franchised: 6 - Franchise Fee: $7,500 - Royalty: 6% gross sales, franchisor pays national advertising - Total Inv: $100,000 inclusive of leaseholds, stock, equipment and fran. fee - Financing: Yes, complete package through franchisor.

GOODYEAR CERTIFIED AUTO SERVICE CENTRE
Goodyear of Canada
10 Four Seasons Place, Etobicoke, ON, M9B 6G2. Contact: Fran. Dir. - Tel: (416) 626-4611. Retail tire sales and automotive services. Franchising Since: 1972 - No. of Units: Company Owned: 113 - Franchised: 45 - Royalty: 3% - Total Inv: $100,000.

HAMILTON RADIATOR SERVICE LTD.
624 Parkdale Ave., N., Hamilton, ON, L8H 5Z3. Contact: Mr. Leigh Hammond, Pres. - Tel: (905) 549-4181. Manufacture, service and repairs to radiators as well as a complete cooling system specialist (includes automotive air conditioning and gas tank repairs). Established: 1955 - Franchising Since: 1983 - No. of Units: Company Owned: 11 - Franchised: 7 - Franchise Fee: $12,000 - Royalty: 5% + 5% adv. - Total Inv: $65,000 - Financing: Bank financing for qualified applicants.

LEBEAU VITRES D'AUTOS
Div. of Autostock
8288 Boul Pie IX, Montreal, PQ, H1Z 3T6. Contact: Lescarbeau S., Dir. - Tel: (514) 593-8000. Sales and installation of windshields, car radio, alarm system, anti-theft system upholstery, cellular phone, sun-roofs, engine remote starter. Established: 1947 - Franchising Since: 1980 - No. of Units: Company Owned: 39 - Franchised: 31 - Franchise Fee: $30,000 - Royalty: 5% plus 2% publicity - Total Inv: $150,000 excl. land & bldg.

MAACO AUTO PAINTING & BODYWORKS
MAACO Systems Canada, Inc.
5915 Airport Rd., Ste. 330, Mississauga, ON, L4V 1T1. Contact: Hermann Delisle, Fran. Dev. Mgr. - Tel: 1-800-387-6780. Production auto painting and bodywork. Established: 1972 - Franchising Since: 1972 - No. of Units: Franchised: 38 in Canada, 440 in US, 5 in Mexico, 2 in Puerto Rico - Franchise Fee: $25,000 - Royalty: 8% - Total Inv: $220,000 - Financing: No.

MASTERMECHANIC, THE
1989 Dundas St. E., Mississauga, ON, L4X 1M1. Contact: Andrew Wanie, Pres. - Tel: (905) 629-3773, Fax: (905) 629-3864. Professional automotive services, general repairs for domestic & imported cars & vans, hi-tech equipment & government licensed mechanics. Established: 1980 - Franchising Since: 1985 - No. of Units: Company Owned: 3 - Franchised: 21 - Franchise Fee: $25,000 - Royalty: 6% on sales - Total Inv: $100,000 - $150,000 - Financing: Assistance with local banks.

MISTER FRONT-END LTD.
192 N. Queen St., Etobicoke, ON, M9C 1A8. Contact: Gerry R. Jones, Pres. - Tel: (416) 622-9999. Automotive and truck alignment, suspension repair and power steering box rebuilding. Established: 1973 - Franchising Since: 1980 - Franchise Fee: $15,000 - Royalty: 5% - Total Inv: $120,000 - Financing: Yes.

OIL GARD ANTI-RUST CANADA LTD.
4056 Meadowbrook Drive, Ste. #101, London, ON, N6L 1E1. Contact: Donald F. Hawken, Pres. - Tel: (800) 887-2304, (519) 652-9944, Fax: (519) 652-9614. Automotive rust protection. Established: 1976 - Franchising Since: 1983 - No. of Units: Franchised: 63 - Franchise Fee: $500 to $25,000 - Total Inv: $5,000 - $50,000 equip, supplies, product, lic. fee. - Financing: On approved applicants.(See our ad on page 181.)

OIL-TECH INDUSTRIES, LTD.
9 Gowan St., Barrie, ON, L4N 2N9. Contact: John Robb, Pres. - Tel: (705) 721-0058. Automotive rust control and appearance for vehicles. Established: 1982 - Franchising Since: 1984 - Franchise Fee: None - Royalty: None - Total Inv: $7,200 and up - Financing: None.

OILTRELL AUTO COSMETIC CENTERS
5 Peacock Bay, St. Catharines, ON, L2M 7N8. Contact: George Kelmer, Owner - Tel: (905) 938-1444. Automotive detailing centres specializing in annual rustproofing (The Neutralizer) and guaranteed five-yr acrylic print glazing (The Shine), plus a host of other exclusive premium quality car care products for the marine and the used and new markets. Established: 1984 - Franchising Since: 1986 - No. of Units: Company Owned: 1 - Franchised: 12 - Franchise Fee: $5,000 - Total Inv: $10,000 - Financing: Yes.

OK TIRE STORES
OK Tire Stores, Inc.
9430 - 198 St., Langley, BC, V1M 3C8. Contact: Denis Marshall, V.P. Fran. - Tel: (604) 888-3000. Tires and mechanical services, brakes, wheel alignments, shocks, exhaust, suspension, front fender repair. Established: 1952 - Franchising Since : 1952- No. of Units: 97 - Franchise Fee: $3,500 - Total Inv: $110,000 equip., inv. - Financing: No.

ONTARIO AUTO COLLISION
1124 Rymal Rd. E., Hamilton, ON, L8W 3N7. Contact: Tony Mercanti, Dir., Fran. Oper. - Tel: (905) 388-2264. Autobody repair and refinishing. Established: 1960 - Franchising Since: 1992 - No. of Units: Company Owned: 6 - Franchised: 5 - Franchise Fee: $25,000 - Royalty: 6%, 1% sales/mktg., 1% finance/acctg. - Total Inv: $215,000 includes fran. fee and $115,000 equip.

PERMA-SHINE
P.O. Box 21129 - 6677 Meadowvale Town Ctr. Cir., Mississauga, ON, L5N 2W0. Contact: Brian Batstone, Pres. - Tel: (905) 877-2403, Fax: (905) 877-8127. Car detailing including permanent shine and rust-protection including oiling. Established: 1974 - Franchising Since: 1976 - No. of Units: Company Owned: 1 - Franchised: 46 - Franchise Fee: $5,000 - Royalty: $200 flat fee monthly - Total Inv: Varies - Financing: No.

RIP N' TEAR VINYL REPAIR *
Rip N' Tear Vinyl Repair Systems, Inc.
P.O. Box 8000 - 596, Abbotsford, BC, V2S 6H1. Contact: Brian Hann, Dir. of Fran. - Tel: (604) 852-6285. Mobile service repairing vinyl, plastics & leather - automotive dashboards, seating. Established: 1993 - Franchising Since: 1994 - No. of Units: Company Owned: 1 - Franchised: 3 - Franchise Fee: $15,000 - Royalty: $250 monthly - Total Inv: $20,000 - Financing: No.

RUST CHECK CENTER
Rust Check Canada Inc.
109 Wilkinson Rd., Brampton, ON, L6T 4X1. Contact: Robert Wowk, Nat'l. Sales Mgr. - Tel: (905) 456-7878, Fax: (905) 456-9027. Rust inhibiting and vehicle detailing. Established: 1976 - Franchising Since: 1981 - No. of Units: Company Owned: 3 - Franchised: 277 - Franchise Fee: $15,000 to $40,000 - Royalty: None - Total Inv: $20,000 to $50,000 - Financing: Limited.

SHINE FACTORY, THE
Shine Factory Systems, Inc.
3519 14th St. S.W., Calgary, AB, T2T 3W2. Contact: Bruce Cousens, Pres. - Tel: (403) 243-3030. Automotive polish and detail state of the art car wash and appearance center location requiring $350,000. Regular appearance centers requires $75,000 - $100,000 investment. Established: 1979 - Franchising Since: 1979 - No. of Units: Franchised: 24 - Franchise Fee: $10,000 - $50,000 - Royalty: 8% gross sales - Financing: No.

SNAP-ON TOOLS OF CANADA LTD.
2325 Skymark Ave., Mississauga, ON, L4W 5A9. - Tel: (800) 665-8665, Fax: (905) 238-9658. Snap-on Tools of Canada Ltd. is the Canadian subsidiary of Snap-on Incorporated, the world's largest independent manufacturer of tools & equipment for the professional technician. We are an established company, with a comprehensive product line, that developed the concept of a "showroom on wheels". A Snap-on franchise offers some unique features: a low initial franchise fee, a low fixed monthly fee, no advertising fee, financing assistance, ongoing training and assistance. Dealer business software and credit assistance programs. Established: 1931 - Franchising Since: 1993 - No. of Units: Company Owned: 22 - Franchised: 324 - Non-franchised: 76 - Franchise Fee: $4,000 - Royalty: no royalty fee, $50 monthly admin. fee - Total Inv: $107,150 to $195,000 - Financing: Financing available for certain components of initial investment.

STOP 'N STEER SHOPS
Northern Investments Ltd.
2841 E. Arthur St., Thunder Bay, ON, P7E 5P5. Contact: George Giba, Owner - Tel: (807) 623-4700. Automotive repair centres specializing in high profit required areas of automotive maintenance, brakes, steering, suspension and alignments. Offers owner training support packages, ongoing training and purchasing power. Management experience or license technician an asset. Established: 1978 - No. of Units: Company Owned: 1 - Franchised: 1 - Franchise Fee: $16,500 - Royalty: 5% - Total Inv: $150,000 - $175,000 - Financing: Assistance.

SUPERIOR TIRE AUTO FITNESS CENTRES
Superior Tire Corp.
5070 Sheppard Ave. E., Scarborough, ON, M1S 4N3. Contact: P. Hyatt, Pres. - Tel: (416) 291-9291. Tires & automotive service. Established: 1942 - Franchising Since: 1991 - No. of Units: Company Owned: 4 - Franchised: 3 - Franchise Fee: $25,000.

SURE STOP BRAKE CENTERS
Motorcade Industries Ltd.
90 Kimcourt St., Toronto, ON, M6M 5G1. Contact: Roger Williams, Fran. Dir. - Tel: (416) 614-6118. Sale of complete brake systems, suspension systems, shocks, etc. Established: 1952 - Franchising Since: 1972 - No. of Units: Franchised: 70 - Total Inv: $20,000 - Financing: Yes.

TINT KING MOTORING ACCESSORIES
Tint King of California Inc.
1950 Hwy 7, Unit #10, Concord, ON, L4K 3B2. Contact: Mr. Allan Starkman - Tel: (905) 738-5020. Tint, accessory and detail shop(s). North America's fastest growing automotive aftermarket service. Now expanding nationwide. Enter the knighthood today! Established: 1982 - Franchising Since: 1983 - No. of Units: Franchised: 29 - Franchise Fee: $25,000 - Royalty: 7% of gross sales - Total Inv: $25,000 includes territory, training, supplies, tools, advertising, field support - Financing: Yes.

TINT MASTER AND AUTO GLASS *
6033 Shawson Dr., Unit 9, Mississauga, ON, L5T 1H8. Contact: James Formosa, Pres. - Tel: (905) 670-TINT (5181), Fax: (905) 670-8468. Automotive window film - energy saver for the 90's. Comfort, image,

safety are three important needs for every driver. Film processing technology and highest quality materials provide optical clarity of film and provide years of comfort and good looks for millions of drivers. Established: 1981 - Franchising Since: 1995 - No. of Units: Company Owned: 1 - Franchised: 5 - Franchise Fee: $15,000 - Royalty: 6% - Total Inv: $80,250 which includes fran. fee - Financing: We assist in obtaining financing.

TIRES ONLY
10 Easton Road, Brantford, ON, N3P 1J5. Contact: Gail Kaufman, Mktg Mgr. - Tel: (519) 753-8487. Multi-faceted retail marketing program specializing in tire sales & service and ride control. Established: 1985 - Franchising Since: 1988 - No. of Units: Company Owned: 5 - Franchised: 9 - Franchise Fee: $10,000 retail store; $5,000 mobile pass. unit; $2,500 mobile comm. unit - Royalty: 2% retail store; 5% mobile pass. unit; 10% mobile comm. unit - Total Inv: $100,000; $65,000; $35,000 - Financing: Assistance in securing.

UNI PRO
Uni-Select, Inc.
170 boul. Industriel, Boucherville, PQ, J4B 2X3. Contact: Luc Charlebois, Dir. - Tel: (514) 641-2440. Automobile parts. Established: 1969 - Franchising Since: 1980 - No. of Units: 160 - Franchise Fee: $2,995 - Royalty: 3% adv.

VITAL PROTECTION SYSTEMS INC.
17 McEwan Dr., Bolton, ON, L7E 1H5. Contact: Curtis D. Johnson, Pres. - Tel: (905) 951-3600. Anti corrosion (rust proofing) of automobiles including undercoating, sound guard, fabric and paint protection plus liquid truck bed liner. Established: 1969 - Franchising Since: 1970 - No. of Units: Company Owned: 3 - Franchised: 15 - Franchise Fee: variable - Royalty: based on purchases - Total Inv: $25,000 - $50,000 - Financing: Yes.

WYNN'S CLASSIC CAR CARE CENTRE
Wynn's Canada Ltd.
1025 Westport Cres., Mississauga, ON, L5T 1E8. Contact: Francis Hong, Mgr. Bus. Dev. - Tel: (905) 670-4260. Automotive detailing centre which includes services such as interior/exterior shampoo, wax, scratch removal, engine shampoo, window tinting, pinstriping, hand wash, etc. Established: 1939 - Franchising Since: 1991 - No. of Units: Company Owned: 1 - Franchised: 1 - Franchise Fee: $10,000 - Royalty: 6% of gross sales - Total Inv: fran. fee plus $15,000 work. cap.

AUTOMOTIVE: TRANSMISSION REPAIR

AALL-TECH TRANSMISSION *
Aall Tech Transmission Systems, Inc.
5651 #3 Rd., Richmond, BC, V6X 2C7. Contact: Bill Byrd, Gen. Mgr. - Tel: (604) 644-0257. Automotive transmission service. Established: 1975 - Franchising Since: 1995 - No. of Units: Company Owned: 4 - Franchised: 1 - Franchise Fee: $25,000 - Royalty: 6% + 6% adv. - Total Inv: $150,000 - Financing: Through bank arrangement.

MISTER TRANSMISSION
Mister Transmission (International) Ltd.
30 Wertheim Ct., Ste. 5, Richmond Hill, ON, L4B 1B9. Contact: Kevin Brillinger, V.P. Corp. Dev. - Tel: (905) 886-1511, Fax: (905) 886-1545. Transmission repair specialists. Established: 1963 - Franchising Since: 1969 - No. of Units: Franchised: 89 - Franchise Fee: $25,000 - Royalty: 7% - Total Inv: $125,000 - Financing: Assistance.

BEVERAGES

BREWING EXPERIENCE, THE
450 Woodlawn Rd. W., #6, Guelph, ON, N1K 1A6. Contact: John Leveris, Dir., Sales & Mktg. - Tel: (519) 837-2304. Consumer do-it-yourself brewery. Traditional specialty grains and fire brewing recipes registered trademark. Established: 1989 - Franchising Since: 1990 - No. of Units: Company Owned: 1 - Franchised: 16 - Franchise Fee: $20,000 - Royalty: fixed annual fee - Total Inv: $190,000 - Financing: No.

PIC-A-POP BEVERAGES
33 Stapleton St., Winnipeg, MB, R2L 1Z9. Contact: Helmut Sass, Gen. Mgr. - Tel: (204) 667-0614. Soft drink beverages. Dealerships. Established: 1971 - No. of Units: Company Owned: 17 - Dealerships: 83.

WINE NOT *
15 Heritage Rd., Unit 1, Markham, ON, L3P 3T1. Contact: Rick Keene or Pat Burden @ (905) 848-5773, Franchising - Tel: (905) 294-6121. A complete wine making operation for both retail sales and the restaurant industry. A turnkey operation. Established: 1993 - Franchising Since: 1994 - No. of Units: Company Owned: 1 - Franchised: 6 - Franchise Fee: $35,000 - royalty: 5%, 2% adv. - Total Inv: $115,000 - Financing: Yes.

WINE WORKS
450 Woodlawn St. W., Unit 6, Guelph, ON, N1K 1A6. Contact: John Leveris, Dir., Sales & Mktg. - Tel: (519) 837-2304. Consumer do-it-yourself winery. Consumers can blend the world's finest grape juice and concentrates to create their own premium wines right in our stores. Established: 1994 - Franchising Since: 1994 - No. of Units: Franchised: 3 - Franchise Fee: $15,000 - Royalty: 5% of gross sales, 3% mktg. - Total Inv: $135,000 - Financing: No.

BUILDING PRODUCTS AND SERVICES

AJUST-A-TRACK LTD.
21 Grenfell Cr., Unit 2, Nepean, ON, K2G 0G3. Contact: Flo Lehmann, Pres. - Tel: (613) 225-7624. Manufacturer of vinyl tracks to convert sashless sliding windows, reusing existing glass at one half the cost of new retrofit windows. Established: 1987 - Total Inv: $2,500 - Financing: No.

AMERICAN RESTORATION SERVICES
284 Northshore Blvd. E., Burlington, ON, L7T 1W9. Contact: D'Arcy Draper - Tel: (905) 632-4585. Building restoration (ext. & int.) with environmentally safe products. High profit, low overhead business. Full Training. Turnkey. Unique marketing program. Ongoing support. Comm. and res. Excellent protected areas still available. Established: 1970 - Franchising Since: 1975 - No. of Units: Company Owned: 1 - Franchised: 250 - Franchise Fee: $12,500 U.S. - Royalty: No royalty payments - Total Inv: $30,000 - $35,000 U.S. - Financing: Yes.

AMERILOK CANADA
110 Chain Lake Dr., Vantage Point, Unit 3I, Halifax, NS, B3S 1A9. Contact: A. Peter Feron, Pres./Owner - Tel: (902) 450-5144 (also fax). Four business opportunities available. 1) Manufacture fiberglass wicker furniture; 2) Perma-Brite bathtub refinishing; 3) Hydro-Bath bathtub whirlpool conversion; 4) Coved-Wal seamless one-piece custom formed bathtub enclosure. Established: 1988 - Franchising Since: 1988 - No. of Units: Licensed: 32 - Franchise Fee: 1) W2000 weaving system $29,000; 2) Perma-Brite/ Hydro-Bath/ Coved-Wal bathroom renovation $12,500 each - Financing: No.

AMERISPEC HOME INSPECTION SERVICES (CANADA) *
AmeriSpec Canada Inc.
223-1433 Lonsdale Ave., N. Vancouver, BC, V7M 2H9. Contact: Murray, Nat. Sales Mgr. - Tel: (800) 665-9558. Home inspections concerning the condition of the property, part of a typical real estate transaction, new industry in Canada, tremendous growth occuring. Established: 1987 - Franchising Since: 1988 - No. of Units: Franchised: 250 - Franchise Fee: $22,900 U.S. urban, $11,900 U.S. rural - Royalty: 7% gross rev., 3% gross rev. adv. - Financing: Yes, O.A.C.

BATH SMITH, THE
Bath Smith, Inc.
26463 - 28th Ave., Aldergrove, BC, V4W 3A6. Contact: George Moore, Fran. Mktg.

VARCON Construction Co. Ltd.
Industrial • Residential • Commercial • Institutional

CUSTOMERS WANTED
Can we build your next franchise store, corporate offices or distribution center? Construction budgets & deadlines are a priority to us.

WE OFFER:
- Turnkey or partial construction
- Project management
- Design and build
- Budget consultations

25 Rutherford Rd. South, Unit 5
Brampton, Ont., L6W 3J3
(800) 581-6729
Tel: (905) 451-7316, Fax: (905) 451-8563

Exec. - Tel: (604) 857-8900, Fax: (604) 856-1149. Unique patented bathtub replacement system leading to complete bathroom renovations. Established: 1993 - Franchising Since: 1993 - No. of Units: Company Owned: 1 - Franchised: 13 - Franchise Fee: $15,000 - Royalty: 5% gross sales - Total Inv: $34,900: $15,000 fee, $10,000 work. cap., $9,900 inven. & equip.

BATHTUB DOCTOR, LE DOCTEUR BAIGNOIRE
Respo-Technik of North America, Ltd.
2814-C Leigh Rd., Victoria, BC, V9B 4G3. Contact: W.C. (Chuck) Parsons, Pres. - Tel: (604) 478-3900, Fax: (604) 478-0045. Bathtub resurfacing and chip repair. Established: 1952 - Franchising Since: 1952 - No. of Units: Company Owned: 1 - Franchised: 36 - Franchise Fee: $15,000 - Royalty: 5% gross - Total Inv: $20,000 min. - Financing: No.

BEAVER LUMBER COMPANY LTD.
7303 Warden Ave., Markham, ON, L3R 5Y6. Contact: Wm. C. Worden, V.P. Admin. - Tel: (905) 479-2255. Retail lumber, building materials and related hard goods. Established: 1906 - Franchising Since: 1977 - No. of Units: Company Owned: 47 - Franchised: 128 - Franchise Fee: $8,000 - $20,000 - Financing: No.

DEC-K-ING
Coast Sundecks Waterproofing Ltd.
19292 60th Ave., Ste. 119, Surrey, BC, V3S 8E5. Contact: Roland P. Houle, Pres. - Tel: (604) 530-0050, Fax: (604) 530-4466. Reinforced vinyl sheeting for waterproofing sundecks, roof decks, garage decks, pool decks, patios. Also aluminum/glass railings. Established: 1978 - Franchising Since: 1981 - No. of Units: Franchised: 96 - Franchise Fee: $2,500 - $15,000 (Initial inv. $1,500) - Total Inv: $5,000 - $15,000 - Financing: No.

DO-IT CENTER STORES
D.H. Howden & Co. Limited
P.O. Box 2485, London, ON, N6A 4G8. Contact: Ron MacDonnell, Franchise Marketing Mgr. - Tel: (519) 686-2200. Complete marketing programme (merchandising, store decor, advertising, etc.) for independent retail building supply dealers. Established: 1901 - Franchising Since: 1984 - No. of Units: Franchised: 60 - Total Inv: variable - Financing: will assist in obtaining.

ENVIRO-SHEILD ENERGY SYSTEMS *
6033 Shawson Dr., Unit 9, Mississauga, ON, L5T 1H8. Contact: John Formosa, Pres. - Tel: (905) 670-5181, Fax: (905) 670-8468. There are millions of square feet of commercial, institutional and residential glass which needs to be retrofitted with our high tech environmental solar film. The retrofit of glass with film results in a reduction of energy usage that surpasses dollar for dollar any other system. Established: 1995 - Franchising Since: 1995 - No. of Units: Company Owned: 1 - Franchise Fee: $20,000 - Royalty: 6% - Total Inv: $79,500 which incl. fran. fee - Financing: We assist in obtaining financing.

EUROPEAN SHARPENING, INC. *
457 - 42 Ave. S.E., Calgary, AB, T2G 1Y3. Contact: Doug McKay, Pres. - Tel: (403) 287-0850. ESI provides sharpening services to wood working, metal, ice arena, paper industry and general public. New tooling in the woodworking, ice arena, paper industry. Established: 1975 - Franchising Since: 1991 - No. of Units: Company Owned: 1 - Franchised: 4 - Franchise Fee: $30,000 - Royalty: 10% incl. adv. - Total Inv: Start up $140,000 - $300,000 - Financing: None at this time.

GRASSROOTS - THE HOME INSPECTION SPECIALISTS
PAIRS Reporting Service, Inc.
214 Martindale Rd., St. Catharines, ON, L2R 6P9. Contact: Harry Salomons, V.P., Fran. Sales - Tel: (800) 774-2538, (905) 687-1925, Fax: (905) 685-8125. Home inspection service with full support, marketing materials, strategy, training, customer service, bookkeeping, and procedures on how to run your own business successfully. Quick generation of inspection reports using our unique, easy-to-use computerized system. Our report is narrative style, not just a checklist. Established: 1991 - Franchising Since: 1991 - No. of Units: Franchised: 7 - Franchise Fee: $15,000 - Royalty: 7%, 3% adv. - Total Inv: $27,500 incl. fran. fee and $7,500 training fee (may be greatly reduced if operating from existing office) - Financing: To qualified candidates - $7,500 prime + 2% (over 24 months).

HECK OF A DECK
Heck Of A Deck Ltd.
1290 Speers Rd., Ste. 13, Oakville, ON, L6L 2X4. Contact: R. Higgins, Owner - Tel: (905) 825-3189. Deck/fence construction. 3 season sunrooms, retaining walls, interlocking patios & driveways, wood staining, finishing and renewing. Established: 1991 - Franchising Since: 1993 - No. of Units: Company Owned: 1 - Franchised: 1 - Franchise Fee: $12,000 - $20,000 - Royalty: 5%, 2% adv. - Total Inv: approx. $5,000 start-up costs plus fran. fee - Financing: No.

IN'FLECTOR CONTROL SYSTEMS INC.
3088 Jefferson Blvd., Windsor, ON, N8T 3G9. Contact: B.D. (Bernie) Rosney, Dir. of Fran. - Tel: (800) 945-7598, Fax: (519) 944-6146. Manufacturer of the revolutionary In'Flector Window Insulator Panels: an innovative, successful, patented system to provide homeowners and businesses with energy savings and comfort 365 days a year. Established: 1983 - Franchising Since: 1991 - No. of Units: Company Owned: 1 - Franchised: 23 - Franchise Fee: Regional $25,000 - Master Representative $100,000 - Royalty: 8% - Total Inv: Regional $29,000 - Master $110,000 - Financing: For master rep. only.

KITCHEN SAVER
Kitchen Saver of Canada
75 Bessemer Rd., London, ON, N6E 1P9. Contact: Craig Jones, Pres. - Tel: (519) 686-8820. Cabinet door manufacturer and ready to assemble cabinets. Established: 1986 - Franchising Since: 1986 - No. of Units: Franchised: 15 - Franchise Fee: $10,000 - $20,000 - Total Inv: variable - Financing: Some.

KITCHEN WIZARDS (CANADA) *
Ste. 3100, 350 7th Ave. S.W., Calgary, AB, T2P 3N9. Contact: Mr. Jon Havelock, Pres. - Tel: (403) 256-6104 or 1-800-491-3323. Kitchen remodeling options: including new, refaced, recolored or revived cabinets; appliance refinishing; counter, floor, tile and other refinishing. Two weeks training in marketing, management and design with ongoing support by phone, fax, conventions and advanced training. Established: Canada: 1994, U.S. parent: 1994 - No. of Units: Company Owned: 1 CAN, 1 US - Franchised: 0 CAN, 4 US - Franchise Fee: $20,000 per 100,000 population - Royalty: 8% on gross sales, 2% adv. - Total Inv: Fran. fee plus $30,000 - $40,000 for operations - Financing: Yes, for qualified purchasers through corporate bank.

LA TUILE EUROPE LTD.
4025-C Boul. Leman, Laval, PQ, H7E 1A2. Contact: Andre Labbe, Owner - Tel: (514) 664-1666. Fibreglass modular roofing tiles. Franchising Since: 1981 - No. of Units: 10 - Franchise Fee: $20,000 - Total Inv: $30,000 - Royalty: 2% adv. - Financing: Assistance.

MEASURE MASTERS FLOOR PLANNING & BLUEPRINT SERVICE
Measure Masters Inc.
2974 Folkway Dr., Mississauga, ON, L5L 1Z6. Contact: John McPhail, Pres. - Tel: (905) 608-0000. Provide computerized floor plan blue prints of existing buildings, residential and commercial. Bonded measurements and certified square footage. All franchises operate from home. Established: 1989 - Franchising Since: 1990 - No. of Units: Franchised: 12 - Franchise Fee: $30,000 - $50,000 - Royalty: 8% - Total Inv: $30,000 - $50,000 incl. all hard & software, training on location - Financing: 3rd party possible.

MONSIEUR DISMAT
Dismat, Inc.
1250 Mobel St., Boucherville, PQ, J4B 5K1. Contact: Robert Dutton, Pres. - Tel: (514) 599-5100. Building supplies. Established: 1966 - No. of Units: 125.

PAL LUMBER AND BUILDING
5 rue Montclair, Hull, PQ, J8Y 2E3. Contact: Ronald Lavoie, Pres. - Tel: (819) 771-5841. Wood and construction materials. Franchisee must currently own an establishment. Franchising Since: 1958 - No. of Units: Company Owned: 12 distribution centers - Franchised: over 100.

PAUL DAVIS SYSTEMS CANADA
5240 Finch Ave. E., Ste. 10, Scarborough, ON, M1S 5A3. Contact: Wm. Robinson, Pres. - Tel: (800) 661-5975. Provides property damage estimates and restoration services to major insurance companies across

North America. Established: 1966 (US) - Franchising Since: 1971 (US), 1986 (CAN) - No. of Units: Franchised: 190 (US), 25 (CAN) - Franchise Fee: $29,000 - $44,500 - Royalty: 3.5% on gross sales - Total Inv: $60,000 - $75,000 - Financing: Yes.

PERMACRETE
Permacrete Systems Ltd.
426 Caldwell Rd., P.O. Box 2697, DEPS, Dartmouth, NS, B2W 4R4. Contact: William G. Cole, Pres. - Tel: (902) 462-1500 or (800) 565-LEAK (5325), Fax: (902) 462-2954. Unique system of basement waterproofing offering protected territories and water control (license-franchise). Two week in-house and on-site training with supervision and ongoing support. Established: 1980 - Franchising Since: 1990 - No. of Units: Company Owned: 1 - Franchised: 20 - Franchise Fee: $18,000 - $30,000 - Royalty: 4% gross, 2% adv. - Financing: No.

PLOMBERIUM
Deschenes & Fils Ltee.
8335 St-Michel Blvd., Montreal, PQ, H1Z 3E6. Contact: Danielle Lamarre, G.M. - Tel: (514) 374-3110. Chain of retail stores in plumbing fixtures and accessories. (Stores must be owned by plumbers). Established: 1980 - Franchising Since: 1980 - No. of Units: Franchised: 15.

PLUMBING MART
P.M.C. Corporation
21 Research Rd., Mississauga, ON, M4G 2G7. Contact: Wm. Gibson, Pres. - Tel: (416) 275-0574. Retail plumbing and bathroom renovation specialists for do-it-yourself, full service and complete bathroom renovation, service and design. Established: 1959 - Franchising Since: 1984 - No. of Units: Company Owned: 1 - Franchised: 12 - Franchise Fee: $50,000 - Royalty: 5% of net sales - Total Inv: $200,000 - Financing: Through conventional means.

RADIXX/WORLD LTD.
Northern Shield Protective Coatings
827 Danforth Place, Burlington, ON, L7T 1S1. Contact: John S. Luckanuck, President - Tel: (905) 522-8111, Fax: (905) 528-4585. Automotive, Industrial and Construction Coatings. Automotive, paint sealants, rust inhibitor, fabric protector, and undercoatings for lifetime warranties. Industrial and construction, fire retardant coatings, insulation and board products. Established: 1992 - Franchising Since: 1994 - No. of Units: Company Owned: 1 - Franchised: 2 - Franchise Fee: $25,000 - Royalty: 5% - Total Inv: $50,000 - Financing: Yes.

STUCCO DOCTOR
Pro-Tech Stucco Corp.
411 Fernhurst Pl., Coquitlam, BC, V3K 5T9. Contact: Franchise Director - Tel: (800) 663-2466. A process, technique and chemical formula to apply a special high density stucco coat over any type of existing stucco, brick, masonry or concrete. Costs approx. the same as paint and can guarantee it for life. Established: 1991 - Franchising Since: 1991 - No. of Units: Franchised: 6 - Franchise Fee: $22,500 - Royalty: 8%, 2% adv. - Total Inv: fee + $30,000 - $60,000 - Financing: No.

STUDENT WORKS PAINTING
Works Corps.
460 McNicol Ave., Willowdale, ON, M2H 2E1. Contact: Chris Thompson, Pres. - Tel: (416) 798-7300. Student operated residential maintenance painting business. Entire business/marketing plans and materials provided, along with ongoing support. Operates only during the summer. Established: 1981 - Franchising Since: 1983 - No. of Units: approx. 1,000 (Incl. Canada & U.S.) - Royalty: 10% of sales - Total Inv: $2,000 an average for summer vehicle - Financing: Yes, depending upon regional gov't programs.

SUPER GARD CANADA LTD. *
4056 Ste. #102 Meadowbrook Dr., London, ON, N6L 1E1. Contact: Donald F. Hawken, Pres. - Tel: (800) 682-6943. The long lasting answer for your outside and inside protection needs. Industrial strength coatings for commercial, agricultural and residential use. Sales, service and application for concrete, masonry, wood, metal, interlocking and natural stone. Your Protective Coatings Specialist. Established: 1988 - No. of Units: Company Owned: 1 - Dealers: 60+ - Dealership Fee: Based on territory - Total Inv: Opportunities start at $1,000 - Financing: Yes, on approved applicants.

SUPER SEAMLESS STEEL SIDING OF CANADA, LTD.
560 Henderson Dr., Regina, SK, S4N 5X2. Contact: Marilyn Mryglod, Dir. of Franc. - Tel: (800) 565-4334, (306) 721-8000. Exclusive franchisor of the ABC Super Seamless siding machines in Canada. Machines jobsite or in-plant manufacture siding in custom lengths up to 200 ft. Company provides PVC Coil for manufacture and supply all necessary trims and accessories, comprehensive business operation manuals. Training, counselling and sales aid. Established: 1978 - Franchising Since: 1985 - No. of Units: Company Owned: 2 - Franchised: 15 - Franchise Fee: $9,750 - Royalty: yearly fee - Total Inv: $52,000 - $100,000.

SURFACE DOCTOR *
200 - 100 Park Royal, W. Vancouver, BC, V7T 1A2. Contact: Fran. Dir. - Tel: (604) 922-4393. Repair & resurface bathtubs, sinks, tiles, countertops, kitchen appliances. Bathroom & kitchen remodeling. Established: 1994 - Franchising Since: 1994 - No. of Units: Company Owned: 2 - Franchised: 70 - Franchise Fee: CN$19,800 (for BC, AB, SK & MB) - Royalty: CN$295 ($260 royalty, $35 adv. fee) - Total Inv: CN$26,700 (Territory fee $19,800; equip., inven. & supply package $6,900).

UNIVERSITY FIRST CLASS PAINTERS *
University Contractors Corp. Ltd.
5687 West St., Ste. 200, Halifax, NS, B3K 1H6. Contact: Mike Benteau, Pres. - Tel: (902) 455-4448. Offering franchises for a full range of painting and cleaning services. We provide marketing, training, leases for equipment, accounting and payroll services and all forms for the operation of the business. Established: 1982 - Franchising Since: 1986 - No. of Units: Company Owned: 1 - Franchised: 30 - Franchise Fee: None - Royalty: 16% - 24% depends on area and experience - Total Inv: $3,000 - $5,000 - Financing: Yes.

SUPER GARD

A WELL ESTABLISHED COMPANY SEEKING MASTER LICENSEES FOR NATIONAL DEVELOPMENT

OFFERING:
- Automotive Rust Prevention Products
- Rust Prevention for stationary equipment and buildings
- Protective Coatings for all cementatious based materials
- We service the Automotive, Agricultural, Industrial, Residential and Retail markets

CONTACT THE NATIONAL OFFICE AT
4056 Meadowbrook Drive, Suite #102
London, Ont. N6L 1E1
(519) 652-5242 OR 1-800-682-6943

DEDICATED TO PRESERVE AND PROTECT

WINDSOR PLYWOOD
Box 560, Surrey, BC, V3T 5M5. Contact: S.R. Jones or A.Wightman, Pres. /Mgr., Mktg.& Opers. - Tel: (604) 581-4661. The wholesale and retail distribution of building material products. Established: 1960 - Franchising Since: 1970 - No. of Units: 61 - Franchise Fee: $35,000.

WINMAR
Winmar Franchise Corp.
P.O. Box 3561, Stn. A, London, ON, N6A 4L4. Contact: John White, Owner - Tel: (519) 451-0000. General contracting, disaster restoration, insurance work specialists. Established: 1977 - Franchising Since: 1991 - No. of Units: Franchised: 9 - Franchise Fee: $20,000 - Royalty: 3% to million gross, 1% over million, .25% adv. - Total Inv: $50,000 - Financing: Yes.

WISE CRACKS® *
Wise Cracks Restoration Ltd.
2 Bluewater Rd., Atlantic Acres Industrial Park, Bedford, NS, B4B 1G7. Contact: Fran. Dir. - Tel: (902) 835-6763. Company developed and field proven systems for the control of foundation water problems catering to residential, commercial and government clients using patented technologies and trade-mark protected products. Offering 100% satisfaction. Exciting opportunity to ethical persons. Established: 1991 - Franchising Since: 1994 - No. of Units: Company Owned: 1 - Franchised: 4 - Franchise Fee: Starting at: $15,000 per unit - Royalty: Low rate, varies - co-op & group advertising programs - Total Inv: Up to $25,000 per unit - Financing: Negotiable.

WORLDWIDE REFINISHING SYSTEMS
10 Foundry St., Dundas, ON, L9H 2V7. Contact: Andy Ross, Master Licensee - Tel: (905) 628-5991. The repair and refinishing of bathtubs, sinks, ceramic tiles, kitchen cupboards, countertops and vanities using a proprietary coating material developed for the space industry. Established: USA 1970/Canada 1990 - Franchising Since: 1970 - No. of Units: Company Owned: 1 - Franchised: 550+ - Franchise Fee: $200 per 1,000 population (Minimum area 100,000 pop.) - Royalty: 7% weekly - Total Inv: $30,000 to $35,000 min. - Financing: No.

BURGLAR & FIRE PREVENTION

ALLIANCE SECURITY SYSTEMS, INC.
6 - 140 McGovern Drive, Cambridge, ON, N3H 4R7. Contact: Hal Gould, Pres. - Tel: (519) 650-5353. Electronic security alarm business. Sales and service of wireless alarm systems - training, products, monitoring. Established: 1970 - Franchising Since: 1972 - No. of Units: Company Owned: 1 - Franchised: 48 - Franchise Fee: $10,000 - Royalty: No - Total Inv: Training, products, start-up package - Financing: Yes.

BRICK FIRE & SAFETY LTD. *
951 Thomas Avenue, Winnipeg, MB, R2L 2C6. Contact: B. Roberts, Pres. - Tel: (204) 668-1594. Sales/service of fire & safety equipment (fire extinguisher, fire hoses, fire systems, fire alarms, fire equipment, safety equipment). Also, fire training services. Established: 1990 - Franchising Since: 1995 - No. of Units: Company Owned: 1 - Franchise Fee: $10,000 - Royalty: 5% of sales - Total Inv: $50,000 + $10,000 fran. fee - Financing: None.

INTERNATIONAL LOSS PREVENTION SYSTEMS INC.
1350 E. 4th Ave., Vancouver, BC, V5N 1O5. Contact: Ian Abramson, Pres. - Tel: (604) 255-5000. The leading Canadian manufacturer and exporter of shoplifting prevention equipment. Established: 1987 - Franchising Since: 1987 - No. of Units: Company Owned: 1 - Franchised: 12 - Franchise Fee: $5,000 - $25,000 - Royalty: .5% - Total Inv: $5,000 - $25,000 inven. - Financing: Yes.

RESCUE ALERT
P.O. Box 270, Campbellford, ON, KOL 1LO. Contact: T. Dodsley, Pres. - Tel: (705) 778-3863. Burglar and medical alarms plus child identification for missing persons. Operated by former police officer. Established: 1989 - Franchising Since: 1992 - Franchise Fee: $3,800 - Royalty: None - Total Inv: $3,800 incl. equip. - Financing: Yes, with money back guarantee. Send a S.A.S.E. for free info-package.

V.I.D.E.O. SECURITY PROCESS
5045 Orbitor Dr., Bldg. 12, Ste. 102, Mississauga, ON, L4W 4Y4. Contact: Ron Hill-Holland, Pres. - Tel: (905) 625-7595, Fax: (905) 625-5888. Professional inventory service (residential & commercial) designed to maximize your insurance dollars in event of claims for loss/damage. Ideal for women/men over 50's. Credibility established with members of Canadian Insurance Industry. A home-based business. Established: 1989 - No. of Units: Company Owned: 1 - Franchised: 1 - Franchise Fee: $25,000 (includes video equip. & training) - Royalty: 5% yr. 1, 6% yr. 2, 7% yr. 3 - Total Inv: From $31,000 to $35,000 - Financing: Ontario govt. loan.

BUSINESS PRODUCTS AND SERVICES

BARTER WORLD INC.
21 Gladstone Ave., Ste. 305, Oshawa, ON, L1J 4E3. Contact: Ken Yeomans, Pres. - Tel: (800) 668-5915. A brokerage firm overseeing business owners trading goods and services between each other. Established: 1993 - No. of Units: Company Owned: 1 - Franchised: 1 - Franchise Fee: $5,000 - $45,000 - Royalty: 2.5% - Total Inv: $10,000 - $55,000 - Financing: Yes.

CAN-AM DIVORCERVICE, (1984) INC.
2615 Mary Hill Rd., Port Coquitlam, BC, V3C 3B5. Contact: Donald Burdney, Pres. - Tel: (604) 942-4549. Divorce kit do-it-yourself and public steno and filing service. Established: 1970 - Franchising Since: 1987 - No. of Units: 1 - Franchise Fee: $15,000 single (masters available) - Royalty: 15% - Total Inv: $29,500 turn-key.

CANADA POST CORPORATION
2701 Riverside Dr., Ste. N0551, Ottawa, ON, K1A 0B1. Contact: Daniel Domitrovic, Mgr., Fran. Dev. - Tel: (613) 734-7575. Retailing of postal products through existing established retail businesses. Franchising Since: 1987 - No. of Units: Franchised: 1,000 urban outlets & 1,200 rural - Royalty: 2%+ 1% adv. - Total Inv: approx. $65,000 (counters, point of sale, leaseholds, decor) - Financing: No.

CANADIAN BARTER EXCHANGE
Canadian Barter Exchange Corp.
6021 Yonge St., Ste. 125, Toronto, ON, M2M 3W2. Contact: Brian Owen, Dir. Bus. Dev. - Tel: (416) 667-0242 or (800) 465-1560. Business to business barter trade exchange. Established: 1993 - Franchising Since: 1994 - No. of Units: Company Owned: 2 - Franchised: 2 - Franchise Fee: $12,500 - $27,500 - Royalty: 4% of trading volume - Financing: Yes.

CANADIAN BUSINESS BROKERS LTD.
201 - 602 11th Ave., S.W., Calgary, AB, T2R 1J8. Contact: Nicholas Stuber, Pres. - Tel: (403) 262-9570. Establishment and operation of business brokerage office by way of franchises, licenses, joint ventures and partnerships. Established: 1985 - Franchising Since: 1987 - No. of Units: Company Owned: 2 - Franchised: 1 - Franchise Fee: $35,000 - Royalty: 2% adv., 6% - Total Inv: $150,000 - Financing: No.

CMC COLLATERAL MANAGEMENT CANADA LTD.
104 - 630 Columbia St., New Westminster, BC, V3M 1A5. Contact: Robert M. Fletcher, Pres. - Tel: (604) 522-8618, Fax: (604) 522-9896. Specialized financial service company offers third party assessments to financial institutions on the assets pledged as collateral for loans. Offers secondary letter of credit financing, successful preparation of financing requests and loan placements. Established: 1983 - No. of Units: Company Owned: 1 - Franchise Fee: $25,000 - Royalty: 5%, 10% adv. - Total Inv: $75,000.

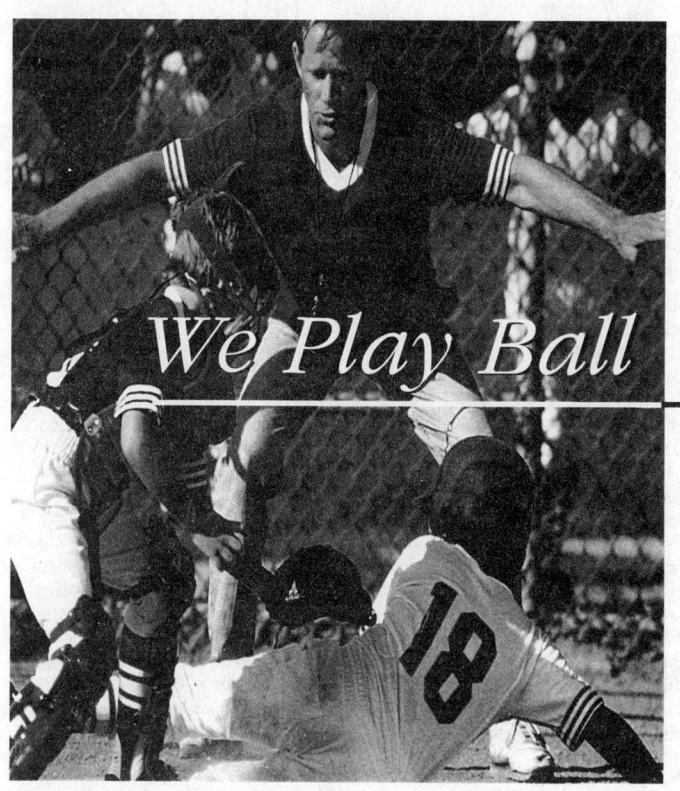

We designed our business to handle the unexpected. Like eleventh-hour additions, deletions and changes. That's why we process payrolls in 23 offices throughout the country. Locally, where our clients are. Our employees work and play in the same community as our customers. Always anticipating the call. On or off the field.

Adding to your expertise

Comcheq
23 offices across Canada

Comcheq

▶ Payroll services for businesses of any size in virtually any industry

▶ Flexible input and output options

Offices throughout Canada
In Winnipeg call (204) 947-9400

COMCHEQ
125 Garry St., Winnipeg, MB, R3C 3P2. Contact: Theresa Romijn, National Sales Support Coordinator - Tel: (204) 946-0770. Comcheq provides payroll services and human resource management systems to businesses in virtually any industry. With branches across Canada, our flexible payroll system ensures personalized service for businesses of all sizes.

E.K. WILLIAMS & CO.
E.K. Williams & Co. (Ontario) Ltd.
6465 Millcreek Dr., Ste. 205, Mississauga, ON, L5N 5R3. Contact: George Kostopoulos - Tel: (905) 567-4180, (800) 387-8335, Fax: (905) 567-5355. Part of world-wide network of 300 offices providing accounting services, management consultation, taxation services, training seminars for management and employees, business software. All services tailored for small business. Established: 1992 - Franchising Since: 1992 - No. of Units: Company Owned: 1 - Franchised: 5 - Franchise Fee: N/A - Royalty: 5% of gross revenue (minimum $400 per month) - Total Inv: $40,000 - $50,000 - Financing: No.

ENVOY BUSINESS SERVICES *
3555 Don Mills Rd., Ste. 6, Willowdale, ON, M2H 3N3. Contact: John Reynolds, Owner - Tel: (416) 496-9189, Fax: (416) 496-9190. Retail outlets providing a full range of business services primarily to the home based business person but also to residential customers. Established: 1990 - Franchising Since: 1990 - No. of Units: Company Owned: 2 - Franchised: 17 - Franchise Fee: $25,500 CDN - Royalty: 6% on gross sales - Total Inv: $70,000 CDN - Financing: Yes.

FILE SECURITY INC. *
661 Justus Dr., Kingston, ON, K7M 2H5. Contact: Tammy MacKenzie, Gordon Cummins, Mgr., Pres. - Tel: (613) 634-FILE, Fax: (613) 384-5304. Optical document scanning onto CD Rom to relieve space constraints and save on overhead expenses. It provides networking to share information that can be accessed in seconds via CD rather than time consuming manual searches. We provide a one stop shop for a paper free environment. Established: 1992 - No. of Units: Company Owned: 3 - Franchised: 3 - Franchise Fee: $35,000 - Royalty: 5%-8% - Total Inv: $180,000 - Financing: OAC.

 **E.K.Williams & Co.**
(ONTARIO) LTD.
BUSINESS MANAGEMENT SERVICES

#1 Business Service Franchise
(As rated by Entrepreneur Magazine in 1990 & 1992)

- Over 55 years experience
- Full training and support
- Prime areas available
- Over 300 offices worldwide
- Ongoing research & development
- Marketing & promotional expertise

For detailed information call now!
First Choice Franchise Services Inc.
1-800-387-8335
Members of the Canadian Franchise Association

IMAGE CONTROL
Recycled Toner Cartridges
1396 Kingston Rd., Toronto, ON, M1N 1R3. Contact: John Connolly, Gen. Mgr. - Tel: (800) 465-4594, (416) 694-7509, E-Mail: image@beachweb.com. Canada's largest inventory of toner cartridges - new, compatible, remanufactured - all at discount from 'Depot' type store prices. Trademark regd. #728213. No royalties, recurring fees or fancy lawyers. Associates receive: 2 days training, on-going support, existing base of corporate and retail customers in protected area. Solid accounting, marketing and dignified proven, telemarketing systems. Meticulously detailed cross reference & guides. You will be the Laser & Jet Printer, fax and small copier toner expert in your area. Inclusion in all national corporate advertising and the most advanced WWW site in the industry. Associates must have sales experience to gain corporate accounts & close leads supplied. Currently 2 retail locations, 3 other home based associates. License fee $12,500. Initial inventory min. $5,000. Image Control will assist with up to 35% financing. Member of Metro To. Better Business Bureau.

INTERFACE FINANCIAL GROUP, THE
Interface Group Ltd., The
180 Renfrew Dr., Ste. 245, Markham, ON, L3R 9Z2. Contact: D.T. Banfield, Pres. - Tel: (905) 475-5701, Fax: (905) 475-8688, from U.S. 1-800-387-0860. Invoice discounting financial service, providing working capital to small business. Established: 1970 - Franchising Since: 1990 - No. of Units: Franchised: 14 - Franchise Fee: $25,000 - Royalty: 10% of gross income - Total Inv: $75,000+ ($25,000 fee, $5,000 equip., $45,000+ work. cap.) - Financing: On fee only.

INTERNATIONAL BUSINESS OPPORTUNITIES
Worldwide Canadian Management Consultants, Inc.
1480 Bayly St., #7, Pickering, ON, L1W 3T8. Contact: Kelly Roger, Dir. - Tel: (905) 831-2832, Fax: (905) 686-0469. Import/export - business network in 32 countries. International sales rep. worldwide. Large profit. Work from home office or have a full office. Established: 1976 - Franchising Since: 1982 - No. of Units: Company Owned: 2 - Franchised: 35 - Franchise Fee: US$20,000 - Total Inv: US$60,000 to $120,000 - Financing: Yes.

INTERNATIONAL HOME OFFICE *
1053311 Ontario Inc.
10 Royal Orchard Blvd., P.O. Box 53037, Thornhill, ON, L3T 7R9. Contact: Vladimir Machlis, Pres. - Tel: (905) 764-7058, Fax: (905) 709-3821. Service of office machines (copiers, fax, printers); sales of supplies for office machines. Established: 1989 - Franchising Since: 1992 - No. of Units: Company Owned: 1 - Franchise Fee: $15,000 - Total Inv: $15,000.

JOBSOURCE CANADA & INTERNATIONAL JOBLINK
Teltech Canada Group Inc.
1057 Steeles Ave. W., #577, North York, ON, M2R 3X1. Contact: L. Burke, Pres. - Tel: (416) 631-7799. Information technologies packages including scanning, computer, fax-on-demand, voice processing and data communications. Software for local and international job matching. Established: 1985 - Franchising Since: 1989 - No. of Units: Company Owned: 3 - Franchised: 8 - Franchise Fee: $2,500 - Royalty: 10% - Total Inv: Hardware & software $1,920 (P.C. & phone line required) - Financing: Joint venture possible.

MAIL BOXES ETC.
MBEC Communications Inc.
505 Iroquois Shore Rd., Unit 4, Oakville, ON, L6H 2R3. Contact: Ron Weston, V.P. Fran. Sales - Tel: (905) 338-9754, Fax: (905) 338-7491. Business and communications services. Established: 1990 - Franchising Since: 1990 - No. of Units: Company Owned: 1 - Franchised: 175 - Franchise Fee: $24,950 - Royalty: 6% - Total Inv. $110,000 - Financing: Yes.

MONEY CONCEPTS (CANADA) LTD.
180 Attwell Dr., Ste. 501, Etobicoke, ON, M9W 6A9. Contact: Jim MacDonald, Franc. Dir. - Tel: (416) 674-0450. Money Concepts is in the business of bringing personal financial planning to the middle income market through individually owned financial planning centres purchased by entrepreneurs under the franchise system. Money Concepts provides a comprehensive business system embodying all aspects of business establishment and continuation. Established: 1984 - Franchising Since: 1985 - No. of Units: Franchised: 72 - Franchise Fee: $30,000 - Total Inv: fee plus $15,000 start up costs - Financing: None.

PACK 'N' SHIP MAILING CENTERS
#3, 844 51st St. East, Saskatoon, SK, S7K 5C7. Contact: Gerry, Pres. - Tel: (306) 931-8881. Custom packing & shipping service in addition to mail preparation. Limited retail of packing supplies. Established: 1981 - Franchising Since: 1981 - No. of Units: Company Owned: 6 - Franchised: 225 - Franchise Fee: $25,000 - Royalty: None - Total Inv: $60,000 - $100,000.

PACKAGING DEPOT
Packaging Depot Inc.
5524 Cambie St., Vancouver, BC, V5Z 3A2. Contact: Jay Bayne, Pres. - Tel: (604) 325-9966. Retail packaging and shipping services for personal effects and commercial goods. We offer a full range of supplies, insurance, pick-up services and everything else needed. Uncomplicated business serving strong market demand. B.C.'s leading firm, expanding nationwide. Established: 1986 - Franchising Since: 1989 - No. of Units: Company Owned: 1 - Franchised: 1 - Franchise Fee: $25,000 - Royalty: 5% of Gross - Total Inv: $95,000 incl. equip., inven., work cap., promo, license, etc. - Financing: From major banks.

PAK MAIL CENTRES *
Pak Mail Canada
6465 Millcreek Dr., Ste. 205, Mississauga, ON, L5N 5R3. Contact: George Kostopoulos - Tel: (905) 567-4180, (800) 387-8335, Fax: (905) 567-5355. Pak Mail is a one-stop centre that provides packaging, shipping, supplies and business support services as well as specialty crating, international shipping, private mailbox rental and mail preparation. While our services are often used by busy residential consumers, much of our business comes from a virtually unlimited market of Business Customers. Full training & support. Established: 1983 - Franchising Since: 1984 - No. of Units: Franchised: 255 - Franchise Fee: $25,000 - Royalty: 6% - Total Inv: $53,000 - $98,000 - Financing: Assistance through financial institutes.

PARALEGAL INVESTIGATION
P.O. Box 270, Campbellford, ON, K0L 1L0. Contact: T. Dodsley, Pres. - Tel: (705) 778-3863. Fifty paralegal opportunities. No experience needed. On-going support by attorney and former police investigators. Established: 1989 - Franchising Since: 1992 - Franchise Fee: $3,800 - Royalty: None - Total Inv: $3,800 incl. all support - Financing: Yes, with money back guarantee. Send a S.A.S.E. for a free info-package.

PAYSTATION *
Paymaster Cheque-Writers (Canada Ltd.)
7 Vulcan St., Etobicoke, ON, M9W 1L3. Contact: Sheila Alianak, Dir. of Operations - Tel: (800) 268-1440. Our business is controlling white collar crime resulting from information technology, computer software. Canada wide home-based opportunity. Established: 1995 - Licensing Since: 1995 - No. of Units: Company Owned: 9 - Licensed: 6 - Franchise Fee: $10,000 - Royalty: None - Total Inv: $15,000 ($10,000 license fee, $3,000 training, $2,000 inventory) - Financing: No.

POSTNET
3383 Sources Rd., Dollard Des Ormeaux, PQ, H9B 1Z8. Contact: Michel Gagnon, Pres. - Tel: (514) 683-4000, (800) 960-7678. Business & communication center offering shipping, packaging, fax, copies, business services and much more. Established: 1994 - Franchising Since: 1992 - No. of Units: Company Owned: 1 - Franchised: 6 (350 in US) - Franchise Fee: $25,000 - Royalty: 6%, 2% adv. - Total Inv: $95,000 - Financing: Yes.

PREVUE ASSESSMENT *
Prevue Resource Group
206 - 7080 River Rd., Richmond, BC, V6X 1X7. Contact: Eric Hoover, Partner - Tel: (604) 278-1231. Sale of Prevue Assessment product to human resource and sales departments. Software-based application enables employees to be benchmarked to overachievers insuring Job Fit. Used for hiring, coaching, training needs and succession planning requirements. Established: 1994 - Offering dealerships since: 1994 - No. of Units: Company Owned: 1 - Dealerships: 5 - Dealership Fee: $16,000 - Royalty: Initial inventory purchase - Financing: None.

PRODUCTIVITY POINT INTERNATIONAL CANADA INC.
116 Albert St., 2nd Fl., Ottawa, ON, K1P 5G3. Contact: Joseph Colvey, Sales Mgr. - Tel: (613) 230-3391. PPI is a powerful consortium of conversion-computer-training franchises across Canada and U.S. Major benefit to conversion - franchisees include: 1) networked national training delivery 2) comprehensive instructor-led courseware portfolio - 300 course title 3) mgmt. support systems 4) save money on ATC applications. Established: 1985 - Franchising Since: 1991 - No. of Units: Company Owned: 1 - Franchised: 52 - Franchise Fee: $15,000 - Royalty: 8% up to $500,000, 7.5% up to $1 million, 7% up to $1.5 million etc. - Total Inv: $15,000 plus monthly royalties based on revenues - Financing: Qualification: must be an existing established instructor-led computer training company to be considered.

PROSHRED SECURITY
Proshred Inc.
2200 Lakeshore Blvd. W., Ste. 102, Toronto, ON, M8V 1A4. Contact: Margaret Graham, Fran. Dev. - Tel: (800) 461-9760. Large mobile document shredding service operating in U.S.A., Canada and Europe. Business to business service for executive types with good management skills. Established: 1986 - Franchising Since: 1990 - No. of Units: Company Owned: 4 - Franchised: 25 - Franchise Fee: $35,000 - Royalty: 8% of sales - Total Inv: $218,000: $55,000 cash plus work. cap. - Financing: Third party: $110,000.

RIBBON XCHANGE
Rynker Ribbon Exchange, Inc.
7550 River Rd., Unit 14, Delta, Vancouver, BC, V4G 1C8. Contact: Heather Benson, Marketing Assoc. - Tel: (604) 946-4367. Manufacture a high speed re-inking/stuffing machine. Established: 1989 - Franchising Since: 1989 - No. of Units: Company Owned: 1 - Franchised: 10 - Franchise Fee: $10,000 - Royalty: $100 per month support/service - Total Inv: $35,000 - Financing: Conditional.

ROSS DIXON FINANCIAL SERVICES
Ross Dixon Financial Corp.
110 Pinnacle Rd., Kitchener, ON, N2P 1C5. Contact: Dave Valenoff, Pres. & CEO - Tel: (519) 895-1513. Offers personal service in sales of a broad range of financial products. RDFS shops the markets for GIC's, RSP's, mutual funds, mortgages, insurance, RIF's, annuities and T Bills. Established: 1978 - Franchising Since: 1989 - No. of Units: Company Owned: 2 - Franchised: 12- Franchise Fee: $15,000 - Royalty: 20% of gross commissions - Total Inv: $25,000 work. cap. - Financing: Rent computer equipment & software to franchisee.

SHRED-TECH
Shred-Tech Ltd.
295 Pine Bush Rd., Cambridge, ON, N1T 1B2. Contact: Sales Dept. - Tel: (519) 621-3560, Fax: (519) 621-0688. Mobile document destruction service. Established: 1976 - No. of Units: Franchised: 122 - Total Inv: $115,000 U.S. - Financing: Yes.

CARPET, DRAPERY AND UPHOLSTERY CLEANING

CHEM-DRY® CARPET & UPHOLSTERY CLEANING
Jandor Enterprises (Canada) Ltd.

8361B Noble Rd., Chilliwack, BC, V2P 7X7. Contact: Peter Snow, Trudy Miller, President, Licensing & Sales - Tel: 1-800-665-9090. LOW INVESTMENT - HIGH RETURN FRANCHISE. Chem-Dry® is a safe, non-toxic alternative for cleaning carpets & upholstery without soaps & detergents. Using patented carbonating cleaning solutions, you can make your dreams of independence & prosperity come true. Your purchase includes the equipment and cleaning product to perform carpet & upholstery cleaning, stain removal and carpet protection services. Optional services include water damage restoration, urine odour & stain removal, leather/vinyl cleaning & protecting, auto interior detailing and fabric protection. A training library is included along with five (5) days in field training. (Travel & accommodation excluded). Established: 1977 - Franchising Since: 1978 - No. of Units: In Canada: 125 - Worldwide: 4,700 - Countries: 50 - Franchise Fee: $14,950+GST - Royalty: $280+GST/mo. - Total Inv: $30,000+GST ($14,950 + $13,900 equipment) - Financing: $13,900 (Leased equipment package).

FABRI-ZONE CLEANING SYSTEMS
Fabri-Zone Canada, Ltd.
3135 Universal Dr. Unit#6, Mississauga, ON, L4X 2E2. Contact: David S. Collier, Pres. - Tel: (800) 667-3357, (905) 602-7691, Fax: (905) 602-7821. Turn key franchise concept for patented purification dry cleaning of carpets & upholstery, ceilings & walls, odour removal, water & smoke damage restoration & Fabri-Restore steam finishing for carpets. Established: 1981 - Franchising Since: 1985 - Number of Units: Company Owned: 1 - Franchised: 65 - Franchise Fee: $2,000 - $5,000 - Royalty: 6% - Total Inv: $2,500 - $30,000 - Financing: Yes.

GOOD LOOKIN' CARPET CLEANING *
GLCC Franchising Inc.
40 Burnbank St., Nepean, ON, K2G 0H4. Contact: Luigi F. Orlando, Fran. Sales - Tel: (613) 831-2604. Carpet and upholstery cleaning; carpet repairs and sales; fire and water damage restoration. A full service company. Make it your business. Established: 1990 - Franchising Since: 1995 - No. of Units: Company Owned: 1 - Franchise Fee: $10,000 - Royalty: Flat monthly fee $500 - $1,000 per month - Total Inv: Approx. Initial Inv: $30,000 to $50,000 - Financing: Not at this time.

ROTO-STATIC CARPET & UPHOLSTERY CLEANING
Robben Industries, Ltd.
100 Leek Cres., Unit 3, Richmond Hill, ON, L4B 3E6. Contact: Richard J. Crispi; Cecilia Murphy, Pres.; Admin./Sales Mgr. - Tel: (905) 886-5560. Unique method of cleaning carpets & upholstery by an advanced technique of static attraction. Low investment, low overhead, high returns. Established: 1977 - Franchising Since: 1977 - No. of Units: Franchised: 117 - Franchise Fee: $8,250 - Royalty: 5% - Total Inv: $18,000 - $27,900 - Financing: Nil.

RUG DOCTOR RENTS
Rug Doctor Canada Ltd.
14 Trottier Bay, Winnipeg, Man, R3T 3Y5. Contact: Gerald Hochman, Exec. V.P. - Tel: (204) 284-1444, Fax:(204) 453-2324. Rug Doctor Rents is at the forefront of carpet and upholstery cleaning systems for the Do-It-Yourself market throughout the world. Exclusiveness is granted for territory in which Rug Doctor Rents rental stations may be set up. Area development is accomplished with the assistance of the franchisor. Full training and support programs are also provided. Many national accounts are available into which the machines may be placed. Established: 1975 - Franchising Since: 1978 - No. of Units: Company Owned: 10 corp.

territories - Franchised 42 - Royalty: 6 - 8% - Total Inv: Dependent on number of machines and size of territory - Financing: Assistance with banking, but no direct financing.

STEAMATIC FRANCHISES LTD.
6535 Millcreek Drive, Unit 2, Mississauga, ON, L5N 2M2. Contact: Tim Smith, Pres. - Tel: (800) 387-0154. Indoor air quality services including hot water extraction processes for carpet-upholstery, complete HVAC (Duct) decontamination, fire and water restoration. 9 profit centers. Established: 1967 - No. of Units: 67-Canada, 150-U.S. - Franchise Fee: $5,000 - $28,500 - Royalty: 10% declining to 5% - Total Inv: $20,000 - $60,000 - Financing: Yes.

VONSCHRADER ASSOCIATE
Vonschrader Canada
9 Antares Dr., Nepean, ON, K2E 7V5. Contact: Douglas Conner, Pres. - Tel: (800) 267-7422. Patented and worldwide manufacturer of state-of-the-art and industry rated #1 dry foam carpet, upholstery, wall and ceiling cleaning systems. Far superior to steam cleaning. Established: 1989 - Franchising Since: 1990 - No. of Associates: 418 - Franchise Fee: $550 - Total Inv: $2,500 - $15,000 - Financing: Yes.

ZIPPY-CLEAN
Derek's Ltd.
582 Hillside Ave., Pembroke, ON, K8A 8B2. Contact: Derek Clark, Pres. - Tel: (613) 732-1196. Carpet and upholstery cleaners offering rental mat service. Established: 1990 - Franchising Since: 1990 - No. of Units: Company Owned: 1 - Financing: Yes.

CHILDREN'S PRODUCTS AND SERVICES

CHILDREN'S MARKETPLACE, THE
P.O. Box 1078, Tottenham, ON, L0G 1W0. Contact: Joan McDonald, Pres. - Tel: (905) 936-2092. A great children's specialty store selling baby furniture, nursery accessories, educational toys, books, wonderful gifts and specially selected clothes. Offers designer consignment of children's items, a great service to parents. Established: 1974 - Franchising Since: 1980 - No. of Units: Franchised: 7 - Franchise Fee: $25,000 - Royalty: 6% + 1% adv. - Total Inv: $89,000.

CREATE-A-BOOK CANADA/INTERNATIONAL
#206, 2916 - 19 St. N.E., Calgary, AB, T2E 6Y9. Contact: Ron Marcolin, Mgr. - Tel: (403) 250-9322, Fax: (403) 250-9448. Dealerships available retailing unique personalized books for both children and adults! Established: 1987 - Franchising Since: 1987 - No. of Units: Franchised: 135 Canada - Internationally represented in 36 countries worldwide - Franchise Fee: $1,995 - Total Inv: $2,495 (CDN) - Financing: Yes.

FUTUREKIDS ONTARIO & QUEBEC
18 Crimson Millway, Willowdale, ON, M2L 1T6. Contact: Dave Jones, V.P. Fran. Sales - Tel: (416) 445-6488, Fax: (416) 445-5750. Computer literacy training for children. We also provide curriculum licensing to private & public schools. We train teacher & adults in computer literacy. Established: 1983 - Franchising Since: 1986 - No. of Units: Company Owned: 2 - Franchised: 34 - Franchise Fee: 35,000 - Royalty: $360/mo. + 10% - Total Inv: $70,000 - $100,000 - Financing: No.

GENIUS KID ACADEMY, INC. *
404 Steeles Ave. W., Ste. 214, Thornhill, ON, L4J 6X3. Contact: Nathan Aryev, Dir. - Tel: (905) 886-1920. Computer learning centre for kids - exciting alternative in a field of education. Established: 1992 - Franchising Since: 1993 - No. of Units: Company Owned: 1 - Franchised: 1 - Franchise Fee: $20,000 - Royalty: $250 1st yr., $500 2nd yr., $1,000 4th - Total Inv: $40,000 to $60,000.

HAND ME DOWNS
DMJ Management
R.R. #1, Enniskillen, ON, L0B 1H0. Contact: Stephanie Jukes, Owner/Founder - Tel: (905) 263-4719, (800) 567-5437. Consignment children's clothing, toys, equipment & nursery furniture and maternity wear. Established: 1991 - Franchising Since: 1993 - No. of Units: Company Owned: 2 - Franchised: 6 - Franchise Fee: $15,000 - Royalty: 5% of gross sales - Total Inv: $30,000 - $40,000 - Financing: Yes.

IDENTIFICATION SERVICES OF CANADA INC.
Ste. 238, 150 Clark Blvd., Brampton, ON, L6T 4Y8. Contact: Joe Marois, Nat'l. Dir. - Tel: (905) 796-2211. Provide laminated child I.D. cards containing a child's photograph, fingerprint, and physical description, on a yearly basis to parents. The program is marketed through public and private schools, using a unique video presentation. Established: 1988 - Franchising Since: 1988 - No. of Units: Company Owned: Can. 2/USA 1 - Franchised: Can. 39/USA 277 - Franchise Fee: $35,000 incl. equip. - Royalty: Nil - Total Inv: $35,000 incl. fran. fee and equip. - Financing: Financial guidance possible.

KIDDIE KOBBLER
68 Robertson Rd., Nepean, ON, K2H 8P5. Contact: Fred Norman, Pres. - Tel: (613) 820-0505, Fax: (613) 820-8250. Children's shoe stores located in major shopping malls. The extensive marketing plan is designed to develop new & repeat business through intensive customer service, selection & value. Established: 1951 - Franchising Since: 1968 - No. of Units: Franchised: 31 - Franchise Fee: $30,000 - Royalty: 4%, .5% adv. - Total Inv: $100,000 - $130,000 - Financing: Franchisor will help prepare loan applications. SBA may be available.

LE BATEAU BLANC
Multiplicant, Inc.
710 Bouvier St., Quebec City, PQ, G2J 1A7. Contact: Pierre Yelle, Pres. - Tel: (418) 627-1846, Fax (418) 627-4125. Children's fashions. Established: 1975 - Franchising Since: 1984 - No. of Units: Company Owned: 2 - Franchised: 15 - Franchise Fee: $24,500 - Total Inv: $125,000: $40,000 leasehold/equip, $65,000 inven. + fran fee - Royalty: 5% - Financing: No.

MAD SCIENCE GROUP, THE *
5460 Royalmount, Ste. 204, Mount Royal, PQ, H4P 1H7. Contact: Ariel Shlien, George Palmer, Pres., Dir. of Fran. - Tel: (800) 586-5231, (514) 344-6691, Fax: (514) 344-6695. Fun and hands-on and educational science activities for children conducted in schools, camps, libraries, scout groups, daycares, resorts, etc... Complete training, support and equipment supplied. Tested systems include operations and program manuals. Established: 1985 - Franchising Since: 1995 - No. of Units: Company Owned: 4 - Franchised: U.S. 8, Canada 1 - Franchise Fee: $20,000 - Royalty: 8% - Total Inv: $40,000 - Financing: Yes.

OUR BABY IMPRESSIONS
Associated Baby Impressions Ltd.
437 Duke Court, Kelowna, BC, V1W 3A2. Contact: Sal or Darlene, Owners - Tel: (604) 764-4888. Imprints of baby's hands and feet, 3 dimensional casting in a frame (8x10) with baby's name and age. Also children up to 12 yrs. Each print reveals all lifelines in hands & feet. Established: 1987 - Franchising Since: 1988 - No. of Units: Company Owned: 1 - Franchised: 74 - Franchise Fee: $6,000 - $9,000 - Royalty: 2% - Total Inv: includes equip., training & supplies (enough to do 100 plaques) - Financing: No.

PANDA - LE SPECIALISTE DU SOULIER POUR ENFANTS
Franchise & Finance
141 Maple, Chateauguay, PQ, J6J 3R1. Contact: Franchise Dir./Pres. - Tel: (514) 692-4936. Children's and preteen shoe specialists, high quality service and merchandise. A turn-key operation. Established: 1938 - Franchising Since: 1973 - No. of Units: Company Owned: 6 - Franchised: 47 - Franchise Fee: $25,000 - Royalty: 3% plus 1% adv - Total Inv: $100,000 incl. working capital.

PANDA SHOES
Panda Franchises Ltd.
305 Marc-Aurele-Fortin Blvd., Laval, PQ, H7L 2A3. Contact: Linda Goulet, V.P. - Tel: (514) 622-4833, Fax: (514) 622-2989. Children shoes specialist, fitting from 0 to 10 yrs. old. Greatest selection from Italy, France, Spain, Brazil, Portugal, USA and Canada. National advertising. Locations in regional malls. Established: 1972 - Franchising Since: 1974 - No. of Units: Company Owned: 5 - Franchised: 55 - Franchise Fee: $25,000 - Royalty: 4% - Total Inv: approx. $150,000 (fran. fee, $60,000 inven., $65,000 lease) - Financing: No.

PEANUT CLUB INDOOR PLAYGROUND, THE *
Peanut Club Franchise Group, The
36 Cranfield Rd., Toronto, ON, M4B 3H3. Contact: Brian Shedden, Treasurer - Tel: (416) 751-7161. Pay for play indoor playground and party facility. Target market: Infant - Age 7. Established: 1991 - Franchising Since: 1993 - No. of Units: Company Owned: 1 - Franchised: 7 - Franchise Fee: $25,000 - Royalty: 7%, 3% adv. - Total Inv: $65,000.

STRETCH-N-GROW OF CANADA INC.
290 Briar Hill Ave., Toronto, ON, M4R 1J2. Contact: Michelle Katz, Pres. - Tel: (416) 483-1436. Classes are conducted in day care facilities and nursery schools teaching physical fitness and good eating habits to kids at an early age. Established: 1993 - Franchising Since: 1993 - No. of Units: Franchised: 12 - Franchise Fee: $7,800 - $8,800 - Royalty: 10% plus administration fees of $100 per mo. - Total Inv: $10,000 - $12,000.

WEE WATCH PRIVATE HOME DAY CARE
Wee Watch Day Care Systems, Inc.
105 Main St., Unionville, ON, L3R 2G1. Contact: Terry Fullerton, V.P. - Tel: (905) 479-4274. Private home day care agencies catering to children aged 6 weeks and older, full time or part time. Largest day care in Canada. Established: 1984 - Franchising Since: 1986 - No. of Units: Franchised: 45 - Franchise Fee: $7,500 - Royalty: 8%, 2% adv. - Total Inv: $20,000 - Financing: No.

CLEANING PRODUCTS AND SERVICES

A PERFECT TOUCH *
1020 Denison St., Ste. 203, Markham, ON, L3R 3W5. Contact: Arlene Bishop, Pres. - Tel: (905) 477-4648. We are a home cleaning business specializing in quality cleaning (housework). Established: 1981 - Franchising Since: 1994 - No. of Units: Company Owned: 1 - Franchised: 2 - Franchise Fee: $9,500 - Royalty: 4% + 2% adv. - Financing: No.

ACTION-THE STUDENT WINDOW CLEANING TEAM
ASI - Academic Systems Inc.
476 Evans Ave., Unit 1, Etobicoke, ON, M8W 2T7. Contact: Rodney Larmand, V.P. - Tel: (416) 291-9990. Seasonal network of student-run residential window cleaning franchises. Franchisor provides full training, administrative/consulting support and established customer base. Established: 1986 - Franchising Since: 1986 - No. of Units: Company Owned: 1 - Franchised: 50 - Royalty: 18.5% - 22.5% of gross sales.

AIRKEM DISASTER SERVICES
100 Huntington Park, Sault Ste. Marie, ON, P6A 3P5. Contact: Jack Moore, Owner - Tel: (705) 759-2255. Insurance restoration work pertaining to floods, fire, smoke etc. Established: 1987 - Franchising Since: 1994 - No. of Units: Company Owned: 1 - Royalty: $5,000 - $10,000 - Total Inv: $15,000 - $25,000 - Financing: No.

AL-VIN SIDING CLEANERS
Al-Vin Products Ltd.
18L 37 Lakeshore Rd., Wainfleet, ON, L0S 1V0. Contact: Keith Schaefer, Owner - Tel: (905) 899-2522 or (800) 263-9746. Cleaning exteriors of homes, business, with aluminum and vinyl siding. Established: 1982 - Franchising Since: 1987 - No. of Units: Company Owned: 2 - Franchised: 38 - Franchise Fee: $17,500 - $50,000 - Royalty: flat royalty payment - Total Inv: $25,000 - $75,000 - Financing: Yes.

ALL AMERICAN SHADE CARE SYSTEM *
25 Coronet Rd., Etobicoke, ON, M8Z 2L8. Contact: Dieter Micheletti, Dir. - Tel: (416) 234-8069, Fax: (416) 234-9718. The company provides a blind cleaning service for all hard window coverings such as venetians, verticals, sunscreens and parabolic louvers. A patented variable hydromatic system cleans more thoroughly so spotting and shrinkage can be controlled. Established: 1989 - Franchising Since: 1995 - No. of Units: Company Owned: 1 - Franchise Fee: $15,000 - Royalty: 5% - Total Inv: $52,500 incl. fran. fee - Financing: For qualified prospects.

ARODAL SERVICES
Arodal International Inc.
6171 Conin Dr., Mississauga, ON, L4V 1N8. Contact: Mr. A.E. Fisher, Pres. - Tel: (905) 678-6888. Contract cleaning of industrial and commercial office buildings. Established: 1971 - Franchising Since: 1990 - No. of Units: Company Owned: 2 - Franchised: 2 - Franchise Fee: $20,000 - Royalty: 7% of gross sales - Total Inv: $80,000; fran. fee plus $60,000 furn., leaseholds & computer - Financing: 50%.

BEE-CLEAN
Bee-Clean Building Maintenance, Inc.
4140-97th St., Edmonton, AB, T6E 5Y6. Contact: Jim Malott, Pres. - Tel: (403) 462-0069. Janitorial service. Established: 1967 - Franchising Since: 1972 - No. of Units: Company Owned: 7 - Franchised: 25 - Franchise Fee: $12,500 - Royalty: scale from 5% to 2% - Total Inv: $15,000 min. for down pymt, work cap, equip. - Financing: Yes.

BLUE DIAMOND WINDOW CLEANING
Blue Diamond Window Cleaning Ltd.
2399 Royal Windsor Dr., Mississauga, ON, L5J 1K9. Contact: Michael J. Kernaghan, Dir. of Franc. Sales - Tel: (905) 823-8400. Power wash cleaning. Established: 1986 - Franchising Since: 1986 - No. of Units: Company Owned: 1 - Franchised: 13 - Franchise Fee: $30,000 - Royalty: $6,671 per truck - Total Inv: $35,000 - $40,000 - Financing: No.

CAN-CLEAN PRESSURE WASHERS *
450 Matheson Blvd. E., #56, Mississauga, ON, L4Z 1R5. Contact: John Drummond, Gen. Mgr. - Tel: (905) 568-4868, Fax: (905) 568-0611. Sales of pressure washers and water/oil separators and recycling units. Established: 1992 - Total Inv: $2,000 - $50,000 - Financing: If qualified.

CEILING BRITE *
Ceiling Brite Distribution Inc.
641 Thornloe Rd., Site 15, Comp. 49, Kelowna, BC, V1Y 8R3. Contact: Deryl Kent, CEO - Tel: (604) 764-8384. Manufacturer of ceiling and wall cleaning products. Established: 1993 - Franchising Since: 1993 - No. of Units: Company Owned: 1 - Franchised: 9 - Franchise Fee: None - Royalty: None - Total Inv: For equip. & product $10,000 - Financing: No.

CLEAN-BRITE *
Clean Brite Canada Ltd.
1025 Winnipeg St., Regina, SK, S4P 1J3. Contact: Steve Yang, Pres. - Tel: (306) 352-9953. Franchise operations in janitorial supply and service. Commercial and residential accounts. Established: 1981 - Franchising Since: 1986 - No. of Units: Company Owned: 2 - Franchised: 3 - Franchise Fee: $5,000 - $25,000 - Royalty: min. 5%, max. 10% - Total Inv: $10,000 - $60,000 - Financing: Yes.

COVERALL OF CANADA
201 Consumers Rd., Ste .303, North York, ON, M2J 4G8. Contact: Karl Robson, Pres. - Tel: (416) 492-8100, Fax: (416) 492-8216. Commercial office cleaning services provided by franchisees who have received full training, equipment and guaranteed customers from Coverall. Established: 1985 - Franchising Since: 1985 - No. of Units: 14 (US parent) - Franchised: 3,100 internationally - Franchise Fee: Six programs, min. $2,550 - Royalty: 10% service, 5% royalty - Total Inv: $6,000 - $17,000 - Financing: Yes.

CRYSTAL MAINTENANCE SYSTEMS
Crystal Maintenance Systems Inc.
1020 Brevik Pl., Mississauga, ON, L4W 4N7. Contact: Al James, V.P. - Tel: (905) 238-8931. Janitorial maintenance serving commercial, industrial, retail, institutional, public and multi-storey offices. Established: 1979 - Franchising Since: 1994 - No. of Units: Company Owned: 1 - Franchised: 1 - Franchise Fee: $15,000 - Royalty: 13%, 3% nat'l. adv. - Total Inv: approx. $45,000 ($5,000 equip., $25,000 work. cap.) - Financing: Partial.

CYNATEC SPECIALTY CLEANING & RESTORATION *
Cynatec Specialty Cleaning & Restoration Inc.
2344 Valleyview Dr., Courtney, BC, V9N 8S5. Contact: Clinton Beck, Pres., Founder - Tel: (800) 265-6332. Cleaning of acoustical ceilings, restaurant cleaning, building maintenance, blind cleaning, fire restoration, chandelier cleaning using atomized chemicals. Established: 1995 - Franchising Since: 1995 - No. of Units: Franchised: 8 - Franchise Fee: $30,000 - Royalty: 7% gross - Total Inv: $30,000 turnkey - Financing: Yes, prime + 4%.

HORIZON MAINTENANCE ASSOCIATES
M.R. Holdings Ltd.
121 Ilsley Avenue, Ste. W, Dartmouth, NS, B3B 1S4. Contact: Mike Blotnicky, Pres. - Tel: (902) 468-1031. Ongoing cleaning services for offices, retail buildings, warehouses etc. Also window and carpet cleaning services, floor finishing and construction clean-ups. Offer a 30 day money back guarantee. Established: 1982 - Franchising Since: 1987 - No. of Units: Company Owned: 1 - Franchised: 9 - Franchise Fee: $10,000 - Royalty: 5.5% + 1% acc. (optional) - Total Inv: $10,000 - Financing: 50%.

HYGENICOMP COMPUTER CLEANING *
Hygenicomp Technology Maintenance Inc.
Ste. 1510, 200 Burrard St., Vancouver, BC, V6C 3L6. Contact: Clinton Beck, V.P. & Founder - Tel: (800) 760-5876. Cleaning & tune-up of computers and other electronics. ATM cleaning, air filtration, mainframe cleaning, fire restoration. Established: 1989 - Franchising Since: 1991 - No. of Units: Franchised: 31 - Franchise Fee: $29,500 turnkey - Royalty: 8% gross - Total Inv: includes equip. & supplies - Financing: Yes, prime + 4%.

JANI-KING CANADA
Renfrew Group Ltd. (c/o)
109 Ilsley Ave., Ste. 9, Dartmouth, NS, B3B 1S8. Contact: Bruce Tupper, Dir. of Franc. - Tel: (800) 565-1873. World's largest commercial cleaning franchise with 26 years of experience. Franchise Fee includes up to $5,000+ initial monthly cleaning contract revenue and a startup equipment package valued at up to $2,500. Federally registered trademark number TMA 324268. Professional training and continuous support while franchisees provide commercial cleaning programs on a long-term contract basis. Accounts receivable and collections function provided by regional office. The program has proven itself many times over and produces hundreds of successful business people each year. Established: 1969 - Franchising Since: 1974 (in Canada since 1986) - No. of Units: Company Owned: 25 - Franchised: 4,210 - Franchise Fee: $9,900 - Total Inv: $9,900 - Financing: Partial, available to qualified individuals.

JDI CLEANING SYSTEMS
JDI Cleaning Systems Inc.
3390 South Service Rd., Burlington, ON, L7N 3J5. Contact: Joseph Imbrogno, Fran. Dir. - Tel: (905) 634-5228, Fax: (905) 634-8790. Commercial janitorial services. Initial contracts, equipment, training, supplies and administrative support to qualified individuals seeking the opportunity to own and operate their own business. Master franchises available. Established: 1992 - Franchising Since: 1992 - No. of Units: Company Owned: 2 - Franchised: 22 - Franchise Fee: $10,500 - Royalty: 13%, 2% adv. - Total Inv: $19,000 - Financing: Yes.

MASTER CARE JANITORIAL
327-555 Sixth St., New Westminster, BC, V3L 5H1. Contact: Christopher Stone, VP - Tel: (604) 525-8221. Provide janitorial services to commercial and retail buildings - via franchising. Established: 1981 - Franchising Since: 1987 - No. of Units: Company Owned: 1 - Franchised: 15 - Franchise Fee: $10,000 - Royalty: 7% - Total Inv: $10,000 - Financing: British Columbia.

MERRY MAIDS
ServiceMaster of Canada
6540 Tomken Rd., Mississauga, ON, L5T 2E9. Contact: David Messenger, Gen. Mgr. - Tel: (905) 670-0000, Fax: (905) 670-0000. North America's largest residential cleaning business. Established: Can 1989, US 1979 - Franchising Since: Can 1989, US 1980 - No. of Units: Franchised: 20 in Canada - Franchise Fee: $18,000 - Royalty: 7% on sales - Total Inv: $20,500 - Financing: Yes.

MINI MAID SERVICES
Mini Maid Service Systems
192 Shorting Rd., Scarborough, ON, M1S 3S7. Contact: Fred Romito, Pres. - Tel: (800) 363-MAID. Residential housecleaning performed by 4-person teams in identified uniforms and company car. Professional advertising, training, and ongoing support ensures profitable success. Established: 1979 - Franchising Since: 1979 - No. of Units: Company Owned: 11 - Franchised: 78 - Franchise Fee: $9,950 - Royalty: 6,5,4% + 2% adv. - Total Inv: $14,000 ($4,000 min. work cap) - Financing: No.

MISS MILLY HOUSE CLEANING *
2273-129 St., Surrey, BC, V4A 7V7. Contact: Peter Myddleton - Tel: (604) 531-5449. BC based franchise offering franchises only in BC. Support & training is ongoing. Personalized approach towards franchise owners & clients needs. Established: 1991 - Franchising Since: 1992 - No. of Units: Company Owned: 1 - Franchised: 10 - Franchise Fee: $10,500 - Royalty: 8% - Total Inv: $10,500 fran. fee/$5,000 - $10,000 work. cap. - Financing: OAC.

MOLLY MAID INTERNATIONAL, INC.
100 Bronte Rd., Oakville, ON, L6L 3B8. Contact: Karen Grantham, Oper. Co-ord. - Tel: (905) 847-6243. Home cleaning service. Established: 1978 - Franchising Since: 1980 - No. of Units: Company Owned: 1 - Franchised: 160 - Franchise Fee: $14,000 - Royalty: 6% - Total Inv: $14,000 - Financing: No.

NATURE TECH SYSTEMS *
Nature Technologies Inc.
900 Hyde Park Rd., London, ON, N6A 4B7. Contact: Larry Boyd, Pres. - Tel: (519) 657-8041. Environmentally friendly process for the maintenance, restoration & preservation for exterior wood, brick, aluminum, vinyl & concrete surfaces. Established: 1994 - Franchising Since: 1994 - Franchise Fee: $20,000 - Royalty: Nil - Total Inv: $20,000 - Financing: No.

ONTARIO DUCT CLEANING LTD.
5635 Finch Ave. E., Ste. 5, Scarborough, ON, M1B 5K9. Contact: Peter Townend, V.P. - Tel: (416) 292-9700, Fax: (416) 292-7600. Residential/commercial high technology duct cleaning. Established: 1979 - Franchising Since: 1988 - No. of Units: Company Owned: 1 - Franchised: 15 - Franchise Fee: $20,000 - Royalty: 7% - Total Inv: $80,000 - Financing: Yes.

ORECK CENTRE, THE *
Axe Houghton Group, Inc.
1129 Paterson St., Winnipeg, MB, R2J 1G7. Contact: Mr. Ben Cohen, Pres. - Tel: (204) 992-2990, Fax: (204) 254-7979. Direct sales of air purification equipment, residential and commercial, sale of commercial cleaning equipment. Established: 1992 - Franchising Since: 1995 - No. of Units: Company Owned: 1 - Franchised: 2 - Franchise Fee: $3,000 - Total Inv: $10,000 to $30,000.

POWER KING CLEANING SYSTEMS *
1 Church St., Unit 5, Keswick, ON, L4P 3E9. Contact: Brenda Payton, Office Mgr. - Tel: (905) 476-6107, Fax: (905) 476-6107. Pressure wash exhaust systems in restaurants. Established: 1986 - Franchising Since: 1994 - No. of Units: Company Owned: 1 - Franchised: 3 - Franchise Fee: $60,000+ - Royalty: 7%, 1% adv. - Total Inv: $50,000 + $10,000 working credit line.

RESTORX CANADA
Restorx Canada Incorporated
100 Nipissing Rd., #13, Milton, ON, L9T 5B2. Contact: Terry Gibbons, Pres. - Tel: (905) 876-4559. Canada's foremost disaster restoration company utilizing patented products and proprietary systems. Established: 1946 - Franchising Since: 1991 - No. of Units: Franchised: 13 - Franchise Fee: $29,900 - Royalty: $700/month - Total Inv: Approx. $60,000 excluding fran. fee - Financing: Small amount available.

SANIBRITE INC.
3045 Southcreek Rd., Unit 19, Mississauga, ON, L4X 2X7. Contact: Hossein Companieh, Acct. Exec. - Tel: (905) 624-4290, Fax: (905) 602-5383. Operation of business dealing in franchising, janitorial and maintenance services and rendering technical assistance in the establishment and or operation of custodial maintenance business. Established: 1987 - Franchising Since: 1989 - No. of Units: Company Owned: 1 - Franchised: 40 - Franchise Fee: $2,500 - $17,000 (vary) - Royalty: 5%, 3%, 12% - Total Inv: vary $2,500 to $17,000 - Financing: Yes.

SERV-U-CLEAN LTD. *
207 Edgeley Blvd., Unit 5, Concord, ON, L4K 4B5. Contact: Rick Katz, Gen. Mgr. - Tel: (905) 660-0899, Fax: (905) 660-0550. Commercial contract janitorial services. Established: 1991 - Franchising Since: 1992 - No. of Units: Company Owned: 4 - Franchised: 45 - Franchise Fee: $5,450+ - Financing: Partial financing available.

SILO CLEAN INTERNATIONAL
4325 Steeles Ave. W., Ste. 110, Downsview, ON, M3N 1V7. Contact: Marvin Lee, Mktg. Dir. - Tel: (905) 660-7022, Fax: (905) 660-1755. World's safest and fastest clean out of industrial silos, tanks, bins and hoppers. Services over 80 industries, worldwide. Company is the inventor and developer of a cleaning process which enables cleaning done by remote control from the outside without sending men in. Avoids all confined space legislation and liability for companies using service as well as providing significant cost savings. Dry cleaning, no water or chemicals used. Established: 1984 - Licensing Since: 1993 - No. of Units: Company Owned: 1 - License Fee: $150,000 approx., depending on size of territory - Royalty: 6% - Total Inv: $150,000 incl. tech. training program, equip., mktg. training - Financing: No.

SOAP EXCHANGE, THE *
Soap Exchange Enviro-Wise Refill Centres
#8, 2241 Hanselman Ave., Saskatoon, SK, S7L 6A7. Contact: Daisy, Mktg. Dir. - Tel: (306) 244-7727. Retail stores which sell quality, concentrated, biodegradable house cleaning products. We use a refill program to shrink our landfill space. We have a personal care line as well. Established: 1988 - Franchising Since: 1993 - No. of Units: Company Owned: 2 - Franchised: 20 - Franchise Fee: E-4 size $7,000, E-1 size $12,000 - Royalty: None - Total Inv: Varies on size, $16,000 - $37,000 - Financing: None.

SPOTLESS OFFICE SERVICES, INC.
1959 Marine Dr., Ste. 1061, N. Vancouver, BC, V7P 3G1. Contact: Bob Mussio - Tel: (604) 985-6569. Building maintenance broker. No trucks, cleaning equip. or office needed. Janitors use own equipment. Can be operated from home, contacting office buildings and sign them up to a janitorial cleaning contract. Established: 1978 - Franchising Since: 1980 - No. of Units: Company Owned: 1 - Franchised: 17 - Total Inv: $3,000 - Royalty: 5% - Financing: No.

UNICLEAN SYSTEMS
Uniclean Systems, Inc.
#460 - 212 Brooksbank Ave., N. Vancouver, BC, V7J 2C1. Contact: Jack Karpowicz, Pres. - Tel: (604) 986-4750. Professional office cleaning on the long term contract basis. Established: 1976 - Franchising Since: 1981 - No. of Units: Company Owned: 1 - Franchised: 346 - Franchise Fee: $7,000 - $12,500 - Royalty: 10% - Total Inv: $8,000 - $15,000 - Financing: No.

WINCH ENTERPRISES
48 Riverside Cr. S.E., Calgary, AB, T2C 3Y1. Contact: Brian Winch, Pres. - Tel: (403) 236-7551. Earn big money in commercial outdoor clean-up. So simple even a child can be successful. Work full or part time from home or office. One year money back guarantee. Established: 1981 - No. of Units: Company Owned: 1 - Total Inv: $30.00 for business manual - Financing: No.

DISTRIBUTORS

ACCU-SPEED MARINE PRODUCTS CORPORATION *
200B 908 - 17th Ave. S.W., Calgary, AB, T2T 0A3. Contact: Bruce Oxley, Brent Bergs, Pres., Proj. Mgr. - Tel: (800) 461-4884, (403) 244-2580, Fax: (403) 244-2582. Turbine marine speedometer pick-up system for licensing and sale. Established: 1994 - Distributing Since: 1995 - Distributor Fee: $25,000 to $200,000 - Financing: Yes.

ADVANCED COATING, INC. *
P.O. Box 670, Hwy. 12, Midland, ON, L4R 4P4. Contact: Mr. Les Shannon - Tel: (705) 534-7219. Distributor of liquid applied coatings for foundations, air/vapour barriers and retrofit metal roofs. Established: 1994 - Franchising Since: 1994 - No. of Units: Company Owned: 1 - Franchised: 15 - Franchise Fee: $1,000 - Royalty: 4% - Total Inv: $20,000 - $25,000 - Financing: None.

ALLSTAR DISTRIBUTING INC.
2115 St-Regis, Dollard des Ormeaux, PQ, H9B 2M5. Contact: Myrna Dorfman, Pres. - Tel: (514) 685-1400, Fax: (514) 685-5038. Manufacturer of "Typhoon" spiral gumball machine, sticker machines and stickers, temporary tattoos & pogs. Corporate accounts available. Established: 1981- No. of Units: Company Owned: 200.

AMERACAR PLATING INT'L. *
Ameracar Instruments Canada
1990 Charest West Blvd., Ste. 118, Quebec City, PQ, G1N 4K8. Contact: Jacques Caron, Pres. - Tel: (418) 688-2024, (418) 688-7058, E-Mail: sale@ameracar.com, WWW: http://ameracar.com. Portable electroplating system for more than 60 metals and 40 alloys on any metallic (chrome, aluminum...) and non metallic surface such as wood, glass, plastic, tissues, rubber, etc. World's only multi-voltage user system (12/24/115/230 volts, 50/60 HZ) and amps/hrs displays (.000001) for 1/1,000,000 inch accuracy of deposit. Established: 1989 - Franchising Since: 1995 - No. of Units: Company Owned: 4 - Dealers: 235 - Fee: $1,500/$9,000 - Total Inv: $7,000: liquid, system, training, technical book, anodes, etc.- Financing: All credit card, leasing, long term financing.

BAG-A-SIGN INC.
145 Falcon St., P.O. Box 6473, Stn. D, London, ON, N5W 4Z2. Contact: Licensing Sales & Marketing, Gary VanderHeide, Richard Veldstra - Tel: (800) 668-2559 in Canada and the U.S.A. or Corporate Fax (519) 455-9514. Master Licenses or Distributorships for states and provinces (excluding Ontario). Own a Master License and set up your own network dealership with Corporate Assistance to service the commercial, industrial, municipal and government sectors in regards to low cost, reusable, pesticide, real estate, general purpose lawn signs protected under copyrights, design, etc... Established: 1990; now limited to selling only State or Provincial Master Licenses. Master License Fees by State or Province $10,000 - $15,000 depending on population - Royalties: 5% - Total Inv: $15,000 - $20,000 - Joint Venture or company financing may be available for qualified applicants.

BREATHPATROL INC. *
P.O. Box 583, Niagara Falls, ON, L2E 6V2. Contact: Gerhard Zielinsky, Pres. - Tel: (800) 361-3284, (905) 354-4448, Fax: (800) 278-8507, (905) 354-4412. Vending & distributor of breath lozenges for eliminating alcohol and other bad breath to bars, restaurants etc. Established: 1993 - Offering Dealerships Since: 1993 - Vending Since: 1995 - No. of Dealers: 20 - Investment: $400 to $15,000 - Financing: No.

CANADIAN TRAINING & DEVELOPMENT GROUP, INC.
7170 W. Credit Ave., Mississauga, ON, L5N 5Z3. Contact: Ted Kemper, Pres. - Tel: (905) 542-0224. C.T.D.G. offers business opportunities in the form of distributorships. This national educational/training company has been providing Canadian businesses with a single source for all their training & development needs for over 20 years. Distributor support includes extensive training in sales/mktg., facilitation, training skills,

product knowledge. Two annual conferences & conventions, monthly training schools, bi-monthly support mailings, two full-time marketing directors, a 1-800 support line etc. Established: 1974 - Offering Distributorships Since: 1975 - No. of Distributorships: 118 - Total Inv: $40,000 - Financing: Yes.

CANMAX MARKETING INC. *
2 Thorncliffe Pk. Dr., Unit 29, Toronto, ON, M4H 1H2. Contact: Nelville Weare, Pres. - Tel: (416) 696-6288, Fax: (416) 696-6226. Set up of distributorships, vending routes including equipment, product, location assistance & training. Exclusive line of equipment includes spiral gumball machines, candy cranes and new "Lifesaver" dispenser dealerships. Established: 1978 - Distributorships Since: 1978 - No. of Distributors: 2,000 - Total Inv: $11,000 - Financing: No.

CHECKROOM SERVICES INC.
1350 East 4th Ave., Vancouver, BC, V5N 1J5. Contact: Don Garden, General Mgr. - Tel: (604) 251-1000. Exclusive distributorships for the Lock 'N' Leave coin-operated coat-checking system & check room concession services. Established: 1993 - Franchising Since: 1993 - No. of Units: Company Owned: 1 - Franchised: 4 - Total Inv: $15,000 - $25,000 - Financing: Canada/USA/Europe/Asia.

COLOURITE FLOORING NETWORK *
465097 BC Ltd.
3352 Dunbar Street, Vancouver, BC, V6S 2C1. Contact: Ron Mendelson, Pres. - Tel: (604) 736-2177, Fax: (604) 736-8862. Shop-at-home flooring dealerships offering all types of flooring at reduced prices direct to the consumer. Little experience req'd. Ongoing support provided. Incredible income possible. Established: 1994 - Offering Dealerships Since: 1994 - No. of Units: Company Owned: 1 - Dealerships: 1 - Fee: $2,000 - Total Inv: $2,000.

CREATE-A-SHOT PRODUCTS CORPORATION *
200A, 908 - 17th Ave. S.W., Calgary, AB, T2T 0A3. Contact: Bruce Oxley, Brent Bergs, Pres., Prov. Mgr. - Tel: (800) 461-4884, (403) 244-2580, Fax: (403) 244-2582. Golf shot simulators and driving range mat surfaces for licensing and sale. Established: 1993 - Distributing Since: 1995 - Distributor Fee: $50,000 to $200,000 - Total Inv: $20,000 to $200,000 - Financing: Yes.

DATOLAB CANADA INC.
14 Verral Ave., Toronto, ON, M4M 2R2. Contact: Mike Cheevers, Dir. - Tel: (416) 465-4674. School of language. Also courses for students to improve marks in school. Established: Can. 1982, USA 1968 - Distributorship Since: 1989 - No. of Units: Company Owned: Can. 1, USA 1 - Distributor Fee: $15,000 + $10,000 - Total Inv: $25,000 - Financing: Yes.

DICKIE DEE ICE CREAM
Good Humor - Dickie Dee Ice Cream
70 Denison St., Markham, ON, L3R 2P5. Contact: Bob Wilson, Dir. of Mobile Vending - Tel: (905) 513-9550. Mobile street vending of frozen novelties. Equipment (tricycles, carts, freezers etc.) is leased to a contracted distributor who then leases to vendors. Ice cream & water ice novelties are sold to the distributor by the company. The company provides training & support. Established: 1959 - Distributorships Since: 1960 - No of Distributors: 240 - Total Inv: Approx. $700 per unit leased - Financing: No.

DRUG TRADING CO. LTD.
P.O. Box 335, Stn. A, 1960 Eglinton Ave., Toronto, ON, M1L 2M5. Contact: Denis Field, Mgr. - Tel: (416) 288-1100. Company is engaged in the wholesale of drugs. Mfg. opers. carried out in small plant in Scarborough. Franchised opers. carried out through IDA, Guardian and Custom Pharmacy stores. Established: 1904 - Offering Distributorships Since: 1933 - No. of Units: 2250 stores.

EASTERN DISPLAY TECHNOLOGIES
R.R. #5, Belleville, ON, K8N 4Z5. Contact: Tom Tyson, Owner - Tel: (613) 962-7920 or (800) 267-2861. Wholesaler of mobile portable signs (and supplies), L.E.D. programmable displays, and neon open signs. Established: 1986 - Franchise Fee: Purchase of inventory only - Financing: No.

ELEGANCE JEWELRY *
PBM Enterprises, Inc.
25 Kenmount Rd., Ste. 202, St. John's, NF, A1B 1W1. Contact: Slade Melvin, Pres. - Tel: (709) 726-1515. Home based fashion jewelry sales. Established: 1995 - Franchising Since: 1995 - No. of Units: Company Owned: 1 - Franchised: 25 - Franchise Fee: $99 (starter kit) - Total Inv: $99 (starter kit) - Financing: N/A.

EUROPEAN SAFETY PRODUCTS (CAN) LTD.
Mitschele Marketing Group
2201-1150 Burnaby St., Vancouver, BC, V6E 1P2. Contact: Max Mitschele, Pres. - Tel: (604) 689-9830. Inexpensive portable home and office security systems with new MLM program. Established: 1991 - Distribution Fee: $49.95 + taxes - Royalty: 5 levels - Total Inv: $49.95.

FABRICLAND/FABRICVILLE
76 Miranda, Toronto, ON, M6E 5A1. Contact: Ron Kimel, Co-Owner - Tel: (416) 703-1877. Fabric, drapery, upholstery, sewing notions, crafts, patterns, etc. Established: 1968 - Distributing Since: 1968 - No. of Units: Company Owned: 110 - Franchised: 16 - Fee: $35,000 - Royalty: 5% - Total Inv: $110,000 - Financing: No.

GALAXY CRYSTAL & CHINA, INC.
11 Latonia Dr., Rexdale, ON, M9W 2J1. Contact: Jake Rumph, Pres. - Tel: (416) 741-1758, Fax: (416) 741-1769. Direct sales of cookware, chinaware crystal, oil cure skillets, woks, extra large pans to 20 quart. Ideal business to operate from home. Low overhead. Established: 1983 - Franchising Since: 1984 - No. of Units: Company Owned: 1 - Franchised: 25 - Franchise Fee: min. $300 - Total Inv: avg. $2,300 secured by inventory - Financing: Yes.

GENUINE PARTS COMPANY LTD.
5530 Third St., S.E., Calgary, AB, T2H 1J9. Contact: Brian Johnson, Mktg. - Tel: (403) 253-2246. Auto parts. Established: 1947 - No. of Units: Company Owned: 17 - Associates: 163 - Distribution Centers: 4.

GUARANTEED MUFFLER SHOPS
Motorcade Industries, Ltd.
90 Kimcourt St., Toronto, ON, M6M 5G1. Contact: Roger Williams, Franc. Dir. - Tel: (416) 614-6118. Auto parts warehouse distributor presently operating in Ontario only. Established: 1950 - Franchising Since: 1972 - No. of Units: Franchised: 70 - Approx. Inv: $20,000 - Royalty: 8% - Financing: Yes.

HORIZON MANAGEMENT SYSTEMS
695 Rupert St., Waterloo, ON, N2V 1Z5. Contact: Larry Humphries, V.P. - Tel: (519) 884-6810. Provides personal management tools and workshops to improve the effectiveness of management and sales people. Many business people are now using this system to organize their activities and information. Established: 1986.

I.L.P.S.
International Loss Prevention Systems Corp.
1350 E. 4th Ave., Vancouver, BC, V5N 1J5. Contact: Don Garden, Dir. Int'l. Sales & Mktg. - Tel: (604) 255-5000. Shoplifting prevention products and systems. Established: 1988 - Offering Distributorships Since: 1988 - No. of Units: Company Owned: 1 - Distributors: 41 - Distributorship Fee: $25,000 - Royalty: 0 - Total Inv: $25,000.

INFL-AD-ABLE IMAGES OF CANADA, INC.
5615-103 St., Edmonton, AB, T6H 2H3. Contact: J.M. Macbeth, Mktg. Mgr. - Tel: (403) 438-6500. Manufacturer of cold air inflated advertising balloon systems and custom shape product replicas plus walkabout costumes. Established: 1986 - Distributing Since: 1986 - No. of Units: Company Owned: 1 - Distributed: 9 - Total Inv: $10,000 - Financing: No.

IRLY BIRD BUILDING CENTRES
Irly Distributors Ltd.
7846 - 128th St., P.O. Box 9010, Surrey, BC, V3T 4X7. Contact: Al Munro, Gen Mgr. - Tel: (604) 596-1551. Complete building supply program including distribution. Established: 1963 - Franchising Since: 1963 - No. of Units: Franchised: 63 - Franchise Fee: $5,000.

KEN-CO INDUSTRIES, LTD.
1070 Heritage Rd., Burlington, ON, L7L 4X9. Contact: Larry Minaker, Pres./G.M. - Tel: (905) 335-1828. Direct marketing of garage supplies and auto parts to the general repair garage and service station industries.

Established: 1963 - Distributing Since: 1963 - No. Distributorships: 31 - Distribution Fee: varies 0 - $10,000 - Total Inv: $15,000 - $30,000 equip., $15,000 - $25,000 inven.

MAC TOOLS CANADA
Division of Stanley Canada, Inc.
237 Brunel Rd., Mississauga, ON, L4Z 1X3. Contact: Mr. Aubrey McCallum, Oper. Mgr. - Tel: (905) 890-6400. Manufactures and distributes tools for the industrial and automotive aftermarket. Our products are only available from authorized mobile distributors. Each distributor has a protected territory assignment. Investment in inventory is also protected by a buyback agreement. Established: 1938 - Distributing Since: 1938 -No. of Distributorships: 2000 Worldwide, 135 Canada - Total Inv: approx. $112, 298 - Financing: Yes, for approved applicants.

MEAN GREEN
Mean Green Manufacturing
110-1772 Broadway, Port Coquitlam, BC, V3C 2M8. Contact: J. D. Cumley, Marketing - Tel: (604) 944-4130. Distributors of Canadian made environmentally friendly hand cleansers. Established: 1987 - Franchising Since: 1987 - No. of Units: Company Owned: 1 - Franchised: 6 - Financing: Not needed.

MISTER MINI POST
Box 131 Place Bonaventure, Montreal, PQ, H5A 1A6. Contact: Murray Black, Pres. - Tel: (514) 397-2214, Fax: (514) 393-1163. Manufacturer and distributor of private postal terminals. Each module contains 60 postal boxes. Ideal traffic builder for supermarkets, drug stores, convenience stores and other mass merchandisers. Self contained, free standing, lockable & private. Brings increased traffic & sales. You can also create your own route. Total Inv: $6,000 per 60 box unit.

MR. TUBE STEAK *
155 West Kent Ave. N., Vancouver, BC, V5X 2X4. Contact: Steve Duff, Dir. of Mktg. - Tel: (604) 322-0005. Area distributors who supply hotels, clubs, convenience stores, gas bars etc. utilizing equipment (counter top version of hot dog vending cart) and our premium hot dogs & smokies. Established: 1988 - Licensing Since: 1988 - No. of Units: 300+ - Licensed: 32 Distributors - Total Inv: $15,900 (includes 10 cooking units with locations, manuals, training, inventory forms, signage, business cards, promotional material etc.) - Franchise Fee: $120/year per unit, includes advertising.

NAUTILUS
Nautilus Canada Fitness Equip. Ltd.
87 George St., Ste. 5, Ottawa, ON, K1N 9H7. Contact: F. Sutcliffe, Pres. - Tel: (613) 762-2030. Fitness centers. Established: 1975 - Franchising Since: 1975 - Total Inv: $100,000 plus - Financing: No.

NEWAYS DISTRIBUTORS *
309 Lawrence St., New Westminster, BC, V3M 5L3. Contact: Tracey DePaoli, Exec. - Promotions - Tel: (604) 526-6721, Fax: (604) 526-6721. High quality toxin free personal care products, safer ingredients used. Also high quality herbal heath formulations. Very lucrative plan & bonus pay out program. No selling required, no stocking, low quotas. Established: 1986 - Distributing Since: 1986 - Fee: max. req. of $150 mth. for pay out of two profit ctrs. - Total Inv: $150/mo. with products on auto-ship program.

NOAH'S ARK LEASING *
Jungleland Mini Putt Inc.
5796 Byng Ave., Niagara Falls, ON, L2J 5E2. Contact: Herb Cowan, Pres. - Tel: (905) 371-1724. Lawn ornaments for special occasions such as birthdays, just arrived, happy retirement, welcome home, congratulations. Established: 1994 - Franchising Since: 1994 - No. of Units: Company Owned: 2 - Franchised: 1 - Franchise Fee: $15,000 - Royalty: None - Total Inv: $15,000 plus advertising - Financing: None.

NSA INDEPENDENT DISTRIBUTOR
235 Martindale Rd., St. Catharines, ON, L2W 1A5. Contact: David Vedova, Owner - Tel: (905) 685-4851. Marketing a complete line of environmental products, water & air treatment systems and educational systems for pre-schoolers. Established: 1970 - Franchising Since: 1980 - No. of Units: Franchised: 50,000+ - Franchise Fee: $25 - Total Inv: Avg. $5,000 - $10,000 - Financing: Yes.

PAGE II FOIL SYSTEMS INC.
169 Dalhousie St., Brantford, ON, N3T 2J6. Contact: Wm. D. Hurley, Pres. - Tel: (519) 759-8200, Fax: (519) 759-7991 . Distributor of Page II system, a fully integrated computerized foil printing system. Established: 1989 - No. of Units: Company Owned: 15 - Total Inv: $4,995.

PARADISE ISLAND
Trophey Foods
6555 Kestrel Rd., Mississauga, ON, L5T 1P4. Contact: Franchise Department - Tel: (905) 670-8050. Food distributor business promoting quality nuts and confectionery products to retail food and convenience stores. Established: 1980 - Franchising Since: 1987 - No. of Units: 360 - Franchise Fee: $10,000 - Total Inv: $87,000 - $125,000 - Financing: Yes, through major banks.

PERSONAL HEALTHCARE PRODUCTS, PHP, INC. *
P.O. Box 74088, Ottawa, ON, K1M 2H9. Contact: Doug Watson, V.P. - Tel: (613) 749-2630. Wholesale distributor of vitamin supplements & skin care products. Established: 1994 - Fee: $1,000 min. for territory - Financing: Yes.

PINGOUIN
Promofil Canada Ltd.
300 Marcellaurin Blvd., Ste. 100, St-Laurent, PQ, H4M 2L4. Contact: Alain Francois, Gen. Mgr. - Tel: (514) 747-2938. Manufacturer and distributor of yarns and accessories, plus new exclusive ready-to-wear fashions from Europe. Established: 1929 - Franchising Since: 1974 - No. of Units: Company Owned: 3 - Franchised: 33 - Total Inv: $40,000 - $50,000 - Financing: No.

PRO-TECT ASPHALT LTD.
100 Buchanan St., Cobourg, ON, K9A 1Z1. Contact: Jim Hartford, Pres. - Tel: (905) 372-3902. Manufacture of driveway sealing equipment and distributor of related asphalt maintenance equipment. Support and assistance given to purchaser in establishing driveway sealing business. Established: 1980 - No. of Distributors: 25 - Total Inv: $2,275 - Financing: No.

PROVINCIAL TABLE PADS
Provincial Table Pads Ltd.
321 Anchor Rd., Unit 1A, Hamilton, ON, L8W 3R1. Contact: Ross DePalma, Pres. - Tel: (905) 383-1343. Shop at home service for custom table pads. Established: 1982 - Franchising Since: 1983 - No. of Units: Company Owned: 2 - Franchised: 5.

SAFE-PAK SUPPLY CANADA, INC.
1638 Kebet Way, Port Coquitlam, BC, V3C 5M5. Contact: Russ MacDonald, Fran. Co-ord. - Tel: (604) 942-1788. Safety and first aid supplies are being marketed primarily to industrial accounts via professional appointed service/display units. Dealership includes a computer data service, sales training, sales aids and catalogues. Established: 1973 - Offering Distributorships Since: 1988 - No. of Units: 4 - Franchise Fee: $25,000 - Total Inv: $96,000 - Financing: Yes.

SECURITY PLUS *
132 Lakeshore Rd. E., Ste. 106 , Mississauga, ON, L5G 1E6. Contact: Neil Tulsiani, Pres. - Tel: (905) 949-6934. Sales and distribution of security products, including pepper sprays, currency detector pens and personal alarms. Established: 1994 - Franchising Since: 1994 - No. of Units: Company Owned: 1 - Franchised: 165 - Franchise Fee: None - Total Inv: $277.50 min.

SERVICEMASTER
Servicemaster Res/Comm.
6540 Tomkin Rd., Mississauga, ON, L5T 2E9. Contact: David Messenger, V.P. Sales & Mktg. - Tel: (905) 670-0000. Professional cleaning services for businesses, government and institution buildings and residences. Cleaning and re-construction after fire or flood damage. Established: (Can) 1953, (US) 1947 - Franchising Since: (Can) 1953, (US) 1952 - No. of Units: Franchised: 125 in Can. - Franchise Fee: $9,300 - $17,300 - Royalty: 8% - 9% depending on type of business - Total Inv: $18,600 - $29,600 Can. funds - Financing: Yes.

SHUR-GAIN
Maple Leaf Foods, Inc.
R.R. #4, James St. S., St. Mary's, ON, N4X 1C7. Contact: Gary Richardson, Manager - Tel: (519) 349-2152, Fax: (519) 349-2675. Livestock & poultry feeds, pet foods, animal health products, birdseed, horse feed. Established: 1929 - Distributing Since: 1938 - No. of Units: Company Owned: 20 - Distributors: 200 - Total Inv: $50,000 - $200,000 - Financing: Yes.

SIGNATURE COMMUNICATIONS INC.
850 Tapscott Rd., Unit 24, Scarborough, ON, M1X 1N4. Contact: Nick Cindea, Pres. - Tel: (416) 754-1511, Fax: (416) 754-9192. Dealership in manufacturing rubber stamps and glazing photos on china. Training, marketing plan, supplies and on going buisness assistance and support provided. Established: 1987 - Franchising Since: 1989 - No. of Units: Company Owned: 1 - Franchised: 56 - Total Inv: $2,500 to $8,500 - Financing: Yes.

SOFTUB CANADA *
2451 Evans Rd., Val Caron, ON, P3N 1L1. Contact: Gary Kingsley, Dir. of Dealer Dev. - Tel: (705) 897-8827. Manufacturer/distributor of lightweight, portable, full featured hydrotherapy hot tub. Softubs plug into standard 110V outlet, and weighing only 60lbs empty adds to the portability. Established: 1990 - Franchising Since: 1990 - No. of Units: Franchised: 100 - Total Inv: $15,000 - Financing: No.

SUNITRON INC.
1170 Sheppard Ave. W., Bldg. #50, Downsview, ON, M3K 2A3. Contact: Jerry Pappa, Pres. - Tel: (416) 630-8811, Fax: (416) 781-5140. Distributor of all kinds of computerized bill board for indoor or outdoor (LED message signs). Established: 1986 - No. of Dealers: Over 350 - Total Inv: Up to negotiation - Financing: No.

SURGEMASTER
P.O. Box 3564, Regina, SK, S4P 3L7. Contact: Ron Brewer, Dir. - Tel: (306) 775-1242. Transient voltage surge suppressor manufacturer. TVSS equipment for homes and business. Protection of all electrical equipment, not just computers. Established: 1984 - No. of Units: 1 - Total Inv: approx. $2,000.

TIME MASTERS
Time Masters, Inc.
47 Redgrave Dr., Etobicoke, ON, M9R 3T9. Contact: Thom Tyson, Seminar Dir. - Tel: (416) 248-5555, Fax: (416) 248-5558. Time management and goal setting seminar at which clients are taught effective time management techniques. Big buyers are governments, large businesses and individuals. Systems for students, sales, executives & general use. A Time Master System is provided for each client. Established: 1984 - Franchising Since: 1987 - No. of Units: Company Owned: 2 - Franchised: 16 - Franchise Fee: $14,500 - Royalty: None - Total Inv: $15,000 to $25,000 - Financing: None.

UAP/NAPA ASSOCIATE PROGRAM
7025 Ontario St., E., Montreal, PQ, H1N 2B3. Contact: Benoit Bouchard, Coordinator, Jobber Programs - Tel: (514) 256-5031, Fax: (514) 256-8469. Wholesale and retail stores for distributing automotive parts and supplies including body shop supplies. UAP Inc. Established: 1926 - Franchising Since: 1955.

WATERSKILL GAMES, INC. *
55 Administration Rd., Unit 29, Concord, ON, L4K 4G9. Contact: Betty Briselle, V.P., Mktg. - Tel: (905) 669-6904. Manufacturer and distributor of Coin Drop Amusement Games. Established: 1994 - Franchising Since: 1994 - No. of Units: 1 - Franchised: 10 - No. of Units: Company Owned: 1 - Franchised: 10 - Franchise Fee: $10,000 avg. - Royalty: None - Total Inv: $10,000 avg.

WEATHER-BOS *
Weather-Bos Canada Ltd.
R.R. 1, Hwy. 22 W., Hyde Park, ON, N0M 1L0. Contact: Eric J. Bos, Pres. - Tel: (519) 641-0357, Fax: (519) 641-4629. Manufacturers of enviro safe stains and paints. Established: 1989.

WEBER SECURITY DISTRIBUTION *
675 Queen St. S., Kitchener, ON, N2G 4H6. Contact: Donald Young, Exec. V.P. - Tel: (519) 888-4290, Fax: (519) 888-4206. Importer and distributor of security, access control, cctv and home automation systems. Established: 1992 - Total Inv: Demo kit $800, initial stock $500 - Financing: Net 30 payment terms.

WINDSHIELD-SMITH
Windshield-Smith Repair Service
P.O. Box 218, Shell Lake, SK, S0J 2G0. Contact: Bryce Smith, Owner - Tel: (306) 427-4825, Fax: (306) 427-2050. Repair stone bruises & cracks on windshields. Established: 1990 - No. of Units: Company Owned: 1 - Distributorships: 8 - Fee: $3,000 - Royalty: None - Total Inv: $3,000 - $3,500 - Financing: No.

EMPLOYMENT & PERSONNEL

500 SELECTION SERVICES INC., THE
615 Rene-Levesque West, Ste. 600, Montreal, PQ, H3B 1P6. Contact: Pauline Lessard, Dir. - Tel: (514) 861-8373. Employment agency offering complete permanent and temporary employees. Established: 1952 - Franchising Since: 1968 - No. of Units: Company Owned: 6 - Franchised: 9 - Franchise Fee: $25,000, terms - Royalty: 7% of perm gross sales, 4% of temp gross sales - Total Inv: 1st year cash flow incl. fran. fee $75,000 - Financing: No.

AACTIVE PERSONNEL SERVICES LTD.
290 William Ave., Winnipeg, MB, R3B 0R1. Contact: M. Peters, Pres. - Tel: (204) 982-4611. Blue collar temporary personnel. Established: 1973 - Franchising Since: 1989 - No. of Units: Company Owned: 1 - Franchised: 1 - Franchise Fee: $20,000 - Royalty: 6% 1st $800,000, 4% 2nd $800,000, 3% thereafter - Total Inv: $50,000: $20,000 fran. fee, $25,000 work. cap., $5,000 office equip. - Financing: Yes, O.A.C.

DRAKE OFFICE OVERLOAD, DRAKE PERSONNEL, DRAKE EXECUTIVE
Drake International Inc.
P.O. Box 800, Stn. F, Toronto, ON, M4Y 2N8. Contact: Judith Pineault, Fran. Dir. - Tel: (416) 216-1000, Fax: (416) 216-1109. Temporary and permanent placement service. Industrial/clerical to executive placement. Full initial training program and on-going support. Training in marketing, budgeting, and new systems through seminars and onsite meetings. Established: 1951 - Franchising Since: 1969 - Number of Units: Company Owned: 42-Cndn. - Franchised: 12-Cndn. - Franchise Fee: $10,000 - $25,000 - Royalty: 7% gross sales (temporary) 18% of gross sales (permanent) - Total Inv: fee + 6-8 mos. operating cost (approx. $60,000).

GET-A-JOB, CANADA! *
Camroux & Company Ltd.
P.O. Box 2006, 5507 River Rd., Niagara Falls, ON, L2E 6Z2. Contact: Chuck/John, Owners - Tel: (905) 358-0688, (800) 565-4732, Fax: (905) 358-0511. Employment databank service for job seekers and employers, advertised nationally on radio and print. Internet e mail: get-a-job@touchtone.com. Established: 1990 - Franchising Since: 1995 - No. of Units: Company Owned: 2 - Total Inv: $295.

HUNT PERSONNEL, TEMPORARILY YOURS
Business Aid, Inc.
365 Bloor St. E., Ste. 1902, Toronto, ON, M4W 3L4. Contact: Ted Turner, Pres. - Tel: (416) 920-4141, Fax: (416) 920-7285, E-Mail: tristed@passport.ca. Personnel services, temporary and permanent. Established: 1967 - Franchising Since: 1974 - No. of Units: Company Owned: 1 - Franchised: 10 - Franchise Fee: $10,000 min. - Total Inv: $50,000 - Royalty: varies with volume and services. WWW site: http://www.barint.on.ca/netwave/hunt/.

SENIORS FOR BUSINESS/ SENIORS FOR SENIORS
Seniors Franchise Systems Inc.
55 Eglinton Ave. E., Ste. 311, Toronto, ON, M4P 1G8. Contact: Peter Cook, Pres. - Tel: (416) 481-4579. Employment agencies for persons 50 plus. Established: 1985 - Franchising Since: 1990 - No. of Units: Company Owned: 1 - Franchised: 4 - Franchise Fee: min. $25,000 - Royalty: 6% of sales - Total Inv: min. $50,000 - Financing: No.

THE RESUME HUT
PenLan Career Group
743 View St., Victoria, BC, V8W 1J9. Contact: H. Landry, Pres. - Tel: (604) 383-3983, Fax: (604) 383-1580, e-mail: penlan@islandnet.com, Home Page: http://www.islandnet.com/penlan. A career consulting business...since 1986. We are the McDonald's of the resume business, with over 9,000 clients served. Resumes, career consulting, outplacement, networking, career testing, business planning and more. Established: 1986 - Franchising Since: 1991 - No. of Units: Company Owned: H.O. - Franchised: 3 - Franchise Fee: $10,000 - Royalty: 2% + 2% adv. - Total Inv: $18,000 max. - Financing: Some possible.

ENTERTAINMENT

CANADIAN POOLPLAYERS ASSOC. INC. *
200 McNab St., Ste. 201, Box 722, Walkerton, ON, N0G 2V0. Contact: Lindsay Dobson, Pres. - Tel: (519) 881-2196, Fax: (519) 881-2520. Amateur pool leagues, organize tournaments. Established: 1989 - Franchising Since: 1989 - No. of Units: Franchised: 13 - Royalty: $5.00 per team or 20%, whichever is greater - Total Inv: $4,500 approx. - Financing: No.

DAVOLI OF NORTH AMERICA
Sunitron Inc. Holding Corp.
1170 Sheppard Ave. W., Downsview, ON, M3K 2A3. Contact: Jerry Rappa, Pres. - Tel: (416) 630-8811 - 12 - 18. Davoli of North America imports from Italy hi fi sound systems for mobile D.J., night clubs and discoteques.. Davoli sells only to dealers, not to the direct public. Established: 1986 - Network Dealer Since: 1988 - Royalty: None - Total Inv: $3,900 - Financing: No.

FOREST HILL VIDEO
Video Party Tyme
55 Northfield Dr., E., Waterloo, ON, N2K 3T6. Contact: Harvey Norris, Pres. - Tel: (519) 746-2704. Video, sales & rentals. Established: 1982 - No. of Units: Company Owned: 2 - Franchised: 6.

GARRY ROBERTSON MUSIC SERVICES
Box 160 St. Boniface P.S., Winnipeg, MB, R2H 3B4. Contact: Garry Robertson, Pres. - Tel: (204) 255-8871. Supply disc jockey services and mobile music entertainment. Established: 1971 - Franchising Since: 1975 - No. of Units: Company Owned: 5 - Franchised: 23 - Total Inv: $15,000 - Royalty: 7.5%.

JUST NEW REELEASES *
80 W. Beaver Creek Rd., Unit 2, Richmond Hill, ON, L4B 1H3. Contact: Brian Kenny - Tel: (905) 882-5200. Video store franchisor. Established: 1990 - Franchising Since: 1990 - No. of Units: Company Owned: 3 - Franchised: 81 - Financing: Yes.

RIDE CO., THE
Greene Flyer Inc.
37 Niagara St., Toronto, ON, M5V 1C2. Contact: Randy Presnaik, Pres. - Tel: (416) 504-0112, Fax: (416) 504-0310. Portable childrens amusement ride, holds 16 kids, takes up 30 feet of space, runs on household current and can be set up by one person in less than one hour and even less to dismantle. Can be towed easily by compact pick-up or minivan. Established: 1990 - Franchising Since: 1990 - No. of Units: Company Owned: 2 - Franchised: 13 - Franchise Fee: $15,000 - Royalty: Only initial franchise fee and purchase of the unit - Total Inv: $15,000 fran. fee, $45,000 purchase unit - Financing: Full assistance to obtain financing & licensing.

TOP GOLF MINIATURE
4232 Bourque Blvd., Rock Forest, PQ, J1N 1W7. Contact: Rene Sckoropad, C.E.O. - Tel: (819) 820-1169. Miniature Golf. Established: 1989 - Franchising Since: 1990 - No. Of Units: Franchised: 5 - Franchise Fee: $20,000 - Royalty: 5% - Total Inv: $200,000 - Financing: 70%.

FOOD: CONVENIENCE STORES, SPECIALTY SHOPS, AND SUPERMARKETS

ACHILLE DE LA CHEVROTIERE LTEE.
333 Ave. Montemurro, P.O Box 940, Rouyn-Noranda, PQ, J9X 5E1. Contact: Levis Trotier, Sales Dir. - Tel: (819) 797-1900. Food retailer (grocery, meat, fruit and vegetables). Established: 1956 - Franchising Since: 1963 - No. of Units: 8.

AG FOODS
Associated Grocers (Div. of the Overwaitea Food Group)
Box 7200, Vancouver, BC, V6B 4E4. Contact: Glenn Barrick, Real Estate Rep. - Tel: (604) 888-1213, Fax: (604) 888-8565. Retail-oriented wholesaler supplying full product listing (grocery, frozen, produce, meat, deli, confectionery, HBA, cigarettes & tobacco) to all types of operations, including gas bars, C-stores, full-line grocery stores. (5,000 - 50,000 sq. ft.) Franchising Since: 1992 - No. of Units: Company Owned: 1 - Franchised/Licensed: 48 - Total Inv: Varies - Financing: Introduction to financial institutions.

ALIMENTATION COUCHE TARD
1600 Boul. St. Martin, E., Tour B., Ste. 280, Laval, PQ, H7G 4S7. Contact: Robert Durand - Tel: (514) 662-3272 or (800) 361-8895. Convenience stores offering gas, banking, videotapes and dry cleaning services. Established: 1979 - Franchising Since: 1979 - No. of Units: Company Owned: 9 - Franchised: 150 - Franchise Fee: $22,000 - Total Inv: $85,000 - Royalty: 11% - Financing: Possible arrangement with commercial banks.

AMI GEM METRO RICHELIEU SUPER CARNAVAL
Metro Richelieu
11011 Maurice Duplessis Blvd., Montreal, PQ, H1C 1V6. Contact: Claude Brunetta, Franc. Dir. - Tel: (514) 643-1000. Grocery and convenience stores. Established: 1976 - No. of Units: 628.

ARENA MEATS
The Beef Place
22 White Oak Ct., Markham, ON, L3P 3Y1. Contact: Amedeo Arena, Owner - Tel: (905) 294-7640. Meat shops. Established: 1979 - Franchising Since: 1990 - No. of Units: Company Owned: 2 - Franchise Fee: $25,000 - Royalty: 6% - Total Inv: $80,000 - $100,000 - Financing: No.

BEAVER TAILS®
Beaver Tails Canada Inc.
112 Nelson Str., Ste. 101C, Ottawa, ON, K1N 7R5. Contact: Robert Libbey - Tel: (613) 789-4940, (800) 704-0351, Fax: (613) 599-5425. Beaver Tails are a fun, wholesome pastry product served fresh at leisure food locations such as stadiums, markets, theme parks, shopping centres & other entertainment venues. Established: 1976 - Franchising Since: 1991 - No. of Units: Company Owned: 20 - Franchised: 10 - Franchise Fee: $20,000 - Royalty: 5% bus. rights, 3% adv. - Total Inv: $50,000 - $75,000 for equip., leaseholds - Financing: Assistance is provided in securing financing.

BECKER MILK CO., LTD.
671 Warden Ave., Toronto, ON, M1L 3Z7. Contact: Franchise Mgr. - Tel: (416) 698-2591. Convenience stores. Established: 1957 - Franchising Since: 1972 - No. of Units: Company Owned: 600 - Franchised: 75 - Franchise Fee: $15,000 - Royalty: 3% - Total Inv: $65,000 - $95,000 - Financing: None.

BULK BARN
55 Leek Cres., Beaver Creek Bus. Pk., Richmond Hill, ON, L4B 3Y2. Contact: Carl Ofield, Pres. - Tel: (905) 886-6756, Fax: (905) 886-3717. Canada's largest bulk food retailer. No. of Units: 43.

CHOCOLATE BAR DESSERT CAFE, THE *
Chocolate Bar, Ltd.
535 Cleveland Cres. S.E., Calgary, AB, T2G 4R8. Contact: Mark Climan, V.P. - Tel: (403) 287-2114, Fax: (403) 287-2117. Dessert & cappuccino bar with lunch, breakfast, gourmet chocolates, gift baskets,

etc. Established: 1986 - Franchising Since: 1992 - No. of Units: Company Owned: 1 - Franchised: 3 - Franchise Fee: $20,000 - Royalty: 4%, 2% adv. - Total Inv: $75,000 equip. + $75,000 - Financing: No.

CHOCOLATERIE BERNARD CALLEBAUT, LTD.
1313 1st St. S.E., Calgary, AB, T2G 5L1. Contact: Robert Ingles, Mktg. Dir. - Tel: (800) 661-8367. High quality chocolates and chocolate related products. Manufactured in Calgary and sold exclusively at Callebaut outlets. Established: 1983 - Franchising Since: 1984 - No. of Units: Company Owned: 1 - Franchised: 13 - Franchise Fee: $15,000 - $25,000 - Total Inv: $150,000 - $170,000 min. $100,000 unencumbered.

CLOVER FARM, FOODLAND
Clover Farm Stores of Canada
P.O.Box 3100, Brantford, ON, N3T 6K2. Contact: Franchise Dir./Pres. - Tel: (519) 751-6000. Grocery and convenience stores. No. ofUnits: Company Owned: 122 - Franchised: 195.

GATEWAY NEWSTANDS/ GATEWAY CIGAR STORES
Tobmar Investments
30 East Beaver Creek Rd., Ste. 206, Richmond Hill, ON, L4B 1J2. Contact: Michael Aychental, C.E.O. - Tel: (905) 886-8900, (905) 886-8904. Tobacco/newsstands and gifts in large office buildings and shopping malls from coast to coast. Established: 1983 - Franchising Since: 1983 - No. of Units: Franchised: 201 - Franchise Fee: $25,000 - $75,000 - Royalty: 3% gross sales - Total Inv: $60,000 - $175,000 - Financing: Yes.

HICKORY FARMS OF CANADA
10 Esna Park Dr., Markham, ON, L3R 1E1. Contact: John Lawson - Tel: (905) 479-3199, Fax: (905) 940-6777. Specialty foods. No. of Units: Company Owned: 20 - Franchised: 11.

IGA
Hudon et Deaudelin Ltee.
11281 Albert-Hudon Blvd., Montreal-Nord, PQ, H1G 3J5. Contact: Gaetan Dufresne, Dir. Dev. - Tel: (514) 324-5700. Voluntary wholesaler supplying affiliated food markets and convenience stores. Established: 1873 - Franchising Since: 1953 - No. of Units: Company Owned: 2 - Affiliated: 855.

IGA
Oshawa Foods
6355 Viscount Rd., Mississauga, ON, L4V 1W2. Contact: Franchise Dir. - Tel: (905) 672-6633. Retail grocery.

JUG CITY
Knechtel Wholesale Grocers
P.O. Box 1358, Kitchener, ON, N2G 4H8. Contact: Mr. Jim Milles, Dir. - Tel: (519) 743-5521. Convenience stores. Established: 1975 - No. of Units: 35.

KERNELS POPCORN (CAN)
Kernels Popcorn, Limited
40 Eglinton Ave., E., Ste. 250, Toronto, ON, M4P 3A2. Contact: Bernice Sinopoli, Oper. Adm. - Tel: (416) 487-4194. Canadian retail popcorn chain operating in regional shopping malls. Over 70 flavours sold in variety of unique packaging. Established: 1983 - Franchising Since: 1984 - No. of Units: Company Owned: 11 - Franchised: 56 - Franchise Fee: $25,000 - Royalty: 8%, 1% adv. - Total Inv: $110,000 - $140,000 incl. fee - Financing: No.

KNECHTEL ASSOCIATE STORES
The Knechtel Corp.
P.O. Box 1358, Kitchener, ON, N2G 4H8. Contact: John Kabucis, Dir. Store Dev. - Tel: (519) 742-3502. Wholesaler of grocery products to independent retailers and convenience stores. Established: 1930 - Franchising Since: 1975 - No. of Units: Franchised: 68 - Total Inv: Varies (depending on store size) - Financing: Corporately assisted.

LES SUCERIES DE GRAND-MAMAN (1987) INC.
133 Trudel, Quebec City, PQ, G1N 3R1. Contact: Claude Gagnon, Pres., Dir. Gen. - Tel: (418) 682-0268, (800) 263-0268, Fax: (418) 682-3124. Manufacturer of chocolates, sucre a la creme and fudge. Established: 1980 - Franchising Since: 1980 - No. of Units: Franchised: 10.

M & M MEAT SHOPS
M & M Meat Shops Ltd.
P.O. Box 2488, 640 Trillium Dr., Kitchener, ON, N2H 6M3. Contact: Christine Freeman, Admin. Assistant - Tel: (519) 895-1075. Sale of frozen foods at the retail level including barbeque items, vegetables, desserts and party items. Established: 1980 - Franchising Since: 1981 - No. of Units: Company Owned: 1 - Franchised: 143 - Franchise Fee: $30,000 - Royalty: 3% + 1.5% adv. - Total Inv: $300,000 turn-key - Financing: $150,000 bank.

METRO - RICHELIEU - AMIX - GEM
Alimentation A.D.L. Enr.
333 Montemurro Ave., P.O. Box 940, Rouyn-Noranda, PQ, J9X 5E1. Contact: Levis Trottier, Sales Mgr. - Tel: (819) 797-1900. Food retailer. Established: 1927 - Franchising Since: 1950 - No. of Units: Franchised: 48 - Royalty: Purchasing Agreement - Total Inv: Depending on store size - Financing: Yes.

MOHAWK OIL CO, LTD.
Mohawk Oil Co Ltd.
1467 Spitfire Pl., Port Coquitlam, BC, V3C 5P1. Contact: Sam Sidhu, Fran. Dept. - Tel: (604) 942-3812. Service station and convenience store. Established: 1961 - No. of Units: Company Owned: 34 - Franchised: 304.

NUTTER'S BULK & NATURAL FOODS
107 - 1601 Dunmore Rd., S.E., Medicine Hat, AB, T1A 1Z8. Contact: Bruce Champion, Fran. Licensing Dir. - Tel: (403) 529-1664, Fax: (403) 529-6507. Nutter's, Western Canada's largest bulk and natural food franchise, offers a unique retail opportunity in one of North America's fastest growing industries. Our unique combination of bulk foods, deli, natural foods and gourmet gift baskets has made Nutter's a leading edge food retailer. Established: 1982 - Franchising Since: 1984 - No. of Units: Company Owned: 5 - Franchised: 27 - Franchise Fee: $15,000 to $30,000 - Royalty: 2% to 4% - Total Inv: $120,000 - $250,000 - Financing: No.

OODLES HOME READY FOODS
Oodles Daily Food Ltd.
P.O. Box 348, Surrey, BC, V3T 5B6. Contact: Steven Jaeger, Pres. - Tel: (604) 888-1121. Frozen home ready foods retail. Established: 1991 - Franchising Since: 1993 - No. of Units: Company Owned: 2 - Franchise Fee: $20,000 - Royalty: 3% sales, 1% adv. - Total Inv: approx. $150,000 turn key - Financing: Royal Bank, Federal Business Development Bank.

POULTRY KING *
Poultry King, Inc.
30 E. Beaver Creek Rd., Ste. 206, Richmond Hill, ON, L4B 1J2. Contact: David Goldman, Pres. - Tel: (905) 886-8900, Fax: (905) 886-8904. Retail of poultry and dairy prepared foods and associated products. Established: 1995 - Franchising Since: 1995 - No. of Units: Franchised: 2 - Franchise Fee: $35,000 - Royalty: 6% - Total Inv: $140,000 - Financing: Up to 25%.

PROVI-SOIR
Division de C Corp., Inc.
3100 Cote Vertu-Bureau 560, St. Laurent, PQ, H4R 2J8. Contact: Franchise Dept. - Tel: (514) 333-5110. Convenience store, gas, and fast food. Established: 1975 - Franchising Since: 1975 - No. of Units: Franchised: 252 - Franchise Fee: $25,000 - Royalty: 11.6% avg. - Total Inv: $75,000 - Financing: No.

REDDI MART CONVENIENCE STORES
Horne & Pitfield Foods, Ltd.
17220 Stoney Plain Rd., Edmonton, AB, T5S 1K6. Contact: Ambrose Micklich, Dir. Conv. Group - Tel: (403) 486-4800. Convenience stores. Established: 1988 - Franchising Since: 1988 - No. of Units: Franchised: 80.

RENAISSANCE, THE CHOCOLATE COMPANY
Benkis Enterprises Ltd.
2404 Woodview Dr., S.W., Calgary, AB, T2W 4X7. Contact: R.A. Benkis, V.P. - Tel: (403) 938-3050. Renaissance produces gourmet handmade and dipped chocolates and chocolate creations. Marketing is through the company's retail outlets, franchised stores in eastern Canada, and through specialty chocolate outlets in western Canada. Established:

1982 - Franchising Since: 1992 - No. of Units: Company Owned: 2 - Franchised: 1 - Franchise Fee: approx. $20,000 - Royalty: approx. 5% of gross sales, depending on circumstances - Total Inv: $45,000 - $50,000 incl. fran. fee - Financing: No.

SAVE-EASY, FOODMASTER, RED & WHITE, QUIK MART, VALU MART AND THE PHARMACY
Atlantic Wholesalers Ltd.
4 Charlotte St., Sackville, NB, E0A 3C0. - Tel: (902) 468-8866. Food, GM and health and beauty pharmacies in The Pharmacy group. Established: 1903 - Franchising Since: 1954 - No. of Units: 16 - Franchised: 434.

SCHNEIDER'S POPCORN PARTIES INC. *
#2 - 2406 Wheaton Ave., Saskatoon, SK, S7L 5Z4. Contact: D.J. Schneider, C.E.O. - Tel: (800) 665-6484. Home parties - popcorn seed, spice, poppers & oil. Entire marketing system geared to the rapidly growing home-based businesss marketplace. Established: 1988 - Franchising Since: 1994 - No. of Units: Company Owned: 4 - Franchised: 9 - Franchise Fee: $15,000 - Royalty: Nil - Total Inv: fran. fee plus $15,000 stock, $5,000 equip. - Financing: No.

SCHWAB'S FINEST IN MEATS
Schwab's Meat Products Ltd.
3690 Sandwich St., W., Windsor, ON, N9C 1B7. Contact: Henry Schwab, Pres. - Tel: (519) 254-4735. Established: 1955 - No. of Units: Company Owned: 1 - Franchised: 8.

SWEET FACTORY INC., THE
Sheppard Sq., 3709 Chesswood Rd., Downsview, ON, M3J 2P6. Contact: P. Friedmann, Pres. - Tel: (416) 638-5687. Retail confectionary. Established: 1988 - Franchising Since: 1989 - No. of Units: Company Owned: 4 - Franchised: 54 - Franchise Fee: $25,000 store, $20,000 - $25,000 kiosk - Royalty: 6% - Total Inv: $50,000 - $120,000.

TABATOUT INC.
1001 University, Ste. C-22, Montreal, PQ, H3B 4L4. Contact: Jean-Gilles Boisvert, Pres. - Tel: (514) 875-7676. Retail outlets selling magazines, books, newspapers, confectionery drinks & tobacco. Established: 1984 - Franchising Since: 1986 - No. of Units: Company Owned: 5 - Franchised: 7 - Franchise Fee: $35,000 - Royalty: 3% - Total Inv: $70,000 - $125,000.

TICKETS 'N THINGS *
Tickets 'N Tobacco, Inc.
210 Central Blvd., Ste. 102, Orleans, ON, K1E 3V7. Contact: Chris Goneau, Pres. & Dir. of Dev. - Tel: (613) 824-5633, Fax: (613) 824-6305. Smoke shops in shopping centres throughout Canada. Lottery tickets, confectionary goods, tobacco products. Established: 1987 - Franchising Since: 1989 - No. of Units: Company Owned: 1 - Franchised: 33 - Franchise Fee: $20,000 - Royalty: less than 1% - Total Inv: leaseholds $10,000 - $12,000, inven. $6,000 - $10,000 - Financing: Yes.

VALU-MART/FRESHMART/MR. GROCER/YOUR INDEPENDENT GROCER
National Grocers Co. Ltd.
6 Monogram Pl., Weston, ON, M9R 4C4. Contact: Leo Bugeja, Dir. Fran. - Tel: (416) 245-5050. Stores featuring in-store bakery and delicatessen within a conventional supermarket format. Established: 1925 - Franchising Since: 1929 - No. of Units: 180.

WINKS
C Corp. (Ontario) Inc. Western Division
#300, 13220 St. Albert Trail, Edmonton, AB, T5L 4W1. Contact: Marian Majeau, Mgr., Winks Admin. - Tel: (403) 455-4747 Ext. 304, Fax: (403) 455-4999. Winks Convenience Stores focus on food service. Hot chicken program - in store bakery - 24 hr - full video and game rentals. Established: 1988 - Franchising Since: 1988 - No. of Units: Company Owned: 5 - Franchised: 22 - Franchise Fee: $25,000 - Royalty: 12.5% - Total Inv: $25,000 fran. fee, $40,000 inven., $10,000 small equip. - Financing: No.

FOOD: DONUT, BAKERY AND COFFEE SHOPS

APOLLO COFFEE HOUSES, INC.
1595 W. Broadway, Vancouver, BC, V6J 1W6. Contact: Norman Mannie, Pres. - Tel: (604) 730-0910. Upscale gourmet coffee houses. Extensive range of espresso based drinks including flavored lattes, Italian sodas, granitas, fresh squeezed juices, European cheesecakes, gourmet sandwiches. Established: 1993 - Franchising Since: 1994 - No. of Units: Company Owned: 2 - Franchise Fee: $20,000 - Royalty: Monthly 7.5% full, 2.5% adv. - Total Inv: Approx. $165,000: build out $145,000, fran. fee $20,000 - Financing: $30,000 down (incl. $20,000 fran. fee), assistance in bank loan.

BAGEL BUILDERS (CANADA) INC.
1115 Sherbrooke St. W., Ste. 2802, Montreal, PQ, H3A 1H3. Contact: Martin Greenspon, Pres. - Tel: (514) 289-8718. Bagel (on premises) bakery restaurant serving bagels (10 different flavours), cheese spreads, bagel sandwiches, soups, desserts and beverages. Average ticket at breakfast $2.00 and at lunch $5.00. Bagel Builders bagels are low in fat and sodium, high in dietary fiber and contain no cholesterol. Established: 1994 - Franchising Since: 1994 - No. of Units: Company Owned: 1 - Franchised: 59 - Franchise Fee: $30,000 - Royalty: 7% - Total Inv: $125,000 - $175,000 incl. license fees, work. cap., inven., rent, deposits, leasehold.

BAKER'S DOZEN DONUTS
Baker's Dozen Donuts Corporation
1224 Dundas Street East, Mississauga, ON, L4Y 4A2. Contact: Joe Farrugia, Fran. Dir. - Tel: (905) 272-1825, (905) 272-0140. Coffee shops. Established: 1977 - Franchising Since: 1984 - No. of Units: Company Owned: 2 - Franchised: 107 - Royalty: 5%, 2% adv. - Total Inv: from $60,000 - Financing: Yes.

BEVCO INTERNATIONAL INC. *
235 Yorkland Blvd., Ste. 504, North York, ON, M3J 4Y8. Contact: V. Villanti, G.M. - Tel: (416) 496-8552, Fax: (416) 496-0683. Baked goods. Established: 1973 - Franchising Since: 1989 - No. of Units: Company Owned: 1 - Franchised: 6 - Franchise Fee: $50,000 - Royalty: 7% - Total Inv: $300,000 - Financing: North America.

BEVERLEY'S WHOLESALE BAKERS
Bevco International Inc.
2706 Slough St., Mississauga, ON, L4T 1G3. Contact: Vince Villanti, Administration - Tel: (905) 677-9377. Sub baking of homestyle tarts to the foodservice industry and retail. Established: 1979 - No. of Units: Company Owned: 1 - Franchised: 1 - Franchise Fee: $50,000 - Royalty: 5%, 2% adv. - Total Inv: $150,000 - $500,000 - Financing: Yes.

BLENZ COFFEE
Blenz Coffee Ltd.
Ste. 300, 535 Thurlow St., Vancouver, BC, V6E 3L2. Contact: Geoffrey Hair, Pres. - Tel: (604) 682-2995. Sale at retail of high quality coffee and coffee related products, in a comfortable, friendly and efficient environment. This business best suits people with high energy and a desire to provide the best and receive the rewards of being the best. Established: 1989 - Franchising Since: 1990 - No. of Units: Company Owned: 1 - Franchised: 9 - Franchise Fee: $20,000 - Royalty: 8%, 2% adv. - Total Inv: All in (turnkey) $150,000 - $175,000 - Financing: To qualified investors.

BREAD KING BAKERIES
103 Guildwood Pky., Westhill, ON, M1E 1P1. Contact: A. Rahim - Tel: (416) 267-1610. Bread, buns, etc. Established: 1981 - Franchising Since: 1981 - No. of Units: 2 - Franchise Fee: $15,000 - Royalty: 5% - Financing: No.

BUN KING BAKERIES
1173 North Service Rd., E., Oakville, ON, L6H 1A7. Contact: Angelo Rizzuti, Pres. - Tel: (905) 842-8770. Bakery of buns & bread. Established: 1979 - Franchising Since: 1979 - No. of Units: Company Owned: 70 - Franchise Fee: $14,000 - Total Inv: $140,000 - Royalty: 4% + 1% adv. - Financing: No, but will assist.

BUNS MASTER BAKERY
Maple Leaf Foods
2 East Beaver Creek Rd., Bldg. 1, Markham, ON, L4B 2N4. Contact: John Mallinick, Pres. - Tel: (905) 764-7066, Fax: (905) 764-7634. Merchandise unique quality buns, rolls, bread and other bakery products on a self-serve basis. Established: 1972 - Franchising Since: 1977 - No. of Units: Company Owned: 2 - Franchised: 113 - Franchise Fee: $25,000 - Royalty: 4% + 1%-3% adv. - Total Inv: $275,000 - $300,000 - Financing: Through chartered banks.

BUSKETT BAKERY
3029 Dundas St., W., Toronto, ON, M6P 1Z3. Contact: Fred Sherri, Pres. - Tel: (416) 763-2562. No. of Units: Company Owned: 1 - Franchised: 6 - Franchise Fee: $15,000 - Royalty: varies - Financing: No.

CAROLE'S CHEESECAKE COMPANY
Carole's Cheesecake Company Ltd.
1272 Castlefield Ave., Toronto, ON, M6B 1G3. Contact: Michael Ogus, Exec. V.P. - Tel: (416) 256-0000. Manufacturer, retailer and food service supplier of 100 flavours of premium brand cheesecakes + 20 other gourmet baked cakes & pies. Manufact. & retailer of a line of low fat salad dressings & marinades. Established: 1979 - Franchising Since: 1980 - No. of Units: Company Owned: 1 - Franchised: 7 - Franchise Fee: $25,000 - Royalty: none - Total Inv: $125,000 - $200,000 - Financing: Assistance thru Cdn. chartered banks.

CHEESECAKE CAFE, THE *
Columbia Licensing Inc.
Ste. 1165, 5555 Calgary Trail South, Edmonton, AB, T6H 5P9. Contact: Alex Lewonink, Secretary-Treasurer - Tel: (403) 436-3399, Fax: (403) 437-2250. Bakery restaurants. Established: 1988 - Franchising Since: 1995 - No. of Units: Company Owned: 5 - Franchised: 1 - Franchise Fee: $40,000 - Royalty: 5% of gross sales, 2% adv. - Total Inv: $600,000 to $700,000 in leased premises - Financing: Through banks.

COFFEE TIME DONUTS
Coffee Time Donuts Inc.
477 Ellesmere Rd., Scarborough, ON, M1R 4E5. Contact: Wendy McKinnon, Dir. of Fran. - Tel: (416) 288-8515. Coffee, donuts, muffins, sweet baked goods, soups, sandwiches and salads. Established: 1982 - Franchising Since: 1989 - No. of Units: Company Owned: 2 - Franchised: 120 - Franchise Fee: $15,000 - Royalty: 4.75%, 1% adv. - Total Inv: $100,000 - $140,000 kiosk locations, $140,000 - $190,000 satellite store, $190,000 - $240,000 full producing - Financing: Arranged through financial institutions.

COFFEE WAY
Coffee Way, Inc., The
123 Rexdale Blvd., Rexdale, ON, M9W 1P3. Contact: Roger G. Garneau, Dir. of Fran. - Tel: (416) 741-4144. Coffee, donuts, muffins, pastries, soup and sandwiches. Established: 1982 - Franchising Since: 1985 - No. of Units: Franchised: 21 - Franchise Fee: Included in turnkey pkg. - Royalty: 5% of gross sales - Total Inv: $160,000 - $225,000 turnkey package - Financing: No.

COMPANY'S COMING BAKERY CAFE
Comac Food Group Inc.
Ste. 440, 1121 Centre St. N., Calgary, AB, T2E 7K6. Contact: Janine Hunka, Fran. Sales - Tel: (403) 230-1151, (800) 361-1151. Featuring over 65 varieties of freshly baked goods including mini loaves, carrot cake, brownies, tarts and over 20 varieties of gourmet coffee. Established: 1987 - Franchising Since: 1989 - No. of Units: Franchised: 22 - Franchise Fee: $25,000 - Royalty: 8% (no adv. royalty) - Total Inv: $100,000 to $150,000 for store development costs - Financing: Royal Bank of Canada.

COOKIES BY GEORGE - CAFÉ BY GEORGE
Great Cookies By George, Inc.
300 Wellington St., Kingston, ON, K7K 2Z3. Contact: Don Landon, Pres. - Tel: (613) 546-3377. Retail sale of fresh baked goods specializing in gourmet cookies, gifts and a wide variety of beverages including specialty coffees and juices. Established: 1981 - Franchising Since: 1983 - No. of Units: Company Owned: 2 - Franchised: 29 - Franchise Fee: $19,000 - Royalty: 6%, 1.5% adv. - Total Inv: $80,000 - $130,000 - Financing: No.

COUNTRY STYLE DONUTS
Country Style Donuts CSD
2 East Beaver Creek Rd., Bldg. One, Richmond Hill, ON, L4B 2N3. Contact: Girts Steinhards, Fran. Mgr. - Tel: (905) 764-7066. Donut shops featuring freshly ground & brewed coffee and a full variety of donuts, pastries, luncheon sandwiches, soups, salads and specialty products. Established: 1962 - Franchising Since: 1963 - No. of Units: Company Owned: 2 - Franchised: 160 - Franchise Fee: $35,000 - Royalty: 4.5% of gross sales - Total Inv: $235,000 (fran. fee $35,000; equip. $105,000; leaseholds $95,000) - Financing: No.

DONUT DELITE CAFE, INC.
77 Bessemer Rd., Unit 19, London, ON, N6E 1P9. Contact: Joe Garagozzo, Fran. Mktg. Dir. - Tel: (519) 668-6868. Donuts, coffee, muffins, soups & sandwiches. Established: 1984 - Franchising Since: 1984 - No. of Units: Company Owned: 1 - Franchised: 30 - Franchise Fee: $20.000 - Total Inv: $127,500 - Royalty: 5% - Financing: Yes.

DUNKIN' DONUTS (CANADA) LTD.
3773 Cote Bertu, Ste. 350, St. Laurent, PQ, H4R 2M3. Contact: Marty Martindale, Dir. of Fran. - Tel: (514) 856-3100. Donut shops, serving coffee, donuts, muffins, croissants, etc. Established: 1950 - No. of Units: Franchised: 124 - Franchise Fee: $40,000 - Total Inv: $200,000 min. - Royalty: 4.9% plus 6% adv. - Financing: Yes.

DUTCH MASTER DONUTS LTD.
747 Don Mills Rd., Toronto, ON, M3C 1T2. Contact: H. Floros, Fran. Dir. - Tel: (416) 424-1010. Donuts, coffee. Established: 1960 - Franchising Since: 1979 - No. of Units: Company Owned: 2 - Franchised: 5 - Royalty: 5% - Financing: Yes.

EDDIE SHACK DONUTS *
Eddie Shack Donuts, Inc.
19 Kenviw Blvd., Unit 42, Brampton, ON, L6T 5G5. Contact: D. Pizzimenti, Pres. - Tel: (905) 799-3640, Fax: (905) 799-3739. Upscale donut shops with drive thru, serving deli sandwiches, soups, salads, specialty cakes & quality coffee. Established: 1993 - Franchising Since: 1994 - No. of Units: Company Owned: 1 - Franchised: 8 - Franchise Fee: $10,000 - Royalty: 5%, 2% adv. - Total Inv: $275,000 drive thru, $250,000 no drive thru, $180,000 satellite store - Financing: Yes.

GOURMET CUP
Gourmet Cup Foods Ltd., The
P.O. Box 490, 2265 W. Railway St., Abbotsford, BC, V2S 5Z5. Contact: T. Hartford, Dir. of Fran. - Tel: (604) 852-8771, Fax: (604) 859-1711. Retail sale of gourmet coffees & teas, beverages (cappuccinos, espressos, juice, hot chocolate), pastries & coffee/tea accessories (grinders, pots, mugs). Established: 1985 - Franchising Since: 1986 - No. of Units: Company Owned: 1 - Franchised: 48 - Franchise Fee: $25,000 - Royalty: 8% - Total Inv: $110,000 - $250,000 - Financing: No.

GRABBAJABBA
Comac Food Group Inc.
Ste. 440, 1121 Centre St. N., Calgary, AB, T2E 7K6. Contact: Janine Hunka, Fran. Sales Mgr. - Tel: (403) 230-1151, (800) 361-1151. Upscale European coffee house featuring over 50 varieties of Arabica coffee and over 12 varieties of specialty coffee plus European style sandwiches, soups, salads, freshly baked goods and decadent desserts. Established: 1988 - Franchising Since: 1990 - No. of Units: Franchised: 47 - Franchise Fee: $25,000 - Royalty: 8% (no adv. royalty) - Total Inv: $150,000 - $175,000 for store dev. cost - Financing: Royal Bank of Canada.

GREAT CANADIAN BAGEL, THE *
Great Canadian Bagel, Ltd., The
8 Beamish Dr., Etobicoke, ON, M9B 3P3. Contact: Brian Leon, V.P., Franchising & Leasing - Tel: (416) 234-2800, Fax: (416) 234-5744. Bakery/restaurant specializing in fresh baked bagels prepared in full view of the customer. Over 17 varieties of bagels & 15 flavours of cream cheese daily. Established: 1993 - Franchising Since: 1994 - No. of Units: Company Owned: 6 - Franchised: 32 - Franchise Fee: $25,000 - Royalty: 6%, 1% adv. - Total Inv: $250,000 turnkey, approx. $80,000 to $100,000 cash required - Financing: Assistance provided.

HEALTH BREAD BAKERY, OPEN WINDOW BAKERY
Open Window Bakery Ltd.
1125 Finch Ave., W., Toronto, ON, M3J 2E8. Contact: Max Feig, Pres. - Tel: (416) 665-8241. Bakeries. Established: 1957 - No. of Units: Company Owned: 21 - Franchised: 20.

HERMES BAKERY LTD.
2885 Bathurst St., Toronto, ON, M6B 3A4. Contact: Herman Maierovits, Pres. - Tel: (416) 787-1234. Bakery. Established: 1955 - No. of Units: Company Owned: 2 - Franchised: 2.

HEWITTS (NEW YORK STYLE) BAGEL BAKERY *
T.H.G. Franchising
54 Easton Rd., Box 20012, Brantford, ON, N3P 2A4. Contact: Ron Hewitt, Fran. Dir. - Tel: (519) 752-5223, Fax: (519) 752-1280. Bagel bakery with a deli and gourmet coffee bar with sit down restaurant. Established: 1995 - Franchising Since: 1995 - No. of Units: Company Owned: 1 - Franchise Fee: $20,000 - Royalty: 4%, 2% adv. - Total Inv: $160,000 - Financing: No.

HUBERT'S EUROPEAN NATURAL BAKERIES, INC. *
35 Alexandra Blvd., Toronto, ON, M4R 1L8. Contact: Fran. Dir. - Tel: (416) 488-3687, Fax: (416) 481-9505. Breads and buns are baked from original and traditional German recipes. We use no additives, fat, sugar, colours or milk. All pastries are made from the finest ingredients. This has been a tradition in Germany since 1647. Established In U.S.: 1993 - Franchising Since: 1995 - No. of Units: Company Owned: 1 - Franchise Fee: $20,000 - Royalty: 6% - Total Inv: $167,500 which includes the fran. fee pays for equip., and leaseholds - Financing: We assist qualified prospects to obtain financing.

JAVA JOE'S *
Java Joe's Inc.
(c/o Rep.) 912 Wilson Ave., North York, ON, M3K 1E7. Contact: Development Mgr. - Tel: (416) 633-7219. Specialty food & beverage concept of gourmet espresso-based & flavoured coffees and teas from world-wide; cold drinks; and freshly prepared delectable foods, baked goods & exotic desserts in a colourful, relaxing & cheerful atmosphere. Established: 1991 - Franchising Since: 1992 - No. of Units: Company Owned: 3 - Franchised: 7 - Franchise Fee: Included - Royalty: 7%, 2% adv. - Total Inv: $125,000 and up - Financing: Will assist with arrangement (O.A.C.).

JUST DESSERTS
A.A.J.J. Investments Inc.
310 Davenport Rd., Toronto, ON, M5R 1K6. Contact: J. Givens, President - Tel: (416) 944-2270. Just Desserts is a dessert cafe, world famous for great tasting desserts i.e., 52 varieties of cakes and light snacks and a variety of coffees. Established: 1978 - Franchising Since: 1992 - No. of Units: Company Owned: 1 - Franchised: 14 - Royalty: yes - Total Inv: $280,000 - Financing: No.

LA MAISON DU CROISSANT
La Maison du Croissant Ltd.
695 Yonge St., Toronto, ON, M4Y 2B2. Contact: Ms. E. Lieberman, Franch. Co-ord. - Tel: (416) 927-1906. Bakery/cafe - croissanterie. Established: 1980 - Franchising Since: 1984 - No. of Units: Company Owned: 3 - Franchised: 1.

LE MUFFIN PLUS
393 St. Jacques, Montreal, PQ, H2Y 1N9. Contact: Tony Elisii, V.P. - Tel: (514) 281-2067. Specializing in muffins baked on site plus sandwiches, gourmet salads, specialized coffees, desserts, cookies, juices. Established: 1982 - Franchising Since: 1983 - No. of Units: Company Owned: 7 - Franchised: 22 - Franchise Fee: $20,000 - Royalty: 7% - Total Inv: between $130,000 & $220,000 - Financing: Program with Royal Bank.

LES BOULANGERIE CANTOR
8575 8th Ave., Montreal, PQ, H1Z 2X2. Contact: Gail Cantor, Fran. Dept. - Tel: (514)374-2700. Wholesale baker with bakery/convenience retail outlets. Established: 1950 - Franchising Since: 1964 - No. of Units: Company Owned: 5 - Franchised: 75 - Royalty: 2% - Total Inv: $80,000 - $150,000. Financing: Through bank.

MCBEANS
Midwest Coffee Systems Inc.
1560 Church Ave., Unit 6, Victoria, B.C., V8P 2H1. Contact: Arne Andersson, Pres. - Tel: (604) 721-2411, Fax: (604) 721-3213. Gourmet coffee, tea and related accessories. Established: 1983 - Franchising Since: 1985 - No. of Units: Company Owned: 1 - Franchised: 16 - Franchise Fee: $25,000 - Royalty: 7% - Total Inv: $135,500 - $173,500 incl. fran. fee - Financing: Will assist through conventional methods.

MICHEL'S BAGUETTE
mmmuffins Canada Corporation
3300 Bloor St. W., Centre Tower, 9th Fl., Etobicoke, ON, M8X 2X3. Contact: Nancy Robinson, Fran. Mgr. - Tel: (416) 236-0055, Fax: (416) 236-0054. Combination French café & bakery stores for either take-out or dine-in consumption includes a sit-down cappuccino bar. Established: 1980 - Franchising Since: 1984 - No. of Units: Company Owned: 2 - Franchised: 9 - Franchise Fee: $40,000 - Royalty: 6%, 2% adv. - Total Inv: $750,000 - $900,000 (with 35% unencumbered cash) - Financing: We will set up bank contacts for potential franchisees.

MINI BITES
3522 Irwin Court, Mississauga, ON, L5L 4W4. Contact: G. Robinson, Owner - Tel: (905) 820-5124. Mobile donut concession. Established: 1992 - Franchising Since: 1994 - No. of Units: Company Owned: 1 - Franchise Fee: $56,000 - Royalty: 3% gross sales - Total Inv: $56,000 turnkey 18' unit - Financing: No.

MMMARVELLOUS MMMUFFINS
MMMuffins Canada Corp.
3300 Bloor St. W., #2910, Etobicoke, ON, M8X 2X3. Contact: Nancy Robinson, Fran. Mgr. - Tel: (416) 236-0055, Fax: (416) 236-0054. Hot, freshly baked mmmuffins, in over 80 mmmarvellous varieties, are produced from scratch at each store. In addition to our mmmuffins, we also have a delicious assortment of freshly baked streusals and cookies, complemented by a selection of natural juices, and gourmet coffees and teas. Established: 1979 - Franchising Since: 1980 - No. of Units: Company Owned: 4 - Franchised: 108 - Franchise Fee: $25,000 - Royalty: 7% - Total Inv: $160,000 - $185,000 - Financing: Introduction to bank.

MONSIEUR FELIX & MR. NORTON COOKIES
4100 Thimens Blvd., St. Laurent, PQ, H4R 1X4. Contact: Normand Ciarlo, Dir. of Fran. Dev. - Tel: (800) 463-7055, Fax: (514) 333-7277. Retail shops specializing in freshly baked gourmet chocolate chunk cookies in 12 varieties, packaged in unique trademarked containers. Delivery and corporate gift services available. Established: 1985 - Franchising Since: 1990 - No. of Units: Company Owned: 8 - Franchised: 21 - Franchise Fee: $25,000 - Royalty: 5%, 6% adv. - Total Inv: $135,000 - $165,000 - Financing: No.

MR. MUGS
149769 Canada, Inc.
P.O. Box 20019, Brantford, ON, N3P 2A4. Contact: Paul Cleave, Fran. Dir. - Tel: (519) 752-9890. Coffee & donut franchise featuring a deli bar with fresh made soup, sandwiches and chili. Donuts and bakery goods made on premises. Established: 1983 - Franchising Since: 1986 - No. of Units: Company Owned: 2 - Franchised: 21 - Franchise Fee: $20,000 - Royalty: 4%, 2% adv. - Total Inv: $40,000 - $190,000 (incl. fran. fee) - Financing: Possible partial.

MRS. POWELL'S BAKERY EATERY
Afton Food Group, Inc.
3380 South Service Rd., Burlington, ON, L7N 3J5. Contact: J. Vaudry, V.P. - Tel: (905) 681-8448. High quality bakery goods specializing in cinnamon rolls, muffins, and variety coffees, deli sandwiches and

gourmet salads. Satellite store concept reduces capital costs for retail development and maximizes production capabilities of producing store kitchens. Established: 1984 - Franchising Since: 1985 - No. of Units: Franchised: 31 - Franchise Fee: $25,000 - Royalty: 5%, 2% adv. - Total Inv: $112,000 - $190,000 (Total investment/incl. fran. fee) - Financing: Third party.

MUFFIN BREAK
Muffin Break Canada Inc.
3300 Bloor St. W, Ste. 2910, Etobicoke, ON, M8X 2X3. Contact: Nancy Robinson, Fran. Mgr. - Tel: (416) 236-0055, Fax: (416) 236-0054. Muffins & pastries baked on premises compliment our gourmet coffees, teas & refreshing fruit juices. Eat in or take out. Established: 1980 - Franchising Since: 1981 - No. of Units: Company Owned: 2 - Franchised: 39 - Franchise Fee: $25,000 - Royalty: 6% - Total Inv: $160,000 - $200,000 - Financing: Indirect.

OMA'S OFEN, THE EUROPEAN BAKERY & CAFE *
J.F. Schmitz Associates...The Finders
500 Rossland Rd. W., P.O .Box 58025, Oshawa, ON, L1J 8L6. Contact: Joseph Schmitz, Fran. Cons. - Tel: (905) 579-9792, Fax: (905) 579-4692. Healthy, out of the ordinary, fresh food concept featuring daily baked breads, buns, bagels and pastry. Outstanding breakfasts, soups and European style sandwiches made from top quality meats and cheeses. OMA's coffee is specially roasted and blended in Vienna. Established: 1990 - Franchising Since: 1990 - No. of Units: Franchised: 4 - Franchise Fee: $25,000 - Royalty: 6% of gross sales - Total Inv: Turnkey $150,000 - $250,000 - Financing: $100,000 to $175,000.

P.A.M.'S COFFEE & TEA CO.
494980 Ontario Ltd.
100 West Beaver Creek, #4, Richmond Hill, ON, L4B 1H4. Contact: Greg MacCormack, Fran. Dir. - Tel: (905) 771-7199. Specialty coffee chain. Established: 1981 - Franchising Since: 1991 - No. of Units: Company Owned: 1 - Franchised: 10 - Franchise Fee: $25,000 - Royalty: 8%, 2% adv. - Total Inv: $110,000 - $165,000 - Financing: No.

PHILINS NATURAL FOOD CREATIONS/BAKES
200 Kent St., Ottawa, ON, K1P 5M9. Contact: Philip Berman, Pres. - Tel: (613) 234-2825. Natural and fast food bakeries. Established: 1979 - Franchising Since: 1982 - No. of Units: Company Owned: 5 - Franchised: 1 - Franchise Fee: $20,000 - Total Inv: $120,000 - Royalty: 5%.

PISTOL & BURNES COFFEE & TEA HOUSE *
Pistol & Burnes Coffee Roastery Corp.
#10 - 8005 Alexander Rd., Delta, BC, V4G 1C6. Contact: Ralph Collins, Sales Mgr. - Tel: (604) 946-7303, Fax: (604) 946-5951. Retailers of specialty coffees and teas in pleasant, comfortable surroundings. Selling cupped and bulk coffees and teas, panini sandwiches and bagels. Roasters and wholesalers since 1978. Canadian owned. Established: 1978 - Franchising Since: 1994 - No. of Units: Franchised: 10 - Franchise Fee: $20,000 - Royalty: Nil - Total Inv: From $60,000 to $130,000 turnkey - Financing: Some O.A.C.

ROASTMASTIR'S - CUSTOM ROASTED ORGANIC COFFEES
Outhwaite Investments Ltd.
12547 19th Ave., Surrey, BC, V4A 9P1. Contact: Bill Outhwaite, Pres. - Tel: (800) 663-2331, (604) 535-7005, Fax: (604) 535-9256. Custom roasted organic coffees. Established: 1993 - Franchising Since: 1993 - No. of Units: Company Owned: 2 - Franchised: 22 - Franchise Fee: $25,000 - Royalty: 6%, 1.5% ad. fund - Total Inv: $150,000 to $180,000.

ROBIN'S DONUTS
Robin's Foods Inc.
725 Hewitson St., Thunder Bay, ON, P7B 6B5. Contact: Ron Whitehead/Ken Ranta, Sales Dept. - Tel: (807) 623-4453, Fax: (807) 623-4682. Coffee house serving donuts, assorted pastries, deli with complete line of soups, sandwiches, salads, full line of hot & cold beverages specializing in coffee, 7 day, 24 hour operation. Established: 1975 - Franchising Since: 1978 - No. of Units: Company Owned: 15 - Franchised: 215 - Franchise Fee: $35,000 - Royalty: 4% - Total Inv: $260,000: equip. $150,000; leaseholds $75,000 plus fran. fee - Financing: No.

SAINT CINNAMON BAKE SHOPPES
Saint Cinnamon Bakery Ltd.
7181 Woodbine Ave. #222, Markham, ON, L3R 1A3. Contact: R. Hassell, V.P. - Tel: (905) 470-1517. Fast food, freshly baked cinnamon rolls & baked products with our freshly brewed coffee. Established: 1986 - Franchising Since: 1986 - No. of Units: Company Owned: 1 - Franchised: 124 - Franchise Fee: $25,000 - Royalty: 6%, 3% adv. - Total Inv: $80,000 - $100,000.

SECOND CUP COFFEE CO.
Second Cup, Ltd., The
175 Bloor St. E., South Twr, #801, Toronto, ON, M4W 3R8. Contact: Robyn Paikin, Fran. Asst. - Tel: (416) 975-5541. Specialty gourmet coffees and teas. Established: 1975 - Franchising Since: 1979 - No. of Units: Company Owned: 6 - Franchised: 180 - Franchise Fee: $20,000 - Royalty: 9% - Total Inv: $170,000 - $225,000 - Financing: Introduction to bank.

SWEET ROSIE'S
Sweet Rosie's Corporation
362 Sumach Street, Toronto, ON, M4X 1V4. Contact: Rosie Gumieniak, C/O - Tel: (416) 923-9113, Fax: 920-9297. Gourmet coffee bar, bake shoppe, sandwiches, muffins, salads, etc. European concepts. Established: 1978 - Franchising Since: 1981 - No. of Units: Company Owned: 2 - Franchised: 14 - Franchise Fee: $25,000 (CAN) - Royalty: 5%, 2% adv. - Total Inv: $135,000 to $165,000 turnkey average - Financing: Up to $50,000 min. investments $45,000.

THE HOT BAGELWORKS BAKERY *
Bagels Franchise Inc.
439 Spadina Rd., Ste. 303, Toronto, ON, M5P 2W3. Contact: Morry Guttman, Dir., Store Dev. - Tel: (416) 322-6613. On site production and baking of bagels complete with sandwiches and "Dreamcheese" cream cheese spreads. We use the traditional boiling and baking method without using any ingredient additives. Established: 1992 - Franchising Since: 1995 - No. of Units: Company Owned: 4 - Franchise Fee: $25,000 - Royalty: 5% yr. 1, 6% yr. 2 and further - Total Inv: $235,000 (up to) turnkey with training - Financing: Will assist.

TIM HORTONS
The TDL Group Ltd.
874 Sinclair Rd., Oakville, ON, L6K 2Y1. Contact: Lilian Longdo, Mgr. of Fran. - Tel: (905) 845-6511. Retail coffee, donuts, and specialty baked goods. Established: 1964 - Franchising Since: 1965 - No. of Units: Company Owned: 25 - Franchised: 1,000 - Franchise Fee: $15,000 - Royalty: 3% based on gross sales - Total Inv: $275,000 to $325,000 - Financing: Through major chartered banks.

TIMOTHY'S COFFEES OF THE WORLD
Timothy's Royal Coffee
400 Steeprock Dr., North York, ON, M3J 3B1. Contact: Becky McKinnon, Pres. - Tel: (416) 638-3333. Retail sale of quality coffees & teas and related products. Established: 1975 - Franchising Since: 1980 - No.of Units: Company Owned: 38 - Franchised: 12 - Franchise Fee: $20,000 - Royalty: 9% of sales - Total Inv: $150,000 - $200,000 includes leaseholds, fixtures, equipment, franchise fee & inventory - Financing: Through C.I.B.C.

TREATS
Treats International
418 Preston St., Ottawa, ON, K1S 4N2. Contact: J. Deknatel, C.O.O. - Tel: (613) 563-4073. Micro bakery operations from 100 - 1800 square feet. Established: 1977 - Franchising Since: 1979 - No. of Units: Company Owned: 5 - Franchised: 175 - Franchise Fee: $25,000 - Royalty: 8%, 2% adv. - Total Inv: $150,000 - $200,000 - Financing: O.A.C.

UNCOMMON GROUND GOURMET COFFEE *
T.H.G. Franchising
54 Easton Rd., Box 20012, Brantford, ON, N3P 2A4. Contact: Ron Hewitt, Dir. of Fran. - Tel: (519) 752-5223, Fax: (519) 752-1280. Upscale gourmet coffee shops combined with a small deli featuring bagel sandwiches and desserts. Established: 1995 - Franchising Since: 1995 - No. of Units: Franchised: 1 - Franchise Fee: $20,000 - Royalty: 4%, 2% adv. - Total Inv: $140,000.

FOOD: ICE CREAM AND YOGURT

Baskin Robbins Ice Cream & Yogurt

BASKIN ROBBINS
50 Ronson Dr., Suite 131, Etobicoke, ON, M9W 1B3. Contact: Kavita Hildenbrand, National Fran. Mgr. - Tel: (416) 245-3131, (800) 268-4923. Ice cream and frozen desserts. Established: 1945 - Franchising Since: 1971(Canada) - No. of Units: Franchised: 219 - Franchise Fee: $25,000 - Royalty: 1% - Total Inv: store costs (leaseholds, equip. & signage) $150,000 - $160,000 - Financing: No.

DAIRY QUEEN CANADA, INC.
5245 Harvester Rd., P.O. Box 430, Burlington, ON, L7R 3Y3 . Contact: Jennifer Lang, Larry Carver, Wayne Vanderhorst, Fran. Dev. Man. - Tel: (905) 639-1492, Fax: (905) 681-3623. Franchising of quick service restaurants specializing in fast food & frozen dairy treats. Established: 1940 - Franchising Since: 1950 - No. of Units: Franchised: 461 - Franchise Fee: $30,000 - Royalty: 4% - Total Inv: $450,000 (plus) - Financing: DQCI will finance 50% of the initial franchise fee of $30,000.

G. WILLIKERS - OLDE WORLD FUDGE *
Olde World Fudge Co. Ltd.
#207, 7475 Hedley Ave., Burnaby, BC, V5E 2R1. Contact: Wanye Wright, Pres. - Tel: (604) 432-9908, Fax: (604) 432-9980. On site candy/yogurt/ice cream manufacturer and retailer. Established: 1982 - Franchising Since: 1984 - No. of Units: Company Owned: 2 - Franchised: 8 - Franchise Fee: $10,000 - Royalty: 8%, 2% adv. - Total Inv: $75,000 to $100,000 depending on size - Financing: No.

GOOD FOR YOU FRUIT AND YOGURT
#6 W. 17th Ave., Vancouver, BC, V5Y 1Z4. Contact: Amir Hemani, Operations Dir. - Tel: (604) 875-1029. Features frozen yogurt and light, nutritious menu items. Established: 1983 - Franchising Since: 1983 - No. of Units: Franchised: 22 - Franchise Fee: $25,000 - Total Inv: $75,000 - $80,000 - Royalty: 5% - Financing: No.

YOGEN FRUZ
Yogen Fruz Int'l Ltd.
8300 Woodbine Ave., Markham, ON, L3R 9Y7. Contact: Garry Gordon, Fran. Dir. - Tel: (905) 479-8762. Retail frozen yogurt cone, milkshakes, pies and other yogurt related. Established: 1986 - Franchising Since: 1987 - No. of Units: Company Owned: 1 - Franchised: 400 - Franchise Fee: $25,000 - Royalty: 6%, 2% adv. - Total Inv: fran. fee, $35,000 leaseholds, $35,000 equip. - Financing: Bank assistance available.

COOL PRODUCT

- Over 600 flavours of ice cream.
- 20 flavours of frozen yogurt.
- Sundaes.
- Milk Shakes.
- Floats.
- Cappuccino Blast.
- Ice cream cakes.
- Ice cream pies.
- Clown Cones.
- Yogurt Gone Crazy.
- Frozen Yogurt Bars.
- Incredibles Cakes.

HOT! FRANCHISE

- Module & full line stores available.
- Turn-key operation
- World's most popular ice cream stores.
- Well established brand name.
- Quality products and service.
- Business Management Training.
- Ongoing Operational support.
- National and Local Marketing support.
- $60,000 unencumbered investment required.

Baskin Robbins Ice Cream & Yogurt
1-800-268-4923 or (416) 245-3131

FOOD: RESTAURANTS AND QUICK SERVICE

241 PIZZA LTD.
557 Dixon Rd., Unit 111, Etobicoke, ON, M9W 6K1. Contact: Clyde Viola, Fran. Officer - Tel: (416) 241-0241. Pizza outlets. Established: 1986 - Franchising Since: 1986 - No. of Units: Franchised: 65 - Franchise Fee: $15,000 - Royalty: 6.5% of net telephone sales + 6.5% - Total Inv: $140,000 - Financing: Assistance.

A & W FOOD SERVICES OF CANADA
#300 - 171 West Esplanade, North Vancouver, BC, V7M 3K9. Contact: J. Graham Cooke, V.P. Fran. - Tel: (604) 988-2141. Hamburger-based fast food restaurants. Established: 1956 - Franchising Since: 1957 - No. of Units: Company Owned: 150 - Franchised: 270 - Franchise Fee: $42,000 - Service Fee: 2.5%, 3.5% adv. - Total Inv: $200,000 - $600,000 depending on concept - Financing: No.

ABC FAMILY RESTAURANTS
Ste. 202, 15373 Fraser Hwy., Surrey, BC, V3R 3P3. Contact: Ron Martens, Pres. - Tel: (604) 583-2919. Family restaurants. Established: 1976 - Franchising Since: 1977 - No. of Units: 14 - Franchise Fee: $25,000 - Royalty: 4% + 1% adv. - Total Inv: $250,000 - $300,000 - Financing: No.

ALBERT'S FAMILY RESTAURANT
Albert's Franchise Inc.
10544 - 114 Street, Edmonton, AB, T5n 2t2. Contact: David Gibson, V.P. - Tel: (403) 429-1259, Fax (403) 426-7391. Successful family restaurant chain, good cash flow, we have a complete training program. We are successful because we have excellent on-going support and a value priced menu. Established: 1980 - Franchising Since: 1989 - No. of Units: Company Owned: 8 - Franchised: 12 - Franchise Fee: $25,000 - Royalty: 5%, 2% adv. - Total Inv: $350,000 - $450,000 - Financing: No.

ARBY'S ROAST BEEF RESTAURANT
Arby's Canada, Inc.
6299 Airport Rd., #111, Mississauga, ON, L4V 1N3. Contact: Mick Hirschler, Dir. of Dev. - Tel: (905) 672-2729, Fax: (905) 672-2755. Roast beef sandwich based fast food concept. Established: 1981 - Franchising Since 1981 - No. of Units: Company Owned: 16 - Franchised: 98 - Franchise Fee: $42,500 - Royalty: 4% plus adv. - Total Inv: $400,000.

ARTHUR TREACHERS FISH & CHIPS
299 Kirby Cres., Newmarket, ON, L3X 1H1. Contact: Zulí Lalani, Pres. - Tel: (905) 836-6431. Fast food, food court & street concept selling fish, chicken, soups & sandwiches. Famous for having the original fish & chips which are not only delicious & nutritious, but low in calories and 99% cholesterol free. Established: 1987 - Franchising Since: 1987 - No. of Units: Company Owned: 2 - Franchised: 10 - Royalty: 6%, 2% adv. - Total Inv: $130,000 to $165,000 depending on location - Financing: Yes, through financial institutions.

AUTHORS MAGAZINE & CAFE *
501 Cambridge St., S.E., Medicine Hat, AB, T1A 0T3. Contact: Philip Murphy, Pres. - Tel: (403) 526-2524. Cafe with magazines & books (including membership-based Authors Magazine), as well as Internet access & computer training facilities geared to writers & journalists. Established: 1992 - Franchising Since: 1995 - Franchise Fee: $25,000 - Royalty: 5%, 2% adv. - Total Inv: $25,000 fran. fee, $40,000+ lease & operating - Financing: Limited.

BAGEL STOP, THE
Zonin Food Corp. Ltd.
601 Magnetic Dr., Unit 24, Downsview, ON, M3J 3J2. Contact: A. Zilberberg, Pres. - Tel: (416) 663-7579, Fax: (416) 663-5539. The sale at retail of bagels and bagel sandwiches, soups, salads, hot and cold non-alcoholic beverages. Established: 1987 - Franchising Since: 1988 - No. of Units: Company Owned: 3 - Franchised: 15 - Franchise Fee: $20,000 - Royalty: 6%, 2% adv. - Financing: Will assist.

BEST CHOICE FALAFEL *
J.F. Schmitz Associates..The Finders
500 Rossland Rd. W., P.O. Box 58025, Oshawa, ON, L1J 8L6. Contact: Joseph Schmitz, Fran. Cons. - Tel: (905) 579-9792, Fax: (905) 579-4692. Middle East Lebanese specialty foods & beverages. Located in food courts and street front locations (latter in university cities). Established: 1989 - Franchising Since: 1995 - No. of Units: Company Owned: 4 - Franchise Fee: $10,000 - Royalty: 6% of sales - Total Inv: $55,000 complete turnkey/move in operation ready - Financing: $50,000 to qualified applicants.

BINO'S FAMILY RESTAURANTS
Bino's Management Corp.
6962 Buller Ave., Burnaby, BC, V5J 4S3. Contact: Kevin Turner, Franc. Dir. - Tel: (604) 435-3044. Wide variety family restaurant serving breakfast, lunch and dinner 24 hrs. Established: 1972 - Franchising Since: 1977 - No. of Units: Franchised: 19 - Franchise Fee: $25,000 - Royalty: 4% + 1% adv. - Total Inv: $300,000 - $350,000 - Financing: Assistance.

BOSTON PIZZA
Boston Pizza International Inc.
200 - 5500 Parkwood Way, Richmond, BC, V6V 2M4. Contact: B.M. Skene, Dir. of Franc. - Tel: (604) 270-1108, Fax: (604) 270-4168. Pizza and pasta restaurants. Full liquor bar service. Menu also includes soup, salads, ribs, steaks, finger foods and gourmet desserts. Established: 1963 - Franchising Since: 1968 - No. of Units: Company Owned: 1- Franchised: 99 - Franchise Fee: $45,000 - Royalty: 7% food sales + 2.5% national adv. - Total Inv: $575,000 - $675,000 - Financing: Yes, with banking, but no direct financing.

BRISKETS LTD.
2055 Bishop Ave., Montreal , PQ , H3D 2E8. Contact: Howard Cohen, Pres. - Tel: (514) 843-3650. Restaurant featuring smoked meats. Established: 1984 - Franchising Since: 1984 - No. of Units: Company Owned: 9 - Franchise Fee: $75,000 ($30,000 fran. fee) - Total Inv: $225,000 - Royalty: 6% + 2% adv.

BURGER BROTHERS
International Burger Brothers
456 Main St., Penticton, BC, V2A 5C5. Contact: Frank Webb, Pres. - Tel: (604) 492-5600. Double drive-thru hamburger fast food, specializing in flame broiled burgers and crispy coated fries. Modular buildings are factory built and shipped to prepared sites. Available worldwide. Established: 1986 - Franchising Since: 1987 - No. of Units: Company Owned: 1 - Franchised: 7 - Franchise Fee: $12,500 - Royalty: 4% - Total Inv: $200,000 - Financing: Third party.

BURGER HEAVEN
D.J.K. (Mural) Holdings
77 - 10th St., New Westminster, BC, V3M 3X4. Contact: Jude Mural, Owner/Pres. - Tel: (604) 522-8339. Burger Heaven restaurant serves the largest selection of burgers anywhere. Soup, salad, sandwiches, desserts alc. bev., beer, wine, liq., coffees etc. A unique experience. Established: 1984 - Franchising Since: 1994 - No. of Units: Company Owned: 1 - Franchise Fee: $40,000 - Royalty: 6% on food sales, 2% local adv., 2% nat'l. adv. - Total Inv: $200,000 - $400,000 - Financing: Bank financing.

BURGER KING
Burger King Restaurants of Canada Inc.
401 The West Mall, 7th Fl., Etobicoke, ON, M9C 5J4. Contact: Susan Cowan, Manager, Fran. Dev. - Tel: (416) 626-6464. Second largest hamburger chain in the world. Over 2,000,000 Whopper Sandwiches are sold each day in over 43 countries worldwide. Established: 1954 - Franchising in Canada Since: 1969 - No. of Units: Company Owned: 76 - Franchised: 120 - Franchise Fee: $40,000 - Royalty: 4% - Total Inv: $450,000 - $950,000.

VARCON Construction Co. Ltd.
Industrial • Residential • Commercial • Institutional

CUSTOMERS WANTED
Can we build your next franchise store, corporate offices or distribution center? Construction budgets & deadlines are a priority to us.

WE OFFER:
- Turnkey or partial construction
- Project management
- Design and build
- Budget consultations

25 Rutherford Rd. South, Unit 5
Brampton, Ont., L6W 3J3
(800) 581-6729
Tel: (905) 451-7316, Fax: (905) 451-8563

CAFE CHRISTOPHE VAN HOUTTE, INC.
8300 19th Ave., Montreal, PQ, H1Z 4J8. Contact: Mario Veronneau, Gen. Mgr., Fran. - Tel: (514) 593-7711. European bistro. Established: 1951 - Franchising Since: 1980 - No. of Units: Company Owned: 1 - Franchised: 9 - Franchise Fee: $50,000 - Total Inv: $150,000 - Royalty: 5% - Financing: No.

CAFE SUPREME
Cafe Supreme F&P Ltd.
1233 Rue de la Montagne, Suite 201, Montreal, PQ, H3G 1Z9. Contact: Sam Huq, Gen. Mgr. - Tel: (514) 875-9803. A European style cafe bistro. Established: 1980 - Franchising Since: 1980 - No. of Units: Company Owned: 5 - Franchised: 35 - Franchise Fee: $25,000 - Royalty: 5% - Total Inv: $150,000 - $250,000 - Financing: Through bank.

CALIFORNIA CREPES *
California Crepes Ltd.
#35 - 12091 Bath Rd., Richmond, BC, V6V 1H2. Contact: Val Usher, Pres. - Tel: (604) 844-4728. Fresh food - fast! Handmade crepes filled with a variety of deli meats, fresh veggies & sauces smothered in melted cheese or fresh fruits, whipped cream & shredded chocolate. Established: 1990 - Franchising Since: 1994 - No. of Units: Company Owned: 2 - Franchised: 1 - Franchise Fee: $10,000 - Royalty: 5% gross sales plus $1.5% adv. - Total Inv: Up to $85,000 - depending on square footage - Financing: SBIP, Private.

CAPT. SUBMARINE
Nemo Foods Ltd.
1179 Finch Ave. W., Downsview, ON, M3J 2G1. Contact: Franchise Dir./Pres. - Tel: (416) 665-0968. Fast food submarine sandwiches & misc. Established: 1972 - Franchising Since: 1972 - No. of Units: Company Owned: 8 - Franchised: 23 - Franchise Fee: $15,000 - Royalty: 5% & 3% Adv. - Total Inv: $90,000 - Financing: If applicable.

CASEY'S GRILLHOUSE & BEVERAGE CO. *
Prime Restaurant Group Inc.
10 Kingsbridge Garden Cir., Ste. 600, Mississauga, ON, L5R 3K6. Contact: Richard Stark, Sr. V.P., Dev. - Tel: (905) 568-0000, Fax: (905) 568-0080. Casual dinner-house designed and themed with imagery of beverage manufacturing plant and open kitchen; menu features grilled foods and stresses freshness and quality. Established: 1979 - Franchising Since: 1984 - No. of Units: Company Owned: 3 - Franchised: 22 - Franchise Fee: $40,000 - Royalty: 5% - Total Inv: $40,000 fran. fee, $25,000 opening team fee, $650,000 to $825,000 development cost, $50,000 working cap. - Financing: No.

CAZ'S FISH & CHIP SHOPPE
Scotco Dist. Ltd.
200 N. Service Rd. W., Unit #1, Ste. 600, Oakville, ON, L6M 2V1. Contact: James H. Clark, Pres. - Tel: (905) 847-7424. Restaurant. Established: 1973 - Franchising Since: 1988 - No. of Units: Franchised: 7 - Franchise Fee: $25,000 - Royalty: 5%, 3% mktg. - Total Inv: $295,000 dep. on location - Financing: No.

CHEZ BETTER
Franchise Chez Better Ltee.
4384 Boul. St. Laurent, Montreal, PQ, H2W 1Z5. Contact: David Better, Pres. - Tel: (514) 286-9842. Restaurant service with liquor license. Established: 1987 - Franchising Since: 1988 - No. of Units: Company Owned: 2 - Franchised: 4 - Franchise Fee: $25,000 - Royalty: 8% - Total Inv: $250,000 - Financing: 40% ($100,000) capital, 60% financed.

CHICK - N - CHICK *
Mayotee Enterprises Inc.
3484 Jeanne Mance, Montreal, PQ, H2X 2J8. Contact: André Savard, Oper. Mgr. - Tel: (514) 982-6075, Fax: (514) 849-3799. Featuring the best fried chicken complemented with fresh salad bar and fixins'. Established: 1994 - Franchising Since: 1994 - No. of Units: Franchised: 3 - Franchise Fee: $30,000 - Royalty: 6% - Total Inv: $150,000 - Financing: SBL.

CHICKEN CHEF
Chicken Chef Canada Ltd.
97 Plymouth St., Winnipeg, MB, R2X 2V5. Contact: Fred Thorgilsson, Pres. - Tel: (204) 694-1984. Family oriented full service restaurants offering dine-in, take-out and catering of pressure cooked chicken, pizza, fish, ribs, salads, and other popular menu items. Annual sales $18 million. Established: 1984 - Franchising Since: 1984 - No. of Units: Franchised: 35 - Franchise Fee: $12,000 - Annual Vol: 19,000,000.

CHICKEN DELIGHT
Chicken Delight of Canada, Ltd.
395 Berry St., Winnipeg, MB, R3J 1N6. Contact: Robert J. Ritchie, Mktg. Dir. - Tel: (204) 885-7570, Fax: (204) 831-6176. Fast food: retail, dine in/take out, delivery, drive-through and catering of deep fried chicken, made-to-order pizza, plus ribs, shrimp, salad, etc. Established: 1958, 1952 U.S.A. - Franchising Since: 1952 - No. of Units: Company Owned: 19 - Franchised: 45 - Franchise Fee: $20,000 per unit only, larger areas negotiable - Royalty: 5% - Total Inv: $125,000 - $650,000 - Financing: No.

CHICO'S 2 IN 1 FAMOUS CHICKEN 'N PIZZA
584 Voutrait Rd., R.R. # 2, Mill Bay, BC, V0R 2P0. Contact: Mr. Zacharopoulos, Fran. Dev. - Tel: (604) 495-3136. Fast food take-out and delivery operation offering special recipe chicken, pan pizza, ribs, pasta, salads and burgers. Established: 1988 - Franchising Since: 1989 - No. of Units: Company Owned: 1 - Franchised: 7 - Franchise Fee: $10,000 - Royalty: 3%, 3% adv. - Total Inv: $90,000 - Financing: Financial assistance given to qualified purchasers.

CHUCK E. CHEESE'S
All Canada Pizza Shows
2452 Sheppard Ave. E., Ste. 2020, Willowdale, ON, M2J 1X1. Contact: Franchise Dir./Pres. - Tel: (416) 497-8855. Pizza restaurants. No. of Units: Franchised: 4 - Franchise Fee: $25,000 - Royalty: 3.25%.

CITY SUBMARINE
SABSCO Corp.
406 -717 Portage Ave, Winnipeg, MB, R3G 0M8. Contact: Steve Sabbagh, Pres. - Tel: (204) 786-8696, Fax: (204) 783-1749. Sandwiches, soups, and salads. Established: 1978 - Franchising Since: 1983 - No. of Units: Franchised: 9 - Franchise Fee: $10,000 - Royalty: 5% - Total Inv: $75,000 to $90,000 - Financing: No.

CORTINA CARRY-OUT LTD.
1323 Martindale, Sudbury, ON, P3E 4J7. Contact: Henry Fay, Manager - Tel: (705) 522-3200. Family restaurant with take-out & delivery. Established: 1964 - Franchising Since: 1969 - No. of Units: Company Owned: 1 - Franchised: 12 - Franchise Fee: Varies - Royalty: 3% adv. - Total Inv: Varies depending on size & location.

COUNTRY KITCHEN
C.K. Franchising Inc.
12425 Jasper Ave., Edmonton, AB, T5N 3K9. Contact: V.L. Humphreys, Pres. - Tel: (403) 496-9225, Fax: (403) 488-8096. Family restaurant. Established: 1990 - Franchising Since: 1990 - No. of Units: Company Owned: 1 - Franchised: 9 - Franchise Fee: $40,000 - Royalty: 5% + 1% adv. - Total Inv: $600,000 - $1,000,000.

CRISPY CREPES
Crepencore Systems, Inc.
35 Alexandra Blvd., Toronto, ON, M4R 1L8. Contact: Franc. Dir. - Tel: (416) 488-3687. Gourmet Breton crepes, large and/or thin, fresh and/or frozen with plain, sweet or salted fillings. Also, spring rolls and many other varieties. Established:1986 - Franchising Since: 1988 - No. of Units : Company Owned: 1 - Franchised: 8 - Franchise Fee: $17,500 - Royalty: 5% - Total Inv: $84,000 incl fran fee - Financing: Assist.

CROISSANT PLUS
5005 Jean Talon W., Ste. 210, Montreal, PQ, H4P 1W7. Contact: Linda Benoit, Fran. Mgr. - Tel: (514) 735-5550, Fax: (514) 735-7564. Restaurant chain selling healthy, fresh food items such as salads, soups and sandwiches in Quebec, Ontario and British Columbia. Established: 1981 - Franchising Since: 1981 - No. of Units: Company Owned: 8 - Franchised: 36 - Franchise Fee: $27,500 - Royalty: 5% gross sales, 2% adv. - Total Inv: $150,000 - $180,000 - Financing: Will assist.

CRUPIZZA *
J.F. Schmitz Associates..The Finders
500 Rossland Rd. W., P.O. Box 58025, Oshawa, ON, L1J 8L6. Contact: Joseph Schmitz, Fran. Cons. - Tel: (905) 579-9792, Fax: (905) 579-4692. Strip centre and street front: 50% off pick-up pizza & limited Italian specialty foods...Food courts have extended Italian specialty

foods. Established: 1986 - Franchising Since: 1986 - No. of Units: Company Owned: 1 - Franchised: 3 - Franchise Fee: $10,000 - Royalty: Flat fee of $200 per week - Total Inv: $55,000 for turnkey ready to move in and operate - Financing: $50,000 to qualified applicants.

CULTURES FRESH FOOD RESTAURANTS
Cultures Restaurants Inc.
Ste. 1605, 20 Bay St., Toronto, ON, M5J 2N8. Contact: John Beauparlant, Gen. Mgr. - Tel: (416) 368-1440. Cultures is a fresh food concept, in which all products are prepared fresh on the premises every day. Salads, soup, sandwiches, a wide variety of baked goods and frozen yogurt specialties make up a healthy menu. Established: 1977 - Franchising Since: 1980 - No. of Units: Company Owned: 11 - Franchised: 33 - Franchise Fee: $35,000 - Royalty: 5%, 3% adv. - Total Inv: $150,000 - $300,000 - Financing: Through bank.

DAVE'S PIZZA RESTAURANTS, LTD.
5579-47th St., #6, Red Deer, AB, T4N 1S1. Contact: Dave Nobes, Pres. - Tel: (403) 346-7511. Pizza restaurants from take out to 100 seat lounges, optional. Pizza, spaghetti, lasagna, ribs, chicken, other pasta. Lunch menu added in some locations. Established: 1971 - Franchising Since: 1980 - No. of Units: Franchised: 14 - Franchise Fee: $3,500-$6,500 - Royalty: 2.5% + 1.5% adv. - Total Inv: $40,000 - $200,000 depending on size of restaurant - Financing: Advising.

DE DUTCH PANNEKOEK HOUSE
De Dutch Pannekoek House Restaurants Inc.
15235 Fraser Hwy., Surrey, BC, V3R 3P3. Contact: W.K. (Bill) Waring, Pres. - Tel: (604) 599-4293, Fax (604) 599-4281. Full service breakfast specialty, menu features many signature items in an ethnic Dutch theme. Emphasis on quality over price. Seating capacity 60 inside, 24 patio (where applicable). The company is currently seeking qualified area developers outside British Columbia and Washington State. Established: 1975 - Franchising Since: 1978 - No. of Units: Franchised: 18 - Franchise Fee: $37,500 - Royalty: 5%, adv. 2% - Total Inv: $230,000 - $270,000.

De Head Office
15235 Fraser Highway
Surrey,
British Columbia,
Canada V3R 3P3
Telephone:
(604) 599-4293
(604) 951-3840
Facsimile:
(604) 599-4281

W.K. (Bill) Waring
President

De Dutch Pannekoek House Restaurants Inc.

DESPERADO'S SALOON AND WESTERN EATERY
T.H.G. Franchising
P.O. Box 20012, Brantford, ON, N3P 2A4. Contact: Ron Hewitt, Dir. of Fran. - Tel: (519) 752-2945. Saloon and western eatery with a neighbourhood bar concept featuring Tex Mex food, western decor, music and dancing. Established: 1993 - Franchising Since: 1993 - No. of Units: Company Owned: 1 - Franchised: 1 - No Franchise Fee - Royalty: 5% - Total Inv: $140,000 - Financing: Partial.

DI LALLO BURGER *
Di Lallo Management
2851 Allard, Montreal, PQ, H4E 2M1. Contact: Lou Di Lallo Sr., Owner - Tel: (514) 767-9921. Established: 1929 - Franchising Since: 1973 - No. of Units: Company Owned: 1 - Franchised: 5 - Franchise Fee: $15,000 - Royalty: $225/mo., supplier rebates - Total Inv: $100,000: $15,000 fran. fee, $85,000 set-up - Financing: None.

DIDGERIDOOS ROTISSERIE CHICKEN
Didgeridoos Canada Corporation
505 Consumers Rd., Ste. 1000, Toronto, ON, M2J 4V8. Contact: Wm. (Bill) Hood, Pres. - Tel: (416) 493-3900, ext. 600. Quick service, eat-in/take-out featuring fresh rotisserie chicken, hot vegetables, salads, prepared fresh daily. No fried products. Established: 1994 - Franchising Since: 1994 - No. of Units: Company Owned: 1 - Franchise Fee: $25,000 - Royalty: 5%.

DIJO'S PIZZA PANZEROTTO *
Dijo's Pizza Holdings, Ltd.
1706 Robson St., Vancouver, BC, V6G 1E2. Contact: Dino Pastore, Pres. - Tel: (604) 685-5555, Fax: (604) 687-7771. Take out - pizza (slices, take out, delivery) wings, panzerotti! Established: 1986 - Franchising Since: 1988 - No. of Units: Company Owned: 2 - Franchised: 2 - Total Inv: $65,000 to $85,000 - Financing: Yes.

DIXIE LEE FRIED CHICKEN
Dixie Lee Food Systems Ltd.
51 Mary St. W., Ste. 205, Lindsay, ON, K9V 5Z6. Contact: Dave Silvester, Pres. - Tel: (705) 324-3145, Fax: (705) 324-8945. Proven fast food chicken concept. Established: 1964 - No. of Units: Company Owned: 3 - Franchised: 116 - Franchise Fee: $20,000 - Royalty: 3% plus 1% adv. fees - Financing: Yes.

DOMINO'S PIZZA *
Domino's Pizza of Canada
3838 Bankers Hall, 855 - 2nd St. S.W., Calgary, AB, T2P 4J8. Contact: Cory Gelmon, V.P. Fran. - Tel: (403) 263-8187, Fax: (403) 266-5813. Pizza delivery and take-out. Franchise Fee: Nil - Royalty: 5.5% royalty; 4% nat'l. ad. fund - Total Inv: $150,000 cdn; equip., leaseholds, op. capital.

DON CHERRY'S GRAPEVINE
Don Cherry's Grapevine Restaurants, Inc.
1233 The Queensway, Etobicoke, ON, M8Z 1S1. Contact: Mr. Richard J. Scully, Pres. - Tel: (416) 253-7717. Canada's premier sports bar. Established: 1985 - Franchising Since: 1989 - No. of Units: Company Owned: 1 - Franchised: 19 - Franchise Fee: $50,000 - Royalty: 6%, 1.5% adv. - Total Inv: $450,000 - $600,000 - Financing: No.

DOUBLE DOUBLE PIZZA & CHICKEN *
2011 Lawrence Ave. W., Unit 10, Weston, ON, M9N 3V3. Contact: Arman Jalili, Pres. - Tel: (416) 241-0088. Central order entry computer assisted fast food. Pickup and delivery of pizza and a complete line of chicken products. Established: 1990 - Franchising Since: 1990 - No. of Units: Company Owned: 4 - Franchised: 40 - Franchise Fee: $10,000 - Royalty: Fixed payments including royalties, advertising and order processing - Financing: Assistance with financing to qualified applicants.

DRUXY'S FAMOUS DELI SANDWICHES
Druxy's Inc.
18 King St. E., Ste. 1500, Toronto, ON, M5C 1C4. Contact: Peter Druxerman, V.P. Mktg. - Tel: (416) 364-8001. Chain of New York style delicatessen restaurants designed as cafeterias. The philosophy is to offer customers the highest quality, service & product possible. Druxy's prides itself in going beyond where other fast food operators would venture, giving customers a unique and unforgettable experience. Established: 1976 - Franchising Since: 1990 - No. of Units: Company Owned: 25 - Franchised: 20 - Franchise Fee: $30,000 - Royalty: 5%, 2% adv. - Total Inv: $260,000; $200,000 construction, $30,000 fran. fee, $30,000 work. cap. - Financing: No.

DYNASTIE DE CHINE
Matoyee Enterprises, Inc.
3484 Yeanne Mance, Montreal, PQ, H2X 2J8. Contact: Stanley Ma, Pres. - Tel: (514) 982-6075. Full license sit down restaurant, featuring the best in Oriental buffet-style cuisine. Established: 1990 - Franchising Since: 1990 - No. of Units: Franchised: 5 - Franchise Fee: $30,000 - Royalty: 4%, 1% adv. - Total Inv: $500,000 - $600,000.

EAST SIDE MARIO'S *
Prime Restaurant Group, In.c
10 Kingsbridge Garden Cir., Ste. 600, Mississauga, ON, L5R 3K6. Contact: Richard Stark, Sr. V.P., Dev. - Tel: (905) 568-0000, Fax: (905) 568-0080. Casual restaurant themed (by decor, method of operation and

choice of menu) to be reminiscent of small family run Italian restaurant in Manhattan's Little Italy in the 1930's. Menu consists of American-Italian favourites (including pizza and pasta). Established: 1979 - Franchising Since: 1984 - No. of Units: Company Owned: 2 - Franchised: 42 - Franchise Fee: $40,000 - Royalty: 5% - Total Inv: $40,000 fran. fee, $25,000 opening team fee, $775,000 to $925,000 development cost, $75,000 working cap. - Financing: No.

EDELWEISS DELI EXPRESS
Edelweiss International Franchise Corp.
#7-3331 Viking Way, Richmond, BC, V7C 4S1. Contact: Duncan Williams, Pres. - Tel: (604) 270-2360, Fax: (604) 270-6560. Delicious subs, quality sandwiches, soups & salads. Full training and support provided on all aspects of the business. Full marketing support, ongoing support programs. Stresses nutritious & delicious food. Established: 1973 - Franchising Since: 1989 - No. of Units: Company Owned: 1 - Franchised: 26 - Franchise Fee: $10,000 - Royalty: 6%, 4% adv. - Total Inv: $55,000 - $85,000 - Financing: Bank.

EDO JAPAN
604 Manitou Rd. S. E., Calgary, AB, T2G 4C5. Contact: S. K. Ikuta, Pres. - Tel: (403) 287-3822, Fax: (403) 243-6143. Original Japanese "Teppan Style" fast food established since 1977. Trained cooks offer a display of showmanship, serving fresh, and nutritious food to happy, repeat customers. Established: 1977 - Franchising Since: 1986 - No. of Units: Company Owned: 6 - Franchised: 76 - Franchise Fee: $20,000 - Royalty: 6% - Total Inv: $170,000 - $225,000.

ELEPHANT & CASTLE
P.O. Box 10240, Pacific Centre, Vancouver, BC, V7Y 1E7. Contact: Mr. Jeffrey M. Barnett, Mng. Dir. - Tel: (604) 684-6451. British/Irish pub atmosphere. Franchise Fee: $50,000 - Royalty: 6%.

FAT ALBERT'S RESTAURANTS/RALPH'S DINING LOUNGES
Randa Food Systems Company Ltd.
Unit #10, 2615 Lancaster Rd., Ottawa, ON, K1B 5N2. Contact: Franchise Dir./Pres. - Tel: (613) 739-3734. Fat Albert's: specializing in submarines and pizzas, licensed, seating 40-60 people; Ralph's: neighborhood licensed lounges (adjacent to Fat Albert's), comfortable atmosphere seating 50-90 people. Established: 1969 - Franchising Since: 1974 - No. of Units: Company Owned: 7 - Franchised: 14 - Franchise Fee: $50,000 - Approx. Total Inv: $600,000 - Royalty: 5%.

FATSO'S HOMEMADE HAMBURGERS, SALADS, SHAKES & FRIES
P.O. Box 700, Don Mills Stn., Don Mills, ON, M3C 2T6. Contact: Steve Georgopoulos, Pres. - Tel: (416) 447-4584. Fast food and homemade hamburgers. Established: 1984 - Franchising Since: 1989 - No. of Units: Company Owned: 1 - Franchised: 5 - Franchise Fee: $20,000 - Royalty: 5% + 2% adv. - Total Inv: 40% of total inv. - Financing: Assistance.

FISH & CHIP SHOPPE, THE
733719 Ontario Limited
200 N. Service Rd. W., #1, Oakville, ON, L6M 2V1. Contact: Jim Clark, Franc. Dir. - Tel: (905) 847-7424. Dining room & take out. (80-90 seats) Specialize in various fish (deep fried) and grilled fish steaks. Established: 1987 - Franchising Since: 1988 - No. of Units: Company Owned: 1 - Franchised: 7 - Franchise Fee: $25,000 - Royalty: 5%, 3% Mktg. - Total Inv: $275,000 - Financing: Via Royal Bank financing package.

FONTAINE SANTE
830 Begin St., St. Laurent, PQ, H4M 2N5. Contact: Faical Farhat, V.P. - Tel: (514) 956-7730. Health fast food. Established: 1981 - Franchising Since: 1983 - No. of Units: Company Owned: 4 - Franchised: 16 - Franchise Fee: $25,000 - Total Inv: $145,000: $60,000 equip.; $60,000 leasehold - Royalty: 5% + 1% promotion - Financing: By small business loan.

FRANX SUPREME
Maytoyee Enterprises Inc.
3484 Jeanne Mance, Montreal, PQ, H2X 2J8. Contact: Stanley Ma, Pres. - Tel: (514) 982-6075. Offers a menu specializing in hot dogs & french fries. Quality, cleanliness, service and ambiance compares with the major fast food outlets in North America. Established: 1990 - Franchising Since: 1990 - No of Units: Franchised: 6 - Franchise Fee: $25,000 - Royalty: 6% - Total Inv: $150,000 to $165,000.

FRIENDLY BANNERS RESTAURANTS
Banners Restaurants of Canada, Ltd.
#203 - 1965 West Fourth Ave., Vancouver, BC, V6J 1M8. Contact: Irwin Woodrow, Pres. - Tel: (604) 737-7748, Fax: (604) 737-7993. A family-oriented restaurant open for breakfast, lunch & dinner featuring selected Baskin-Robbins products. Established: 1972 - Franchising Since: 1972 - No. of Units: Franchised: 7 - Franchise Fee: $30,000 - Royalty: 4%, 2% adv. - Total Inv: equip., leaseholds $300,000; work. cap. $100,000 - Financing: Will assist franchisee in obtaining financing.

GOLDEN GRIDDLE FAMILY RESTAURANTS
Golden Griddle Corporation, The
505 Consumers Rd., Ste. 1000, Willowdale, ON, M2J 4V8. Contact: W.W. (Bill) Hood, Exec. V.P. - Tel: (416) 493-3800, Ext. 600, Fax: (416) 493-3889. Full service family restaurants. Licensed, extensive menu for all occasions. Some units opened 24hrs. Established: 1964 - Franchising Since: 1976 - No. of Units: Franchised: 56 - Franchise Fee: $10,000 - Royalty: 5%, 3% adv. - Total Inv: $100,000 - $400,000 incl. fran fee - Financing: No.

GOLPHIS RESTAURANTS LTD.
3209 Post Meridian, Pt. Coquitlam, BC, V3B 1A5. Contact: Golphis Caramonolis, Pres. - Tel: (604) 941-4067. Established: 1973 - Franchising Since: 1975 - No. of Units: Company Owned: 2 - Franchised: 3 - Franchise Fee: $50,000 - Approx. Total Inv: $250,000 - Royalty: 3% gross on food only - Financing: Yes.

GRANDMA LEE'S RESTAURANT AND BAKERY
Grandma Lee's Inc.
1200 Aerowood Dr., Unit 30, Mississauga, ON, L4W 2S7. Contact: Sun Lee, V.P. Fran. - Tel: (905) 625-5055, Fax: (905) 625-1481. Restaurants featuring homestyle baked products, chili, stews, soups, sandwiches made on fresh baked bread on the premises. A full line of desserts and specialty products are also available. Established: 1972 - Franchising Since: 1977 - No. of Units: Company Owned: 1 - Franchised: 104 - Franchise Fee: $25,000 - Royalty: 6.5% + 1.5% mktg. - Total Inv: $75,000 - $150,000 - Financing: Yes.

GRECO PIZZA DONAIR
Grinner's Food Systems Ltd.
105 Walker St., P.O. Box 1040, Truro, NS, B2N 5G9. Contact: Christopher MacDougall, Dir. of Dev. - Tel: (902) 893-4141. Pick-up and delivery restaurant chain, specializing in pizza, donair, salads, oven sub sandwiches and pita wrap sandwiches. Established: 1977 - Franchising Since: 1981 - No. of Units: Company Owned: 2 - Franchised: 54 - Franchise Fee: $15,000 - Royalty: 5%, 3% adv. - Total Inv: $140,000 - $160,000 - Financing: No.

HAN MONGOLIAN BARBECUE *
Han Mongolian Barbecue Ltd.
P.O. Box 1913, Vernon, BC, V1T 8Z7. Contact: Martin Hunziker, Pres. - Tel: (604) 558-3558, Fax: (604) 558-5510. Fantastic and healthy fresh food buffet and dining room cooking concept. Established: 1994 - Franchising Since: 1995 - No. of Units: Company Owned: 1 - Franchise Fee: $30,000 - Royalty: 3.5%, 1.5% adv. - Total Inv: $160,000 - $220,000 avg., min. cash req'd. $120,000 - Financing: No.

HARVEY'S RESTAURANT
Cara Operations Ltd.
230 Bloor St., W., Toronto, ON, M5S 1T8. Contact: Mgr. of Franchise Admin. - Tel: (416) 962-4571. Fast food restaurant serving charbroiled hamburgers, hot dogs, chicken fingers, salads, chicken salads, chicken sandwiches & breakfast items. Established: 1883 - Franchising Since: 1962 - No. of Units: Company Owned: 8 - Franchised: 284 - Franchise Fee: $50,000 - Harvey's with Churchs Chicken $57,000 - Harvey's Plus (Harvey's serving Swiss Chalet chicken) $75,000 - Royalty: 5% (1.5% covenant fee if Cara on head lease) - Total Inv: $550,000 to $700,000 depending on extent of ownership - Financing: No.

HEAVY DUTY PIZZA
Heavy Duty Pizza Inc.
113-115 Cushman Rd., Unit 21, St. Catharines, ON, L2M 6S9. Contact: Denis Blanchard, Pres. - Tel: (905) 641-1117. Retail pizza and subs, commissary at head office. Established: 1975 - Franchising Since: 1975 - No. of Units: Company Owned: 4 - Franchised: 6 - Franchise Fee: $10,000 - Royalty: 4%, 3% adv. - Total Inv: $70,000 - $80,000 - Financing: No.

HECTOR
Casse Croute "Hector" Inc.
270, 76ieme Rue Est, Charlesbourg, PQ, G1H 1G7. Contact: Georges Fontaine, Pror. - Tel: (418) 623-8849. Fast foods (Cuisine rapide same as Burger King, etc.) Our speciality is Pain a La Viande. Meat in hotdog bread with special sauce. Franchise or Licence available. Established: 1954 - Franchising Since: 1984 - No. of Units: Company Owned: 1 - Franchised: 2 - Franchise Fee: $25,000/ Licensor/ $5,000.- Fournitore sauce and photo menu and operator manuel - Total Inv: $150,000 - $200,000 - Royalty: 3%/400,000, 4%/500,000.

HO-LEE-CHOW
GCF Food Services Inc.
320 Danforth Ave., Ste. 202, Toronto, ON, M4K 1N8. Contact: Jake Cappillo, Pres. - Tel: (416) 778-6660, Fax: (416) 778-6694. Great Chinese food delivered fast & fresh. Pick-up available too. Each entré cooked to order - Hot! - Fast! and Fresh! within 45 min. Established: 1989 - Franchising Since: 1989 - No. of Units: Company Owned: 1 - Franchised: 17 - Franchise Fee: included in turnkey package - Royalty: 6%, 3% adv. - Total Inv: $125,000 + $25,000 fran. fee - Financing: Yes.

HOUSTON PIZZA FAMILY RESTAURANT *
Houston Pizza Franchises Ltd.
3422 Hill Ave., Regina, SK, S4S 0W9. Contact: John Kolitsas, Pres. - Tel: (306) 584-0888. Family restaurant, specializes in pizza, pasta & steak house, eat-in, take out and delivery. Established: 1970 - Franchising Since: 1983 - No. of Units: Company Owned: 1 - Franchised: 10 - Franchise Fee: $10,000 - Royalty: 7%, 3% for adv. included - Total Inv: $200,000 ($70,000 equip., $130,000 leasehold improvement) - Financing: No.

HUMPTY'S FAMILY RESTAURANTS
Humpty's Restaurants International, Inc.
2505 Macleod Tr. S., Calgary, AB, T2G 5J4. Contact: Don Koenig, Pres. - Tel: (403) 269-4675. A full service family restaurant providing large portions of quality food at reasonable prices. A unique menu provides extensive selection and a 24 hour breakfast. Established: 1977 - Franchising Since: 1983 - No. of Units: Company Owned: 2 - Franchised: 32 - Franchise Fee: $25,000 - Royalty: 2% - 5% - Total Inv: $200,000 - $350,000 - Financing: Assistance with sourcing.

HUSKY ROADHOUSE / HUSKY HOUSE RESTAURANT *
Husky Oil Marketing Co.
707 - 8th Ave. S.W., Calgary, AB, T2P 3G7. Contact: C. Perry Bloxom, Food Svcs. Mgr. - Tel: (403) 298-6712. Restaurants & food stores. Franchising Since: 1990 - No. of Units: Company Owned: 42 - Franchised: 3 - Franchise Fee: varies - Royalty: varies - Total Inv: varies.

J. KWINTER GOURMET HOT DOGS
3130 Bathurst St., #214, Toronto, ON, M6A 2A1. Contact: Debbie Alexander, Dir. of Oper. - Tel: (416) 781-4299. Kwinters features 4 types of hot dogs, fries & drinks. Our own factory produces the hot dogs from 100% beef or 100% veal. No by-products, no fillers, no MSG. Independently rated as the best hot dog in Canada. Established: 1984 - Franchising Since: 1985 - No. of Units: Franchised: 18 - Franchise Fee: $20,000 - Royalty: 6% - Total Inv: ranges from $60,000 - $120,000 - Financing: Yes.

JACQUES CARTIER PIZZA, INC.
2419 Chemin Chambly, Longueuil, PQ, J4L 1L8. Contact: Stella Lagiorgia, V.P. - Tel: (514) 647-5334. Fast food Italian restaurant featuring pizza, pasta & submarine sandwiches. Dining room, delivery & pick-up counter. Established: 1961 - Franchising Since: 1985 - No. of Units: Company Owned: 1 - Franchised: 4 - Franchise Fee: $50,000 - Royalty: 6% - Total Inv: $150,000 - Financing: Yes.

JIMMY THE GREEK
181 Bay St., Toronto, ON, M5J 2T3. Contact: Jim Antonopoulos, Pres. - Tel: (416) 214-4794, Fax: (416) 362-0827. Greek cuisine served in a fast food environment. Established: 1985 - Franchising Since: 1985 - No. of Units: Company Owned: 3 - Franchised: 14 - Franchise Fee: $25,000 - Royalty: 5% - Total Inv: $125,000 to $160,000 - Financing: Yes.

JOEY'S ONLY SEAFOOD RESTAURANT
Joey's Only Franchising Ltd.
514 42nd Ave. S.E., Calgary, AB, T2G 1Y6. Contact: David Mossey, Fran. Dir. - Tel: (403) 243-4584. Operation of full-service seafood restaurants. Established: 1985 - Franchising Since: 1991 - No. of Units: Franchised: 11 - Franchise Fee: $25,000 - Royalty: 4.5% - Total Inv: $119,000 - $150,500 (equip., supplies and re-dec). For further details please contact: Consultants America Corp., 12279 US Highway 64, EADS, TN, 38028.

JOEY'S ONLY SEAFOOD RESTAURANTS (ONTARIO)
9301 Yonge St., #2A, Richmond Hill, ON, L4C 1V4. Contact: Perry Wong, C.A., V.P. Mktg. - ON Master Franchisor - Tel: (905) 770-3474. Canada's largest and fastest growing seafood franchise. Full service, affordable, family-style seafood restaurant. Dine-in & take-out. Protected territories. Small cash requirement. Excellent financing package. Established: 1985 - Franchising Since: 1992 - No. of Units: Company Owned: 1 - Franchised: 50 - Franchise Fee: $25,000 - Royalty: 4.5%, 2% adv. - Total Inv: $150,000 - $175,000 TTL - Financing: Small cash requirement.

KEG RESTAURANTS LTD.
#150-10760 Shellbridge Way, Richmond, BC, V6X 3H1. Contact: Kelly Nordin, Michael Graydon, Fran. Dir., V.P. Mktg. & Bus. Dev. - Tel: (604) 276-0242. Full service, full menu, licensed steak houses. Actively pursuing franchise opportunities. Established: 1971 - Franchising Since: 1973 - No. of Units: Company Owned: 66 - Franchised: 14 - Franchise Fee: $50,000 - Royalty: 5% gross, 2.5% mktg. - Total Inv: $1,800,000, stand-alone building, and start up - Financing: No.

KELSEY'S RESTAURANTS
450 South Service Rd. W., Oakville, ON, L6K 2H4. Contact: Patricia Phelan, Dir. of Fran. - Tel: (905) 842-5510, Fax: (905) 842-5603. Casual dining dinner house with lounge. "Your neighbourhood bar and grill." Established: 1977 - No. of Units: Company Owned: 25 - Franchised: 20 - Franchise Fee: $27,500 - Royalty: 4% - Total Inv: $500,000 to $700,000 - Financing: No.

KFC
KFC Canada, div. of Pepsi Cola Canada Ltd.
10 Carlson Court, Ste. 300, Rexdale, ON, M9W 6L2. Contact: Ian Johnstone, Bus. Dev. Mgr. - Tel: (416) 674-0367. Quick service restaurant specializing in chicken. No. of Units: Company Owned: 240 - Franchised: 580.

KOJAX
Kojax Souvlaki
8150 Marco Polo, Montreal, PQ, H1E 5Y7. Contact: Giovanni Fiorino, Pres. - Tel: (514) 494-2526. Greek fast food specializing in souvlaki & yero (donair). Established: 1977 - Franchising Since: 1985 - No. of Units: Company Owned: 2 - Franchised: 15 - Franchise Fee: $38,500 - Royalty: 5%, 2% adv. - Total Inv: $250,000 turn key - Financing: No.

KOYA JAPAN
Koya Japan, Inc.
717 Portage Ave., Ste. 406, Winnipeg, MB, R3G 0M8. Contact: Steve Sabbagh, Pres. - Tel: (204) 783-4433, Fax: (204) 783-1749. Japanese fast food restaurants. Established: 1985 - Franchising Since: 1986 - No. of Units: Company Owned: 1 - Franchised: 20 - Franchise Fee: $25,000 - Royalty: 6% - Total Inv: $125,000 - Financing: No.

LA CAGE AUX SPORTS
Sportscene Restaurants Inc.
426 Rue Ste-Helene, Montreal, PQ, H2Y 2K7. Contact: Michel Bedard, Fran. & Dev. - Tel: (514) 849-9376. Sports bar and restaurant. Established: 1984 - Franchising Since: 1987 - No. of Units: Company Owned: 1 - Franchised: 3 - Franchise Fee: $75,000 - Royalty: 5% - Total Inv: $750,000 approx. - Financing: None.

LA TORTILLERIA
La Tortilleria Holdings
145 - 1669 Johnston St., Vancouver, BC, V6H 3R9. Contact: Boris Schaffer, Pres. - Tel: (604) 327-0070, Fax: (604) 327-0272. Mexican fast food. Established: 1984 - Franchising Since: 1992 - No. of Units: Company Owned: 2 - Franchised: 2 - Franchise Fee: $15,000 - Royalty: 4% sales, 2% adv. - Total Inv: $100,000 - $140,000 - Financing: No.

LES PRES RESTAURANT
Restaurants Les Pres Canada Ltee.
3224-Jean Beraud, Bureau 200, Laval, PQ, H7T 2S4. Contact: Christian Beaulieu, Dir. Gen. - Tel: (514) 973-2010. Semi fast food restaurants with table service and liquor licence. Established: 1982 - Franchising Since: 1982 - No. of Units: Company Owned: 9 - Franchised: 16 - Franchise Fee: $50,000 - Royalty: 5% + 4% adv.

LICK'S RESTAURANTS
1962A Queen St. E., Toronto, ON, M4L 1H8. Contact: Frank Peruzzi, Fran. Dir. - Tel: (416) 362-5425. Gourmet fast food and ice cream. Established: 1979 - Franchising Since: 1991 - No. of Units: Company Owned: 6 - Franchised: 5 - Franchise Fee: $35,000 - Royalty: 6%, 2% mktg., 1% accounting - Total Inv: $275,000 - $375,000 - Financing: No.

LIL' JULI SNACK BARS
300 King George Rd., Brantford, ON, N3R 5L8. Contact: Victor Bielik, Pres. - Tel: (519) 753-7211. Fast food. Established: 1972 - Franchising Since: 1974 - No. of Units: Company Owned: 1 - Franchised: 2 - Franchise Fee: $25,000 - Approx. Total Inv: $40,000 - $60,000 - Royalty: 3%.

LITE-WAY SUBS & DELI INC. *
150 Britannia Rd. E., Ste. 14, Mississauga, ON, L4Z 1W6. Contact: Paul Aneja, Pres. - Tel: (905) 890-7111, Fax: (905) 890-5400. Submarine sandwiches, pasta & salad using low fat meats, cheeses & sauces. Established: 1994 - Franchising Since: 1994 - No. of Units: Company Owned: 2 - Franchised: 11 - Franchise Fee: $10,000 - Royalty: 5%, 2% adv. - Total Inv: $85,000 turnkey: $55,000 equip. & leasehold; $10,000 fran. fee; $10,000 admin; $10,000 cash, rent, insurance, misc. exp. - Financing: Yes.

LONG JOHN SILVER'S SEAFOOD SHOPPES
Nelron Restaurants Ltd.
384 King St. N., Waterloo, ON, N2J 2Z3. Contact: Norman Steele, Pres. - Tel: (519) 888-7650. Quick service restaurant. Fish and seafood plus quality chicken products. Established: 1977 - Franchising Since: 1977 - No. of Units: 4 - Franchise Fee: $22,500 - Royalty: 4 -5.5% - Total Inv: $750,000 includes land/building.

LOS RIOS MEXICAN FOODS
The SLC Corporation
3710 Chesswood Drive, Ste. 220, Downsview, ON, M3J 2W4. Contact: Gabe Sarracini, President - Tel: (416) 636-9348, Fax: (416) 636-9162. Mexican Fast Food Restaurants located in Regional Shopping Centres and Downtown Office Towers. Established: 1983 - Franchising Since: 1985 - No. of Units: Franchised: 10 - Franchise Fee: $20,000 - Royalty: 6% on monthly gross sales - Total Inv: $125,000 - $140,000 - Financing: No, but will assist in packaging a BIL for prospective franchisee.

MADE IN JAPAN - A TERIYAKI EXPERIENCE
Made In Japan Japanese Restaurants Limited
2133 Royal Windsor Dr., Ste. 23, Mississauga, ON, L5J 1K5. Contact: Nik Jurkovic, Dir. of Fran. Dev. - Tel: (905) 823-8883. Serving Teriyaki dishes, operating in food courts of major shopping centres across Canada in over 42 locations. Established: 1986 - Franchising Since: 1987 - No. of Units: Franchised: 42 - Franchise Fee: $25,000 - Royalty: 6% - Total Inv: leaseholds $80,000, equip. $60,000 - Financing: Yes.

MANCHU WOK
S.C. Food Services (Canada) Inc.
500 Hood Road, Markham, ON, L3R 0P6. Contact: Gavin Swartzman, Vice Pres. Fran. & New Bus. Dev. - Tel: (905) 946-7205. Oriental quick service restaurant chain operating primarily in shopping mall food courts. Established: 1981 - Franchising Since: 1981 - Number of Units: Company Owned: 36/CND, 93/US - Franchised: 64/CND, 53/US - Franchise Fee: $30,000 - Royalty: 6%, 2% adv. - Total Inv: Varies - Financing: Yes.

MANDARIN
Mandarin Restaurant Franchise Corp.
239 Queen St. E., #18, Brampton, ON, L6W 2B6. Contact: George Chiu, V.P. - Tel: (905) 451-4100. Chinese licensed restaurant and take-out. Established: 1979 - No. of Units: Company Owned: 1 - Franchised: 9 - Franchise Fee: 10% - Royalty: 5% - Total Inv: $1,400,000 turnkey - Financing: Assistance provided.

MARY BROWN'S FRIED CHICKEN
Can Skillet Systems, Inc.
250 Shields Crt., Markham, ON, L3R 9W7. Contact: N. Beattie, V.P. Fran. Dev. - Tel: (905) 513-0044. Chain of chicken restaurants with products such as chicken fillet sandwiches, taters, salads etc. Established: 1977 - Franchising Since: 1977 - No. of Units: Franchised: 69 - Franchise Fee: $20,000 - Royalty: 4% of gross sales - Total Inv: $150,000 - $200,000 - Financing: Bank.

MCDONALD'S RESTAURANTS OF CANADA LTD.
McDonalds Place, Toronto, ON, M3C 3L4. Contact: John Piper, Mgr. of Lic. - Tel: (416) 443-1000. Fast food. Established: 1967 - Licensing Since: 1971 - No. of Units: Company Owned: 236 - Licensed: 230 - Approx. Initial Inv: $250,000 - Approx. Total Inv: $650,000 - Financing: No.

MIGHTY TACO & SUBS *
5232 Woodside Dr., Niagara Falls, ON, L2E 7G1. Contact: Wm. Siarto, Fran. Dev. - Tel: (905) 356-4242, Fax: (905) 356-9373. Preparation of taco & subs with special sauces & ingredients. Established: 1996 - Franchising Since: 1996 - Franchise Fee: $5,000 - Royalty: 4%, 2% adv. - Total Inv: $60,000 approx. - Financing: No.

MIKE'S RESTAURANTS
M-Corp., Inc.
8250 Decarie Blvd., Ste. 310, Montreal, PQ, H4P 2P5. Contact: Daniel Harvey, Dir. Franc. - Tel: (514) 341-5544. Italian style restaurants. Established: 1967 - Franchising Since: 1969 - No. of Units: 131 - Franchise Fee: $45,000 - Approx. Total Inv: $225,000-$575,000 - Royalty: 8% adv. incl. - Financing: Yes.

MINI DONAL LTD.
74 Main St., Ste. Anne de Mad, NB, E0L 1G0. Contact: Hermel Cormier, Pres./Owner - Tel: (506) 445-2742. Franchise for small restaurant. Established: 1979 - Franchising Since: 1979 - No. of Units: Company Owned: 32 - Franchise Fee: $1,000 per yr.

MR. MIKE'S STEAKHOUSE RESTAURANTS
Megalicious Food Corp.
#5 - 8765 Ash St., Vancouver, BC, V6P 6T3. Contact: Roger Newton, Pres. - Tel: (604) 322-7044, 1-800-668-MIKE. A semi service restaurant, featuring steak, burgers, chicken and seafood. Extensive salad bar offering over 60 items of hot food, salads, soups, desserts. Established: 1960 - Franchising Since: 1964 - No. of Units: Franchised: 22 - Franchise Fee: $25,000 CDN - Royalty: 4% - Total Inv: $100,000 to $225,000: Leaseholds $50,000 to $150,000, Equip. $75,000, Inventory $15,000 - Financing: Assistance to Royal Bank.

MR. SUB
Mr. Submarine Ltd.
720 Spadina Ave., Ste. 300, Toronto, ON, M5S 2T9. Contact: Kerry T. Shirakawa, V.P. Bus. Dev. - Tel: (416) 962-6232, Fax: (416) 962-9995. Fast food submarine sandwiches, salads, soups, baked goods, desserts, beverages. Established: 1968 - Franchising Since: 1972 - No. of Units:

Company Owned: 1 - Franchised: 501 - Franchise Fee: up to $10,000 - Royalty: 5%, 3% adv. - Total Inv: Equip. $60,000; Leaseholds $50,000; Fran. Fee $10,000 - Financing: N/A.

MR. TUBE STEAK
155 West Kent Ave. N., Vancouver, BC, V5X 2X4. Contact: Steve Duff, Dir. of Mktg. - Tel: (604) 322-0005. Franchise of mobile food vending carts & food prep. system using premium hot dogs & smokies. Established: 1988 - Franchising Since: 1988 - No. of Units: Company Owned: 20 - Franchised: 160 - Franchise Fee: $8,000 - $9,000 (incl. equip.) - Royalty: $750/yr - Total Inv: $8,000 - $9,000 - Financing: Partial.

MRS. VANELLI'S PIZZA & ITALIAN FOODS
Mrs. Vanelli's Restaurant Ltd.
23-2133 Royal Windsor Dr., Mississauga, ON, L5J 1K5. Contact: Nik Jurkovic, Franc. Dir. - Tel: (905) 823-8883. Serving traditional Italian style dishes. Operating in food courts of shopping centres across Canada with over 86 locations. Established: 1981 - Franchising Since: 1983 - No. of Units: Company Owned: 2 - Franchised: 84 - Franchise Fee: $25,000 - Royalty: 6% - Total Inv: leaseholds $80,000, equip. $60,000 - Financing: Assistance.

MYSTERY PIZZA & CHICKEN *
Mystery Pizza & Chicken Ltd.
3300 McNicoll Ave., Ste. 301A, Scarborough, ON, M1V 5J6. Contact: Poopak Safarian, Mktg. Mgr. - Tel: (416) 693-9394, Fax: (416) 292-9660. Pizza & chicken take out & delivery outlets. Established: 1990 - Franchising Since: 1990 - No. of Units: Company Owned: 2 - Franchised: 23 - Royalty: 5% - Total Inv: $75,000 - Financing: Assistance.

NEW ORLEANS PIZZA
316 Marsland Dr., Waterloo, ON, N2J 3Z1. Contact: John Cossay, Pres. - Tel: (519) 885-4600, Fax: (519) 746-2526. Pizza, submarines & wings, menu in take out, delivery units. Some counter service seating available. Established: 1978 - Franchising Since: 1982 - No. of Units: Company Owned: 5 - Franchised: 12 - Franchise Fee: $7,000 - Royalty: 3% - Total Inv: $75,000 to $100,000 - Financing: Yes.

NEW YORK FRIES
122164 Canada Inc.
1220 Yonge St., Ste. 400, Toronto, ON, M4T 1W1. Contact: L. Meade Helman, Exec. V.P. - Tel: (416) 963-5005, Fax: (416) 963-4920. A quick service concept providing consumer with a fresh cut fried potato with skins on and the nutritional value intact. Offer a high quality product cooked according to a unique recipe and served in a clean, fresh environment. Established: 1984 - Franchising Since: 1985 - No. of Units: Company Owned: 10 - Franchised: 91 - Franchise Fee: $25,000 - Royalty: 6%, 1.5% nat'l. ad fund - Total Inv: Fran. fee $25,000; leaseholds & equip. $100,000 to $150,000 - Financing: No.

NOODLE DELIGHT INC.
85 W. Wilmot St., #6, Richmond Hill, ON, L4B 1K7. Contact: Alfred P. Lam, Pres. & CEO - Tel: (905) 886-9700. Authentic Chinese Noodle and Rice dishes in Western convenience restaurant setting. Special feature is the open kitchen where patrons can watch their food being cooked in front of them in giant woks and served piping hot. Established: 1983 - Franchising Since: 1986 - No. of Units: Company Owned: 1 - Franchised: 4 - Franchise Fee: $25,000 - Royalty: 5% gross - Total Inv: 3% gross - Financing: None.

O'DONALS FAMILY RESTAURANTS
O'Donals Restaurants of Canada Ltd.
332 Rosehill Wynd, Delta, BC, V4M 3L9. Contact: Don Michel, Pres. - Tel: (604) 943-5052. Family style full service restaurant featuring quality menu items including senior & kids menus. Offer support & purchasing programs. Established: 1981 - Franchising Since: 1987 - No. of Units: Company Owned: 4 - Franchised: 3 - Franchise Fee: $25,000 - Royalty: 4% + 2% adv. - Total Inv: $150,000 cash, Total cost $500,000 - Financing: Package through Royal Bank.

OK HOT DOGS *
5232 Woodside Drive, Niagara Falls, ON, L2E 7G1. Contact: William Sijarto, Fran. Dev. - Tel: (905) 356-4242, Fax: (905) 356-9373. Hot dog carts. Established: 1995 - Franchising Since: 1995 - Franchise Fee: $1,000 - Royalty: 3%, 2% adv. - Total Inv: Turnkey from $9,900.

OK SUBMARINE LTD.™
5232 Woodside Drive, Niagara Falls, ON, L2E 7G1. Contact: Franchise Dept. - Tel: (905) 356-4242, Fax: (905) 356-9373. Foremost submarine sandwiches, salads, home-made style soups and custom sandwiches etc. Optional grill for steak subs, OK Western burgers etc. Deep fryer for french fries, onion rings, breaded mushrooms, zucchini & cheese stix and clams & shrimp, deep fried fish, and Buffalo-style chicken wings etc. Minimum turnkey operation $69,000 for 400-500 sq. ft. take-out concept (may vary); or $89,000 for Grill & fryer system which may vary, 400-500 sq. ft. take-out concept. Established: 1989 - Franchising Since: 1995 - No. of Units: Company Owned: 2 - Franchise Fee: $5,000 - Royalty: 5%, 2.5% adv. - Total Inv: $69,000 basic, $89,000 grill concept - Financing: Can assist in obtaining for qualified applicants.

ORANGE JULIUS
Orange Julius Canada, Ltd.
5245 Harvester Rd., Box 430, Burlington, ON, L7R 3Y3. Contact: Mark Ferguson, Dir. of Leasing - Tel: (905) 639-1492. Fast food franchisor with restaurants in enclosed malls, selling orange fruit drinks and hot dogs. Established: 1977 - Franchising Since: 1977 - No. of Units: Franchised: 103 - Franchise Fee: $15,000 - Royalty: 6% - Total Inv: $150,000.

ORIGINAL PANZEROTTO AND PIZZA
Il' Panzerotto and Pizza Ltd., The
234 Parliament St., Toronto, ON, M5A 3A4. Contact: Joe Schiavone, Franc. Dir. - Tel: (416) 362-5555. Fast food take out specializing in pizza, panzerotto, Italian sandwiches and wings ordered through a central number. Established: 1976 - Franchising Since: 1980 - No. of Units: Franchised: 36 - Franchise Fee: $20,000 - Royalty: 5% + 3% adv. - Total Inv: $145,000 turn-key - Financing: Yes.

P-WEE'S PIZZA, PASTA & MORE
P-Wee's Pizzeria Holdings Ltd.
591 Trinity Rd., Route 1, Jerseyville, ON, L0R 1R0. Contact: Dan Fratoni, Pres. - Tel: (905) 648-1434. Pizza, pasta and licensed dining rooms, unique system of ready, pre-prepared dishes. Looking for area franchisee. Established: 1958 - Franchising Since: 1970 - No. of Units: Company Owned: 3 - Franchised: 4 - Franchise Fee: $10,000 - Royalty: 4% gross - Total Inv: $150,000 - $200,000 - Financing: No.

PACINI
Les Restaurants Pacini Inc.
2550 Daniel Johnson, Ste. 600, Laval, PQ, H7T 2L1. Contact: Pierre Bourassa, Mgr., Bus. Dev. - Tel: (514) 973-2010. Italian-style, full-service family restaurant. Attractive atmosphere. Very popular concept in province of Quebec. (Licensed). Established: 1980 - Franchising Since: 1986 - No. of Units: Company Owned: 15 - Franchised: 18 - Franchise Fee: $35,000 - Royalty: 5% gross sales - Total Inv: $650,000.

PANAGOPOULOS PIZZA *
#1 - 32868 Ventura Ave., Abbotsford, BC, V2S 6J3. Contact: Brian Rooke, Dir. - Tel: (604) 859-6621. Take out and delivery of pizza. Established: 1986 - Franchising Since: 1986 - No. of Units: Company Owned: 6 - Franchised: 80 - Franchise Fee: $15,000 - Royalty: 5%, 5% adv. - Total Inv: $130,000 to $150,000 - Financing: No.

PANINI - PIZZA PASTA *
Mayotee Enterprises, Inc.
3484 Jeanne Mance, Montreal, Pq, H2X 2J8. Contact: André Savard, Oper. Mgr. - Tel: (514) 982-6075, Fax: (514) 849-3799. Featuring the best in pizza and pasta with salads, submarines and fries. Established: 1994 - Franchising Since: 1994 - No. of Units: Franchised: 1 - Franchise Fee: $30,000 - Royalty: 6% - Total Inv: $150,000 - Financing: SBL.

PANTRY FAMILY RESTAURANTS, THE
Pantry Hospitality Corporation, The
10607 King George Hwy., Surrey, BC, V3T 2X6. Contact: Mike Hoffmann, Pres. - Tel: (604) 536-4111. A full menu family restaurant chain offering breakfast, lunch or dinner served any time of day, seven days a week. Established: 1975 - Franchising Since: 1976 - No. of Units: Company Owned: 1 - Franchised: 23 - Franchise Fee: $40,000 - Royalty: 4.5% of gross, 2.5% adv. - Total Inv: Depends on site and area of restaurant - Financing: No.

PASTEL'S CAFE
Comac Food Group Inc.
#440, 1121 Centre St. N., Calgary, AB, T2E 7K6. Contact: Janine Hunka, Fran. Sales Mgr. - Tel: (403) 230-1151, (800) 361-1151. Pastel's features a full menu of the finest quality gourmet sandwiches, mouth watering array of specialty salads and hearty homemade soups, all prepared with fresh, healthy ingredients. Established: 1980 - Franchising Since: 1982 - No. of Units: Franchised: 17 - Franchise Fee: $25,000 - Royalty: 5% (no adv. royalty) - Total Inv: $150,000 - $175,000 for store development costs - Financing: Royal Bank of Canada.

PITA PAZZAZ
Pita Pazzaz Inc.
5339 Richborough Dr., Mississauga, ON, L5R 3J9. Contact: Ray Gauthier, Pres. - Tel: (905) 568-4477. Fast food for the 90's - (exemplary sales performance). Variety of low fat/low calorie foods in pita bread. Donairs, salads, falafal, kabobs. Located in food courts - major shopping centres. Established: 1991 - Franchising Since: 1992 - No. of Units: Company Owned: 1 - Franchised: 15 - Franchise Fee: $20,000 - Royalty: 6% (no adv. fee) - Total Inv: $85,000 - $125,000 - Financing: Yes. Master or multi-unit franchise available.

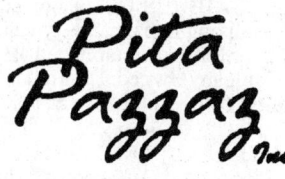

"Catch The Jazz"

Pita Pazzaz Inc.
- Top Sales Performer
- Complete Training & Support System
- Low Fat Food For The 90's

5339 RICHBOROUGH DR., MISSISSAUGA, ONTARIO L5R 3J9
PHONE: (905) 568-4477 / FAX: (905) 568-3910

PIZZA DELIGHT
Pizza Delight Corp.
P.O. Box 23070, Moncton, NB, E1A 6S8. Contact: Malcolm Houser, Exec. V.P. - Tel: (506) 853-0990. Full service licensed casual restaurants. Established: 1968 - Franchising Since: 1969 - No. of Units: Company Owned: 3 - Franchised: 147 - Franchise Fee: $30,000 - Royalty: 6%, 3% adv. - Total Inv: $275,000 - $450,000 - 40% equity - Financing: Through banks.

PIZZA DONINI
Donini Restaurant Inc.
9520 De L'Acadie, Suite 420, Montreal, PQ, H4N 1L8. Contact: Morton Jaquays, V.P. Fran. - Tel: (514) 383-6060; Fax (514) 385-6620. Full service restaurants featuring pizza and Italian style dishes as well as other menu items. One number system and 30 min. delivery guarantee. Donini counters (5-10 seats) or restaurants (45-55 seats). Established: 1986 - Franchising Since: 1986 - No. of Units: Franchised: 34 - Franchise Fee: $35,000 - Royalty: 9% (incl. adv.) - Total Inv: $185,000 to $240,000.

PIZZA HUT CANADA
5600 Explorer Dr., Mississauga, ON, L4W 4Y2. Contact: Humphrey Kadaner, Dir. Franchise - Tel: (905) 602-2769. Family dine-in, carryout & delivery pizza restaurant. Established: 1958 - Franchising Since: 1968 - No. of Units: Company Owned: 239 - Franchised: 148 - Franchise Fee: $40,000 - Royalty: 5%, 4% adv. - Total Inv: Excluding land/lease costs, Inline - $575,000, Free standing - $925,000 - Financing: No. No longer offering franchises in Canada. Contact name for Pizza Hut U.S. Wilma Jarboe, Tel: (316) 681-9806.

PIZZA NOVA
Pizza Nova Take-Out Ltd.
2100 Ellesmere Rd., Scarborough, ON, M1H 3B7. Contact: Frank Macri, Fran. Dir. - Tel: (416) 439-0051. Take-out and delivery of pizza and pasta. Established: 1963 - Franchising Since: 1968 - No. of Units: Company Owned: 1 - Franchised: 58 - Franchise Fee: $8,000 - Royalty: 6% - Total Inv: $100,000-$125,000.

PIZZA PIZZA
Pizza Pizza Limited
580 Jarvis St., Toronto, ON, M4Y 2H9. Contact: Sebastian Fuschini, V.P. Fran. - Tel: (800) 263-5556, (416) 967-1010, Fax: (416) 967-0891. Take-out and delivery of fresh stone-baked pizza, subs, wings, Italian dinners and salads. Some dine-in units. Established: 1968 - Franchising Since: 1975 - No. of Units: Company Owned: 16 - Franchised: 240 - Franchise Fee: $20,000 - Royalty: 6%, 6% adv. fund - Total Inv: $100,000 to $175,000, 30% - 35% cash down - Financing: Some assistance provided.

PIZZA ROYALE
650 Graham Bell, Ste. 217, Ste. Foy, PQ, G1N 4H5. Contact: Rejean Samson, Pres. - Tel: (418) 682-5744, Fax: (418) 682-2684. Italian restaurant. Pizza cooked in an open-fire wood oven in the serving area with salad and pasta bar, take-out orders and delivery available. Established: 1980 - Franchising Since: 1985 - No. of Units: Company Owned: 3 - Franchised: 12 - Franchise Fee: $30,000 - Total Inv: $350,000: $290,000 leasehold, equip, $60,000 fees + others. - Royalty: 3.9%-1.8% adv. - Financing: Yes.

PIZZAVILLE - PIZZA & PANZEROTTO
741 Rowntree Dairy Rd., Unit 1, Woodbridge, ON, L4L 5T9. Contact: A. Contardi, Pres. - Tel: (905) 850-0070. Pizza take out and delivery. Established: 1979 - Franchising Since: 1979 - No. of Units: 45 - Franchise Fee: $15,000 - Approx. Total Inv: $100,000 - Royalty: 5% of sales, 3% advertising - Financing: Introduction to bank.

PIZZERIA DI LORENZO'S
2201 Arch St., Ottawa, ON, K1G 2H5. Contact: Dan Fascinato, Mgr. - Tel: (613) 737-3737. Italian/Canadian restaurant with Ottawa's favourite pizza. Established: 1976 - Franchising Since: 1990 - No. of Units: Company Owned: 2 - Franchised: 5 - Franchise Fee: $25,000 - Royalty: 6% (First year free of royalties) - Total Inv: $50,000 - $100,000 depending on location - Financing: Some.

RESTAURANT NORMANDIN *
2335 Boul. Bastien, Quebec City, PQ, G2B 1B3. Contact: Denis Pigeon, Gen. Mgr. - Tel: (418) 842-9160. Family restaurant. Established: 1969 - Franchising Since: 1990 - No. of Units: Company Owned: 21 - Franchised: 5 - Franchise Fee: $30,000 - Royalty: 3%.

RICKY'S RESTAURANTS
104-12824 Anvil Way, Surrey, BC, V3W 8E7. Contact: Ron Hildebrand, Sr. V.P. - Tel: (604) 597-7273. Family restaurant chain. Established: 1979 - Franchising Since: 1987 - No. of Units: Company Owned: 5 - Franchised: 25 - Franchise Fee: $40,000 - Royalty: 3%, 2.5% adv. - Total Inv: $150,000 - $475,000.

RISTORANTE GIORGIO / LE STEAK FRITES ST PAUL / COQ & BROUE
Restaurants Giorgio (Amerique) Ltee.
222 Saint-Laurent Blvd., Montreal, PQ, H2Y 2Y3. Contact: Sylvie Paradis, Dir. Corp. Affairs - Tel: (514) 845-4221, Fax: (514) 844-0071. Restaurants. Established: 1977 - Franchising Since: 1985 - No. of Units: Company Owned: 11 - Franchised: 18 - Franchise Fee: $30,000 - Royalty: 5%, 4% adv. - Total Inv: $300,000 - Financing: None.

ROCCO RACCOON'S INDOOR PLAYGROUNDS INC. *
12-111 Fourth Ave., Ste. 350, Ridley Square, St. Catharines, ON, L2S 3P5. Contact: Mr. Varlis, Fran. Dept. - Tel: (905) 984-5115. U.S. Inquiries: 27 Minard St., Lockport, NY, 14094, Tel: (716) 434-7553, Contact: Mr. Varlis, Fran. Dept. We specialize in opening Fun Family Play Centers with Indoor supervised play areas, with a full menu (including pizza), gift shops, skill testing games and animated characters. Established: 1994 - Franchising Since: 1994 - Franchise Fee: $40,000 - Royalty: 3% of gross annual sales - Total Inv: $500,000 to $850,000 -

Financing: Reality, comp., acct., admin., complete training program and ongoing support. "Where Kids Of All Ages Have Fun"™. Our concept welcomes those who are looking for this fastest growing industry sweeping North America.

ROMEO'S PLACE, LTD.
760 Johnson St., Victoria, BC, V8W 1N1. Contact: Dimitrios Mavrikos, Pres. - Tel: (604) 383-2121. Family restaurants specializing in Italian food and pizza. Licensed bar. Established: 1974 - Franchising Since: 1981 - No. of Units: Company Owned: 3 - Franchised: 2 - Approx. Inv: $275,000 - $300,000 - Royalty: 3.5% - Financing: No.

RUFFAGE
Ruffage International Inc., c/o Ashton Food Group, Inc.
3380 South Service Rd., Burlington, ON, L7N 3J5. Contact: R. MacDonald, Pres. - Tel: (905) 681-8448. Specializes in upscale fresh food, specifically soups, salads, sandwiches with some hot foods. Served in both sit-down and take-out facilities. Stores generally operate Monday - Friday 7am - 5 pm. Established: 1986 - Franchising Since: 1986 - No. of Units: Company Owned: 2 - Franchised: 16 - Franchise Fee: $29,500 - Royalty: 5%, 2% adv. - Total Inv: $125,000 - $250,000 all inclusive - Financing: Third party.

SAILOR STEAMER HOT DOGS
#2201, 10104 103rd Ave., Edmonton, AB, T5J 0H8. Contact: David Hardy, V.P. Franchising - Tel: (403) 448-9099. Featuring both inline and kiosk locations in major shopping centers in Alberta, Sailors markets premium hot dogs, french fries, chicken fillets and a fresh salad option. Established: 1985 - Franchising Since: 1987 - No. of Units: Franchised: 5 - Franchise Fee: $25,000 - Royalty: 5% of gross sales - Total Inv: $125,000 - Financing: Yes.

SAKKIO JAPAN *
95 Royal Crest Ct., Unit 5, Markham, ON, L3R 9X5. Contact: Danny Cheung, Mng., Fran. - Tel: (905) 474-0710. Japanese fast food restaurant chain with 70 stores in food courts of super regional malls. Established: 1986 - Franchising Since: 1993 - No. of Units: Company Owned: 64 - Franchised: 6 - Franchise Fee: $30,000 - Royalty: 6% - Total Inv: $160,000 to $200,000 (turnkey basis) - Financing: Yes.

SAKURA JAPANESE FAST FOOD INC.
645 Sir Richards Rd., Mississauga, ON, L5C 1A3. Contact: Lisa Ough, Franc. Dir. - Tel: (905) 897-8795 or (905) 497-7786. Established: 1979 - Franchising Since: 1988 - No. of Units: Company Owned: 1 - Franchised: 5 - Franchise Fee: $25,000 - Royalty: 5% + 2% adv. - Total Inv: $145,000 Min. Financing: Yes.

SANDWICH BOARD, THE
Nova Sandwich Corp.
10 Plastics Ave., Etobicoke, ON, M8Z 4B7. Contact: R.D. Hoefel, Pres. - Tel: (416) 255-0898. Gourmet style sandwich bar serving a wide variety of salads, sandwiches, baked goods and catering. Established: 1981 - Franchising Since: 1985 - No. of Units: Company Owned: 2 - Franchised: 20 - Franchise Fee: $25,000 - Royalty: 5% of sales weekly, 2% of sales weekly for advertising - Financing: Up to 25% of construction costs.

SANDWICH TREE
Rest-Con Management Systems Ltd.
#300-535 Thurlow St., Vancouver, BC, V6E 3L2. Contact: Joanne Green, Dir. of Franchising - Tel: (604) 684-3314, Canada 1-800-663-TREE. Real food, fast & friendly, made to order sandwiches, soups & hot food. Eat-in, take-out and catering services. Food fair or sit-down locations in malls, office complexes & industrial parks. Established: 1976 - Franchising Since: 1977 - No. of Units: Franchised: 75 - Franchise Fee: $27,500 - Royalty: 5% + 3% adv. - Total Inv: $95,000 - $110,000 - Financing: Partial.

SAUSAGE HOUSE, THE
David Houghton & Associates
508 Ridgewood Crt., Oakville, ON, L6M 2E8. Contact: David Houghton, Pres. - Tel: (905) 847-5719. Fast food and frozen retail sausage on a bun and french fries located in shopping mall food courts. Established: 1982 - Franchising Since: 1984 - No. of Units: Company Owned: 3 - Franchised: 3 - Franchise Fee: $21,000 - Royalty: 5%, 3% adv. - Total Inv: $125,000 - Financing: Yes.

SBARRO
Scott's Management Services Inc.
500 Hood Rd., Markham, ON, L3R 0P6. Contact: Mr. Miles Summers, V.P. - Tel: (905) 946-7150. Three models featuring pizza and authentic Italian offerings in food courts, restaurants and high traffic sites. Established: 1992 - Franchising Since: 1992 - No. of Units: Company Owned: 2 - Franchised: 7 - Franchise Fee: $30,000 - $40,000 - Royalty: 6%, 1% mktg. - Total Inv: $180,000 - $450,000 - Financing: Assistance.

SELECT SANDWICH
Select Food Services, Inc.
1090 Don Mills Rd., Ste. 401, Don Mills, ON, M3C 3R6. Contact: Carol Kahn, Dir. of Franc. - Tel: (416) 391-1244. Custom made sandwiches, soups, salads, frozen yogurt, homemade muffins plus hot specials. Established: 1980 - Franchising Since: 1982 - No. of Units: Company Owned: 3 - Franchised: 31 - Franchise Fee: $30,000 - Royalty: 6% + 2% adv. - Total Inv: $160,000 - $275,000 - Financing: Yes.

SIZZLING WOK INTERNATIONAL INC.
P.O. Box 1038, Saskatoon, SK, S7K 4R6. Contact: G. Jeff Mack, Pres. - Tel: (306) 955-3667, Fax: (306) 955-3666. Gourmet oriental fast food outlets in shopping mall food courts. Established: 1984 - Franchising Since: 1987 - No. of Units: Company Owned/Joint Ventured: 9 - Franchised: 38 - Franchise Fee: $25,000 - Royalty: 5% of gross - Initial Inv: $75,000; Approx. Total Inv: $200,000 - Financing: Available OAC.

SMITTY'S FAMILY RESTAURANT
Smitty's Canada Ltd.
501-18th Ave. S.W., 6th Floor, Calgary, AB, T2S 0C7. Contact: W. Chan, Pres. - Tel: (403) 229-3838. Specializing in pancakes & waffles, featuring lunch & dinner items with liquor lounge. Established: 1960 - Franchising Since: 1960 - No. of Units: Company Owned: 15 - Franchised: 113 - Franchise Fee: $35,000 - Royalty: 5% - Total Inv: $300,000 - $400,000 - Financing: Yes.

SNO-BIZ *
Sno-Biz International
9 Antares Dr., Nepean, ON, K2E 7V5. Contact: Douglas Conner, President Operations - Tel: (613) 727-1795. World's highest profit fast food business, Wal-Mart vendor approved, portable store concept, patented equipment. Established: 1994 - No. of Associates: 15 - Cash Inv: $5,000 - Total Inv: $5,000 - $25,000 - Financing: Yes.

SQUARE BOY PIZZA AND SUBS
Waymar Food Service
728 Oxford St., Oshawa, ON, L1J 3V9. Contact: Ted Crandall, Reg. Opers. Mgr. - Tel: (905) 434-4444. Pizza and submarine take-out and delivery only. Established: 1979 - Franchising Since: 1980 - No. of Units: 35 - Franchise Fee: $10,000 - Approx. Total Inv: $85,000 approx.- Royalty: 5% - Financing: Assistance.

ST. HUBERT BAR-B-Q
St. Hubert Bar-B-Q Ltd.
1515 Chomedey Blvd., Ste. 250, Laval, PQ, H7V 3Y7. Contact: Jacques Guilbert, Fran. & Real Est. Dir. - Tel: (514) 688-6500, Fax: (514) 688-3900. Family style restaurant offering roasted chicken and Bar-B-Q ribs. Table service, take-out and home delivery in certain areas. Established: 1951 - Franchising Since: 1967 - No. of Units: Company Owned: 20 - Franchised: 76 - Franchise Fee: $40,000 - Royalty: 4% - Total Inv. - $700,000 - $1,300,000 - Financing: No.

ST. JEROME'S CHICKEN & RIBS *
St. Jerome Restaurant Ltd.
313 Prince Albert Rd., Dartmouth, NS, B2Y 1N3. Contact: Dan Patfield, Pres. - Tel: (902) 461-2308, Fax: (902) 469-5859. Family restaurant with speciality in chicken(bar-b-q) & ribs. Established: 1989 - Franchising Since: 1990 - No. of Units: Company Owned: 2 - Franchised: 12 - Franchise Fee: $29,000 - Royalty: 5%, 2% adv. - Total Inv: $200,000 to $250,000 - Financing: No.

STUDEBAKER'S
1418 Wakehurst Cres., Oakville, ON, L6J 6T6. Contact: Phil Passy, Pres. - Tel: (905) 829-0040. Restaurant/bar with unique nostalgic entertainment format. Established: 1986 - Franchising Since: 1987 - No. of Units: Company Owned: 2 - Franchised: 2 - Franchise Fee: $50,000 - Royalty: 5%, 1% adv. - Total Inv: $200,000 - $500,000 - Financing: No.

SUBS PLUS
Subs Plus Inc.
173 Queenston St., St. Catharines, ON, L2R 3A2. Contact: Robert Dumas, Pres. - Tel: (905) 641-4404. Fast food outlet specializing in submarine sandwiches along with delicious fresh cakes & pastries baked fresh on the premises. "We will train you in the skills you need." Established: 1985 - Franchising Since: 1990 - No. of Units: Company Owned: 1 - Franchised: 3 - Franchise Fee: $12,000 - Royalty: 3.5%, 2% adv. - Total Inv: $100,000 + $12,000 - Financing: Assistance.

SUKIYAKI - A JAPANESE DELIGHT
Matoyee Enterprises Inc.
3484 Jeanne Mance, Montreal, PQ, H2X 2J8. Contact: Stanley Ma, Pres. - Tel: (514) 982-6075. Exciting teppan style Japanese fast food featuring beef, chicken, shrimp, rice & noodles. Established: 1988 - Franchising Since: 1988 - No. of Units: Company Owned: 1 - Franchised: 9 - Franchise Fee: $25,000 - Royalty: 6% - Total Inv: $150,000 to $175,000.

SWISS CHALET CHICKEN & RIBS
Cara Operations Ltd.
230 Bloor St., W., Toronto, ON, M5S 1T8. Contact: Mgr. of Franchise Admin. - Tel: (416) 962-4571. Licensed family restaurant serving char-broiled chicken and barbecued pork ribs. Established: 1883 - Franchising Since: 1980 - No. of Units: Company Owned: 20 - Franchised: 126 - Franchise Fee: $75,000 - Royalty: 5% (1.5% covenant fee if Cara on head lease) - Total Inv: $750,000 to $950,000 depending on extent of ownership - Financing: No.

TACO TIME CANADA INC.
#301, 740 4th Ave. S., Lethbridge, AB, T1J 0N9. Contact: Ken Pattenden, Pres. - Tel: (403) 329-1156. Franchising quick service Mexican fast food. Established: 1977 - Franchising Since: 1977 - No. of Units: Franchised: 90 - Franchise Fee: $20,000 - Royalty: 5%, 5% adv. - Total Inv: $250,000 - Min. Cash Req'd.: $80,000.

TAKE 2 CAFÉ
The Bavaras Group
130 Bloor St. West, Toronto, ON, M5S 1N5. Contact: Brian Breslin, Pres. - Tel: (416) 920-4178. Café concept focusing on coffees, teas and gourmet sandwiches. Established: 1991 - Franchising Since: 1994 - No. of Units: Company Owned: 1 - Franchised: 1 - Franchise Fee: $5,000 - Royalty: 5%, 1.5% co-op adv. - Total Inv: $180,000 - Financing: Yes.

THE ARROW...A NEIGHBORHOOD PUB *
Neighborhood Pub Group
6465 Millcreek Dr., Ste. 205, Mississauga, ON, L5N 5R3. Contact: George Kostopoulos - Tel: (905) 567-4180, (800) 387-8335, Fax: (905) 567-5355. The Arrow...A Neighborhood Pub, captures the atmosphere of traditional British Pubs but in a distinctly North American fashion which is designed to appeal to the whole family with emphasis on locally produced beverages and produce. Strong commitment to the community and the environment are integral aspects of the overall concept. Complete training and support. Established: 1991 - Franchising Since: 1995 - No. of Units: Company Owned: 3 - Franchised: 1 - Franchise Fee: $35,000 - Royalty: 5% - Total Inv: $290,000 to $340,000 - Financing: Assistance through financial institutes.

TIKI MING
Matoyee Enterprises Inc.
3484 Jeanne Mance, Montreal, PQ, H2X 2J8. Contact: Stanley Ma, Pres. - Tel: (514) 982-6075. Featuring the best in Chinese fast food. Established: 1983 - Franchising Since: 1983 - No. of Units: Company Owned: 4 - Franchised: 30 - Franchise Fee: $25,000 - Royalty: 6% - Total Inv: $150,000 to $175,000.

TOBY'S GOODEATS
83 Bloor St. W., 2nd Flr., Toronto, ON, M5S 1M1. Contact: Mr. Jody Ortved, Franc. Dir. - Tel: (416) 927-0323. Gourmet hamburger restaurants featuring table service in an atmosphere of comfort and nostalgia. Established: 1976 - Franchising Since: 1990 - No. of Units: Company Owned: 9 - Franchise Fee: $45,000 - Royalty: 5% gross sales + 2% adv. - Total Inv: $550,000 (approx.) turn-key includes fran.fee.

TOM'S HOUSE OF PIZZA
7730 MacLeod Trail S., Calgary, AB, T2H 0L9. Contact: John H. Windle, Pres. - Tel: (403) 252-0111. Family atmosphere pizza restaurant with small intimate sports lounge. Established: 1963 - Franchising Since: 1964 - No. of Units: Company Owned: 1 - Franchised: 3.

TROLL'S SEAFOOD RESTAURANTS
#602-535 Thurlow St., Vancouver, BC, V6E 3L2. Contact: Geoffrey Hair, Pres. - Tel: (604) 684-3331. Highly successful fresh food concept (500 - 2,500 sq. ft). Features high quality fish and chips, chowders and salads. Established: 1946 - Franchising Since: 1984 - No. of Units: Franchised: 16 - Franchise Fee: $25,000 - Royalty: 5% - plus 2% adv.

VALENTINE
Groupe Valentine, Inc.
6495 Boul. Choquette, St. Hyacinthe, PQ, J2S 8L2. Contact: Jean-Pierre Robin, Pres. - Tel: (514) 773-1276. Fast food operation serving hot dogs, hamburgers and french fries. Established: 1979 - Franchising Since: 1984 - No. of Units: Company Owned: 3 - Franchised: 105 - Franchise Fee: $25,000 - Royalty: 5%, 2.5% adv. - Total Inv: $150,000 - Financing: National Bank.

WENDY'S RESTAURANTS
Wendy's Restaurants of Canada, Inc.
6715 Airport Rd., Ste. 301, Mississauga, ON, L4V 1X2. Contact: Edgar Mayne, Dir. of Dev. - Tel: (905) 677-7023. Quick service restaurants serving hamburgers, french fries, chicken sandwiches, salads, chili, and baked potatoes. Established: 1975 - Franchising Since: 1979 - No. of Units: Company Owned: 94 - Franchised: 77 - Franchise Fee: $40,000 - Royalty: 4% of monthly sales + 2% adv. - Total Inv: $500,000 - $1,000,000 - Financing: No.

WESTERN PIZZA & FAMILY RESTAURANTS
Western Pizza & B.B.Q. Chicken 1979 Ltd.
6 Wood Cres., Regina, SK, S4S 6J7. Contact: Jim or Spiro Bonis, Pres. & V.P. Mktg. - Tel: (306) 924-8391. Pizza, pasta, chicken, take-out, delivery & dining. One of the top franchises in Saskatchewan looking to expand in Manitoba. Established: 1976 - Franchising Since: 1979 - No. of Units: Company Owned: 2 - Franchised: 14 - Franchise Fee: $10,000 which goes to the promotion of new location - Royalty: 4% of gross sales - Total Inv: $100,000.

WHITE SPOT RESTAURANTS
White Spot Ltd.
1126 S.E. Marine Dr., Vancouver, BC, V5X 2V7. Contact: Linda Swartos, Qualification Specialist - Tel: (604) 321-6631. White Spot is an up-scale family style restaurant business in the west. Established: 1928 - Franchising Since: 1993 - No. of Units: Company Owned: 18 - Franchised: 28 - Franchise Fee: $75,000 - Royalty: 5%, 2% adv., 1% local mktg. - Total Inv: $500,000 - $900,000 dependent on location - Financing: No.

WILLY DOG
829 Norwest Road, Unit 823, Kingston, ON, K7P 2N3. Contact: Will R. Hodgskiss, Sandy Stewart, Pres. - Tel: (613) 531-7384. Hot dog, sausage, chicken & ribs sold off a vending cart. Established: 1989 - Franchising Since: 1993 - No. of Units: Company Owned: 12 - Franchised: 31 - Franchise Fee: $2,500 - $2,995 - Royalty: $299 monthly for eight months a year - Total Inv: $2,500 - $2,995 for turn key operation - Financing: In some instances.

WILLY'S OLD STYLE HAMBURGERS *
3916 McLeod Trail S., Calgary, AB, T2G 2R5. Contact: Will Danek, Pres. - Tel: (403) 243-1175, Fax: (403) 233-7205. Fast food restaurant. Established: 1977 - Franchising Since: 1989 - No. of Units: Company Owned: 2 - Franchised: 6 - Franchise Fee: $20,000 - Royalty: 4% - Total Inv: $150,000 to $180,000 - Financing: No.

WING MACHINE, INC.
156 Willowdale Ave., Willowdale, ON, M2N 4Y6. Contact: Frank Schiavone, Mgr. - Tel: (416) 961-1000. Fast food chicken, specializing in wings. Established: 1986 - Franchising Since: 1987 - No. of Units: Franchised: 10 - Franchise Fee: $25,000 (CAN) - Royalty: 6%, 6% adv. - Total Inv: $150,000 - $180,000 (CAN) - Financing: Negotiable.

FRANCHISE CONSULTANTS AND FRANCHISE SERVICES

ACCOUNTING & CONSULTING SERVICES OF CANADA INC.
1454 Dundas St. E., Ste. 125, Mississauga, ON, L4X 1L4. Contact: Douglas Steen, V.P. - Tel: (905) 848-6202. Professional accounting & consulting expertise for the franchisee & franchisor. Financial business planning statements. Franchise analysis, assistance for financing, evaluation and selection services. Established: 1984.

ANDREW L. CHIN, C.A.
7220-6 Kennedy Road, Suite 1002, Markham, ON, L3R 0N4. Contact: Andrew Chin, Proprietor - Tel: (416) 609-9663, Fax: (416) 297-8454. Assistance to prospective and existing franchisees in the following areas: Business plans, franchise assessments, cash flow forecasts, preparation of financial statements, tax returns and computerization of accounting systems.

ASEN VITKO ASSOCIATES ARCHITECT
19 Yorkville Ave., Toronto, ON, M4W 1L1. Contact: Asen Vitko - Tel: (416) 928-0220. Specialists in serving the franchise industry in Canada. Architecture, engineering, interior design, project management.

ATLANTIC & PACIFIC HOLDINGS LTD.
P.O. Box 8748, Victoria, BC, V8W 3S3. Contact: Brian F. Johnson, Pres. - Tel: (604) 361-4658. Franchisor consultant. Experienced in franchise systems, commercializing technologies via franchising, venture capital, public companies, government assistance & master franchising. Established: 1993.

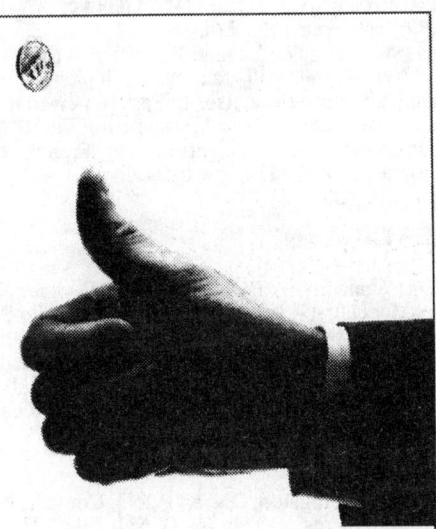

Heads you win, tails you win.

Don't take a chance, you can significantly increase your odds for business success when you invest in an established, reputable franchise organization. So, instead of flipping a quarter, use it to call The Canadian Franchise Association today.

Before you invest, investigate.
1-800-665-4232

5045 Orbitor Dr., Bldg. 12, Mississauga, Ont. L4W 4Y4
Tel: (905) 625-2896 Fax: (905) 625-9076

BANK OF MONTREAL
National Franchising Services, 15th Fl., 55 Bloor St. W., Toronto, ON, M4W 3N5. Contact: J.F. (Jim) Holloway or S.Z. (Steve) Iskierski, Senior Mgr., Mgr. Senior Accts. - Tel: (416) 927-6020 or (416) 927-6026, Fax: (416) 927-6369. Established in 1817, major Canadian chartered bank, providing a full range of domestic and international banking services, including a specialized group which deals exclusively with franchisors and their franchise networks.

BRIEF ROTFARB WYNBERG CAPPE
3845 Bathurst St., Ste. 402, Downsview, ON, M3H 3N2. Contact: M. Rotfarb, Partner - Tel: (416) 635-9080, Fax: (416) 635-0462. Chartered Accountants - services include preparation of business plans, financing proposals, exploring business opportunities and accounting and tax planning services. Established: 1980 - No. of Units: One head office.

BUSINESS CONNECTIONS INT'L.
1454 Dundas St. E., Ste. 125, Mississauga, ON, L4X 1L4. Contact: William Gay, Franc. Dir. - Tel: (905) 848-6202. Offering professional, comprehensive franchise services to the franchisor & franchisee with an experienced staff, covering all services, representing 30 different opportunities. Established: 1983.

BY LAW TRADENAME, CLEARANCE INC.
Box 12109 - Ste. 2200, 555 West Hastings, Vancouver, BC, V6B 4N6. Contact: Sandra Wright or Trisha Dore - Tel: (604) 669-6023, (800) 663-1444. Trade mark searching and development for Canada and foreign countries. Trade mark registration referral. Established: 1985.

CANADIAN FRANCHISE ASSOCIATION
Association Canadienne de la Franchise
5045 Orbitor Dr., Bldg. 12, Unit 201, Mississauga, ON, L4W 4Y4. Contact: Sue McSherry - Tel: (800) 665-4232 or (905) 625-2896, Fax: (905) 625-9076. Established: 1967. The Canadian Franchise Association is the national association of franchisors and firms providing products and services to franchisors. CFA is dedicated to promoting and strengthening ethical franchising in Canada. As a condition of membership, members agree to abide by the CFA Code of Ethics and undergo the scrutiny of their peers upon application for membership in the Association. CFA provides seminars and meetings to assist franchisors in networking and learning from each other. For prospective franchisees, CFA provides numerous materials to help in the selection process.

CANADIAN IMPERIAL BANK OF COMMERCE
Commerce Court Postal Station, Toronto, ON, M5L 1A2. Contact: Charles Scrivener, General Mgr. National Franchising - Tel: (416) 980-3225, Fax: (416) 980-3229. One of Canada's largest full service banks, CIBC provides specialized financial services to franchise businesses. Franchise Services.

Charles M. Scrivener
General Manager
National Franchising Services

Commerce Court West, 3rd Floor
Toronto, Ontario
M5L 1A2

Fax: (416) 980-3229
Tel: (416) 980-3225

CASTELANE CONSULTING
48 Dunblaine Avenue, Toronto, ON, M5M 2R9. Contact: Karen Castelane, Pres. - Tel: (416) 322-5924 (also fax). Franchise program set-up and improvement, including manuals; training programs; sales strategy and materials; market, competitor, customer and store research; local marketing programs; and performance audits.

COMMERCIAL CONSULTANTS INC.
2911 A Cleveland Ave., Saskatoon, SK, S7K 8A9. Contact: Lorne Horning, Pres. - Tel: (306) 931-2131, Fax: (306) 931-2323. Act as advisor to franchisors in establishing program, operation of the system and sales of franchises. Established: 1983.

COMPUSEARCH MARKET & SOCIAL RESEARCH LTD.
330 Front Street West, Ste. 1100, Toronto, ON, M5V 3B7. Contact: Ian Caminsky, Dir. Mktg. - Tel: (416) 348-9180, Fax (416) 348-9195. Provide demographic, socio-economic and consumer expenditure data for any area in Canada. Established: 1976.

EXPAND your business

North America is hot for franchise concepts. And First Choice Franchise Services has the experience and resources to successfully expand your business.

First Choice Franchise Services is a full-service franchise marketing company that specializes in the development, promotion and sale of quality franchises regionally, nationally and internationally.

Our service retains the flavor and effectiveness of an in-house franchise division, but at a much lower cost and risk to the franchisor. More importantly, we know the franchise market—what works and what does not.

This means that we are able to provide you with results that count—closed sales. Our qualified franchise specialists, with extensive sales and marketing experience, will guide you through the process of successfully expanding your concept into new territories!

For more information call, or write to: George Kostopoulos, President
1-800-387-8335

6465 Millcreek Drive,
Suite 205,
Mississauga, Ontario,
Canada, L5N 5R3

FIRST CHOICE FRANCHISE SERVICES INC.®

Member of The Canadian Franchise Association

CONTEMPORARY COMMUNICATIONS
Contemporary Communications Ltd.
2605 Alma St., Vancouver, BC, V6R 3S1. Contact: Perry Goldsmith, Pres. - Tel: (604) 224-2384. Public relations & communications. Services for franchisors. Established: 1974.

CUTCOST CONSULTANTS LTD.
912 Wilson Avenue, Downsview, ON, M3K 1E7. Contact: Nino G. Cutruzzola, Pres. - Tel: (416) 633-7219, Fax: (416) 636-6487. Retail and franchise development including: expansions, management, operations, construction, design & locations. Established: 1988.

DAREN, MARTENFELD, CARR & CO., CHARTERED ACCOUNTANTS
1 Eglinton Ave. E., Ste. 302, Toronto, ON, M4P 1A1. Contact: Marvin B. Martenfeld, FCA, Partner - Tel: (416) 322-1650. Franchise consultants, accounting, audit and taxation services, Acquisitions and private investment banking. Established: 1970.

DAVID HOUGHTON & ASSOCIATES, INC.
508 Ridgewood Crt., Oakville, ON, L6M 2E8. Contact: David Houghton, Pres. - Tel: (905) 847-5739. Franchisee Consultant. Established: 1989.

DEAN CONSULTING GROUP
350 Burnhamthorpe Rd. W., Ste. 202, Mississauga, ON, L5B 3J1. Contact: Ernest Anderson, Pres. - Tel: (905) 273-DEAN (3326). Middle East franchise facilitators, finding investors to obtain master franchises in the Middle East.

DYNAMIC PERFORMANCE SYSTEMS, INC.
170 Evans Ave., Ste. 301, Toronto, ON, M8Z 1J7. Contact: Fred Berni, Pres. - Tel: (416) 201-0202, Fax: (416) 201-0808. Consultants to the franchise industry providing assessments of prospective franchisees or employees and predicting their future performance. Established: 1988.

ERNST & YOUNG
Ernst & young Twr., P.O.Box 251, TD Center, Toronto, ON, M5K 1J7. Contact: Art Good, Fran. Dir./Partner - Tel: (416) 864-1212. One of Canada's pre-eminent professional accounting and management consulting firms offering a complete range of services to organizations expanding through franchising/licensing in domestic and international forums. Services include feasibility reviews, profitability analysis, marketing plans and positioning, strategic planning, growth and distribution strategies, systems and operations reviews, turn around strategies, financing plans, franchisee relations, productivity, training and more, are offered through 30 offices from coast to coast. Established: 1964.

F.D.C. (FRANCHISE DEVELOPMENT) *
89 Queensway W., Ste. 314, Mississauga, ON, L5B 2V2. Contact: Rick Keene, Pat Burden, Pres. - Tel: (905) 848-5773. A complete franchise management and marketing program for franchisors including financing proposals for franchisees. Established: 1978.

FEDERAL BUSINESS DEVELOPMENT BANK
3660 Hurontario St., 8th Floor, Mississauga, ON, L5B 3C4. Contact: Bill Heynings, Mgr., Management Svcs. - Tel: (905) 566-6417. Providing consulting and financial services to small and medium sized businesses.

FHG INTERNATIONAL INC. *
2510 Yonge St., Ste. 325, Toronto, ON, M4P 2H7. Contact: Doug Fisher, M.Sc, CMC, Pres. - Tel: (416) 489-6996. Management consulting firm specializing in foodservice & retail franchise development including: strategic planning, manual development, promotional material, business plans, litigation support and arbitration. Established: 1984.

FINANCIAL FOCUS, INC.
P.O. Box 1735, 23 Cashin Ave., St. John's, NF, A1C 5P5. Contact: Terence W. Pike, Pres. - Tel: (709) 754-1847, Fax: (709) 754-1943. Management consultants specializing in franchise search and evaluation. Established: 1989 - No. of Units: Company Owned: 1.

FIRST CALL MANAGEMENT SOLUTIONS
81 Fincham Ave., Markham, ON, L3P 4C9. Contact: John R. Clarke, Pres. - Tel: (905) 471-5532. Business and franchise development, franchise sales, results oriented management team. Established: 1980.

FIRST CHOICE FRANCHISE SERVICES
First Choice Franchise Services Inc.
6465 Millcreek Drive, Ste. 205, Mississauga, ON, L5N 5R3. Contact: George Kostopoulos, Pres. - Tel: (905) 567-4180, (800) 387-8335, Fax: (905) 567-5355. A full service franchise development and marketing company that specializes in the promotion and sale of quality franchise concepts regionally, nationally and internationally. Our qualified franchise specialists, with extensive sales and marketing background can ensure successful expansion of your concept. Established: 1988 - No. of Units: Company Owned: 1. (See our ad on page 215.)

FOUNDATION BUSINESS BROKERS
Ste. 2201, Canada Trust Twr., 10104 - 103 Ave., Edmonton, AB, T5J 0H8. Contact: David Hardy, President - Tel: (403) 448-9099, Fax: (403) 425-0530. Specializing in the sale of businesses, including those in the franchise industry. Experienced in the franchise industry as a franchisee and master franchise. Have a national network of business intermediaries who can assist in selling territorial or master franchises. Offices also located at: Ste. 600, Bow Valley Square IV, 250 - 6th Ave. S.W. Calgary, AB, T2P 3H7, Tel: (403) 262-4224, Fax: (403) 262-6002.

FRANCHISE AFFAIRES 1701, INC.
55 Lorne Ave., St. Lambert, PQ, J4P 2G7. Contact: Norbert Lemieux, Pres. - Tel: (514) 466-9538, Fax: (514) 466-9430. Specialized franchise development and franchisees' recruitment for the Quebec market and marketing consultation. Established: 1986 - Franchising Since: 1987.

FRANCHISE CANADA DEVELOPERS INC.
10 Baby Point Terrace, Toronto, ON, M6S 4S4. Contact: Frank A. Rush, Pres. - Tel: (416) 769-6430, Fax: (416) 769-6429. Franchise Consultant. Established: 1981.

FRANCHISE CONCEPTS & RECRUITING
10150 - 117 St., Ste. 102, Edmonton, AB, T5K 2J2. Contact: John S. Horsley, Pres. - Tel: (403) 496-9489 or (800) 661-7682. Marketing of franchises in Alberta with a team of lawyers and accountants, assisting franchisors through the registration requirements of Alberta. Specialize in the Franchise Evaluation Test for use in recruiting the best franchisees. Established: 1984.

FRANCHISE FINANCIAL SERVICES
1124 Bridalwood Tr., Oakville, ON, L6H 1K8. Contact: Bill Harris, Pres. - Tel: (905) 847-5125. Life insurance plans designed for the franchisee. His/her company and employees including key person insurance, health and disability, business continuation, collateral life insurance, partnerships and buy-sell funding. Also available are flexible group plans, seminars and employee counselling. Established: 1982.

FRANCHISE REALTY, INC.
10150 - 117 St., Ste. 102, Edmonton, AB, T5K 2J2. Contact: John S. Horsley, Pres. - Tel: (403) 496-9489 or (800) 661-7682. Specializing in site selection, lease negotiations, demographic studies in Alberta for Franchisors. Established: 1988.

FRANCHISE RECRUITERS
William J. Coke and Associates Ltd.
20 Holly St., Ste. 203, Toronto, ON, M4S 3B1. Contact: George Kinzie, Pres. - Tel: (416) 322-5730, Fax: (416) 322-0648. An international executive search corporation dedicated to franchising. Unconditional guarantee. Excellent client references. Placement of franchise professionals in sales, operations, marketing, executive training, finance, legal and international development. Established: 1984.

FRANCHISE REGISTRY & EXCHANGE, INC.
704 Woodpark Blvd. SW, Calgary, AB, T2W 3R7. Contact: Douglas J. Queen, C.A., Pres. - Tel: (403) 251-7321. Author of Low-Risk Franchising and franchise consultant with particular emphasis on the assistance to franchisees in the evaluation of franchise opportunities in Canada and preparation of filings for franchisors to the Alberta Securities Commission in the province of Alberta.

FRANCHISE SUPPORT SERVICE
Box 2000, Squamish, BC, V0N 3G0. Contact: Mary Jane Charman, Pres. - Tel: (604) 898-5157, Fax: (604) 898-5107. Assisting franchisors in establishing their systems and networking in Canada. In depth experience in Operational Support Systems for franchisors and franchisor/franchisee relations. Established: 1988.

FRANK BAKER & ASSOCIATES, INC.
Provincial Development Corp.
486 Albert St., Ottawa, ON, K1R 5B5. Contact: F. Baker, Pres. - Tel: (613) 230-8055, Fax: (613) 237-9660. Advice to franchisors, franchisees, including real estate investments, hospitality industry (hotel & restaurant), contracts, sales & marketing. Established: 1975 - No. of Units: Company Owned: 1.

FREELANCE PROFESSIONAL SERVICES
P.O. Box 742, 800 Place Victoria, Montreal, PQ, H4Z 1J9. Contact: Barbara Etcovitch, Dir./Pres. - Tel: (514) 361-9186 or (613) 834-3791, Fax: same or (613) 824-0119. Development, promotion, sales, copy and design of promotional literature for franchisors/franchisees and small businesses, etc. Workshops in how to promote your own business with emphasis on marketing, copy and design. Established: 1986.

GEIST & ASSOCIATES INC.
327 Renfrew Dr., Ste. 301, Markham, ON, L3R 9S8. Contact: Rene Geist, Sr. Sales Mgr. - Tel: (905) 475-1022. Advertising & marketing specialists, consultants, customized seminars to the franchising and retail industries. Established: 1980.

GEORGIAN OAKS INTERNATIONAL
1952 Ludgate Cres., Ottawa, ON, K1J 8L2. Contact: William P. Marsden, C.E.O. - Tel: (613) 741-0267. Assemble, analyze and evaluate franchises and business marketing plans. Largest independent franchise brokers east of Toronto and west of St. John's. Established: 1984 - No. of Units: Company Owned: 2.

GOLDMAN, SLOAN, NASH & HABER
181 University Ave., Ste. 2100, Toronto, ON, M5H 3M7. Contact: Ron Miller - Tel: (416) 777-5010, Fax: (416) 862-9953. Franchisor Consultant.

HERTZBERG & ASSOCIATES LTD.
30 Wertheim Ct., Unit 20, Richmond Hill, ON, L4B 1B9. Contact: Jack Hertzberg, Pres. - Tel: (905) 764-8004. Franchise and business advisors who work with franchisors and franchisees to conduct and prepare feasibility assessments and business plans; design and implement control systems including tailored manuals; and provide training in the use of these systems. Established: 1982.

HINSPERGER FRANCHISE CONSULTANTS / NETWORK LEASING
2 Cullen Dr., St. Catharines, ON, L2T 3H1. Contact: Scott Hinsperger, Pres. - Tel: (905) 687-8554, Fax: (905) 687-9050. Complete franchise development & marketing services for new and established franchisors. Equipment and vehicle financing for franchisors and franchisees. Established: 1987.

INFORMATION PLUS
2 Bloor St. W., #404, Toronto, ON, M4W 3E2. Contact: D.C. Sawyer, Pres. - Tel: (416) 968-1062 in the US call (716) 852-2220. Provides qualitative research to support business location decisions, industry and market trends information and related business development data, for Canada and the U.S. Established: 1979.

J. F. SCHMITZ ASSOCIATES..THE FINDERS *
500 Rossland Rd. W., P.O. Box 58025, Oshawa, ON, L1J 8L6. Contact: Joseph Schmitz, Pres. - Tel: (905) 579-9792, Fax: (905) 579-4692. In depth consulting service to both franchisor & franchisee. Franchisor:

Franchise, site development & operations. Franchisee: Franchise acquisitions, specializing in new franchises and out of Canada franchise representation. Established: 1963 - Franchising Since: 1989.

JOHN H. DELL & ASSOCIATES, INC.
4195 Dundas St, W., Ste. 200, Toronto, ON, M8X 1Y4. Contact: John H. Dell, Pres. - Tel: (416) 239-2860, Fax: (416) 233-7037. Assists franchisors on how to set up franchise packages including financial, banking, legal and corporate assistance. Assists franchisees with evaluation of franchise package including financial, corporate, legal and banking advice. Established: 1981.

LARKIN INVESTMENTS LTD.
32-4318 Emily Carr Dr., Victoria, BC, V8X 5E7. Contact: Richard Larkin, Pres. - Tel: (604) 658-1258. Marketing one of the best opportunities today - "The People's Franchise". Free information package available. Established: 1988.

M-FOUR CANAM INTERNATIONAL
1115 Sherbrooke St. W., Ste. #2802, Montreal, PQ, H3A 1H3. Contact: Martin Greenspon, Pres. - Tel: (514) 289-8718, Fax: (514) 499-8553. Canada's most comprehensive franchise marketing strategists, providing consultancy services to franchisors planning to expand in Canada or Internationally. Specializing in franchise development, feasibility projections, marketing plans and franchisee recruiting. • Master Licensees •Area Franchisees • Multiple Unit Networks • Site location and lease negotiation services. Established: 1981. Also contact: M-Four International, 63 St. Clair Ave. W., Ste. 1903, Toronto, ON, M4V 2Y9, Tel: (416) 969-8657, Fax: (416) 969-9754.

MANAGEMENT 2000
10150 - 117 St., Ste. 102, Edmonton, AB, T5K 2J2. Contact: John S. Horsley, Exec. V.P. - Tel: (403) 496-9489 or (800) 661-7682. Franchise Consulting Company. A series of franchise related seminars geared towards Franchisor and Franchisee conventions. Specializes in customized in-house seminars for Franchisor and staff, creation or update of operations and training manuals, and the formation of Franchise Advisory Councils.

MARTIN INTERNATIONAL
500 Place d'Armes, Ste. 2910, Montreal, PQ, H2Y 2W2. Contact: Serge Martin, Pres. - Tel: (514) 288-3931. Organizer of the Business Start-Up Expo held in Montreal (65,000 visitors) and in Quebec City (25,000 visitors) each year in January. Also organizer of the Business World Exhibition with its section on Franchises & Business Opportunities each year at the end of September (30,000 visitors). Established: 1967.

MCGOVERN, HURLEY, CUNNINGHAM
#503 - 2005 Sheppard Ave. E., North York, ON, M2J 5B4. Contact: W. David Sanderson, C.A., Partner - Tel: (416) 496-1234. Public accounting firm providing consulting services to franchisors & franchisees, taxation, accounting and financial planning to entrepreneurial companies and individuals. Established: 1984.

MEDIA THREE MARKETING SERVICES LTD.
431 Alden Rd., Ste. 20, Markham, ON, L3R 3L4. Contact: Brock Weir, Pres. - Tel: (905) 475-6611. Offers expert marketing and communication planning, video and audio productions, interactive video training and speciality programming, event management and graphic design. Established: 1973.

NATIONAL FRANCHISE CONSULTANTS *
51 Hurricane Rd., Fonthill, ON, L0S 1E3. Contact: Andre Champagne, Canada - Tel: (905) 892-8404, Fax: (905) 892-9934. Franchise consulting, Canada and the U.S., full service, specializes in franchise development and franchise sales. Established: 1986 - No. of Offices: 2.

OFF THE BEATEN PATH MARKETING
Main St., Box 1138, Osoyoos, BC, V0H 1V0. Contact: W. Schmidt, Pres. - Tel: (604) 446-2455 or Fax (604) 446-2862. Consulting to establish master franchises in Canada and the USA. Includes packaging first step marketing efforts with advertising and screen interview, arranging local supply, feasibility studies and marketing research. Established: 1967.

PACIFIC FRANCHISE ASSOCIATION
Ste. 523, 409 Granville St., Vancouver, BC, V6C 1T2. - Tel: (604) 669-3177 or (604) 669-5343. P.F.A. is a regional franchise association with strong focus on ethical and professional franchising. Membership consists of franchisors and companies or individuals doing business with franchisors. The association holds monthly breakfast meetings that are open to member and non-member franchisors. Members must commit to the P.F.A. Code of Ethics. Formed in 1990 membership is approximately 100.

PACIFIC MENTOR GROUP
2nd Fl., 848 West Hastings, Vancouver, BC, V6C 1C8. Contact: Jim Eagles, Pres. - Tel: (604) 682-8383. Assist in the sale of operating companies. Assist in structuring mergers and acquisitions. Help raise capital for expansion of operating companies. Established: 1991.

PARAGON RESOURCE GROUP, IN.C *
385 Beverley Glen Blvd., Thornhill, ON, L4J 7S5. Contact: Cliff Horwitz, Pres. - Tel: (905) 881-4825. Franchise consulting services to both franchisors and franchisees. Established: 1994.

PRICE WATERHOUSE
1 1st Can. Pl., Ste. 3300, Box 190, Toronto, ON, M5X 1H7. Contact: Ralph Selby, Partner - Tel: (416) 863-1133. A national accounting and consulting firm providing an extensive range of professional services to franchisors and franchisees. Services include accounting and management information systems; preparation of forms and policies with respect to royalties and advertising; preparation of operation and training manuals; business plan development; feasibility studies; consultation with solicitors, financing packages, tax planning and review; audit and accounting services.

QUALITY CREDIT SERVICES LTD. *
500 Hood Rd., Ste. 200, Markham, ON, L3R 0P6. Contact: Jeff Riddall, Manager - Tel: (800) 655-9564, (905) 946-6855. Licensed consumer reporting agency providing financial background reports on both individuals and corporations to franchisors & franchisees alike. Established: 1992.

RETAILINK
265 - 16 Midlake Blvd. S.E., Calgary, AB, T2X 2X7. Contact: Ken Purris, Pres. - Tel: (800) 567-9389. We are a new franchise development and management firm in Western Canada and we offer a comprehensive program that allows you to carefully take a look at franchising as a method of business expansion. Established: 1994.

ROBBINEX INC.
41 Stuart St., Hamilton, ON, L8L 1P5. Contact: Doug Robbins, Pres. - Tel: (905) 523-7510, Fax: (905) 523-4998. In-depth knowledge of all aspects of franchising with emphasis on the buying/selling of businesses, set up of new franchises, advising prospective franchisees on purchasing or starting a business. Established: 1972.

ROYAL BANK OF CANADA
Head Office, Business Banking, 200 Bay St., 9th Fl., South Twr., Toronto, ON, M5J 2J5. Contact: Tony DePascal, Manager, Franchising Markets, Franchise Banking Group - Tel: (416) 974-8301 or Toll Free 1-800-268-FRAN (3726). Provider of financial services meeting the unique needs of the franchising market since 1973. Wide variety of economic and financial services provided by dedicated franchising network across the country. Supplier of "Franchisor/Franchisee - Doing It Right" a how-to booklet on setting up or buying into a franchise system.

ROYAL BANK

A. M. (Tony) DePascal
Manager, Franchise Banking

Franchise Banking Group, Business Banking
200 Bay Street, 9th Floor, South Tower
Toronto, Ontario M5J 2J5

Tel: (416) 974-8301
Fax: (416) 974-8320

S & H REALTY CORPORATION
BCE Place, 181 Bay St., Ste. 1620, Toronto, ON, M5J 2T3. Contact: Danny Klempfner, Pres. - Tel: (416) 364-7810. A real estate broker and consultant specializing in retail leasing and site selection on behalf of expanding franchisors. Services offered include finding a site and negotiating transactions as well as preparing market analysis reports. Established: 1982.

SCOTIABANK
Bank of Nova Scotia
44 King St. W., Toronto, ON, M5H 1H1. Contact: R.D. (Roger) Roy, Manager, Franchising - Tel: (416) 866-4377. One of North America's premiere financial institutions with assets of more than $107 billion. Scotiabank offers a full spectrum of services in retail, commercial, corporate and investment banking including financing for franchisors and their franchisees. Established: 1832 - No. of Units: Company Owned: 1,400.

SMITH, NIXON & CO.
320 Bay St., Ste. 1600, Toronto, ON, M5H 4A6. Contact: John C. Sinclair, Manager - Tel: (416) 361-1622. Full range of accounting, taxation and business advisory services to franchisors and franchisees. Established: 1961.

SOCIETE NATIONALE DE LA FRANCHISE INC.
2800 Rue Einstein, Ste.145, Sainte-Foy, PQ, G1X 4N8. Contact: Julien Riou, Pres. - Tel: (418) 652-0898. Franchise Consultant. Specialist of development for English franchisees in Quebec. Established: 1986 - Franchising Since: 1990 - No. of Units: Company Owned: 1 - Franchise Fee: $5,000 - Royalty: 10% - Total Inv: $20,000 - Financing: No.

TORONTO DOMINION BANK
Toronto Dominion Centre, 55 King St., W., Toronto, ON, M5K 1A2. Contact: Denise Lepard, Mgr. Fran. Banking Services - Tel: (416) 982-7887. Providing financial products and services tailored to the needs of franchisors and franchisees.

TORONTO FINANCIAL & BUSINESS CONSULTANTS
3410 Midland Ave., Ste. 12, Scarborough, ON, M1V 4V5. Contact: Mr. M. Hafeez, Pres. - Tel: (416) 609-1526 or Fax: (416) 609-1529. Business and financial consultants specializing in financing, business analysis and turn-around, acquisitions, resolving serious operational problems, personnel motivation, etc. Established: 1982 - No. of Units: Company Owned: 1.

VARCON CONSTRUCTION CO. LTD. *
25 Rutherford Rd., S., Unit 5, Brampton, ON, L6W 3J3. Contact: Angelo Riccio, General Manager - Tel: (800) 581-6729. General Contractors.

VINCENT TUCKER LTD.
55 University Ave., Suite 340, Toronto, ON, M5J 2H7. Contact: Peter Buchanan, Dir. - Tel: (416) 363-3200. Provide assistance to franchisor organizations in the areas of franchise development and franchise packaging.

VR BUSINESS BROKERS (CANADA) INC.
2 Lansing Square, Ste. 101, North York, ON, M2J 4P8. Contact: Serge DeConinck, Pres. - Tel: (416) 497-1545. Business and franchise professionals specializing in the design and development of the complete franchise program for your business. Services include: business plan development, financial analysis, franchise marketing, etc. Established: 1984.

W.H. PUNT ENTERPRISES INC.
356 King St. W., Kingston, ON, K7L 2X4. Contact: W. H. Punt, Pres. - Tel: (613) 549-4475, Fax: (613) 549-4475. Franchise consulting, system development & marketing. Business review, evaluation and interim management. Established: 1983.

WALT HAMBROCK, FRANCHISE & BUSINESS BROKER
35 Waterman Ave., Ste. 102, London, ON, N6C 5T8. Contact: Walt Hambrock, Pres. - Tel: (519) 686-8117, Fax: (519) 686-9322. Specializing in marketing and selling of new and existing franchises in Ontario and specifically in Southern Ontario. Program aids franchisor/franchisee with maintaining a direct cost program with the sale of each outlet.

ZAREX CONSULTING GROUP
225 East Beaver Creek Rd., Ste. 300, Richmond Hill, ON, L4B 3P4. Contact: Les Rupf or Robin Wilson, Pres./V.P. - Tel: (905) 886-0215. Franchise consultants specializing in strategic planning for established franchisors, franchise system design, franchise selling, franchise system trouble shooting, operations manuals, franchisor financing and assisting in the purchase or sale of franchisor companies. Established: 1978.

R. D. (Roger) Roy

Manager
The Bank of Nova Scotia
Independent Business & Franchising
Scotia Plaza
44 King Street West, 10th Floor
Toronto, Ontario M5H 1H1

Tel: (416) 866-4377
Fax: (416) 866-4839

FRANCHISE CONSULTANTS - LEGAL

BEALLOR & PARTNERS
28 Overlea Blvd., Toronto, ON, M4H 1B6. Contact: Barry Flodder, Partner - Tel: (416) 423-0707. Provide complete franchisor and franchisee service. Established: 1968.

BUCHWALD ASPER GALLAGHER HENTELEFF
2500 - 360 Main St., Winnipeg, MB, R3C 4H6. Contact: A.D.M. Ogaranko, Q.C., Lawyer - Tel: (204) 956-0560. Law firm - franchise consultants.

BULL, HOUSSER & TUPPER
3000-1055 West Georgia St., Vancouver, BC, V6E 3R3. Contact: Gini Staab, Mktg. Coord. - Tel: (604) 687-6575. Law firm. Established: 1890.

COHEN, MARKUS, Q.C., LL.M.
Ste. 1010, 22 St. Clair Ave. E., Toronto, ON, M4T 2S3. Contact: Mark Cohen, Owner - Tel: (416) 961-5355. Legal franchise consultant concentrating on franchise law matters since the early 80's. Trade-mark agent since 1969.

CONNELL LIGHTBODY
1055 West Georgia St., Ste. 1900, Vancouver, BC, V6E 4J2. Contact: Philip G. Ferber - Tel: (604) 684-1181. Full service law firm, including franchising and trade marks. Established: 1961.

DAVID N. KORNHAUSER *
Conway, Kleinman, Kornhauser & Gotlieb
390 Bay St., 5th Fl., Toronto, ON, M5C 2W7. Contact: David Kornhauser, Lawyer - Tel: (416) 366-6000, Fax: (416) 366-9808. Full service law firm. Practical advice for both franchisors and franchisees.

DAVID WIZINSKY *
Coglan, Wizinsky
930 - 800 W. Pender St., Vancouver, BC, V6C 2V6. Contact: David Wizinsky, Principal - Tel: (604) 688-3800. Franchise legal services with emphasis on public financing of franchise concepts. Established: 1989.

DEMIANTSCHUK LARSEN & SINGER
700 4th Ave. S.W., Ste. 1400, Calgary, AB, T2P 3J4. Contact: Nikolaus Demiantschuk, Partner - Tel: (403) 262-8888. Gen. practise of law including franchising, acquisitions, financing, leasing, trade marks, corp. and commercial.

DOUGLAS, SYMES & BRISSENDEN
Ste. 2100, One Bentall Ctr., 505 Burrard St., Vancouver, B.C., V7X 1R4. Contact: John L. Rogers, Partner - Tel: (604) 683-6911. Law firm. Established: 1925.

EKLIND, LIPTON & JACOBS
1 Queen St. E., Ste. 1900, Toronto, ON, M5C 2W6. Contact: S.W. Eklind, Sr. Partner - Tel: (416) 367-0871. Attorneys representing franchisors and franchisees on an international basis.

EYRE, GEORGE C.
2 Sheppard Ave. E., Ste. 900, North York, ON, M2N 5Y7. Contact: George C. Eyre, Barrister & Solicitor & Trade Mark Agent - Tel: (416) 226-0096. Legal and consulting services for franchisors and franchisees.

FLEMING KAMBEITZ
1500, 736-6th Ave. S.W., Calgary, AB, T2P 3T7. Contact: Larry Yuzda, Partner - Tel: (403) 266-5550, Fax: (403) 265-6910. Lawyers. Established: 1955.

FRASER & BEATTY
P.O. Box 100, 1 First Canadian Place, Toronto, ON, M5X 1B2. Contact: Barbara Conway, Lawyer - Tel: (416) 863-4753. Fraser & Beatty is a full service law firm with many specialty areas, including franchising, competition law, high technology, international trade, mergers and acquisitions, securities and intellectual property. Offices in Toronto, North York, Ottawa, Vancouver, and affiliated in Montreal with McMaster, Meighen.

G. STEWART BAKER LAW OFFICE *
57 King St., P.O. Box 6279, Stn. A., Saint John, NB, E2L 4R7. Contact: Stewart Baker - Tel: (506) 646-1199. Law firm providing complete legal services for franchisors and franchisees.

GARY J. MATALON, BARRISTER & SOLICITOR
403 St. Clements Ave., Toronto, ON, M5N 1M2. Contact: Gary J. Matalon - Tel: (416) 481-8596, Fax: (416) 481-3789. In practice since 1984. Franchise and business law. Sole practitioner with experience at one of Canada's largest law firms as in-house counsel.

GERALD SAMUEL FIELDS
Ste. 1002, Aetna Canada Ctr., 145 King St. W., Toronto, ON, M5H 3X6. Contact: Gerry Fields, Mng. Partner - Tel: (416) 862-8000, Fax (416) 862-8001, E-Mail: counsel@thewire.com. Law firm specializing in franchise financing in Canada, the United States and internationally. Advises on all laws, including all offering documentation; taxation; international trade; franchising and master agreements. Assists clients with strategic and organizational planning. Provides financing. Established: 1974.

GOODMAN LAPOINTE FERGUSON
200 King St. W., Ste. 2300, Toronto, ON, M5H 3W5. Contact: Sheldon Disenhouse, Attorney - Tel: (416) 595-2300. Goodman Lapointe Ferguson is a national legal consulting firm providing a full range of professional services to the franchise industry, including structural consultations, advising with respect to document package and other legal elements of franchising. Other offices are located at: 1010 Sherbrooke St. W., Ste. 1100, Montreal, PQ, H3A 2R7 - Contact: Alex S. Konigsberg, Partner - Tel: (514) 288-7390; and 666 Burrard St., Ste. 500, Vancouver, BC, V6C 3H3 - Contact: Leonard Polsky, Partner - Tel: (604) 687-3216.

GORMAN NASON LJUNGSTROM
121 Germain St., P.O. Box 7286, Station A, Saint John, NB, E2L 4S6. - Tel: (506) 634-8600. Full service law firm providing complete legal services for franchisors and franchisees.

HARRISON, ELWOOD *
450 Talbot St., P.O. Box 3237, London, ON, N6A 4K3. Contact: Peter Macrae Dillon, Partner - Tel: (519) 661-6740, Fax: (519) 667-3362. Full service business law firm with extensive experience in franchising,

VARCON Construction Co. Ltd.
Industrial • Residential • Commercial • Institutional

CUSTOMERS WANTED
Can we build your next franchise store, corporate offices or distribution center? Construction budgets & deadlines are a priority to us.

WE OFFER:
• Turnkey or partial construction
• Project management
• Design and build
• Budget consultations

25 Rutherford Rd. South, Unit 5
Brampton, Ont. L6W 3J3
(800) 581-6729
Tel: (905) 451-7316, Fax: (905) 451-8563

FRANCHISING IS NOT A LICENSE TO PRINT MONEY. BUT IT'S A McSTART.

Providing the concept's good. And providing the legal agreement is drawn up so it's a win-win deal for both franchisee and franchisor: all the i's dotted and the t's crossed, with no room for snags or snarls down the road.

So, call us. Let's talk about how we can help make your franchise a household name.

Client First Service ™ is our Trademark.

MacKIMMIE MATTHEWS
BARRISTERS • SOLICITORS

(403) 232-0611

---

licensing and distribution. Members of the Canadian Franchise Association. Established: 1930.

HOLDEN DAY WILSON
Box 52, Ste. 2400, Toronto Dominion Bank Tower, T-D Centre, Toronto, ON, M5K 1E7. Contact: Mr. John Hall, Partner - Tel: (416) 361-1444. Providing full legal services to franchisors/franchisees including franchise agreements, real estate, litigation and intellectual property. Established: 1900.

J. JOHN O'DONOGHUE *
2200 Yonge St., Ste. 1301, Toronto, ON, M4S 2C6. Contact: John O'Donoghue, Lawyer - Tel: (416) 932-4945, Fax: (416) 932-0541. The provision of legal services to franchisors/franchisees including preparation of and negotiation of franchise agreements, real estate acquisitions through purchase and/or leasing/subleasing, financing, sales and acquisitions, and dispute resolution. Established: 1967 - Franchising Since: 1969.

LEVALLIANT, TED
155 Queen St., Ste. 900, Ottawa, ON, K1P 6L1. Contact: Ted LeValliant, Lawyer - Tel: (613) 736-8915. Law Firm.

LEVITT, BEBER
Scotia Plaza, 40 King St. W., Toronto, ON, M5H 3Y4. Contact: Edward N. Levitt - Tel: (416) 367-6630, Fax: (416) 367-6631. Franchise law for franchisors and franchisees. Established: 1975.

MACKIMMIE MATTHEWS
700, 401-9 Avenue S.W., Calgary, AB, T2P 2M2. Contact: John Houghton, Lawyer - Tel: (403) 232-0611. MacKimmie Matthews is a major Calgary law firm that believes in always doing what's best for the client by delivering the highest quality legal services, promptly and at a fair price. Established: 1920.

MENDELSOHN ROSENTZVEIG SHACTER
1000 Sherbrooke St. W., Ste. 2700, Montreal, PQ, H3A 3G4. Contact: Michael Ludwick, Partner - Tel: (514) 987-5024, Fax: (514) 987-1213. Lawyers. A business-oriented, full service, mid-sized law firm providing service in English and French to thousands of local, national and international clients.

MILNER FENERTY
30th Fl., Fifth Ave. Pl., 237-4th Avenue S.W., Calgary, AB, T2P 4A7. Contact: Gail L. Harding, Partner - Tel: (403) 268-7139, Fax: (403) 268-3100. Law firm.

OGILVY RENAULT
1981 Ave. McGill College, Ste. 1100, Montreal, PQ, H3A 3C1. Contact: R.J.F. Bowie, Partner - Tel: (514) 847-4403. Full legal services relating to franchising.

LEVITT, BEBER
BARRISTERS & SOLICITORS

EDWARD N. LEVITT

Franchise Law for Franchisors and Franchisees

SCOTIA PLAZA
40 KING STREET WEST
TORONTO, ONTARIO CANADA M5H 3Y4
TELEPHONE: (416) 367-6630 DIRECT: 367-6623 FAX: (416) 367-6631

OSLER, HOSKIN & HARCOURT

Advisors to International Franchise Organizations

Franchisors setting up business in Canada or expanding operations here and abroad have turned to Osler, Hoskin & Harcourt for more than 20 years.

We provide advice in an array of business issues including: agreements, licensing, finance, tax, employment and competition/trade. And our experience can bring additional value: significant industry expertise; in depth knowledge of cross border concerns; a network of other professionals for additional counsel.

Contact: Frank Zaid at (416) 862-6415
Counsel to the Canadian Franchise Association

TORONTO	OTTAWA	CALGARY	NEW YORK
Tel: (416) 362-2111	Tel: (613) 235-7234	Tel: (403) 260-7000	Tel: (212) 867-5800
Fax: (416) 862-6666	Fax: (613) 235-2867	Fax: (403) 260-7024	Fax: (212) 867-5802

Internet Address: counsel@osler.com

OSLER RENAULT
LONDON • PARIS • HONG KONG • SINGAPORE

OSLER, HOSKIN & HARCOURT
P.O. Box 50, 1 First Canadian Place, Toronto, ON, M5X 1B8. Contact: Frank Zaid, Partner - Tel: (416) 862-6415. Law Firm. Franchise Law Group specializes in advising CNDN/US & international franchisors, as well as franchise investors and franchise associations in all aspects of franchise law. Members of Canadian Franchise Assoc., International Franchise Assoc., International Bar Assoc. (Franchise Committee) and American Bar Assoc. Franchise Forum. General Counsel to Canadian Franchise Association.

POULIOT MERCURE, S.E.N.C.
CIBC Tower, 1155 West Rene Levesque Blvd., 31st Flr., Montreal, PQ, H3B 3S6. Contact: Jean H. Gagnon, Lawyer/Partner - Tel: (514) 875-5210, Telecopier: (514) 875-4308. A major Canadian law firm practicing mainly in the field of commercial and civil law comprising a group of lawyers which specialized itself in the field of franchising (both domestic and international) and intellectual property matters. Affiliated with Cassels Brock & Blackwell (Toronto), Douglas Symes & Brissenden (Vancouver) and Noriega y Escobedo (Mexico). Established: 1952.

RICHARDS & RICHARDS
10325 150th St., Surrey, BC, V3R 4B1. Contact: Jeffrey Andrews, Lawyer - Tel: (604) 588-6844, Fax: (604) 588-8800. Full service law firm with expertise in franchising. Established: 1967.

SCARLETT MANSON ANGUS
1200-777 Hornby St., Vancouver, BC, V6Z 1S4. Contact: Douglas W. Scarlett, Partner (Lawyer) - Tel: (604) 684-4777. Law firm. Established: 1992.

SHIBLEY RIGHTON
401 Bay St., Ste. 1800, Toronto, ON, M5H 2Z1. Contact: Jonathan H. Flanders, Partner - Tel: (416) 363-9381. Law firm. Established: 1964.

SOTOS, KARVANIS BARRISTERS AND SOLICITORS
Ste. 1250, 180 Dundas St. W., Toronto, ON, M5G 1Z8. Contact: John Sotos, Liisa Kaarid, Solicitor/Partner, Solicitor - Tel: (416) 977-0007. All aspects of franchising including dispute resolution for franchising industry. Established: 1980.

OSLER, HOSKIN & HARCOURT

P.O. BOX 50
1 FIRST CANADIAN PLACE
TORONTO, ONTARIO
CANADA M5X 1B8
TEL: (416) 362-2111
FAX: (416) 862-6666

BARRISTERS & SOLICITORS · PATENT & TRADE-MARK AGENTS
TORONTO · OTTAWA

FRANK ZAID
DIRECT DIAL: (416) 862-6415

INTERNATIONALLY · OSLER RENAULT · NEW YORK · LONDON · PARIS · HONG KONG · SINGAPORE

Sotos Karvanis
BARRISTERS & SOLICITORS

John Sotos, B.A., LL.B.

Suite 1250,
180 Dundas Street West,
Toronto, Ontario, Canada
M5G 1Z8

Telephone: (416) 977-0007
Telecopier: (416) 977-0717

STEWART ROPER & ASSOCIATES
95 Wellington St. W., Ste. 906, P.O.Box 40, Toronto, ON, M5J 2N6. Contact: A. Stewart, Partner - Tel: (416) 368-7881. Franchise Law. Established: 1969.

WITTEN BINDER
2500 10303 Jasper Ave., Edmonton, AB, T5J 3N6. Contact: Daniel Zalmanowitz, Partner - Tel: (403) 428-0501, Fax: (403) 429-2559. Full service Alberta law firm, Alberta Franchise Act compliance, franchise litigation. Established: 1925.

GREETING SERVICES

GETEM CARDS
P.O.Box 741, Sarnia, ON, N7T 7J7. Contact: Henry Maas, Principal - Tel: (519) 869-8072. Sale of life size greeting card rental outlets. Cards can be custom lettered for any occasion. Twelve various characters. There are 3 foot and 6 foot signs. Superb home business. Established: 1989 - Franchising Since: 1989 - No. of Units: Franchised: 8 - Franchise Fee: $3,500 complete package - Total Inv: $3,500 - Financing: No.

NORTHERN CARD PUBLISHING COMPANY
Northern Card Publishing Company Ltd.
Commercial Ste. 104, 66 Isabella St., Toronto, ON, M4Y 1N3. Contact: Hugh Clarkson, Pres. - Tel: (416) 924-8183. A greeting card publisher, distributing their own cards in the Toronto area and with protected territories available across Canada for wholesalers/distributors. Established: 1991 - Franchising Since: 1992 - No. of Units: Company Owned: 7 - Franchised: 3 - Total Inv: $10,000 - $60,000 dependent on territory size - Financing: Yes.

ORIGINAL BASKET BOUTIQUE *
Original Basket Boutique, Ltd.
4200 Frirway Pl, N. Vancouver, BC, V7G 1X9. Contact: S. Chandler, Pres. - Tel: (604) 929-8552. Home based gift basket company. Established: 1986 - Franchising Since: 1989 - No. of Units: Franchised: 21 - Franchise Fee: $6,500 - $9,500 - Royalty: 7% - Financing: No.

PARTY HUT
922928 Ontario Inc.
6625 Kitimat Rd., Unit 49, Mississauga, ON, L5N 6J1. Contact: Luigi, Pres. - Tel: (905) 542-1555. Novelty gifts and special greeting cards for the life of the party, especially those turning 30, 40, 50 etc. Established: 1987 - Franchising Since: 1990 - No. of Units: Company Owned: 1 - Franchised: 7 - Franchise Fee: $20,000 - Royalty: 6%, 2% adv. - Total Inv: $100,000 - $125,000.

YOUR EXPRESSION PERSONALIZED GREETINGS
20 Holly St., #206, Toronto, ON, M4S 3B1. Contact: Steve Parker, Fran. Dir. - Tel: (416) 322-3626. Our uniqueness comes from the in-store personalization process of a wide range of social greeting products such as greeting cards, invitations, stationery, cartoon panels, certificates, tributes, etc. Established: 1988 - Franchising Since: 1989 - No. of Units: Company Owned: 1 - Franchised: 7 - Franchise Fee: $25,000 - Royalty: 6% - Total Inv: $150,000 - $175,000.

HAIRSTYLING & COSMETICS

BODY SHOP, THE
33 Kern Rd., Don Mills, ON, M3B 1S9. Contact: Franchise Dept. - Tel: (416) 441-3202. Retailer of naturally-based cosmetic products for men and women in refillable containers. An environmentally responsible company, whose franchisees work closely with their community to effect positive social change. Established: 1976 - Franchising in Canada Since: 1980 - No. of Units: Company Owned: 16 - Franchised: 97 - Franchise Fee: $15,000 - Royalty: $200/mo. admin. costs - Total Inv: $275,000 - $300,000 - Financing: No.

CALL N' CUT
Call N' Cut Inc.
880 Wilson Ave., North York, ON, M3K 1E7. Contact: Joseph Pampena, Exec. Pres. - Tel: (416) 630-5001. In-home hairdressing services, specializing in seniors, disabled and handicapped people. Established: 1980 - Franchising Since: 1989 - No. of Units: Company Owned: 50 - Franchised: 4 - Franchise Fee: $4,000 U.S. - Royalty: 9%, 3% adv. - Financing: Interest free financing available worldwide.

CARYL BAKER VISAGE
Visage Cosmetics Ltd.
801 Eglinton Ave., W., Downsview, ON, M5N 1E3. Contact: Alan Baker, V.P. - Tel: (416) 789-7191. Retail cosmetic salons. Established: 1969 - Franchising Since: 1975 - No. of Units: Company Owned:1 - Franchised: 31 - Franchise Fee: $12,500 - Approx. Total Inv: $75,000 approx. Financing: Not from company.

COSMETIC ISLAND
Cosmetic Island, Inc.
35 Martinridge Pl., Calgary, AB, T3J 3B8. Contact: Frank Webb, Fran. Dir. - Tel: (403) 280-6966. Small island shaped cosmetic counters selling an exclusive line of cosmetics and skin care products. Established: 1993 - Franchising Since: 1994 - No. of Units: Company Owned: 1 - Franchise Fee: $2,500 - Royalty: 4%, 2% adv. - Total Inv: $18,500.

DESIGNER FRAGRANCES *
369 Queen St. W., Toronto, ON, M5V 2A4 . Contact: John Tuli, Fran. Dir. - Tel: (416) 585-2730 . Discount retail chain of genuine designer fragrances for men & women. Established: 1991 - Franchising Since: 1995 - No. of Units: Company Owned: 6 - Franchise Fee: $50,000 - Royalty: 6% - Total Inv: $200,000 - Financing: Yes.

FABUTAN SUN TAN STUDIO
Bldg. 101, 208 57th Ave. S.W., Calgary, AB, T2H 2K8. Contact: Doug McNabb, Pres. - Tel: (403) 640-2100. Sun tanning studios; 5 - 8 tanning beds approx. Established: 1979 - Franchising Since: 1984 - No. of Units: Company Owned: 10 - Franchised: 39 - Franchise Fee: $5,000 to $15,000 - Royalty: 5% - Total Inv: approx. $45,000 to $65,000 - Financing: No.

FACES
Ligi Inc.
5-3425 Laird Rd., Mississauga, ON, L5L 5R8. Contact: Pierre LeBlanc, Pres. - Tel: (905) 569-8989, Fax: (905) 569-8998. Cosmetic retail colour makeup, skincare, bodycare. Established: 1974 - Franchising Since: 1983 - Franchise Fee: $15,000 - Royalty: 5% 1st yr., 6% 2nd yr. & 7% 3rd yr. - Total Inv: $15,000 fran. fee + $37,000 fixed assets ($12,000 inven.) - Financing: Yes.

FIRST CHOICE HAIRCUTTERS
First Choice Haircutters, Ltd.
6465 Millcreek Dr., Ste. 210, Mississauga, ON, L5N 5R6. Contact: Linda Craig, Dir.Franchise Sales - Tel: (905) 821-8555, Fax: (905) 567-7000. Our business grows 24 hours a day! High volume, price value, retail haircutting & haircare services for the entire family. Fully guaranteed services. Staffed with licensed stylists. Strong base of corporate stores allows for extensive R&D and ongoing support unprecedented in the industry. Established: 1980 - Franchising Since: 1981 - No. of Units: Company Owned: 103 - Franchised: 133 - Franchise Fee: $25,000 - Royalty: 6% US, 7% CDN - Total Inv: $69,000 (incl. fran. fee) - Financing: Assistance through financial institutes.

FRAGRANCE
La Parfumerie Duquin Ltd.
9610 F. Ignace, Brossard, PQ, J4Y 2R4. Contact: Alain Quintal, Pres. - Tel: (514) 444-1806. Perfumes and cosmetics stores. Established: 1972 - Franchising Since: 1986 - No. of Units: Company Owned: 3 - Franchised: 17 - Franchise Fee: $15,000 - Royalty: 3%, 1.5% adv. - Total Inv: approx. $150,000 - Financing: Yes.

HEAD SHOPPE, GOLDEN CLIPPER, THE
Box 8, 1465 Brenton St., Halifax, NS, B3J 3T3. Contact: Peter Mahoney, Pres. & Owner - Tel: (902) 455-1504. Hairstyling salons. Established: 1977 - No. of Units: 15 Head Shoppes, 2 Golden Clippers.

INTERBEAUTE COIFFURE
1225, rue de la Montagne, Montreal, PQ, H3G 1Z2. Contact: M. Vidal Salvo, Pres. - Tel: (514) 876-4020. Interbeaute Coiffure is an upscale hair salon for men and women. Also offers cosmetic services and related retail products. Established: 1975 - Franchising Since: 1990 - No. of Units: Company Owned: 12 - Franchised: 4 - Franchise Fee: $20,000 - Royalty: 5% or minimum fee per year $10,000 - Total Inv: 20% cost.

JOSEPH'S HAIR SALONS (JOSEPH COIFFURES)
18 Hollywood Ave., Ste. 303, North York, ON, M2N 6P5. Contact: Don Bumbaca, Franc. Dir. - Tel: (416) 733-3525. Hairstyling salons. Established: 1955 - No. of Units: Company Owned: 11 - Franchised: 5.

MAGICUTS
3780 14th Ave., Ste. 106, Markham, ON, L3R 9Y5. Contact: Kim Huxhold, Dir. of Fran. Dev. - Tel: (905)470-2887 . Reasonably priced full service haircare salons. Established: 1981 - Franchising Since: 1982 - No. of Units: Company Owned: 17 - Franchised: 165 - Franchise Fee: $25,000 - Royalty: 7% , 1.5% adv. - Total Inv: $60,000 - $80,000 - Financing: Yes, to qualified investors.

NAIL QUEEN
Nail Queen Ltd.
6465 Millcreek Dr., Ste. 205, Mississauga, ON, L5N 5R3. Contact: George Kostopoulos - Tel: (905) 567-4180, (800) 387-8335, Fax: (905) 567-5355. Nail Queen is a unique combination of product and technique, developed with quality in mind resulting in Canada's first complete turnkey nail care salon, specializing in the application of artificial nails and manicures. Your staff of skilled nail technicians, trained by our own Nail Academy, will free you up to concentrate on the operations and promotions of your business. Established: 1985 - Franchising Since: 1987 - No. of Units: Company Owned: 1 - Franchised: 3 - Franchise Fee: $25,000 - Royalty: 5% - Total Inv: $60,000 - $75,000 - Financing: Assistance through financial institutes.

NAILS 'N LASHES STUDIO
Box 340, Sharon, ON, L0G 1V0. Contact: Irving Fine, Pres. - Tel: (905) 473-5774. Application of acrylic fingernails. Established: 1970 - Franchising Since: 1972 - No. of Units: Franchised: 23 - Franchise Fee: $5,000 - $20,000 (depending on territory) - Total Inv: $15,000 - $30,000. Financing: Subject to credit.

NECTAR CANADA
Alberton Natural Resources Inc.
3397 American Dr., Unit 23 , Mississauga, ON, L4V 1T5. Contact: Richard Tremblay, Fran. Dept. - Tel: (905) 678-7092. A complete range of quality natural based body and bath products for the entire family at affordable prices. Established: 1981 (Ireland) - Franchising Since: 1995 - No. of Units: Company Owned: 51 Bay locations, 1 Corporate - Franchise Fee: $10,000 - Royalty: 2%, 1% adv. - Total Inv: $150,000 - $175,000 - Financing: No.

SUNBANQUE ISLAND TANNING
2533 A Yonge St., Toronto, ON, M4P 2H9. Contact: Joel Guisto, Pres. - Tel: (416) 488-5838, Fax: (416) 488-3712. Suntanning salons, aesthetics and cosmetic/skin care products. Established: 1983 - Franchising Since: 1983 - No. of Units: Company Owned: 1 - Franchised: 12 - Franchise Fee: $10,000 - Royalty: 4% for adv. - Total Inv: $40,000 - Financing: Yes.

SUR VISAGE COSMETICS
Sur Visage, Inc.
9050 Charels de la Tour, Montreal, PQ, H4N 1M2. Contact: J. Bassali, Franc. Dir. - Tel: (514) 733-3465. Exclusively designed cosmetics studio in regional malls and fashionable street locations, offering its own full line of high fashion, high quality cosmetic products and accessories. A unique concept in the art of makeup application by highly trained owner and makeup consultants. Also aesthetics, nails and make-up courses. Established: 1979 - Franchising Since: 1981 - No. of Units: Company Owned: 3 - Franchised: 6 - Franchise Fee: $15,000 - Total Inv: approx. $60,000 - $120,000 - Royalty: 5%.

TRIZZ HAIR ALTERNATIVES
Trizz Hair Alternatives, Ltd.
14 Mendota Rd., Etobicoke, ON, M8Y 1E8. Contact: Mr. Steve Yoksimovich, Gen. Mgr. - Tel: (416) 252-9591. Trizz stores offer a wide selection of wigs, hairpieces, hair additions and hair accessories, such as brushes, combs and shampoos. Stores and kiosks are located in high profile locations in regional malls and mixed use, commercial complexes. Established: 1964 - Franchising Since: 1992 - No. of Units: Company Owned: 6 - Franchised: 1 - Franchise Fee: $25,000 - Royalty: 6% - Total Inv: $49,500 - $145,000 - Financing: Yes.

WIGGY'S NAIL PLACE
Nudex Int'l, Inc.
20 Edgecliffe Golf Way, Unit 1815, Don Mills, ON, M3C 3A4. Contact: Derek Newell, Pres. - Tel: (416) 439-2960. The application of artificial fingernails and associated services. Established: 1974 - Franchising Since: 1977 - No. of Units: Company Owned: 2 - Franchised: 2 - Franchise Fee: $15,000 - Total Inv: approx. $25,000.

YVES ROCHER CANADA LTD.
1001 Renaude La Pointe, Ville Anjou, PQ, H1J 2W2. Contact: Marc Lauerdiere, Fran. Dept. - Tel: (514) 355-5333. Beauty products. Established: 1985 - Franchising Since: 1985 - No. of Units: Company Owned: 7 in Canada, 1200 outside Canada.

HEALTH AIDS AND SERVICES

BEVERLY HILLS WEIGHT LOSS CLINIC
Beverly Hills Weight Loss Clinics of Canada Inc.
200-94 Bridgeport Rd. E., Waterloo, ON, N2J 2J9 . Contact: Gloria Foertsch, Coord., Admin. - Tel: (519) 746-3444 or (800) 668-5798. Weight loss services, offering a behavioral based program. Various weight management programs available, with all client programs selected by a doctor. Established: 1988 - Franchising Since: 1988 - No. of Units: Company Owned: 2 - Franchised: 60 - Franchise Fee: $25,000 - Royalty: 7.5% - Total Inv: $40,000; fee, lease, furnishings, supplies - Financing: Yes, must qualify.

OUR BUSINESS GROWS 24 HOURS A DAY

Since 1980, we have offered the entire family convenience; clean & comfortable surroundings; first class haircare and a fair price. Guaranteed.
A First Choice Haircutters franchise offers affordable, unlimited growth potential and a solid market.
Join the team of 200+ successful stores.
Call or write: Director of Franchising, First Choice Haircutters
6465 Millcreek Dr., Ste. 210
Mississauga, ON, L5N 5R6
Tel: (905) 821-8555, Fax: (905) 567-7000

HEALTH CARE INVESTMENT OPPORTUNITIES

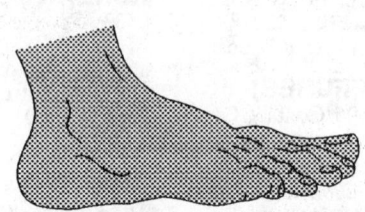

WANTED!!!
MASTER FRANCHISEE
(QUEBEC & E. CANADA)

- Exclusive Territory subject to Performance Criteria
- Capital to finance 10 centres within 5 - 7 years
- Initial Master Fee (negotiable)
- Individual Location Fee
- 5% Royalty on Gross Sales

Franchisor will Provide:
- Initial Training
- Translation
- Technical Support
- Marketing Support
- System Manuals

FOLLOW IN OUR FOOTSTEPS !!!

- Franchising since 1985
- Canadian owned & operated
- 21 Locations
- 14 Franchises
- 7 Corporate Centres

- Gross Sales of $7 million
- North America's largest provider of Prescription Footwear and Orthoses
- Industry Leader in New Technology

LOCATIONS AVAILABLE IN 1996

ONTARIO
- Barrie
- S.S. Marie
- Thunder Bay
- Sarnia

CORPORATE EMPLOYMENT OPPORTUNITIES

- Profit Sharing
- Full Benefit package
- Annual earnings of $40,000 - $80,000

Qualifications
Degrees in:
- Physiotherapy
- Occupational Therapy
- Human Kinetics
- Kinesiology
- Chiropody

(Or Equivalent Experience)

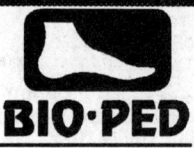

BIO·PED FOOT CARE CENTRES

2150 WINSTON PARK DRIVE; UNIT 2, OAKVILLE, ONTARIO L6H 5V1; TEL (905) 829-0505 FAX (905) 829-5199

BIO PED FOOT CARE CENTERS
1170 Burnhamthorpe Rd. W., Ste. 16, Mississauga, ON, L5C 4E6. Contact: Greg Heller, V.P. - Tel: (905) 896-4824. Foot care centre specializing in custom made orthopedic appliances, specialized footwear and custom modification for persons with foot problems. 6,000 units to U.S. and Europe. Established: 1985 - Franchising Since: 1985 - No. of Units: Company Owned: 7 - Franchised: 14 - Franchise Fee: $30,000 - $100,000 - Royalty: 8% + 2% adv. - Total Inv: $150,000 - $200,000 turnkey - Financing: Assistance.

CLOUTHIER, ESSAIN
McMahon Essain Inc.
10301 Colbert, Anjou, PQ, H1J 2G5. Contact: Denise Martin, V.P. - Tel: (514) 355-8350. Drug stores. Established: 1979 - No. of Units: 119.

DENTRIX DENTAL CARE
Ste. 300, 222 - 58th Ave., S.W., Calgary, AB, T2H 2S2. Contact: Dr. Roger Watson, Pres. - Tel: (403) 255-6211. Dental centres. Established: 1984 - No. of Units: 6.

DR. SPECS OPTICAL *
C & G Optical
2280A Leckie Rd., Kelowna, BC, V1X 6G6. Contact: Cathy Goheen, Pres. - Tel: (604) 861-7731. Chain of retail optical outlets. Established: 1987 - Franchising Since: 1994 - No. of Units: Company Owned: 7 - Franchised: 7 - Franchise Fee: $15,000 - Royalty: 5% of gross sales (monthly) - Total Inv: $89,000 (incl. fran. fee) - Financing: No.

HALE OPTICAL EYE-CRAFTERS/ LONDON OPTICAL / PRESCRIPTION OPTICAL
Prescription Optical Company Ltd.
7060 Waltham Ave., Burnaby, BC, V5J 4V5. Contact: Ron Phillip, Franc. Dir. - Tel: (604) 430-1501. Established: 1924 - No. of Units: 45.

JEAN COUTU GROUP
530 Beriault, Longueuil, P.Q. J4G 1S8. Contact: Mr. Yvon Bechard, Sr. Exec. V.P. - Tel: (514) 646-9760. Drug stores. Established: 1969 - No. of Units: 146.

MEDICHAIR LTD.
2506 Southern Ave., Brandon, MB, R7B 0S4. Contact: Scott Third, Dir. of Operations - Tel: (204) 726-1245. MEDIchair Ltd. is one of Canada's largest chain of franchised home health care stores. MEDIchair offers as the exclusive Canadian distributor quality DME products like Pacesave Plus, Scooter, Aquatic Bathlifts, Swedish Nova Rollator, Pegasus walk-n-rest walkers along with a complete line of ADL products. Established: 1985 - Franchising Since: 1986 - No. of Units: Franchised: 24 - Franchise Fee: $37,500 - Royalty: 5% - Total Inv: $90,000 - Financing: No.

MIGRAINE CLINIC *
Energy Medicine Developments (N.A.) Inc.
104 - 630 Columbia St., New Westminster, BC, V3M 1A5. Contact: Bob Fletcher, V.P. - Tel: (604) 522-8618, Fax: (604) 522-9896. Electro magnetic medical device which is used to suppress pain. Established: 1994 - No. of Units: Company Owned: 1 - Franchise Fee: $25,000 - Royalty: 10% of sales, incl. adv. - Total Inv: $50,000 - $75,000 - Financing: Major Canadian cities.

PHARMASAVE DRUGS LTD.
Forewest Holdings, Inc.
6350 203rd St., Langley, BC, V2Y 1L9. Contact: Gordon Barefoot, Bus. Dev. Mgr. - Tel: (604) 532-2250. Retail drug stores. Established: 1981 - No. of Units: Company Owned: 4 - Franchised: 187 - Total Inv: variable - Royalty: percentage of sales to cover advertising.

R.X. SOLEIL, INC.
2466 Belanger St., Montreal, PQ, H2G 1ES. Contact: Pres. - Tel: (514)729-8859. Suntanning studio with accessory sale of complementary products such as sun-tanning gel & lotion, promotional material (e.g. lighters and garments) with logo. Established: 1981 - Franchising Since: 1981 - No. of Units: Company Owned: 6 - Franchised: 64 - Franchise Fee: $10,000 - $30,000 - Approx. Total Inv: $75,000 - $155,000 - Royalty: 5%, 5% adv. - Financing: Yes, bank package.

SANGSTERS HEALTH CENTRE
Box 996, Yorkton, SK, S3N 2X3. Contact: Roy Sangster, Pres. - Tel: (306) 783-9177, Fax: (306) 783-3331. Retail vitamins, herbs, natural cosmetics, diet products, body building supplies, snacks & foods. Established: 1971 - Franchising Since: 1978 - No. of Units: Company Owned: 2 - Franchised: 23 - Franchise Fee: $15,000 - Royalty: 5% - Total Inv: $60,000 - $80,000 - Financing: Will assist.

"MAKE HEALTH A HABIT"
- ROY SANGSTER -

Canadian Franchise Head Office
Darwen Holdings Ltd., P.O. Box 996
Yorkton, Sask. S3N 2X3
Tel.: (306) 783-9177
Fax: (306) 783-3331

SLIM WITHIN LIFESTYLE CONSULTING OFFICES
Slim Within Lifestyle Franchises, Inc.
2 Bloor St. W., Ste. 700, Toronto, ON, M4W 3R1. Contact: George Fluter, Dir. of Fran. Dev. - Tel: (416) 944-2200, Fax: (416) 960-5863. Consulting offices providing councilling & products in health, wellness & weight control. Established: 1992 - Franchising Since: 1992 - No. of Units: Company Owned: 1 - Franchised: 68 - Franchise Fee: $15,000 - Royalty: 5% ongoing support, 5% adv. - Total Inv: $40,000 turnkey - Financing: Assistance in business plan and leasing company will provide $20,000 on equip. pkg. on approved credit.

SUNRIDER INTERNATIONAL
455 Hilldale Rd., Thunder Bay, ON, P7B 5N1. Contact: Jon Essa, Director - Tel: (807) 683-6885. Herbal foods and natural cosmetic, skin-and-hair-care. Sunrider's Mission "To help people throughout the world enjoy better health, prosperity and financial independence by providing superior herbal food products and a motivating compensation plan." Established: 1982 - Franchising Since: 1982 - No. of Distributors: approx. 375,000 worldwide and growing rapidly - Distributor Fee: $49. - Start-up investment $100. - $1,000.

SUNSTREAM TAN & SKIN CARE
Sunstream Canada
44 Charles St., W., Ste. 2809, Toronto, ON, M4Y 1R7. Contact: Maurice Shpur, Pres. - Tel: (416) 964-6424. Sun tan equipment. Established: 1984 - Franchising Since: 1984 - No. of Units: Company Owned: 3 - Franchised: 7 - Franchise Fee: $15,000 - Approx. Total Inv: $75,000 - Royalty: 5% - Financing: Yes.

SUPER THRIFTY DRUG MARTS
381 Park Ave., E., Brandon, MB, R7A 7A5. Contact: Greg Skura, Pres. - Tel: (204) 728-1522. Drug stores. Established: 1978 - Franchising Since: 1980 - No. of Units: 11.

VARCON Construction Co. Ltd.
Industrial · Residential · Commercial · Institutional

CUSTOMERS WANTED
Can we build your next franchise store, corporate offices or distribution center? Construction budgets & deadlines are a priority to us.

WE OFFER:
- Turnkey or partial construction
- Project management
- Design and build
- Budget consultations

25 Rutherford Rd. South, Unit 5
Brampton, Ont. L6W 3J3
(800) 581-6729
Tel: (905) 451-7316, Fax: (905) 451-8563

VITAL ENERGY HEALTH TRAINING INC. *
4630B Muir Rd., Courtenay, BC, V9N 9A9. Contact: Grant Gibson, Pres. & Founder - Tel: (800) 828-4825. Training seminars for people who work in front of computer terminals dealing with eye strain, carpel tunnel syndrome. Established: 1994 - Franchising Since: 1995 - No. of Units: Company Owned: 1 - Franchised: 2 - Franchise Fee: $15,000 - Royalty: 8% - Total Inv: $15,000 - Financing: Yes.

WE CARE HOME HEALTH SERVICES
We Care Health Services Inc.
601 Scotia Towers, 1011 Rosser Ave., Brandon, MB, R7A 0L5. Contact: Joan Plante, Dir. Fran. Sales - Tel: (204) 725-4222, Fax: (204) 728-8146. Professional nursing, homemaking, home support, companion sitting and respite care. Established: 1984 - Franchising Since: 1988 - No. of Units: Franchised: 43 - Franchise Fee: $25,000 - Royalty: 5%, 2% nat'l. adv., .5% computer - Total Inv: $50,000 - Financing: No.

HOME FURNISHINGS

BETONEL LTEE.
8600 De L'Epee, Montreal, PQ, H3N 2G6. Contact: Franchise Director - Tel: (514) 273-8855. Paint, wallpaper, stain, varnish. Established: 1959 - Franchising Since: 1985 - No. of Units: Company Owned: 8 - Franchised: 18 - Franchise Fee: $5,000 - Total Inv: $50,000 - Financing: For half inventory.

CEDAR CHEST, THE
Creations By Dean, Inc.
9 Duke Street, St. Catharines, ON, L2R 6W8. Contact: Dean Maguire, Pres. - Tel: (905) 688-2665. Handcrafted, exquisitely designed pine furniture, where the customer provides desired dimensions, style and type of stain, and the furniture is made to suit within 2 weeks. Full support, training manual and exclusive territory provided. Established: 1991 - Franchising Since: 1993 - No. of Units: Company Owned: 1 - Franchised: 10 - Franchise Fee: $10,000 - Royalty: 4% of gross, 2% adv. - Total Inv: $45,000 - Financing: Yes.

CERTA PROPAINTERS CANADA
5397 Eglington Ave., W., Ste. 109, Toronto, ON, M9C 5K6. Contact: Scott Mossip, VP - Tel: (800) 446-6840, Fax: (416) 620-9622. Painting and decorating service company. Residential and commercial work. Basic painting, wallpapering, spraying and decorative finishes. Established: 1989 - Franchising Since: 1991 - No. of Units: Franchised: 40 - Franchise Fee: $16,000 - Royalty: $700 - $1,200/month depends on size of the territory - Total Inv: $35,000: $16,000 fee, $19,000 start up & equip. - Financing: Some with Certa ProPainters and Suppliers.

COLOR YOUR WORLD, CORP.
10 Carson St., Toronto, ON, M8W 3R5. Contact: Ms. Denise Weishar, Fran. Mgr. - Tel: (416) 259-3251. Retailers of paint and wallcoverings. Established: 1932 - Franchising Since: 1969 - No. of Units: Franchised: 100 - Franchise Fee: 7 1/2% of previous year's sales - Royalty: 0-17% of gross profit/rent & adv. 28% of gross profit combined - Total Inv: $150,000 - $250,000 - Financing: For smaller volume stores.

DECOR DISTINCTION
1122 Finch Ave. W., Ste. 7, Downsview, ON, M3J 3J5. Contact: S. Belanger, V.P. - Tel: (416) 736-0003. Large Canadian owned franchise operation offering complete interior design service in the comfort of your home. Established: 1982 - Franchising Since: 1990 - No. of Units: Company Owned: 1 - Franchised: 14 - Franchise Fee: $15,000 - $25,000 - Royalty: 9.5% - 8% - Total Inv: $22,000 - $35,000 - Financing: Yes.

DECORATING DEN
25 Orchard Parkway, Grimsby, ON, L3M 3B1. Contact: Heather MacDougall, Reg. Dir. - Tel: (905) 945-8344. Affordable, international shop-at-home decorating service. Each franchise is operated by a professionally trained decorator who brings 4,000 to 5,000 samples of fabrics, draperies, wall coverings, floor coverings, furniture & accessories to the customer's home in a specially equipped Colour Van. The customer enjoys the convenience of reviewing generous samples in the lighting conditions which exist in the home. Established: 1970 - Franchising Since: 1970 - No of Units: Franchised: over 1,200 - Franchise Fee: $8,900 - $20,900 - Royalty: 11% - 7% (decreasing) - Total Inv: Fran. fee plus $15,000 work. cap.

DUNBAR CARPET BY COLOUR *
465097 BC Ltd.
3352 Dunbar St., Vancouver, BC, V6S 2C1. Contact: Ron Mendelson, Pres. - Tel: (604) 736-2177, Fax: (736-8862). A) Retail flooring outlet, unique concept, complete turn-key operation - not much experience required. Incredibly high income potential - exclusive territory B) Mobile dealership (similar to above) exclusive territory. Established: 1994 - Franchising Since: 1994 - No. of Units: Company Owned: 1 - Franchise Fee: A) $10,000, B) $5,000 - Total Inv: A) $20,000, B) $10,000 - Financing: No.

FERPLUS DECORATION, FERPLUS QUINCAILLERIE, FERPLUS RENOVATION
Marchands Unis, Inc.
915 Paradis St., Duberger, PQ, G1N 4E3. Contact: Norma Fortin, V.P. Dev. - Tel: (418) 687-3050. Retail stores specializing in wallpaper, paint and hardware. Established: 1950 - No. of Units: 125.

KIT ATOUT
Group Cantrex, Inc.
4445 Garand, St-Laurent, PQ, H4R 2H9. Contact: Pierre Vezina, Franchise Dir. - Tel: (514) 335-0260. Unassembled furniture. Established: 1984 - Franchising Since: 1984 - No. of Units: 46 - Franchise Fee: $10,000 - Royalty: $1,200 - Total Inv: $150,000 - Financing: Special program with Royal Bank of Canada.

KITCHEN CRAFT CONNECTION, THE
1180 Springfield Rd., Winnipeg, MB, R2C 2Z2. Contact: Herb Buller, Pres. - Tel: (204) 224-3211. Kitchen and bathroom furnishings and accessories. Established: 1981 - No. of Units: 4.

LEON'S FURNITURE LTD.
88 Gordon MacKay Rd., Weston, ON, M9N 3T4. Contact: Bruce Stevens, Mgr. Franc. Div. - Tel: (416) 243-7880. Furniture, appliances and carpet retail. Established: 1909 - Franchising Since: 1983 - No. of Units: 16 - Franchise Fee $10,000.

MAX PIES CARPET
A Max Pies Carpet Canada Inc.
3650 Weston Rd., Unit 22, Toronto, ON, M9L 1W2. Contact: Leo Dos Reis, Fran. Dir. - Tel: (416) 748-9242. Floor covering shop at home franchise with very low overhead. Customer saves money and franchisee makes more money. Call to find out how you too can make $3,300 avg./hr. Established: 1982 - Franchising Since: 1992 - No. of Units: Company Owned: 1 - Franchised: 8 - Franchise Fee: $7,900 to $29,500 - Royalty: 1.5% advertising - Total Inv: $8,000 - $30,000 - Financing: Yes.

PAINT SHOP
P.S. Paint Shop, Inc.
979 Topsail Rd., Mount Pearl, NF, A1N 3K1. Contact: Paul Burt, Pres. - Tel: (709) 364-1021. Home decorating retail. Offering paint, wallpaper, blinds & related products. Servicing retail and contractor. Established: 1973 - Franchising Since: 1975 - No. of Units: Company Owned: 1 - Franchised: 13 - Franchise Fee: $10,000 - Royalty: 5% - Total Inv: varies.

PANHANDLER, RAFTERS, POT POURRI, LIVING LIGHTING
LIV Canada
4699 Keele St., #1, Downsview, ON, M3J 2N8. Contact: M. Mayerson, V.P., Leasing - Tel: (416) 661-9916, Fax: (416) 661-9706. Retail kitchenware, giftware, residential lighting. Established: 1968 - Franchising Since: 1972 - No. of Units: Company Owned: 4 - Franchised: 125 - Franchise Fee: $25,000 - Royalty: 6% - Total Inv: $25,000 - $250,000 - Financing: No.

ST. CLAIR PAINT & WALLPAPER, WALLPAPER WORLD
2600 Steeles Ave., W., Concord, ON, L4K 3C8. Contact: Harry Litwin, V.P., Real Est. and Fran. - Tel: (905) 738-0080. Retail sale of paint, wallpaper and other decorating accessories. Established: 1939 - Franchising Since: 1970 - No. of Units: 146 St. Clair - 1 Wallpaper World.

ZIP INTERNATIONAL LTD.
1400 St-Jean Baptiste, Quebec, PQ, G2E 5B7. Contact: Benoit Dery, Pres. - Tel: (418) 871-2221. Furniture. Established: 1979 - No. of Units: Company Owned: 1 - Franchised: 6.

HOUSE/PET SITTING SERVICES

CUSTOM HOME-WATCH INTERNATIONAL
Custom Home-Watch International, Inc.
2094 Tomat Ave., Kelowna, BC, V1Z 3C5. Contact: Terry Bates, Pres. - Tel: (604) 769-4329, Fax: (604) 769-4329. Looking after absent home-owner's premises, pets, plants, yard, mail, repairs, maintenance, maid service. Franchisees receive all start up supplies, training, equipment and operations manual. Many group benefits and ongoing assistance. Established: 1988 - Franchising Since: 1989 - No. of Units: Franchised: 42 - Franchise Fee: $1,950 - $4,950 (depending on population) - Royalty: 3% + 2% nat'l adv. - Total Inv: $3,000 - $10,000 - Financing: Yes.

HOUSESITTERS, THE
Housesitters Franchise Corp., The
530 Queen St., East, Toronto, ON, M5A 1V2. Contact: Cameron Dalsto, Vice Pres. - Tel: (416) 947-1295; Canada (800) 387-1337; US (800) 388-1814. Full service home, family, and pet care, maid service, corporate relocation and property management. Established: 1981 - Franchising Since: 1986 - No. of Units: Company Owned: 4 - Franchised: 38 - Franchise Fee: $25,000 min. - Royalty: 8%, 2% adv. - Financing: O.A.C.

Full-time owner-operators with marketing and management background required to open select franchises
Home and pet sitting for travellers • Residential house cleaning
Property Management for financial institutions
Complete turnkey inventory • Training and on-going support
Fully computerized • Existing customer base • Offices coast-to-coast
CAMERON DALSTO (416) 947-1295 or 1-800-387-1337

LAUNDRY & DRY CLEANING

1 HOUR DRYCLEANERS *
J.F. Schmitz Associates..The Finders
500 Rossland Rd. W., P.O. Box 58025, Oshawa, ON, L1J 8L6. Contact: Joseph Schmitz, Fran. Cons. - Tel: (905) 579-9792, Fax: (905) 579-4692. On site drycleaning, shirt laundry, repairs plant. Established: 1988 - Franchising Since: 1988 - No. of Units: Company Owned: 1 - Franchised: 4 - Franchise Fee: $10,000 - royalty: 6.5% of sales - Total Inv: $230,000 complete turnkey, move in ready for operation - Financing: $200,000 for qualified applicants.

CHATEL VOTRE NETTOYEUR (YOUR CLEANER)
1200 boul. Rome, Local M, Brossard, PQ, J4W 3H3. Contact: Andre Demers or Rock Potheir, Pres./V.P. - Tel: (514) 671-5642, Fax: (514) 671-5243. Drycleaning and related services. Established: 1984 - Franchising Since: 1984 - No. of Units: Company Owned: 6 - Franchised: 90 - Franchise Fee: $15,000 - Royalty: 3% - Total Inv: $135,000 to $145,000 - Financing: Via S.B.L.

CLEANING BY PAGE
10547 116 Street, Edmonton, AB, T5H 3L8. Contact: Sara Hunter, Fran. Dir. - Tel: (403) 429-3600. Full service professional drycleaning company located throughout Edmonton & area. Established: 1933 - Franchising Since: 1986.- No. of Units: Company Owned: 13 - Franchised: 23 - Franchise Fee: $10,000 - Royalty: 7.5% on plant production - Total Inv: $100,000+ depending on new or established, pre-owned locations - Financing: No.

CONVENIENT DRY CLEANING DEPOT *
J.F. Schmitz Associates..The Finders
500 Rossland Rd. W., P.O. Box 58025, Oshawa, ON, L1J 8L6. Contact: Joseph Schmitz, Fran. Cons. - Tel: (905) 579-9792, Fax: (905) 579-4692. Drycleaning, shirt laundry, shoe repair depot. Established: 1988 - Franchising Since: 1988 - No. of Units: Franchised: 6 - Franchise Fee: $10,000 - Royalty: 6.5% of sales - Total Inv: $67,000 for complete turnkey, ready for business outlet - Financing: $50,000 to qualified applicants.

HILLARY'S CLEANERS
1235 Bank St., Ottawa, ON, K1S 3Y2. Contact: David Hillary, Pres. - Tel: (613) 733-3070. Innovative environmentally sound dry cleaning concept. Established: 1950 - Franchising Since: 1989 - No. of Units: Company Owned: 5 - Franchised: 9 - Franchise Fee: $25,000 - Royalty: $600 per month - Total Inv: $150,000 - Financing: Yes.

LONDON CLEANERS
London Cleaners Inc.
21 Amber St., Unit 12, Markham, ON, L3R 4Z3. Contact: Marc Kuzu, V.P. - Tel: (905) 475-1350. Dry cleaners. Established: 1929 - Franchising Since: 1982 - No. of Units: Company Owned: 2 - Franchised: 18 - Franchise Fee: $20,000 - Royalty: 5% - Total Inv: $40,000 - $125,000 - Financing: Ontario, B.C., and U.S.A.

MAYTAG
Lavoir Libre-Service Maytag
10301 Ray Lawson, Anjou, PQ, H1J 1L6. Contact: Pierre Bourcheix, Pres. - Tel: (514) 351-1212. Self-service laundry. Franchising Since: 1958 - No. of Units: 400 Canada, 2,500 US, - Approx. Inv: $80,000 - Financing: Partial.

MICHON CLEANERS
Franchise & Finance
141 Maple, Chateauguay, PQ, J6J 3R1. Contact: Franchise Dir./Pres. - Tel: (514) 692-4936. Dry cleaning. Turn-key operation. Established: 1938 - Franchising Since: 1982 - No. of Units: Company Owned: 3 - Franchised: 16 - Franchise Fee: $10,000 - Total Inv: $128,000 - Royalty: 5% - Financing: Through Franchise & Finance.

NETTOYEUR MICHEL FORGET
Nettoyers Michel Forget Ltée.
2285 Michelin, Sainte-Rose, Laval, PQ, H7L 5B8. Contact: Antoine Cairlo, Gen. Dir. - Tel: (514) 681-8373. Nettoyage à sec. Established: 1984 - Franchising Since: 1984 - No. of Units: Franchised: 46 - Franchise Fee: $20,000 - Royalty: $355.25/mo. - Total Inv: $125,000 - Financing: $100,000.

PLATIS & SONS 1 HOUR CLEANERS
1 Bedford Rd., Toronto, ON, M5R 2J7. Contact: C. Platis, Pres. - Tel: (416) 923-2785. No. of Units: Company Owned: 3 - Franchised: 11.

SKETCHLEY
Three Penguins Inc.
290 Old Weston Rd., Toronto, ON, M6N 3A4. Contact: Don Schell, Fran. Dir. - Tel: (416) 656-5606. Service/dry cleaning. Established: 1956 - Franchising Since: 1987 - No.of Units: Company Owned: 125 - Franchised: 58 - Franchise Fee: $25,000 - Royalty: 5% - Total Inv: $55,000 - $200,000 - Financing: Yes.

SOAP'S GOODTIME LAUNDRY
Soap's Goodtime Laundry (Canada) Inc.
18 Concorde Pl., Ste. 919, North York, ON, M3C 3T9. Contact: Norman D. Dynes, Pres. - Tel: (416) 444-6246. Excellent business opportunity of unique nature, combining a modern version fabric care facility, with a licensed café/entertainment centre focused for all age groups. Traditionally unpleasant tasks can be performed in an attended, coin-op, state-of-the-art laundromat or dropped off for drycleaning and/or professional wash/dry/fold service. Established: 1990 - Franchising Since: 1994 - No. of Units: Company Owned: 1 - Franchise Fee: $25,000 - Royalty: 6% royalty/service fee & 2% advertising/promotion - Total Inv: Initial down payment: $50,000 to $80,000, total investment: $200,000 to $250,000 - Financing: Will assist. For franchise information, contact: Head Office or Soap's Development Manager, c/o 921 Wilson Ave., Downsview, ON, M3K 1E7, Tel: (416) 633-7219, Fax: (416) 636-6487.

LAWN, GARDEN CARE AND FLORISTS

BOBBY LAWN CARE / BOBBY PEST CONTROL
Bobby Lawn, Inc.
P.O. Box 6473, London, ON, N5W 5S4. Contact: Ron VanderHeide, Henry Vandenberg, Licensing Division - Tel: U.S. & Canada (800) 265-7521. We offer the finest lawn care services available using the exclusive Bobby Lawn Care System designed and manufactured exclusively by Bobby Lawn Inc. and supplemented by a broad range of cultural provided services to produce a healthy, beautiful lawn with enhanced sales. We practice Integrated Pest Management and environmentally responsible lawn care services for weed and insect control as well as structural pest control. Established Since: 1979 - Restricted Number of Licensees Issued Since: 1981 - No. of Units (trucks) Company Owned: 45 - Licensed 52 - Royalties: 5% - Total Inv: $15,000 - $25,000 - Financing: No.

CLINTAR GROUNDSKEEPING SERVICES
Clintar Limited
4210 Midland Ave., Scarborough, ON, M1V 4S6. Contact: Robert Goodwin, V.P. - Tel: (416) 291-1611 or Fax: (416) 291-6792. Clintar provides high quality groundskeeping services to Fortune 500 clients. Our year-round service includes: landscape maintenance, snow removal, power sweeping, light construction and irrigation maintenance. Established: 1973 - Franchising Since: 1983 - No. of Units: Franchised: 8 - Franchise Fee: $30,000 - Royalty: 8% of sales - Total Inv: $100,000, 50% financed. Financing: Assistance provided.

ENVIRO MASTERS LAWN CARE
P.O. Box 178, Caledon East, ON, L0N 1E0. Contact: Martin Fielding, Pres. - Tel: (905) 584-9592. Organic and Environmentally considerate lawn care programs. Established: 1987 - Franchising Since: 1991 - No. of Units: Company Owned: 2 - Franchised: 24 - Franchise Fee: $15,000 - Royalty: 5% - Total Inv: $25,000 - Financing: No.

GREENLAND IRRIGATION *
150 Ambleside Dr., London, ON, N6G 4R1. Contact: Barry Smith, Pres. - Tel: (519) 439-4235. Sales & service to existing clients. Guaranteed income. Established: 1986 - Franchising Since: 1990 - No. of Units: Company Owned: 10 - Franchised: 2 - Franchise Fee: $25,000 - Royalty: 8% to 17% - Financing: 5 years, 12% interest.

HERBU
Herbu, Inc.
1433, rue Du Cap, Beloeil, PQ, J3G 5M2. Contact: Claude Gagnon, Pres. - Tel: (514) 464-5755. Lawn care. Franchised: 15 - Franchise Fee: $12,500 - Royalty: fixed (to be determined) - Total Inv: $45,000 - Financing: No.

LAWN CARE THE PROFESSIONAL WAY
Nutrite Inc.
P.O. Box 1000, Brossard, PQ, J4Z 3N2. Contact: Jacques Cardinal, Mgr. - Tel: (514) 462-2555. Lawn care. Nutrite Inc. is also a manufacturer of fertilizer. Established: 1984 - Franchising Since: 1984 - No. of Units: Franchised: 42 - Franchise Fee: $15,000 - Royalty: $3,550 per year - Total Inv: $40,000 - Financing: No.

NUTRILAWN INTERNATIONAL INC.
Ste. 110, 5397 Eglinton Ave. W., Etobicoke, ON, M9C 5K6. Contact: Derek Riley, Pres. - Tel: (416) 620-7100, Fax: (416) 620-7771. Franchisor of Ecology Friendly lawncare territories. A wide range of marketing methods used to sell and grow healthy lawns that include cultural management techniques, customer education, and plant health care. Established: 1985 - Franchising Since: 1987 - No. of Units: Franchised: 42 - Franchise Fee: $15,000 - $50,000 - Royalty: 6%, 2% nat'l. adv. fund - Financing: To qualified candidates.

NUTRITE, INC.
7005 boul. Taschereau, Brossard, PQ, J4Z 3N2. Contact: Jacques Cardinal, Mgr. - Tel: (514) 462-2555, Fax: (514) 462-3634. Lawn care. Established: 1984 - Franchising Since: 1985 - No. of Units: Franchised: 42 - Franchise Fee: $15,000 - Royalty: $3,550 - Total Inv: $50,000 - Financing: No.

O'TOOLE LAWN CARE *
Unit 3, 167 Lexington Ct., Waterloo, ON, N2J 4R9. Contact: Patrick O'Toole, Owner - Tel: (519) 746-2555. Full program of lawn care services including fertilizer and aeration that encourages the minimal use of pesticides. Established: 1993 - Franchising Since: 1995 - No. of Units: Company Owned: 4 - Franchise Fee: $15,000 - Royalty: 5% - Total Inv: $35,000: $15,000 fran. fee, $12,000 truck, $5,000 equip., $3,000 aerator - Financing: Yes.

SERVICEMASTER LAWN CARE
Servicemaster Lawn Care Canada
4210 Midland Ave., Scarborough, ON, M1V 4S6. Contact: Robert C. Wilton, Pres. - Tel: (416) 291-2596, (800) 668-5140, Fax: (416) 291-6792. Lawn care and tree and shrub care services to residential customers. Established: 1973 - Franchising Since: 1991 - No. of Units: Franchised: 22 - Franchise Fee: $18,000 - Royalty: 8% - Total Inv: $50,000 - Financing: Yes.

WEED MAN
Turf Management Systems, Inc.
2399 Royal Windsor Dr., Mississauga, ON, L5J 1K9. Contact: Michael J. Kernagha, V.P. - Tel: (905) 823-8550. Lawn care. Established: 1970 - Franchising Since: 1976 - No. of Units: Company Owned: 4 - Franchised: 118 - Franchise Fee: $25,000 - Royalty: 6% - Total Inv: $30,000 - Financing: No.

WEEDTECH ENVIRONMENTAL LAWN CARE
Weedtech
2 Perth St., St. Catharines, ON, L2P 3C9. Contact: J.R. Asma, Franc. Dir. - Tel: (905) 682-9333. Environmentally oriented lawn care service for weed and insect control. Established: 1989 - Franchising Since: 1990 - No. of Units: Company Owned: 1 - Franchise Fee: $16,000 - Royalty: 8% on gross sales, 2% adv. - Total Inv: Approx. $30,000 - Financing: Yes.

MOTELS, HOTELS AND CAMPGROUNDS

CHOICE HOTELS CANADA
5090 Explorer Dr., 6th Floor, Mississauga, ON, L4W 4T9. Contact: Jim Baldassari, V.P., Fran. Dev. - Tel: (905) 602-2222. Franchisor of 7 brands: Clarion, Quality Inn, Comfort Inn, Sleep Inn, Rodeway Inn, Econo Lodge and Friendship Inn. Established: 1993 - Franchising Since: 1949 - No. of Units: Franchised: 192 - Franchise Fee: Economy brands $25,000+, $250/rm. min.; Others min. $35,000 or $300/rm. - Royalty: Approx. 6.5% to 8.5% dep. on brand, incl. mktg. & res. fees - Total Inv: Affiliation & start-up only $50,000 to $75,000 - Financing: No.

DAYS INNS - CANADA
Realstar Hotel Services Corp.
2 St. Clair Ave. W., Ste. 700, Toronto, ON, M4V 1L5. Contact: Dennis Ricci, Dir., Fran. Sales & Dev. - Tel: (800) 840-8162. Hotel/motel franchises - establishing franchised properties in all major cities across the country in the moderate priced segment of the market. Providing extensive and dedicated franchise services to franchisees, including a reservation system which is scheduled to process more than 11,000,000 calls in 1995. Established: 1992 - Franchising Since: 1992 - No. of

Units: Franchised: 42 - Royalty: 5% of gross room revenue (grr), adv. 1.5% grr, reservation 2.3% grr - Total Inv: Equip. cost (reservation software) $1,800, franchise fee $350/room - Financing: No.

HOTEL DES GOUVERNEURS
Auberges des Gouverneurs Inc.
777 University St., Ste. 800, Montreal, PQ, H3C 3Z7. Contact: Dominique Labelle, Dir. of Sales - Tel: (514) 875-8822, Fax: (514) 875-6711. Full service hotel chain offering deluxe accommodation, restaurants, bars, meeting facilities and swimming pools, located throughout Quebec. Established: 1963 - Franchising Since: 1969 - No. of Units: Company Owned: 6 - Franchised: 4.

HOWARD JOHNSON HOTELS IN CANADA
Accommodex Franchise Management, Inc.
940 The East Mall, Etobicoke, ON, M9B 6J7. Contact: Bill Durnford, V.P., Fran. Dev. - Tel: (416) 620-4656, (800) 249-4656, Fax: (416) 620-1697. Hotels, motor lodges, restaurant. Established: 1971 - Franchising Since: 1971 - No. of Units: Franchised: 37 - Franchise Fee: $15,000 - Royalty: 5% gross room revenue - Total Inv: Varies - Financing: Varies.

RAMADA INNS, HOTELS, SUITES
Ramada Franchise Canada Ltd.
15 Toronto St., Ste. 400, Toronto, ON, M5C 2R1. Contact: Warren Adamson, Exec. V.P. - Tel: (416) 361-1010, Fax: (416) 361-9050. Franchisor of Ramada Inns, Hotels, Suites, Resorts, Ramada Ltd., Ramada Plaza for Canada. Established: 1992 - Franchising Since: 1992 - No. of Units: Franchised: 30 - Franchise Fee: $35,000 - Royalty: 3% mktg. assessment, 4% (calc. on room revenue) - Financing: No.

TRAVELODGE / THRIFTLODGE *
Royco Hotels and Resorts Ltd.
500, 5940 Macleod Tr. S., Calgary, AB, T2H 2G4. Contact: Leanne Bannon, Dir. of Fran. Dev. - Tel: (403) 259-9800, Fax: (403) 255-6981. Exclusive franchisor of Travelodge and Thriftlodge in Canada - in association with Forte Hotels, Inc. Established: 1992 - Franchising Since: 1992 - No. of Units: Franchised: 78 - Franchise Fee: $30,000 - Royalty: 8% - Financing: Assistance available.

VENTURE INNS INC.
925 Dixon Rd., Etobicoke, ON, M9W 1J8. Contact: Michael Jackson, Regional V.P. - Tel: (416) 674-2222, Fax: (416) 674-8641. To manage, market, license and grow a chain of hotels in the luxury budget sector of the hospitality business. Established: 1983 - Franchising Since: 1986 - No. of Units: Company Owned: 7 - Franchised: 2 - Franchise Fee: $100 per room, $20,000 minimum - Royalty: 1.5% gross guest room revenues, 2.4% adv.

VILLAGER LODGE *
940 The East Mall, Etobicoke, ON, M9B 6J7. Contact: Bill Durnford, V.P., Fran. Dev. - Tel: (800) 249-4656, (416) 620-4656, Fax: (416) 620-1897. Economy level motels focusing on extended stay market. Canadian franchise established Feb., 1995. Established: 1989 - Franchising Since: 1989 - No. of Units: Canadian: 0 - U.S.: 45 - Franchise Fee: $10,000 - Royalty: 5% of gross room revenue - Total Inv: Varies - Financing: Varies.

WANDLYN INNS
58 Prospect St., P.O. Box 430, Fredericton, NB, E3B 5P8. Contact: Gary Llewellyn, Pres. - Tel: (506) 452-0550. Mid-market motor inns, highway locations, 50-150 units per location, full facility. Established: 1955 - Franchising Since: 1970 - No. of Units: 18.

PET PRODUCTS AND SERVICES

DOGHOUSE KENNEL SUPPLY LTD.
2004 - 80th Ave., N.W., Edmonton, AB, T6P 1N2. Contact: Florence Becter, Pres. - Tel: (403) 440-1692. Pet supplies. Established: 1975 - No. of Units: Company Owned: 5 - Franchised: 2.

GLOBAL PET FOODS
Global Pet Food Sales Inc.
84 Doney Cres., Concord, ON, L4K 3A8. Contact: Morris Manna, Pres. - Tel: (905) 738-3663, Fax: (905) 738-9885. Specialty pet food stores specializing national, premium and our own private labels. Complete range of accessories. Established: 1973 - Franchising Since: 1986 - No. of Units: Company Owned: 6 - Franchised: 29 - Franchise Fee: $25,000 - Royalty: 6% - Total Inv: $90,000 - Financing: No.

PAULMAC'S PET FOOD, PAULMAC'S PLUS
Paulmac's Pet Food Inc.
2365 Whittington Dr., Peterborough, ON, K9J 6X4. Contact: Mike Everson, Fran. Dev. Mgr. - Tel: (705) 745-9405. One of Canada's largest distributors and retailers of quality pet food, pet supplies and pets. Established: 1983 - Franchising Since: 1987 - No. of Units: Company Owned: 13 - Franchised: 33 - Franchise Fee: $12,500 5 year term - Royalty: 3% - Total Inv: $85,000 to $160,000 - Financing: No.

PAWS & CLAWS PET NUTRITION CENTRES
Falwyn Investors Group Ltd.
6465 Millcreek Dr., Ste. 205, Mississauga, ON, L5N 5R3. Contact: George Kostopoulos, Pres. - Tel: (905) 567-4180, (800) 387-8335, Fax: (905) 567-5355. Paws & Claws is a retail chain of specialty pet food and accessory stores, dedicated to providing for the total nutritional needs of pets. We offer a complete line of pet foods and supplies for animal care and maintenance. We have achieved a balance with our inventory which ensures that Paws & Claws satisfy our consumers as well as their owners. Established: 1986 - Franchising Since: 1990 - No. of Units: Company Owned: 2 - Franchised: 4 - Franchise Fee: $25,000 - Royalty: 6% - Total Inv: $93,000 - $125,000 - Financing: Assistance through financial institutes.

PET HABITAT
International Bio Research Ltd.
6921 Heather St., Vancouver, BC, V6P 3P5. Contact: Ernest Ang, Pres. - Tel: (604) 266-2721; Fax (604) 266-5880. Upscale retail pet shop. Established: 1979 - Franchising Since 1981 - No. of Units: Company Owned: 3 - Franchised: 8 - Franchise Fee: $15,000 & up - Royalty: 5% on gross sales - Total Inv: $125,000 and up - Financing: Yes.

PET PARADISE
Pet Paradise Inc.
1111 Davis Dr., Unit 11A, 404 Shopping Centre, Newmarket, ON, L3Y 7Y1. Contact: Mr. Andrew Goodman, RFD Consultants, Ltd., Fran./Real Est. Mgr. - Tel: (905) 853-7387 or (905) 695-3942. Offers a full line of pets, pet foods and pet related accessories. Large outlets and diverse product lines distinguish us from the competition. Pet Paradise stores carry 7000 to 9000 items, depending on store size. The typical size of stores range from 1,500 sq. ft. to 3,000 sq. ft., depending upon enclosed or strip Shopping Centre locations. Established: 1959 - Franchising Since: 1991 - No. of Units: Company Owned: 27 - Franchised: 4 - Franchise Fee: $25,000 - Royalty: 5% on new stores, 6% on corporate stores changed to franchises - Total Inv: $135,000 - Financing: Yes.

PET VALU
Pet Valu Inc.
7300 Warden Ave., Ste. 400, Markham, ON, L3R 9Z6. Contact: David J. Wheat, V.P. Fran. Dev. - Tel: (905) 946-1200. Sale of pet foods and pet supplies. Established: 1976 - Franchising Since: 1987 - No. of Units: Company Owned: 29 - Franchised: 186 - Franchise Fee: $12,000 (6 years) - Royalty: 6%, 10% rent - Total Inv: $75,000+ - Financing: No.

PETLAND
Clifford Agencies Ltd.
164 Goulet Street, Winnipeg, MB, R2H 0R7. Contact: Robert Brissette, Pres. - Tel: (204) 989-7600, Fax: (204) 237-7756. Retail pet stores. Established: 1979 - Franchising Since: 1990 - No. of Units: Company Owned: 6 - Franchised: 11 - Franchise Fee: $25,000 - Royalty: 4.5% - Total Inv: $150,000 - $250,000 - Financing: Yes.

RUFFIN'S PET CENTER, INC.
P.O. Box 155, Dunnville, ON, N1A 2X5. Contact: Mark Reynolds, Pres. - Tel: (905) 774-7079, Fax: (905) 774-1096. Unique retailer of pets, pet supplies and discount pet foods. Established: 1981 - Franchising Since: 1987 - No. of Units: Franchised: 16 - Franchise Fee: $10,000 - Royalty: 4%, 1% adv. - Total Inv: $25,000-Inventory; $10,000-fix. & equip.; $5,000-leaseholds; $5,000-deposits/hydro/rent/etc. - Financing: Assistance in obtaining.

RYAN'S PET FOODS
Ryan's Pet Food Inc.
6315 Kestrel Rd., Mississauga, ON, L5T 1Z4. Contact: Brian Doran, Dir. of Dev. - Tel: (905) 795-8900, Fax: (905) 795-8903. Retail business selling pet foods and an extensive line of accessories such as leashes, collars, toys, kennels, litters, fish foods, various pet hygiene products and miscellaneous cages. Established: 1979 - Franchising Since: 1993 - No. of Units: Company Owned: 27 - Franchised: 14 - Franchise Fee: $25,000 - Royalty: Flat fee escalates with years in business - Total Inv: $95,000 incl. initial fee, opening inventory, buildout of retail facility and working cap. - Financing: Limited amount based upon inventory.

PHOTO, FRAMING AND ART

ATHENA
Athena International Canada Ltd.
1040 Stacey Crt., Mississauga, ON, L4W 2X8. Contact: David Bishop, V.P. Retail Opers. - Tel: (905) 629-1022. Retailer of prints (photographic & fine art), posters, greeting cards, framed prints and laminates, custom framing and lamination. No. of Units: Company Owned: 16 - Franchised: 34 - Franchise Fee: $25,000 - Royalty: 7% - Total Inv: leaseholds $50,000 - $80,000, $25,000 - $30,000 inventory - Financing: No.

CAMERA EXPERT
5000 Armand-Frappier, St. Hubert, PQ, J3Z 1G5. Contact: M. Lemyre, Dir. of Oper. - Tel: (514) 856-7750, Fax: (514) 656-4338. Photo finishing, cameras, accessories and services. Established: 1974 - Franchising Since: 1994 - No. of Units: Company Owned: 106 - Franchised: 2 - Franchise Fee: $20,000 - Royalty: 0, but 4% for nat'l. adv. - Total Inv: $40,000 - $50,000 cash, $180,000 - $195,000 to finance - Financing: yes.

FRAMING EXPERIENCE / FRAMING & ART CENTRE
Framing Experience Ltd.
1800 Appleby Line, Burlington, ON, L7L 6A1. Contact: John Williams, Dir. of Fran. - Tel: (905) 332-6116. Custom and do-it-yourself picture framing and art galleries serving residential and corporate clients. Established: 1974 - Franchising Since: 1974 - Number of Units: Franchised: 45 - Franchise Fee: $18,000 - Royalty: 5.5%, 1% - 2% adv. - Total Inv: $40,000 - $100,000: equip. $10,000 - $30,000, inven. $7,000 - $15,000, leaseholds $0 - $20,000, millwork $7,000 - $15,000, plus fran. fee - Financing: Bank and franchisor.

FUTURE STARS SPORTS PHOTOGRAPHY *
325 Barton St. E., Stoney Creek, ON, L8E 2K8. Contact: Joe Bruno, Pres. - Tel: (905) 664-9511 or (800) 461-6575. Photography of youth sports organizations from hockey to baseball to dance and karate. Offering such products as trading cards, photo pennants and digitally produced sport posters! Established: 1987 - Franchising Since: 1991 - No. of Units: Company Owned: 7 - Franchised: 10 - Franchise Fee: $2,500 - $5,000 - Royalty: N/A - Total Inv: $10,000 approx. ($6,000 equip.) - Financing: No.

JAPAN CAMERA 1 HOUR PHOTO
Japan Camera Centre Ltd.
205 Riviera Dr., Unit 1, Markham, ON, L3R 5J8. Contact: Kim Foster, Fran. Sales Mgr. - Tel: (416) 445-1481, (800) 268-7740. On-site photofinishing services, combined with retail camera and photographic merchandise. Established: 1959 - Franchising Since: 1981 - No. of Units: Company Owned: 33 - Franchised: 117 - Franchise Fee: $20,000 - Royalty: 7% - Total Inv: 40% of purchase price - Financing: Assistance to qualified applicant.

MAGNI FRAME CUSTOM FRAMING & ART STUDIOS
1800 Sheppard Ave. E., Unit L-167, Willowdale, ON, M2J 5A4. Contact: Leon Dagon, Mng. Dir. - Tel: (416) 730-9672. Custom framing, art conservation & restoration, memorabilia conservation & framing. Specializing in all custom framing of specialty items such as tapestries, needlework, silk screens. Established: 1988 - Franchising Since: 1989 - No. of Units: Company Owned: 1 - Franchised: 3 - Franchise Fee: $25,000 - Royalty: 5% + 2% - Total Inv: Depending on location - Financing: Yes.

NORTHERN IMAGES
Arctic Cooperative
1645 Inkster Blvd., Winnipeg, MB, R2X 2W7. Contact: Jim McMillan, Fran. Dir. - Tel: (204) 942-5501. Arts and crafts. Established: 1972 - No. of Units: 5.

ONE HOUR MOTO PHOTO & PORTRAIT STUDIO
Canadian Industrial Services Ltd.
1315 Lawrence Ave., E., #509, Don Mills, ON, M3A 3R3. Contact: Sam Hamam, Pres. - Tel: (416) 443-1900. On-site photo finishing and portrait studios. Sale of photo related merchandise, film, frames, albums & all photo related services. Established: 1987 - Franchising Since: 1987 - No. of Units: Company Owned: 2 - Franchised: 54 - Franchise Fee: $35,000 - Royalty: 6% - Total Inv: $225,000+ - Financing: Will assist with bank financing to approved applicants.

PICTURES
I.T.M. Holdings Inc.
560 Finley Ave., Ajax, ON, L1S 2E3. Contact: Terry Mulholland, Dir. Fran. - Tel: (905) 428-2538. A unique wall decor store featuring framed art, gallery prints, limited-edition prints and custom framing. Established: 1981 - Franchising Since: 1990 - No. of Units: Company Owned: 5 - Franchised: 30 - Royalty: 5% - Total Inv: $60,000 - $75,000 - Financing: Financial, realty, comp., full training.

PORTRAITS NOW INTERNATIONAL LTD.
135 Bank St., Ottawa, ON, K1P 5N7. Contact: Amin Amlani, Pres. - Tel: (613) 235-4164. One hour portrait studio: Established: 1986 - No. of Units: Company Owned: 1 - Franchised: 2 - Royalty: 10% of sales.

SOOTER STUDIOS LTD.
88 Sherbrook St., Winnipeg, MB, R3C 2B3. Contact: John Kresz, Pres. - Tel: (204) 775-8188. Portrait studios, photofinishing and photo related products. Established: 1960 - Franchising Since: 1966 - No. of Units: Company Owned: 142 - Franchised: 180 - Franchise Fee: $1.50 per population, Royalty: 5% + - Total Inv: $30,000 - $60,000 - Financing: Yes.

TADDICK CORP.
Box 3171, Station B, Fredericton, NB, E3A 5G9. Contact: Jack Lamey, Pres. - Tel: (506) 453-1476. Dealership (exclusive) - Art & craft supplies combined with framing shop. Excellent money maker & unique retail set-up. Training provided. Very competitive retail pricing. Established: 1991 - Franchising Since: 1991 - No. of Units: Company Owned: 2 - Franchised: 5 - Franchise Fee: none - Royalty: none - Total Inv: $35,000 - $40,000 (equip., stock, set-up) - Financing: No, but will do projections etc. for loan applications.

U FRAME IT, FLAIR U FRAME IT, FLAIR CUSTOM FRAMING CENTRES
Flair Franchise Systems, Inc.
2-1391 St. James St., Winnipeg, MB, R3H 0Z1. Contact: Garth Rogerson, Gen. Mgr. - Tel: (204) 987-9006, Fax: (204) 987-9010. Custom & do-it-yourself picture framing with retail sales of posters, prints & art work. Established: 1972 - Franchising Since: 1974 - No. of Units: Company Owned: 4 - Franchised: 27 - Franchise Fee: $15,000 - Royalty: 5% - Total Inv: $90,000 (equip., fix., leaseholds, inven.) - Financing: Assistance.

ZELLERS PORTRAIT STUDIO
St-A Photo Corp.
3 Picardie, Gatineau, PQ, J8T 1N3. Contact: J. St. Amour, V.P. - Tel: (819) 561-7113. Personalized family portraits as well as children, graduation etc. Complete photo studio service plus lamination, framing

and photographic restoration. Established: 1988 - Franchising Since: 1989 - No. of Units: Franchised: 32 - Franchise Fee: $25,000 - Royalty: 2.5 % Sales - Total Inv: $85,000 - Financing: Yes.

PRINTING AND COPYING SERVICES

HENRY ARMSTRONG'S INSTANT PRINTING
Armstrong Printing Ltd.
955 Portage Ave., Winnipeg, MB, R3G 0R2. Contact: Greg Armstrong, V.P. Mktg. - Tel: (204) 958-4230. Instant printing and copying. Established: 1968 - Franchising Since: 1982 - No. of Units: 14 - Franchise Fee: $12,500.

KWIK-KOPY PRINTING
Kwik-Kopy Printing Canada Corp.
15900 Yonge St., Aurora, ON, L4G 3G8. Contact: John Johnson, V.P. Sales - Tel: (800) 387-9725, Fax: (905) 727-1952. Full service quick printing operation featuring offset printing, photocopying, design, typesetting and fax service and much more. Fast, reliable and quality assurance. Established: 1979 - Franchising Since: 1979 - No. of Units: Franchised: 82 - Franchise Fee: $20,000 - Royalty: 6%, 3% adv. - Total Inv: $166,000 approx. - Financing: Portion of franchise fee.

LASERNETWORKS
Noreco Inc.
785 Pacific Rd., Unit #1, Oakville, ON, L6L 6M3. Contact: Chris Stoate, Pres. - Tel: (905) 847-5990. Recycling laser printer and photocopier toner cartridges. Established: 1987 - Franchising Since: 1990 - No. of Units: Company Owned: 2 - Franchised: 34 - Franchise Fee: $20,000 - Royalty: 7.5%, 5% adv. - Total Inv: $35,000 - $45,000 plus one year income.

LE PRINT EXPRESS
160 Nashdene Rd., Toronto, ON, M1V 4C4. Contact: Mike Shriqui, V.P., Fran. Dev. - Tel: (800) 263-1723. Prime retail locations in major shopping malls offering instant "while you wait" service for business cards, labels, stickers, signs, banners, posters, invitations, barcode labels, colour copies. Full printing and fax services. Established: 1990 - Franchising Since: 1993 - No. of Units: Franchised: 25 across Canada - Franchise Fee: Nil - Royalty: Flat rate - Total Inv: $54,500 + equipment package of $130,000 - Financing: Yes, for $130,000 equip. pkg.

MADE 'N-A-MINUTE PRINTERS
Made 'N-A-Minute Printers, Ltd.
2050 Rosser Ave., Burnaby, BC, V5C 5Y1. Contact: Paul McCrea, Sec/Treas. - Tel: (604) 291-7266. Instant print shops. Established: 1979 - Franchising Since: 1985 - No. of Units: Company Owned: 1 - Franchised: 8 - Royalty: 4% 1st $250,000, then 3% - Total Inv: $35,000 - Financing: No.

MINUTEMAN PRESS
6299 Airport Rd., Ste. 704, Mississauga, ON, L4V 1N3. Contact: Don Greeder, V.P. - Tel: (905) 677-6015, Fax: (905) 677-6061. Full service printing & graphics franchise. Established: 1973 - Franchising Since: 1975 - No. of Units: Franchised: 814 - Franchise Fee: US$44,500 - Royalty: 6% of gross - Total Inv: US$110,000 - Financing: Approx. 2/3 can be financed.

PRINTING NETWORK
418 Hanlan Rd., Woodbridge, ON, L4L 4Z1. Contact: Joe Osiel, Pres. - Tel: (905) 850-8151. Electronic black and colour printing and laser desktop publishing. Established: 1989 - Franchising Since: 1989 - No. of Units: Company Owned: 1 - Franchised: 14 - Franchise Fee: $20,000 - Royalty: 5%, first 6 months-royalty free - Total Inv: $115,000 set-up + franc. fee - Financing: Yes.

SCREEN PRINTING NORTH AMERICA INC.
Ste. 100, 627 Lyons Lane, Oakville, ON, L6J 5Z7. Contact: J.H. Miller, Fran. Dir. - Tel: (905) 338-9229, Fax: (905) 338-8874. A full service silk screening production operation with laser computerized new technology from T-shirts to posters, low costs, high profits. Established: 1988 - Franchising Since: 1988 - No. of Units: Franchised: 37 - Franchise Fee: $28,000 - Royalty: 6% - Total Inv: varies approx. $28,000 - Financing: No.

SIGARANT CANADA
165 Delayne Dr., Aurora, ON, L4G 5B7. Contact: George Lockhart, Pres. - Tel: (905) 727-5044. Home-based enterprises such as hot stamping, engraving, signs, pad printing and bumper stickers. Established: 1974 - Franchising Since: 1974 - No. of Units: Franchised: 1,200 - Total Inv: $1,000 to $10,000 - Financing: OAC.

SIR SPEEDY PRINTING
2800 Fourteenth Ave., #24, Markham, ON, L3R 0E4. Contact: Michael McKittrick, Pres. - Tel: (905) 475-9394. Full service printing and copy centres with desk top publishing facilities. Unique niche as "The Business Printer". Established: 1985 - Franchising Since: 1985 - No. of Units: Company Owned: 1 - Franchised: 6 - Franchise Fee: $20,000 - Royalty: 6%, 3% adv. - Total Inv: $110,000 - $170,000 plus working capital - Financing: N/A.

SPEEDY PRINTING CENTERS
13521 55 A Avenue, Surrey, BC, V3X 3B5. Contact: Joan Stewart, V.P. - Tel: (800) 726-9050, (604) 572-1352, Fax: (604) 572-9119. Full service printing, copying, business service centers. Full color printing, copying, desktop publishing, typesetting & faxing, local region support. Established: 1986 - Franchising Since: US 1987 - No. of Units: Franchised: US 403, Canada 33 - Franchise Fee: $19,500 - Royalty: 6% on receipts - Total Inv: $150,000 turnkey - Financing: Yes.

SURE GRAPHICS LTD.
101, 12465 - 82 Ave., Surrey, BC, V3W 3E8. Contact: Zul Mitha, Pres. - Tel: (604) 594-8334, Fax: (604) 594-8320. Copying, printing, desktop publishing and fax services. Established: 1986 - Franchising Since: 1988 - No. of Units: Company Owned: 2 - Franchised: 47 - Total Inv: $96,500 - Financing: Yes, up to 80%.

ZIPPY PRINT ENTERPRISES LTD.
408 N. Service Rd. E., Oakville, ON, L6H 5R2. Contact: Dir. of Fran. Dev. - Tel: (905) 849-7401. Full service quick print and fast copy outlets offering related services such as binding, desktop publishing, fax, etc. Established: 1979 - Franchising Since: 1981 - No. of Units: Franchised: 65 - Franchised Fee: $40,000 - Royalty: 5% declining scale from $500,000 annual sales - Total Inv: $150,000 - Financing: 50%.

REAL ESTATE SERVICES

AMERICA'S CHOICE® / CANADA'S CHOICE® *
Preferred Realty Concepts, Inc.
646 N. French Rd., Amherst, NY, 14228. Contact: Kathy Akey, Pres. - Tel: (800) 831-2493 (US/Canada), (716) 691-0596. Owner-assisted real estate marketing. No license needed. Full service owner assisted marketing - owner shows home. Full franchisee training and support. High profit per unit. Established: 1991 - Franchising Since: 1993 - No. of Units: Company Owned: 1 - Franchised: 17 units, 1 state - Franchise Fee: $5,000 option 1, $13,000 option 2, state/prov. options avail. - Royalty: 10%, 1% na'l. adv. - Financing: Yes, options 2 & state/prov. option.

CENTURY 21 REAL ESTATE CANADA, LTD.
700, 1199 West Pender St., Vancouver, BC, V6E 2R1. Contact: C. Brian Rushton, V.P. & Reg. Dir. - Tel: (604) 606-2100. World's largest real estate franchisor located in 11 countries with approximately 6,000 franchised outlets and 80,000 sales associates. Established: 1975 - Franchising Since: 1976 - No. of Units: Franchised: 300 - Franchise Fee: $20,000 metro areas; $10,000 rural areas - Royalty: Per person & transaction fees - metro areas; percentage royalty option - rural areas - Total Inv: $75,000 - $100,000 metro areas; $30,000 - $50,000 rural areas - Financing: Franchise fee only, under some circumstances.

GROUP TRANSACTION BROKERAGE SERVICES INC.
550 Sherbrooke W., #775, Montreal, PQ, H3A 1B9. Contact: J.L. Bernard, Gen. Mgr. - Tel: (514) 288-6777. Real Estate Services. Established: 1980 - Franchising Since: 1982 - No. of Units: Franchised: 55 - Franchise Fee: $16,500 - Royalty: $85/month/ agent service fee, $50/month/agent adv. fee - Total Inv: $50,000 - $100,000 - Financing: Yes.

HOMELIFE
Homelife Realty Services, Inc.
28 Drewry Ave., Willowdale, ON, M2M 1C8. Contact: Dennis Goldberg, Franc. Sales & Mktg. - Tel: (800) 668-0186. Real estate offices. Established: 1985 - Franchising Since: 1985 - No. of Units: Franchised: 285 - Franchise Fee: from $9,000 - Royalty: from $575. per month - Total Inv: from $10,000 - Financing: In some cases.

NATIONAL REAL ESTATE SERVICE
9th Fl., 1188 W. Georgia St., Vancouver, BC, V6E 4M9. Contact: Jack Gancher, Dir. of Marketing - Tel: (604) 685-3474. Residential and commercial brokerage franchise; international computerized listing service; advertising agency, printing division. Established: 1955 - Franchising Since: 1980 - No. of Units: Company Owned: 25 - Franchised: 360 - Franchise Fee: $5,000 - $22,500 - Royalty: Fixed fee.

PILLAR TO POST *
5805 Whittle Rd., Ste. 211, Mississauga, ON, L4Z 2J1. Contact: Gordon Williams, Dir. of Fran. - Tel: (800) 294-5591, Fax: (905) 568-8137. The Pillar To Post professional home inspection program was developed by specialists for persons wanting to be in a business for themselves that is home based and does not require a large capital investment, expensive inventories, accounts receivable or employees. Extensive technical, marketing and operations training provided at company's training facility. Strong ongoing corporate support. Established: 1994 - Franchising Since: 1994 - No. of Units Franchised: 41 - No. of Area Developers: 3 - Franchise Fee: $10,900 to $20,900 - Royalty: 7% - Total Inv: Unit Franchise: $16,000 to $30,000; Area Developer: $40,000 to $70,000 - Financing: OAC.

PRO JET
Pro Jet Courtier, Inc.
2800 Einstein #145, Quebec City, PQ, G1X 4N8. Contact: Julien Riou, Pres. - Tel: (418) 652-7887. Real estate. Established: 1987 - Franchising Since: 1990 - No. of Units: Company Owned: 1 - Franchised: 2 - Franchise Fee: $5,000 - Royalty: variable - Total Inv: $5,000 - $45,000 - Financing: Yes.

PROPERTY LINE HOME MARKETING CONSULTANTS *
P.O. Box 34008, Highland Hills P.O., Kitchener, ON, N2N 3G2. Contact: Blain Miller, Pres. - Tel: (519) 745-8461, Fax: (519) 744-7621. A real estate consulting service that provides homeowners a professional "for sale by owner" marketing system as an alternative to agent commissions. A real estate license is not required for this marketing service and our company provides all necessary training and ongoing support. Established: 1992 - Franchising Since: 1995 - No. of Units: Company Owned: 1 - Franchise Fee: $7,500 - $25,000 - Royalty: 7%, 3% adv. - Total Inv: $7,500 (home-based), $25,000+ (store-front lease) - Financing: Minimum start-up cost and balance of franchise fee paid in installments.

REALTY WORLD CANADA
Real Estate World Services (1978) Ltd.
#430, 6450 Roberts St., Burnaby, BC, V5G 4E1. Contact: Harold L. Waddell, Pres. - Tel: (604) 294-2321. Full service real estate franchisor. Established: 1974 Canada, 1975 US - No. of Units: 200 Canada, 1,300 U.S. - Franchise Fee: $2,900 - $15,900 - Royalty: 6% gross - Financing: Improvements, furnishings and operating credit line available.

SUTTON GROUP *
Canwest Marketing Ltd.
1700 Varsity Estates Dr. N.W., Calgary, AB, T3B 2W9. Contact: Chris Bolt, Pres. - Tel: (403) 286-5863. 100% commission, fee for service real estate brokerage. Average franchise has 60 realtors. Established: 1989 - Franchising Since: 1989 - No. of Units: Company Owned: 1 - Franchised: 24 - Franchise Fee: $20,000 - Royalty: $60 per month per salesperson - Total Inv: $120,000 - $150,000 - Financing: No.

TRANS-ACTION REAL ESTATE SERVICES
Group Trans-Action Brokerage Services, Inc.
550 Sherbrooke, West, Ste. 775, Montreal, PQ, H3A 1B9. Contact: J. L. Bernard, Gen. Mgr. - Tel: (514) 288-6777. Complete real estate services. Established: 1979 - Franchising Since: 1982 - No. of Units: Franchised: 54 - Franchise Fee: $8,000 to $16,500 - Royalty: $135 per agent/mnth. - Total Inv: $8,000 - $50,000 - Financing: Yes.

WILDWOOD CAPITAL INC.
5218 Yonge St., Willowdale, ON, M2N 5P6. Contact: Ehud Estreicher, Pres. - Tel: (416) 223-8111, (800) 461-8111, Fax: (416) 223-4645. Low overheads, excellent income. Corporate training and support. Established: 1975 - Correspondents Since: 1992 - No. of Units: Company Owned: 1 - Correspondents: 3 - Correspondents Fee: $9,995 - Royalty: % of income (commission) - Financing: No.

RENTAL SERVICES

INN TENTS
Inn Tents Canada Inc.
466 Elgin St., P.O. Box 2142, Brantford, ON, N3T 5Y6. Contact: Rick St. Amand, Co-Owner - Tel: (519) 752-2000. Businesses are set up as home base operations. Franchises receive an inventory of party canopies to be rented out in the market that the franchise has bought the rights to. Established: 1993 - Franchising Since: 1993 - No. of Units: Company Owned: 1 - Franchise Fee: $10,000 - Royalty: Per year is based on the amount of rental cost of each canopy in inventory - Total Inv: $25,000 - Financing: Possible.

JOE LOUE TOUT RENT ALL, INC.
28 Vanier, Chateauguay, PQ, J6J 3W8. Contact: J.M. Bissonnette, P.D.G. - Tel: (514) 692-6268. Renting of tools & equipment and recreational vehicles. Established: 1979 - Franchising Since: 1982 - No. of Units: Franchised: 65 - Franchise Fee: starting at $17,500 - Royalty: 4%, 3% publicity - Total Inv: From $40,000 to $250,000 - Financing: Yes.

JOE RENT ALL, INC.
28 Vanier, Chateauguay, PQ, J6J 3W8. Contact: J.M. Bissonnette, Pres.. Tools and equipment, party goods, recreational vehicles and boats, etc. Established: 1982 - Franchising Since: 1982 - No. of Units: Franchised: 66, 1 master franchise in Winnipeg, MB - Franchise Fee: $17,500 - Royalty: 4% + 3% publicity - Financing: Yes.

RETAIL

A BUCK OR TWO STORES LTD.
350 Creditstone Rd., Ste. 201, Concord, ON, L4K 3Z2. Contact: Lorriane Waldman, Fran. Dir. - Tel: (905) 738-3180. 2,000 or 3,000 sq. ft. locations in enclosed shopping malls coast to coast selling general merchandise ranging from $1 to $5 with a bright and vibrant dollar store traffic oriented concept. Established: 1986 - Franchising Since: 1988 - No. of Units: Company Owned: 3 - Franchised: 79 - Franchise Fee: $50,000 - Royalty: 6%, 1% adv. - Total Inv: Turn-key complete $150,000 - Financing: Yes in-house.

AUSTRALIAN CLOTHING & GIFT IMPORTS
374 Brookdale Ave., Toronto, ON, M5M 1R2. Contact: John Keating, Owner - Tel: (416) 783-5780. Australian outlet for a wide range of Down Under products. Established: 1967 - Franchising Since: 1989 - No. of Units: Company Owned: 1 - Franchise Fee: $10,000 - Total Inv: approx. $20,000 - $30,000 - Financing: No.

BALLOON EXPRESS COMPANY
Balloon Express Co., Inc.
312 Lakeshore Rd. W., Mississauga, ON, L5H 1G8. Contact: John - Tel: (905) 271-8606. Retail outlets specializing in party goods, balloons and balloon deliveries, children's parties and balloon decorating. Established: 1979 - Franchising Since: 1983 - Franchise Fee: $10,000 - Total Inv: $30,000 - $90,000 - Royalty: 5% - Financing: Royal Bank.

BESTSELLERS
Hazelton Lanes, 55 Avenue Rd., Ste. 2700, Toronto, ON, M5R 3L2. Contact: Brian Melzack, CEO - Tel: (416) 927-7810, (800) 361-3181, Fax: (416) 927-1789. North America's first multi-media home entertainment retail operation selling the best of books, music and movie videos. Established: 1990 - Franchising Since: 1990 - No. of Units: Company Owned: 6 - Franchised: 31 - Franchise Fee: $25,000 - Royalty: 5% - Total Inv: $100,000 to $120,000 - Financing: Relationship with a Chartered Bank.

BIRDERS NATURE STORE
265 Eglinton Ave. W., Toronto, ON, M4R 1B1. Contact: William Schyuem, Pres. - Tel: (416) 481-2431. Wild bird centered nature gift stores, retailing bird feeders, bird houses, bird baths, bird seed, books, binoculars, garden accessories & gifts. Established: 1991 - Franchising Since: 1991 - No. of Units: Company Owned: 1 - Franchised: 8 - Franchise Fee: $15,000 - Royalty: 3%, 2% adv. - Total Inv: $60,000 to $120,000 - Financing: Will assist with obtaining.

BIZOU
Bizou International Inc.
615 Cameron, Ste-Marie, Beauce, PQ, G6E 1B1. Contact: Roger Pomerleau, Pres. - Tel: (418) 387-8481. Sales at retail of costume jewellery, fashion jewellery and accessories. Established: 1988 - Franchising Since: 1989 - No. of Units: Company Owned: 47 - Franchised: 5 - Franchise Fee: $10,000 - Total Inv: $75,000 - Financing: No.

BOOK BANK LTD.
5 Roberta Cres., Nepean, ON, K2J 1G5. Contact: Ted MacMillan, Pres. - Tel: (613) 825-4746, Fax: (613) 825-9611. Retail bookstores. Established: 1977 - Franchising Since: 1986 - No. of Units: Franchised: 7, now licensing territories! - Initial territorial licence fee: $10,000 max. $25,000 - Set-up cost approx: $20,000 - $30,000 - Royalty: flat monthly fee - Total Inv: $46,500 (avg).

BUCK-A-ROO DOLLAR STORES
206 Sherwood Ct., Oshawa, ON, L1G 6R8. Contact: Mr. L. DuPuis, Pres. - Tel: (905) 436-1330. Dollar stores that sell 8 categories of product from 50¢ to $3.00. Established: 1992 - Franchising Since: 1992 - No. of Units: Franchised: 9 - Franchise Fee: $15,000 - Royalty: 5% of gross sales - Total Inv: $50,000 for 1,000 sq. ft. store (incl. stock, shelving, fee) - Financing: None, $15,000 new venture loan.

CALENDAR CLUB *
Paris Southern Lights
266 Mile Hill Rd., Paris, ON, N3L 3T5. Contact: John Edgar - Tel: (519) 442-2294, Fax: (519) 442-4602. Seasonal retailing of calendars. Established: 1989 - Franchising Since: 1992 - No. of Units: Company Owned: 30 - Security Deposit: $3,500 - Total Inv: $3,500.

CANADIAN TIRE CORP. LTD.
P.O. Box 770, Station K, 2180 Yonge St., Toronto, ON, M4P 2V8. Contact: Marilyn Rubin, Dealer Section Mgr. - Tel: (416) 480-3365. Comprehensive customer service driven retail operation: automotive, auto service, seasonal, hardware and houseware. Established: 1922 - Franchising Since: 1927 - No. of Units: Franchised: 425+ - Financing: Yes.

CRAFT TREE CENTRES *
461 N. Service Rd. W., Oakville, ON, L5M 2V5. Contact: Bill Fitzpatrick, Gen. Mgr. - Tel: (905) 825-1249. Craft Tree Centres operates a chain of full line craft and art supply stores. Picture framing classes and children craft parties gives Craft Tree a viable & exciting retail environment. Established: 1990 - Franchising Since: 1992 - No. of Units: Company Owned: 5 - Franchised: 2 - Franchise Fee: $20,000 - Royalty: 5%, 2% adv. - Total Inv: $106,000: store equip. $22,000, inven. $45,000, decorating & working. cap. $19,000, fran. fee $20,000 - Financing: Yes.

DOLLAR BILL'S
Dollar Bill's Ltd.
1290 Central Pkwy. W., Ste. 707, Mississauga, ON, L5C 4R3. Contact: Andy Stevenson, Dir., Fran. Sales - Tel: (905) 896-7117. Retail store offering a wide and ever changing variety of value priced merchandise up to $5.00 in the following retail departments or categories: housewares, kitchenwares, giftwares, health & beauty, toys, party goods, stationery, pre-packaged foods and confectionary. Established: 1986 - Franchising Since: 1992 - No. of Units: Company Owned: 9 - Franchised: 18 - Franchise Fee: $25,000 - Royalty: 5% of gross sales payable weekly - Total Inv: $160,000 - $200,000 incl. inventory - Financing: $50,000 - $70,000 (inventory portion of total inv.).

DOLLAR DEPOT
A.W. Associates Ltd.
55 Seaforth Rd., Kingston, ON, K7M 1E1. Contact: W.H. Punt, Fran. Dev. - Tel: (613) 542-1242 or Fax/Tel: (613) 549-4475. Retail stores selling everything for one dollar or less. Intending to expand to $1.00, $2.00 and $3.00 stores. Established: 1975 - Franchising Since: 1991 - No. of Units: Company Owned: 2 - Franchised: 3 - Franchise Fee: $15,000 - $25,000 - Royalty: 4% per month on Net Sales - Total Inv: $20,000 leaseholds, $30,000 inventory - Financing: Via Royal Bank of Canada and Toronto Dominion Bank.

DUFFERIN GAME ROOM STORE
Dufferin Game Room Store Ltd.
3770 Nashua Dr., Mississauga, ON, L4V 1M6. Contact: Catherine Selinger, Pres. - Tel: (905) 677-7665, Fax: (905) 677-5322. A unique Family Fun concept specializing in Game Room products for the home. Canadian owned and operated, for 28 yrs, the Dufferin Group of Companies manufactures a complete line of billiard tables and accessories as well as other recreation products such as bars and game tables. Franchising opportunities available across Canada. Owner operators preferred. Established: 1986 - Franchising Since: 1986 - No. of Units: Company Owned: 22 - Franchised: 26 - Franchise Fee: $20,000 - Royalty: 5%, 2% adv. - Total Inv: $200,000z - Financing: None.

DYNAMIC DAVE'S BARGAIN HOUSE
Dolphin Consulting Group
6150 Starfield Cres., Mississauga, ON, L5N 1X1. Contact: Carl Maynard, Fran. Dir. - Tel: (905) 542-3313. Variety merchandise, priced at $1, $2, $3, $5, $10. Discount pricing, health & beauty products, clothing, gifts, toys, housewares, hardware, confectionary. Established: 1992 - Franchising Since: 1993 - No. of Units: Franchised: 6 - Franchise Fee: $20,000 - Royalty: 5% - Total Inv: $150,000 - Financing: Yes.

ENGLISH BUTLER *
Brunswick Square, 39 King St., Saint John, NB, E2L 4W3. Contact: Bill Randell - Tel: (506) 652-4110, Fax: (506) 634-6980. Retail sale of giftware and home decor catering to traditional tastes. Established: 1984 - Franchising Since: 1994 - No. of Units: Company Owned: 5 - Franchised: 5 - Franchise Fee: $25,000 - Royalty: 6%, Adv. .5% - Total Inv: $220,000, Min. of $75,000 cash.

FLAG SHOP, THE
Vancouver Flag Shop, Inc., The
1755 W. 4th Ave., Vancouver, BC, V6J 1M2. Contact: Doreen Braverman, Fran. Dir. - Tel: (604) 736-8161, Fax: (604) 736-6439. Flags, banners, flagpoles, pins, crests, books. Custom sewing of flags, banners and windsocks done on the premises. Established: 1975 - Franchising Since: 1988 - No. of Units: Company Owned: 1 - Franchised: 5 - Franchise Fee: $15,000 (US) - Royalty: purchasing surcharge - Financing: No.

THE FLAG SHOP

FLAGS • BANNERS • FABRIC DESIGN • FLAG POLES

DOREEN BRAVERMAN
President

1755 W. 4TH AVENUE
VANCOUVER, BC V6J 1M2

TEL: (604) 736-8161
FAX: (604) 736-6439

FUTON FACTORY OUTLET
64 Grand Ave. S., Cambridge, ON, N1S 2L8. Contact: John McCutcheon, Pres. - Tel: (519) 622-5030. Manufacturer and retailer of Futon mattresses and related bedding items. Established: 1983 - Franchising Since: 1984 - No. of Units: 10 - Franchise Fee: $15,000 - Total Inv: $25,000 - Financing: Yes.

GIANT TIGER STORES LTD.
98 George St., Ottawa, ON, K1N 5W2. Contact: Svend Pedersen, V.P. Admin. - Tel: (613) 241-1201. Family discount stores: clothing, shoes, health & beauty aids, toys, novelties. Established: 1961 - Franchising Since: 1965 - No. of Units: Company Owned: 1 - Franchised: 73.

GREAT CANADIAN DOLLAR STORE *
#201 - 321 St. Julian St., Duncan, BC, V9L 3S5. Contact: Bud Walker - Tel: (604) 748-1090. We offer a retailer the opportunity to sell selected housewares, toys, health and beauty aids, novelties, tools, leisure products at $1.00 to $2.00. Established: 1992 - Franchising Since: 1992 - No. of Units: Franchised: 12 - Franchise Fee: $10,000 - Royalty: 2% of gross sales - Total Inv: $30,000 - $60,000 depending on size of store: $10,000 fran. fee, $20,000 - $30,000 stock, $5,000 - $10,000 leasehold etc. - Financing: N/A.

GREAT WILDERNESS COMPANY *
Great Wilderness Co., Inc.
113 Edgewater Dr., Stoney Creek, ON, L8E 4Z2. Contact: J. Miller & Assoc., Agents - Tel: (905) 643-0628, Fax: (905) 643-0804, or J. Miller & Assoc. Tel: (905) 338-9229. Retail giftware with a nature/wildlife theme. Established: 1989 - Franchising Since: 1991 - No. of Units: Company Owned: 1 - Franchised: 18 - Franchise Fee: $30,000 - Royalty: 5% - Total Inv: $200,000 inven., $125,000 L.H. - Financing: B.I.L.

GROWER DIRECT FRESH CUT FLOWERS INC.
#301, 4220-98 Street, Edmonton, AB, T6E 6A1. Contact: John Paton, V.P. of Oper. - Tel: (403) 436-7774. Grower Direct Fresh Cut Flowers Inc. is the supplier of high quality fresh cut flowers to its 133 retail franchise outlets across Canada. Established: 1990 - Franchising Since: 1991 - No. of Units: Franchised: 133 - Franchise Fee: $20,000 - Royalty: $240 per week/$15 per week nat'l. adv. - Total Inv: $55,000 ($20,000 fran. fee, $35,000 start-up) - Financing: No.

HERBRAND TOOLS & EQUIPMENT
Herbrand Tools Corporation
340 Dufferin St., Toronto, ON, M6K 1Z9. Contact: E.D. Brooks, Mktg. Mgr. - Tel: (416) 534-7943, Fax: (416) 537-1642. Hand tools, pneumatic tools, hydraulic equip., tool boxes, measuirng tools, diagnostic equip., and specialized tools for automotive and industrial uses. Established: 1930 - Franchising Since: 1950 - No. of Units Franchised: 100 - Total Inv: $28,000 - Financing: $14,000.

HOLLYWOOD STORES, THE
Hollywood Stores of Movies & Memorabilia, The
100 City Centre Dr., Mississauga, ON, L5B 2C9. Contact: Peter Bordignon, Pres. - Tel: (416) 376-6289. Unique concept, movie studio store carrying video movies for sale, cartoon clothing & accessories. We buy direct from all major movie studios for maximum industry g.p. Established: 1993 - Franchising Since: 1994 - No. of Units: Company Owned: 2 - Franchised: 2 - Franchise Fee: $15,000 - Royalty: 5% - Total Inv: $150,000 - $250,000 turn-key - Financing: No.

HOME HARDWARE, HOME BUILDING CENTRE, HOME HARDWARE BUILDING CENTRE, HOME FURNITURE
Home Hardware Stores, Limited
34 Henry St., St. Jacobs, ON, N0B 2N0. Contact: Terry Davis, V.P. Mktg. - Tel: (519) 664-4913, Fax: (519) 664-2865. Canada's largest chain of independently owned hardware, home improvement and furniture retailers. Established: 1964 - Franchising Since: 1964 - No. of Units: Company Owned: 1 - Franchised: 936 - Franchise Fee: Investment in share/ownership - Royalty: Addition to purchases - Total Inv: Minimum $100,000 - Financing: Independantly arranged.

HOUSE OF KNIVES, THE EDGE
House of Knives Ltd.
61 McBrine Place, P.O. Box 9024, Kitchener, ON, N2G 4X2. Contact: Larry Margetts, Leasing Mgr. - Tel: (519) 748-2211. Established: 1979 - No. of Units: Company Owned: 28 - Franchised: 14 - Royalty: $100,000.

IMPRESSIONS *
First Impressions Treasures Inc.
331 Main St., P.O. Box 2080, Picton, ON, K0K 2T0. Contact: Lane Befus, Pres. - Tel: (613) 476-1093, Fax: (613) 476-1100. After more than a decade of selling 'faxu' rings, we have distilled our experience into a unique system. No more guessing as to which styles will sell. From literally hundreds of styles, we have chose a dozen all time classic best sellers. We know what styles sell and in which sizes. Established: 1985 - Franchising Since: 1995 - No. of Units: Company Owned: 7 - Franchise Fee: $15,000 - Royalty: 6% - Total Inv: $36,800 which includes fran. fee - Financing: We assist obtaining financing.

....IT STORE
1111 Flint Road, Unit 36, Downsview, ON, M3J 3C7. Contact: Jack Green, CEO - Tel: (416) 665-3471, Fax: (416) 665-8839. Gifts from the perfectly practical to the absolutely ridiculous.™ Established: 1981 - Franchising Since: 1981 - No. of Units: Company Owned: 19 - Franchised: 31 - Franchise Fee: $25,000 - Royalty: 6%, 2% adv. - Total Inv: $155,000+: $70,000 leaseholds, $60,000 inventory, $25,000 fran. fee - Financing: No.

R.E.M. INC.
Retail Entertainment Merchandising

1111 Flint Road, Unit #36
Downsview, Ontario. M3J 3C7
Tel: 416 IT STORE   Fax: 416.665.8839

OVER 50 STORES ACROSS CANADA

L. A. MUSIC
60 Green Lane, Unit 1, Thornhill, ON, L3T 7P5. Contact: Lon Appleby, Pres. - Tel: (905) 889-5096. Records and tapes. Established: 1973 - No. of Units: 2.

LE NATURIST JEAN-MARC BRUNET
1351-H rue Ampere, Boucherville, PQ, J4B 5Z5. Contact: Denis Goyette, V.P. - Tel: (514) 655-7826 or (800) 361-6521. Natural products. Established: 1968 - Franchising Since: 1970 - No. of Units: Company Owned: 38 - Franchised: 35 - Approx. Inv: $5,000 - $25,000 - Royalty: 1-2%.

MARCHANDS UNIS, INC.
915 Paradis St., Quebec City, PQ, G1N 4E3. Contact: Jean-Pierre Drewitt, V.P. - Tel: (418) 687-3050. Hardware, sporting goods, paint and wallpaper.

MIGHTY DOLLAR *
528 Hood Rd., Markham, ON, L3R 3K9. Contact: John MacKenzie, Pres. - Tel: (905) 513-8191, Fax: (905) 513-6387. Dollar store with 20% of stock over a dollar. Established: 1992 - Franchising Since: 1992 - No. of Units: Company Owned: 22 - Franchised: 9 - Franchise Fee: $25,000 - Royalty: 5% - Total Inv: $100,000+ - Financing: Yes.

MUSIC CITY
National Record Distributors
30 Plymouth St., Winnipeg, MB, R2X 2V7. Contact: Richard Drysdale, Pres. - Tel: (204) 633-1412. Pre-recorded music and related accessories. Established: 1947 - No. of Units: Company Owned: 12 - Franchised: 8 - Franchise Fee: $5,000 - Royalty: 5% - Total Inv: $50,000 - $150,000 - Financing: No.

PAPER FACTORY, THE
Paper Factory, Inc., The
811 Victoria St. N., Kitchener, ON, N2B 3C3. Contact: J. White, G.M. - Tel: (519) 742-7340. Retail party shop. Established: 1984 - Franchising Since: 1986 - No. of Units: Company Owned: 4 - Franchised: 17 - Franchise Fee: $25,000 - Royalty: 4% - Total Inv: $100,000 - Financing: Yes.

PERSONALIZED PICTURES INC.
#206, 2916 19 St. N.E., Calgary, AB, T2E 6Y9. Contact: Ron Marcolin, Mgr. - Tel: (403) 250-9322, Fax: (403) 250-9448. New dealerships available retailing unique cartoon pictures which are personalized, matted and framed! Established: 1994 - Franchising Since: 1994 - No. of Units: 65 Canada - Franchise Fee: $1,995 - Total Inv: $2,495 CDN - Financing: Yes.

PHARM-ESCOMPTES JEAN COUTU
Services Farmico, Inc.
530 Beriault St., Longueuil, PQ, J4G 1S8. Contact: Jacques Masse, V.P. Exec. - Tel: (514) 646-9760. Retail pharmaceutical. Established: 1969 - Franchising Since: 1974 - No. of Units: 127 - Approx. Inv: $750,000/ store stock, fixtures - Royalty: 5% 1st $2 million and 4% thereafter.

POT POURRI COFFEE & TEA *
4699 Keele St. #1, Downsview, ON, M3J 2N8. Contact: M. Mayrson, VP-Leasing - Tel: (416) 661-9916. Combination store selling complete line of kitchenware combined with cozy gourmet coffee & tea cafe. Established: 1995 - Franchising Since: 1995 - No. of Units: Franchised: 2 - Franchise Fee: $25,000 - Royalty: 6% - Total Inv: Leaseholds $25,000 - $60,000, Inven. $40,000 - Financing: Business plan & cash flow prepared for banking.

PRO HARDWARE
D.H. Howden & Co. Ltd.
3232 White Oak Rd., London, ON, N6A 4G8. Contact: Ron MacDonnell, Fran. Mktg. Mgr. - Tel: (519) 686-2200. Retail hardware. Established: 1901 - Franchising Since: 1964 - No. of Units: Company Owned: 1 - Franchised: 358 - Total Inv: $150,000 inven., $50,000 fixtures & equip. - Financing: Will assist in obtaining.

RECORDS ON WHEELS / WHEELS ENTERTAINMENT / ROW
ROW Entertainment
255 Shields Court, Markham, ON, L3R 8V2. Contact: Rosie Knapp, Fran. Dir. - Tel: (905) 475-3550. Retail sales of cassettes, compact discs, video, T-shirts & related accessories. Established: 1974 - Franchising Since: 1975 - No. of Units: Company Owned: 19 - Franchised: 14 - Franchise Fee: $7,500 - Royalty: None - Total Inv: Min. $75,000 - Financing: None.

RO-NA L'ENTREPOT, RO-NA HOME CENTRE, RO-NA HARDWARE
Le Groupe Ro-Na Dismat, Inc.
1250, Nobel, Boucherville, PQ, J4B 5K1. Contact: Michel Mérineau, Dev. Dir. - Tel: (514) 599-5124, Fax: (514) 599-5157. Retail chain, hardware, buying and selling group specialized in hardware, L.B.M. horticultural prod. Established: 1939 - No. of Units: Franchised: 450 - Franchise Fee: $6,000 for share + $90,000 investment - Royalty: No, advertising program - Total Inv: $96,000 (company shares) - Financing: Agreements with banks.

ROCKING HORSE, THE
843 2nd Ave., E., Owen Sound, ON, N4K 2H2. Contact: Dianne Mattice, Franc. Dir. - Tel: (519) 371-9921. Trend setting toy boutique, exclusive products for tots and adults. Established: 1975 - Franchising Since: 1991 - No. of Units: Company Owned: 2.

SHAKRAS HOUSEWARES
Shakras Housewares Inc.
3814 Bloor St. W., Etobicoke, ON, M9B 6C2. Contact: Franchise Director - Tel: (416) 231-0707. Sales and service of small household appliances. Established: 1977 - No. of Units: Company Owned: 2 - Franchised: 1 - Franchise Fee: $25,000 - Royalty: 6%, 3% adv. - Total Inv: $110,000 - $135,000.

SHEFIELD & SONS
Shefield & Sons Tobacconists Inc.
P.O. Box 490, 2265 W. Railway St., Abbotsford, BC, V2S 5V5. Contact: T. Hartford, Dir. of Fran. - Tel: (604) 859-1014, Fax: (604) 859-1711. Retail sale of tobacco and related products, lottery, reading material, confectionery and unique giftware and souvenirs. Established: 1976 - Franchising Since: 1976 - No. of Units: Company Owned: 1 - Franchised: 60 - Franchise Fee: $10,000 - Royalty: 2% - Total Inv: $69,000 - $150,000 - Financing: No.

SHOPPERS DRUG MART
225 Yorkland Blvd., Willowdale, ON, M2J 4Y7. Contact: Marvin Goldberg - Tel: (416) 493-1220. Retail pharmacies. Shoppers Drug Mart associate program open and available only to licensed pharmacists. Established: 1968 - Franchising Since: 1968 - No. of Units: approx. 675.

SIMPLY CHARMING / RODAN JEWELLERS
Rodan Enterprises (1994) Ltd.
4259 Canada Way, Ste. 246, Burnaby, BC, V5G 1H1. Contact: Merl Rice, Gen. Mgr. - Tel: (604) 438-1625, Fax: (604) 438-1635. Fine jewellery stores on key corner locations in major regional shopping centres - British Columbia, Canada only. Established: 1976 - Franchising Since: 1982 - No. of Units: Franchised: 13 - Franchise Fee: $50,000 Simply Charming, $75,000 Rodan Jewellers - Royalty: 5% - Total Inv; $250,000 Simply Charming, $500,000 Rodan - Financing: Yes.

SOAPBERRY SHOP
50 Galaxy Blvd. #12, Toronto, ON, M9W 4Y5. Contact: Susan Whyte, Dir. of Fran. - Tel: (416) 674-0248, Fax: (416) 674-0249. Retailer of high quality herbal environment friendly skin, hair and bath preparations for men, women and children. Established: 1983 - Franchising Since: 1988 - No. of Units: Company Owned: 6 - Franchised: 4 - Franchise Fee: $25,000 - Royalty: None - Total Inv: Fran. fee $25,000, Leaseholds $60,000 to $100,000, Inven. $60,000 - Financing: No.

SPECIAL CELEBRATIONS *
Special Celebrations Inc.
210 Centrum Blvd., Unit 102, Orleans, ON, K1E 3V7. Contact: C. Goneau, Pres. & Dir. of Dev. - Tel: (613) 824-5633, Fax: (613) 824-6305. Party specialty stores, also retailing accessories & party services, limo rental service, hot air balloon ride bookings, clown rentals, etc. Established: 1995 - Franchising Since: 1995 - No. of Units: Franchised: 1 - Franchise Fee: $25,000 - Royalty: 5% of net sales + 5% of service commissions - Total Inv: Leaseholds $15,000 - $25,000, Inven., $30,000 - Financing: Yes.

SPORTS TRADERS
Traders International
#1400 - 400 Burrard, Vancouver, BC, V6C 3G2. Contact: Ted Van Samang, V.P. Fran. Dev. - Tel: 1-800-643-1764. Used & new discount sports equipment stores. Established: 1983 - Franchising Since: 1987 - No. of Units: Company Owned: 1 - Franchised: 24 - Franchise Fee: $25,000 - Royalty: 4% - Total Inv: $120,000 - $140,000, cash required $80,000 - Financing: Yes.

SUMMUM CREATIVE JEWELLERY
Bijouteries L'Erudit Inc.
1550 Ampere #406, Boucherville, PQ, J4B 7L4. Contact: Jérôme Côté, Dir. - Tel: (514) 641-9898, Fax: (514) 641-3989. Jewelleries outlets specialized in silver jewels and semi-precious stones. Established: 1991 - Franchising Since: 1992 - No. of Units: Company Owned: 2 - Franchised: 3 - Franchise Fee: $15,000 - $25,000 - Royalty: 5% + 3% publicity - Total Inv: $50,000 inventory, $25,000 kiosk, fran. fee, $5,000 turn key operation - Financing: Yes.

TANDY LEATHER CO.
Tandy Crafts Ltd.
P.O. Box 13000, 120 Brock St., Barrie, ON, L4M 4W4. Contact: Doug Black, Pres. - Tel: (705) 728-2481. Do-It-Yourself leathercrafts. Retail of leather skins and all hardware for same. Can be done from home base or store if already an established business. Established: 1919 - Franchising Since: 1975 - No. of Units: Company Owned: 9 - Franchised: 110 - Franchise Fee: $1,000 - Total Inv: $3,500 - $10,000 - Financing: No.

TOY TRADERS
Traders International
#1400 - 400 Burrard, Vancouver, BC, V6C 3G2. Contact: Ted Van Samang, V.P. Fran. Dev. - Tel: 1-800-643-1764. Used & new toys and other affordable kids stuff. Established: 1993 - Franchising Since: 1993 - No. of Units: Company Owned: 1 - Franchised: 2 - Franchise Fee: $25,000 - Royalty: 4% - Total Inv: $60,000 - $80,000, cash required $40,000 - Financing: Yes.

TOYS FOR TIKES
Litl' Tots Franchising Inc.
546 Memorial Dr., Fenwick, ON, L0S 1C0. Contact: Brock Muir, Pres. - Tel: (905) 688-2665. Retail toy stores. Complete training & support. Established: 1992 - Franchising Since: 1992 - No. of Units: Company Owned: 1 - Franchised: 3 - Franchise Fee: $10,000 - Royalty: 12% - Total Inv: $23,000: fran. fee + work. cap. & equip. - Financing: Assistance.

TRIDENT KEY MART
Trident Management Ltd.
I-650 Clyde Ave., W, Vancouver, BC, V7T 1E2. Contact: Herbert W. Beaverstone, Pres. - Tel: (604) 926-0725. Key cutting, engraving, locksmithing, knife and scissor sharpening. Sales of gift items, trophies, key fobs, mugs, security items, personalized gifts. Established: 1978 - Franchising Since: 1978 - No. of Units: 33 - Approx. Inv: $65,000 - $95,000 - Royalty: management fee - Financing: Yes.

TRINKETS FINE JEWELLERY
150 Spinnaker Way, Unit 12, Concord, ON, L4K 1N1. Contact: Sara Benaim, Fran. Admin. - Tel: (905) 660-3369, Fax: (905) 660-3295. Affordable fine 10K, 14K, 18K jewellery for all ages. "Where your investment is as good as gold." Established: 1980 - Franchising Since: 1989 - No. of Units: Company Owned: 6 - Franchised: 2 - Franchise Fee: $25,000 - Royalty: 6%, 2% adv - Total Inv: $25,000 fran. fee, $65,000 min. cash, $110,000 total - Ongoing support and assistance. 3 week training (in-store), including 1 week with Canadian Jewellers Association.

TRUE VALUE HARDWARE STORES
Cotter Canada Hardware and Variety Cooperative, Inc.
1530 Gamble Place, P.O. Box 6800, Winnipeg, MB, R3C 3A9. Contact: Hugh Matson, Recruiting & Training Specialist - Tel: (800) 665-5085, Fax: (204) 453-9477. Member owned Cooperative serving 425 stores in Canada. Established in USA in 1948, 6000+ stores. Total True Value stores in Canada - 170. Established: 1992 - Franchise Fee: $2000 - Total Inv: approx. $250,000 - Financing Available: National Bank Packages.

U-PAWN & SMILE
Domphaff Corp. Ltd.
1820 S. Sheridan Way, Mississauga, ON, L5J 2M2. Contact: Ralph Conty, Fran. Dir. - Tel: & Fax: (416) 252-8936 . Pawnbroker and discount outlet for retailing, buying, selling and collateral lending. Dealing in a large variety of new, reconditioned and used consumer goods. Neighbourhood oriented operation doing all cash business by providing services to constant market demands. Low cost group purchasing power combined with inventory networking assures relatively quick merchandise turn-around at high profit margins. Training and operating manuals are provided along with ongoing market consultation. Franchise Fee: $5,000 - $20,000 (depending on territory) - Royalty: 8%, 2% adv. of gross sales - Total Inv: $135,000 - $175,000 (min. $100,000 unencumbered).

V & S DEPARTMENT STORES
Cotter Canada Hardware and Variety Cooperative, Inc.
1530 Gamble Place, P.O. Box 6800, Winnipeg, MB, R3C 2A9. Contact: Hugh Matson, Recruitment & Training Specialist - Tel: (800) 665-5085, Fax: (204) 453-9477. Membered owned Cooperative serving 425 stores in Canada. Established in USA in 1948. Serving 6000+ stores. Total V & S stores in Canada 183. - Year Established: 1992 - Franchise Fee: $2000 - Total Inv: $175,000 - Financing Available: National Bank Packages.

VIVAH JEWELRY
Vivah Franchise, Inc.
3715 Chesswood Dr., Downsview, ON, M3J 2P6. Contact: Mr. Z. Goodbaum, Pres. - Tel: (416) 631-6513. Retail sale of exclusive fashion jewelry namely earrings, pins, necklaces, and bracelets with a strong emphasis on sterling silver jewelry, fashion watches and bridal lines. Established: 1976 - Franchising Since: 1989 - No. of Units: Company Owned: 9 - Franchised: 1 - Franchise Fee: $25,000 - Total Inv: $20,000 - $25,000 merch., $40,000 - $75,000 store fix. - Financing: $80,000 min. invest. with bal. thru bank.

WENDI T'EEZE FANTASY BOUTIQUE *
10 Holland St. E., Box 69, Bradford, ON, L3Z 2A7. Contact: Tony Natale, Pres. - Tel: (905) 775-1409, Fax: (905) 775-8903. An upscale adult boutique selling lingerie, swimwear, clubwear, novelties, xxx movies and magazines. Established: 1990 - Franchising Since: 1995 - No. of Units: Company Owned: 1 - Franchised: 1 - Franchise Fee: $7,000 - Total Inv: $40,000.

WINE KITZ *
Wine Kitz Canada Inc.
785 Wonderland Rd., London, ON, N6K 1M6. Contact: John R. DeHondt, Pres. - Tel: (519) 471-5144. Retail outlet for beer & wine making ingredients, related equipment & giftware. Established: 1992 - Franchising Since: 1993 - No. of Units: Company Owned: 2 - Franchised: 2 - Under Development: 2 - Franchise Fee: $18,500 - Royalty: flat fee $420 per month offset by buying group rebates - Total Inv: $55,000 turnkey with stock - Financing: 50% franchise fee by franchisor.

RETAIL: CLOTHING AND SHOES

AGNEW, AGGIES
Agnew Group Inc.
825 Bradley Ave., London, ON, N6E 3C2. Contact: Franchise Director - Tel: (519) 685-2227. Retail footwear group. Established: 1877 - Franchising Since: 1988 - No. of Units: 350+ - Franchise Fee: $30,000 - Royalty: 6% + 3% nat'l adv. - Total Inv: Min. $100,000 with $35,000 cash. Financing: No.

BACKSTAGE PASS *
Backstage Pass Franchising, Inc.
740 Supertest Rd., Downsview, ON, M3J 2M5. Contact: Brian Stutz, Mktg. Dir. - Tel: (800) 463-4858(416) 665-8890, Fax: (416) 665-4904. Retail chain specializing in music and entertainment related clothing & fashion accessories. Directed towards the teem market. Established: 1987 - Franchising Since: 1994 - No. of Units: Company Owned: 7 - Franchised: 3 - Franchise Fee: $25,000 - Royalty: 5% - Total Inv: $150,000 total turnkey - Financing: Yes.

BLUE JUNCTION
590 Gordon Baker Rd., Willowdale, ON, M2H 3B4. Contact: Raj Tanna, G.M. - Tel: (416) 490-1719. Retail sales of casual wear for guys and gals. Established: 1974 - Franchising Since: 1978 - No. of Units: Company Owned: 1 - Franchised: 5 - Franchise Fee: $25,000 - Total Inv: $25,000 F.F, $25,000 inven., $40,000 leasehold - Financing: No.

CENTMIL CHEMISES
5650 Cypihot St., St. Laurent, PQ, H4S 1V7. Contact: Jean-Guy LeBlanc, Pres. - Tel: (514) 334-8203. Men's accessories. Established: 1984 - No. of Units: 15 - Royalty: 2% of sales.

ESCADA CANADA INC.
409 King St. W., 4th Fl., Toronto, ON, M5V 1K1. Contact: Fran. Dir. - Tel: (416) 595-0107. Ladies' wear. No. of Units: 5.

FOSTER'S SHOES CLAPP SHOES
Foster's Shoes
1892 Lawrence Ave., E., Scarborough, ON, M1R 2Y5. Contact: William Foster, C.E.O. - Tel: (416) 759-5610. Retail shoes. Established: 1953 - No. of Units: Company Owned: 8 - Franchised: 2.

KETTLE CREEK CLOTHING CO.
Canada Trans Limited
456 Albert St., P.O. Box 261, Strathroy, ON, N7G 3J2. Contact: Doug Hamilton, Pres. - Tel: (519)245-4811. Womens & mens clothing in natural fabrics, Canadian design. Established: 1979 - Franchising Since: 1981 - No. of Units: Company Owned: 1- Dealers: 17 - Royalty: included in the price of goods - Total Inv: Leaseholds - $40,000 Inventory - $85,000.

LA CACHE
Cornell Trading Ltd.
1619 William St., Montreal, PQ, H3Z 1R1. Contact: Chris Cornell, Pres. - Tel: (514) 935-9295. Ladies clothing collection, soft home furnishing, gifts, pottery, jewelry, etc. Established: 1973 - Franchising Since: 1986 - No. of Units: Company Owned: 16 - Franchised: 6 - Franchise Fee: $5,000 - Total Inv: $100,000-$150,000 turn-key (fix, inven., leasehold) - Financing: No.

LEGS BEAUTIFUL HOSIERY BOUTIQUES
1875 Leslie St., Unit 20, Don Mills, ON, M3B 2M5. Contact: Ian Collins - Tel: (416) 449-7444. Retailer of women's specialty hosiery. Established: 1978 - No. of Units: Company Owned: 23 - Franchised: 17 - Franchise Fee: $25,000 - Royalty: 8% - Total Inv: $120,000 - Financing: Assistance.

MONEYSWORTH & BEST QUALITY SHOE REPAIR
Moneysworth & Best Quality Shoe Repair, Inc
80 Galaxy Blvd., Unit 11, Toronto, ON, M9W 4Y8. Contact: Dean McCann, Director Franc. Dev. - Tel: (416) 674-6148. While-you-wait shoe repair plus full line of branded shoe care merchandise with guaranteed customer satisfaction. Locations in major shopping malls. Established: 1984 - Franchising Since: 1986 - Number of Units: Company Owned: 23 - Franchised: 56 - Franchise Fee: $10,000 - Royalty: 8% - Total Inv: $110,000: fee $10,000 - equip $50,000 - furn, fix, leaseholds - $40,000, inven. - $10,000 - Financing: No.

MS. EMMA DESIGNS LTD.
134 Peter Street, Toronto, ON, M5V 2H2. Contact: Sofia Verna, Owner - Tel: (416) 598-2466. Hand crafted clothing in natural fibers, with custom fittings. Established: 1973 - Franchising Since: 1986 - No. of Units: Franchised: 2 - Royalty: 2% - Total Inv: flexible - Financing: Partly.

NORMA PETERSON
Norma Peterson Fashion Enterprises Inc.
20 Steelcase Rd., W., #3, Markham, ON, L3R 1B2. Contact: Jane Bishop, V.P. - Tel: (905) 470-2424. Ladies fashion (casual elegance). Established: 1975 - Franchising Since: 1985 - No. of Units: Company Owned: 1 - Franchised: 8 - Franchise Fee: None - Royalty: None - Total Inv: Opening stock $15,000 - $25,000, fixtures etc. $7,000 - $15,000 - Financing: None.

PETTICOAT BOX, THE
103 - 1515 Pemberton Ave., North Vancouver, BC, V7P 2S3. Contact: Maria Cullen, Franchisor - Tel: (604) 985-4996, Fax: (604) 985-3937. European style lingerie retail outlets (stores). Established: 1989 - Franchising Since: 1991 - No. of Units: Company Owned: 1 - Franchised: 6 - Franchise Fee: $25,000 incl. lawyer's fees & lease negotiations - Royalty: 5% of gross sales - Total Inv: $130,000 - $160,000 turnkey (incl. fran. fee) - Financing: Across Canada.

PLEASE MUM *
Elia Fashions Ltd.
1121 William St., Vancouver, BC, V6A 2J1. Contact: Kevin Jewson/ Cristie Palmer, V.P. Sales/Fran. Dev. Mgr. - Tel: (604) 254-1998, Fax: (604) 254-0831. Canadian made children's wear ages NB-10 years. Bright, fun clothing in styles kids love, at a price Mums will adore! Established: 1986 - Franchising Since: 1987 - No. of Units: Company Owned: 13 - Franchised: 27 - Franchise Fee: $50,000 - Royalty: 6% gross sales - Total Inv: $50,000 fran. fee, $50,000 inven., $50 sq. ft. leaseholds - Financing: N/A.

WORK WORLD
Western Workwear World
#101, 12827 76th Ave., Surrey, BC, V3W 2V3. Contact: Bernie Bielby, Fran. Sales Dir. - Tel: (604) 590-1841, Fax: (604) 590-0880. Sale of work wear, casual wear, foot wear & accessories. Established: 1978 - Franchising Since: 1978 - No. of Units: Company Owned: 7 - Franchised: 145 - Franchise Fee: $25,000 - Royalty: 4.75% of gross sales - Total Inv: $170,000 - Financing: Yes, require $75,000 min. inv., balance financed.

RETAIL: COMPUTER, ELECTRONICS AND VIDEO

A PLUS SOFTWARE *
Wohar Holdings
111 Gordon Baker Rd., North York, ON, M2H 3R1. Contact: Cindy Naigle/Cindy Petrow, Fran. Dev. - Tel: (416) 492-4499. Dedicated to the sale of IBM compatible computer software and accessories to the home and small business users. Established: 1988 - Franchising Since: 1990 - No. of Units: Company Owned: 2 - Franchised: 19 - Franchise Fee: $60,000 - Royalty: 2.5% - Total Inv: $295,000 - Financing: N/A.

COMPUCENTRE
Hartco Enterprises, Inc.
9001 Louis H. Lafontaine, Anjou, PQ, H4W 2Y1. Contact: Myer Hart, V.P. Franchising - Tel: (514) 354-3810, Fax: (514) 354-2299. Compucentre is made up of retail stores selling personal computers, peripherals, t.v. games, software, calculators and accessories located in high traffic regional malls. Established: 1976 - Franchising Since: 1982 - No. of Units: Company Owned: 6 - Franchised: 50 - Franchise Fee: $25,000 - Royalty: None - Financing: Bank franchise package.

COMPUTERLAND CANADA INC.
2000 Clark Blvd., Brampton, ON, L6T 4M7. Contact: Raymond Andre, Leasing Mgr. - Tel: (905) 793-9000. Computer retail stores. Established: 1977 - Franchising Since: 1977 - No. of Units: 77 - Franchise Fee: $10,000+ - Royalty: 8% + 1% adv. fund/mo. - Total Inv: $250,000 - Financing: No.

CYBERMIND *
Cybermind Canada, Inc.
40 West Pearse St., Unit 6, Richmond Hill, ON, L4B 1E3. Contact: Mr. Israel Ellis, Pres. - Tel: (905) 707-8787. Location based virtual realty entertainment and retail outlets, offering everything in VR and interactive technology to learn, experience & purchase. Professional training and continuous support from head office. Established: 1994 - Franchising Since: 1994 - No. of Units: Company Owned: 2 - Franchised: 3 - Franchise Fee: $15,000 - $35,000 - Royalty: 7% licensing, 3% adv. - Total Inv: Avl. equip. $250,000, leaseholds $50,000 - Financing: If qualifies.

DIGITCOM TELECOMMUNICATIONS
Digitcom Canada, Inc.
21 St. Clair Ave. E., Ste. 300, Toronto, ON, M4T 1L9. Contact: J. Wiener, Pres. - Tel: (416) 969-7890. Call processing, telecommunications, voice mail, interactive voice response, computer telephone integration. Established: 1991 - Franchising Since: 1993 - No. of Units: Company Owned: 1 - Franchised: 1 - Franchise Fee: $40,000 - Total Inv: $75,000 - Financing: Yes.

FEATURE PRESENTATION
Feature Presentation Inc.
Hazelton Lanes, 55 Avenue Rd., Ste. 2700, Toronto, ON, M5R 3L2. Contact: Brian Melzack, C.E.O. - Tel: (416) 927-7810, (800) 361-3181, Fax: (416) 927-1789. Canada's first retail sales only movie video operation, selling box office, classics, children's, exercise, sports and new release videos. Either a kiosk-style or traditional store design. Established: 1993 - Franchising Since: 1993 - No. of Units: Company Owned: 4 - Franchised: 3 - Franchise Fee: $25,000 - Royalty: 5% - Total Inv: $80,000 - $100,000 - Financing: Relationship with a Chartered Bank.

LASER LAND
Laser Land Canada
2200 Dundas St. E., Mississauga, ON, L4X 2V3. Contact: Diane Jones, Pres. - Tel: (905) 566-0800, Fax: (905) 566-5890. Retail laser video discs and accessories for sale and rental. Franchise kiosks available for existing store owners. Established: 1987 - Franchising Since: 1988 - No.

of Units: Company Owned: 1 - Franchise Fee: $1,200 and up - Royalty: 6% of sales - Total Inv: $10,000 and up: $5,000 inven., $1,200 fran. fee, $1,000 fixtures, $2,800 work. cap. - Financing: No.

MICROPLAY VIDEO GAME STORES
MicroPlay of America, Inc.
918 Dundas St. E., 5th Fl., Mississauga, ON, L4Y 4H9. Contact: Mason Copeland, Pres. - Tel: (905) 949-2580. Video game retail specialty stores. Established: 1987 - Franchising Since: 1993 - No. of Units: Company Owned: 8 - Franchised: 140 - Franchise Fee: $29,500 - Royalty: varies 0% - 6% - Total Inv: $120,000 - $150,000 - Financing: Yes, by qualified individuals.

MOVIE SELLER
9350 Yonge St., Richmond Hill, ON, L4C 5G2. Contact: Richard Sadowski, V.P. Fran. Sales - Tel: (905) 737-1108. Entertainment one stop shop. Strong emphasis on video sell through with 3,500-5,000 different titles. No rental stores. Also retail full line of licensed products. Established: 1992 - Franchising Since: 1994 - No. of Units: Company Owned: 4 - Franchise Fee: $25,000 - Royalty: 6%, 2% adv. - Total Inv: $30,000 leaseholds & fixtures, $10,000 equip., $50,000 inven. - Financing: Yes, up to 80%.

MULTIVIDEO
Le Centre Videofilm Multivideo, Inc.
1510 boul. Henri-Bourassa Ouest, Montreal, PQ, H3M 3E3. Contact: Sylvie Sauriol, Pres. - Tel: (514) 333-7257. Films, videos and video accessories. Franchising Since: 1982 - No. of Units: Company Owned: 5 - Franchised: 17 - Franchise Fee: $10,000 - Total Inv: $140,000 - Royalty: $5,000/year - Financing: Yes, partial.

PLANET INTERNET LOGON CENTER *
Planet Internet Corporation
5507 River Rd., Niagara Falls, ON, L2E 6Z2. Contact: John Clarke, V.P. & G.M. - Tel: (905) 358-0688, Fax: (905) 358-0511. Logon Centers are high profile centers designed for the sale of internet on line time. Computers, peripherals, software and internet publications, as well as conducting learning seminars for business and personal use of the Internet to make money. Established: 1995 - Franchising Since: 1995 - No. of Units: Company Owned: 1 - Franchise Fee: $15,000 - Royalty: None, no advertising - Total Inv: $75,000 to $100,000 - Financing: Yes.

RADD MULTIMEDIA *
5072 Kingsway, Burnaby, BC, V5H 2E7. Contact: Walter Morel, Fran. Dir. - Tel: (604) 451-1544, 1-800-985-9444. Video game specialty retail store concept, buy, sell and trade of new and previously played interactive games and hardware. Operation and marketing support along with site selection and construction available. Established: 1994 - Franchising Since: 1994 - No. of Units: Company Owned: 4 - Franchised: 2 - Franchise Fee: $25,000 - $10,000 (multiple store development) - Royalty: 2% on new product, 5% on previously played - Total Inv: Hard Costs: $45,000; Inventory $30,000 - $50,000; plus working cap. and fran. fee - Financing: Will assist with business plan.

RADIO SHACK AUTHORIZED SALES CENTRE (CANADA)
A Division of Tandy Corporation
279 Bayview Dr., Barrie, ON, L4M 4W5. Contact: Joe Dombroski, Dir., Dealer Division - Tel: (705) 728-6242, Fax: (800) 665-5650. Retail electronics for the complete catalogue line of Radio Shack products including TRS-80 computers and peripherals. Established: 1972 - Franchising Since: 1972 - No. of Units: Company Owned: 492 - Franchised: 391 - Approx. Inv: varies with size of market area.

ROBOSOFT ELECTRONIC SOFTWARE STORE *
RoboSoft Technology, Inc.
P.O. Box 251, Stn. B., Toronto, ON, M5T 2W1. Contact: Gregory Yankelovich, Pres. - Tel: (416) 368-0539, Fax: (416) 368-8446. Fully automated computer software vending machines installed in shopping malls, airports and other high traffic locations. RoboSoft distribution method allows to bring to the consumer valuable computer programs at deeply discounted prices. Established: 1992 - Franchising Since: 1995 - No. of Units: Company Owned: 15 - Franchise Fee: Min. $20,000 (equip. cost) - Royalty: 5% electronic inventory updates - Total Inv: $20,000 - Financing: Yes.

STAR VIDEO
190 Harwood Ave., S., Ajax, ON, L1S 2H9. Contact: David Kang, Mgr. - Tel: (905) 427-7799. Established: 1983 - Franchising Since: 1984 - No. of Units: Company Owned: 2 - Franchised: 6 - Franchise Fee: negotiable - Total Inv: $300,000 - Financing: No.

STEREO DEN
Steve O'Bryan Holdings Ltd.
2300 Lawrence Ave., E., Ste. 14, Scarborough, ON, M1P 2R2. Contact: Stephen Yap, Pres. - Tel: (416) 288-8998. Retailer of home electronic entertainment. Offering car & home stereos, televisions, video recorders, camcorders, telephone and accessories etc. Established: 1977 - Franchising Since: 1981 - No. of Units: Company Owned: 6 - Franchised: 16 - Franchise Fee: $25,000 - Royalty: 6% includes advertising - Total Inv: $150,000 - Financing: No.

STEREO PLUS
5715 boul. Royal, Ste. 3, Trois-Rivieres, PQ, G9A 4N9. Contact: Richard Roy, Pres. - Tel: (819) 378-2303, Fax: (819) 376-2554. Retail electronics. Established: 1982 - Franchising Since: 1982 - No. of Units: Company Owned: 7 - Franchised: 55 - Franchise Fee: $15,000 - Royalty: 2% of purchase - Total Inv: $60,000 - Financing: Bombardier Credit.

TOP FORTY / TFM
Top Forty Music Ltd.
10333 - 174 St., Edmonton, AB, T5S 1H1. Contact: Al Herfst, V.P. - Tel: (403) 489-2324. Retailer of pre-recorded music products, video and other paraphernalia. Established: 1975 - Franchising Since: 1983 - No. of Units: Company Owned: 22 - Franchised: 17 - Franchise Fee: $15,000 - Royalty: 5% - Total Inv: $120,000 - $160,000 - Financing: 60% thru bank.

VIDEO CUBE, INC.
2255 Markham Rd., Scarborough, ON, M1V 2W3. Contact: Garson Hoffman, Pres. - Tel: (416) 299-3625. Video outlet open 24 hours operating with video vending machines. Takes cash or charge on Visa or Master Card. Franchising Since: 1986 - No. of Units: Company Owned: 15 - Franchised: 30 - Royalty: $300. per month - Total Inv: $10,000 - Financing: Yes-80%.

VIDEOFLICKS CANADA LTD.
1654 Avenue Rd., Toronto, ON, M5M 3Y1. Contact: Beverly Kavanagh, Pres. - Tel: (416) 782-4438. Videotape rental with rental of machinery as well as sale of VCR's and related accessories. Established: 1981 - Franchising Since: 1981 - No. of Units: 40 - Franchise Fee: $15,000 - Royalty: 5% - Total Inv: $60,000 - $80,000.

VIDEOMATIC 24 HR
Videomatic 24 hr. Movie Rentals, Inc.
760 King Rd., Burlington, ON, L7T 3K6. Contact: David Cranston, Pres. - Tel: (905) 681-0238. Operate a fully automatic video store utilizing two patented video vendors. Complete computer records, no payroll, store open 24 hours every day. First store opened in 1985. Exclusive licenses available. Established: 1985 - No. of Units: Company Owned: 2 - Franchised: 54 - Total Inv: $25,000 -Financing: No.

SCHOOLS AND TEACHING

ACADEMY FOR MATHEMATICS
Academy For Mathematics & Science, Inc.
30 Glen Cameron Rd., Thornhill, ON, L3T 1N7. Contact: Balti Sauer, Pres. - Tel: (905) 709-3233. Franchising of learning centres teaching mathematics & science. Established: 1993 - Franchising Since: 1993 - No. of Units: Company Owned: 2 - Franchised: 20 - Franchise Fee: $18,500 - Royalty: 15% - Total Inv: $30,000 - Financing: Can be arranged.

ACADEMY OF LEARNING
9011 Leslie St., Unit 205, Richmond Hill, ON, L4B 3B6. Contact: Les Prosser, Dir. of Mktg. - Tel: (905) 886-8973, Fax: (905) 886-8591. Computer and business skills training centres. A unique "Integrated Learning™" system of self paced, flexible training. Established: 1987 - Franchising Since: 1987 - No. of Units: Company Owned: 1 - Franchised: 120 - Franchise Fee: $60,000 - Royalty: Nil - Total Inv: $100,000: $60,000 fran. fee; $20,000 equip. & furniture; $20,000 work. cap. - Financing: No.

ALPINE DRIVING SCHOOL LTD.
#77 - 1089 W. Broadway, Vancouver, BC, V6H 1E5. Contact: Russ, Pres. - Tel: (604) 970-8677. Driver education and training for cars (not trucks i.e. class 4 & 5 only) including classroom instructions. Established: 1992 - Franchising Since: 1994 - No. of Units: Company Owned: 1 - Franchised: 2 - Franchise Fee: $30,000 - Royalty: 6% of gross, 2% adv. - Total Inv: $50,000 - Financing: Yes.

BROADBELT & FONTE MODEL CENTRE *
Broadbelt & Fonte Model Centre, Inc.
696 Dufferin St., Toronto, ON, M6K 2B5. Contact: Manuel Fonte, V.P. - Tel: (416) 588-8806. Modelling school. Established: 1990 - Franchising Since: 1994 - No. of Units: Company Owned: 1 - Franchised: 1 - Franchise Fee: $15,000 - Royalty: 10% - Total Inv: $5,000 - $10,000 - Financing: No.

BUSINESS TELEVISION (CAN. OFFICES)
2800 John St., Ste. 11, Markham, ON, L3R 0E2. Contact: Richard Simpson, Pres. - Tel: (905) 475-1316. Franchisor custom development training educational, informational video based programming and support materials. Full service from budgeting, design, scripting and production to build a well trained, informed franchise system. Established 1980.

COMPUTERPALS *
21 Meadowglade Cres., Willowdale, ON, M2J 1C6. Contact: Ray Catzel, Pres. - Tel: (416) 490-9698. Teaching computer literacy in fun-filled environment. Established: 1992 - Franchising Since: 1994 - No. of Units: Company Owned: 1 - Franchised: 3 - Franchise Fee: from $10,000 - Royalty: 10% - Total Inv: from $30,000 - Financing: Yes.

EXECUTRAIN
Canadian Training Associates
5140 Yonge St., Ste. 800, North York, ON, M2N 6L7. Contact: Sondra Kiss, Pres. - Tel: (416) 221-5353. World's largest computer training company with over 100 locations in more than 15 countries. Executrain specializes in the education of business professionals. Established: 1984 - Franchising Since: 1986 - No. of Units: Company Owned: 1 - Franchised: 100+ - Franchise Fee: $35,000 - Royalty: Ranges from 6% to 9% - Total Inv: $200,000 to $300,000 work. cap. - Financing: Yes.

GRADE EXPECTATIONS LEARNING CENTRES
Grade Expectations Learning Systems Inc.
105 Main St., Unionville, ON, L3R 2G1. Contact: Graham Ballantine, Gen. Mgr. - Tel: (905) 513-9434, Fax: (905) 479-9047. Specializing in supplementary education from grades 1 through OAC. Established: 1994 - Franchising Since: 1994 - No. of Units: Company Owned: 2 - Franchised: 4 - Franchise Fee: $15,000 - Royalty: 10% - Total Inv: $60,000 - Financing: No.

INTERNATIONAL INSTITUTE OF TRAVEL
907687 Ontario Inc.
98 Dupont St., Toronto, ON, M5R 1V2. Contact: Rudolph Nareen, Pres. - Tel: (416) 924-4888. The Institute offers a practical training program in travel and tourism and works together with instructors and course advisors from airlines and other travel related companies. Established: 1983 - No. of Units: Company Owned: 2 - Franchised: 5 - Franchise Fee: $25,000 - Royalty: 7% - Total Inv: $110,000 - Financing: No.

LEARNING MAGAZINE, THE
Partners In Education
Box 2268, Stony Plain, AB, T7Z 1X7. Contact: June Ruest, Dir. of Fran. - Tel: (403) 963-6922, Fax: 9403) 963-6922. The Learning Magazine offers a unique publishing experience for both part-time and full time opportunities. The company provides complete editorial content where required along with the flexibility for adjustment to suit local communities, complete training, equipment and head office support is provided. Established: 1982 - Franchising Since: 1994 - No. of Units: Company Owned: 1 - Franchised: 1 - Franchise Fee: $25,000 - Royalty: 5% - Total Inv: $25,000 - Financing: 50%.

MATH PLUS LEARNING CENTRES
62 Carden St., Guelph, ON, N1H 3A2. Contact: Marc Hurwitz, Pres. - Tel: (519) 822-3536, Fax: 763-4809. Specialized learning centres with the top quality in mathematics enhancement and remediation by individualized tuition. Extensive staff training, computerized management system, and tried marketing plan. Established: 1993 - Franchising Since: 1994 - No. of Units: Company Owned: 8 - Franchised: 1 - Franchise Fee: U.S. $15,000 - Royalty: 15% - Total Inv: U.S. $34,000 (incl. work. cap) - Financing: No.

MUSIC TRENDS TEACHING STUDIOS *
Music Trends Teaching Studios, Inc.
1071 Midland Ave., Scarborough, ON, M1K 4G7. Contact: Rick Maidment - Tel: (416) 285-4990, Fax: (416) 285-8834. Music education & sale of related material. Established: 1986 - No. of Units: Company Owned: 1 - Fees: Subject to arrangement.

OXFORD LEARNING CENTRES
Oxford Learning Centres Inc.
6465 Millcreek Dr., Ste. 205, Mississauga, ON, L5N 5R3. Contact: George Kostopoulos - Tel: (905) 567-4180, (800) 387-8335, Fax: (905) 567-5355. Oxford Learning Centres is a franchisor of private educational centres, specializing in improving students academic skills, by teaching them how to think and learn. We cover a full curriculum of subjects for students between 3 and 23 years of age. Established: 1981 - Franchising Since: 1990 - No. of Units: Company Owned: 1 - Franchised: 21 - Franchise Fee: $25,000 - Royalty: 9% - Total Inv: $80,000 - $95,000 - Financing: Assistance through financial institutes.

Invest In *Our* Future

Reap the financial rewards of running an educational centre while building your own franchise business. Founded in 1983, Oxford Learning Centres are a privately owned business dedicated to helping students improve their learning skills. Our unique Oxford Program helps students achieve better grades and attain higher levels of self esteem.

- Personal teaching experience is not required.
- Take advantage of extensive training and support.
- Capitalize on our name and reputation.
- Realize tangible results in a service-oriented business.
- Provide the "gift of learning" to our children.

Take an active role in your future by becoming part of Oxford Learning Centres. Call today – only a limited number of franchise opportunities are available!

For more information call: 1-800-387-8335, in Toronto (905) 567-4180 or write to: First Choice Franchise Services, 6465 Millcreek Drive, Suite 205, Mississauga, ON L5N 5R3.

SANDLER SALES INSTITUTE (CANADA) LTD.
3625 McGill St., Vancouver, BC, V5K 1J3. Contact: Franchise Director - Tel: (800) 670-1400, (604) 681-2212, Fax: (604) 683-3579. Sales and service management. Our philosophy is training through reinforcement versus one day seminars. Established: 1967 - Franchising Since: 1984 - No. of Units: Franchised: 165 - Franchise Fee: $36,000 - Royalty: $908 per month - Total Inv: $36,000 - Financing:No.

SEARS DRIVER TRAINING *
A. OK Road Safety Systems Ltd.
247 N. Service Rd., Ste. 301, Oakville, ON, L6M 3E6. Contact: Luba Castracane, Pres. - Tel: (416) 363-7483. A full service driver training school with national name recognition. Turnkey operation with ongoing training & support. Low overhead, high traffic exposure with classrooms conveniently located in selected Sears stores. Established: 1976 - Franchising Since: 1994 - No. of Units: Company Owned: 12 - Franchised: 4 - Franchise Fee: $20,000 - Royalty: 6%, 5% nat'l. adv. - Total Inv: $25,000 - $45.000 - Financing: No.

SKILLSET TRAINING
SKILLSET Training Systems Inc.
69 Yonge St., Ste. 1200, Toronto, ON, M5E 1K3. Contact: Ted Turner, Pres. - Tel: (416) 920-4141, Fax: (416) 920-7285. Corporate computer training centers. Established: 1990 - Franchising Since: 1994 - No. of Units: Company Owned: 2 - Franchise Fee: $15,000 - $30,000 depending on market - Royalty: 10% reducing to 5% - Total Inv: $100,000 plus salaries other than franchisees (if necessary) minimum - Financing: No, hardware might be leased if qualified. Web site: http://www.barint.on.ca/netwave/skillset/franchise.html

TECHNOKIDS - TECHNOPLUS COMPUTER LEARNING CENTRE
461-B27 North Service Rd. W., Oakville, ON, L6M 2V5. Contact: Scott Gerard, Pres. - Tel: (905) 847-1605, Fax: (905) 847-1934. A complete PC computer learning centre for both kids and adults which teaches all popular software applications. Stand alone locations in upscale business complexes. Established: 1993 - Franchising Since: 1993 - No. of Units: Company Owned: 1 - Franchised: 4 - Franchise Fee: $20,000 - Royalty: 6%, 0% adv. - Total Inv: $75,000: fran. fee plus $40,000 equip., $15,000 work. cap. - Financing: None, will assist in bank application.

TECHNOPLUS MOBILE COMPUTER TRAINING *
461-B27 North Service Rd. W., Oakville, ON, L6M 2V5. Contact: Scott Gerard, Pres. - Tel: (905) 847-1605, Fax: (905) 847-1934. A home based business from where you travel to a clients home or office and teach all the popular software applications using a mobile classroom, i.e. notebook computers. Established: 1993 - Franchising Since: 1995 - No. of Units: Company Owned: 1 - Franchised: 1 - Franchise Fee: $20,000 - Royalty: 6%, 0% adv. - Total Inv: $50,000: fran. fee plus $20,000 equip., $10,000 work. cap. - Financing: None, will assist in bank application.

TECNIC DRIVING SCHOOL GROUP
2195 La Piniere Blvd., Brassard, PQ, J4W 1M2. Contact: Donald O'Hara, Franchise Director - Tel: (514) 443-6360. Driving school. Established: 1957 - Franchising Since: 1984 - No. of Units: Company Owned: 1 - Franchised: 146 - Franchise Fee: $15,000 - Royalty: 4% + 2% adv. - Total Inv: $40,000 - Financing: Yes, in Quebec and Ontario, may expand elsewhere.

TORONTO SCHOOL OF BUSINESS, COMPUCOLLEGE SCHOOL OF BUSINESS
International Business Schools Inc.
5650 Yonge St., Ste. 1400, North York, ON, M2M 4G3. Contact: Lorne Karasik, Exec. V.P. - Tel: 416-733-4452. Private career training schools. Provides short term courses to enable students to obtain entry level job positions. Established: 1976 - Franchising Since: 1983 - No. of Units: Company Owned: 14 - Franchised: 32 - Franchise Fee: $50,000 - $75,000 depending on size of location - Total Inv: $200,000 - $300,000 incl. fran. fee - Royalty: 7% - Financing: No, but will assist in bank presentation.

URBAN AND RURAL SCHOOLS
U & R Tax Services Ltd.
1345 Pembina Hwy., Winnipeg, MB, R3T 2B6. Contact: Greg Davenport, V.P. Oper. - Tel: (204) 949-3636, Fax: (204) 949-3668. Basic, advanced and professional tax training courses and bookkeeping courses by homestudy or in classroom. Includes training, advertising, supplies and on-going supervision to ensure maximum profitability. Currently available in Canada only. Additional courses, seminars and newsletters under development. Established: 1972 - Franchising Since: 1973 - No. of Units: Company Owned: 23 - Franchised: 97 - Franchise Fee: $3,500 - $7,500 (partially refundable) - Royalty: 13.3% - 50% based on type and volume of revenue - Total Inv: $5,000 - $11,500 (partially refundable) - Financing: Yes.

YOUNG DRIVERS OF CANADA / YOUNG DRIVERS OF AMERICA
Commerce Place Phase II, 21 King St. W., Ste. 890, Hamilton, ON, L8P 4W7. Contact: Peter Christianson, Pres. - Tel: (905) 529-5501. Driver training. Established: 1970 - Franchising Since: 1976 - No. of Units: Franchised: 71 - 150 classrooms - Franchise Fee: $6,000 - Royalty: 4% of student fees, 4% of student fees for adv. - Total Inv: $25,000.

SIGN PRODUCTS & SERVICES

1 HOUR SIGNS
1 Hour Signs Inc.
485 Silvercreek Pkwy. N., Unit 4, Guelph, ON, N1H 7K5. Contact: Shan Jamal, Pres. - Tel: (519) 824-2832. The most technologically advanced sign shop franchise - specializing in large or small signs. Ready made

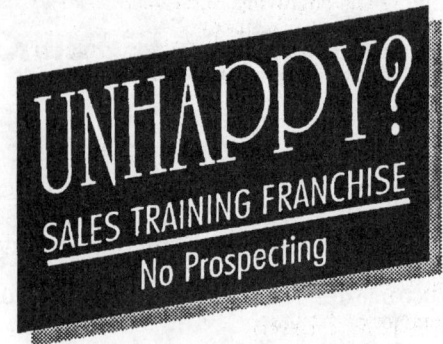

We are looking for an entrepreneur to own and operate a sales training business in your area:

* Join a winning team with 29 years of success
* Control your own schedule
* Be part of a $210 billion per year industry
* Join the #1 Sales Training Franchise in North America
* Over 150 Franchises in North America

Call or write today for our Franchise Kit. 1-800-670-1400

Sandler Sales Institute (Canada) Ltd.
3625 McGill Street, Vancouver BC V5K 1J3
Phone: (604) 681-2212 Fax: (604) 683-3579

signs, screen printing and engraving. Established: 1991 - Franchising Since: 1992 - No. of Units: Company Owned: 1 - Franchised: 5 - Franchise Fee: $20,000 - Royalty: 5%, 1.5% adv. - Total Inv: $139,000; min. cash req. $55,000 - Financing: Assistance.

CALL-A-SIGN LTD.
R.R. #1, Belmont, ON, N0L 1B0. Contact: George Van Colen, Pres. - Tel: (519) 644-0272. Manufacture, sale, rental and long-term leasing of high quality illuminated, changeable copy, mobile signs equipped with a colored headliner section. Established: 1974 - Franchising Since: 1978 - No. of Units: Company Owned: 12 - Franchised: 1 - Franchise Fee: $35,000 - Total Inv: $100,000 - $500,000 - Royalty: 3% - 7% dep. on territory - Financing: Assistance.

INSTANT CUSTOM SIGNS
Brickell & Associates Ltd.
349 Jelley Ave., Newmarket, ON, L3X 1S4. Contact: Gary J. Brickell, Pres/Founder - Tel: (905) 836-9406. Full service commercial sign shop. Design, manufacture & retail all types of signage & lettering. Each shop utilizes the finest computerized sign makers available...for fast, quality results. Established: 1983 - Franchising Since: 1985 - No. of Units: Company Owned: 1 - Franchised: 8 - Franchise Fee: $27,000 - Royalty: 4% 1st yr., 3% 5th yr., no adv. royalties - Total Inv: $85,000: fran. fee plus $30,000 equip./stock, $8,000 other, $20,000 work. cap. - Financing: Assist in acquiring 3rd party funding.

PORT-A-SIGN
R. R. #1, Belmont, ON, N0L 1B0. Contact: George Van Colen - Tel: (519) 644-1188. Mobile signs. Established: 1970 - Franchising Since: 1976 - No. of Units: Company Owned: 12 - Franchised: 12 - Approx. Inv: $300,000 - Financing: Yes.

SIGNS NOW
Signs Now Canada
#100 - 2000 West 12th Ave., Vancouver, BC, V6J 2G2. Contact: John Pozer, Pres. - Tel: (604) 733-8669, Fax: (800) 733-5344. The original instant sign & graphics company. Computer generated vinyl sign & graphics company. Four weeks franchise training, on-going workshops, monthly newsletter. Established: USA 1983, Canada 1991 - Franchising Since: USA 1986 - No. of Units: Franchised: 25 in Canada, 190 in USA - Franchise Fee: $22,000 - Royalty: Reducing Scale 7% - Total Inv: $71,300 incl. $10,000 work. cap. - Financing: Yes.

SPEEDPRO SIGN & PRINT CENTERS
Speedpro Systems Inc.
Ste. 18, 19912 96th Ave., Surrey, BC, V4N 3R1. Contact: Mr. Dave Crawford, District Manager - Tel: (604) 882-5115, Fax: (604) 882-3626. A one-stop advertising center, providing signs & printed products - produced same day. Established: 1991 - No. of Units: Franchised: 21 - Total Inv: $76,500.

VINYLGRAPHICS CUSTOM SIGN CENTRES
Vinylgraphics, Inc.
1733 Keele St., Toronto, ON, M6M 3W7. Contact: Tony Baxby, Dir., Fran. Dev. - Tel: (416) 656-9988, (416) 656-3676. Custom sign centres that offer full service interior/exterior signage, window lettering, vehicle and boat lettering, special event banners, magnetic signs, illuminated exterior signs, etc., to today's business community. The sign graphics are computer generated, utilizing state-of-the-art technology and proven vinyl films. Established: 1983 - Franchising Since: 1988 - No. of Units: Company Owned: 1 - Franchised: 10 - Franchise Fee: $25,000 - Royalty: 8% - Total Inv: $90,720 ($25,000 fran. fee, $5,000 adv. launch package, $60,720 inven., equip., supplies & leaseholds) - Financing: Equipment.

SPORTS & RECREATION

AL'S DIVEMASTER SERVICES
Al's Dive Shop, Inc.
9 Duke St., St. Catharines, ON, L2R 6W8. Contact: Allen J. Marsh, Founder & Pres. - Tel: (905) 688-2665, Fax: (905) 688-7728. All aspects of the diving sport are offered: teaching, retailing and dive outings. Established: 1994 - Franchising Since: 1994 - No. of Units: Company Owned: 1 - Franchised: 1 - Franchise Fee: $15,000 - Royalty: 5%, 2% adv. - Total Inv: $100,000 incl. fran. fee - Financing: No.

CALHOUN SPORTSWEAR
Catfish Calhoun, Inc.
250 Bunting Rd., St. Catharines, ON, L2M 3Y1. Contact: M. Myers, Pres. - Tel: (905) 688-6100. Manufacturer of imprinted active sportswear, infants to adult sizes; screen printing, computerized embroidery, instant heat press printing. Established: 1973 - Franchising Since: 1984 - No. of Units: Company Owned: 5 - Franchise Fee: $10,000 - $15,000 - Total Inv: $40,000 up depending on store size.

CYCLEPATH, THE
Anything Cycle, Inc.
6760 Pacific Circle, Mississauga, ON, L5T 1N8. Contact: John L. Watson, Fran. Dir. - Tel: (905) 564-8488, (800) 722-2793. The Cyclepath is Canada's largest bicycle, in-line-skate and fitness retail franchise. We carry an extensive selection of brand name (many exclusive) bicycles, parts and accessories and offer full service on all products. Fully computerized systems. Established: 1981 - Franchising Since: 1987 - No. of Units: Company Owned: 1 - Franchised: 56 - Franchise Fee: $40,000 - Royalty: None - Total Inv: $150,000 - $200,000 (including inventory) - Financing: Assistance through financial institutes.

DARKZONE *
Darkzone Technologies Inc.
230 Osborne St., Winnipeg, MB, R3L 1Z5. Contact: L.A. O'Connor, Pres. - Tel: (204) 287-8776, Fax: (204) 287-8703. The Ultimate Laser Adventure™. Suitable for all ages. Features 3 team format interactive laser game played in custom designed theme maze. Full support systems to all sites from pre-opening. Turnkey sites available. Established: 1993 - Franchising Since: 1994 - No. of Units: Company Owned: 1 - Franchised: 5 - Franchise Fee: $35,000 to $50,000 - Royalty: Varies (3%-8% approx.) - Total Inv: Varies with size/number 350-600,000 - Financing: None.

DOG'S EAR T-SHIRT CO., THE
6584 Golden Eagle Way, Nanaimo, BC, V9V 1P8. Contact: Mr. B. Giraud, Pres. - Tel: (604) 390-1981. Retail sales of t-shirts and imprinted sportswear. Established: 1974 - Franchising Since: 1978 - No. of Units: Franchised: 11 - Franchise Fee: $15,000 - Royalty: 4%, 2% adv. - Total Inv: Turn Key $75,000 - Financing: No.

DYNAMO POOL LEAGUE
Canadian Pool Players Assoc. Inc.
200 McNab St., Ste. 201, Walkerton, ON, N0G 2V0. Contact: Lindsay Dobson, Pres. - Tel: (519) 881-2196. Organizing amateur pool leagues using a unique copyright handicap system - directing tournaments. Established: 1988 - Franchising Since: 1989 - No. of Units : Franchised: 10 - Franchise Fee: None - Royalty: $5 per team or 20% whichever is greater - Total Inv: $4,500 seminar, software, office supplies - Financing: None.

EXCELLENCE SPORTS
Marchands Unis, Inc.
CP 1377 Terminus, Quebec, PQ, G1K 7G7. Contact: Mr. Simon Boulanger, Dir. Mktg. - Tel: (418) 687-3050. Sporting goods. No. of Units: 75.

FLYAWAY INDOOR SKYDIVING
165417 Canada Ltd.
Box 1234, Cornwall, ON, K6H 5R9. Contact: Cliff Tessier, V.P. - Tel: (613) 933-2443, Fax: (613) 932-3518. Closed system vertical wind tunnel in which participants perform skydiving maneuvers. Spectator gallery can hold up to 60 people. Revenues derive from participants and spectators. Relatively simple business to operate. High returns possible. Exciting, fun, thrilling recreational activity. Established: 1980 - Franchising Since: 1984 - Franchise Fee: $50,000 - Royalty: 6% - Total Inv: $450,000 - Financing: Yes.

GOLF USA
Off Course Pro Shops Ltd.
9675 Macleod Tr. S., Calgary, AB, T2J 0P6. Contact: Toby Racette, Dir. of Fran. - Tel: (403) 640-2000, Fax: (403) 640-2426. Golf equipment specialty store offering golf equipment and related clothing, accessories,

supplies and services. Established: 1993 in Canada - Franchising Since: 1986 in U.S.A. - No. of Units: Company Owned: 1 - Franchised: 5 - Franchise Fee: $48,000 - Royalty: 3%, 1% ad. fund - Total Inv: $225,000 to $300,000 - Financing: No.

JERSEY CITY
Jercity Franchises, Ltd.
824 - 41 Ave. N.E., Calgary, AB, T2E 3R3. Contact: Tim Walsh, Fran. Licensing - Tel: (403) 230-5587. Jersey City sells the highest quality authentic & replica sports apparel & gifts from all the major leagues. Our stores sell items from toddler to adults; of interest to men & women. Established: 1983 - Franchising Since: 1989 - No. of Units: Company Owned: 3 - Franchised: 27 - Franchise Fee: $20,000 for first, $10,000 for subsequent - Royalty: 5% of gross, 1% adv. royalty - Total Inv: $145,000 - $195,000 - Financing: Royal Bank of Canada.

MUSCLEMAG INTERNATIONAL
6465 Airport Rd., Mississauga, ON, L4V 1E4. Contact: Marianne Butler, Licensing Mgr. - Tel: (905) 678-7311. Exercise stores selling to the skyrocketting fitness, health and bodybuilding market. Established: 1974 - Franchising Since: 1993 - No. of Units: Company Owned: 4 - Franchised: 12 - Franchise Fee: $4,500 - Royalty: 5% - Total Inv: $45,000 - $65,000 (start-up costs) - Financing: No.

NEVADA BOB'S GOLF AND RACQUETS
Dimarco Golf
5170 Dixie Rd., Mississauga, ON, L4W 1E3. Contact: Bill Dimarco, Pres. - Tel: (905) 624-5077. Franchise operation specializing in golf and racquet goods, repair services, footwear and athletic sportswear. Established: 1985 (Eastern Can.) - Franchising Since: 1987 (Eastern Can.) - No. of Units: Company Owned: 2 (Eastern Can.) - Franchised: 10 (Eastern Can.) - Franchise Fee: $15,000 - $40,000 assessed on local population & potential sales vol. - Royalty: 3.5% on first ($1M) gross sales - Total Inv: $150,000 min. (incls. fran. fee, leaseholds & inventory).

RODIER, RODIER HOMMES
Promafil Canada Ltd.
300 Marcellaurin Blvd., Ste. 100, St. Laurent, PQ, H4M 2L4. Contact: Alain Francois, Gen. Mgr. - Tel: (514) 747-1837. Ladies' and men's sportswear. Established: 1942 - Franchising Since: 1948 - No. of Units: 50 - Franchised: 550 - Total Inv: $100,000 store layout, $70,000 inven. - Financing: No.

SPORTS EXPERTS
4141 Autoroute 440, Laval, West, PQ, H7P 4W6. Contact: Mr. Louis Gourdeau, Dir. of Fran. Dev. - Tel: (514) 687-5200. Sporting goods and leisure products. Established: 1967 - Franchising Since: 1972 - No. of Units: Company Owned: 48 - Franchised: 159 - Franchise Fee: $30,000- Royalty: 4.5% - Total Inv: $600,000 .

SPORTS RECRUITS INTERNATIONAL
Sports Recruits International Inc.
128 Queen St. S., Box 42277, Mississauga, ON, L5M 5Z5. Contact: Terry Glenister, Dir. of Fran. - Tel: (905) 821-0040. International recruiting organization which provides exposure of above average student/athletes to American/Canadian colleges/universities for purpose of obtaining a funded college/university education. Established: 1990 - Franchising Since: 1990 - No. of Units: Franchised: 10 - Franchise Fee: Varies according to location based on size of territory - Total Inv: Varies based on size of territory - Financing: No.

TRIPLE AAA SPORTS PHOTOGRAPHY INC.
P.O. Box 80808, Burnaby, BC, V5H 3Y1. Contact: Rob Johnson, Pres. - Tel: (604) 451-1111. Sports team photography. Established: 1977 - Franchising Since: 1992 - No. of Units: Company Owned: 1 - Franchised: 4 - Franchise Fee: $25,000 - Royalty: 10% - Total Inv: $40,000 includes all (fee & equip.) - Financing: No.

WACKYPUTT *
Le Rigolfeur Inc.
7 Boul. J.F. Kennedy, Loc. 12, St. Jerome, PQ, J7Y 4B4. Contact: P. Desjardins, Pres. - Tel: (514) 438-2070, Fax: (514) 438-8478. Patented gags 'n pranks exterior electronics miniature golf with interchangable cup, tee & platform. Established: 1993 - Franchising Since: 1993 - No. of Units: Company Owned: 3 - Franchised: 15 - Franchise Fee: $2,500 to $35,000+ - Royalty: 50¢ per ball after 10,000/yr. - Total Inv: $185,000 to $300,000 - Financing: No.

TRAVEL

ALGONQUIN TRAVEL
Ottawa Algonquin Travel Corp.
657 Bronson Ave., Ottawa, ON, K1S 4E7. Contact: Katrina Rourke, Dir. of Fran. - Tel: (613) 233-7713, (613) 233-7805. Full service travel agencies. Locations available coast to coast in Canada. Highest average sales per franchise travel agency in Canada. Established: 1964 - Franchising Since: 1979 - No. of Units: Company Owned: 1 - Franchised: 52 - Franchise Fee: $35,000 - Royalty: 6% - 10%, 5% adv. - Total Inv: $115,000 - $150,000 - Financing: National franchise banking program with CIBC.

CRUISE VACATIONS
101 - 2025 W. Broadway, Vancouver, BC, V6J 1Z6. Contact: Gordon Froese, Dir. of Mktg. & Sales - Tel: (604) 731-5546, (800) 665-1882. Cruise only travel agencies. Established: 1978 - Franchising Since: 1991 - No. of Units: Company Owned: 1 - Franchised: 4 - Franchise Fee: $39,900 - Royalty: 1% of gross sales - Total Inv: $95,000 incl. computer hardware, license fee, work. cap., leasehold, rent, deposits - Financing: Secured by applicant.

CRUISESHIPCENTERS
Pacific Northwest Cruiseshipcenters Ltd.
Ste. 555, 1111 W. Hastings St., Vancouver, BC, V6E 2J3. Contact: Eunice LaRocque, Dir. of Fran. Sales - Tel: (604) 685-1221, (604) 685-1245. Retail travel centers specializing in cruise vacation sales. Established: 1989 - Franchising Since: 1989 - No. of Units: Franchised: 31 - Franchise Fee: $40,000 - Royalty: 9% of commissioned revenue - Total Inv: $125,000 - Financing: No.

CRUISESHIPCENTERS (ONTARIO)
125 Lakeshore Rd. E., Oakville, ON, L6J 1H3. Contact: Bill Courian, Reg. Dir. - Tel: (905) 338-8083. Cruise travel agency. Established: 1987 - Franchising Since: 1987 - No. of Units: Company Owned: 1 - Franchised: 28 - Franchise Fee: $40,000 - Royalty: approx. 1% of sales - Total Inv: fran. fee, $20,000 furn. & equip., $40,000 work. cap. - Financing: Yes.

GOLIGER'S TRAVEL LTD.
5025 Orbitor Dr., Bldg. 4, Ste. 300, Mississauga, ON, L4W 4Y5. Contact: Mara Pagotto, Franchise Dept. - Tel: (905) 625-8374. Retail travel agencies. Established: 1955 - Franchising Since: 1979 - No. of Units: Company Owned: 5 - Franchised: 84 - Franchise Fee: $49,000 - Royalty: $1,100 a month - Total Inv: fran fee, $40,000 office & leasehold, $40,000 working cap. - Financing: Yes, thru normal channels.

ROBERT Q'S TRAVEL
Robert Q's Travel Mart Inc.
105 Wharncliffe Rd. S., London, ON, N6J 2K2. Contact: Dana Jarvis, Fran. Dept. - Tel: (519) 672-9020. Full service travel agency, airport transportation service throughout Southwestern Ontario serving Toronto and Detroit airports, as well as escorted tour companies. Established: 1969 - Franchising Since: 1975 - No. of Units: Company Owned: 2 - Franchised: 15 - Franchise Fee: $15,000 - $25,000 - Royalty: 1% of commissionable sales - Total Inv: approx. $75,000 - Financing: Yes.

THOMAS COOK / MARLIN TRAVEL
10711 Cambie Rd., Richmond, BC, V6X 3G5. Contact: Mrs. Mikki Dorn, V.P. & Dir. of Franc. - Tel: (604) 278-3454. Travel agency. Established: 1967 - No. of Units: Company Owned: 104 - Franchised: 111 - Franchise Fee: $5,000 - Royalty: 0.75% on sales plus 0.5% adv. - Total Inv: $40,000, fee, $35,000 working capital, $20,000 furniture and fixtures.

TRAVEL PROFESSIONALS INTERNATIONAL
Chia Chia Communications Inc.
8th Fl., 1661 Portage Ave., Winnipeg, MB, R3J 3T7. Contact: Lewis Sovereign, Dir. of Bus. Dev. - Tel: (800) 757-8580, (204) 987-3521, Fax: (204) 987-3338. Full service travel agency with unique central

support office linked to home, office and business based associates. Low overhead, high profit structure. Established: 1976 - Franchising Since: 1987 - No. of Units: Company Owned: 4 - Franchised: 500+ - Franchise Fee: $14,995 - Total Inv: $3,500 training, $1,500 manuals, balance fee - Financing: Yes.

UNIGLOBE TRAVEL
Uniglobe Travel (International) Inc.
1199 W. Pender St., Ste.900, Vancouver, BC, V6E 2R1. Contact: Dir. Fran. Licensing - Tel: (800) 590-4111. Large travel franchise. A franchisee receives a vast array of services. National TV advertising, brand image, profitability software programs, one-on-one agency consultations, owners and managers meetings, preferred override programs, plus the equivalent of 125 days of training per month system-wide, all to gain a competitive edge in the travel market. Established: 1979 - Franchising Since: 1980 - No. of Units: Franchised: 1165 - Franchise Fee: $3,000 - $47,000 - Royalty: 0.5 - 1%, $735/mo. adv. - Total Inv: $3,000 - $150,000 - Financing: Varies according to region.

WILDWOOD TRAVEL INC.
5218 Yonge St., Willowdale, ON, M2N 5P6. Contact: Ehud Estreicher, Pres. - Tel: (416) 223-8111, (800) 461-8111, Fax: (416) 223-4645. A unique work from your home travel business. Low overheads, excellent income. Corporate training & support. Established: 1990 - Franchising Since: 1990 - No. of Master Correspondents: 11 - Correspondents: 200 - Franchise Fee: $12,500 - Equipment: $2,500 - Financing: No. Franchise: Franchise Fee $50,000 for each territory of one million in population.

WATER TREATMENT

CULLIGAN OF CANADA LTD.
2213 N. Sheridan Way, Mississauga, ON, L5K 1A5. Contact: Carmen Scione, Pres. - Tel: (905) 822-1601. Manufacturing and distributing of water conditioning equipment, domestic and commercial/industrial through franchised dealers. Established: 1947 - Franchising Since: 1952 - No. of Units: Company Owned: 1 - Franchised: 55 - Franchise Fee: $10,000 - $18,000 - Royalty: 5% Bottled Water - Total Inv: $75,000 - $100,000.

INTEGRA ENVIRONMENTAL
Integra Environmental Inc.
5035 North Service Rd., #C7, Burlington, ON, L7L 5V2. Contact: Marc Bajzik, V.P., Mktg. - Tel: (905) 336-2096. Water filtration equipment sold to residential, industrial & commercial applications. We have approx. 500 distributors. Average start-up package is $2,000. Established: 1983 - Franchising Since: 1985.

MISCELLANEOUS

ACTION PARALEGAL
61 Sheppard Ave. W., North York, ON, M2N 1M4. Contact: Wayne P. Morrison, Pres. - Tel: (416) 590-0253, Fax: (416) 733-9715. Paralegal services. Established: 1988 - Franchising Since: 1994 - No. of Units: Company Owned: 2 - Franchised: 2 - Franchise Fee: $18,000 - Royalty: 1st year nil, 2nd year 5% - Total Inv: $18,000 - Financing: Yes.

ACTUAL REALITY INTERNATIONAL, INC. *
8630 - 53rd Ave., Edmonton, AB, T6L 1V9. Contact: Tim Healey, Sales & Mktg. - Tel: (403) 440-3706. Sells interactive laser games / dealership. Established: 1992 - Franchising Since: 1993 - No. of Units: Company Owned: 1 - Franchised: 9 - Franchise Fee: $85,000 US - Royalty: .30 per game played (5% on gross) - Total Inv: Turnkey $200,000 to $250,000.

BEVINCO
Bevinco Bar Systems, Ltd.
235 Yorkland Blvd., #409, Toronto, ON, M2J 4Y8. Contact: Barry Driedger, Pres. - Tel: (416) 490-6266, (800) 665-1743, Fax: (416) 490-6899. Liquor inventory control service for bars and restaurants utilizing our computerized system of weighing and counting stock on hand and used. Then comparing it to sales and producing detailed variance reports to control "shrinkage". Established: 1987 - Franchising Since: 1990 - No. of Units: Company Owned: 1 - Franchised: 55 - Franchise Fee: $15,000 - Royalty: $10/audit - Total Inv: $20,000, $5,000 equip. - Financing: No.

CANADIAN CHEQUE CASHING CORP. *
185 E. Hastings St., Vancouver, BC, V6A 1N5. Contact: Pat Hughes, Gen. Mgr. - Tel: (604) 683-2222, Fax: (604) 683-2384. Cheque cashing business, foreign exchange, money orders, Western Union agents. Established: 1985 - Franchising Since: 1995 - No. of Units: Company Owned: 2 - Franchise Fee: $15,000 - Royalty: Negotiable - Total Inv: Applicant should have $100,000 unencumbered capital.

CASH-A-CHEQUE
Cash Plus Services Inc.
360 Bayfield St., Unit 3, Barrie, ON, L4M 3C4. Contact: Barry C. Luke, Gen. Mgr. - Tel: (705) 725-7680, Fax: (705) 725-7687. Cheque cashing and currency exchange. Established: 1990 - Franchising Since: 1992 - No. of Units: Company Owned: 1 - Franchised: 19 - Franchise Fee: $25,000 or $60,000 - $65,000 turnkey - Royalty: fixed $350 + GST - Total Inv: additional $20,000 - $50,000 operating cash - Financing: Some.

CROPCO INC.
P.O. Box 880, Hwy. 21, Kincardine, ON, N2Z 2Z4. Contact: Murray King, Gen. Mgr. - Tel: (519) 523-4231. A crop consulting company selling their service to farmers and agribusiness. Established: 1987 - Franchising Since: 1992 - No. of Units: Company Owned: 1 - Franchised: 1 - Franchise Fee: $10,000 - Royalty: 10%, 1% adv. - Total Inv: $15,000 operating - Financing: Leasing package.

DFD TELEBROADCASTING
163 Limestone Cr., Downsview, ON, M3J 2R1. Contact: Marvin D. Fine, Pres. - Tel: (416) 665-7997, Fax: 665-2958. Notification service bureau of voice messages. Established: 1984 - Franchising Since: 1986 - No. of Units: Company Owned: 1 - Franchised: 2 - Royalty: mthly. software license fee $5 line/day - Total Inv: $4,000 - Financing: Yes.

DRIVER'S ADVOCATE
4158 Sheppard Ave. E., Scarborough, ON, M1S 1T3. Contact: Susan McDonald, Franc. Sales Dir. - Tel: (416) 292-1888. To the franchisee with experience as police, prosecutor or Justice of the Peace, Driver's Advocate offers in-depth training in court procedures, marketing and business administration. We use our business experience to provide ongoing educational updates and continued support of your financial objectives. Established: 1987 - Franchising Since: 1992 - No. of Units: Company Owned: 2 - Franchised: 1 - Franchise Fee: $30,000 - Royalty: flat mthly. rate $1,000 + mthly. adv. $500. - Total Inv: $55,000: start up costs (inc.fee) $40,000, work. cap. $15,000 - Financing: We can help obtain financing.

EDWARD D. JONES & CO. *
Sussex Ctr., Ste. 902, 90 Burnhamthorpe Rd. W., Mississauga, ON, L5B 3C3. Contact: Wally Rawlinko, Sales Hiring - Tel: (905) 273-8400. A full service investment firm specializing in single-representative, community-based branch offices. Established: 1994 (CAN), 1871 (US) - No. of Units: Company Owned: 3,300.

FAST-FIX JEWELRY REPAIRS
1115 Sherbrooke St. W., Ste. 2802, Montreal, PQ, H3A 1H3. Contact: Martin Greenspon, Pres. - Tel: (514) 289-8718, Fax: (514) 499-8553, or (416) 969-8657, Fax: (416) 969-9754. A jewelry and watch repair service chain that offers fast, efficient, quality work in regional malls throughout North America. Chain soldering, remounting, ring sizing, engraving and replacement of watch batteries and watch bands. Established: 1984 - Franchising Since: 1987 - No. of Units: Company Owned: 3 - Franchised: 62 - Franchise Fee: $25,000 - Royalty: 7% - Total Inv: $75,000 - $95,000 incl. license fee, work. cap., inven., rent, deposits, leasehold - Financing: Conventional sources.

FIBRENEW INDUSTRIES LTD. *
1407 Acadia Dr., Calgary, AB, T2J 4C6. Contact: Michael Wilson, Pres. - Tel: (403) 278-1448, Fax: (403) 278-1434. Repair & re-dye leather, plastic, vinyl & fabric with specific applications in automobile, aviation, marine & residential industries. Established: 1985 - Franchising Since: 1985 - No. of Units: Company Owned: 4 - Franchised: 31 - Franchise Fee: $25,000+ - Royalty: flat rate - Financing: No.

J&M COIN, STAMP & JEWELLERY LTD.
106 W. Broadway St., Vancouver, BC, V5Y 1P3. Contact: Joseph Iorio, Pres. - Tel: (604) 876-7181. Coin, stamp, jewellery, foreign exchange buying & selling. Established: 1967 - No. of Units: Company Owned: 4 - Franchise Fee: $25,000 - Royalty: $1,000 per month - Total Inv: $25,000 fran. fee, $50,000 - $150,000 furniture & equip., $150,000 & up inventory - Financing: Yes.

LORMIT PROCESS SERVICES *
Lormit Management Systems, Inc.
310, 10232 - 112 St., Edmonton, AB, T5K 1M4. Contact: Tim Haworth, Pres. - Tel: (403) 424-4442, Fax: (403) 426-4917. Delivery of notice in legal proceedings. Established: 1979 - Franchising Since: 1985 - No. of Units: Franchised: 33 - Royalty: 20% of cash receipts inclusive of advertising and centralized accounts collection - Total Inv: approx. $300 for stationery - Financing: No.

MAGI SEAL SERVICES
Magi Seal Services, Inc.
1065 Clarkside Rd., London, ON, N5V 3B3. Contact: James Harris, CEO - Tel: (800) 388-2640. Furniture stores sell fabric protection to customers and contract Magi Seal to do the actual spraying of the furniture. Established: 1983 - Franchising Since: 1983 - No. of Units: Company Owned: 1 - Franchised: 22 - Franchise Fee: $10,000 to $90,000 - Royalty: None - Total Inv: Typical $15,000 - Financing: 80% company financing.

MONEY MART
National Money Mart, Inc.
3rd Floor, 1640 Oak Bay Ave., Victoria, BC, V8R 1B2. Contact: Jim Wilson, Fran. Lic. Consultant - Tel: (604) 595-5211. The franchise business offers financial and related services including cheque cashing, sale of money orders, cash wire service, mail box rentals, sale of photo identification, fax and copy service, currency exchange (optional) and other products and services developed by the franchisor from time to time. Established: 1982 - Franchising Since: 1982 - No. of Units: Company Owned &/or Operated: 32 - Franchised: 104 - Franchise Fee: $25,000 - Royalty: 6.75% of gross rev., 2% adv. - Total Inv: $120,000 min. - Financing: No.

MR. CRISPY'S HOT FRIES
Pro Fries Inc.
#530, 510 5th St. S.W., Calgary, AB, T2P 3S2. Contact: Kenneth J. Small, Pres. - Tel: (403) 237-9758. Design and manufacture of patented french fry vending machine that services a 4.5 oz. of traditionally-cooked real potato fries in 45 seconds. CSA, UL, ULC and NAMA listed. Established: 1986 - Franchising Since: 1989 - No. of Units: Company Owned: 120 - Franchised/Sold: 550 - Franchise Fee: $15,600 - Royalty: 10¢ vend - Total Inv: $13,900 per machine - Financing: No.

MR. WIZARD (R) GLASS TINTING SHOWROOM
Mr. Wizard (R) Glass Tinting
P.O. Box 486, Victoria, B.C., V8W 2N8. Contact: J.A. Haskett, Franc. Dir. - Tel: (604) 475-2404, Fax: (604) 475-2405. Offering 2 separate franchises: Vehicle and a Residential/Commercial franchise. Both involve applying our unique 5-ply polyester films to vehicle or building windows. Vehicle franchise operates from a minimum 1-bay shop. Res/Com franchise can be started from home office. Established: 1987 - Franchising Since: 1989 - No. of Units: Company Owned: 1 - Franchised: 2 - Franchise Fee: $25,000 for 10 yr. term - Royalty: 7% max. declining to 5.5% - Total Inv: $25,000 + inv. pkg. of $19,500 vehicle, $14,500 res.com - Financing: Possibly up to 50% of fran. fee.

PARALEGAL ASSOCIATES
Paralegal Associates Inc.
80 Bradford St., Ste. 125, Box 7, Barrie, ON, L4N 6S7. Contact: Frank J. Laird, Pres. - Tel: (705) 721-9422, Fax: (705) 721-9423. Providing full range of paralegal services including (highway traffic & provincial offences, small claims, landlord/tenant, family matters, business incorporation, criminal pardons). Established: 1987 - Franchising Since: 1987 - No. of Units: Company Owned: 2 - Franchised: 10 - Franchise Fee: $15,000 - Royalty: 5%, 1% adv. - Total Inv: $15,000 - Financing: Yes.

PERSONAL PROTECTION SYSTEMS *
200 Steelcase Rd., E., #3, Markham, ON, L3R 1G2. Contact: Helen Fischer, Franchising - Tel: (800) 861-4777, (905) 940-9777, Fax: (905) 940-9701. Women's personal protection courses. Established: 1993 - Franchising Since: 1995 - No. of Units: Company Owned: 1 - Franchise Fee: $7,500 - Royalty: 15% - Total Inv: $11,000 - Financing: No.

POINTTS
Pointts Advisory Ltd.
304 The East Mall, Ste. 370, Toronto, ON, M9B 6E2. Contact: Brian J. Lawrie, Pres. & C.E.O. - Tel: (416) 234-9200. Firm of ex-police officers who represent citizens in court charges under the Highway Traffic Act. Established: 1984 - Franchising Since: 1985. No. of Units: Company Owned: 3 - Franchised: 30 - Franchise Fee: $60,000 + - Royalty: 9% - Total Inv: Fran. fee plus set-up - Financing: Yes.

SCHARECORP
Scharecorp Marketing Ltd.
228 Carlton St., Toronto, ON, M5A 2L1. Contact: Susan Milligan, Dir.Franc. - Tel: (416) 968-7418. Operation of Good Turn System coin-operated vendors bearing the Muscular Dystrophy Association name & logo. Established: 1984 - Franchising Since: 1986 - Number of Units: Franchised: 8,500 - Franchise Fee: $17,500 - Total Inv: $17,500 fran.fee $17,500 product & equip. - Financing: Yes.

SHRED-IT
Shred-It Franchise, Inc.
2359 Royal Windsor Dr., Unit 15, Mississauga, ON, L5J 1K5. Contact: John Prittie, V.P. Fran. Dev. - Tel: (905) 855-2540. Mobile paper shredding and recycling business serving hospitals, medical facilities, banks and financial institutions, government, large and small business. A mobile franchise operating business to business. Established: 1989 - Franchising Since: 1992 - No. of Units: Company Owned: 2 - Franchised: 2 - Franchise Fee: $35,000 - Royalty: 5%, 1.5% ad. fund - Total Inv: $80,000 - $90,000 + work. cap. $80,000 - $100,000 - Financing: 3rd party - trucks leased.

STRIPPERS!, THE
SAW Creations Inc.
427 Gage Ave., Unit 2, Kitchener, ON, N2M 5E1. Contact: Margery Smith, Mktg. Dir. - Tel: (519) 576-8282. Complete restoration of antiques and all types of furniture. Retail store front and shop with on-site stripping and finishing service. Minimum one month training in the marketing and hands on aspects of the business. Established: 1982 - Franchising Since: 1989 - No. of Units: Company Owned: 1 - Franchised: 5 - Franchise Fee: $27,500 - Royalty: None - Total Inv: $35,000 - Financing: No.

T.D.I. SYSTEMS CANADA *
11 - 1393 Border St., Winnipeg, MB, R3H 0N1. Contact: Wilson Wong, Pres. - Tel: (204) 697-9612, Fax: (204) 697-9615. Large format printing (artist canvas, watercolor, vinyl, translite, photo papers, etc.) from one printer. Enlarge images as small as 1"x2" into any size on any media. Established: 1994 - No. of Units In Canada: 25 - Total Inv: $50,000 - Financing: Yes.

TELE-TECH COMMUNICATIONS INC.
1350 E. 4th Ave., Vancouver, B.C., V5N 1J5. Contact: Ian Abramson, Pres. - Tel: (604) 255-5000. Cordless pay phones. Established: 1987 - Franchising Since: 1987 - No. of Units: Company Owned: 1 - Franchised: 2 - Franchise Fee: $15,000 - Financing: No.

ZEMBIK OPEN AIR PROTECTION INC. *
Zembiko Innovations Ltd.
#2, 293 17 St. West, Prince Albert, SK, S6V 3X6. Contact: Allen, Pres. - Tel: (306) 922-3390. Instant portable shelters. Box extender. Established: 1992 - Franchising Since: 1994 - No. of Units: Company Owned: 1 - Franchised: 2 - Franchise Fee: $150,000 US funds - Royalty: 10% on sales - Total Inv: $150,000 fran. fee, hoop building $40,000 - Financing: No.

OVERSEAS LISTINGS

AUTOMOTIVE PRODUCTS AND SERVICES

ADD-ITT FRANCHISING LTD.
The Old Freight Depot, Roberts Rd., Balby, Doncaster, S. Yorks., England, DN4 0JU. Contact: Mr. Mercer, U.K. Fran. Dev. Mgr. - Tel: (0302) 320269. Van based sales business selling full range of automotive products to the garage trade. Structured computerized sales program and stock management system. Comprehensive in-house and field training provided. Established: 1984 - Franchising Since: 1986 - No. of Units: Company Owned: 1 - Franchised: 7 - Franchise Fee: £8,500 includes £2,000 initial stock and starter pack - Royalty: None - Total Inv: £8,500 initial fee, equip., stock, training, etc.

AUTELA
Autela Components Ltd.
Regal House, Birmingham Rd., Stratford-Upon-Avon, Warwickshire, England, CV37 OBN. Contact: Mr. R. B. Taylor, Nat. Fran. Mgr. - Tel: (01789) 414545, Fax: (01789) 414580. Automotive aftermarket parts distributor. Wholesale motor component distributor to the motor and allied industries from commercial property sites. Established: 1971 - Franchising Since: 1982 - No. of Units: Company Owned: 77 - Franchised: 20 - Franchise Fee: £5,000 - Royalty: 5% mgmt. fee and 0.5% adv. fee - Total Inv: £50,000 to $60,000 - Financing: Yes, through all major banks.

AUTO 5
GB-INNO-BM sa
Ave. des Olympiades 20, Brussels Brabant, Belgium, 1140. Contact: H.J. Ruys, Expansion Manager - Tel: (02) 243-24 31 and 36. Sales of car accessories with workshop. Specializing in tires, exhausts, batteries, shock absorbers, lubricants, maintenance products. Established: 1966 - Franchising Since: 1986 - No. of Units: Company Owned: 42 - Franchised: 5 - Franchise Fee: 300.000 F - Royalty: 6.6% on turnover - Total Inv: 6.000.000+ BF - Financing: 1.700.000 BF.

AUTO COLORMATCH
P.A. Research Ltd.
28 Glen Road Boscombe, Bournemouth, Dorset, U.K., BH5 1HS. Contact: Peter Addison, M.D. - Tel: 0202-396002. Car paint shop in a small van repairing small dings, rust marks scratches etc. on cars for trade & public at 1/2 price of spraying whole panel. Established: 1986 - Franchising Since: 1988 - No. of Units: Franchised: 12 - Franchise Fee: require area - Royalty: master franchisees for Canada & US - Financing: Yes.

AUTOPREP LTD.
Old School, The Common, Redbourne, St. Albans, Herts, England, AL3 7NG. Contact: G. N. Hustings, Dir. - Tel: 0805-770697. Car cleaning and valet service. Established: 1978 - Franchising Since: 1978 - No. of Units: 2 - Franchise Fee: £4,500 - Total Inv: £5,500 - Royalty: 15%.

AUTOPRO LTD.
1A Badminton Rd., Trading Estate, Yate, Bristol, England, BS17 5JS. Contact: Nick Brayshaw, Mng. Dir. - Tel: 0454-314971, Telex: 44202. Supply of hand tools and equipment to garage trade out of mobile vans. Established: 1977 - Franchising Since: 1977 - No. of Units: 47 - Franchise Fee: £2,500 - Total Inv: £8,500.

AUTOSHEEN LIMITED
21-25 Sanders Rd., Finedon Rd. Ind. Estate, Wellingborough, Northants, England, NN8 4NL. Contact: Graham Bullock, Mktg. Dir. - Tel: 0933 272347. Mobile automotive valeting to private and corporate customers in U.K. Established: 1984 - Franchising Since: 1985 - No. of Units: Company Owned: 2 - Franchised: 55 - Franchise Fee: £4,995 - £8,995 depending on area covered - Royalty: 8% management fee + 2.5% mktg. - Total Inv: work. cap. £900, launch exps. £500 + fran. fee - Financing: Through major banks.

AUTOSMART LIMITED
Lynn Lane, Shenstone, Staffordshire, UK, WS14 0DH. Contact: Sophie Atkinson, Dir. - Tel: 0543 481616. Autosmart franchisees have a 'mobile showroom' from which they sell vehicle cleaning products to car dealers and hauliers. Established: 1978 - Franchising Since: 1978 - No. of Units: Franchised: 85 - Franchise Fee: £3,500 - Royalty: None - Total Inv: £18,000 - £30,000 work. cap. - Financing: From all big 5 banks.

AVIS RENT-A-CAR LTD.
Trident House, Station Rd., Hayes, Middlesex, England, UB3 4DJ. Contact: Tony Brewer, Lic. Rel. Mgr. - Tel: (01) 848-8765. Auto rentals. Established: 1946 (in USA) - No. of Units: 3,500 locations in 110 countries, 90 in UK - Inv: £55,000.

BATTERYMAN BY CHLORIDE
Chloride Automotive Batteries Ltd.
Chequers Lane, Dagenham, , Essex , England, RM9 6PX. Contact: Geoff Dean, Mktg. Mgr. - Tel: 01-592-4560. Selling of dry batteries and allied products. Established: 1920 - Franchising Since: 1982 - No. of Units: 28 - Franchise Fee: £5,000/vehicle - Royalty: 1% gross - Financing: to suitable applicants through major banks.

BUDGET RENT A CAR INT. INC.
41 Marlowes, Hemel Hempstead Herts., England, HP1 1XJ. Contact: Bernard Glover, Fran. Sales Mgr. - Tel: (44) 1442 276000, Fax: (44) 1442 276100. Car, van and truck rental. Established: 1966 in UK - Franchising Since: 1960 - No. of Units: Company Owned: 11 - Franchised: 142 - Franchise Fee: £25,000 - Royalty: 7.5% + 2.5% adv. - Total Inv: £75,000 (£25,000 fee + £50,000 work. cap.) - Financing: For fleet but not for investment.

BUMPA T BUMPA AUTOMART
17 Glentanna St., Kedron, Brisbane, Australia, 4031. Contact: Mr. Andrew Harrison, Gen. Mgr. - Corporate - Tel: (07) 3301577. Retail automotive spare parts, accessories, and car stereo. Established: 1973 - Franchising Since: 1984 - No. of Units: Company Owned: 4 - Franchised: 32 - Franchise Fee: $40,000 to $70,000 - Royalty: 4% + 3% adv. - Total Inv: $400,000 - $730,000 - Financing: 50%.

CARNOISSEUR
Carnoisseur (Retail) Ltd.
Brittany Court, High St. S., Dunstable, Bedfordshire, England, LU6 3HR. Contact: Neville Crow, Chairman - Tel: (0582) 471700. Retail specialist car accessories. Established: 1986 - Franchising Since: 1993 - No. of Units: Company Owned: 1 - Franchised: 5 - Franchise Fee: £3,000 - Royalty: 6% sales - Total Inv: £30,000 - Financing: Yes.

CLEAN PARK
Clean Park GmbH
Amselweg 6/1, Winnenden, Germany, 71364. Contact: Thomas Idler, Fran. Mgr. - Tel: 07195/6902-0. Selling and installation of franchised self service washing plants and additional installations for car care. Established: 1986 - Franchising Since: 1986 - Franchise Fee: DM 70, - per bay and month - Royalty: approx. DM 50,000 per bay and year - Total Inv: approx. DM 150,000 - DM 1,200,000 - Financing: No, but support in obtaining and securing a credit.

COMPUTA TUNE
9 Petre Rd., Clayton Le Moors, Accrington, Lancs., England, BB5 5JB. Contact: A. Whittaker, Mng. Dir. - Tel: 01254 391792, Fax: 01254 390361. Mobile vehicle servicing and fixed site mot centres. Established: 1981 - Franchising Since: 1986 - No. of Units: Company Owned: 1 - Franchised: 108 - Franchise Fee: £3,500 - Royalty: 10% on sales - Total Inv: £7,500 - Financing: Yes, up to 70%.

ELEPHANT BLEU
Hypromat France S.A.
15, rue du Travail Z.I., BP 147, Hoerdt, France, 67720. Contact: M. Bruno Palmino, Export Mgr. - Tel: (33) 88.51.78.51. Self-service car wash centres under high pressure. Construction, distribution and maintenance. Established: 1973 - Franchising Since: 1987 - No. of Units: Company Owned: 84 - Franchised: 314 - Franchise/Entry Fee: 50.000 FF - Royalty: 520 FF per bay and per month - Total Inv: 5 bays' centre: 1.400.000, FF + civil works + site.

FITTAPART LTD.
1 Southwell Rd., W., Mansfield, Nottinghamshire, England, . Contact: J. R. Buckley, Dir. - Tel: 0623-759331. Retail auto parts and accessories. Established: 1977 - Franchising Since: 1978 - No. of Units: 4 - Approx. Inv: £25,000 - £50,000 - Royalty: 5%.

FORSLUNDS GUMMI AB/AB SVENSKA GUMMICENENTRALEN
Forslunds Gummi AB
Box 1105, Industrigatan 11 Linköping, S-581 11, Sweden, . Contact: Lorentz Österlund, Managing Director . Tyre Business. Established: 1923 - Franchising Since: 1980 - No. of Units: Company Owned: 2 - Franchised: 14.

HIGHWAY WINDSCREENS & GLAZING
Highway Windscreens (UK) Ltd.
Cathedral House, 16 Cathedral St., Norwich, Norfolk, U.K., NR1 1LX. Contact: Marianne Ashford, Fran. Coord. - Tel: 0603 667058. Windscreen repair and replacement. 24 hour emergency glazing, security film. Established: 1973 - Franchising Since: 1980 - No. of Units: Company Owned: 4 - Franchised: 61 - Franchise Fee: £12,000 - Royalty: 12% reducing to 6.25% - Total Inv: £38,000 (full cash flow available) - Financing: Via banks subject to status.

HOMETUNE *
Hometune Motoring Services
Carlton House, Nantwich Rd., Calveley, Cheshire, U.K., CW6 9JW. Contact: Bryan Fretton, Fran. Dev. Mgr. - Tel: (0) 1829 260030. Mobile vehicle servicing and tuning services. On site work for vehicle maintenance and efficient running. Car security products fitting on site, caravan servicing, insured and guaranteed. Established: 1968 - Franchising Since: 1968 - No. of Units: Franchised: 110 - Franchise Fee: £9,000 plus tax - Royalty: 12.5% of labour.

IDENTICAR SECURITY SYSTEMS
Identicar Worldwide Ltd.
International House, Wolverhampton Rd., Warley, West Midlands, U.K., B69 4RJ. Contact: John Harris, C.E.O. - Tel: (021) 544-7022. Security marking systems. Established: 1980 - Franchising Since: 1980 - Franchise Fee: £5,000 - £125,000 - Total Inv: £10,000 - £150,000 (incl. equipment, depending on size of country) - Royalty: 3% - 10% subject to market factors - Financing: 70% subject to status.

IMI MARSTON RADIATOR SERVICES.
Sandhill Dr., Narborough, Leicester, England, . Contact: P. E. Richardson, Commercial Dir. - Tel: 0533-866551. Radiator sales and service. Established: 1969 - Franchising Since: 1982 - Franchise Fee: £12,000 - Total Inv: £20,000 - Royalty: 6% - Financing: possible.

LASALIGN
Auto-Tek Lasalign Ltd.
O.S.B. House, 135 High St., Bromley Kent, England, . Contact: Graham Ross, Bus. Dev. Dir. - Tel: (01) 4666021/2/3. Mobile laser assisted trailer axle alignment working with road haulage industry and companies running trailer fleets. Established: 1982 - Franchising Since: 1983 - No. of Units: Company Owned: 2 - Franchised: 7 - Franchise Fee: £2,200 - Total Inv: £10,500 - Royalty: 20%

MIDAS LE SILENCIEUX
108, avenue Jean Moulin, 78170 La Celle Saint Cloud, France, . Contact: Jean-Pierre Dassieu - Tel: (1) 30 82 56 56. Automotive repairs. Established: 1976 - Franchising Since: 1979 - No. of Units: Company Owned: 75 - Franchised: 162 - Franchise Fee: 100,000 FF - Total Inv: 1,000,000 FF - Royalty: 5% + 5% adv.

MOBILE RADIATOR SERVICES *
80 Abbotsford Rd., Bowen Hills, Qsld., Australia, 4006. Contact: David Geers, Gen. Mgr. - Tel: (0011) 61 7 252 4500. Specializes in exchanging, cleaning out and repairing automobile radiators, with free pick up and delivery. Each franchise has a central workshop, fully maintained and using the most up to date equipment and computers with control of a specified territory. Established: 1986 - Franchising Since: 1987 - No. of Units: Franchised: 6 - Franchise Fee: $10,000 - Royalty: Nil - Total Inv: $10,000 - $80,000 - Financing: Yes.

MOBILETUNING LTD.
The Gate House, Lympne Industrial Park, Lympne, Hythe, Kent, England, CT21 4LR. Contact: Derrick Morley, Dir. - Tel: (0303) 48473. Mobile car engine tuning service. Established: 1976 - Franchising Since: 1976 - No. of Units: Company Owned: 2 - Franchised: 63 - Franchise Fee: £4,100 - Royalty: 10% - Total Inv: £10,500 - Financing: 70% to suitable applicants.

MR. CLUTCH
Clutch International Ltd.
2 Priory Rd., Strood, Rochester, Kent, England, ME2 2EG. Contact: Mr. M. Daniels, Sales & Mktg. Mgr. - Tel: (0634) 717747. Chain of garages specializing in the fast-fit replacement of clutches, brakes & gearboxes. Established: 1978 - Franchising Since: 1986 - No. of Units: Company Owned: 10 - Franchised: 39 - Franchise Fee: £12,500 - Royalty: 10% on turnover - Total Inv: £49,000 breakdown upon request - Financing: Yes, details upon request.

PLEIN POT S.A.
166 ave. Georges Clemenceau, 92000 Nanterre, France, . Contact: Alain Marmonnier - Tel: 204.30.72. Automotive repairs. Established: 1979 - Franchising Since: 1981 - No. of Units: Company Owned: 33 - Franchised: 70 - Approx. Inv: 600,000 FF - Royalty: 4% - Financing: 200,000 FF.

PRACTICAL CAR & VAN RENTAL
Practical Car & Van Rental Ltd.
Practical House 23/25 Little Broom Street, Camp Hill, Birmingham, England, B12 0EU. Contact: Bolton Agnew, Mng. Dir. - Tel: (0121) 772-8599, Fax: (0121) 766-6229. System/insurance and vehicle based franchise using the rental experience and ability to offer competitive insurance and leasing rates. Applicable to all aspects of motor trade. Established: 1984 - Franchising Since: 1984 - No. of Units: Franchised: 200 approx. - Franchise Fee: £4,000 - £9,000 - Royalty: 7%, 2% mktg. - Total Inv: Franchise fee only - Financing: Leasing package for vehicle supply.

PROTEXCAR LTD.
International House, Wolverhampton Rd., Worley, England, B69 4RJ. Contact: J.A. Jackson, Sec. - Tel: 021 5447022. Vehicle security - permanent vehicle identification and ignition isolation. Established: 1977 - Franchising Since: 1980 - No. of Units: Company Owned: 2 - Franchised: 19 - Approx. Inv: £10,000 - Financing: to suitable applicants.

RUST CHECK
Rust Check Central Corp.
00-451 Warszawa. u. Rozbrat 44a, Warsaw, Poland, . Contact: Franchise Director - Tel: 29-88-66. Rust prevention franchise in area of automotive and industrial application. Sale and distribution of leading corrosion prevention and protecting materials, technology and chemicals for all

applications. Established: 1990 - Franchising Since: 1990 - No. of Units: Franchised: 72 - Total Inv: $US 10,000, incl. equip., training, etc. - Financing: Yes.

SERCK MARSTON
International Radiator Services Ltd.
Silvertown House, Vincent Square, London, England, SW1P 2PL . Contact: Miss Gail Latham (0527) 510111, Adv. & Promo. - Tel: (0507) 510111. Supply of radiators for all types of vehicle and engine cooling systems, industrial heat exchangers, heater radiators, oil coolers, number plates, clutches, brake shoes, air brakes, power steering, water pumps, turbochargers, road springs and seat belts.

SILVER SHIELD AUTOMOTIVE GLAZING
Silver Shield Screens Ltd.
Wheler Rd., Whitley, Coventry, England, CV3 4LA. Contact: John A. Oliver, Mng. Dir. - Tel: 0203 307755. 24 hour mobile automotive glass replacement and repair service, nationwide. Established: 1972 - Franchising Since: 1978 - No. of Units: Franchised: 65 - Franchise Fee: from £15,000 - Royalty: 10% - Total Inv: £50,000 - Financing: Yes, 50%.

TAC DEVELOPMENT
Parking porte de la Development Villette, Paris, France, 75019. Contact: Mr. Leon-Dufour - Tel: (1) 48.34.74.00. Rapid automobile painting. Established: 1973 - Franchising Since: 1979 - No. of Units: Company Owned: 2 - Franchised: 37 - Franchise Fee: 90,000 FF - Total Inv: 700,000 FF - Royalty: 3% + 3% adv. - Financing: Finance et Europe.

THRIFTY CAR RENTAL *
Flightform Ltd.
The Old Court House, Hughenden Rd., High Wycombe, Bucks., England, HP1 35DT. Contact: A. Burton, Sales Dir. - Tel: 01494 474767. Car & van rental. Established: 1991 - Franchising Since: 1991 - No. of Units: Company Owned: 2 - Franchised: 52 - Franchise Fee: £17,000 + VAT - Royalty: 5% Thrifty, 2% adv. - Total Inv: £50,000 (£17,000 fee, £33,000 work. cap) - Financing: Yes for vehicles, no for working capital.

TUNE-UP
23 High Street, Bagshot, Surrey, England, GU19 5AF. Contact: Mr. A.H. Stevens, Dir. - Tel: (0276) 451199. Mobile engine tuning and servicing franchise. Established: 1988 - Franchising Since: 1988 - No. of Units: Franchised: 65 - Franchise Fee: £3,500 - Royalty: 10% - Total Inv: £15,000 - £20,000 - Financing: Depending on status.

TYREFIX
Tyrefix Ltd.
Taylors Piece, 9-11 Stortford Rd., Dunmow, Essex, England, CM6 1DA. Contact: Carol Mackaoui, Dir. - Tel: (0371) 876640. Specialists in on-site plant puncture repairs. Offering a within the hour service from time of call. Established: 1988 - Franchising Since: 1990 - No. of Units: Company Owned: 1 - Franchised: 9 - Franchise Fee: £10,000 - Royalty: 10% mgt., 1% adv. - Financing: Yes.

ULTRATUNE SYSTEM (AUST) PTY.
299 Canterbury Rd., Canterbury, Victoria, Australia, . Contact: Franchise Director - Tel: (03) 8364511. Ultra-tune has the latest equipment, software and training to cater for the ever growing technological advancements of the modern vehicle.

WASH N' WAX
Wash N' Wax Ltd.
11 Randolph Place, Edinburgh, Lothian, U.K., EH3 7TA. Contact: Colin McCraith, Dir. - Tel: (031) 226-2823. Mobile contract car care specialists offering the executive driver a regular valeting service from one of our unique self sufficient vehicles. Seeking distributor/licensor. Established: 1986 - Franchising Since: 1987 - No. of Units: Company Owned: 1 - Franchised: 57 - Franchise Fee: £3,500 - Royalty: 10% - Total Inv: £9,750 incl. F.F. & equip. - Financing: 80%.

BUILDING PRODUCTS AND SERVICES

1ST CALL
First Call Ltd.
Chandos Mews, 34B Chandos Rd., , Redland, Bristol, Avon, England, BS6 6PF. Contact: Christopher Greaves, Fran. Dir. - Tel: (0117) 9232525, Fax: (0117) 9445251. Immediate building repairs 24 hour covering all basic trades, plumbing, carpentry, roofing, glazing, insurance repairs. Mainly business to business. Established: 1989 - Franchising Since: 1990 - No. of Units: Franchised: 38 - Franchise Fee: £7,000 to £12,000 - Royalty: 15% (3% which is mktg. levy) - Total Inv: £15,000 to £30,000 (subject to type of start-up) - Financing: Via most High Street banks.

BATH WIZARD, THE
Bath Transformations Ltd.
Victory House, Somers Rd., N., Portsmouth, Hants, U.K., PO1 1PJ. Contact: Geoff Jenkins-Lover - Tel: 0705-753719 or 861622. Bathroom renovation service. Established: 1985 - Franchising Since: 1986 - No. of Units: Company Owned: 1 - Franchised: 16 - Franchise Fee: £5,000 - Royalty: 5% management, 5% adv. - Total Inv: £25,000.

BLANKHOUT (HOLLAND) CLAIRBOIS (FRANCE) BLANKHOLZ (GERMANY)
Blankhout Nederland Franchising bv
Noolseweg 14, Blaricum, The Netherlands, 1261 EC. Contact: Carlo M. Andreoli, Mktg. Mgr. - Tel: 035 53 18758, Fax: 035 53 80314. Wood and metal stripping, furniture stripping, furniture restoration. Established: 1977 - Franchising Since: 1979 - No. of Units: Franchised: 42 - Franchise Fee: $6,500 - Royalty: 5.25% for publicity - Total Inv: $50,000 - Financing: Yes, 60%.

BUF-A-TUB
Newlook Services
Business & Technology Centre, Bessemer Dr., Stevenage, Herts, U.K., SG1 2DX. Contact: Raymond Kray, Dir. - Tel: 0438-310008. Bathroom renovation services. A new unique system called refacing of enamel bathtubs, that can transform a dull, shabby bathroom into a new sparkling shiny bathroom within 3 hours. No spraying or plumbing. Established: 1967 - No. of Units: Company Owned: 1 - Franchised: 3 - Franchise Fee: £5,750 - Royalty: 5% - Total Inv: £5,750 - Financing: Yes.

CICO CHIMNEY LININGS LTD.
Westleton, Suffolk, England, IP17 3B3. Contact: R. J. Hadfield, Mng. Dir. - Tel: (01) 728-648-608, Fax: (01) 728-648-428. The lining of domestic & non domestic chimneys using the Cico cast-in-site refractory lining system. No points to work loose & non distallic so no corrosion. Established: 1980 - Franchising Since: 1982 - No. of Units: Franchised: 20 - Franchise Fee: £8,000 (sterling) - Royalty: 7.5% + 2.5% sales promo. - Total Inv: fran. fee plus £8,000 equip., £6,000 working cap.

CLENTECH
Abbotts Barton House, Worthy Rd., Winchester, Hants, U.K., S023 7SJ. Contact: Derek Anling, Bus. Dev. Mgr. - Tel: 0962-63577. Reconditioning and refurbishment of suspended acoustic ceilings. Established: 1981 - Franchising Since: 1981 - No. of Units: Company Owned: 2 - Franchised: 14 - Franchise Fee: £12,500 - Total Inv: £20,000 - Royalty: 20% - Financing: yes.

COVERITE
Cover Right Ltd.
Great Western Trading Estate, Martock, Somerset, U.K., . Contact: Patrick M. O'Leary, Mng. Dir - Tel: 0935-824866. Seamless floor and wall coverings in different grades and in a wide range of colours and designs. Established: 1970 - Franchising Since: 1981 - No. of Units: Company Owned: 1 - Franchised: 6 - Approx. Inv: £7,500.

CRETEPRINT PAVING SYSTEMS
Auckland House, Perry Way, Witham, Essex, England, CM8 3SX. Contact: Leonard Edney (UK) or Len Edney (Int'l), Nat'l Mgr/Mng. Dir. - Tel: (0376) 517766. The franchise and supply of decorative paving system suitable for both residential and commercial markets. Established: 1972 - Franchising Since: 1976 - No. of Units: Franchised: approx. 135 - Franchise Fee: £5,500 - Royalty: £1.30 per M of paving laid - Total Inv: £17,500 + VAT - Financing: To 100% given asset backing.

CUPBOARD LOVE (U.K.) LTD.
Unit 8, Premier Trading Estate, Dartmouth Midleway, Birm., England, B74AT. Contact: P.J. Upton, Mng. Dir. - Tel: 021 333 3342. Manufacturer and retailer of made to measure doors for refurbishing existing kitchens, bedrooms, bathrooms, lounge/dining furniture. New doors for old cupboards. Established: 1987 - Franchising Since: 1990 - No. of Units: Company Owned: 3 - Franchised: 1 - Franchise Fee: £5,000 - Royalty: 9% mgmt. fee on sales turnover - Total Inv: £20,000: displays, fee, legals, van, etc - Financing: No.

CURADRAFT (GB) LTD.
Delmae House Home Farm, Ardington Wantage, Oxfords., U.K., OX12 8PN. Contact: Mr. C. O'Connell, Director - Tel: 0235-833022. Curadraft - The Window Seal Craft. Established: 1985 - Franchising Since: 1988 - No. of Units: Company Owned: 2 - Franchised: 1 - Franchise Fee: £12,000 has VAT @ 15% - Royalty: 10% plus 2 1/2% adv - Financing: yes.

DAMPCURE-WOODCURE/30
Dampcure-Woodcure/30 Ltd.
4 Merton Road, Watford, Herts, U.K, WD1 7BU. Contact: Carole Darley, Dir. - Tel: (0923) 663322, Fax : (0923) 223842. Timber and damp treatment service. Established: 1959 - Franchising Since: 1982 - No. of Units: Company Owned: 2 - Franchised: 22 - Franchise Fee: £16,500 - Royalty: 15% graduating to 10% - Total Inv: £16,500 - Financing: Through leading banks.

DYNO PLUMBING
Dyno Rod Developments Ltd.
143 Maple Rd., Surbiton, Surrey, England, KT6 4BJ. Contact: M. Simms, Fran. Dept. - Tel: 081-481 2200, Fax: 081-481 2288. Emergency plumbing, installation and repair work. Offers 24 hour cover - 365 days a year. Established: 1985 - Franchising Since: 1985 - No. of Units: Franchised: 22 - Franchise Fee: £8,000 - Royalty: 22 1/2% includes: mktg., communications, credit control, mgmt. support, PR, adv., sales report - Total Inv: A.O.R. - Financing: up to 75%.

DYNO-ELECTRICS
Dyno Rod Developments Ltd.
143 Maple Rd., Surbiton Surrey, England, KT6 4BJ. Contact: M. Simms, Franc. Dept. - Tel: 081-481 2200, Fax: 081-481 2288. Emergency electrical installation and repair work offering 24 hour cover 365 days a year. Established: 1983 - Franchising Since: 1983 - No. of Licensed Contractors: 4 - Franchised Units: 20 - Franchise Fee: £8,000 - Royalty: 22 1/2% includes mktg., communication, credit control, mgmt. support, PR, adv., sales support - Total Inv: A.O.R. - Financing: up to 75%.

FERSINA INTERNATIONAL
Cestrum House, Industry Rd., Carlton, Barnsley, S. Yorks, England, S70 3NH. Contact: I. Woodward, Nat'l Fran. Mgr. - Tel: 0226-728310. Sales of UPVC window and door systems. Established: 1981 - Franchising Since: 1981 - No. of Units: Company Owned: 1 - Franchised: 50 - Approx. Inv: £20,000 - Royalty: 2.5% - Financing: no.

FLORENSE *
Fabrica de Moveis Florense Ltda.
Rua John Kennedy, no 2509, Flores da Cunha, Rio Grande do Sul - RS, Brazil, 95270-000. Contact: Jose Braga, Fran. Coord. - Tel: (054) 292-1300. Manufacturers of home and office furniture. Specialized in kitchen cabinetes, closets and office furniture. Established: 1953 - Franchising Since: 1988 - No. of Units: Company Owned: 1 - Franchised: 119 - Franchise Fee: None - Royalty: None - Total Inv: US$80,000 in first six months - Financing: No.

GARAGE DOOR COMPANY, THE
Unit 7, Russel Rd. Industrial Estate, Edinburgh, Scotland, EH11 2NN. Contact: Allan MacReath, Fran. Mgr. - Tel: 031-337-3332. The supply, installation and repair of all types of garage doors, remote control operators and access systems to both the domestic and industrial markets. The fitting of automatic gate systems is a further service. Established: 1977 - Franchising Since: 1984 - No. of Units: Franchised: 11 - Franchise Fee: £500 - Royalty: 6% of total weekly sales (excl. VAT) - Total Inv: £19,500.

GSS
GSS (UK) Ltd.
2 Southernhay West, Exeter, Devon, England, EX1 4JG. Contact: Graham Sclater, Gen. Mgr. - Tel: (0392) 499889. Property maintenance specialists carrying out day to day reactive and planned maintenance in the commercial and retail property sector. Established: 1991 - Franchising Since: 1991 - No. of Units: Company Owned: 1 - Franchise Fee: £15,000 - Royalty: 7.5% - Total Inv: £40,000 - Financing: Yes.

GUN-POINT LTD.
Gun Point Ltd.
Thavies Inn House, 3/4 Holborn Circus, London, England, EC1N 2PL. Contact: Hugh Chamberlain, Dir. - Tel: UK 071-353-1759. The franchising of mechanised brickwork repointing cleaning and waterproofing. Pressure pointing, grouting, wall tie replacement, epoxy crack repairs. Established: 1980 - Franchising Since: 1984 - No. of Units: Franchised: 17 - Franchise Fee: £7,000 - Royalty: 9%, 3% adv. - Total Inv: £17,100 plus £6,000 work. cap. - Financing: No.

HIRETECH AT SAINSBURYS HOMEBASE
Hire Technicians Group Ltd.
Chalk Hill House, Chalk Hill, Watford, Hertfordshire, England, WD1 4BH. Contact: Neville Selwood, Fran. Dir. - Tel: (0923) 52230. Tool and equipment hire centre offering a wide range of industrial equipment for hire to the homeowner, do it your-selfer, builder and industrial user customer. UK operation only. Established: 1955 - Franchising Since: 1984 - No. of Units: Company Owned: 30 - Franchised: 3 - Franchise Fee: £3,000 - Total Inv: £27,000 - Royalty: 5% mgmt. service fee - Financing: through normal banking channels to suitable applicants.

HUNTER DOUGLAS LTD.
338 Victoria Rd., Rydalmere, NSW, Australia, 2116. Contact: Franchise Director - Tel: (02) 6388000. A multinational industrial group engaged in the manufacture marketing and distribution of a wide range of window coverings, packaged home improvement and architectural products.

INTOTO KITCHENS
Wakefiled Road, Leeds, W. Yorkshire, England, LS27 7JZ. Contact: D. Watts, Mktg. Dir. - Tel: 0532-524131. Retailing fitted kitchens and bedrooms from High St. retail premises. Established: 1980 - Franchising Since: 1980 - No. of Units: Company Owned: 2 - Franchised: 34 - Franchise Fee: $25,000 - Total Inv: $240,000+ - Financing: Yes.

JET - ROD FRANCHISING, LTD.
Irwell House, 89 Barton Lane, Manchester, England, M30 0ET. Contact: Roy Jackson, Mng. Dir. - Tel: (061) 788- 7672. Offers territorial area franchises in the field of drain & pipe cleaning. Both domestic and industrial. Established: 1986 - Franchising Since: 1987 - No. of Units: Franchised: 20 - Franchise fee: £6,800 - £13,000 - Royalty: 15% - 20% - Total Inv: £45,000 - Financing: All major U.K. banks.

LAKESIDE SECURITY SHUTTERS
Unit 8, Beaufort Crt., Beaufort Rd, Plasmarl, Swansea, South Wales, SA6 8JG. Contact: Phil Lake, Dir. - Tel: (0792) 77-1117. Manufacture and installation of continental style, maintenance-free aluminum security shutters for homes, commercial premises and garage doors. Established: 1988 - Franchising Since: 1990 - No. of Units: Company Owned: 4 - Franchised: 10 - Franchise Fee: £5,000 - £10,000 depending on area - Total Inv: £10,000 - £15,000 - Financing: Yes.

MEND-A-BATH INT'L (PTY) LTD.
9 Haupt St., P.O. Box 10347, Linton Grange, Port Elizabeth, Cape Prov., South Africa, 6014. Contact: Ivor Benn, Mng. Dir. - Tel: (041) 432499. Bathtub refinishing. Established: 1977 - No. of Units: Company Owned: 1 - Franchised: 26, 7 master - Master License Fee: up to $150,000.

MIXAMATE CONCRETE
Mixamate Holdings Ltd.
Beddington Lane, Croydon, Surrey, England, CR9 4QD. Contact: Peter Slinn, Man. Dir. - Tel: 081-689-5500. Offer the real alternative to ready-mixed concrete. A super convenient service with unique patented vehicle supplying concrete when where and in whatever quantities you want it. Established: 1978 - Franchising Since: 1982 - No. of Units: Company Owned: 2 - Franchised: 27 - Franchise Fee: £5,000 - Total Inv: from £20,000 - Financing: 70%.

RENUBATH SERVICES LTD.
Cottleborough Ltd.
76/78 Cricklade St., Cirencester, Glos., England, GL7 1JN. Contact: D. Townsend, Mng. Dir. - Tel: (0285) 656624. Renovation of sanitary ware including resurfacing of baths and chip damage repair. Established: 1965 - Franchising Since: 1965 - No. of Units: Franchised: 3 - Franchise Fee: £10,000 - £15,000 - Royalty: 5% of turnover - Financing: Yes.

SENSORTROL *
197 Attercliffe Rd., Sheffield, England, S4 7XF. Contact: G. White, Dir. - Tel: (0114) 2701543. Energy management controls systems - a simple plug-in electronic controller for boilers of all sizes which cuts fuel consumption by as much as 30%. Established: 1983 - Franchising Since: 1992 - Franchise Fee: £900 U.K. Sterling - Royalty: None - Total Inv: £900 U.K. Sterling - Financing: No.

SOLAR-MESH®
Solar-Mesh Pty, Ltd.
49 Boyland Ave., Coopers Plains, Brisbane, Queensland, Australia, 4108. Contact: Ken Ivory, Mng. Dir. - Tel: (07) 2777 692. Sun control device, also quarantine insect screening. Established: 1984 - Franchising Since: 1986 - No. of Units: Company Owned: Multiple - Franchised: Multiple - Franchise Fee: varies - Royalty: Built into product costings - Total Inv: From $150,000 Australian$ - Financing: T.A.P.

STANAIR INDUSTRIAL DOOR SERVICES LTD.
Stanair House, The Crescent, Kettering, Northants, U.K., NN15 7HW. Contact: John Standoloft or Martin Wall, Chairman/Director - Tel: (0536) 82187. The repair and installation of industrial doors. Established: 1974 - Franchising Since: 1990 - No. of Units: Company Owned: 2 - Franchise Fee: £7,000 - £12,000. Van operated or business franchise available - Total Inv: £22,000 (van, tools, adv., first 3 months salary) - Financing: Midland Bank.

VENTROLLA LTD.
51 Tower St., Harrogate, N. Yorkshire, England, HG1 1HS. Contact: Mr. R.W. Tunnicliffe, Mng. Dir. - Tel: 0423 567004. Conservation and renovation of sash windows. Established: 1984 - Franchising Since: 1988 - No. of Units: Company Owned: 1 - Franchised: 12 - Franchise Fee £19,000 approx. - Royalty: 10% on sales - Total Inv: £32,000 approx. - Financing: N/A.

WORLDWIDE REFINISHING SYSTEMS
Acre Business Park, Acre Rd., Reading, Berks., England, RG2 OSA. Contact: Nigel Dunnett, Man. Dir. - Tel: (UK) 0734 462140. Refurbishment of bathrooms, washrooms, kitchens in both domestic and commercial markets using unique products and renovation techniques. Established: US 1988, UK 1990 - Franchising Since: US 1988, UK 1990 - No. of Units: Company Owned: 1 - Franchised: 26 - Franchise Fee: £6,000 - Royalty: 8% net turnover, 2% net turnover adv. - Total Inv: £17,500 (excl. work. cap.) complete business package - Financing: Through all UK Clearing banks.

BUSINESS PRODUCTS AND SERVICES

A.I.M.S.
A.I.M.S. Partnership Plc.
24 Red Lion St., London, England, WC1R 4SA. Contact: M. O'Brien, Nat'l. Dev. Mgr. - Tel: 0171 831 0775, Fax: 0171 404 2325. Provision of accountancy, taxation and general business advisory services to owner-managed businesses. Established: 1992 - Franchising Since: 1992 - No. of Units: Company Owned: 1 - Franchised: 29 - Franchise Fee: £5,650 - Royalty: 12.5% falling to 8.5% - Total Inv: Fran. fee plus office setup - varies - Financing: No.

ACCOUNTING CENTRE, THE
Elscot House, Arcadia Ave., Finchley, London, England, N3 2JE. Contact: Tony Partis, Managing Dir. - Tel: (081) 349-3191. Provision of monthly management accounts to small/medium sized businesses. Franchisees generate clients on a local basis, supervise their bookkeeping, assist in interpreting their accounts and provide advice. Established: 1972 - Franchising Since: 1983 - No. of Units: Company Owned: 3 - Franchised: 4 - Franchise Fee: £7,500 - Total Inv: £15,000 - Royalty: 10% - Financing: No.

ALFAL CONSULTANTS SA
6 Cours de Rive, Geneva, Switzerland, 1204. Contact: Al-Fallouji Ikbal, Chairman - Tel: (022) 28 84 39. Promotions, contacts, public relations; setting up and development of companies management, legal and fiscal advice and other activities. Established: 1984 - Franchising Since: 1987.

AMTRAK EXPRESS PARCELS LTD. *
Company House, Tower Hill, Bristol, England, BS2 0EQ. Contact: Franchise Dept. - Tel: 0117 927 2002. Overnight parcel service throughout UK and international delivery service throughout the world. Established: 1987 - Franchising Since: 1987 - No. of Units: Company Owned: 1 - Franchised: 341 - Franchise Fee: from £12,500 - Total Inv: £19,000 incl. work. cap - Financing: Yes.

ANC
Parkhouse East Industrial Estate, Chesterton, Newcastle-Under-Lyme, Staffordshire, England, ST5 7RB. Contact: Antony Flood, Fran. Acct. Mgr. - Tel: (0782) 563322. Express parcel, freight and courier services - local, national and international. Established: 1981 - Franchising Since: 1981 - No. of Units: Company Owned: 3 - Franchised: 75 - Franchise Fee: P.O.A. - Royalty: Trunking charge - Total Inv: P.O.A. - Financing: Yes.

APOLLO DESPATCH
Apollo Despatch Plc
Apollo House, 28/30 Hoxton Sq., London, England, N1 6NN. Contact: Norman Grossman, Fran. Dir. - Tel: 011-44-171-739-8444, Fax: 011-44-171-739-6463. Urgent same-day courier service by motorcycle and van plus overnight and international facilities. Established: 1980 - Franchising Since: 1990 - No. of Units: Company Owned: 6 - Franchised: 6 - Franchise Fee: £15,000 - Royalty: 10% incl. 2% adv. - Total Inv: £15,000 fran. fee, £15,000 set-up, £12,000 working cap. = £42,000 - Financing: 70% of total through major banks.

ASC NETWORK, PLC
24 Red Lion St., London, England, WC1R 4SA. Contact: Josef Sucharewicz, Mng. Dir. - Tel: 071 831 0775. Commercial finance brokers. Established: 1977 - Franchising Since: 1989 - No. of Units: Company Owned: 1 - Franchised: 30 - Franchise Fee: £50,000 - Royalty: 15% - Total Inv: £50,000 - Financing: By arrangement.

AUDIDCELL
CRA
65 Queens Walk, Ruislip, Middlesex, England, HA4 0LX. Contact: S. Harding, Sec. - Tel: 081 845 5993. Cost reduction consultancy aimed at telecoms expenditure. Established: 1993 - Franchising Since: 1993 - No. of Units: Company Owned: 1 - Franchise Fee: £5,950 - Royalty: None - Financing: No.

BOOK-KEEPING NETWORK, THE *
90 Woodhall St., Stirling, Western Australia, 6021. Contact: Alex Polglaze, C.E.O. - Tel: (+619) 349-9189. Computerised book-keeping service for small and medium businesses and other organisations looking after payables, receivables, profit & loss etc. & payroll. Established: 1984 - Franchising Since: 1990 - No. of Units: Company Owned: 1 - Franchised: 7 - Franchise Fee: $AUD 13,500 - Royalty: 12% support, 3% adv. - Total Inv: $42,000 - Financing: Yes.

BUREAU OF CREDIT MANAGEMENT, THE
28 Gilman St., Hanley, Stoke-on-Trent, Staffordshire, England, . Contact: M. Peake, Dir. - Tel: 0782-28770. Credit management. Established: 1980 - Franchising Since: 1983 - No. of Units: Company Owned: 1 - Franchised: 2 - Approx. Inv: £3,000 - Financing: company assisted plan.

BUSINESS POST LTD.
Business Post Holdings Ltd.
Nat'l Hub Ctr., Express House, Spitfire Rd., Erdington, Birmingham, England, B249PB. Contact: Mr. Peter Tompkins, Fran. Mgr. - Tel: (021) 328 4555. An established national overnight parcel distribution company. Established: 1970 - Franchising Since: 1988 - No. of Units: Company Owned: 12 - Franchised: 54 - Franchise Fee: £4,500 - Royalty: 2% adv. - Total Inv: £20,000 - £100,000.

CITY LINK
City Link Transport Holdings Ltd.
Batavia Rd., Sunbury-on-Thames, Middlesex, England, TW16 5LR. Contact: David Kennard, Mng. Dir. - Tel: 44+(0)932 788799. National/international express/courier collection and delivery services. Established: 1969 - Franchising Since: 1980 - No. of Units: Company Owned: 3 - Franchised: 48 - Franchise Fee: upon application, subject to territory - Royalty: 10% - Total Inv: upon application - subject to territory - Financing: Yes, subject to status of applicant.

COUNTRY BUSINESS SALES LTD.
9A Churchgate St., Soham, Ely, Cambridgeshire, England, CB7 5DS. Contact: Richard Armstrong-Tait, Dir. - Tel: (0353) 723350. Business transfer agents, valuers, and stocktakers. Established: 1986 - Franchising Since: 1986 - No. of Units: Company Owned: 1 - Franchised: 10 - Franchise Fee: £12,950 - Royalty: 10% - Total Inv: fran. fee + £10,000 work cap. - Financing: 50% - 100%.

COUNTRY PROPERTIES AND ROGERS
Country Rose Management Franchise Ltd.
41 High St. Baldock, Herts, England, SG7 5NP. Contact: Gerald Dale, Consultant - Tel: 0462-896148. Estate agents. Established: 1974 - Franchising Since: 1982 - No. of Units: Company Owned: 2 - Franchised: 16 - Franchise Fee: £3,000 - Royalty: 7 1/2% - Total Inv: £20,000 - Financing: yes.

DATAPRO
Datatrend Cursos E Sistemas S/C Ltda.
Av. Dr. Nelson D'Avila, 390, Sao Jose Dos Campos, Sao Paulo, Brazil, 12245-031. Contact: Mr. Luis Namura, Pres. - Tel: (0123) 22-8011. Computer training company. Established: 1976 - Franchising Since: 1983 - No. of Units: Company Owned: 1 - Franchised: 39 - Franchise Fee: US$35,000 - Royalty: 10% - Total Inv: US$70,000 - Financing: 6 months to a year.

DE MAINE INSURANCE SERVICES
27 Bridge St., St. Ives, Huntingdon, Cambridgeshire, England, . Contact: P. Theakston - Tel: 0480-63969. Automobile insurance. Established: 1983 - Franchising Since: 1984 - No. of Units: Company Owned: 3 - Franchised: 1 - Franchise Fee: £1,500 - Total Inv: £7,000 - Royalty: approx. 1.5% - Financing: yes.

DRIVER HIRE
Driver Hire Group Services Ltd.
Castlefields Lane, Crossflatts, Bingley, W. Yorkshire, England, BD16. Contact: J.P. Bussey, Mng. Dir. - Tel: (0274) 551166. Employment agencies specializing in LGV & non-LGV drivers, and blue collar workers. Established: 1984 - Franchising Since: 1985 - No. of Units: Company Owned: 2 - Franchised: 56 - Franchise Fee: £22,500 - Royalty: 5%, 2% admin., 1% admin. - Total Inv: £35,000: £22,500 fran. fee, £12,500 work. cap. - Financing: Up to 60%.

ELLUS
Ellus Ind. E Com. Ltda.
Rua Coronel Luis Barroso 151, Sao Paulo S.P., Brazil, 04750. Contact: Joe Lago, Dir. - Tel: (011) 521-9133, Fax:(011) 246-9984. A design enterprise. Creativity guided by a universal fashion concept, for fixed target, in each cycle or moment. Modern marketing based on the franchising and licensing systems. Selective marketing, based on the principle of line segmentation, products, public and life styles. Established: 1972 - Franchising Since: 1979 - No. of Units: Franchised: 115 - Royalty: 10% - Total Inv: min. cash requirement - Financing: for qualified individuals.

EUROGRANT
EuroGrant Search Ltd.
Eamam Wharf, Blackburn Waterside, Blackburn, Lancs., England, BB1 5BL. Contact: J. B. Bishop, M.D. - Tel: 0245 56557. To assist companies to identify grants and soft loans and then to apply for those incentives for the company. Established: 1991 - Franchising Since: 1993 - No. of Units: Company Owned: 1 - Franchised: 12 - Franchise Fee: £2,500 - Royalty: None - Total Inv: £6,000 - Financing: Yes.

EVERETT MASSON & FURBY
EMF Group Ltd.
3 Cornhill, Ottery, St. Mary, Devon, England, EX11 1DW. Contact: Kathie Carr, Dir. - Tel: (01404) 813762, Fax: (01404) 815236. Business transfer agents. Established: 1963 - Franchising Since: 1971 - No. of Units: Company Owned: 1 - Franchised: 25 - Franchise Fee: £25,000 - Royalty: 10% of commissions rec'd. - Total Inv: £25,000 plus WIP £20,000 - Financing: Yes.

FLAT SHOP FRANCHISING
Property Rentals
2 The Avenue, The Cross, Worcester, England, WR1 3QA. Contact: Mr. Mio Blagojevic, Fran. Dir. - Tel: 0905-24856. Residential letting agents and property management agents. Established: 1984 - Franchising Since: 1990 - No. of Units: Company Owned: 1 - Franchise Fee: $2,500 - Royalty: $1,000 mnth. service fee - Total Inv: $12,500 (equip., work cap., fran. fee, lease, etc.) - Financing: Yes.

FOXMEAD SERVICES
British Credit Recovery Club
Bookfield House, Selby Rd., Garnforth, Leeds, England, LS25 1NB. Contact: B. Wagstaff, Mng. Dir. - Tel: 0532-868565. Credit control service, aiding companies in collection of overdue accounts. Established: 1980 - Franchising Since: 1981 - No. of Units: Company Owned: 1 - Franchised: 8 - Approx. Inv: £7,500 - Royalty: negotiable - Financing: yes.

FUTURE TRAINING SERVICES
The Old Mill, Northgrove Rd., Hawkhurst, Kent, England, TN18 4AP. Contact: Mark Meakings, M.D. - Tel: (0580) 752-619. Secretarial, computer and bookkeeping training systems which can run along side existing business or stand alone. Using self-teach method of learning, allowing student to work independently, starting any day from 2hrs. per/wk to fulltime. Established: 1988 - Franchising Since: 1989 - No. of Units: Company Owned: 1 - Franchised: 15 - Franchise Fee: £1,500 - £3,000 - Total Inv: £3,000 - £8,540.

HUMANA INTERNATIONAL
Alexander House, 9-11 Fulwood Pl., London, England, WC1V 6HG. Contact: Douglas Bugie, Mng. Dir. - Tel: (071) 242-1234. Executive recruitment and general human resources network including temporary management and out placement consulting. Established: 1992 - Franchising Since: 1992 - No. of Units: Franchised: 52 - Franchise Fee: £20,000 - Royalty: 10% incl. 1% for adv./p.r. - Total Inv: £30,000: £15,000 fran. fee, £5,000 start-up, £10,000 running costs.

IB YOUR OFFICE *
IB Your Office Int'l. Ltd.
Industrie Straße ibic, 50999 Cologne, Germany, . Contact: (49) 2236-962460, Jaapjan Fenijn - Tel: Assst. Mng. Dir.. IB Your Office is one of the largest business center networks worldwide. It offers not only office space, the clients can use the full supporting infrastructure and manpower. They can also use the international network that the system is based on. Established: 1989 - Franchising Since: 1990 - No. of Units: Company Owned: 1 - Franchised: 95 - Franchise Fee: Depending per county, approx. DM 50,000 - Total Inv: approx. DM 400,000 - Financing: Yes.

INTERLINK EXPRESS PLC
Mabel St., The Meadows, Nottingham, England, NG2 3ED. Contact: R.A.M. Bugden, Fran. Dir., At: Brunswick Court, Brunswick Square, Bristol BS2 8PE. Carriage of overnight parcels throughout UK & Europe. Established: 1981 - Franchising Since: 1981 - No. of Units: Company Owned: 118 - Franchised: 118 - Total Inv: £100,000 - £250,000 re-sale of existing businesses only.

INTERNATIONAL BUSINESS CONSULTANTS ASSOCIATION
Cedar Lodge, Norwich Rd., Tasburgh, Norwich, Norfolk, England, NR15 1NS. Contact: Peter Coe, Partner - Tel: 0508-470686. Business and management consultants. Established: 1982 - Franchising Since: 1983 - No. of Units: Company Owned: 1 - Franchised: 5 - Approx. Inv: £50,000 - Royalty: 20% plus 5% adv. - Financing: Yes.

MAIL BOXES ETC.
Mail Boxes Europe Ltd.
84 Marylebone High St., London, England, W1M 3DE. Contact: Serena Lang, Mktg. Mgr. - Tel: 071-935-9411. Established in 1992, Mail Boxes Europe Ltd. is the master licensee of Mail Boxes Etc. in the United Kingdom. MBE is the world's largest network of postal, business & communications centres, with more than 2,000 franchised locations throughout the U.S. and 11 other countries. Established: 1992 - Franchising Since: 1980 in the USA - No. of Units: Company Owned: 11 - Franchised: 2,000 worldwide - Franchise Fee: £12,500 incl. training, opening support, design & site selection - Royalty: 6%, 2% mktg. - Total Inv: £60,000 incl. fran. fee - Financing: Yes, through High St. banks.

MAIL BOXES ETC.
Mail Boxes Etc. (Thailand) Co. Ltd.
44/1-3 Sukhumvit 21 Asoke Rd., Bangkok, 10110, Thailand, . Contact: Surasak Sawangrut, Mng. Dir. - Tel: (66-2) 259-8456-7, Fax: (66-2) 259-8455. The world's largest franchisor of postal, business and communications franchise service network. Each MBE center provides the customer a total one stop shop, while the master franchisor provides product support, store design and layout, training, systems and procedures. Established: 1980 US - Franchising Since: 1980 US - No. of Units: Franchised: 2,750 centers in 44 countries - Total Inv: $20,000 US - Royalty: 6%, 2% adv. - Total Inv: US$ 80,000 to US$ 120,000.

MAIL BOXES ETC.
Mail Boxes Etc. (Australia) Pty Ltd.
273 Alfred St., North Sydney, NSW, Australia, 2060. Contact: Michael Larkins, Dir. - Tel: (02) 9955 8922, Fax: (02) 9954-9556. World's largest network of postal, business & communications centers with over 3,100 centers in 45 countries. Established: 1980 USA, 1993 AUS - Franchising Since: 1993 Australia - No.of Units: Company Owned: 1 - Franchised: 19 - Franchise Fee: A$25,000 - Royalty: 6%, 2% adv. - Total Inv: A$115,000 incl. fran. fee - Financing: Yes.

MAIL BOXES ETC. BRAZIL
Rua Oscar Freire, 953, Cerquiera Cesar, Sao Paulo, SP, Brazil, 01426-001. Contact: Jairo Adriano, Master Licensee - Tel: 011-55-11-851-0214. MBE is the world's largest network of franchised postal, business and communication service centers with more than 2,400 centers in 29 different countries. Established: 1992 - Franchising Since: 1980 in the U.S. - Franchise Fee: US$20,000 - Royalty: 6%, 2% adv. - Total Inv: US$75,000 incl. fran. fee.

MAIL BOXES ETC. FRANCE
4 Rue de Berri, 75008 Paris, France, . Contact: Michele Schaub, Pres. - Tel: 011-33-1-45-62-2000. MBE is the world's largest network of franchised postal, business and communication service centers with more than 2,400 centers in 29 different countries. Established: 1992 - Franchising Since: 1980 in the U.S. - Franchise Fee: francs 200,000 (incl. training & site selection) - Royalty: 6%, 2% adv. - Total Inv: francs 1,000,000 incl. fran. fee - Financing: Yes.

MAIL BOXES ETC. ITALY
Piazza IV Novembre, 1, 20124, Milan, Italy, . Contact: Graziano Fiorelli, Master Licensee - Tel: 011-39-2-669-2661. MBE is the world's largest network of franchised postal, business and communication service centers with more than 2,400 centers in 29 different countries. Established: 1992 - Franchising Since: 1980 in the U.S. - Franchise Fee: Liras 28,000,000 (incl. training & site selection) - Royalty: 6%, 2% adv. - Total Inv: Liras 130,000,000 (incl. fran. fee).

MAIL BOXES ETC. MEXICO
Platero #39, C.P. 03900, Mexico, D.F., Mexico, . Contact: Blaine Roberts, Pres. - Tel: 011-525-598-0222. MBE is the world's largest network of franchised postal, business and communication service centers with more than 2,400 centers in 29 different countries. Established: 1990 - Franchising Since: 1980 in the U.S. - Franchise Fee: US$27,500 - Royalty: 6%, 2% adv. - Total Inv: US$70,000.

MAIL BOXES ETC. PHILIPPINES
#105, Twr. Ground 1st Fl., Makati Cinema Sq. Twr., Pasong Tamo, Cor. Pasay Rd., Makati, Metro Manilla, Philippines, . Contact: Hector Yango, Mng. Dir. - Tel: 011-632-811-1685. MBE is the world's largest network of franchised postal, business and communication service centers with more than 2,400 centers in 29 different countries. Established: 1994 - Franchising Since: 1980 in the U.S. - Franchise Fee: US$20,000 - Royalty: 6%, 2% adv. - Total Inv: US$85,000 incl. fran. fee.

MAIL BOXES ETC. TURKEY
Hekimsuyu Cad. No. 42, Kucukkoy, Istanbul, Turkey, . Contact: Aydin Turkmen, Master Licensee - Tel: 011-90-212-535-7352. MBE is the world's largest network of franchised postal, business and communication service centers with more than 2,400 centers in 29 different countries. Established: 1993 - Franchising Since: 1980 in the U.S. - Franchise Fee: US$14,500 - US$21,500 - Royalty: 6%, 2% adv. - Total Inv: US$50,000 (incl. fran. fee) - Financing: Yes.

MAIL BOXES ETC. VENEZUELA
Torre Centuria, Local Commercial N#2 P.B., Av. Venezuela con calle, Mohedano, Urb. El Rossal, Caracas, Venezuela, . Contact: Kenneth Landau, Master Licensee - Tel: 011-582-952-7444. MBE is the world's largest network of franchised postal, business and communication services centers with more than 2,400 centers in 29 different countries. Established: 1993 - Franchising Since: 1980 in the U.S. - Franchise Fee: US$32,600 - Royalty: 6%, 2% adv. - Total Inv: US$90,000 (incl. fran. fee).

MORTGAGE ADVICE CENTER LTD., THE
Mortgage Franchise Ltd.
298 Ewell Rd., Surbiton, Surrey, U.K., . Contact: Barry Clayton, Chairman - Tel: (081) 390-9990. Offering independent mortgage advice to clients. Choose from 250 leading sources. Established: 1987 - Franchising Since: 1988 - No. of Units: Franchised: 9 - Franchise Fee: $5,000 - Royalty: $5,000 per yr., $433 per mnth., V.A.T. - Total Inv: $60,000 ($20,000 refurb. + $40,000 cash flow) - Financing: Yes.

NATIONWIDE INVESTIGATIONS
Nationwide House, 86 Southwark Bridge Rd., London, England, SE1 0EX. Contact: Mr. K. Walker, Head of Fran. - Tel: 44-1-928-1799. Private investigation. Established: 1963 - Franchising Since: 1978 - No. of Units: Company Owned: 3 - Franchised: 22 - Franchise Fee: $10,500 min. - Royalty: 10% - Total Inv: $15,000 min. - Financing: Up to one third.

OPENSHOP
Systems Consultancy
34 Elm Tree Ct., King St., Cottingham, Hull, U.K., . Contact: Anthony Hodge, Principal Consul.. Low-cost information processing systems for small businesses. Established: 1972 - Franchise Fee: £30,000 - Total Inv: £150,000.

PITMAN TRAINING CENTRE *
Pitman Training Ltd.
154 Southampton Row, London, England, WC1B 5AX. Contact: James O'Brien, Fran. Mgr. - Tel: (44) 0171 837 4481, Fax: (44) 0171 837 9272. The computer and office training network. Training in pc applications and office skills. Established: 1992 - Franchising Since: 1992 - No. of Units: Company Owned: 3 - Franchised: 67 - Franchise Fee: £10,000 min. - Total Inv: £50,000 incl. fran. fee, equip., materials & opening stock - Financing: Via UK banks.

PRIORITY MANAGEMENT SYSTEMS PTY. LTD. *
11 Averill St., Rhodes, Sydney, NSW, Australia, 2138. Contact: Greg Sparks, Mng. Dir. - Tel: (02) 736 3999. Recognized as a leader in management training, and named the number one franchise training organization in North America, Priority Management is involved in helping all staff increase productivity and effectiveness. Established: 1988 - Franchising Since: 1988 - No. of Units: Franchised: 22 - Franchise Fee: $27,500 initial - Royalty: Nil - Total Inv: $50,000 - Financing: No.

RIBBON REVIVAL
Caslon Crt., Pitronnerie Rd., St. Peter Port, Guernsey, U.K., . Contact: Colin Carnachan, Mng. Dir. - Tel: (0481) 729552. Recycling of the full range of print technologies including photocopier, telefax, laser toner, ink jet cartridge and line printer, cash register and typewriter ribbons. Full technical training and support given. Established: 1992 - Franchising Since: 1993 - No. of Units: Company Owned: 1 - Franchised: 16 -

Franchise Fee: £10,000 - £30,000 - Royalty: 9% on gross turnover for UK, negotiable overseas - Total Inv: £30,000 - £60,000 incl. work. cap. - Financing: Possibly.

ROMANO CENTER
Romano S/A Materials Pl Construcofs
Chucri Zaidan St, 230 - Morumbi, Sao Paulo, Brazil, 04583. Contact: Oswaldo Romano Jr., Dir. - Tel: (011) 543 4011. Home center - All products for home, office, buildings. More then 30,000 items stored. All stores are connected by computers and sell the same items and same price. Established: 1956 - Franchising Since: 1988 - No. of Units: Company Owned: 4 - Franchised: 16 - Franchise Fee: (US)$100,000 - Royalty: 7% - Total Inv: (US)$200,000 - Financing: some.

S.O.S. COMPUTADORES
Rua Estela, 112, Sao Paulo, Brazil, 04011-000. Contact: Luiz Carlos Izzo, Dir. - Tel: (011) 575-5005. Treinamento em informatica. Established: 1983 - Franchising Since: 1984 - No. of Units: Company Owned: 1 - Franchised: 22 - Franchise Fee: $18,000-$28,000 - Royalty: Embutido no material didatica fornecido - Total Inv: $36,000, 1% fase, $10,000-$15,000 2% fase.

SDR SVENSK DIREKTREKLAM
P.O. Box 1524, Uppsala, Sweden, S-75145. Contact: Tom Bruno, Mgr. Int'l Oper. - Tel: (46) (0) 18-10 01 80. Distribution of unaddressed direct advertising. Established Since: 1973 - Franchising Since: 1976 - No. of Units: Company Owned: 1 - Franchised: 63 - Franchise Fee: SEK 75,000 - Total Inv: SEK 250,000 - Royalty: 17.5% gross.

SEEKERS
234 The Broadway, London, England, NW9 6AS. Contact: Nyman, Dir. - Tel: (081) 202-7882. Estate agency. Established: 1979 - Franchising Since: 1979 - No. of Units: Franchised: 80+ - Franchise Fee: from £5,000 - Royalty: 10%, 5% mktg. fund - Total Inv: £15,000 - £40,000 - Financing: Yes.

SMALL BUSINESS ADVISORY CENTRES
1213 Stratford Rd., Hall Green, Birmingham, England, B28 9AD. Contact: R. Hogg, Chairman - Tel: 021-778-5106. Accounting and business consulting services to small businesses. Established: 1983 - Franchising Since: 1984 - No. of Units: 5 - Approx. Inv: £12,500 - Royalty: 12.5%.

START INFORMATIQUE
B.P. 09, Salies-de-Bearn, France, 64270. Contact: J.F. Idiart, Pres. - Tel: (59) 382666. Information. Established: 1978 - Franchising Since: 1981 - No. of Units: 20 - Aprox. Initial Inv: 100,000 FF - Total Inv: 250,000 FF - Royalty: 1% publicity.

STOCKCHECK
John Gilpin Ltd.
Harewood Courtyard, Harewood, Leeds, W. Yorkshire, England, LS17 9LF. Contact: Mr. Chris J. Brown, Opers. Dir. - Tel: 0532-886565. Computerized stock control systems. Established: 1983 - Franchising Since: 1983 - No. of Units: 10 - Approx. Inv: £10,000 - £12,500 - Royalty: 7.5% + 2.5% adv. - Financing: no.

SWINTON INSURANCE
Swinton Insurance Group
Swinton House, 6 Great Marlborough St., Manchester, England, M1 5SW. Contact: Mr. P.W. Lowe, Fran. Dir. - Tel: (061) 236-1222. High Street insurance specialist. Established: 1959 - Franchising Since: 1984 - No. of Units: Company Owned: 450 - Franchised: 300 - Franchise Fee: £3,000 (plus V.A.T.) - Royalty: 6% commission share - Total Inv: £30,000 plus work. cap. - Financing: Yes.

TELE-PAGES DIRECTORIES
8A High St., Marlborough, Wiltshire, England, SN8 1AA. Contact: Diedre McCarthy, Mktg. Mgr. - Tel: (0672) 515551. Directory publishing franchise. Established: 1979 - Franchising Since: 1993 - No. of Units: Company Owned: 15 - Franchise Fee: £2,500 + approx. £7,000 work. cap - Total Inv: £9,500 - Financing: Assistance through Barclays Bank.

TNT PARCEL OFFICE
TNT Express (UK) Ltd.
Abeles Way, Athgerstone, Warwickshire, U.K., CV9 2RY. Contact: Franchise Dept., - Tel: 0827 303030. Fractional franchises added to existing businesses. Franchisees provide a drop off and collection facility for convenient local access to TNT's worldwide transport operation. They receive a commission on all traffic. Established: 1946 - Franchising Since: 1981 - No. of Units: Company Owned: 18 - Franchised: 205 - Franchise Fee: £3,500 - Financing: No.

TRAVAIL EMPLOYMENT GROUP
24 Southgate St., Gloucester, Glos., England, GL1 2DP. Contact: Mr. Steve Mills, Fran. Mgr. - Tel: (01452) 307645, Fax: (01452) 303197. Temporary, contract & permanent recruitment services in most skill disciplines. Established: 1977 - Franchising Since: 1985 - No. of Units: Company Owned: 8 - Franchised: 34 - Franchise Fee: £10,000 - Royalty: 7.25% of sales, wholly inclusive - Total Inv: £60,000 - £65,000: £10K fee, £20K start-up, £30-£35K work. cap. - Financing: From all major banks to a corporate scheme.

WETHERBY TRAINING SERVICES LTD.
Flockton House, Audby Lane, Wetherby, West Yorkshire, England, LS22 7FD. Contact: Ray Shuttleworth, Partner. Business and computer training courses. Established: 1977 - Franchising Since: 1978 - No. of Units: Franchised: 200 - Franchise Fee: £4,950 - Royalty: sale of workbooks + annual lic. fee £750 P.A. - Total Inv: £15,000 - Financing: Yes.

WHITE KNIGHT *
White Knight Franchising (U.K.) Ltd.
Hi-Point, Thomas St., Taunton, Somerset, England, TA2 6HB. Contact: Richard Pape, Fran. Dev. Officer - Tel: 01823 251223. Value added tax accounting bureau. Established: 1989 - Franchising Since: 1991 - No. of Units: Company Owned: 1 - Franchised: 19 - Franchise Fee: £8,000 per county - Royalty: 10% of turnover, paid monthly, calculated quarterly - Total Inv: £8,000 fran. fee plus computer hardware (£1,500) - Financing: Up to £4,000 at 8% over 39 mos.

CLEANING PRODUCTS AND SERVICES

CHEM-DRY SOUTHERN SERVICES LTD.
Chem-Dry
2 The Metro Centre, St. Albans, Herts., England, AL4 9QT. Contact: Lynn Joyce, Sales Mgr. - Tel: 0727 852030. Carpet, upholstery and fabric cleaning and restoration services. Established: 1988 - Franchising Since: 1978 - No. of Units: Franchised: over 400 in U.K. - Franchise Fee: £14,250 - Royalty: None, £149 monthly service/support fee - Total Inv: £20,000 - Financing: Yes.

CHEMICAL EXPRESS
Chemical Express Group Ltd.
Ninian Way, Wilnecore, Tamworth, Staffs, England, B775DZ. Contact: Les Gray, Managing Dir. - Tel: 01827 2514131. Mobile showrooms supplying full range of cleaning, maintenance & hygiene chemicals plus janitorial supplies direct to every type of business & industry. Established: 1985 - Franchising Since: 1986 - No. of Units: Franchised: 83 - Franchise Fee: £7,900 - Royalty: 7.5% - Total Inv: £15,000 - Yes, through major banks.

CINDERELLA HOME SERVICES
323 Kirkdale, Sydenham, London, England, SE23 2RT. Contact: Mrs E. A. Rowland, Dir.. Employment agency dealing with placing nannies, domestic cleaners and offering a membership service for babysitting and all temporary childcare and household services. Established: 1982 - Franchising Since: 1990 - No. of Units: Company Owned: 1 - Franchised: 2 - Franchise Fee: £5,750 - Royalty: 7% annual sales - Total Inv: £7,614 - Financing: Yes.

DIAL-A-DUSTER (UK) LTD.
263A Rose Lane, Mossley Hill, Liverpool, Merseyside, England, L18 5UJ. Contact: L.D. Hollis, Dir. - Tel: 0151-729-0215. Mobile domestic cleaning service fully stocked and equipped micro van calling on 50 regular clients and offering spring cleans. This single van franchise offers particular benefits to lady or husband/wife teams to multi van

level. Established: 1990 - Franchising Since: 1993 - No. of Units: Company Owned: 3 - Franchised: 2 - Franchise Fee: £2,350 - Total Inv: £10,000 - Financing: Via major banks.

DIVERSEY MOBILE SALES
Weston Favell, Norhants, England, NN3 4PD. Contact: A.D.C. Wilding, Opers. Mgr. - Tel: 0604-405311. Supplying cleaning and maintenance materials to garages, factories and workshops. Established: 1958 - Franchising Since: 1983 - No. of Units: 4 - Franchise Fee: £2,500 - Royalty: 11% plus 1% adv. - Total Inv: £4,000 - Financing: Yes.

GLOBAL CLEANING CONTRACTS LTD.
8-10 High St., Sutton, Surrey, England, SM1 1HN. Contact: Kevin Wearn, Mng. Dir. - Tel: 01-642-0054. Managerial agency which provides its clients with higher standards of cleaning than conventional cleaning companies. Established: 1975 - Franchising Since: 1979 - No. of Units: Company Owned: 1 - Franchised: 24 - Franchise Fee: £10,000 - Royalty: 14% G.P., plus 6% adv. - Total Inv: £50,000 - Financing: yes.

JET CLEEN LIMITED
P.O. Box 44, Dunstable, Bedfordshire, England, LU6 2QT. Contact: Philip Lloyd, Mng. Dir. - Tel: 0852 873530. Jet Cleen provides a mobile contract steam cleaning service for commercial transport, industry and agriculture. Established: 1981 - Franchising Since: 1981 - No. of Units: 10 - Franchise Fee: £5,000 - Total Inv: £14,000 - Royalty: 15% - Financing: yes.

LAVITA
Lavanderia Lavita Ltda.
Av. Dr. Cardoso De Mello, 878, Sao Paulo, Brazil, 04548. Contact: Jim Sato, Mgr. - Tel: 011 543 7088. The difference of the original is that we have just 3 franchised units, and we have been established since 1952. Established: 1952 - Franchising Since: 1982 - No. of Units: Company Owned: 12 - Franchised: 3.

LIMPIDUS *
Rua Clodomiro Amazonas, 1427-2 andar, Sao Paulo, SP, Brazil, 04537-012. Contact: Fernando Sodre, Dir. - Tel: (55) 11 820 8894, Fax: (55) 11 820 2438. Janitorial service. Established: 1980 - Franchising Since: 1992 - No. of Units: Company Owned: 3 - Franchised: 15 - Franchise Fee: 5.500 - 26.000 - Royalty: ^^,5 - Total Inv: 2.500 - 5.000 - Financing: Partial, depending on location.

MAIDS, THE
Global Group, The
8-10 High St., Sutton, Surrey, England, SM1 1HN. Contact: Kevin Wearn, Mng. Dir. - Tel: (01) 643-0138. Fast and efficient home cleaning service. Established: 1983 - Franchising Since: 1984 - No. of Units: Company Owned: 2 - Franchised: 14 - Franchise Fee: £8,000 - Royalty: 14% + 6% adv. - Total Inv: £35,000 - Financing: yes.

MINSTER CLEANING SERVICES
Minster House, 948 - 952 Kingsbury Rd., Birmingham, W.M., England, B24 9PZ. Contact: Alan Haigh, Managing Partner - Tel: 0121-386 1186, Fax: 0121 386 1191. Marketing & management of office cleaning serivces. Established: 1982 - Franchising Since: 1992 - No. of Units: Company Owned: 2 - Franchised: 15 - Franchise Fee: £12,000 - Royalty: 7% - Total Inv: £65,000 inc. £45,000 work. cap. - Financing: Subject to status.

MISTER KOOL'S
Joysound Limited
82 High St., Albrighton, Wolverhampton, England, WV7 3JA. Contact: Theo Kool, Dir. - Tel: 0902 374111. Carpet & upholstery cleaning service, using new process, no shampoos, dry powders or steam. Fibres dry & go minutes after cleaning. Established: 1990 (UK) - Franchising Since: 1987/88 (Continent) - No. of Units: Company Owned: 3 - Franchised: 50+ - Franchise Fee: £8500 plus vat per 1 million inhabitants - Royalty: £105 per month - Total Inv: £12000 (includes leased van & stock) - Financing: Various banks.

MOLLY MAID UK
Agostpolar, Ltd.
Hamilton Rd., Slough, Berks, England, SL1 4QY. Contact: Pam Bader, Chief Executive - Tel: 0753 523388. Domestic cleaning franchise. Established: 1982 international - Franchising Since: 1982 - No. of Units:

Company Owned: 2 - Franchised: over 200 - Franchise Fee: £7.800 plus VAT - Royalty: 8%, 2% - Total Inv: £3.500 franchise fee, the rest set up costs - Financing: National banks.

MOPPS CLEANING SERVICES
Mopps Plc.
P.O. Box 1055, Paisley, Renfrenshire, U.K., PA3 2SH. Contact: Jennifer, Co. Secretary - Tel: 041 887 7848. Commercial & industrial contract cleaning. Established: 1988 - Franchising Since: 1992 - No. of Units: Company Owned: 4 - Franchised: 2 - Franchise Fee: £8,950 - Royalty: 7.5% reducing - Total Inv: £14,000 - Financing: Yes.

MR. SLADE DRYCLEANING
Maritime Chambers, 1 Howard St., North Shields, Tyne & Wear, England, NE30 1AR. Contact: R.P. Slade, Chairman - Tel: 091 2596421. Retail drycleaning shops offering standard cleaning plus range of specialized services including suede and leather, carpet cleaning hire, curtains, silk tie and permanent creasing/pleating. Established: 1977 - Franchising Since: 1981 - No. of Units: Company Owned: 20 - Franchised: 2 - Franchise Fee: £13,000 - Total Inv: £30,000 - Royalty: 10%.

PVC VENDO
Vendo plc
215 East Lane, Wembley, Middlesex, England, HA0 3NG. Contact: Ivan Calhoun, Mng. Dir. - Tel: (081) 908 1234. Commercial vehicle fleet powerwashing to preplanned contract frequencies. Also hygiene-sanitation powercleaning food vehicles. Other countries: France, Holland, Belgium, Ireland, Luxembourg. Established: 1981 - Franchising Since: 1989 - No. of Units: Company Owned: 12 - Franchised: 82 - Franchise Fee: £1,000 sterling - Royalty: 12.5% continuous mktg. & mgmt. Total Inv: £11,500 sterling (mktg., database, equip., vehicle, training) - Financing: Yes.

RAINBOW CARPETS
Rainbow Corner Ltd.
140-142 Caversham Rd., Reading, Berkshire, England, . Contact: David Staples, Mng. Dir. - Tel: 0734-585032. Retailing and supplying of carpets and floor coverings. Established: 1966 - Franchising Since: 1976 - No. of Units: Company Owned: 6 - Franchised: 1 - Franchise Fee: £5,000 - Total Inv: £20,000 - £50,000 - Royalty: 7% plus 7.5% adv. - Financing: yes.

SAFECLEAN
10 Blacklands Way, Abington, Oxfordshire, England, OX14 1DY. Contact: Ron Patmore, Sales Mgr. - Tel: (0235) 833022. Carpet, upholstery and curtain cleaning & protection. Established: 1969 - Franchising Since: 1974- No. of Units: Company Owned: 1 - Franchised: 45 - Franchise Fee: £9,500 - Royalty: 10% - Total Inv: £9,500.- Financing: Yes.

SQUARE 1 CLEANING SERVICES
Square 1 Environmental Services Ltd.
2 Cranleigh Ave., Rottingdean, Brighton, E. Sussex, England, BN2 7GT. Contact: Anthony Delow, Mng. Dir. - Tel: 0273-305016, Fax: 0273-301787. Domestic & commercial cleaning as well as carpet & upholstery cleaning & protecting. Established: 1987 - Franchising Since: 1987 - No. of Units: Franchised: 14 - Franchise Fee: £9,750 - Royalty: 7% - 10% - Total Inv: £15,000 incl. work. cap. - Financing: Yes.

TRAFALGAR CLEANING CHEMICALS
Unit 4, Gillmans Ind. Est., Billingshurst, W. Sussex, England, RH14 9E2. Contact: John Thompson, Mng. Dir. - Tel: 0403 785111. The supply of cleaning and maintenance chemicals to the motor and transport industries. Established: 1984 - Franchising Since: 1987 - No. of Units: Company Owned: 2 - Franchised: 21 - Franchise Fee: £9,900 - Royalty: 2% (mktg. support & adv.) - Financing: Yes.

FOODS AND BEVERAGES

7-ELEVEN CONVENIENCE STORES
7-Eleven Stores Pty. Ltd.
321 - 355 Ferntree Gully Rd., Mount Waverley, Victoria, Australia, 3149. Contact: Mr. Len Campbell, Real Est. & Fran. Mgr. - Tel: (03) 544-2722. 24 hour convenience stores selling basic food & household

needs such as newspapers & magazines, milk, bread, confectionery, soft drinks, take-away food & beverages, groceries, cleaning products etc. Many stores also offer self serve petrol. Established: 1977 - Franchising Since: 1978 - No. of Units: Company Owned: 3 - Franchised: 156 - Franchise Fee: $20,000 - $60,000 - Royalty: 46% to franchisee, 54% to franchisor - Total Inv: fran. fee, stock min. $50,000, goodwill (if applicable) $50,000 - $250,000 - Financing: For part stock only.

ALFONSO'S
3 Prince Albert Rd., London, U.K., NW1 7SN. Contact: Philip Smith, Dir. - Tel: (071) 267-2828. Alfonso's offers the consumer a wide choice of eat-in or take-away high quality dairy soft serve ice cream treats in an entertaining store environment. Established: 1993 - Franchising Since: 1994 - No. of Units: Company Owned: 1 - Franchised: 1 - Franchise Fee: Dependent on territory - Royalty: 6%, 4% mktg. - Total Inv: From £70,000 to £140,000.

ALPINE SOFT DRINKS (UK) LTD.
McAlpine House, Pytchley Lodge Rd., Kettering, Northants., England, NN15 6JN. Contact: M. Meredith, Deputy Mng. Dir. - Tel: (0536) 415115. Manufacturer & distributor of soft drinks & allied products direct to the customer's door. Established: 1975 - Franchising Since: 1987 - No. of Units: Company Owned: 20 approx. - Franchised: 180+ - Franchise Fee: Total cost between £1,000 and £7,000.

AMPOL ROAD PANTRY *
Ampol Road Pantry Pty Ltd.
620 Macauley St., Albury, NSW, Australia, 2640. Contact: Gary Tuck, Fran. Mgr. - Tel: (060) 582000. Convenience stores, always open, providing fuel & food at all hours. Established: 1987 - Franchising Since: 1987 - No. of Units: Company Owned: 1 - Franchised: 50 - Franchise Fee: $80,000 3+3+3 year tenure - Royalty: 5% of shop sales.

ARBY'S ROAST BEEF RESTAURANTS
Arby's U.K. Ltd.
24 Hay Market, London, England, SW1Y 4DG. Contact: Larry M. Lion - Tel: (071) 930-7171. America's largest and most successful roast beef restaurant chain. Established: 1992 - Franchising Since: 1992 - No. of Units: Company Owned: 1 - Franchised: 1 - Franchise Fee: £35,000 - Royalty: 6% - Financing: Possibly.

BANANA FRITZ
Rhondda, Eastdon, Starcross, Exeter, Devon, U.K., EX6 8RJ. Contact: Mrs. Pat Tibbs, M.D. - Tel: 0626 890093. Banana Fritz is a piece of banana, coated in a delicious batter and served on a stick. A sweet sensation that everyone loves. Established: 1960 - Franchising Since: 1992 - No. of Units: Company Owned: 1 - Franchised: 2 - Franchise Fee: £10,800 - Royalty: 8% - Total Inv: fran. fee plus premises & mobile unit.

BEWLEY'S CAFES AND SHOPS
Bewley's Franchising Ltd.
Mary St., Dublin 1, Dublin, Ireland, . Contact: C. O'Brien, Dev. Mgr. - Tel: 01-6776761. Cafes and shops with 150 year tradition offering full range of branded tea, coffee and confectionery products. Established: 1840 - Franchising Since: 1988 - No. of Units: Company Owned: 6 - Franchised: 29 - Total Inv: approx. £350,000 - Financing: No.

BREAD ROLL COMPANY, THE
Units 3,4,6, Verulam Ind. Est., 224 London Rd., St. Albans, Herts., England, AL1 1JF. Contact: Stephen Ville, Mng. Dir. - Tel: (0727) 835291. Manufacturer & distributor of bread rolls & morning goods throughout southern and central England. Established: 1983 - Franchising Since: 1983 - Number of Units: Company Owned: 2 - Franchised: 21 - Franchise Fee: £2,500 - Total Inv: £30,000 (£10,000 work. cap.) - Financing: No.

BRIOCHE GOURMANDE
LeGrand Et Cie
#3 rue Fon de Rache, Agen, France, 47000. Contact: Jacques-Henri Gardiel - Tel: (53) 66.34.75. Pastry shop. Established: 1980 - Franchising Since: 1981 - No. of Units: 35 - Inv: 1,200,000 FF.

BURGER STAR
206 Bath Rd., Cheltenham, Glos., U.K., GL52 7NE. Contact: Simon Daws - Tel: (0242) 528884. Fast food hamburger and pizza take-away. Established: 1981 - Franchising Since: 1989 - No. of Units: Company Owned:1 - Franchised: 3 - Franchise Fee: £6,000 - Royalty: 5% gross sales, 1% adv. levy - Total Inv: £50,000 - £65,000 - Financing: Yes.

CAFE DO PONTO *
Cafe Do Ponto S.A. Ind. Com. E Exp.
Av. Cafe do Ponto, 336 - Jd. dos Camargos, Barueri, SP, Brazil, 06410-900. Contact: Franchising Dept. - Tel: (55 11) 422.4122. Coffee shops, specialty coffee. Established: 1950 - Franchising Since: 1977 - No. of Units: Company Owned: 11 - Franchised: 175.

CANADIAN MUFFIN COMPANY, THE
19 Rotterdam Dr., London, England, E14 3JA. Contact: Garry Rowse, Mng. Dir. - Tel: 071 538 1667. Wholesome vegetarian fast food. Established: 1989 - Franchising Since: 1991 - No. of Units: Company Owned: 1 - Franchised: 5 - Franchise Fee: £60,000 - Royalty: 6% mgmt. fee, 2% mktg. - Total Inv: £25,000 shopfitting, £25,000 equip., £10,000 fees & legal - Financing: Yes.

CARTONS BOULANGERIES
Unit 2, Telegraph Hill Estate, Laundry Rd., Minster, Ramsgate, Kent, England, CT12 4HJ. Contact: Bob Peel, Consultant - Tel: (0843) 821940. French bakery, patisserie, delicatessen. Take out or eat in. Established: 1981 - Franchising Since: 1984 - No. of Units: Company Owned: 1 - Franchised: 7 - Franchise Fee: £5,000 - Total Inv: £35,000 - £75,000 - Financing: yes.

CHANTEGRILL, JARDIN BRESILIEN, PASCALINE, PASTA-FACTORY
Groupe Nouvelle Restauration Francais
40 Av. du Lac, Crespieres, France, 78121. Contact: Daniel Majonchi, C.E.O. - Tel: (1) 30 5437 12. Four different concepts of restaurants: Changegrill: French garden restaurant. Jardin Bresilien: cocktail bar with live music and light food. Pascaline: traditional French bistro and brasserie. Pasta-Factory: fresh pasta and rock music. Established: 1980 - Franchising Since: 1980 - No. of Units: Company Owned: 9 - Franchised: 35 - Franchise Fee: $30,000 U.S. - Royalty: 5% - Total Inv: $250,000 - $1,000,000 U.S. - Financing: 70%.

CHICAGO PIZZA PIE FACTORY
My Kinda Town Plc.
195-197 Kings Rd., Chelsea, London, England, SW3 5ED. Contact: Stephen Gee, Deputy Chairman - Tel: 44 (0) 171 351 6996. The Chicago Pizza Pie Factory creates a feeling of actually being in Chicago. Every bit of wall space is covered with a vast amount of authentic Chicago memorabilia, i.e. street signs. Posters of cinema & theatre. Its menu offers a wide choice of deep dish pizzas and other classic dishes such as chicken, caesar salad, stuffed mushrooms, aubergine parmigiana and bruschetta. Established: 1977 - Franchising Since: 1985 - No. of Units: Company Owned: 20 - Franchised: 24 - Franchise Fee: £55,000 - £85,000 - Royalty: 5% - 7% - Total Inv: £300,000+ - Financing: No.

CIRCLE C CONVENIENCE STORES
137-139 Crawley Rd., Roffey, Horsham, W. Sussex, England, RH10 6AA. Contact: Richard Perkins, Dir. - Tel: (0403) 268888, Fax: (0403) 257682. Retail shop to offer neighbourhood wide range to cope with most day to day needs. Established: 1982 - Franchising Since: 1984 - No. of Units: Company Owned: 18 - Franchised: 40 - Franchise Fee: £8,000 ($12,000) - Royalty: 3% of gross sales - Total Inv: shop £20,000, fitting £20,000, stock £20,000 - Financing: Yes.

CIRCLE K
Circle K (UK) Licensing Ltd.
Fareham Point, Wickham Rd., Fareham, Hampshire, England, PO16 7BU. Contact: D.C. Ellis-Jones, Dir. Licensing Dev. - Tel: 0329 822666. Convenience Stores. Specialist chain with central merchandise distribution and advanced I.T. systems and epos. Established: 1965 - Franchising Since: 1984 - No. of Units: Company Owned: 140 - Franchised: 71 - Franchise Fee: £14,000, £15,000 petrol stations - Royalty: 3% of merchandise sales excluding VAT, .5% adv. - Total Inv: £80,000 - £160,000 - Financing: Major UK banks finance up to 70%.

COFFEEMAN
Coffeeman Management Ltd.
Unit 29, Trent Lane Ind. Est., Castle Donnington, Leics., England, DE74 2NP. Contact: Brian Hardiman, Fran. Mgr. - Tel: 0332-850221. Delivery of fresh ground coffee & other products to catering and office customers. Established: 1976 - Franchising Since: 1984 - No. of Units: Franchised: 75 - Franchise Fee: £5,500 - Total Inv: Fran. Fee + £5,400 stationery/equip. etc. - Financing: Yes.

COMTESSE DU BARRY S.A.
32200 Gimont, France, . Contact: Francis LaCroix - Tel: 62.67.70.10. Restaurant. Established: 1908 - Franchising Since: 1974 - No. of Units: Company Owned: 6 - Franchised: 34 - Franchise Fee: 30,000 - 80,000 F - Total Inv: 1,000,000 F.

COUNTRY GOODNESS
Gannel Rd., Newquay, Cornwall, England, . Contact: Michael Pearce - Tel: (063) 73 4870. A full range of exclusive gift food products. Inv: £1,500 in-store, £12,000 for complete shop.

COURTE-PAILLE
Serare SA
Z1 - Petite Montagne Nord, CE 1412, 910 19, Evry Cedex, France, . Contact: Gilles Pelisson, Dir. - Tel: (6) 077-92-20. Restaurant which is a small and round house with thatched or tile roof and private parking. Half-timbered, the fireplace shelters a fire on which meat and sausages are grilled. Established: 1959 - Franchising Since: 1959 - No. of Units: Company Owned: 97 - Franchised: 1.

CREPELITO
Crepelito-Comercio de Maqs. Gen. Alimenticious Ltda.
Rua Oscar Freire, 1784, Sao Paulo, Sao Paulo, Brazil, 05409. Contact: Cyro Augusto Baffi, Owner - Tel: (055) 011-280-1299. A fast food, which offers a product with no competitors. Crepes served on a pick with different kinds of stuffings such as sweets, fruit, ham, sausage and others as well as ice cream, espresso and soft drinks. Established: 1986 - Franchising Since: 1987 - No. of Units: Company Owned: 9 - Franchised: 32 - Franchise Fee: US $39,000 - Royalty: 7% - Financing: 4 x US $9,750.

DELI FRANCE
Whitworths Restaurants Ltd.
166 Bute St. Mall, Arndale Centre, Luton, Beds., England, LU1 2TU. Contact: Mr. M.J.B. Ward, Mng. Dir. - Tel: 0582-422781. French-style coffee shop & retailer of bakery products. Established: 1991 - Franchising Since: 1992 - No. of Units: Company Owned: 1 - Franchised: 3 - Franchise Fee: £10,000 - Royalty: 6% - Total Inv: £140,000 - Financing: 75%.

DELIFRANCE *
La Petite Croissanterie Ltd.
3 Woodside Pl., Glasgow, U.K., G3 7QF. Contact: Steve Dinnes, Dir. - Tel: 0141-353-5200. Chain of authentic French cafe/bakeries with both a sit-in and take-away facility. Established: 1985 - Franchising Since: 1990 - No. of Units: Company Owned: 3 - Franchised: 3 - Franchise Fee: £10,000 - Royalty: 6% of net sales - Total Inv: fran. fee plus £120,000 - £140,000 shopfit, £40,000 - £60,000 equip., £10,000 start-up costs - Financing: Yes, from banks with franchise dept.

DIAMOND CHOPSTICKS
Ste. 1 50-52 Urunga Parade, Miranda, NSW, Australia, 2228. Contact: Franchise Director - Tel: (02) 5261444. Chinese home delivery franchise.

DINKUM DOG
Plumcourt Ltd.
88-92 Wallis Rd., Hackney, London, U.K., E9 5LN. Contact: John Drage, M.D. - Tel: (081) 985-3623. Fast food sales and marketing. UK and European sites only. Established: 1986 - Franchising Since: 1990 - Franchise Fee: £10,900 - Royalty: 5% man. fee, 3% adv. levy - Financing: Yes.

DISTRIBUIDORA CORY *
Industria De Prod. Alimenticios Cory Ltda
R: Antonio Fernandes Figueiroa, 1056, Ribeirao Preto, Sao Paulo, Brazil, 14095-280. Contact: Arimatea, Fran. Mgr. - Tel: (016) 627,1550 Ramal 230. Distributors of cookies, biscuits and candies. All the products are made by Cory Industries. Established: 1969 - Franchising Since: 1991 - No. of Units: Company Owned: 1 - Franchised: 22 - Franchise Fee: US$10,000 - Royalty: 0.5% over gross sales - Total Inv: US$40,000 - Financing: No.

DIXY FRIED CHICKEN
185 Town Rd., Edmonton, London, U.K., N9 0HL. Contact: Mr. A. Mahmood, Mng. Dir. - Tel: 081-345-6675. Fast food take away and sit down units offering fried chicken and associated products, fries, side dishes and desserts. Established: 1986 - Franchising Since: 1986 - No. of Units: Company Owned: 10 - Franchised: 28 - Franchise Fee: £5,000 - Royalty: 4% - Total Inv: £100,000 - Financing: Yes.

DOMINOS
Dominos Pizza Group
Unit 10, Maryland Road, Tongwell, Milton Keynes, England, MK15 8HF. Contact: Bill Ewbank, Dev. Dir. - Tel: 0908-618-222. Pizza home delivery and take-away. Established: 1985 - Franchising Since: 1985 - No. of Units: Company Owned: 4 - Franchised: 82 - Franchise Fee: initial fee £10,000, £8,000 fran. fee per store - Royalty: 5.5% of turnover + 4% adv. - Total Inv: £90,000 (1st store).

DON MILLERS HOT BREAD KITCHENS
Whitworths Bakeries Ltd.
166 Bute Street Mall, Arndale Centre, Luton, England, LU1 2TL. Contact: Mr. M. J. B. Ward, Mng. Dir. - Tel: 0582-422781. Produce & retailer of bakery products including take-away. Established: 1973 - Franchising Since: 1983 - No. of Units: Company Owned: 92 - Franchised: 34 - Franchise Fee: £10,000 - Royalty: 8% - Total Inv: £70,000 - Financing: 75%.

DONUT KING
464 St. Kilda Rd., 3rd floor, Melbourne, Victoria, Australia, 3004. Contact: Mark Lewis, Mgr. Fran. Selection - Tel: 8677666. Specialty food retailer, retailing donuts, hot & cold beverages and ice cream. All outlets located in major shopping centres. Established: 1981 - Franchising Since: 1982 - No. of Units: Franchised: 75 - Franchise Fee: $55,000 - Royalty: 6% gross sales, 2% adv. levy of gross sales - Total Inv: $150,000 - $200,000 incl. fran. fee, fixtures, fittings - Financing: To suitable applicants.

EAGLE BOYS DIAL-A-PIZZA *
Eagle Boys Dial-A-Pizza Australia Plc.
232 Arthur St., Fortitude Valley 406, Brisbane, Queensland, Australia, 4006 . Contact: Mr. Tom Potter, Mng. Dir. - Tel: (07) 3254-1799, Fax: (07) 3254 1960. Franchise home delivery pizza business. Established: 1987 - Franchising Since: 1989 - No. of Units: Company Owned: 1 (training store) - Franchised: 70 - Franchise Fee: A$25,000 - Royalty: 6% of turnover - Total Inv: A$150,000 - A$200,000 - Financing: Bank or financial institution only.

ESPETINHOS CAMPINAS *
Rua Eldorado, 586/630, Campinas, SP, Brazil, . Contact: Andre, Pres./Dir. - Tel: (0192) 47-7733. Barbecue (in sticks) production and sales. Barbecue accessories. Parties organization and services. Established: 1984 - Franchising Since: 1989 - No. of Units: Company Owned: 3 - Franchised: 4 - Franchise Fee: US$7,000 - Royalty: 4% - Total Inv: US$22,000 - Financing: No.

FATTY ARBUCKLES AMERICAN DINER
Fatty Arbuckles Franchise Ltd.
Arbuckle House, High Street, Poole, Dorset, England, BH15 1BP. Contact: Adrian Lee, Mng. Dir. - Tel: (0202) 668909 or Fax (0202) 660334. Themed American style diner/restaurant serving very generous portions of quality food at affordable prices in a friendly relaxed atmosphere. The central theme being eating should be fun. Established: 1983 - Franchising Since: 1990 - No. of Units: Company Owned: 11 - Franchised: 17 - Franchise Fee: £10,000 - Royalty: 6% mgmt., 2% adv. - Total Inv: £100,000 - £250,000 - Financing: 70% thru Nat'l Westminster Bank Plc.

FAVORITE FRIED CHICKEN
7 Davy Rd., Gorse Lane, Clacton-On-Sea, Essex, U.K., C015 4XD. Contact: Sholto Williamson, Fran. Mgr.. Pressure fried chicken fast food retail shops. Established: 1986 - Franchising Since: 1987 - No. of Units: Company Owned: 7 - Franchised: 41 - Franchise Fee: $4,500 - Royalty: 4% - Total Inv: $45,000 equip. & shopfitting.

GOOD GOOD *
Trident Adm. Empreend. E Part. Ltda.
Rua D. Mariana 133 casa 2, Rio de Janeiro, RJ, Brazil, 22280-020. Contact: Moises, Partner-Director - Tel: (021) 286-6016. Chain of fast food pizza restaurants with 27 stores. Menu: pizza, beverages and desserts. Food service: Dine-in, takeout and delivery. There are stores in Rio de Janeiro (the majority), Brasilia, Salvador, Belo Horizonte, Sao Paulo e Vila Velha. Established: 1983 - Franchising Since: 1988 - No. of Units: Company Owned: 4 - Franchised: 23 - Franchise Fee: US$12,000 - Royalty: 6% - Total Inv: US$75,000.

GREAT AUSTRALIAN ICE CREAMERY
Ice Creameries of Australia
Ice Creamery Hse., 271 Bong Bong St., Bowral, NSW, Australia, 2576. Contact: J. Johnson, Sales & Mktg. Coord. - Tel: (048) 622299. Sit down or take-away ice cream parlours offering wide range of flavours, cones, sundaes & spiders plus milkshakes, hot drinks & hot food located around Australia. Franchisees are usually married couples. Established: 1977 - Franchising Since: 1982 - No. of Units: Company Owned: 1 - Franchised: 93 - Franchise Fee: $37,500 - Royalty: none, percentage rebate paid on stocks purchased - Total Inv: $170,000 - $180,000 incl. fran. fee - Financing: Assistance with bank finance available.

HARRER MEINE EISDIELE *
Toni Harrer Systemz Entrale
Ungargasse 8, 2700 Wr. Neustadt, Austria, 2700. Contact: Mr. Harrer, System Mgr. - Tel: 02622/29084. Production and distribution of ice cream. Established: 1988 - Franchising Since: 1990 - No. of Units: Company Owned: 4 - Franchised: 4 - Franchise Fee: 5% - Total Inv: US$300,000 - Financing: No.

HARRY RAMSDEN'S
Harry Ramsden's PLC
Larwood House, White Cross, Guiseley, Leeds, W. Yorkshire, England, LS20 8LZ. Contact: John Barnes, Chairman - Tel: 0943 879531. Fish and chip restaurants & takeaways. Established: 1928 - Franchising Since: 1991 - No. of Units: Company Owned: 1 - Franchised: 11 - Franchise Fee: $150,000 - Royalty: 7% of sales - Total Inv: Build. $1,200,000, Equip. $350,000.

HEMGLASS SVERIGE AB
Box 53, 64521 Strangnas, Sweden, . Contact: Jan Hallgren, Mng. Dir. - Tel: 0152-18020, Fax: 0152-15704. Home delivery of ice cream. Established: 1968 - Franchising Since: 1968 - No. of Units: Company Owned: 22 - Franchised: 14 - Franchise Fee: SEK 5,000 - 20,000 - Total Inv: SEK 100,000 - 300,000.

HENRY J. BEAN'S BAR & GRILL
My Kinda Town Plc.
195-197 Kings Road, Chelsea, London, England, SW3 5ED. Contact: Steven Gee, Deputy Chairman - Tel: 44 (0) 171 351 6996. A typical 1950's style American neighborhood bar & grill offering a menu of potato skins, nachos, hamburgers, hot dogs & chili as well as a large range of drinks. Memorabilia includes autographed photos and quantities of old American advertising signs. Established: 1983 - Franchising Since: 1989 - No. of Units: Company Owned: 17 - Franchised: 12 - Franchise Fee: £45,000 - £75,000 - Royalty: 5% - 7% - Total Inv: £100,000 - Financing: No.

HOGGIES
Hoggies Ltd.
Stowupland Hall, Stowmarket Suffolk, England, IP14 4BE. Contact: Chris Knock, Franc. Admin. - Tel: 0449 674289. Spit-roast and outside catering. Established: 1985 - Franchising Since: 1990 - No. of Units: Company Owned: 3 - Franchised: 3 - Franchise Fee: £4,000 - Royalty: £100 per month maintenance contract on equipment - Total Inv: £19,500 (equipment £15,500 franchise fee £4,000) - Financing: Yes, subject to status.

KFC
KFC (GB) Ltd.
88-97 High Street, Brentford, Mddx., England, TW8 8BG. Contact: S. Bartholomew, District Mgr. - Tel: 081 569 7070. Fast food. Established: 1965 - Franchising Since: 1965 - No. of Units: Company Owned: 82 - Franchised: 215 - Franchise Fee: £10,000 - Royalty: 5% - Total Inv: £200,000 - Financing: No.

KWIK BITE
Kwik Bite (UK) Ltd.
187-189 Seabourne Rd., SouthBourne, Bournemouth, Dorset, England, BH5 2HH. Contact: C.R. Page, Mng. Dir. - Tel: 0202 421200. Delivery of leading brands of confectionery; crisps and snacks to places of work. We service the end user by providing a fully merchandised tray of product plus collection facility. Established: 1993 - Franchising Since: 1990 - No. of Units: Franchised: 65 - Franchise Fee: £11,500 - Royalty: £1 per week in site - Total Inv: £2,000 retail value stock/P.O.S. matl./uniform/stationery/training etc. - Financing: Yes, subject to status, house equity etc.

L'HERBIER DE PROVENCE *
I.M.T. Ges.m.b.H
Schumannpasse 3B, Perchtoldsdorf, Austria, 2380. Contact: Mr. Legerer, G.M. - Tel: 865-40-73. Import & export of nutrition foods, cosmetics. Established: 1984 - Franchising Since: 1988 - No. of Units: Company Owned: 2 - Franchised: 8 - Franchise Fee: $10,000 - Royalty: 7% - Total Inv: $39,000 - Financing: 100%.

LATE LATE SUPERSHOP, THE
P.O. Box 53, New Century House, Manchester, England, M60 4ES. Contact: J.M Campbell, Dir. - Tel: 061-834-1212. A convenience retailer selling a wide range of products including groceries, wines and spirits, delicatessen, greengrocery, books and magazines, confectionery. Established: 1985 - Franchising Since: 1985 - No. of Units: Franchised: 10 - Franchise Fee: £8,000 start up fee - Royalty: 2% - Total Inv: £70,000 - Financing: up to 70% through banks.

LENARD'S POULTRY SHOPS *
Poultry Shop Pty. Ltd., The
Ste. 2, 50 Cleveland St. Stones Corner, Brisbane, Queensland, Australia, 4120. Contact: Maitland Bardwell, Fran. & Leasing Mgr. - Tel: (07) 397-2345. Retailing of value added fresh poultry. Operate predominantly in shopping centres anchored by good supermarket. Established: 1987 - Franchising Since: 1987 - No. of Units: Company Owned: 2 - Franchised: 81 - Franchise Fee: $40,000 - $50,000 depending on site - Royalty: 4% fran. fee, 3% mktg. fee - Total Inv: $40,000 fran. fee, plus approx. $135,000 for plant, equipment, etc. - Financing: Major banks.

LES ROIS MAGES
Turfait Et Cie S.A.
210 rue Louis Armand - Z-1- Aix en Provence, 13794 Aix. en. Pr. Cedex 3, France, . Contact: Turfait Pierre, Directeur - Tel: 42.24.42.57. Torrefaction et degustation cafes thes chocolats. Established: 1950 - Franchising Since: 1977 - No. of Units: Company Owned: 10 - Franchise Fee: 70,000 FRS. - Royalty: 1% - Total Inv: 400,000 FRS - B.P. 132,000.

LOBSTER VILLAGE
Loeberenstreet 19, Z U G, Suisse, 8125. Contact: Claude Haari, Owner/Pres. - Tel: (01) 391 9160, Fax: (01) 391-2796. Restaurant - the motto "Have fun - have Lobster". Dining room/bar with service. Established: 1986 - Franchising Since: 1990 - No. of Units: Company Owned: 1 - Franchised: 4 - Franchise Fee: CH-Fr. 35,000 - Royalty: 4% - Total Inv: from 80,000 to 250,000 Swiss Francs - Financing: Yes.

LOVE TOAST
Crepelito Com. Maqs. Gen. Alimenticios, Ltda.
Rua Oscar Freire, 1784, Sao Paulo, Brazil, 05409. Contact: Cyro Augusto Baffi, Owner - Tel: (055) 011-280-1299. Love Toast offers many different products such as waffles, sweet and salted picks, ice cream, espresso and soft drinks. Established: 1986 - Franchising Since: 1989 - No. of Units: Company Owned: 1 - Franchised: 3 - Franchise Fee: $39,000 US - Royalty: 7% - Total Inv: $39,000 US - Financing: 4 X $9,750 US.

MASTER BREW LTD.
Beverages House, 7 Ember Centre, Hersham, Surrey, England, KT12 3PT. - Tel: 01932 253787. Franchisees sell and deliver fresh roast and ground coffee and a complete range of beverage products to offices and catering outlets. Established: 1986 - Franchising Since: 1990 - No. of Units: Company Owned: 1 - Franchised: 65 - Total Inv: £9,900 + VAT + £7,000 work. cap. - Financing: Most banks.

MCDONALD'S RESTAURANTS
McDonald's Restaurants Ltd.
11-59 High Rd., East Finchley, London, England, N2 8AW. Contact: Wendy Ayling, Fran. Coord. - Tel: (0181) 700 7153, Fax: (0181) 700 7055. Quick service restaurants. Established: 1974 in UK - Franchising Since: 1986 in UK - No. of Units: Company Owned: 609 - Franchised: 134 - Franchise Fee: $30,000.

MISTER DONUT
353 North End Road, London, England, SW6 1NN. Contact: Mr. E. Saheb, Man. Dir. - Tel: (071) 386-9133. Fast food, donuts, pastry, muffins, cookies....brownies. Established: 1955 - Franchising Since: 1956 - No. of Units: Company Owned: 1 - Franchised: 1,000 - Franchise Fee: Based on the size of the region or country in Europe - Royalty: 3% and 2% adv. - Total Inv: £150,000, will depend on the size of region - Financing: The company may help finance through the banks.

MISTER PIZZA
Pizzarias Mister Pizza Ltd.
rue da Quitanda, 50 and/or 6 centro, Rio de Janerio - RJ, Brazil, 20011-030. Contact: Mrs. Eliane Bernardino, Vice-Pres. - Tel: (021) 224-4477, Fax: (021) 262-6364. Fast food pizza shops, thin and thick crust pizza as main menu item, special assorted sandwiches, giant hot-dogs with special sauces. Established: 1981 - Franchising Since: 1983 - No. of Units: Company Owned: 26 - Franchised: 59 - Franchise Fee: $15,000 U.S. - Royalty: 6% + 2% publicity - Total Inv: $120,000 U.S.

MONGOLIAN BARBEQUE *
68 Home Park Rd., London, England, SW19 7HN. Contact: John Dodds, Fran. Mgr. - Tel: 0181-947-7500. Restaurants/catering. Established: 1988 - No. of Units: Company Owned: 6 - Franchised: 3 - Franchise Fee: £10,000 sterling - Royalty: 6.5% mgmt. svc. fee, 1% adv. levy - Total Inv: circa £25,000 sterling + fit out costs & property costs (£100,000 min.) - Financing: Assistance with preparation of business plan.

MORLEY'S FAST FOODS
207 - 209 Worton Rd., Isleworth, Middlesex, England, TW7 6DS. Contact: John von Ahlefeldt - Tel: 01-568-4343. Established: 1985 - No. of Units: Company Owned: 1 - Franchised: 7 - Approx. Inv: £60,000 - £70,000 - Royalty: 4% + 3% adv. - Financing: yes.

MR. BIG (UK) LTD.
18 Fairfax St., Coventry, England, CU1 5RY. Contact: Franchise Director - Tel: (0203) 57722/29238. Mr. Big giant sized hamburgers, counter or waitress service units.

MR. COD
Mr. Cod Ltd.
6/7 High St., Woking, Surrey, England, GU21 1BG. Contact: J. Brewer, Mng. Dir. - Tel: 0483-755407. Fast food fish and chip take away and restaurant. Established: 1980 - Franchising Since: 1985 - No. of Units: Company Owned: 3 - Franchised: 5 - Franchise Fee: £5,000 - Royalty: various - Total Inv: £50,000 - £100,000 - Financing: Yes.

NATURAL LIFE HEALTH FOODS
15 Queen St., Salisbury, Wilts., England, SP1 QEY. Contact: Bob Peel, Consultant - Tel: 0722 335965. Health food stores. Established: 1983 - Franchising Since: 1986 - No. of Units: Company Owned: 1 - Franchised: 6 - Franchise Fee: £7,500 - Royalty: 4.5% - Total Inv: £40,000 - £90,000 dependant on size - Financing: yes 50%.

NICECREAM
Nicecream Comercio de Alimentos Ltda
Rua Gaivota, 987, Sao Paulo, Brazil, 04522. Contact: Bernard Jeger, Pres. - Tel: (5511) 542-5988, Fax: (5511) 240-0936. Frozen yogurt and other products such as: specialty sandwiches, quiche, pizzetta, salad bar. Established: 1986 - Franchising Since: 1989 - No. of Units: Company Owned: 8 - Franchised: 8 - Franchise Fee: $ 11,000.00 (US) - Royalty: 5% on gross sales - Total Inv: $ 50,000 (US).

NOPRI
8 Rue d'Argent, Brussels, Belgium, 1000. Contact: Maurice Boisdenghien, Mng. Dir. - Tel: (02) 212 8111. Full line supermarkets. Established: 1928 - Franchising Since: 1934 - No. of Units: Franchised: 188 - Inv: varies.

O'BRIEN'S IRISH SANDWICH BARS *
1st Fl., 16 Exchequer St.,, Dublin 2, Ireland, . Contact: Brody Sweeney, Mng. Dir. - Tel: 353 1 671 5176. Upmarket made to order sandwich and cappucino bar with a contemporary Irish theme. Established: 1988 - Franchising Since: 1994 - No. of Units: Company Owned: 4 - Franchised: 4 - Franchise Fee: £7,500 - Royalty: 6%, 2% mktg. - Total Inv: £50,000 Irish pounds - Financing: Yes.

P & C PAO E COMPANHIA *
Pao & Companhia Servicos Ltda.
Rua Itapema, 326, Belo Horizonte, Minas Gerais, Brazil, 30330-490. Contact: Helio Valadao, Mktg. Dir. - Tel: (55) 31 225-4751. Franchising of bakery - bread without chemical additives - natural style. Established: 1984 - Franchising Since: 1986 - No. of Units: Company Owned: 2 - Franchised: 60 - Franchise Fee: US$75 per sq. meter - Royalty: 3% on gross - Total Inv: Avg. US$120,000 - Financing: Possibility of banking financing up to 50%.

PERFECT PIZZA
Perfect Pizza House, The Forum, Hanworth Lane, Chertsey, Surrey, England, KT16 9JX. Contact: Martin Clayton, Fran. Sales Dir. - Tel: 0932-568000. Pizza delivery and take-away. Established: 1978 - Franchising Since: 1982 - No. of Units: Company Owned: 20 - Franchised: 210 - Franchise Fee: £8,000 - Royalty: 8%, includes mktg. - Total Inv: £75,000 incl. construction, equip., legal fees, smallwares - Financing: Through all of the main lending banks.

PICCOLO PIZZA *
Fast Food Systems Ltd.
Unit 1, Headley Pk. 9, Headley Rd. E., Reading, Berks., England, RG5 4SQ. Contact: A.J. Withers, Mng. Dir. - Tel: 01734 441100, Fax: 01734 441080

PIERRE VICTOIRE, PIERRE LAPIN, CHEZ JULES, BEPPE VITTORIO
Pierre Victoire Ltd.
48 Albany St., Edinburgh, Scotland, EH1 3QR. Contact: Fiona Lawrence, Fran. Dir. - Tel: (0131) 479-0011, Fax: (0131) 479-0012. Bistro style French restaurants offering excellent quality cuisine at value for money prices. Established: 1988 - Franchising Since: 1992 - No. of Units: Company Owned: 10 - Franchised: 82 - Franchise Fee: £12,500 - Royalty: 5% turnover - Total Inv: £50,000 - £80,000.

PIZZA 2/4
Franchise Development Services, Castle House, Castle Meadow, Norwich, England, NR2 1PJ. Contact: D. Mayers, Cons. - Tel: 0603-620301. Pizza restaurant with Italian style decor suitable for husband/wife operation with part time staff. Established: 1978 - Franchising Since: 1985 - No. of Units: Company Owned: 1 - Franchised: 1 - Franchise Fee: £10,000 - Total Inv: £30,000 - Royalty: 5% - Financing: possible.

PIZZA EXPRESS
29 Wardour St., Soho, London, England , W1V 3HB. Contact: Jonathan Dell, Fran. Dir. - Tel: 071-437-7215. Italian style pizzerias following a common theme but still retaining a uniquely individual design providing a haven for the genuine pizza lover. Thin pizza bases, carefully sourced ingredients, twenty-seven years experience, keeps Pizza Express the leading force in the UK pizza market. Established: 1965 - Franchising Since: 1972 - No. of Units: Company Owned: 15 - Franchised: 52 - Franchise Fee: £20,000 - Royalty: 4% of net sales - Total Inv: approx. £250,000.

PIZZA HAVEN
464 St. Kilda Rd., Melbourne, Victoria, Australia, 3004. Contact: Franchise Director - Tel: (03) 2677666. Food service outlet specializing in home delivered pizzas and a variety of side dishes.

PIZZA HUT *
Pepsico do Brazil Ltda.
Av. Brig. Faria Lima 1815 - 6th Fl., Sao Paulo, SP, Brazil, 01451-001. Contact: Dilson J.O. Santos, Fran. Dir. - Tel: (011) 815-3933. Fast food business, restaurants and quick service. Established: 1989 (in Brazil) - Franchising Since: 1989 - No. of Units: Company Owned: 54 - Franchised:

65 - Franchise Fee: US$20,000 territorial fee, US$25,000 initial fee - Royalty: 6% gross monthly sales - Total Inv: Average $600,000 per unit - Financing: No.

PIZZA HUT (UK) LTD.
149 Earl's Court Rd., London, England, . Contact: Peter A. Bassi, Area V.P. - Tel: 370 6443. Restaurants selling freshly prepared pizza, pasta, salad, desserts, wine and lager. Established: 1973 - Franchising Since: 1979 - No. of Units: Company Owned: 12 - Franchised: 1 - Franchise Fee: $25,000 US - Total Inv: £135,000 - Royalty: 5%.

PIZZA-MANN *
Ruflingerstraße 17, 4060 Leonding, Austria, . Contact: Mr. Platzl, Owner - Tel: 43/732/67 06 46. Pizzamann is doing Pizza-business in Austria. We are in outdoor, indoor and delivery service. We are market-leader in that business in Austria. Established: 1986 - Franchising Since: 1987 - No. of Units: Company Owned: 25 - Franchised: all - Franchise Fee: 5% of net turnover - Total Inv: $50,000 per unit for franchisee.

POPPINS RESTAURANTS
21 King St., Frome, Somerset, England, . Contact: A.L. Robinson, - Tel: 0243-864647. Restaurants. Established: 1979.

PRISUNIC
102 rue de Provence, P.O. Box 351.09, 75426 Paris Cedex 09, France, . Contact: J. Blanchard, Mgr. Int'l Oper. - Tel: (1) 42 82 49 66. Distribution de produits alimentaires et non alimentaires repondant aux besoins courants du plus grand nombre de consommateurs. Established: 1932 - Franchising Since: 1934 - No. of Units: Company Owned: 109 - Franchised: 302.

QUICK HAMBURGER RESTAURANT
Motorest S.A.
Grote Steenweg 224 Bus 5, 2600 Berchem, Anvers, France, . Contact: M. Van Keymeulen - Tel: 03/280 28 11 . Fast food. Established: 1971 - Franchising Since: 1978 - No. of Units: Company Owned: 25 - Franchised: 9 - Franchise Fee: 250,000 FB - Total Inv: 430,000,000 FB - Royalty: 8% - Financing: 300,000 FB.

SEVEN-ELEVEN CONVENIENCE STORES
Seven-Eleven (Japan) Co. Ltd.
4-14 Shibakoen 105, Tokyo, Japan, . Contact: Tsumie Yamaguchi, Sec. - Tel: (03) 459-3711. Convenience stores. Established: 1973 - Franchising Since: 1974 - No. of Units: Company Owned: 68 - Franchised: 3327 - Franchise Fee: ¥3 million - Total Inv: ¥23 million (including ¥20 million for store construction) - Royalty: 45% gross profit - Financing: ¥20 million.

SOUTHERN FRIED CHICKEN & SFC EXPRESS
Fast Food Systems Ltd.
Unit 1, Headley Pk 9, Headley Rd. E., Reading, Berks., England, RG5 4SQ. Contact: A.J. Withers, Mng. Dir. - Tel: 01734 441100, Fax: 01734 441080. Turnkey concept for chicken burgers & pizzas. Primarily fast food. Equipment manufacturers and owners of registered trade marks worldwide. Established: 1980 - Franchising Since: 1984 - No. of Units: Franchised: 600 - Franchise Fee: Commitment to disposables & spices - Total Inv: min. £30,000, max. £100,000- Financing: Up to 50% on leasing.

SPUDULIKE
Spudulike Ltd.
34/38 Standard Rd., Park Royal, London, England, NW10 6EU. Contact: Ron Snipp, Dir. - Tel: 081 965-0182, Fax: 081 965-6102. Specialist baked potato restaurants. Established: 1981 - Franchising Since: 1981 - No. of Units: Company Owned: 20 - Franchised: 23 - Franchise Fee: £10,000 - Royalty: 5% mgmt. 3% adv. - Total Inv: £80,000 - Financing: Up to 50%.

ST. PIERRE'S CORP.
1 Bidwell St., Wellington, New Zealand, . Contact: Perry Katsoulis, Pres. - Tel: (04) 844-431. Specialty food retailer, specializing in gourmet seafood, poultry, and delicatessen. Established: 1985 - Franchising Since: 1989 - No. of Units: Company Owned: 3 - Franchised: 12 - Franchise Fee: $25,000 - Royalty: 7% - Total Inv: $180,000 - $230,000 - Financing: yes.

STANDA SPA-AFFILIAZIONE-FRANCHISING-IMPROSSO
Strada 4 Palazzo Q1, 20085 Rozzano Hilano, Italy, . Contact: Maurizio Rotta Gentile, Director - Tel: (02) 83212 741. Franchising Food/Non Food. Franchising Since: 1970.

STROUD CREAMERY
Lansdown, Stroud, Glos., England, . Contact: Pat Smith, Dir. - Tel: 04-536-2351. Dairy products. Established: 1967 - Franchising Since: 1967 - No. of Units: Company Owned: 10 - Franchised: 46 - Approx. Inv: £1,000 - Royalty: £9 per week.

THORNTONS PLC
Thornton Park, Somercotes Derbyshire, England, DE55 4XJ. Contact: R.E. Smith, Commercial Executive - Tel: 0773 608822. A fractional franchise established in existing High St. shops selling a compatible product mix (quality sugar and chocolate confectionery). Established: 1977 - Franchising Since: 1977 - No. of Units: Company Owned: 207 - Franchised: 162 - Inv: £15,000.

TICKLE MANOR TEAROOM - LAVENHAM
Tickle Manor Tearoom Ltd.
18 High St., Lavenham, Sudbury, Suffolk, England, CO10 9PT. Contact: James Blake, Chairman - Tel: (0787) 248216. Franchise tearooms, serving morning coffee, light lunch, and afternoon tea, of a very special kind. Professional catering. Service & ambiance with a curious theme which proves irresistible to customers new and regular. Established: 1988 - Franchising Since: 1990 - No. of Units: Franchised: 1 - Franchise Fee: £7,000 - Royalty: 5% total: 1% trouble shooting, 1.5% menu provision, 1% recipe dev., 1.5% mktg. - Total Inv: £7,000 fran. fee, £25,000 fixtures/fittings - Financing: No.

TOASTY KITCHENS
Old George Brewery, Rollestone St., Salisbury, Wiltshire, England, SP1 1BB. Contact: Charles Bartlett, Dir. - Tel: (0722) 327456. Our specially designed gas operated cooking system enables franchisees to prepare, seal, and then sell thousands of crispy, freshly baked roasted sandwiches a day. The equipment is fitted in custom built catering trailers for use at all outdoor events and shows. Established: 1981 - Franchising Since: 1983 - No. of Units: Company Owned: 1 - Franchised: 14 - Franchise Fee: £12,000 + VAT incl. fully equip. catering unit - Royalty: £78 per mon. - Total Inv: £12,000 + £3,000 work cap. - Financing: Yes, in UK.

UNIGATE DAIRIES LTD.
14/40 Victoria Rd., Aldershot, Hants, England, GU1 11TH. Contact: K.R. House - Tel: (0252) 24522. Distribution of milk and dairy products and soft drinks.

WATNEY MANN & TRUMAN BREWERS
The Brewery, 91 Brick Lane, London, England, E1 6QN. Contact: P. Robinson - Tel: 01 377-0020. Licensed house (pub).

WENDY'S SUPA SUNDAES *
209 Fullarton Rd., Eastwood, South Australia, Australia, 5063. Contact: Michelle Pech, Nat'l. Fran. Mgr. - Tel: (08) 373 3944. Wendy's Supa Sundaes is a chain of specialised impulse treat outlets. The bright shops and tempting range of products including ice cream, vitari, hot dogs, fruit salad and drinks promote on image of a "busy little ice cream shop". Established: 1979 - FranchisingSince: 1980 - No. of Units: Company Owned: 24 - Franchised: 256 - Franchise Fee: Variable - Royalty: 6%, 3% adv. - Total Inv: $100,000 - $300,000 - Financing: Package available.

WILTSHIRE FARM FOODS
Ladydown, Trowbridge, Wiltshire, U.K., BA14 8RJ. Contact: Gary Rigby, Fran. Mgr. - Tel: 0225 753636, Fax: 0225 777084. Established: 1928 - Franchising Since: 1991 - No. of Units: Company Owned: 1 - Franchised: 39 - Franchise Fee: £8,000 plus vat - Royalty: None - Total Inv: £10,000 - £15,000 - Financing: No.

FRANCHISE CONSULTANTS

A F L DEESON PARTNERSHIP LTD., THE
Ewell House, Faversham, Kent, England, ME13 8UP. Contact: Dominic Deeson, Mng. Dir. - Tel: 0795 535468. Franchise Consultants. Established: 1959.

ARENDORFF & PARTNERS
Amaliegade 37, 1256 Copenhagen K, Denmark, . Contact: Peter A. Arendorff, Lawyer - Tel: (45) 33 91 00 60. International law firm that runs the secretariat of the Danish Franchisor's Association. Lawyers.

CALTAIN ASSOCIATES
Golitha Cottage, Draynes, Nr. Liskeard, Cornwall, England, PL14 6RX. Contact: Dick Crook, Chairman - Tel: (01579) 321 060, Fax: (01579) 321 502. An American with 30 yrs. of franchise experience in European markets where he has the most successful track record for building ethical, profitable and long-lasting franchises.

CFM CONSULTING
P.O. Box 748, Caterham, Surrey, England, CR3 7YQ. Contact: David C. Taube - Tel: (44) 1883 65 3178, Fax: 44 1883 65 3287. Everything for the U.S. or Canadian franchisor with serious intentions on Europe: market studies, competitor search, outline recommendations, detailed business plans, finding master licensee, helping with start-up, problem solving. All counsellors are highly experienced and have many years of experience as CEO's of franchise businesses.

COMMERCIAL DEVICES
5 Farm Bldgs., Palmers Moor, Thornborough, North Bucks., England, MK18 2DJ. Contact: Derek Ayling and Alison Rushworth, Sr. Partners - Tel: (0280) 824100. Franchise and marketing counselling and trainers, specializing in bringing North American operations into Europe. Established: 1977 - Franchising Since: 1981.

CORRS CHAMBERS WESTGARTH
Bourke Pl., 600 Bourke St., Melbourne, Victoria, Australia, 3000. - Tel: (613) 672-3000, Fax: (613) 602-5544. Commercial law firm.

DAVID BIGMORE & CO.
36 Whitefriars St., London, England, EC4Y 8BH. Contact: David Bigmore, Principal - Tel: 44-171-583-2277, Fax: 44-171-583-2288. Franchise Solicitors. Established: 1978 - Franchising Advice Since: 1985.

EDARA
#11, 26 July St, Midan Lobnan, Mohandessin, Cairo, Egypt, 12411. Contact: Mr. M. Azmi, Chairman - Tel: (202) 345-3340, Fax: 302-1870. Franchise consultants/brokers in the Middle East. Established: 1991.

EDWARD J. EVANS & CO. (C.P.A.)
Ste. 1/122 Gardenvale Rd., Gardenvale, Victoria, Australia, 3185. Contact: Edward Evans, Principal - Tel: 61 03 596 7688, Fax: 61 03 596 7791. Franchise consultants-financial & accounting services. Full establishment of franchise system, evaluation, feasibility, business plan, site selection, franchisee recruitments. Sale of master licence. (Introduce Overseas franchisors to Aust. S.E. Asia.) Established: 1986.

EUROPEAN FRANCHISE CONSULTANTS INTERNATIONAL
EFC Holding B.V.
Postbus 5039, 3008 AA Rotterdam, The Netherlands, . Contact: Rolf J. L. Schot, Man. Dir./CEO - Tel: 31 10 241 5090, Fax: 31 10 241 5099. Consultancy for business formula e.g. franchising in the Netherlands and in other European countries. Established: 1969 - No. of Units: Company Owned: 2.

FIELD FISHER WATERHOUSE
41 Vine St., London, England, EC3N 2AA. Contact: Mark Abell, Partner - Tel: 071-481-4841, Fax: 071-488-0084. Solicitors specializing in international franchising. Established: 1820.

FMM CONSULTANTS INTERNATIONS LTD.
83, Victoria Rd., Horley, Gatwick Airport, Surrey, England, RH6 7QH. Contact: Graham Tinsley, Int'l. Dir. - Tel: (44) 1293-820200, Fax: (44) 1293-821122. Europe's largest specialist franchise consultancy that has divisions for, property services, accountancy, information technology, public relations, management services, training, insurance, design, conferences & seminars, manual writing including ISO 9000. Established: 1981 - Franchising Since: 1963.

FRANCHISE COUNSELLING CENTRE
130 Pretoria Parade, P.O. Box 738, Hornsby, N.S.W., Australia, 2077. Contact: Garry Williamson, Mng. Dir. - Tel: (02) 482 7233, Fax: (02) 482 7339. Established: 1985 - Franchising Since: 1989 - No. of Units: Company Owned: 1 - Franchised: 3 - Franchise Fee: $35,000 - Royalty: 7% mgmt. fee, 2% adv. - Total Inv: $50,000 - Financing: No.

FRANCHISE DESIGN CONSORTIUM LTD.
12 Peterborough Mews, London, England, SW6 3BL. Contact: Mr. Graham Jones, Mgr. - Tel: (071) 736-0646. A supplier of creative services dedicated to serving the branding and marketing objectives of franchises. It is composed of two leading companies; David Loch Design (graphic & corp. design) - Tilney Lumsden Shane (interior design). Established: 1990.

FRANCHISE DEVELOPMENT
2 Heathfield Rd., Sea Point, Cape Town, South Africa, 8001. Contact: Franchise Director, - Tel: (021) 44 6710/44-2723. Franchise program developers, franchise marketing.

FRANCHISE DEVELOPMENT SERVICES LTD.
Franchise Development Services Int'l.
Castle House, CastleMeadow, Norwich, Norfolk, England, NR2 1PJ. Contact: Mr. R. Seaman, Chairman - Tel: (44) 603-620301. A Christian company, providing service to established and prospective franchisors and franchisees. Altogether we have seven divisions. Services to international, established, prospective franchisors and franchisees, publishing, advertising, seminars & exhibitions. Established: 1981 - Franchising Since: 1983 - No. of Units: Company Owned: 3 - Franchised: 7 - Franchise Fee: US$75,000 - $150,000 - Royalty: 10% service mgmt. fee + 5% adv. - Total Inv: approx. x2 of fran. fee to establish & develop the business to its fullest potential - Financing: Joint venture operations considered.

FRANCHISE DEVELOPMENTS PTY
464 St. Kilda Rd., Melbourne, Victoria, Australia, 3004. Contact: Franchise Director - Tel: (03) 2677666. Franchise Consultants.

FRANCHISE FACTORS
1 Howard St., North Shields, Tyne & Wear, U.K., NE30 1AR. Contact: John Scott, Dir. - Tel: (0632) 595287. Franchise and marketing consultants. Established: 1979.

FRANCHISE FINANCING AND MARKETING
27 Aetorahis St., Thessaloniki 54640, Greece, . Contact: M.H. Sarantoglou, Dir. Gen. - Tel: (**30) 31-821742, Fax: (**30) 31-819424. Providing services to franchisors/parent companies as representatives. Broker. Finding areas, locations, (Master) franchisees, partners. Undertake expansion of firms through franchising, partnerships, branches. Personal experience of organizing approx. 2000 outlets, subsidiaries. Financing services to franchisors worldwide through direct lenders/funding. Marketing and sales of franchises, distributorships.

FRANCHISE KOLLEGIET
P.O. Box 6589, Stockholm, Sweden, S-113-83. Contact: Tom Bruno, Fran. Dir. - Tel: 46 (0) 8 612 30 50. Consultants in national and international franchising and licensing (Sweden). Established: 1988.

FRANCHISE RESOURCES
5 Glenwood Way, Castle Hill, NSW, Australia, . Contact: Chris Dent, Partner - Tel: (02) 634-1634 or 868-4777. Consultancy for franchisors on aspects of franchising in Australia including real estate selection, legal, manuals, staff selection, marketing, business plans, financing, etc. Established: 1982.

FRANCHISE SHOP LTD, THE
6 Old Hillside Close, Winchester, Hampshire, U.K., SO22 5LW. Contact: Mr R. J. Childs, Mgr/Dir. - Tel: (0962) 855530. Franchise industry service supplier, franchise development and promotion, using a wide range of cost saving marketing programmes. A portfolio of at least 10 franchisors and maintains computer data bases of over 14,000 prospective franchisees. Established: 1984.

FRANCHISE SYSTEMS LIMITED
Ste. 2/14 Kenthurst Rd., Dural 2156, Sydney NSW, Australia, . Contact: Michael Padden, Man. Dir. - Tel: 61 2 651 3644, Fax: 61 2 651 4187. Franchise consultants, marketing and accounting services, market evaluations, feasibility and research programs, franchise recruitment, activities and consultants throughout Australia and SE Asia.

FRANCHISE SYSTEMS LIMITED *
17A Jalan Sctiapuspa, Medan Damansara, Kuala Lumpur, Malaysia, 50490. Contact: Su Thoo, Man. Dir. - Tel: (03) 255 9345, Fax: (03) 255-4750. Franchise consultants, marketing and accounting services, market evaluations, feasibility and research programs, franchise recruitment, activities and consultants throughout Australia and SE Asia.

GOLDSMITH WILLIAMS
42-44 Stanley St., Liverpool, Merseyside, England, L1 6AL. Contact: Edward R. Goldsmith, Sr. Partner. Solicitors dealing in franchising. Established: 1984 - Franchising Since: 1984.

HOPKINS & WOOD
2-3 Cursitor St., London, England, EC4A 1NE. Contact: Simon Rendell, Kieran F. O'Connor, Partner, Solicitor - Tel: 071 404 0475. Legal advisers to domestic and cross border franchisors and franchisees; European network, strong European law department.

HORWATH FRANCHISING SERVICES
10th Flr., BT Tower, 1 Market St., Sydney, NSW, Australia, 2000. Contact: C. Jugmans/R.W. Fitzgerald, Director/Manager - Tel: (02) 372-0777, Telefax: (02) 372-0606. Management consultants offering specialist services to franchisors. Specialize in feasibility studies and investigation of franchisees for compliance with financial aspects of franchise agreements. Established: 1988.

'IMTIYAZ'
Franchise Development and Marketing
P.O. Box 4520, Jeddah, Saudi Arabia, 21412. Contact: Khaled H. El-Zarka, Gen. Mgr. - Tel: (02) 660-7517. Developing sales, and marketing of franchise systems and distributorships in the Middle East. Established: l988.

ING BANK
P.O. Box 1800, NL-1000 BV, Amsterdam, The Netherlands, . Contact: Jan C. Bezemer, Mgr. Fran. Finance - Tel: +31 20 652 2993. NMB Bank has unprecedented experience since 1962 and a leading position in franchise finance. It offers a comprehensive financial and insurance package to both franchisor and franchisee. Established: 1926 (successor of NMB Bank) - No. of Units: Company Owned: 400.

JOHN PERKINS & ASSOCIATES
Avon House, High Street, Welford-Upon-Avon, Warwickshire, England, CV37 8EA. Contact: John S. Perkins, Principal - Tel: (0789) 750439. The only franchise advisor (not a consultant) in the U.K. Also involved with licensing & valuations to intellectual assets. Established: 1984.

LADAS & PARRY
52 High Holborn, London, U.K, WC1V 6RR. Contact: Iain C. Baillie, Partner - Tel: (0171) 242-5566, Fax: (0171) 405-1908. International intellectual property, licensing and franchising lawyers, U.K. and European Trademark Agents.

LEATHES PRIOR(SOLICITORS & NOTARIES)
74 The Close, Norwich, Norfolk, England, MR35 2JE. Contact: Jonathan Chadd, Partner - Tel: (0603) 610911. Solicitors and notaries providing legal advice to the franchise industry on all aspects of franchising. Also, members of Eu-Lex network of European law firms, able to advise on European level. Advisors.

LUCAS BARON *
26 Station St., Fern Tree Gully, Victoria, Australia, 3156. Contact: David Lucas, Principal - Tel: 03 758 7055. Lawyers. Established: 1977.

M K C -MICHEL KAHN CONSULTANTS
58 avenue des Vosges, Strasbourg, France, 67000. Contact: Michel Kahn - Tel: (33) 88 36-56-16. Consultant in franchise and partnership.

MACPHERSON & KELLEY SOLICITORS
229 Thomas St., Dandenong, Melbourne, Victoria, Australia, 3175. Contact: Stephen Giles, Partner - Tel: (613) 7916444. Legal practice providing a full range of legal services and specializing in franchise law and franchise consulting in Australia. Recognized as one of Australia's leading franchise law firms. Established: 1905 - Franchising Since: 1984 - No. of Units: Company Owned: 2 - Franchised: 2 - Franchise Fee: depends upon location - Royalty: 50% of franchisee's net profit before personal drawings - Total Inv: $40,000 - $200,000 depending upon location - Financing: Franchisor financed.

MACROBERTS
27 Melville St., Edinburgh, Scotland, EH3 7JF. Contact: Michael J. Bell, Partner - Tel: (031) 226-2552. Established for 130 years.

MENZIES - CHARTERED ACCOUNTANTS
Ashby House, 64 High St., Walton-on-Thames, Surrey, England, KT12 1BW. Contact: Andrew Denley, Partner - Tel: (01932) 247611. Chartered accountants advising business generally, financial planning, taxation advice and other specialist areas including franchising. Established: 1912 - Franchising Since: 1985.

MEXICAN FRANCHISE ASSOCIATION, AC
Ave. Insurgentes Sur 1783 - 303, 01020, Mexico, D.F.. Contact: German Fernandez-Del Busto, Chairman - Tel: 5 6610655, 6632198. The Mexican Franchise Association was founded in 1989, servicing a group of pioneering franchise companies and in response to those seeking information and guidance in the then newly discovered franchise way of business. After 5 years, membership has grown to over 175 franchisor members, and an ever growing number of suppliers who can respond to the special needs of these companies. Established: 1989.

MODERN ARAB ENTERPRISES, JEDDAH SKYE'S N.A. VIZION AMSTERDAM
Xpekt Resources Ltd. Middle East
P.O. Box 1226., 4 Annis Komninis St., Nicosia, Cyprus, . Contact: Jason Saba, Mng. Dir. - Tel: (2) 456430/31. Localization of franchises to suit local taste and trends, marketing and feasibility studies, project development, implementation and design. Turn key operations, training and continuous support. Established: 1984 - Franchising Since: 1984 - No. of Units: Company Owned: 8 - Franchised: 5 - Franchise Fee: $30,000 - Total Inv: $170,000 - Royalty: 5 - 6%.

MUNDAY'S ATTORNEYS
Crown House, Church Road, Claygate, Esher, Surrey, England, KT10 0LP. Contact: Ray Walley & Manzoor G.K. Ishani, Partners - Tel: (044) 372 467272, Fax (044) 372 463782. Attorneys and notaries public.

NAT WEST BANK
Franchise Section, Level 10, Drapers Gdns., 12 Throgmorton Ave., London EC2N 2DL, England, . Contact: Peter Stern or Jean Blair, Sr.Fran.Mgr./Secretary - Tel: 171-920-5256, Fax: 171-920-5217. Largest retail bank in U.K. Providers of finance for franchisors & franchisees since 1981. Established: 1826 - Franchising Since: 1981 - No of Units: Company Owned: 2500 - Financing: for franchisors & franchisees in UK & Europe.

NETHERLANDS FRANCHISE ASSOCIATION
Boomberglaan 12, Hilversum, The Netherlands, 1217 RR . Contact: A.W.M. Brouwer, Exec. Dir. - Tel: (31) 35 624 34 44, Fax: (31) 35 6249194. National association for franchisors and companies, affiliated with franchising. Established: 1972.

NEW CENTURY SOFTWARE LIMITED
Southampton, Hampshire, U.K., SO3 1LJ. Contact: Richard Pelly, Dir. - Tel: (+44) 962-771811. Develop and support computer software for business systems. Multi-lingual applications. Emphasis on single systems for use by both franchisor and franchisee. Established: 1980 - Franchising Since: 1982 - No. of Units: Company Owned: 1.

OWEN WHITE
Senate House, 62-70 Bath Rd., Slough, Berkshire, U.K., SL1 3SR. Contact: Anton Bates, Partner - Tel: (0753) 536846. Legal advice. Solicitors specializing in the provision of legal services to master licensors, franchisors & franchisees.

PAISNER & CO.
Bouverie House, 154 Fleet St., London, England, EC4A 2DQ. Contact: Linda Fazzani, Partner - Tel: 44 (0) 71 353 0299. Law firm advising on all aspects of franchising including document preparation, competition law, tax planning, intellectual property franchise litigation, EC law, property for franchisors and franchisees. Established: 1932.

PEAT MARWICK MAIN & COMPANY
England Branch Aquis Court, 31, Fishpool St., St. Albans, Hertfordshire, U.K., AL3 4RF. Contact: Gerry W. Hopkinson, Principal - Tel: 0727-43000. An international accounting, auditing, taxation and management consulting firm with over 300 offices worldwide. Established: 1895.

PHILIPPE LOUSBERG & ASSOC. S.P.R.L.
1521 Chaussee de Waterloo, Bte. 9, 1180 Brussels, Belgium, . Contact: Philippe Lousberg, Mgr. - Tel: 32 2 374 70 87; Fax: 32 2 374 47 59. Franchisor/Franchisee Consultant.

REES POLLOCK
7 Pilgrim Street, London, England, EC4V 6DR. Contact: W.A.J. Pollock, Partner - Tel: 071 329 6404. Chartered accountants: advice on UK tax & accounting, franchising in the UK and master licenses, & general business advice. Established: 1990.

STOY HAYWARD FRANCHISING SERVICES
8 Baker St., London, England, W1M 1DA. Contact: Amanda Engge, Dir. - Tel: (071) 486-5888. Europes leading franchise consultants, with 270 offices in 70 countries. Expert at overseas market studies and finding master licensees or joint venture partners. Established: 1987.

SWEDISH FRANCHISE ASSOCIATION
P.O. Box 5512, S 114 85 Stockholm, Sweden, . Contact: Stig H. Sohlberg, CEO - Tel: (46) 86608610, Fax (46) 86627457. The only trade association for franchisors. Established: 1972.

SYNCON GMBH *
Nonntaler - Hauptstr 48, Salzburg, Austria, 5020. Contact: Waltraud Frauenhuber, Manager - Tel: (43) 662-825670, Fax: (43) 662-825671. Franchising consultants. Development of franchise systems, adapt foreign franchise systems. Established: 1972.

WILKINSON & GRIST *
6/F Prince's Building, Chater Rd., Central, Hong Kong, . Contact: Ms. Ella Cheong, Sr. Partner - Tel: (852) 2524-6011. Franchising Lawyer.

GENERAL

ACCASTILLAGE DIFFUSION
Intermer S.A.
Zi du Bois de Leuze, BP 41, Saint-Martin de Crau, France, 13552. Contact: Monnoyeur, Pres. - Tel: 90 47 01 10, Fax: 90 47 01 12. Purchasing center and group management. All equipment for nautical leisure, mainly sailing. Includes electronics. Established: 1977 - Franchising Since: 1975 - No. of Units: Franchised: 36 - Franchise Fee: 35,000 F - Royalty: 1% net turnover, 1.5% adv. - Total Inv: 700,000 F.

ALEXANDER INTERNATIONAL
Athena/Alexander Language Institute
27 Aetorahis St., Thessaloniki, Greece, 54640. Contact: Men. H. Sarantoglou, Dir. Gen. - Tel: (**30)31-827106, Fax: (**30) 31 819424. Small to medium sized language teaching centers/schools. Also, private tuition centers. Internationally since 1994. Established: 1966 - Franchising Since: 1970 - No. of Units: Company Owned: 89 - Franchised: 25 master franchises available - Franchise Fee: $4,000 - $10,000 - Royalty: 6% - 15% gross - Total Inv: $10,000 US - $100,000 US - Financing: Small initial capital loan.

ALL-GOLD OF SWITZERLAND
84 Marylebone High St., London, England, W1M 3DE. Contact: Jane Clark, All-Gold Principal - Tel: 0302 360007. A mobile 24K gold plating service for gold plating car emblems, golf clubs, bathroom and kitchen fittings & jewellery etc. The profit potential is excellent and there is a superb system to expand your new business. Established: 1994 - Franchising Since: 1994 - No. of Units: Company Owned: 1 - Franchised: 51 - Franchise Fee: £3,000 - Total Inv: £3,000 - Financing: Yes.

ANICARE VETERINARY GROUP
23 Buckingham Rd., Shoreham-by-Sea, Brighton, W. Sussex, U.K., BN3 5UA. Contact: J. P. Sheridan, Mng. Dir. - Tel: 0273-463022. Provision of professional veterinary services to the owners of domestic pet animals. Franchisees are self-employed, graduate veterinary surgeons utilizing a corporate image and a range of management support systems under franchise agreements with the franchisor. Established: 1971 - Franchising Since: 1977 - No. of Units: Franchised: 8 - Franchise Fee: £4,750 - Royalty: 5.5% - 7% - Total Inv: £50,000 - Financing: Yes.

AREA TENT HIRE
185 Great Tattenhams, Tattenham Corners, Epsom Downs, Surrey, U.K., . Contact: Raye Elliott. - Tel: 07313-59419. Marquee tent hire service for social and commercial events. Approx. Inv: £11,000.

ASHBY'S
Paulig (UK) Ltd.
658 The Crescent, Colechester Bus. Pk., Colechester, Essex, England, CO4 2YB. Contact: Nigel Weekes, Fran. Business Mgr. - Tel: 0206 851500. Sales and distribution of fine tea, coffee and allied products to the independent caterer and business sector. Local hot beverage specialist providing quality at the right value with an excellent service. Established: 1987 - Franchising Since: 1990 - No. of Units: Franchised: 15 - Franchise Fee: £5,000 - Total Inv: £11,500 (fran. fee, £2,000 stock, £1,500 coffee brewers, £2,000 work cap.) - Financing: Front leading commercial banks.

BREWER & TURNBULL LTD. *
Hargreaves St., Burnley, Lancs., England, BB11 1BV. Contact: Alvin Mowe, Fran. Sales Mgr. - Tel: 01282 830 830, Fax: 01282 838 004. One of UK's leading national and international removals and storage organization. Established: 1931 - Franchising Since :1982 - No. of Units: Franchised: 30 - Franchise Fee: From £4,000 - Royalty: 8% - Total Inv: from £4,000.

BUILDING ENGENHARIA *
Rua Recife, 51, Curitiba, Parana, Brazil, 80035-110. Contact: Evilasio, Director - Tel: (041) 252-0726. Structural designs based on system totally informatized with data input extremely easy. Formworks and other details are automated outputs from the data input. Real estate products and services. Established: 1985 - Franchising Since: 1991 - No. of Units: Company Owned: 1 - Franchised: 74 - Franchise Fee: $1,000 - Royalty: 10% over the projects price - Total Inv: approx. $10,000 .

C 'N C WINDOW CENTRES
Window & Door Manufacturing Co. Ltd.
Waterfall Lane Trading Estate, Waterfall Lane, Cradley Heath, W. Midlands, England, B64 6PU. Contact: B. Chamberlain, Joint M.D. - Tel: (021) 561-4191. Manufactures and retails the sale of UPWC/aluminum doors and windows. Established: 1980 - Franchising Since: 1987 - No. of Units: Company Owned: 10 - Franchised: 3 - Franchise Fee: none - Royalty: 5% of total sales - Total Inv: approx. £10,000 (initial stock, setting up showroom).

CARD CONNECTION
Card Connection Ltd.
Park House, South St., Farnham, Surrey, England, GU9 7QQ. Contact: Simon Hulme, Mng. Dir. - Tel: (0252) 733177. Card connection publishes a range of high quality greeting cards which are distributed through a network of franchisees who operate their own exclusive area. Established: 1992 - Franchising Since: 1992 - No. of Units: Franchised: 75 - Franchise Fee: £9,950 (initial package) - Royalty: None - Total Inv: £18,000 (incl. £6,000 work. cap.) - Financing: Yes.

CENTURY 21 UK LTD.
Roberts House, Station Close, Potters Bar, Herts., England, EN6 3JW. Contact: Bill Pegram, Mng. Dir. - Tel: 0707-646465. Estate agency/real estate franchise. Established: 1971 - Franchising Since: 1971 - No. of Units: Franchised: 50 - Franchise Fee: £1,000 - Royalty: 6% on turnover, 2% ad. fund - Financing: No.

CHOICES HOME SALES
Choice Home Sales, Ltd.
6 High St., Crawley, West Sussex, England, RH10 1BJ. Contact: Simon Shingrock, Mgn. Dir. - Tel: (0293) 565644. Estate agency. Established: 1989 - Franchising Since: 1990 - No. of Units: Company Owned: 1 - Franchised: 1 - Franchise Fee: £15,000.

CINDERELLA DESIGNER GOWNS
Cinderella Designer Gowns Ltd.
Lochrin House, Coatbank St., Coatbridge, Strathclyde, U.K., ML5 3SS. Contact: Jill Greenhalgh, Mng. Dir. - Tel: (0236) 40957. Home run second income, ladies dress hire, ball gowns and cocktail dresses. Established: 1987 - Franchising Since: 1989 - No. of Units: Company Owned: 1 - Franchised: 8 - Total Inv: £10,000.

CLIMAT DE FRANCE
B.P. 93, Avenue des Andes, 91943 Les Ulis Cedex, France, . Contact: Christian Henneman, Intern. Dev. Mgr. - Tel: 16 (1) 69 28 58 60. French hotel chain. (2 stars chain). Established: 1980 - Franchising Since: 1980 - No. of Units: Company Owned: 20 - Franchised: 140 - Franchise Fee: FF 3,500 per room and FF 50,000 for restaurant - Royalty: 4% C.A. H.T. - Total Inv: FF 12,000,000 - 15,000,000 TTC - Financing: FF 2 - 3,000,000.

COLOUR COUNSELLORS LTD.
3 Dovedale Studios, 465 Battersea Park Road, London, England, SW11 4LR. Contact: Virginia Stourton, Dir. - Tel: (071) 978-5023. Interior decoration and soft furnishings. Established: 1970 - Franchising Since: 1978 - No. of Units: Company Owned: 1 - Franchised: 58 - Franchise Fee: £10,000 - Royalty: fixed mgmt. service fee - Total Inv: £10,000 - Financing: No.

COMPLETE WEED CONTROL
Complete Weed Control Ltd.
7 Astley House, Cromwell Bus. Pk., Banbury Rd., Chipping Norton, Oxfordshire, England, OX7 6SR. Contact: R.W. Turner, Mng. Dir. - Tel: 0608 644044. Amenity and industrial weed control specialists offering a service to local authorities, public utilities, industrial and commercial customers or anyone with a ground maintenance problem. Established: 1972 - Franchising Since: 1982 - Number of Units: Company Owned: 1 - Franchised: 20 - Franchise Fee: £8,000+ (according to area) plus £4,750 start up costs - Royalty: 10% incl. 3% nat'l adv. - Financing: 70% through leading banks.

COUNTRYWIDE GARDEN MAINTENANCE SERVICES
164-200 Stockport Rd., Cheadle, Stockport, Cheshire, England, SK8 2DP. Contact: Simon Stott, Dir. - Tel: (061) 428-4444. Franchise operation providing landscape maintenance services on a yearly contract basis to commercial and domestic customers, supported by a strong corporate identity, direct mail, telesales, and advertising. Master licenses are available. Established: 1984 - Franchising Since: 1986 - No. of Units: Company Owned: 2 - Franchised: 28 - Royalty: 8%, 2% mktg levy (based on total turnover) - Financing: Yes.

CROWN DOMESTIC APPLIANCES
6 Railway Approach, E, Grinstead, Sussex, England, . Contact: Franchise Director - Tel: 0342-25273. Repair of major brands of domestic electrical appliances (vacuum cleaners, washing machines, etc.) and the reconditioning and sale of rebuilt models. No. of Units: 5 - Approx. Inv: £5,000.

CRYSTAL GALLERIES LTD.
Rombalds, Rombalds Lane, Benrhydding, Ilkley, Yorks, U.K., . Contact: Dorothy Bailey, Dir. - Tel: 0943-600344. Personalized engraving process. Established: 1983 - No. of Units: 1 - Approx. Inv: £2,500 - Royalty: 5% - Financing: none.

CULLIGAN INTERNATIONAL COMPANY
Unit 3, Bleinheim Rd., Cressex Ind. Estate, High Wycombe, Bucks., England, HP12 3RD. Contact: R. W. Fitzwilliam, Sales Mgr. - Tel: 0494-36484. Service and operation of your own water treatment company. Established: 1936 - Franchising Since: 1937 - No. of Units: Company Owned: 30 - Franchised: over 1,000 worldwide - Approx. Inv: £2,500.

DECORATING DEN (UK)
Decor Systems (SW) Ltd.
Bowditch Membury, Axminster, Devon, U.K., EX137TY. Contact: Sarah Bell, Mktg. Dir. - Tel: UK 404 881789, Fax: 404 881786. Mobile interior decorating business. Established: UK 1989 - Franchising Since: 1970 USA - No. of Units: Company Owned: 3 - Franchised: 30 - Franchise Fee: £10,900 - £13,900 - Royalty: 11% - 7%, 2% adv. - Financing: Yes, UK Banks.

DIFUSAO DE EDUCACAO E CULTURA S/A
Yazigi International
Av. 9 de Julho, 3166, Sao Paulo, Sao Paulo, Brazil, 01406-000. Contact: Claudia Bueno, Mgr., Fran. Dept. - Tel: (011) 884.9600. Yazigi is a large Brazilian language teaching instruction, which was the pioneer to organize a franchise system in Brazil (1963). Today Yazigi teaches languages to approximately 70,000 students yearly in its 170 franchised schools. Established: 1950 - Franchising Since: 1963 - No. of Units: Company Owned: 3 - Franchised: 167 - Franchise Fee: $5,000 (US) - Total Inv: $40,000 (US) incl. fran. fee and installation of the school.

DOGS' WORLD
R.G.V. Enterprises S.A.
1411 Chee de Wavre, B-1160 Bruxelles, Belgium, . Contact: Vuye Raymond - Tel: 02-6737381. Dog grooming and school. Established: 1972 - Franchising Since: 1976 - No. of Units: 2 - Franchise Fee: 500,000 FB - Total Inv: 1,000,000 FB - Royalty: 25% school only.

DOR-2-DOR *
Zone Marketing (UK) Ltd.
Clare Lodge, 41 Holly Bush Lane, Harpenden, Herts., England, AL5 4AY. Contact: Jeff Frankling, Fran. Dir. - Tel: 44 1582 460977, Fax: 44 1582 462727. Leaflet distribution to residential households. Comprehensive package includes manuals, sales support, freefone sales enquiry line, hotline telephone support & backup. Established: 1987 - Franchising Since: 1995 - No. of Units: Company Owned: 1 - Franchised: 10 - Franchise Fee: None - Royalty: £35 per month or 5% of sales, whichever greater.

DUDS 'N SUDS
Duds 'n Suds UK Ltd.
141 Strand Rd., Derry, Northern Ireland, BT48 7RB. Contact: Damian Nicell, Dir. - Tel: 01504 262615. Duds 'n Suds laundromats feature, in addition to modern washers and dryers, a big screen TV, an attended snack bar, plenty of comfortable seating, games and more. Duds 'n Suds UK Ltd. is the franchisor of the Duds 'n Suds laundry system for the UK and Ireland. Established: 1991 - Franchising Since: 1992 - No. of Units: Company Owned: 1 - Franchised: 6 - Franchise Fee: £15,000 - Royalty: 5% franchise, 2% adv. - Total Inv: £145,000: £40,000 personal investment - Financing: Yes.

DUREX VENDING
LRC Products Ltd.
North Circular Rd., London, England, E4 8QA. Contact: Mr. A Donney, G.M. - Tel: (081) 527-2377. Condom vending. Established: 1968 - Franchising Since: 1990 - No. of Areas: Franchised: 24 - Franchise Fee: £12,500 - Total Inv: £64,000 (vending machines & stock £30,000, lic. fee £12,500, fran. pkg. £10,000, equip. £3,000, V.A.T. £8,000) - Financing: N/A.

DUSKIN CO., LTD.
Sekaicho Building, 6-24 Nakatsu, 1-Chome Kita-ku, Osaka, 531, Japan, . Contact: Eiichi Tominaga, Mgr. Int'l Div. - Tel: (06) 372-8771. Manufacturing, selling and renting of dust control and household products. Fast food and seafood chain. Established: 1963 - Franchising Since: 1963 - No. of Units: Company Owned: 136 - Franchised: 5,000 - Franchise Fee: Varies - Royalty: Varies.

DUTY DRIVER LTD.
42 Station Rd., Twyford, Berks., England, RG10 9N. Contact: T.M. Bedford, Mng. Dir. - Tel: (0734) - 320200. Executive agency for part and full time chauffeurs. Established: 1985 - Franchising Since: 1988 - No. of Units: Company Owned: 3 - Franchised: 5 - Royalty: 21% of turnover, marketing & factoring - Total Inv: £15,000: first 2 yrs. adv. & set up - Financing: Yes.

DYNO LOCKS
Dyno-Rod Developments Ltd.
143 Maple Rd., Surbiton, Surrey, England, KT6 4BJ. Contact: Peter Curtis, Business Manager - Tel: 081-481 2200, Fax: 081-481 2288. Emergency door/lock opening service. Lock fitting and repair. Mobile service, 24 hours a day, 365 days a year. Established: 1986 - Franchising Since: 1988 - No. of Units: Franchised: 40 - Franchise Fee: £6,500 - Royalty: A.O.R. - Total Inv: £16,500 - Financing: Up to 70% can be financed.

EXCHANGE TRAVEL AGENCY LTD.
Exchange House, Parker Rd., Hastings, E. Sussex, U.K, TN34 3UB. Contact: A. Scott, Fran. Dev. Mgr. - Tel: 0424-423571. Travel agencies in England and Wales. Established: 1890 - Franchising Since: 1983 - No. of Units: Company Owned: 31 - Franchised: 62 - Franchise Fee: £8,500- Royalty: 12.5%/annum mgmt. fee - Total Inv: £70,000 - £100,000 - Financing: Yes.

EXPRESS DAIRY (UK) LTD.
Northern Division, Broadfield Rd., Sheffield, U.K., . Contact: K. Hunt - Tel: 0274-640318. Manufacture, processing, packaging, marketing and distribution of milk and dairy produce.

FASTSIGNS
European Fastsigns Ltd.
36 High Street, New Malden, Surrey, England, KT3 4HE. Contact: D. Birnie, Mng. Dir. - Tel: (0181) 336-0802. Fast service, fully computerized sign shops. Established: 1992 - Franchising Since: 1993 - No. of Units: Company Owned: 1 - Franchised: 5 - Franchise Fee: £15,000 to £19,500, Royalty: 8% of gross sales exc. tax - Total Inv: £70,000 - Financing: Yes.

FELICITAS
58 Ave. des Vosges, Strasbourg, France, 67000. Contact: Michel Kahn, Mgr., Chairman - Tel: 88.36.56.17. Established: 1972 -Franchising Since: 1973 - No. of Units: 60.

FISK SCHOOLS LIMITED
Av. Lins de Vasconcelos, 2594, Sao Paulo, Sao Paulo, Brazil, 04112-001. Contact: Bruno Caravati, V.P. - Tel: (55) 011 573 7000, Fax: (55) 11 549-2144. English course as a second language. Group and individual classes. English for all ages. Courses basic through advanced in three years maximum. 35 years of experience. Established: 1958 - Franchising Since: 1960 - No. of Units: Company Owned: 31 - Franchised: 450.

FLOWER BARROW COMPANY, THE
3 Orchard Crt., Heron Rd., Sowton, Exeter, Devon, U.K., EX2 7LL. Contact: Mrs. S. Taylor, Partner - Tel: (0392) 444788. Manufacturer of dried flower arrangements to sell through franchises. Established: 1985 - Franchising Since: 1990 - No. of Units: Company Owned: 7 - Franchised: 2 - Total Inv: £8,000: barrow & display-£2,000; Stock-£3,000; stationery-£500; set-up-£1,500; training course-£1,000 - Financing: National Westminster Bank, Lloyds Bank.

FORMATIVE FUN
Formative Fun Ltd.
33 South St., Bridport, Dorset, U.K., DT6 3NY. Contact: Jane or Dinah, Mng. Dir., Co. Sec. - Tel: 0308 421811. Marketing and advising parents on an exclusive range of educational games, toys and books. Established: 1989 - Franchising Since: 1991 - No. of Units: Company Owned: 1 - Franchised: 11 - Franchise Fee: £4,000 - Royalty: 10%, 2% adv. - Total Inv: £5,000 + £5,000 overdraft facility - Financing: No.

GB BRICOCENTRE ET GARDEN CENTER
GB-Inno-BM S.A.
20 Ave. des Olympiades, 1140 Bruxelles, Brabant, Belgium, . Contact: Mr. Willocq. Do-it-yourself garden. Established: 1973 - Franchising Since: 1978 - No. of Units: Company Owned: 57 - Franchised: 23 - Franchise Fee: 300,000 FB - Total Inv: 16,000,000 FB - Royalty: 6.6% du C.A. TVAC - Financing: 3,500,000 FB.

GEM TRAVEL
Nevill House, 15 Nevill St., Tunbridge Wells, Kent, England, TN2 5RV. Contact: John Neville, Partner - Tel: 0892-516660. Retail travel agencies. Established: 1972 - Franchising Since: 1989 - No. of Units: Company Owned: 1 - Franchised: 30 - Franchise Fee: £10,400 - Royalty: Nil - Total Inv: £15,000 - Financing: Yes.

GIGANTAGRAM
Sunset House, 178B West Malvern Rd., Malvern, Worcs., U.K., WR14 4AZ. Contact: K. Buchmann, M.D. - Tel: (0684) 562661, Fax: (0684) 893271. A business from your own home producing banners, signs and gigantagrams. Established: 1985 - Franchising Since: 1986 - No. of Units: Company Owned: 1 - Franchised: 41 - Franchise Fee: £2,900 - Royalty: £50 per month - Total Inv: £4,950: Fee: £2,900 + £2,050.

GOLD VAULT LTD., THE
26 Shetty Park Rd., Shetty Swansea, England, . Contact: S. A. Ramsey-Williams, Dir. - Tel: 0792-469639. Dental suppliers. Established: 1985 - Franchising Since: 1986 - No. of Units: Company Owned: 1 - Franchised: 1 - Approx. Inv: £5,000 - Financing: Possible.

GRAPEVINE DISCOUNT TRAVEL
4, Heathfield Rd., Kings Heath, Birmingham, England, B14 7DB. Contact: Rod Gethins, Principal - Tel: (0121) 444-1666, Fax: (0121) 444-8226. Telephone sales - travel agency. Established: 1991 - Franchising Since: 1992 - No. of Units: Company Owned: 1 - Franchised: 4 - Franchise Fee: £11,950.

GREENALLS INN PARTNERSHIP
Greenalls Ave., P.O. Box #2, Warrington, Cheshire, U.K., WA46RH. Contact: Dennis Whiteley, Bus. Dev. Executive - Tel: 0925-51234. Public house retailing. Established: 1762 - No. of Units: Company Owned: 500 - Franchised: 750 - Royalty: 1% of turnover - Total Inv: £15,000 - £20,000 - Financing: Yes.

HELEN O'GRADY CHILDREN'S DRAMA ACADEMY *
Helen O'Grady International Pty. Ltd.
5/82 Reserve St., Wembley, Perth, W.A., Australia, 6014. Contact: Steve Griffiths, Mng. Dir. - Tel: (619) 3837800, Fax: (619) 3837810. The Helen O'Grady Children's Drama Academy holds after school classes for children in over 400 locations throughout the U.K., Australia , New Zealand, South Africa and Singapore. Will now consider expressions of interest from suitable organizations for the master licence of U.S.A. and other countries. A unique program aimed at developing confidence, self-esteem and communication skills. Established: 1979 - Franchising Since: 1989 - No. of Units: Company Owned: 1 - Franchised: 48 - Franchise Fee: $35,000 - Royalty: 10% of gross fees - Total Inv: Fran. fee $35,000, set-up costs $5,000 - Financing: Yes.

HESTIA
Pluri-Publi S.A.
33, rue Mozart, Paris, France, 75016. Contact: Jessica Duros, Int. Dev. - Tel: 33 1 42 24 88 88. Real Estate. Established: 1974 - Franchising Since: 1977 - No. of Units: Company Owned: 8 - Franchised: 28 - Franchise Fee: 135,000 FF - Royalty: 10% declining scale, 4% adv. declining scale - Total Inv: 300,000 FF.

HOLIDAY INN, HOLIDAY INN RESORT, HOLIDAY INN EXPRESS, HOLIDAY INN GARDEN COURT, HOLIDAY INN CROWNE PLAZA, HOLIDAY INN CROWN PLAZA RESORT
Holiday Inn Worldwide Europe - Middle East - Africa (EMEA)
Woluwe Office Park 1, Rue Neerveld 101, 1200, Brussels, Belgium, . Contact: Reas Kondraschow, V.P. Franchising EMEA - Tel: 32 2 777 5523, Fax: 32 2 777 5603. Hotels. Established: 1952 - Franchising Since: 1954 - No. of Units: Company Owned: 54 - Franchised: 152 - Application Fee: US$400 per room - Minimum Royalty Fee (per annum): $20,000 to $50,000 - Mktg./Res. Assessment Fee: 2% to 2.5% - Special Mktg. Contribution: 8% or fixed charge $250 25 points - Bank Guarantee: $50,000 for duration of license.

HOMEBUYERS ADVICE CENTRE
Homebuyers Advice Centre Plc.
Ste. 401, India Bldgs., Water St., Liverpool, England, L2 0QT. Contact: John C. Cartlidge, Sales Dev. Mgr. - Tel: (051) 236-2872. Domestic mortgage and re-mortgage advice and arrangement-counselling of clients need and provision of impartial friendly advice. Established: 1985 - Franchising Since: 1988 - No. of Units: Company Owned: 3 - Franchised: 17 - Royalty: none - Total Inv: main office: $50,000, community office: $30,000 (incl. work cap.) - Financing: Interest paid by franchisor subject to acceptance.

HOUSE OF COLOUR LTD.
28 The Avenue, Watford, Herts., England, WD1 3NS. Contact: Lynn Elvy, Fran. Dir. - Tel: 01923 211188. Colour analysts & image consultants. Established: 1986 - Franchising Since: 1986 - No. of Units: Company Owned: 1 - Franchised: 80 - Franchise Fee: £5,000 + V.A.T. - Total Inv: £7,500 + V.A.T.

HYDE-BARKER TRAVEL
Market St., Mansfield, Notts., England, NG18 1SR. Contact: M. A. Hyde-Barker, Mng. Dir. - Tel: 0623-31121. Travel agencies. Established: 1948 - Franchising Since: 1985 - No. of Units: 1 - Approx. Inv: £1,500 - Royalty: 1% plus 4% adv. - Financing: no.

IMAGINE TRANSFERS LTD.
Broomhills, Braintree, Essex, England, CM7 7RW. Contact: Tony Merrington, Mng. Dir. - Tel: 0376-320354. Heat transfers and fusion presses for printing T-shirts. Established: 1972 - Franchising Since: 1972 - No. of Units: Company Owned: 5 - Franchised: 100+ - Franchise Fee: £5,000 - Total Inv: £5,000 - Financing: No.

INDOOR CRICKET STADIUMS
Bluerise Ltd.
24 Wainman Rd., Woodston, Peterborough, England, PE2 OBX. Contact: Neil Sinclair, G.M. - Tel: 0733-238800. Operator of 8-a-side indoor cricket stadiums. Established: 1985 - Franchising Since: 1985 - No. of Units: Company Owned: 3 - Franchised: 1 - Franchise Fee: negotiable - Royalty: 5% - Approx. Inv: £125,000 - Financing: no.

INFOPOINT
Infopoint Ltd.
8 Kings Meadow, Ferry Hinksey Road, Oxford, England, OX9 7PP. Contact: Philip Flookm, M.D.. Network of vending machines on outskirts of towns selling town centre maps. Established: 1985 - Franchising Since: 1987 - No. of Units: Company Owned: 10 - Franchised: 6 - Royalty: 2.5% - Total Inv: Min. £2,250 - Financing: yes.

INTACAB LTD.
West Mayne, Basildon, Essex, England, SS15 6RW. Contact: Mel Lilley, Fran. Dir. - Tel: (0268) 415891. Taxi and private hire service based on the operating methods of the Yellow Cab Company of Chicago. Franchisee benefits from unique computer control and monitoring systems. Established: 1975 - Franchising Since: 1982 - No. of Units: Company Owned: 1 - Franchised: 10 - Franchise Fee: £6,000 - Total Inv: £40,000 min. - Royalty: 7.5% - Financing: 50%.

JARDILAND
Tripode
26 rue de la Maison Rouge Lognes, Marne La Vallee Cedex 2, 77323, France,. Contact: Daniel Metivet, Pres. Dir. General - Tel: (1) 60.05.81.63. Telex: 691 169F. Garden centers. Established: 1973 - Franchising Since: 1982 - No. of Units: Company Owned: 76 - Franchised: 46 - Royalty: 1.60% - Total Inv: 5,000,000 FF.

JUST WILLS PLC.
46-50 Chertsey Rd., Byfleet, Surrey, England, KT14 7AN. Contact: Justian de Frias, Chairman & Mng. Dir. - Tel: (0932) 336390. A home visit last will & testament business. A work from home white collar franchise opportunity with positive cash flow and no bad debts, staff or stock. Seven out of ten people die without writing a will giving a huge untapped market. Established: 1989 - Franchising Since: 1991 - No. of Units: Company Owned: 1 - Franchised: 51 - Franchise Fee: £2,000 - £15,000 - Royalty: Maximum of £7.50p - Total Inv: £20,000 maximum - Financing: No.

KWIK STRIP
Kwik Strip (U.K.) Ltd.
P.O.Box 1087, Church Road, Winscombe, Avon, England, BS25 1BH. Contact: Ivor Chivers, Mng. Dir. - Tel: 0934 843100. Furniture stripping and restoration. Established: 1982 - Franchising Since: 1983 - No. of Units: Company Owned: 1 - Franchised: 28 - Franchise Fee: £5,000 - Royalty: 5% gross t/o, 2.5% adv. - Total Inv: £20,500; fran. fee plus £9,500 equip., £6,000 work. cap.

L'ECOLE BUISSONNIERE
Jouets d'Art International
25 Bis Rue Judaique, Bordeaux, 33000, France,. Contact: Boris Dinard, Mgr. - Tel: 56.52.46.20. Toys and gifts for children. Established: 1972 - Franchising Since: 1979 - No. of Units: Company Owned: 2 - Franchised: 7 - Franchise Fee: 300,000 FF - Total Inv: 500,000 FF - Royalty: 3% - Financing: no.

LE CLUB FRANCAIS
Language Clubs (Int.) Ltd.
18/19 High St., Twyford, Hampshire, England, SO21 1RF. Contact: John Ellis, Dir. - Tel: (44) 962-714036. Fun language clubs for children between 3 & 11 years old. Courses available in French, Spanish & German. Established: 1988 - Franchising Since: 1990 - No. of Units: Franchised: 300 U.K. - Franchise Fee: $3,000 - Royalty: 10% - Total Inv: $3,000 - Financing: No.

LIFE TIME TROPHIES
Life Time Sporting Products & Services
397 Dorset Rd., Boronia, Australia,. Contact: John Young, Mgr. Dir.. Trophies and badges, direct importing, manufacturing plant (wood). Screen printing - Giftware - Plastics. Established: 1980 - Franchising Since: 1984 - No. of Units: Franchised: 12 - Franchise Fee: $20,000 - Royalty: 2.5% gross receipts - Total Inv: $50,000/display, machinery, etc. $30,000 + fran. fee - Financing: No.

M & B MARQUEES
M & B Marquees Ltd.
Premier House Tennyson Drive, Pitsea, Basildon, Essex, U.K., SS13 3BT. Contact: John D. Mansfield, Mng. Dir. - Tel: 01268-558002, Fax: (01268) 552783. Offer a marquee hire service plus a full range of accessories and supporting services. Distinctively designed marquees can be erected quickly on all surfaces. Franchisees are given full training and a defined area. Established: 1976 - Franchising Since: 1985 - No. of Units: Company Owned: 1 - Franchised: 35 - Franchise Fee: Dependant on state/territory - Royalty: 9% of turnover + from year two 1% of nat'l adv. - Total Inv: from £50,000 - Financing: Available subject to status.

MASTERSHARP
P.A. Research Ltd.
28 Glen Rd., Boscombe, Bournemouth, Dorset, England, BH5 1H5. Contact: P. Addison, M.D. - Tel: 202-396002, Fax: 202-300111. Mobile tool renovation/sharpening/sales. Established: 1988 - Franchising Since: 1989 - No. of Units: Company Owned: 1 - Franchised: 25 - Franchise Fee: £4,000 - Royalty: £750 per year - Total Inv: £10,500 - Financing: Yes.

MED-PED S.A.
Plaza Med-Ped, Palma Nova, Mallorca, Spain,. Contact: Cecil Brown, Fran. Dir. - Tel: (3471) 68 16 32. Moped and scooter rentals to tourists in sunny Mediterranean tourist resorts. Established: 1976 - Franchising Since: 1980 - No. of Units: Company Owned: 4 - Franchised: 6 - Franchise Fee: $12,000 US - Total Inv: $75,000 US - Royalty: 6% gross monthly sales - Financing: no.

MERCERIE PLUS
Mercatique et Distribution
58110 Brinay, Brinay, France,. Contact: Michel Rady, Chairman - Tel: 86.84.91.00. Sew Product-Button; embroidery. Established: 1977 - Franchising Since: 1980 - No. of Units: Franchised: 46 - Franchise Fee: 20,000 FF - Total Inv: 300,000 FF.

METRO ROD SERVICES
Metro House, Churchill Way, Macclesfield, Cheshire, England, SK11 6AY. Contact: J.L.B. Harris, Man.Dir. - Tel: (0625) 3444. Drain and pipe cleaning specialists. Established: 1983 - Franchising Since: 1983 - No. of Units: Company Owned: 8 - Franchised: 39 - Franchise Fee: $10,000 - Royalty: 23% - Total Inv: $45,000 - Financing: yes.

MEXICAN CONTACT, THE
R.I.A.M. International
Jupiter St., #41, Cot. Tecamachalco, Mexico City, D.F., Mexico, 53950. Contact: Manager - Tel: 2-51-10-65, Fax: 2-51-28-35. Mexican business directories, English/Spanish publications, literature and information about producers and manufacturers of products and services, from various regions of Mexico. Public and private sources. For retailers,

distributors, importers and exporters. Representation and agents. Established: 1990 - Franchising Since: 1991 - Franchise Fee: US $350.00 - Total Inv: Variable - Financing: None.

MODULAR MARQUEES LTD.
Modular Marquees (Nationwide) Ltd.
The Yard, High Green, Catterick Village, Richmond, N. Yorks., England, DL10 7LN. Contact: Jeremy Howie, Man. Dir. - Tel: 0748-812385. Tent and marquee rental. Established: 1978 - Franchising Since: 1984 - No. of Units: Company Owned: 1 - Franchised: 9 - Franchise Fee: £3,000 - Royalty: 5% on turnover + fixed fee based on number of units held - Total Inv: £24,500 approx.

MONSIEUR BRICOLAGE
A.N.P.E.
2 et 4 rue Pierre et Marie Curie, Ingre, France, 45 140. Contact: Jean Claude Lapotre, Responsable de l'Expansion - Tel: 38 43 50 00. Magasin de bricolage et de decoration. Partnership. Established: 1965 - Franchising Since: 1980 - No. of Units: Company Owned: 1 - Franchised: 230.

MORTAR MASON WALL POINTING
Westleton, Saxmundham, Suffolk, England, 1P17 3BS. Contact: R.J. Hadfield, Director - Tel: (072) 873-608. The mechanical repointing of masonry walls, the mortar being injected into the joint through a nozzle from a ground level pumping unit. Established: 1989 - Franchising Since: 1991 - No. of Units: Company Owned: 1 - Franchised: 1 - Franchise Fee: £8,000 - Royalty: 7.5%, 2.5% adv. - Total Inv: fran. fee plus equip. £6,000, work cap. £6,000, deposit on van £3,000.

MOSTYNS
Avon Works, Bridge St., Christchurch, Dorset, England, BH23 1DY. Contact: Paul Levein, Fran. Dir.. Custom-made soft furnishing concept. Developed over the last 40 yrs. All fabrics are exclusive, representing the latest styles at realistic prices. Established: 1950 - Franchising Since: 1965 - No. of Units: Company Owned: 120 - Franchised: 10 - Franchise Fee: £6,000 - Total Inv: upwards from £20,000 (negotiable) - Financing: No.

MR. LIFT LTD.
The Lifthouse, Gloucester Rd., Almondsbury, Bristol, Avon, U.K., BS12 4HY. Contact: Rupert Crook, Fran. Dev. Mgr. - Tel: (0454) 618181. Sales, hire and service of new and used fork lift trucks from a modern industrial unit on an industrial estate. Established: 1975 - Franchising Since: 1985 - No. of Units: Company Owned: 3 - Franchised: 3 - Franchise Fee: £7,500 - Total Inv: £75,000 - Royalty: 5% mng. serv. fee, 2.5% adv. - Financing: up to 2/3 from major UK clearing banks.

NATURAL WAY, THE
Leeds House, 79a High St., Newcastle Under Lyme, Staffs, England, ST5 1PS. Contact: M. Taylor, Comm. Dir. - Tel: (01782) 711122, Fax: (01781) 711717. Individual weight loss company providing a personal and confidential service based on a one to one consultancy. No drugs involved. All natural foods. Established: 1987 - Franchising Since: 1993 - No. of Units: Company Owned: 22 - Franchised: 32 outlets - Franchise Fee: £7,500 - Royalty: No royalty - Total Inv: £7,500 fran. fee, £7,500 work. cap.

NATURAMA
Naturama School of Drama, The
42 Pinner Crt. Pinner Rd., Pinner, Middlesex, England, HA5 5RJ. Contact: Ms D. Brookens - Tel: (081) 866-5046. Drama school franchise specializing in nature and drama for 5-7 yr. olds and 8-12 yr. olds. Supplemental income part-time with full-time potential. The drama school of the future firmly rooted in the present. Children's emotional and spiritual development of paramount importance. Fun, adventure and knowledge leading to a love of life. Established: 1985 - Franchising Since: 1992 - Franchise Fee: equiv. of £450 - Royalty: 5% mgmt, 5% adv. - Total Inv: £450 fee plus £100 to £250 start-up - Financing: Educational grants.

NISBETS CHEFSHOP
Nisbets
Kelso House, Waterloo St., Old Market, Bristol, Avon, England, BS2 0PH. Contact: Andrew Nisbet, Mng. Dir. - Tel: (0272) 555843. Supplies equipment, utensils and clothing to college students about to embark on training to be chefs, at the catering colleges around the country, through mobile showrooms. Established: 1983 - Franchising Since: 1993 - No. of Units: Company Owned: 4 - Franchised: 4 - Franchise Fee: £5,500 - Royalty: 10% - Total Inv: £9,870 - Financing: Up to two thirds from High St. banks.

ONSITE TRAINING
Grove House, Great North Rd., Little Paxton, Cambs., U.K., PE19 4EL. Contact: Margaret James, Admin. Mgr.. Computer training. Established: 1985 - Franchising Since: 1989 - No. of Units: Company Owned: 1 - Franchised: 6 - Franchise Fee: £12,000 at present - Royalty: 12.5% - Total Inv: approx. £25,000 - Financing: Banking approval.

PANIC LINK P/C
Control Sortation Centre, Melbourne Rd., Lount, Leics., U.K., LE6 5RS. Contact: Heather Wilkinson, Nat. Franc. Mgr. - Tel: 0530 411111. Nationwide parcel delivery and collection service, on a franchised basis. Established: 1987 - Franchising Since: 1988 - No. of Units: Franchised: 95 - Franchise Fee: $10,000 - $20,000 - Royalty: ongoing fees directly linked to turnover of franchise - Total Inv: franchise fee, working capital of $5,000 - $10,000 - Financing: Through major clearing banks.

PASS & CO. TIMBER PRESERVATION
Pass & Co. Services Ltd.
Passco House, 635 High Rd., Leystonstone London, England, E11 4RD. Contact: Allen Winter, Fran. Mgr. - Tel: (081) 539 1105. Treatment of timbers against insect & fungal infestation. Also damp control & plasterwork. Established: 1958 - Franchising Since: 1983 - No. of Units: Company Owned: 1 - Franchised: 51 - Franchise Fee: £7,500 (pounds sterling) + tax - Royalty: 10% of turnover - Total Inv: FF £7,500/equip. & stationary £2,500 - Financing: yes.

PERSIANAS COLUMBIA S/A
Rua Thabor, 593, Sao Paulo, Sao Paulo, Brazil, 04202. Contact: Mr. Ubirajara C. Daura, Presidents Staff - Tel: (011) 272-2000. Industry of blinds-vertical and horizontal. Established: 1942 - Franchising Since: 1988 - No. of Units: Company Owned: 2 - Franchised: 5 - Franchise Fee: $30,000 (US) - Royalty: 12% - Financing: about $200,000 (US).

PETS PARADISE
464 St. Kilda Rd, Melbourne, Victoria, Australia, 3004. Contact: Franchise Director - Tel: (03) 2677666. Pet shops.

PIRTEK
Pirtek (UK) Ltd.
35 Acton Park Estate, The Vale Acton, London, W3, England, . Contact: Forbes Petrie, M.D. - Tel: (081) 749-8444. Hydraulic hose supply and replacement via depots and mobile workshops. A 24 hr., 7 days a week service. Established: 1988 - Franchising Since: 1989 - No. of Units: Company Owned: 1 - Franchised: 18 - Franchise Fee: £10,000 - Total Inv: £140,000: £70,000 cash, £70,000 financed - Financing: Through main banks.

PIRTEK FLUID SYSTEMS, PTY. LTD. *
1/163 Prospect Hwy., Sydney, N.S.W., Australia, 2147. Contact: W. Davey, Mktg. Dir. - Tel: (02) 838 7888. Established: 1980 - Franchising Since: 1985 - No. of Units: Company Owned: 2 - Franchised: 48 - Franchise Fee: A$20,000 - Royalty: 1.5% mgmt, .75% adv. - Total Inv: $260,000 - $800,000 - Financing: No.

POMME DE PAIN
SA. Bretonniere
173, Rue St. Martin, 75003 Paris , France, . Contact: B. Vaillans, Directeur . Restauration Rapide. Established: 1980 - Franchising Since: 1985 - No. of Units: Company Owned: 35 - Franchised: 4 - Franchise Fee: 5% - Total Inv: 2 M.F.

RAPEL RADIO ALARM SYSTEMS (ADMAX) LTD.
39 Church St., Weybridge, Surrey, England, KT13 8DG. Contact: M.A. Webb, Mng. Dir. - Tel: 0932-56526. Radio alarm systems that are flexible, reliable, cost effective and easy to install. Established: 1979 - Franchising Since: 1980 - No. of Units: Company Owned: 1 - Franchised: 12 - Approx. Inv: £160,000.

RE-NU PLC
489A London Rd., North Cheam, Surrey, England, SM3 8JW. Contact: Mr. Mal Weeraratne, Mgn. Dir. - Tel: (081) 786-7171. Kitchen door replacement. Established: 1987 - Franchising Since: 1988 - No. of Units: Company Owned: 1 - Franchised: 60 - Franchise Fee: £6000 - Total Inv: £15,000 - £20,000 - (init. training £2,000, cont. training £2,000, work cap. £5,000 - £10,000) - Financing: All UK.

REAL ESTATE SIGNS LTD.
Meriden Hall, Meriden,, Coventry, Warks, England, CV7 7LA. Contact: Mr. S.C. Breese, Mng. Dir. - Tel: 0676-23944 . Management of estate agency for sale boards. Established: 1988 - Franchising Since: 1992 - No. of Units: Company Owned: 1 - Franchised: 15 - Franchise Fee: £11,500 + VAT - Royalty: None - Total Inv: Fran. fee plus £18,500 work. cap. - Financing: Usually 50% through banks subject to security.

RECOGNITION EXPRESS
Recognition Express ltd.
P.O. Box 7, Rugby Rd., Hinckley, Leicestershire, England, LE10 2NE. Contact: Mr. Terry Howorth, Managing Dir. - Tel: 01455 238133. Manufacture and sale of personalized lapel badges, interior & exterior signs and vehicle livery, on a business to business basis. Established: 1979 - Franchising Since: 1980 - No. of Units: Company Owned: 1 - Franchised: 26 - Franchise Fee: £8,000 - Royalty: 10% of gross mthly. sales - Total Inv: £35,000 (£22,000 equip.) - Financing: Royal Bank of Scotland 70% & leasing (equip.).

REFACE-A-DOOR
Hilmar House, 5 Girton St., Manchester, England, M7 9UR. Contact: P. Jackson, Fran. Mgr. - Tel: (061) 839-1189. Kitchen and bedroom door panels made to measure to fit and reface existing doors. Rigid panels including wood finishes. Established: 1989 - Franchising Since: 1989 - No. of Units: Franchised: 20 - Franchise Fee: £2,950 - Financing: Yes.

ROAD RUNNER SCOOTER HIRE
Shop 2 Picnic Bay Arcade, Picnic Bay, Magnetic Island, Queensland, Australia, . Contact: Franchise Director, - Tel: (077) 785222. Specialty scooter rental.

ROMAN SPA HYDROMASSAGE
Roman Spa Health & Leisure Products Ltd.
3 Britannia Blgd., Merchant Rd. Hotwells, Bristol, Avon, England, BS8 4QD. Contact: M.J. Fedeczvo, Chairman/Dir. - Tel: (0272) 250120. Direct sales of a unique portable hydromassage system complete with accessories and herbal bath additives. Established: 1986 - Franchising Since: 1988 - No. of Units: Company Owned: 2 - Franchised: 6 - Franchise Fee: £6,500 - Total Inv: £14,500 + V.A.T. - Financing: Up to 100% depending on status.

SAFEWAY MOTORING SCHOOL
25 Weston Rd., Long Ashton, Bristol, England, BS18 SLA. Contact: A. Otten, Dir. - Tel: (0275) 392582. A motoring school franchise. Established: 1978 - Franchising Since:1984 - No. of Units: Company Owned: 6 - Franchised: 80 - Franchise Fee: £4,000 - Total Inv: £1,000 plus finance facilities - Financing: Yes.

SECURITAL
Group 4 Securital
Farncombe House, Broadway, Worcs., England, WR12 7RJ. Contact: G. Shopland, Tech. Dir. - Tel: (0684) 295250. Residential and small business premises alarm market. Established: 1982 - Franchising Since: 1982 - No. of Units: Company Owned: 1 - Franchised: 13 - Approx. Inv: £6,500+l - Royalty: 6% - Financing: partial.

SELECTAMARK SECURITY SYSTEMS LIMITED
5 Locks Court, 429 Crofton Rd., Locksbottom, Kent, England, BR6 8NL. Contact: J. G. Brown, Mng. Dir. - Tel: 0689-860757. Permanent security marketing. Established: 1978 - Franchising Since: 1979 - No. of Units: Company Owned: 1 - Franchised: 8 - Franchise Fee: £2,000 - Royalty: 3% adv. - Total Inv: £2,000 - Financing: 80%.

SIGN EXPRESS *
Techsign Franchising Participacoes Ltda.
Calcada Das Rosas 43, Barveri, Sao Paulo, Brazil, 06453-000. Contact: Susan Berger, V.P. - Tel: (011) 725-2055. Sign making franchise (master franchisee for Brazil). Established: 1991 - Franchising Since: 1992 - No. of Units: Company Owned: 1 - Franchised: 20 - Franchise Fee: $20,000 - Royalty: 5%, 2% publicity - Total Inv: $100,000 - Financing: No.

SKILL ALIANCA INGLESA *
Skill Alianca Inglesa S/C Ltda.
Av. Indianopolis, 3356, Sao Paulo, SP, Brazil, 04062-003. Contact: Alderlei, Mktg. Dir. - Tel: 011 581-09-22. English as a foreign language franchise schools. Established: 1973 - Franchising Since: 1985 - No. of Units: Company Owned: 3 - Franchised: 146 - Franchise Fee: US$3,500 (minor cities) and US$6,500 (major cities) - Royalty: None - Total Inv: US$20,000 - FInancing: No.

SOFITEL
Schema
2 rue de la Mare Neuve, Evry, 91021, France, . Contact: Jean Breville - Tel: (6) 077-93-20. Hotels. Established: 1964 - Franchising Since: 1964 - No. of Units: 5 - Franchise Fee: 100,000 FF per room - Total Inv: 600,000 FF per room - Royalty: 3%.

SOMERFORD CLAIMS PLC.
Somerford Hall, Somerford, Stafford, England, ST19 9DQ. Contact: Bernard Sullman, Fran. Dir. - Tel: 0902 850721. Uninsured loss recovery. Loss of earnings for the taxi industry when a taxi is involved in a non-fault accident. Established: 1987 - Franchising Since: 1989 - No. of Units: Company Owned: 1 - Franchised: 23 - Franchise Fee: £7,500 - Royalty: Percentage of total L.O.E. - Total Inv: Computer equip. £3,000 - Financing: Depending on area.

SOVEREIGN SERVICES
39 Osborne Rd., Eastbourne, E, Sussex, England, . Contact: B. R. Southon, Dir. - Tel: 0293-547932. Private ambulance service. Established: 1978 - Franchising Since: 1982 - No. of Units: 13 - Approx. Inv: £12,500 - Royalty: 10%, £1,200 adv. - Financing: bank facility.

SPACEAGE PLASTICS
Spaceage Plastics Ltd.
Spaceage House, 85 Ringwood Rd., Parkstone, Poole, Dorset, England, BH14 0RH. Contact: Dalziel, Dir. - Tel: 0202-732053. Distributors of rigid & foam plastic building profiles, solid & structured polycarbonate sheets, glazing bars, aerated pvc sheet, rigid pvc sheet, thermoformed pvc door panels. Established: 1982 - Franchising Since: 1990 - No. of Units: Company Owned: 4 - Franchised: 1 - Franchise Fee: £6,000 - Royalty: 5% sales, 1% adv. - Total Inv: £50,000 stock above £6,000 - Financing: Barclays Bank, Plc.

SPICE - THE ADVENTURE GROUP
Spice UK Ltd.
18 Henrietta St., Old Trafford, Manchester, England, M16 9GA. Contact: Dave Smith, M.D. - Tel: 061 872 2213. Adventure sports and social group members pay an annual subscription for monthly newsletter packed full of events, local, national & international. Consultancy available for independent operators. Established: 1980 - Franchising Since: 1986 - No. of Units: Company Owned: 1 - Franchised: 9 - Franchise Fee: £10,000 - Financing: Yes.

STAR TRAVEL
All Star Travel B.V.
W.G. Plein 472, Amsterdam, The Netherlands, 1054SH. Contact: J.P. Peerenboom, Consultant - Tel: (020) 127754. Travel agency. Established: 1988 - Franchising Since: 1988 - No. of Units: Company Owned: 1 - Franchised: 7 - Franchise Fee: 1% - DFL 30.000 - Total Inv: DFL 100.000 incl. royalties - Financing: yes.

STONEASE PAVING PATTERN IMPRINTED CONCRETE LTD.
71 Chapel Rd., Tiptree, Nr. Colchester, Essex, England, 105 ORD. Contact: Paul Wagner, Mng. Dir. - Tel: (0621) 816083. Concerned with selling and maintaining franchises in pattern imprinted concrete. Established: 1988 - Franchising Since: 1988 - No. of Units: Company Owned: 1 - Franchised: 10 - Franchise Fee: £9,000 + VAT - Royalty: £1 per sq. meter concrete layed - Financing: Have loan companies interested in assisting.

SWINGTIME GOLF CENTRES
Swingtime (Golf Centres) Ltd.
4th Flr., Knightsbridge House, 197 Knightbridge, London, England, SW7 1RB. Contact: Jonathan Snellgrove, Managing Dir. - Tel: 071 973 8866. Golf driving ranges, public access golf courses, retail golf shops & associated leisure activities. Established: 1991 - Franchising Since: 1992 - No. of Units: Company Owned: 2 - Franchised: 6 - Franchise Fee: £25,000 - Royalty: 5% plus 3% adv. - Total Inv: £350,000 - Financing: Yes, up to 80%.

TIGHTS MACHINE, THE
Tight Fit Ltd.
P.O. Box 48, Beyton, Bury St. Edmunds, Suffolk, England, IP30 9HS. Contact: T.D. Elliot, Dir. - Tel: 0359 71629. Supply of hosiery vending machines and products for sale through them. Established: 1987 - Franchising Since: 1989 - No. of Units: Company Owned: 1 - Franchised: 20 - Total Inv: £3,750.

TIOLI
Calligraphics Ltd.
2 Royal Bldg., The Parade, Liskeard, Cornwall, England, PL14 6AF. Contact: R. A. Bragger, Dir. - Tel: 0579-44029. Custom glass engraving while-you-wait. Established: 1981 - Franchising Since: 1985 - No. of Units: Company Owned: 5 - Franchised: 1 - Approx. Inv: £10,000 minimum - Royalty: 10% - Financing: no.

TRAVEL BAZAAR, THE
Dooley Travel Group PLC
221 Westbourne Park Rd., London, U.K, W11 1EA. Contact: Riaz Dooley, Mng. Dir. - Tel: (071) 221-6095/1729, Fax: 229-3595. Air ticket brokers/seat sale specialist on discounted air fares worldwide. Package holidays/special interest tours/conferences. Hotel booking agents/theater and sporting events bookings. Established: 1979 - Franchising Since: 1981 - No. of Units: Company Owned: 5 - Franchised: 59 - Franchise Fee: £1500 - Royalty: None, once training provided, with all the knowhow and contacts, they are fully responsible to run their business - Total Inv: £2000 - £6000 - Financing: Yes, secured against assets and personal guarantees.

TROPHY UK
Riverside House, St. Simon St., Salford, Manchester, England, M3 7ET. Contact: David Mooney, Mng. Dir. - Tel: 01144 61 839 5737. Mobile pet food franchise. Professional door-to-door pet food service throughout the UK with an enormous market. Trophy offers its customers a variety of tinned dog and cat food, complete food in a variety of protein levels, brawn, biscuits. Established: 1992 - Franchising Since: 1992 - No. of Units: Franchised: 300+ - Franchise Fee: £6,995 plus VAT - Royalty: £25 per week plus VAT first year, £15 per week plus VAT thereafter - Financing: Advice and assistance available to home-owners.

UNICIS
B.P. 237, 16 rue Faidherbe, Lille Cedex, France, 59002. Contact: Henri Masson - Tel: 20-55-42-14. Dating services. Established: 1973 - Franchising Since: 1975 - No. of Units: Company Owned: 2 - Franchised: 86 - Approx. Inv: 300,000 FF - Royalty: 10%.

UTICOLOR
Uticolor (Great Britain) Ltd.
30-32 Chase Rd., London, England, NW10 6QN. Contact: John Court - Tel: 081 965 6869. Leather and vinyl repair, reconditioning and renovation service. Established: 1974 - Franchising Since: 1977 - No. of Units: Company Owned: 1 - Franchised: 24 - Franchise Fee: £10,000 - £12,000 - Royalty: 10% - 7% - Total Inv: £10,000 - £12,000 - Financing: Yes.

VA SIGNS
The Sign Franchise
Hennisfield, Sutton-on-the-Hill, Ashbourne, Berbts., England, DE6 5JF. Contact: Bob Potter, Co. Prop/Partner - Tel: 0283 733961. Sign making business and vehicle livery/graphics. Established: 1986 - Franchising Since: 1991 - No. of Units: Company Owned: 1 - Franchised: 21 - Franchise Fee: £5,000 - Royalty: 5% of gross turnover - Total Inv: £20,000 - Financing: Part.

VAL-U-PAK
Zone Marketing (UK) Ltd.
Clarke Lodge, 41 Holly Bush Lane, Harpenden, Herts., England, AL5 4AY. Contact: Jeff Frankling, Fran. Dir. - Tel: 44 1582 460977, Fax: 44 1582 462727. Packs of discount vouchers promoting local shops & businesses distributed to local residential households. Established: 1987 - Franchising Since: 1989 - No. of Units: Company Owned: 1 - Franchised: 1 - Royalty: £50 per month or 5% of sales, whichever greater - Financing: Package now being relaunched with no up front franchise fee.

VERLAG DEUTSCHER STADTPLANE GMBH
Gustener Straße 1818, Titz -Ameln, Germany, 52445. Contact: Mr. Karl-Heinz Rolka, Mgr. - Tel: 0 2463-6772, Fax: 0 2463-6777. Distribution of maps and guides in over 400 cities worldwide. Special editions for various targeted groups, guest guides, guides for building and construction, guides for cultural events, automobile guides and cartographical present items. Established: 1973 - Franchising Since: 1975 - No. of Units: Company Owned: 12 - Franchised: 172 - Franchise Fee: DM 50.000,00 - 120.000,00 - Royalty: 3% - Total Inv: DM 60.000.000 - DM 140.000.000 - Financing: Eventually.

VIAPLAN BV
Dr.-Jaegersstraat 39, Heerlen, The Netherlands, NL-6417 GJ. Contact: Karl-Heinz Rolka, Dir. - Tel: (045) 71 65 72. Drawing, manufacturing and marketing of cartographies in special editions, f.i. as guides of events, guest guides, guides for home and living, automobile guides etc. Established: 1984 - Franchising Since: 1985 - No. of Units: Company Owned: 4 - Franchised: 37 - Franchise Fee: HFL 60.000 - HFL 135.000 - Royalty: 3% - Total Inv: HFL 170.000 - Financing: Eventually.

VIAPLAN S.A.R.L.
Route de Stavelot 117, Weisswampach, Luxembourg, L 9991. Contact: Ronald Rolka, Asst. Mgr. - Tel: (00352) 97 90 29. Drawing, manufacturing and marketing of cartographies in special edition, f.i. as guides of events, guest guides, guides for home and living, automobile guides etc. Established: 1990 - Franchising Since: 1991 - No. of Units: Company Owned: 1 - Franchised: 3 - Franchise Fee: LFR 1.000.000 - 2.400.000 - Royalty: 3% - Total Inv: LFR 3.000.000.

VINYL MASTER (UK) LTD.
Unit 2A, Vulcan Works, 205 Leckhampton Rd., Cheltenham, Gloucestershire, England, GL53 0AL. Contact: Nick Scanlan, Mng. Dir. - Tel: (0242) 584511. Vinyl repair process. Established: 1980 - Franchising Since 1981 - No. of Units: Company Owned: 1 - Franchised: 12 - Franchise Fee: £4,500 - Royalty: £1,000 per annum - Total Inv: £8,000.

WASTE WHACKER LTD.
Holbrook, Ipswick, Suffolk, England, IP9 1PT. Contact: Andrew Rodwell, Dir. - Tel: 0473-328272. Design, production and marketing of waste disposal equipment. Established: 1982 - Franchising Since: 1982 - No. of Units: Company Owned: 1 - Franchised: 5 - Approx. Inv: £670 min.

WHITEGATES ESTATE AGENCY
Legal and General
4 Bruntcliffe Way, Morley, Leeds, Yorks, England, LS27 0JG. Contact: R. Ellison, Fran. Dir. - Tel: 0532 539166. Sales of all types of properties, commercial and residential. Property letting and management, sale of financial services. Established: 1978 - Franchising Since: 1986 - No. of Units: Company Owned: 80 - Franchised: 40 - Franchise Fee: £5,000 - Royalty: 10% of gross turnover - Total Inv: £40,000 - Financing: Bank.

HEALTH AND BEAUTY AIDS AND SERVICES

APPLEWOODS INTERNATIONAL, LTD. *
Heathfield Ind. Estate, Newton Abbot, Devon, England, TQ12 6RY. Contact: Roger Buoy, Chairman - Tel: 01626 832283. Natural soaps & toiletries, production of natural toiletries. Established: 1992 - No. of Units: Franchised: 30 - Total Inv: $120,000 - Financing: No.

ASSOCIATION FOR APPLIED HYPNOSIS, THE
33 Abbey Park Rd., Grimsby, South Humbs., England, DN32 0HS. Contact: Franchise Director - Tel: Grimsby 47702. Persons with acceptable medical-psychology qualifications trained to use specially developed, complimentary natural therapy techniques for the purpose of relieving and resolving a variety of stress related psychosomatic, psychoneurotic, habit and other problems. Supervised Practices. Established: 1980 - Franchise Fee: $6,000 (includes training and subsequent supervision) - Royalty: $1,500 p.a. (includes membership fees) - Total Inv: Normal office costs; travelling and accommodation costs extra.

BEKA COIFFEUR'S *
Beka International
Rua Oscar Freire 565, Sao Paulo, SP, Brazil, 01426-001. Contact: Metairon, Dir. - Tel: (011) 881-0355. Hair's beauty cosmetic franchise hairdressers, make up, esthetic. Established: 1967 - Franchising Since: 1991 - No. of Units: Company Owned: 1 - Franchised: 4 - Franchise Fee: US$ 5,000 - Royalty: 5% F.B. - Total Inv: US$ 120,000 - Financing: 50%.

BODY & FACE PLACE, THE
12 Glenthrone Mews, 115 Glenthrone Rd., London, England, W6 0LJ. Contact: Don Kennedy/ Tim MacAndrews, Directors. Natural beauty retailers and manufacturers. Established: 1986 - Franchising Since: 1986 - No. of Units: 5 - Franchised: 71 - Franchise Fee: Approx: £70,000 - Royalty: 4% mgmt. fee - Financing: Bank loan.

BODY REFORM
Natural Beauty Products Ltd.
Western Ave., Bridgend Ind. Estate, Bridgend, Mid Glamorgan, Wales, U.K., CF31 3RT. Contact: D. Bushell, Mktg. Dir. - Tel: 0656 766 566, Fax: 0656 650456. Natural cruelty free toiletries & cosmetics manufactured at above address marketed through corporate style detail outlets - Body Reform Shops. Master licenses available internationally. Established: 1985 - Franchising Since: 1990 - No. of Units: Company Owned: 3 - Franchised: 60 - Total Inv: £80,000 to £100,000 sterling.

BODY SHOP, THE
Body Shop International, Plc.,
Watersmead Bus. Park, Littlehampton, W. Sussex, England, BN17 6L7. Contact: Peter Tyson, Gen. Mgr., Mew Markets - Tel: 44 903 731500. Retailing of naturally based cosmetics and toiletries. Established: 1976 - Franchising Since: 1977 - No. of Units: Company Owned: 32 - Franchised: 922 - Franchise Fee, Royalty, Total Inv. & Financing: Vary per market.

COMMUNITY CARELINE SERVICES *
Sandringham House, 22-28 Chirstopher St., Salford, England, M5 4PT. Contact: Giulia Kaff, PR & Support Exec. - Tel: 0161 877 4477, Fax: 0161 877 6700. Provisions of home care services to the elderly & people with disabilities. Supply of monitoring services to the community. Client base: private, social services & housing associations. Established: 1990 - Franchising Since: 1993 - No. of Units: Company Owned: 1 - Franchised: 200 - Franchise Fee: £9,000 - Royalty: 2% turnover (yr. 1), 4% turnover (yr. 2), 6% turnover (yr. 3) - Total Inv: £9,000 + work. cap. (approx. £15,000).

CROWN OPTICAL CENTRE
Crown Eyeglass Plc.
Blakewater Rd., Glenfield Park, Blackburn, England, BB1 5QH. Contact: Ms. D. Singer, Fran. Dir. - Tel: 0254 51535. Manufacturers, distributors and retailers via franchised outlets of prescription glasses & readymade reading glasses. Established: 1984 - Franchising Since: 1984 - No. of Units: Company Owned: 4 - Franchised: 54 - Franchise Fee: £40,000 - Royalty: Nil - Total Inv: £40,000 - Financing: By arrangement.

DOLLOND & AITCHISON
Dollond & Aitchison Group, Plc.
1323 Coventry Rd., Yardley, Birmingham, England, B23 8LP. Contact: Victor Howitt, Fran. Dir. - Tel: 021-706-6133, Night Line: 021-706-8996. Retail opticians with 650 branches in the U.K., Spain, Italy, and Switzerland. Established: 1750 - Franchising Since: 1988 - No. of Units: Company Owned: 650 - Franchised: 44 (40 UK, 4 Italy) - Franchise Fee: £3,000 for existing branches, £6,000 from scratch - Royalty: 7.5% of sales, 2.5% of sales for adv. & mktg. - Total Inv: £20,000 - £100,000 - Financing: Local banks and company in selected cases.

FIRST IMPRESSIONS
The Coach House, Ramsey Manor, 37 High St., Burwell, Cambridge, England, CB5 0HD. Contact: P.P.B. Halpin, Owner - Tel: 01638 741166, Fax: 01638 742253. Personal image consultancy. Established: 1987 - Franchising Since: 1987 - No. of Units: Company Owned: 1 - Franchised: 150 - Franchise Fee: £2,750.

FRANCESCO GROUP
Francesco Group Holdings Ltd.
Woodings Yard, Bailey St., Stafford Staffordshire, U.K., ST17 4BG. Contact: Frank Dellicompagni, Co. Dir. - Tel: (0785) 47175. Ladies and gentlemen's hairdressing. Established: 1969 - Franchising Since: 1983 - No. of Units: Company Owned: 4 - Franchised: 17 - Franchise Fee: £6,000 - Royalty: 10% net takings - Total Inv: £45,000 - Financing: Assistance.

HOMEOPATIA DR. WALDEMIRO PEREIRA *
Homeopatia Waldemira Pereria Lab. Indl. F. Ltda
Av. Mal. Floriano Peixoto, 7709, Curitiba, Parana, Brazil, 81.650-000. Contact: Pereira/Waldemiro, Director - Tel: (041) 276-9622. Farmaceutical industries homeopatic Brazilian natural products - franchising to drug stores. Established: 1933 - Franchising Since: 1991 - No. of Units: Company Owned: 6 - Franchised: 3 - Franchise Fee: US$3,500 - Royalty: 5% - Total Inv: US$ 25,000 - Financing: No.

J.T. LAZARTIGUE (UK) LTD.
20 James St., London, England, W1M 5HN. Contact: G. Makhoul, Dir. - Tel: (071) 629-6487. Diagnostic and advisory hair centre. Also, market and sell own brand of hair products and cosmetics. Established: 1975 - Franchising Since: 1975 - No. of Units: Company Owned: 22 - Franchised: 120 - Royalty: 7% of turnover, 5% adv. - Total Inv: £60,000 - Financing: No.

JACQUES JANINE *
Jacnine Comp. Imp. Exp. Ltda
Rua Augusta, 2763 - conj. 21, Sao Paulo, SP, Brazil, 01413-100. Contact: Nelson Chemin, Finance Admin. Dir. - Tel: (011) 883-7088. Jacques Janine company, specializing in beauty care, develops a professional and efficient work in service of beauty, in the fields of hair, facial and corporal esthetics, make up, manicure, pedicure, eetc. using what is most advanced in equipments, prdoucts and specialized staff. Established: 1957 - Franchising Since: 1990 - No. of Units: Company Owned: 6 - Franchised: 14 - Franchise Fee: US$10,000 - Royalty: 7% - Total Inv: US$155,000.

KARL SWITZERLAND
19 The South-Yarra Corporate Center, 209 Toorak Rd., South-Yarra, Victoria, Australia, 3144. Contact: Karl Scherer, Pres.. Ladies' and men's hair fashions. Upmarket positioning with beautician services available. Positioned only in major regional shopping centres and malls. Established: 1961 - Franchising Since: 1984 - No. of Units: Company Owned: 5 - Franchised: 10 - Franchise Fee: $20,000 - Total Inv: $100,000 - $120,000 - Royalty: 8% - Financing: yes.

LABORATOIRES SIMONE MAHLER
106 Quai Des Chartrons, Bordeaux, Gironde, France, 33082. Contact: Francois Xavier Beraud, Export Mgr. - Tel: (33) 5639 3765. Manufacturers and distributors of cosmetics and perfumes. Established: 1952 - Franchising Since: 1962 - No. of Units: Company Owned: 30 - Franchised: 86 - Franchise Fee: 50,000 FF - Royalty: 3% - Total Inv: 500,000 - 900,000 FF - Financing: 50%.

LADY K SALON SUPPLIES
Hairdressing Franchising Ltd.
Ancaster House, Ancaster, N. Grantham, Lincolnshire, England, . Contact: B. G. Singleton, Fran. Exec. - Tel: 0400-30674. Suppliers of hairdressing products from mobile units. Established: 1982 - Franchising Since: 1984 - No. of Units: Company Owned: 1 - Franchised: 2 - Approx. Inv: £12,000 - Financing: yes.

LAMBOURN COURT INTERNATIONAL PLC
Lambourn Court International
The Manor Barn, Keysoe, Bedfordshire, England, MK44 2HR. Contact: David M. Hinds, Founder/Chairman - Tel: 0234 708848, Fax: (0234) 708702. Stress Management Consultants. Established: 1987 - Franchising Since: 1991 - No. of Units: Franchised: 75 - Franchise Fee: £18,500 plus VAT @ 17.5% sterling - Royalty: 10%.

NATIONAL SLIMMING CENTRES
3, Trinity House, 161, Old Christchurch Rd., Bournemouth, Dorset, England, BH1 1JW. Contact: Mr. S. Hass, Exec. Dir. - Tel: (0202) 555233. Professional medically supervised weight loss method. Established: 1981 - Franchising Since: 1987 - No. of Units: Company Owned: 20 - Franchised: 5 - Franchise Fee: £25,000 - Royalty: nil - Total Inv: £25,000 - Financing: No.

NECTAR BEAUTY SHOPS
The Nectar Group
95a Belfast Rd., Carrickfergus, Co. Antrim, Northern Ireland, BT38 8XX. Contact: Mr. W. B. Waring, Mng. Dir. - Tel: 01960 351580, Fax: 01960 351740. Manufacturer of natural beauty products sold only through their franchised and company owned shops worldwide. Established: 1981 - Franchising Since: 1984 - No. of Units: Company Owned: 1 - Franchised: 311 - Franchise Fee: By agreement - Royalty: None - Total Inv: Fran. fee plus opening stock £20,000 approx. plus shopfitting £20,000 approx.

PRICE ATTACK *
Price Attack Franchising Pty. Ltd.
39 Leopard St., Kangaroo Point, Qsld., Australia, 4169. Contact: Gary Jackson, Mng. Dir. - Tel: (0011) 61 7 891 1822. Haircare & cosmetics & hair salons. Established: 1985 - Franchising Since: 1986 - No. of Units: Company Owned: 3 - Franchised: 72 - Franchise Fee: Aus$50,000 - Royalty: 5% fran. fee, 2% adv. - Total Inv: Aus$250,000 - $300,000 - Financing: No.

SPLASHDANCE
Splashdance Fitness
Splashdance House, 5 Dymoke Road, Hornchurch, Essex, England, RM11 1AA. Contact: Ms. Y. Peters , Sales - Tel: (0708) 747013. Water fitness franchise running classes in your own area, part-time or full-time. Established: 1985 - Franchising Since: 1989 - No. of Units: Company Owned: 40 - Franchised: 14 - Franchise Fee: £650 - Royalty: 7.5% of gross - Total Inv: £1,000 - Financing: Yes.

TRIMLINE HEALTH & FITNESS CENTRES
Kreativ Properties Ltd.
6 Burwell Close, Healey, Rochdale, Lanchester, England, OL12 6DQ. Contact: Mr. S. K. Fogo, Mng. Dir. - Tel: (0706) 33797. Health and fitness centres. Established: 1976 - Franchising Since: 1989 - No. of Units: Franchised: 4 - Franchise Fee: £5,000 - Royalty: 8% per annum - Total Inv: £80,000 new site basic scheme + initial fee - Financing: Yes, existing clubs on some occasions can be acquired at less the cost.

PHOTO, PRINTING AND ART

CHROMA COPY
42-44 Broadwick St., London, England, W1V 3DF. Contact: Franchise Director - Tel: (01) 734-0744/5. Printing and copying services. Established: 1979 - No. of Units: 25+.

FASTFRAME
Fastframe Franchises Ltd.
Int'l. Ctr., Netherton Park, Stannington, Morpeth Northumberland, England, NE61 6EF. Contact: Margaret Hewison, Fran. Dir. - Tel: (0670) 789797. Retailer of picture framing, prints, posters etc. in a high profile city centre location. Established: 1983 - Franchising Since: 1984 - No. of Units: Company Owned: 20 - Franchised: 71 - Franchise Fee: £10,000 - Royalty: 6.25% mktg. + 6.25% mgmt. fee - Total Inv: £55,000 - Financing: Yes.

FLETCHERS FOTOGRAPHS NAI FLETCHERS FOTOGRAPHICS PTY. LTD.
317 Pitt St., Sydney, NSW 2000, Australia, . Contact: David Buching, Gen. Mgr. - Tel: (02) 2618354. Photographic retailing. Established: 1977 - Franchising Since: 1985 - No. of Units: Company Owned: 3 - Franchised: 25 - Franchise Fee: $10,000 - Royalty: 2% Corp. adv., l/2% lic. fee (gross sales) - Total Inv: $150,000 - Financing: No.

FOTOQUELLE NEDERLAND B.V.
Noorderdreef 70, Nieuw Vennep, The Netherlands, 2153LL. Contact: E. Knappe, Mng. Dir. - Tel: (0252673209). Photo retail trade. Established: 1975 - Franchising Since: 1975 - No. of Units: Company Owned: 4 - Franchised: 370 - Total Inv: HFL 3,000, fixture and Hfl. 5,000, inv. Mdse.

KALL-KWIK PRINTING
Kall-Kwik House, 106 Pembroke Rd., Ruislip, Middlesex, England, HA4 8NW. Contact: Clive Sawkins - Tel: 08956-32700. Printshop franchise. Established: 1979 - Franchising Since: 1979 - No. of Units: Company Owned: 1 - Franchised: 196 - Franchise Fee: £14,000 - Total Inv: £115,000 - Royalty: 10% - Financing: Yes.

PDC COPYPRINT
PDC International PLC
1 Church Lane, East Grinstead, West Sussex, U.K., RH19 3AZ . Contact: Michael Marks, Director - Tel: (01342) 315321, Fax: (01342) 327117. Printing, design & copying. Established: 1965 - Franchising Since: 1982 - No. of Units: Company Owned: 1 - Franchised: 34 - Franchise Fee: £7,500 - Royalty: 6% + 4% adv. reducing to 5% - Total Inv: £111,000 includ. £31,000 working cap. - Financing: 70%.

PHOTO CERAMICS PTY. LTD.
137 Regent St., Chippendale, Sydney, Australia, 2008. Contact: Franchise Director - Tel: (02) 690-1633. Customized glazing of photos onto porcelain.

PIP PRINTING
Printnet Ltd.
15 Newman St., London, England, W1P 3HD. Contact: Mr. C. Bowman, Chairman - Tel: 071-636 2571. Printing of business and personal stationery - letterheads, visiting cards, leaflets, forms, invoices - copying, colour copying & printing - artwork & design. Established: 1993 - Franchising Since: 1993 - No. of Units: Franchised: 17.

PRINTDESIGNS
Chester Rd., Kelsall, Tarperley, Cheshire, U.K., CLO6 0RJ. Contact: C. David Gattie, M.D. - Tel: 0829-52095. Graphic design, artwork, typesetting, and printing. Established: 1978 - Franchising Since: 1989 - No. of Units: Company Owned: 2 - Franchised: 2 - Franchise Fee: £6,000 - Royalty: 6%, 4% adv. levy - Total Inv: initially £60,000 - phased inv. - Financing: Yes.

PRONTAPRINT LTD.
Pontaprint Plc
Coniscliffe House, Coniscliffe Rd., Darlington Co Durham, England , DL3 7EX. Contact: Liz Pollard, Fran. Man. - Tel: 0325 483333. Business service centre offering printing, copying, office supplies, and services to the modern business. Established: 1971 - Franchising Since: 1973 - No. of Units: Company Owned: 2 - Franchised: 295 - Franchise Fee: £5,550 - Royalty: 5% + 5% mktg. services fund - Total Inv: £80,000: £15,000 franchise pkg. + licence fees £20,000 sundry expenses £45,000 equip. + Shopfit - Financing: all major High St. Banks.

SHOP PHOTO VIDEO
16 Rue au Pain, Versailles, France, 78000. Contact: Mr. Ferrero, Dir. - Tel: 1-39-50-02-36. Photographic, movie and video material. Established: 1962 - Franchising Since: 1966 - No. of Units: Company Owned: 4 - Franchised: 45 - Royalty: 1%.

SNAP PRINTING *
Snap Franchising Ltd.
105 Hay St., Subiaco, W.A., Australia, 6008. Contact: Tim Hantke, C.E.O. - Tel: (09) 382 3599. Franchising quick printing. Established: 1967 - Franchising Since: 1979 - No. of Units: Company Owned: 1 - Franchised: 140 - Franchise Fee: Aus$42,000 - Royalty: 6% x sales yr. 1, 8% thereafter - Total Inv: Aus$240,000 - Financing: from banks.

SNAPPY SNAPS
Snappy Snaps Franchises Ltd.
11/12 Glenthorne Mens, Glenthorne Road, Hammersmith, London, U.K., W60LJ. Contact: Tim MacAndrews, Dir. - Tel: (081) 741-7474. One hour film developing processing and photographic retail products. Established: 1983 - Franchising Since: 1986 - No. of Units: Franchised: 51 - Franchise Fee: £12,500 - Royalty: 6%, 2% Adv. - Total Inv: £107,000 - Financing: yes.

RETAIL

ACTUA-SA
16 Cite Joly, 75011, Paris, France, . Contact: Daniel Dorra - Tel: (1) 48.05.23.16. Furniture sofa and gift stores. Established: 1974 - Franchising Since: 1976 - No. of Units: Company Owned: 5 - Franchised: 30 - Franchise Fee: 40,000 FHT, Total Inv: 300,000 - 800,000 F - Royalty: 5% - Financing: 50%.

ALBIE FOX PERSONALIZED EMBROIDERY
Fox House, Redhill Dr., Hook-A-Gate, Shrewsbury, Salop, U.K., SY5 8BW. Contact: Albie Fox, M.D. - Tel: 1743-860093. Mobile embroidery business. Purpose built unit travels to sporting events, exhibitions etc. and caters to the impulse buyer. Established: 1988 - Franchising Since: 1993 - No. of Units: Company Owned: 1 - Franchised: 2 - Franchise Fee: £36,000 - £50,000 - Royalty: 12.5% turnover - Total Inv: £31,000 machinery & hardware, £5,000 license - Financing: Lease on machinery.

APC ALARMS LTD.
181C Barrack Rd., Christchurch, Dorset, England, BH23 2AR. Contact: M.A. O'Brien, Dir. - Tel: 0202-21722. Retail domestic burglar alarm systems and security equipment. Established: 1983 - Franchising Since: 1983 - No. of Units: Company Owned: 2 - Franchised: 3 - Approx. Inv: £12,000 plus working capital - Royalty: 7.5%.

APOLLO WINDOW BLINDS
Fountain Crescent, Inchinnan, Renfrewshire, England, PA4 9RE. Contact: Kate Wilson, Franchise Dev. Mgr. - Tel: (041) 812-3322. Manufacture and retail of blinds and curtains through shop premises. Established: 1973 - Franchising Since: 1975 - No. of Units: Franchised: 75 - Franchise Fee: £6,000 shop based - Total Inv: £40,000 shop based (incl. £7,000 w.c.) - Financing: 70% through all major banks.

AT COMPUTER WORLD
Computer World House, 43 Calthorpe Rd., Edgbaston, Birmingham, England, . Contact: Mr. Carvin, Appoint. Dir. - Tel: 021-455-8484. Sale of microcomputers and supplies. Established: 1984 - No. of Units: Company Owned: 1 - Franchised: 20 - Approx. Inv: £30,000 - £100,000 per store - Royalty: 2% adv. - Financing: yes.

BABYBOTTE BEVERLY
Bidegain SA
Avenue Montardon, Pau, 64000 Cedex, France, . Contact: Jean-Jacques Schott - Tel: (59) 32-01-25. Children's shoes. Established: 1980 - Franchising Since: 1982 - No. of Units: Company Owned: 4 - Franchised: 15 - Approx. Inv: 700,000 FF - Royalty: 2%.

BERGER DU NORD
Laines Berger du Nord S.A.
50, rue de l'Epideme, Tourcoing, 59200, France, . Contact: Francois Maestripieri - Tel: 20-26-92-29. Yarn shop. Established: 1925 - No. of Units: Company Owned: 1 - Franchised: 184 - Approx. Inv: 600,000 FF - Financing: 300,000 FF.

BIZARRE *
Bizarre Ind. e Com. de Roupas Ltda.
Estrada do Campo Limpo, 3464, Sao Paulo, SP, Brazil, 05744.000. Contact: Rufino, Bus. Dir. - Tel: 55.011.511.6162. Bizarre is a youth wear company. Rt products jeans, t-shirts, jackets, shirts, dresses and etc. It's a casual clothing company. Established: 1988 - Franchising Since: 1990 - No. of Units: Company Owned: 11 - Franchised: 4 - Franchise Fee: US$15,000 - Royalty: 2%, 3% publicity - Total Inv: US$60,000 - Financing: US$15,000.

BOB'S TILE CENTERS
Unit 48, Shand Kydd Ind. Estate, Somerford Rd., Christchurch, Dorset, England, . Contact: L.Platt , Dir. - Tel: 0202-474222 . Retail tiles and ancillary lines. Established: 1970 - Franchising Since: 1983 - No. of Units: Company Owned: 15 - Franchised: 2 - Approx. Inv: £15,000 - Royalty: 10%.

BRICO
New G.I.B., S.A
Chee De Charleroi 239, (1060) Brussels, Belgium, . Contact: H. J. Ruys, Dev. Mgr. - Tel: (02) 536 57 71. One stop shopping D.I.Y. centers for home improvement, home beautification and gardening with specialized assortments and customer services. Established: 1973 - Franchising Since: 1978 - No. of Units: Company Owned: 47 - Franchised: 61 - Franchise Fee: 450,000 BF - Royalty: 6.60% on turnover - Financing: 5,000,000 BF.

BUMPSADAISY MATERNITY STYLE
Bumpsadaisy Ltd.
1606 High St., Knowle, Solihull, W. Midlands, England, B93 0JU. Contact: Diana Ellis, Dir. - Tel: 0564-775438. Retail outlets for maternity wear and/or hire outlets based at home. Established: 1982 - Franchising Since: 1984 - No. of Units: Retail Outlets: 3 - Franchised: 1 retail, 12 home-based - Franchise Fee: Retail £2,000 - Home-based £500 - Royalty: Retail 5% turnover, Home-based £50/month - Total Inv: Retail-dependent on rent etc., Home-based £500 fee, £3,000 45 garments, £500 local adv. - Financing: No.

CAPT'N SNOOZE PTY LTD.
Capt'n Snooze Pty. Ltd.
21A Shierlaw Ave., Canterbury, Victoria, Australia, 3126. Contact: Ray King, Mng. Dir. - Tel: (03) 830 4166. Specialty bedding stores. Established: 1974 - Franchising Since: 1976 - No. of Units: Franchised: 85 - Franchise Fee: $50,000 - Royalty: 4% adv. fee, 3.5% mng. fee - Total Inv: Minimum $175,000 - $200,000 - Financing: No.

CAROLL
Caroll International
30 Rue de Calebrai, Paris, France, 75019. Contact: Henri Foare, Directeur Commercial - Tel: (33-1) 53 26 53 26, Fax: (33-1) 53 26 53 00. Women's apparel. Caroll stores sell goods belonging to Caroll International, and get a commission on the basis of the turnover. Deliveries of new styles every week. Target = active women aged 30-40 looking for the best value of their money and style. Established: 1963 - Franchising Since: 1980 - No. of Units: Company Owned: 100 - Franchised: 90 - Franchise Fee: FF 50,000 - Total Inv: FF 400,000/80 sq. meters.

CASH CONVERTERS
15-17 Gentlemens Field Westmill Rd, Ware, Herts., England, SG12 0EF. Contact: Marie Hare, Mng. Dir. - Tel: 0920 485696. Pawnbrokers/ retailers of high quality secondhand goods in an upmarket high profile, sophisticated environment. Established: 1991 - Franchising Since: 1992 - No. of Units: Company Owned: 3 - Franchised: 28 - Franchise Fee: £25,000 - Royalty: fixed fee £250/wk. - Total Inv: £80,000 - Financing: Partial.

CATIMINI
94 Rue Choletaise, BP 67, Saint Macaire-en-Mauges, France, 49450. Contact: Catherine Rochais, Fran. Dir. - Tel: 41.55.33.55. Children's clothing and accessories. (0 - 12 yrs). Established: 1972 - Franchising Since: 1982 - No. of Units: Company Owned: 22 - Franchised: 45 - Franchise Fee: 65,000 F - Total Inv: 550,000 F - Royalty: 3% C.A. H.T. (1.5% for training, 1.5% for adv. - Financing: 50% of total inv.

CHRISTIAENSEN
GB-Immo-BM
B.P. 999, 1000 Bruxelles, Brabant, Belgium, . Contact: Foret Marcel - Tel: (02) 582-29-17. Toys and games. Established: 1982 - No. of Units: Company Owned: 73 - Franchised: 62 - Franchise Fee: $200,000.

CINERENT BENELUX
Schiestraat 38, Noordwijk, Zuid, The Netherlands, 2201AS. Contact: Mr. N. Broersen, Dir. - Tel: (01719) 56222. Rent videos. Established: 1987 - Franchising Since: 1987 - No. of Units: Company Owned: 2 - Franchised: 80 - Franchise Fee: 3%.

CLARKS SHOP, THE
C&J Clark Ltd.
40 High St., Street, Somerset, England, BA16 0YA. Contact: Paul Monaghan, Fran. Mktg Mgr. - Tel: 01458-43131. Retailing of branded footwear for men, women, and children. Established: 1825 - Franchising Since: 1984 - No. of Units: Company Owned: 400+ - Franchised: 125 - Franchise Fee: £7,500 - Royalty: management services charge approx. 1% of turnover - Total Inv: fixtures-fittings £45,000; stock £45,000; w.cap./fees £20,000 - Financing: Yes, guaranteed loan scheme through major bank. U.K. availability only at present.

COLCCI *
Colcci Ind. e Com. do Vestuario Ltda.
Av. Otto Renaux, 377, Brusque, SC, Brasil, 88350-000. Contact: Ricardo Habitzreuter, Supervisor - Tel: (0055) 47 351-3399, Fax: 47 355-0668. Manufaction and commercialization of "Fashion & Sportswear" clothing (also accessories) for both sexes on the adult and childish segments. Established: 1986 - Franchising Since: 1989 - No. of Units: Company Owned: 4 - Franchised: 206 - Franchise Fee: R$ 20,000 - Total Inv: R$70,000 (fran. fee plus R$20,000 standard furniture, R$30,000 initial clothing stock) - Financing: No.

COLLECTION 5
Mercatigue et Distribution
58110, Brinay, France, . Contact: Michel Rady - Tel: 16 (86) 84 91 00. Haberdasher's shop. Established: 1970 - Franchising Since: 1975 - No. of Units: Company Owned: 20 - Franchised: 30 - Approx. Inv: 250,000 FF.

COMPUTER KINETICS
P & G Enterprises Ltd.
15 Warwich Dr., Greenham, Newbury, England, RG14 7TT. Contact: F.M. Smith, Mng. Dir. - Tel: 0823-358611. Specializes in F.M.S. electronics. Established: 1983 - No. of Units: 1 - Approx. Inv: £13,500 - Royalty: 10% - Financing: To suitable locations.

COUNTER INTELLIGENCE
7/170 Forster Rd., Mount Waverley, Victoria, Australia, . Contact: Franchise Director - Tel: (03) 543-2822. Specialists in computer aided retailing.

COVINET WIJN & DRANKENGROEP
Covin B.V.
Branderijstraat 1, 's-Hertogenbosch, Noord Brabant, The Netherlands, 5201 AK. Contact: H.F.A. Vugs, Dir. - Tel: (073) 217445. Established: 1973 - Franchising Since: 1982 - No. of Units: Company Owned: 32 - Franchised: 22 - Franchise Fee: 1.5% - Royalty: n.v.t.

CREATE-A-BOOK
Diss Business Centre, Diss, Norfolk, U.K., IP21 4EY. Contact: J. Hutton-Williams, Owner - Tel: 0379 641444. Personalized books, pictures, cards etc. Made in a few minutes using our software, computer & laser printer. Established: 1989 - Franchising Since: 1980 U.S. - No. of Units: Company Owned: 1 - Franchised: 50 - Franchise Fee: from £995 - Total Inv: from £2,500 - Financing: No.

DISMARINA *
Cia - Vidraria Santa Marina
DPD, Ave. Santa Marina U 482, Sao Paulo, SP, Brazil, 05036903. Contact: Thierry Jean, Franchise & Commercial Mgr. - Tel: 55 11 874 79 54, Fax: 55 11 86q 17 20. Wholesale/distribution of warehouse products in retail shops. Technology is informatics/force sale administration/logistic. Established: 1987 - Franchising Since: 1987 - No. of Units: Franchised: 90 - Royalty: 10% - Total Inv: $10,000 US - Financing: None.

DOGSBODY & CAT TAILS
17 High St., Staple Hill, Bristol, England, BS16 5HA. Contact: Shirley Britton - Tel: 0272 560672. High Street retail and/or pet grooming stores. Retail stores sell wide range of pet accessories and pet foods - leading brands and own brand natural foods. Our products are tested on humans for animals. Established: 1989 - Franchising Since: 1993 - No. of Units: Company Owned: 3 - Franchised: 1 - Franchise Fee: £10,000 + VAT - Royalty: 10% from gross sales (6% mgmt. fee, 2% local adv., 2% nat'l. adv.) - Total Inv: from £25,000 - £35,000, incl. fran. fee, stock, shopfitting, signage, etc. - Financing: Subject to status, 50% banks.

DORBER COLLECTION, THE *
110 Saltergate, Chesterfield, Derbyshire, England, S4) 1NE. Contact: Jim Scott, Fran. Mgr. - Tel: 1246 551755. Greeting cards and add-on products supplied to retailers on sale or return. Full training, extensive product range, good returns. Established: 1990 - Franchising Since: 1994 - No. of Units: Company Owned: 1 - Franchised: 5 - Franchise Fee: £1,650 - Royalty: None - Total Inv: £8,500 - Financing: No.

DREAMS (PREMIER BED CENTRES)
Crusader House, Halifax Rd.,, High Wycombe, Bucks., England, HP12 3SD. Contact: Martin England, Oper. Dir. - Tel: (0494) 461146. Bed and sofa-bed retailer. Dreams is an easy to run, very profitable retail franchise, which sells all types of beds and sofa-beds. Two people can run a showroom, (2,000 sq. ft.). Market leaders with substantial group discounts and a proven successful franchise formula! Established: 1981 - Franchising Since: 1991 - No. of Units: Company Owned: 16 - Franchised: 2 - Franchise Fee: £8,000 - £15,000 - Royalty: 5% of turnover - Total Inv: £40,000 - £50,000 dependent on store & stock size.

DURHAM PINE
137 High St. W., Gateshead, Tyne & Wear, England, NE8 1EJ. Contact: Mr. D. Pitt, Chief Exec. - Tel: (0191) 4771402, Fax: (0191) 4775418. Retailers of pine furniture. Established: 1986 - Franchising Since: 1991 - No. of Units: Company Owned: 11 - Franchise Fee: £6,750 - Royalty: 5% of gross sales - Total Inv: £42,000 - Financing: Yes.

DYMOCKS BOOKSTORES *
428 George St., Sydney, Australia, 2000. Contact: Mr. P. Allen, Int'l. Dev. - Tel: (612) 224 0411. Bookstore retailing. Established: 1885 - Franchising Since: 1986 - No. of Units: Company Owned: 1 - Franchised: 74 - Franchise Fee: $37,500 min. dependant on store size - Royalty: 5% of gross sales - Total Inv: $400,000.

ELIO CECCHINI L'ART DE LA FROMAGERIE
57 bd de Souville, Carpentras, Vaucluse, France, 84200. Contact: Elio Cecchini - Tel: 1690 63 28 20. Retail cheese shop. Established: 1981 - Franchising Since: 1982 - No. of Units: Company Owned: 7 - Franchised: 4 - Franchise Fee: 50,000 FF - Total Inv: 200,000 - 400,000 F H.T. - Royalty: 2 - 1.5%.

FOCUS MICROSYSTEMS
Focus Office Equipment Ltd.
Sherlock House, Bayswater Farm Rd., Headington, Oxford, U.K., OX3 8BX. Contact: Mr. Duncan Samuel, Man. Dir. - Tel: (01865) 66241, Fax: (01865) 750937. Focus are a computer systems house providing full systems for specialist market sectors. Complete with their own software team. Established: 1981 - Franchising Since: 1993 - No. of Units: Company Owned: 1 - Franchised: 1 - Franchise Fee: £10,000 - Royalty: 10% of turnover - Total Inv: £10,000 - Financing: Yes.

GARDEN BUILDING CENTRES LTD.
Keilworth Rd., Hampton in Arden, Warks., U.K., . Contact: Ian Jackson, Sales Dir. - Tel: 0299-266361. Units sell a wide range of garden sheds, summerhouses, greenhouses and conservatories. No. of Units: Company Owned: 10 - Franchised: 2 - Approx. Inv: £24,000 depending on location.

GENEVIEVE LETHU
BP 22-5 Passage du Cotre-Le Gabut, F17002 La Rochelle, France, . Contact: Jean-Pierre Gousseau, Gen. Man. - Tel: 46.68.40.00. Franchising Since: 1972 - No. of Units: Company Owned: 5 - Franchised: 60 - Franchise Fee: 70,000 FF HT - Royalty: 5% Ht du CA HT.

GOLF GALORE
Golf Galore Ltd.
50 Walsworth Rd., Hitchin, Hertfordshire, England, SG4 9SU. Contact: Alyson Coyle - Tel: (0462) 435660. Golf retail. Established: 1989 - Franchising Since: 1989 - No. of Units: Company Owned: 2 - Franchised: 14 - Franchise Fee: £10,000 - Royalty: 7.5% - Total Inv: approx. £60,000 - Financing: Yes.

GRANNY MAY'S MANAGEMENT *
25-27 Waterloo St., Surry Hills, N.S.W., Australia, 2010. Contact: John Kurz, Gen. Mgr. - Tel: (02) 281-7978, Fax: (02) 281-9539. Retail sales of cards, gifts, licensed merchandise, stationery, wrapping paper, novelties, partyware, confectionary, apparel, prints, posters, and all goods sold as per the Granny May's concept or included in any Granny

May's catalogue. Established: 1980 - Franchising Since: 1983 - No. of Units: Company Owned: 8 - Franchised: 69 - Franchise Fee: $50,000 - Royalty: 5% - Total Inv: $200,000 - $250,000 approx. - Financing: Franchisees directed to various banks.

HAMILTONS
Hamiltons Confectioners Ltd.
Stanton Court, Stanton, Nr. Broadway, Worcs., England, WR12 7NE. Contact: Andrew Campbell, Chairman - Tel: (0386) 584551. Old fashioned sweet shops. Established: 1986 - Franchising Since: 1993 - No. of Units: Company Owned: 2 - Franchised: 1 - Franchise Fee: £5,000 - Total Inv: £28,000 - Financing: No.

HARRIET WEBSTER'S
Unit 8, Moor Lane Trading Est., Sherburn In Elmet, Leeds, England, LS25 6ES. Contact: T. Webster, Mng. Dir. - Tel: 0977-681141. Retail of quality toffee & fudge, manufactured & sold in traditional way. Established: 1991 - Franchising Since: 1991 - No. of Units: Company Owned: 8 - Franchised: 6 - Total Inv: £1,000 + £5,000 work. cap. - Financing: 50%.

HIGH LEVEL PHOTOGRAPHY
Mount Pleasant, Elm Corner Ockham, Guildford, Surrey, U.K., GU23 6PX. Contact: John Power, Bus. Dev. Mgr. - Tel: (0483) 222-666. Elevated video and photographic services. Established: 1983 - Franchising Since: 1989 - No. of Units: Company Owned: 3 - Franchised: 1.

HOUSE OF SOMETHING DIFFERENT
12/16 Church Hill, Loughton, England, . Contact: Ron Padwick, Fran. Dir. - Tel: 01-502-2286 or 01-502-0215. Fireplaces & grates. Also gas, coal and electric fires. Established: 1980 - Franchising Since: 1984 - No. of Units: Company Owned: 5 - Franchised: 3 - Approx. Inv: £40,000 - Royalty: 2.5% plus 2% adv. - Financing: yes.

HUGO BOSS
Hugo Boss Moda Ltda.
AV. Reboucas, 3995, Sao Paulo, Brazil, 05401. Contact: Willy H. Herrmann, General Mgr. - Tel: (011) 210-3200. Men's fashion. Established: 1988 - Franchising Since: 1988 - No. of Units: Franchised: 40 - Royalty: 21% - Total Inv: US$ 500,000 - Financing: No.

IN TOTO KITCHENS
Wakefield Rd., Gildersome, Morley, N. Leeds, England, LS27 7JZ. Contact: Malcolm Eccleston, Fran. Oper. Mgr. - Tel: 0532-524131. Retailing fitted kitchens. Established: 1980 - Franchising Since: 1980 - No. of Units: Company Owned: 1 - Franchised: 32 - Franchise Fee: £5,000 - Total Inv: approx. £35,000 - Financing: subject to status.

INFINITIF
26, rue du Caire, 75 002 Paris, France, . Contact: David Edmond, P.D.P. - Tel: 43-39-97-03. Ladies ready to wear garments. Established: 1970 - Franchising Since: 1970 - No. of Units: Company Owned: 19 - Franchised: 16 - Franchise Fee: 50.000 F - Royalty: 2% of sales - Total Inv: 8,000 F - Financing: No.

INSPORT
Sportsforum UK, Ltd.
Hemel Hempstead Ski Centre, St. Albans Hill, Hemel Hempstead, Herts., U.K., HP3 9NH. Contact: Alan Deeprose, Fran. Dir. - Tel: (0442) 241321. General sports retailing of equipment and clothing. Established: 1974 - Franchising Since: 1988 - No. of Units: Franchised: 7 - Franchise Fee: £6,000 - Royalty: 8% of turnover - Total Inv: £60,000 (£20,000 cap. required) - Financing: No.

JULIO *
Grupo Julio SA de CV
Calz. de Tlalpan 509-Col. Alamos, Mexico, DF, Mexico, 03400. Contact: Sabrina Bernardini, Fran. Mgr. - Tel: (525) 538-4291 Fax: (525) 538-2323. Women apparel and accessories stores. Established: 1975 - Franchising Since: 1992 - No. of Units: Company Owned: 19 - Franchised: 12 - Total Inv: $60,000 approx. store set up, $50,000 inven. - Financing: No.

K.A.S. *
2405, Brasilio Itibere, Curitiba, PR, Brazil, 80.230-050. Contact: Sergio Daitschman, Owner - Tel: 55.41.3220661, Fax: 55.41.2232590. Fitness and dance wear. Established: 1981 - Franchising Since: 1991 - No. of Units: Company Owned: 8 - Franchised: 4 - Franchise Fee: US$10,000 - Royalty: 10% - Total Inv: US$50,000 - Financing: No.

KLEINS *
Kleins Franchising Pty. Ltd.
1 Abbotts Rd., Dandenong, Victoria, Australia, 3175. Contact: Greg Campbell, Mng. Dir. - Tel: (03) 706 4966. Fashion accessory retailer specializing in fashion jewellery. Established: 1982 - Franchising Since: 1990 - No. of Units: Company Owned: 34 - Franchised: 166 - Franchise Fee: On application - Royalty: 15%, 5% adv. - Total Inv: Dependant on site - Financing: On application.

LEADERS HEALTH FOOD STORES
105 London Rd., Brighton, Sussex, England, BN1 4JG. Contact: Roy Harris, Fran. Dir. - Tel: (0273) 695001. Health food stores. Established: 1955 - Franchising Since: 1983 - No. of Units: Company Owned: 32 - Franchised: 4 - Franchise Fee: £4,000 - Total Inv: £20,000 - £40,000 including stock - Royalty: 4% net.

LPC - LIVROS PERSONALIZADOS PARA CRIANCAS *
J.E.J. Editora E. Comercio Ltda.
Rua Tatui, No. 94, Sao Paulo, SP, Brazil, 01409-010. Contact: Judy Schechtmann, Pres. - Tel: (011) 883-1582, Fax: (011) 883-1582. Personalized childrens books - with a computer and a laser printer we personalized the book with the name of the children in 5 minutes. Established: 1991 - Franchising Since: 1991 - No. of Units: Franchised: 25 - Franchise Fee: US$ 4,000 - Royalty: None - Total Inv: US$8,000.

MASTER THATCHERS LTD.
Rose Tree Farm, 29 Nine Mile Ride, Finchampstead, Berkshire, England, RG11 4QD. Contact: Mr. R West, M.D. - Tel: (0734) 734203. Roof thatching and retailing of thatched products. Established: 1974 - Franchising Since: 1982 - No. of Units: Franchised: 30 - Franchise Fee: £15,000 + VAT - Royalty: 10% on turnover - Total Inv: £15,000 + VAT - Financing: 2/3.

MIDLAND WATERLIFE FRANCHISING
154 High St., Bromsgrove, Worcestershire, England, BG1 8AR. Contact: R. Miles, Dir. - Tel: 0527-70676. Retail aquatic outlets located in garden centers and other selected outlets. Established: 1983 - Franchising Since: l983 - No. of Units: Company Owned: 3 - Franchised: l0 - Franchise Fee: £4,000 - Royalty: 2% adv. on net sales - Total Inv: fixture & fittings £20,000 - £25,000, stock £20,000 - Financing : Yes, help to finance.

MOSTLY MOVIES *
Mostly Movies Management Pty. Ltd.
41 Murriverie Rd., North Bondi, Sydney, NSW, Australia, 2026. Contact: Marsha Weinskin, Dir. - Tel: (02) 365-1256. The retail sale of video movies and movie memorabilia from all mostion picture studios including Disney, Warner, Paramount. Established: 1990 - Franchising Since: 1991 - No. of Units: Franchised: 12 - Franchise Fee: $30,000 - Royalty: 5%, 2% adv. - Total Inv: On 100 sm shop $90,000 fitout & $70,000 stock - Financing: As per bank requirements.

NATALY'S
18 Avenue du General Gallieni, Nanterre, France, 92007. Contact: Miss Clair, Exp. Man. - Tel: 47.25.24.74. Offer a wide range of products (furniture, clothes, toys) for children from 0 to 6 and the pregnant women through a channel of similar shops decorated to create a special Nataly's concept. Established: 1953 - Franchising Since: 1960 - Number of Units: Company Owned: 185 - Franchised: 165 - Total Inv: min. cash requirement.

NATURE'S WAY
10 Devonshire Rd., Bexhill, Sussex, England, . Contact: Derek Howell, Chairman - Tel: (04) 24-222125. Health food retail. Established: 1971 - Franchising Since: 1978 - No. of Units: Company Owned: 25 - Franchised: 18 - Franchise Fee: £13,000 plus stock of £8,000 - Total Inv: £21,000 - Royalty: goods must be purchased from franchisor - Financing: up to 33% via franchisor's bank.

NEVADA BOB
The Rotunda, Broadgate Circle, London, England, EC2M 2QS. Contact: Philip Smith, Fran. Dir. - Tel: 071 628 4999. Golf retailers. Established: 1989 - Franchising Since: 1990 - No. of Units: Company owned: 1 - Franchised: 15 - Franchise Fee: £25,000 - Royalty: 3.5% of gross turnover - Total Inv: £180,000 (£25,000 fran. fee, £35,000 lease improv. on premises, £120,000 of stock) - Financing: Links with 4 major banks.

OLIVER
H.C.B. Manufaturer De Roupas
Rua D. Mariano 225, Rio De Janeiro, Brazil, 22280. Contact: Marcelo Amarante, Franc. Dir. - Tel: (021) 2868422/2, Fax: 2269232. Fine sportsmen clothing. Established: 1979 - Franchising Since: 1981 - No. of Units: Company Owned: 8 - Franchised: 70 - Royalty: 3%, 3% adv. - Total Inv: (US) $35,000.

OSCAR PET FOOD *
Oscar Business, The
Bannister Hall Mill, Higher Walton, Preston, Lancs., England, PR5 4DB. Contact: Mark Frampton, Sales & Mktg. Dir. - Tel: 44 (0) 1772-626789. Pet food home delivery, direct from the manufacturer to your door, with free advice from Dr. Frape and Dr. Peter Neville and with products (Best) supported by Linda McCartney. Established: 1993 - Franchising Since: 1993 - No. of Units: Franchised: 100 - Franchise Fee: £5,950 ex. VAT - Royalty: Support fee £5 per week - Total Inv: £5,950 plus vehicle cost.

OXIGENIO *
Oxigenio Ind. Do Vest. Ltda
Rua Prof. Stroele, No 99, Petropolis, RJ, Brazil, 25680-170. Contact: Mr. Nelson, Fran. Mgr. - Tel: (55) 242 43 3376. Clothing and accessories for teenager, young people and children. More than 800 types of products. T-shirts, shorts, backpacks, wallets, tennis shoes, hats, jeans, bikinis, handbags, others. Established: 1964 - Franchising Since: 1988 - No. of Units: Company Owned: 4 - Franchised: 11 - Franchise Fee US$10,000 - Royalty: None - Total Inv: US$50,000 - Financing: Yes.

PETIT BOY
Desmazieres S.H.
Chemin des Coteaux, Nau, France, 64800. Contact: Bernard Boutin, Fran. Mgr. - Tel: 59.61.15.43. French ready-to-wear manufacturer with high quality products for the 0-14 year old child. Established: 1942 - Franchising Since: 1979 - No. of Units: Company Owned: 4 - Franchised: 36. Partners sought to introduce franchises to U.S.

PINE STORE, THE
Pine Plus Ltd.
Unit 1, Brockhampton Lane, Havant, Hants, England, PO9 1LU. Contact: Robin Sutherland, Mng. Dir. - Tel: (0705) 498018. Pine furniture specialists. Established: 1982 - Franchising Since: 1994 - No. of Units: Company Owned: 10 - Franchised: 4 - Franchise Fee: £12,500 - Royalty: 5% of sales - Total Inv: Up to £70,000 dependent on location (£40,000 stock) - Financing: Yes.

PRIMETIME VIDEO LTD.
Primetime Video Group Ltd.
Trafalga House, 5/7 High Lane, Chorlton, Manchester, England, M21 1DJ. Contact: M. Hulme, Dir. - Tel: 061-860-4853. Home entertainment centers, hiring, renting and selling videos, games, books, computers, confectionery. Established: 1982 - Franchising Since: 1991 - No. of Units: Company Owned: 36 - Franchised: 1 - Franchise Fee: £50,000 - £150,000 - Royalty: £10,000 legal fees & contract cost - Total Inv: £10,000 royalty, £30,000+ stock, £10,000 lease, £20,000 fittings - Financing: Yes.

PRONUPTIA YOUNGS
Cupio Plc.
Metcalf Dr., Altham, Accrington, Lancs., England, BB5 5TU. Contact: Robert Devlin, Mng. Dir. - Tel: 0282-772577. Bridal fashions including accessories = Pronuptia. Mens formal wear and hire service = Youngs. Established: 1948 - Franchising Since: 1978 - No. of Units: Company Owned: 40 - Franchised: 43.

RAMSEY GAS
Ramsey Gas Ltd.
Forth Street, Bootle, Merseyside, England, L20 8JW. Contact: Mr. M. Ramsey, Dir. - Tel: 051 922 6611. Liquified petroleum gas (L.P.G.) distributor (own label "Ramsey Gas") together with natural gas (mains) appliance sales through showrooms. Established: 1972 - Franchising Since: Pilot 1989, Full 1993 - No. of Units: Company Owned: 2 - Franchised: 3 - Franchise Fee: £7,000 incl. training, pounds sterling - Royalty: 7% mgmt. svc. fee, 1% adv. - Total Inv: Avg. £39,500: stock £13,500 + £7,000 setting up premises, £3,000 misc., £4,000 work. cap., £5,000 admin. & prom., plus fran. fee - Financing: Yes.

ROBIN HOOD GOLF CENTRE
Robin Hood Golf, PLC
200 Robin Hood Lane, Hall Green, Birmingham, England, B28 0LG. Contact: Paul Walton, Mng. Dir. - Tel: (021) 778-4161. Golf equipment retail sales. Established: 1978 - Franchising Since: 1985 - No. of Units: Company Owned: 2 - Franchised: 14 - Franchise Fee: £10,000 - Royalty: 3% of turnover (net) - Total Inv: £50,000 - Financing: Available thru Midland Bank.

ROCHE-BOBOIS
18, rue de Lyon, Paris, 75012, France, . Contact: J. E. Chouchan - Tel: 344-18-18. Furniture. Established: 1960 - Franchising Since: 1960 - No. of Units: 72 in France, 69 other.

ROSE BENEDETTI
Rose Benedetti Modas Ltda.
R. Padre Joao Manoel, 1055, Sao Paulo, Sao Paulo, Brazil, 01411. Contact: Luis Felipe Beneditti, Dir. - Tel: (011) 881 1744, Fax: 282 8005. Creates, produces and sells costume jewelry such as earrings, necklaces, rings, belts and bracelets. Known and admired by Brazilian men and women as a role model of success. Established: 1973 - Franchising Since: 1985 - No. of Units: Company Owned: 6 - Franchised: 5 - Franchise Fee: $30,000.00 - Royalty: 3%,5% adv. - Total Inv: $95,000.00

RUSPA - LEATHER GOODS DIV. *
Via C. Colombo, 2, Robassomero (TO), Italy, 10070. Contact: L. Ruspa, Mng. Dir. - Tel: (011) 9241066. Producer of leather goods. Worldwide license for Giueiaro Design, Pinineraina, Vinci brands. Established: 1948 - Franchising Since: 1993 - No. of Units: Company Owned: 1 - Franchised: 20 - Franchise Fee: US$100,000 - Royalty: 2% - Total Inv: US$60,000 per single shop - Financing: No.

RYMAN
Swallowfield Way,, Hayes, Mddx., England, UB3 1DQ. Contact: Chris Hurdle, Fran. Mgr. - Tel: 081-569-3000. Retail stationers. Established: 1893 - Franchising Since: 1986 - No. of Units: Company Owned: 87 - Franchised: 24 - Franchise Fee: £10,000 - Total Inv: £100,000 - Financing: No.

SCOOP-A-MARKET
Bonnington Rd. Lane, Edinburgh, Scotland, EH6 5PX. Contact: G. Gunn, Trading Dir. - Tel: (031) 555-0545. Bulk and natural food retailing. Established: 1975 - Franchising Since: 1987 - No. of Units: Company Owned: 1 - Franchised: 20 - Franchise Fee: £3,000 sterling - Royalty: nil - Total Inv: fittings $10,000, stock $5,000, others $10,000 - Financing: No.

SMOKES 'N' THINGS GIFT SHOPS
464 St. Kilda Rd., Melbourne, Victoria, Australia, 3004. Contact: Mark Beaconsfield - Tel: (03) 2677666. Retail gift shop and specialist tobacconists.

SNAP-ON-TOOLS LTD.
Dunham House, 85-99 Cross St., Sale, Cheshire, England, M33 1FU. Contact: M. Lancaster, Mng. Dir. - Tel: (061) 969-0126. Mobile sales of tools and equipment. Established: 1926 - Franchising Since: 1966 - No. of Units: 280 - Approx. Inv: £5,000.

SOLOMON CARPETS
31 Gouger St., Adelaide, S.A., Australia, 5000. Contact: Franchise Director - Tel: (08) 2316151. Specialists and retail in the carpet industry.

SPAR CONVENIENCE STORES
332 Clepington Rd., Dundee, Tayside, DD3 8SJ. Contact: Mr. Jim Carroll, Franchise Mgr. - Tel: 0382 818771. Retail convenience stores trading seven days a week, from 7AM - 10PM, selling alcohol, fresh foods, confectionery, soft drinks and groceries. Established: 1922 - Franchising Since: 1988 - No. of Units: Franchised: 21 - Franchise Fee: £2,000 - £5,000 + stock (approx. £20,000) - Royalty: 1.5% of gross weekly turnover - Total Inv: £25,000 - £30,000 - Financing: Yes.

STRAP-ON WRISTWEAR
1 Sharman Ave., St. Annes-on-Sea, Lancs., England, FY8 3AR. Contact: Mr. B.B. Sergeant, Sr. Partner - Tel: (0253) 726186. The sale and repair of watches and accessories such as batteries, straps, bracelets, etc. Sites are provided in major hypermarkets and shopping centres. Established: 1969 - Franchising Since: Aug. 1991 - No. of Units: Company Owned: 3 - Franchise Fee: £5,000 - Royalty: none - Total Inv: £15,000 - Financing: £10,000.

TALASSIO
Angmering House, Sea Lane, Angmering on Sea, W. Sussex, England, BN16 1NB. Contact: David F. Harris, M.D. - Tel: (0903) 782121. Retail sales and hire of ladies, gentlemen and children's wedding attire. Established: 1981 - Franchising Since: 1989 - No. of Units: Company Owned: 3 - Franchised: 6 - Franchise Fee: on application - Financing: Yes, full support 5 year forecast.

TEAM (AUDIO) LTD.
Haverscroft Industrial Estate, New Road, Attleborough, Norfolk, U.K., NR17 1YE. Contact: David Fossey, Mng. Dir. - Tel: (0953) 454544. Wholesale distribution of audio/video products to retail outlets by customized mobile showroom. Franchise operates from home. Established: 1978 - Franchising Since: 1983 - No. of Units: Company Owned: 3 - Franchised: 15 - Franchise Fee: £5,000 - Royalty: 3-5% - Total Inv: £30,000 - Financing: Yes, 2/3.

TIE RACK
Tie Rack PLC
Captial Interchange Way, Brentford, Middlesex, England, TW8 0EX. Contact: Andrew Potter, Fran. Mgr. - Tel: (01) 995-1344. Tie Rack is a specialist retailer of ties, scarves, wraps, belts and accessories for men and women. The company sells a vast range of quality merchandise at low prices through it's franchised network of distinctive shops. Established: 1981 - Franchising Since: 1982 - No. of Units: Company Owned: 20 UK, 95 Overseas - Franchised: 105 UK, 8 Overseas - Franchise Fee: £8,000 initial fee - Total Inv: From - £80,000 - Royalty: 8% - Financing: no.

TRAMLINES SPORTS LTD.
1 East St., Tonbridge, Kent, England, TN9 1HP. Contact: Duncan H. Robinson, Dir.. Sports shops. Established: 1983 - Franchising Since: 1985 - No. of Units: 1.

TRIPODE JARDILAND
26 eur de la Maison Rouge, Lognes, 77323 Marne la Vallee Cedex 2, France,. Contact: Daniel Metivet, Dir. - Tel: 60 05 81 63. Telex: 691 169. Franchise garden centers. Established: 1973 - Franchising Since: 1982 - No. of Units: Company Owned: 73 - Franchised: 41 - Royalty: 1.60% du CA - Total Inv: 4 Million FF.

TRUST PARTS LTD.
7 Groundwell Ind. Estate, Swindon, U.K, SN2 5AY. Contact: Robin Bourne, Mng. Dir. - Tel: (0793) - 723 749. Engineering workshop consumables and tools. Over 900 individual lines, sold from specially equipped Mercedes or Renault panel van. Established: 1979 - Franchising Since: 1986 - No. of Units: Company Owned: 65 - Franchised: 10 - Franchise Fee: £5,000 - Royalty: 5% up to max. £5,000 - Total Inv: approx. £20,000 - Financing: Yes.

TWIST
35 Kensington Church St., London, England, W8 4LL. Contact: D. Gilbert, Dir. - Tel: 071 938 3806. Innovative own label ladies fashion outlets. Complete clothing system which appeals to wide age/socio-economic groups due to its easy styles and simple styles. Perfect for 90's women. Established: 1987 - Franchising Since: 1988 - No. of Units: Company Owned: 6 - Franchised: 1 - Franchise Fee: £10,000 - Total Inv: £40,000 - Financing: No.

VET, DIDI, YANK'S, SUPERSTAR
Coltex B.V.
2 Celsiusstraat, Heerhugowaard, The Netherlands, 1704 RW. Contact: J. Elzas, Gen. Mgr. - Tel: (31) 02207-51500. Vet: jeans and leisurewear, Didi: ladies fashions, Yank's: mens fashions. Superstar: ladies fashions. Established: 1903 - Franchising Since: 1975 - No. of Units: Company Owned: 126 - Franchised: 43.

VIDEOLAND
Videoland Nederland B.V.
Schiestraat 38, Noordwijk, Zuid, The Netherlands, 2200 AB. Contact: N.J.M. Broersen, Comm. Dir. - Tel: (1719) 56222. Rental of videos. Established: 1984 - Franchising Since: 1984 - No. of Units: Company Owned: 5 - Franchised: 150 - Franchise Fee: 5% turnover - Royalty: Hfl. 5.000,00 - Total Inv: Hfl. 250,000 - Financing: No.

WAND & BODEN
Budapester Str. 7-9, 1000 Berlin 30, Germany, . Contact: Theo Sindern, Managing Dir. - Tel: (030) 25 00 87 0. Retailers for wallpaper, fabrics, carpeting, painting, floor-covering. Established: 1968 - Franchising Since: 1972 - No. of Units: Company Owned: 16 - Franchised: 17 - Franchise Fee: 1,5 - 2.9% - Total Inv: 200-bis 500 TDM - Financing: no.

WEIDER
Greenroyd Mill, Sutton in Craven, KLY.BD20 7LW, England, . Contact: P.Sutton, Retail Div. Mgr. - Tel: (0535) 632294. Retailer of health & fitness equipment, clothing and other products. Franchising Since: 1985 - No. of Units: Company Owned: 5 - Franchised: 16 - Franchise Fee: £5000 + vat - Royalty: percentage of net sales - Total Inv: variable according to site.

INDEX

Symbols

$AVE-A-BUCK   2
1 HOUR DRYCLEANERS   227
1 HOUR PHOTO   137
1 HOUR SIGNS   240
1 HOUR SIGNS INC.   *240*
1 POTATO 2, INC.   69
1-DAY RESUME   23
1053311 ONTARIO INC.   *188*
122164 CANADA INC.   *210*
13-BELOW   154
14 KARAT PLUM, THE   *145*
149769 CANADA, INC.   *201*
165417 CANADA LTD.   *241*
1ST CALL   247
20/20 VIDEO   155
2001 FLAVORS OF AMERICA   65
2001 FLAVORS PLUS POTATOES   65
21ST CENTURY AUTOMOTIVE MARKETING   10
241 PIZZA LTD.   203
256 OPERATING ASSOCIATES   69
3 DAY BLINDS   127
4-SALE HOTLINE   141
465097 BC LTD.   *194*, *226*
494980 ONTARIO LTD.   *202*
500 SELECTION SERVICES INC., THE   196
6 TWELVE CONVENIENT MART   56
7-ELEVEN CONVENIENCE STORES   253
7-ELEVEN FOOD STORES   56
7-ELEVEN STORES PTY. LTD.   *253*
733719 ONTARIO LIMITED   207
907687 ONTARIO INC.   *239*
922928 ONTARIO INC.   *222*

A

A & M FOOD STORES, INC.   56
A & W FOOD SERVICES OF CANADA   204
A & W RESTAURANTS   69
A & W RESTAURANTS, INC.   *69*
A BUCK OR TWO STORES LTD.   232
A CHOICE NANNY   33
A CORPORATE A'FAIR, INC.   23
A DIVISION OF TANDY CORPORATION   238
A DREAM HOME FOR YOU CORP.   *144*
A F L DEESON PARTNERSHIP LTD., THE   259
À JAMAIS INC.   154
A MAX PIES CARPET CANADA INC.   *226*
A NOVEL IDEA BOOKSTORE   146
A PERFECT TOUCH   191
A PLUS SOFTWARE   237
A REAL NEW YORK BARGAIN   154
A REAL NEW YORK BARGAIN FRANCHISE CORP.   *154*
A SHADE BETTER, INC.   127
A WONDERFUL WEDDING   168
A WORLD OF DECORATING   127
A+ FINANCIAL SERVICES LTD.   *176*
A-1 EMPLOYMENT SERVICES   50
A-1 WINDOW CLEANING   37
A-1 WINDOW RESIDENTIAL & COMMERCIAL CLEANING   37
A-PRO SERVICES   32
A-PRO SERVICES INC.   *32*
A. OK ROAD SAFETY SYSTEMS LTD.   *240*
A.A.J.J. INVESTMENTS INC.   *201*
A.B. FRANCHISE CORP.   *69*
A.F. TECHNOLOGIES   10
A.I. AUTOMOTIVE CORP.   *12*
A.I.M.S.   249
A.I.M.S. PARTNERSHIP PLC.   *249*
A.I.N. LEASING CORP.   *6*
A.J. BARNES BICYCLE EXPRESS   146
A.N.P.E.   265
A.W. ASSOCIATES LTD.   *233*
AAA DYE AND CHEMICALS CO.   45
AAA FRANCHISE FINDERS   102

AAA VENDING   23
AACTIVE PERSONNEL SERVICES LTD.   196
AALL TECH TRANSMISSION SYSTEMS, INC.   *183*
AALL-TECH TRANSMISSION   183
AAMCO TRANSMISSIONS   16
AAMCO TRANSMISSIONS, INC.   *16*
AARON'S RENTAL PURCHASE   144
AB BROKERS   *141*
ABBEY CARPET CO.   146
ABBOTT'S FROZEN CUSTARD, INC.   65
ABBY'S PIZZA INNS   69
ABC FAMILY RESTAURANTS   204
ABC PHONETIC READING SCHOOL INC.   158
ABC SEAMLESS, INC.   17
ABC SEAMLESS, INC.   *17*
ABERDEEN BARNS   69
ABOFF'S   127
ABRA AUTO BODY & GLASS   10
ABRAHAM, PRESSMAN & BAUER, PC   112
ABX - ASSOCIATES BUSINESS XCHANGE   102
ACADEMY FOR MATHEMATICS   238
ACADEMY FOR MATHEMATICS & SCIENCE, INC.   *238*
ACADEMY OF LEARNING   158, 239
ACC SOLUTIONS, INC.   *121*
ACC-U-TUNE & BRAKE   7
ACCASTILLAGE DIFFUSION   261
ACCENT HAIR SALON   118
ACCENT HAIR SALONS, INC.   *118*
ACCESSORIES FOR HER   146
ACCOMMODEX FRANCHISE MANAGEMENT, INC.   *229*
ACCOUNTABILITIES ACCOUNTING AND TAX SERVICE   *1*
ACCOUNTANT'S CHOICE   *1*
ACCOUNTANTS INC.   50
ACCOUNTANTS INC. SERVICES   *50*
ACCOUNTING & CONSULTING SERVICES OF CANADA INC.   214
ACCOUNTING CENTRE,THE   249
ACCTCORP INTERNATIONAL   23
ACCU-SPEED MARINE PRODUCTS CORPORATION   193
ACCURATE LEGAL OPINIONS   112
ACE HARDWARE, ACE HARDWARE HOME CENTER   146
ACHILLE DE LA CHEVROTIERE LTEE.   197
ACN FRANCHISE SYSTEMS, INC.   *33*
ACOUSTIC CLEAN   38
ACTION PARALEGAL   243
ACTION SPORTS PHOTOS   137
ACTION-THE STUDENT WINDOW CLEANING TEAM   191
ACTIVE TIRE & AUTO CENTRES, INC.   *180*
ACTUA-SA   270
ACTUAL REALITY INTERNATIONAL, INC.   243
AD COM EXPRESS   168
AD-COMM INTERNATIONAL   *4*
ADD-ITT FRANCHISING LTD.   245
ADDRA MEDICAL, INC.   *121*
ADIA PERSONNEL SERVICES   50
ADIA SERVICES, INC.   *50*
ADMIRAL OF THE FLEET CRUISE CENTERS   165
ADSF INC.   *17*
ADVANCED COATING, INC.   *193*
ADVANCED FRANCHISING WORLDWIDE   102
ADVANCED SALES AND MANAGEMENT COURSES   23
ADVANCED SALES TRAINING CORP.   *23*
ADVANTAGE PAYROLL SERVICE   *1*
ADVANTAGE RADON CONTROL CENTERS   141
ADVENTURENT, INC.   *163*
ADVENTURES IN ADVERTISING   23
ADVENTURES IN ADVERTISING FRANCHISE, INC.   *23*
ADVERTISING SOLUTION   2
AERO-COLOURS, INC.   *10*
AERO-COLOURS® FRANCHISES   10
AF&G SUPPLY INC.   *153*
AFFORDABLE CAR RENTAL   6
AFFORDABLE LUXURY HOMES, INC.   17
AFTCO ASSOCIATES   121
AFTCO ASSOCIATES, LTD.   *121*
AFTER THE GOLD RUSH, INC.   55
AFTERMARKET APPEARANCE INDUSTRIES INC.   *10*
AFTON FOOD GROUP, INC.   *201*
AG FOODS   197
AG-MART   168
AG-MART, INC.   *168*

A'GACI 154
AGI SOFTWARE 43
AGNEW, AGGIES 236
AGNEW GROUP INC. 236
AGOSTPOLAR, LTD. 253
AGWAY, INC. 146
AHH-SOME GOURMET COFFEE INC. 60
AHRENS CHIMNEY TECH., INC. 17
AID AUTO STORES, INC. 10
AIM MAIL CENTERS 23
AIR BOINGO INC. 162
AIR BROOK LIMOUSINE, INC. 6
AIRBORNE FOR MEN 155
AIRBORNE FOR MEN LTD. 155
AIRCHEK 10
AIRE SERV CORPORATION 17
AIRE SERV HEATING & AIR CONDITIONING 17
AIRE-MASTER OF AMERICA 38
AIRE-MASTER OF AMERICA, INC. 38
AIRKEM DISASTER SERVICES 191
AIT FREIGHT SYSTEMS, INC. 169
AJ TEXAS HOTS 69
AJ TEXAS HOTS FAST FOOD FRANCHISE 69
AJUST-A-TRACK LTD. 183
AL-VIN PRODUCTS LTD. 191
AL-VIN SIDING CLEANERS 191
ALBERTON NATURAL RESOURCES INC. 223
ALBERT'S FAMILY RESTAURANT 204
ALBERT'S FRANCHISE INC. 204
ALBIE FOX PERSONALIZED EMBROIDERY 270
ALEXANDER & ALEXANDER OF MINNESOTA, INC. 102
ALEXANDER INTERNATIONAL 261
ALFAL CONSULTANTS SA 249
ALFONSO'S 254
ALGONQUIN TRAVEL 242
ALIMENTATION A.D.L. ENR. 198
ALIMENTATION COUCHE TARD 197
ALL AMERICAN FROZEN YOGURT AND ICE CREAM SHOPS 65
ALL AMERICAN FROZEN YOGURT CO., INC., THE 65
ALL AMERICAN SHADE CARE SYSTEM 191
ALL AMERICAN SIGNS SHOPS INC. 160
ALL CANADA PIZZA SHOWS 205
ALL MY MUFFINS 60
ALL STAR TRAVEL B.V. 266
ALL TUNE AND LUBE 7
ALL-GOLD OF SWITZERLAND 261
ALL-V'S SUBMARINE SANDWICH SHOPPES 69
ALLAN & PARTNERS 51
ALLAN COHEN & ASSOC., INC. 102
ALLEN'S FLOWERS & PLANTS 131
ALLEN'S FLOWERS, INC. 131
ALLENTOWN VINYL INC. 43
ALLERCLEAN INC. 19
ALLIANCE SECURITY SYSTEMS, INC. 186
ALLIED BROKERS 141
ALLSTAR DISTRIBUTING INC. 193
ALLSTAR RENT-A-CAR 6
ALMOST HEAVEN, LTD. 146
ALOE SHOPPE 43
ALOETTE COSMETICS, INC. 118
ALPHA LASER CARTRIDGE INC. 24
ALPHABETLAND 33
ALPHAGRAPHICS, INC. 139
ALPHAGRAPHICS® PRINTSHOPS OF THE FUTURE 139
ALPINE DRIVING SCHOOL LTD. 239
ALPINE SOFT DRINKS (UK) LTD. 254
AL'S BAR-B-QUE INC. 69
AL'S DINER 69
AL'S DINER INC. 69
AL'S DIVE SHOP, INC. 241
AL'S DIVEMASTER SERVICES 241
AL'S FORMAL WEAR 144
AL'S FORMAL WEAR, INC. 144
AL'S POTTERY, CHINA & SILVER 146
AL'S POTTERY FRANCHISE SYSTEMS 146
ALTA MERE WINDOW TINTING & AUTO ALARMS 10
ALTAMAR GROUP LTD. 102
ALTERNATIVE MEDIA GROUP 3, 5
ALTERNATIVE VIRTUAL MALL 169
ALTRACOLOR SYSTEMS 10

ALWAYS OPEN 56
ALWAYS OPEN FRANCHISE CORP. 56
AMACADE AMUSEMENT & ENTERTAINMENT CENTERS 55
AMAILCENTER FRANCHISE CORPORATION 23
AMALISA SERVICES 24
AMATEUR BOWLERS TOUR 162
AMATEUR BOWLERS TOUR, INC. 162
AMAVEND VENDING SYSTEMS 43
AMBIC BUILDING INSPECTION CONSULTANTS 17
AMC SERVICE MANAGEMENT, CO. 24
AMC SERVICE MANAGEMENT INTERNATIONAL, LLC 24
AMECI IN & OUT, INC. 69
AMECI PIZZA AND PASTA 69
AMERACAR INSTRUMENTS CANADA 193
AMERACAR PLATING INT'L. 193
AMERASIA GROUP, INC. 43
AMERICA ONE 24
AMERICA ONE INC. 24
AMERICAN AIR CARE, INC. 38
AMERICAN BRAKE SERVICE 10
AMERICAN BROKERS NETWORK, INC. 141
AMERICAN BUSINESS GROUP, INC. 102
AMERICAN CONCRETE RAISING INC. 17
AMERICAN DARTERS ASSOCIATION, INC. 55
AMERICAN DARTERS ASSOCIATION, INC. 162
AMERICAN DECK & SUNROOM COMPANY 17
AMERICAN ENTERPRISES, INC. 32
AMERICAN ENTERPRISES INC. 33
AMERICAN EXTERIOR CLEANING CORP. 38
AMERICAN FAST PHOTO & CAMERA 137
AMERICAN FASTSIGNS, INC. 160
AMERICAN FLUID TECHNOLOGY™ AFT™ MOBILE ON-SITE FLUID 10
AMERICAN FOOD LINES, INC. 62
AMERICAN FRANCHISEE ASSOCIATION 102
AMERICAN GRAFFITI 38
AMERICAN HARDWARE SUPPLY CO. 145
AMERICAN HERITAGE SHUTTERS 146
AMERICAN HERITAGE SHUTTERS INC. 146
AMERICAN INSTITUTE OF SMALL BUSINESS 158
AMERICAN LEAD CONSULTANTS 169
AMERICAN LEAD CONSULTANTS, INC. 169
AMERICAN LEAK DETECTION 17
AMERICAN LENDERS SERVICE CO. 24
AMERICAN LINCOLN HOMES AMERLINK 17
AMERICAN MEDICAL WEIGHT ASSOCIATION 121
AMERICAN MOBILE SOUND 55
AMERICAN NAME-JEWELRY 43
AMERICAN NURSING CARE 121
AMERICAN PHYSICAL REHABILITATION NETWORK 121
AMERICAN POOLPLAYERS ASSOCIATION 162
AMERICAN RESTORATION SERVICES 38, 183
AMERICAN ROOF-BRITE 38
AMERICAN SECURITY FINANCE 169
AMERICAN SECURITY FINANCIAL CORP. 45
AMERICAN SIGN SHOPS 160
AMERICAN SINGING TELEGRAMS 117
AMERICAN SPEEDY PRINTING CENTERS 139
AMERICAN SPEEDY PRINTING CENTERS, INC. 139
AMERICAN TRANSMISSIONS 16
AMERICAN VENTURES GROUP 2
AMERICAN VIDEO INC. 155
AMERICAN VIDEO, INC. 157
AMERICAN VISION CENTERS, INC. 121
AMERICAN WHOLESALE FLORAL 131
AMERICAN WHOLESALE THERMOGRAPHERS, INC. 139
AMERICANDY 56
AMERICARE DENTAL CENTERS, U.S.A. 121
AMERICARE DENTAL SYSTEM 121
AMERICA'S CARPET GALLERY 127
AMERICA'S CHOICE® / CANADA'S CHOICE® 231
AMERICA'S CHOICE® CANADA'S CHOICE® 141
AMERICA'S DOCTORS OF OPTOMETRY 121
AMERICA'S FAVORITE CHICKEN CO. 75, 93
AMERICA'S STEAK EXPERTS, INC. 78, 88
AMERICINN INTERNATIONAL, INC. 133
AMERICINN MOTEL 133
AMERICOUNT BUSINESS CONSULTANTS, INC. 1
AMERICOUNTS 24
AMERICUTS FAMILY BARBER SHOP 118

AMERICUTS FRANCHISE SYSTEMS, INC.   *118*
AMERIDIAL INC., FRANCHISE SERVICES   *102*
AMERILOK CANADA   *183*
AMERISEAL, INC.   *17*
AMERISPEC CANADA INC.   *183*
AMERISPEC HOME INSPECTION SERVICE, INC.   *141*
AMERISPEC HOME INSPECTION SERVICES (CANADA)   *183*
AMERIVEND CORP.   *130*
AMI FRANCHISING INC.   *10*
AMI GEM METRO RICHELIEU SUPER CARNAVAL   *197*
AMI PIZZA WHOLESALE   *43*
AMIGO MOBILITY CENTER   *121*
AMM LICENSING INC.   *60*
AMMARK CORPORATION   *16*
AMPOL ROAD PANTRY   *254*
AMPOL ROAD PANTRY PTY LTD.   *254*
AMRON SCHOOL OF THE FINE ARTS   *158*
AMS FRANCHISE CORP.   *55*
AMT INC.   *63*
AMTRAK EXPRESS PARCELS LTD.   *249*
AMUSEMENT PRODUCTS, LLC   *162*
AMUSEMENT PRODUCTS LLC   *163*
ANAGO INTERNATIONAL, INC.   *38*
ANAGO INTERNATIONAL, INC., ANAGO OF DETROIT, INC.   *38*
ANC   *249*
ANDREW L. CHIN, C.A.   *214*
ANDREX CONSULTING SERVICES   *102*
ANDY'S OF AMERICA   *70*
ANDY'S RESTAURANT   *70*
ANGELICA UNIFORMS GROUP   *154*
ANGELO'S PIZZA, INC.   *70*
ANGILO'S PIZZA   *70*
ANICARE VETERINARY GROUP   *261*
ANNE L. KLEINDIENST   *112*
ANYTHING CYCLE, INC.   *241*
APARTMENT SEARCH   *144*
APARTMENT SEARCH INTERNATIONAL   *144*
APARTMENT SELECTOR   *145*
APC ALARMS LTD.   *270*
APOLLO COFFEE HOUSES, INC.   *199*
APOLLO DESPATCH   *249*
APOLLO DESPATCH PLC   *249*
APOLLO WINDOW BLINDS   *270*
APPARELMASTER, INC.   *129*
APPEARANCE RECONDITIONING CO.   *10*
APPLE AUTO GLASS LTD.   *180*
APPLE POLISHING SYSTEMS   *180*
APPLE POLISHING SYSTEMS CANADA INC.   *180*
APPLE SIDRA COSCO FLAVORS   *17*
APPLEBEE'S INTERNATIONAL, INC.   *70*
APPLEBEE'S NEIGHBORHOOD GRILL & BAR/RIO BRAVO CANTI   *70*
APPLEWOODS INTERNATIONAL, LTD.   *267*
APRAT MART   *56*
APRN, INC.   *121*
AQUAPURA CORPORATION, THE   *43*
ARABICA CAFES INC.   *70*
ARBY'S CANADA, INC.   *204*
ARBY'S, INC.   *70*
ARBY'S ROAST BEEF RESTAURANT   *204*
ARBY'S ROAST BEEF RESTAURANTS   *254*
ARBY'S U.K. LTD.   *254*
ARCHADECK   *18*
ARCTIC CIRCLE RESTAURANTS, INC.   *70*
ARCTIC COOPERATIVE   *230*
AREA TENT HIRE   *261*
ARENA MEATS   *197*
ARENDORFF & PARTNERS   *259*
ARMAND'S CHICAGO PIZZERIA; ARMAND'S PIZZA EXPRESS   *70*
ARMAND'S RESTAURANT FRANCHISING   *70*
ARMOLOY CORP., THE   *169*
ARMSTRONG PRINTING LTD.   *231*
ARMSTRONG, TEASDALE, SCHLAFLY & DAVIS   *112*
ARMSTRONG WORLD INDUSTRIES   *18*
ARNI'S FRANCHISING INC.   *70*
ARNI'S INC.   *70*
ARNOLD COHEN   *112*
ARODAL INTERNATIONAL INC.   *191*
ARODAL SERVICES   *191*
AROPI INC.   *152*

ARRIBA FRANCHISE MARKETING, INC.   *102*
ART AVENUE   *137*
ART SOURCE AND DESIGN   *127*
ARTECH WINDOW TINTING & AUTO SECURITY   *169*
ARTEK, INC.   *108*
ARTHUR ANDERSEN & CO.   *102*
ARTHUR RUTENBERG HOMES, INC.   *141*
ARTHUR TREACHERS FISH & CHIPS   *204*
ARTHUR TREACHER'S FISH & CHIPS   *70*
ARTHUR TREACHER'S, INC.   *70*
ARTISTIC HORIZONS, INC.   *2*
ASC NETWORK, PLC   *249*
ASEN VITKO ASSOCIATES ARCHITECT   *214*
ASGAT AGENCY, INC.   *103*
ASHBY'S   *261*
ASHLEY AVERY'S COLLECTABLES   *146*
ASI - ACADEMIC SYSTEMS INC.   *191*
ASI SIGN SYSTEMS, INC.   *160*
ASSET ONE   *24*
ASSOCIATED BABY IMPRESSIONS LTD.   *190*
ASSOCIATED CANADIAN CAR RENTAL OPERATORS (A.C.C.R.O   *178*
ASSOCIATED GROCERS (DIV. OF THE OVERWAITEA FOOD GRO   *197*
ASSOCIATION CANADIENNE DE LA FRANCHISE   *214*
ASSOCIATION FOR APPLIED HYPNOSIS, THE   *268*
ASTRO-PURE WATER PURIFIERS   *167*
ASUKA CORPORATION   *43*
AT COMPUTER WORLD   *270*
ATEC GRAND SLAM U.S.A.   *163*
ATHENA   *230*
ATHENA INTERNATIONAL CANADA LTD.   *230*
ATHENA/ALEXANDER LANGUAGE INSTITUTE   *261*
ATHENEUM LEARNING CORP. OF AMERICA   *158*
ATHLETE'S FOOT GROUP INC., THE   *154*
ATHLETE'S FOOT, THE   *154*
ATHLETIC ATTIC MARKETING, INC.   *154*
ATHLETIC ATTIC MARKETING, INC.   *154*
ATHLETIC LADY   *154*
ATL INTERNATIONAL, INC.   *7*
ATLANTIC & PACIFIC HOLDINGS LTD.   *214*
ATLANTIC MOWER PARTS & SUPPLIES, INC.   *146*
ATLANTIC WHOLESALERS LTD.   *199*
ATLAS TRANSMISSION   *16*
ATTIC LTD, THE   *127*
ATWORK   *51*
ATWORK PERSONNEL SERVICES   *51*
AU BON PAIN   *60*
AUBERGES DES GOUVERNEURS INC.   *229*
AUDIDCELL   *249*
AUGIES, INC.   *87*
AUNTIE ANNE'S HAND-ROLLED SOFT PRETZELS   *60*
AUNTIE ANNE'S INC.   *60*
AURELIO'S PIZZA, INC.   *70*
AUSTIN HARDWOODS   *146*
AUSTRALIAN CLOTHING & GIFT IMPORTS   *232*
AUTELA   *245*
AUTELA COMPONENTS LTD.   *245*
AUTHENTIC LOG HOMES CORP.   *44*
AUTHORS MAGAZINE & CAFE   *204*
AUTO 5   *245*
AUTO ACCENTS, INC.   *10*
AUTO AMERICA   *11*
AUTO APPEARANCE CENTRE   *180*
AUTO APPEARANCE CENTRE LTD.   *180*
AUTO ARTISTRY, INC.   *11*
AUTO ARTISTRY, INC.   *11*
AUTO COLORMATCH   *245*
AUTO DINER, INC.   *70*
AUTO DRIVEAWAY CO.   *169*
AUTO EXAM, INC.   *11*
AUTO LAB FRANCHISE MGT. CORP.   *7*
AUTO ONE GLASS & ACCESSORIES   *11*
AUTO SHOW MAGAZINE   *2*
AUTO VALET   *44*
AUTO-LAB DIAGNOSTIC & TUNE-UP CENTERS   *7*
AUTO-TEK LASALIGN LTD.   *246*
AUTOLIST   *11*
AUTOLIST CORPORATION   *11*
AUTOMAX   *180*

AUTOMOTIVE TECHNOLOGIES, INC. *153*
AUTOPREP LTD. *245*
AUTOPRO LTD. *245*
AUTOPRO REPAIR CENTRE *180*
AUTOSHEEN LIMITED *245*
AUTOSMART LIMITED *245*
AUTOSTOCK, INC. *180*
AUTOTECH FRANCHISE SYSTEMS, INC. *16*
AVANTI VENDING MACHINES *44*
AVIS CAR & TRUCK RENTAL *178*
AVIS RENT-A-CAR LTD. *245*
AVISCAR, INC. *178*
AWC COMMERCIAL WINDOW COVERINGS *129*
AWC COMMERCIAL WINDOW COVERINGS, INC. *129*
AXE HOUGHTON GROUP, INC. *192*

B

B-DRY SYSTEM *18*
B-DRY SYSTEM, INC. *18*
B.V. PARAGON, INC. *165*
BAB SYSTEMS, INC. *60*
BABBITT BASEBALL CAMPS *162*
BABBITT BASEBALL CAMPS, INC. *162*
BABCOCK & SCHMID ASSOCIATES, INC. *103*
BABY NEWS CHILDRENS STORES *33*
BABY TOWN INC. *33*
BABY-TENDA CORP. *33*
BABYBOTTE BEVERLY *270*
BABY'S AWAY *145*
BABY'S AWAY INTERNATIONAL, INC. *145*
BABY'S ROOM USA, INC. *37*
BAC FRANCHISING INC. *133*
BACK YARD BURGERS *70*
BACK YARD BURGERS, INC. *70*
BACKSTAGE PASS *236*
BACKSTAGE PASS FRANCHISING, INC. *236*
BADGE MAKER, LE BADGE *177*
BAG-A-SIGN INC. *193*
BAGEL BUILDERS (CANADA) INC. *199*
BAGEL BUILDERS FAMOUS OVEN FRESH BAGELS *60*
BAGEL CONNECTION, THE *70*
BAGEL FRANCHISE SYSTEMS, INC. *70*
BAGEL SHOPPE, INC., THE *71*
BAGEL STOP, THE *204*
BAGELS ARE FOREVER! *60*
BAGELS FRANCHISE INC. *202*
BAGELSMITH FRANCHISING COMPANY, INC. *71*
BAGELSMITH RESTAURANTS & FOOD STORES *71*
BAGS & SHOES *154*
BAHAMA BUCK'S FRANCHISE CORPORATION *65*
BAHAMA BUCK'S ORIGINAL SHAVED ICE COMPANY *65*
BAIN'S DELI *71*
BAIN'S DELI FRANCHISE ASSOCIATES *71*
BAKER'S DOZEN DONUTS *199*
BAKER'S DOZEN DONUTS CORPORATION *199*
BALDINOS GIANT JERSEY SUBS, INC. *71*
BALLOON BOUQUETS *117*
BALLOON BOUQUETS, INC. *117*
BALLOON EXPRESS CO., INC. *232*
BALLOON EXPRESS COMPANY *232*
BALLOON WRAP, INC. *169*
BALLOONS + BEARS *117*
BANANA FRITZ *254*
BANANAS *65*
BANK OF MONTREAL *214*
BANK OF NOVA SCOTIA *218*
BANNERS RESTAURANTS OF CANADA, LTD. *207*
BAR-MASTER INTERNATIONAL *44*
BARBECUES GALORE *146*
BARBEQUE COUNTRY FRANCHISING *71*
BARBEQUE COUNTRY JAMBOREE RESTAURANTS *71*
BARBERS, HAIRSTYLING FOR MEN & WOMEN, INC., THE *118*
BARBERS, HAIRSTYLING FOR MEN & WOMEN, INC., THE *118*
BARBIER & BARBIER *112*
BARBIZON INTERNATIONAL, INC. *158*
BARISTA BRAVA COFFEE *60*
BARTER EXCHANGE, INC. *24*
BARTER WORLD INC. *186*
BARTKO, TARRANT & MILLER *112*
BASEMENT DE-WATERING SYSTEMS, INC. *18*
BASEMENT DE-WATERING/SAFE-AIRE INC. *18*
BASKIN ROBBINS *203*
BASKIN-ROBBINS '31' ICE CREAM AND YOGURT *65*
BASSETT MANAGEMENT CO., INC. *71*
BASSETT'S ORIGINAL TURKEY *71*
BATES BURGERS, INC. *71*
BATH FITTER *18*
BATH FITTER FRANCHISING INC. *18*
BATH GENIE, INC. *170*
BATH SMITH, INC. *183*
BATH SMITH, THE *183*
BATH TRANSFORMATIONS LTD. *247*
BATH WIZARD, THE *247*
BATHCREST *18*
BATHCREST, INC. *18*
BATHTUB DOCTOR, LE DOCTEUR BAIGNOIRE *184*
BATTERIES PLUS - AMERICA'S BATTERY STORES *146*
BATTERYMAN BY CHLORIDE *245*
BAVARIAN WAX ART *137*
BCT (BUSINESS CARDS TOMORROW) *139*
BCX PRINTING *139*
BDL ENTERPRISES, INC. *169*
BE SOME BODY *121*
BEADWORKS *146*
BEADWORKS INTERNATIONAL, INC. *146*
BEALLOR & PARTNERS *219*
BEAUTY BY SPECTOR, INC. *44*
BEAVER LUMBER COMPANY LTD. *184*
BEAVER TAILS CANADA INC. *197*
BEAVER TAILS® *197*
BECK, VILLATA & CO., P.A. CERTIFIED PUBLIC ACCOUNTA *1*
BECK, VILLATA & CO., P.C. CERTIFIED PUBLIC ACCOUNTA *1*
BECKER MILK CO., LTD. *197*
BECKETT & STEINKAMP, ATTORNEYS AT LAW *112*
BEE-CLEAN *191*
BEE-CLEAN BUILDING MAINTENANCE, INC. *191*
BEEFSTEAK CHARLIE'S *71*
BEKA COIFFEUR'S *268*
BEKA INTERNATIONAL *268*
BELLINI JUVENILE DESIGNER FURNITURE *33*
BELLINI JUVENILE DESIGNER FURNITURE CORP. *33*
BEN & JERRY'S *65*
BEN & JERRY'S HOMEMADE, INC. *65*
BEN FRANKLIN CRAFTS *146*
BEN FRANKLIN STORES INC. *146*
BEN FRANKS *71*
BENCH AD *2*
BENCHMARK GROUP *103*
BENEFICIAL HEALTH & BEAUTY, INC. *121*
BENEFICIAL INTERNATIONAL *121*
BENIHANA, INC. *71*
BENIHANA OF TOKYO *71*
BENKIS ENTERPRISES LTD. *198*
BENNETT'S BAR-B-QUE *71*
BERGER DU NORD *270*
BERGSON'S ICE CREAM & FOOD SHOPS *71*
BERLITZ FRANCHISING CORP. *170*
BERLITZ INTERNATIONAL, INC. *170*
BEST BAGELS IN TOWN *60*
BEST CHOICE FALAFEL *204*
BEST INNS OF AMERICA *133*
BEST PERSONALIZED BOOKS, INC. *36*
BEST WESTERN *133*
BEST WESTERN INTERNATIONAL, INC. *133*
BESTSELLER RETAIL GROUP, INT'L. *151*
BESTSELLERS *232*
BETONEL LTEE. *226*
BETTER BACK STORE *122*
BETTER BIRTH FOUNDATION *122*
BETTER HOMES AND GARDENS REAL ESTATE *141*
BETTER HOMES REALTY *141*
BETTER HOMES REALTY, INC. *141*
BETWEEN ROUNDS BAGEL DELI & BAKERY *71*
BETWEEN ROUNDS FRANCHISE CORP. *71*
BEVCO INTERNATIONAL INC. *199*
BEVERLEY'S WHOLESALE BAKERS *199*
BEVERLY HILLS INTERNATIONAL, INC. *122*
BEVERLY HILLS WEIGHT LOSS CLINIC *122*

BEVERLY HILLS WEIGHT LOSS CLINIC   223
BEVERLY HILLS WEIGHT LOSS CLINICS OF CANADA INC.   223
BEVINCO   243
BEVINCO BAR SYSTEMS, LTD.   243
BEWLEY'S CAFES AND SHOPS   254
BEWLEY'S FRANCHISING LTD.   254
BICYCLE FRANCHISORS, INC.   146
BIDEGAIŃ SA   270
BIG APPLE BAGELS   60
BIG BOB'S USED CARPET SHOPS   146
BIG BOB'S USED CARPET SHOPS OF AMERICA, INC.   146
BIG BOY FAMILY RESTAURANTS   71
BIG CITY BAGELS   60
BIG ED'S HAMBURGER   71
BIG FRANK'S CHICAGO STYLE HOT DOGS   71
BIG MIKE'S FLAVORS UNLIMITED   44
BIG MIKE'S FROZEN DESSERT BLENDING MACHINE   44
BIG O TIRES   11
BIG O TIRES, INC.   11
BIG ORANGE, INC.   17
BIG SKY BREAD COMPANY   60
BIG TOWN HERO FRANCHISING INC.   71
BIG TOWN HERO SANDWICHES   71
BIGHORN SHEEPSKIN CO.   147
BIJOUTERIES L'ERUDIT INC.   235
BIKE LINE   162
BIKER'S DREAM SUPERSTORES   147
BILL'S SANDWICH SHOPS   71
BINGO BUGLE NEWSPAPER   2, 177
BINO'S FAMILY RESTAURANTS   204
BINO'S MANAGEMENT CORP.   204
BIO PED FOOT CARE CENTERS   225
BIOGIME SKIN CARE CENTERS   122
BIRDERS NATURE STORE   233
BIRDS OVER AMERICA   170
BISS, INC.   65
BIX FURNITURE STRIPPING   117
BIXBY'S BAGEL CO.   60
BIXBY'S FOOD SYSTEMS, INC.   60
BIZARRE   270
BIZARRE IND. E COM. DE ROUPAS LTDA.   270
BIZOU   233
BIZOU INTERNATIONAL INC.   233
BJ'S KOUNTRY KITCHEN   72
BLACK FILMMAKERS ASSOCIATION   55
BLACK MAGIC CHIMNEY SWEEPS, INT'L.   44
BLACK MAGIC PRESSURE WASHING   38
BLACKBERRY COTTAGE   147
BLACKSTONE DETECTIVE AGENCY   170
BLADERUNNER MOBILE SHARPENING SYSTEMS   170
BLAKE GROUP, INC., THE   103
BLANKHOUT (HOLLAND) CLAIRBOIS (FRANCE) BLANKHOLZ
  (G   247
BLANKHOUT NEDERLAND FRANCHISING BV   247
BLENZ COFFEE   199
BLENZ COFFEE LTD.   199
BLIMPIE INTERNATIONAL, INC.   72
BLIMPIE SUBS & SALADS   72
BLOMMER'S ICE CREAM/SAM'S SUBS/OLLIE'S OVENS   65
BLUE CHIP COOKIES   61
BLUE CHIP FRANCHISES CORP.   61
BLUE DIAMOND WINDOW CLEANING   191
BLUE DIAMOND WINDOW CLEANING LTD.   191
BLUE JUNCTION   236
BLUE MILL ENTERPRISES CORP.   63
BLUE NOTE INTERNATIONAL   55
BLUERISE LTD.   264
BOARDWALK FRANCHISE CORP.   56
BOARDWALK FRIES, INC.   72
BOARDWALK PEANUT SHOPPE, THE   56
BOBBY LAWN CARE / BOBBY PEST CONTROL   228
BOBBY LAWN, INC.   228
BOBBY RUBINO'S PLACE FOR RIBS   72
BOBBY RUBINO'S USA, INC.   72
BOB'S TILE CENTERS   270
BOCA BEAUTY CLUB   118
BOCA BEAUTY CLUB FRANCHISE, INC.   118
BODY & FACE PLACE, THE   268
BODY & SOUL, INC.   120
BODY REFORM   268

BODY SHOP INTERNATIONAL, PLC.,   268
BODY SHOP, THE   222, 268
BODY SHOP, THE   118
BODYCUES   122
BODYLOG INC.   122
BOJANGLES' FAMOUS CHICKEN 'N BISCUITS®   72
BOJANGLES' RESTAURANTS, INC.   72
BOMBAY PALACE RESTAURANTS   72
BOMBAY PALACE RESTAURANTS, INC.   71
BON APPETIT INTERNATIONAL GOURMET FOODS, INC.   56
BONANZA RESTAURANTS   72
BONJOUR BAGEL CAFE   61
BOOK BANK LTD.   233
BOOK RACK   147
BOOK RACK FRANCHISING CORP.   147
BOOK SHELF, THE   170
BOOK-KEEPING NETWORK, THE   249
BOOMERANG   155
BOOMERANG GAMEWARE   155
BORVIN BEVERAGE   17
BORVIN BEVERAGE FRANCHISE CORP.   17
BOSCO JEWELERS INC.   44
BOSTON BARTENDERS SCHOOL ASSOCIATES INC.   158
BOSTON BARTENDERS SCHOOL OF AMERICA   158
BOSTON BEANERY RESTAURANT & TAVERN   72
BOSTON BEANERY RESTAURANTS, INC.   72
BOSTON MARKET   72
BOSTON PIZZA   204
BOSTON PIZZA INTERNATIONAL INC.   204
BOTTOM LINE CONSULTANTS   103
BOULDER BLIMP COMPANY   2
BOURBON STREET CANDY CO.   57
BOVERIE INVESTMENTS, INC.   117
BOWINCAL INTERNATIONAL INC.   72
BOX BROS. CORP.   170
BOX LUNCH, INC.   72
BOXIES CAFE   72
BOY BLUE OF AMERICA, INC.   65
BOZ HOT DOGS   72
BRAKE CENTERS OF AMERICA   11
BRAKE SHOP, THE   11
BRAKE WORLD   11
BRAVO RESTAURANTS, INC.   77
BREAD & CHEESE CUPBOARD   57
BREAD BOX, THE   2
BREAD KING BAKERIES   199
BREAD ROLL COMPANY, THE   254
BREADEAUX PIZZA, INC.   72
BREADSMITH   61
BREADSOUL CAFE   61
BREADSOUL FRANCHISE, INC.   61
BREATHPATROL INC.   193
BRESLER'S ICE CREAM AND YOGURT SHOPS   65
BRESLER'S INDUSTRIES, INC.   65
BREWER & TURNBULL LTD.   261
BREWING EXPERIENCE, THE   183
BREWSTER'S COFFEE   61
BREWSTER'S COFFEE FRANCHISE COMPANY   61
BRICE GROUP, THE   72, 76
BRICK FIRE & SAFETY LTD.   186
BRICKELL & ASSOCIATES LTD.   241
BRICKKICKER HOME INSPECTION   141
BRICO   270
BRIDE'S DAY FRANCHISE CORP.   168
BRIDE'S DAY MAGAZINE   168
BRIDGEMAN'S RESTAURANTS, INC.   65
BRIDGEMAN'S, THE ORIGINAL ICE CREAM RESTAURANTS, BR   65
BRIEF ROTFARB WYNBERG CAPPE   176, 214
BRIGGS AND MORGAN, PROFESSIONAL ASSOCIATION   112
BRIGHT BEGINNINGS   2
BRILLIANT IDEAS!   24
BRILLIANT IDEAS! INC.   24
BRINKER INT'L.   75
BRIOCHE GOURMANDE   254
BRISKETS LTD.   204
BRITE SITE   38
BRITISH CREDIT RECOVERY CLUB   250
BROADBELT & FONTE MODEL CENTRE   239
BROADBELT & FONTE MODEL CENTRE, INC.   239
BROADWAY   72

BROADWAY PIZZA 72
BRODY'S YOGURT CO. 66
BROKER ONE SECURITIES CORP. 24, 28, 29
BROUGHTON & HARRELL CORP. 69
BROWN & STADFELD 112
BROWNING GROUP, THE 103
BROWN'S CHICKEN & PASTA 73
BROWN'S CHICKEN & PASTA, INC. 73
BROWNSTEIN & ZEIDMAN 112
BRUCE S. SCHAEFFER, ESQ. 113
BRUEGGER FRANCHISE CORP. 61
BRUEGGER'S BAGEL BAKERY 61
BRUSTERS ICE CREAM 66
BTI AMERICAS PARTNER GROUP 165
BUBBA'S BREAKAWAY 73
BUBBA'S BREAKAWAY FRANCHISE SYSTEMS INC. 73
BUCHANAN INGERSOLL, P.C. 113
BUCHWALD ASPER GALLAGHER HENTELEFF 219
BUCK-A-ROO DOLLAR STORES 233
BUCKET BRIGADE, INC. 38
BUCK'S PIZZA 73
BUD LIGHT DART LEAGUE 162
BUDDY'S BAR-B-Q, INC. 73
BUDGET BLINDS, INC. 127
BUDGET BRAKE & MUFFLER 180
BUDGET HOST INNS 133
BUDGET HOST INTERNATIONAL 133
BUDGET PEST CONTROL 170
BUDGET PRINTING CENTERS 139
BUDGET RENT A CAR CORPORATION 6
BUDGET RENT A CAR INT. INC. 245
BUDGET RENT A CAR OF CANADA LTD. 178
BUDGETEL INNS 133
BUF-A-TUB 247
BUFFALO PHIL'S 73
BUFFALO WILD WINGS & WECK 73
BUFFALO'S CAFE 73
BUFFALO'S FRANCHISE CONCEPTS INC. 73
BUILDING BLOCKS, INC. 34
BUILDING ENGENHARIA 261
BUILDING INSPECTION CONSULTANTS 17
BUILDING SERVICE AND MAINTENANCE 38
BULK BARN 197
BULL, HOUSSER & TUPPER 219
BULLETS 73
BULLETS CORP. OF AMERICA, INC. 73
BULLHIDE LINER 11
BULLHIDE LINER CORP. 11
BUMPA T BUMPA AUTOMART 245
BUMPER-TO-BUMPER 11
BUMPSADAISY LTD. 270
BUMPSADAISY MATERNITY STYLE 270
BUN KING BAKERIES 200
BUNDY & MORRILL, INC., P.S. 113
BUNDY AMERICAN CORP. 6
BUNING THE FLORIST 131
BUNS MASTER BAKERY 200
BUREAU OF CREDIT MANAGEMENT, THE 249
BURGER BROTHERS 204
BURGER HEAVEN 204
BURGER KING 204
BURGER KING CORPORATION 73
BURGER KING RESTAURANTS OF CANADA INC. 204
BURGER STAR 254
BURKE AND ASSOCIATES 44
BURNETT COMPANIES CONSOLIDATED 51
BURNETT PERSONNEL SERVICES 51
BURTSON CORPORATION 101
BUSCEMI'S INTERNATIONAL 73
BUSCEMI'S PIZZA & SUB SHOPPES 73
BUSINESS ADVERTISING SPECIALTIES CORP. (BASCO) 2
BUSINESS AID, INC. 196
BUSINESS AMERICA 103
BUSINESS AMERICA ASSOCIATES, INC. 103
BUSINESS BROKERS HAWAII, INC. 24
BUSINESS CARDS TOMORROW, INC. 139
BUSINESS CONNECTION, INC. 25
BUSINESS CONNECTIONS INT'L. 214
BUSINESS CONSULTANTS OF AMERICA 24
BUSINESS EXPANSIONS INTERNATIONAL 104

BUSINESS GOLF ASSC. 175
BUSINESS IMAGES DISTRIBUTING 26
BUSINESS INFORMATION INTERNATIONAL, INC. 24
BUSINESS OPPORTUNITIES OF AMERICA, INC. 106, 108
BUSINESS POST HOLDINGS LTD. 249
BUSINESS POST LTD. 249
BUSINESS TELEVISION (CAN. OFFICES) 239
BUSKETT BAKERY 200
BUSY BEE MAID SERVICE INC. 38
BUTH-NA-BODHAIGE 118
BUTLER ASSOCIATES INC. 44
BUTLER LEARNING SYSTEMS 44
BUTTERFIELDS DEVELOPMENT, INC. 147
BUTTERFIELD'S ETC.® 147
BUTTONS BY BOBBY 44
BUY OWNER INTERNATIONAL 141
BUYER'S AGENT, INC., THE 141
BUYER'S RESOURCE REAL ESTATE 141
BUYING & DINING GUIDE 2
BW-3 FRANCHISE SYSTEMS INC. 73
BXC PRINTING CENTERS INC. 139
BY LAW TRADENAME, CLEARANCE INC. 214
BY OWNER, INC. 141
BY OWNER REALITY NETWORK 141
BYOB WATER STORE, THE 167
BYWAYS AUTOMOTIVE GROUP LTD. 178
BYWAYS RENT A CAR 178
BZIRCUS 34
BZIRCUS FRANCHISE CORPORATION 34

C

C & G OPTICAL 225
C CORP. (ONTARIO) INC. WESTERN DIVISION 199
C 'N C WINDOW CENTRES 261
C&J CLARK LTD. 271
C.K. FRANCHISING INC. 205
C.S.C. INC. 102
C.Y.C., INC. 32
CA$H PLUS 24
CA$H PLUS, INC. 24
CADILLAC PLASTIC 44
CAFE BRESLERS 73
CAFE CHRISTOPHE VAN HOUTTE, INC. 205
CAFE DO PONTO 254
CAFE DO PONTO S.A. IND. COM. E EXP. 254
CAFE INTERNATIONAL, INC. 73
CAFE ON MAIN 73
CAFE SUPREME 205
CAFE SUPREME F&P LTD. 205
CAFFE CLASSICO 73
CALCULATED COUPLES 170
CALDWELL ENTERPRISES, INC. 79
CALENDAR CLUB 233
CALHOUN SPORTSWEAR 241
CALIDO CHILE TRADERS 147
CALIDO CHILE TRADERS SYSTEMS INC. 147
CALIFORNIA CLOSET COMPANY 18
CALIFORNIA CREPES 205
CALIFORNIA CREPES LTD. 205
CALIFORNIA CUSTOM CLEANING 180
CALIFORNIA PUBLICOM, INC. 26
CALIFORNIA RESTAURANT SYSTEMS INC. 74
CALL N' CUT 222
CALL N' CUT INC. 222
CALL-A-SIGN LTD. 241
CALLANETICS 122
CALLANETICS FRANCHISE CORPORATION 122
CALLIGRAPHICS LTD. 267
CALORIE SHOP WEIGHT LOSS CENTERS OF AMERICA, INC. 122
CALTAIN ASSOCIATES 259
CAM SYSTEMS INC. 39
CAMERA EXPERT 230
CAMI RESTAURANT CORP. 73
CAMI'S THE SEAFOOD PLACE 73
CAMPTOWN U.S.A. 133
CAMROUX & COMPANY LTD. 196
CAN SKILLET SYSTEMS, INC. 209
CAN-AM DIVORCERVICE, (1984) INC. 186

CAN-CLEAN PRESSURE WASHERS *191*
CANADA POST CORPORATION *186*
CANADA TRANS LIMITED *236*
CANADIAN BADGE MAKER LTD., THE *177*
CANADIAN BARTER EXCHANGE *186*
CANADIAN BARTER EXCHANGE CORP. *186*
CANADIAN BUSINESS BROKERS LTD. *186*
CANADIAN CHEQUE CASHING CORP. *243*
CANADIAN FRANCHISE ASSOCIATION *214*
CANADIAN IMPERIAL BANK OF COMMERCE *214*
CANADIAN INDUSTRIAL SERVICES LTD. *230*
CANADIAN MUFFIN COMPANY, THE *254*
CANADIAN POOL PLAYERS ASSOC. INC. *241*
CANADIAN POOLPLAYERS ASSOC. INC. *197*
CANADIAN TIRE CORP. LTD. *233*
CANADIAN TRAINING & DEVELOPMENT GROUP, INC. *193*
CANADIAN TRAINING ASSOCIATES *239*
CANCORP *44*
CANDLEMAN *147*
CANDLEMAN CORP. *147*
CANDY BLOSSOMS *57*
CANDY BLOSSOMS, INC. *57*
CANDY BOUQUET *57*
CANDY BOUQUET INTERNATIONAL, INC. *57*
CANDY EXPRESS *147*
CANDY EXPRESS FRANCHISING, INC. *147*
CANDY HEADQUARTERS, INC. *57*
CANDY HQTRS *57*
CANDY MAGIC, INC. *150*
CANDYLAND *57*
CANDYMEN INC. *57*
CANINE COUNSELORS *136*
CANINE COUNSELORS INC. *136*
CANMAX MARKETING INC. *194*
CANTEEN CORP. *57*
CANWEST MARKETING LTD. *232*
CAP-IT FRANCHISE INTERNATIONAL, INC. *180*
CAP-IT LIGHT TRUCK IMPROVEMENT CENTRES (CAP-IT ACCE *180*
CAPERS COMPANY *74*
CAPITAL CARPET CLEANING *32*
CAPITAL FUNDING SERVICES *104*
CAPITAL SALES CORP. *32*
CAP'N TACO *74*
CAPT. SUBMARINE *205*
CAPTAIN D'S SEAFOOD *74*
CAPTAIN TONY'S PIZZA & PASTA EMPORIUM *74*
CAPTAIN'S COTTAGE FRANCHISE INC. *90*
CAPTAIN'S COTTAGE FRANCHISE, INC. *89*
CAPTEC FINANCIAL GROUP, INC. *104*
CAPT'N NEMO'S *74*
CAPT'N NEMO'S FRANCHISE SYSTEMS, INC. *74*
CAPT'N SNOOZE PTY LTD. *270*
CAPT'N SNOOZE PTY. LTD. *270*
CAR-X MUFFLER & BRAKE/SPEEDY MUFFLER KING *9*
CARA OPERATIONS LTD. *207, 213*
CARBONE & SONS *74*
CARD CONNECTION *261*
CARD CONNECTION LTD. *261*
CARD SENDERS *117*
CARDIAC CARR CO. *36*
CAREER ADVANCEMENT SCIENCES *51*
CAREER BLAZER RESUME SERVICES *24*
CAREER BLAZERS *24*
CAREER BLAZERS LEARNING CENTERS *158*
CAREER BLAZERS STAFFING SERVICES *51*
CAREER EMPLOYMENT SERVICES *52*
CAREERS U.S.A., INC. *51*
CARL KARCHER ENTERPRISES, INC. *74*
CARLINE MUFFLERS & MORE *179*
CARL'S JR. RESTAURANTS *74*
CARLSON HOSPITALITY WORLDWIDE *133*
CARNOISSEUR *245*
CARNOISSEUR (RETAIL) LTD. *245*
CAROL BLOCK, LTD. *118*
CAROLE RIGGS DANCE STUDIOS *162*
CAROLE RIGGS HARRIS *162*
CAROLE'S CHEESECAKE COMPANY *200*
CAROLE'S CHEESECAKE COMPANY LTD. *200*
CAROLINA BEVERAGE CORP. *17*

CAROLL *270*
CAROLL INTERNATIONAL *270*
CAROUSEL SYSTEMS *34*
CARPET NETWORK *127*
CARPETERIA *147*
CARPETERIA, INC. *147*
CARROUSEL WOOD PRODUCTS *18*
CARROUSEL WOOD PRODUCTS LTD. *18*
CARROWS RESTAURANT *74*
CAR'S THE STAR FRANCHISE SYSTEMS *137*
CARSTAR AUTOMOTIVE, INC. *11*
CARTER & TANI *113*
CARTER INVESTMENT CO. *74*
CARTEX LIMITED *12*
CARTONS BOULANGERIES *254*
CARTOON CARTOGRAPHICS & CALENDARS *3*
CARTOON CLASSICS *147*
CARVEL CORP. *66*
CARVEL ICE CREAM BAKERY *66*
CARYL BAKER VISAGE *222*
CASA MIA RESTAURANTS *74*
CASA OLE RESTAURANT & CANTINAS *74*
CASEY'S GENERAL STORES, INC. *57*
CASEY'S GRILLHOUSE & BEVERAGE CO. *205*
CASEY'S SPORTS *162*
CASEY'S SPORTS CARDS & COLLECTIBLES *162*
CASH CONNECTION *104*
CASH CONVERTERS *270*
CASH PLUS SERVICES INC. *243*
CASH-A-CHEQUE *243*
CASI *55*
CASSANO'S, INC. *74*
CASSANO'S PIZZA & SUBS *74*
CASSE CROUTE "HECTOR" INC. *208*
CASTELANE CONSULTING *214*
CASTLE ROSE, INC. *87, 92*
CASTLETON *142*
CASTLETON HOME CORP., INC. *142*
CASUALTY ADJUSTER'S GUIDES *3*
CASWELL-MASSEY *147*
CATERINA'S *57*
CATERINA'S FRANCHISE COMPANY, INC. *57*
CATFISH CALHOUN, INC. *241*
CATFISH KITCHEN *74*
CATHEDRAL DIRECTORIES FRANCHISES, INC. *3*
CATHOLIC STORE *147*
CATIMINI *270*
CAZIER ENTERPRISES *152*
CAZ'S FISH & CHIP SHOPPE *205*
CBSI *25*
CD WAREHOUSE *147*
CEDAR CHEST, THE *226*
CEILING BRITE *191*
CEILING BRITE DISTRIBUTION INC. *191*
CEILING CLEAN *38*
CEILING DOCTOR *38*
CEILING DOCTOR INC. *38*
CEILTECH *38*
CEILTECH CEILING CLEANING *38*
CELEBRITY SPORTS ASSOC. *95*
CELEX *152*
CELLULAND, INC. *170*
CEN-TA GROUP *176*
CENTER FOR BUSINESS REGENERATION, INC. *104*
CENTMIL CHEMISES *236*
CENTRAL PARK *74*
CENTRAL PARK USA, INC. *74*
CENTRIX GROUP, THE *60*
CENTURY 21 REAL ESTATE *142*
CENTURY 21 REAL ESTATE CANADA, LTD. *231*
CENTURY 21 REAL ESTATE CORP. *142*
CENTURY 21 UK LTD. *261*
CERTA PROPAINTERS CANADA *226*
CERTA PROPAINTERS LTD. *127*
CERTIGARD CAR REPAIR (PETRO-CANADA) *180*
CFC FRANCHISING COMPANY *74*
CFM CONSULTING *259*
CGI, INC. *170*
CHALL-AIDE MEDICAL PRODUCTS *122*
CHAMPION AUTO STORES *11*

CHAMPION AUTO STORES, INC. *11*
CHANTEGRILL, JARDIN BRESILIEN, PASCALINE, PASTA-FAC *254*
CHARLEY'S STEAKERY *74*
CHARLIE'S CHICKEN *74*
CHARLIE'S CHICKEN OF AMERICA *74*
CHART CORPORATION *122*
CHART REHABILITATION *122*
CHATEL VOTRE NETTOYEUR (YOUR CLEANER) *227*
CHECK EXPRESS, INC. *24*
CHECK EXPRESS USA, INC. *24*
CHECK MART *25*
CHECK PATROL *25*
CHECKCARE SYSTEMS, INC. *25*
CHECKERS DRIVE-IN RESTAURANTS, INC. *74*
CHECKERS PIZZA *74*
CHECKERS PIZZA, INC. *74*
CHECKERS SIMON & ROSNER *104*
CHECKMATE *51*
CHECKMATE SYSTEMS, INC. *51*
CHECKROOM SERVICES INC. *194*
CHEEBURGER CHEEBURGER *75*
CHEEBURGER CHEEBURGER RESTAURANTS INC. *75*
CHEERWINE BOTTLERS *17*
CHEESE VILLA *75*
CHEESECAKE CAFE, THE *200*
CHEF'S FRIED CHICKEN *75*
CHEF'S FRIED CHICKEN, INC. *75*
CHEF'S TAKEOUT *75*
CHEM-DRY *252*
CHEM-DRY SOUTHERN SERVICES LTD. *252*
CHEM-DRY® CARPET & UPHOLSTERY CLEANING *189*
CHEM-DRY® CARPET, DRAPERY AND UPHOLSTERY CLEANING *32*
CHEM-MARK INTERNATIONAL *44*
CHEMICAL EXPRESS *252*
CHEMICAL EXPRESS GROUP LTD. *252*
CHEMSTATION *38*
CHEMSTATION INTERNATIONAL *38*
CHERYL LENTS EXERCISE DANCE, INC. *121*
CHESAPEAKE BAGEL BAKERY *61*
CHESAPEAKE KNIFE & TOOL *147*
CHESTER E. BACHELLER, ESQ. *113*
CHEZ BETTER *205*
CHIA CHIA COMMUNICATIONS INC. *242*
CHIC CHICK *75*
CHIC CHICK, INC. *75*
CHICAGO PIZZA PIE FACTORY *254*
CHICAGO'S PIZZA *75*
CHICAGO'S PIZZA FRANCHISES *75*
CHICK - N - CHICK *205*
CHICKEN CHARLIES *75*
CHICKEN CHEF *205*
CHICKEN CHEF CANADA LTD. *205*
CHICKEN DELIGHT *205*
CHICKEN DELIGHT OF CANADA, LTD. *205*
CHICKS NATURAL *75*
CHICKS NATURAL, INC. *75*
CHICO'S *75*
CHICO'S 2 IN 1 FAMOUS CHICKEN 'N PIZZA *205*
CHILD CARE & SCHOOL PUBLISHING CO. *3*
CHILD ENRICHMENT SERVICES, INC. *33*
CHILDREN'S MARKETPLACE, THE *190*
CHILDREN'S ORCHARD *34*
CHILDREN'S ORCHARD, INC. *34*
CHILI COMPANY, THE *75*
CHILI'S,OTB, SPAGGEDDIES, GRADY'S, COZYMEL'S, RAMAN *75*
CHIMNEY RELINING INTERNATIONAL, INC. *21*
CHISHOLM TRAIL BUILDERS *44*
CHLORIDE AUTOMOTIVE BATTERIES LTD. *245*
CHOCOLATE BAR DESSERT CAFE, THE *197*
CHOCOLATE BAR, LTD. *197*
CHOCOLATE GROUP, THE *44*
CHOCOLATERIE BERNARD CALLEBAUT, LTD. *198*
CHOICE HOME SALES, LTD. *262*
CHOICE HOTELS CANADA *228*
CHOICE HOTELS INTERNATIONAL *133, 134, 135*
CHOICES HOME SALES *262*
CHRISTIAENSEN *270*
CHROMA COPY *269*
CHROMATECH LABORATORIES INC. *137*

CHS HOLDINGS INC. *142*
CHUBBY'S DINER *75*
CHUBBY'S FOOD SERVICE, INC. *75*
CHUCK E. CHEESE'S *205*
CHUNOWITZ, TEITELBAUM & BAERSON, LTD., CERTIFIED PU *1, 104*
CHURCHS CHICKEN *75*
CIA - VIDRARIA SANTA MARINA *271*
CICI ENTERPRISES, INC. *75*
CICI'S PIZZA *75*
CICO CHIMNEY LININGS LTD. *247*
CINDERELLA DESIGNER GOWNS *262*
CINDERELLA DESIGNER GOWNS LTD. *262*
CINDERELLA HOME SERVICES *252*
CINDY'S CINNAMON ROLLS *61*
CINERENT BENELUX *270*
CIRCLE C CONVENIENCE STORES *254*
CIRCLE K *254*
CIRCLE K (UK) LICENSING LTD. *254*
CITIZENS AGAINST CRIME *23*
CITY LINK *250*
CITY LINK TRANSPORT HOLDINGS LTD. *250*
CITY LOOKS SALONS INTERNATIONAL *118*
CITY SUBMARINE *205*
CKC *74*
CLAFLIN HOME HEALTH CENTERS, INC. *122*
CLARION INNS *133*
CLARKE'S CHARCOAL BROILER *75*
CLARKE'S FRANCHISING, INC. *75*
CLARKS SHOP, THE *271*
CLASSIC CHINA *147*
CLASSIC CHINA FRANCHISING, INC. *147*
CLASSY CLOSETS ETC. *18*
CLASSY MAIDS *38*
CLASSY MAIDS USA, INC. *38*
CLEAN BRITE CANADA LTD. *191*
CLEAN MACHINE POWERWASH INC. *41*
CLEAN PARK *246*
CLEAN PARK GMBH *246*
CLEAN-AIRE INTERNATIONAL, INC. *44*
CLEAN-BRITE *191*
CLEANCO, INC. *11*
CLEANING BY PAGE *227*
CLEANING CONSULTANT SERVICES, INC. *158*
CLEANNET USA *39*
CLENTECH *247*
CLENTECH ACOUSTIC CLEAN *39*
CLIFFORD AGENCIES LTD. *229*
CLIMAT DE FRANCE *262*
CLINTAR GROUNDSKEEPING SERVICES *228*
CLINTAR LIMITED *228*
CLOSET CLASSICS *44*
CLOSET FACTORY FRANCHISE CORP., THE *18*
CLOSET FACTORY, THE *18*
CLOSETS TO GO *18*
CLOSETS TO GO, INC. *18*
CLOSETTEC *18*
CLOSETTEC FRANCHISE CORP. *18*
CLOUTHIER, ESSAIN *225*
CLOVER FARM, FOODLAND *198*
CLOVER FARM STORES OF CANADA *198*
CLUB NAUTICO INTERNATIONAL POWERBOAT RENTALS *163*
CLUB SANDWICH *57*
CLUB SANDWICH FRANCHISING, INC. *57*
CLUBHOUSE INNS OF AMERICA, INC. *133*
CLUCK-U-CHICKEN *75*
CLUCK-U-CHICKEN, INC. *75*
CLUTCH INTERNATIONAL LTD. *246*
CMC COLLATERAL MANAGEMENT CANADA LTD. *186*
COACHMAN DRY CLEANING & LAUNDRY *130*
COAST SUNDECKS WATERPROOFING LTD. *184*
COAST TO COAST COLLISION CENTRES *181*
COAST TO COAST ENGINEERING SERVICES, INC. *18*
COAST TO COAST FRANCHISE SERVICES INC. *181*
COAST TO COAST HARDWARE *147*
COAST TO COAST STORES, INC. *147*
COASTAL CHOCOLATE CO. *44*
COBBLESTONE FRANCHISING, INC. *170*
COBBLESTONE QUALITY SHOE REPAIR *170*
COBRA CAR PROTECTION CENTRES *181*

COCK OF THE WALK   *75*
COFFEE BEANERY LTD., THE   *61*
COFFEE TIME DONUTS   *200*
COFFEE TIME DONUTS INC.   *200*
COFFEE WAY   *200*
COFFEE WAY, INC., THE   *200*
COFFEEMAN   *255*
COFFEEMAN MANAGEMENT LTD.   *255*
COGLAN, WIZINSKY   *219*
COHEN, MARKUS, Q.C., LL.M.   *219*
COIT DRAPERY AND CARPET CLEANERS   *32*
COLCCI   *271*
COLCCI IND. E COM. DO VESTUARIO LTDA.   *271*
COLDWELL BANKER RESIDENTIAL AFFILIATES   *142*
COLEMAN-GARVIN REALTY, INC.   *104*
COLLECTION 5   *271*
COLLEGE PROSPECTS OF AMERICA®, INC.   *163*
COLLISION SHOP, THE   *11*
COLOR COMPUTER PORTRAITS   *137*
COLOR SPECIALTIES, INC.   *170*
COLOR TILE & CARPET   *127*
COLOR TILE, INC.   *127*
COLOR YOUR CARPET   *32*
COLOR YOUR WORLD, CORP.   *226*
COLOR-GLO   *170*
COLOR-PRO   *44*
COLOR/MATCH   *45*
COLORFAST MARKETING SYSTEMS INC.   *25*
COLORS ON PARADE   *12*
COLORTYME   *145*
COLORWORKS   *12*
COLORWORKS FRANCHISE GROUP   *12*
COLOUR COUNSELLORS LTD.   *262*
COLOURITE FLOORING NETWORK   *194*
COLTEX B.V.   *274*
COLUMBIA LICENSING INC.   *200*
COLUMBIA STEAK HOUSE   *76*
COMAC FOOD GROUP INC.   *200, 211*
COMCHEQ   *187*
COMET CLEANERS   *130*
COMFORT INNS   *133*
COMMAND PERFORMANCE STYLING SALONS   *118*
COMMERCIAL CONSULTANTS INC.   *214*
COMMERCIAL DEVICES   *259*
COMMUNICATIONS WORLD INTERNATIONAL, INC.   *25*
COMMUNITY CARELINE SERVICES   *268*
COMMUNITY PUBLICATIONS OF AMERICA, INC.   *2, 4, 5*
COMMWORLD   *25*
COMP-U-MED SYSTEMS, INC.   *122*
COMPACT DISCS INTERNATIONAL, LTD.   *147*
COMPANY CORPORATION, THE   *104*
COMPANY'S COMING BAKERY CAFE   *200*
COMPLETE MUSIC   *55*
COMPLETE WEED CONTROL   *262*
COMPLETE WEED CONTROL LTD.   *262*
COMPLETESEAL FABRIC PROTECTION   *32*
COMPOSIL OF SOUTH TEXAS   *32*
COMPREHEND! COMPUTER EDUCATION CENTERS   *158*
COMPREHEND! FRANCHISE CORP.   *158*
COMPREHENSIVE BUSINESS SERVICES   *1, 176*
COMPREHENSIVE BUSINESS SERVICES OF CANADA   *176*
COMPREHENSIVE FRANCHISING, INC.   *104*
COMPREHENSIVE FRANCHISING SYSTEMS, INC.   *18*
COMPREHENSIVE PAINTING   *18*
COMPRI HOTEL   *133*
COMPUCENTRE   *237*
COMPUQUEST EDUCATIONAL SERVICES   *158*
COMPUSEARCH MARKET & SOCIAL RESEARCH LTD.   *214*
COMPUTA TUNE   *246*
COMPUTEMP, INC.   *51*
COMPUTER BUSINESS SERVICES, INC.   *25*
COMPUTER KINETICS   *271*
COMPUTER MAINTENANCE SERVICE   *155*
COMPUTER POWER SUPPLY   *156*
COMPUTER RENAISSANCE   *156*
COMPUTERLAND   *156*
COMPUTERLAND CANADA INC.   *237*
COMPUTERPALS   *239*
COMPUTERTOTS   *34*
COMREAL INTERNATIONAL, INC.   *142*

COMTESSE DU BARRY S.A.   *255*
CONCEPT INDEPENDENT TRAVEL AGENCY (CITA)   *165*
CONCEPTUAL EDGE, THE   *104*
CONCORD FRANCHISE CORP.   *148*
CONDOMINIUM TRAVEL ASSOCIATES, INC.   *145*
CONDOTELS   *133*
CONDOTELS INTERNATIONAL, INC.   *133*
CONES & COFFEE   *66*
CONES & COFFEE INC.   *66*
CONEY AMERICA CORPORATION   *87*
CONEY'S CORP.   *76*
CONEY'S EXPRESS   *76*
CONFIDENTIAL BUSINESS CONNECTION   *25*
CONGRESS ROTISSERIE   *76*
CONNECTICUT RESTAURANT GROUP, INC.   *76*
CONNELL LIGHTBODY   *219*
CONNEX INTERNATIONAL, INC.   *104*
CONNOISSEUR FRANCHISE CORP.   *148*
CONNOISSEUR, THE   *148*
CONROY'S FLOWERS   *131*
CONSIGN & DESIGN FRANCHISE CORP.   *127*
CONSIGN & DESIGN FURNISHINGS   *127*
CONSOL CARPET CLEANING   *32*
CONSOL CARPET CLEANING FRANCHISE CORPORATION   *32*
CONSULTANTS AMERICA CORP.   *172*
CONSULTANTS OF AMERICA PROFESSIONAL CORP.   *109*
CONSULTANTS, THE   *104*
CONSUMER DENTAL NETWORK   *122*
CONSUMER NETWORK OF AMERICA   *3*
CONSUMERHEALTH, INC.   *122*
CONTEMPO PORTRAITS   *137*
CONTEMPORARY CLASSIC LOG HOMES BY AMERICAN LINCOLN   *17*
CONTEMPORARY COMMUNICATIONS   *215*
CONTEMPORARY COMMUNICATIONS LTD.   *215*
CONTINENTAL INDOOR SOCCER LEAGUE   *163*
CONTINENTAL TELEFAX   *26*
CONTROL-O-FAX   *25*
CONTROL-O-FAX SYSTEMS, INC.   *25*
CONVENIENCE MONEY CENTERS, INC   *25*
CONVENIENT DRY CLEANING DEPOT   *227*
CONVENIENT FOOD MART   *57*
CONVENIENT FOOD MART INC.   *57*
CONWAY, KLEINMAN, KORNHAUSER & GOTLIEB   *219*
COOKIE BOUQUET FRANCHISING CORP.   *61*
COOKIE BOUQUET/COOKIES BY DESIGN   *61*
COOKIE MUG INC., THE   *61*
COOKIE MUG, THE   *61*
COOKIES BY GEORGE - CAFÉ BY GEORGE   *200*
COOKIES IN BLOOM   *61*
COOKIES IN BLOOM, INC.   *61*
COOPER'S TURKEY PLACE   *76*
CORN DOG 7   *76*
CORN DOG 7, INC.   *76*
CORNELL TRADING LTD.   *237*
CORNERSTONE FUELS   *170*
CORNERSTONE FUELS INTERNATIONAL, INC.   *170*
CORPORATE HOUSING SERVICES   *142*
CORRS CHAMBERS WESTGARTH   *259*
CORTINA CARRY-OUT LTD.   *205*
COSCO INTERNATIONAL, INC.   *17*
COSMETIC ISLAND   *222*
COSMETIC ISLAND, INC.   *222*
COST CUTTERS FAMILY HAIR CARE   *118*
COTTAGE INN PIZZA   *76*
COTTAGECARE   *39*
COTTER CANADA HARDWARE AND VARIETY COOPERATIVE, INC   *236*
COTTLEBOROUGH LTD.   *249*
COTTMAN TRANSMISSION CENTERS   *16*
COTTMAN TRANSMISSION SYSTEMS, INC.   *16*
COUCH'S CORNER BARBECUE   *76*
COUCH'S CORNER BBQ FRANCHISING SYSTEMS, INC.   *76*
COUNTER INTELLIGENCE   *271*
COUNTRY BUSINESS SALES LTD.   *250*
COUNTRY CLUTTER   *148*
COUNTRY GOODNESS   *255*
COUNTRY HEARTH INN   *133*
COUNTRY HOSPITALITY CORP.   *76*
COUNTRY INN & SUITES BY CARLSON   *133*

COUNTRY KITCHEN 205
COUNTRY KITCHEN RESTAURANTS 76
COUNTRY PROPERTIES AND ROGERS 250
COUNTRY ROSE MANAGEMENT FRANCHISE LTD. 250
COUNTRY STYLE DONUTS 200
COUNTRY STYLE DONUTS CSD 200
COUNTRY VISIONS 148
COUNTRYWIDE GARDEN MAINTENANCE SERVICES 262
COUPON-CASH SAVER 3
COUPON-CASH SAVER FRANCHISE CORP. 3
COURTE-PAILLE 255
COUSINS SUBS 76
COUSIN'S SUBS SYSTEMS, INC. 76
COUSTIC-GLO 39
COUSTIC-GLO INTERNATIONAL, INC. 39
COVALT ENTERPRISES, INC. 83
COVER RIGHT LTD. 247
COVERALL CLEANING CONCEPTS 39
COVERALL NORTH AMERICA, INC. 39
COVERALL OF CANADA 191
COVERITE 247
COVIN B.V. 271
COVINET WIJN & DRANKENGROEP 271
COWBOY CHICKEN 76
COZZOLI'S PIZZA 76
COZZOLI'S PIZZA SYSTEMS, INC. 76
CP ENTERPRISES INC. 137
CRA 249
CRAFT TREE CENTRES 233
CRAFTERS BOUTIQUE 148
CRATERS & FREIGHTERS 170
CRATERS & FREIGHTERS FRANCHISE COMPANY 170
CRAZY BENZY'S FRANCHISE CORP. 148
CRAZY PIZZA INC. 84
CREATE-A-BOOK 271
CREATE-A-BOOK - PRESTO BOOKS - GRACE CHRISTION 3
CREATE-A-BOOK CANADA/INTERNATIONAL 190
CREATE-A-SHOT PRODUCTS CORPORATION 194
CREATIONS BY DEAN, INC. 226
CREATIVE AMUSEMENT SERVICES INC. 55
CREATIVE ASSET MANAGEMENT, INC. 25
CREATIVE ASSET MANAGEMENT™ 25
CREATIVE COLORS INTERNATIONAL 12
CREATIVE COLORS INTERNATIONAL, INC. 12
CREATIVE CROISSANTS 76
CREATIVE DISPLAY OF FLORIDA, INC. 137
CREATIVE SALES SOLUTIONS 104
CREATIVE SALES SOLUTIONS, INC. 104
CREATIVE VENTURES CORP. 50
CREDIT PLUS CARD 45
CREPELITO 255
CREPELITO COM. MAQS. GEN. ALIMENTICIOS, LTDA. 256
CREPELITO-COMERCIO DE MAQS. GEN. ALIMENTICIOUS LTDA 255
CREPENCORE SYSTEMS, INC. 205
CREST GROUP, THE 25
CRESTCOM INTERNATIONAL, LTD. 25
CRESTLINE VENTURES CORPORATION 181
CRETEPRINT PAVING SYSTEMS 247
CRISPY CREPES 205
CRITERIUM ENGINEERS 18
CRITTER CARE 129
CRITTER CONTROL 171
CROISSANT PLUS 205
CRONER COMPANY, THE 104
CROPCO INC. 243
CROWE & DUNLEVY 113
CROWN DOMESTIC APPLIANCES 262
CROWN EYEGLASS PLC. 268
CROWN OPTICAL CENTRE 268
CROWN TROPHY, INC. 148
CRUISE CENTERS OF AMERICA 165
CRUISE HOLIDAYS 166
CRUISE HOLIDAYS INTERNATIONAL, INC. 166
CRUISE LINES RESERVATION CENTER 166
CRUISE SHOPPE LTD., THE 166
CRUISE SHOPPES AMERICA, LTD. 166
CRUISE VACATIONS 242
CRUISESHIPCENTERS 242
CRUISESHIPCENTERS (ONTARIO) 242
CRUPIZZA 205
CRYSTAL GALLERIES LTD. 262
CRYSTAL MAINTENANCE SYSTEMS 191
CRYSTAL MAINTENANCE SYSTEMS INC. 191
CSS FRANCHISE NETWORK 104
CSS FRANCHISING 42
CSS FRANCHISING NETWORK 104
CTP INTERNATIONAL, INC. 76
CUB FOODS 57
CULLIGAN INTERNATIONAL CO. 167
CULLIGAN INTERNATIONAL COMPANY 262
CULLIGAN OF CANADA LTD. 243
CULTURES FRESH FOOD RESTAURANTS 206
CULTURES RESTAURANTS INC. 206
CULVER FRANCHISING SYSTEMS, INC. 66
CULVER'S FROZEN YOGURTS 66
CUMULUS INC. 100
CUPBOARD LOVE (U.K.) LTD. 248
CUPIO PLC. 273
CURADRAFT (GB) LTD. 248
CURBMATE CORP. 45
CURTIS MATHES HOME ENTERTAINMENT CENTERS 156
CURTIS SYSTEM - THE ADVANCED AUTOMOTIVE CARE 12
CUSTOM AUTO RESTORATION SYSTEMS 12
CUSTOM CASE SUPPLY CO. 171
CUSTOM HOME-WATCH INTERNATIONAL 227
CUSTOM HOME-WATCH INTERNATIONAL, INC. 227
CUSTOM MAID, INC. 39
CUSTOM MUFFLER SERVICE CENTER 9
CUT ONLY 131
CUTCO INDUSTRIES, INC. 119
CUTCOST CONSULTANTS LTD. 215
CWI INCORPORATED 75
CYBER EXCHANGE 156
CYBERMIND 237
CYBERMIND CANADA, INC. 237
CYCLEPATH, THE 241
CYGNUS SYSTEMS INC. 137
CYNATEC SPECIALTY CLEANING & RESTORATION 191
CYNATEC SPECIALTY CLEANING & RESTORATION INC. 191

D

D & K ENTERPRISES INC. 139
D & K ENTERPRISES INC. 36
D & K OPTICAL 125
D&K ENTERPRISES INC. 35, 150, 175
D. M. COUGHLIN, INC. 39
D.F.P. FRANCHISING INC. 77
D.F.S., INC. 117
D.H. HOWDEN & CO. LIMITED 184
D.H. HOWDEN & CO. LTD. 235
D.J. GILL ASSOCIATES, INC. 45
D.J. GILL ASSOCIATES INC. 50
D.J.K. (MURAL) HOLDINGS 204
D.L.M. 171
D.O.C OPTICAL 122
D.O.C OPTICS CORP. 122
D.P.L. ENTERPRISES, INC. 38
D.W.I. ALTERNATIVES 172
DADDY-O'S EXPRESS DRIVE-THRU 76
DAIRY BELLE FREEZE DEVELOPMENT CO., INC. 76
DAIRY MART CONVENIENCE STORES 57
DAIRY MART CONVENIENCE STORES, INC. 57
DAIRY QUEEN 77
DAIRY QUEEN CANADA, INC. 203
DAIRY QUEEN, KARMELKORN SHOPPES, ORANGE JULIUS 77
DAMAS & ASSOCIATES 105
DAMON'S INTERNATIONAL INC. 77
DAMON'S, THE PLACE FOR RIBS/DAMON'S CLUBHOUSE 77
DAMPCURE-WOODCURE/30 248
DAMPCURE-WOODCURE/30 LTD. 248
DAN HANNA AUTO WASH 12
D'ANGELO SANDWICH SHOPS 76
D'ANGELO'S SANDWICH SHOPS, INC. 76
DAN'S FAN CITY 148
DAN'S FAN CITY, INC. 148
DAREN, MARTENFELD, CARR & CO., CHARTERED ACCOUNTANT 215

DARKZONE 241
DARKZONE TECHNOLOGIES INC. 241
DATABAR INC. 25
DATAPRO 250
DATATREND CURSOS E SISTEMAS S/C LTDA. 250
DATOLAB CANADA INC. 194
DAVE'S PIZZA RESTAURANTS, LTD. 206
DAVEY LAW CORPORATION 113
DAVID BIGMORE & CO. 259
DAVID E. HOLMES 113
DAVID HOUGHTON & ASSOCIATES 212
DAVID HOUGHTON & ASSOCIATES, INC. 215
DAVID N. KORNHAUSER 219
DAVID WIZINSKY 219
DAVOLI OF NORTH AMERICA 197
DAWN DONUT SYSTEMS, INC. 61
DAYLIGHT CORPORATION 62
DAYLIGHT DONUTS 62
DAYS EASE, INC. 39
DAYS INNS - CANADA 228
DAYS INNS OF AMERICA 134
DCAP INSURANCE 171
DE DUTCH PANNEKOEK HOUSE 206
DE DUTCH PANNEKOEK HOUSE RESTAURANTS INC. 206
DE MAINE INSURANCE SERVICES 250
DE/MAR 18
DEAN CONSULTANTS 105
DEAN CONSULTING GROUP 215
DEC-K-ING 184
DECK THE WALLS 137
DECO HOME STORES, INC. 127
DECOR-AT-YOUR-DOOR 127
DECOR DISTINCTION 226
DECOR SYSTEMS (SW) LTD. 262
DECORATING DEN 128, 226
DECORATING DEN (UK) 262
DECORATING DEN SYSTEMS, INC. 128
DECORATIVE ARTS, INC. 127
DECOWALL 128
DEL TACO 77
DEL TACO, INC. 77
DELCO CLEANING SYSTEMS 45
DELI CORPORATION OF AMERICA, INC. 86
DELI FRANCE 255
DELIFRANCE 255
DELOITTE & TOUCHE 1, 177
DELTA JANITORIAL SYSTEMS, INC. 39
DEMIANTSCHUK LARSEN & SINGER 219
DEMOMETRICS CORP. 105
DENNY'S INC. 77
DENNY'S INC. 78
DENT DOCTOR 12
DENT DOCTOR, INC. 12
DENTAL STORE, LTD. THE 122
DENTAL STORE, THE 122
DENTPRO 12
DENTPRO FRANCHISE CORP. 12
DENTRIX DENTAL CARE 225
DER WEINERSCHNITZEL 77
DEREK'S LTD. 190
DERMACULTURE CLINIC 122
DESCHENES & FILS LTEE. 185
DESIGN SHOP, THE 3
DESIGNER FRAGRANCES 222
DESI'S FAMOUS PIZZA 77
DESMAZIERES S.H. 273
DESPERADO'S SALOON AND WESTERN EATERY 206
DETAIL PLUS SYSTEMS, INC. 12
DETAIL PLUS CAR WASH & AUTO APPEARANCE CENTERS 12
DEUTSCH GROUP, THE 105
DEVELOPING CONCEPTS, INC. 35
DFD TELEBROADCASTING 243
DI LALLO BURGER 206
DI LALLO MANAGEMENT 206
DIAL A MAID 39
DIAL-A-DUSTER (UK) LTD. 252
DIAL-A-GIFT 117
DIAL-A-GIFT, INC. 117
DIAL-A-TILE 171
DIAMOND CHOPSTICKS 255
DIAMOND DAVE'S TACO CO. 77
DIAMOND DAVE'S TACO CO., INC. 77
DIAMOND QUALITY TRANSMISSION CENTERS OF AMERICA, IN 16
DIAMONFLAIR CORP. 148
DIAMONTRIGUE 148
DIANA CRAFTERS, LTD. 148
DICKIE DEE ICE CREAM 194
DIDGERIDOOS CANADA CORPORATION 206
DIDGERIDOOS ROTISSERIE CHICKEN 206
DIET CENTER 122
DIET CENTER INC. 122
DIET LIGHT WEIGHT LOSS SYSTEM 122
DIET WORKSHOP 123
DIFUSAO DE EDUCACAO E CULTURA S/A 262
DIGIAD 177
DIGITAL ADVERTISING, INC. 177
DIGITAL MESSAGE SYSTEMS, CORP. 47
DIGITCOM CANADA, INC. 237
DIGITCOM TELECOMMUNICATIONS 237
DIJO'S PIZZA HOLDINGS, LTD. 206
DIJO'S PIZZA PANZEROTTO 206
DIMARCO GOLF 242
DINKUM DOG 255
DIP 'N STRIP, INC. 117
DIRECT OPINIONS FRANCHISING, INC. 25
DIRECT OPINIONS™ 25
DISC GO ROUND 148
DISCOUNT BRIDAL SERVICE INC. 168
DISCOUNT CAR & TRUCK RENTALS LTD. 178
DISCOUNT CAR AND TRUCK RENTALS 178
DISCOUNT PARTY WAREHOUSE 148
DISMARINA 271
DISMAT, INC. 184
DISTRIBUIDORA CORY 255
DIV. AUTOSTOCK INC. 180
DIV. OF ACE NOVELTY CO. INC. 55
DIV. OF AUTOSTOCK 181
DIV. OF BLANKENSHIP ENTERPRISES 87
DIV. OF BP OIL CO. 15
DIV. OF WALKER EXHAUSTS 179
DIVERSEY MOBILE SALES 253
DIVERSIFIED ARTS 137
DIVERSIFOODS, INC. 60
DIVISION DE C CORP., INC. 198
DIVISION OF STANLEY CANADA, INC. 195
DIXIE LEE FOOD SYSTEMS LTD. 206
DIXIE LEE FRIED CHICKEN 206
DIXON COMMERCIAL INVESTIGATORS, INC. 25
DIXON'S CHILI, INC. 77
DIXON'S FAMOUS CHILI 77
DIXY FRIED CHICKEN 255
DMJ MANAGEMENT 190
DO-IT CENTER STORES 184
DOCTOR VIDEO TECHNOLOGY, INC. 157
DOCTOR'S ASSOCIATES, INC. 98
DOG WASH 136
DOGHOUSE KENNEL SUPPLY LTD. 229
DOG'S EAR T-SHIRT CO., THE 241
DOGS' WORLD 262
DOGSBODY & CAT TAILS 271
DOLLAR BILL'S 233
DOLLAR BILL'S LTD. 233
DOLLAR DEPOT 233
DOLLAR RENT A CAR 178
DOLLAR RENT A CAR (CANADA) LTD. 178
DOLLAR RENT A CAR SYSTEMS, INC. 6
DOLLOND & AITCHISON 268
DOLLOND & AITCHISON GROUP, PLC. 268
DOLLY'S PIZZA 77
DOLLY'S PIZZA FRANCHISING CORP. 77
DOLPHIN CONSULTING GROUP 233
DOLPHIN PUBLICATIONS OF AMERICA, INC. 3
DOLPHIN PUBLICATIONS OF AMERICA, INC. 4
DOMINOS 255
DOMINO'S PIZZA 77, 206
DOMINOS PIZZA GROUP 255
DOMINO'S PIZZA, INC 77
DOMINO'S PIZZA OF CANADA 206
DOMPHAFF CORP. LTD. 236

DON CHERRY'S GRAPEVINE 206
DON CHERRY'S GRAPEVINE RESTAURANTS, INC. 206
DON MILLERS HOT BREAD KITCHENS 255
DON RICARDO'S MEXICAN RESTAURANT 77
DONALD J. FOLTZ & ASSOCIATES, INC. 106
DONATOS PIZZA, INC. 77
DONINI RESTAURANT INC. 211
DONNA JEAN'S UNIQUE COUNTRY GIFTS 148
DONUT DELITE CAFE, INC. 200
DONUT INN 62
DONUT INN, INC. 62
DONUT KING 255
DONUT MAN, THE 62
DONUTLAND 62
DONUTLAND USA LTD. 62
DOOLEY TRAVEL GROUP PLC 267
DOR-2-DOR 262
DORACO 19
DORBER COLLECTION, THE 271
DOUBLE DOUBLE PIZZA & CHICKEN 206
DOUBLE RAINBOW CAFE 66
DOUBLE RAINBOW GOURMET ICE CREAMS INC. 66
DOUBLETREE HOTELS CORP. 133
DOUGHERTY & ASSOCIATES 113
DOUGLAS, SYMES & BRISSENDEN 219
DOWNEY AUTOMOTIVE WAREHOUSE 11
DOWNEY'S AUTO STORES / BUMPER TO BUMPER AUTO STORES 12
DR. JOHN A. BERGER & ASSOCIATES 105
DR. NICK'S TRANSMISSIONS 16
DR. PERSONNEL 51
DR. PERSONNEL, INC. 51
DR. SPECS OPTICAL 225
DR. VINYL 12
DR. VINYL AND ASSOCIATES, LTD. 12
DRAIN TECH, INC. 39
DRAKE INTERNATIONAL INC. 196
DRAKE OFFICE OVERLOAD, DRAKE PERSONNEL, DRAKE EXECU 196
DRAPERY FACTORY, THE 148
DRAPERY WORKS SYSTEMS, LTD. 171
DRAPERY WORKS, THE 171
DREAMS (PREMIER BED CENTRES) 271
DRIVER HIRE 250
DRIVER HIRE GROUP SERVICES LTD. 250
DRIVER'S ADVOCATE 243
DRUG CASTLE FRANCHISES, INC. 148
DRUG EMPORIUM, INC. 148
DRUG TRADING CO. LTD. 194
DRUXY'S FAMOUS DELI SANDWICHES 206
DRUXY'S INC. 206
DRY CLEANING STATION 130
DRY CLEANING WORLD & LAUNDRY WORLD 130
DRYCLEAN-USA 130
DRYCLEAN-USA FRANCHISE COMPANY 130
DRYCLEANING SYSTEMS INTERNATIONAL INC. 130
DUCHESS WORLDWIDE, INC. 77
DUCTBUSTERS 39
DUDS 'N SUDS 262
DUDS 'N SUDS UK LTD. 262
DUFFERIN GAME ROOM STORE 233
DUFFERIN GAME ROOM STORE LTD. 233
DUN & BRADSTREET 25
DUN & BRADSTREET RMS FRANCHISE CORP. 25
DUNBAR CARPET BY COLOUR 226
DUNHILL PERSONNEL SYSTEM, INC. 51
DUNKIN' DONUTS (CANADA) LTD. 200
DUNKIN' DONUTS INC. 62
DURA-BUILT FRANCHISE SYSTEM, INC. 16
DURA-BUILT TRANSMISSIONS 16
DURACLEAN INTERNATIONAL, INC. 32
DURASTILL, INC. 45
DUREX VENDING 262
DURHAM PINE 271
DUSKIN CO., LTD. 262
DUTCH MASTER DONUTS LTD. 200
DUTY DRIVER LTD. 262
DYKEMA, GOSSETT, SPENCER, GOODNOW & TRIGG 113
DYMOCKS BOOKSTORES 271
DYNACO, INC. 81
DYNAMARK SECURITY CENTERS, INC. 23
DYNAMIC DAVE'S BARGAIN HOUSE 233
DYNAMIC DEVELOPMENT ASSOCIATES 45
DYNAMIC PERFORMANCE SYSTEMS,INC. 215
DYNAMIC TEMPORARY SERVICES,INC. 51
DYNAMO POOL LEAGUE 241
DYNASTIE DE CHINE 206
DYNO LOCKS 263
DYNO PLUMBING 248
DYNO ROD DEVELOPMENTS LTD. 248
DYNO-ELECTRICS 248
DYNO-ROD DEVELOPMENTS LTD. 263

E

E-Z TAN FRANCHISE SYSTEMS, INC. 123
E-Z TAN TANNING SALONS 123
E. K. WILLIAMS & CO. 25
E. K. WILLIAMS & CO. LTD. 177
E.K. WILLIAMS & CO. (ONTARIO) LTD. 187
E.P.I.C. SYSTEMS, INC. 39
EAGLE BOYS DIAL-A-PIZZA 255
EAGLE BOYS DIAL-A-PIZZA AUSTRALIA PLC. 255
EAGLE CLEANERS 130
EAST OF CHICAGO PIZZA COMPANY, INC. 77
EAST SIDE MARIO'S 206
EASTERN DISPLAY TECHNOLOGIES 194
EASY HAIR 118
EASYRIDERS FRANCHISING INC. 148
ECHOLS INTERNATIONAL TRAVEL/TRAINING COURSES/ INTERN 159
ECONO LODGES OF AMERICA, INC. 134
ECONO LUBE N' TUNE, INC. 7
ECONOMY LODGING SYSTEMS, INC. 134
ECONOTAX 1
ECOWATER SYSTEMS 167
ECOWATER SYSTEMS, INC. 167
ECW CORP. 34
EDARA 259
EDDIE SHACK DONUTS 200
EDDIE SHACK DONUTS, INC. 200
EDELWEISS DELI EXPRESS 207
EDELWEISS INTERNATIONAL FRANCHISE CORP. 207
EDO JAPAN 207
EDUCATIONAL RESOURCE CENTERS OF AMERICA 159
EDWARD D. JONES & CO. 243
EDWARD J. EVANS & CO. (C.P.A.) 259
EDWARD M. DOLSON 113
EDWARDO'S NATURAL PIZZA RESTAURANT 77
EDWIN K. WILLIAMS & CO. 25
EFC HOLDING B.V. 259
EFFECTIVE DIRECT MARKETING SYSTEMS, INC. 3
EFFECTIVE MAILERS 3
EGRESS ENTERPRISES INC. 178
EIRTEN'S PARLORS, INC. 89
EKLIND, LIPTON & JACOBS 219
EKW SYSTEMS 177
EL CENTRO FOODS, INC. 92
EL CHICO 78
EL CHICO RESTAURANTS, INC. 78
EL POLLO LOCO 78
EL TACO RESTAURANTS 78
ELDORADO BANK 105
ELDORADO STONE CORP. 19
ELECTRO MAGIC 171
ELECTRON PURE LTD. 45
ELECTRONIC REALTY ASSOCIATES, L.P. 142
ELECTRONIC TAX FILERS, INC. 1
ELEGANCE JEWELRY 194
ELEGANT IMAGES 118
ELEGANT IMAGES FRANCHISE CORP. 118
ELEPHANT & CASTLE 207
ELEPHANT BLEU 246
ELIA FASHIONS LTD. 237
ELIAS BROTHERS RESTAURANTS, INC. 71
ELIO CECCHINI L'ART DE LA FROMAGERIE 271
ELIZABETH GRADY, FACE FIRST 118
ELLIOTTS' OFF BROADWAY DELI, INC. 78
ELLUS 250

ELLUS IND. E COM. LTDA. *250*
ELMER'S PANCAKE & STEAK HOUSE *78*
ELS EDUCATIONAL SERVICES *159*
ELS INTERNATIONAL (ELSI) *159*
EMACK & BOLIO'S *66*
EMBASSY SUITES HOTELS *134*
EMBASSY SUITES, INC. *134*
EMERALD GREEN, INC. *131*
EMERALD GREEN LAWN CARE *131*
EMERY WATERHOUSE CO., THE *153*
EMF GROUP LTD. *250*
EMPRESS CHILI *78*
EMPRESS FOOD PRODUCTS, INC. *78*
EMPRESS TRAVEL FRANCHISE CORP. *166*
EMSAR *123*
ENCORE NAILS *119*
ENCORE NAILS, LLC *119*
END-A-FLAT TIRE SAFETY SEALANT *45*
ENDRUST AUTO APPEARANCE SPECIALISTS *12*
ENDRUST INDUSTRIES *12, 45*
ENECON *171*
ENECON CORPORATION *171*
ENERGY AUTOMATION SYSTEM, INC. *45*
ENERGY MEDICINE DEVELOPMENTS (N.A.) INC. *225*
ENERGY MISER WINDOWS *171*
ENERGY PRODUCTS, INC. *45*
ENGLISH BUTLER *233*
ENTERTAINMENT CONCEPTS, LTD. *55*
ENTOURAGE INTERNATIONAL, INC. *122*
ENTRECEPT, INC. *69*
ENTREES ON TRAYS *78*
ENTREPRENEUR EXPO, THE *105*
ENTREPRENEUR'S SOURCE, THE *105*
ENVIRO MASTERS LAWN CARE *228*
ENVIRO-SHEILD ENERGY SYSTEMS *184*
ENVIROBATE, INC. *19*
ENVIRONMENTAL AIR SERVICES *171*
ENVIRONMENTAL AIR SERVICES, INC. *171*
ENVIRONMENTAL BIOTECH, INC. *171*
ENVIRONMENTAL HEALTH SERVICES *167*
ENVOY BUSINESS SERVICES *187*
EQUALITY PLUS TELECOMMUNICATIONS *26*
EQUALITY PLUS TELECOMMUNICATIONS CORP. *26*
EQUIFAX MARKETING DECISION SYSTEMS *105*
EQUIPMENT MANAGEMENT SERVICES & REPAIR *123*
ERA MID-AMERICA LTD. *142*
ERA® - (NAME OF FRANCHISE) *142*
ERBERT & GERBERT & FRIENDS, INC. *78*
ERBERT & GERBERT'S SUBS & CLUBS *78*
ERIK'S DELICAFE FRANCHISES INC. *78*
ERNST & YOUNG *105, 215*
ESCADA CANADA INC. *236*
ESCAPE ENTERPRISES INC. *97*
ESKIMO PIE CORP. *66*
ESPETINHOS CAMPINAS *255*
EURO-WALL STYLES *128*
EUROGRANT *250*
EUROGRANT SEARCH LTD. *250*
EUROPEAN BODY WRAP INTERNATIONAL *45*
EUROPEAN FASTSIGNS LTD. *263*
EUROPEAN FRANCHISE CONSULTANTS INTERNATIONAL *259*
EUROPEAN SAFETY PRODUCTS (CAN) LTD. *194*
EUROPEAN SHARPENING, INC. *184*
EUROPEAN TAN SPA, INC. *123*
EVER VISION INC. *12*
EVER-DRY WATERPROOFING *19*
EVERETT MASSON & FURBY *250*
EVERLASTING EXPRESSIONS *149*
EVERYTHING YOGURT & SALAD CAFE *66*
EXCELLENCE SPORTS *241*
EXCHANGE TRAVEL AGENCY LTD. *263*
EXECUTIVE, THE *3*
EXECUTRAIN *26, 239*
EXPLORATIONS *34*
EXPLORATIONS FRANCHISE GROUP, INC. *34*
EXPRESS DAIRY (UK) LTD. *263*
EXPRESS MART CONVENIENT STORES *57*
EXPRESS OIL CHANGE *7*
EXPRESS PERSONNEL SERVICES *51*
EXPRESS POSTAL CENTERS FRANCHISING, INC. *26*

EXPRESS SERVICES, INC. *51*
EXPRESSIONS CUSTOM FURNITURE *128*
EXPRESSIONS IN FABRICS, LTD. *128*
EXPRESSO TERMINI *62*
EXQUISITE CRAFTS *148*
EXQUISITE CRAFTS, INC. *148*
EYEGLASS EMPORIUM *123*
EYESUPPLY EYEWEAR & EYECARE CENTERS *123*
EYEWEAR HOUSE, THE *153*
EYRE, GEORGE C. *219*

F

F & A, INC. *46*
F-O-R-T-U-N-E PERSONNEL CONSULTANTS *51*
F.C.I.A. *105*
F.D.C. (FRANCHISE DEVELOPMENT) *215*
FABRI-ZONE CANADA, LTD. *189*
FABRI-ZONE CLEANING SYSTEMS *32, 189*
FABRICA DE MOVEIS FLORENSE LTDA. *248*
FABRICLAND/FABRICVILLE *194*
FABRION REPAIR SYSTEMS *12*
FABUTAN SUN TAN STUDIO *222*
FACES *222*
FACTUAL DATA *26*
FACTUAL DATA CORP. *26*
FAJITA WILLIE'S CAFE & CANTINA *78*
FALWYN INVESTORS GROUP LTD. *229*
FAMILY HAIRCUT STORE *119*
FAMILY INNS OF AMERICA *134*
FAMILY RESTAURANTS *78*
FAMILY STEAK HOUSES OF FLORIDA *78*
FAMOUS DILL BURGER, INC., THE *78*
FAMOUS DILL BURGER, THE *78*
FAN FAIR CORP. *155*
FANTASTIC SAM'S INTERNATIONAL, INC. *119*
FANTASTIC SAM'S, THE ORIGINAL FAMILY HAIRCUTTERS *119*
FANTASY PUBLICATIONS, INC. *2*
FARO'S FRANCHISE SYSTEMS *78*
FARO'S PIZZA *78*
FAS GRAS INTERNATIONAL, INC. *131*
FASGRAS INTERNATIONAL, INC. *131*
FASHION, LTD. *154*
FASHIONS UNDER $10 *154*
FAST AID FRANCHISE CORP. *174*
FAST FOOD SYSTEMS LTD. *257, 258*
FAST PLATES + PLUS *12*
FAST TRAK DEVELOPMENT COMPANY, INC. *61*
FAST-FIX JEWELRY REPAIRS *171, 244*
FASTFRAME *137, 269*
FASTFRAME FRANCHISES LTD. *269*
FASTFRAME USA, INC. *137*
FASTSERV CENTRAL *123*
FASTSERV MEDICAL *123*
FASTSIGNS *160, 263*
FAT ALBERT'S RESTAURANTS/RALPH'S DINING LOUNGES *207*
FAT BOYS BAR-B-Q *78*
FAT BOYS' BAR-B-Q FRANCHISE SYSTEMS, INC. *78*
FAT T, INC. *17*
FAT TUESDAY *17*
FATBURGER *78*
FATBURGER NORTH AMERICA, INC. *78*
FATSO'S HOMEMADE HAMBURGERS, SALADS, SHAKES & FRIES *207*
FATTY ARBUCKLES AMERICAN DINER *255*
FATTY ARBUCKLES FRANCHISE LTD. *255*
FAVORITE FRIED CHICKEN *255*
FAX-9 *26*
FAX-9 HOLDING CORP. *26*
FEATURE PRESENTATION *237*
FEATURE PRESENTATION INC. *237*
FEDERAL BUSINESS DEVELOPMENT BANK *215*
FELDMAN, WALDMAN & KLINE *113*
FELICITAS *263*
FELIX RUSLIN DIRECT RESPONSE, INC. *3*
FERN LABORATORIES, INC. *119*
FERPLUS DECORATION, FERPLUS QUINCAILLERIE, FERPLUS *226*
FERSINA INTERNATIONAL *248*
FHG INTERNATIONAL INC. *105, 215*

FIBER SEAL 32
FIBER SEAL, INC. 32
FIBRE TECH, INC. 19
FIBRE TECH POOL COATINGS 19
FIBRENEW INDUSTRIES LTD. 244
FIELD FISHER WATERHOUSE 259
FIELD OF DREAMS 148
FIESTA CARTOON MAPS 3
FIGARO'S FRESH-TO-BAKE-PIZZA 78
FIGARO'S ITALIAN PIZZA INC. 78
FILE SECURITY INC. 187
FILTERFRESH 57
FINANCIAL FOCUS, INC. 215
FINDERBINDER™ & SOURCE BOOK™ DIRECTORIES 26
FINE ART RENTALS 137
FINE ART RENTALS FRANCHISING INC. 137
FINE THREADS 154
FINE THREADS, INC. 154
FIRE DEFENSE INTERNATIONAL, INC. 23
FIRE GLAZED HAM BY THE SWISS COLONY 57
FIREGRILL 78
FIREHOUSE SUBS 79
FIRESTONE TIRE AND AUTOMOTIVE CENTRES 181
FIRST CALL LTD. 247
FIRST CALL MANAGEMENT SOLUTIONS 216
FIRST CHOICE FRANCHISE SERVICES 216
FIRST CHOICE FRANCHISE SERVICES INC. 105
FIRST CHOICE FRANCHISE SERVICES INC. 216
FIRST CHOICE HAIRCUTTERS 222
FIRST CHOICE HAIRCUTTERS, LTD. 222
FIRST DISCOUNT TRAVEL 166
FIRST DISCOUNT TRAVEL & DISCOUNT TRAVEL 166
FIRST IMPRESSIONS 268
FIRST IMPRESSIONS TREASURES INC. 234
FIRST OPTOMETRY EYECARE CENTERS, INC. 123
FIRSTAFF, INC. 51
FIRSTAT NURSING SERVICES 123
FIRSTAT OF AMERICA 123
FISH & CHIP SHOPPE, THE 207
FISK SCHOOLS LIMITED 263
FIT-BY-FIVE 34
FITNESS ON WHEELS 123
FITNESS ON WHEELS, INC. 123
FITTAPART LTD. 246
FIXX ENTERPRISES INC. 13
FIXX-A-DENT 13
FIZZ KIDS 34
FIZZ KIDS OF AMERICA FRANCHISING, INC. 34
FKA AM MARKETING 26
FLAG SHOP, THE 233
FLAGSTAR 77
FLAIR FRANCHISE SYSTEMS, INC. 230
FLAMERS CHARBROILED HAMBURGERS 79
FLAMERS CORPORATION 79
FLAT SHOP FRANCHISING 250
FLEAPRUF 365 19
FLEET FEET, INC. 154
FLEET FEET SPORTS/FLEET FEET TRIATHLETE 154
FLEET SERVICE, INC. 7
FLEETMASTERS 7
FLEMING KAMBEITZ 219
FLETCHERS FOTOGRAPHS NAI FLETCHERS FOTOGRAPHICS PTY 269
FLEX TEAM, INC. 51
FLEX-TEAM 51
FLIGHTFORM LTD. 247
FLOOR COVERINGS INTERNATIONAL 128
FLOORS TO GO 149
FLORENSE 248
FLORIDA TROPICALS 131
FLOWER BARROW COMPANY, THE 263
FLOWERAMA 131
FLOWERAMA OF AMERICA, INC. 131
FLUKY'S 79
FLYAWAY INDOOR SKYDIVING 241
FLYER NETWORK 178
FLYER NETWORK, INC. 178
FMM CONSULTANTS INTERNATIONS LTD. 259
FMS MANAGEMENT SYSTEMS, INC. 79
FOCUS MICROSYSTEMS 271

FOCUS OFFICE EQUIPMENT LTD. 271
FOLIAGE DESIGN SYSTEMS 131
FOLIAGE DESIGN SYSTEMS FRANCHISE CO. 131
FONTAINE SANTE 207
FONTANO'S SUBS 79
FONTANO'S SUBS FRANCHISE SYSTEM INC. 79
FOOD-N-FUEL 57
FOOD-N-FUEL, INC. 57
FOODEE'S INC. 79
FOODEE'S PIZZA 79
FOODMAKER, INC. 83
FORD GUM & MACHINE COMPANY 45
FORESIGHT ENGINEERING, INC. 19
FOREST HILL VIDEO 197
FOREVER LEARNING, INC. 159
FOREWEST HOLDINGS, INC. 225
FORM-YOU 3 WEIGHT LOSS CENTERS 123
FORM-YOU-3 INTERNATIONAL, INC. 123
FORMACOURSE 163
FORMATIVE FUN 263
FORMATIVE FUN LTD. 263
FORSLUNDS GUMMI AB 246
FORSLUNDS GUMMI AB/AB SVENSKA GUMMICENENTRALEN 246
FORTE HOTELS, INC. 134
FORTE HOTELS, INC. 136
FORTH FINANCIAL NETWORK FRANCHISE 26
FORTH FINANCIAL RESOURCES, LTD. 26
FORTUNE FRANCHISE CORP. 51
FORTUNE FRANCHISE CORPORATION 52
FORTUNE PRACTICE MANAGEMENT 171
FOSTER, PEPPER & SHEFELMAN 114
FOSTERS FREEZE INTERNATIONAL, INC. 79
FOSTERS FREEZE/FOSTERS FREEZE JR. 79
FOSTER'S SHOES 236
FOSTER'S SHOES CLAPP SHOES 236
FOTOQUELLE NEDERLAND B.V. 269
FOUNDATION BUSINESS BROKERS 216
FOUNTAIN RHOADES, P.C. 114
FOUR EVERGREEN SILK PLANT STORES 149
FOUR SEASONS MARKETING CORP. 19
FOUR SEASONS SUNROOMS 19
FOUR STAR PIZZA 79
FOURTH R, THE 159
FOURTH R. INC. 159
FOX MEYER HEALTH CORP. 123
FOXMEAD SERVICES 250
FOX'S PIZZA DEN 79
FPI 104
FRAGRANCE 223
FRAME & SAVE 138
FRAME IT YOURSELF 137
FRAME KING, INC. 138
FRAMING EXPERIENCE / FRAMING & ART CENTRE 230
FRAMING EXPERIENCE LTD. 230
FRANCESCO GROUP 268
FRANCESCO GROUP HOLDINGS LTD. 268
FRANCHISE & FINANCE 190, 227
FRANCHISE ACQUISITION DIVESTMENT CONSULTANTS LTD. 105
FRANCHISE ADVISORS WORLDWIDE 109
FRANCHISE AFFAIRES 1701, INC. 216
FRANCHISE ARCHITECTS, THE 105
FRANCHISE ASSOCIATES 105
FRANCHISE ASSOCIATES INC. 82
FRANCHISE ASSOCIATES, THE 105
FRANCHISE AXIS 106
FRANCHISE BROKER NETWORK OF ILLINOIS 106
FRANCHISE BUILDERS 106
FRANCHISE BUSINESS INTERNATIONAL 106
FRANCHISE BUSINESS SYSTEMS INC. 106
FRANCHISE CANADA DEVELOPERS INC. 216
FRANCHISE CENTRE™, THE(DBA) 106
FRANCHISE CHEZ BETTER LTEE. 205
FRANCHISE CONCEPTS & RECRUITING 216
FRANCHISE CONSORTIUM, LTD. 106
FRANCHISE CONSULTANTS, INC. 104
FRANCHISE CONSULTANTS INTERNATIONAL ASSOCIATION 105
FRANCHISE CONSULTING GROUP, THE 106
FRANCHISE CONSULTING SERVICES 106
FRANCHISE COUNSELLING CENTRE 259
FRANCHISE DESIGN CONSORTIUM LTD. 259

FRANCHISE DEVELOPERS *107*
FRANCHISE DEVELOPMENT *259*
FRANCHISE DEVELOPMENT AND MARKETING **260**
FRANCHISE DEVELOPMENT INTERNATIONAL, INC. *107*
FRANCHISE DEVELOPMENT SERVICES INT'L. *259*
FRANCHISE DEVELOPMENT SERVICES LTD. *259*
FRANCHISE DEVELOPMENTS, INC. *107*
FRANCHISE DEVELOPMENTS PTY *259*
FRANCHISE FACTORS *259*
FRANCHISE FINANCIAL SERVICES *216*
FRANCHISE FINANCING AND MARKETING *259*
FRANCHISE FOUNDATIONS *107*
FRANCHISE FOUNDATIONS, DIVISION OF *102*
FRANCHISE GROUP, THE *107*
FRANCHISE KOLLEGIET *259*
FRANCHISE LAW TEAM *114*
FRANCHISE LEARNING & CONSULTING CENTER LTD. *107*
FRANCHISE MARKETING NETWORK *107*
FRANCHISE MASTERS *107*
FRANCHISE NETWORK INTERNATIONAL (DBA) *107*
FRANCHISE OPPORTUNITIES, INC. *108*
FRANCHISE PERFORMANCE PARTNERS *108*
FRANCHISE PROFILES INTERNATIONAL *106*
FRANCHISE REALTY, INC. *216*
FRANCHISE RECRUITERS *216*
FRANCHISE RECRUITERS LTD. SM *108*
FRANCHISE REGISTRY & EXCHANGE, INC. *216*
FRANCHISE RESOURCE DEVELOPMENT CORP. *108*
FRANCHISE RESOURCES *259*
FRANCHISE SALES CENTER *108*
FRANCHISE SEARCH, INC. *108*
FRANCHISE SHOP LTD, THE *259*
FRANCHISE STORE, THE (C/O) *151*
FRANCHISE STORES INTERNATIONAL *108*
FRANCHISE SUPPORT SERVICE *216*
FRANCHISE SYSTEMS CORPORATION *108*
FRANCHISE SYSTEMS LIMITED *260*
FRANCHISING BOARD, LTD., THE *108*
FRANCHISING BUSINESS CONCEPTS, LTD. *108*
FRANCHISING WORKS, INC. *108*
FRANCHISINTERNATIONAL, INC. *108*
FRANCORP, INC. *108*
FRANDATA *108*
FRANDATA CORP. **108**
FRANK & STEIN DOGS & DRAFTS *79*
FRANK BAKER & ASSOCIATES, INC. *216*
FRANKFURTER RESTAURANTS, THE *79*
FRANKFURTER USA, INC., THE *79*
FRANKIE FOOK-LUN LEUNG, ATTORNEY AT LAW *114*
FRANKIE'S FAMILY RESTAURANTS *79*
FRANKLIN TRAFFIC SERVICE, INC. *26*
FRANKLIN'S PRINTING, DIGITAL IMAGING & COPYING *139*
FRANKLIN'S SYSTEMS, INC. *139*
FRANWAY INTERNATIONAL *108*
FRANX SUPREME *207*
FRASER & BEATTY *219*
FREELANCE PROFESSIONAL SERVICES *216*
FRENCH TOAST *34*
FRIDAY NITE LIVE! INC. *34*
FRIDAY'S FRONT ROW SPORTS GRILL *79*
FRIDAY'S HOSPITALITY WORLDWIDE *98*
FRIEND OF THE FAMILY *52*
FRIENDLY BANNERS RESTAURANTS *207*
FRIJOLES RESTAURANTS, INC. *78*
FRONT PAGE CAFE *79*
FRONT PAGE, INC. *79*
FRULLATI CAFE *79*
FRULLATI FRANCHISE SYSTEMS, INC. *79*
FUDDRUCKERS *79*
FUDGE CO., THE *57*
FUN SERVICES *55*
FUN TIME PIZZA - WORLD OF ENTERTAINMENT *80*
FUNCTION JUNCTION *149*
FUNDAZZLE *34*
FUNTIME INTERNATIONAL *80*
FURNITURE MEDIC *117*
FURNITURE WEEKEND *128*
FURNITURE WEEKEND FRANCHISING, INC. **128**
FUTON FACTORY OUTLET *233*
FUTURE CORPORATION *133*
FUTURE STARS SPORTS PHOTOGRAPHY *230*
FUTURE TRAINING SERVICES *250*
FUTUREKIDS, INC. *34*
FUTUREKIDS ONTARIO & QUEBEC *190*

G

G. STEWART BAKER LAW OFFICE *219*
G. WILLIKERS - OLDE WORLD FUDGE *203*
G.D. RITZY'S INC. *76*
GALARDI GROUP FRANCHISE CORP. *77*
GALARDI GROUP, INC. *101*
GALAXSEA ASSOCIATES INC. *166*
GALAXSEA CRUISES *166*
GALAXY CRYSTAL & CHINA, INC. *194*
GALLERY 92 INC. *138*
GALLUCCI'S INTERNATIONAL, INC. *80*
GALLUCCI'S PIZZERIA, INC. *80*
GAME PLAYER *149*
GAME PLAYER FRANCHISING INC. *149*
GAMES TO GO *163*
GAPPA & KIRKHAM, INC. *109*
GARAGE DOOR COMPANY, THE *248*
GARDEN BUILDING CENTRES LTD. *271*
GARRY ROBERTSON MUSIC SERVICES *197*
GARY J. MATALON, BARRISTER & SOLICITOR *219*
GAS TANK RENU-USA *13*
GATEWAY APPAREL *45*
GATEWAY NEWSTANDS/ GATEWAY CIGAR STORES *198*
GB BRICOCENTRE ET GARDEN CENTER *263*
GB-IMMO-BM *270*
GB-INNO-BM S.A. *263*
GB-INNO-BM SA *245*
GCF FOOD SERVICES INC. *208*
GCO, INC. *149*
GEIST & ASSOCIATES INC. *216*
GELATO AMARE *66*
GEM TRAVEL *263*
GENDRON GIFTS *149*
GENERAL BUSINESS SERVICES, INC. *26*
GENERAL ELECTRIC CREDIT CORP. *108*
GENERAL NUTRITION CENTER *123*
GENEVIEVE LETHU *271*
GENIUS KID ACADEMY, INC. *190*
GENUINE PARTS COMPANY LTD. *194*
GEORGIA CARPET OUTLETS *149*
GEORGIAN OAKS INTERNATIONAL *216*
GEPPETTO'S PIZZA & RIBS *80*
GERALD SAMUEL FIELDS *219*
GET-A-JOB, CANADA! *196*
GETEM CARDS *222*
GIANT TIGER STORES LTD. *234*
GIFF'S SUB SHOP *80*
GIFF'S SUB SHOP FRANCHISE SYSTEM INC. *80*
GIGANTAGRAM *263*
GILBERT E. HISCOTT, ESQ. *114*
GILBREATH'S INFORMATION SERVICES, INC. *26*
GILROY, CRAMER, MCLAUGHLIN & GELSON, P.C. *114*
GINGISS FORMALWEAR CENTERS *145*
GINGISS INTERNATIONAL, INC. *145*
GINO'S EAST RESTAURANT CORP. *90*
GIOVANNI'S PIZZA *80*
GIOVANNI'S PIZZA INC. *80*
GLAMOUR GIRL AND BOY BEAUTY CONTESTS *55*
GLAMOUR SHOTS LICENSING, INC. *138*
GLASS MAGNUM *171*
GLASS TECHNOLOGY WINDSHIELD REPAIR *13*
GLCC FRANCHISING INC. *189*
GLEDHILL ENTERPRISES *82*
GLOBAL CLEANING CONTRACTS LTD. *253*
GLOBAL GROUP, THE *253*
GLOBAL NUTS & FRUITS, INC. *59*
GLOBAL PET FOOD SALES INC. *229*
GLOBAL PET FOODS *229*
GLOBAL TRAINING NETWORK *30*
GLORIA JEAN'S GOURMET COFFEES *62*
GNC FRANCHISING, INC. *123*
GODDARD SCHOOL, THE *34*
GODFATHER'S PIZZA *80*

GODFATHER'S PIZZA, INC. *80*
GOFAX PUBLIC PHONE/FAX STATIONS *26*
GOLD COAST DOGS *80*
GOLD COAST DOGS FRANCHISE SYSTEMS, INC. *80*
GOLD MEDAL PRODUCTS *45*
GOLD STAR CHILI *80*
GOLD STAR CHILI, INC. *80*
GOLD VAULT LTD., THE *263*
GOLDEN BEAR GOLF CENTERS, INC. *163*
GOLDEN BEAR INTERNATIONAL *163*
GOLDEN CHICKEN FRANCHISES *80*
GOLDEN CORRAL CORP. *80*
GOLDEN CORRAL FAMILY STEAKHOUSE *80*
GOLDEN FRANCHISING CORPORATION *80*
GOLDEN FRIED CHICKEN *80*
GOLDEN GRIDDLE CORPORATION, THE *207*
GOLDEN GRIDDLE FAMILY RESTAURANTS *207*
GOLDIE'S PATIO GRILL *80*
GOLDMAN, SLOAN, NASH & HABER *216*
GOLDSMITH WILLIAMS *260*
GOLF GALORE *271*
GOLF GALORE LTD. *271*
GOLF PLAYERS INC. *165*
GOLF USA *149, 241*
GOLF USA, INC. *149*
GOLFOMAT CORP. *45*
GOLIGER'S TRAVEL LTD. *242*
GOLPHIS RESTAURANTS LTD. *207*
GOOD FOR YOU FRUIT AND YOGURT *203*
GOOD GOOD *256*
GOOD HUMOR - DICKIE DEE ICE CREAM *194*
GOOD LOOKIN' CARPET CLEANING *189*
GOOD NEWS ADVERTISING & MAILING INC. *178*
GOODEAL DISCOUNT TRANSMISSIONS *16*
GOODMAN LAPOINTE FERGUSON *219*
GOODTURN MANAGEMENT, INC. *181*
GOODTURN RIDE CENTRES *181*
GOODYEAR CERTIFIED AUTO SERVICE CENTRE *181*
GOODYEAR OF CANADA *181*
GOODYEAR TIRE & RUBBER CO. *13*
GOODYEAR TIRE CENTERS *13*
GORIN'S HOMEMADE, INC. *66*
GORMAN NASON LJUNGSTROM *219*
GOSH ENTERPRISES, INC. *74*
GOUBAUD *119*
GOURMET CUP *200*
GOURMET CUP COFFEE *62*
GOURMET CUP FOODS LTD., THE *200*
GOURMET CUP OF AMERICA, INC. *62*
GOURMET SPECIALTY GOURMET *58*
GRABBAJABBA *200*
GRADE EXPECTATIONS LEARNING CENTRES *239*
GRADE EXPECTATIONS LEARNING SYSTEMS INC. *239*
GRAHAM & DUNN *114*
GRAND SLAM U.S.A. *163*
GRANDMA LEE'S INC. *207*
GRANDMA LEE'S RESTAURANT AND BAKERY *207*
GRANDY'S, INC. *80*
GRANNY FEEL GOOD'S NATURAL FOOD *80*
GRANNY MAY'S MANAGEMENT *271*
GRAPEVINE DISCOUNT TRAVEL *263*
GRAPHIC INFORMATION SYSTEMS, INC. *140*
GRASSROOTS - THE HOME INSPECTION SPECIALISTS *184*
GREASE MONKEY *7*
GREASE MONKEY INTERNATIONAL, INC. *7*
GREASE PIT, THE *179*
GREAT AMERICAN BAGEL, THE *80*
GREAT AMERICAN CLEANERS INC. *130*
GREAT AMERICAN COOKIE COMPANY *62*
GREAT AUSTRALIAN ICE CREAMERY *256*
GREAT CANADIAN BAGEL, LTD., THE *201*
GREAT CANADIAN BAGEL, THE *201*
GREAT CANADIAN DOLLAR STORE *234*
GREAT CLIPS *119*
GREAT CLIPS, INC. *119*
GREAT COOKIES BY GEORGE, INC. *200*
GREAT CUTS *119*
GREAT EARTH VITAMIN STORES *123*
GREAT EXPECTATIONS PRECISION HAIRCUTTERS *119*
GREAT FRAME UP SYSTEM, INC., THE *138*

GREAT GOLF LEARNING CENTERS *163*
GREAT HARVEST BREAD CO. *62*
GREAT HARVEST FRANCHISING *62*
GREAT OUTDOOR SUB SHOPS, INC. *80*
GREAT STEAK & FRY CO., THE *81*
GREAT VIDEO SHOPPE, INC., THE *156*
GREAT WILDERNESS CO., INC. *234*
GREAT WILDERNESS COMPANY *234*
GREAT WRAPS! *81*
GRECO PIZZA DONAIR *207*
GREEK'S PIZZERIA *81*
GREENALLS INN PARTNERSHIP *263*
GREENBERG TRAURIG *114*
GREENE FLYER INC. *197*
GREENLAND IRRIGATION *228*
GREETINGS *3*
GREETINGS INC. *3*
GREGORY J. ELLIS, ESQ. *114*
GRETEL'S PRETZELS *62*
GREY FOX LTD. *53*
GRINDERS & SUCH, INC. *81*
GRINDERS AND SUCH RESTAURANTS *81*
GRINNER'S FOOD SYSTEMS LTD. *207*
GROUND ROUND INC., THE *81*
GROUND ROUND RESTAURANTS *81*
GROUP 4 SECURITAL *266*
GROUP CANTREX, INC. *226*
GROUP TRANS-ACTION BROKERAGE SERVICES, INC. *232*
GROUP TRANSACTION BROKERAGE SERVICES INC. *231*
GROUPE NOUVELLE RESTAURATION FRANCAIS *254*
GROUPE VALENTINE, INC. *213*
GROVE RECREATIONS INC. *163*
GROVE RECREATIONS, INC. *165*
GROW BIZ INTERNATIONAL *36, 148, 150, 156, 164*
GROWER DIRECT FRESH CUT FLOWERS INC. *234*
GRUPO JULIO SA DE CV *272*
GSS *248*
GSS (UK) LTD. *248*
GUARANTEED MUFFLER SHOPS *194*
GUARANTEED TUNE UP *7*
GUARANTEED TUNE UP, INC. *7*
GUARDIAN INTERLOCK SYSTEMS *13*
GUARDSMAN PRODUCTS, INC. *117*
GUARDSMAN WOODPRO *117*
GUN POINT LTD. *248*
GUN-POINT LTD. *248*
GUNSTER, YOAKLEY, VALDES-FAULI & STEWART P.A. *114*
GWYNNE LEARNING ACADEMY *159*
GWYNNE SYSTEMS, INC. *159*
GYM DANDY FOR TOTS *35*
GYM ROMPERS *35*
GYM ROMPERS FRANCHISE, INC. *35*
GYMBOREE *35*
GYMNASTICS IN MOTION/KANGAROO KIDS, INC. *35*
GYMSTERS INC. *35*

H

H & R BLOCK CANADA, INC. *177*
H & R BLOCK, INC. *1*
H-P PRODUCTS, INC. *50*
H.C.B. MANUFATURER DE ROUPAS *273*
H.D. FRANCHISING SYSTEMS, INC. *19*
H.E.L.P. HEAT & ENERGY LOSS PREVENTION *19*
H.M.S. BROWN BAGGERS *81*
H.M.S. FRANCHISING, INC. *81*
H.O.M.E. *142*
H20 + *149*
HAAGEN-DAZS *66*
HAAGEN-DAZS SHOPPE COMPANY, INC., THE *66*
HAIR ASSOCIATES, INC. *119*
HAIR N' THINGS INC. *119*
HAIR REPLACEMENT CENTERS INT. INC. *119*
HAIR REPLACEMENT SYSTEMS / HRS *119*
HAIRCRAFTERS *119*
HAIRDRESSING FRANCHISING LTD. *268*
HAIRLINES FRANCHISE SYSTEMS, INC. *119*
HAKKY, INC. *171*
HAKKY INSTANT SHOE REPAIR *171*

HALDORN & MANN, INC. *38*
HALDORN & MANN, INC./BLACK MAGIC SUPPLY *12, 44*
HALE OPTICAL EYE-CRAFTERS/ LONDON OPTICAL / PRESCRI *225*
HAM SUPREME SHOPS *58*
HAM SUPREME SHOPS, INC. *58*
HAMILTON RADIATOR SERVICE LTD. *181*
HAMILTON-RYKER COMPANY, THE *52*
HAMILTONS *272*
HAMILTONS CONFECTIONERS LTD. *272*
HAMPTON INN HOTELS *134*
HAN MONGOLIAN BARBECUE *207*
HAN MONGOLIAN BARBECUE LTD. *207*
HAND ME DOWNS *190*
HANDLE WITH CARE PACKAGING STORE *26*
HANDYMAN CONNECTION *19*
HANDYMAN HOUSE CALLS, INC. *39*
HANNA AUTO WASH FRANCHISE, INC. *12*
HAPPI HOUSE *81*
HAPPI HOUSE FRANCHISING CORP. *81*
HAPPI-NAMES *149*
HAPPI-STORES, INC. *149*
HAPPY & HEALTHY PRODUCTS INC. *45*
HAPPY CHEF SYSTEMS, INC. *81*
HAPPY JOE'S PIZZA & ICE CREAM PARLORS, INC. *81*
HAPPY STEAK, THE *81*
HARDEE'S FOOD SYSTEMS, INC. *81*
HAROLD L. KESTENBAUM, ESQ. *114*
HARRER MEINE EISDIELE *256*
HARRIET WEBSTER'S *272*
HARRIS RESEARCH INC. *32*
HARRISON, ELWOOD *219*
HARRY A. HALKOWICH *114*
HARRY RAMSDEN'S *256*
HARRY RAMSDEN'S PLC *256*
HARTCO ENTERPRISES, INC. *237*
HARTZ KRISPY CHICKEN *81*
HARTZOG, INC. *81*
HARVEY WASHBANGERS® *130*
HARVEY WASHBANGERS® FRANCHISE CORPORATION *130*
HARVEY'S RESTAURANT *207*
HAT ZONE FRANCHISING CO. LTD., THE *149*
HAT ZONE, THE *149*
HAUNTED HAYRIDES ™ *55*
HAUNTREPRENEURS, LTD. *55*
HAWKIN'S PRO-CUTS, INC. *120*
HAWTHORN SUITES *134*
HAYES GROUP, INC., THE *108*
HEAD OVER HEELS *35*
HEAD OVER HEELS FRANCHISE SYSTEM, INC. *35*
HEAD SHOPPE, GOLDEN CLIPPER, THE *223*
HEADQUARTERS COMPANIES *26*
HEALTH BREAD BAKERY, OPEN WINDOW BAKERY *201*
HEALTH FORCE, INC. *52*
HEALTH MART *123*
HEALTH SYSTEMS PLUS WELLNESS & WEIGHT MANAGEMENT *123*
HEALTHCARE RECRUITERS INT'L *52*
HEALTHMART, INC. *123*
HEARTLAND RETIREMENT SERVICES, INC. *176*
HEAVENLY HAM *58*
HEAVEN'S BEST CARPET & UPHOLSTERY CLEANING *32*
HEAVY DUTY PIZZA *208*
HEAVY DUTY PIZZA INC. *208*
HECK OF A DECK *184*
HECK OF A DECK LTD. *184*
HECTOR *208*
HEEL QUIK! HEEL/SEW QUIK! *171*
HEEL QUIK!, INC. *171*
HEFTY PUBLISHING *3*
HEIDI'S FROGEN YOZURT SHOPPE *66*
HEIDI'S FROGEN YOZURT SHOPPES, INC. *66*
HEID'S DEVELOPMENT CO. *81*
HEID'S OF LIVERPOOL *81*
HELEN HUTCHLEYS *66*
HELEN HUTCHLEYS INC. *66*
HELEN O'GRADY CHILDREN'S DRAMA ACADEMY *263*
HELEN O'GRADY INTERNATIONAL PTY. LTD. *263*
HELEN ROWE *114*
HELP U MOVE *171*
HELP-U-SELL REAL ESTATE *142*

HELPING OTHERS PURSUE EDUCATION *52*
HEMGLASS SVERIGE AB *256*
HEMORRHOID CLINICS OF AMERICA *123*
HENNING'S FISH HOUSE *81*
HENNING'S FISH HOUSE LTD. *81*
HENRY ARMSTRONG'S INSTANT PRINTING *231*
HENRY J. BEAN'S BAR & GRILL *256*
HER PLACE *154*
HER PLACE FRANCHISING, INC. *154*
HER REAL ESTATE INC. *142*
HER REALTORS *142*
HERBRAND TOOLS & EQUIPMENT *234*
HERBRAND TOOLS CORPORATION *234*
HERBU *228*
HERBU, INC. *228*
HERITAGE LOG HOMES, INC. *19*
HERMES BAKERY LTD. *201*
HERTZ CANADA LTD. *178*
HERTZBERG & ASSOCIATES LTD. *216*
HESSIAN, MCKASY & SODERBERG, P.A. *114*
HESTIA *263*
HEWITTS (NEW YORK STYLE) BAGEL BAKERY *201*
HI-SHOTS AERIAL PHOTOGRAPHY LTD. *45*
HICKORY FARMS *58*
HICKORY FARMS, INC. *58*
HICKORY FARMS OF CANADA *198*
HIGH LEVEL PHOTOGRAPHY *272*
HIGH TOUCH - HIGH TECH *35*
HIGH TOUCH INVESTMENT CORP. *35*
HIGH WHEELER INC., THE *66*
HIGH WHEELER RESTAURANT & ICE CREAM PARLOUR *66*
HIGHWAY WINDSCREENS & GLAZING *246*
HIGHWAY WINDSCREENS (UK) LTD. *246*
HILLARY'S CLEANERS *227*
HILLARY'S GOURMET ICE CREAM & YOGURT PARLORS *66*
HILLARY'S GOURMET ICE CREAM CO. *66*
HILTON HOTELS *134*
HINSPERGER FRANCHISE CONSULTANTS / NETWORK LEASING *216*
HIRE TECHNICIANS GROUP LTD. *248*
HIRETECH AT SAINSBURYS HOMEBASE *248*
HIS & HERS IRONING SERVICE *130*
HISTORICAL RESEARCH CENTER, INC., THE *172*
HISTORICAL RESEARCH CENTER INTERNATIONAL, INC., THE *172*
HMS FRANCHISE, INC. *142*
HO-LEE-CHOW *208*
HOBBYTOWN UNLIMITED *172*
HOBBYTOWN USA *172*
HOGGIES *256*
HOGGIES LTD. *256*
HOGI YOGI FRANCHISING CORPORATION *67*
HOGI YOGI SANDWICHES AND FROZEN YOGURT *67*
HOJ CAR AND TRUCK RENTALS/LEASING *178*
HOJ FRANCHISE SYSTEMS *178*
HOLDEN DAY WILSON *220*
HOLE-IN-ONE ADVERTISING *3*
HOLIDAY INN, HOLIDAY INN RESORT, HOLIDAY INN EXPRES *263*
HOLIDAY INN WORLDWIDE EUROPE - MIDDLE EAST - AFRICA *263*
HOLIDAY INNS, INC. *134*
HOLLAND & KNIGHT *113*
HOLLYWOOD STORES OF MOVIES & MEMORABILIA, THE *234*
HOLLYWOOD STORES, THE *234*
HOLLYWOOD WEIGHT LOSS CLINICS *124*
HOME CLEANING CENTERS OF AMERICA *39*
HOME ENVIRONMENT CENTER FRANCHISE, INC. *167*
HOME GROWN INDUSTRIES *87*
HOME HARDWARE, HOME BUILDING CENTRE, HOME HARDWARE *234*
HOME HARDWARE STORES, LIMITED *234*
HOME INSTEAD, INC. *124*
HOME INSTEAD SENIOR CARE *124*
HOME MARKETING SPECIALISTS, INC. /THE NO-COMMISSION *142*
HOME RATERS OF AMERICA, INC. *19*
HOME RATERS OF... *19*
HOME SERVICES ALLIANCE *19*
HOMEBUYERS ADVICE CENTRE *263*
HOMEBUYERS ADVICE CENTRE PLC. *263*
HOMEBUYERS' ASSISTANCE PROGRAM, INC. *142*
HOMELIFE *232*

HOMELIFE REALTY SERVICES, INC. *232*
HOMEOPATIA DR. WALDEMIRO PEREIRA *268*
HOMEOPATIA WALDEMIRA PERERIA LAB. INDL. F. LTDA *268*
HOMEOWNERS CONCEPT, INC. *142*
HOMES & LAND MAGAZINE *3*
HOMES & LAND PUBLISHING CORPORATION *3, 5*
HOMESTEADER ENTERPRISES, INC. *4*
HOMESTEADER, THE *4*
HOMETEAM INSPECTION SERVICE, THE *142*
HOMETUNE *246*
HOMETUNE MOTORING SERVICES *246*
HOMEWATCH INTERNATIONAL, INC. *129*
HOMEWOOD SUITES HOTELS *134*
HOMEWOOD SUITES, INC. *134*
HONEY DEW ASSOCIATES *81*
HONEY DEW DONUTS *81*
HONORS LEARNING CENTER, THE *159*
HOOTERS OF AMERICA, INC. *81*
HOPE CAREER CENTERS *52*
HOPKINS & WOOD *260*
HOPPER AND KANOUFF, P.C. *114*
HORIZON MAINTENANCE ASSOCIATES *192*
HORIZON MANAGEMENT SYSTEMS *194*
HORIZONS OF AMERICA, INC. *24*
HORNE & PITFIELD FOODS, LTD. *198*
HORWATH FRANCHISING SERVICES *260*
HOSPITALITY CORPORATION INTERNATIONAL *134*
HOSPITALITY FRANCHISE SYSTEM *135*
HOSPITALITY FRANCHISE SYSTEMS *134, 136*
HOSPITALITY FRANCHISE SYSTEMS, INC. *134*
HOSPITALITY INTERNATIONAL, INC. *135*
HOST HELPERS *172*
HOSTESS HELPER *52*
HOT DOG CHARLIE ENTERPRISES *82*
HOT LOOKS HIGH FASHION PORTRAITS *138*
HOT LOOKS INTERNATIONAL, INC. *138*
HOT N' FAST *172*
HOT SAM FRANCHISE DEVELOPMENT, INC. *62*
HOT SAM PRETZEL BAKERY *62*
HOT STUFF PIZZA, SMASH HIT SUBS, CINNAMON STREET BA *82*
HOTEL DES GOUVERNEURS *229*
HOULIHAN'S *82*
HOULIHAN'S RESTAURANT GROUP *82*
HOUSE DOCTORS HANDYMAN SERVICE *19*
HOUSE OF BLINDS & MORE *128*
HOUSE OF BLINDS & MORE FRANCHISE CORP. *128*
HOUSE OF COFFEE INC. *62*
HOUSE OF COLOUR LTD. *264*
HOUSE OF KNIVES LTD. *234*
HOUSE OF KNIVES, THE EDGE *234*
HOUSE OF SOMETHING DIFFERENT *272*
HOUSE OF STENO, INC. *26*
HOUSEMASTER - "THE HOME INSPECTION PROFESSIONALS" *142*
HOUSESITTERS FRANCHISE CORP., THE *227*
HOUSESITTERS, THE *227*
HOUSTON PIZZA FAMILY RESTAURANT *208*
HOUSTON PIZZA FRANCHISES LTD. *208*
HOWARD & HOWARD ATTORNEYS *114*
HOWARD JOHNSON FRANCHISE SYSTEMS *134*
HOWARD JOHNSON HOTELS IN CANADA *229*
HOWARD JOHNSON'S RESTAURANTS *82*
HOWE CEILING CLEANING *39*
HQ BUSINESS CENTERS *26*
HQ NETWORK SYSTEMS, INC. *26*
HSA INTERNATIONAL, INC. *19*
HUB COMMUNICATIONS LTD. *46*
HUBB'S *82*
HUBB'S DEVELOPMENT, INC. *82*
HUBERT'S EUROPEAN NATURAL BAKERIES, INC. *201*
HUDDLE HOUSE, INC. *82*
HUDDLE HOUSE RESTAURANT *82*
HUDON ET DEAUDELIN LTEE. *198*
HUDSON'S GRILL *82*
HUDSON'S GRILL OF AMERICA, INC. *82*
HUGO BOSS *272*
HUGO BOSS MODA LTDA. *272*
HUMANA INTERNATIONAL *250*
HUMPTY'S FAMILY RESTAURANTS *208*
HUMPTY'S RESTAURANTS INTERNATIONAL, INC. *208*
HUNGRY HOWIE'S PIZZA & SUBS, INC. *82*

HUNT BROTHERS, INC. *48*
HUNT PERSONNEL, TEMPORARILY YOURS *196*
HUNTER DOUGLAS LTD. *248*
HUNTINGTON LEARNING CENTER, THE *159*
HUNTINGTON LEARNING CENTERS, INC. *159*
HUNTINGTON RESTAURANT *82*
HURDY GURDY INTERNATIONAL *67*
HUSKY OIL MARKETING CO. *208*
HUSKY ROADHOUSE / HUSKY HOUSE RESTAURANT *208*
HYCITE CORPORATION *149*
HYDE-BARKER TRAVEL *264*
HYDRO-CHEM SYSTEMS, INC. (EST. 1971) *39*
HYGENICOMP COMPUTER CLEANING *192*
HYGENICOMP TECHNOLOGY MAINTENANCE INC. *192*
HYPROMAT FRANCE S.A. *246*

I

I CAN'T BELIEVE IT'S YOGURT *67*
I HAVE A WONDERFUL MAID *40*
I TO THE FUTURE, LTD. *35*
I. ROBOTICS, INC. *48*
I.C.C.C.C. *62*
I.L.P.S. *194*
I.M.T. GES.M.B.H *256*
I.T.M. HOLDINGS INC. *230*
IB YOUR OFFICE *250*
IB YOUR OFFICE INT'L. LTD. *250*
IBIS *134*
ICE CREAM & YOGURT CLUB, THE *67*
ICE CREAM CHURN *67*
ICE CREAM CHURN INC. *67*
ICE CREAM CLUB, INC., THE *67*
ICE CREAMERIES OF AUSTRALIA *256*
ICN *108*
IDENT-A-KID PROGRAM *35*
IDENT-A-KID SERVICES OF AMERICA *35*
IDENTICAR SECURITY SYSTEMS *246*
IDENTICAR WORLDWIDE LTD. *246*
IDENTIFICATION SERVICES OF CANADA INC. *190*
IDRS, INC. *20*
IGA *198*
IHOP, INC. *82*
IKE'S DELI & BAKERY INC. *62*
IL' PANZEROTTO AND PIZZA LTD., THE *210*
ILLUSIONS JEWELRY COMPANY *149*
ILLUSIONS REPLICA JEWELRY *149*
I'M SMART *172*
IMAGE CONTROL *188*
IMAGE IN TIME *46*
IMAGES IN TIME *172*
IMAGIMAZE FAMILY FUN CENTERS *35*
IMAGINE TOMORROW® *35*
IMAGINE TRANSFERS LTD. *264*
IMI MARSTON RADIATOR SERVICES. *246*
IMPAC FRANCHISING *108*
IMPRESSIONS *234*
IMPRESSIONS ON HOLD INTERNATIONAL *27*
IMTEC (INTERNATIONAL MANAGEMENT TECHNOLOGY CORPORAT *109*
'IMTIYAZ' *260*
IN TOTO KITCHENS *272*
INACOM CORP. *156*
INACOMP COMPUTER CENTERS *145*
INCHES-A-WEIGH *124*
INCREDIBLE CHOCOLATE CHIP COOKIE COMPANY *62*
INDEPENDENT LIGHTING FRANCHISE CORP. *46*
INDIVIDUAL *78*
INDOOR CRICKET STADIUMS *264*
INDUSTRIA DE PROD. ALIMENTICIOS CORY LTDA *255*
INDY LUBE 10-MINUTE OIL CHANGE *8*
INDY LUBE SERVICE CO., INC. *8*
INFINITIF *272*
INFL-AD-ABLE IMAGES OF CANADA, INC. *194*
IN'FLECTOR CONTROL SYSTEMS INC. *184*
INFOPOINT *264*
INFOPOINT LTD. *264*
INFORM *139*
INFORM INTERNATIONAL INC. *139*

INFORMATION PLUS 216
INFRANGIBLES, INC. 73
ING BANK 260
INK WELL OF AMERICA, INC., THE 139
INK WELL, THE 139
INKY DEW, LLC 46
INN TENTS 232
INN TENTS CANADA INC. 232
INNOVATIONS IN CORPORATIONS, INC. 170
INNOVATIVE MOVING STYTEMS, INC. 46
INNSUITES HOTELS 134
INQUIRY PLUS 27
INQUIRY PLUS FRANCHISING CORP. 27
INSPECTECH 19
INSPORT 272
INSTANT CUSTOM SIGNS 241
INSTY-PRINTS 139
INSTY-PRINTS , INC. 139
INSULATED DRY-ROOF SYSTEM 20
INTACAB LTD. 264
INTEGRA ENVIRONMENTAL 243
INTEGRA ENVIRONMENTAL INC. 243
INTELLIGENT ELECTRONICS 157
INTERBEAUTE COIFFURE 223
INTERFACE FINANCIAL GROUP, THE 188
INTERFACE GROUP LTD., THE 188
INTERIM HEALTHCARE 52
INTERIM PERSONNEL 52
INTERIM SERVICES INC. 52
INTERIM SERVICES, INC. 52
INTERLINK EXPRESS PLC 250
INTERMER S.A. 261
INTERNATIONAL AMERICAN GRAFFITI FRANCHISING CORP. 38
INTERNATIONAL BARTENDING INSTITUTE 159
INTERNATIONAL BIO RESEARCH LTD. 229
INTERNATIONAL BOARD OF DIRECTORS 109
INTERNATIONAL BURGER BROTHERS 204
INTERNATIONAL BUSINESS CONSULTANTS ASSOCIATION 250
INTERNATIONAL BUSINESS OPPORTUNITIES 188
INTERNATIONAL BUSINESS SCHOOLS INC. 240
INTERNATIONAL CLEANING SERVICES 40
INTERNATIONAL DIRECT RESPONSE INC. 4
INTERNATIONAL ENTERTAINMENT SYSTEMS (IES) 46
INTERNATIONAL FRANCHISE ASSOCIATION 109
INTERNATIONAL FRANCHISE DEVELOPMENT 109
INTERNATIONAL FRANCHISING 136
INTERNATIONAL GOLF 163
INTERNATIONAL GOLF ENTERPRISES INC. 163
INTERNATIONAL HOME MARKETING SYSTEMS, INC. 128
INTERNATIONAL HOME OFFICE 188
INTERNATIONAL HOUSE OF PANCAKES RESTAURANTS 82
INTERNATIONAL INSTITUTE OF TRAVEL 239
INTERNATIONAL LOSS PREVENTION SYSTEMS CORP. 194
INTERNATIONAL LOSS PREVENTION SYSTEMS INC. 186
INTERNATIONAL MARKETING SYSTEMS, INC. 110
INTERNATIONAL MERGERS & ACQUISITIONS 27
INTERNATIONAL POULTRY COMPANY 82
INTERNATIONAL PUBLISHING SERVICES, INC. 168
INTERNATIONAL RADIATOR SERVICES LTD. 247
INTERNATIONAL SUN SHADE, INC. 152
INTERNATIONAL TELEVISION PRODUCTIONS, INC. 172
INTERNATIONAL TOURS, INC. 166
INTERNATIONAL VIDEO YEARBOOKS, INC. 156
INTERNATIONAL VOICE EXCHANGE (IVX) 27
INTERSTATE DAIRY QUEEN CORP. 77
INTOTO KITCHENS 248
INVENTION SUBMISSION CORP. 27
INVESTORS GROUP FINANCIAL SERVICES INC. 177
INVIRO 143
INVISIONS 119
INVISIONS INTERNATIONAL CORP. 119
IOWA REALTY COMPANY, INC. 143
IOWA REALTY MEMBERS 143
IPC FRANCHISING CORP. 82
IRLY BIRD BUILDING CENTRES 194
IRLY DISTRIBUTORS LTD. 194
IRV H. KAUFMAN & ASSOCIATES 109
IRVINGS FOR RED HOT LOVERS 82
IRVINGS FRANCHISE SYSTEMS 82
ISCO, LTD. 75

ISLAND FREEZE FRANCHISE SYSTEMS, INC. 67
ISLAND WATER SPORTS 149
ISLAND WATER SPORTS FRANCHISE GROUP INC. 149
ISLANDMANIA 35
ISLANDMANIA FRANCHISE CORP. 35
ISU INTERNATIONAL 27
IT STORE 234
ITALIAN EXPRESS FRANCHISE CORP. 82
ITALIAN EXPRESS FRANCHISE CORP. 93
ITALIAN OVEN, INC. 82
ITALIAN OVEN, THE 82
ITALIAN PLACE, THE 82
ITALIANNI'S 83
ITALO'S PIZZA SHOP, INC. 83
IT'S DENTS OR US 13
ITT SHERATON CORP. 135
IVY GATE ASSEMBLY 172
IVY GATE FURNITURE ASSEMBLY 172
IZZY'S PIZZA RESTAURANTS 83

J

J&H FOODS 96
J&M COIN, STAMP & JEWELLERY LTD. 244
J. F. SCHMITZ ASSOCIATES..THE FINDERS 216
J. JOHN O'DONOGHUE 220
J. KWINTER GOURMET HOT DOGS 208
J. MICHAEL DADY & ASSOCIATES, P.A. 114
J. ROBERTS & ASSOCIATES 27
J.C.M. CONSULTING 109
J.D. BYRIDER SALES 13
J.D. BYRIDER SYSTEMS 13
J.E.J. EDITORA E. COMERCIO LTDA. 272
J.F. SCHMITZ ASSOCIATES...THE FINDERS 202
J.F. SCHMITZ ASSOCIATES..THE FINDERS 204, 205, 227
J.F.M., INC. 58
J.L. HAMMETT CO. 159
J.P. LEE'S INTERNATIONAL 83
J.T. LAZARTIGUE (UK) LTD. 268
J.W. TUMBLES LICENSING CORP. 35
J.W. TUMBLES®, A CHILDREN'S GYM 35
JACK GODFREY & SONS, INC. 130
JACK IN THE BOX 83
JACKI'S, INC. 124
JACKPOT CONVENIENCE STORES, INC. 58
JACKPOT FOOD MART 58
JACK'S COPY CENTER 139
JACKSON DIGITAL IMAGING CORP. 139
JACKSON HEWITT TAX SERVICE 1
JACNINE COMP. IMP. EXP. LTDA 268
JACQUES CARTIER PIZZA, INC. 208
JACQUES JANINE 268
JADE SECURITY, INC. 23
JAKE'S PIZZA 83
JAKE'S PIZZA INTERNATIONAL 83
JAMES A. MEANEY 114
JAN-PRO 40
JAN-PRO CLEANING SYSTEMS 40
JANDOR ENTERPRISES (CANADA) LTD. 189
JANI-KING CANADA 192
JANI-KING INTERNATIONAL, INC. 40
JANTIZE AMERICA INC. 40
JANUZZI FRANCHISING INC. 83
JANUZZI'S PIZZA & SUBS 83
JAPAN CAMERA 1 HOUR PHOTO 230
JAPAN CAMERA CENTRE LTD. 230
JARDILAND 264
JAVA CENTRALE 62
JAVA CENTRALE, INC. 62
JAVA JOE'S 201
JAVA JOE'S INC. 201
JAY ROBERTS & ASSOCIATES, INC. 28
JAZZERCISE 124
JBS, INC. 53
JB'S RESTAURANTS 83
JDI CLEANING SYSTEMS 192
JDI CLEANING SYSTEMS INC. 192
JEAN COUTU GROUP 225
JEANNE PIAUBERT COSMETICS, LTD. 149

JENNINGS, STROUSS & SALMON, P.L.C. *112*
JENNY CRAIG INTERNATIONAL INC. *124*
JENNY CRAIG WEIGHT LOSS CENTERS *124*
JERCITY FRANCHISES, LTD. *242*
JERKY HUT *58*
JERKY HUT INTERNATIONAL, INC. *58*
JERRY'S SUBS AND PIZZA *83*
JERRY'S SYSTEMS, INC. *83*
JERSEY CITY *242*
JERSEY MIKE'S FRANCHISE SYSTEMS INC. *83*
JERSEY MIKE'S SUBMARINES *83*
JET - ROD FRANCHISING, LTD. *248*
JET CLEEN LIMITED *253*
JET, INC. *46*
JET PRESS - BIZWIZ *140*
JET-BLACK INTERNATIONAL, INC. *172*
JET-BLACK SEALCOATING & REPAIR *172*
JEWELRY REPAIR ENTERPRISES *172*
JEWELRY REPAIR ENTERPRISES, INC. *171*
JEWELRY-BY-THE-INCH *46*
JIFFY SHINE USA, INC. *14*
JIM DANDY CLEANERS *130*
JIM DANDY INTERNATIONAL, INC. *130*
JIMBOY'S TACOS *83*
JIMMY JOHN'S *83*
JIMMY THE GREEK *208*
JJB ENTERPRISES *145*
JOAN M. CABLES LA FEMMINA BEAUTY SALONS, INC. *119*
JOB BANK USA *46*
JOBSOURCE CANADA & INTERNATIONAL JOBLINK *188*
JOE LOUE TOUT RENT ALL, INC. *232*
JOE RENT ALL, INC. *232*
JOEY'S ONLY FRANCHISING LTD. *208*
JOEY'S ONLY SEAFOOD RESTAURANT *208*
JOEY'S ONLY SEAFOOD RESTAURANTS (ONTARIO) *208*
JOHN & JOE FASHIONS, INC. *158*
JOHN CASABLANCAS MODELING AND CAREER CENTERS *159*
JOHN GILPIN LTD. *252*
JOHN H. DELL & ASSOCIATES, INC. *217*
JOHN L. HAY *114*
JOHN MOHR, ATTORNEY AT LAW *114*
JOHN PERKINS & ASSOCIATES *260*
JOHN ROBERT POWERS FINISHING, MODELING, AND CAREER *159*
JOHN ROBERT POWERS SCHOOL SYSTEM, INC. *159*
JOHN SIMMONS *149*
JOHN T'S UNIQUE GIFTS *149*
JOHNNY APPLESEED RESTAURANTS *84*
JOHNNY QUIK FOOD STORES, INC. *58*
JOHNNY ROCKETS *84*
JOHNSON HYDRO SEEDING CORP. *131*
JOLLY PIRATE ENTERPRISES *63*
JON SMITH ENTERPRISES, INC. *84*
JON SMITH SUBS *84*
JOS. A. BANK CLOTHIERS *154*
JOSEPH'S HAIR SALONS (JOSEPH COIFFURES) *223*
JOSLIN DIABETES AFFILIATED CENTERS *124*
JOSLIN DIABETES CENTER, INC. *124*
JOUETS D'ART INTERNATIONAL *264*
JOYSOUND LIMITED *253*
JR. FOOD MART *58*
JRECK SUBS, INC. *84*
JTC MANAGEMENT, INC. *102*
JUG CITY *198*
JUGS RANGE-PRO *163*
JUICE WORLD *58*
JUICY LUCY'S DRIVE-THRU *84*
JUICY LUCY'S, INC. *84*
JULIE ANN'S CORPORATION *67*
JULIE ANN'S FROZEN CUSTARD *67*
JULIO *272*
JULIO'S *84*
JULIO'S ENTERPRISES *84*
JUNGLELAND MINI PUTT INC. *195*
JUST DESSERTS *201*
JUST KIDDING, INC. *36*
JUST NEW REELEASES *197*
JUST REMINISCING *172*
JUST REMINISCING, INC. *172*
JUST WILLS PLC. *264*
JUST-A-BUCK *149*

JUSTICE NETWORK FRANCHISE CORP, THE *172*
JUSTICE NETWORK, THE *172*

K

K & N MOBILE DISTRIBUTION SYSTEMS *46*
K & O PUBLISHING, INC. *2*
K-BOB'S CAPITAL RESOURCE GROUP, LTD. *84*
K-BOB'S STEAKHOUSES *84*
K.A.S. *272*
KALI'S BOUTIQUE *154*
KALI'S COTTONS INC. *154*
KALL-KWIK PRINTING *269*
KAMEHAMEHA CARPET CLEANERS *33*
KAMPGROUNDS OF AMERICA, INC. *134*
KANALY TRUST COMPANY *109*
KANGAKAB INC. *35*
KARL SWITZERLAND *268*
KATIE MCGUIRE'S, INC. *84*
KEEP THE CHANGE! *172*
KEESAL, YOUNG & LOGAN *114*
KEG RESTAURANTS LTD. *208*
KELLY'S COFFEE & FUDGE FACTORY *58*
KELLY'S SPECIALTY GROUP, INC. *58*
KELSEY'S RESTAURANTS *208*
KEMMONS WILSON *136*
KEMP STRATEGIES *109*
KEMPER INTERNATIONAL INC. *46*
KEN-CO INDUSTRIES, LTD. *194*
KENNEDY A. BROOKS *115*
KENNEDY FRANCHISING, INC. *16*
KENNEDY STUDIOS, INC. *138*
KENNEDY TRANSMISSION *16*
KENNETH F. DARROW, PA *115*
KENNETH P. ROBERTS *115*
KENNETH P. ROBERTS, A PROF. LAW CORP. *115*
KENNY ROGERS ROASTERS *84*
KERNELS POPCORN (CAN) *198*
KERNELS POPCORN, LIMITED *198*
KETTLE CREEK CLOTHING CO. *236*
KETTLE RESTAURANTS, INC. *84*
KEVIN BRENDAN MURPHY, A PROF. CORP. *112*
KEY ASSOCIATES, INC. *143*
KEY WEST ALOE *119*
KEY WEST COSMETIC & FRAGRANCE FACTORY *119*
KFC *84, 208, 256*
KFC (GB) LTD. *256*
KFC CANADA, DIV. OF PEPSI COLA CANADA LTD. *208*
KFC CORPORATION *84*
KID KINGDOM *35*
KID SECURE OF AMERICA *35*
KID TO KID *36*
KID TO KID FRANCHISE SYSTEM, INC. *36*
KIDDIE ACADEMY INTERNATIONAL, INC. *36*
KIDDIE ACADEMY LEARNING CENTERS *36*
KIDDIE KOBBLER *190*
KIDDING AROUND *36*
KIDS AGAIN *36*
KIDS AGAIN, INC. *36*
KIDS FRANCHISE CORP. *150*
KID'S KAB *36*
KID'S KAB, INC. *36*
KIDS TEAM *150*
KILWIN'S CHOCOLATES AND ICE CREAM *58*
KILWIN'S CHOCOLATES FRANCHISE *58*
KINDERDANCE INTERNATIONAL *36*
KING KOIL BEDQUARTERS *150*
KING KOIL SLEEP PRODUCTS *150*
KIP MCGRATH EDUCATION CENTERS *159*
KIRBY TOURS *166*
KIRBY TOURS, INC. *166*
KIT ATOUT *226*
KITCHEN CRAFT CONNECTION, THE *226*
KITCHEN SAVER *184*
KITCHEN SAVER OF CANADA *184*
KITCHEN SOLVERS *20*
KITCHEN TUNE-UP *20*
KITCHEN WIZARDS (CANADA) *184*
KITCHENPRO *20*

KLEIN, HEISLER & KLARREICH P.C. *115*
KLEINS *272*
KLEINS FRANCHISING PTY. LTD. *272*
KNECHTEL ASSOCIATE STORES *198*
KNECHTEL WHOLESALE GROCERS *198*
KNIGHTS INN, KNIGHTS COURT *134*
KNOCKOUT INSPECTIONS *172*
KNOCKOUT PEST CONTROL INC. *172*
KNOWLEDGE DEVELOPMENT CENTERS *28*
KNOWLEDGE DEVELOPMENT CENTERS, INC. *28*
KOACH ENTERPRISES, INC. *109*
KOHR BROS. FROZEN CUSTARD *67*
KOHR BROS., INC. *67*
KOJAX *208*
KOJAX SOUVLAKI *208*
KOPY GRAPHICS INTERNATIONAL, INC. *140*
KOPY RITE *140*
KOSDALE CORP. *4*
KOTT KOATINGS INC. *172*
KOYA JAPAN *208*
KOYA JAPAN, INC. *208*
KRASSENSTEIN & SAUER PROFESSIONAL CORP. *115*
KREATIV PROPERTIES LTD. *269*
KRISPY KREME DOUGHNUT CORP. *63*
KRON CHOCOLATIER *58*
KRONAN CORP. *96*
KRUG'S BIG & TALL *154*
KRUMBLY BURGER INC. *84*
KRYSTAL COMPANY, THE *84*
KTC INTERNATIONAL, INC. *172*
KTU WORLDWIDE *20*
KUMON EDUCATIONAL INSTITUTE INC. *159*
KUSHELL ASSOCIATES, INC. *109*
KUSTOM CARDS INTERNATIONAL, INC. *46*
KWIK BITE *256*
KWIK BITE (UK) LTD. *256*
KWIK KOPY CORPORATION *140*
KWIK STRIP *264*
KWIK STRIP (U.K.) LTD. *264*
KWIK-KOPY PRINTING *231*
KWIK-KOPY PRINTING CANADA CORP. *231*

L

L. A. MUSIC *234*
L.A. SMOOTHIE FRANCHISES, INC. *58*
L.A. SMOOTHIE HEALTHMART AND CAFE *58*
LA CACHE *237*
LA CAGE AUX SPORTS *209*
LA CASITA RESTAURANTS *84*
LA MAISON DU CROISSANT *201*
LA MAISON DU CROISSANT LTD. *201*
LA PARFUMERIE DUQUIN LTD. *223*
LA PETITE CROISSANTERIE LTD. *255*
LA PIZZA LOCA *84*
LA SALSA *84*
LA SALSA HOLDING CO. *84*
LA SENORITA MEXICAN RESTAURANTS *84*
LA TORTILLERIA *209*
LA TORTILLERIA HOLDINGS *209*
LA TUILE EUROPE LTD. *184*
LABOR FINDERS / OFFICE FORCE *52*
LABOR FINDERS INTERNATIONAL, INC. *52*
LABOR WORLD *52*
LABORATOIRES SIMONE MAHLER *268*
LADAS & PARRY *260*
LADY K SALON SUPPLIES *268*
LADY OF AMERICA *124*
LAINES BERGER DU NORD S.A. *270*
LAKESIDE SECURITY SHUTTERS *248*
LAMBOURN COURT INTERNATIONAL *269*
LAMBOURN COURT INTERNATIONAL PLC *269*
LAMPPOST FRANCHISE CORPORATION *84*
LAMPPOST PIZZA *84*
LAMY GROUP, LTD., THE *109*
LAND MARK PRODUCTS *92*
LANDA CORPORATION *119*
LANGENWALTER CARPET DYEING *33*
LANGENWALTER INDUSTRIES INC. *33*

LANGUAGE CLUBS (INT.) LTD. *264*
LARGE LTD. *18*
LARKIN, HOFFMAN, DALY & LINDGREN, LTD. *115*
LARKIN INVESTMENTS LTD. *217*
LAROSA'S PIZZERIAS *85*
LARRY'S GIANT SUBS® *85*
LARRY'S ICE CREAM AND YOGURT PARLOURS *67*
LARRY'S INDUSTRIES, INC. *67*
LARUE MARKETING CONSULTANTS *109*
LAS VEGAS DISCOUNT GOLF & TENNIS *163*
LASALIGN *246*
LASER CHARGE, INC. *156*
LASER CHEM ADVANCED CARPET AND UPHOLSTERY DRYCLEANI *33*
LASER CHEM INTERNATIONAL CORP. *33*
LASER LAND *237*
LASER LAND CANADA *237*
LASER PRODUCT CONSULTANTS *140*
LASER PROFESSOR FRANCHISING CORP. *159*
LASER PROFESSOR LEARNING CENTERS *159*
LASERNETWORKS *231*
LASERQUEST *172*
LASERQUIPT *156*
LASERQUIPT INTERNATIONAL LTD. *156*
LASORDA'S DUGOUT, INC. *85*
LASTING IMPRESSIONS, INC. *43, 46*
LATE LATE SUPERSHOP, THE *256*
LATONIA SALES & SUPPLY CO. *151*
LAUND-UR-MUTT *136*
LAVANDERIA LAVITA LTDA. *253*
LAVITA *253*
LAVOIR LIBRE-SERVICE MAYTAG *227*
LAW ENFORCEMENT ASSOCIATES *46*
LAW OFFICE OF KENNETH G. PROTONENTIS, P.A. *115*
LAWN CARE THE PROFESSIONAL WAY *228*
LAWN DOCTOR *131*
LAWN DOCTOR, INC. *131*
LAZERQUICK COPIES *140*
LE BATEAU BLANC *190*
LE CENTRE VIDEOFILM MULTIVIDEO, INC. *238*
LE CLUB FRANCAIS *264*
LE CROISSANT SHOP *63*
LE GROUPE RO-NA DISMAT, INC. *235*
LE MUFFIN PLUS *201*
LE NATURIST JEAN-MARC BRUNET *234*
LE PEEP RESTAURANTS, INC. *85*
LE PRINT EXPRESS *231*
LE RIGOLFEUR INC. *242*
LEADERS HEALTH FOOD STORES *272*
LEADERSHIP MANAGEMENT, INC. *159*
LEAN LINE, INC. THIN LIFE CENTERS FRANCHISE CORP. *124*
LEARNING MAGAZINE, THE *239*
LEARNRIGHT CORPORATION *160*
LEARNRIGHT® *160*
LEATHER SOLUTION, THE *117*
LEATHES PRIOR(SOLICITORS & NOTARIES) *260*
LEAVERTON AUTO *9*
LEBEAU VITRES D'AUTOS *181*
L'ECOLE BUISSONNIERE *264*
LEDGERPLUS *1*
LEDO PIZZA *85*
LEDO PIZZA SYSTEMS, INC. *85*
LEE MYLES CORP. *16*
LEE MYLES TRANSMISSIONS *16*
LEE'S ICE CREAM *67*
LEES INN *134*
LEES INNS OF AMERICA, INC. *134*
LEGAL AND GENERAL *267*
LEGRAND ET CIE *254*
LEGS BEAUTIFUL HOSIERY BOUTIQUES *237*
LEISURE SYSTEMS, INC. *136*
LEMON TREE A UNISEX HAIRCUTTING ESTABLISHMENT, THE *119*
LEMONBUSTERS *13*
LEMSTONE BOOKS *150*
LEMSTONE, INC. *150*
LENARD'S POULTRY SHOPS *256*
LENTZ USA *9*
LEON'S FURNITURE LTD. *226*
LEOTARDI EXERCISEWEAR *155*

LEROS ASSOCIATES, INC. *172*
LEROS POINT TO POINT *172*
LES BOULANGERIE CANTOR *201*
LES PRES RESTAURANT *209*
LES RESTAURANTS PACINI INC. *210*
LES ROIS MAGES *256*
LES SUCERIES DE GRAND-MAMAN (1987) INC. *198*
LETTER WRITER, THE *28*
LETTUCE LEAF *85*
LEVALLIANT, TED *220*
LEVITT, BEBER *220*
LEWIS & TRATTNER *115*
LEWIS D'AMATO BRISBOIS & BISGAARD *114*
LGC *177*
LGC CORP. *177*
L'HERBIER DE PROVENCE *256*
LICK'S RESTAURANTS *209*
LIC'S *68*
LIFE TIME SPORTING PRODUCTS & SERVICES *264*
LIFE TIME TROPHIES *264*
LIFE TRENDS WEIGHT LOSS & TONING CENTERS *124*
LIFESAFE SECURITY *172*
LIGI INC. *222*
LIL' JULI SNACK BARS *209*
LIL' ORBITS INC. *46*
LIL' ORBITS MINI DONUTS *46*
LIL' PEACH *58*
LIMPIDUS *253*
LINC CORPORATION,THE *20*
LINDA'S FLAME ROASTED CHICKEN *85*
LINK STAFFING SERVICES *52*
LION SECURITY PRODUCTS *46*
LIP-N-LOR'S ENTERPRISES, INC. *42*
LIQUI-GREEN LAWN CARE CORP. *132*
LITE OFFICE *28*
LITE-WAY SUBS & DELI INC. *209*
LITL' TOTS FRANCHISING INC. *236*
LITTLE CAESAR'S PIZZA *85*
LITTLE CHEF ENTERPRISES *85*
LITTLE FUN STATION, INC. *34*
LITTLE GYM INTERNATIONAL, INC., THE *36*
LITTLE GYM, THE *36*
LITTLE KING INC. *85*
LITTLE KING OF TOPEKA *85*
LITTLE PROFESSOR BOOK CENTER / LITTLE PROFESSOR BOO *150*
LITTLE PROFESSOR BOOK CENTERS, INC. *150*
LITTLE WEDDING CHAPEL, THE *168*
LIV CANADA *226*
LIVING GREEN *132*
LIZIO'S SPAGHETTI VENDORS *85*
LLOYD PERSONNEL SYSTEMS, INC. *52*
LLOYD'S ICE CREAM, INC. *68*
LOARD'S ICE CREAM & CANDIES *68*
LOBSTER VILLAGE *256*
LOCAL MERCHANT DISPLAY CENTERS *4*
LOCKE PURNELL RAIN HARRELL *115*
LOCKLIER CO., INC. *100*
LOCKS & KEYS, INC. *150*
LOGAN FARMS HONEY GLAZED HAMS *173*
LOGAN FARMS, INC. *173*
LOGOS AND LABELS *150*
LOLLYTGOS LTD. *34*
LOMMA ENTERPRISES, INC. *163*
LOMMA GOLF *163*
LONDON CLEANERS *227*
LONDON CLEANERS INC. *227*
LONG JOHN SILVER'S SEAFOOD SHOPPES *85, 209*
LONGBRANCH STEAKHOUSE & SALOON *85*
LORD'S AND LADY'S HAIR SALONS *120*
LORMIT MANAGEMENT SYSTEMS, INC. *244*
LORMIT PROCESS SERVICES *244*
LORRAINE'S TROPI-TAN *124*
LORRAINE'S TROPI-TAN, INC. *176*
LOS RIOS MEXICAN FOODS *209*
LOSURDO'S FOODS, INC. *46*
LOSURDO'S RESTAURANT *46*
LOVE TOAST *256*
LOVE'S GROUP *68*
LOVE'S YOGURT *68*
LOX OF BAGELS *63*

LPC - LIVROS PERSONALIZADOS PARA CRIANCAS *272*
LRC PRODUCTS LTD. *262*
LUBE FACTORY INTERNATIONAL INC., THE *179*
LUBE FACTORY, THE *179*
LUBE WAGON, THE *8*
LUBEPRO'S *8*
LUBEPRO'S INTERNATIONAL, INC. *8*
LUBRICHEK INDUSTRIES, INC. *179*
LUCAS BARON *260*
LUYE AQUAFIT INTERNATIONAL, INC. *163*

M

M & B MARQUEES *264*
M & B MARQUEES LTD. *264*
M & M MEAT SHOPS *198*
M & M MEAT SHOPS LTD. *198*
M K C -MICHEL KAHN CONSULTANTS *260*
M&S ENTERPRISES *92*
M-CO., INC. *32*
M-CORP., INC. *209*
M-FOUR CANAM INTERNATIONAL *217*
M.G.M. INTERNATIONAL *150*
M.G.M. LIQUOR WAREHOUSE *150*
M.L.U.S. INC. *8*
M.R. HOLDINGS LTD. *192*
M.T.C. MANAGEMENT, INC. *100*
MAACO AUTO PAINTING & BODYWORKS *13, 181*
MAACO ENTERPRISES, INC. *13*
MAACO SYSTEMS CANADA, INC. *181*
MAC BIRDIE GOLF GIFTS *164*
MAC BIRDIE GOLF GIFTS, INC. *164*
MAC TOOLS CANADA *195*
MAC TOOLS, INC. *46*
MACAYO MEXICAN RESTAURANTS *85*
MACKALL, CROUNSE & MOORE, PLC *115*
MACKIMMIE MATTHEWS *220*
MACPHERSON & KELLEY SOLICITORS *260*
MACPHERSON MEISTERGRAM *47*
MACRI'S DELI FRANCHISE, INC. *85*
MACROBERTS *260*
MAD HATTER CAR CARE CENTERS, INC. *9*
MAD SCIENCE GROUP, THE *190*
MADE 'N-A-MINUTE PRINTERS *231*
MADE IN JAPAN - A TERIYAKI EXPERIENCE *209*
MADE IN JAPAN JAPANESE RESTAURANTS LIMITED *209*
MADE 'N-A-MINUTE PRINTERS, LTD. *231*
MAGI SEAL SERVICES *244*
MAGI SEAL SERVICES, INC. *244*
MAGIC MARKETING, INC. *127*
MAGIC WOK *85*
MAGICUTS *223*
MAGIS FUND RAISING SPECIALISTS, INC. *173*
MAGNI FRAME CUSTOM FRAMING & ART STUDIOS *230*
MAGNUM PIERING *20*
MAID BRIGADE SYSTEMS , INC. *40*
MAID BRIGADE SERVICES *40*
MAID EASY *40*
MAID TO PERFECTION *40*
MAIDS AHOY, INC. *40*
MAIDS AHOY! *40*
MAIDS INTERNATIONAL, THE *40*
MAIDS, THE *40, 253*
MAIL BOXES ETC. *28, 188, 251*
MAIL BOXES ETC. (AUSTRALIA) PTY LTD. *251*
MAIL BOXES ETC. (THAILAND) CO. LTD. *251*
MAIL BOXES ETC. BRAZIL *251*
MAIL BOXES ETC. FRANCE *251*
MAIL BOXES ETC. ITALY *251*
MAIL BOXES ETC. MEXICO *251*
MAIL BOXES ETC. PHILIPPINES *251*
MAIL BOXES ETC. TURKEY *251*
MAIL BOXES ETC. VENEZUELA *251*
MAIL BOXES EUROPE LTD. *251*
MAIN EVENT LAWN SIGN INC. *161*
MAIRS, INC. *130*
MAISON DU POPCORN *58*
MAJESTIC YACHTS INC. *176*
MAJOR MAGIC'S ALL STAR PIZZA REVUE INC. *85*

MAK'N WAVES, INC.   *138*
MALIBU GALLERY   *138*
MALIBU GALLERY FRANCHISE, INC.   *138*
MAMA LENA'S SPAGHETTI EXPRESS   *86*
MAMA LENA'S SPAGHETTI EXPRESS, INC.   *86*
MAMA ROSA'S PIZZA   *86*
MAMAR, INC.   *19*
MAMMA ILARDO'S PIZZERIA   *86*
MANAGEMENT 2000   *109, 217*
MANAGEMENT ACTION PROGRAMS   *109*
MANAGEMENT CONSULTANTS   *28*
MANAGEMENT RECRUITERS / SALES CONSULTANTS   *52*
MANAGEMENT RECRUITERS INTERNATIONAL, INC.   *52*
MANCHU WOK   *86, 209*
MANDARIN   *209*
MANDARIN RESTAURANT FRANCHISE CORP.   *209*
MANDY'S MATCHING DEVELOPMENT CORP.   *173*
MANDY'S MATCHING SERVICE   *173*
MANHATTAN BAGEL CO.   *86*
MANHATTAN BAGEL CO., INC.   *86*
MANPOWER TEMPORARY SERVICES   *52*
MANUFACTURING MANAGEMENT ASSOCIATES   *28*
MAP   *109*
MAPLE LEAF FOODS   *200*
MAPLE LEAF FOODS, INC.   *196*
MAR-KAL PRODUCTS CORP.   *47*
MARBLE RENEWAL   *173*
MARBLE SLAB CREAMERY   *68*
MARBLE SLAB CREAMERY, INC.   *68*
MARBLELIFE   *20*
MARBLELIFE, INC.   *20*
MARBLES MUSIC & VIDEO   *156*
MARCHANDS UNIS, INC.   *234*
MARCHANDS UNIS, INC.   *226, 241*
MARCO'S INC.   *86*
MARCO'S PIZZA   *86*
MARCUS CORP.   *133*
MAREMONT EXHAUST PRODUCTS   *180*
MARK PI'S CHINA GATE/MARK PI'S FEAST OF THE DRAGON/   *86*
MARK PI'S FRANCHISE CORP.   *86*
MARKET STREET BUFFET & BAKERY   *86*
MARKET TARGET RESEARCH   *109*
MARKETING CONSULTANTS OF AMERICA 'MCA'   *109*
MARKETING RESOURCES GROUP   *109*
MARKETING SERVICES BY VECTRA, INC.   *47*
MARRIOTT CORP.   *134*
MARSHALL GROUP, THE   *109*
MARTEK LTD.   *173*
MARTEK LTD.   *46, 138, 172*
MARTIN FRANCHISES INC.   *130*
MARTIN INTERNATIONAL   *217*
MARTING FRANCHISE CORP.   *156*
MARTING RADIO DIAGNOSTIC SERVICES   *156*
MARTY WOLF GAME CO.   *55*
MARY ANN'S GOLDEN FRIED CHICKEN   *86*
MARY BROWN'S FRIED CHICKEN   *209*
MARY-LEE CO., INC.   *67*
MARY'S PIZZA SHACK   *86*
MASH HOAGIES INC.   *86*
MASH HOAGIES/MASH SUBS & SALADS   *86*
MASTER BREW LTD.   *256*
MASTER CARE JANITORIAL   *192*
MASTER HOSTS INNS & RESORTS / RED CARPET INN / SCOT   *135*
MASTER STROKE   *40*
MASTER SUPPLY SYSTEMS INTERNATIONAL, INC.   *15*
MASTER THATCHERS LTD.   *272*
MASTERMECHANIC, THE   *182*
MASTERSHARP   *264*
MATCO TOOLS   *13*
MATH PLUS LEARNING CENTRES   *239*
MATOYEE ENTERPRISES INC.   *213*
MATOYEE ENTERPRISES, INC.   *206*
MAURICE'S GOURMET BARBEQUE/PIGGIE PARK RESTAURANTS   *86*
MAVERICK FAMILY STEAK HOUSE   *86*
MAX PIES CARPET   *226*
MAX'S DELI & RESTAURANT   *86*
MAYOTEE ENTERPRISES INC.   *205*
MAYOTEE ENTERPRISES, INC.   *210*
MAYTAG   *227*
MAYTAG HOMESTYLE LAUNDRIES   *130*
MAYTOYEE ENTERPRISES INC.   *207*
MAZZIO'S CORPORATION   *86, 93*
MAZZIO'S PIZZA   *86*
MBEC COMMUNICATIONS INC.   *188*
MCBEANS   *201*
MCCOLLA ENTERPRISES, LTD.   *152*
MCDONALD'S   *87*
MCDONALD'S CORP.   *87*
MCDONALD'S RESTAURANTS   *257*
MCDONALD'S RESTAURANTS LTD.   *257*
MCDONALD'S RESTAURANTS OF CANADA LTD.   *209*
MCGOVERN, HURLEY, CUNNINGHAM   *217*
MCGROW CONSULTING   *110*
MCGUIRE, WOODS, BATTLE & BOOTHE   *115*
MCMAHON ESSAIN INC.   *225*
MCMAID, INC.   *40*
MCQUIK'S OILUBE   *8*
MCQUIK'S OILUBE, INC.   *8*
MEALS TO YOU   *87*
MEAN GREEN   *195*
MEAN GREEN MANUFACTURING   *195*
MEASURE MASTERS FLOOR PLANNING & BLUEPRINT SERVICE   *184*
MEASURE MASTERS INC.   *184*
MED-PED S.A.   *264*
MEDELA, INC.   *126*
MEDIA MARKETING   *47*
MEDIA THREE MARKETING SERVICES LTD.   *217*
MEDICAL INSURA FORM SERVICE   *124*
MEDICAP PHARMACIES INC.   *124*
MEDICAP PHARMACY   *124*
MEDICHAIR LTD.   *225*
MEDICINE SHOPPE INTERNATIONAL INC., THE   *124*
MEDICINE SHOPPE, THE   *124*
MEDICLEAN   *33*
MEDIPOWER   *124*
MEGA VIDEO, INC.   *156*
MEGALICIOUS FOOD CORP.   *209*
MEINEKE DISCOUNT MUFFLER SHOPS   *9*
MEINEKE DISCOUNT MUFFLER SHOPS, INC.   *9*
MELCO EMBROIDERY SYSTEMS   *173*
MELLOW MUSHROOM   *87*
MELTING POT RESTAURANT, THE   *87*
MELTING POT RESTAURANTS, INC., THE   *87*
MEND-A-BATH INT'L (PTY) LTD.   *248*
MENDELSOHN ROSENTZVEIG SHACTER   *220*
MEN'S HAIR NOW   *120*
MENZIES - CHARTERED ACCOUNTANTS   *260*
MERCATIGUE ET DISTRIBUTION   *271*
MERCATIQUE ET DISTRIBUTION   *264*
MERCERIE PLUS   *264*
MERCHANT ADVERTISING SYSTEMS, INC.   *4*
MERCHANT, GOULD, SMITH, EDELL, WELTER & SCHMIDT, P.   *115*
MEREDITH CORPORATION   *141*
MERIDIAN REGULATORY ACUPUNCTURE   *125*
MERISEL F.A.B.   *156*
MERLE HARMON'S FAN FAIR   *155*
MERLE NORMAN COSMETICS, INC.   *120*
MERLIN SERVICES CORP.   *52*
MERLIN'S FRANCHISING, INC.   *9*
MERLIN'S MUFFLER AND BRAKE   *9*
MERMAID CAR WASH   *13*
MERMAID MARKETING, INC.   *13*
MERRY MAIDS   *40, 192*
MESSAGE ON HOLD NETWORK, THE   *47*
METRO - RICHELIEU - AMIX - GEM   *198*
METRO OFFICE SUITES & BUSINESS CENTER AT THE WOODBR   *28*
METRO RICHELIEU   *197*
METRO ROD SERVICES   *264*
METROMEDIA RESTAURANT GROUP   *93*
METROMEDIA STEAKHOUSES, INC.   *72*
MEXICAN CONTACT, THE   *264*
MEXICAN FRANCHISE ASSOCIATION, AC   *260*
MFP FRANCHISE SYSTEMS, INC.   *88*
MHN FRANCHISING, INC.   *120*
MIAMI SUBS   *87*
MIAMI SUBS CORPORATION   *87*
MICHEL'S BAGUETTE   *201*

MICHEL'S BAKERY & CAFE 63
MICHON CLEANERS 227
MICKEY FINN'S SPORTS CAFE 87
MICRO-REALITY INDOOR STOCK CAR RACING 164
MICROAGE COMPUTER CENTERS 156
MICROAGE, INC. 156
MICROPLAY OF AMERICA, INC. 238
MICROPLAY VIDEO GAME STORES 238
MICROTEL 135
MICROWAVE CLINIC 173
MID STATE MAILERS INC. 4
MIDAS 9
MIDAS (CANADA), INC. 180
MIDAS INTERNATIONAL CORP. 9
MIDAS LE SILENCIEUX 246
MIDAS MUFFLER SHOP 180
MIDLAND WATERLIFE FRANCHISING 272
MIDWAY MOTOR LODGES 135
MIDWEST COFFEE SYSTEMS INC. 201
MIGHTY DISTRIBUTING SYSTEM 13
MIGHTY DISTRIBUTING SYSTEM OF AMERICA, INC. 13
MIGHTY DOLLAR 234
MIGHTY TACO & SUBS 209
MIGRAINE CLINIC 225
MIKE ANDERSON'S SEAFOOD RESTAURANT CONSULTING, INC. 87
MIKE ANDERSON'S SEAFOOD RESTAURANTS 87
MIKE SCHMIDT'S PHILADELPHIA HOAGIES 87
MIKE'S RESTAURANTS 209
MILFORD HEIRLOOM INC. 138
MILITARY RENT-ALL, INC. 145
MILLION AIR INTERLINK, INC. 173
MILNER FENERTY 220
MING AUTO BEAUTY CENTERS 13
MING INTERNATIONAL, INC. 13
MINI BITES 201
MINI DONAL LTD. 209
MINI MAID 41
MINI MAID SERVICE SYSTEMS 192
MINI MAID SERVICES 192
MINI SERVICES COMPANY, INC., THE 41
MINI-GOLF, INC. 164
MINIT-LUBE ONTARIO INC. 179
MINIT-TUNE & BRAKE AUTO CENTRES 179
MINIT-TUNE INTERNATIONAL CORP. 179
MINSTER CLEANING SERVICES 253
MINUTE MAN 87
MINUTE MAN OF AMERICA 87
MINUTE MUFFLER AND BRAKE 180
MINUTEMAN FURNITURE RESTORATION 117
MINUTEMAN PRESS 231
MINUTEMAN PRESS & INTERNATIONAL MINUTE PRESS 140
MINUTEMAN PRESS INTERNATIONAL 140
MIRACLE AUTO PAINTING AND BODY REPAIR 14
MIRACLE AUTO PAINTING, INC. 14
MIRACLE METHOD BATHROOM RESTORATION 20
MIRACLE METHOD OF THE U.S. 20
MIRACLE-EAR 125
MISS ARISTA PAGEANT, U.S.A. 55
MISS MILLY HOUSE CLEANING 192
MISTER DONUT 257
MISTER FRONT-END LTD. 182
MISTER KOOL'S 253
MISTER MINI POST 195
MISTER MONEY - USA 150
MISTER PIZZA 257
MISTER SOFTEE, INC. 68
MISTER TRANSMISSION 183
MISTER TRANSMISSION (INTERNATIONAL) LTD. 183
MITEY INC. 9
MITSCHELE MARKETING GROUP 194
MIXAMATE CONCRETE 248
MIXAMATE HOLDINGS LTD. 248
MJB INTERNATIONAL REAL ESTATE 143
MMMARVELLOUS MMMUFFINS 201
MMMUFFINS CANADA CORP. 201
MMMUFFINS CANADA CORPORATION 201
MOBILE AUTO SYSTEMS 14
MOBILE CHEF 87
MOBILE CONTAINER SERVICE 173

MOBILE CONTAINER SERVICE, INC. 173
MOBILE MECHANIC 14
MOBILE MONETARY SERVICES 28
MOBILE MONETARY SERVICES INTERNATIONAL 28
MOBILE RADIATOR SERVICES 246
MOBILETUNING LTD. 246
MOBILITY CENTER, INC. 121
MODEL MERCHANDISING INTERNATIONAL, L.P. 159
MODERN ARAB ENTERPRISES, JEDDAH SKYE'S N.A. VIZION 260
MODULAR MARQUEES (NATIONWIDE) LTD. 265
MODULAR MARQUEES LTD. 265
MOE'S ITALIAN SANDWICHES 87
MOESTOGO CORP. 87
MOHAWK OIL CO, LTD. 198
MOHAWK OIL CO LTD. 198
MOLE HOLE, THE 150
MOLLY MAID 41
MOLLY MAID INC. 41
MOLLY MAID INTERNATIONAL, INC. 192
MOLLY MAID UK 253
MOMA'S FAMILY FAVORITE INC. 87
MOM'S BAKE AT HOME PIZZA 87
MOM'S FAMILY FAVOURITE U BAKE PIZZA 87
MONDAY MORNING AMERICA, INC. 36
MONDAY MORNING MOMS 36
MONEY BROKER ONE 28
MONEY CONCEPTS (CANADA) LTD. 188
MONEY MAILER 4
MONEY MAILER, INC. 4
MONEY MART 244
MONEY MASTERS 28
MONEY MASTERS FRAN. DEV. CORP. 28
MONEY STORE INVESTMENT CORPORATION, THE 110
MONEY STRETCHERS 47
MONEY TIME ACCOUNTING & TAX OFFICES 177
MONEY TIME, INC. 177
MONEYSWORTH & BEST QUALITY SHOE REPAIR 237
MONEYSWORTH & BEST QUALITY SHOE REPAIR, INC 237
MONFRIED OPTICAL, KINDY OPTICAL, DULING OPTICAL 125
MONGOLIAN BARBEQUE 257
MONITORNET 173
MONOGRAMS TO GO, INC. 47
MONOTAG CORP. 161
MONSIEUR BRICOLAGE 265
MONSIEUR DISMAT 184
MONSIEUR FELIX & MR. NORTON COOKIES 201
MONSIEUR MUFFLER 180
MONTANA SUNDOWN, INC. 21
MOORE BUSINESS FORMS & SYSTEMS DIVISION 110
MOPPS CLEANING SERVICES 253
MOPPS PLC. 253
MORALL BRAKE CENTER 14
MORALL BRAKE CENTER, INC. 14
MORLEY'S FAST FOODS 257
MORTAR MASON WALL POINTING 265
MORTGAGE ADVICE CENTER LTD., THE 251
MORTGAGE FRANCHISE LTD. 251
MOSTLY MOVIES 272
MOSTLY MOVIES MANAGEMENT PTY. LTD. 272
MOSTYNS 265
MOTO PHOTO, INC. 138
MOTOR KOTE 47
MOTORCADE INDUSTRIES LTD. 182
MOTORCADE INDUSTRIES, LTD. 194
MOTOREST S.A. 258
MOTORWORKS, INC. 14
MOTORWORKS REMANUFACTURED ENGINE INSTALLATION CENTR 14
MOUNTAIN COMFORT FURNISHINGS 128
MOUNTAIN COMFORT FURNISHINGS, INC. 128
MOUNTAIN MAN NUT & FRUIT CO. 47
MOUNTAIN MARKETING 47
MOUNTAIN MIKE'S PIZZA 87
MOVIE EXCHANGE 156
MOVIE SELLER 238
MOVIE WAREHOUSE 156
MOVIE WAREHOUSE MANAGEMENT, INC. 156
MOXIE JAVA 63
MOXIE JAVA INTERNATIONAL 63
MR. BIG (UK) LTD. 257

MR. BULKY TREATS & GIFTS 59
MR. BULKY TREATS & GIFTS LIMITED PARTNERSHIP 59
MR. BURGER, INC. 87
MR. CD-ROM 156
MR. CD-ROM STORES, INC. 156
MR. CHECKOUT DISTRIBUTORS 47
MR. CHECKOUT DISTRIBUTORS, INC. 47
MR. CLUTCH 246
MR. COD 257
MR. COD LTD. 257
MR. CONEY 87
MR. CRISPY'S HOT FRIES 244
MR. ELECTRIC 20
MR. GATTI'S, INC. 88
MR. GOODCENTS FRANCHISE SYSTEMS, INC. 88
MR. GOODCENTS SUBS & PASTAS 88
MR. HERO 88
MR. HOT DOG 88
MR. JIM'S PIZZA 88
MR. LIFT LTD. 265
MR. LUBE 179
MR. LUBE, A DIVISION OF IMPERIAL OIL 179
MR. LUBE U.S. 8
MR. MIKE'S STEAKHOUSE RESTAURANTS 209
MR. MOVIES 157
MR. MUGS 201
MR. PAYROLL CORPORATION 28
MR. ROOTER CORP. 20
MR. SLADE DRYCLEANING 253
MR. STEAKS 88
MR. SUB 209
MR. SUBB 88
MR. SUBB FRANCHISE CORP. 88
MR. SUBMARINE LTD. 209
MR. SUBMARINE OF BERWYN INC. 88
MR. TRANSMISSION 16
MR. TREES 132
MR. TREES FRANCHISE CORP. 132
MR. TUBE STEAK 195, 210
MR. WISE CLEANERS 130
MR. WIZARD (R) GLASS TINTING 244
MR. WIZARD (R) GLASS TINTING SHOWROOM 244
MRS. FIELDS COOKIES 63
MRS. FIELDS INC. 63
MRS. MARTY'S DELI RESTAURANT 88
MRS. POWELL'S BAKERY EATERY 63
MRS. POWELL'S BAKERY EATERY 201
MRS. POWELL'S INC. 63
MRS. SPOON'S FRESH BURGERS/ICE CREAM 88
MRS. VANELLI'S PIZZA & ITALIAN FOODS 210
MRS. VANELLI'S RESTAURANT LTD. 210
MS. EMMA DESIGNS LTD. 237
MSA NATIONWIDE FIELD SERVICE 143
MSI INTERNATIONAL 54
MUFFIN BREAK 202
MUFFIN BREAK CANADA INC. 202
MUFFIN TIN, THE 63
MUFFLER HOUSE CANADA LTD. 180
MULTI MANAGEMENT SYSTEMS, INC. 8
MULTI-TUNE & TIRE 8
MULTIPLICANT, INC. 190
MULTISTATE TRANSMISSIONS 16
MULTIVIDEO 238
MUNCHABLE BOUQUET 150
MUNDAY'S ATTORNEYS 260
MURPHY MANAGEMENT CORPORATION 53
MURTAUGH, MILLER, MEYER & NELSON 114
MUSCLEMAG INTERNATIONAL 242
MUSIC CITY 234
MUSIC GO ROUND 150
MUSIC TRENDS TEACHING STUDIOS 239
MUSIC TRENDS TEACHING STUDIOS, INC. 239
MUZAK 56
MY FAVORITE MUFFIN 63
MY FAVORITE MUFFIN TOO, INC. 63
MY FRIEND'S PLACE 88
MY KINDA TOWN PLC. 254, 256
MY MOTHER'S DELICACIES, INC. 63
MY MOTHER'S DELICACIES™ CAFE 63
MY PIE - UNIQUE PIZZA IN THE PAN 88
MY VERY OWN CLOCK 150
MYSTERY PIZZA & CHICKEN 210
MYSTERY PIZZA & CHICKEN LTD. 210

N

N & J MEDICAL CORP. 121
N.S. & T. 85
NACHO NANA'S 88
NACHO NANA'S INTERNATIONAL 88
NACOMEX USA 29
NAFCO 110
NAIL QUEEN 223
NAIL QUEEN LTD. 223
NAILS 'N LASHES STUDIO 223
NAKED FURNITURE 128
NAMCO SYSTEMS, INC. 4
NANETTE CREATIONS 47
NAT WEST BANK 260
NATALY'S 272
NATGO, INC. 173
NATHAN'S 88
NATHAN'S FAMOUS, INC. 88
NATION-WIDE GENERAL RENTAL CENTERS, INC. 145
NATIONAL 9 INNS, SUITES, MOTELS 135
NATIONAL ASSOCIATION OF BUSINESS LEADERS 47
NATIONAL ASSOCIATION OF FRANCHISE COMPANIES 110
NATIONAL AUTO/TRUCKSTOPS INC. 173
NATIONAL CHEMICALS AND SERVICES INC. 41
NATIONAL COLLEGE RECRUITING ASSOC. INC. 164
NATIONAL CONSULTANT REFERRALS, INC. 110
NATIONAL COOPERATIVE BANK 110
NATIONAL FINANCIAL COMPANY 29
NATIONAL FRANCHISE ASSOCIATES 110
NATIONAL FRANCHISE CONSULTANTS 110
NATIONAL FRANCHISE CONSULTANTS 217
NATIONAL FRANCHISE SALES 110
NATIONAL GROCERS CO. LTD. 199
NATIONAL HYGIENE FRANCHISE CORP. 41
NATIONAL HYGIENE SERVICE 41
NATIONAL INTERNATIONAL ROOFING 20
NATIONAL INTERNATIONAL ROOFING CORPORATION 20
NATIONAL LEAK DETECTION INC. 173
NATIONAL MAIL ORDER ASSOCIATION, L.L.C. 173
NATIONAL MAINTENANCE CONTRACTORS 41
NATIONAL MAINTENANCE FRANCHISE CORP. 41
NATIONAL MONEY MART, INC. 244
NATIONAL PROPERTY INSPECTIONS 143
NATIONAL PROPERTY REGISTRY 173
NATIONAL PROTECTIVE ASSOCIATION 47
NATIONAL REAL ESTATE SERVICE 232
NATIONAL REAL ESTATE SERVICE, INC. 143
NATIONAL RECORD DISTRIBUTORS 234
NATIONAL SLIMMING CENTRES 269
NATIONAL SURVIVAL GAME 47
NATIONAL TELE-COMMUNICATIONS 29
NATIONAL TENANT NETWORK 29
NATIONAL TENANT NETWORK, INC. 29
NATIONAL TRADE EXCHANGE 173
NATIONALITIES 150
NATIONALITIES FRANCHISING INC. 150
NATIONWIDE FRANCHISE MARKETING SERVICES 110
NATIONWIDE INCOME TAX SERVICE COMPANY 2
NATIONWIDE INVESTIGATIONS 251
NATIONWIDE MARKETING 47
NAT'L RESTAURANT SEARCH, INC. 52
NATURAL BEAUTY PRODUCTS LTD. 268
NATURAL CANADIAN SPRING WATER 167
NATURAL LIFE HEALTH FOODS 257
NATURAL WAY, THE 265
NATURALAWN OF AMERICA 132
NATURALLY YOGURT & SPEEDSTER'S CAFE'S 68
NATURAMA 265
NATURAMA SCHOOL OF DRAMA, THE 265
NATURE INDOORS 20
NATURE INDOORS, INC. 20
NATURE OF THINGS STORE, THE 150
NATURE TECH SYSTEMS 192
NATURE TECHNOLOGIES INC. 192

NATURE'S 10 *150*
NATURE'S CHOICE *43*
NATURE'S REFLECTIONS *173*
NATURE'S REFLECTIONS INC. *173*
NATURE'S TABLE *89*
NATURE'S TABLE SYSTEMS, INC. *89*
NATURE'S WAY *272*
NATURE'S WAY CAFE *89*
NATURE'S WAY FRANCHISING GROUP, INC. *89*
NAUT-A-CARE *173*
NAUT-A-CARE FRANCHISING, INC. *173*
NAUTILUS *195*
NAUTILUS CANADA FITNESS EQUIP. LTD. *195*
NCC PROMOTIONS *4, 178*
NECTAR BEAUTY SHOPS *269*
NECTAR CANADA *223*
NECTAR USA, INC. *120*
NEIGHBORHOOD PUB GROUP *213*
NELRON RESTAURANTS LTD. *209*
NEMO FOODS LTD. *205*
NENDELS CORPORATION *135*
NESS STUDIOS *47*
NETHERLANDS FRANCHISE ASSOCIATION *260*
NETTOYERS MICHEL FORGET LTÉE. *227*
NETTOYEUR MICHEL FORGET *227*
NEUBAUER RESTAURANTS CORP. *89*
NEVADA BOB *273*
NEVADA BOB'S DISCOUNT GOLF *164*
NEVADA BOB'S GOLF AND RACQUETS *242*
NEVADA BOB'S PROS SHOP, INC. *164*
NEW BUSINESS INV CORP. *126*
NEW CENTURY SOFTWARE LIMITED *260*
NEW ENGLAND FOOD, INC. *89*
NEW ENGLAND PASTRY MILL *63*
NEW ENGLAND PIZZA *89*
NEW G.I.B., S.A *270*
NEW HORIZONS COMPUTER LEARNING CENTER *160*
NEW HORIZONS FRANCHISING, INC. *160*
NEW ORLEANS PIZZA *210*
NEW ORLEANS SNOWBALLS, INC. *68*
NEW TOWNE DINER *89*
NEW YORK FRIES *210*
NEWAYS DISTRIBUTORS *195*
NEWCHOICES FRANCHISE MARKETING, INC. *174*
NEWCHOICES RELATIONSHIP CENTER *174*
NEWCOMERS OF AMERICA HOME INSPECTION SERVICE, INC. *20*
NEWLOOK SERVICES *247*
NEXUS - CONSULTANTS TO MANAGEMENT *110*
NIAGARA CYCLO MASSAGE *47*
NIAGARA OF AMERICA INC. *47*
NICAR FRANCHISING, INC. *81*
NICE 'N GREEN FRANCHISE SYSTEMS *132*
NICE 'N GREEN FRANCHISE SYSTEMS, INC. *132*
NICECREAM *257*
NICECREAM COMERCIO DE ALIMENTOS LTDA *257*
NICHOL & COMPANY PUBLIC RELATIONS *110*
NIGHTSHIFT INTERNATIONAL, INC. *151*
NISBETS *265*
NISBETS CHEFSHOP *265*
NITRO-GREEN CORP. *132*
NITRO-GREEN PROFESSIONAL LAWN & TREE CARE *132*
NIX CHECK CASHING *174*
NMTC, INC. *13*
NO APPOINTMENT FAMILY HAIRCUTTERS, INC. *120*
NOAH'S ARK LEASING *195*
NOEL LOG HOMES, INC. *20*
NOODLE DELIGHT INC. *210*
NOPRI *257*
NORECO INC. *231*
NORMA PETERSON *237*
NORMA PETERSON FASHION ENTERPRISES INC. *237*
NORRELL TEMPORARY SERVICES *53*
NORTHERN CARD PUBLISHING COMPANY *222*
NORTHERN CARD PUBLISHING COMPANY LTD. *222*
NORTHERN IMAGES *230*
NORTHERN INVESTMENTS LTD. *182*
NORTHERN SHIELD PROTECTIVE COATINGS *185*
NORWALK - THE FURNITURE IDEA *128*
NOTS, INC. *150*
NOVA MEDIA INC. *140*
NOVA MEDIA MULTI MEDIA PRESUME SHOP™ *140*
NOVA SANDWICH CORP. *212*
NOVUS GLASS REPAIR & REPLACEMENT *14*
NOVUS INC. *14*
NPR SERVICES, INC. *173*
NSA INDEPENDENT DISTRIBUTOR *195*
NSG, INC. *47*
NU-CONCEPT BODY WRAP, INC. *48*
NU-VENTURES INC. *96*
NU-WAY WEINERS *89*
NU-WAY WEINERS, INC. *89*
NUDEX INT'L, INC. *223*
NUMERO UNO *89*
NUMERO UNO FRANCHISE CORP. GELET ENTERPRISES, INC. *89*
NURSEFINDERS *125*
NUTMEG PANTRY INC. *59*
NUTMEG PANTRY SUPERETTE *59*
NUTRI/SYSTEM WEIGHT LOSS CENTERS *125*
NUTRILAWN INTERNATIONAL INC. *228*
NUTRITE, INC. *228*
NUTRITE INC. *228*
NUTTER'S BULK & NATURAL FOODS *198*
NUVISION, INC. *125*
NUVISION OPTICAL *125*
NY CORP. *68*

O

O. T. HODGE CHILI PARLORS *89*
O.P.E.N. CLEANING SYSTEMS *41*
O.P.T.I.O.N. CARE, INC. *125*
O2 EMERGENCY MEDICAL CARE SERVICE *125*
OA FRANCHISE SALES, INC. *29*
O'BRIEN BUDD, INC. *48*
O'BRIEN'S IRISH SANDWICH BARS *257*
OCH INTERNATIONAL, INC. *8*
OCTO FREINS SILENCIEUX, OCTO BRAKES MUFFLERS *180*
O'DONALS FAMILY RESTAURANTS *210*
O'DONALS RESTAURANTS OF CANADA LTD. *210*
OFF COURSE PRO SHOPS LTD. *241*
OFF THE BEATEN PATH MARKETING *217*
OFFICE 1 SUPERSTORE *151*
OFFICE 1 SUPERSTORE, INTERNATIONAL *151*
OFFICE ALTERNATIVE, INC., THE *29*
OFFICE OASIS *29*
OFFICE OASIS, INC. *29*
OFFICE ONE *29*
OGILVY RENAULT *220*
OHIO STATE WATERPROOFING *19*
OIL BUTLER *8*
OIL BUTLER INTERNATIONAL, CORP. *8*
OIL CAN HENRY'S QUICK LUBE CENTER *8*
OIL CAN VAN, INC. *8*
OIL EXPRESS NATIONAL, INC. *8*
OIL EXPRESS® *8*
OIL GARD ANTI-RUST CANADA LTD. *182*
OIL-TECH INDUSTRIES, LTD. *182*
OILTRELL AUTO COSMETIC CENTERS *182*
OK COFFEE TIME *63*
OK FOOD MANAGEMENT US CORP. *90, 174*
OK FOOD MANAGEMENT USA CORP. *58, 167*
OK HOT DOGS *210*
OK SUBMARINE CORPORATION *90*
OK SUBMARINE LTD.™ *210*
OK TIRE STORES *182*
OK TIRE STORES, INC. *182*
OKY-DOKY FOODS *59*
OLD FASHIONED EGG CREAM CO. INC. *59*
OLD STYLE HAMBURGERS *90*
OLDE WORLD FUDGE CO. LTD. *203*
OLIVE INDUSTRIES LTD., INC. *90*
OLIVER *273*
OLIVER'S PIZZA INC. *90*
OLIVE'S GOURMET PIZZA *90*
OLYMPIC GOLD SPORTING GOODS *48*
OLYMPUS ONE PRICE DRY CLEANING, INC. *130*
OMA'S OFEN, THE EUROPEAN BAKERY & CAFE *202*
OMEX *41*
OMEX INTERNATIONAL, INC. *41*

ON & OFF ROAD OPTIONS *15*
ON TARGET GOLF CENTERS *164*
ON TARGET, INC. *164*
ON-HOLD INTERNATIONAL *29*
ON-TARGET! MARKETING & MEDIA, INC. *4*
ONCE UPON A CHILD *36*
ONE ACCORD, INC. *151*
ONE HOUR MARTINIZING DRY CLEANING *130*
ONE HOUR MOTO PHOTO & PORTRAIT STUDIO *230*
ONE HOUR MOTO PHOTO & PORTRAIT STUDIO® *138*
ONE INVESTOR ONE *29*
ONE PRICE DRY CLEANERS *130*
ONE STOP KITCHEN SHOP *151*
ONE STOP UNDERCAR, INC. *14*
ONSITE TRAINING *265*
ONTARIO AUTO COLLISION *182*
ONTARIO DUCT CLEANING LTD. *192*
OODLES DAILY FOOD LTD. *198*
OODLES HOME READY FOODS *198*
OPEN WINDOW BAKERY LTD. *201*
OPENSHOP *251*
OPTION CARE *125*
OPTION CARE, INC. *125*
ORANGE JULIUS *210*
ORANGE JULIUS CANADA, LTD. *210*
OREAN THE HEALTH EXPRESS *90*
ORECK CENTRE, THE *192*
ORENSTEIN & PARTNERS CHARTERED ACCOUNTANTS *177*
ORIENTAL FURNITURE WAREHOUSE *48*
ORIGINAL BASKET BOUTIQUE *222*
ORIGINAL BASKET BOUTIQUE, LTD. *222*
ORIGINAL EGG CREAM CO. *59*
ORIGINAL GINO'S EAST OF CHICAGO, THE *90*
ORIGINAL HAMBURGER STAND *90*
ORIGINAL OIL PAINTINGS FRANCHISE CORP. *137*
ORIGINAL PANCAKE HOUSE, THE *90*
ORIGINAL PANZEROTTO AND PIZZA *210*
ORIGINAL PITA SUB SHOP *90*
ORIGINAL TACO CABANA MEXICAN PATIO CAFE, THE *90*
ORION FOOD SYSTEMS *82*
OSCAR BUSINESS, THE *273*
OSCAR PET FOOD *273*
OSHAWA FOODS *198*
OSLER, HOSKIN & HARCOURT *221*
O'TOOLE LAWN CARE *228*
OTTAWA ALGONQUIN TRAVEL CORP. *242*
OTTO COOL, INC. *10*
OTTOMANELLI'S CAFE FRANCHISING CORP. *90*
OUR BABY IMPRESSIONS *190*
OUR WEIGH *125*
OUTDOOR CONNECTION *164*
OUTDOOR FUN SIGNS *161*
OUTHWAITE INVESTMENTS LTD. *202*
OUTSOURCE INTERNATIONAL *52*
OVERSIZE CLOTHING FRANCHISE CORP. *154*
OWEN WHITE *260*
OWNERS' ALLIANCE, INC. *129*
OXFORD LEARNING CENTRES *239*
OXFORD LEARNING CENTRES INC. *239*
OXIGENIO *273*
OXIGENIO IND. DO VEST. LTDA *273*
OXYGEN THERAPY INSTITUTE, INC. *125*
OYSTER KRACKER, THE *90*

P

P & C PAO E COMPANHIA *257*
P & G ENTERPRISES LTD. *271*
P-WEE'S PIZZA, PASTA & MORE *210*
P-WEE'S PIZZERIA HOLDINGS LTD. *210*
P.A. RESEARCH LTD. *245*, *264*
P.A.M.'S COFFEE & TEA CO. *202*
P.A.S.S. PACKAGING AND SHIPPING SPECIALISTS *29*
P.J.'S COFFEE AND TEA *64*
P.J.'S USA, INC. *64*
P.M.C. CORPORATION *185*
P.S. PAINT SHOP, INC. *226*
PACER GO-KARTS *162*
PACIFIC FRANCHISE ASSOCIATION *217*

PACIFIC FUNDING GROUP, INC. *110*
PACIFIC MENTOR GROUP *217*
PACIFIC NORTHWEST CRUISESHIPCENTERS LTD. *242*
PACIFIC PRODUCTS *48*
PACIFIC TRADE RESOURCES, INC. *48*
PACINI *210*
PACK 'N' SHIP MAILING CENTERS *188*
PACKAGING DEPOT *188*
PACKAGING DEPOT INC. *188*
PACKAGING STORE, INC., THE *26*
PACKY THE SHIPPER/ PACK 'N SHIP *29*
PADGETT BUSINESS SERVICES *2*, *177*
PADGETT BUSINESS SERVICES OF CANADA, LTD. *177*
PADGETT BUSINESS SERVICES USA, INC. *2*
PADOW'S DELI SHOPS *90*
PAGE II FOIL SYSTEMS INC. *195*
PAINT SHOP *226*
PAINTER ONE CORP. *174*
PAIRS REPORTING SERVICE, INC. *184*
PAISNER & CO. *261*
PAK MAIL CANADA *188*
PAK MAIL CENTERS OF AMERICA, INC. *29*
PAK MAIL CENTRES *188*
PAL LUMBER AND BUILDING *184*
PALMER VIDEO *157*
PALMER VIDEO CORP. *157*
PANAGOPOULOS PIZZA *210*
PANCAKE COTTAGE FAMILY RESTAURANTS *90*
PANCAKES-A-PLENTY *90*
PANCHERO'S FRANCHISE CORPORATION *90*
PANCHERO'S MEXICAN GRILL *90*
PANDA - LE SPECIALISTE DU SOULIER POUR ENFANTS *190*
PANDA EXPRESS *90*
PANDA FRANCHISES LTD. *190*
PANDA SHOES *190*
PANDA SYSTEMS, INC. *90*
PANHANDLER, RAFTERS, POT POURRI, LIVING LIGHTING *226*
PANIC LINK P/C *265*
PANINI - PIZZA PASTA *210*
PANTRY FAMILY RESTAURANTS, THE *210*
PANTRY HOSPITALITY CORPORATION, THE *210*
PAO & COMPANHIA SERVICOS LTDA. *257*
PAOLI BIKE & SPORTS *162*
PAPA JOHN'S INTERNATIONAL, INC. *91*
PAPA JOHN'S PIZZA *91*
PAPA MURPHY'S INTERNATIONAL, INC. *91*
PAPA ROMANO'S *91*
PAPACHINO'S FRANCHISE CORP., INC. *91*
PAPACHINO'S RISTORANTE & PIZZA RESTAURANTS *91*
PAPA'S PIZZA TO-GO *91*
PAPER BY DESIGN *151*
PAPER FACTORY, INC., THE *235*
PAPER FACTORY, THE *235*
PAPER FIRST AND PARTY *151*
PAPER FIRST FRANCHISING, INC. *151*
PAPER FIRST/PAPERTOWN *151*
PAPER WAREHOUSE *151*
PAPYRUS *117*
PAPYRUS FRANCHISE CORP. *117*
PARA-LEGAL OFFICE *29*
PARA-SAILING UNLIMITED, INC. *164*
PARADISE BAKERY & CAFE *64*
PARADISE BAKERY, INC. *64*
PARADISE FOODS, INC. *58*
PARADISE ISLAND *195*
PARAGON RESOURCE GROUP, IN.C *217*
PARAGRAVE CORP. *174*
PARALEGAL ASSOCIATES *244*
PARALEGAL ASSOCIATES INC. *244*
PARALEGAL INVESTIGATION *188*
PARALLAX PRODUCTIONS *157*
PARCEL PLUS *29*
PARCEL PLUS, INC. *29*
PARCOM TECHNOLOGIES, INC. *48*
PARCOURSE LTD. *125*
PARIS SOUTHERN LIGHTS *233*
PARKER INTERIOR PLANTSCAPE *132*
PARKER PEST CONTROL, INC. *170*
PARKWAY MACHINE CORP. *48*
PARTNERS IN EDUCATION *239*

PARTNERS IN SMALL BUSINESS *177*
PARTY ANIMALS *56*
PARTY ANIMALS, INC. *56*
PARTY CITY *151*
PARTY CITY CORP. *151*
PARTY FAIR FRANCHISING CO. *151*
PARTY HUT *222*
PARTY LAND *151*
PASQUALE'S PIZZA & PASTA *91*
PASS & CO. SERVICES LTD. *265*
PASS & CO. TIMBER PRESERVATION *265*
PASSPORT GETAWAY MAGAZINE *4*
PASSPORT PUBLISHING CORPORATION *4*
PASTA EXPRESS *91*
PASTA EXPRESS SYSTEMS, INC. *91*
PASTA TO GO *91*
PASTEL'S CAFE *211*
PATTER MARKETING SERVICES *110*
PAUL DAVIS SYSTEMS CANADA *184*
PAUL, HASTINGS, JANOFSKY & WALKER *115*
PAUL REVERE'S PIZZA *91*
PAUL REVERE'S PIZZA INT'L., LTD. *91*
PAUL W. DAVIS SYSTEMS, INC. *20*
PAULIG (UK) LTD. *261*
PAULMAC'S PET FOOD INC. *229*
PAULMAC'S PET FOOD, PAULMAC'S PLUS *229*
PAWS & CLAWS PET NUTRITION CENTRES *229*
PAYLESS CAR RENTAL SYSTEM, INC. *6*
PAYMASTER CHEQUE-WRITERS (CANADA LTD.) *188*
PAYSTATION *188*
PBD INTERNATIONAL, INC. *151*
PBM ENTERPRISES, INC. *194*
PC PARAMEDIC COMPUTER REPAIR *29*
PC PROFESSOR COMPUTER TRAINING WORKSHOPS *160*
PCR - PERSONAL COMPUTER RENTALS, INC. *157*
PDC COPYPRINT *269*
PDC INTERNATIONAL PLC *269*
PEAK PERFORMERS *125*
PEAK PERFORMERS FRANCHISE CORP. *125*
PEANUT CLUB FRANCHISE GROUP, THE *191*
PEANUT CLUB INDOOR PLAYGROUND, THE *191*
PEAR SPERLING EGGAN & MUSKOVITZ, P.C. *115*
PEARLE, INC. *125*
PEARLE VISION *125*
PEARTREE HOME MARKETING *174*
PEARTREE HOME MARKETING CONSULTANTS *174*
PEAT MARWICK MAIN & COMPANY *261*
PEDRO'S TACOS *91*
PEDRO'S TACOS OF CALIFORNIA, INC. *91*
PEE WEE WORKOUT *36*
PEGGY LAWTON KITCHENS, INC. *91*
PENGUIN POINT *91*
PENGUIN POINT FRANCHISE SYSTEMS, INC. *91*
PENLAN CAREER GROUP *197*
PENN BROTHERS ENTERPRISES INC. *76*
PENN STATION *91*
PENN STATION, INC. *91*
PENNSYLVANIA PRETZEL FRANCHISE CORPORATION *64*
PENNYSAVER *4*
PEPE'S, INCORPORATED *91*
PEPE'S MEXICAN RESTAURANTS *91*
PEPPERIDGE FARM, INC. *64*
PEPSICO DO BRAZIL LTDA. *257*
PERFECT PIZZA *257*
PERFECT PRETZEL, INC. *59*
PERFECT PRETZEL, THE *59*
PERFORMANCE GROUP LTD. *110*
PERFORMANCE MARKETING STRATEGISTS INC. *110*
PERFORMANCE SALON SYSTEMS, INC. *118*, *120*
PERKINS FAMILY RESTAURANT & BAKERY *91*
PERKINS FIT BY FIVE INC. *34*
PERKINS RESTAURANTS OPERATING COMPANY, L.P. *91*
PERKITS YOGURT SHOPS *68*
PERMA CERAM *20*
PERMA CERAM ENTERPRISES, INC. *20*
PERMA-GLAZE *21*
PERMA-GLAZE, INC. *21*
PERMA-JACK CO. *21*
PERMA-SHINE *182*
PERMACRETE *185*

PERMACRETE SYSTEMS LTD. *185*
PERMAFLU *21*
PERMANENT, INC. *125*
PERMANENT WEIGHT CONTROL CENTER *125*
PERSIANAS COLUMBIA S/A *265*
PERSONAL HEALTHCARE PRODUCTS, PHP, INC. *195*
PERSONAL PROTECTION SYSTEMS *244*
PERSONALIZED BOOKS *36*
PERSONALIZED CHILDREN'S BOOKS *36*
PERSONALIZED DREAM SCENES *151*
PERSONALIZED PICTURES INC. *235*
PERSONET, INC. *53*
PERSONNEL CONCEPTS, INC. *52*
PERSONNEL NETWORK, THE - PERSONET *53*
PET HABITAT *229*
PET NANNY OF AMERICA, INC. *129*
PET NANNY® *129*
PET PALS *136*
PET PALS INC. *136*
PET PARADISE *229*
PET PARADISE INC. *229*
PET PIONEERS, INC. *136*
PET VALU *229*
PET VALU INC. *229*
PET-TENDERS® *129*
PET-TENDERS® INTERNATIONAL, INC. *129*
PETER I. HOPPENFELD *115*
PETER PIPER INC. *91*
PETER PIPER PIZZA *91*
PETIT BOY *273*
PETLAND *136*, *229*
PETLAND, INC. *136*
PETR-ALL PETROLEUM CORP. *57*
PETROLON SLICK 50 *48*
PETS ARE INN *129*
PETS ARE INN, INC. *129*
PETS PARADISE *265*
PETTICOAT BOX, THE *237*
PEYRON ASSOCIATES, INC. *2*
PEYRON TAX SERVICES *2*
PHARM-ESCOMPTES JEAN COUTU *235*
PHARMASAVE DRUGS LTD. *225*
PHILADELPHIA BAR & GRILL *92*
PHILINS NATURAL FOOD CREATIONS/BAKES *202*
PHILIPPE LOUSBERG & ASSOC. S.P.R.L. *261*
PHILLIPS, NIZER, BENJAMIN, KRIM & BALLON *115*
PHILLY CONNECTION *92*
PHILLY FRANCHISING CO., THE *92*
PHILLY'S FAMOUS SOFT PRETZEL CO. INC. *64*
PHILLY'S FINEST *92*
PHILLY'S FINEST, INC. *92*
PHIL'S FOOD SERVICE *73*
PHIL'S FOOD SERVICE, INC. *92*
PHOENIX CAR & TRUCK RENTALS *178*
PHOTO ADVERTISING INDUSTRIES INC. *48*
PHOTO CERAMICS PTY. LTD. *269*
PHOTO DRIVE-UP FRANCHISING, INC. *138*
PHOTO DRIVE-UP, INC. *138*
PHX. ED. FRANCHISE SYS. INC. *158*
PHYSICIAN DISPENSING SYSTEMS, INC. *125*
PHYSICIANS WEIGHT LOSS CENTERS *125*
PIC-A-POP BEVERAGES *183*
PICASSO'S PIZZA EXPRESS *92*
PICCADILLY CIRCUS PIZZA *92*
PICCOLO PIZZA *257*
PICCOLO'S PIZZA *92*
PICTURES *230*
PIERRE VICTOIRE LTD. *257*
PIERRE VICTOIRE, PIERRE LAPIN, CHEZ JULES, BEPPE VI *257*
PIETRO'S PIZZA PARLORS *92*
PIG-N-0UT *92*
PIGGIE PARK ENTERPRISES, INC. *86*
PIGGLY WIGGLY *59*
PIGGLY WIGGLY CORPORATION *59*
PILDES MANAGEMENT CORP. *125*
PILDES OPTICAL *125*
PILLAR TO POST *232*
PILLSBURY, MADISON & SUTRO *115*
PILOT AIR FREIGHT CORP. *174*
PINCH A PENNY, INC. *151*

PINE PLUS LTD. *273*
PINE STORE, THE *273*
PINGOUIN *195*
PIP PRINTING *140, 269*
PIRTEK *265*
PIRTEK (UK) LTD. *265*
PIRTEK FLUID SYSTEMS, PTY. LTD. *265*
PISTOL & BURNES COFFEE & TEA HOUSE *202*
PISTOL & BURNES COFFEE ROASTERY CORP. *202*
PITA PAZZAZ *211*
PITA PAZZAZ INC. *211*
PITEGOFF, OCKO & HARRINGTON *115*
PITMAN TRAINING CENTRE *251*
PITMAN TRAINING LTD. *251*
PIZZA 2/4 *257*
PIZZA COLORE *92*
PIZZA COLÓRE FRANCHISING, INC. *92*
PIZZA DELIGHT *211*
PIZZA DELIGHT CORP. *211*
PIZZA DEPOT *92*
PIZZA DEPOT INC. *92*
PIZZA DONINI *211*
PIZZA EXPRESS *257*
PIZZA FACTORY, INC *92*
PIZZA HAVEN *257*
PIZZA HOUSE PIZZA *48*
PIZZA HUT *257*
PIZZA HUT (UK) LTD. *258*
PIZZA HUT CANADA *211*
PIZZA HUT, INC. *92*
PIZZA INN *92*
PIZZA INN, INC. *92*
PIZZA JOE'S *92*
PIZZA JOE'S, INC. *92*
PIZZA MAN - HE DELIVERS *92*
PIZZA NOVA *211*
PIZZA NOVA TAKE-OUT LTD. *211*
PIZZA PIPELINE INC., THE *92*
PIZZA PIPELINE, THE *92*
PIZZA PIT *92*
PIZZA PIT INVESTMENT ENTERPRISES, INC. *92*
PIZZA PIZZA *211*
PIZZA PIZZA LIMITED *211*
PIZZA RANCH *93*
PIZZA ROYALE *211*
PIZZA, U.S.A. *93*
PIZZA USA FRANCHISE CORP. *93*
PIZZA-MANN *258*
PIZZARIAS MISTER PIZZA LTD. *257*
PIZZAS BY MARCHELLONI *93*
PIZZAVILLE - PIZZA & PANZEROTTO *211*
PIZZERIA DI LORENZO'S *211*
PIZZERIA MANAGEMENT SYSTEMS, INC. *95*
PIZZERIA UNO *93*
PIZZETTI'S PIZZA *93*
PLAINS REFRIGERANT RECLAIM CORP. *174*
PLAINS REFRIGERANT RECLAIM OF (NAME OF CITY) *174*
PLANET INTERNET CORPORATION *157, 238*
PLANET INTERNET LOGON CENTER *238*
PLANET INTERNET LOGON CENTER *157*
PLATIS & SONS 1 HOUR CLEANERS *227*
PLAY IT AGAIN SPORTS *164*
PLEASE MUM *237*
PLEIN POT S.A. *246*
PLOMBERIUM *185*
PLUM INTERNATIONAL, INC. *145*
PLUMBING M.D. *174*
PLUMBING MART *185*
PLUMCOURT LTD. *255*
PLURI-PUBLI S.A. *263*
PLUS 1 PIZZA *93*
PLUS COMPANIES, THE *155*
PNS, INC. *29*
POCO-LOCO WESTERN TOWNS, INC. *56*
POFOLKS *93*
POINTS FOR PROFIT *4*
POINTTS *244*
POINTTS ADVISORY LTD. *244*
POLLO TROPICAL *93*
POLLO TROPICAL, INC. *93*

POLY-TUB RESTORATION *21*
POMME DE PAIN *265*
PONDEROSA *93*
PONTAPRINT PLC *269*
PONY MAIL BOX & BUSINESS CENTER *29*
POOCH PROTECTORS® *129*
POOL CLEAR *164*
POOL CLEAR FRANCHISE CORP. *164*
POPCORN PLUS *48*
POPEYES FRIED CHICKEN & BISCUITS *93*
POPPINS RESTAURANTS *258*
PORPOISE POOL & PATIO *151*
PORT OF SUBS *93*
PORT OF SUBS, INC. *93*
PORT-A-SIGN *241*
PORTRAIT MASTERS *138*
PORTRAIT MASTERS, INC. *138*
PORTRAITS NOW INTERNATIONAL LTD. *230*
POSTAL ANNEX *30*
POSTAL ANNEX, INC. *30*
POSTNET *30, 189*
POSTNET INTERNATIONAL FRANCHISE CORP. *30*
POT POURRI COFFEE & TEA *235*
POTATO SACK FRANCHISE CORP. *93*
POTATO SACK, THE *93*
POTIONS & LOTIONS *120*
POTTS' HOT DOGS *93*
POTTY DOCTOR FRANCHISE SYSTEMS *21*
POTTY DOCTOR PLUMBING SERVICE *21*
POULIOT MERCURE, S.E.N.C. *221*
POULTRY KING *198*
POULTRY KING, INC. *198*
POULTRY SHOP PTY. LTD., THE *256*
POUR LA FRANCE! *93*
POWER KING CLEANING SYSTEMS *192*
POWERBASE, INC. *110*
PRACTICAL CAR & VAN RENTAL *246*
PRACTICAL CAR & VAN RENTAL LTD. *246*
PRACTICAL RENT-A-CAR *6*
PRACTICAL RENT-A-CAR SYSTEMS, INC. *6*
PRACTICAR SYSTEMS, INC. *179*
PRAIRIE HOUSE RESTAURANT *93*
PRE-FIT FRANCHISES, INC. *36*
PRE-FIT, INC. *36*
PRECIOUS IMAGE JEWELERS *151*
PRECIOUS PLACES *36*
PRECIOUS PLACES, LTD. *36*
PRECISION POWERWASH 2000 *41*
PRECISION TUNE, INC. *8*
PREFERRED REALTY CONCEPTS, INC. *141, 231*
PREMIER PUBLISHERS, INC. *48*
PREMIUM PLUS MOBILE OIL CHANGE INC. *179*
PREMIUM SHOPPING GUIDE *4*
PRESCRIPTION OPTICAL COMPANY LTD. *225*
PRESIDENT TUXEDO *145*
PRESSED 4 TIME *130*
PRESSED 4 TIME, INC. *130*
PRETZEL TIME *64*
PRETZEL TIME, INC. *64*
PRETZEL TWISTER, THE *64*
PRETZEL WORLD *64*
PRETZEL WORLD INC. *64*
PRETZELMAKER *64*
PRETZELMAKER, INC. *64*
PRETZELS PLUS *64*
PRETZELS PLUS, INC. *64*
PREVENT-A-CRACK *14*
PREVENT-A-CRACK, INC. *14*
PREVUE ASSESSMENT *189*
PREVUE RESOURCE GROUP *189*
PRICE ATTACK *269*
PRICE ATTACK FRANCHISING PTY. LTD. *269*
PRICE WATERHOUSE *217*
PRIMARK INTERNATIONAL, INC. *141*
PRIME RESTAURANT GROUP, IN.C *206*
PRIME RESTAURANT GROUP INC. *205*
PRIME TIME GUIDE & T.V. LISTINGS *4*
PRIMETIME VIDEO GROUP LTD. *273*
PRIMETIME VIDEO LTD. *273*
PRIMROSE SCHOOL *160*

PRIMROSE SCHOOL FRANCHISING, CO. *160*
PRINCETON ENERGY PARTNERS, INC. *21*
PRINCETON REVIEW MANAGEMENT CORP., THE *160*
PRINCETON REVIEW, THE *160*
PRINTDESIGNS *269*
PRINTHOUSE EXPRESS, INC. *140*
PRINTHOUSE EXPRESS, THE *140*
PRINTING NETWORK *231*
PRINTING ONE *140*
PRINTING ONE CORPORATION *140*
PRINTNET LTD. *269*
PRIORITY MANAGEMENT SYSTEMS, INC. *30*
PRIORITY MANAGEMENT SYSTEMS PTY. LTD. *251*
PRISUNIC *258*
PRIVATE POSTAL CENTERS *30*
PRO CUTS *120*
PRO FRIES INC. *244*
PRO GOLF DISCOUNT *164*
PRO GOLF OF AMERICA, INC. *164*
PRO HARDWARE *235*
PRO IMAGE, THE *151*
PRO JET *232*
PRO JET COURTIER, INC. *232*
PRO-LITE, INC. *48*
PRO-PAINT INTERNATIONAL *14*
PRO-PAINT REPAIR *14*
PRO-TECH STUCCO CORP. *185*
PRO-TECT ASPHALT LTD. *195*
PRO-TEM, FLEX-STAFF *53*
PRO-TOUCH *41*
PROCARE VISION CENTERS INC. *126*
PRODUCTIVITY POINT INTERNATIONAL *30*
PRODUCTIVITY POINT INTERNATIONAL CANADA INC. *189*
PROFESSIONAL CARPET SYSTEMS *33*
PROFESSIONAL DYNAMETRIC PROGRAMS/PDP, INC. *53*
PROFESSIONAL HOUSE DOCTORS *21*
PROFESSIONAL HOUSE DOCTORS, INC. *21*
PROFESSIONAL LEGAL ASSISTANCE ASSOCIATES *30*
PROFESSIONAL POLISH INC. *174*
PROFESSIONAL POLISH JANITORIAL MAINTENANCE/LAWN MAI *174*
PROFESSIONAL RECYCLED BOOKSELLERS ASSOCIATION *146*
PROFESSIONAL SITTER SERVICE *126*
PROFESSIONAL WAY CORP. *48*
PROFILES *53*
PROFILES - SECURITY & PERSONNEL RISK ASSESSMENTS *53*
PROFIT ASSOCIATES *48*
PROFIT-ON-HOLD *4*
PROFORCE USA - COMMERCIAL CLEANING SYSTEMS, INC. *41*
PROFORMA, INC. *30*
PROFUSION SYSTEMS *117*
PROFUSION SYSTEMS INC. *117*
PROHOME *21*
PROHOME INCORPORATED *21*
PROMAFIL CANADA LTD. *242*
PROMISES FULFILLED *37*
PROMISES MARKETING INT'L. *37*
PROMOFIL CANADA LTD. *195*
PROMOTIONS ETCETERA, INC. *55*
PROMPTO 10 MINUTE OIL LUBE & FILTER *8*
PROMPTO SYSTEM, INC. *8*
PRONTAPRINT LTD. *269*
PRONUPTIA YOUNGS *273*
PROPAINT PLUS, INC. *14*
PROPERTY DAMAGE APPRAISERS *174*
PROPERTY DAMAGE APPRAISERS, INC. *174*
PROPERTY LINE HOME MARKETING CONSULTANTS *232*
PROPERTY RENTALS *250*
PROSHRED INC. *189*
PROSHRED SECURITY *189*
PROSOURCE WHOLESALE FLOORCOVER *48*
PROTEXCAR LTD. *246*
PROTOCOL *174*
PROVENTURE *30*
PROVENTURE BUSINESS GROUP, INC. *30*
PROVI-SOIR *198*
PROVINCIAL DEVELOPMENT CORP. *216*
PROVINCIAL TABLE PADS *195*
PROVINCIAL TABLE PADS LTD. *195*
PRUDENTIAL REAL ESTATE AFFILIATES, INC., THE *143*

PTR TUB & TILE RESTORATION *48*
PUDGIE'S FAMOUS CHICKEN *94*
PUDGIE'S PIZZA & SUBS *94*
PUDGIE'S PIZZA FRANCHISING, INC. *94*
PUDLEY'S *94*
PULL-OUT SHELF COMPANY, INC. *21*
PULL-OUT SHELF COMPANY, THE *21*
PUROFIRST *21*
PUROFIRST INTERNATIONAL, INC. *21*
PUTT-PUTT® GOLF & GAMES *164*
PUTT-PUTT® GOLF COURSES OF AMERICA, INC. *164*
PVC VENDO *253*
PWLC OF AMERICA, INC. *125*
PYTHON'S *174*
PYTHON'S INC. *174*

Q

Q LUBE *8*
Q LUBE, INC. *8*
Q&S MANAGEMENT *87*
Q-PON BOOK, THE *4*
Q.M. MARKETING, INC. *110*
QUAKER STATE MINIT-LUBE *179*
QUALITY CREDIT SERVICES LTD. *217*
QUALITY INNS *135*
QUALITY MARKETING ASSOCIATES, INC. *170*
QUICK HAMBURGER RESTAURANT *258*
QUICKWAY CONVENIENCE STORES *59*
QUICKWAY, INC. *59*
QUIJAS ENTERPRISES *94*
QUIK PRINT *140*
QUIK STOP MARKETS *59*
QUIK STOP MARKETS, INC. *59*
QUIKAVA *64*
QUINN, KULLY & MORROW *115*
QUINZI'S GOLF DOCTOR SHOPS, INC. *164*
QUIZNO'S CLASSIC SUBS *94*

R

R & R ENTERPRISES, INC. *14*
R & S INDUSTRIES CORP. *48*
R.C. KNOX AND COMPANY, INC. *111*
R.D.F. DEVELOPMENTS, INC. *93*
R.F.F. ENTERPRISES, INC. *168*
R.G.V. ENTERPRISES S.A. *262*
R.I.A.M. INTERNATIONAL *264*
R.J. GATOR'S INC. *94*
R.J. GATOR'S RAW BAR & SEA GRILLE *94*
R.X. SOLEIL, INC. *225*
RACO CAR WASH SYSTEMS, INC. *15*
RACS INTERNATIONAL *41*
RACS INTERNATIONAL INC. *41*
RADD MULTIMEDIA *238*
RADIO SHACK *157*
RADIO SHACK AUTHORIZED SALES CENTRE (CANADA) *238*
RADISSON HOTELS WORLDWIDE *135*
RADIXX/WORLD LTD. *185*
RAGER AND ASSOCIATES *111*
RAHSCO MANUFACTURING CO, INC. *45*
RAINBORN, INC. *167*
RAINBOW CARPET CENTERS INC. *128*
RAINBOW CARPET COLOR CENTERS *128*
RAINBOW CARPETS *253*
RAINBOW CORNER LTD. *253*
RAINBOW INTERNATIONAL CARPET DYEING AND CLEANING CO *33*
RAINBOW SNOW, INC. *68*
RAINBOWLAND, INC. *37*
RAINSOFT WATER CONDITIONING *167*
RALLY'S INC. *94*
RALPH ROTTEN'S NUT POUND *59*
RAMADA FRANCHISE CANADA LTD. *229*
RAMADA FRANCHISE SYSTEMS *135*
RAMADA INNS, HOTELS, SUITES *229*
RAMS HORN RESTAURANTS INC. *94*
RAMSEY GAS *273*
RAMSEY GAS LTD. *273*

RANCAR CORPORATION *119*
RANCH *1 *94*
RANCH *1 GROUP, THE *94*
RANDA FOOD SYSTEMS COMPANY LTD. *207*
RAPEL RADIO ALARM SYSTEMS (ADMAX) LTD. *265*
RAPIT MAIL & SERVICES INC. *30*
RAY ENTERPRISES INC. *132*
RAYNE CORPORATION *167*
RCI, INC. *126*
RDGS FRANCHISE CORPORATION *164*
RE-BATH *21*
RE-BATH CORPORATION *21*
RE-NU PLC *266*
RE-SELL-IT SHOPS, INC. *151*
RE-SSIDE AMERICA *21*
RE/MAX *143*
RE/MAX INTERNATIONAL, INC. *143*
READING GLASSES TO GO *126*
REAL ESTATE ONE LICENSING CO. *143*
REAL ESTATE SIGNS LTD. *266*
REAL ESTATE WORLD SERVICES (1978) LTD. *232*
REALSTAR HOTEL SERVICES CORP. *228*
REALTY 500 *143*
REALTY EXECUTIVES *143*
REALTY EXECUTIVES INTERNATIONAL, INC. *143*
REALTY ONE *143*
REALTY ONE CORP. *143*
REALTY WORLD CANADA *232*
REALTY WORLD CORP. *143*
RECOGNITION EXPRESS *4, 266*
RECOGNITION EXPRESS INT'L., INC. *4*
RECOGNITION EXPRESS LTD. *266*
RECORD SWAP *151*
RECORDS ON WHEELS / WHEELS ENTERTAINMENT / ROW *235*
RECYCLED PAPER GREETINGS *152*
RECYCLED TONER CARTRIDGES *188*
RED BOY PIZZA *94*
RED BOY PIZZA FRANCHISING CORP. *94*
RED CARPET KEIM REAL ESTATE *143*
RED GIRAFFE VIDEO *157*
RED HOT & BLUE *94*
RED ROBIN BURGER & SPIRITS EMPORIUM *94*
RED ROBIN INTERNATIONAL, INC. *94*
RED WING SHOES *155*
REDDI MART CONVENIENCE STORES *198*
REDDING'S BESTSELLER AUDIOBOOKS *151*
REED, SMITH, SHAW & MCCLAY *115*
REES POLLOCK *261*
REFACE IT KITCHEN SYSTEMS INC. *21*
REFACE-A-DOOR *266*
REGIONAL NETWORK OF PERSONNEL CONSULTANTS, THE *53*
RELAX THE BACK FRANCHISING CO. *126*
RELAX THE BACK STORE *126*
REMEDY STAFFING SERVICES *53*
REMEDYTEMP, INC. *53*
REMERICA *144*
REMERICA REAL ESTATE CORP. *144*
REMODELING CONTRACTING & CLEANING SERVICE, INC. *41*
RENAISSANCE EXECUTIVE FORUMS, INC. *30*
RENAISSANCE, THE CHOCOLATE COMPANY *198*
RENFREW GROUP LTD. (C/O) *192*
RENNSPORT *14*
RENNSPORT FRANCHISING INC. *14*
RENT A DENT CORP. *6*
RENT A VETTE *6*
RENT A VETTE INTERNATIONAL *6*
RENT-A-CENTER STORES *145*
RENT-A-DENT *6*
RENT-A-ROBOT *48*
RENT-A-WRECK *179*
RENT-A-WRECK OF AMERICA, INC. *6*
RENTAL GUIDE MAGAZINE *5*
RENTAL NETWORK *144*
RENTAL REFERRAL PROS *145*
RENTALAND *145*
RENTALAND, INC. *145*
RENUBATH SERVICES LTD. *249*
RENZIOS INC. *94*
RESCUE ALERT *186*
RESIDENCE INNS BY MARRIOTT, THE *135*

RESIDENTIAL BUILDING INSPECTORS *21*
RESORT MAPS FRANCHISE, INC. *5*
RESORT PUBLICATIONS *5*
RESPO-TECHNIK OF NORTH AMERICA, LTD. *184*
RESPOND FIRST AID SYSTEMS *126*
REST-CON MANAGEMENT SYSTEMS LTD. *212*
RESTAURANT DEVELOPERS CORP. *88*
RESTAURANT NORMANDIN *211*
RESTAURANT SYSTEMS INTERNATIONAL *62, 65, 66*
RESTAURANTS GIORGIO (AMERIQUE) LTEE. *211*
RESTAURANTS LES PRES CANADA LTEE. *209*
RESTORX CANADA *193*
RESTORX CANADA INCORPORATED *193*
RESTORX, INC. *41*
RESTORX, INC. *33*
RETAIL RECRUITERS *53*
RETAIL RECRUITERS INTERNATIONAL, INC. *53*
RETAIL TECHNOLOGIES INTERNATIONAL *111*
RETAILINK *218*
RETIREE SKILLS, INC. *53*
RETRAC CORPORATION *85*
REVA S. BAUCH, ATTORNEY AT LAW *115*
REX. P. CORNELISON, III, ATTORNEY AT LAW, P.C. *116*
RG PARTNERS, INC. *111*
RIBBON REVIVAL *251*
RIBBON XCHANGE *189*
RICH PLAN *174*
RICH PLAN CORP. *174*
RICHARDS & RICHARDS *221*
RICHMOND SALES INC. *48*
RICHY'S RESTAURANTS *94*
RICKSHAW CHINESE FOOD *94*
RICKSHAW RESTAURANTS, INC. *94*
RICKY'S RESTAURANTS *94*
RICKY'S RESTAURANTS *211*
RIDE CO., THE *197*
RIDEABLE BICYCLE REPLICAS INC. *48*
RIP N' TEAR VINYL REPAIR *182*
RIP N' TEAR VINYL REPAIR SYSTEMS, INC. *182*
RIPLEY'S ATTRACTIONS INC. *56*
RIPLEY'S BELIEVE IT OR NOT *56*
RISTORANTE GIORGIO / LE STEAK FRITES ST PAUL / COQ *211*
RITA'S WATER ICE & RITA'S ITALIAN ICES *68*
RITA'S WATER ICE FRANCHISE CORP. *68*
RIVER-DIEGO INV. CORP. *100*
RJF FINANCIAL SERVICES, INC. *111*
RO-NA L'ENTREPOT, RO-NA HOME CENTRE, RO-NA HARDWARE *235*
ROAD RUNNER SCOOTER HIRE *266*
ROADWAY MUFFLER & BRAKE CENTERS *9*
ROASTERS CORP. *84*
ROASTMASTIR'S - CUSTOM ROASTED ORGANIC COFFEES *202*
ROBBEN INDUSTRIES, LTD. *189*
ROBBINEX INC. *218*
ROBBINS' RETIREMENT COMMUNITIES *126*
ROBERT J. BAER MARKETING *111*
ROBERT Q'S TRAVEL *242*
ROBERT Q'S TRAVEL MART INC. *242*
ROBIN C. CARTER, ATTORNEY AT LAW, P.C. *116*
ROBIN HOOD GOLF CENTRE *273*
ROBIN HOOD GOLF, PLC *273*
ROBIN ROSE AMERICA, INC. *68*
ROBIN ROSE ICE CREAM & CHOCOLATE *68*
ROBIN'S DONUTS *202*
ROBIN'S FOODS INC. *202*
ROBOSOFT ELECTRONIC SOFTWARE STORE *238*
ROBOSOFT TECHNOLOGY, INC. *238*
ROCCO RACCOON'S INDOOR PLAYGROUNDS INC. *211*
ROCCO RACCOON'S INDOOR PLAYGROUNDS, INC. *95*
ROCHE-BOBOIS *273*
ROCHE-BOBOIS U.S.A. LTD. *128*
ROCKING HORSE, THE *235*
ROCKPORT INSTITUTE *53*
ROCKY MOUNTAIN CHOCOLATE FACTORY, INC. *59*
ROCKY MOUNTAIN LOG HOMES *21*
ROCKY ROCOCO PAN STYLE PIZZA *95*
ROCS CARDS AND GIFTS *152*
RODAN ENTERPRISES (1994) LTD. *235*
RODENTVELT RACEWAY *56*
RODEWAY INNS INTERNATIONAL *135*

RODIER, RODIER HOMMES 242
ROGER CLEMENS FLAME ROASTED CHICKEN 95
ROGER DUNN GOLF SHOPS 164
ROGER J. MCLAUGHLIN, ESQ. 116
ROHR'S RESTAURANT FRANCHISING, INC. 174
ROHR'S RESTAURANT SERVICE 174
ROJOS POPCORN CO. 49
ROJO'S U.S.A., INC. 49
ROL-A-DECOR 128
ROLL-A-WAY, INC. 21
ROLL-A-WAY STORM AND SECURITY SHUTTERS 21
ROLLING PIN KITCHEN EMPORIUM 152
ROLLO POLLO 95
ROMA CORPORATION 100
ROMAN SPA HEALTH & LEISURE PRODUCTS LTD. 266
ROMAN SPA HYDROMASSAGE 266
ROMANCO PUBLISHERS 49
ROMANO CENTER 252
ROMANO S/A MATERIAS PL CONSTRUCOFS 252
ROMEO'S PLACE, LTD. 212
ROMP AROUND 37
ROMP AROUND FUN CENTERS, INC. 37
RONALD N. ROSENWASSER, P.A. 116
RONLEN ENTERPRISES, INC. 141
RON'S PIZZA DELIVERY/RON'S PIZZA HOUSE/A & R PIZZA 95
RONZIO PIZZA 95
ROOFTOP BALLOONS 5
ROOM-MATE REFERRAL SERVICE CENTER, INC. 144
ROOM-MATE REFERRAL SERVICE CENTERS & ROOM-MATE REGI 144
ROSATI'S FRANCHISE SYSTEMS, INC. 95
ROSATI'S PIZZA 95
ROSE BENEDETTI 273
ROSE BENEDETTI MODAS LTDA. 273
ROSE VALENTI FRAGRANCES 152
ROSE VALENTI, INC. 152
ROSS DIXON FINANCIAL CORP. 189
ROSS DIXON FINANCIAL SERVICES 189
ROTH YOUNG PERSONNEL SERVICES, INC. 53
ROTO-ROOTER CORP. 22
ROTO-STATIC CARPET & UPHOLSTERY CLEANING 189
ROUND TABLE FRANCHISE CORP. 95
ROUND TABLE PIZZA 95
ROUND THE CORNER RESTAURANTS, INC. 95
ROW ENTERTAINMENT 235
ROWE & ASSOCIATES 114
ROYAL APPLES 59
ROYAL APPLES, INC. 59
ROYAL BANK OF CANADA 218
ROYAL GUARD FISH & CHIPS 95
ROYAL PRESTIGES 149
ROYCO HOTELS AND RESORTS LTD. 229
RPL SUPPLIES INC. 138
RUBY'S DINER 95
RUBY'S FRANCHISE SYSTEMS, INC. 95
RUDNICK & WOLFE 116
RUDOLPH'S BAR-B-Q 95
RUFFAGE 212
RUFFAGE INTERNATIONAL INC., C/O ASHTON FOOD GROUP, 212
RUFFIN'S PET CENTER, INC. 230
RUG DOCTOR CANADA LTD. 189
RUG DOCTOR LP 33
RUG DOCTOR PRO 33
RUG DOCTOR RENTS 189
RUNZA DRIVE INN RESTAURANTS 95
RUSPA - LEATHER GOODS DIV. 273
RUSS AUTO 14
RUSS AUTO INC. 14
RUSSELL JOHNS ASSOCIATES, LTD. 5
RUSSOLI TEMPS 53
RUST CHECK 246
RUST CHECK CANADA INC. 182
RUST CHECK CENTER 182
RUST CHECK CENTRAL CORP. 246
RX SURGICAL SERVICES 49
RYAN HOMES, INC. 22
RYAN'S FAMILY STEAK HOUSE 95
RYAN'S PET FOOD INC. 230
RYAN'S PET FOODS 230
RYAN'S SOCCER INTERNATIONAL, INC. 164
RYMAN 273
RYNKER RIBBON EXCHANGE, INC. 189

S

S & H REALTY CORPORATION 218
S.C. FOOD SERVICES (CANADA) INC. 209
S.C. FOOD SERVICES INC. 86
S.O.S. COMPUTADORES 252
SA. BRETONNIERE 265
SABSCO CORP. 205
SAF-T AUTO CENTERS 14
SAFARI ANIMAL CARE CENTERS 136
SAFE-PAK SUPPLY CANADA, INC. 195
SAFE-T-CHILD 37
SAFE-T-CHILD, INC. 37
SAFECLEAN 253
SAFEWAY MOTORING SCHOOL 266
SAILOR STEAMER HOT DOGS 212
SAINT ANDREWS GOLF CORP. 163
SAINT CINNAMON BAKE SHOPPES 202
SAINT CINNAMON BAKERY LTD. 202
SAKKIO JAPAN 212
SAKURA JAPANESE FAST FOOD INC. 212
SALADALLEY RESTAURANTS, INC. 95
SALE BY OWNER SYSTEMS 144
SALSBURY 175
SALSBURY INDUSTRIES 30
SALVATORE SCALLOPINI 95
SAMMI'S DELI 96
SAMMI'S DELI INC. 96
SAMPA CORP. 140
SAM'S HOT DOGS 95
SAM'S HOT DOGS, INC. 95
SAM'S ITALIAN FOODS 95
SAMUEL MANCINO'S ITALIAN EATERY 96
SAN JUAN POOLS 165
SAN JUAN PRODUCTS 165
SANDERSON & ASSOCIATES 111
SANDLER SALES INSTITUTE (CANADA) LTD. 240
SANDLER SYSTEMS INC. 160
SANDWICH BOARD, THE 212
SANDWICH SPECIALISTS, INC. 72
SANDWICH TREE 212
SANDY HOOK SCIENTIFIC, INC. 30
SANDY'S ASSOCIATES, INC. 96
SANFORD ROSE ASSOCIATES 53
SANGSTERS HEALTH CENTRE 225
SANIBRITE INC. 193
SANVITA PROGRAMS 126
SANWA BUSINESS CREDIT CORPORATION 111
SAS TAX PAC DISTRIBUTORS 49
SAUSAGE HOUSE, THE 212
SAVE-EASY, FOODMASTER, RED & WHITE, QUIK MART, VALU 199
SAW CREATIONS INC. 244
SBARRO 212
SBARRO, INC. 96
SBARRO THE ITALIAN EATERY 96
SBK FRANCHISE SYSTEMS, INC. 97
SC PROMOTIONS, INC. 105
SCALLOPINI VENTURES 95
SCANDIA DOWN CORP. 152
SCANDIA DOWN SHOPS 152
SCARLETT MANSON ANGUS 221
SCHARECORP 244
SCHARECORP MARKETING LTD. 244
SCHEMA 266
SCHLOTZSKY'S DELI RESTAURANT 96
SCHLOTZSKY'S INC. 96
SCHNADER, HARRISON, SEGAL & LEWIS 116
SCHNEIDER'S POPCORN PARTIES INC. 199
SCHOOP'S HAMBURGERS 96
SCHOOP'S HAMBURGERS, INC. 96
SCHWAB'S FINEST IN MEATS 199
SCHWAB'S MEAT PRODUCTS LTD. 199
SCIENCE SHOP, INC., THE 152
SCIENTIA CORP. 48
SCIENTIFIC SEARCH ASSOCIATES, INC. 53

SCM 175
SCOOP-A-MARKET 273
SCOOPERS ICE CREAM 68
SCOOPERS ICE CREAM INC. 68
SCORECARD PLUS 165
SCOTCO DIST. LTD. 205
SCOTIABANK 218
SCOTTO PIZZA 96
SCOTT'S MANAGEMENT SERVICES INC. 212
SCREEN PRINTING NORTH AMERICA INC. 231
SCREEN PRINTING USA 140
SCREEN PRINTING USA, INC. 140
SCRUBWAY INC. 41
SCUBA NETWORK 165
SCUBA NETWORK STORES 165
SDR SVENSK DIREKTREKLAM 252
SEAGA MANUFACTURING CORPORATION 175
SEALMASTER 175
SEARS DRIVER TRAINING 240
SEARS REALTY PROFESSIONALS HAS A DREAM HOME FOR YOU 144
SEATTLE'S BEST COFFEE 64
SEAWEST SUB SHOPS, INC. 98
SECOND CUP COFFEE CO. 202
SECOND CUP, LTD., THE 202
SECOND SOURCE COMPUTER CENTERS 157
SECURITAL 266
SECURITY ALLIANCE CORP., THE 23
SECURITY PLUS 195
SEEKERS 252
SELECT FOOD SERVICES, INC. 212
SELECT INNS FRANCHISING INC. 135
SELECT SANDWICH 212
SELECTAMARK SECURITY SYSTEMS LIMITED 266
SELECTIVE BOOKS INC. 49
SELL YOUR OWN HOME 144
SELL YOUR OWN HOME OF AMERICA 144
SEMET, LICKSTEIN, MORGENSTERN, BERGER, FRIEND, BROO 116
SENIORS CHOICE NEWSMAGAZINE, THE 178
SENIORS FOR BUSINESS/ SENIORS FOR SENIORS 196
SENIORS FRANCHISE SYSTEMS INC. 196
SENSIBLE CAR RENTAL, INC. 6
SENSOMATIC SAVER SYSTEM DEALERS 49
SENSORMATIC ELECTRONICS CORP. 49
SENSORTROL 249
SERARE SA 255
SERCK MARSTON 247
SERGIO'S MEXICAN RESTAURANT 96
SERV U-1, INC. 41
SERV U-1ST 41
SERV-U-CLEAN LTD. 193
SERVICE CENTER 30
SERVICE ONE COMMERCIAL CLEANING SYSTEMS, INC. 41
SERVICE ONE JANITORIAL 41
SERVICE-MAID INDUSTRIES, INC. 42
SERVICE-TECH CLEANING 42
SERVICE-TECH CORPORATION 42
SERVICEMASTER 42, 195
SERVICEMASTER COMPANY, LP, THE 132
SERVICEMASTER LAWN CARE 228
SERVICEMASTER LAWN CARE CANADA 228
SERVICEMASTER LAWNCARE 132
SERVICEMASTER OF CANADA 192
SERVICEMASTER RES/COMM. 195
SERVICES FARMICO, INC. 235
SERVING BY IRVING, INC. 175
SERVISTAR 145
SERVISTAR CORPORATION 22
SERVPRO INDUSTRIES 38
SERVPRO INDUSTRIES, INC. 42
SEVEN-ELEVEN (JAPAN) CO. LTD. 258
SEVEN-ELEVEN CONVENIENCE STORES 258
SEVERSON & WERSON 116
SGD COMPANY 163
SGO DESIGNER GLASS OF... 152
SHAKE A PAW PUPPIES 136
SHAKEY'S, INC. 96
SHAKEY'S PIZZA RESTAURANTS 96
SHAKRAS HOUSEWARES 235
SHAKRAS HOUSEWARES INC. 235

SHAMPOO CHEZ 136
SHAMPOO CHEZ, INC. 136
SHAN INVESTMENT CO. 88
SHAPIRO, ROSENFELD & CLOSE 116
SHARI'S MANAGEMENT CORP. DBA SHARI'S RESTAURANTS 96
SHARP-N-LUBE 132
SHEFIELD & SONS 235
SHEFIELD & SONS TOBACCONISTS INC. 235
SHEFSKY FROELICH & DEVINE LTD. 116
SHELLAR CORP. 28
SHERATON HOTELS AND INNS 135
SHE'S FLORISTS 132
SHE'S FLOWERS INC. 132
SHIBLEY RIGHTON 221
SHINE FACTORY SYSTEMS, INC. 182
SHINE FACTORY, THE 182
SHINE-A-BLIND 42
SHIP SHAPE CAR WASHES INC. 14
SHIPPING CONNECTION 30
SHIPPING CONNECTION, INC. 30
SHIPPING DEPARTMENT, THE 31
SHOE FIXERS 155
SHOES FOR HER/SHOES FOR HIM 155
SHOESMITH/SHOEFIXERS 175
SHONEY'S 74
SHOOTERS INTERNATIONAL, INC. 96
SHOOTERS ON THE WATER 96
SHOP PHOTO VIDEO 269
SHOPPERS DRUG MART 235
SHOPPING DELIVERY SERVICE OF AMERICA 43
SHOPPING SERVICE OF AMERICA 43
SHOW PLACE FRANCHISING CORP. 68
SHOW PLACE ICE CREAM PARLOURS 68
SHOWBIZ PIZZA PLACE AND CHUCK E. CHEESE'S 96
SHOWBIZ PIZZA TIME, INC. 96
SHRED-IT 31, 244
SHRED-IT AMERICA, INC. 31
SHRED-IT FRANCHISE, INC. 244
SHRED-TECH 189
SHRED-TECH LTD. 189
SHUR-GAIN 196
SICILY'S, THE PIZZA PLACE, INC./SICILY'S PIZZA JR. 96
SIEGEL BUSINESS SERVICES, INC. 111
SIESTA SLEEP SHOPS INC. 128
SIGARANT CANADA 231
SIGN BIZ, INC. 161
SIGN EXPRESS 161, 266
SIGN EXPRESS, INC. 161
SIGN IT QUICK 161
SIGN IT QUICK INTERNATIONAL, INC. 161
SIGNAL GRAPHICS PRINTING 140
SIGNATURE ANALYSIS 175
SIGNATURE COMMUNICATIONS INC. 196
SIGNATURE ENTERPRISES 118
SIGNATURE INNS 135
SIGNATURE INNS, INC. 135
SIGNED, SEALED AND REMEMBERED 118
SIGNS & MORE IN 24 162
SIGNS & MORE IN 24, INC. 162
SIGNS BY TOMORROW 161
SIGNS FIRST 161
SIGNS NOW 162
SIGNS NOW 241
SIGNS NOW CANADA 241
SIGNS NOW CORPORATION 162
SIGNWORLD 162
SILK PLANT FOREST 132
SILO CLEAN INTERNATIONAL 193
SILVER FREEDMAN & TAFF 116
SILVER SHIELD AUTOMOTIVE GLAZING 247
SILVER SHIELD SCREENS LTD. 247
SIMIAN COMMERCIAL 149
SIMONIZ EXPRESS DETAIL CENTERS 14
SIMPLE SIMON'S PIZZA 96
SIMPLICITY SEWING & CRAFT CENTER 37
SIMPLICITY SEWING & CRAFT CENTERS INT'L. 37
SIMPLY CHARMING / RODAN JEWELLERS 235
SINGER, LEWAK, GREENBAUM, & GOLDSTEIN 111
SINGER SPECS., INC. 126
SINGER/SPECS DISCOUNT VISION CENTERS 126

SINGING MACHINE COMPANY INC., THE 56
SIP 'N SPIN 131
SIP 'N SPIN FRANCHISE INC. 131
SIR GEORGE'S ROYAL BUFFET 96
SIR GOONY MINIATURE GOLF 165
SIR PIZZA 96
SIR SPEEDY, INC. 140
SIR SPEEDY PRINTING 231
SIR SPEEDY PRINTING CENTERS 140
SIRLOIN STOCKADE FAMILY RESTAURANTS 96
SIRLOIN STOCKADE INTERNATIONAL, INC. 96
SITE FOR SORE EYES 126
SITTERS ON SITE 37
SITTERS UNLIMITED 129
SIZZLER 97
SIZZLER RESTAURANTS INTERNATIONAL, INC. 97
SIZZLER SANTA CLARA, INC. 97
SIZZLIN' QUICK HAMBURGERS, INC. 97
SIZZLING WOK INTERNATIONAL INC. 212
SKEETER'S GROOMING FACILITY 136
SKETCHLEY 227
SKILL ALIANCA INGLESA 266
SKILL ALIANCA INGLESA S/C LTDA. 266
SKILLSET TRAINING 240
SKILLSET TRAINING SYSTEMS INC. 240
SLACK'S HOAGIE SHACK 97
SLEEP INNS 135
SLEEPING GIANT WITHIN, INC., THE 160
SLEEPING GIANT WITHIN, THE 160
SLENDER CENTER 126
SLIDE SHOTS INC. 175
SLIM WITHIN LIFESTYLE CONSULTING OFFICES 225
SLIM WITHIN LIFESTYLE FRANCHISES, INC. 225
SLUMBERLAND INTERNATIONAL 128
SMALL BUSINESS ADVISORY CENTRES 252
SMALL BUSINESS CLUB 49
SMALL CITY BUSINESS JOURNALS INC. 141
SMITH & UNDERWOOD, P.C. 116
SMITH, GILL, FISHER & BUTTS 113
SMITH, NIXON & CO. 218
SMITTY'S CANADA LTD. 212
SMITTY'S FAMILY RESTAURANT 212
SMOKEETER ELECTRONIC AIR CLEANERS & INDOOR AIR QUAL 49
SMOKERS EXPRESS 152
SMOKES 'N' THINGS GIFT SHOPS 273
SMOKEY ENTERPRISES, INC. 22
SMOKEY MOUNTAIN HOMES 22
SMOOTHIE KING 126
SMOOTHIE KING FRANCHISES 126
SNAP FRANCHISING LTD. 269
SNAP PRINTING 269
SNAP SHOTS 138
SNAP-ON TOOLS OF CANADA LTD. 182
SNAP-ON-TOOLS CORPORATION 15
SNAP-ON-TOOLS LTD. 273
SNAPPY SNAPS 270
SNAPPY SNAPS FRANCHISES LTD. 270
SNC FRANCHISE CORP. 120
SNELLING AND SNELLING, INC. 54
SNELLING PERSONNEL SERVICES 54
SNIP N' CLIP HAIRCUT SHOPS 120
SNO-BIZ 212
SNO-BIZ INTERNATIONAL 212
SNYDER DRUG STORES, INC. 152
SOAP EXCHANGE ENVIRO-WISE REFILL CENTRES 193
SOAP EXCHANGE, THE 193
SOAPBERRY SHOP 235
SOAP'S GOODTIME LAUNDRY 228
SOAP'S GOODTIME LAUNDRY (CANADA) INC. 228
SOBIK'S SUBS 97
SOCIETE NATIONALE DE LA FRANCHISE INC. 218
SOFITEL 266
SOFTUB CANADA 196
SOFTWARE CITY 157
SOL ABRAMS, PUBLIC RELATIONS AND MARKETING CONSULTA 111
SOLAR-MESH PTY, LTD. 249
SOLAR-MESH® 249
SOLID/FLUE CHIMNEY SYSTEMS, INC. 49
SOLOMON CARPETS 273
SOMERFORD CLAIMS PLC. 266
SONIC DRIVE-IN RESTAURANTS 97
SONIC INDUSTRIES INC. 97
SONITROL 23
SONITROL CORPORATION 23
SONNY'S FRANCHISE CO. 97
SONNY'S REAL PIT BAR-B-QUE, INC. 97
SOOTER STUDIOS LTD. 230
SOS SALES, INC. 37
SOTOS, KARVANIS BARRISTERS AND SOLICITORS 221
SOUNDSATION ENTERTAINMENT 56
SOUPER SALAD, INC. 97
SOUTHEAST COMPANIES 8
SOUTHEASTERN DIRECTORY ASSOCIATION, INC. 3
SOUTHERN FRIED CHICKEN & SFC EXPRESS 258
SOUTHERN MAID DONUT SHOP 64
SOUTHERN MANAGEMENT ASSOC. 97
SOUTHLAND CORP., THE 56
SOUTHWEST PET, INC. 136
SOUTHWEST PROMOTIONAL CORPORATION 4
SOVEREIGN SERVICES 266
SP UNITED, INC. 96
SPACEAGE PLASTICS 266
SPACEAGE PLASTICS LTD. 266
SPAD'S PIZZA, INC. 97
SPAGHETTI JACK'S 97
SPAGHETTI SHOP, THE 97
SPAGHETTI VENDORS FRANCHISE SYSTEM INC. 85
SPAR CONVENIENCE STORES 274
SPARKLE INTERNATIONAL INC. 42
SPARKLE WASH 42
SPARKLING MAID 42
SPARKLING MAID, INC. 42
SPECIAL CELEBRATIONS 235
SPECIAL CELEBRATIONS INC. 235
SPECIAL SELECTIONS 175
SPECIALTY BAKERIES, INC. 60
SPECTRUM WEST FRANCHISE SALES & MARKETING CONSULTAN 111
SPEED FAB-CRETE CORP. 22
SPEEDEE OIL CHANGE & TUNE-UP 8
SPEEDPRO SIGN & PRINT CENTERS 241
SPEEDPRO SYSTEMS INC. 241
SPEEDY AUTO GLASS 15
SPEEDY CAR-X, INC. 9
SPEEDY KEYS 175
SPEEDY KEYS, INC. 175
SPEEDY LUBE / QUIK MARTS 8
SPEEDY MUFFLER KING CANADA LTD. 180
SPEEDY MUFFLER KING INC. 180
SPEEDY PRINTING CENTERS 231
SPEEDY SIGN A RAMA, USA, INC. 162
SPEEDY SIGN* A*RAMA, USA, INC. 162
SPEEDY TRANSMISSION CENTERS 16
SPHERE NORTH AMERICA CORP. 134
SPICE - THE ADVENTURE GROUP 266
SPICE UK LTD. 266
SPINNER'S PIZZA & SUBS 97
SPLASHDANCE 269
SPLASHDANCE FITNESS 269
SPOONER'S SNAPPY TOMATO PIZZA COMPANY 97
SPORT CLIPS 120
SPORT IT 152
SPORT IT, INC. 152
SPORT SHOE MARKETING, INC. 155
SPORT SHOE, THE 155
SPORTS EXPERTS 242
SPORTS FANTASY MARKETING, INC. 152
SPORTS RECRUITS INTERNATIONAL 242
SPORTS RECRUITS INTERNATIONAL INC. 242
SPORTS SECTION, THE 138
SPORTS TRADERS 235
SPORTSCENE RESTAURANTS INC. 209
SPORTSFORUM UK, LTD. 272
SPORTSLIFE ENTERPRISES 152
SPORTSMAN'S CLUB INTERNATIONAL 165
SPORTSMAN'S CLUB OF AMERICA 165
SPOT-NOT CAR WASHES 15
SPOTLESS OFFICE SERVICES, INC. 193

SPR CHIP REPAIR *117*
SPR COUNTERTOP & TUB REPAIR *22*
SPR DETAIL MAGIC *49*
SPR INTERNATIONAL *21*
SPR INTERNATIONAL INC. *22, 48, 117*
SPR INTERNATIONAL, INC. *38, 40, 49*
SPRING CREST COMPANY, INC. *152*
SPRING CREST DRAPERY CENTERS *152*
SPRING-GREEN LAWN CARE *132*
SPRING-GREEN LAWN CARE CORP. *132*
SPUDULIKE *258*
SPUDULIKE LTD. *258*
SQUARE 1 CLEANING SERVICES *253*
SQUARE 1 ENVIRONMENTAL SERVICES LTD. *253*
SQUARE BOY PIZZA AND SUBS *212*
SRA INTERNATIONAL, INC. *53*
ST- A PHOTO CORP. *230*
ST. CLAIR DEVELOPMENT CORP. *76*
ST. CLAIR PAINT & WALLPAPER, WALLPAPER WORLD *227*
ST. ELIZABETH CORP., THE *122*
ST. HUBERT BAR-B-Q *212*
ST. HUBERT BAR-B-Q LTD. *212*
ST. JEROME RESTAURANT LTD. *212*
ST. JEROME'S CHICKEN & RIBS *212*
ST. PIERRE'S CORP. *258*
STAFF BUILDERS HOME HEALTH CARE *54*
STAINED GLASS OVERLAY, INC. *152*
STAN EVANS BAKERIES, INC. *64*
STAN EVANS BAKERY *64*
STANAIR INDUSTRIAL DOOR SERVICES LTD. *249*
STANDA SPA-AFFILIAZIONE-FRANCHISING-IMPROSSO *258*
STANLEY STEEMER CARPET CLEANER *33*
STAR CLEANERS, INC. *131*
STAR LUBE *9*
STAR TRAVEL *266*
STAR VALLEY INSTALLATIONS *152*
STAR VIDEO *238*
STARLOG - THE COMIC & SCIENCE FICTION UNIVERSE *152*
STARLOG FRANCHISE CORP. *152*
START INFORMATIQUE *252*
STARTECH INC. *128*
STARVING STUDENTS *175*
STEAK & EGGER *97*
STEAK & HOAGIE SHOP, THE *97*
STEAK ESCAPE, THE *97*
STEAK 'N SHAKE *97*
STEAK N SHAKE, INC. *97*
STEAK-OUT *98*
STEAK-OUT FRANCHISING, INC. *98*
STEAKS TO GO *98*
STEAKS TO GO FRANCHISE CO. *98*
STEAM BROTHERS INC. *33*
STEAMATIC *33*
STEAMATIC FRANCHISES LTD. *190*
STEAMATIC, INC. *33*
STEIN & KAHAN, A LAW CORPORATION *116*
STELLARVISION/STARROOMS *128*
STEREO DEN *238*
STEREO PLUS *238*
STERLING OPTICAL CORP. *126*
STEVE O'BRYAN HOLDINGS LTD. *238*
STEVEN A. CHASE, ATTORNEY AT LAW *116*
STEVEN S. RAAB LAW OFFICE *116*
STEVE'S HOMEMADE ICE CREAM, INC. *68*
STEVE'S ICE CREAM *68*
STEWART'S DRIVE-IN *98*
STEWART'S RESTAURANTS, INC. *98*
STOCKCHECK *252*
STOICO FOOD SERVICES, INC. *97, 98*
STONE CRAB INN *98*
STONEASE PAVING PATTERN IMPRINTED CONCRETE LTD. *266*
STOP 'N STEER SHOPS *182*
STOP SMOKING PLAN *126*
STORE PACK, INC. *111*
STORK NEWS OF AMERICA, INC. *118*
STOUT & CO. *98*
STOY HAYWARD FRANCHISING SERVICES *261*
STRAP-ON WRISTWEAR *274*
STRASBURGER & PRICE *116*
STRATEGIC BUSINESS DEVELOPMENT CORP. *111*

STRATEGIC BUSINESS SYSTEMS, INC. *31*
STRATEGIC CREATIVE SERVICES *111*
STRAW HAT COOPERATIVE CORPORATION *98*
STRAW HAT PIZZA *98*
STREET CORNER NEWS *152*
STRETCH-N-GROW OF CANADA INC. *191*
STRINGS FRANCHISES INC. *98*
STRINGS ITALIAN CAFE *98*
STRIPPERS!, THE *244*
STROUD CREAMERY *258*
STS, INC. *149*
STUCCO DOCTOR *185*
STUCKEY'S *59*
STUCKEY'S CORPORATION *59*
STUDEBAKER'S *212*
STUDENT SUPER-SAVER® *5*
STUDENT WORKS PAINTING *185*
STUDIO PLUS *135*
STUDIO PLUS OF AMERICA INC. *135*
STUFF 'N TURKEY *98*
STUFF'N TURKEY, INC. *98*
STUFT PIZZA FRANCHISE CORP. *98*
STUFT PIZZA FRANCHISE CORP. *98*
SUB & STUFF SANDWICH SHOP *98*
SUB SHOPS *98*
SUB STATION II *98*
SUB STATION II, INC. *98*
SUBS PLUS *213*
SUBS PLUS INC. *213*
SUBURBAN LODGE *136*
SUBURBAN LODGES OF AMERICA, INC. *136*
SUBWAY SANDWICHES AND SALADS *98*
SUCCESS CENTERS INTERNATIONAL *31*
SUCCESSORIES *152*
SUGAR CREEK STORES INC. *59*
SUGARLOAF CREATIONS, INC. *175*
SUKIYAKI - A JAPANESE DELIGHT *213*
SULLIVAN & COGLIANO *54*
SUMMIT FAMILY RESTAURANTS, INC. *83*
SUMMIT TRAVEL *166*
SUMMIT TRAVEL GROUP, INC. *166*
SUMMIT-NAKED FURNITURE, INC. *128*
SUMMUM CREATIVE JEWELLERY *235*
SUN SCREEN INTERNATIONAL *15*
SUN SHADE OPTIQUE *152*
SUNBANQUE ISLAND TANNING *223*
SUNBELT BUSINESS BROKERS *31*
SUNDAY BEST! *131*
SUNGLASS BOUTIQUE *153*
SUNITRON INC. *196*
SUNITRON INC. HOLDING CORP. *197*
SUNQUEST SYSTEMS *98*
SUNQUEST SYSTEMS, INC. *98*
SUNRIDER INTERNATIONAL *225*
SUNSHINE CAFE RESTAURANTS *98*
SUNSHINE PROPERTIES INC. *137*
SUNSHINE PROPERTIES INT'L INC. *56*
SUNSHINE PROPERTIES INT'L. INC. *165*
SUNSPLASH *68*
SUNSTREAM CANADA *225*
SUNSTREAM TAN & SKIN CARE *225*
SUPER 8 MOTELS *136*
SUPER ADS INC. *5*
SUPER COUPS *5*
SUPER GARD CANADA LTD. *185*
SUPER INDUSTRIES, INC. *132*
SUPER KING CATFISH *98*
SUPER KING CATFISH, INC. *98*
SUPER SEAMLESS STEEL SIDING OF CANADA, LTD. *185*
SUPER THRIFTY DRUG MARTS *225*
SUPERCUTS *120*
SUPERGLASS WINDSHIELD REPAIR *15*
SUPERGLASS WINDSHIELD REPAIR, INC. *15*
SUPERIOR MARKETING SERVICES, INC. *2*
SUPERIOR TIRE AUTO FITNESS CENTRES *182*
SUPERIOR TIRE CORP. *182*
SUPERLAWNS *132*
SUPPLY MASTER USA® *15*
SUPREME PRODUCTS INC. *98*
SUR VISAGE COSMETICS *223*

SUR VISAGE, INC. 223
SURE GRAPHICS LTD. 231
SURE STOP BRAKE CENTERS 182
SUREWAY AIR EXPRESS 31
SUREWAY AIR TRAFFIC CORP. 31
SURF FOTO 138
SURF-SHIELD CORP. 22
SURFA SHIELD 22
SURFACE DOCTOR 175, 185
SURFACE SPECIALISTS 22
SURFACE SPECIALISTS SYSTEMS, INC. 22
SURGEMASTER 196
SUTTON GROUP 232
SVI INC. 173
SWEDISH FRANCHISE ASSOCIATION 261
SWEET CITY 59
SWEET CITY INTERNATIONAL, INC. 59
SWEET FACTORY INC., THE 199
SWEET ROSIE'S 202
SWEET ROSIE'S CORPORATION 202
SWING SYNC 175
SWINGTIME (GOLF CENTRES) LTD. 267
SWINGTIME GOLF CENTRES 267
SWINTON INSURANCE 252
SWINTON INSURANCE GROUP 252
SWISHER HYGIENE FRANCHISE CORPORATION 42
SWISHER INTERNATIONAL 42
SWISS CHALET CHICKEN & RIBS 213
SWISS COLONY SEASONALS 59
SWISS COLONY STORES INC. 57, 59
SYD SIMONS COSMETICS, INC. 120
SYLVAN LEARNING CENTERS 160
SYLVAN LEARNING SYSTEMS, INC. 160
SYNCON GMBH 261
SYSTEMS CONSULTANCY 251

T

T & G CRAFTS 175
T & P HOAGIE SYSTEMS, INC. 97
T-SHIRTS PLUS 155
T.D.I. SYSTEMS CANADA 244
T.G.I. FRIDAY'S RESTAURANTS 98
T.H.G. FRANCHISING 201, 202, 206
T.J. CINNAMONS BAKERY 64
T.J. CINNAMONS, INC. 64
T.T. ADS MARKETING INC. 178
T.T. FOODS, INC. 99
TABATOUT INC. 199
TAC DEVELOPMENT 247
TACO BELL CORP. 99
TACO CABANA, INC. 90
TACO CASA 99
TACO CASA INTERNATIONAL, LTD. 99
TACO CONCEPTS, INC. 99
TACO GRANDE 99
TACO HUT 99
TACO HUT AMERICA INC. 99
TACO JOHN'S 99
TACO JOHN'S INTERNATIONAL, INC. 99
TACO LOCO 99
TACO MAKER, INC., THE 99
TACO MAKER, THE 99
TACO MAYO 99
TACO MAYO FRANCHISE SYSTEMS, INC. 99
TACO TICO, INC. 99
TACO TIME 99
TACO TIME CANADA INC. 213
TACO TIME INTERNATIONAL 99
TACO TREAT 99
TACO TREAT INC. 99
TACO VIA 99
TACO VIA FRANCHISE SYSTEMS INC. 99
TACO VIVA 99
TADDICK CORP. 230
TAKE 2 CAFÉ 213
TAKE-A-CARD 178
TAKE-A-CARD ONTARIO 178
TAKEOUT TAXI 99
TAKEOUT TAXI FRANCHISING SYSTEMS, INC. 99
TALASSIO 274
TALENT TREE PERSONNEL SERVICES 54
TALKING ADS 5
TALKING ADS OF AMERICA 5
TALKING BOOK INC. 145
TALKING BOOK WORLD 145
TANDY CORPORATION 157
TANDY CRAFTS LTD. 235
TANDY LEATHER CO. 235
TANGIBLE RESEARCH & DEVELOPMENT CORP. 38, 39, 42
TARGET BUSINESS CONSULTANTS, INC. 111
TASTEE-FREEZ 68
TASTEE-FREEZ INTERNATIONAL 68
TASTY TACOS 99
TAX MAN INC. 2
TAXPRO INC. 1
TCBY 68
TD INC. 31
TEAM (AUDIO) LTD. 274
TEAM GOLF 165
TEAM WORKS CLEANING SERVICES 42
TEAM-WORKS 42
TECH SYSTEMS INC. 44
TECH SYSTEMS, INC. 137
TECHNOKIDS - TECHNOPLUS COMPUTER LEARNING CENTRE 240
TECHNOPLUS MOBILE COMPUTER TRAINING 240
TECHSIGN FRANCHISING PARTICIPACOES LTDA. 266
TECHSTAFF 22
TECHSTAFF, INC. 22
TECNIC DRIVING SCHOOL GROUP 240
TELE-PAGES DIRECTORIES 252
TELE-TECH COMMUNICATIONS INC. 245
TELECHECK SERVICES, INC. 31
TELTECH CANADA GROUP INC. 188
TEMPACO 49
TEMPACO, INC. 49
TEMPS & CO. 54
TERMINIX INTERNATIONAL 175
TERMINIX INTERNATIONAL CO. L.P. 175
TERRA SYSTEMS 132
TERRA SYSTEMS FRANCHISE CORP. 132
TEXACO REFINING & MARKETING INC. 9
TEXAS LOOSEY'S CHILI PARLOR AND SALOON 100
TEXAS STATE OPTICAL 126
TFM, CO. 59
THE ARROW...A NEIGHBORHOOD PUB 213
THE BAVARAS GROUP 213
THE BEEF PLACE 197
THE BRICE GROUP 67
THE CAR PHONE STORE 153
THE GENDRON CORP. 63, 149
THE GREAT AMERICAN BAGEL, INC., 80
THE GYMBOREE CORPORATION 35
THE HOT BAGELWORKS BAKERY 202
THE KNECHTEL CORP. 198
THE MAILHOUSE, INC. 5
THE MILL 65
THE NECTAR GROUP 269
THE QUIZNO'S CORP. 94
THE RESUME HUT 197
THE RIGHT WAY BY POLLY 126
THE SERVICEMASTER COMPANY 42
THE SIGN FRANCHISE 267
THE SLC CORPORATION 209
THE TDL GROUP LTD. 202
THEE CHIMNEY SWEEP, INC. 175
THELEN, MARRIN, JOHNSON & BRIDGES 116
THEMED PUTTING COURSES 165
THERMAL-ATION 175
THIRD DIMENSION CUTS, INC. 120
THIRTEEN-ONE, INC. 111
THOMAS, BALLENGER, VOGELMAN & TURNER, P.C. 116
THOMAS BLANTZ ENTERPRISES INC. 122
THOMAS COOK / MARLIN TRAVEL 242
THOMAS NIX DISTRIBUTOR, INC. 174
THOMASON ENTERPRISES, INC. 168
THOMPSON & NIGHT, P.C. 116
THOMPSON, HINE & FLORY 114
THORNTONS PLC 258

THREE DOG BAKERY *137*
THREE DOG BAKERY, INC. **137**
THREE PENGUINS INC. **227**
THRIFTY CANADA, LTD. **179**
THRIFTY CAR RENTAL *179, 247*
THRIFTY RENT-A-CAR SYSTEM, INC. *7*
THRUWAY MUFFLERCENTRE *180*
THUNDERCLOUD SUBS *100*
TICKETS 'N THINGS *199*
TICKETS 'N TOBACCO, INC. **199**
TICKLE MANOR TEAROOM - LAVENHAM *258*
TICKLE MANOR TEAROOM LTD. **258**
TIE RACK *274*
TIE RACK PLC **274**
TIGHT FIT LTD. **267**
TIGHTS MACHINE, THE *267*
TIKI MING *213*
TILDEN FOR BRAKES CARE CARE CENTERS *15*
TILDEN RENT-A-CAR SYSTEMS LTD. *179*
TILL-TAPE ADS® *178*
TIM HORTONS *202*
TIMBER LOG BUILDING SYSTEMS *49*
TIMBERMILL STORAGE BARNS INC. *22*
TIME & TEMPERATURE ADVERTISING *5*
TIME MASTERS *196*
TIME MASTERS, INC. **196**
TIME SERVICES, INC. **54**
TIME TEMPORARY SERVICES *54*
TIMOTHY'S COFFEES OF THE WORLD *202*
TIMOTHY'S ROYAL COFFEE **202**
TIMS MANAGEMENT SYSTEMS, INC. *54*
TINDER BOX AND TINDER BOX GOURMET CAFE *59*
TINDER BOX INTERNATIONAL, INC. **59**
TINT KING MOTORING ACCESSORIES *182*
TINT KING OF CALIFORNIA INC. **182**
TINT MASTER AND AUTO GLASS *182*
TIOLI *267*
TIPPY'S TACO HOUSE *100*
TIRE CENTRES *15*
TIRES ONLY *183*
TIX TRAVEL & TICKET AGENCY *166*
TKO REAL ESTATE ADVISORY GROUP *111*
TNT EXPRESS (UK) LTD. **252**
TNT PARCEL OFFICE *252*
TO HAWAII ONLY *166*
TO HAWAII ONLY FRANCHISE, INC. **166**
TOASTY KITCHENS *258*
TOBMAR INVESTMENTS **198**
TOBY'S GOODEATS *213*
TODAYS COMPUTERS BUSINESS CENTERS *157*
TODAY'S SENIORS NEWSPAPER *178*
TODAYS TEMPORARY *54*
TODDLIN' TIME *37*
TODDLIN' TIME, INC. **37**
TOGETHER DATING SERVICE *175*
TOGETHER DEVELOPMENT CORP. **175**
TOGO'S EATERY *100*
TOM & JERRY'S BURGERS & BEER *100*
TOM & JERRY'S, INC. **100**
TOM'S FOOD, INC. *49*
TOM'S HOUSE OF PIZZA *213*
TONI HARRER SYSTEMZ ENTRALE *256*
TONY ROMA'S, A PLACE FOR RIBS *100*
TOP DRAWER CUSTOM CLOSETS *22*
TOP FORTY / TFM *238*
TOP FORTY MUSIC LTD. **238**
TOP GOLF MINIATURE *197*
TOP VALUE EXHAUST SYSTEMS *9*
TOP VALUE MUFFLER SHOPS *9*
TOPSY'S POPCORN & ICE CREAM SHOPPE *68*
TORONTO DOMINION BANK *218*
TORONTO FINANCIAL & BUSINESS CONSULTANTS *218*
TORONTO SCHOOL OF BUSINESS, COMPUCOLLEGE SCHOOL OF *240*
TORRENCE ENTERPRISES (BROKER) *111*
TOTAL CAR FRANCHISING CORPORATION **12**
TOTAL SHAVING SOLUTION, THE *49*
TOTAL SOLUTIONS, INC. **49**
TOWER CLEANING SYSTEMS *42*
TOWN AND COUNTRY OFFICE & CARPET CARE SYSTEMS *42*

TOWN PUMP FOOD STORES, INC. *100*
TOWNSEND, O'LEARY, SUMAN AND MCKEE, INC. *111*
TOY TRADERS *37, 236*
TOY TRADERS FRANCHISE, INC. **37**
TOYS FOR TIKES *236*
TPI TRAVEL SERVICES *166*
TRADE LABOR *176*
TRADE SECRET *121*
TRADE SECRET, INC. **121**
TRADERS INTERNATIONAL *235, 236*
TRADING FACES *139*
TRADITIONS, LTD. **154**
TRAFALGAR CLEANING CHEMICALS *253*
TRAMLINES SPORTS LTD. **274**
TRANEX RESIDENTIAL LENDING NETWORK *144*
TRANS PACIFIC INVESTMENT CORP. **107**
TRANS-ACTION REAL ESTATE SERVICES *232*
TRANS/PACIFIC RESTAURANTS, INC. *100*
TRANSERV, INC. *7*
TRANSMARK GROUP, THE *31*
TRANSMISSION USA, DIV. OF MORAN INDUSTRIES, INC. **16**
TRANSWORLD IMPORT/EXPORT CORP. **29**
TRANSWORLD INDUSTRIES *49*
TRAVAIL EMPLOYMENT GROUP *252*
TRAVEL AGENTS INTERNATIONAL *166*
TRAVEL AGENTS INTERNATIONAL, INC. **166**
TRAVEL BAZAAR, THE *267*
TRAVEL CENTER LTD. *166*
TRAVEL IMPRESSIONS **166**
TRAVEL NETWORK *166*
TRAVEL NETWORK LTD. **166**
TRAVEL PROFESSIONALS INSTITUTE *160*
TRAVEL PROFESSIONALS INTERNATIONAL *166, 242*
TRAVEL PROFESSIONALS INTERNATIONAL, INC. **166**
TRAVEL PROS INC. **166**
TRAVEL SUCCESS *166*
TRAVEL TRADE SCHOOL, THE *160*
TRAVELHOST AGENCIES, INC. **167**
TRAVELHOST TRAVEL AGENCY *167*
TRAVELODGE *136*
TRAVELODGE / THRIFTLODGE *229*
TRAVELPLEX *167*
TRC STAFFING SERVICES, INC. **54**
TREASURE CACHE, THE *153*
TREATS *202*
TREATS INTERNATIONAL **202**
TRIAD EQUIPMENT MAINTENANCE SYSTEMS, INC. *42*
TRIDENT ADM. EMPREEND. E PART. LTDA. *256*
TRIDENT KEY MART *236*
TRIDENT MANAGEMENT LTD. **236**
TRIMARK, INC. **5**
TRIMLINE HEALTH & FITNESS CENTRES *269*
TRINKETS FINE JEWELLERY *236*
TRIPLE AAA SPORTS PHOTOGRAPHY INC. *242*
TRIPLE CHECK INCOME TAX SERVICE *2*
TRIPODE **264**
TRIPODE JARDILAND *274*
TRIZZ HAIR ALTERNATIVES *223*
TRIZZ HAIR ALTERNATIVES, LTD. **223**
TROLL'S SEAFOOD RESTAURANTS *213*
TROPHEY FOODS **195**
TROPHY UK *267*
TROPI-TAN, INC. **124**, *176*
TROPIK SUN FRUIT & NUT *60*
TROTTER'S BARBECUE *100*
TROTTER'S CORP. **100**
TRUCK OPTIONS *15*
TRUCKSTOPS OF AMERICA FRANCHISE SYSTEMS, INC. *15*
TRUE VALUE HARDWARE STORES *236*
TRUST PARTS LTD. *274*
TRUSTWORTHY HARDWARE STORES *153*
TSO, INC. **126**
TSW THE SIGN WASHERS *162*
TUBBY'S SUB SHOPS *100*
TUBBY'S SUB SHOPS, INC. **100**
TUFFY ASSOCIATES CORP. **15**
TUFFY AUTO SERVICE CENTERS *15*
TUMBLEWEED MEXICAN RESTAURANT *100*
TUNE-IN *5*
TUNE-IN PUBLICATIONS, INC. **5**

TUNE-UP 247
TUNEX AUTOMOTIVE/DIAGNOSTIC SPECIALISTS 9
TUNEX INTERNATIONAL, INC. 9
TURF MANAGEMENT SYSTEMS, INC. 228
TURFAIT ET CIE S.A. 256
TUTOR TIME CHILD CARE LEARNING CENTERS 37
TUTOR TIME CHILD CARE SYSTEMS, INC. 37
TV FACTS MAGAZINE 5
TV FACTS OF NORTH AMERICA 5
TV NEWS MAGAZINE 5
TWIGLAND FASHIONS INC. 154
TWIST 274
TWO MEN AND A TRUCK 176
TYPING TIGERS 31
TYREFIX 247
TYREFIX LTD. 247

U

U & R TAX SERVICES LTD. 177
U & R TAX SERVICES LTD. 240
U FRAME IT, FLAIR U FRAME IT, FLAIR CUSTOM FRAMING 230
U-PAWN & SMILE 236
U-SAVE AUTO RENTAL 7
U-SAVE AUTO RENTAL OF AMERICA INC. 7
U.S. LAWNS, INC. 133
U.S. ROOTER CORP. 22
U.S. ROOTER SERVICE 22
U.S. SCHOOL OF PROFESSIONAL PAPERHANGING, INC. 160
U.S. STRUCTURES, INC. 18
U.S.A CANDY, INC. 56
UAP INC. 180
UAP/NAPA ASSOCIATE PROGRAM 196
UGLY DUCKLING RENT-A-CAR 7
ULTIMATE TAN, THE 126
ULTRA BOND, INC. 49
ULTRATUNE SYSTEM (AUST) PTY. 247
ULTRAZONE, INC. 165
UNCLE TONY'S INTERNATIONAL, INC. 100
UNCLE TONY'S PIZZA & PASTA RESTAURANTS 100
UNCO INDUSTRIES, INC. 50
UNCOMMON GROUND GOURMET COFFEE 202
UNDER WARES FOR HIM 155
UNI PRO 183
UNI-SELECT, INC. 183
UNICIS 267
UNICLEAN SYSTEMS 193
UNICLEAN SYSTEMS, INC. 193
UNIFIED MANAGEMENT CORP. 28
UNIFORCE STAFFING SERVICES 54
UNIGATE DAIRIES LTD. 258
UNIGLOBE TRAVEL 243
UNIGLOBE TRAVEL (INTERNATIONAL) INC. 243
UNISHIPPERS ASSOCIATION INC. 176
UNISON MARKETING COMMUNICATIONS 5
UNISON SYNDICATIONS 5
UNITED AIR SPECIALISTS, INC. 49
UNITED BUSINESS GROUP, INC. 156
UNITED BUSINESS GROUP, INC. 145
UNITED CHECK CASHING 31
UNITED CHECK CASHING CO. INC. 31
UNITED CONSUMERS CLUB 43
UNITED CONSUMERS CLUB FRANCHISING CORP. 43
UNITED COUPON CORP. 6
UNITED COUPON OF...(LOCATION OF FRANCHISE TERRITORY 6
UNITED FRANCHISE CONSULTANTS 111
UNITED PRINTING UNLIMITED 141
UNITED PRINTING UNLIMITED INC. 141
UNITED STATES SEAMLESS 22
UNITED STUDIOS OF SELF DEFENSE 165
UNITED STUDIOS OF SELF DEFENSE, INC. 165
UNITED VENTURES, INC. 46
UNITED WORTH HYDROCHEM CORP. 167
UNIVERSAL PRODUCTS CO. 162
UNIVERSAL TRAINING 111
UNIVERSITY CONTRACTORS CORP. LTD. 185
UNIVERSITY FIRST CLASS PAINTERS 185
UNIVERSITY PAINTERS 129
UNIVERSITY PAINTERS, INC. 129

UNIWAY MANAGEMENT CORP. 43
UNO RESTAURANT CORP. 100
UNO RESTAURANTS CORP. 93
UPLAND & ASSOCIATES 112
UPPER KRUST 100
URBAN AND RURAL SCHOOLS 240
US-1 AUTOPARTS FRANCHISE CORP. 15
USA AUTOMOTIVE SYSTEMS 10
USA BABY 37
USA DORACO 19
USA MUFFLER AND BRAKES 10
UTICOLOR 267
UTICOLOR (GREAT BRITAIN) LTD. 267

V

V & S DEPARTMENT STORES 236
V.I.D.E.O. SECURITY PROCESS 186
V.I.P. COMPANION-CARE, INC. 54
VA SIGNS 267
VAC SET SIGN SHOP 162
VACATIONBOUND GLOBAL MOTORHOME TRAVEL 7
VACATIONBOUND, INC. 7
VACUFLO - CENTRAL VACUUM CLEANING SYSTEMS 50
VAL-PAK COUPONS 6
VAL-PAK DIRECT MARKETING SYSTEMS, INC. 6
VAL-U-PAK 267
VALDCO T-SHIRTS 176
VALENTINE 213
VALENTINO'S INC. 100
VALET EXPRESS 31
VALET EXPRESS FRANCHISING INC. 31
VALMONT INDUSTRIES, INC. 156
VALU-MART/FRESHMART/MR. GROCER/YOUR INDEPENDENT GRO 199
VALUE LINE MAINTENANCE SYS. 42
VALVOLINE INSTANT OIL CHANGE 9
VALVOLINE INSTANT OIL CHANGE FRANCHISING, INC. 9
VANCOUVER FLAG SHOP, INC., THE 233
VANN MANN CORP. 170
VARCON CONSTRUCTION CO. LTD. 218
VARSITY, THE 100
VCR DOCTOR 157
VENDO PLC 253
VENDOR$ CHOICE™, THE 50
VENTROLLA LTD. 249
VENTURE INNS INC. 229
VENTURE MARKETING ASSOC. 112
VERLAG DEUTSCHER STADTPLANE GMBH 267
VERN'S DOG HOUSE, INC. 100
VET, DIDI, YANK'S, SUPERSTAR 274
VIAPLAN BV 267
VIAPLAN S.A.R.L. 267
VICORP 101
VICTORIAN PAPERS 153
VICTORIAN PAPERS' - LEGACY 153
VICTORY LANE QUICK OIL CHANGE 9
VIDE-O-GO, INC. 157
VIDE-O-GO TAPE LEARNING CENTERS OF AMERICA 157
VIDEO 5000 168
VIDEO BIZ, INC. 157
VIDEO CUBE, INC. 238
VIDEO DATA SERVICES 31
VIDEO EDITOR 157
VIDEO GALAXY FRANCHISE, INC. 157
VIDEO GAME SWAPPERS 157
VIDEO GAME SWAPPERS, INC. 157
VIDEO GAMER 157
VIDEO PARTY TYME 197
VIDEO STOP 157
VIDEO STOP UNLIMITED INC. 157
VIDEO THRILLS FAMILY ENTERTAINMENT 158
VIDEO UPDATE 158
VIDEO UPDATE, INC. 158
VIDEOFLICKS CANADA LTD. 238
VIDEOGENICS 158
VIDEOLAND 274
VIDEOLAND NEDERLAND B.V. 274
VIDEOMATIC 24 HR 238

VIDEOMATIC 24 HR. MOVIE RENTALS, INC. *238*
VIE DE FRANCE BAKERY/CAFÉ *65*
VIE DE FRANCE YAMAZAKI, INC. *65*
VIKING MANAGEMENT CORPORATION *112*
VILLA ENTERPRISES MANAGEMENT LTD., INC. *100*
VILLA PIZZA *100*
VILLAGE INN RESTAURANTS *101*
VILLAGER LODGE *229*
VINCENT TUCKER LTD. *218*
VINYL MASTER (UK) LTD. *267*
VINYLGRAPHICS CUSTOM SIGN CENTRES *241*
VINYLGRAPHICS, INC. *241*
VIP BOAT CLUB *145*
VIP BOAT CLUBS OF FLORIDA INC. *145*
VIRTROPOLIS *56*
VIRTROPOLIS CORPORATION, THE *56*
VIS CONSULTANTS, INC. *112*
VISAGE COSMETICS LTD. *222*
VISTA RESTAURANTS *101*
VITAL ENERGY HEALTH TRAINING INC. *226*
VITAL PROTECTION SYSTEMS INC. *183*
VITAMIN POWER *50*
VITAMIN POWER INCORPORATED *50*
VIVAH FRANCHISE, INC. *236*
VIVAH JEWELRY *236*
VLOCK & BROWN *116*
VOICE-TEL *31*
VOICE-TEL ENTERPRISES, INC. *31*
VOICESMART CORP. *31*
VOICESMART CORP. *31*
VOLPE NAILS, INC. *121*
VONSCHRADER ASSOCIATE *190*
VONSCHRADER CANADA *190*
VR BUSINESS BROKERS *31*
VR BUSINESS BROKERS (CANADA) INC. *218*

W

W.H. PUNT ENTERPRISES INC. *218*
W.O.T.R. FRANCHISING, INC. *101*
WACKYPUTT *242*
WAFFLETOWN U.S.A. LTD. *101*
WALK & JOG/WALK & ATHLETIC FOOTWEAR *155*
WALL-FILL WORLDWIDE INC. *22*
WALLPAPERS TO GO *129*
WALLPAPERS TO GO, INC. *129*
WALT HAMBROCK, FRANCHISE & BUSINESS BROKER *218*
WALT'S ROAST BEEF INT'L, INC. *101*
WAND & BODEN *274*
WANDLYN INNS *229*
WARD'S FOOD SYSTEMS, INC. *101*
WAREHOUSE RESTAURANT *101*
WASCOMAT OF AMERICA *50*
WASH N' WAX *247*
WASH N' WAX LTD. *247*
WASH ON WHEELS *42*
WASHINGTON GOLF CENTER *165*
WASTE WHACKER LTD. *267*
WAT-A-HEATER WATER PRE-HEATING SYSTEM *50*
WATCH GALLERY *153*
WATCH WHAT DEVELOPS FRANCHISE CONCEPTS, INC. *137*
WATER MART *153*
WATER MART INC. *153*
WATER RESOURCES INTERNATIONAL *167*
WATER SYSTEMS *167*
WATER SYSTEMS MANAGEMENT CORP. *167*
WATERBED EMPORIUM *129*
WATERBED EMPORIUM FRANCHISING CO. *129*
WATERCARE CORPORATION *167*
WATERCHEF FRANCHISING, INC. *168*
WATERCHEF WATER CENTER *168*
WATERSKILL GAMES, INC. *196*
WATNEY MANN & TRUMAN BREWERS *258*
WATSCO, INC. *176*
WATSCO INC. *50*
WAYMAR FOOD SERVICE *212*
WAYNE'S SCREEN MACHINE *22*
WAYNE'S SCREEN MACHINE INC. *22*
WCP FRANCHISING INC. *176*

WE CARE HAIR *121*
WE CARE HAIR DEVELOPMENT *121*
WE CARE HEALTH SERVICES INC. *226*
WE CARE HOME HEALTH SERVICES *226*
WE LOVE YOGURT & DELI *69*
WE LOVE YOGURT FRANCHISE, INC. *69*
WE TOSS'EM, THEY'RE AWESOME PIZZA FACTORY *92*
WEAR MASTER COMPANY *10*
WEAR MASTER MUFFLER AND BRAKE CENTERS *10*
WEATHER-BOS *196*
WEATHER-BOS CANADA LTD. *196*
WEBER SECURITY DISTRIBUTION *196*
WEBSCO, INC. *168*
WEDDING BELLES, INC. *168*
WEDDING EXPRESSIONS *168*
WEDDING GOWN SPECIALISTS RESTORATION LABS *168*
WEDDING GUIDE, THE *168*
WEDDING INFORMATION NETWORK, INC. *168*
WEDDING PAGES, THE *168*
WEE WATCH DAY CARE SYSTEMS, INC. *191*
WEE WATCH PRIVATE HOME DAY CARE *191*
WEED MAN *228*
WEEDTECH *228*
WEEDTECH ENVIRONMENTAL LAWN CARE *228*
WEIDER *274*
WELCOME HOST *118*
WELCOME HOST OF AMERICA, INC. *118*
WELTY & BLAIR *116*
WELTY & BLAIR P.C. *116*
WENDI T'EEZE FANTASY BOUTIQUE *236*
WENDY'S *101*
WENDY'S INTERNATIONAL, INC. *101*
WENDY'S RESTAURANTS *213*
WENDY'S RESTAURANTS OF CANADA, INC. *213*
WENDY'S SUPA SUNDAES *258*
WESLEY BERRY FLOWERS *133*
WEST APP. INC. *31*
WEST COAST ENTERTAINMENT *158*
WEST SANITATION SERVICES, INC. *43*
WESTERN APPRAISERS *31*
WESTERN AUTO *15*
WESTERN AUTO SUPPLY COMPANY *11, 15*
WESTERN MAINTENANCE CO. *42*
WESTERN MEDICAL SERVICES *54*
WESTERN PIZZA & B.B.Q. CHICKEN 1979 LTD. *213*
WESTERN PIZZA & FAMILY RESTAURANTS *213*
WESTERN SIZZLIN *101*
WESTERN SIZZLIN, INC. *86, 101*
WESTERN STAFF SERVICES *54*
WESTERN STAFF SERVICES, INC. *54*
WESTERN STEER FAMILY RESTAURANTS *101*
WESTERN WORKWEAR WORLD *237*
WESTLAND OF (NAME OF TERRITORY) *176*
WESTLAND SERVICES CORPORATION *176*
WESTROCK ICE CREAM *50*
WETHERBY TRAINING SERVICES LTD. *252*
WHATABURGER *101*
WHATABURGER, INC. *101*
WHEELCHAIR GETAWAYS, INC. *7*
WHISKEY DUST *153*
WHITE HEN PANTRY *60*
WHITE HORSE LTD. *101*
WHITE KNIGHT *252*
WHITE KNIGHT FRANCHISING (U.K.) LTD. *252*
WHITE MOUNTAIN CREAMERY *69*
WHITE SPOT LTD. *213*
WHITE SPOT RESTAURANTS *213*
WHITEGATES ESTATE AGENCY *267*
WHITWORTHS BAKERIES LTD. *255*
WHITWORTHS RESTAURANTS LTD. *255*
WHOLE DONUT, THE *65*
WICKENHAUSER, INC. *150*
WICKS 'N' STICKS *153*
WICKS 'N' STICKS, INC. *153*
WIENER KING SYSTEMS, INC. *101*
WIENERSCHNITZEL *101*
WIFE SAVER *101*
WIGGY'S NAIL PLACE *223*
WILD BIRD CENTERS *153*
WILD BIRD CENTERS OF AMERICA, INC. *153*

WILD BIRD CROSSING 153
WILD BIRD MARKETPLACE 153
WILD BIRDS UNLIMITED 153
WILD BIRDS UNLIMITED, INC. 153
WILDERNESS LOG HOMES, INC. 22
WILDWOOD CAPITAL INC. 232
WILDWOOD TRAVEL INC. 243
WILKINSON & GRIST 261
WILLIAM J. COKE AND ASSOCIATES LTD. 216
WILLIAM TELL EVENT SPECIALISTS 31
WILLIAMS, MULLEN, CHRISTIAN & DOBBINS 116
WILLY DOG 213
WILLY'S OLD STYLE HAMBURGERS 213
WILSON HOTEL MANAGEMENT CO. INC. 136
WILTSHIRE FARM FOODS 258
WIMBERLEY HOMES 50
WINCH ENTERPRISES 193
WINDO VANGO 129
WINDOW & DOOR MANUFACTURING CO. LTD. 261
WINDOW WORKS 129
WINDOW WORKS INTERNATIONAL, INC. 129
WINDOW WORLD INTERNATIONAL 153
WINDOWEAR 153
WINDOWEAR INC. 153
WINDQUEST (FORMERLY LAMINATIONS, INC.) 44
WINDSHIELD-SMITH 196
WINDSHIELD-SMITH REPAIR SERVICE 196
WINDSOR PLYWOOD 186
WINE KITZ 236
WINE KITZ CANADA INC. 236
WINE NOT 183
WINE WORKS 183
WING MACHINE, INC. 213
WING WAGON 101
WING-IT OF WATERTOWN, INC. 101
WINGS TO GO 101
WINGS TO GO, INC. 101
WINKS 199
WINMAR 186
WINMAR FRANCHISE CORP. 186
WINSTON FRANCHISE CORP. 53
WINZER CORP. 15
WINZER FRANCHISE COMPANY 15
WISE CRACKS RESTORATION LTD. 186
WISE CRACKS® 186
WITTEN BINDER 222
WIZ TECHNOLOGY INC. 158
WIZARD OF ADS 6
WOHAR HOLDINGS 237
WOK ON THE RUN 101
WOMEN IN FRANCHISING,INC. 112
WOMEN'S HEALTH BOUTIQUE 127
WOMEN'S HEALTH BOUTIQUE FRANCHISE SYSTEM, INC. 127
WOMEN'S WORKOUT WORLD 127
WOODFIN SUITES 136
WOODWORKERS CLUB FRANCHISING, INC. 22
WOODWORKERS CLUB, THE 22
WOODY'S BAR-B-Q 101
WOODY'S BAR-B-Q FRANCHISE SALES, INC. 101
WORK WORLD 237
WORKS CORPS. 185
WORLD CLASS PARKING 176
WORLD FRANCHISE CONSULTANTS 112
WORLD FRANCHISES, INC. 130
WORLD GYM 165
WORLD GYM LICENSING, LTD. 165
WORLD INSPECTION NETWORK 144
WORLD INSPECTION NETWORK INTERNATIONAL, INC. 144
WORLD OF DECORATING, INC. 127
WORLD OF WARES 50
WORLD ROBOTIC BOXING ASSOCIATION 165
WORLDWIDE CANADIAN MANAGEMENT CONSULTANTS, INC. 188
WORLDWIDE INFORMATION SERVICES, INC. 176
WORLDWIDE INFORMATION SERVICES INC. 158
WORLDWIDE PRODUCTS - REHEATER LTD. 50
WORLDWIDE REFINISHING SYSTEMS 186
WORLDWIDE REFINISHING SYSTEMS 249
WORLDWIDE REFINISHING SYSTEMS, INC. 23
WORLDWIDE WASHINGTON GOLF CENTER, INC. 165

WORM WAREHOUSE 50
WOVENHEARTS® 176
WRITE-1 CORPORATION 50
WRITERS' BLOC, THE 112
WRY ENTERPRISES INC. 102
WSE FRANCHISING INC., DBA TRAVELPLEX INTERNATIONAL 167
WSMP, INC. 101
WYNN'S CANADA LTD. 183
WYNN'S CLASSIC CAR CARE CENTRE 183

X

X-BANKERS CHECK CASHING 32
X-BANKERS EXPRESS, INC. 32
XEROGRAPHIC COPY CENTERS FRANCHISING 139
XPEKT RESOURCES LTD. MIDDLE EAST 260

Y

YACHT SALES DEALERSHIP 176
YAMAHA MOTOR CORP., USA 50
YARD CARDS®, INC. 118
YASIN'S FAST SUPREME 102
YASIN'S FRANCHISE SYSTEMS INC. 102
YAYA'S FLAME BROILED CHICKEN 102
YAZIGI INTERNATIONAL 262
YELLOW JACKET DIRECT MAIL ADVERTISING 6
YELLOW JACKET FRANCHISE CORPORATION 6
YELLOWSTONE LOG HOMES 50
YOGEN FRUZ 203
YOGEN FRUZ INT'L LTD. 203
YOGI BEAR'S JELLYSTONE PARK CAMP-RESORTS 136
YOGURT & SUCH 69
YOGURT & SUCH FRANCHISE SYSTEMS INC. 69
YOGURTERIA 69
YOGURTERIA FRANCHISE CORP. 69
YOUNG DRIVERS OF CANADA / YOUNG DRIVERS OF AMERICA 240
YOUNG MANAGEMENT COMPANY 102
YOUR EXPRESSION PERSONALIZED GREETINGS 222
YUMMY YOGURT, INC. 69
YVES ROCHER CANADA LTD. 223

Z

ZACK'S FAMOUS FROZEN YOGURT, INC. 69
ZANIE'S COMEDY SHOWPLACE 102
ZAREX CONSULTING GROUP 218
ZELLERS PORTRAIT STUDIO 230
ZEMBIK OPEN AIR PROTECTION INC. 245
ZEMBIKO INNOVATIONS LTD. 245
ZEPPE'S PIZZERIA 102
ZIEBART INTERNATIONAL CORP. 15
ZIEBART TIDYCAR 15
ZIP FOOD STORES 60
ZIP INTERNATIONAL LTD. 227
ZIPPY PRINT ENTERPRISES LTD. 231
ZIPPY-CLEAN 190
ZONE MARKETING (UK) LTD. 262, 267
ZONIN FOOD CORP. LTD. 204
ZUZU FRANCHISING CORP. 102
ZUZU HANDMADE MEXICAN FOOD RESTAURANTS 102

1996 Franchise Annual Directory Advertisers

Aamco Transmissions
Academy of Learning
American Association of Franchisees & Dealers
American Franchisee Association
Arnold Cohen
AWC Commercial Window Coverings
Babcock & Schmid Associates, Inc.
Bank of Montreal
Baskin Robbins
Bath Fitter
Berlitz International
Bio Ped Foot Care Centers
Bobby Rubino's Place For Ribs
Brewster's Coffee
Buchwald Asper Gallagher Henteleff
Business Expansions International
Bzircus Franchise Corp.
Canadian Franchise Association
Canadian Imperial Bank of Commerce
Cash-A-Cheque
Century 21 Real Estate
Chem-Dry Carpet & Upholstery Cleaning
Comcheq
Computemp
Cooper's Turkey Place
Critter Care
Cyclepath, The
De Dutch Pannekoek House
Decor-At-Your-Door
Deloitte & Touche
Digiad
E.K. Williams & Company
Entrepreneur's Source
Fabutan Sun Tan Studio
Fastsigns, Inc.
Fire Defense International
First Choice Franchise Services
First Choice Haircutters
Flag Shop
Franchise Developments
Francorp
Fun Services
Handyman Connection
Housesitters
Howard & Howard
Hungry Howie's Pizza & Subs
Image Control
Impressions On Hold
Inviro
...it Store
Jani-King (Canada)
Jani-King (U.S.)
Kohr Bros.
Lawn Doctor
Levitt Beber
Little Wedding Chapel
Lox of Bagels
Maaco Auto Painting & Bodyworks
Mackimmie Matthews
Mail Boxes Etc.
Matco Tools
Mike's Restaurant
Mini Maid Services
Mr. Subb
Nail Queen
National Franchise Consultants
National Franchise Sales
Oil Gard Canada
Osler, Hoskin & Harcourt
Oxford Learning Centres
P.A.S.S.
Pak Mail
Paws & Claws
Paystation
Performance Marketing Strategists
Pita Pazzaz
Productivity Point
Remerica
Rent-A-Wreck
Rocco Raccoon's Indoor Playground
Royal Bank of Canada
Sandler Sales Institute
Sangster's Health Centres
Scotiabank
Signs Now
Snip N' Clip
Sotos Karvanis
Sport Shoe, The
Super Gard
The Arrow...Neighborhood Pub
Thrifty Car Rental
Tutor Time Child Care Centers
United Consumers Club
Varcon Construction
Wear Master Muffler & Brake Centers
Women In Franchising

THE FRANCHISE ANNUAL DIRECTORY QUESTIONNAIRE

"THE ORIGINAL FRANCHISE HANDBOOK AND DIRECTORY"

Name(s) of Outlets: _____

Corporate Company Name (if different from above): _____

Corporate Address: (Street) _____

(City) _____ (State/Prov.) _____ (Zip/Postal Code) _____

Telephone: ( ) _____ Fax: ( ) _____

Name of Person to Contact: _____ Position: _____

Brief Description of Business: _____

_____

_____

_____

Year Established: _____ Franchising Since: _____

Number of Units: Company Owned: _____ Franchised: _____

Franchise Fee: _____

Royalty: (Breakdown): _____

Total Investment: (Breakdown): _____

Financing Available: _____

Addresses of Corporate Headquarters in Other Countries:

_____   _____

_____   _____

_____   _____

_____   _____

Date: _____ Approved by: _____ Title: _____

Complete and Return to: INFO FRANCHISE NEWS, INC.   INFO FRANCHISE NEWS, INC.
728 Center St., Box 550   or   9 Duke St., Box 670
Lewiston, NY, 14092   St. Catharines, ON, L2R 6W8
Phone: (716)754-4669   Phone: (905) 688-2665
               Fax: (905) 688-7728

MAILING LIST RENTALS

Jani-King
Attn: Jerry L. Crawford
4950 Keller Springs Rd., #190
Dallas, TX, 75248

Lawn Doctor, Inc.
Attn: Edward L. Reid
142 Highway 34, Box 401
Holmdel, NJ, 07733

Mail Boxes Etc.
Attn: Rick Milner
6060 Cornerstone Ct., W.
San Diego, CA, 92121

Mr. Subb
Attn: Gary Sheehan
601 Columbia St.
Cohoes, New York, 12047

Pita Pazzaz
Attn: Ray Gauthier
5339 Richborough Dr.
Mississauga, ON, L5R 3J9

...it Store
Attn: Jack Green
1111 Flint Rd., Unit 36
Downsview, ON, M3J 3C7

Mini Maid
Attn: Fred Romito
192 Shorting Rd.
Scarborough, ON, M1S 3S7

Comcheq
Attn: Theresa Romijn
125 Garry St.
Winnipeg, MB, R3C 3P2

Remerica
Attn: James Courtney
44523 Ann Arbor Rd.
Plymouth, MI, 48170

List A: Franchisors interested in contacting our directory purchasers (the hottest list of prospective franchisees in the world) can rent our list at 25¢ per name. Individual states/provinces are available. The rental fee is for a one time use only. Many franchisors have paid as much as $5.00 per lead for prospective franchisees and INFO offers an extraordinary value at only 25¢ per lead. We believe our directory purchasers will also benefit from reviewing detailed franchisor presentations.

List B: INFO also rents a mailing list of all the franchisors listed in this directory plus any new franchisors which we have discovered since the January date of publication. (We usually find hundreds of new franchises per year.) This list contains all the new franchisors plus any address changes of the companies listed in the directory. If you are interested in marketing a product/service to these franchisors then this is the list for you. Cost for this unique list rental is $350.00.

Both lists come on pressure sensitive labels in zip code/postal code order.

INFO FRANCHISE NEWS
728 Center St., P.O. Box 550
Lewiston, NY, 14092
(716) 754-4669

INFO FRANCHISE NEWS
9 Duke St., P.O. Box 670
St.Catharines, ON, L2R 6W8
(905) 688-2665

FAX (905) 688-7728

GUARANTEED ACCURATE • COMPLETELY UPDATED • 27TH YEAR

The 1996 Franchise Annual
"The Original Franchise Directory and Franchise Handbook for the Prospective Investor"

MasterCard — **MAIL THIS NO-RISK COUPON TODAY!** — **VISA**

❏ Please send..........copy (ies) of *The 1996 Franchise Annual Directory* at $39.95.
        (shipping, handling & applicable taxes included - 10 day money back guarantee)
❏ I wish to receive *The Info Franchise Newsletter* at $96.00 per year (only $8.00 per month).
    (Full refund if you are not satisfied after receiving three issues.)
❏ I wish to receive *The Info Franchise Newsletter* at the special two year rate of $175.00.
❏ **Overseas** (Non-North-American Directory orders) $44.95 total includes Air Mail Delivery.
    Newsletter $120.00 per year. **International checks must be drawn in U.S. Dollars on a U.S. Bank.**

Name _____

Address _____

City _____ State/Prov. _____ Code _____

❏ Payment enclosed.   Please charge to my   ❏ Visa   ❏ Mastercard

Card # _____ Expiry Date _____

Cardholder Name: _____ Signature: _____

Info Franchise News,   **Fax: 905-688-7728**   **Info Franchise News,**
728 Center St., Box 550,   9 Duke Street, Box 670,
Lewiston, New York, 14092-0550   St. Catharines, Ontario, L2R 6W8
Tel: 716-754-4669   Tel: 905-688-2665
                  E-Mail: infopress@infonews.com
               WWW Site: http://infonews.com/franchise

MasterCard — **MAIL THIS NO-RISK COUPON TODAY!** — **VISA**

❏ Please send..........copy (ies) of *The 1996 Franchise Annual Directory* at $39.95.
        (shipping, handling & applicable taxes included - 10 day money back guarantee)
❏ I wish to receive *The Info Franchise Newsletter* at $96.00 per year (only $8.00 per month).
    (Full refund if you are not satisfied after receiving three issues.)
❏ I wish to receive *The Info Franchise Newsletter* at the special two year rate of $175.00.
❏ **Overseas** (Non-North-American Directory orders) $44.95 total includes Air Mail Delivery.
    Newsletter $120.00 per year. **International checks must be drawn in U.S. Dollars on a U.S. Bank.**

Name _____

Address _____

City _____ State/Prov. _____ Code _____

❏ Payment enclosed.   Please charge to my   ❏ Visa   ❏ Mastercard

Card # _____ Expiry Date _____

Cardholder Name: _____ Signature: _____

Info Franchise News,   **Fax: 905-688-7728**   **Info Franchise News,**
728 Center St., Box 550,   9 Duke Street, Box 670,
Lewiston, New York, 14092-0550   St. Catharines, Ontario, L2R 6W8
Tel: 716-754-4669   Tel: 905-688-2665
                  E-Mail: infopress@infonews.com
               WWW Site: http://infonews.com/franchise